A GLOSSARY
of the
Construction, Decoration and Use
of Arms and Armor

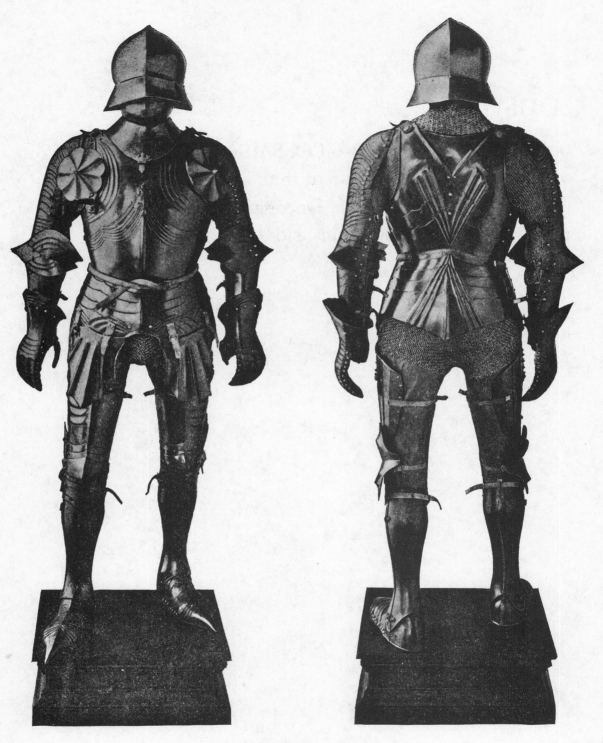

Gothic armor with blackened surface, German, 1490.
From the Collection of Dr. Bashford Dean.

A GLOSSARY

OF THE

Construction, Decoration and Use
of Arms and Armor

IN ALL COUNTRIES AND IN ALL TIMES

Together with
Some Closely Related Subjects

By GEORGE CAMERON STONE

JACK BRUSSEL, *Publisher*
NEW YORK , N. Y.

Introduction

THIS book started as a series of notes for my own information. I had for years been collecting Oriental arms and armor, and had found the published accounts both widely scattered and very contradictory. I also found that while the development of arms East and West often paralleled each other, practically no attention had been paid to this by those who had written about either.

As with other subjects the pioneer writers made many mistakes, most of which have been corrected by those who came later; but many have been copied and reprinted as though proved. Much has been published about arms and armor that is very contradictory. Not only do different writers disagree with each other, but they frequently disagree with themselves and call the same things by different names, and different things by the same one. I know of no book that treats of arms as a whole or attempts to point out the relationship between those of different times and places.

Very few of those who have written on the subject give consideration to the conditions under which armor and weapons were used, which is usually the controlling factor. Those who have written about European armor are usually scornful of the Oriental because much of it is unsuitable for the method of fighting used in Europe in the early times; the converse is also true but that they ignore.

The dating of arms and armor is very difficult. Most of the experts tell us that anyone familiar with European specimens should be able to date a piece within ten or fifteen years. This is both true and false. It is quite true that they usually agree; but they do not consider that changes did not occur everywhere at the same time. A particular type might have been made, say at Milan, at a certain time, then copied at the main points of manufacture in other countries and finally produced as something new at a small and remote place fifty, or more, years later. The present method of dating is probably as good as is possible; but it would be more correct to give more latitude and say "not earlier than" the date given.

The dating of oriental armor is more difficult. In the East styles changed less often and the same styles were worn for centuries and over much larger areas and by a greater variety of races. Also they spread more irregularly. The best makers and workers of metals in the middle East were Persians, and the best work done in Persia, the Turkish Empire and Northern and Central India was by them. This has led to considerable confusion of styles and often makes it difficult to say to what country a given piece should be attributed.

The Japanese is also difficult to date. Not that we do not know the different forms and when they originated, but much armor of early forms was made and worn in the Tokugawa period. At this time, from the middle of the 17th to the middle of the 19th century, every daimio was obliged to spend a part of each year at the Shogun's court, where they vied with each other in the elaborateness of their equipment. As the Tokugawa organization was feudal, arms and armor formed the most conspicuous items. It became the fashion to wear at court armor copied from the old suits preserved in the temples. These were made by men who, at the same time, were making armor for contemporary use. Most of it gives a much better idea of how the old armor looked than the faded and ragged remnants preserved in the temples and museums. Then, too, in Japanese armor the elements of each part, as well as the parts, were laced together with silk cords which chafed badly and soon wore out, so that they had to be frequently renewed, making it impossible to say whether a suit was an early one that had been relaced, or a later one, when both were of the same style. The Japanese experts who have carefully studied the most minute details can do it but few others are able to do so.

The experts and museums have never agreed on any system of classification, and many do not seem to consider that one is necessary or desirable. In this they are a depressing contrast to the biological museums all of which are arranged on the same system which is logical, extensible and flexible, being based on ascertainable physical characteristics. It has the added advantage of providing for any new and peculiar specimens which at once take their proper places.

The same confusion exists in the photographic departments. No attempt is usually made to take the objects to the same or any definite scale. Usually everything is taken as large as possible on the plate used. They all appear to think that the larger the picture the better. They need to take a course under some microscopist who would teach them that magnification without definition is worse than waste, in other words that the smallest picture that will show the desired detail is the best. It would be no more trouble to take things to definite scales than the present haphazard fashion. All that is needed is to have a fixed position for the object to be taken and to mark circles on the floor at suitable distances on which to place the camera. Plain screens should always be used for backgrounds; decorated backgrounds are very confusing. The longer the focus of the lens used the less it will distort the perspective.

In this book I have endeavored to bring together descriptions, methods of constructing, decorating and using the weapons of all countries and all times. Unfortunately the information with regard to many of them is very meagre. It was impossible to arrange it by classes as there is no agreement on, or definition of, the classes to be used. To propose a new one was only to add to the present confusion. I have therefore arranged it alphabetically—first giving the English name, if there was one—or the name most used by English writers—or the name used in the country of its origin as the main heading. I have followed this by all of the synonyms I could find, and cross referenced the latter. This has involved a certain amount of repetition but is, I believe, the easiest for the reader.

In the course of time I have accumulated a fairly complete library of books on the subject. This not only includes those devoted exclusively to arms and armor but many more that only mention them occasionally and give short, but frequently important, items of information regarding them. I have also visited the principal museums, and many private collections, in most parts of the world. I have given particular attention to the methods of making arms and armor in various countries. Whenever possible I have watched and talked to the workers. In several cases I have bought the special tools used and specimens of unfinished work showing the methods of construction. I believe that I am better qualified to do this than many of those who have written about it. I am a metallurgist and have made and studied metals during the greater part of my life. For many years I was in charge of shops working metals and am therefore familiar with most of the materials, tools and methods used.

I have included a number of subjects that seemed to me closely enough allied to the main one to warrant it. These include fencing, fortification, early military organization, hawking, and, to a limited extent, hunting, and the capture of the larger marine mammals.

The illustrations are mostly from my own photographs, some from my drawings; many are from various museums, and a few from books. In all cases all of the objects in any figure are to scale unless the contrary is stated. Where the provenance is not given the objects are from my own collection.

There is not, and could not be, any consistency in the spelling as most of the names are quotations. Many are transliterations from many languages, many of which are into languages other than English. They are made in all sorts of systems, or in none at all. I had to take them as I found them. In all cases they are followed by all of the synonyms that I could find, all of which have been cross referenced.

I am fully aware that this book is far from complete or perfect, but I trust that it may be an incentive to some one better qualified than I to write another on similar lines that will give more accurate information.

In conclusion I wish to express my thanks to the following institutions and individuals for pictures and information that have been of the greatest assistance to me: The American Museum of Natural History, for several pictures; The Field Museum of Chicago, for pictures; Mr. S. V. Grancsay, Curator of Armor, Metropolitan Museum of Art, who has selected and described most of the European specimens illustrated; Mr. C. O. Kienbusch who has given me pictures, lent me books and given much information; Mr. L. W. Jenkins, Director of the Peabody Museum, Salem, who has given me many pictures and much valuable information; The Metropolitan Museum of Art, for many pictures; The Museum of the American Indian, for pictures; Mr. W. Renwick for many pictures of objects in his unique collection of late firearms; Mr. Robert H. Rucker who has placed his unequalled knowledge of things Japanese at my disposal and who has given me valuable suggestions and most helpful criticism; The Smithsonian Institution, U. S. National Museum, for many pictures; The Ameria Reale, Turin, for pictures from its unique collections; The Victoria and Albert Museum, South Kensington, which has taken a number of pictures especially for me; The Wallace Collection, London, for pictures; Mr. A. McM. Welch, for pictures from his very complete collection of Scottish weapons.

A GLOSSARY
of the
Construction, Decoration and Use
of Arms and Armor

A GLOSSARY OF THE
Construction, Decoration and Use of Arms and Armor in All Countries and in All Times

'ABBASI. A straight-bladed Rajput sword strengthened at the back by perforated supports. (Egerton 400, 401).

A Persian scimeter. (Wallace Orient).

'ABBASAI TALWAR. A Punjabi sabre with a slightly curved blade. (Egerton 653).

crossing rivers. These were called *suiba abumi*, literally "crossing a river on horseback stirrups."

The later stirrups differed from all others in having no sides. In rare cases there is a rod from the upper end of the front to the foot plate near the heel; this prevents the foot from slipping out sideways. The foot plate is large enough for the entire

FIGURE 1. *Abumi. 1. Pre-Yamato type with hooded toes. 2. Frames only. Iron inlaid with brass vines; originally they were filled in with wood. 3. Early and simple type; all iron. 4. Gold lacquer with hawks in relief. Late Tokugawa. 5. Suiba abumi. Perforated treads. 18th century. 6. Iron inlaid with silver. Tokugawa. 7. All iron, early type. It has a stay, from the foot plate up to the loop for the stirrup leather, to keep the foot from slipping out sideways.*

ABUMI, BATTO. A stirrup, Japan. The very early Japanese stirrups had hooded toes and quite long iron straps for the stirrup leathers. Some had long foot plates, like the later ones, of which some were perforated to let out water picked up when foot to rest on, and curves up and back at the front so as to bring the loop for the stirrup leather over the instep. They are usually made entirely of iron, but sometimes have iron frames filled in with wood. Occasionally they have perforated foot plates. Fig. 1.

ABUMI-ZURE. A leather guard fastened to the inner side of the Japanese *suneate* (shin guard) to protect the leg from the stirrup. (Garbutt 140). Fig. 759.

ACINACES, AKINAKES. A short, straight-bladed, double-edged dagger worn at the right side by the Persians, 500-400 B.C. (Burton Sword 210, 212, 227).

FIGURE 2. *Adaga.* 1. *Steel, 15th century.* 2. *Spanish, 1590, guard of Philip II.* 3. *Spanish, 15th century.* 1 *and* 3. *Collection of Dr. Bashford Dean.* 2. *Metropolitan Museum. Not to scale.*

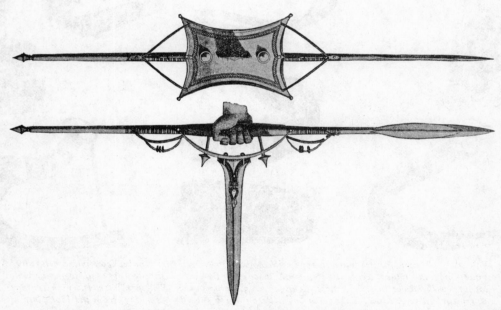

FIGURE 3. *Adaga, after Jubinal, Armeria Real, Madrid*

ACHICO. A bolas with three balls. See Bolas.

ACIES. Roman steel; or, more properly, the steel edge of a weapon or tool the body of which is made of iron. (Burton Sword 107).

ACLYS. A Roman weapon usually described as a dart. Burton, however, considers it to have been a species of throwing stick or boomerang. (Burton Sword 35).

ACTON. See Aketon.

ADAGA, ADARGA, ADARGUE. A shield or parrying weapon. It is of Arabic origin and the name is derived from the Arabic *el-darakah*, a shield.

The weapon usually called by this name is a shield made of two ellipses with their longer sides overlapping. Frequently it is made of two oval plates riveted to a straight bar, I fig. 2. It is made of metal, leather or wood covered with leather. It was used, mainly in Spain, from the latter part of the 14th to well into the 16th century. Fig. 2.

Under this name Jubinal illustrates a weapon of quite different character, fig. 3, which, he says, was used by the Moors in the 15th century.

ADAYA. An arrow that has missed its mark, Japan.

ADSCRIPTII. One of the divisions of the Roman light infantry. They were irregular troops and not considered trustworthy. (Burton Sword 245).

ADZE. The adze is a carpenter's tool something like an axe but with the edge at right angles to the handle. The Maoris were the only people who used it regularly as a weapon. Their war adzes had jade blades and elaborately carved handles, while those used as tools had plain ones. Fig. 4.

whether it is a tool or a weapon, probably the former. (Hewitt I, 45, 48).

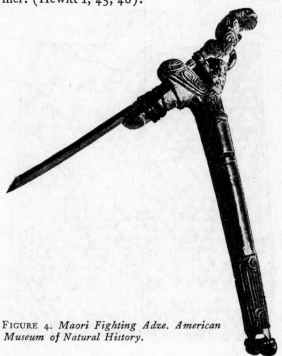

FIGURE 4. *Maori Fighting Adze. American Museum of Natural History.*

AEN. Zinc, Japan.

AFGAN KNIFE. See Khyber Knife.

AFGAN STOCK. The very much curved gun

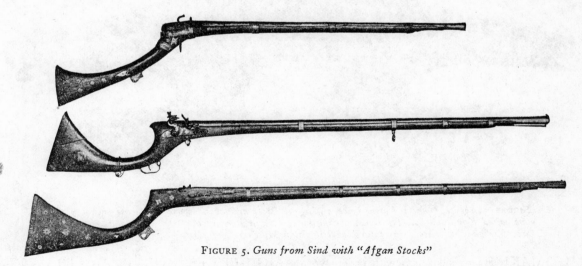

FIGURE 5. *Guns from Sind with "Afgan Stocks"*

ADZE-AXE. An implement with an adze blade on one side of the head and an axe blade on the other. One was found in a Frankish grave at Parfondeval by the Abbé Cochet. It is uncertain

stock with a very deep, narrow butt, used particularly in Sind. It received its name from the English because Sind was under Afgan rule at the time they first entered it. Fig. 5.

AFUT, AFUST. A gun carriage. (ffoulkes Armourer 153).

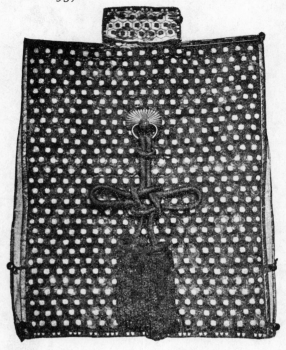

FIGURE 6. *Age-Maki. Purple silk cords and tassels on a Japanese brigandine of the 17th century.*

on the back and to its loops cords from the *sode* (shoulder guards) were tied to keep the latter from swinging forward when the wearer stooped over. (Conder 267).

AGGER. Mounds of earth which the Romans raised in front of positions that they were attacking to give commanding locations for their projectile engines; and also as a shelter for the troops forming for an attack. (Violet le Duc, Hist. 361).

AGLET. See Aiguilette.

AGLIGAK, AGILIGAK. A seal harpoon with a bone point, Point Barrow. (Murdoch 214).

AGNY ASTRA. A rocket, or fire tipped dart, used by the early Hindus. It was discharged horizontally from a bamboo tube and used against cavalry. (Egerton, p. 10).

AGRAPES, AGGRAPES. Hooks and eyes used with ordinary dress or with armor. (Fairholt 408).

AHIR. A curved Mahratta sword (Sinclair, I.A. II, 216).

AIGOTE. Kote, Japanese armored sleeves, connected by cloth or leather. See Kote. There are several varieties. (Garbutt 140). Fig. 7.

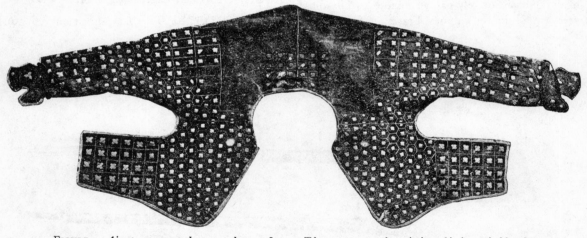

FIGURE 7. *Aigote, connected armor sleeves, Japan. There are several varieties, this is probably the one called Kogusoku-kote (little armor-like kote) because it is so complete. The sleeves and body are of brigandine. Late 15th century. Metropolitan Museum.*

AGE-MAKI. Heavy silk cords with tassels worn as ornaments on Japanese armor. They were usually red but sometimes purple for the higher ranks. They were generally tied in a peculiar bow, fig. 6, but sometimes with other knots. The largest was

AIGUILETTE, AGLET, AIGLET, ANGLET. The metal tag on the end of a point or lace, sometimes the point itself. Points were used during the middle ages to fasten together the pieces of plate armor, and also the portions of the civil dress.

At first the armor for the arm was supported by points fastening to the shoulders of the arming doublet, later the arm pieces were hung from pins on the gorget. Fig. 8.

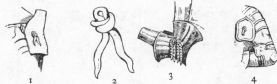

FIGURE 8. *Aiguilettes. 1. From the effigy of a knight of the Pembridge family. Temp. Ed. II. 2. The same, larger scale. 3. End of the 15th century. 4. From the Harlein MSS. 4826. After Planche.*

AIGUNIA. Machines, or engines, of war. (ffoulkes Armourer 153).

AJIRO GAKE. See Anda Tsudzumi.

AIKUCHI, KUSUNGOBU. A dagger without a guard, Japan. The second name is the older and refers to the length of the blade which was originally— *ku* (nine) *sun, go* (five) *bu,* 0.95 of a Japanese foot, equal to about 10.8 English inches. Apparently this type of knife was not carried by persons of rank until the later Tokugawa times; it then became popular and was used by old men, by men living in semi-religious retirement, and by those rewarded with the titles of *Hoin, Hokyo, Hogen,* etc. In the early part of the Tokugawa period the end of the scabbard was usually protected by a ring of buffalo horn which had a shoulder on it that locked into a similar ring on the hilt. Later, when this kind of knife became more popular with the higher classes, these pieces were often made of metal decorated like the other fittings. The decora-

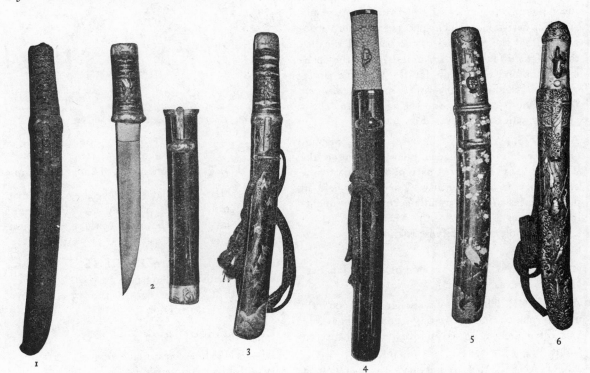

FIGURE 9. *Aikuchi. 1. Blade 8.75 inches long, unsigned. Scabbard and hilt mountings of iron inlaid with gold. Kozuka and kogai of shakudo with shishi partly of gold. 2. Blade signed Tomohide, 17th century. All mounts of silver carved with waves and inlaid with gold dragon flies. Scabbard of black lacquer with incised snow crystals. 3. Blade 9 inches long of diamond section, signed Nagamichi, 16th century. All mounts of gold. Menuki peonies, others with trees in relief in shakudo and silver. 4. Finely watered blade signed Kaneuji. Same hilt with gold menuki. Hilt and scabbard fittings black horn or lacquer of fine quality. Kozuka, shakudo nanako with borders and flowers in relief in gold. 5. Silver mounts finely engraved. Scabbard and hilt of fine gold lacquer with a tree, flower vases, storks, etc., in high relief in shell and lacquer. A cabinet piece and not for use. 6. Blade 9.625 inches long, engraved with a ken and bonji characters. Hilt and mountings all silver waves. Scabbard covered with shibuichi chased with a wave design with fish, lobsters, etc., in high relief in gold, silver, shakudo and copper.*

tion was partly on each so that the two appeared as one when the knife was sheathed. The ring on the hilt was sometimes called the *fuchi*, and the one on the scabbard the *koi-guchi kanagu*. Usually the two, collectively, were called the *koi-guchi*. Sometimes the koi-guchi was a special fitting with a projecting flange, if it was attached to the hilt the flange fitted over a plain cap on the scabbard; if it was attached to the scabbard a plain cap on the hilt fitted into it. See Koi-Guchi.

These knives were used in committing ceremonial suicide, *harakiri* or *seppuku*. When used for this purpose they were fitted with hilts and scabbards of plain white wood. (Joly, Naunton xvii).

The aikuchi was carried by those whose fighting days were over, apparently as a notice that while the wearer was no longer seeking trouble, he was still prepared to defend himself. One of the old meanings of the name is "a pleasant companion." Another derivation, which appears to be more probable, is that the open end of the scabbard is called the *koi-guchi* (literally carp mouth), and the opening in the end of the hilt for the tang the *tsuka-guchi* (hilt mouth), the knife is called *ai-kuchi* (meet mouth), the two not being separated by a guard as with other knives. Fig. 9.

AILETES, ALETES. Square, round, pentagonal, shield or cross-shaped guards worn on the shoulders from the latter part of the 13th to the middle of the 14th century. They were held in place by laces and were usually decorated, frequently with the coat of arms of the wearer. Fig. 10.

No example of this defense is known to be in existence.

AINAKA-GOTE. A variety of kote, Japanese armored sleeve.

AKAGANE. Copper, Japanese. It was frequently used in making and decorating sword fittings; and was often pickled so as to give it a brilliant red patine.

AKAGANE-GASA. A hat-shaped copper helmet worn by the lower classes of Japanese retainers. Like the "tin hat" of the late war it was often used as a cooking pot.

There is said to have been a special kind worn in the eastern provinces which had a loose piece on the crown that revolved when struck by a weapon or missile. (Conder 280).

AKEDAMA. The rim of the hachimanza.

AKETON, ACTON, AUQUETON, GAMBESON, HACKETON, HAQUETON, WAMBAIS, WAMBESIUM, WAMS. A quilted garment much used as armor in the 12th and 13th centuries. The knights wore it under their hauberks, and it was the sole defense of the foot soldiers. When worn under armor it was sometimes without sleeves.

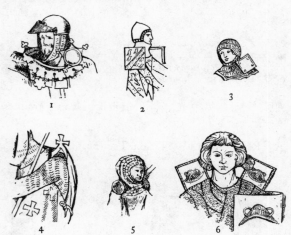

FIGURE 10. *Ailettes. 1, 2, 3, 4. From contemporary manuscripts. 5. From an ivory carving. 6. From the brass of a Septvans, Chartham, Kent. After Planche.*

AKINAKES. See Acinaces.

AKURIO. Evil demon, a type of Japanese menpo.

ALAMANI. An Indian sabre like the old German hussar sword. It was probably used by Hyder's German cavalry in the 17th century. (Egerton, 745 and p. 11).

A LA POULAINE SOLERETS. Foot guards (solerets) with very long pointed toes. They were worn with Gothic armor in the 15th century. (ffoulkes 70). Fig. 11.

ALBLAST. See Arbalest.

ALBORIUM. A bow made of hazel, 11th century. (ffoulkes Armourer 153).

ALCATO. A collar or gorget, 13th century. (Planche 5).

ALFANGE. The Spanish form of the Persian word *khanjar*, a knife or dagger. (Burton Sword 29).

ALI-ALI. A kind of Malay knife. (Skeat & Blagden II, 643).

ALKINDE. The Spanish name for Indian watered steel, *wootz*. (Burton Sword 110).

ALKIR. See Kalka.

ALLECRET, HALECRET. Body armor of the 16th century of uncertain character. Some authorities describe it as a light back and breast. (Planche 5).

ALLIGOLES. Rohilla mercenaries much employed in the Indian wars. (Tod I, 558).

ALLONGE. A thrust with a rapier or small sword.
A long rein used for exercising horses. (Hoyt 351).

Yamato Dake. He was once trapped by his enemies in a field of burning grass, but mowed a space clear with his sword and so escaped. After this the sword was called the *Kusunagi no Tsurugi*, or grass quelling sword. Yamato Dake consecrated it to the temple of Atsuta, where it is still said to be. (Joly Leg. 345, 367, 395).

AMAOI. Stiffening plates on the edges of the scabbard of a tachi. They are held in place by bands. (Joly Int. 8). Fig. 386.

AMBALANG. The sling of the Toba Battaks, Sumatra. (Arc. f. Eth. VI, 121).

FIGURE 11. *A la Poulaine Solerets. Probably German, 15th century. Metropolitan Museum. Not to scale.*

ALMAIN RIVETS. Modern writers frequently use this name for sliding rivets, that is, rivets that slide in slots in one or both of the pieces that they join, thus allowing a considerable amount of flexibility. In the early inventories, however, it always indicates a suit of light armor. "2000 complete harnesses called Almayn rivets according to a pattern in the hands of John Dawney, accounting always a salet, a gorget, a breastplate, a backplate and a pair of splints for every complete harness at 18s. the set." Payment for them was made in the King's behalf to a certain merchant of Florence, Sept. 13th, 1512. (ffoulkes Armouries 49).

ALVAU-UL. See Bo-Un.

AMA-GOI-KEN. A Japanese sword in the form of the ancient one used by Kobo Daishi. It represents the Amakurikara, or rain dragon. (Jap. Ex. 71).

AMAKURIKARA. A dragon wound around a sword. Used as a decoration on Japanese blades. Fig. 12.

AMA NO MURAKUMO TSURUGI. The mythical sword that was drawn from the tail of the eight-headed dragon by Susano-O no Mikoto, and was kept in the temple of Ise until given to

AMENTUM, ANKULE, MESANKULE. The first is the Latin name, the others are Greek. A loop of cord attached to the shaft of a spear to assist in throwing it. The Greeks fastened it close to the butt end of the spear; but, in parts of Central Africa where it is still used, it is placed near the middle of the shaft. (Cowper 229).

FIGURE 12. *Amakurikara. Japanese temple sword. Straight, double-edged blade 13 inches long, with a dragon carved winding around it. Vajra hilt. Tibetan scabbard set with coral, turquoise and shell.*

AMERA. A kind of spear thrower used by the Arunta, Luritja, Urmatjera and Kaitish tribes of Australia. It consists of a broad lanceolate blade of mulga wood (*Acacia Aneura*), tapering off at both ends. It is almost always decidedly concave, but sometimes nearly flat. At one end it has a small wooden point attached by means of a lump of resin firmly bound by sinew. At the opposite end there is a still larger mass of the same material which not only makes a handle, but holds a flake of flint which forms the most useful cutting implement of the tribes that use this form of thrower. The broad surface makes it inefficient as a thrower, but, on the other hand it serves a treble purpose. First as a thrower, second as a cutting implement, and third as a receptacle for certain things, such as decorative materials and blood, used during ceremonies. (Spencer & Gillen 687). See Spear Throwers 2, fig. 744.

AMIDA TAGANE, AMIDA YASURIME. Decorations of radiating lines on a Japanese guard, fig. 13. Frequently it is used in connection with other forms of ornament.

FIGURE 13. *Amida Tagane. Tsuba decorated with radiating lines.*

AMUKTA. One of the divisions, or classes, of weapons recognized by the ancient Hindus. It means the "unthrown," and comprises 20 species.

According to Hindu tradition "Jaya a daughter of primeval Daksha (one of the Rishis or sacred sages), became, according to a promise of Brahma, the creator, the mother of all weapons, including missiles. They are divided into four great classes. The *Yantramukta* (thrown by machines); the *Panimukta* (hand thrown); the *Muktasandharita* (thrown and drawn back) and the *Mantramukta* (thrown by spells, and numbering six species), form the *Mukta* or thrown class of twelve species. This is opposed by the *Amukta* (unthrown) of twenty species, to the *Muktamukta* (either thrown or not) of ninety-eight varieties, and to the *Bahuyuddha* (weapons which the body provides for personal struggles). All are personified." (Burton Sword 214).

AMUSETTE. A gun mounted like a cannon but fired like a musket. It is said to have been invented by Marshal Saxe and used by the French horse artillery. (Hoyt 352).

AN, KURA. A saddle, Japan. The Japanese saddles had wooden trees made of four pieces laced together and shaped much like our army saddles. The wood was almost always decorated with lacquer. I, 11 Fig. 680.

ANAK, PANAH. An arrow, Malay.

ANAK TOUMIANG. The inner tube of the blowpipe of the Orang Mantra of the Malay Peninsula. (Arc. f. Eth. IV, 266). See Toumiang.

ANCUS, ANKUS, FURSI, GUSBAR, HENDOO. The Indian elephant goad. It is shaped much like a modern boathook, with a spike on the end and a sharp hook on the side.

When used by a man riding on the elephant the handles are comparatively short and the hooks vary much in size; when carried by a man walking beside the elephant the handles are about five feet long and the hooks always small. Most are plain and solely for use; but many are mainly for display and are finely chiseled, or have handles of ivory or jade, or are covered with goldsmith's work and jewels. They vary in length from about fifteen inches to nearly four feet. Figs. 14, 15.

ANDANICUM, ANDAINE. A name for Indian watered steel used by Marco Polo. See Ondanique.

ANDARMA, BAR-NGA. A spear with a bamboo shaft and a head of acacia. Princess Charlotte Bay. (Roth, Aust. Mus. VII, 194).

ANDA TSUDZUMI, AJIRO GAKE. Japanese corselets covered with cane work. The two are different. (Conder 263).

ANDREA FERRARA. A celebrated Italian swordsmith, 1550-1583. The Highland broadswords are often called Andrea Ferrara because his blades were so much used and highly valued in Scotland.

ANELEC, ANALACE. See Cinquedea.

ANGIRK'HA. A surcoat, a long robe worn over armor in India in the 16th century. (Egerton, p. 23).

ANGLET. See Aiguilette.

ANGON. The barbed spear or javelin of the Franks in the 7th century. (Hewitt I, 25).

AN-GORA. A club with a broad, square end and sharp edges. It is used for killing fish at night when

FIGURE 14. *Decorated Ancus. The whole is practically covered with diamonds, only the point and hook being bare. Part of the decoration on the handle is in enamel. South Kensington Museum.*

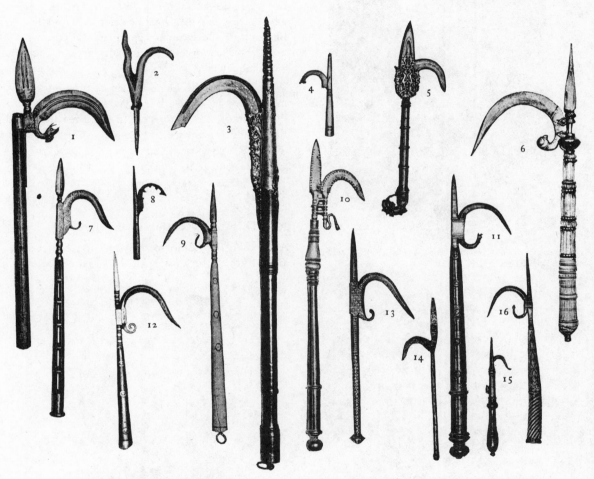

FIGURE 15. *Ancus. 1. Tanjore XVII. Steel head and wooden handle. 2. Java XVIII. Head only, all steel. 3. Ceylon XVII. Steel head inlaid with brass and silver, wood shaft. 4. Ceylon, head only. Steel inlaid with silver. 5. Central India. Carved steel head and shaft with a brass monster on the end. 6. Southern India XVII. Steel head, ivory handle, shaft carved and fluted cylinders of crystal separated by gilt rings. 7. Rajput XVIII. Blackened steel inlaid with gold. 8. Ceylon, head only, all steel. 9. Silver plated head and ivory handle. 10. Southern India. Carved steel head and wooden handle separated by an ivory ornament. 11. Ceylon XVIII. Steel head, handle painted with bands of bright colored lac. 12. India. Steel head, flat shaft and butt forged in one piece; wood covers riveted to the shaft. 13. All steel inlaid with silver. 14. Mysore. Very rough iron forging. 15. Very small, probably made for some mahout's child. Steel socketed with a ring on the back, short wooden handle painted red. The points have been rebated so that it could not injure the elephant. Length 10 inches. 16. Central India, XVIII. Steel head, carved ivory handle.*

they are attracted by a light by the Koko-Minni blacks of Queensland.

FIGURE 16. *Anime (Venetian?), second half of the 16th century. Metropolitan Museum.*

century. The plates are horizontal and lap so that the open joints are upwards. While this makes it very flexible it is not good as a defence. Fig. 16.

ANKULE. See Amentum.

ANNEAU. A ring guard. It was used on one, or both, sides of the guards of swords and knives in the early 16th century and later. (Dean Handbook 67).

ANLAS. Burton says, Sword 263: "The peculiarly English anelace or anlas, more or less conical and sharp-pointed." This description is totally unlike that of the weapon commonly called an anelace; which, moreover, is Italian and not English. See Cinquedea.

ANTEPILANI. The first two lines of the Roman heavy infantry. They were so called because they were placed before the three divisions called Pilus. (Burton Sword 247).

ANTESIGNANI. Roman light infantry who preceded the standards. (Burton Sword 247).

ANTIA. The iron handle of a shield. (Fairholt 412).

AOBIE. A short bamboo sword, Japan.

AOI TSUBA. A form of guard much in vogue in the 12th century in Japan. It is made up of four

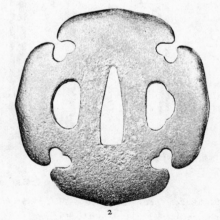

FIGURE 17. *Aoi Tsuba. 1. Iron mokume (wood grain) surface. Collection of Mr. C. O. Kienbusch. 2. Iron plain.*

ANGUSHTANA. An archer's ring, India. (South Kensington). See Archer's Ring.

ANGUVIGANG. A whale lance, Cumberland Sound Eskimo. (U. S. N. M. 1900, 265).

ANIME. Laminated body armor of the late 16th

lobes like the heart-shaped leaves of the *Aoi* (Assarum), or has heart-shaped openings in it, or both. Fig. 17.

AOR. One of the Homeric names for the sword. (Burton Sword 222).

AORI. A shape of tsuba parallel top and bottom with the former considerably shorter than the latter. (Weber I, 202). 17, fig. 805.

Saddle flaps, Japan. (M. M. S. II, 234).

APNINIAP, CHININIAP. An Ainu fish spear with a forked shaft, each branch of which is fitted with a barbed head loosely fastened to the shaft by a long cord. The butt end of the shaft has a short fork in which the line is laid when the spear is thrown. (Batchelor 154). Fig. 18.

APPELS. In fencing, accentuating a feint by a slight movement of the foot. (Castle 155).

APRON. In gunnery, a square plate of lead covering the vent of a cannon to keep the charge dry and the vent clean and open. (Hoyt 353).

APSARAS. Hindu goddesses "who summon the chosen from the field of battle and convey them to the 'mansions of the sun.'" (Tod I, 461).

AQUANDE-DA. The leather bracer of the Omaha. (Dorsey 287).

ARAI-KAWA-ODOSHI. Cords of light red leather used for lacing together the parts of Japanese armor.

ARAME. An unfinished sword blade, Japan.

ARBALEST, ARBALETE, ALBLAST, ARBLAST. The European crossbow of the middle ages. All of the varieties consist essentially of a heavy bow mounted on a stock with a groove in the top for the arrow, and a mechanical arrangement for holding and releasing the string. The earlier bows were made of wood or whalebone; the later of steel. Sometimes they had wood backs and bellies separated by about twenty thin plates of horn or whalebone; these were so placed that they were bent in the direction of their greatest width, not like a leaf spring. The entire bow was covered with a wrapping of sinew.

The earliest crossbows had comparatively light bows that could be drawn by hand, the stock being braced against the body. As they became stronger the bow was placed on the ground, and the feet on

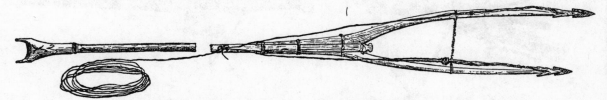

FIGURE 18. *Apniniap. Ainu salmon spear. U. S. National Museum, 1890, p. 70.*

ARABAS. A kind of arquebus, India. (Tod I, 220).

ARAI-I. A kind of spear thrower that is also used as a spear guard on the Pennyfather River, Queensland. The blade varies greatly in width. It is made of any one of five kinds of hard wood which has been seasoned by burying it in the ground for two or three months to prevent its splitting. The peg is a cylindrical piece of ironwood fixed in the vertical edge of the end of the blade, which is split to receive it. It is fastened by twine passing through holes in the blade, and is covered with resin. The shell haft is made of two pieces of *pera* shell (*Melo diadema*) attached by beeswax. The handle is called *to-o*, the opposite end *kwanna*, the blade *a-rar*, the peg *ko-kan*, the edge of the blade *bu-ni*, the shell shaft *pe-ra*, and the extreme end beyond the shell *teriwan* (tail). (Roth, Aust. Mus. VII, 197. See Spear Throwers 18, fig. 744).

it holding it down, while both arms and back were used to pull the string. Up to this time the bow had been lashed to the end of the stock; later it was passed through a mortise a few inches from the end of the stock and a metal stirrup was added to place the foot in when drawing the bow. The stirrup was also used in drawing the bow with the cord and pulley, belt and claw (graffle), or by the windlass. When using the cord and pulley—one end of the cord was fastened to the belt and the other hooked to the stock, the user then stooped down, bending his knees, and fastened the hook on the pulley to the string. He bent the bow by rising and straightening his legs. By belt and claw—a long hook, the graffle, was fastened to the belt and hooked to the string, the bow was drawn by pushing with the leg, the foot being placed in the stirrup. When using the windlass the stirrup was merely used to steady the arbalest while the bow was drawn by a windlass and pair of tackles hooked to the stock. Very powerful bows were sometimes drawn by a screw passing through a hole in the rear end of the stock and hooked to the string, a wing nut on the screw

an arrangement of articulated levers that hooked to the string and stock. Sometimes it was permanently attached to the stock, more often it was separate and was carried hung from the belt. Fig. 305.

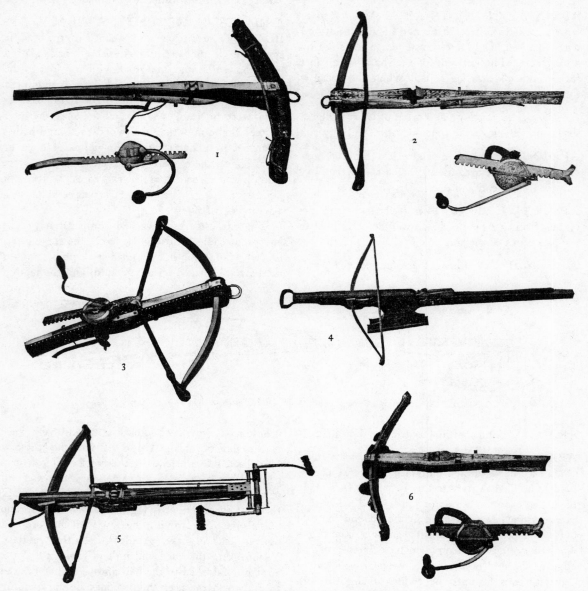

FIGURE 19. *Arbalestes. 1. German, 15th century. 2. German, dated 1584. 3. German, about 1550. 4. French(?) wall crossbow, 16th century. 5. French stirrup crossbow with its windlass, 16th century. 6. Flemish, 16th century. Metropolitan Museum. Not to scale.*

being turned to draw the bow. A rack and pinion turned by a crank (cranequin or cric), or the windlass and tackles (moulinet) was carried hung from the belt. The most popular arrangement for the lighter crossbows was the goat's foot, or pied de biche,

The largest crossbows had very complicated locks; some having as many as six scears between the trigger and the nut (catch for the string). Either, or both, ends of this train could be locked by a pin inserted in a hole in the stock.

In order to put the string on the bow the latter had to be partially bent which was done by means of a "bastard string." This was a cord shorter than the regular string with clamps on the ends by means of which it could be fastened to the bow. By its use the bow could be sufficiently bent to permit of putting the regular string in its place.

largely used in the English army in the time of Elizabeth, and were said to have been used by the English at the attack of the Isle of Rhee in 1627. Light crossbows shooting either bolts, stones, clay pellets or bullets were used for shooting game until the end of the 18th century.

The stock of the crossbow was called the tiller

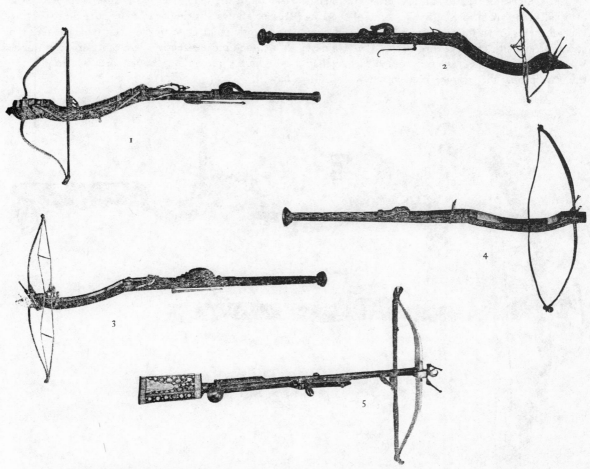

FIGURE 20. *Arbalestes a Jalets.* 1. *German, about* 1520. 2. *Italian, 16th century.* 3. *Italian, end of the 16th century.* 4. *French, early 17th century.* 5. *German, about 1700. Metropolitan Museum. Not to scale.*

The large crossbows were much more powerful than any long bow, but could not be fired as rapidly and were more difficult to protect from damage by rain or dampness. They were mainly used in the attack and defense of fortified places, the attacking crossbowmen being protected by large shields, pavis or mantlet, carried by attendants. The lighter crossbows were used in the field by men protected only by their armor. Crossbows were

or arbrier, and the catch for holding the string the nut. The arrows were called bolts or quarrels, and were much shorter and heavier than those used with the long bow. Fig. 19.

ARBALETE A CRIC. A crossbow drawn by a rack and pinion, or cric. Fig. 19, nos. 1, 2, 3 and 6.

ARBALETE A JALET, PELLET CROSSBOW, PRODD. A crossbow with a long, light wooden stock, frequently ending in a ball or knob, and arranged to shoot stones or bullets instead of bolts. The string was double and had a small pouch in the middle to hold the missile. Many were elaborately decorated with carving and inlaying as they were intended mainly for sport. They were used for game until well into the 18th century. Fig. 20.

The Chinese used, and still use, crossbows firing clay balls that are surprisingly like some of the European forms, even to the front sights, a bead on a string stretched across a wire arch. The Chinese back sights are, however, very much larger than the European. The trigger mechanism is also dif-

ARCHER'S GUARD. See Bracer.

ARCHER'S RING. Throughout the greater part of the East the method of drawing and loosing the bow differs radically from those used in Europe. In it the thumb is put around the string and a ring is worn on it to protect it from the pressure and friction of the string when it is drawn and released. It also allows of bringing the pressure on the string at a single point close to the nock which makes the bow much more effective than the European method where three or four fingers are used to pull the bow.

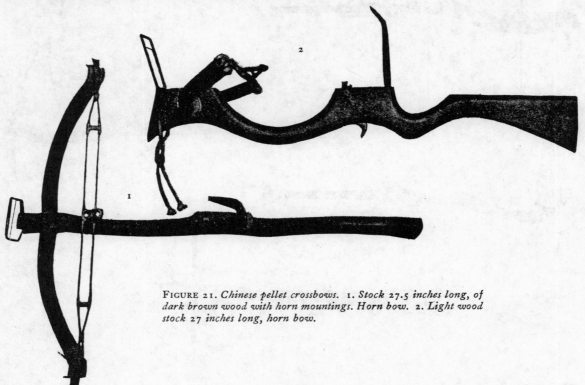

FIGURE 21. *Chinese pellet crossbows. 1. Stock 27.5 inches long, of dark brown wood with horn mountings. Horn bow. 2. Light wood stock 27 inches long, horn bow.*

ferent, being composed of two levers that lock together without a spring and are held in place by the pressure of the string until the trigger is pulled. Fig. 21.

ARBALEST A TOUR. A crossbow drawn by a windlass. 5, fig. 19.

ARBALESTINA. A cross-shaped opening in a wall from which to shoot with a crossbow. (Payne-Gallwey, The Crossbow 9).

ARBRIER. The stock of a crossbow. (Boutell 138).

These rings vary considerably in shape in different countries, and even in the same one. In Turkey, Persia, India and Korea the part that bears on the string is much wider than the other parts. In some of the Indian rings it is also wider on the back of the thumb than at the sides. In India the part of the ring on which the string slides is quite convex. In some of the Indian rings the upper end turns out in a hook. In Turkey, Persia and the few Chinese rings of this shape it is almost always highly convex. Nearly all Chinese rings are cylindrical

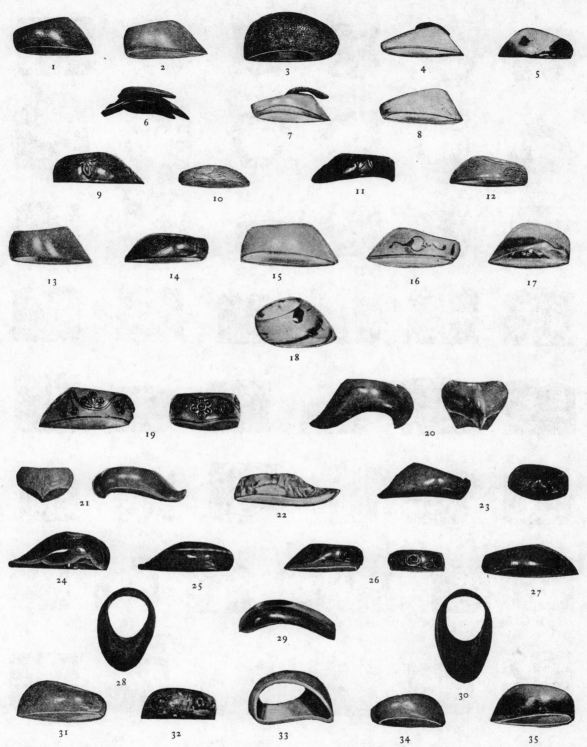

FIGURE 22. *Archer's Rings. 1. Turkey. Gray jade. 2. Turkey. Light jade . 3. Turkey. Very large ring of bone inlaid with brass. 4. Turkey. Bone with a leather guard. 5. Turkey. Red and white agate. 6. Turkey. Tortoise shell with a leather guard.. 7. Turkey. Ivory with a leather guard. 8. Turkey. Bone with a flat end. 9. Persia. Carved gray-green jade. 10. Persia. Carved white jade. 11. Persia. Carved dark green jade. 12. Persia. Carved white jade. 13. Indo-Persia. Gray jade. 14. Indo-Persia. Jade. 15. Indo-Persia. White jade. 16. Indo-Persia. Jade inlaid with gold. 17. Indo-Persia. Yellow and white agate. 18. Indo-Persia. Yellow, brown and white translucent agate. 19. India, side and back. Light jade inlaid with jewels set in gold. 20. India. Light jade with dark veins. Very high arch, upturned end and large ridge at the back. 21. India. Light jade similar to the preceding. 22. India. Rock crystal. It has been set with jewels which have been picked out. 23. India, side and back. Ivory with a heart-shaped ornament on the back. 24. India, turned up end. Gray agate with curved white lines. 25. India. Gray agate with straight white lines. 26. India, end and side. White jade, flat inlay of gold, three jewels on the back. 27. India. Mottled green jade. 28, 29, 30. Korea. Black and white cow's horn. 31. Probably Chinese, ivory. 32. Probably Chinese, ivory with incised rings at the back. 33. Ivory with a very high arch. 34. Probably Chinese. Gray jade. 35. Probably Chinese. Black and white stone.*

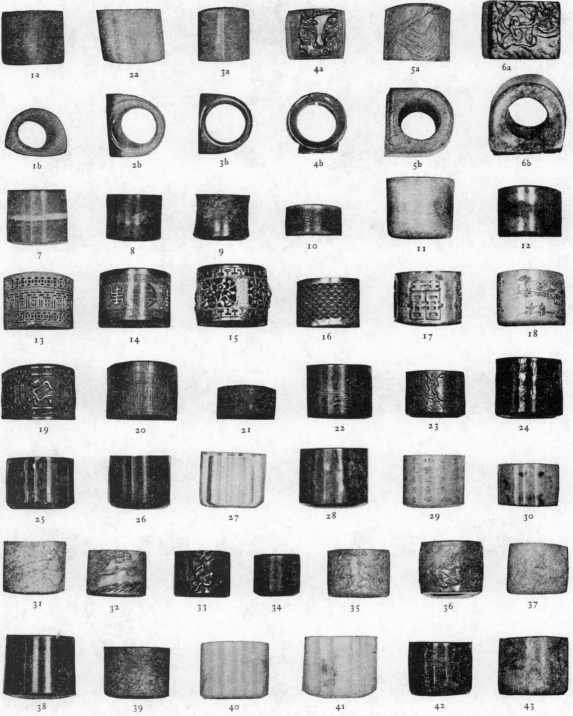

FIGURE 23. *Chinese Archer's Rings. The first six are of D section; the upper line shows the sides and the second the ends.* 1 *a, b. Light jade, curved red face.* 2 *a, b. White jade with a flat, red face inclined to the axis.* 3 *a, b. Green jade vertical red face.* 4 *a, b. Small ring of translucent jade with a carved vertical face.* 5 *a, b. White jade vertical face. The curved side is carved with waves.* 6 *a, b. Very large ring of mottled jade with the vertical face carved in high relief.* 7. *Agate with a white band in the middle.* 8. *Agate(?) with black ends.* 9. *Yellow and white stone with concave sides.* 10. *Stag horn, unusually narrow.* 11. *Stag horn.* 12. *Stag horn.* 13. *Pottery pierced.* 14. *Metal enameled in colors, blue ends.* 15. *Metal pierced and enameled in colors, gilt ends.* 16. *Silver, sides woven wires.* 17. *Ivory with characters in relief.* 18. *Ivory, very finely carved with an incised landscape and inscription.* 19. *Wood carved in high relief.* 20. *Wood with a silver lining.* 21. *Wood, very narrow.* 22. *Wood, inlaid with silver flowers and an inscription.* 23. *Composition, carved and lined with silver.* 24. *Yellow and brown mottled wood with a horn lining.* 25. *Amber.* 26. *Jet.* 27. *Rock crystal.* 28. *"Tomb" jade.* 29. *White jade with a very finely incised poem.* 30. *White jade with yellow spots.* 31. *Gray stone.* 32. *White jade carved in low relief.* 33. *Black stone with a kirin in high relief.* 34. *Very small ring of dark green jade.* 35. *Mottled white jade carved in low relief.* 36. *Greenish jade carved in low relief.* 37. *White jade carved in high relief.* 38. *Black glass.* 39. *Stone.* 40. *White jade.* 41. *White jade with a green spot.* 42. *Stone green, yellow and red.* 43. *Gray jade.*

All of the varieties of "archer's rings" are not used by bowmen. At the present time only those made of deer horn or wood are used in shooting. Amiot says, p. 387, "anneau de corne ou de cerf ou de quelque pierre precieuse (presumably jade)." The much decorated rings are worn simply as ornaments.

with one end convex and the other concave. Some Chinese rings are of D section like the old Assyrian. Many of the cylindrical Chinese rings are not for archers but were worn as ornaments, many of these are much smaller than the archer's rings. The Korean rings are much wider where the string bears than any others. They are always made of cow horn. It is uncertain whether the Japanese ever wore rings. As far back as we have information they wore gloves with an extra thickness of leather where the string bears; or they lined the thumb with some hard material which practically forms a ring.

Archer's rings are made of any hard, tough material — metals, horn, bone, ivory, jet, amber, tortoise shell and many kinds of stone, jade being the most popular. Some are ornamented with inlaying and jewels, occasionally to such an extent as to render them useless for their legitimate purpose. This type was worn only as an ornament for parade. Figs. 22, 23.

The Chinese sometimes carried their rings in small cases of ivory or embroidered materials; the cover slides on the suspension cords. They were carried hung from the belt. Fig. 24.

In use the point is turned towards the end of the thumb and not towards the hand as some descriptions would indicate. The shapes of some of them show this to have been impossible. The Chinese cylindrical rings are worn with the convex end towards the hand.

ARCIONES. The high peaks, back and front, of the war saddles of the middle ages. They were covered with steel plates which were often forged so as to be highly decorative. Fig. 679.

ARMED. In the middle ages, and up to the 17th century, "armed" meant wearing armor and had no reference to carrying arms. A man without armor was said to be "unarmed," even though carrying a number of weapons.

ARMET. A type of closed helmet that conforms to the shape of the head and covers it completely. It first appeared on the Continent in the third quarter of the 15th century, and was a very distinct advance on any of its predecessors, being lighter and at the same time completely protecting the head, face and neck. It was soon further improved by adding a gorget wide enough to bring the weight on the shoulders instead of the head. As it fitted

closely to the shape of the head it was necessary to open it in order to put it on. In the earliest forms this was accomplished by hinging the cheek pieces immediately below the visor pivots so that they could open outwards. The cheek pieces joined in front of the chin, and the visor fitted over them when low-

FIGURE 24. *Cases for archer's rings. 1. Box covered with blue silk studded with bright steel disks. It has a gilded hook by which to hang it from the belt, 17th century. 2. Box for two rings; it is divided in the middle and has two caps. Covered with brocade, 19th century. 3. Embroidered silk case for a single ring, 18th century. 4. Carved ivory box for one ring. The bottom is in two pieces and must be taken apart to get the ring out, 18th century.*

ered. The skull piece was continued down the back in a strip about an inch wide which was overlapped by the cheek pieces when closed. A short stem with a disk or roundel, sometimes called a volet, on it projected from the back of the helmet. This was probably intended to protect the joint. A specimen in the Churburg has a crescent-shaped piece fastened to the skull at the back of the neck so as to overlap both cheek pieces and hold them in place. The roundel gave the name of armet a rondelle to this type. Fig. 25.

The English armet was somewhat different, being modeled more closely to the shape of the head. The skull piece covered the back of the head and ears while the movable chinpiece revolved on the same pivots as the visor. It was firmly closed by a hook or spring bolt on the side. This type gradually displaced the armet a rondelle. Fig. 26.

The buffe, a reinforcing piece covering the chin and lower part of the face, was often worn with early armets. It was fastened in place by a strap, or straps, passing around the neck and buckling below the rondelle. As no means were provided in the early armets for holding the visor down the buffe projected above it and prevented its being forced up by a lance or sword thrust. 3 fig. 25, fig. 195.

Although the armet did not come into use rapidly it had nearly displaced the other types of helmet by the year 1500. Some time before this the gorget had become large enough to transfer the weight of the headpiece to the shoulders. Later it was made a separate piece with a bead at its upper edge which fitted into a corresponding bead on the lower edge of the helmet. This made a joint that was perfectly tight at the neck and allowed the head to be turned freely while the weight of the helmet was supported by the shoulders, a combination never found in any other helmet. It continued to be the most popular type for both war and the tournament until the end of the 16th century. (Laking Armour II, 71).

ARMET A RONDELLE. See Armet.

ARMIL, ARMILAUSA, ARMYLL. Believed to have been a garment worn over armor, its exact nature is uncertain. (Planche 12).

ARMINS. Velvet or cloth coverings for the shafts of pikes, halbards and similar weapons. They were primarily intended to keep the hand from slipping, but were later used mainly for ornament.

ARMING DOUBLET. A padded garment of some heavy material, usually leather, worn under armor to protect the person and ordinary clothes from stains and chafing. It was padded to act as a cushion to blows struck on the armor. When mail gussets were worn to protect the joints they were fastened to the arming doublet; aiguilettes for hold-ing the arm pieces in place were also attached to it. (ffoulkes 61). See Pourpoint.

ARMING GIRDLE. The sword belt worn with armor. (Planche 13).

ARMING HOSE. Heavy hose worn with armor. (Planche 13).

ARMING POINTS. Laces, or cords, for fastening the parts of the armor together, or for supporting it from the doublet. (ffoulkes 38).

ARMING SPURS. Spurs worn with armor. When the horses wore plate armor the spurs had to have very long shanks in order to reach the animal under the flanchards.

ARMING SWORD. The estoc. (Planche 14).

A short sword worn at the right side. (ffoulkes Armourer 154).

ARM KNIFE. A small knife carried on the left arm near the shoulder by many Sudanese tribes. It has a blade about six inches long, straight and double-edged. A loop fastened to the scabbard passes around the arm and holds the knife in place. Fig. 27.

The Tuaregs carry a longer knife on the left wrist. See Telek.

ARMLET. Armlets are used as weapons in many parts of the world. The Tankuls of Assam wear heavy brass armlets with which they are said to strike crushing blows downwards. (Hodson 37).

"In addition to his other weapons a Tewarik usually wears a heavy stone ring on his right arm above his elbow. This weapon, if such it can be called, is intended to give greater weight to his arm when wielding sword or lance, and is also used, when he gets to close quarters and enfolds his enemy in a kind of bear's hug, to press against his head in order to crush in his temples." (King 272). 3, 4 fig. 28.

The Irengas of the Upper Nile wear disk-shaped arm rings, the sharp edges of which are covered with leather sheaths except when fighting. (Ratzel I, 100, 102). 1, fig. 28. Of a similar nature are the rings of their neighbors the Jurs, which are fitted with a pair of spikes. (Ratzel I, 100). 1, fig. 461.

The natives of the Nuhr and the Latookas (Central African tribes from the vicinity of Gondokoro) wear "an ugly iron bracelet armed with knife blades

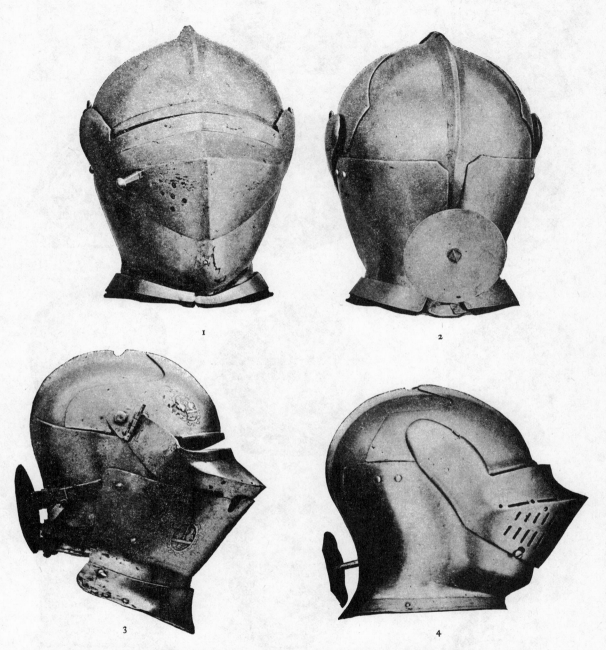

FIGURE 25. *Armets a Rondelles.* 1, 2. *Italian, about* 1480. 3. *Armet and buffe. Italian, about* 1475. *Arms of the Piombini family of Treviso.* 4. *Italian,* 1475-1500. *Metropolitan Museum. Not to scale.*

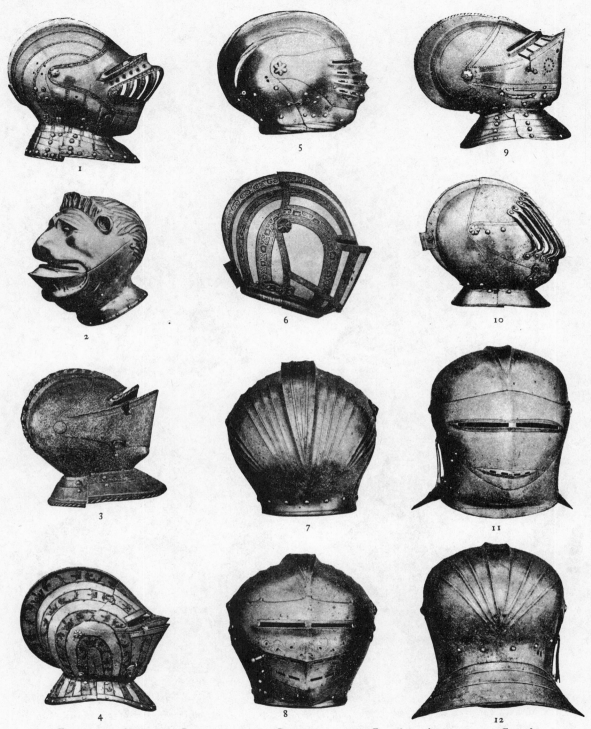

FIGURE 26. *Armets.* 1. *German,* 1540. 2. *German,* 1535. 3. *French,* 16th *century.* 4. *French,* 1600. 5. *German,* 1520. 6. *Italian,* 1580. 7-8. *German,* 1515. 9. *French,* 17th *century.* 10. *Pisan,* 17th *century.* 11-12. *German, about* 1500. *Metropolitan Museum. Not to scale.*

FIGURE 27. *Arm Knives. 1. Sudan. Blade 7.5 inches long, wood hilt. Red leather scabbard with a braided arm loop. 2. Blade 6.5 inches long, ebony hilt. Scabbard of black stamped leather with filigree silver mounts. 3. Sudan. Blade 7.75 inches long. Hilt and scabbard covered with stamped leather and snakeskin. 4. Sudan. Blade 4.875 inches long, wood hilt. Scabbard leather, with a flat arm loop. 5. Sudan. Blade and hilt forged in one piece, hilt covered with leather. Stamped leather scabbard and arm loop. 6. Sudan. Blade 6.5 inches long, wood hilt with cross guard. Scabbard of brown and white leather, round arm loop.*

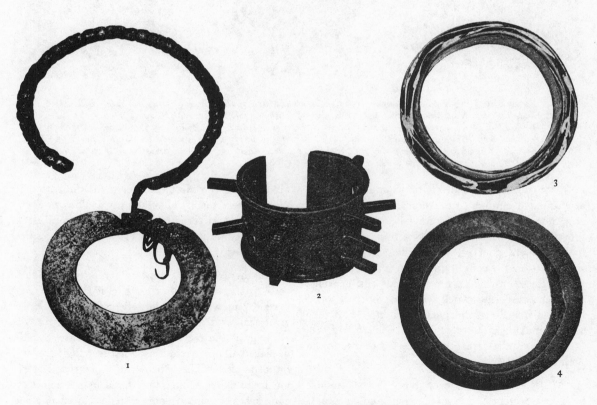

FIGURE 28. *Armlets. 1. Irenga, Upper Nile. Circular steel knife with a leather sheath covered with iron and brass. 2. Ouled Nail woman's fighting bracelet. Silver, 1.875 inches wide with 13 spikes three-sixteenths of an inch square and thirteen-sixteenths long. 3. Tuareg armlet of black and white obsidian. Inside diameter 3.375 inches. 4. Tuareg armlet of granite. Inside diameter 3.25 inches.*

about four inches long by half an inch broad; the latter is used to strike with if disarmed and to tear with when wrestling with an enemy." (Baket, Albert Nyanza 143). ". . . the men wear . . . a horrible kind of bracelet of massive iron with spikes about an inch in length, like leopard's claws, which they use for a similar purpose . . . He (the chief of the Neuhr) exhibited his wife's arms and back covered with jagged scars, in reply to my question as to the use of the spiked bracelet." (Baker, *loc. cit.* 42, 43).

The women of the Ouled nail, a North African Arab tribe, usually become prostitutes as soon as

has not gone equally far in all countries. The first armor was undoubtedly the skins of beasts, and such armor has been used within a very few years in the Philippines, 1, fig. 82. The next step was probably to fasten scales or rings of some harder material on it, fig. 29. In the earlier armor of this type the strengthening pieces were always put on the outside, later they were often riveted or quilted between layers of cloth or leather. This type of armor is called brigandine and was largely used in Europe from the 10th to the 16th century, at first for war and later as light armor. In China it has

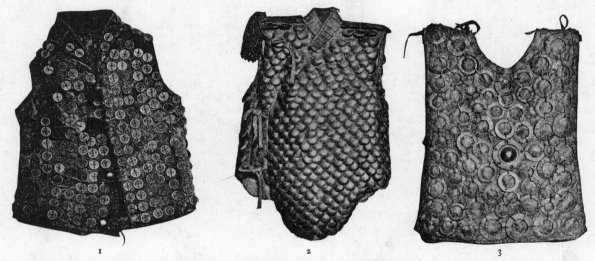

1   2   3

FIGURE 29. *Ring and Scale Armor. 1. Sitka, Alaska. Made of three layers of tanned hide hardened, and with the front and part of the back covered with modern Chinese and Japanese coins. U. S. N. M. No. 18,927. 2. Chinese corselet of brass scales sewed on heavy cotton cloth. 3. Corselet from northeastern Asia(?). The base is padded leather on which rings are fastened by narrow strips of leather. The center ornament and the three rings nearest to it are of brass, all of the others are of iron. The last two only are to scale.*

they are old enough and continue until they have accumulated enough to make an attractive dowry, and then marry and no stigma is attached to the life they have been leading. Not unnaturally they have frequent quarrels among themselves and on such occasions wear fighting bracelets until peace returns. These bracelets are wide bands of silver quite well decorated and armed with a number of spikes about an inch long and over an eighth of an inch square, making quite effective weapons. 2, fig. 28.

Even in India arm guards are sometimes found with semicircular knives on the wrists. 3, fig. 59.

ARMOR. Armor has been worn by all nations with any pretentions to civilization, and its evolution has been along the same lines everywhere, but

always been the most used form for the better armor. Where the art of weaving was known, armor made of pads covered with cloth, or of several thicknesses of cloth quilted together, was used even after scale armor was given up. Fig. 30.

Another very early type of armor was made of rods, or slats, of wood or bone lashed together with cord or sinew. It was largely used by the North American Indians and in Eastern Siberia, fig. 87. As soon as the metals became known they rapidly displaced all other materials wherever their cost was not prohibitive. The difficulty of making and working large pieces of metal confined its use at first to comparatively small plates fastened to each other, or to cloth or leather. Armor of this kind was very heavy as it was necessary to have the plates overlap to secure complete protection. The Greeks and Romans used bronze, but its use was restricted by the scarcity of the tin required to produce it. Mail, a fabric of interlaced links, is logically the next step rope and probably in the East. The most elaborate and complete armor of plate ever used was in Europe during the 15th and 16th centuries.

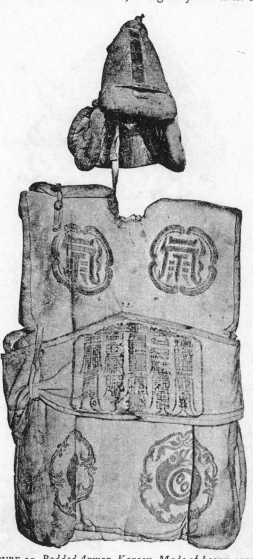

FIGURE 30. *Padded Armor. Korean. Made of heavy, coarse, brown cotton cloth padded to a thickness of about an inch and a half. The belt is a separate piece and less padded. The helmet is strapped with tinned iron and brass. The decorations are letters and scrolls stenciled in black.*

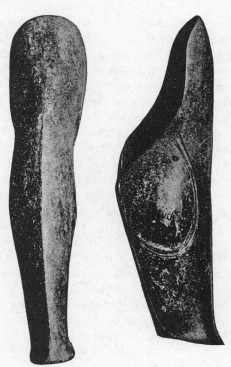

FIGURE 31. *Greek Greaves, probably 6th century* B.C. *Metropolitan Museum.*

FIGURE 32. *Greek Helmet, 6th-5th century* B.C. *Metropolitan Museum.*

and almost certainly antedates plate. Its very perishable nature has prevented much of early date from surviving, and our knowledge of early armor is too incomplete to enable us to be sure on this point. Certainly mail was worn before plate in Eu-

We have a fair knowledge of the armor of Greece and Rome. The former was very simple for the light troops, consisting of beautifully modeled greaves, fig. 31, which covered the legs from the knee to the ankle, a well modeled helmet, fig. 32, fitting closely to the head and leaving the face wholly or partly uncovered, and a huge shield. The heavy armed troops wore corselets in addition. Sometimes they were of bronze but, more often, of some form of ring or scale armor. The Roman armor was more elaborate and varied. It included body armor of most of the then known kinds. Bronze corselets for the officers and better armed troops, fig. 33. The arms and legs were generally unprotected. Some of the Roman helmets were very large with high and broad crests; but the legionaries probably wore helmets like 3, fig. 33. Shields were almost universal. They were of a great variety of shapes and sizes. The small ones were almost always round, and many of the larger ones also. Others were elliptical or rectangular, the latter often being curved to fit around the body.

The armor of the Northern Nations that overran Europe at the close of the Roman Empire approximated that of the Romans. But little of it remains and our knowledge of it is extremely fragmentary.

From the 10th to the 13th century mail was so prominent in Europe that this period is often called the "Age of Mail," not that other forms of armor were not used, for padded, scale and ring armor were far more common, but the higher classes wore mail almost exclusively. Fig. 34. See also Mail. The helmets of this time were the only part of the equipment regularly made of plate. They were heavy pots worn only when fighting, being ordinarily car-

FIGURE 35. *Norman Helmet, 11th century. Metropolitan Museum.*

ried at the saddle bow. The head was covered by a padded hood, then by a hood of mail, and over these the helmet. The earliest helmets were pointed and either left the face entirely unprotected, or had a bar, the nasal, projecting downwards in front of the nose. This was the Norman helmet, fig. 35.

1   2   3

FIGURE 33. *Roman Armor.* 1. *Body armor, 7th century* B.C. 2. *Body armor, 4th-3rd century* B.C.
3. *Helmet, 4th-3rd century* B.C. *Metropolitan Museum. Not to scale.*

FIGURE 34. *Armor of the Age of Mail, after Shaw.* 1. *Spanish warriors of the latter part of the 11th century. From a manuscript in the British Museum.* 2. *A knight of the 12th century. He wears a complete suit of mail, partly covered by a surcoat ornamented with crosses. His helmet is held above his head by an attendant.* 3. *Knights fighting, from a manuscript of the middle of the 13th century.* 4. *Effigy of Charles D'Estampes in the Royal catacombs at St. Denis. Charles comte D'Estampes was killed at the siege of Pimorain September 5, 1336. The style of armor in the effigy is of rather earlier date than his death.*

During the 12th century the helmets were made larger with curved sides and flat tops. Because of their shape these were called barrel helms. A little later these were abandoned for the sugar-loaf helms

The hauberk had skirts reaching to the feet and was split up, back and front, for use on horseback. The sleeves were long enough to cover the hands. Mail gauntlets were sometimes worn. The com-

1   2

FIGURE 36. *Transition Armor.* 1. *Brigandine of large plates covered with velvet, mail with much plate on the arms and legs. Metropolitan Museum.* 2. *Plate and mail about 1450. Higgins Armory, Worcester. Not to scale.*

with pointed tops which caused a blow to glance instead of being transmitted to the head. The entire weight of all of these helmets rested on the head. The higher classes wore a heavily padded garment, the gambeson, and over it the hauberk of mail.

mon soldier wore the gambeson as the sole protection of his body.

In the next, or Transition Period (1277-1410), padded and scale armor as well as mail were still worn, but the latter was reinforced by plate, fig. 36.

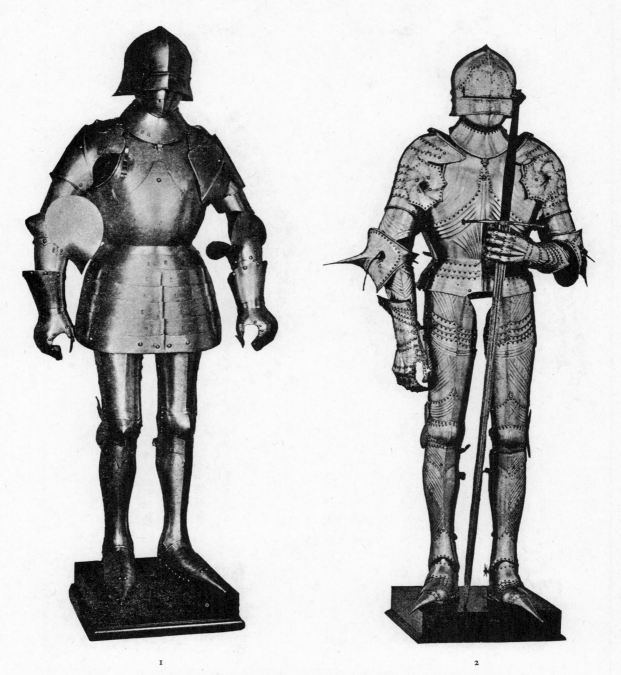

1   2

FIGURE 37. *Gothic Armor. 1. Italian of about 1460. It is one of the earliest complete suits
known and was made by the Missaglia of Milan. It is homogeneous, except that the salade
is of German rather than Italian type. 2. German, latter part of the 15th century. It is of
flamboyant gothic and extremely elaborate. Metropolitan Museum. Not to scale.*

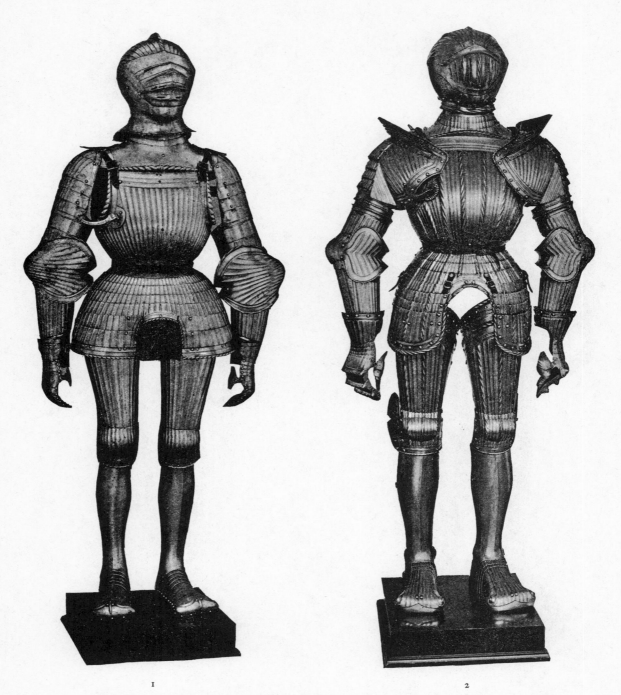

FIGURE 38. *Maximilian Armor.* 1. *Nuremberg, 1510-1525.* 2. *Milan, 1525. Metropolitan Museum. Not to scale.*

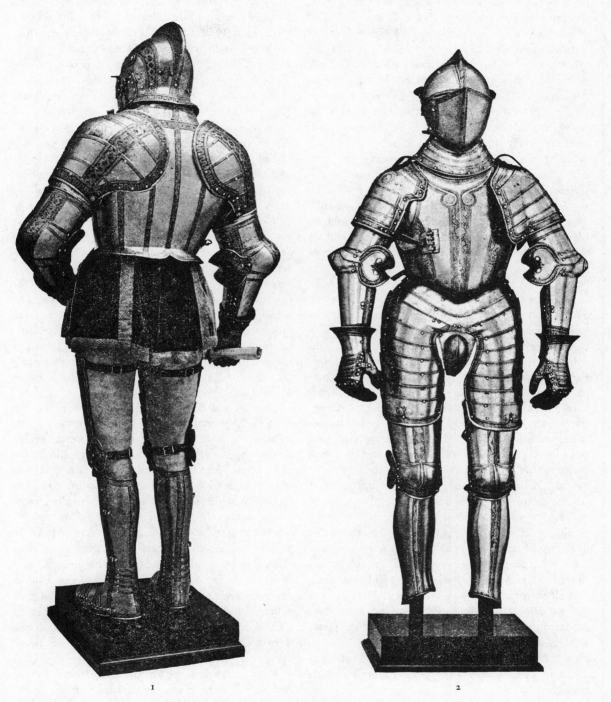

FIGURE 39. *Armor of the 16th century.* 1. *English, made for Sir James Scudamore by Jacobe.* 2. *German. Metropolitan Museum. Not to scale.*

Brigandines of large plates were often worn in place of hauberks. The first additions of plate were the knee cops, the next the wing-like guards, called ailettes, worn on the shoulders. By the end of the 13th century the entire leg below the knee was frequently covered by plate or boiled leather. The addition of plates gradually proceeded until, by the beginning of the 15th century, the entire person was protected by it except for the openings at the joints, which were only covered by gussets of mail fastened to the undergarments. The great heaume worn at this time rested on the shoulders and was often fastened to the backplate by a hasp and staple. These large helmets gradually gave way to the lighter pointed basinets which had capes of mail (the camail) attached which covered the shoulders. Some left the face bare, some had flaps of mail on the camail which could be hooked up at the forehead covering all of the face but the eyes, others had movable plate visors. See Basinet.

Complete armor of plate was in use at the beginning of the 15th century, and during the next hundred years reached its greatest perfection. This was the period of Gothic armor (frontispiece and fig. 37) which for beauty of form, dignity and perfect adaptation to its purpose has never been surpassed at any time or in any country. Every detail was carefully studied, and any change that increased the efficiency was worked out with painstaking care. It was for this purpose that the two sides were made quite unlike each other to adapt them to the different functions of the right, or sword, arm and those of the left, or bridle, arm. The breastplate was made in two or more pieces overlapping in a long point and connected by straps or sliding rivets, thus giving a certain amount of flexibility. The feet were covered by laminated solerets with long, pointed toes which could be removed when the wearer was on foot. The shoulder and elbow cops were very large in order to guard the openings at the joints, and the hands were covered by mitten gauntlets. The thickness of the plates was regulated for the strains they would have to bear; not only did the different pieces vary but different parts of the same plate differed considerably in thickness.

In the early part of the century the heaume was still worn, but it soon gave way to the lighter basinet, with or without a visor; this, in turn, was displaced by the chapel de fer and the salade. The most popular helmets were the deep salades with fixed or movable visors. These were either of the Italian form (barbute or celata) which fitted closely to the head and neck; or of the German which projected backwards in a rather long tail.

For light armor brigandines of plates covered with cloth were frequently worn, figs. 36, 190.

Towards the end of the 15th century heavy ridges were often placed around the armpits and the upper edges of the breastplate, and fluting became common. The compact, closed armet displaced the heavier and less efficient chapel de fer and salade, and the use of a greater number of articulated plates did away with the necessity of the very large guards formerly worn at the joints.

By the beginning of the 16th century these changes resulted in the elaborately fluted type of armor known as Maximilian, fig. 38. It is characterized by radiating fluted channels, generally spreading from a point on the breastplate, and by the more rounded outlines of all of its parts. The breastplates became more globose and the feet were protected by broad-toed sabatons instead of pointed solerets. The Maximilian armor is fine though rather clumsy and lacks the dignified simplicity and thoroughbred air of the Gothic. The Maximilian period lasted from about 1500 to 1540.

During, and for some time after, this period the design of the armor showed much of the Gothic influence and the best suits of the 16th century are extremely fine. Fig. 39. The armor gradually became more complicated in construction and was often decorated by embossing, etching and fire gilding, all of which impaired its defensive value. Some of the suits were made of an immense number of pieces elaborately articulated together so as to completely enclose the wearer, and at the same time allow him the full use of all of his muscles and joints. The two most elaborate suits of this kind in existence are the Genouilhac armor in the Metropolitan Museum, fig. 40, and the suit of Henry VIII for fighting on foot in the lists, now in the Tower of London. Each is a marvel of mechanical design and construction.

Even in the early part of the 16th century armor was occasionally made for parade, without, however, losing its efficiency as a protection. The suit, fig. 41, is a remarkable example of this type. It is elaborate to grotesqueness but its excessive ornamentation does not sensibly decrease its usefulness.

The half suit, fig. 42, is a particularly good example of the parade armor of the middle of the 16th century. It is superbly decorated but the plates are light and have been seriously weakened by the frequent annealing necessitated by the excessive embossing.

FIGURE 40. *This magnificent suit was made in 1527 for the Sieur Jacques Gourdon de Genouilhac, who commanded the French artillery at the battle of Pavia under Francis I. He was a very large man; when the picture was taken the armor was worn by a man over six feet tall and weighing over 225 pounds, and it was much too large for him. It is made of an immense number of plates flexibly connected to permit of easy movement. The entire surface is covered with etched designs and gilded. In places where the plates were protected from wear the gilding is as fresh as when first put on. Many of the reinforcing pieces for tilting are still with it; others have disappeared as the attachments for them show. Metropolitan Museum.*

FIGURE 41. *Parade Armor. German, about 1520. It is a marvelous example of forging and is probably the finest suit of its kind in existence. Metropolitan Museum.*

Special types were evolved such as the pikeman's armor, fig. 43, which continued in use as long as armor was worn. It consisted of an open headpiece, a sort of chapel de fer, and a back and breast with very wide bell-shaped taces worn over a buff coat. This suit is an unusually elaborate one and undoubtedly belonged to the guard of some prince.

The war armor became simpler and more clumsy and the parade armor more overdecorated and useless, fig. 44. These changes in the character of the armor were undoubtedly due mainly to the changes in tactics which gave greater importance to the infantry, and to masses of men, and less to the individual cavalier who had been the most important factor heretofore. The greater use of firearms and their increasing force and range made it impossible for a man to carry the weight of armor necessary

FIGURE 43. *Pikeman's armor, English, about* 1610. *Metropolitan Museum.*

for complete protection, and it was lightened by discarding the less essential parts. The armor for the leg below the knee was the first to be abandoned, fig. 45, next that for the arms, then the thigh pieces were shortened, and finally given up. The breast and back remained in use for some time longer; but at last they were dropped and nothing remained but the gorget and, sometimes, the helmet. The closed helmets had practically disappeared by the end of the 16th century and a great variety of open ones took their place.

The armor worn at tournaments was rarely the same as that used in battle after the end of the 14th

FIGURE 42. *Parade Armor. Half armor made for the Duke of Sessa. Milanese work of about* 1560. *The rondache is Italian of about* 1600. *Metropolitan Museum.*

FIGURE 44. *Late Armor. 1. German, about 1590. Bands of elaborate etched work separated by broad bands of blued steel. 2. German, "black and white" suit, 17th century. Metropolitan Museum. Not to scale.*

century. In the 15th century the ordinary armor was frequently adapted for the tournament by adding extra pieces which were put on over the regular suit; but special armor for jousting was also made that was totally unlike anything worn in battle. The jousting helmets were often of the type of the heaume, but heavier. They were very large with only a narrow slit across the upper part to see through, below this the face guard projected in a sharp ridge to deflect the lance. They rested on the shoulders and were solidly bolted to the breastplate. The most typical form was made of three pieces

closed the door, and went it blind. These openings were always on the right side because in jousting at the barrier, the most popular form, it was not possible to hit the right side of the head with the lance.

The breastplates were frequently unsymmetrical, projecting on the right side in a square "box" to carry the rest to support the heavy lance, fig. 48. A special form, fig. 49, was used in some forms of joust. In it the legs were uncovered as the barrier protected them. For other forms of joust the thighs were covered by large plates fastened to the saddle,

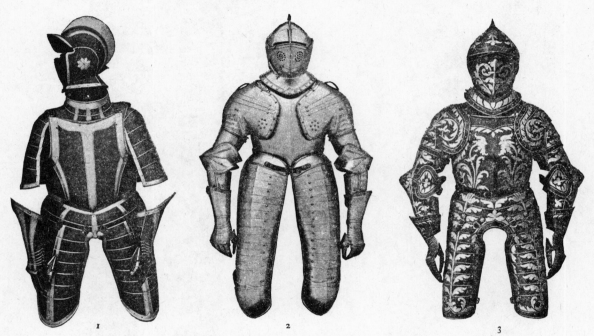

FIGURE 45. *Three-Quarter Suits.* 1. *German, about* 1570. 2. *French, about* 1580. 3. *German, about* 1590. *Metropolitan Museum. Not to scale.*

riveted together with the opening for the neck large enough to go over the head, fig. 46. A heavy padded leather hood was first laced on the jouster's head. It covered both head and neck and had only sufficient opening to allow the wearer to see and breathe. Leather straps were fastened to the hood and passed through holes in the helmet and tied on the outside so as to prevent the helmet from touching the head, no matter how much the wearer was knocked about. Some tilting helmets had an opening on the right that was guarded by a projecting flange, 1, fig. 47. Others had an opening closed by a hinged door, 2, fig. 47. The wearer took a look,

fig. 458. There were many different forms of tournament and each required special armor, so that a complete suit for war and the tournament sometimes had as many as a hundred extra pieces to adapt it for the various forms of combat in the lists.

It is comparatively easy to determine the age of a piece of European armor, as the patterns were constantly changing and many specimens are in existence. The old pictures are also of great assistance as the artists invariably dressed their characters in the style of armor worn at the time the picture was painted regardless of the time it represented. A person familiar with European armor can usually date

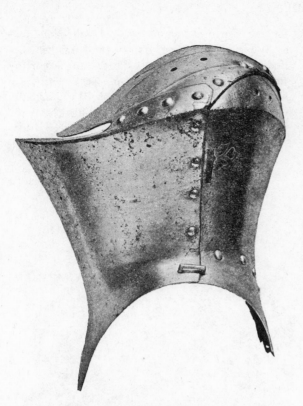

FIGURE 46. *Jousting Helm, German, end of the 15th century. Metropolitan Museum.*

FIGURE 48. *Jousting Armor with "box" breastplate, German, about 1500. Metropolitan Museum.*

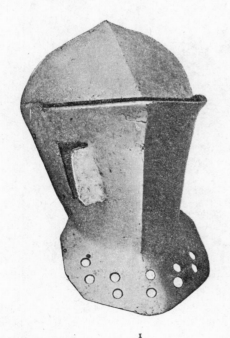

1

2

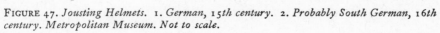

FIGURE 47. *Jousting Helmets. 1. German, 15th century. 2. Probably South German, 16th century. Metropolitan Museum. Not to scale.*

it within ten to fifteen years. It is quite different with Oriental armor; the styles changed very seldom and the same types were worn for centuries with only slight variations in decoration. There are no adequate collections and but few pictures. Most of the great fighting races of the East are Mohammedans and their religion, if they are orthodox, forbids their making a picture of any living thing. The Persians are not orthodox and did make pictures, but they are conventional and all show the same types of armor regardless of the time or place represented. Their descriptions are always figurative and it does not help much to read, for instance, that a certain warrior was dressed in armor "like the shining full moon." An exception must be made for the Japanese who have fine collections and many pictures showing the armor of different periods with great accuracy. There are also many Japanese books on arms and armor, several of which have been translated into English. The difficulty with Japanese is the danger of getting lost in the maze of words. They have names for every slightest variation in every detail of each thing and the differences are often so slight that they are almost impossible to recognize. This is particularly bad as every character can be written in from two to four ways and each can be translated in from two to four ways. When there are pictures there is very little difficulty; but when there are not there is often much.

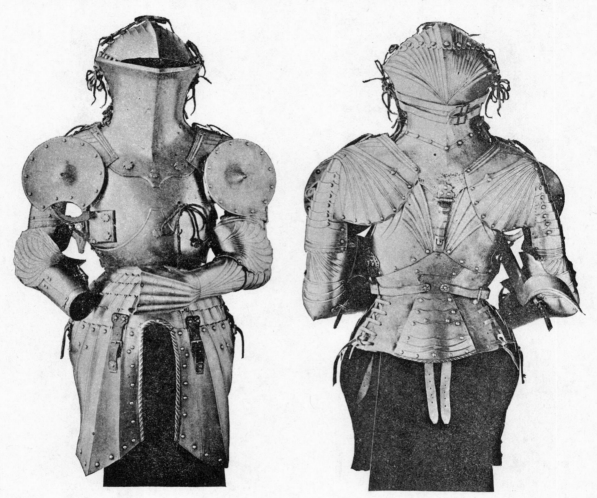

FIGURE 49. *German Gothic jousting armor, about 1500. It shows the cords for holding the padded cap in the helmet and also those for fastening the tilting shield on the breastplate. Collection of Dr. Bashford Dean.*

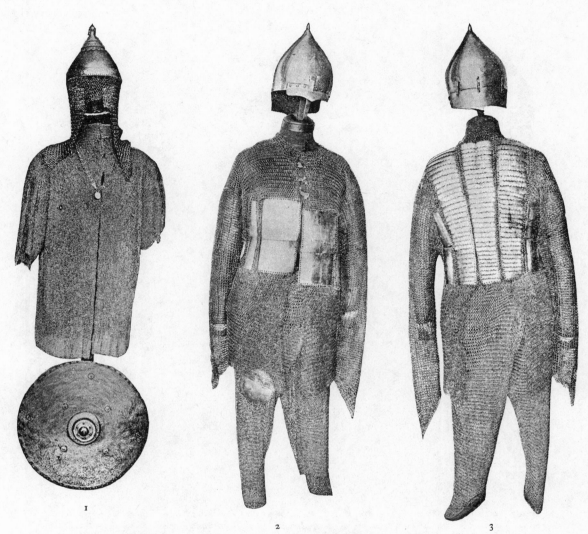

FIGURE 50. *Turkish Armor. 1. Shirt of fine riveted mail with the collar and chest of double mail. Pointed steel helmet with a neck guard of heavy riveted mail. The cap and band of silver decorated with niello have probably been added later. The suit and the shield of engraved steel are all of the 15th century. 2, 3. Back and front of a suit of about 1600. Coat of heavy riveted mail with four large plates on the front and rows of small ones with scalloped edges on the back. Legs of riveted mail with large round plates at the knees. Conical helmet with a hinged plate neck guard, the ear guards are missing.*

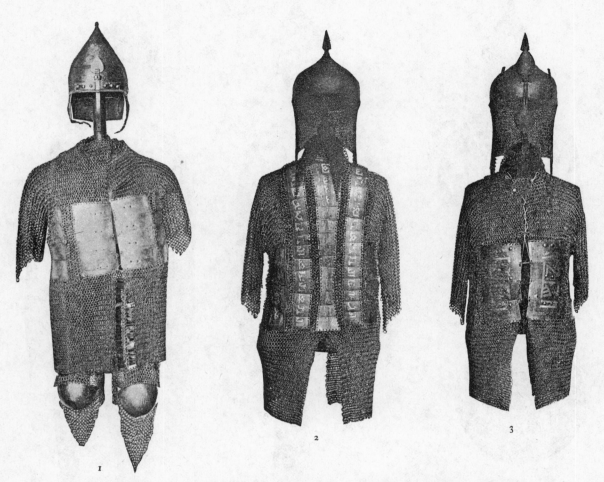

FIGURE 51. *Turkish Armor, 16th century. 1. Plates engraved and inlaid with silver, connected by riveted mail. Conical helmet with plate ear and neck guards, engraved, gilded and bound with silver. 2, 3. Body of plates connected by riveted mail. The plates are engraved and inlaid with cufic inscriptions in silver. Large turban helmet with gold inscriptions in cartouches.*

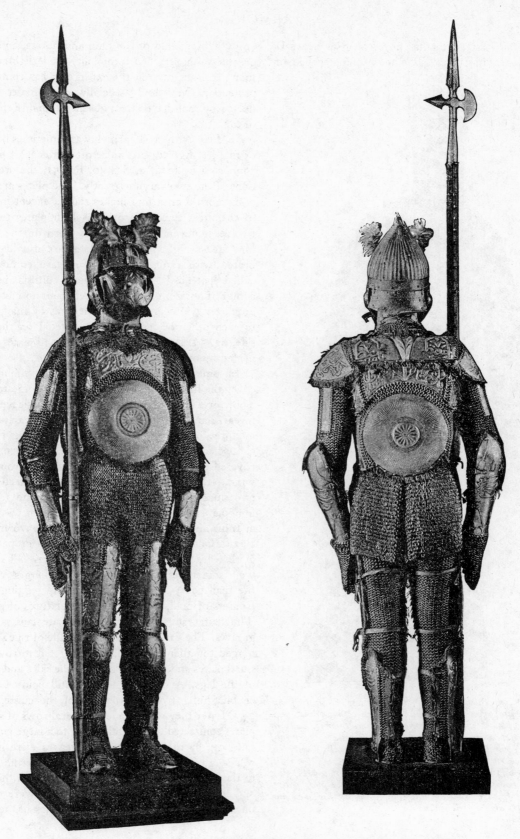

FIGURE 52. *Turkish Armor ("Pot lids"). Turkey, 16th century. All of the plates are embossed in high relief. Reale Armeria di Torino.*

In the East armor has never been as heavy or complete as in Europe. The hotter climate, the gen-

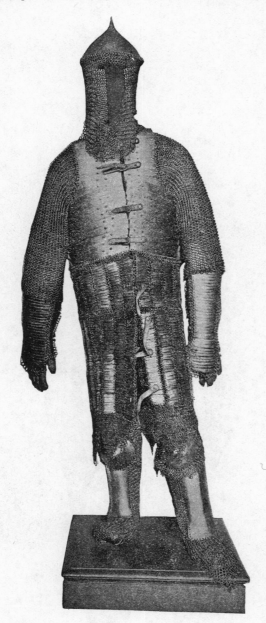

FIGURE 53. *Turkish Armor, 15th century. Helmet of one piece with four ridges running to a projecting point; neck guard of mail hung by clevises with rosette ends. Body of horizontal lames riveted to straps on the inside; short mail sleeves; skirts of small plates connected by mail. Vambraces of three rows of overlapping plates connected by mail. Cuisses of two hinged plates and two rows of overlapping plates, conical knee cops. Greaves of a single plate covering the front of the leg, and mail covering the back and foot. All of the mail is riveted.*

erally lighter build of the men and horses, and the greater value attached to mobility made lighter armor necessary even at the expense of less complete protection. Mail and especially small plates connected by mail have always been the main reliance of the East.

In Turkey the body armor was sometimes a shirt of mail, 1, fig. 50, but more often a coat of plates connected by mail, 2, fig. 50, fig. 51, the proportions of the two varying greatly. The plates are seldom more than a few inches square except in one of the most typical forms in which plates ten or twelve inches in diameter were worn on the back and breast, fig. 52. These plates are usually decorated with radiating flutes, and are commonly called "pot-lids." A very early form consists of body armor of horizontal strips of steel about an inch and a quarter wide connected at the ends by mail, and to each other by leather straps riveted on the inside, fig. 53. It has a skirt of many small plates connected by mail and short mail sleeves.

In some suits the mail sleeves are long enough to cover the hands, more often they only come to the elbow or a little above it. With the short sleeves the forearm and hand were protected in the early suits by three or five lines of small overlapping plates connected by mail. Later the outside of the arm was covered by a single curved plate reaching from the wrist to the elbow, while the wrist was protected by two small plates joined to each other and to the long plate by mail. This style of arm guard was used in India and Persia as long as armor was worn. See Bazu Band. Gauntlets of mail, scales or padded cloth were attached to these arm pieces. The legs were sometimes covered only by the long skirts of the mail coat; sometimes by separate leggings, or trousers of mail, with or without mixtures of plate. The better suits usually had separate cuisses and greaves. The earlier cuisses were made of two plates hinged together in front and connected to rows of small plates and mail that covered the sides and back of the legs. A conical knee cop and pointed mail curtain hung from the bottom of the cuisse, fig. 247. Later they were made of several rows of small plates connected to each other and to a large curved knee cop by mail. The earlier greaves were made of a single plate reaching from just below the knee to the instep, and mail covering the back of the leg and foot. Later, apparently, two plates were used, one at the front and the other at the back of the leg.

FIGURE 54. *Turkish "turban" helmets, 15th century. Metropolitan Museum of Art*

FIGURE 55. *Turkish Helmets, 15th to 17th century. The two in the middle originally had mail neck guards; the others had hinged plates like the second on the left. All had sliding nasals.*

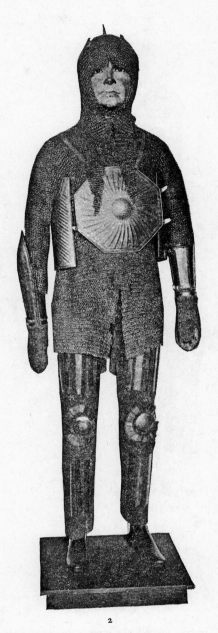

1

2

FIGURE 56. *Indian and Persian Armor.* 1. *Mogul officer's suit, 18th century. Coat of plates and mail with very long sleeves to cover the hands. Four plates in front, four on each side and three lines of scales down the back. Lined throughout with quilted and padded green silk. Helmet of plates and mail with a mail neck guard; very large silver plated nasal. The edges of the neck guard and the mail of the helmet were covered with red velvet. All mail riveted. 2. Persian, 17th-18th century. Bowl-shaped helmet with a mail neck guard. The arm guards and the char aina are fluted and they, and the helmet, have borders of inscriptions inlaid in gold. The shirt is of mail. The legs, which are of later date, are made up of many small plates elaborately inlaid with gold and connected by fine mail. All of the mail is riveted.*

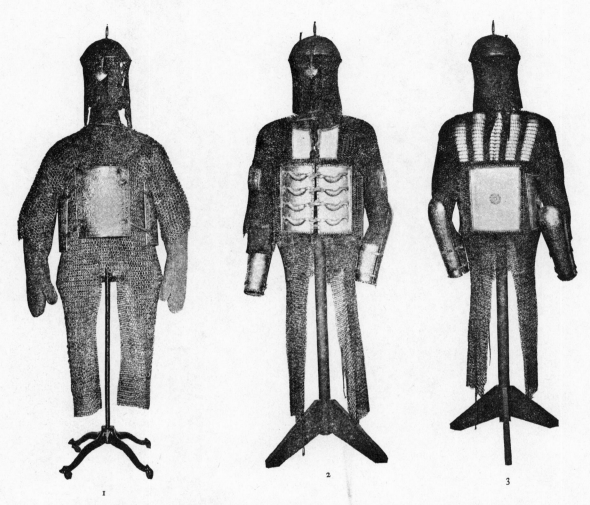

FIGURE 57. *Indian Armor. 1. Northern India, 17th-18th century. Shirt of double riveted mail with each link stamped with an inscription and the reverse side with concentric rings. Weight 23 pounds. Helmet and char aina of steel covered with an arabesque pattern in relief. Steel and brass neck guard. Elbow length gauntlets of bar-link mail over heavy pads of striped silk. 2, 3. Front and back of a Central Indian suit. Body of plates and mail with long skirts to cover the legs. The links on the shoulders are very heavy and graduate to very light ones at the ends of the skirts. The strings for tieing the mail around the legs are still attached. Sleeves of copper bar-link mail with silver plates with Hindu gods in high relief on the upper arms. There are five body plates with moulded silver borders. The two large plates in front each have four silver fish in high relief with rings in their mouths for the straps. The back plate has a silver rosette in the center. The helmet and arm guards are of steel inlaid with gold in a flower pattern carved in relief.*

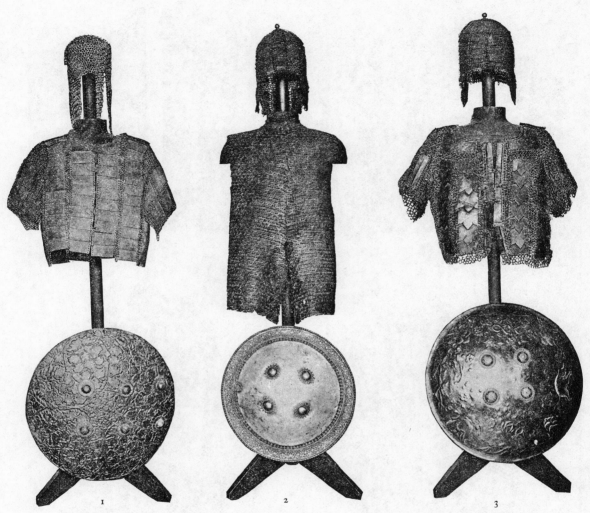

FIGURE 58. *Indian Half Suits.* 1. *Hood of heavy riveted mail with four short chains hanging from the crown. Coat of rectangular plates connected by riveted mail. Persian hide shield 20.5 inches in diameter with six bosses and three handles so that it can be carried on the arm or held in the hand. It is carved with a flower pattern in low relief and colored green on a brown ground.* 2. *Mogul helmet of overlapping scalloped scales and riveted mail. Heavy mail chin strap. Body; shoulders of riveted mail, remainder of hexagonal plates connected by riveted rings, leaving no openings between. Steel shield 17.75 inches in diameter with an applied openwork border of gilded copper, four bosses and inlaid ornaments at the center. It is lined with red velvet with patterns in gilt studs.* 3. *Helmet of small, pierced plates and riveted mail. It has ear tabs but no neck guard. Short coat of elaborately scalloped plates and bands of riveted mail. Hooks and eyes are forged on the front plates for fastening. Hide shield 20.75 inches in diameter, Shakpura Rajestan. It has four silver bosses and is painted with hunting scenes in lac, partly in relief. Painted border around the inside.*

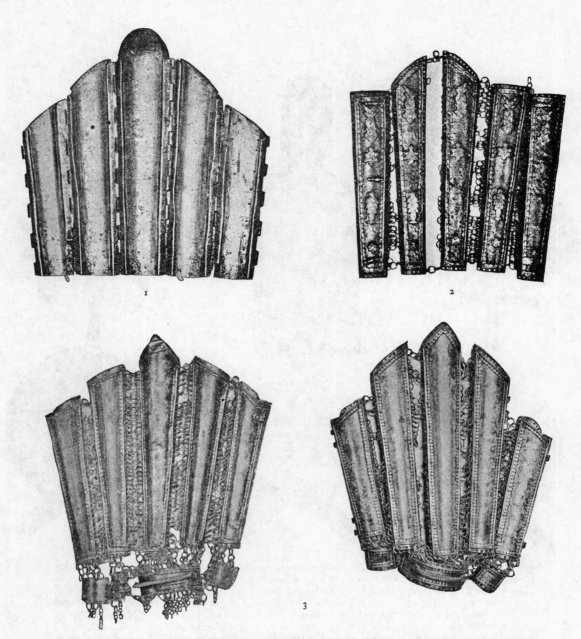

FIGURE 59. *Indian Splinted Arm Guards.* 1. *Five plates hinged together and inlaid with inscriptions in silver.* 2. *Five plates connected by mail and decorated with applied brass ornaments.* 3. *A pair. Five arm plates and three wrist plates with brass borders, all connected by mail. One wrist plate has a curved knife on it, the other has a roped bar.*

The earliest helmets were conical with plate, mail or padded neck guards. From the 14th to the 16th century the helmets were often very large and elaborately fluted and decorated, fig. 54. They were worn over turbans and were called "turban helmets." Overlapping these in time and continuing in use later were ogival, ogee and conical helmets, fig. 55. The latest Turkish armor was essentially the same as that worn in Persia and India. The helmet nos. 2, 3, fig. 51, is intermediate in form between the "turban helmets" and the Persian.

The horse armor included chanfrons, fig. 214, of a single plate covering the front of the head with cheek pieces of a single plate or of a number of small ones. The crinets and body armor were made up of a large number of very small plates connected by mail. Fig. 124.

We have no very accurate knowledge of the armor worn in India and Persia prior to the 17th century. Apparently the earliest types were padded, scale and brigandine armor as in Europe. These gradually gave way to mail and mixed plate and mail; and at the time of which we first have definite examples there were several varieties, all of which were used as long as armor was worn. The body was protected by mail alone, or by small plates connected by mail. In the north one of the commonest forms of body armor was a long coat of mail with plates four to six inches square on the breast, and with the back covered with small overlapping plates. The skirts were generally long enough to cover the legs and the sleeves reached to the wrists or even covered the hands. Such suits were worn over padded garments, or had padded linings permanently fixed in them, 1, fig. 56. Rough suits of this kind were used by Mogul troopers, and better ones by the officers. The helmets worn with them were frequently made of many small plates connected by mail, 1, fig. 56, 2, 3, fig. 58. Another very common style, which was worn throughout India and Persia, was a coat, or shirt, of mail over which four plates, the char aina, were hung, 2, fig. 56, 1, fig. 57. The front and back plates were generally rectangular, occasionally octagonal, and the side plates were also rectangular but with the tops cut away to give room under the arms. When the front plate was unusually large it was also sometimes cut out at the neck. Often the plates were directly connected to the mail instead of being

hung over it by straps, 2, 3, fig. 57. Half suits of small plates of a great variety of shapes and sizes connected by mail were also worn, fig. 58.

The arms were protected in a variety of ways. Frequently the mail sleeves were long enough to cover them, sometimes they even reached beyond the fingers. Usually the mail sleeves only came to the elbow and the forearms were protected by plate bazu bands which had gauntlets of mail, scales

FIGURE 60. *Indian leg plates of blued steel with gold inlaid borders. They have holes around the edges so that they can be attached to mail chausses.*

or pourpointerie connected to them. Occasionally gauntlets of mail, or of splints connected by mail, were worn, fig. 59.

The legs were often unprotected; but generally the skirts of the hauberk were long enough to cover them. They were split up for use on horseback and tied around the legs. When the skirts were short separate mail chausses were sometimes worn, 1, 3, fig. 61. The mail legs were generally two separate pieces that covered the front and outside of the leg from the waist to the ankle and the inside also below the knee; occasionally they were joined in front of mail, 1, 3, fig. 61. These suits frequently have patterns worked in brass or copper links, 1, fig. 61. Usually these patterns are geometrical, but occasionally they are inscriptions in Arabic characters,

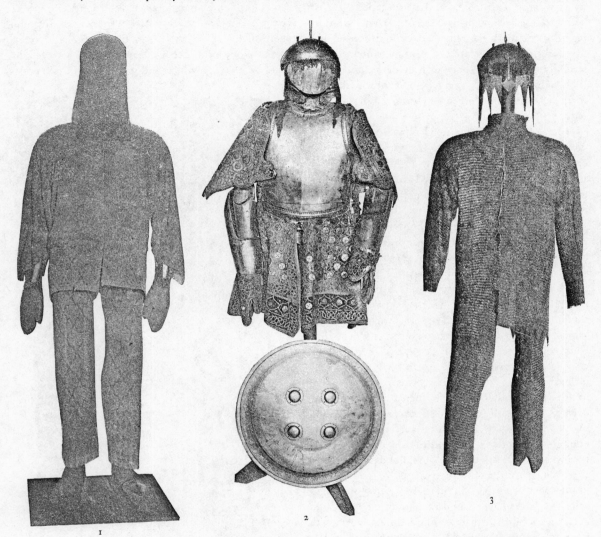

FIGURE 61. *Indian Suits. 1. Central India, 18th century. Suit of ganga-jamni mail, open links with patterns in brass and copper links. The shoes and bars on the wrist plates of the gauntlets are inlaid with gold. 2. Central India, 18th century. Steel helmet, arm guards and shield of the usual types inlaid with gold. The breast and back of European patterns are similarly inlaid and have borders of pierced and gilded brass. The shoulder guards and skirts are of heavily padded red velvet with gilt studs and small round plates. 3. Central India, 17th century. Coat and chausses of bar-link mail. The lower edge of the coat is vandyked with brass links, and the back has two rows of small plates. The helmet is plain and the links of the neck guard are riveted though less than ⅛ of an inch in diameter.*

for a few inches below the belt. Rarely plates were worked into the mail to give additional protection to the fronts of the thighs and shins, fig. 60.

Other suits, helmets and all, were made entirely fig. 543. These decorated pieces of mail are called Ganga-Jamni, and typify the meeting of the dark waters of the Jamna with the muddy ones of the Ganges. The links of the suits so decorated are never riveted. The helmets may be open hoods, with or without sliding nasals, or have a movable flap of mail with which the entire face can be covered. The movable flap always has a pocket in the middle so as not to press too hard on the nose.

In some cases the entire body is protected by a garment made up of small plates with just enough mail to connect them, 1, fig. 58. Solid backs and

FIGURE 62. *Indian Armor. Mogul helmet inlaid with gold; with a mail neck guard and* three *sliding nasals. Arm guards of russet steel inlaid with gold, gauntlets of quilted green jazerant work. Lahore. Remainder of suit Rajput. Leather lined with quilted kincob, and faced with green velvet with gilt studs. The plates are of bright steel with the borders inlaid with gold. The belt, kamr, is of leather covered with velvet embroidered with gold. The sword, khanda, and its belt are Mahratta. All but the kamr are of the 18th century. Wallace Collection nos. 1789 to 1794.*

FIGURE 63. *Armor, Sind 18th century. The entire suit is of steel plates with applied brass borders embossed, and alternate rows of steel and brass scales, except the arm guards which are of plate with applied brass decoration.*

breasts copied from European forms, or even of European make, were worn during the 17th century and later. With these the upper part of the arms

FIGURE 64. *Indian Helmets.* 1. *Three plates connected by mail. Riveted mail neck guard.* 2. *Steel, made of three pieces riveted together and decorated with very crude engraved designs. Strong European influence.* 3. *Similar to no. 1, but it has a sliding nasal and padded cloth ear and neck guards.* 4. *Central India. Steel "turban" helmet with a very large sliding nasal and plate ear and neck guards.* 5. *Mahratta, 17th century. Steel, the lower part gilded.* 6. *Steel and brass. Evidently copied from a Scotch bonnet but made to be worn wrong side before. It has rings for the attachment of ear and neck guards.* 7. *Northern India, 17th-18th century. Padded red velvet lined with mail.* 8. *Similar to no. 7, but it has a much longer neck guard and a large, silver plated nasal.*

FIGURE 65. *Helmets, Caucasus, 18th century.* 1. *Flat steel crown and a long neck guard of riveted mail with an opening for the face.* 2. *Conical steel crown partly covered by a silver plate with a gilded border. Long neck guard of riveted mail that covers the entire face.*

and legs were generally covered with pads of velvet decorated with gilt studs, 2, fig. 61. Entire suits were also made of this kind of pourpointerie, usually with metal plates inserted at important points, fig. 62.

FIGURE 66. *Tibetan Armor. Helmet of eight overlapping plates and a knob on the top, all laced together with strips of leather. The neck guard and body armor are made of small iron scales laced together; the bottom of the skirt is formed of leather flaps. This is the earliest type of Tibetan armor, and was formerly called "willow leaf."*

In Sind very elaborate suits were worn. They were made up of many small plates framed with brass mouldings and decorated with embossed brass ornaments; in parts rows of decorated, overlapping scales, alternately of iron and brass, were sub-

stituted for the plates; all were connected by mail. The helmets, gauntlets and shoes were of the same construction. Fig. 63.

The Persian armor was similar to much of the Indian but seldom had such large admixtures of plate, except on the legs. The Persians made leg armor of mail with a great number of small plates arranged in patterns, 2, fig. 56, which are different from anything used in India. They rarely used any but the bowl-shaped helmets with spiked tops,

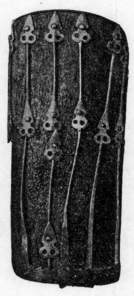

FIGURE 67. *Tibetan arm guard of leather strapped with iron.*

small nasals and chain neck guards. The Persians were the best armorers in the East and worked not only in their own country but also in Turkey and India.

The commonest helmet in India and Persia was the *top* (India) or *kulah khud* (Persia). It is bowl-shaped, either low and flat, or high and pointed, usually with a spike on the top and two or three plume holders on the front. It has a sliding nasal with both ends expanded into plates. When not in use the nasal could be fastened up out of the way by a link and hook, or by a set screw. The helmet shown in fig. 62 is remarkable in having three of these sliding bars, one in front of the nose, and one on each temple. In some of the Indian helmets the lower end of the nasal is enormously enlarged in a crescent so that it covers most of the face below the eyes, 1, fig. 56, and 4, fig. 64. The neck guards may be of padded cloth, but are usually of mail, sometimes riveted but generally of open links with patterns in brass and copper links. They are very short over the forehead, moderately short over the shoulders, and come down in long points at the sides in front and all across the back. They vary greatly in details and decoration but are recognizably of the same type. Other helmets are hoods,

Shields, *sipar* (Persia), *dhal* (India), were universally used. They were made of steel or hide, occasionally of several thicknesses of cloth and vary greatly in size, see Dhal. Some of the early Persian shields were made of concentric rings of cane with silk woven over them in patterns. In Malabar and

FIGURE 68. *Armor of Sikkim and Bhutan. Steel helmet with a knob and peak both engraved and gilded. The neck and ear flaps are of heavily lined brocade. Riveted mail shirt with the collar covered with red flannel and stiffened by leather lacings. Four circular plates cn the breast, sides and back. They are of steel lined with leather; each has a border of the Greek fret and an ornament in the center of two crossed vajras in a circle, all engraved and gilded. Belt of overlapping strips of steel with raised edges; all riveted to leather straps.*

usually of mail, which is occasionally padded and covered with velvet, 7, 8, fig. 64. A number of other forms are occasionally found, some of which are shown in fig. 64.

FIGURE 70. *Koryak Armor, western Siberia. The helmet and body armor are made of strips of steel laced together. The wide pieces protecting the back and neck are of wood covered with leather. American Museum of Natural History.*

the south the shields are more conical and have handles of wood or iron.

Horse armor was rarely used. The few chanfrons that are known are made of steel and approximate the European forms. The body armor was probably made mainly of leather. There are two complete suits of Tibetan horse armor in the India Museum, South Kensington, fig. 125, that show a mixture of Indian and Chinese forms. They probably give a fair idea of the general appearance of the horse armor of southern and eastern Asia.

The main difference in the armor of different parts of India is in the decoration and not in the forms, although certain places have characteristic types. In the north the arm guards have rounded ends like the Persian, further south they become more pointed, and still further south the end turns out and often has a knob on it. See Bazu Band.

fig. 66, which is much like the prehistoric Japanese armor. The helmet is made of eight well forged plates, four plain, and four with scalloped edges and raised ribs, that overlap the others and are laced to them. There is a small round plate with a knob on it at the crown. The neck guard, like the body armor, is made of small round-ended scales laced together with leather. The Tibetans also used mail shirts, most of which probably came from Persia or India; but some are apparently of native make

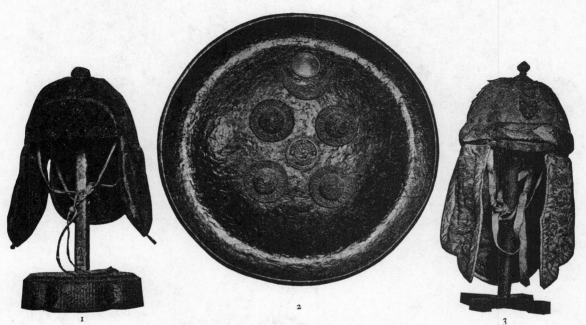

FIGURE 69. *Shield and Helmets, Bhutan, 18th-19th century. 1. Helmet of dark green velvet lined with pieces of hardened leather. 2. Shield of the royal guard. Very heavy leather with a deeply rolled edge; the shield is black and the edge red. Brass bosses and ornaments, the center one set with coral and turquoise. Diameter 21.75 inches. 3. Helmet and neck guard of padded silk of many brilliant colors. The brim and the knob at the top are of engraved brass.*

In the Caucasus the armor was, in the main, a mixture of Turkish, Persian and Tartar types. About the only characteristic feature is the later helmets which have nearly flat, conical crowns usually covered with silver, and very long mail curtains which sometimes cover the entire face except for small openings opposite the eyes. They were worn over high padded caps that raised the plate several inches above the head. Fig. 65.

The earliest Tibetan armor of which we have any account was called "willow leaf" because it was made of long narrow scales laced together. It may, or may not, be the same as the suit shown in

and very heavy. Arm guards of leather strapped with iron were sometimes used, fig. 67. Helmets of semi-Chinese type like those of Sikkim and Bhutan were common.

In Sikkim, Bhutan and Nepal the usual armor was a coat of mail over which four round plates, a sort of char aina, were worn and also broad belts made of narrow, ribbed steel plates riveted to leather straps, fig. 68. The helmets are generally low, wide bowls with small peaks in front, knobs on the top and padded ear and neck guards. Sometimes the whole helmet is of velvet padded and lined with hard leather, 1, fig. 69. Others are made of col-

FIGURE 71. *Chukchi Armor. The body is of wooden hoops, and the neck guard of flat boards, both covered with hide. U. S. National Museum.*

1   2

FIGURE 72. *Chinese, Armor of officers of the Imperial Palace Guard.* 1. *18th century. Black velvet
lined with small iron plates fastened with rivets with gilded heads. The helmet, cuffs and knee guards
are of steel inlaid with gold. The helmet is decorated with raised scrolls and the Buddhist prayer
Om mani padme hum in raised gold letters several times repeated.* 2. *About 1840. Gold brocade
embroidered in colors and edged with black velvet. Gilt rivet heads but no plates. The shoulder
pieces are gilded dragons. The helmet is plain steel with gilded ornaments.*

ored silks, padded and fitted with brass peaks, 3, fig. 69. In all of these types of helmet the ear guards were usually turned up over the head and only turned down when actually fighting. The whole arrangement is very like the caps with reversible ear tabs worn in winter in New England. The mail collars throughout this region are generally stiffened by leather thongs run through the links. The shields are similar to the Indian but are

narrow strips of steel like the Tibetan, but unlike it, the principal guard for the head is a peculiar and inconvenient projection from the back that stands up around the neck and shoulders, fig. 70. This is probably intended to protect the wearer from stones thrown by his friends. We know that all of these nomads are habitual users of the sling, and it is probable that only the strongest and wealthiest wore armor and formed the first line, while the rest be-

FIGURE 73. *Skirt for fighting on foot and extra sleeves of no. 1, fig. 72. The skirt is of jazerant with half of the length of each strip showing on the outside and half hidden by the band of brocade below. The borders are of gold brocade. The sleeves are made of strips of steel about 0.1 inch wide and 0.05 thick riveted to strips of brocade. The cuffs are of steel finely inlaid with gold. The brocade of skirts and sleeves is the same. Not to scale.*

heavier, more convex and have very deep rolled edges, 2, fig. 69.

In Mongolia and northern Asia the armor is generally like that of the most closely surrounding nations. In the north we find rod and hide armor like that worn in northern America, figs. 87, 88. In the east it is more like some of the Chinese. The only really characteristic armor is worn by some of the Siberian tribes, and even this resembles the Tibetan in some respects and that worn in the South Seas in others. This armor is made by lacing together

came the second line of slingers and archers. If this is so it is easy to see that the front rank would require some protection from stones thrown into a crowd having a rough and tumble fight where both parties were inextricably mixed. The fact that in parts of the South Seas similar defenses were worn for this purpose makes it at least probable that this contrivance has the same object.

The U. S. National Museum has some armor of this general type from this region. In it the body armor is made of hoops and the neck defense of boards, both covered with hide. The appearance is quite different from the Koryak, but the effect is the same. It was worn by the Chukchis, fig. 71.

The Tartar armor was much like the Turkish and Russian. The helmets, however, were almost always pointed, in fact pointed helmets were considered as characteristic of the Tartars. Their arms and armor were largely copied by those with whom they fought, and both the Chinese and the Russians were greatly influenced by them.

In China armor changed but little. Various forms of ring, scale, padded and brigandine armor have been used from the earliest times. Mail and plate were apparently unknown and very rarely used, and the little found there is probably of Persian make. The best and most characteristic Chinese suits have always been of brigandine, made of two thicknesses of cloth with small iron plates between them. This was frequently reinforced by round metal plates on the breast, back and knees. The helmets were of steel with neck guards of brigandine like the body armor, 1, fig. 72. These suits had leg pieces like those shown for riding and large divided skirts of jazerant for fighting on foot, fig. 73. In this suit the body, shoulders and upper arms are covered by brigandine, but the lower arms only by padded cloth with gilt rivets to make it look like brigandine. It has, however, another pair of arms of light steel hoops with steel cuffs, fig. 73. Later the entire suits were made of padded cloth with gilt rivets; the only actual armor being the helmet, the round metal plates on the back and breast and the huge and elaborate shoulder guards, 2, fig. 72. The earlier shoulder guards were larger and contained more metal than the later.

Some of the light armor looked like the ordinary garments but was lined with lacquered steel plates riveted on the inside, fig. 74. Scale armor precisely like some of the Roman was sometimes worn, 2, fig. 29.

The parts of a suit of Chinese armor are shown separately in fig. 75.

In the U. S. National Museum and in the Field Museum, Chicago, there are some suits of Lolo (Szechuan, China), that look much like some of the Japanese armor. They are made of leather painted in colors, fig. 76. Shields made of metal, leather, wood or cane were in general use. They are mainly round and three feet or more in diameter.

In Korea the armor of the higher classes was similar in construction to the Chinese but was generally more elaborately decorated. That of the lower classes was commonly a very heavy padded gar-

FIGURE 74. *Chinese Light Armor. Red silk embroidered in colors with dragons, clouds, etc. 18th. century. The right side is thrown back to show the lining of steel plates.*

ment covering only the body and leaving the arms and the lower part of the legs bare. The helmets were of similar material but strapped with metal, fig. 30. Cloth coats with large scales of hardened leather riveted to them were also common, fig. 77. The helmets were quite similar in shape to the Chinese and were made of leather or iron with brig-

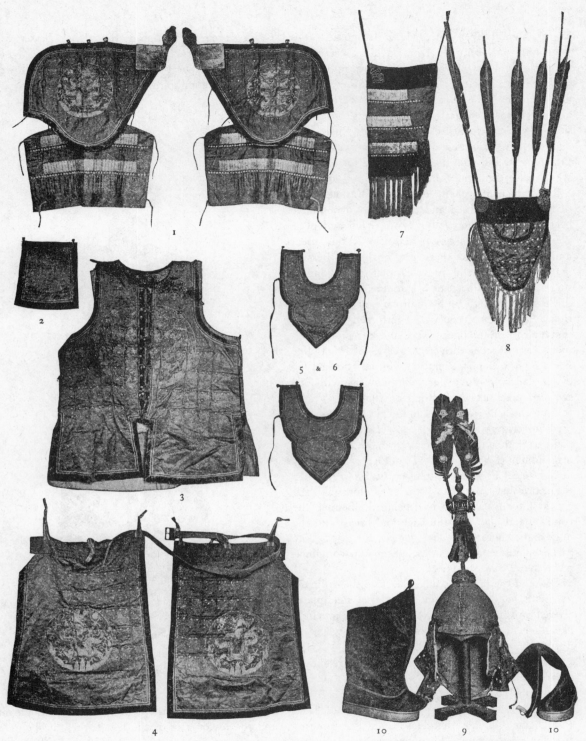

FIGURE 75. *The parts of a suit of Chinese armor of the time of Shun Chih, second half of the 17th century. The suit is mainly of brigandine but partly of jazerant and is covered with blue silk with velvet borders.* 1. *Shoulders and arms of separate pieces buttoned together. The shoulders are of brigandine with a gold dragon embroidered on each. The arms are of jazerant.* 2. *The usual small square to cover the abdomen.* 3. *Body of brigandine.* 4. *The apronlike pieces for the legs; each is embroidered with a gold dragon.* 5, 6. *The armpit guards.* 7. *The armored bow case of jazerant with wide velvet bands top and bottom, and long blue fringe.* 8. *The quiver for the five ceremonial arrows of yellow willow with spiral goose feathers. It also has a wide velvet top and long fringe.* 9. *The helmet of steel with gilded mounts set with ruby, coral, malachite and turquoise. The pink coral indicates that it belonged to an official of the second class. The plumes are decorated with characters and dragons of kingfisher feathers. The upper characters mean "sun" and "moon"; and the lower "pursuance" and "heaven," and indicate "in pursuance of heaven's order to found new dynasty." The dragons have four claws as only the emperor and heir apparent have the right to wear five-clawed ones.* 10. *The boots of black silk with the usual heavy cord soles. The ring and case* 1, *fig.* 24, *the saddle, fig.* 680, *and the bridle* 7-10, *fig.* 188 *belong to this suit.*

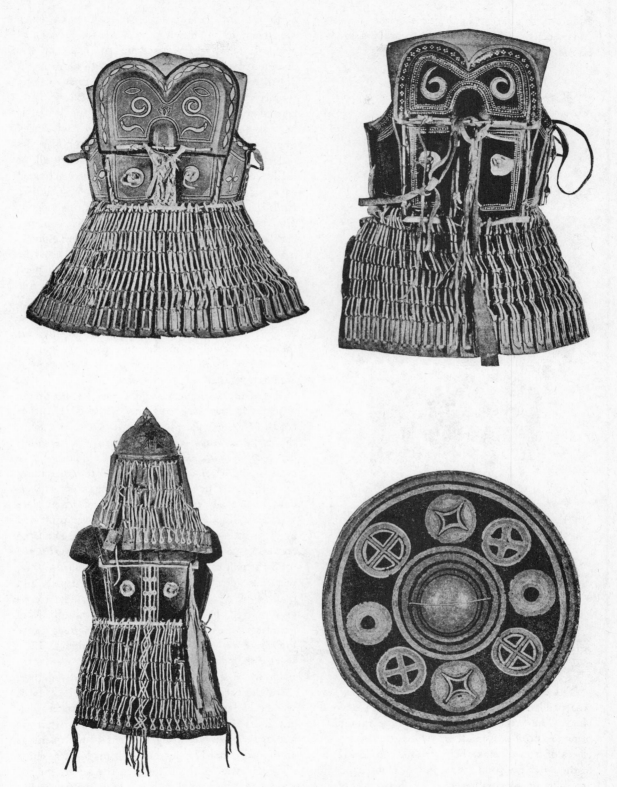

FIGURE 76. *Lolo Armor, Szechuan, China. Three suits of armor and a shield of leather painted in bright colors. Field Museum, Chicago.*

andine neck guards. At the time of the wars with Japan considerable Japanese armor was used in Korea.

FIGURE 77. *Korean Armor, 18th, 19th century. A heavy blue cotton garment covered with scales of hardened leather. Helmet of leather with iron mounts; neck guard lined with plates.*

The earliest armor used in Japan, as elsewhere, was padded or made of scales or rings sewn on cloth. The armor found in the grave mounds of prior to 400 B.C. is made by riveting together small pieces of iron to make helmets and cuirasses. Some of the latter give quite the effect of plate armor but are built up of small pieces. See Kake Yoroi and Tanko.

By the 10th century, the earliest time of which we have definite knowledge, it had assumed a characteristic form which it retained until armor was abandoned in the middle of the 19th century. A Japanese suit, fig. 78, consists of a helmet, *kabuto*, usually made of a large number of narrow plates riveted together with raised edges at the joints. It has a small peak, *maizashi*, in front and a wide neck guard, *shikoro*, made of strips of steel or of scales of leather or steel laced together with heavy silk or leather cords. One or more of these pieces is turned back in front to form ear guards, *fukigayeshi*. The front is usually decorated with two horn-like pieces, *kuwagata*, representing the leaves of a water plant; between them is an ornament, *maidate*, corresponding to the European crest. The face is covered by a steel mask, *menpo*, to which a laminated neck guard, *yodare-kake*, is attached. There are five varieties of menpo—covering the entire face—all of the face below the eyes—the forehead and cheeks only—and two for the cheeks and chin only. Of these the second is much most used. A gorget, *nodowa*, was sometimes worn but was not considered as a regular part of the suit.

The body was enclosed in a corselet, *do*, made of plates or strips laced together with silk or leather cords. It either opened at the side, *do-maru*, or at the back, *haramaki-do*. Attached to it were shoulder pieces, *watagami*, from which it hung. The taces, *kusazuri*, made of strips laced together hung from the do. Under these was worn an apron, *haidate*, of brocade covered with mail or mixed plate and mail. The legs below the knee were protected by close fitting greaves, *sune-ate*, of plate; and the feet were covered with bearskin shoes, *tsurumaki*, or with mail or plate *tabi*. The arm guards, *kote*, were brocade sleeves covered with mixed plate and mail. They usually ended in gauntlets which covered only the backs of the hands and thumbs. Mail gauntlets were rare but were sometimes used. Large guards, *sode*, were hung on the shoulders. They were either single plates, two hinged together or made up of strips or rows of scales laced together.

In the early suits the neck and shoulder guards were very large and the taces few in number, usually four. There were also guards, *hato-wo-no-ita* and *sen-dan-no-ita*, hung in front of the openings at the armpits. The former was made of a single plate and was hung on the left, the latter, for the right side, was made of three plates laced together so as to be more flexible and less apt to get in the way when drawing the bow. In the Kamakura period (1100-1336) the greaves had wide pieces extending upwards and backwards on the outside of the leg to protect the thighs when on horseback, fig. 79. In later times the neck guards were made became more an object of decoration; this was due to the peaceful times in Japan and to the fact that every daimio had to spend a part of each year at court where each tried to outshine the others, and not to the development of firearms or to changes in tactics. Figs. 80, 81.

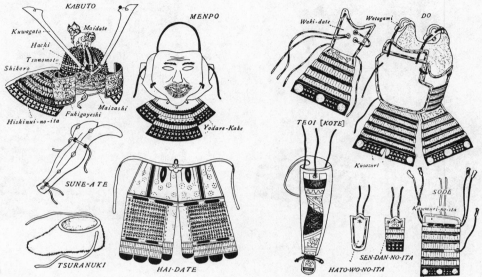

FIGURE 78. *Japanese Armor, after Dr. Dean. The different parts are shown separately with their names.*

smaller, and the taces narrower and more numerous. There was a greater tendency to use larger plates for the breast and to use strips made of a single piece of steel instead of built up of scales laced together. Less plate and more mail was used in the sleeves. In the Tokuwaga period (1600-1868) armor became more elaborate and varied, particularly the helmets, some of which were made of the most extraordinary shapes. As in Europe it

FIGURE 79. *Japanese Greaves, probably the 14th century. Metropolitan Museum.*

Folding armor, including folding helmets, was made to be carried when traveling, figs. 776, 777. Entire suits of mail were worn on occasions, sometimes under the ordinary clothing. In fact complete suits were rarely worn except on parade or when serious fighting was expected.

The armor of the lower classes was similar in general design but was simpler and often made of leather instead of steel. The retainers wore hoods of mixed plate and mail or flat open helmets called jingasa. Even among the upper classes the closeness of the lacing varied with the rank, the higher the rank the closer the lacing.

The Japanese made more varieties of mail than all of the rest of the world put together. It is not only very light but has openings left in it which sometimes amount to half the area. This open mail was used for the inner side of sleeves and other points requiring but little protection. Japanese armor was always as light as was consistent with the desired amount of security. The workmanship of the better suits is excellent, that of the helmets is

FIGURE 80. *Japanese Armor.* 1. *Half suit (O-Yoroi) about 1200.* 2. *Cuirass and taces (Do-Maru) late 15th century. Metropolitan Museum. Not to scale.*

1   2   3

FIGURE 81. *Japanese Armor.* 1. *Suit of a general serving under the daimio of Sakai (Izumi). Mark, Yoshi-Fusa. A remodeled suit of 1550.* 2. *Armor of a Yamabushi, about 1575.* 3. *Suit of plate, early 18th century, signed Miochin Munesuke. Metropolitan Museum. Not to scale.*

FIGURE 82. *Malayan Armor.* 1. *Moro, helmet and corselet of kabau hide; the neck and armholes are bound with burlap.* 2. *Jacket woven of heavy cord.* 3. *Nias. Body armor of cloth covered with scales of bark. The last two are from the U. S. National Museum and are to scale.*

FIGURE 83. *Moro Armor.* 1. *Hauberk of brass plates connected by heavy unriveted brass mail. Brass helmet.* 2. *Hauberk and helmet of plates of kabau horn connected by heavy brass mail. Not to scale.*

FIGURE 84. *Armor from the Kingsmill Islands. The main part of the suit is woven of heavy cord twisted from the fibre of the cocoanut. The helmet is the skin of a spiny fish. The backs of the gauntlets are armed with rows of shark's teeth. This is believed to be the most complete suit known of its kind. Peabody Museum, Salem.*

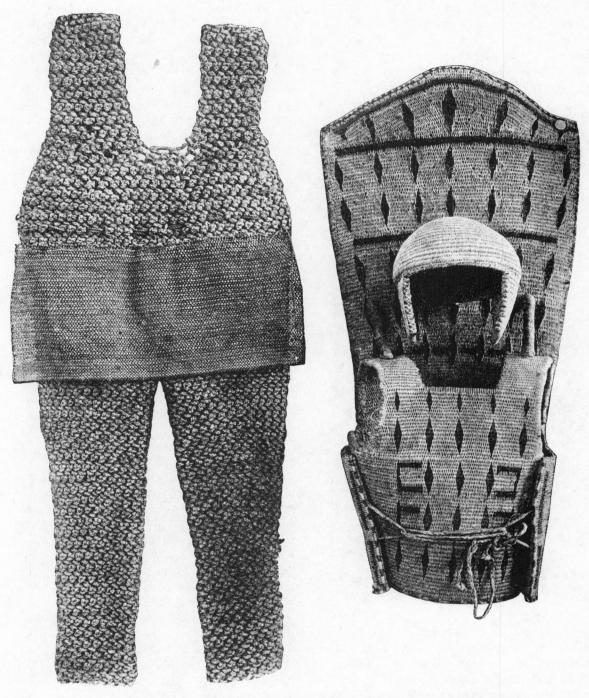

FIGURE 85. *Armor from the Gilbert (Kingsmill) Islands made entirely of cocoanut fibre. American Museum of Natural History.*

marvelous, and the decoration in carving, embossing and inlaying could hardly be surpassed.

In general the Japanese armor is lighter and more flexible than the European. It is characterized by the small size of the individual plates, the greater use of mail and leather, and by the universal use of silk cords, not only to fasten the main parts to each other, but to join the elements of each part. The different colors of these cords had definite meanings. Thus *hiodoshi*, flame color and gold, was

FIGURE 86. *Armor woven of cane and cord from the interior of the North Coast of New Guinea. Field Museum, Chicago.*

restricted to the five great princely families up to the end of the 16th century; white cords indicated that the wearer was engaged in a forlorn hope, etc.

In Malaya armor was not much worn. The Dyaks wore the skins of goats or leopards hanging down before and behind which were probably adequate as a protection from blowpipe darts. The wilder Moros wore hide armor, 1, fig. 82, or jackets of heavy cord, or covered with scales of bark,

2, 3, fig. 82. Those who could afford a better equipment wore armor of brass, or horn, plates connected by heavy brass mail of peculiar design, fig. 83, probably copied from Spanish models. The helmets were generally of brass shaped like the 17th-century Spanish casques. Occasionally they were made of plates of horn connected by mail like the hauberks, or entirely of horn, fig. 378. At Tampassook in Borneo Marryatt met a number of natives equipped for war and says: "One costume was quite novel, being a suit of armor made of buffalo leather scaled with oyster shells."

Few of the natives of the South Pacific use armor. The Kingsmill Islanders are an exception as they occasionally wore armor woven of cocoanut fibre cord. This was necessary as their weapons were generally edged with shark's teeth. This armor covered the body and occasionally the arms and legs. It had a wide flap at the back that curved up and forward protecting the back of the head, figs. 84, 85. This guard for the back of the head was to protect it from the misdirected efforts of the women of the party who followed the men into the fight throwing stones at the enemy.

D'Albertis found a somewhat similar suit in New Guinea in a deserted village. He says (II, 125-6): "One very important (discovery), because, so far as I know, it is the first one found in New Guinea. It consists of a cuirass of armor made of rattang." Others have been found since, fig. 86. It also has a high guard for the back of the head.

The North American Indians of the east and northeast used rod and slat armor made of sticks or pieces of bone tied together so as to make a flexible garment, fig. 87. They also used a variety of forms of hide armor, fig. 88. The Pawnees are said to have made armor of two thicknesses of hide with a lining of sand (?), also helmets of similar construction. The latter are said to have covered the back of the head and forehead. The Plains Indians, who generally fought on horseback, rarely used armor, their only defense being a shield. (Dorsey 288). For a most complete description of aboriginal armor see Hough, *Primitive American Armor*, U. S. N. M., 1893, p. 627. The Aztecs wore armor of similar types but more elaborately decorated. Our knowledge of it is extremely fragmentary, being derived mostly from their sculptures.

In Africa the later Egyptians wore Turkish and Persian armor almost exclusively. Some of the hel-

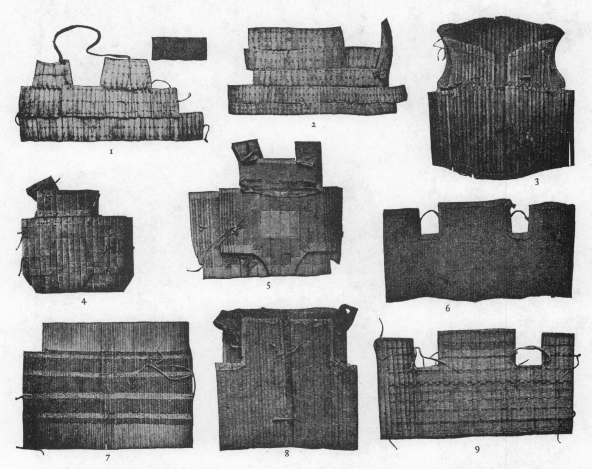

FIGURE 87. *Rod and Slat Armor.* 1. *Eskimo. Cape Prince of Wales, Alaska. Made of three rows of ivory plates, averaging 1 inch by 6, laced together with rawhide. The upper row consists of two sections; one of 10 plates protecting the breast, the other of 8 protecting the upper part of the back. The spaces between the sections form openings for the arms. The middle row is of 38 plates and the lowest of 43. In the upper right hand corner is shown a fragment of similar armor but made of iron plates. It was dug from a bog near where the ivory armor was found.* 2. *Eskimo of Diomede Island, Alaska. Armor of similar construction of walrus ivory. Width extended 49 inches, height 24.* 3. *Prehistoric Aleutian rod armor. Made of two series of cedar rods half an inch in diameter and of different lengths. The rods are perforated at each end and held together by a double lacing of plaited sinew cord. The upper and lower parts are united by a rickrack lashing engaging with the horizontal sewing. The rods are perforated from side to side and a thin rod of whalebone drawn through, rendering the armor flexible. There are two wooden toggles on the right side.* 4. *Tlingit slat armor. Made of 32 slats of cedar and other wood connected by fine weaving of sinew and other cord. A band of weaving 3 inches wide is carried along the front of the top and is continued downward in two places to meet a band crossing the bottom. The front and back are distinct and are joined by elk skin cords at the sides. A section of 8 short slats rises above the rest to protect the throat, and a similar section of 7 guards the back. The armor is held in place by a broad band of elk skin over the right shoulder, and fastened on the left side by a loop and thong.* 5. *Tlingit armor of rods and slats. Made of rods of hard wood 1.25 to 1.5 inches wide and 5/16 of an inch thick woven together with sinew cord.. The neck portions are made of short slats and sewed on by means of a strip of rawhide. The front and back are woven separately and connected by leather cords on the left side and by a loop and double toggle on the right. The shoulder pieces are of heavy elk skin, the one on the right being fastened by a slash and toggle. Width of back piece 24 inches, height 20; width of front 18 inches, height 19.* 6. *Hupa rod armor. Made of 118 peeled rods woven together with native twine and bound with buckskin at the upper and lower edges and armholes. Leather shoulder straps. Six horizontal stripes of red cord cross the front; these indicate the rank of the wearer and the number of enemies killed or captured.* 7. *Taku Indians, Alaska. Made of 72 peeled rods of uniform length and diameter held together by alternate bands of weaving of woolen and sinew cord. Decorated with 4 vertical strips of red paint equally spaced. This was probably worn over a skin coat, both specimens having been secured from the same native.* 8. *Shasta, California. Made of 74 strips of wood made by splitting branches, woven together with native cord of wild hemp. The checkered portion in black is woven with human hair cord. All of the rods are split at both ends and cords drawn into the splits to secure the weaving; and in addition the edges are bound with skin sewed with sinew. The shoulder straps are of otter(?) fur. There are 4 horizontal bands of red paint. Width 38 inches, height 30.* 9. *Klamath rod armor, modern. Made of 44 oval pine rods laced together with cords, some of which are red or yellow. Shoulder straps and binding of buckskin. Width 38 inches, height 21. Not to scale. U. S. National Museum.*

FIGURE 88. *Hide Armor.* 1. *Chilcat Indians, Alaska. Made of tanned caribou hide folded and reinforced; the leather has apparently been stiffened with glue. Two heavy pieces of hide go over the shoulders and form a slit in front for the neck. Width 32 inches, height 37.* 2. *Tlingit, Alaska. Made of thick tanned hide in imitation of an old-fashioned waistcoat, the resemblance being exact in particulars of cut and sewing. Four lappets for fastening in front with brass buttons of English manufacture.* 3. *Tlingit, Alaska. Made of two thicknesses of caribou hide, scarfed regularly to secure flexibility. It was worn under a rod band. Width 21 inches, length 28. A very early specimen.* 4. *Taku Indians, Alaska. Made of thick tanned elk skin or moose skin folded twice like a sheet of note paper. Sewed over the shoulders and strengthened by hinge pieces. Open along the right side; a short slit on the left below the shoulder leaves a passage for the left arm.* 5. *Tlingit. Made of one piece of heavy elk skin apparently smoke tanned, lined inside with another piece sewed around the lower part. It has a heavy guard over the left shoulder; the band over the right shoulder is buttoned over a wooden toggle. Fastened by thongs on the right side.* 6. *Tlingit. Made of two thicknesses of tanned hide and reinforced at the lower part by two more. Sewed with sinew. Width 25 inches, height 33.* 7. *Hupa Indians, California. Made of a large elk skin doubled upon itself. The outer portion reaches to the ankles, the inner only to the knees. Joined over the shoulders by leather straps worked through a series of slashes. Decorated with lines and triangles in red and blue paint which are intended to denote the number of enemies killed and captives taken.* 8. *Alaska. Made of very heavy corrugated hide, single thickness. A strip of lighter leather cut from a painted garment has been sewed to the left side. A double shoulder protector has been sewed to the left side of the neck opening, and the skin has been cut and enlarged by gussets to protect the right shoulder.* 9. *Rear view of 8. Width 30 inches, height 37.5 U. S. National Museum, not to scale.*

mets are bowl-shaped and made of two pieces, a comparatively shallow crown and relatively deep side piece. In the Sudan armor was used until the battle of Omdurman proved it to be useless when

FIGURE 89. *Sudanese Armor. Steel bowl-shaped helmet with a sliding nasal. It is worn over a heavy padded cap, the back and sides of which reach down to the shoulders. Skirt of heavy riveted mail with long skirts to protect the legs, collar of leather stamped with Arabic inscriptions. It has silver buttons on each side of the breast and on each shoulder with Solomon's seal and an Arabic inscription. 19th century.*

opposed to modern firearms. It usually consisted of a well made shirt of riveted mail and a bowl-shaped helmet with a sliding nasal. Some had, and some had not, neck guards of mail. In either case it was worn over a heavy quilted hood, the sides and back of which came down to the shoulders, fig. 89. The mail was probably of English or German make

as it is so regular it must have been made by machines. Pieces of Turkish armor of the 15th and 16th centuries were sometimes used, occasionally in curious ways, as when a knee cop with a part of the mail attached was used as a helmet. Horse armor was also used, the chanfrons were covered with brass, and heavy pads were worn on the body. In Bornu, judging from the pictures that have been published, they used horse armor that looks much

FIGURE 90. *Bornu cuirass. Steel with leather bindings and copper and brass burrs under the rivet heads.*

like the Japanese. They also used cuirasses, well designed and well made, fig. 90. They are built of strips of steel riveted together.

For the various parts and kinds of armor, except helmets, see: Age-Maki, Agrapes, Aigote, Aiguilettes, Ailettes, Ainaka-Gote, Aketon, Akurio, A la Poulaine Solerets, Alcato, Allecret, Almain Rivets, Anda Tsudzumi, Anime, Arai-Kawa-Odoshi, Arming Doublet, Arming Nayles, Arming Points, Arriere Bras, Asahi Odoshi, Ase-Nagashi No Ana, Avant-Bras, Awase-Gote, Bachteretz, Back and Breast, Bainbergs, Baju Tilam, Banded Mail, Baru Sinali, Bases, Baticole, Bazu Band, Bear's Paw Solerets, Beko Tsudzumi, Beni-Odoshi, Besagues, Bezanted Armor, Bhanju, Bishamon Sune-Ate, Bishop's Mantle, Black Armor, Botan Gake, Bouchette, Brachiere, Braconiere, Braconiere a Tonnelet, Brassard, Brayette, Breast and Back, Breastplate, Bregander Nayles, Brene, Brichettes, Brigandine, Brugne, Bruny, Buff Coat, Buffe, Bukhtar, Bumbawe Tefao, Bungakuodori, Byrnie, Caligae, Camail, Carda, Cargan, Chain Mail, Champons, Char Aina, Chausses, Chausson, Chigakushi, Chujak, Clemal, Coat of Defense, Coat of Mail, Cod Piece, Cognizance, Colleret, Cors, Corselet, Coudes, Coutes, Croissants, Cubitiere, Cuirass, Cuirassine, Cuirie, Cuisses, Culet, Curat, Dastana, Defaut de la Cuirasse, Demi-Brassarts, Demi-Jambes, Demi-Placcate, Demi-Poulaine Solerets, Dilge, Do, Do-Maru, Doublet of Fence, Dueling Gauntlet, Ecrevisses, Elbow Cop, Elbow Gauntlet, Elbow Guard, Elbow Piece, Emboitment, Epaul de Mouton, Epauliere, Eriwa, Escaupilles, Espallieres, Etcheu, Falconer's Gauntlet, Faudes, Fencing Gauntlet, Fendace, Flotternel, Forbidden Gauntlet, Front Appendage, Fukuro Gote, Fushi-Nawa-Me-Odoshi, Gadlings, Gagong, Gakido, Gaku-No-Ita, Gaku Sode, Gambeson, Garde de Bras, Garde de Cuisses, Garde de Reins, Gaudichet, Gauntlet, Genbet, Genouilliere, G'hug-'hwah, Giyo-Yo-Ita, Godbertum, Gonjo, Gorget, Gorget Plate, Gousset, Grand Guard, Greave, Gusoku, Gusoku Shi, Gusset, Habergeon, Hai-Date, Half Armor, Hamata, Hanairo-Odoshi, Hanamusubi, Hansho-Gote, Hara-Ate, Haramaki, Haramaki-Do, Harness, Harnois Blanc, Ha-Sode, Hatomune-Do, Hato-Wo-No-Ita, Haubergeon, Hauberk, Hausse Col, Hiji-Gane, Hikiawase, Himo-Tsuki, Hiodoshi, Hishinui, Hishinui-Ita, Hishi-Nui-No-Ita, Hishi-Toji, Hiyotan-Sode, Hiza-Yoroi, Ho-Ate, Hodo-Hai-Date, Hodo-Ita, Hoguine, Horn Armor, Horo, Hosting Harness, Hotoke-Do, Hu Sin King, Ichcahuipilli, Igo-Hai-Date, Ikada, Imbricate Armor, Iroiro-Odoshi, Ita, Ita-Hai-Date, Ita Jikoro, Jack, Jack Boot, Jambeau, Jamboys, Jambs, Jazerant, Jesseraunt, Jubangote, Jowo-Gashira, Kaki Yoroi, Kakudzuri, Kamuri-Ita, Kana-Makari, Kant'hah Sobha, Kara-Aya-Odoshi, Karoenkoeng, Kasa-Jiruchi-No-Kuwan, Kata-Ate, Katchu, Kawadzutsumi, Kawa-Odoshi, Kawara, Kawara Sode, Kawa Tsuchumi, Kawa Tsudzumi, Kebiki, Kabeki Do-Maru, Kegetsu, Kia, Kigomi, Kigote, Kinkaku, Ki-No-Ha-Sode, Kiyo, Knee Cop, Knee Guard, Knemides, Kogane-Majiri-No-Yoroi, Kogusoku-Kote, Kohaze-Gake, Kohire, Kon

Odoshi, Korai-Bo, Korazin, Koshi-Tsuki-No-O, Kote, Kote Haramaki, Kotetsuke, Ko-Zakura-Odoshi, Kozane, Krug, Kujaki, Kurdaitcha Shoes, Kurijimi-No-O, Kurisage-No-O, Kurtani, Kusari, Kusari Gote, Kusari Katabira, Kusari Kiahan, Kusari Sode, Kusari Toji, Kusari Wakibiki, Kusazuri, Kushi Gata, Kutsu, Kyubi-No-Ita, Lames, Laniers, Leg Shield, Leni Croich, Lobster-Tail Tassets, Locking Gauntlet, Lorica Catenata, Mail, Mainfaire, Main Guard, Mamelieres, Manjiyuwa, Manteau d'Armes, Maru Sode, Mascle, Maximilian Armor, Mayewari-Gusoku, Meguriwa, Mempo, Menpo, Mentoniere, Mika-Dzuki-No-Ita, Milled Armor, Moji Tsudzumi, Moko Ita, Mononogu, Moriyo, Moyegi-Nioi-Odoshi, Muchi-Gashi-No-Ana, Mukabaki, Mukashi Jikoro, Muna-Ita, Murasaki Odoshi, Namban-Bo, Namban Sode, Neck Guard, Nerinuki Odoshi, Nimai Kana No Do, Niwo-Sune-Ate, Nodowa, Nuko, Oarame, Ocrea, Odate-Agayemon, Odawara-Inari, Odoshi, Odoshi-Ge, Odoshi-Tosei, Oikago, Oke-Gawa-Do, O-Kinna-Men, Onna-Men, Oshi-No-Gote, Oshitsuke, O-Yoroi, Pair of Plates, Pair of Splints, Pansiere, Passguard, Pauldron, Peascod Breastplate, Pectoral, Peti, Pieces of Advantage, Pizaine, Placard, Plastron, Plate Armor, Poincon, Poldermitton, Poleyne, Pollet, Pots and Mops, Pourpoint, Puffed Armor, Quilted Armor, Renjaku-Do, Rerebrace, Ringed Armor, Rokogu, Rondelle, Sabaton, Saku-Bo, Same Tsudzumi, Sane, Saru-Bo, Sata-Ita, Sayo, Scale Armor, Sei-Ita, Sena-Ate, Sendan-No-Ita, Sentan-Ita, Serzala, Sewari Gusoku, Shells, Shida-Kawa-Odoshi, Shimai-Kane-No-Do, Shino-Dzutsu, Shino-Gote, Shino-Odatsugi, Shinotate-Sune-Ate, Shirogake, Shiwari-Gusoku, Shiwazura, Shoulder Cop, Shoulder Shield, Simong, Sinegaglia, Socket, Sode, Sollerets, Spandrel, Splints, Splinted Armor, Squamata, Standard of Mail, Sudare-Sune-Ate, Sugake-Do-Maru, Sune-Ate, Tabi, Taces, Taka-No-Ha-Sode, Take-Gusoku, Takle, Tanko, Tapul, Tassets, Tatami-Do, Tatami-Gusoku, Tatami Yoroi, Tate-Nashi-Do, Tatewari, Tayui, Tangu, Tentsuki, Teoi, Tetsu Gai, Thabmok, Thorax, Tilting Cuisse, Ting Kia, Tominaga-Gote, Tonlet, Tonoi-No-Haramaki, Tori-Tengu, Tosei, Trellice Coat, Trumelieres, Tscherewza, Tsubame-Bo, Tsudzumi, Tsugi-Gote, Tsutsu-Gote, Tsutsu-Sune-Ate, Tsuyo-Otoshi No Kubo, Tuilles, Turning Pins, Ubu-Dzutsu, Uchi-Awase-Gusoku, Uked

Zutsu, Unchana Odoshi, Upper Pourpoint, Usu-gane-No-Yoroi, Vambrace, Vif de l'Harnois, Volant Piece, Voyders, Wai-Date, Waistcoat Armor, Waki-Biki, Waki-Ita, Wambais, Waraji, Warawazura, Wari Jikoro, Watagami, White Armor, Wire Armor, Yadome, Yama-Gata, Yechiu-Hai-Date, Yeri Mawari, Yetchiu-Gote, Yodare-Kake, Yoroi, Yoroi-Haramaki, Yoroi Kayeshi, Yu-Gote, Yurigi-Ito, Zira, Zirah Baktah, Zirah Korta Saktou.

ARMYLL. See Armil.

ARNACHELLAN. A celebrated modern armorer of Salem, India. (Egerton, p. 58).

ARREST. The lance rest; at first it did not support the lance but distributed the shock over the breastplate. See Lance Rest.

ARRIERE BRAS. Armor for the upper arms. See Brassard.

ARRIERE-GARDE. In the 14th century an army was arranged in three "battles," or divisions, the *avant-garde, bataille* and *arriere-garde,* the arriere-garde thus constituting the modern reserve. Sometimes the three formed in line, the avant- and arriere-gardes forming the wings but retaining their names. This accounts for the apparently contradictory statement sometimes met with in the old chron-

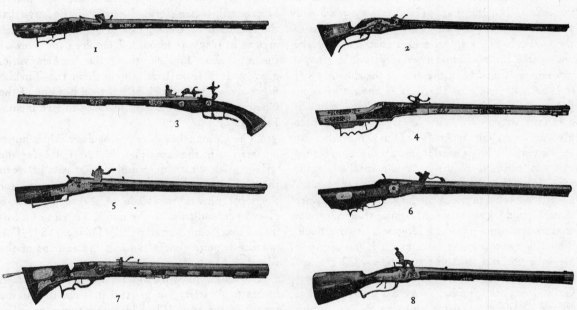

FIGURE 91. *Arquebuses. 1. German, end of the 16th century. 2. French, end of the 17th century. 3. Italian by Lazarino Cominazzo of Brescia, early 17th century. 4. German, early 17th century. The stock is by Hieronymus Borstorffer (d. 1637) and the lock and barrel by Daniel Sadeler of Munich (d. 1632). 5. Rifle, South German, 1637. 6. The barrel is signed G. Grissianus Herold, Dresden, 17th century. 7. Rampart arquebus, German, 1687. 8. German, 17th century. Metropolitan Museum.*

ARQUEBUS, HARQUEBUS. Originally a heavy matchlock gun, later the name was applied to wheel-lock guns, and finally came to mean a gun of fine workmanship as distinguished from the musquet, or common military arm. One of the earliest mentions of the arquebus was its use by the Swiss at the capture of Neuregensberg in 1386, in the war with Sempach. It was also used at the siege of Rapperswill in 1388. Fig. 91. See Matchlock. Fig. 560.

icles, that the army advanced and its rear guard opened the battle. (Hewitt II, 84).

ARROW. The missile shot from a bow. An arrow is composed of three, and usually of four, parts. The head or pile—among the more civilized races this is always made of metal; many savages, however, frequently use bone, stone, horn, shell or any hard material. In Formosa some of the arrows have two roughly forged barbed heads lashed to opposite sides of the shaft. These were probably poisoned as the relatively light bows they used could not have driven the wide head and blunt end of the shaft in far enough to do much damage. The size and shape of arrow heads varies almost without limit. The Japanese war arrows had quite small and simple heads, but some of those carried for parade had huge heads, some of which were made and signed by celebrated artists. See Yano-Ne. A few Turkish and Japanese arrows have heads with movable barbs that remain close to the shaft when the arrow enters the wound but swing out nearly at right angles to it if an attempt is made to withdraw it, 10, fig. 862. Arrow heads are fastened to the shaft in three ways—by a tang which fits into the end of the shaft. This is always used with reed shafts. It is notched at the back and lashed to the shaft. It has a metal socket that fits over the end of the shaft. With target arrows it is often a pointed cap that fits on the end of the shaft.

The body, stele or shaft. It is always of some light wood or of reed. Most arrows have cylindrical shafts, except when they are made of reed which always has a slight taper. The Turkish arrows are an exception. They are largest at about one-third of their length from the nock and smallest at the head. The diameters are roughly as 16 at the head, 22 at the nock and 32 at the largest part. They are almost cylindrical between points at about one-quarter and one-half their length from the nock. There is a slight curve here but it is too slight to measure without micrometer calipers. This shape offers the least possible resistance to the air. Payne-Gallwey says that he has measured many and that all are of the same shape and size. I have found the same.

The nock, or notch for the string. It is frequently cut in the end of the shaft; but in the better ones in a piece of horn glued on. In the Turkish arrows it is made of two pieces of wood having a natural curve that makes the opening at the end considerably smaller than close to the shaft, so that the ends have to be sprung apart to admit the string. This is done to enable the archer, even on horseback, to carry an arrow in place ready for instant use. The pieces of the nock are glued and lashed with sinew to the shaft and it is much stronger than the usual horn nocks.

There is almost always a fourth part—the feathers, which are glued or tied to the shaft, to steady its flight. In the South Seas, and in some parts of South America, very long reed arrows are used without feathers; only, however, at very short ranges. The feathers are usually placed as nearly as possible in the line of the shaft. Some Chinese arrows have them placed in a spiral which is said to increase their power. Some Turkish flight arrows have single vanes from feathers arranged in spirals to cause the arrow to rotate. I have a Japanese arrow, 7, fig. 94, that has both straight and spiral feathers. Some arrows have but two feathers, most have three of which one is of a different color from the others and is placed upward when fired. A few Japanese arrows have four feathers, two of which are always much narrower than the others, and are placed horizontally when fired. Cowper, p. 189, says that the Veddahs of Ceylon use five. I saw no such arrows in Ceylon although I inquired for them at the museums. The length of the feathers varies greatly. It is from barely an inch in the Turkish flight arrows to as much as fourteen in some of the Chinese; in general it is from three to five inches. Figs. 92, 93, 94.

"The Comanches place the blades of their hunting arrows in the same plane as the notch for the string, so that they may more easily pass between the ribs of an animal which are up and down; for the same reason, the blade of the war arrow is placed perpendicular to the notch, the ribs of a human being being horizontal." (Dodge 418). This practice is quite general among the Indians of the Plains.

The length of arrows varies from about eighteen inches to five feet; in general it is about half the length of the bow. The old English rule was that the bow should be of the length of the user, and the arrows half the length of the bow. As six feet was about the maximum length of the bows, the arrows issued to the armies were made three feet long and cut off for those that required shorter ones. In recent years some of the books on archery have stated that "the English cloth yard was twenty-eight inches." This is entirely wrong and any standard dictionary, or book on standards of length, defines the English cloth yard as—"of four quarters, each of four nails of two and a quarter inches; that is thirty-six inches." There were two or three "ells" also used for measuring cloth that were shorter. The statement is probably made to excuse the short arrows and ranges used in modern archery.

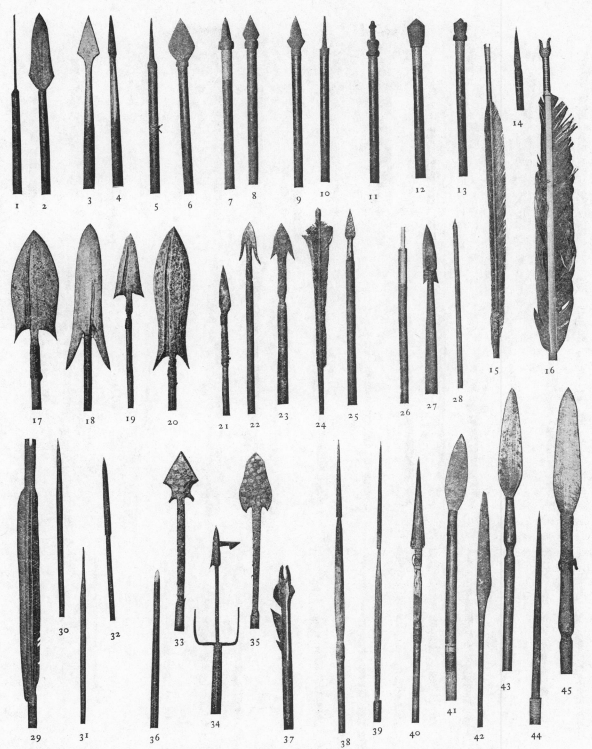

FIGURE 92. *Arrows. 1 to 16 Chinese. The first ten are in pairs, each pair showing two views of the same head. 3 and 4 are military arrows of the end of the 19th century. 15. Feathering of an ordinary arrow. 16. The feathering of a large whistling arrow. 17 to 21. Cashmere, iron heads. 22 to 25. Sikkim. 26. Korea, square iron head. 27. Ainu, bamboo head with a recess for poison. 28. Cambodia. 29 to 32. Java, round iron heads. 33 to 37. Turkey, 17th century. 36 and 37 are the point and feathering of a flight arrow. 38. Mindoro, wooden head. 39. Silkiot, wooden head. 40. Mangayan, wooden head reed shaft. 41, 43, 45. Ilongot, iron heads. 42. New Guinea, triangular head and round shaft cut from a single piece of wood. 44. Tiruray, wooden head, reed shaft*

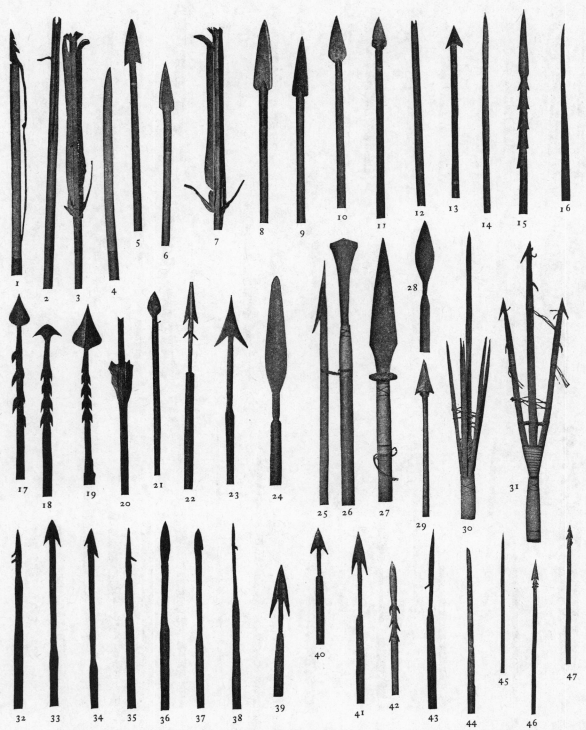

FIGURE 93. *Arrows.* 1. *Eskimo.* 2, 3. *North American Indian.* 4, 5. *Pima.* 6. *Cheyenne.* 7, 8. *Apache.*
9. *Sioux.* 10. *Navaho.* 11. *Sioux, stone head.* 12. *California, notched to receive a stone head.* 13.
Tosahumac, Mexico. 14. *Michol, Mexico.* 15. *South America.* 16. *Guagignon.* 17 to 20. *Besanji,*
Congo. The heads are of iron and the barbs below them are of wood. 21. *Congo.* 22. *Pigmy,*
Congo. 23. *Dahomey.* 24. *East Coast, Africa.* 25 to 28 and 30, 31. *Guiana.* 29. *Terra del Fuego,*
obsidian head. 32 to 38. *Central Africa.* 39. *Mandingo.* 40. *Somali.* 41. *Central Africa.* 42. *Masai.*
43. *Central Africa.* 44, 45. *Bushman.* 46, 47. *Congo, dwarf tribes.*

For the various kinds and parts of arrows see: Adaya, Anak, Bedor, Bitla, Bolt, Boson, Broad Arrow, Carreau, Chado-Kake, Chakra, Chodo-Kake, Cloth Yard Arrow, Curare, Da, Diwal, Dondaine, Ela (Da), Fletcher, Flo, Fore Shaft, Hage-Ro, Hao Shi, Hazu, Hide-Tace, Hikime, Hiki-Ya, Himekabura, Hipa, Hi-Ya, Hyoto, Igurumi, Ipoh, Ipudligadlin, Ja-Qude-Hi, Kabura, Yanagi-Ha, Yano, Ya-No-Ha, Yano-Ne, Ya-Saki, Yassaghi-Ya, Ya-Tsugi, Ya-Zuka, Yoppiki.

ARROW. In fortification — a work placed at the salient angle of the glacis. (Hoyt).

ARTILLATOR. A maker of bows, arrows, darts and other military stores, 14th century. (Hewitt II, 285).

FIGURE 94. *Arrows. 1, 2, 3. Formosan arrows each with two roughly barbed heads lashed to opposite sides of the shaft and projecting about 2.25 inches beyond it. 4, 5, 6, 10. Turkish arrows with steel heads. 8, 9. Persian arrows. Steel heads with designs in black on a gold ground. 7. Japanese arrow with both straight and spiral feathers. 11, 12, 13, 14. Turkish flight arrows with spiral feathering. The length of the feathering is from 3 to 4 inches.*

Kaidaliki, Karimata, Ki-Hoko, Ki Khnam, Kixodwain, Kukiksadlin, Kuri-Ya, Kutsumaki, Kyusen, Li-Pun, Ma, Ma-Ciqade, Mahi-Si, Makagoya, Malleolus, Masaqtihi, Mato-Ya, Mawida, Meiteki, Ming-Ti, Moriankatu, Muschettae, Musquet Arrow, No, Nock, Nutkodlin, Omodake, Otsuba, Paspati, Peacock Arrow, Quarrel, Rama Isihn, Rankling Arrow, Rochette, Roda-Dedali, Sa, Satsu Ya, Savidlin, Severgi, Shaft, Sheaf of Arrows, Shishi-Ya, Shuri, So-Ya Spright, Sresni, Stele Strely, Tako, Teer, Tir, Togari-Ya, Tol-Bod(Da), Tomarki, Trisula, Tsumaguro, Tsunogi, Tugalin, Umla, Ush, Viraton, Vires, Warayang, Wata-Kusi, Whistling Arrow, Ya, Yabane, Ya-Bumi, Yabusuma, Ya-Dame, Yagara, Ya-Hazu, Yajiri,

ARTILLERY. Originally the artillery meant the "gyns," machines for throwing stones and other missiles. Later it was applied to cannon and all guns too large to be managed by one man.

AS, ASI. See Khadga.

ASA-GAO. Morning glory (convolvulus). A form of Japanese helmet shaped like the flower. Fig. 423.

ASAHI ODOSHI. "Dawn-Lacing," a style of lacing together the parts of Japanese armor.

ASANODZUKIN. A Japanese skull cap worn under the helmet. (Garbutt 169). An early fashion as all of the later helmets have the caps fastened in them.

ASE NAGASHI NO ANA. (Sweat running hole). The opening under the chin of a menpo to allow the perspiration to escape.

ASHI. The collars on the scabbard of a tachi by which it is suspended. (Gilbertson, Dec. 81).

The lugs by which a tachi is hung. (Joly. Hawk-shaw xiv). Fig. 95.

The space between these lugs is called Ashima.

ASHIKAWA. A hawk's jesses, Japan. (Harting 214).

ASHIMA. The space between the slings of a tachi scabbard. (Joly, S. & S. 23). Fig. 95.

ASIDEVATA. The mythical sword of the Hindu gods Shiva, Vishnu and finally Indra. It was "fifty thumbs long and four thumbs broad." (Burton Sword 214).

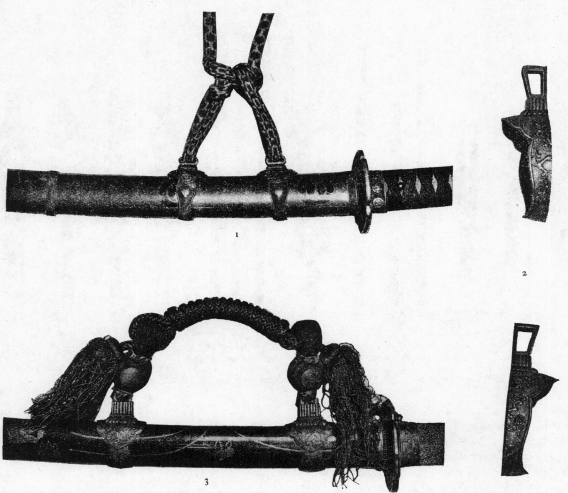

FIGURE 95. *Ashi. 1. Shakudo, nanako surface with gold mon. 2. Shibuichi, vines and gold flowers in relief. 3. Engraved and gilded copper.*

ASHI GARU. Feudal retainers of the lowest rank, Japan.

ASHIKAGA PERIOD. In Japan everything is classed as belonging to one of four periods, of which this is the third, or medieval. It extends from 1336 to 1600. (Dean Jap. 31).

ASIL. A kind of Mahratta sword. Sir G. Malet says, "many seldom encumber themselves with anything but a pair of swords; one of a hard temper, consequently brittle and very sharp, called 'seyre' (Sirohi); the other tough but less sharp named 'asseel' (asil)." (Egerton p. 113).

ASPIS. The Greek shield, it was of huge size, well arched, and frequently made of bronze. (Dean Europ. 15).

FIGURE 96. *Signatures of Assad Ullah on sword blades. Both read the same, "Assad Ullah, the servant of Shah Abbas."*

ASSAD ULLAH. The most celebrated of the Persian swordsmiths. He lived in Ispahan in the time of Shah Abbas, 1587-1628. He is the best known of the Persian sword makers and his blades are of the most beautiful sweep and balance, besides being of very finely watered steel. Egerton spells his name both Asad and Assad. (52, 53, 57). The name in Arabic is Assad ul Allah, the lion of God. Fig. 96.

ASSEGAI, HASSEGAI. The spear of the Kafirs and other allied tribes of South Africa. It usually has a leaf-shaped head, though other shapes are by no means uncommon. The head is fixed to the shaft by a tang, the end of the shaft being wound with cord made of twisted hide to prevent its splitting. The assegai is made mainly for throwing and, when made for this purpose, always has a rather light wooden shaft. Heavier ones are made especially for thrusting, "stabbing" assegais, these sometimes have iron shafts. The name assegai is unknown to the tribes that use them but is Portuguese. Fig. 97.

ASTARA. A boomerang, Sandscrit. (Jaehns 203).

ASTRAGAL. In gunnery, any moulding on a cannon. (Hoyt 357).

ASWAR. A colloquial name for the sword. Rajput. (Tod I, 541).

ATASH BAZI. Fire throwing machines, India 18th century. (Hime 65).

ATLATL. A Mexican spear thrower. The older ones are quite elaborate with large loop handles carved on the lower side. The modern form is usually a straight, flat stick with cord loops at the handle end to give the fingers a purchase. (Arc. f. Eth. III, 137). Some widen out at the handle and have

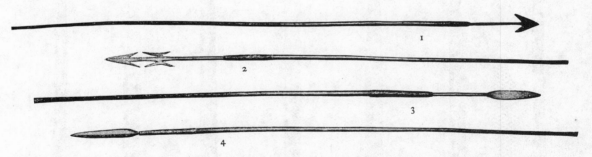

FIGURE 97. *Assegais. 1. Iron head on a shank 7.5 inches long; total length 4 feet 7 inches. 2. Head 12.5 inches long; total length 4 feet 1 inch. 3. Head and shank 12 inches long. 4. Head 7 inches long.*

two holes for the fingers. See Spear Thrower. Figs. 746, 748.

ATOBUSA. A crupper with large tassels, frequently used in war in Japan.

ATO-OSAE. The rear guard of an army, Japan.

ATSU-BUSA. A bridle ornamented with tassels, Japan.

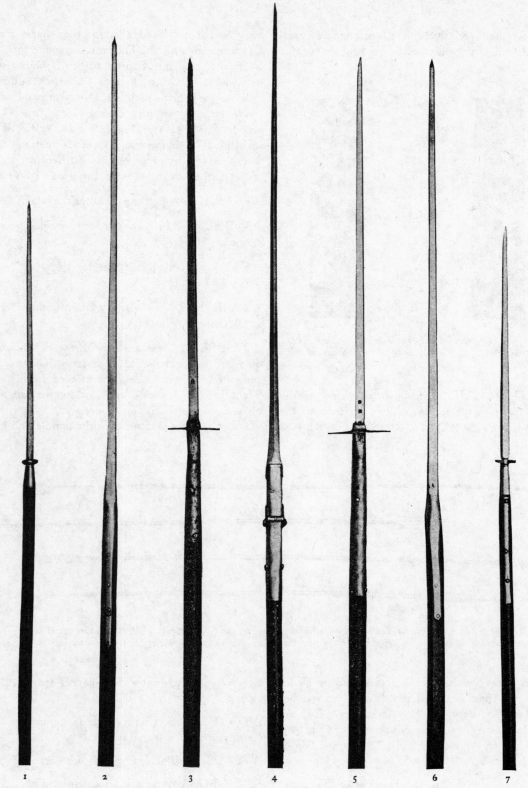

FIGURE 98. *Awl Pikes.* 1. *French(?), 16th century.* 2. *German, 1480, Austrian, 15th century.* 3. *German, 15th century.* 4. *German, 1560.* 5. *Swiss, 15th century.* 6. *German, 1480.* 7. *French(?), 16th century. Metropolitan Museum.*

ATSU-NIKU-BORI. Carving in high relief, Japan.

AUNURGITCH. A type of spear, Melville Island. A typical one measures ten feet six inches in length and has twenty-four barbs, all on one side; the first is nine and the last forty-six inches from the point. The greatest width across the barbs is two inches, and the longest barb is four and three-quarters inches long. The barbs are shaped like the scales of a pine cone. (Spencer North. Ter. 361).

AWL-PIKE. A shafted weapon with a long, slim, straight, square head and, usually, a round or octagonal guard between the head and shaft, 15th century. It is of German origin and the English name is a phonetic rendering of the German *ahlspiess* (eel spear). Fig. 98.

AXE. In most countries of Europe, and many of the East, the axe was a favorite weapon as long as armor was worn; and it was retained in European navies long after it was abandoned on land. At first

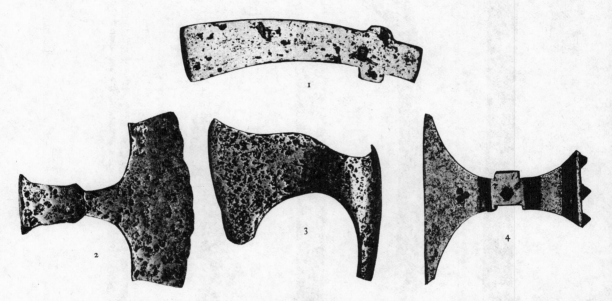

FIGURE 99. *Early European Axes.* 1. *Third to seventh century.* 2. *Seventh to thirteenth century.* 3. *Tenth to fourteenth century.* 4. *Fifteenth century. Metropolitan Museum. Not to scale.*

AUQUETON. See Aketon.

AVANT-BRAS. Armor for the forearm. See Brassard.

AVANT-GARDE. One of the divisions of an army in the 14th century. See Arriere-Garde.

AVANT-PLAT. See Vamplate.

AVENTAILLE. The movable front piece of a helmet, or of the hood of a hauberk. It succeeded the nasal of the 11th and preceded the visor of the 14th century. (Planche 23).

AWASE-DO. A small whetstone used in grinding blades in Japan.

AWASE-GOTE. See Shino-Gote.

the ordinary hatchet or axe of civil life was used as a weapon, but special varieties were soon developed for fighting. War axes were of all sizes from light weapons intended solely for throwing, to heavy pole axes requiring the use of both arms. Most have a single cutting edge, though double axes have been used in many ages and countries. The blade is generally balanced by a hammer head or point on the opposite side of the handle, and the latter is frequently terminated by a spike. The Indian axes are generally lighter than the European and often have the handle made of a flat plate of steel with pieces of wood riveted to each side. Occasionally they have a dagger concealed in the handle; and, sometimes, a sharp-edged hook projects from one side. This was probably intended for cutting the

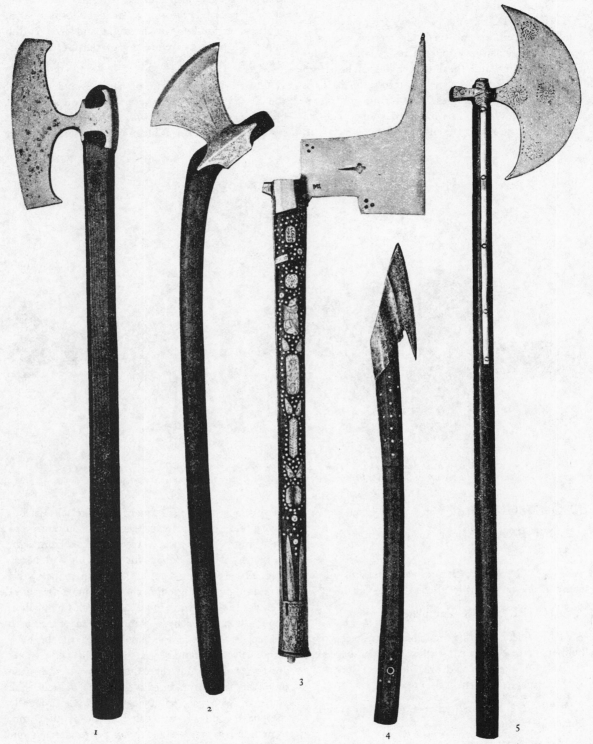

FIGURE 100. *European Axes. 1. German, 14th century. 2. Swedish, 15th century. 3. Saxon miners'*
guild axe, 17th century. 4. German, 14th century. 5. Polish, 17th century. Metropolitan Museum.

FIGURE 101. *Oriental Axes*. 1. *Northern India, XVIII. Steel head with a square pean and crescent blade 15 inches long; adze-eye for handle. Rather light handle with a leather sling.* 2. *Hammer, Persia, XVIII. Blued steel heavily inlaid with silver. The middle of the handle is covered with leather.* 3. *Southern India, XVII. Moulded steel head, wooden handle with ring. Length 2 feet.* 4. *Tanjore, XVII. Moulded steel head with a long, flat tang inserted in the ebony handle and riveted to it.* 5. *Central India, XVIII. Heavy head; handle covered with velvet with embossed silver bands.* 6. *Ceylon or Malabar, XVIII. Crescent blade with a hammer head opposite and a hook for cutting reins projecting from the side. Wooden handle painted in rings with colored lac. Length 23 inches.* 7. *Northern India, XVIII. Light head inlaid with copper and silver, spike on the end. The wooden handle is reinforced by a steel plate in the middle riveted with brass burrs.* 8. *Persia, XVII. Heavy head with a square pean, very finely engraved. Length 20.75 inches.* 9. *State axe, Travancore, XVIII. Pierced steel blade set in finely worked brass inlaid with silver plaques. The spearhead can be slid back into the handle and the opening closed by the conical brass cap shown at the side. Length, including spearhead, 2 feet 11.25 inches.* 10. *North India, XVIII. Crescent blade with an openwork pean in the shape of a pagoda; engraved and inlaid with gold. Wood handle with a central steel plate riveted with brass burrs and mounts. Length 30.125 inches.* 11. *Sind, XVIII. Crescent blade and hollow steel handle containing a knife. The entire handle and most of the blade are covered with a diaper pattern in gold.* 12. *North India, XVIII. Very heavy head with a square pean; chased in low relief and inlaid with silver. Steel shaft with a spiral band of floral decoration inlaid in silver.* 13. *Central India, XVIII. Engraved blade curved back and terminated by a conventional antelope's head.* 14. *Processional axe, Northern India, XVIII. Two light crescent blades engraved with inscriptions. Width 15.5 inches, height 15.* 15. *Persia, XVIII. Narrow blade and long pick point with broad straps on the shaft, chape on butt. All steel work well inlaid with a gold pattern in gold and silver. Length 26.625 inches.* 16. *Herzegovinia. Head inlaid with a runic pattern in silver. It has an adze-eye for the shaft, which is flat. Length 32.25 inches.*

FIGURE 102. *Savage Axes.* 1. Upper Congo, ceremonial axe. Copper blade and copper covered handle. 2. Nzappa Zap. Upper Congo. Iron head with three human faces, handle covered with lizard skin. 3. Nzappa Zap. Iron head with three faces, handle covered with copper. 4. Congo, iron with turned over edges, wooden handle. 5. Nzappa Zap. Handle covered with copper; head with two human faces. 6. Naga Assam. Black wooden handle with a tassel of red and black goat hair. 7. Naga. The cutting edge is only on the side opposite the rounded projection. Wood handle and hair tassel. 8. Naga, Kalyo Kangyu type. Handle wound with cane, length 21 inches. 9. Naga, Chang. This shape shows the transition from the axe to the sword.

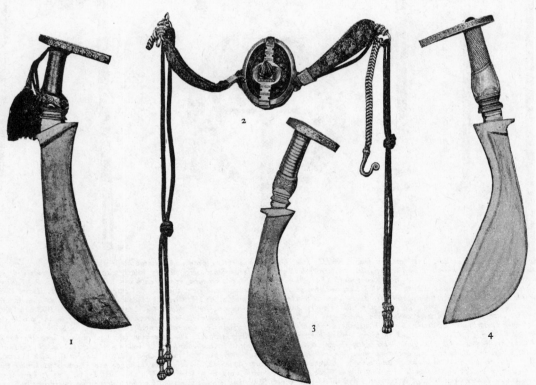

FIGURE 104. *Ayda Katti.* 1. Wooden hilt partly painted red and decorated with silver rosettes. 2. Belt, Todunga, centerpiece of polished brass, other metal parts of silver. 3. Silver hilt. Length of blade 12.75 inches. 4. Ivory hilt, length of blade 15.25 inches.

bridle reins of an opponent. Combinations of axes and pistols were fairly common in both Europe and the East; in these the barrel of the pistol is often the handle of the axe. See Combined Weapons. Japan was almost the only armor-wearing nation that did not ordinarily use axes. In Japan purely smashing

Crowbill, Doloire, Francisca, Fuetsu, Galraki, Godenda, Halbard, Head Axe, Hippe, Hortuk, Jedburg Axe, Kama Yari, Keerli, Kigalee, Kodelly, Lochaber Axe, Lohar, Lucerne Hammer, Masa Kari, Oncin, O-No, Palta, Pareh, Parusa, Patati, Pattisha, Pole-Axe, Raifu, Saber, Sabre Halbard,

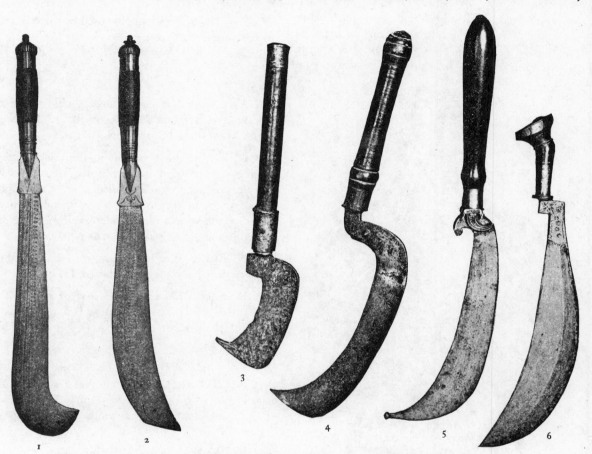

FIGURE 103. *Sacrificial Axes.* 1, 2. *Ram Dao(?), Nepal. Both have heavy, engraved blades, checkered handles and brass mounts. Each has a gold eye inlaid in the blade. Length 19 inches. 3, 4, 5, 6. Malabar. All have rough blades and wooden handles. The blade of no. 5 is 13.5 inches long and the overall length is 2 feet and half an inch. It is doubtful if some, at least, of these Malabar "axes" are not agricultural implements.*

weapons were not considered proper for the samurai. Axes were only used there by the fighting priests, and are very rare. See O-No and Masa-Kari. European Axes figs. 99, 100; Oriental 101; Savage 102.

For the different varieties see: Adze, Adze-Axe, Axe-Knife, Axe (Sacrificial), Ay-Balta, Balinung, Balta, Battle-Axe, Beaked Axe, Berdiche, Bhuj, Biliong, Brandestoc, Buckie, Bullova, Catri, Celt, Chandra-Husa, Chatu Katu, Combined Weapons,

Scorpion, Seko, Shoka, Silepe, Sparte, Stari, Taavish, Taber, Tabar-I-Zin, Taper Axe, Toki, Toki Kakauroa, Toki Poto, Tomahawk, Tongia, Toporok, Tuagh-Catha, Tungi, Udlimau, Uncin, Venmuroo, Voulge, Zaghnal.

AXE-KNIFE. A broad knife blade on the end of a long, straight handle. See Bhuj.

AXE, SACRIFICIAL. Many weapons, especially those from India, are commonly called "sacrificial axes," although they more nearly resemble swords. For instance the sickle-shaped tools from Malabar and the ram dao of Nepal, fig. 103. Some of the former are probably agricultural implements.

AYDA KATTI. The national sword of the Coorgs of Coorg (Malabar). It has a very broad, heavy, curved, single-edged blade very much wider at the end than at the hilt, and sharp on the concave side. The hilt has no guard but has a large kite-shaped pommel. It is carried, unsheathed, on

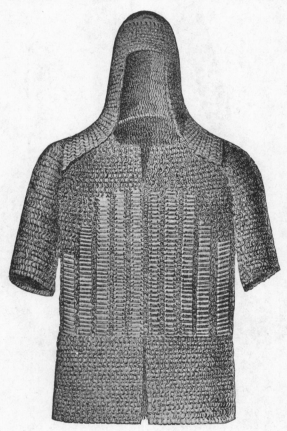

FIGURE 105. *Bachteretz. Russian, a coat of mail. Rockstuhl, plate LXXXIV.*

the back passed through a flattened brass ring with a spike projecting from the center (called the todunga) which is fastened to the belt which is fastened in front by massive silver chains. (Egerton 109 to 123). Fig. 104.

AY-BALTA. A variety of Turkish battle-axe. (Moser XXXIII).

AYRI. Cutting implements of the early Peruvians.

AZAGAI. A lance or javelin, Spanish and Portuguese, 15th century. (Burton Sword 42). The name assegai which we apply to the Kafir spear is undoubtedly derived from this.

AZUCHI. A bank of earth against which a target is placed, Japan.

AZUSA-YUMI. A small bow used by sorcerers in their incantations, Japan.

B

BABANGA. A leaf-shaped sword with a square end, made at Batta on the Gaboon River, and used by the Mpangwe. (Burton Sword 165).

BACELE. "Bardin says that in the middle ages cavalry were divided into groups of ten 'lances' (fifty or sixty horsemen) called *bacele*, and that five of them united to form a regiment of fifty lances, or about 300 men, under the command of a knight banneret." (Denison 155).

BACHELOR. The lower grade of knight, the banneret being the higher. (Hewitt II, 9).

BACHTERETZ. A Russian coat of mail with many rows of very small plates. It is much like many of the Indian coats. Fig. 105. (Rockstuhl LXXXIV).

BACINET. See Basinet.

BACK AND BREAST. The usual description of body armor worn in the 17th century. It consisted of a cuirass, back plate, and some sort of an open helmet. (Planche 27).

BACK SWORD. A kind of sabre. A sword having a straight, or very slightly curved, single-edged blade. The hilts varied greatly. (Castle 242).

BACUL. See Crupper.

BACYN. See Basinet.

BADE-BADE, BATTIG, ROENTJAU. A Malayan knife with a narrow, incurved, single-edged blade sharp on the concave side. It has no guard and the shapes of the hilts and scabbards vary greatly. Fig. 106. It is very widely distributed, being used in most of the islands of the Malay Archipelago.

BADELAIRE. A 16th-century sabre with a short, broad, falchion-shaped blade, a straight hilt with an ornamental pommel and flat quillons. The one towards the edge curves back in the direction of the pommel and the other towards the back of the blade. Fig. 107.

BADGE. A device to distinguish the followers of a king, or private chieftain. The badge was the per-

BADIK. A Javan sword with a short blade having a curved edge and a straight back. It has a pistol hilt, Borneo. (Raffles I, 296 and pl. 296/297).

BADIQ LOKTIGA. A knife with a short, tapering blade and an elaborately carved hilt, Borneo. (Arc. f. Eth. V, 238).

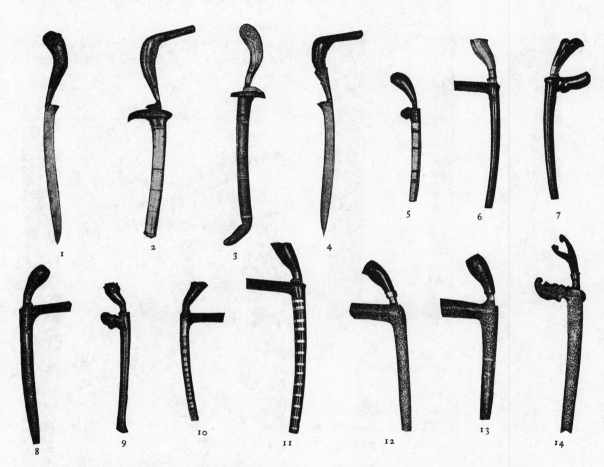

FIGURE 106. Bade-Bade. 1. Acheen. Blade 10.5 inches long, carved horn hilt. 2. Acheen. Scabbard covered with silver. Ivory hilt. 3. Acheen ivory hilt. Carved wood scabbard. 4. Acheen. Blade 10 inches long set in a gold inlaid mount. 5. Blade 5.5 inches long. Wood hilt, silver bands on scabbard. 6. Tringanau. Ivory hilt, wood sheath. 7. Celebes. Brass blade. Horn hilt and scabbard top. 8. West Borneo. Wood hilt. Horn ends on scabbard. 9. Hilt and ends of scabbard of carved horn. 10. Celebes. Blade 6.5 inches long. Horn hilt inlaid with bone. Scabbard with horn top and silver bands. 11. Deeply fluted blade. Horn hilt and scabbard top. Silver bands on scabbard. 12. Menangkabau, Sumatra. Black horn hilt set in silver; blade 9.25 inches long. Scabbard covered with embossed gold plated metal. 13. Menangkabau. Plain wood hilt; heavy grooved blade 9 inches long. Scabbard covered with embossed silver. 14. Scroll hilt set in brass. Double-edged blade 11 inches long. Scabbard of black wood with a scroll top, covered with embossed gold plated metal.

sonal distinction of the middle ages, and was the origin of the armorial insignia. It was a family distinction as hereditary as the coat of arms. (Planche 27,525).

BAGGORO. A flat, sharp-edged club, Queensland. "The wooden sword, the necessary companion of the shield, is about five inches wide up to the point, which is slightly rounded, and usually reaches from the foot to the shoulder. It is made of hard wood with a short handle for only one hand, and is

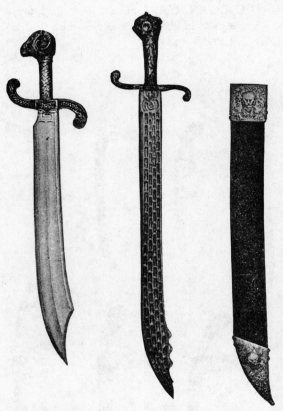

FIGURE 107. *Badelaires. Metropolitan Museum.*

so heavy that any one not used to it can scarcely balance it perpendicularly with half extended arm — the position always adopted before the battle begins." (Lumholtz 121). Fig. 108. Compare Barkur.

BAGH NAKH, BAG'HNAK, NAHAR-NUK, WAGHNAKH, WAGNUK, WAHAR-NUK. An Indian weapon. The name means tiger's claw. It consists of four or five curved blades fixed to a cross bar or glove and carried concealed in the palm of the hand. On the opposite side of the bar there are two rings for the fingers. Occasionally it is made of two plates hinged together instead of a bar; the one for the thumb has one ring and one claw, the longer one for the palm has three claws and two rings. It was never considered a legitimate weapon and, in later days, has only been used by thieves and assassins. Sivaji, the founder of the

Mahratta Empire, used one like 4 when he killed Afzal Khan, the general of the army of Bijapur. (Egerton 476, 477, 479 and p. 27). Fig. 109.

BAGSACAY. See Simbilan.

BAGU. Horse trappings etc. Japan.

BAHLA. A hawking glove, Persia. (Phillott 175, note).

BAHUYDDHA. In the ancient classification of Hindu weapons, those "which the body provides for personal struggles." (Burton Sword 214). See Amukta.

FIGURE 108. *Baggoro. 1. Queensland native with baggoro dancing before a duel. Lumholz, p. 122. 2. Baggoro, Peabody Museum, Salem.*

BAILEY, BALLIUM, BAYLE. The court, or courts, of a castle in the middle ages. The outer bailey was entered through a portcullis and bridge over the moat, and was divided from the inner bailey by a strong embattled wall and towered gate, often with a second portcullis. The inner bailey usually contained the quarters of the garrison, chapel, stables and hospital. The keep, or donjon, was also in the inner bailey. (Grose II, 3).

BAINBERGS, BEINBERGS. Coverings for the front of the legs. They were occasionally made of

taiah, or padded war jacket of the Sea Dyaks. It is made of quilted or padded cotton, usually sleeveless and collarless. (Ling Roth II, 131).

BAKIN. A kind of spear used by the Sea Dyaks. (Ling Roth II, 128).

BAKUDAN. A bomb shell, Japan.

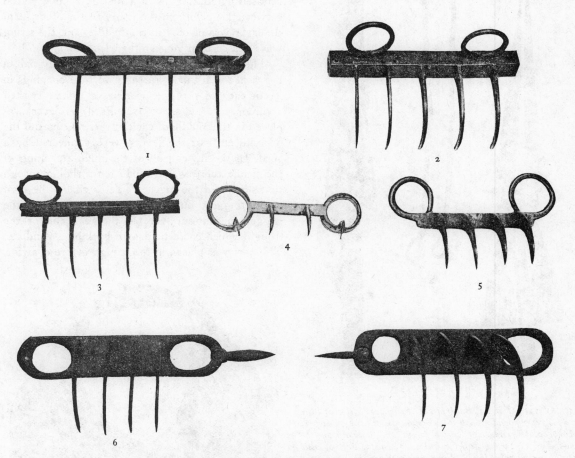

FIGURE 109. *Bagh Nakh.* 1. *Rings and four claws riveted to a flat bar.* 2. *Rings and five claws mortised and riveted in a square bar.* 3. *Five claws and scalloped rings mortised in a square bar.* 4. *A copy of the one Sivaji used when he murdered Afzal Khan. For the left hand.* 5. *Four claws, rings formed by forging down and curving the ends of the bar.* 6, 7. *A pair, right and left, flat plates with holes punched in the ends for the fingers. Four claws and a spearhead riveted to each.*

plate, but more often of boiled leather, 13th century. The name indicates that they were of German origin.

BAJU EMPERAU. A Dyak war coat made of some sort of soft, bast-like material covered with large fish scales sewed on. (Ling Roth II, 100).

BAJU TILAM. The Malay name for the *klambi*

BALASAN. The Menangkabau (Sumatra) blow-pipe. It is rather short and made of a single joint of bamboo. The tube is called *bulau kasoq* and the darts *damak* or *djuing*, the latter being made of the hard fibres that cover the trunk of the *saga-anau*. The butts of the darts are provided with pieces of reed, *timbaru*, which are covered with raw cotton before shooting. (Arc. f. Eth. IV, 267).

BALATOE. A sword, class name, Nias. (Leiden IV, 39). Compare Ballatu.

BALDRIC, BALDRICK, BAUDRICK. A collar or shoulder belt, worn either as a support for a

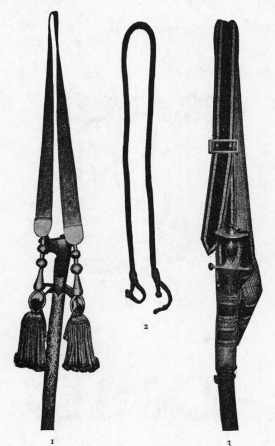

FIGURE 110. *Oriental Baldrics.* 1. *Morocco. Sling of blue and silver brocade with silver mounts on the ends.* 2. *Morocco. Worsted cord with loops and buttons on the ends. For a powder flask or knife.* 3. *India. Belt of blue velvet with gold braid, lined with silver brocade, gilt buckle.*

sword or other weapon, or simply as an ornament, 14th century and later. (Planche 30). Figs. 110, 111.

BALEMBENG. The wide upper part of a kris scabbard, Celebes. (Arc. f. Eth. XVIII, 65).

BALESTARIUS, BALESTAEUS. The large Batak (Sumatra) axe. (Arc. f. Eth. VI, 120). It is of the ordinary Malay type, see Biliong.

BALISTA. An engine for throwing darts and stone balls. In some cases it was merely a huge

crossbow which was drawn by two handwheels working a worm wheel that turned a long screw working in a traveling nut on a block carrying the catch for the string and the trigger mechanism. Two forms of trigger release were used. In the first the hook for the string was at one end of a lever which was pivoted at the other end, and was released by striking, with a mallet, a knob placed between the pivot and the hook. In the other form the lever was pivoted in the middle, and the string was released by prying up the back end.

The earlier, and more common form, of balista had a heavy frame with three vertical openings in it; in each of the side openings a tightly twisted skein of cord or sinew was fixed. A lever was placed in the middle of each of these skeins and the opposite ends of the levers were connected by a cord. In the lower part of the middle opening of the frame there was a guide for a sliding trough that supported the missile. The catch for the cord connecting the outer ends of the levers, and the trigger mechanism were in the rear end of the trough, which could be drawn back by a windlass. The dart was placed in the trough before drawing

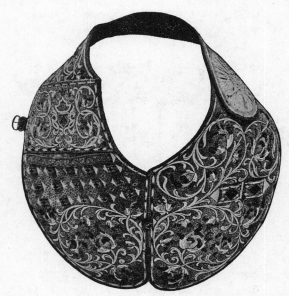

FIGURE 111. *State baldric with holders for knives and other small objects. Spanish, 17th century. Worn by a member of the Ocagna family who was master of the hunt to the king. Metropolitan Museum.*

the string and, as the trigger mechanism traveled with the trough, it could be fired whenever desired regardless of whether it was drawn to its fullest extent. This allowed the users to control the range; in this it differed radically from the crossbow. Fig. 112.

Balistas were made of all sizes, from those with arms three or four feet long and skeins six or eight inches in diameter down to those scarcely larger than a crossbow. In some cases there was a pocket

BALLOK KNIFE. A knife worn at the girdle by priests in the 14th century. (Planche 32).

BALLUR. A peculiar kind of spear thrower used only between the Bloomfield River and Cape Grafton, Queensland. It is a thin, flat piece of wood very much curved, with the wide sides flat and the peg in the plane of the blade. It is used when spear-

FIGURE 112. *Balista. From Payne-Gallwey, Projectile-Throwing Engines, p. 21.*

in the middle of the string so that stones could be thrown. The largest balistas could throw arrows weighing five or six pounds, or stones weighing rather more for a distance of four hundred and fifty to five hundred yards.

The balls used by the ancients were often made of pebbles enclosed in baked clay. They were used because they shattered on striking and therefore could not be used again by the enemy. (Payne-Gallwey, Throwing Engines 21).

BALLAM. A short spear with a broad head used by the infantry of Mysore about 1800. (Egerton, p. 123).

BALLATU. A sword, class name, Nias. (Modigliani, Nias 239). Compare Balatoe.

BALLIUM. See Bailey.

ing fish or birds, especially anything at very close quarters. In using it the blade is held between the first finger and thumb instead of between the first and second fingers, as is done with all other kinds. (Roth, Aust. Mus. VII, 199). See Spear Throwers.

BALTA. Turkish, a battle axe. It did not differ materially from the contemporary European forms except in decoration.

BALUSE. The Nias shield. It is a narrow, oval shield with a central boss covering the hand hole and a heavy rib that projects beyond the ends. It is made of a single piece of wood and is strengthened by transverse lashings of cane. Fig. 113. (Modigliani, Nias 229).

BALWA-NAL. See Jowala-Mookhi.

BAMEROOK. See Giam.

BAN. The first line of the national militia of France in the 13th and 14th centuries. (Hewitt I, 98).

A rocket, India. See Bhan.

BANDANG. A Javan spear with the ordinary Malay type of head and a knob and tassel at the butt to which a cord is fastened. (Raffles plate p. 296/297).

BANDCROLL. A small flag used to indicate the limits of a camp.

FIGURE 113. *Baluse, a Nias shield. Made from a single piece of wood. Length 4 feet 1 inch.*

BANDED MAIL. A variety of mail shown in the illustrations of the 12th and 13th centuries. These indicate alternate rows of links and solid disks, a

FIGURE 114. *Banded Mail. King Arthur from a manuscript of the commencement of the 14th century. (Hewitt II, 148). It is a good example of the armor of the transition period.*

construction that is manifestly impossible. Fig. 114. Many attempts have been made to explain its character but none have been generally accepted. That of Mr. Waller, that this is ordinary mail through alternate lines of the links of which leather thongs have been drawn, may be correct. Certainly the specimens of Oriental mail of this character bear considerable resemblance to some of the old pictures. Mr. C. B. Lewis, who drew the illustrations for De Cosson's Helmets & Mail, suggested a new solution. "According to his idea this banded mail was made by sewing rings on linen, so that they overlapped one another in rows, like the edge mail of Sir S. Meyrick (some examples having the rings

FIGURE 115. *Japanese Bandoliers.* 1. *The charge cases are of red paper with gold spots. In addition there are two red boxes for chargers and a small black primer.* 2. *Precisely like 1 but with only one box for chargers.*

closer than others). It was then covered on both sides by sewing on strips of leather, the stitching passing between the rows of rings, the lower edges of the leather being turned up and covering the upper edges of the strips beneath, thus increasing the thickness of leather between the rings to six folds." (De Cosson, Helmets & Mail, 115). The accompanying illustrations look more like the old ones than any other attempts to imitate them.

There is one serious defect in all of these explanations. All of the proposed methods of construction tend strongly to destroy the flexibility of the mail, and in the old illustrations it is usually shown in the parts where flexibility is most important, as the arms, legs and neck guards. Some of the Oriental bar-link mail with small links looks somewhat like some of the old pictures, and it is flexible. It is sometimes used for the arms of Indian

coats, the bodies of which are of ordinary mail. The fact that no mail looking like the pictures has ever been found makes it unlikely that they were intended to show the actual construction.

It is probable that Laking's suggestion is the true explanation, and that the different methods of representing mail all mean the same thing and were only used to prevent monotony.

BANDELEER. See Bandolier.

BANDEROLLE, BANNEROLE. A small streamer attached to the head of a lance. It is still used in modern armies. In the middle ages it was often called a pencil. (Grose II, 277).

BANDOL, BANDUL. A Javan sword with a hooked point. (Raffles I, 296 and plate p. 296/297).

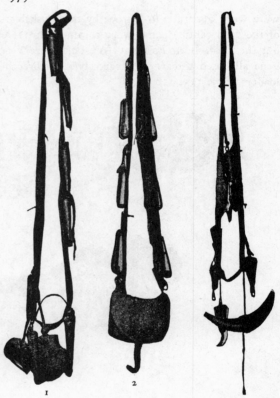

FIGURE 116. *Oriental Bandoliers.* 1. *Tibet. Eight brass powder chargers, bullet pouch and horn primer.* 2. *Turkish, twelve chargers in pairs and a bullet bag.* 3. *Tibet, eight powder chargers of iron and brass and of different sizes and shapes, and a horn primer.*

BANDOLIER, BANDELEER. A baldric, or waist belt, from which hung a number of cases of wood or metal each containing a measured charge of powder for a gun or pistol. It also often carried a primer, or a bullet pouch, or both. Bandoliers

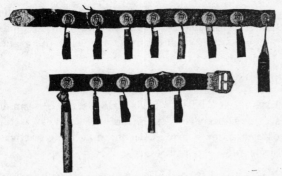

FIGURE 117. *Saxon bandolier, 1580. Guard of Christian I. In addition to the powder chargers it carries a primer and match pipe. Metropolitan Museum.*

were worn generally in Europe by the musketeers of the 17th century; and were common throughout the East. Both East and West they are very generally used to carry the cartridges for breechloaders. Figs. 115, 116, 117.

BANDOLIER BELTS. The more common form of bandolier is a baldric, or shoulder belt; those made to fasten around the waist are sometimes called bandolier belts. Figs. 118, 119.

BANDRING. A sling, Java. (Raffles I, 296 and plate p. 296/297).

BANDUK, BANDOOK, BANDAQ, BUNDUK, BUNDOOK. India, a gun. The Hindustanee name is *banduk* from the Arabic *bunduk*. In Hobson-Jobson the name is said to be derived from *banadik*, the Arabic name for filberts, because they came from Venice (Arab Banadik). The name was transferred to the nut-like pellets shot from the crossbow, thence to the crossbow itself, and finally to firearms. In Hobson-Jobson it is defined as a musket or matchlock. The Handbook to the Ethnological Collections of the British Museum, p. 49, says that it means a flint lock as distinguished from a matchlock (toradar): Egerton uses the two names for either indiscriminately; and the Catalogue of the Wallace Collection calls either kind of a gun a Bunduk-Toradar.

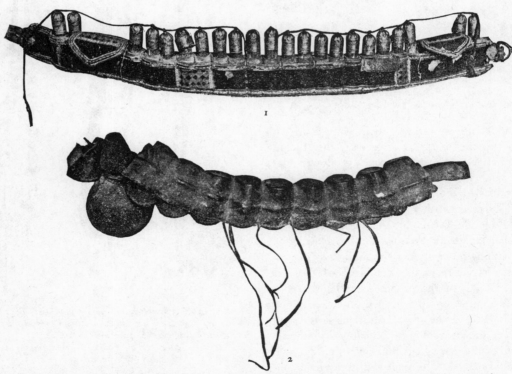

FIGURE 118. *African Bandolier Belts.* 1. *Zanzibar Arab. Belt and pouches covered with red cloth and colored leather. Twenty-two brass chargers with embossed silver caps.* 2. *Central Africa.* **Leather** *belt with nine wooden chargers, a gourd for priming powder and a bullet pouch.*

BANDUK DORAHA. Two guns, one complete-
ly enclosed in the other; the outer gun is a flint
lock, and the inner a percussion, Rajput. (Egerton 801).

BANDUK JAUHADAR. Under this name Egerton and the Wallace Catalogue describe some
guns from Sind with Afgan stocks and flint locks.
It simply means guns with barrels of watered steel
(jauhar).

BARBACAN, BARBICAN. An outwork covering the approach to the drawbridge or gateway of
a fortress or castle. (Grose II, 2).

BARBUTE. A variety of salade, 15th century.
Fig. 121. It fits closely to the head and is precisely
like the Greek casque. It is usually considered the
same as the Italian *celata*. Some authorities question this.

FIGURE 119. *Bandolier belt and breastplate of heavy embossed silver. The belt and shoulder straps
are of yellow silk and silver. Probably Turkish, 18th century.*

BAN-GEEK. See Barngeet.

BAN-GUSOKU. See Nuko.

BANK. A Mahratta knife with a sickle-shaped
blade and straight handle. Fig. 120. (Egerton 480,
481). The Wallace Catalogue describes other forms
of knife under this name.

BANQUI, HANQUI. A short bow wound with
rattan, Japan. (Gilbertson Archery 113).

BANNER. Originally a small square flag carried
before a knight banneret. His arms were embroidered on it. (Grose II, 52). At present it usually
means a flag hung from a horizontal pole hung
from a staff.

BANUWAYA. A kris scabbard, Celebes. (Arc. f.
Eth. XVIII, 65).

BARA JAMDADU. A Mahratta form of katar
intermediate between the usual ones and the gauntlet sword. It has a long blade and a short hand
guard. (Egerton 512, 513). See Katar.

BARB. A backwardly turned point on a spear or
arrow to prevent its being withdrawn from a
wound.

   A variety of horse bred by the North African
Arabs.

Some have a large opening in the front leaving
most of the face uncovered; others have fixed nasals; others again have a T-shaped opening that
allows the wearer to see and breathe well, and still
completely protects the face. Fig. 121. It is the best
of the open helmets of the time as it covers the head
and face completely, is light and not likely to be
knocked out of place.

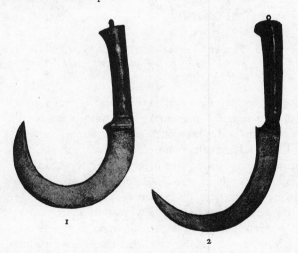

FIGURE 120. *Bank.* 1. *Blade 3.25 inches from hilt to
point, and 9 around the curve. Steel hilt; both it and the
blade are inlaid with silver.* 2. *Blade 5.5 inches from hilt
to point and 8 around the curve. Ivory grip riveted to the
flat tang.*

BARCHI. A Mahratta spear or pike used by foot soldiers. It has a spiked butt and a long, narrow square head with no edge. (Sinclair, I. A. II, 216). Compare Birchi.

BARDINGS. Armor for horses. Horse armor went through the same evolution as that for men and reached its highest development in the 15th and 16th centuries, and then degenerated into mere parade decoration. The earliest was of mail, later

only cover the back of the horse and must have had pieces hanging from the sides that have disappeared.

The most complete suits known consist of: the headpiece or chanfron; some authorities make a distinction between the chanfron, which covered the sides as well as the front of the head; and the frontal, which covered only the front. Sometimes a demi-chanfron, covering only the upper half of the front was used. The upper side of the neck was

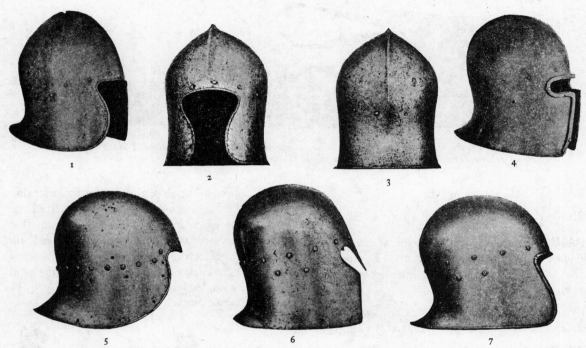

FIGURE 121. *Barbuttes. 1, 2, 3, 4, 5, Italian, 15th century. 6. Spanish, about 1450. 7. Milanese, about 1450. Nos. 1 and 4 from the Collection of Dr. Dean, remainder Metropolitan Museum. Not to scale.*

boiled leather was used very generally, even after plate armor for men had practically displaced all other kinds. But little of the leather armor remains. The Salzburg suit is immensely heavy, some of the pieces being nearly two inches thick; the chanfron is made partly of wood and partly of leather. Both were evidently made for a very large horse. There are a few pieces in the Tower of London, and at the Metropolitan Museum; the most complete one I have seen is in Turin, 1, fig. 122. As with most leather suits the chanfron and crinet are made of steel. Leather is so stiff and difficult to articulate that it is doubtful if cuello were ever made of it. The Turin crupper is unusually complete as most

covered by the crinet, a series of articulated plates, or by alternate narrow plates and strips of mail. This was sometimes supplemented by the much rarer cuello, a similar arrangement of plates and mail covering the lower side of the neck. The peytral, or poitrel, of plate covered the chest and shoulders as far back as the saddle. On many peytrals there are large hemi-spherical bosses on the sides. In the early ones these are smooth and would have caused a lance to glance; but, in some of the later ones they are elaborately embossed so that they would have held a lance instead of making it glance.

Below the saddle the sides were generally protected by plates, called flanchards. The crupper, if of steel, was formed of several plates riveted, or hinged together. It also had a tubular plate, the tail guard, attached at the root of the tail to allow the latter some motion. Some of the later cruppers were much lighter, being made up of a circular plate in the middle of the back with narrow radiating straps covered with short steel plates. All of

In the East horse armor was far less common than in Europe, the generally hotter climate and lighter build of the men and horses made it unsuitable. The Turks, who came in contact with the heavily armed horsemen of Europe more often than any other Orientals, were the principal users. In the 15th and 16th centuries they used plate chanfrons, fig. 214, and complete coverings of

1

2

FIGURE 122. *Horse Armor. 1. Leather poitrel and crupper. The chanfron and crinet are of steel. 2. All steel, 16th century, Italian. It belonged to a member of the Colleoni family of Brescia. Reale Armeria di Torino.*

these were usually much decorated, the round plate having a moulded knob on it and the others being covered with etched ornaments. Fig. 245. The legs were rarely covered, although examples of beautifully articulated defenses for a horse's legs are in existence. The styles of horse armor followed very closely those of armor for men, both reached their highest development at about the same time and then degenerated into mere parade decoration. No. 2 fig. 122, fig. 123.

small plates connected by mail, fig. 124. In Persia and India horse armor was worn but none of it remains and we have very little information regarding it. The chanfrons were of steel and approximated the European forms. The horses' bodies were probably covered by small plates connected by mail.

There are two good sets of Tibetan horse armor in the India Museum, South Kensington, which probably give a fair idea of the horse armor of

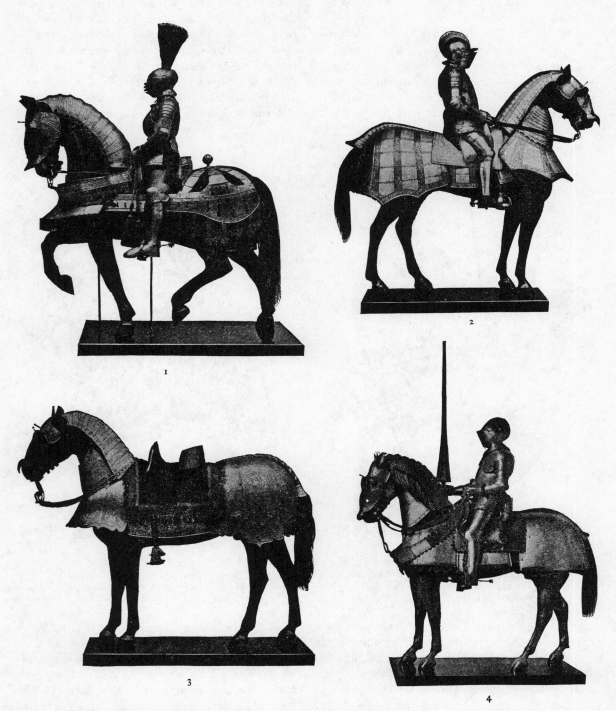

FIGURE 123. *Bardings, Horse Armor. 1. Armor for horse and man. German, 1515. 2. Armor for horse and man. Italian, 1560. 3. Italian, 1560. 4. Armor for horse and man. Italian, 1575. 1. From the collection of Dr. Bashford Dean, remainder Metropolitan Museum. Not to scale.*

FIGURE 124. *Turkish, 16th century. Complete armor for man and horse of small plates connected by mail. Reale Armeria di Torino.*

FIGURE 125. *Tibetan Horse Armor. 1. The chanfron and the front of the poitrel are of leather with iron studs. The saddle and saddle cloths, which act as flanchards, are Chinese. The crupper and back part of the poitrel are of very small plates laced together like the suit, fig. 66. 2. The chanfron, crinet and lower part of the body armor are of leather with iron studs. The upper part of the body is of laced scales which appear much like Japanese armor. The flanchards are of leather. Both suits have long fringes of silk and hair hanging below them. South Kensington Museum. No. 2 is a loan by Sir C. A. Bell.*

southern and eastern types. The heads are protected by steel chanfrons and they have crinets, poitrels and cruppers of small plates laced together. Some resemble the armor for men, fig. 66, others are more like the Japanese. The middle of the horse's body is only protected by the saddle cloths which are heavy rugs, fig. 125.

The Chinese horse armor, like that worn by men, was usually brigandine, or padded silk. The chanfrons were often of the same material and

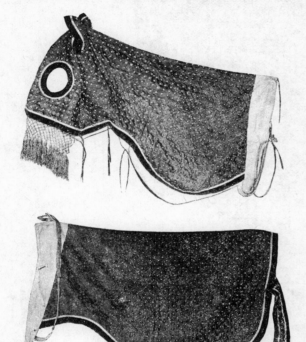

FIGURE 126. *Chinese Horse Armor. Padded blue satin with velvet borders. The upper piece is for the head and neck, a net and fringe over the lower part of the face. Lower, crupper with a broad crupper strap of the same material.*

covered, not only the head but the entire neck, fig. 126. Steel chanfrons were also used. This armor was strong enough to resist cuts from Chinese swords, which are notoriously bad; but would not be effective against spears and arrows.

In Japan horse armor was not used before the 17th century, after which time there was very little serious fighting, and it was apparently never used in battle. The chanfrons were usually the heads of more or less fabulous monsters, fig. 215. They were generally made of paper or leather, though some are of steel; few have any protective value.

The body armor was light, being made of small squares of leather, moulded, lacquered and sewn on cloth. The crupper was a large rectangle that covered the quarters, and has a smaller rectangle, the tail guard, fastened to the middle of one of the longer sides. The flanchards are large oval pieces of leather, moulded and gilded. They were hung from the saddle and were often carried without other armor but merely as decoration. There are also two triangular pieces, sometimes joined together, and made of small squares like the crupper. The use of these is very uncertain; they cannot cover both neck and chest, and it is difficult to see how they would fit on either. There are no bardings in place in any of the Japanese museums, and the only picture I have been able to find is a small one in the Yushu-Kwan (Museum of Arms) in Tokyo. It is very small and does not show any armor on the neck of the horse, and does not indicate clearly what is on its chest. Fig. 127.

Chanfrons were used until very recently in the Sudan. They are padded brass or steel. See Chanfron. In Bornu and parts of the Sudan horse armor was used that looks much like the Japanese according to the pictures that have been published.

BAREN. A large, long fringe used as a banner in Japan.

BARGEERS. Troops employed temporarily, mercenaries, India. (Tod II, 343).

BARKAL. A generic name for club, Rockhampton, Queensland. (Roth, Aust. Mus. VII, 208).

BARKUR, WORRAN. A flat club (sword) about six inches wide and four or five feet long with a short handle joined to the blade with a square shoulder. The handle is only large enough for one hand and is wound with cord covered with beeswax. It was split from the trunk of a small tree and may be either straight or curved. In use it is held in one hand stretched over the shoulder, the weapon hanging down the back, and brought forward from above down with a more or less sudden jerk. A well directed blow from one can split a man's skull. Queensland. (Roth, Aust. Mus. VII, 210). Compare Baggoro.

BAR-NGA. See Andarma.

BARNGEET, BAN-GEEK, BARN-GEEK, PRAAH-WITTOO-AH. The war boomerang

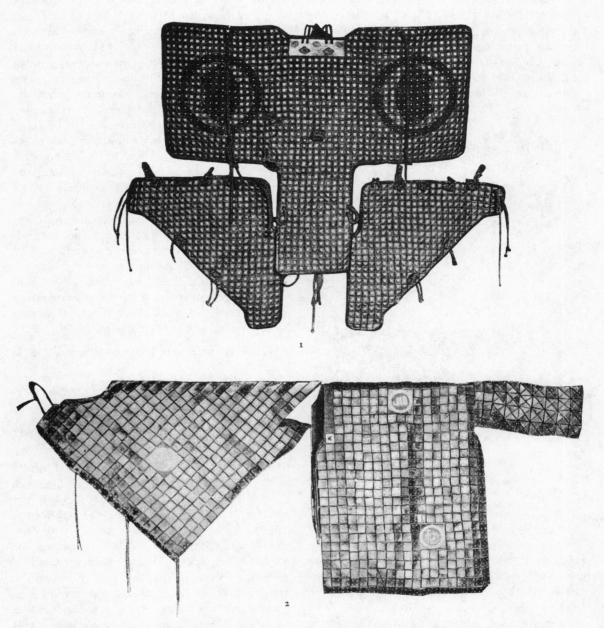

FIGURE 127. *Japanese Horse Armor. 1. Pieces of leather about an inch square moulded, gilded and sewn on cloth. Heavy cords of red silk. The crests are in black. 2. Squares and triangles of leather about an inch on a side, lacquered brown; gold crests lacquered on each piece. The "neck guard" is made in one piece instead of two as usual. Not to scale.*

of Victoria. It is seldom as much curved as the returning boomerang and, if twisted at all, not in the same way. Most are about thirty inches long, an inch and three-quarters wide, and weigh eight or ten ounces; but they vary much in size and shape. It is thrown forwards and up to one hundred and fifty yards. (Brough Smyth I, 313). See Boomerang.

are beautifully balanced weapons, a blow from which can easily sever a man's arm. They are carried in flat wooden scabbards decorated with simple but effective carving.

BARRAGAN. A returning boomerang, New South Wales. (Vic. Mus. 21).

BARRED BURGONET. A burgonet having a

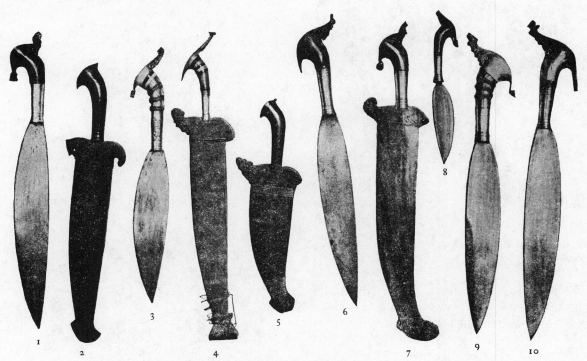

FIGURE 128. *Barongs. 1. Blade 17 inches long. Wood hilt with a brass ferule. 2. Hilt of horn and wood. A fighting barong. 3. Silver hilt with an ivory pommel. 4. Blade 12 inches long. Very light ivory hilt with bands of black horn. 5. Subanun, blade 7.875 x 3.125 inches, wood hilt. 6. Silver grip with wood pommel inlaid with ivory and horn. 7. Battingingi. Wood hilt, silver ferule. 8. Sulu, blade 6.25 inches long. Probably a boy's knife. 9. Zamboanga, back-edged blade 15 inches long. Hilt of gold and silver, ivory pommel. 10. Sulu, silver pommel separated from the gold grip by a band of black horn.*

BARONG. The national weapon of the Moros of Sulu, Mindanao and North Borneo. They have broad, heavy blades about sixteen inches long, nearly three inches wide in the middle and curve to the hilt and point on both edge and back. Usually they are single-edged, but occasionally have a back edge for about half their length. They have no guards and the pommels are often elaborate and characteristic. The more elaborate pommels are on weapons carried largely for show; those intended solely for fighting are simple like 2 and 5 fig. 128. They

fixed face guard of vertical bars. These helmets are purely heraldic and were only used for mortuary purposes. Fig. 129.

BARREL HELM. The large barrel-shaped helmet of the 13th century. It enclosed the head and, at first, the only opening was the ocularium, or vision slit. Later extra breathing holes were added in the lower part. The barrel helm was worn over a light helmet or hood of mail. The entire weight rested on the head and it was only worn when actually fighting.

BARU SINALI. A corselet woven of heavy cord like a sleeveless vest. It was used in Nias. Fig. 130. (Modigliani, Nias 233).

FIGURE 129. *Barred Burgonet. German, 17th century. Metropolitan Museum.*

BARUTDAN. The Indo-Persian powder flask for charge powder. They vary greatly in size, shape and material, none of which seems to be entirely characteristic of the locality from which they come. The decoration is slightly more distinctive as the Persian designs and workmanship are generally better than the Indian. When figures are introduced it is easier to differentiate. Barutdans are made of metal, bone, horn, ivory, paper, shell, wood, leather and stone, and are decorated in all of the ways known. Fig. 131.

BACINET. See Basinet.

BASELARD, BASILARD. A short sword, or dagger, carried by civilians in the 15th century. (ffoulkes 103).

A short sword with a straight, tapering blade of diamond section, straight quillons and a cross pommel. Sometimes it has a straight hilt without a guard, 13th and 14th centuries. (Laking Armour III, 10).

BASEN. The back part of a saddle, Japan.

BASES, LAMBOYS. Steel skirts in folds to imitate the civilian dress of the 16th century. (ffoulkes 75, 77). See Tonlet.

Skirts of fabric or steel worn with armor. (ffoulkes Armourer 155).

BASILISK. See Cannon.

BASINET, BACINET, BACYN, BASCINET, BASNET. The most popular of the lighter helmets of the 14th century. It was evolved from the archer's skull by raising the back of the crown and extending the lower edge to cover the sides and back of the head. The earliest had high, ogival crowns and straight lower edges; they were probably worn over mail hoods. By the middle of the century the crowns had been lowered, the skull piece extended to cover the sides and back of the head, and the camail added. The camail was a cape of mail fastened to the headpiece by a lacing passing through staples (vervelles) on the latter. It covered the neck and shoulders. In some of the basinets of the second quarter of the 14th century there is a

FIGURE 130. *Baru Sinali. Malayan armor of woven cord.*

triangular piece of mail projecting from the middle of the camail that could be hooked up to the forehead so as to cover most of the face. In the third quarter of the century plate visors were added. They projected very strongly in a point and the helmets provided with them were called "pig-faced" or "dog-faced" basinets. The first visors were hinged to the forehead of the helmets but, by the end of the century, they were pivoted at the

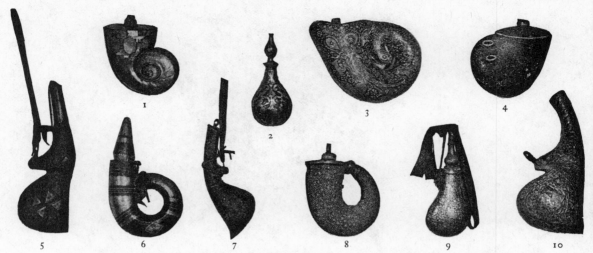

FIGURE 131. *Barutdan.* 1. *India, 18th century. Flask made of a large pearl shell with the large end built out with a mosaic of the same material.* 2. *Persia, 18th century. Brass with applied silver scrolls. Flat back and convex front.* 3. *India, 19th century. Moulded paper decorated with designs in white on black.* 4. *Persia, 18th century. Moulded paper lacquered with gold scrolls on green.* 5. *Persia, about 1800. Wood inlaid with bone. This is called the "camel's intestine" shape.* 6. *Indian Arab, early 18th century. Iron decorated with silver bands and coils of brass and silver wire.* 7. *Afgan, about 1800. Leather decorated in colors with an inscription.* 8. *India, 18th century. Wood flask covered with shark skin, ivory mounts.* 9. *Persia, about 1800. Iron elaborately inlaid with gold and silver.* 10. *Persia, about 1800. Stamped leather decorated in colors.*

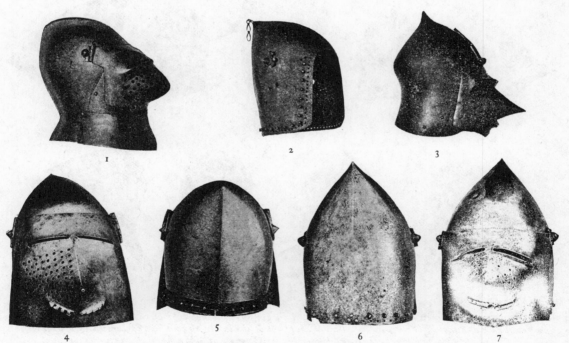

FIGURE 132. *Basinets.* 1. *German, early 15th century.* 2. *French, about 1400. Ex voto in the church of St. Pierre du Martroi, Orleans. Believed to have belonged to Jeanne d'Arc.* 3. *German, about 1350.* 4, 5. *Italian, late 14th century.* 6, 7. *French, about 1400. Metropolitan Museum. Not to scale.*

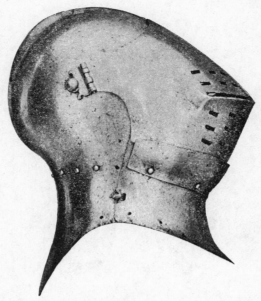

FIGURE 133. *Great Basinet, German, 1400. Metropolitan Museum.*

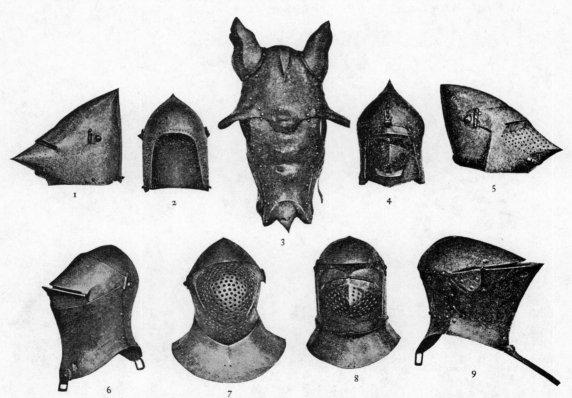

FIGURE 134. *Basinets and Jousting Helms.* 1. *A forgery of a French type of basinet of about 1400.*
2. *French basinet of about 1400.* 3. *Italian chanfron of the late 15th century redecorated in France
in 1539 for the Dauphin, afterwards Henri II.* 4. *German of the end of the 14th century.* 5.
Italian basinet of about 1380. 6. *Jousting helm, French (Burgundian) second half of the 15th century.* 7. *Great basinet. German, early 15th century.* 8. *Great basinet, German(?), first half of the
15th century.* 9. *Jousting Helm. Italian, second half of the 15th century. Metropolitan Museum.*

temples. The pivots were on separate pieces hinged to the visors so that the latter could be raised or, by removing one of the hinge pins, swung out sideways. By removing both pins the visor could be taken off the helmet. Figs. 132, 134.

FIGURE 135. *Batardeau, Italian, about 1500. Metropolitan Museum.*

Early in the 15th century the camail was replaced by plate neck guards forming the "great" basinet, figs. 133, 134. This was used for some time longer for tilting; but, for war, was gradually displaced by the armet.

BASKET HILT. A sword hilt in which the hand is completely enclosed by a system of connected bars extending from the guard to the pommel. It was particularly used for the Scotch broadswords from the 16th to well into the 18th century. Fig. 192.

BASNET. See Basinet.

BASQUES. From the 13th to the 15th century mercenary troops were frequently employed in European wars. Among these the Basques were so conspicuous that the name Basque became synonymous with professional soldier. (Hewitt I, 99, 219).

BASTARD CANNON. See Cannon.

BASTARD CULVERIN. See Cannon.

BASTARD STRING. A string temporarily fastened by clamps to the bow of a crossbow by means of which it was bent enough to permit of putting the regular string in its place. (Payne-Gallwey, The Crossbow 114).

BASTARD SWORD. See Hand-and-a-Half Sword.

BASTION. An earthwork with the exterior faced with masonry projecting from a fortification. It showed two faces, two flanks and a throat in order to flank the curtains. Bastions are full, when the platform is at the level of the curtain walls on each side — empty, when the platform is lower than this — armed with a cavalier, when an earth mound for

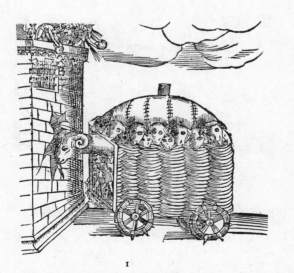
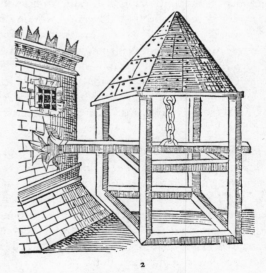

1   2

FIGURE 136. *Battering Rams.* 1. *A movable battering ram on a carriage that shelters the men working it.* 2. *A different kind having a hardened steel cutting bar. From Colliado.*

a battery is raised above the platform. (Violet le Duc, Hist. 361).

BASTON. A mace with a polygonal head. (ffoulkes Armourer 155). See Baton.

BASWA KNIFE. A large, broad-bladed knife with a waved edge and no guard. Upper Congo. (Burton Sword 170).

BATAILLE. The main division of an army in the 14th century. See Arriere-Garde.

BATARDEAU. A knife with the hilt and blade in one piece, otherwise much like a Scotch dirk. It was carried in a pocket in the sword sheath in the late 16th century. Fig. 135.

BATICOLE. Breeches of steel worn under lamboys. They were "articulated with great skill and precision, so as to defend the body without hindering the movements." Spain, 16th century. (Calvert 89).

BA-TO. A stirrup, Japan. See Abumi.

BATON, BASTON. A truncheon carried by a leader, and now the peculiar distinction of a field marshal. From the 12th century on. These names were also used for any kind of a club or staff.

BATTERING RAM. A heavy beam hung from an overhead frame and swung by the united efforts of several men. It was used to break in a wall or gate. It is one of the oldest military engines and continued in use until cannon became sufficiently strong to be more effective. The men working it were usually protected by a movable roof. The striking end of the beam was shod with metal, frequently in the form of a ram's head, hence the name. Colliado illustrates a different form in which the end of the beam is armed with a hardened steel star drill; this, he says, was much more effective. Fig. 136.

BATTERY AND BEATING. Terms of the 17th century fencing masters. "The difference between them being that *battery* is striking with the edge and feeble of your sword upon the edge and feeble of your adversarie, whereas *beating* is done with the forte of your sword on the feeble of your adversaries, and therefore secureth his sword a great deal better than battery doth." (Castle 192).

BATTIG. See Bade-Bade.

BATTLE-AXE. See Axe.

BATTLEMENTS. A wall having in its upper line a range of indentations separated by solid parts. In common usage the entire wall so protected was spoken of as the battlements.

BATWAL TUMBI. A powder flask of leather embroidered with colored thread and strips of porcupine's quills, Nepal. (Egerton 356).

A horn-shaped wooden flask covered with velvet. (Wallace Orient).

BAUDRICK. See Baldric.

BAVIERE. See Beavor.

BAYLE. See Bailey.

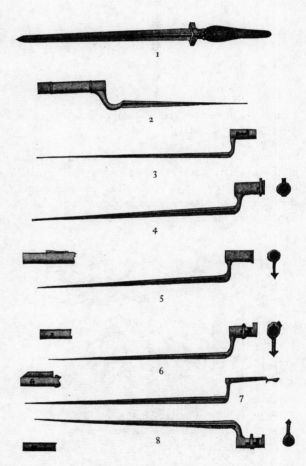

FIGURE 137. *Bayonets; Schoen plate* 11. 1. *French,* 1640. 2. *French, model of* 1747. 3. *Saxon, about* 1750. 4. *French, about* 1768. 5. *French, about* 1774. 6. *French, about* 1800. 7. *For the Swiss carbine of* 1851. 8. *Bayonet that locks on the barrel so that it forms a front sight.*

BAYONET. The bayonet undoubtedly originated in some soldier finding that the handle of his dagger would fit in the muzzle of his gun and convert

FIGURE 138. *Plug Bayonets. Italian, 17th century. Metropolitan Museum.*

it into a fair substitute for a pike. According to Planche the bayonet was invented in Spain about 1580. ffoulkes says it was introduced in France in 1647. Schmidt (Armes a Feu Portative, 29, 30) says: "1571. On donne le nom de bayonette a de long poignards qu'on plante au bout du canon." He also says that triangular plug bayonets were in use in the French army in 1640, and detachable sword bayonets in 1641-2. The latter had short cross guards with a ring on one side that fitted over the end of the barrel, and the latter had a ring fastened to it into which the handle of the bayonet fitted. In 1690 Sweden and England adopted the bayonet. Figs. 137, 138.

The earliest bayonets fitted into the barrel and were held only by friction; the first improvement was to screw them in. While this held them more securely it took much more time to fix and unfix them. These early types were known as plug bayonets, fig. 138. The earliest detachable bayonet is probably the French one already described. Early in the 18th century bayonets were used that had substantially the form of attachment that is in use at the present time.

Bayonets were never used in the East except where they were introduced by Europeans. They were quite common in India in the 18th century in the native armies commanded by European adventurers. Fig. 139.

BAYU. A Bornean knife with a hilt like a mandau and a symmetrical double-edged blade like that of a barong. (British Museum).

BAZDAR. A falconer, India and Persia. (Burton Falconry 9).

BAZU BAND, DASTANA. The arm guard used throughout the Turkish Empire, Persia and India for hundreds of years. It consists of a curved plate covering the outside of the arm from wrist to elbow; this is either fastened to two narrow wrist plates by mail, or hinged to a short plate that protects the inside of the wrist. The hand is covered by a gauntlet fastened to the end of the long plate. In Turkey the arm plate was relatively short, rounded at the upper end, and very slightly curved lengthwise. It nearly always had two narrow wrist plates connected to each other and to the arm plate by mail, the gauntlets were generally of mail over leather. The Persian guards were longer, also rounded at the end, and much more curved length-

FIGURE 139. *Bayonet, India, 18th century. It is of the triangular section usual in Europe. It is fastened to the gun by a spring catch and a screw. Length of blade 13 inches.*

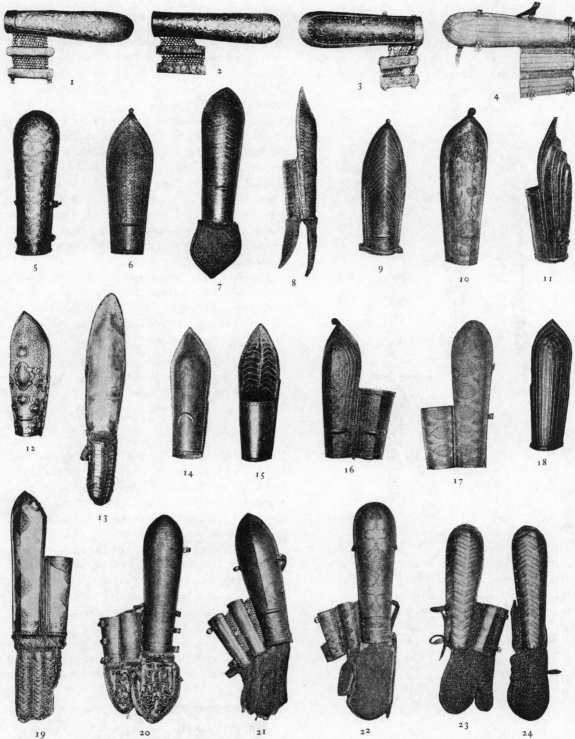

FIGURE 140. *Bazu Band.* 1. *Turkish, XVII. Decorated with a pattern in incised lines.* 2. *Turkish, XVII. Decorated with chiseling in low relief.* 3. *Turkish, XVII, XVIII. Inlaid with an inscription in gold; borders of engraved white metal.* 4. *Indo-Persian, about 1700. Plain steel paneled by lines in low relief.* 5. *Persian, late XVII. Steel with a flower pattern carved in medium relief.* 6. *Southern India, XVII. Elaborately carved and pierced.* 7, 8. *Central India, XVIII. Arms chiseled in low relief and inlaid with gold. Gauntlets of two flaps of padded velvet decorated with gilt studs arranged in patterns. These flaps guard both the palm and back of the hand whether it is open or closed around the reins or a weapon.* 9. *Southern India, XVII. Steel deeply carved with ribs in relief; monsters' heads on the wristbands.* 10. *Southern India, XVII. Steel carved in relief and silvered.* 11. *Central or Southern India, XVII. Steel embossed in steps and pierced.* 12. *Kutch, XIX. Steel covered with a pattern inlaid in silver and ornaments in high relief.* 13. *Sind (Kutch), XVIII. Steel with brass borders and ornaments. Gauntlets of steel scales scalloped and connected by mail.* 14, 15. *Northern India, XVII. Steel etched and gilded. They have their original linings of quilted green velvet.* 16. *Southern India, XVII. Steel very finely chiseled with a diaper pattern in medium relief.* 17. *Persian, XVIII. Steel chiseled in low relief with a pattern of ovals. A favorite design.* 18. *Central India, XVII. Steel carved with lines in low relief; it has been gilded.* 19. *Kutch, XVIII. Steel with applied ornaments of chased brass. Gauntlet of alternate scales of iron and brass connected by riveted mail.* 20. *Indo-Persian, XVII. Steel covered with gold inlay in low relief. Gauntlets of padded silk with gilt studs arranged to form Arabic letters.* 21. *Northern India, XVII, XVIII. Russet steel carved in low relief. Mail gauntlet.* 22. *Persian, XVII. Steel with inscriptions in low relief in cartouches. The ground of the cartouches still shows some of the original gilding. Mail gauntlet.* 23, 24. *Mogul, XVI, XVII. Steel with gilded chevrons in low relief. Gauntlets of riveted mail. Arms and gauntlets have their original linings of red leather.*

wise. They also usually had two narrow plates at the wrist and mail gauntlets. In India the upper end of the arm plate was pointed and, in the south, frequently curved out and ended in a knob or acorn. In place of the two small plates and mail there was generally a single curved plate hinged to the long one. The gauntlets were sometimes of mail or overlapping scales, but usually of padded cloth, frequently velvet, decorated with gilt studs. Fig. 140. Some of the gauntlets are formed of two symmetrical stiff flaps that leave the hand free to grasp sword or reins, while still protecting it.

With very slight modifications this form of arm guard has been used in the East since the 15th century. In India and Persia in later times often but one was worn, on the bridle hand if on horseback, and on the sword hand if on foot and carrying sword and shield.

BEAKED AXE. A variety of bill with a hook, or beak, on the back. It was a favorite in Scandinavia in the 15th and 16th centuries. (Burton Sword 96).

BEAKED BOOMERANG. See Watilikiri.

BEAR'S PAW SOLERETS, DUCK-BILLED SOLERETS, SABATONS. The very broad-toed foot guards of the first half of the 16th century. See Sabatons. Fig. 38.

BECA CESA. A guard in fencing at the end of the 15th century. (Castle 43).

BECCA POSSA. Another guard of the same period. "After this thou wilt make thy scholar move his left foot forward and drop his sword-point towards the ground, turning the pummel upwards, and thou wilt see that he extends his arm and turns his thumb under and towards the point of his sword." (Castle 41).

BEC-DE-CORBIN. A type of war hammer used about 1400. It has a long point like a crow's beak. (Dean Europ. 37). Fig. 141.

BEC-DE-FAUCON. A tower built on two galleys for the purpose of assaulting a town defended by rivers or the sea. (Hewitt II, 328).

BEDHINDI. Mercenary troops in India in the 16th century. There were always a large number available and they were employed by the Indian princes whenever they needed an army.

BEDOR, PANA. The ordinary Javan arrow with a leaf-shaped, or barbed head. (Raffles I, 295 and plate p. 296/297).

FIGURE 141. *Bec de Corbin. 1, 2. Italian, 16th century. 3. German, 15th century. Metropolitan Museum. Not to scale.*

BEDOUH. An Arabic talisman often found on sword blades. It is a square divided into four or nine smaller squares, each enclosing a letter or even number. (Egerton, p. 53).

BEEVOR, BEVOR. See BEAVER.

BEHOURD, BEHOURT, BEHORDICUM, BEHOURDICUM. A species of tournament. "The behourt was a species of bastion or castle constructed of wood or other material, which the holders undertook to defend against all who should attack it. The military exercise was again an adjunct of the tournament, a term which included all exercises practiced by the nobility to fit themselves for the profession of arms, and seemed to have been invented to teach the way to attack and escalade fortified places." (Cripps Day, Appendix II, xvi).

BEINBERGS. See Bainbergs.

BEIRUK. A standard of black, white and yellow cloth, one of which was allowed for each thousand men in the Mysore army under Hyder Ali. (Egerton, p. 33).

BEKO TSUDZUMI. A Japanese corselet covered with tortoise shell. (Conder 263).

BEL. A small bow used by Nicobar children for shooting fish. (Man, A. & N. 8).

BELADAH, BELABANG. A Bornean sabre with a guard and finger guard. (Arc. f. Eth. V, 233). See Parang Nabur.

the first are said to have been twenty stories high. Grose says: "The towers or belfreys of modern times were not so large, they rarely exceeded three or four stages or stories, and were covered with hides to protect them from fire; in them was a

FIGURE 142. *Berdiches. 1. South German (Swiss), 14th, 15th century. Length blade 15 inches. 2. Russian(?), 15th, 16th century. Length blade 22 inches. 3. Slavic, 17th century. Length blade 26.1 inches. 4. Slavic, 15th century. Length blade 23.4 inches. 5. Turkish, 16th, 17th century. Steel handle 32.5 inches long. 6. Turkish, 15th, 16th century. Blade 30.125 inches long inlaid with an inscription in gold. The handle is not the original. Nos. 1 to 4 Metropolitan Museum.*

BELANDA. A kind of Malay knife. (Sk. & Bl.).

BELANGAH. A Dyak blowpipe with an ornamental spearhead and sheath. (Arc. f. Eth. III, 240).

BELAU. A Sakai blowpipe, also its dart, Malay Peninsula. (Skeat & Blagden 537).

BELFREY. A movable tower used in sieges. Belfreys were used from the earliest times and some of

bridge to let down on the parapet, when the works were to be stormed. The lowest stage or ground floor was occupied by a ram; the upper stories by archers and crossbowmen." The last of which we have certain knowledge was built, but not used, by the royalists in 1645. (Grose I, 385).

BELIER. A battering ram. (Boutell 213).

BELLOWS VISOR. A visor with deep transverse flutes. Late 15th and early 16th centuries. 5, fig. 26.

BELLS OF ARMS. Bell tents in which the arms of a company were kept in the field. (Hoyt 354).

BELT HOOK, SASH HOOK. A long, flat hook on the side of a pistol or flask by which to hang it from the belt. The pistols were so bulky that if the belt was loose enough to put them inside it, it was too loose when they were removed. See Flask.

BELT OF KNIGHTHOOD. The elaborate belts of the middle ages. They were not worn by

middle of the blade and the lower end of the latter has a projection that is screwed or riveted to the shaft. In some cases the blade extends far enough beyond the shaft to allow of its being used for thrusting. Fig. 142.

BESAGUES, BESAGNE, CROISSANT, MOTON. Circular, oval, square or cross-shaped plates attached by laces to cover the openings between the plates of the armor at the armpits in the 15th century. (ffoulkes 39).

BEUGLE. See Bible.

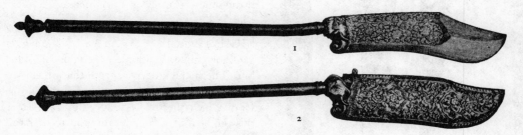

FIGURE 143. *Bhuj. 1. Sind, 17th century. Blade with a panel of chased flowers in silver parcel gilt. Handle silver plated and engraved. Length 26 inches. 2. Sind, 18th century. The blade is partly and the handle entirely covered with engraved silver. The knob on the end of the handle and the elephant's head are of copper, the latter set with colored stones. The sheath is of finely embossed copper. There is a small knife concealed in the handle.*

persons under the rank of knight; but were worn as much with civil as military dress. (Planche 39).

BEMARUK. An Australian shield used for turning aside spears. It is made of wood, pointed at both ends, and the length is three or four times the width. (Howitt 337, 347).

BENDI. See Leonile.

BENDI UTER. A toy crossbow in which the arrow is shot from a bamboo tube. Flores. A slur bow. (Arc. f. Eth. VIII, 10).

BENDO. See Golok.

BENI-ODOSHI. Japanese armor laced with red cords.

BERDICHE. A type of pole axe used in Europe from the 15th to the 17th century. It was also used by the Turks and in the near East. The cutting edges are from fifteen to thirty inches long and the blades are only about three or four inches wide. The staff is fitted in an eye projecting from the

BEVOR. See Beavor.

BEZANTED ARMOR. Armor made of small, round plates of metal riveted or sewed on cloth or leather, 14th century. (Hewitt I, 255). The name is due to the resemblance of the pieces of metal to coins (bezants).

BEWIT. A short leather strap by which a hawk's bell is fastened to its leg or tail. (Michelle 42).

BHAGWA JHANDA. The national flag and emblem of the Mahrattas. It is swallow-tailed and of a deep orange color, emblematic of the followers of Mahadeo. (Egerton, p. 27).

BHALA. The long spear of the Mahratta horsemen. (Sinclair, I. A. II, 216). The Wallace catalogue describes it as a spear of Northern India with a blade ridged or grooved, and sometimes forked.

BHAN, BAN. A rocket or grenade thrown among the horses of an enemy to frighten them, Mogul India, 17th century. (Egerton, p. 25).

BHANDARS. Rocket men of the Mysore army under Hyder Ali. (Egerton, p. 31).

BHANJU. A coat with a gorget attached, India, 16th century. (Egerton, p. 23).

1   2   3

FIGURE 144. *Bichaq. 1. Blade 8 inches long. Scabbard covered with silver plated embossed brass. 2. Watered blade 7.5 inches long inlaid with silver stars. Ivory hilt mounted in silver gilt and set with coral. Black leather scabbard with embossed silver mounts. 3. Blade 8.25 inches long. Hilt of brown wood inlaid with silver. Scabbard covered with embossed silver.*

BHAWANI. Sivaji's sword. It was a Genoa blade of great length and fine temper. (Burton Sword 8). The Mahrattas invoked its assistance before fighting.

It is said to be at Satara, but the sword there does not appear to be of good enough quality to have belonged to Sivaji. It is a firangi. There are at least two other swords said to have been Sivaji's at other places.

BHIROO. The Hindu god of war. (Tod II, 523).

BHUJ, KUTTI. A short, heavy, single-edged knife blade mounted in line with a straight handle about twenty inches long. It was quite common in India, particularly in Sind and the north. It is

sometimes called an "elephant knife" because there is usually an elephant's head at the base of the blade. It frequently has a small knife concealed in the handle. Fig. 143.

BIBLE, BEUGLE, BUGLE. An engine for throwing large stones, 12th and 13th centuries. (Grose I, 382).

BICHAQ. A knife with a straight, single-edged blade and a straight handle made of two plates of bone or ivory riveted to the flat tang. The scabbards are usually partly or entirely covered with embossed metal, frequently silver. It is used throughout Turkey and Armenia. (Moser XI). Fig. 144.

BICH'HWA, BICHWA. An Indian dagger with a doubly curved, double-edged blade and a loop hilt. The shape is derived from that of the old horn daggers which had the curve of the buffalo horns from which they were made, fig. 145. In spite of this the bich'hwa is generally said to be named for its resemblance to the sting of a scorpion (bichwa). It has never been very highly regarded in India, possibly because one was used by Sivaji when he murdered Afzal Khan. Bich'hwas are made both right- and left-handed, and sometimes have forked blades. Fig. 146.

FIGURE 145. *Horn Daggers, Dravidian Central India. Each is made of a single piece of polished horn. Lengths 12.5 and 13.5 inches.*

It is occasionally combined with a bagh nakh, the claws being fastened to the handle of the knife. Fig. 147.

BIDAG. The dirk of the Scotch Highlanders. (Planche 162). See Dirk.

BILIONG. The Malay axe used throughout the Archipelago. The head has a square tang fitting in a mortise in the handle; it can therefore be placed with the edge in line with the handle for use as an axe, or at right angles to it for use as an adze. The

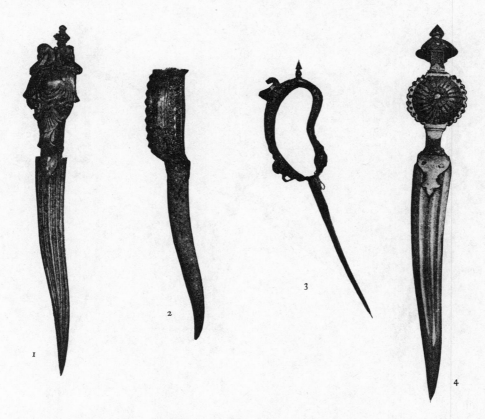

FIGURE 146. *Bich'hwas.* 1. *Mahratta Tanjore, 17th century. Ribbed blade 8.625 inches long, copper hilt. 2. Central India, 18th century. All iron. 3. Blade 6 inches long, moulded hilt inlaid with silver. 4. Heavy fluted blade 9.5 inches long. Silvered steel hilt with projecting bosses on guard and pommel.*

BIDRI WORK. A kind of pewter stained black and inlaid with silver. It is frequently used for sword and knife hilts in India. It is named after Bider, a city sixty miles northwest of Hyderabad, where it is made. (Egerton, pp. 65, 70).

BIFFA. A variety of trebuchet in which the counterpoise is movable. (Hewitt I, 349).

BILARI. An unbarbed and unhafted hunting spear used with a thrower in West Australia. (Vic. Mus. 31).

BILBO. A small rapier. (ffoulkes Armourer 155).

handle is cut from a tree where a branch joins, the mortise for the tang being cut in the part from the trunk, while the branch forms the handle. The handle frequently has quite a large grip, the part between which and the blade being much smaller, making it very flexible. Around the socket it is usually bound with complicated lashings of rattan. Fig. 148.

BILL, BROWN BILL. This is one of the earliest weapons mentioned in medieval warfare, and it was especially favored by the Anglo-Saxons. One of the earliest rallying cries of the English was

"Bows and Bills." It started as an agricultural implement, was modified in many ways for war, and still survives as an agricultural implement in England. The bill has a broad blade with a cutting edge and a variety of spikes and hooks projecting from the back and end. It is mounted on a long

BINI-I-'ASAKIR. Persian, the advance guard, literally the "nose of the army." (Egerton, p. 31).

BINNOL. A chain flail with a spiked ball, Delhi. (Wallace Orient).

BIR-BEN. See Kul-Luk.

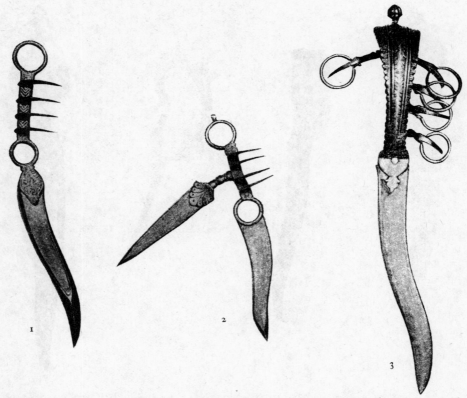

FIGURE 147. *Bich'hwa-Bagh Nakh.* 1. *Watered blade 6.5 inches long. Hilt forged in one piece with the blade. It has a ring at each end and four claws, all inlaid with gold.* 2. *Two blades at right angles and four claws on the grip which has a ring at each end.* 3. *Blade 8 inches long with five claws with ringed handles hinged to them.*

shaft. Bills were also used in Turkey in the 15th century; the Turkish bills are much like the Italian and were sometimes inlaid with silver in characteristic patterns. Fig. 149.

The bill is the original of the family of pole arms variously called bills, guisarmes and fauchards.

BINAUKAN. A Moro hunting spear with a broad, leaf-shaped head of diamond section. (Arc. f. Eth. IV, 70).

BIND, TRUSS. When a hawk strikes and clutches its quarry in the air and retains its hold until they reach the ground, it is said to bind or truss.

BIRCH'HA. A heavy, slightly curved spear from Mysore. (Egerton, p. 123). It sometimes has a forked head. (Wallace Orient).

BIRCHI, BIRCHEE. An Indian lance. (Tod I, 148, II, 91).

BIRRA JUNGEE. A throwing stick, Hyderabad. (Tower 475, p. 10).

BISACUTA, BASAGUE. Believed to have been a double-pointed pick of the 14th century. (Hewitt I, 155, II, 268).

BISHAMON. Generally considered as one of the

Japanese gods of war, Weber says that this is incorrect. He is frequently represented with Daikoku and either Benten or Marashiten as one of the trinity of gods of war.

A variety of kote, Japanese armored sleeve.

BISHAMON SUNE-ATE. Japanese greaves of three metal plates, the middle one being long enough to cover and protect the knee. The upper portion of this plate is called the *kakudzuri*. (Conder 276).

BIT. The two principal kinds are *snaffles*, having a plain, or jointed, bar in the horse's mouth with the reins fastened to rings at the ends; and *curbs*, having an arch or plate in the mouth and vertical bars at the ends. The reins are fastened to the lower ends of these bars, and the upper ends are connected by a chain passing back of the jaw. As the bit is hung from points between the two very heavy pressure can be brought to bear with it. The Spanish and Arab bits have a ring hinged to the top of the

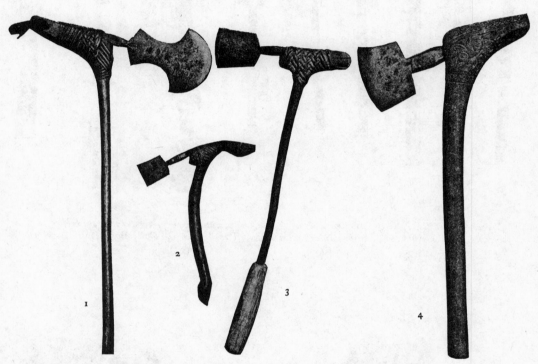

FIGURE 148. *Biliong. 1. Borneo. Straight wooden handle 3 feet 11 inches long. 2. Sulu. Unusually small. Probably for use as a carving adze. 3. Sarawak, Borneo. Length 24.5 inches. This is the usual shape of handle. 4. Sulu, very heavy. The handle is carved near the insertion of the blade.*

BISHANSWAMI, GOSENS. Militant monks, the priests of Hur or Bel. Tod calls them the "Templars of Rajes'than." They were sought as allies by the Rajputs, especially in defensive warfare. (Tod I, 60, II, 108).

BISHOP'S MANTLE. A long tippet, or cloak, of mail worn alone or over armor from the latter part of the 15th to the middle of the 16th century. Fig. 150. (Laking Armour II, 187).

Precisely similar mail cloaks were worn in India in the 18th century.

port (the arch in the mouth) in place of the jaw chain. The curb is much more severe than the snaffle and is always used for military riding. The curb is almost universally used in Spain, the Spanish-American countries and by the Arabs. The Persians, Chinese, Japanese, Malays and the Central Asiatics use snaffles. In India both are used. The Romans used curbs, but the barbarians that overran Europe at the close of the Roman Empire used jointed snaffles. With the coming of heavy armed horsemen the curbs again came into general use,

FIGURE 149. *Bills.* 1, 2, 3, 4, 15th *century, to scale.* 6, 7, 16th *century.* 5, 8, 17th *century.* 5 *to* 8 *to scale.* 9. *Turkish,* 16th *century. Inlaid with silver.* 1 *to* 8 *from the Collection of Dr. Bashford Dean.*

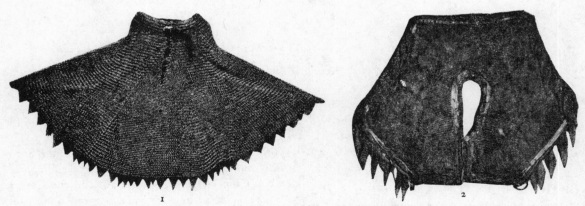

FIGURE 150. *Bishop's Mantle.* 1. *Italian(?) about* 1500. *Metropolitan Museum.* 2. *India,* 18th *century. The dark pattern is in brass links. Not to scale. The European one is of about twice the width of the Indian.*

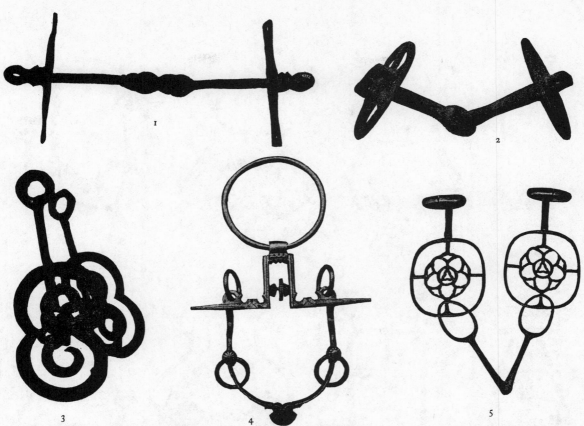

FIGURE 151. *Bits.* 1. *Greek, probably 6th century B.C.* 2. *Classical.* 3. *Japanese from a tumulus in the Prefecture Gumma, 6th century or earlier.* 4. *Arabian, 18th-19th century.* 5. *Japanese, 18th century. Metropolitan Museum. Not to scale.*

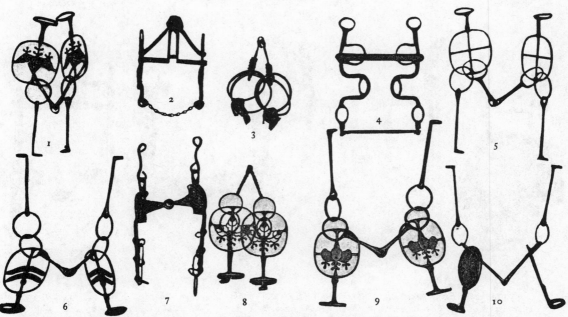

FIGURE 153. *Japanese Bits.* 1. *Broken snaffle with kiri crests.* 2. *Curb bit with a large port.* 3. *Broken snaffle without side bars. Toothed rollers on bar.* 4. *Horse trainer's bit.* 5. *Broken snaffle with light crosses in the side rings.* 6. *Broken snaffle with dragon flies in the side rings.* 7. *Curb bit with solid bosses on the ends of the bar.* 8. *Broken snaffle with fine openwork kiri crests in the side rings.* 9. *Broken snaffle with kiri crests in the side rings.* 10. *Bit with solid bosses in place of side rings.* 17th to 19th century.

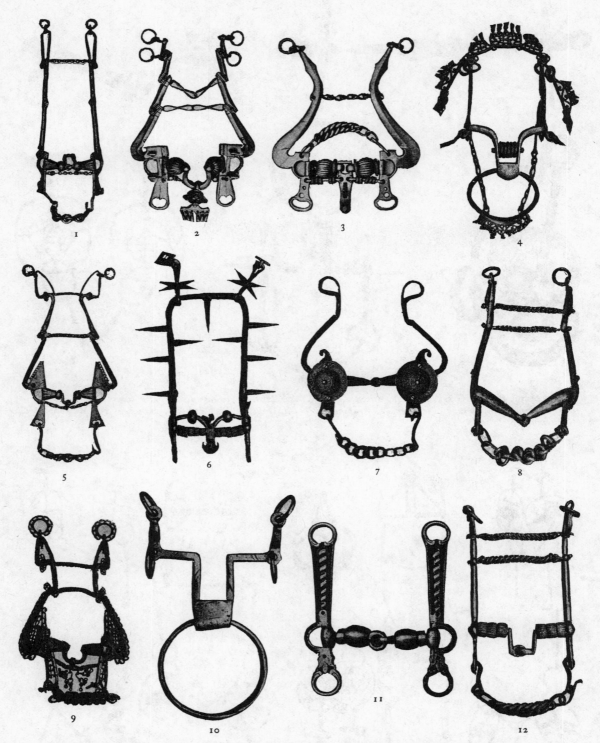

FIGURE 152. *European Bits.* 1. *German, XVIII.* 2. *French, XVIII.* 3. *Spanish, XVII.* 4. *French, about 1600.* 5. *German, end of the XVI.* 6. *French, XVI.* 7. *French, XVI.* 8. *French, XVI.* 9. *French, XVI.* 10. *French, XVI.* 11. *French, XVI.* 12. *German jousting bit, XVI. Metropolitan Museum. Not to scale.*

and were often used in conjunction with snaffles, the bridles having two sets of reins. Figs. 151, 152, 153. See also Bridles.

BI-TERAN, BITTERGAN. A club having a round, straight handle and a curved, flattened end

BLETTA. A type of Australian spear thrower. See Wanmaiia.

BLOWPIPE. A long tube of wood or cane through which darts are propelled by the breath of the user. Blowpipes are common in parts of Brazil,

FIGURE 154. *Blowpipe quiver and darts, Upper Amazon. Quiver of basketwork with the Greek fret around the middle, and the lower part covered with a shining black gum. The darts have wads of cotton on the butts. The blowpipe is nearly ten feet long, covered with bark and with a large mouthpiece and a sight made of two teeth fastened on with gum.*

like a boomerang, Queensland. (Roth, Aust. Mus. VII, 208).

BITLA. An arrow with a point of hard wood, Travancore. (Egerton 80).

BLACK ARMOR. Armor that was blackened, or painted, to keep it from rusting.

Guiana and many Malayan countries, but are rare in Japan. The more common form in South America is very long (eight to ten feet) and is made of a single piece of wood wound with bark and fitted with a bell-shaped mouthpiece of wood. It usually has a sight made of two peccary's teeth fastened with gum about three or four feet from the mouth-

FIGURE 155. *Blunderbusses. 1. Wheel lock, Dutch, 17th century. Length 38.75 inches. 2. Wheel lock, German, 17th century. Length 37 inches. 3. Miquelet lock, Spanish, 18th century. Length 37 inches. 4. Flintlock, Italian, Lazarino Cominazzo, 18th century. Length 42.25 inches. 5. Flintlock, with hinged stock. European, 18th century. Length 35 inches. 6. Flintlock with brass barrel. English, R. Slek, 18th century. Length 28 inches. 7. Flintlock, English, Sir Robert Stewart, 18th century. Length 43 inches. 8. Flintlock, Italian, 18th century. Length 43 inches. From the Collection of Mr. William G. Renwick.*

piece. When used it is held with both hands grasping the tube close to the mouth. The darts are splinters of a tough wood about eight to ten inches long and about one-sixteenth of an inch in diam-

Sumpit, Sumpitan, Taharan, Tanggiri, Telenga, Telep, Tembilan, Tepus, Tolor, Tulup, Tulupan, Ultup, Zarabatana.

FIGURE 156. *Blunderbuss guns and pistols, 19th century. From the Collection of Mr. Charles Noe Daly.*

eter. The butt is wrapped with cotton to make it fit the bore tightly. As the darts are very light and are not propelled with much force, it is necessary to poison them in order to make them effective. In South America *curare*, a strongly narcotic alkaloid, is used. The darts are carried in quivers neatly woven of cane with the lower part covered with gum. Fig. 154.

In parts of South America they make blowpipes of reed, sometimes with inner and outer tubes like some of the Malayan..For the Malayan blowpipes see Sumpitan; and for the Japanese, Fukidake.

For the different varieties, parts and accessories see: Anak Toumiang, Balasan, Belangah, Belau, Cerbotana, Curare, Damaoq, Fukidake, Fuki Ya, Hengot, Hina, Hung, Ipoh, Jemperang, Jowing, Kahuk, Kahuk Isin, Ke-Non, Klahulon, Ladjau, Langa, Paser, Penichul, Poeot, Pubu, Pubu Isi, Pucuna, Punglu, Sabarcane, Sipet, Siren, Sopok,

BLUNDERBUSS. A short gun or pistol of large bore with a bell mouth. Figs. 155, 156, 157. They were not regularly used as military weapons, but were kept and carried for protection against thieves. For this purpose they were used by the guards of

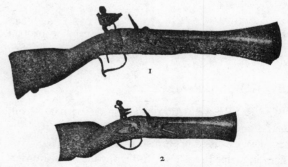

FIGURE 157. *Turkish blunderbuss pistols. 1. Carved wood stock. Length 19.5 inches. 2. Stock inlaid with brass and ivory. Length 13 inches.*

stage coaches as late as 1840. They frequently had bayonets attached, these were hinged at the muzzle and folded back on the barrel when not in use; if

BO-BIYA. An iron case in which to carry a charge for a gun, Japan.

BOCE. A buckler.

FIGURE 158. *Boar Spears.* 1. *Probably English, 16th century.* 2. *Saxon, 1596.* 3. *German, 16th century.* 4. *Probably German, 16th century.* 5. *German, about 1500.* 6. *German, 16th century.* 7. *German, about 1600.* 8. *German, about 1550.* 9. *German, 16th century.* 10. *German, about 1500. Metropolitan Museum. Not to scale.*

required, they were thrown forward by a spring when the catch holding them was released. These bayonets were used on both guns and pistols.

Blunderbusses were introduced in England, probably from Holland, in the latter part of the 16th century. They were occasionally used in most parts of the East. Small ones shaped like guns, but used like pistols, were quite common in Turkey, Persia and Syria. See Pistol and Bukmar.

BLUNTS AND SHARPS. Fencing terms to distinguish the pointless weapons used in practice from the sharpened ones used in actual fighting. (Castle 198).

BOAR. A movable roof, or shed, used to protect the assailants when attacking fortified places. See Cat.

BOARD. See Bord.

BOAR SPEAR. A hunting spear with a broad, leaf-shaped head and a crosspiece below it. The crosspiece was to prevent the animal attacked from running up the shaft and injuring the hunter. About the end of the 16th century similar spears, called by the same name, were used in war. (Hewitt III, 603). Fig. 158.

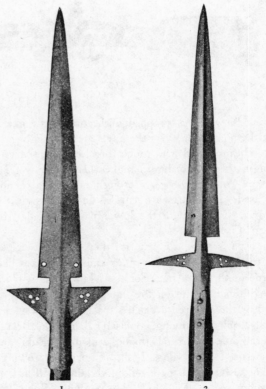

FIGURE 159. *Bohemian Ear-Spoons.* 1. *German, 1490.* 2. *Italian, 16th century. Metropolitan Museum. Not to scale.*

BODKIN. A small dagger. (Fairholt 439).

BOHEMIAN EAR-SPOON. A type of pike with a long, broad point with two triangular projections at the base, 15th century. Fig. 159.

passed around a groove cut in the balls and tied. Usually a second cord with a stone ball attached is fastened to the middle of the first. In such cases the third ball is often smaller than the other two and is

FIGURE 160. 1. *Rosewood Dragon 20.5 inches long.* 2. *Stick carved with a lotus plant in high relief; silver caps and gold mon.* 3, 4. *Wood, shaped like a dagger but with a pen case in place of a blade.* 5. *Solid wood with the mountings of a sword.* 6. *Shaped like a sword with metal mountings representing the tools used in preparing drugs.* 7. *The side of the scabbard that slides off uncovering pockets for packages of drugs.* 8. *The kogai with a spoon on the end and an inscription which reads "If medicine does not make you dizzy it will not cure you."*

BOIS D'ARC. (Bow wood), the osage orange (*toxylon pomiferum*) was so named by the French voyageurs because the Indians of the Southwest made their bows of its wood. The name became corrupted to "bow dark." (Dodge 417).

BOJIRI-MUSHI. The mantis, the Japanese emblem of courage.

BOKU-TO, BOKKEN. An imitation sword or dagger carried by Japanese medical men. It is either a solid piece of wood carved to represent a dagger, or of some fanciful shape. It may be shaped like a dagger but with a drawer for writing brushes instead of a blade. Sometimes it is hollow and contains compartments for medicines which are covered by slides. Fig. 160.

BOLAS. The characteristic weapon of the Indians of the South American plains. It consists of a cord, or thong, with a stone ball fastened to each end. The balls are either sewed up in pieces of leather which are fastened to the cord, or the latter is

held in the hand when the weapon is used. When used it is whirled around the head until the outer ball has attained sufficient velocity and then thrown

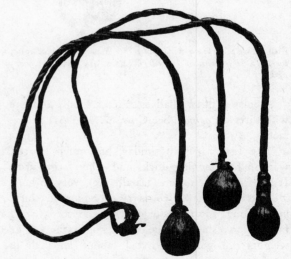

FIGURE 161. *Bolas, Tehuelche, Southern Patagonia. Museum of the American Indian, Heye foundation.*

so as to strike the legs of the animal it is desired to catch. The balls tangle the cords about the victim and disable it. Fig. 161.

are carved in the shape of animals. They are often made of single teeth of the walrus instead of tusk ivory. When not in use the strings are shortened for convenience of carrying, and to prevent their tangling, by tying them in slip knots as follows. All of the strings are straightened out and laid parallel to each other, they are doubled in a bight, with the end under the standing part, the bight of the end passed through the preceding bight which is drawn up close, and so on, usually five or six times, till the cords are sufficiently shortened. They are carried, knotted, in a pouch slung around the neck, a native frequently carrying several sets. When a flock of

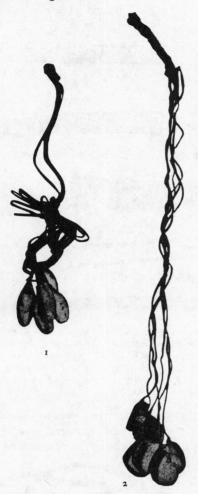

FIGURE 162. *Eskimo Bird Bolas. 1. Five ellipsoidal ivory weights. It is braided for carriage. 2. Six wrought ivory disks.*

A bolas with two balls is called a *somai*, and one with three an *achico*. See Cowper, The Art of Attack, p. 199.

The Eskimo use a similar, but much lighter, weapon for catching ducks and other large birds. It has from four to ten (usually six) ivory or bone weights fastened to cords twenty-four to thirty inches long, the opposite ends of the cords being fastened to a short handle of grass or feathers. The weights are generally ovoid, about an inch in diameter and one and a half to two inches long. Sometimes they are spherical, and occasionally they

FIGURE 163. *Bolos. 1. Broad engraved blade 14 inches long. Hilt and scabbard of carved and pierced horn with silver mountings. 2. Blade 15.375 inches long, carved horn hilt decorated with silver. Stamped leather scabbard with silver mountings. 3. Luzon. Heavy, single-edged blade 17 inches long and 2 inches wide. Black horn handle with a brass guard.*

ducks is seen approaching, the handle is grasped in the right hand, the balls in the left, and the strings straightened by a quick pull. Letting go with the left hand, the balls are whirled around the head and let fly at the passing flock. This weapon is effective up to thirty to forty yards (others say forty to sixty) but the natives often throw it to longer distances, frequently missing their aim. Near Point Barrow it is called *kalauitautin*. (Murdoch 244). It is used from Point Barrow at least as far south

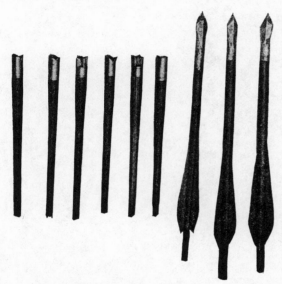

FIGURE 164. *Crossbow Bolts, 16th and 17th centuries. Metropolitan Museum. The two groups are not to the same scale.*

as the Yukon delta, on the intermediate islands, and on the Siberian coast as far as Cape North. Fig. 162.

BOL-LAIR. See Lil-Lil.

BOLO. A general name in the Philippines for a sword or long knife. The name is Spanish and means knife. As used it is nearly equivalent to the Malay word *parang*, a chopper or jungle knife. Fig. 163.

BOLT, CARREAU, QUARREL. The arrow for the crossbow. They are very much shorter and heavier than the arrows for the long bow. The heads are usually square (carré) and the names "carreau" and "quarrel" are derived from the French names for the shape. Fig. 164.

Curiously enough the Chinese crossbow bolts also usually have square heads. Fig. 229.

BOMB. A shell filled with an explosive mixture and fired by a time fuse or by impact. Grose says that they were first used at the siege of Vakterdonc, a town in Holland, in 1588. He also quotes Valturinus (1472) at second hand, describing a bomb made in halves hinged together. He does not appear to be certain of the correctness of the description. (Grose I, 404, 408).

BOMBARD. An early name for cannon. Grose says that it is derived from the Greek *bombos*, expressing the sound made by firing it. Bombards were the beginning of heavy artillery and, at first, were only used in the attack and defense of fortified places. They were certainly used in the 14th century, and possibly earlier.

BOMB LANCE. An explosive shell used to kill whales. The earlier American ones were an inch in diameter and about a foot long. The front of the bomb was a small spear point which could be unscrewed to allow the bomb to be loaded; the middle section, which was much the largest, held the powder, the rear section contained the lock which had a hammer that moved in the line of the axis, and a trigger hinged at the back so that it could be folded flat against the bomb when it was put into the gun. When fired the trigger of the bomb swung out and was pulled when the missile entered the body of the whale. They were very effective weapons but were seldom used, partly on account of their cost, but mainly because the comparatively light guns kicked so badly that they were apt to knock the user overboard. Fig. 165.

Later European types combine the bomb with a harpoon; some explode on entering the body of the whale, and others only when a strain is put upon the line.

BONASPATTI. A Hindu-Malayan god whose head is often used as a decoration on kris sheaths, especially in Bali. Fig. 166.

BONNET. In fortification, a work placed before the salient angle of the ravelin; it consists of two faces parallel to those of the ravelin. (Hoyt 404).

BOOMERANG. The boomerang is commonly supposed to be purely an Australian weapon and as always returning to the thrower when properly handled. Both of these ideas are entirely wrong. It is true that the returning boomerang is unknown outside of Australia, but most boomerangs used there cannot be made to return; and as weapons boomerangs were quite common in ancient Egypt, and are still used in many parts of Africa, India and other countries. The returning boomerang is mainly and lighter than the one made for war and hunting. It has a spiral twist which is often so slight as to be difficult to distinguish. When used it is held vertically and thrown overhand. The length and curve vary greatly; the size depends on the pur-

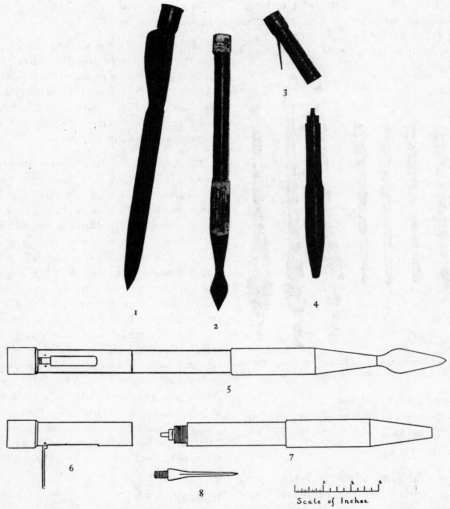

FIGURE 165. *Bomb Lances. 1. Triangular point made by cutting three wide grooves in the end. Three leather feathers. 2. The usual form with a folding trigger. 3. The lock section with the trigger half out. 4. The middle section that carries the explosive charge. 5. A drawing of the complete bomb put together. 6. The lock section. 7. The middle section. 8. The spearhead at the end. Total length 15.75 inches; weight unloaded, one and a half pounds — one-tenth of the weight of the gun from which it is fired. The two bands of largest diameter are of lead.*

a plaything, though it is sometimes used to kill birds.

Boomerangs are flat, curved pieces of wood (occasionally horn or iron) with sharp edges and are generally slightly more convex on one side than on the other. The returning boomerang is thinner pose for which it is to be used and the fancy of the maker. The curve depends on the natural curve of the piece of wood from which it is made. In Australia it is often a piece cut from the slab-like buttress roots of a living tree. Fig. 167.

For the different varieties of boomerangs see: Aclys, Astara, Ban-Geek, Barngeet, Barragan, Beaked Boomerang, Chaku-I, Charal-Jego, Collery, Kandri, Katari, Katariya, Keili, Knili, Kulbeda, Kurupatu, Kylie, Leowel, Lil-Lil, Nyaral,

FIGURE 166. *Head of Bonaspatti in silver on a Bali kris scabbard.*

Parkan, Patshkohu, Praah-Ba-Witto-Ah, Quirriang-An-Wun, Rabbit Stick, Singa, Tjukuli, Tombat, Trombash, Tundiwung, Uramanta, Wadna, Wa-Ngal, Watilikiri, Wittoo-Ah-Will, Wongala, Wonguim, Yachi, Yalma, Yural-Bara.

BOORJ. A tower for the defense of a village, Rajput. (Tod II, 267).

BORD, BOARD. A shield, Anglo-Saxon. It was round, either flat or convex, and made of wood with a metal boss in the center. (Laking Armour I, 3).

BORNA. A spear thrower of the Koko-Minni blacks, Queensland. The blade is long and slightly wider in the center than at the ends. The peg is long, placed in the plane of the blade, and has a deep transverse nick in it to catch the extremity of the spear butt. The lower end of the peg is flat-tened and has two holes drilled in it through which cords pass to two holes in the end of the blade; the cords are covered with resin, but the back of the peg is not. The handle is made of two pieces of *melo* shell set at any sort of an angle, or else of a lath of wood doubled on itself. Compare Bo-Un. See Spear Thrower.

BORRAL. See Gid-Jee.

BOSHI. The shape of the yakiba at the point of a Japanese blade. Fig. 168. See Japanese Blades.

BOSHI-MONO, YAKI-NAOSHI-MONO. A retempered blade, Japan. Such blades are always inferior. (Gilbertson, Blades).

BOSON. An arrow with a round knob on the end from which a sharp point projects. (Planche 48).

BOSS. A projection from a flat, or nearly flat, surface — as the central part of a shield. (Planche 49).

A round metal ornament, as the boss of a bridle.

BOSSOIRS. See Glancing Knobs.

BOTAN GAKI. Fastened with buttons, a type of wakibiki.

FIGURE 167. *Boomerangs, Australia.* 1. *Fighting boomerang 24.75 inches long. One end is roughened to form a handle. It is entirely painted with red ochre.* 2. *Dark wood 22.125 inches long. Both sides are convex, one very slightly.* 3. *Returning boomerang of light wood 19.75 inches long.* 4. *Length 17.5 inches. One end has a long, sharp point and the other has been cut to an obtuse angled point.* 5. *Fighting boomerang of dark wood with the curvature mainly at one end; length 26.875 inches.* 6. *Very light returning boomerang of black wood curved at a very sharp angle. Length from point to point 20.75 inches.*

BOTTA LUNGA. In old fencing an attack much like the modern lunge. (Castle 113).

BOTT, BOTTA. An old fencing term nearly equivalent to the French *coup*. It comprises the action of an attack from its commencement to its completion. (Castle 137).

England in the early part of the 15th century. (ffoulkes 45). Fig. 169.

BOUCHETTE. A large buckle used to fasten together the upper and lower parts of the Gothic breastplate. (Fairholt 46).

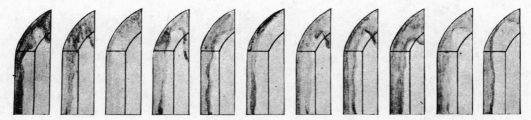

FIGURE 168. *Boshi, shapes of the yakiba at the points of Japanese blades. From a drawing by Mr. T. T. Hoopes.*

BOTTE SECRETE. In the early days of fencing each teacher claimed to have some infallible *botte secrete*, which he taught his pupils when they paid sufficiently well. Every well-known swordsman was supposed to owe his success to one, or more, of such secrets. (Castle 5, 55).

BOUGE, BOULGE. See Voulge.

BOULATS. Watered steel, Persia. (Moser, p. v).

BO-UN, ALVAU-UL. The Princess Charlotte Bay spear thrower. It has a long, thin blade widest in the middle, with a shell handle fixed at any

FIGURE 169. *Shields with bouches. German, Nuremberg, about 1450. Metropolitan Museum. Not to scale.*

BOUCHE. A notch in the upper right-hand corner of a shield to admit of pointing the lance without exposing the arm or body. It was first used in

angle. The peg is in the plane of the blade and is flattened at its attachment; if it is drilled it is only partly covered with cement, if tied it is wholly cov-

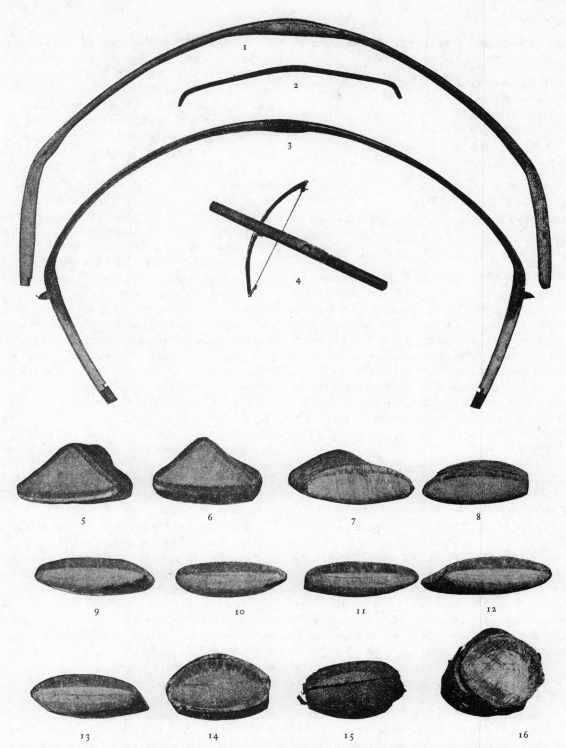

FIGURE 170. *Chinese Bows. 1. Frame of a half made bow. The long piece of bamboo has blocks of deciduous wood glued to the ends, handle and sharp bends near the ends. The horn back is glued on and is scarfed in the middle. All of the pieces are rough. 2. Short bow for a small crossbow. It is complete with the horn back and sinew belly but is not finished. 3. A bow of fine quality said to have been looted from the palace during the Boxer troubles. The horn back is in one piece the full length of the bow. The middle is covered with bark and the ends with shark skin. 4. A toy slur bow with a horn or whalebone bow. 5 to 16. Sections of a bow made in halves and hinged in the middle. 5 is next the end and the others follow in order to 16 which is next the middle. The dark layer at the top of the sections is horn; and the one at the bottom sinew. The light layer at the bottom of section 5 and that around section 16 is the leather cover.*

ered. (Roth, Aust. Mus. VII, 200). Compare Borna. See Spear Thrower.

BOURDONASSE, BOURDON. A light, hollow lance of the 15th century. (Hewitt III, 429).

Light halbards with hollow shafts, carried on state occasions. (Fairholt 461).

A type of tilting lance of the 15th century. It was of very large size but hollow. (Laking Armour III, 84).

BOURGINOT. See Burgonet.

BOUZDYKAN. The Polish mace of the 17th century. It was like those used in western Europe and Turkey at the same period. (Rockstuhl CLXXI).

BOW. The oldest, most used and most widely distributed of projectile weapons. The simplest and commonest kind of bow is a piece of wood tapering in both directions from the middle and having the ends connected by a string shorter than the wood. The side of the bow away from the archer when shooting is called the *back*, and is usually nearly flat; the opposite side is called the *belly*, and is generally more rounded. The middle of the bow is called the *handle* and the ends the *tips*. The latter are frequently made of horn. The notches for the string are called *nocks*.

A bow made from a single piece of wood is called a *self* bow; and one made of several pieces glued together a *built* bow; and one made of wood or bone with sinew stretched on the back a *backed* bow. One made of wood, horn and sinew a *composite* bow. The bows of most savages and those used in western Europe are usually self bows. Backed, or built, bows are not found among early European specimens, and are rare among savages. Backed bows were used in places in which it was difficult to get suitable wood. They are used by the northern Eskimo whose bows are of bone heavily backed by sinew and some owe their whole power to it. In war the Japanese used built bows of the highest class. While built bows are not common they are better than self bows provided the materials and workmanship are first-class. The composite bow is believed to have originated in Turkey and the Turks made the best bows ever produced. They are small and light but have more power than any others. They, or some modification of them, are used in all of the countries as far east as China. In China they also used composite bows but

of a different design. They are far larger and heavier than the Turkish, being made to shoot very large and heavy arrows, while the Turkish were made to send very light arrows for the greatest possible distance. Each does what it is intended to but neither can do the work of the other.

The cross section of self bows varies greatly; most are considerably wider than they are thick, the back being flatter than the belly. Some are almost round, while others have a wide, shallow groove in the back. The Andaman Island bow has a handle of an ordinary size and becomes much wider and thinner and tapers to the tips. In some the limbs are nearly five inches wide in the middle. As a rule the handle of a bow is so placed that the arrow is held very close to the middle of the length. The Japanese bows are an exception as the handle is much below the center. They are very long and the Japanese are short and much of their shooting was done from horseback, or when kneeling on one knee; both positions in which their very long bows could not have been used if held in the middle. In spite of this they are powerful and effective. For any type of bow the power increases with the size up to a certain point, which varies for each. The size alone is no certain indication of the power. The shapes of the arrows and the methods of release have great effects on the performances of bows. Each should be used with the arrows designed for it and using the release it was designed for if it is to show its full power.

In western Europe self bows were used almost exclusively. In England they were the principal weapon. On the Continent they were not as popular, the more powerful, but slower working, crossbow being preferred for war. The old English long bow was preferably made of yew, but many other kinds of wood were also used. "Yew at length became so scarce," writes Grose, "that to prevent its immoderate consumption, bowyers were directed to make four bows of witch-hazel, ash or elm, to one of yew; and no one under seventeen, unless possessed of movables worth forty marks, or the son of parents having an estate of ten pounds per annum, might shoot in a yew bow." (Brand 456). There were many laws regulating the prices and use of bows. Merchants were required to bring in a certain number of bow staves with each ton of goods or cask of wine. The law provided that the highest price a bowyer might charge for a yew bow was three shillings and four pence; or for a sheaf (24) arrows with steel heads, one shilling and two pence.

There are no records of the distances shot in England in early times but the laws indicate that they must have been very long. "That young archers might acquire an accurate eye and a strength of arm, none under 24 years of age might shoot at any standing mark, except it was a rover, and then he was to change his mark at every shot, under penalty of four pence for every shot made contrary to the regulation. It was also enacted that no person above the said age should shoot at any mark not above eleven score yards distant under pain of forfeiting for each shot, six shillings and eight pence." (Grose I, 135). The fine equals the price of two yew bows.

The greatest ranges shot by English bowmen of which we have accurate record are 340 yards by Mr. Trower in 1789, and 308 yards by Mr. Horace Ford in 1858. The record in this country was made by Mr. Ingo Simon, June 6, 1914. The distance was 462 yards, 9 inches; the pull of the bow is said to have been 80 pounds. He told me that he had used a rather small Turkish bow and gear. The Secretary of the Turkish Ambassador in London shot a flight arrow 482 yards. He said that he was not satisfied with the performance as he and his bow were stiff and out of condition, and that with some practice he could shoot very much further. This record was made and certified by the Toxophilites Society. The records carved on the columns in the shooting grounds in Constantinople vary from 625 to 838 yards.

In Africa the bows are generally small and weak. There are two reasons for this; first the bow-using people live mainly in heavily wooded regions where all shooting is necessarily done at short ranges, secondly the arrows are usually poisoned and the injury does not depend on the force of the missile.

The more civilized Malayan people seldom use bows; the Javans did but have practically abandoned them for the last couple of centuries. Their bows and arrows were rather light but well made.

Many of the South Sea Island and South American bows are large and powerful, some are six feet or more long. The arrows used with them are frequently without feathers; they were, however, rarely used except at very short ranges.

The Eskimo use mainly bows of wood heavily backed by twisted sinew and depend mainly on the latter for their strength. They sometimes use bows of pieces of bone lashed together and backed by sinew; these depend entirely on the sinew.

The North American Indians use short, and rather light bows of wood, sometimes backed by sinew. Their range is short and the Indian is not a good shot though he can shoot very rapidly. Dodge, p. 147, says "The most highly prized (bows) among the Indians of Central North America are ingeniously fabricated by carefully fitting together pieces of elk horn, the whole glued together and tightly wrapped with strips of the smaller intestines of deer, or slender threads of sinew, used wet and which, when dry, tighten and unite all the parts into one compact and homogeneous whole, said to be stronger, tougher, more elastic, and more durable than a bow of any other materials. The great difficulty of its construction, the fact that it is liable to become useless in wet, or even in damp weather, and the more general use of firearms, have rendered obsolete this particular make of weapon." Fig. 171.

Built bows have been used occasionally in many parts of the world, but about the only people who have used them consistently are the Japanese whose war bows were made of a piece of deciduous wood between two of bamboo, both of which have their bark outwards. These bows are of nearly uniform section from end to end and are wound with coils of cane at intervals. They are warped to permanent curves at both ends; these reverse when the bow is strung. The Japanese bows are very long; "At the temple of Itasukushima there are two bows. One of these belonged to Yuasa Matashichiro, and is 8 feet 9 inches long; the other belonged to Ihara Koshiro, 8 feet 5 inches, and the diameters of the extreme ends of both is 2.5 inches." (Gilbertson Archery 113). Gilbertson also mentions bows in other temples that are 7 feet 3 inches, two of 7 feet 6, 7-7, 7-8, two of 7-9, 7-10 and 8-6. Count Tokugawa in Tokio showed me a bow fully seven feet long with a cross section of at least two square inches at the handle. Such bows were needed as some of the arrows weighed as much as half a pound and had shafts 40 inches long with diameters up to three-quarters of an inch. See Yumi.

The ceremonial bows are similar in construction but are made in two pieces joined by a metal sleeve at the handle. They are elaborately decorated with

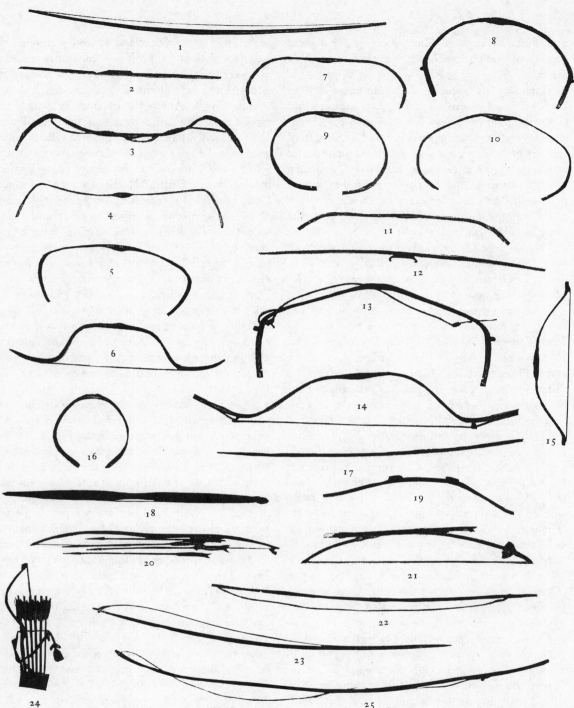

FIGURE 171. *Bows.* 1. *Ceylon, self bow, 5 feet 11.5 inches long painted in several colors.* 2. *India, self bow, painted with peacock's feathers.* 3. *India, composite bow, lacquered yellow and decorated with red and gold.* 4. *India, steel bow, with lacquered borders.* 3 feet 4 inches from tip to tip, unstrung. 5. *India, composite bow, painted black, red and yellow.* 6. *India, painted green, red and gold. Length 3 feet 6 inches, strung.* 7. *Turkish, composite bow, 29 inches from tip to tip in a straight line and 44.5 around the curve. The back is covered with red leather and is signed and dated 1197 Hegira (A.D. 1774).* 8. *Bhutan, composite bow. It is covered with red cloth sewed on.* 9. *Persian, XVII composite bow, painted inside and out with figures of men and horses.* 10. *Persian, very broad composite bow, 4 feet 8 inches around the curve and 18.5 inches from tip to tip, unstrung.* 11. *Persian, entirely covered with miniatures painted in colors on a gold ground. Length 3 feet 4 inches.* 12. *Cashmere, self bow, painted with patterns in red, green and gold. The tips are ivory bird's heads.* 13. *Very heavy Chinese composite bow. The back is painted in red, yellow and green. The sinew string is over a quarter of an inch in diameter.* 14. *Chinese, composite bow, 5 feet 5.5 inches long. The back is painted and the ends are covered with shagren. This and the previous one are of the Manchu type.* 15. *Bow of pure Chinese type, length 2 feet 7.5 inches. It is hinged in the middle and does not reverse when unstrung.* 16. *Korean, sinew wrapped bow, probably for a crossbow. Length around the curve 3 feet 4.25 inches.* 17. *Self bow from the upper Orinoco. It is half round in section with a grooved back, length 5 feet 1.25 inches.* 18. *Alaska, sinew backed wooden bow. The back is shown in the illustration.* 19. *Greenland Eskimo. It is made of pieces of bone lashed together and backed with sinew.* 20. *Sioux, self bow and four arrows. Length 4 feet.* 21. *Bensanji, Upper Congo. Self bow with one end covered with grass cloth. Three arrows.* 22. *Tiruray, Mindanao, of dark wood wound with rattan, rattan string.* 23. *New Guinea. broad bow of black wood. Length 6 feet.* 24. *Japanese, whalebone bow, 2 feet long in a case with 11 arrows.* 25. *Japanese, composite bow, 7 feet and 0.5 inch long.*

lacquer while the fighting bows are plain. The fighting bows were often carried in a frame that held two bows and usually a case for arrows.

The Japanese also made smaller bows of horn or whalebone. Most of those made of horn are about three feet long and are of elliptical section. Like the large bows, they reverse when unstrung. The whalebone bows were much shorter, of rectangular section and shaped like a "cupid's" bow, but with the handle much below the center. They had to be very short as they were carried when traveling in a litter, and therefore were used by men in very cramped positions. They were carried

Practically all of the other nations used composite bows; that is bows built up of a wooden core that is merely a support to hold the other parts together, a horn belly and a sinew back. This type of bow is said to have originated in Turkey and the Turks made the finest bows and arrows ever produced. Their bows will send the light arrows intended for them further than any others and are much smaller and lighter than any others of anything like equal power. They are also very durable and many over one hundred years old are still in serviceable condition. The better Turkish bows are generally signed and dated.

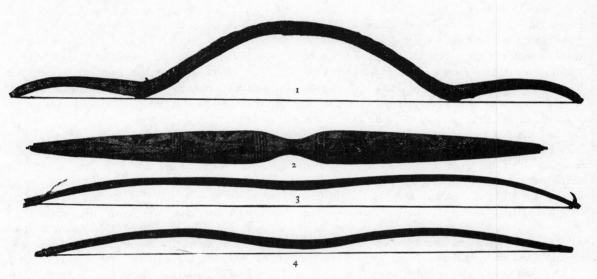

FIGURE 172. *North American Indian Bows.* 1. *Eskimo, Canada.* 2. *Modok, Oklahoma.* 3. *Sioux.* 4. *Apache. Museum of the American Indian, Heye Foundation.*

in small cases, *rimankyu*, fig. 676, which also held the arrows. The Japanese bows are frequently signed.

The Sanju-San-Gen-Do temple in Kyoto has always been a favorite place for archers to test their ability in. The object was to send as many arrows as possible the length of a covered gallery 132 yards long, and only about 22 feet high, low enough to require a very flat trajectory. The difficulty of doing this is proved by numerous arrows sticking in the roof beams and the marks of many others that struck the roof before reaching the target. The record was made by Wasa Daichiri in 1696. It is said that he shot 8,133 arrows in one night of which, however, 3,213 only reached the mark.

The best account of making these bows is given in Payne-Gallwey, Turkish and other Oriental Bows. I have checked this by the account of the only bow maker left in Constantinople. He was highly recommended to me and I was told that he had made bows as long as there was any demand for them; and then, for some years, had enough work repairing bows to keep him busy. At the time that I met him he was teaching in the Government School of Arts and Crafts. As he spoke nothing but Turkish of which I knew nothing we kept our interpreter busy, fortunately he was a good one.

In all but one point he agreed with Payne-Gallwey. The latter says that the frame is made of three pieces of wood, one for the handle and two similar ones for the ends. My Turk said it was made of five. Payne-Gallwey gives as the reason for making it of three the difficulty of shaping the deep and narrow end and the broad and thin limbs and the thick and narrow handle from one piece. This applies with as much force to the difficulty of making the ends and limbs of the same piece and I am inclined to believe that my Turk was right. He also said that they were made from three kinds of wood, tough and stiff for the ends and handle, and very elastic for the limbs. Both say that they were joined by V scarfs of the entire width of the bow.

When the frame was glued together it was warped by heat to the natural curve of the pieces of horn to be used and the latter was next glued to the wood. Two pieces of horn were used each reaching from the middle of the handle, where they are separated by a very thin piece of ivory, to within three or four inches of the ends. The sinew back was next put on. This my Turk said was the most difficult part of making a bow. The sinew is from the great neck tendon of an ox or stag. It was carefully shaped and glued to the frame. It must have been put on under considerable tension as he said that when it was in place the bow curved so much that the ends crossed. He said that it was then baked. Just what he meant by this I could not find out; but probably that it was warped by heat to the shape of an unstrung bow. The sinew was then covered with decorated leather to protect it from moisture and the bow was finished.

The Persian and Tartar bows are similar in general construction to the Turkish but are much wider and curve more when unstrung, with many the ends almost meet. They are also decorated on both back and belly. Their arrows are similar to the Turkish but are not as well shaped and appear clumsy when compared with them.

In India the bows vary tremendously in materials, design and construction. Self bows are used by the wilder people, but most of the bows are composite. Some are made of steel with blocks of wood at the handles. They are of the shape of composite bows and reverse when strung. Some of these are plain, others are lacquered elaborately. It is said that bows were made of nine layers, alternately of wood and horn, but this does not appear probable.

In Tibet and Central Asia the bows are either of Chinese make or close copies of them. In Formosa light self bows are used. In Korea most of the bows are closely related to the Chinese. I have a bow that is probably Korean that is composite like the Chinese but the back is of sinew and the belly of short pieces of ivory wrapped at the joints with coils of cane like the Japanese. It is nearly straight and four feet seven inches long.

The Chinese bows are more complicated. The frame is a piece of bamboo with pieces of a deciduous wood glued on at the handle ends and sharp bends near the ends. Horn is then glued on the belly. A single piece for the length of the bow for the finer ones; and two meeting at the handle for the others. The back has sinew glued on it. The ends and handle are covered with leather or shark skin which goes entirely around the bow. The back only of the parts between is covered with a thin layer of bark which is frequently decorated. Narrow blocks are glued and doweled on the belly of the bow about nine inches from each end; the string bears on these when the bow is not in use. Many of the handles are covered with cork. Figs. 170, 171, 172.

The Chinese bows are large and powerful. Amiot says, p. 387, that the bows made for the army were made of four sizes, 70, 80, 90, and 100 pounds pull. Larger ones were made for exceptional men, or for parade. Bows of 150 pounds are by no means rare in China. The arrows used at the siege of the Legations in 1900 are 3 feet 5.5 inches long and 7/16 of an inch in diameter with heavy socketed steel heads. Some of the whistling arrows are 4 feet 2 inches long with heads four inches in diameter and six inches long. The bows that I saw in Peking that were used with such arrows were huge, about six feet long strung, with a cross section at the handle of nearly two square inches. They were said to have a pull of about 200 pounds and looked it.

The Chinese and Japanese made sectional bows that can be folded up or taken apart for convenience of carriage. The Japanese bows are of two or more pieces that are joined by tenons that fit in metal sleeves. Most of them have very little power and are used mainly for parade or amusement. The Chinese bows are of two pieces joined by a hinge in the middle of the handle. Each half is built up of horn, wood and sinew like their usual bows.

There are several forms of arrow release. In the simplest the arrow is held between the thumb and first finger which surround the string, and the latter is pulled by the pressure of the arrow, 1, fig. 173. This is only possible with a very light bow and is only used by a few savage races. Professor Morse calls this the primary release (Bull. Essex Inst. 1885, 1922). In the secondary release the arrow is held as before but the string is pulled mainly by the tips of the second and third fingers which are placed against it, 2, fig. 173. The tertiary release is much like the secondary, the only difference being that the first finger is nearly straight and its tip also bears on the string and helps pull it, 3, fig. 173.

of our bowmen also." (Hansard 820). The Eskimo also uses this form of release. The Mongolian release is used in Turkey and throughout Asia. In it a ring is worn on the thumb which is passed around the string and under the forefinger, the base of the finger pressing against the arrow, 5, fig. 173. When using this release the arrow is placed to the right of the bow, with the secondary and Mediterranean to the left. Some Japanese bowmen use a combination of the secondary and Mediterranean releases.

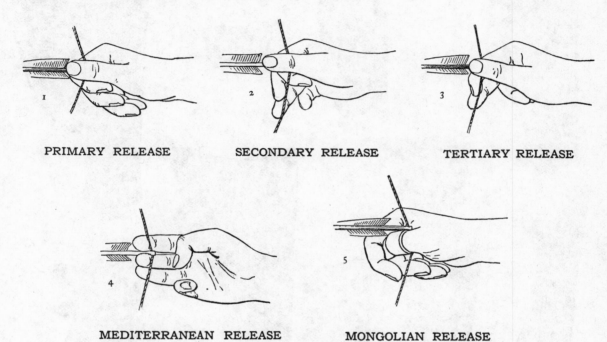

PRIMARY RELEASE   SECONDARY RELEASE   TERTIARY RELEASE

MEDITERRANEAN RELEASE   MONGOLIAN RELEASE

FIGURE 173. *Arrow Releases, Morse.*

These two forms of release are used by the greater part of the North American Indians, by the Siamese and Andaman Islanders among others. The next Professor Morse calls the Mediterranean release, because he says, "It has been in vogue among the northern Mediterranean nations for centuries, and among the southern Mediterranean nations for tens of centuries." In this the string is drawn by the tips of the first two or three fingers, the arrow being held between the first two, 4, fig. 173. This is the method used in Europe throughout the middle ages, two fingers only being used. "Modern English bowmen generally use three fingers. The Flemish the first and second only—a method adopted by some

For the different parts, varieties and accessories of bows (except arrows) see: Adaya, Alborium, Angushtana, Aquande-Da, Archer's Guard, Archer's Ring, Archer's Ring Case, Artillator, Azuchi, Azusa-Yumi, Banqui, Bel, Bois d'Arc, Bow Case, Bow String, Bracer, Butt, Chado-Kake, Challa, Chodo-Kake, Corytus, Daikyu, Dhanu, Dhanurvida, Dornlach, Dzu, Ebira, Endong, Fujihanashi, Gendawa, Ghulel, Gi-ghet, Godha, Gokyu, Gulail, Hage-Ro, Hamayumi, Han-Kyu, Hira Yanagui, Hoko-Yumi, Horn Groove, I-Ba, Igurumi, I-Iru, Ika, Ikuba, Ipoh, Ishiyumi, Ite, Juhatsu, Kachi-Yuki, Kachi-Yumi, Kaku Uchi, Kaman, Kari-Ebira, Ka Ryntich, Kasun, Kiri, Koltschan, Kumtas, Kuro-Boshi, Kusune, Kyu, Kyujutsu, Kyusen, Langkap, Lepa, Lezam, Long Bow, Lumo, Maji-ha, Makiwara, Maktah, Malali, Mande, Marishi-ten, Maru-Ki, Mato, Mato-Ba, Meigen, Mosha-Kina, Motohazu, Nakhuna, Nalutsch, Nigiri, Nu-kigomedo, Otogane, Otokane, Ouruma, Panah, Pellet Bow, Pizikse, Piziksezax, Querquer, Quiver, Rama Ina, Rimankyu, Ronga, Sadak, Saghdach, Saghdak, Satsu Yumi, Sefin, Self Bow, Sha, Shagei,

busuma, Yadate, Ya-Dane, Yadzutsu, Yag, Ya-Gakari, Yagoro, Yama-Gata, Yanagi, Yanagi To Ha, Ya-Omote, Ya-Tsugi, Ya-Zama, Ya-Zutsu, Yo-Kyu, Yoppiki, Yubukuro, Yudame, Yu Gake, Yu-Gote, Yu-Hazu, Yukaeri, Yukaeshi, Yuki, Yumi, Yumi Dame, Yumi Gote, Yumi Gumi, Yumi Mato, Yumi No Tsuru, Yumi Shi, Yumitori, Yumi Yari, Yumi Zira, Yunde, Yuzuka, Yuzuru, Zhoo, Zhooskat, Zuboshi.

FIGURE 174. *Bow Cases and Quivers, Asia.* 1, 2. *Korean bow case and quiver of black enameled leather with borders of cloth embroidered in colors and gilded metal mounts.* 3, 4. *Korean bow case and quiver similar to the last but the embroidery is in brighter colors and the metal mounts are of plain silver.* 5, 6. *Tibet. Bow case and quiver. Both are covered with red cloth trimmed with blue striped braid, and leather edges with silver studs and bosses.* 7, 8. *China. Bow case and quiver covered with black velvet and green leather, with gilded brass mounts.* 9, 10. *China. Bow case and quiver of brown leather trimmed with black, bronze mountings.*
All of these quivers are of the Chinese type with hinged pockets on the back for special arrows.

Sha-Ho, Shateki, Shigeto-Yumi, Shiko, Shingeto, Si Or, Stake (Archer's), Subeki, Suzume Yumi, Tanuki, Tarkash, Tebukoro, Tempat Damak, Thakroo, Tomeang, Tomo, Tribulus, Tsubo Yan-agui, Tsukura, Tsura, Tsuresashi, Tsurumaki, Tsurusuberi, Ulapa, Uma Yumi, Umla, Urahazu, Usuzuru, Utsobo, Yaba, Ya-Bako, Yabusame, Ya-

BOW. The finger guard of a sword or knife.

BOW CASE. Throughout the East the composite bows are always carried strung in cases that only cover the lower half. These cases are usually made of leather, often covered with cloth, silk or velvet, and decorated with inlays of leather or applied metal work, sometimes set with jewels. Some of the bow cases in the palace in Constantinople are a blaze of gems. In China the quiver and bow case were sometimes armored, that is made of brigandine or jazerant, 7, 8, fig. 75. The bow case is hung from the belt and generally has a quiver to match. Fig. 174.

The Plains Indians and several other savage races also use bow cases but more to protect the bow from wet than as carriers. They are generally simple bags of skin or leather, usually with quivers of the same material attached. They were carried slung from the shoulders. Fig. 175, 653.

BOW STRING. The old English bow string was made of cord; and cord is the commonest material for the purpose in most parts of the world. The few Malayans that use the bow are apt to make the string of a piece of rattan. Where bamboo is used for bows the string is often made of a strip of the same material. The Turkish, Indian and Persian bow strings are bundles of silk threads wrapped with silk in the middle and tied to loops of sinew at the ends. The sinew is less apt to chafe and fits better in the nocks of the bow than the soft and bulky string. The lighter Chinese bow strings are of elaborately wound and knotted cotton threads. They are made in sections joined by interlocking loops and are very stiff except at the loops. The heavier strings are made of twisted sinew, sometimes over a quarter of an inch in diameter. Sinew though often used is not a desirable material for bow strings as it stretches badly when wet. The Chinese sometimes make the strings for pellet bows of two paddle-shaped pieces of wood with loops for the nocks at one end, and with their other ends connected by a short length of doubled cord carrying a pouch for the missile. The Japanese strings are either of sinew or of bundles of threads covered with lacquer. In either case the loops at the ends are tied quite differently, generally one is white and the other red. The one that is slipped on last has a short piece of fine cord fastened to it that is held in the teeth while the bow is being bent for stringing. Fig. 176.

BRACER, ARCHER'S GUARD. A covering for the left wrist to protect it from the recoil of the bow string. Guards of this kind have been used in all ages and countries where bows have been used. One is necessary except where the bow is very

highly braced, that is, has such a short string that it cannot hit the arm on the recoil.

In medieval Europe and parts of the East they were generally made of horn, leather or ivory. They were generally quite plain, but were sometimes highly ornamented. In Persia "a quilted half sleeve of crimson velvet, or fine cloth, thickly embroidered with gold flowers protects the arm from being bruised by the return of the cord. . . . The weight of the gold of one which I wore on my arm for a short time was remarkable; it probably amounted to three or four ounces." (Hansard

FIGURE 175. *North American Indian Bow Case. Buckskin bow case and quiver decorated with fringe and red cloth. It contains a sinew backed bow which is badly sprung from being kept unstrung.*

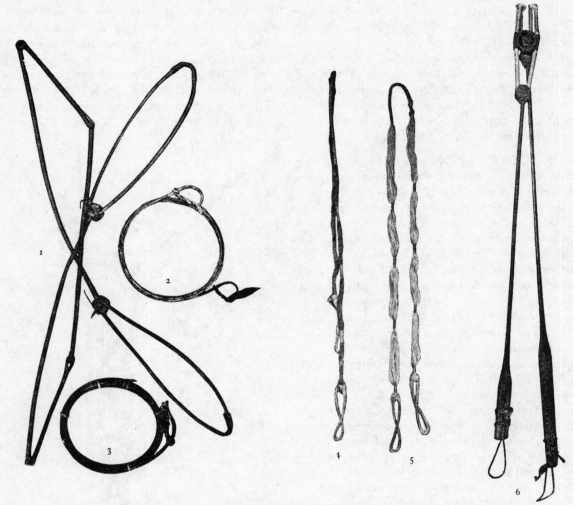

FIGURE 176. *Bow Strings.* 1. *Chinese. It is made of a bundle of threads tightly wound with thread; and is very stiff except where the sections are connected by interlocking loops.* 2. *Japanese, sinew.* 3. *Japanese, cord covered with black lacquer. Each of the last two has a loop at one end and a slipknot at the other.* 4. *Turkish, silk with sinew loops for the nocks.* 5. *Turkish, similar to 4 but longer.* 6. *Chinese, for a pellet bow. Two paddle-shaped sticks, with loops of sinew to go in the nocks, at one end. The other ends are connected by a short doubled cord carrying a pouch for the missile.*

137). One of the time of Henry IV found at Boulton hall, Yorkshire, is also described by Hansard, p. 102. "There is also an ancient leather bracer in the possession of the Honorable Miss Grimstone,

The Japanese formerly used bracers (see Tomo) but centuries ago adopted the practice of easing the grip on the bow as the arrow was discharged. This allows the bow to turn in the hand so that the string

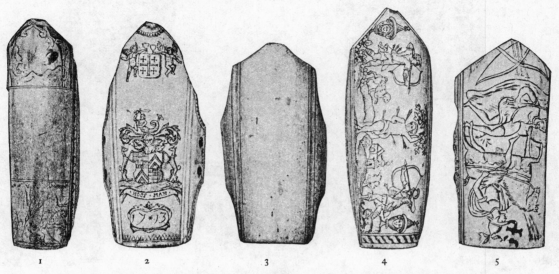

FIGURE 177. *European Bracers.* 1. *Dutch, early 17th century.* 2. *Dutch, dated 1713.* 3. *French, dated 1699.* 4. *Dutch, late 16th century.* 5. *Italian, about 1580. From the Collection of Dr. Dean. All ivory.*

which exactly illustrates the motto of Chaucer ('And on his arm he wore a gai bracer'). It resembles a half sleeve; the part frayed by the bow string (the marks of which are still visible) being without ornament, but a rose, with many curious devices beautifully embossed cover the other portions, and the words JESUS HELPE are inserted on a gilt ground."

There are very few leather bracers in existence. The oldest is in the Egyptian Museum in Cairo. There is also one of much later date in the British Museum. Nearly all of the early bracers that have survived are of ivory, generally decorated with engraving. Fig. 177.

In Burma very curious bracers are used. They are made of wood, very well carved. The part hit by the string is curved and quite large; and they are held to the wrist by two curved prongs on the back. The whole has a decided resemblance to a saddle. Fig. 178.

The Chinese usually dispensed with bracers, their bows being very highly braced. They are said to have used guards made of bamboo and oiled paper, and also occasionally an old sleeve.

strikes the outside of the arm when the force is almost expended. This is called yukaeri or yukaeshi. This makes a bracer unnecessary.

Many savages use pieces of skin or bark bound to the wrist. Some of the North American Indians

FIGURE 178. *Burmese Bracer. Carved wood. South Kensington Museum.*

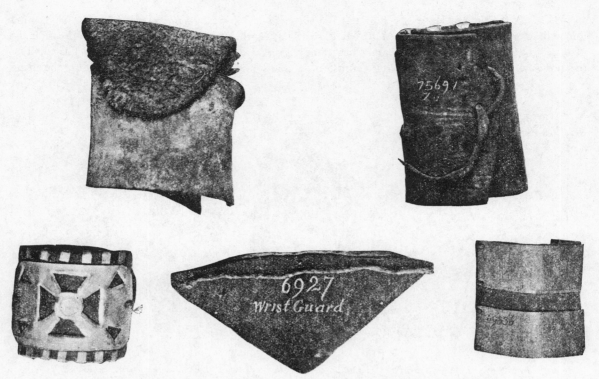

FIGURE 179. *Bracers. North American Indian, Navajo. U. S. National Museum.*

FIGURE 180. *Eskimo Bracers of horn and ivory. U. S. National Museum.*

use fox and badger skins; others use leather bracers, some of which are of complicated shapes. The Navajo wear a broad band of leather with a silver plate for the string to strike against, fig. 179. On the other side of the world bracers woven of split cane are quite common.

"The Matryas, a nation of Brazil, are said by Dr. Southey to twist plaited horsehair around the arm. A number of quill feathers from the macaw or parroquet's wing constitute the bracer of another South American tribe. These encircle the wrist, their quills pointing towards the hand, the

elliptical plates of bone about four inches long and two wide. (Murdoch 210). Some are much smaller and curved, fig. 180. In the South Seas the commonest bracer is a vine, creeper or piece of bark wound around the arm from the wrist to the elbow. (Cayley-Webster 339, Brown Mel. & Pol. 157). "I remarked no ornaments, except the bracelet worn to protect the arm from the bow string. They use this as a bag or purse, and put tobacco or a spare string for their bow, or other little things in it." Fly River, New Guinea. (D'Albertis II, 173). Fig. 181.

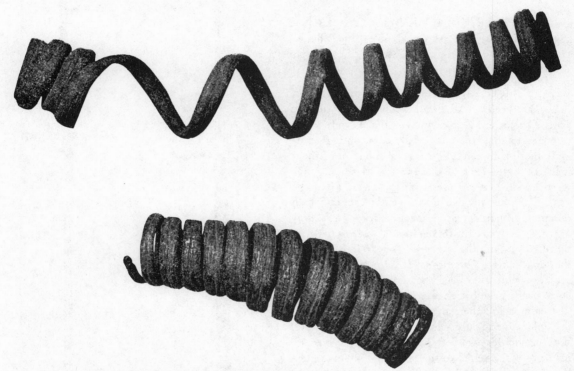

FIGURE 181. *Bracers. Sir Charles Hardy Group. They are coils of bark.*

plumed ends towards the elbow." (Hansard 102).

The Eskimo wears bracers "made of three pieces of bone about four inches long, hinged together and fastened to the wrist by a button and loop." (Wood 1344, 1353). The natives of Point Barrow use bracers made of a mountain sheep's horn curved to fit the wrist. They have long slots in the middle for no obvious purpose, and shorter slots on each of the long sides for the straps that attach them to the wrist. Exactly similar bracers made of bone or copper were used on St. Lawrence Island at Kotzebue Sound. In Greenland bracers are flat

BRACHIERE. An arm guard, 14th century. (Hewitt I, 240, II, 162, 225).

BRACKETS. The cheeks of the traveling carriage of a mortar. This name is also given to the part of the mortar bed where the trunnions are placed. (Hoyt 370).

BRACONIERE. A narrow plate at the lower edge of a breastplate from which the tassets were hung, 16th century.

BRACONIERE A TONNELET, GRANDE BRACONIERE. See Tonnelet.

BRAIL. A strip of leather widest in the middle with a longitudinal slit in the widest part. It is used to secure a hawk that fidgets with her wings. The slit is slipped over the pinion joint, and the ends crossed inside the wing, brought around the body and tied outside the other wing in a bowknot and the ends passed through the bow. (Michel 49).

BRAND. A kind of sword carried hung from the saddle, probably the estoc. (Planche 52).

BRANDESTOC. A hatchet or war hammer with a long blade concealed in the handle. (Dean Hdbk. 68). Fig. 182.

BRAQUEMAR, BRAQUEMART. A kind of sword with a broad, short, double-edged blade, 16th century. (Boutell 177, Castle 54, 229). Its exact nature is unknown.

BRASSARD, BRACHIERE, BRASER, GARDE DE BRAS. Plate armor for the entire arm. The earliest European arm guards were made of boiled leather, the later of plate, becoming gradually more complete. The earliest mention of them is in the latter part of the 13th century, but they were not in general use until the 14th. (Planche 53). They are divided into several parts of which the most important are—the *vambrace* or *avant-bras* for the forearm, the *elbow cop* or *coudiere* for the elbow; and the *rerebrace* or *arriere-bras* for the upper arm. The *shoulder cop, pauldron* or *epauliere* which covered the shoulder, and often a large part of the breast and back, was usually considered a part of the arm guard. In the earliest ones the joints were only partly covered by the plate. The remainder was left bare or was protected by mail gussets fastened to the arming doublet. Later, in the Gothic period, the elbow and shoulder cops were made very large so as to overlap the other plates and protect the joints, fig. 37. The elbow cop was sometimes drawn out in a long point, 2, fig. 37. Still later the arms were covered by a large number of narrow plates articulated together so as to completely enclose the arm and at the same time allow it to be moved in any direction, fig. 725. At first the entire arm guard was hung from points fastened to the arming doublet; these were passed through holes in the shoulder cop and tied on the outside. Later the entire arm hung from pins on the breastplate or gorget.

In the 15th and 16th centuries the Turks used

FIGURE 182. *Brandestocs, all Italian, late 16th century. Metropolitan Museum. Not to scale.*

arm guards made of several rows of overlapping plates connected by mail, these reached from the knuckles to well above the elbow. For other oriental arm guards see Bazu Band and Kote.

BRASS KNUCKLES. See Knuckle Duster.

to protect the privates. Though of no obvious defensive value it was considered of great importance and, by English law, every man above a certain rank was required to have one. The skirt, or breech, of mail was also called a brayette. Fig. 183. (ffoulkes 62, 93).

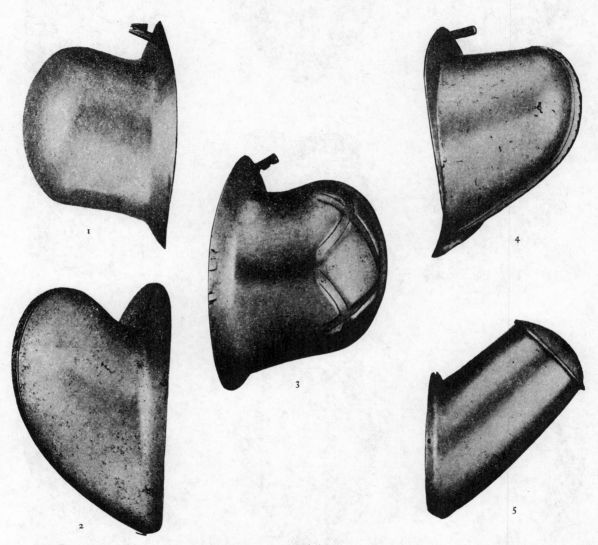

FIGURE 183. *Brayettes.* 1. *German, 1540.* 2. *Swiss(?), 1540.* 3. *German, 1546.* 4. *German, 1550.* 5. *Swiss, 1570. Metropolitan Museum. Not to scale.*

BRAY, BRAYE. A low wall outside the ramparts to prevent the enemy from approaching them. (Violet le Duc, Hist. 362).

BRAYETTE, COD PIECE, FRONT APPENDAGE. A piece copied from the civil dress of the time (16th century) and nominally intended

BREAST AND BACK. See Back and Breast.

BREASTPLATE. A plate, or set of plates, covering the front of the body from the neck to a little below the waist. It is one of the oldest pieces of body armor and was used before history. It was one of the earliest pieces of plate worn in the mid-

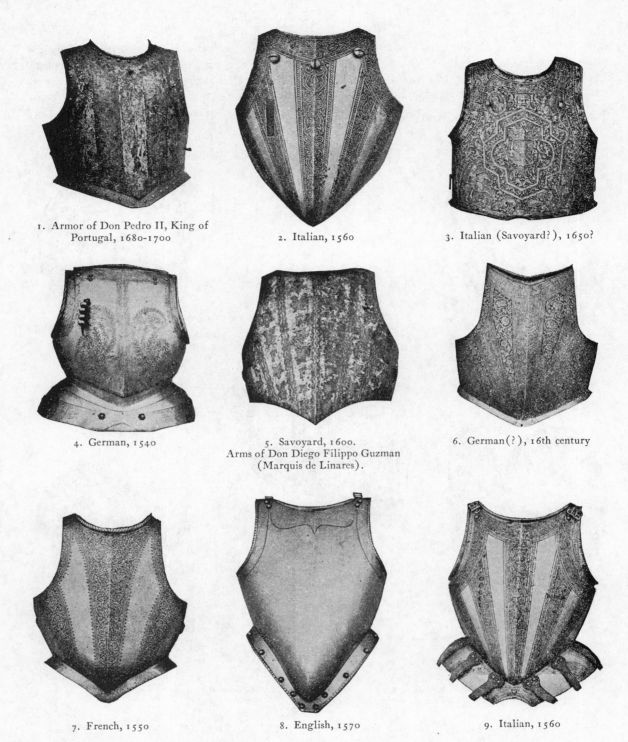

1. Armor of Don Pedro II, King of Portugal, 1680-1700

2. Italian, 1560

3. Italian (Savoyard?), 1650?

4. German, 1540

5. Savoyard, 1600.
Arms of Don Diego Filippo Guzman
(Marquis de Linares).

6. German(?), 16th century

7. French, 1550

8. English, 1570

9. Italian, 1560

FIGURE 184. *Breastplates.* 1. *Arms of the King of Portugal, 1680-1700.* 2. *Italian, 1560.* 3. *Italian (Savoyard?), 1650.* 4. *German, 1540.* 5. *Savoyard, 1600. Arms of Don Diego Filippo Guzman (Marquis di Linares).* 6. *German(?), 16th century.* 7. *French, 1550.* 8. *English, 1570.* 9. *Italian, 1560. Metropolitan Museum. Not to scale.*

dle ages and is still in use. At first it was made of a single piece; but in the 15th century it was often made in two, and sometimes in three parts. The lower overlapped the upper and was connected to it by a strap, or sliding rivets, so as to give it some flexibility. Later it was again made of a single plate. In the 16th century the type of breastplate called anime, fig. 16, was made of narrow horizontal plates fastened together by sliding rivets. Many breastplates have a pronounced ridge, called the *tapul*, in the center. About 1500 it had a projecting point a little below the center, later the point

BREASTSTRAP. A broad strap crossing a horse's chest and fastened to the saddle to keep it from slipping back. It was used as much for decoration as utility and many are very ornate. They were used both in Europe and throughout the East. Fig. 188.

BREECH LOADERS. Firearms that are loaded from the breech. Breechloading firearms were made as early as the 16th century; and there is one in the Tower Collection believed to have belonged to Henry VIII. They were not common or popular

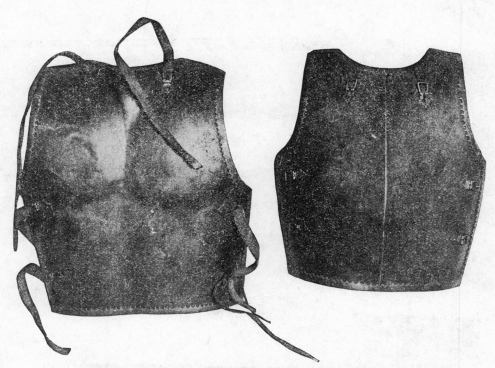

FIGURE 185. *Indian back and breast of watered steel with brass borders, 18th century.*

was placed lower down, and still later it was enlarged to form the "peascod" immortalized by Mr. Punch. The backplate was commonly included when the name breastplate was used. To a large degree the shape of the breastplate followed the fashion of the civil dress of the period. Fig. 184.

The solid breastplate was never common in the East, though it was occasionally worn in India and Japan during the 17th and 18th centuries. In both countries it was apparently copied from the European forms and was often of European make. Fig. 185, and Hatomune-Do, fig. 360.

as they were complicated and expensive. Most of them carried the supply of powder in the stock, and it was sometimes ignited when the gun was fired, destroying both weapon and user.

Although many attempts were made to construct breechloaders, none of them had any success until the latter part of the 18th century. It is true that the celebrated Cookson gun is marked 1586, but this is evidently a mistake, as the type of both stock and lock are very much later. In it the charge is contained in two cavities in the stock. The loading is done by revolving a horizontal cylinder which

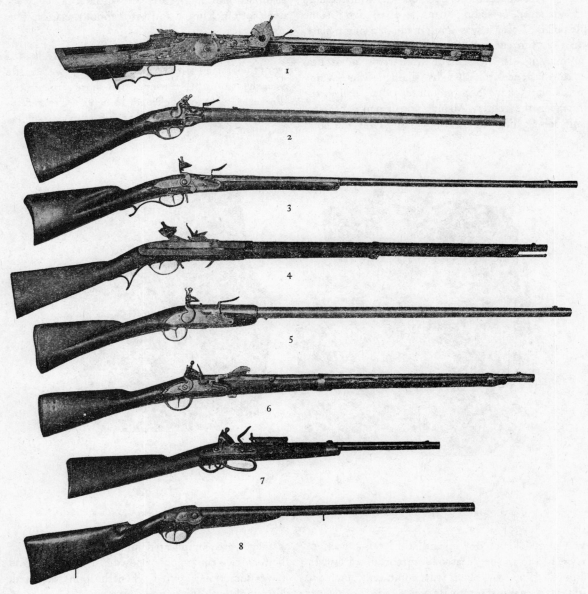

FIGURE 186. Breechloaders. 1. Wheel lock, German, 17th century. Stock signed: Andress Lescribe, Auspugh, 1658. 2. Flintlock, special hair trigger, Austrian, 1757. Length 46.75 inches. 3. Flintlock, removable cartridge, European, 18th century. Length 54.75 inches. 4. Flintlock, Hall, American, 18th century. Length 52.5 inches. 5. Flintlock, German or French, 1775. Length 52.5 inches. 6. Flintlock musket, European, 1750. Length 48.75 inches. 7. Flintlock carbine, French, 1800. Length 36.75 inches. 8. French, 19th century. Length 44.125 inches. No. 1 from the Bashford Dean Memorial Collection. Remainder from the Collection of Mr. William G. Renwick.

forms the recoil block. This cylinder has two cavities in it which receive the ball and charge of powder from the magazine in the stock when the gun is held muzzle down and the cylinder revolved. The ball drops into the barrel and the chamber containing the powder remains in line with it. The powder chamber has a vent through the axis of the cylinder to the pan which revolves with it and is primed as it passes the magazine. Pistols with the

About the middle of the 18th century an Englishman named Warsop invented a breechloading gun in which a screw plug slightly larger than the bore closed the breech. This plug entered the barrel from below and did not extend entirely through it. It was fastened to the trigger guard which formed a lever by which it could be turned. The action was too slow as it required a very large number of turns to remove or replace the plug. It was

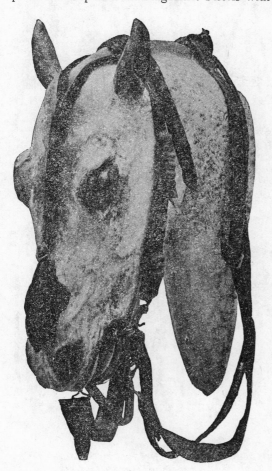

1   2

FIGURE 187. *European Bridles.* 1. *Saxon, 16th century.* 2. *French, about* 1740. *Metropolitan Museum.*

same mechanism were made in the latter part of the 18th century.

Another and practical gun opened at the breech so that loaded chambers could be placed in the barrel which was counterbored to receive them. Each of these chambers had a complete flintlock attached; while practical this gun was much too expensive for general use.

improved by Lieutenant-Colonel Ferguson of the British army in 1776. In his gun the plug came entirely through the barrel and was actuated by a multi-thread screw to give quick travel. Threequarters of a turn made the plug descend below the bore so that the gun could be loaded. His gun was used by the British during the Revolutionary War. At a trial at Woolwich "Notwithstanding a heavy

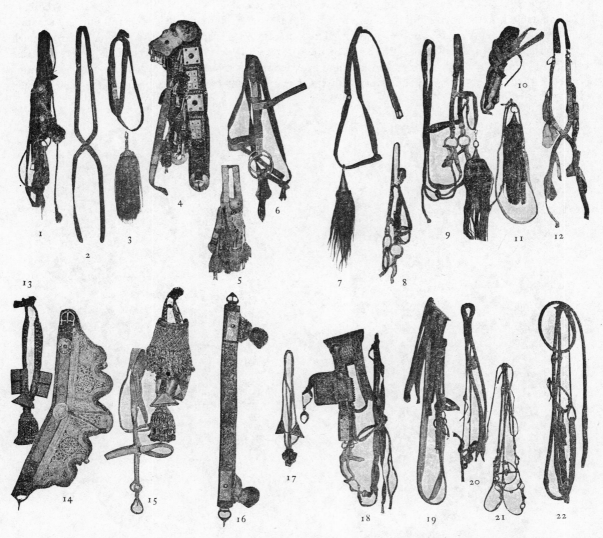

FIGURE 188. *Oriental Bridles.* 1. *Chinese, late 17th century. All mountings of pierced and gilded metal set with turquoise and carnelian. Plain broken snaffle bit.* 2. *Crupper, 17th century. Covered with cloisonee plates.* 3. *Breast strap with yak tail tassel. The mounts match no. 2.* 4. *Sudanese breast strap, 19th century. Decorated with embossed and inscribed gold plates.* 5. *Bridle to match also decorated with gold plates.* 6. *Tibet, 17th century. Silk braid, all mounts of pierced and gilded iron.* 7. *Breast strap to match. It has a yak tail tassel.* 8. *Korean bridle decorated with silver plates enameled in colors. Broken snaffle bit with silver rings on the ends. They are also decorated with colored enamels.* 9, 10, 11, 12. *Belong with the suit of armor, no. 75, China, late 17th century. It is decorated with cloisonee.* 13. *The neck amulet.* 14. *The breast strap and* 15 *the bridle of a Moroccan harness of the 18th century. All are of red cloth embroidered in gold.* 16. *Breast strap.* 17. *Neck amulet and* 18 *the bridle of a Tunisian harness of the early 18th century. All are of red velvet heavily embroidered with gold, gilded metal mounts.* 19. *Persian bridle of about 1800. Leather covered with embroidery of colored silks. Plates and bosses set with carnelians and covered with a mosaic of turquoise.* 20. *Moro bridle. Broken snaffle bit, light headstall of braided hair and heavy rope reins wound with cord.* 21. *North American Indian. Spanish bit, braided rawhide headstall and quirt.* 22. *South American, West Coast. Very heavy bridle of braided leather with a long whip attached.*

rain and the high wind, he fired during the space of four or five minutes at the rate of four shots a minute, and also fired (while advancing at the rate of four miles an hour) four times a minute. He then poured a bottle of water into the pan and barrel of the piece when loaded so as to wet every grain of powder, and in less than half a minute he fired it as well as ever, without extracting the ball. Lastly he hit the bull's-eye lying on his back on the ground, incredible as it seems to many, considering the variations of the wind and the wetness of the weather. He only missed the target three times during the whole course of his experiments." Fig. 186.

BREECH OF MAIL. A short skirt of mail worn in the latter part of the 16th century. It was sometimes called a brayette. (ffoulkes 62).

BREGANDER NAYLES. Rivets for making brigandines. (ffoulkes 33).

BRENE, BROIGNE, BRUNY, BYRNE. A variety of armor of undetermined character worn during the 11th and 12th centuries. (Planche 59).

BRETECHE. A covered passage constructed of wood on top of a wall or tower. It was carried on a series of corbels called machicoulis. It was usually removed in times of peace as it was easily rebuilt when needed. (Hewitt I, 357).

A wooden defense designed to protect the front of a salient. (Violet le Duc, Hist. 462). Compare Hourd.

BRICHETTES. The collective name for armor protecting the loins and hips. It was composed of culettes and tassets that hung from the breast and back. (Planche 58).

BRICOLE. An engine for throwing heavy stones, 14th century. (Hewitt II, 327).

BRIDLE. The simplest form of bridle is the hackamore, a halter with the lead strap hitched around the lower jaw. Bits which were much more effective were invented before history began and have been used ever since. The essential parts of the bridle are—the headstall, an arrangement of straps or cords to hold the bit in the mouth—the bit—and the reins. The North American Indians have reduced the bridle to its essential parts and generally use the lightest and simplest bridles known. They

also sometimes used very elaborate bridles made of horsehair braided in patterns. The bridle readily lends itself to display and, particularly in the East, the purely ornamental parts frequently form a larger part than the essential. Figs. 187, 188. See also Bardings.

FIGURE 189. *Bridle of a Gunlock. Interior of a European flintlock of the late 18th century, showing the bridle.*

BRIDLE CUTTER. A sharp hook-shaped blade on the back or side of an axe with which to cut the reins of an enemy, 16th century and later. (Hewitt III, 604). It was also used in the East. 6, fig. 101.

BRIDLE OF A GUN LOCK. A frame on the inside of the lock plate to hold the inner ends of the pins on which the different links and levers work. (Greener 268). According to Schoen, p. 69, it was a French invention of the middle of the 17th century. Fig. 189.

BRIDOON. A snaffle and its reins acting with, or independently of, the curb and its reins.

BRIGANDINE, BRIGANDYRON, BRIGANTAYLE. A kind of armor much used in Europe from the 13th to the 15th centuries and much longer throughout the East.

In Europe it was made of plates of iron or steel overlapping upwards and riveted to a canvas garment usually covered with silk or velvet. The plates were tinned to prevent their rusting and ruining the cloth. The plates were on the inside in most cases, the rivet heads which showed on the outside were often gilded, producing a very brilliant effect. In the early European specimens, which were used in war, the plates were quite large, sometimes as much as three or four by eight to ten inches. In the later ones, which were used as light armor, they were seldom more than one by two inches. The brigandine was usually a sleeveless vest; but some of the later ones had arms and occasionally legs. Fig. 190.

In Tewkesbury Abbey there is a door covered with plates said to have come from brigandines worn at the battle of Tewkesbury in 1472. Some of them are as large as twenty-eight by four inches, the smallest is four and five-tenths by seven, and the widest is five and five-tenths inches. They are from brigandine is made of hardened leather plates.

In Japan brigandines were often used. The plates were of steel or hard leather. They were generally small hexagons with holes in the middle. They were quilted between layers of cloth and often tied through the holes in the centers. They were mainly used for the minor pieces of armor—neck guards, etc. Occasionally they covered the whole body. Figs. 6, 191.

FIGURE 190. *Brigandines.* 1. *Italian, early 16th century.* 2. *Spanish, 16th century. Metropolitan Museum. Not to scale.*

an eighth to a sixteenth of an inch thick. There are sixty-eight in all.

In India the plates were tinned and generally quilted between two layers of cloth. In some Chinese suits larger steel plates are fastened on the outside of the suit over the knees and breast. Fig. 72.

In China and Korea brigandine was the usual armor. The plates were of iron or steel, usually lacquered to prevent their rusting. They varied greatly in size; if large they were riveted only at the top, if small in the middle. Some Korean

BROAD ARROW. An arrow with a broad, barbed head. At sea arrows of this kind were used for the purpose of injuring the sails and rigging of an enemy in the 14th and 15th centuries. (Hewitt II, 274, 275). A conventional representation of it is still used to designate the property of the British navy.

BROADSWORD. A sword with a straight, wide, single-edged blade. It was the military sword of the 17th century as distinguished from the civil sword, the rapier. It was also the usual weapon of the common people. It generally had a basket hilt with a complicated guard of loops and shells. Fig. 192.

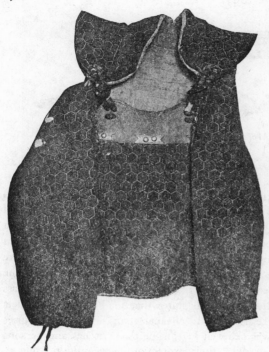

FIGURE 191. *Japanese Brigandine. Cloth with hexagonal plates quilted in but not tied as usual.*

BROCHIERO, BROQUEL. A small target or buckler used in fencing in the first half of the 16th century. (Castle 236).

BROCKET. A spear thrower made partly of wood and partly of cord. (Hor. Mus. 32). See Spear Thrower.

BROIGNE. See Brene.

BROQUEL. See Brochiero.

BROWN BILL. See Bill.

BRUGNE. See Hauberk.

BRUNY. See Brene.

BUCKIE. India, an axe, or axe knife. Egerton illustrates three radically different weapons under this name, calling them all Mahratta. (Egerton 471, 473, 474). The Wallace Catalogue gives this name to an axe from Kutch with a heavy head and crescent blade.

BUCKLER. A shield, more especially the small, round shield held in the left hand when fencing, and used from the 13th to the 17th century.

Meyrick defines a buckler as a shield with a handle (or two close together) in the center and held in the hand; and a target as a shield with two rather widely separated loops through which the arm is passed. While it is by no means certain that

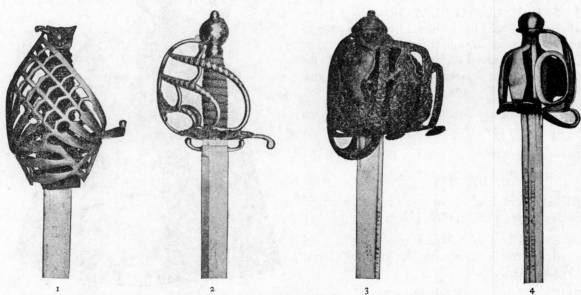

1   2   3   4

FIGURE 192. *Broadswords. 1. Schiavona, Venetian, 17th century. 2. Italian, 17th century. 3. Scotch, about 1750. 4. Scotch, 18th century. Metropolitan Museum. Not to scale.*

these were the original meanings of these names the distinction is a convenient one.

A round shield with two handles close together in the middle is the usual type in Persia and India. See Dhal.

BUKMAR. A musquetoon with a bell mouth, tiger pattern, India. (Egerton 585). Fig. 196.

BULAWA. A mace, Russia. (Scheremetew 107, 108, 109).

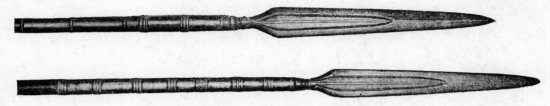

FIGURE 193. *Budiak, Moro spears.*

BUDGE BARREL. A barrel that holds 40 to 60 pounds of powder and has a leather bag fastened to one end with brass nails. They were used in the batteries to keep the powder from being fired by accident. (Hoyt 358).

BUDIAK. A Moro spear with a long, paneled head. Fig. 193. (Arc. f. Eth. IV, 70).

BUFF COAT. A heavy leather coat worn as armor in the 16th and 17th centuries. It was a long skirted coat, frequently without a collar, fig. 194. It was originally made of buffalo leather, hence the name. The ordinary equipment of a trooper in the 17th century was a buff coat, jack boots, a lobster-tailed helmet and a back and breast.

BUFFE, FALLING BEAVOR. A face guard of plate worn with open helmets from the 15th century on. It was either held in place by a strap, or straps passing around the neck, or was bolted to the breastplate. The latter fastening was always used when jousting. Fig. 195.

BUGEI. Military arts, Japan. The use of the sword, spear, bow, etc.

BUGLE. See Bible.

BUGU GURA. See Buki Gura.

BUISINE. A kind of trumpet of bent form and made of brass, 14th century. (Hewitt II, 310).

BUKHTAR. A solid Persian breastplate modeled closely to the human form like the old Greek. (Wallace Orient).

BUKI GURA, BUGU GURA. An arsenal, Japan.

BULLET. Bullets are generally made of lead, and are spherical or ogival in shape. Those of an irregular, elongated shape are called slugs; they are often made by uncivilized peoples and are then made of all sorts of scrap material. The bullets for most modern high powered rifles are jacketed with an alloy of copper and nickel, as lead is too soft to take the rifling properly at the high velocities used. The French, and a few other armies, use solid brass bullets. Rockhill states that in Tibet silver bullets were used, being cheaper than lead. For centuries it was believed in Europe that witches and persons favored by their protection, were invulnerable to

FIGURE 194. *Buff Coat, 17th century. Metropolitan Museum.*

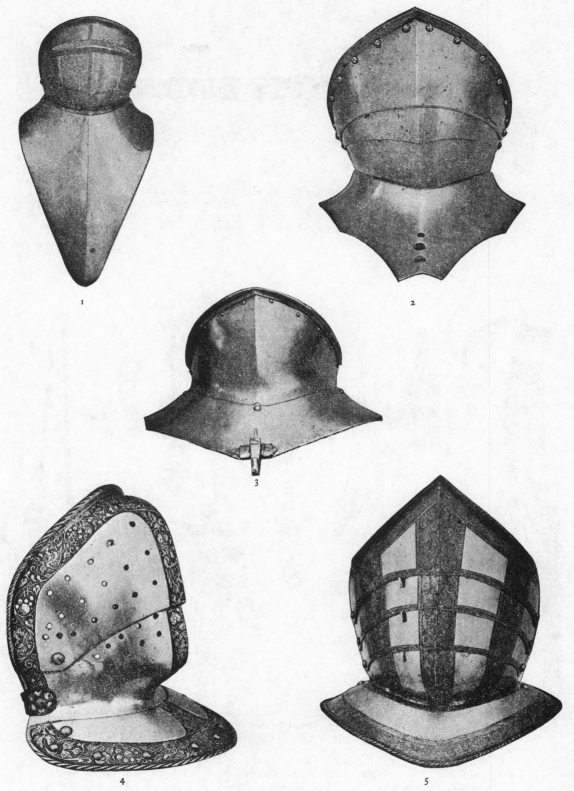

FIGURE 195. *Buffes. 1. French, 15th century. 2. Italian, 15th century. 3. Italian, 15th century.
4. German, 1545. 5. French, 1570. Metropolitan Museum. Not to scale.*

FIGURE 196. *Bukmar. Blued barrel with gold "tiger stripes" and an Arabic inscription reading: "This matchless gun belongs to the King of Ind (Hyder Ali) which equals the flashing lightning, it can decide the fate of the enemy if it finds its mark on his forehead." Silver mounts stamped Hyder Ali, and Seyd Ma Sun (the maker). Flintlock, the cock a tiger's head. Length 3 feet 1.625 inches.*

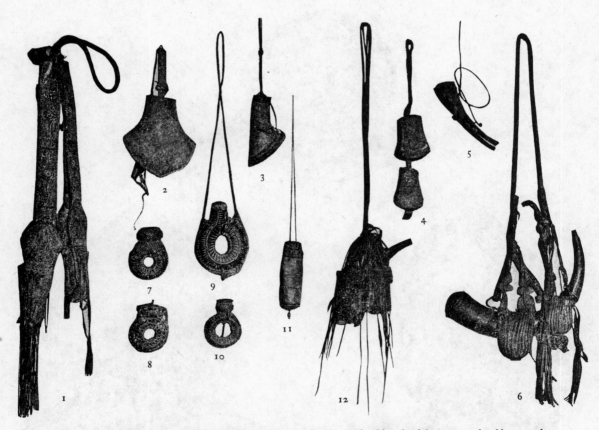

FIGURE 197. *Bullet Carriers. 1. Morocco. Brown leather embroidered with green and white, tassels of colored leather. 2. Tibet. Pouch of brown leather trimmed with green. Attached to the sling are a long iron match pipe and a horn plug. 3. Tibetan. Leather pouch. 4. Tibet. Leather pouch and cover; the latter slides up and down on the slings. 5. Battak, Sumatra. Black wood with long jaws that can be sprung apart to let the bullet come out. 6. Morocco. Powder horn with brass caps and two leather bullet pouches. 7, 8, 9, 10. Cambodian ring-shaped baskets for bullets. 11. Morocco. Leather pouch. 12. North Central Africa. Powder flask covered with leather and two bullet pouches with flaps.*

lead, and sometimes to steel. In such cases the only way of killing them was to use a silver bullet, and they were often used for this purpose. In the old chronicles the diameter of a bullet is often spoken of as its height, the two being the same with the round bullets then universally used.

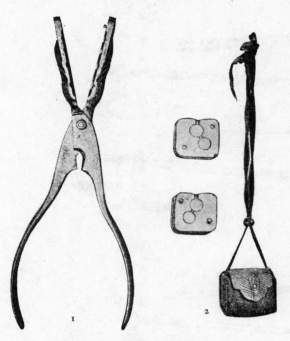

FIGURE 198. *Bullet Moulds. 1. French, 17th century. Metropolitan Museum. 2. Tibet. Soapstone mould in a leather case. Not to scale.*

BULLET BAG, BULLET POUCH. A bag or pouch in which to carry bullets. In Europe they were almost always made of leather and were frequently combined with a flask or primer. In the East they often had silver plates on the outside, or were otherwise decorated. In Siam the bullets were carried in ring-shaped baskets of such a size that only one bullet could come out at a time. The Battaks of Sumatra made wooden bullet carriers with long jaws that had to be sprung apart to let a bullet pass. As a rule the Oriental bullet pouches are of leather, usually bags with drawing strings at the tops. Fig. 197.

BULLET MOULD. A mould in which to cast bullets. Generally it has the form of a pair of pliers, the recesses for the bullets being in the jaws. Some cast but one bullet but many cast several at once. In Tibet bullet moulds are made of talc. Fig. 198.

BULLOVA. The fighting axe of the wild tribes of Chota Nagpur (India). They vary greatly in size and shape. (Mervin Smith 102). Fig. 199.

BUMBAWE TEFAO. An iron face guard, Nias. It consists of a piece across the upper lip with short branches projecting downwards and long ones upwards in front of the ears. (Modigliani, Nias 226). Fig. 765.

BUNCHUK. The horse-tail standard used by the Poles who copied it from their eastern neighbors. It was the insignia of a commander, and was sometimes sent by a subordinate to insure obedience. In Turkey the number of tails indicated the rank of the bearer, the more tails the higher the rank.

BUNDI KATARI. A dagger with a narrow, grooved blade and a transverse hilt, Vizianagram. (Egerton 510).

BUNDOOK, BUNDUK. See Banduk.

BUNGAKUODORI. Padded armor of Chinese-Korean type used in very early times in Japan. The style survives in the costumes of the temple dances. (Dean Hdbk. 119, 120).

BUN-JUL. See Lil-Lil.

BUNYARI, FURIZUMBAI. A sling, Japan.

BURGEE. See Pendant.

FIGURE 200. *Three-combed Burgonet. Florentine, middle of the 16th century. State Guard of Cosimo di Medici. Metropolitan Museum.*

BURGONET, BURGINOT. The burgonet is an open helmet, the salient parts of which are the umbril, or brim, projecting over the eyes, and the neck. As the name implies it is of Burgundian origin and was used in the 16th century. Many are elaborately decorated. Figs. 201, 202.

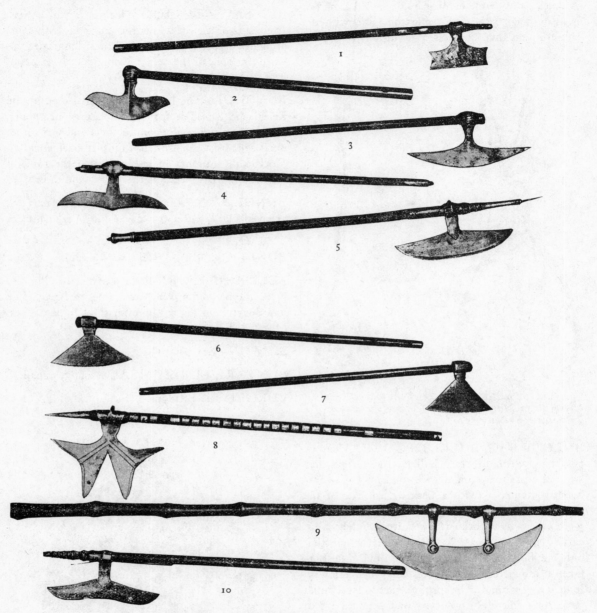

FIGURE 199. *Bullova, Chota Nagpur. Nos. 6 and 7 are Kol. Nos. 8 and 10 are Khond. The heads are from 5 to 14.25 inches long.*

upstanding comb, or occasionally three combs, fig. 200. Ear flaps are sometimes hinged to the sides and a panache, or plume holder, is fixed to the base of the skull. The buffe was commonly used with this type of helmet and was strapped around the

BURR. A broad ring on a lance back of the vamplate, 14th century. It struck the lance rest and distributed the shock over the breastplate.

A washer placed under a rivet, or bolt, head to give it more bearing.

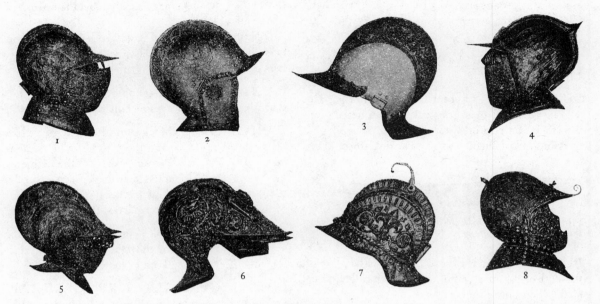

FIGURE 201. *Burgonets. 1. Italian, 1590. 2. German, 1530-1550. 3. French, 1540. 4. English, 17th century. 5. French, 1550. 6. Italian, 1543. 7. German, 1550. 8. French, 1640. Metropolitan Museum. Not to scale.*

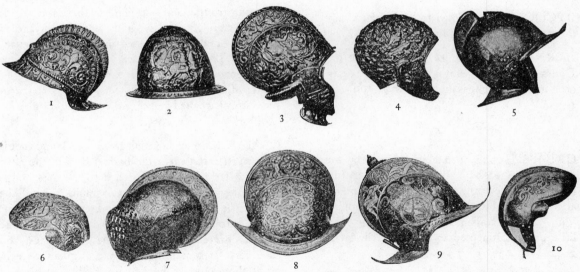

FIGURE 202. *Burgonets and other Helmets. 1. Burgonet, Florentine, middle of the 16th century. State Guard of Cosimo di Medici. 2. Cabasset, Italian, middle of the 16th century. 3. Burgonet, middle of the 16th century. 4. Parade Burgonet, Milanese, 16th century. 5. Burgonet, Venetian, early 16th century. 6. Pate-Plate, German, first half of the 16th century. 7. Burgonet, French, about 1580. Believed to have been worn by Henry III of France. 8. Morian, Italian, 1560. 9. Burgonet, middle of the 16th century. State Guard of Jean Marie del Monte, afterwards Pope Julian III. 10. Pate-Plate, German, about 1550. Work of Wolf of Landshut. Metropolitan Museum.*

BURRONG, PAROOM. A striking club of nearly uniform section throughout, and with a head almost at right angles to the handle. Richmond and Clarence River natives, Australia. (Arc. f. Eth. X, 13).

BUSAR, BUSUR. A crossbow, Malay. (Arc. f. Eth. IV, 278).

BUTT. The end of a spear farthest from the point.

The rear end of a gunstock, sometimes the entire stock of a gun or pistol.

A mound of earth used as a backing for a target.

FIGURE 203. *Buyo Knife, Jolo. Plain bone handle 7 inches long, blade 8 inches long.*

BUTT PLATE, HEEL PLATE. The plate on the butt of a gun or pistol. It is never called a heel plate when on a pistol.

BUYO KNIFE. A Malay knife with a blade nearly straight on the back and curved on the edge, with a long curved handle, fig. 203. It is used as a carpenter's tool.

BYCOCKET. Supposed to have been a helmet of the 14th century. Nothing certain is known of it.

BYRNIE, BYRNE. Body armor worn by the Danes in the 10th century. It is supposed to have been a sort of gambeson. (Hewitt I, 109). See also Brene.

C

CABASSET. An open helmet worn by foot soldiers in the second half of the 16th century and throughout the 17th. It has a narrow brim and usually a curious little point projecting from the top. The name is Italian and means "pear," and the little point is supposed to represent the stem. Fig. 204.

CADGE. A device for carrying a number of hawks at once. It is a round, square or oblong frame of wood, three or four feet wide; and is hung by straps from the shoulders of a man who walks or stands in the middle. At each corner of the frame there is a jointed leg which can be hooked up to the frame when it is being carried or let down when it is de-posited on the ground. The bars that form the body of the frame are padded on top, and on these the hawks, hooded, are fastened by their leashes. (Michell 51).

The man who carried it was called a "cad" and was chosen because he was good for nothing else, hence the modern meaning of the name.

CALIGAE. Military sandals with spiked soles, worn by the Romans. (Fairholt 26).

CALIVER. A matchlock gun intermediate in size between the musquet and the carbine. The name is believed to be derived from "caliber," the diameter of the bore, and is supposed to have been given to the guns of certain regiments because they were all of the same caliber. Latter part of the 16th century.

CALOTE. A steel coif worn under the cavalry hat in the latter part of the 17th century. (Laking Armour II, 66). See Pate Plate. Fig. 202.

CALTHROP, CALTHORP, CALTRAP. Spikes, either planted singly in the ground or radiating from a common center, and strewn on the ground to prevent the advance of cavalry; or in a breach in fortifications to hinder the attacking troops. One of the commonest forms is four spikes radiating from a common point so that in any position one stands vertically. This was the usual form in Europe and was also used in China and Japan, fig. 205. They date from very early times and are the direct ancestors of the barbed wire entanglements of the present day. Many of the Malayan races use sharpened stakes, called *ranjaus* and *panjies*, for the same purpose.

CAMAIL. A guard of mail for the neck and shoulders worn fastened to the basinet during the 14th century. It had a strap fastened to the upper edge with holes in it that fitted over staples around the opening in the front of the headpiece. A lacing was passed through the staples to hold it in place. The camail covered the sides of the head, neck and shoulders. It sometimes had a triangular piece in front that could be hooked up to the forehead of the helmet so as to cover most of the face but the eyes. The camail was sometimes held down at the back by a strap bolted to the back plate. (ffoulkes 41). Fig. 206.

CAMEL GUN. Swivel guns carried by camels. See Shutrnal, Trilhoen and Zamburak.

CAMELIO, VITTORE. A Venetian armorer of the second half of the 15th century. He was especially noted for his light steel armor of high temper. (ffoulkes Armourer 131).

celebrated work was a suit of parade armor presented to Charles V by the Duke of Urbino. It is pseudo Roman and elaborately decorated; it is now in Madrid. (ffoulkes Armourer 132).

FIGURE 204. *Cabassets. 1. Milanese, second half of the 16th century. 2. Probably Flemish, about 1590. 3. Italian, about 1585. 4. French, late 16th century. Decorated by Gauvin (Paris) about 1870. 5. Venetian, 17th century. Painted with the arms of Venice. 6. Italian, bright steel, 17th century. Metropolitan Museum. The first three are to scale, the others are not.*

CAMISADE. A night attack, 16th century. (Hewitt III, 688).

CAMPI, BARTOLOMEO. An Italian armorer born at Pesaro. Most of his work was done between 1545 and 1573, when he was killed, March 7 by an arquebus shot at the siege of Haarlem. His most

FIGURE 205. *Calthrops, Japanese. Much corroded forgings, each with four points about an inch long.*

CAMPILAN, KAMPILAN. A Malayan sword, apparently originally the national weapon of the Sea Dyaks of Borneo, which has been adopted by the Moros of Sulu and Mindanao. It has a carved hilt, usually of wood, with a forked pommel and guard of the same material as the hilt, with wire staples projecting from it on one or both sides. It is usually decorated with tufts of hair dyed either red or black. It has a long, straight, single-edged blade much wider at the point than at the hilt, frequently with a scroll-shaped projection from the back near the point. The usual scabbard is made of two pieces of wood shaped like the blade and only held together by a fastening at the lower end and another a short distance above it. These allow the two parts of the scabbard to spring apart sufficiently to admit the blade, the lower end of which is much wider than the upper end of the scabbard. This peculiar construction of the scabbard makes it possible to clear the blade without drawing it; as when a blow is struck the upper lashing is cut and the scabbard drops off. This makes the campilan a favorite for court wear. It would have been an unforgivable

FIGURE 206. *Camail. Basinet with camail. From the Collection of Dr. Bashford Dean.*

offense for a subject to have appeared at court with a bare weapon, but there were occasions when an attack was likely immediately after leaving; on such occasions a sword that would clear itself had obvious advantages.

In some parts of Mindanao a different type of scabbard is sometimes used. It is made of a single piece of hard wood, straight sided and in section a flattened hexagon. At the middle of one side it has a loop handle cut from the solid and can be used as a parrying shield. Fig. 207.

CANISTER, CASE SHOT. Cannon shot consisting of a metal case containing numerous balls of lead or iron. The balls were smaller than those used in grapeshot.

CANNELURE. The grooving of a blade to lighten it without impairing its stiffness. (Burton Sword 132).

CANNON. "Heavy cannon are first mentioned in the year 1301, when the town of Amberg, in Germany, had constructed a large gun. Ghent had them in 1313, Florence in 1325 and the Germans in 1328. Edward III used them at the siege of Cambrai in 1339, and at Crecy in 1346. In Switzerland they were not introduced till a later date. The first cannon cast at Basle were made in 1371; at Berne in 1413. Cannon were introduced in Russia in 1389, and the Tabourites used howitzers in 1434." (Denison 225). The Swiss accounts differ slightly from this. L'Armee Suisse, p. 9, says that Basle had cannon and *"maitres canoniers"* in 1373, and that St. Gall possessed eleven cannon in 1377. Cannon were used in 1383 in the Burgundian wars. In 1387 the weight of a *gros cannon* was given as eight quintals, fifty-four pounds. The earliest Swiss cannon were made of iron bars welded together and strengthened by bands, later they were cast. In 1413 Berne bought a gros cannon in Nuremberg which was used at the capture of l'Angovie in 1415.

It was not, however, until the 15th century that they were sufficiently developed to be of much practical use except at sieges. Italy and Germany made most of the early cannon, later they were made in France, but not in England until the 16th century.

In 1551 the artillery of the French army consisted of six classes of guns. 1st. The *Cannon*, nearly nine feet ten inches long, which weighed 5,300 pounds and carried a ball of 33.25 pounds. It was drawn upon a carriage by twenty-one horses. 2nd. The *Great Culverin*, which was nearly ten feet long, weighed 4,000 pounds, carried a ball of fifteen pounds and was drawn by seventeen horses. 3rd. The *Bastard Culverin*, nine feet long, weighed 2,500 pounds, carried a ball of seven pounds two ounces and was drawn by eleven horses. 4th. The *Small Culverin* which weighed 1,200 pounds, and carried a ball of two pounds. 5th. The *Falcon* weighed 700 pounds, and carried a ball of one pound ten ounces. 6th. The *Falconet*, six feet four inches long, weighed 410 pounds and carried a fourteen-ounce ball. All of these guns were made of bronze containing ninety per cent of copper and ten of tin.

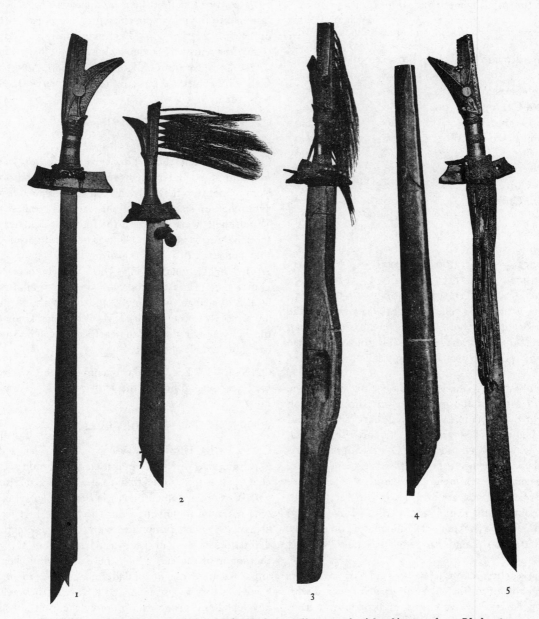

FIGURE 207. *Campilans.* 1. *Blade 29.5 inches long. Hilt covered with white metal.* 2. *Blade 18.75 inches long, inlaid with white metal in lines. Carved wood hilt.* 3. *Unusual type of sheath that can be used as a shield.* 4. *The usual type of sheath. It belongs to no. 5.* 5. *Blade 28 inches long. It has not the usual wire loops on the guard, nor the holes for the tufts of hair.*

The following is a list of the English ordnance of the time of Elizabeth and James I.

Name	Bore of Gun *inches*	Weight of Gun *pounds*	Weight Shot *pounds*	Weight Powder *pounds*
Cannon Royal	8.50	8,000	66.0	30.0
Cannon	8.00	8,000	60.0	27.0
Cannon Serpentine	7.00	5,500	53.5	25.0
Bastard Cannon	7.00	4,500	41.0	20.0
Demi-Cannon	6.75	4,000	33.5	18.0
Cannon Petro	6.00	4,000	24.5	14.0
Culverin	5.50	4,500	17.5	12.0
Basilisk	5.00	4,000	15.0	10.0
Demi-Culverin	4.00	3,400	9.5	3.0
Bastard Culverin	4.00	3,000	5.0	5.75
Sacar	3.50	1,400	5.5	5.5
Minion	3.50	1,000	4.0	4.0
Falcon	2.50	660	2.0	3.5
Falconet	2.00	500	1.5	3.0
Serpentine	1.50	400	.75	1.5
Rabinet	1.00	300	.5	.75

The weights of solid spherical lead shot of the diameters of these bores are, in some cases, less than the weights given above; probably the weights are the maximum permissible for special shot. (Greener 31).

ffoulkes (Armouries 83, 84) differs as to the sizes of some of the guns. For instance—Cannon of eight 8,000 pounds, eight inch bore, sixty pound shot. Cannon of seven 7,000 pounds, seven inch bore, forty-two pound shot. Demi-cannon 3,300 pounds. Culverin 3,000 pounds, 4.5 inch bore. Demi-culverin 5.2 inch bore, length ten feet three inches. Saker 1,500 pounds, 3.5 inch bore, 5 pound ball, point blank range 360 yards. Minion 1,100 pounds. Falcon 800 pounds. Falconette 500 pounds. Rabinette 200 pounds, 1.5 inch bore, five feet six inches long.

The earliest cannon were made of iron bars welded and strengthened by hoops and covered with leather, later they were cast of bronze and iron. The technique was excellent and many of the methods of sweeping, gating and venting might be studied to advantage by modern foundrymen. At the present time the larger guns are made of steel forgings; the very small ones sometimes are made of bronze.

The first cannon were only semi-portable, being mounted on stands which were loaded on carts when the guns had to be moved. Wheeled carriages were probably introduced in the early part of the 16th century. At first the guns appear to have been fastened to them by a pin through a loop cast on the under side of the gun. Trunnions were invented soon after and were in general use by the beginning of the 17th century. All of the cannon shown in Colliado, Prattica Manuale dell'Artiglieria, 1606, have them.

CANNON. The cylindrical portion of an arm guard.

CANNON BALLS. The earliest missiles were made of stone, later they were made of lead and iron. Sometimes the early cannon were loaded with a number of small stones, the original grapeshot. When shells were first used the fuse was lighted before the gun was fired; this was very dangerous as the shell exploded in the gun in case of a misfire. In his book, written in 1580, Senfftenberg of Dantzig describes the construction of a shell fired by the discharge of the gun, and his method must have rapidly come into use. Many curious kinds of missiles were fired from the early guns—chain shot, bar shot, double shot, etc.

CANONIERES. Circular openings in the walls of fortresses for cannon in the 15th century. (Hewitt II, 301).

CANTLE. The rear peak of a saddle.

CAP, PERCUSSION. A copper cap filled with a fulminating mixture and used for igniting the charge in a gun. The first to use such a mixture was Alexander John Forsyth, a Scotch clergyman, who patented the invention in 1807. The first firearms with which fulminates were used were called detonators, the cap proper was a later invention, for the honor of making which there are many claimants. Joshua Rose of Philadelphia is said to have been the first to use it in 1814. It was, however, developed and brought into use by the English gun makers Manton, Egg, Wilkinson, Westley Richards and others. It was first applied to muzzle-loaders and today is used in all classes of breech-loaders, which were only made possible by its invention.

Fulminate of mercury is usually the principal ingredients, but it is often mixed with sulphite of antimony, chlorate of potash or other salts to regulate the rapidity of ignition. See also Fulminates.

CAPELINE, CHAPPELINE. An iron or steel cap worn by light troops in the 13th and 14th centuries. (Planche 83).

CAP OF MAINTENANCE. A cap surmounted by the family crest, worn on the helmet by knights in the 14th century. (Hewitt II, 203).

CAPUCINE. A band holding the barrel of a gun or pistol to the stock. The word is French and there does not appear to be any English equivalent. Capucines are almost universally used in the East and their shapes and decoration are often characteristic of the place of origin. In Morocco and North Africa the Kabyle guns usually have one very wide band of iron near the breech and many narrower ones extending almost to the muzzle. They are generally made of brass or silver, embossed or niello, and often almost cover the barrel. Some also have bands of coiled wire. Wherever the Arab type of gun is used it has a rather small number of bands which are much wider under the stock than over the barrel. They are generally made of brass or silver embossed. In Turkey and the Balkans the bands are widest on the upper side; the widening may be on one or both sides of the band that goes around the stock. The number varies greatly, there being from three to twenty. When a large number are used they are generally more for ornament than use. They are chased, embossed or pierced. In the Caucasus there are usually only two or three very wide silver bands niello. Occasionally the entire barrel is almost covered by somewhat narrower bands. In Afganistan the capucines have a narrow, half-round or flat, band extending around the stock and much widened out over the barrel where it is engraved, embossed or pierced. In Sind the capucines are much like the one-sided ones of the Balkans, but not so wide. On the finer guns they are sometimes made of gold decorated with colored enamels. In India the capucines are generally coils of wire or rawhide, frequently passing over silver saddles on the barrel. In China, in most cases, there are only one or two heavy, half-round bands. Some of the guns have a much larger number of narrow, flat bands of brass or silver, either close together or in groups. In Japan they have simple, heavy brass bands; often there is only one, but occasionally as many as six or eight. In Malaya many of the guns have no capucines, if there are any they are plain brass bands about half an inch wide. Fig. 208.

CAPULUS. The pommel of the Roman dagger. (Burton Sword 257).

CARBAD SCARDA. The scythed car of the Irish. (Burton Sword 277).

CARBINE, CARABEN, CARABINE. A gun of smaller bore than the musquet, introduced in England in the 16th century. In the next century it is described as having a barrel thirty inches long, a flintlock and shooting balls of twenty-four to the pound. At that time it was of about the same length as the musquet but of smaller bore. Still later the carbine became the horseman's gun and was made considerably shorter and lighter than the infantry musquet. (Hewitt III, 715).

CARCAS. A bomb filled with combustible materials and designed to set fire to buildings. (Grose I, 407). It was said to have been invented in 1672 by a German in the employ of Christopher Van Galen. (Hime 195).

CARDA. A kind of cloth used in making padded armor in the 13th century. (Hewitt I, 240, 368).

CARGAN. A collar or tippet of mail, 13th century. (Hewitt I, 241).

CARNET. A name given by Froissart to the visor of a basinet. (ffoulkes 42).

CARPENTUM. The Latin name given to the Gaulish war chariot. (Burton Sword 269).

CARREAU. See Bolt.

CARROCIUM. A chief's standard of the 14th century which was carried on a staff set in a small, four-wheeled cart. The cart was called by the same name. (Hewitt II, 304).

CARRONADE. A short cannon carrying a ball of twelve to sixty-eight pounds. It was much shorter and lighter than the regular guns of the same caliber, and had a chamber for the powder smaller than the bore, like a mortar. It was first made at Carron in Scotland, after which it takes its name. It was mainly used for broadside guns on the smaller ships where great range was not necessary. (Hoyt 378).

CARRY, CARRYING. A hawk is said to carry when she takes her quarry away from the place where she killed it before commencing to eat it. It is a bad fault as it often leads to the loss of the hawk.

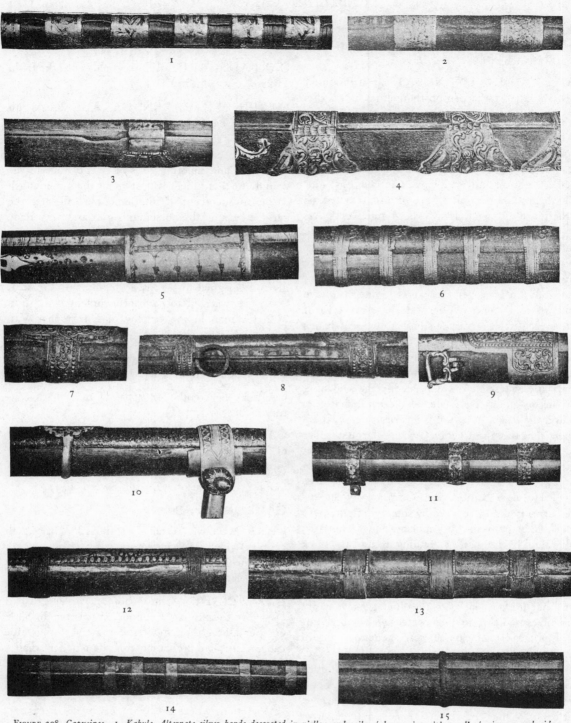

FIGURE 208. *Capucines.* 1. *Kabyle. Alternate silver bands decorated in niello; and coils of brass wire with a roll of wire on each side.* 2. *Kabyle. Silver bands decorated in niello.* 3. *Arab. Embossed band of brass.* 4. *Arab. Embossed silver bands. The Arab capucines are placed with the wide side downwards; all other capucines have it upwards.* 5. *Caucasus. Wide band of silver decorated in niello.* 6. *Turkish. Many embossed and pierced bands of silver gilt.* 7. *Balkans. Embossed silver.* 8. *Balkans. Embossed silver. Two bands are shown; one single ended, the usual type, and one double.* 9. *Balkans. Embossed silver. Both 8 and 9 show sling loops for the strap by which the gun is carried from the shoulder.* 10. *Afgan. To the left is a heavy pierced silver capucine. To the right a silver band for the pin on which the rest is swiveled.* 11. *Sind. Gold bands decorated with flowers in colored enamel.* 12. *India. Rawhide cord over silver saddles.* 13. *India. Wire coils over silver saddles.* 14. *China. Many flat silver bands.* 15. *China. A half-round band of brass.*

CARTE, QUARTE. A position in fencing in which the sword hand is held with the palm up. (Castle 137).

CARTRIDGE, CARTOUCHE. A charge of powder and a bullet in an envelope. At first the envelope was made of paper, now it is made of brass. Cartridges date from the end of the 16th century and largely superceded bandoliers. The early cartridges did not contain any means of igniting the charge, their advantages were quicker loading and making it easier to protect the charge from the wet.

CARTRIDGE BOX. A box in which to carry cartridges. The earlier ones were called patrons and were made of wood, leather, tin, or iron. The latter were preferred—"because they are not so apt to break as the wooden ones, and in wet weather or lying in the tents relax." (Planche 84). The later cartridge boxes are almost always made of leather. See also Patron.

CASCABEL. A knob, or breeching loop, behind the breech of a cannon to facilitate handling, sometimes all back of the base ring. A heavy cable was fastened to it to check the recoil.

CASE OF RAPIERS. A pair of rapiers carried in one sheath. Each sword was flattened on the inside, but as they were held in the right and left hands they were provided with outside guards. (Castle 236).

CASE SHOT. See Canister.

CASQUE. An open helmet modeled on classic lines, a burgonet. They were frequently elaborately decorated with embossed work and gilding. Some of the Italian casques are among the finest examples of this kind of work in existence. Unfortunately, as armor, they are apt to be weak.

CASQUE NORMAND. The Norman helmet of the 12th century. It was conical with a broad, straight, fixed nasal. (Hewitt I, 130). Fig. 35.

CASQUETEL. Meyrick gives this name to an open helmet with an umbril and a laminated neck guard. Other authorities have not accepted this definition.

CASSIS. The Roman helmet of the 1st century. It fitted the head closely and was provided with heavy cheek guards and a very large crest. (Dean Europ. 15).

CAST. A hawk eats feathers, fur and pieces of skin and bone with its food. These are not digested but are vomited as a ball. The material thrown up is called a cast, and the act casting. It is necessary for hawks to cast in order to keep in good health; they are therefore given feathers, etc., with their food.

CASTLE. Grose gives this as a general name for a closed helmet. (Grose II, 243).

CAST OF HAWKS. Two hawks flown together, not necessarily a pair. (Phillott 6).

CAT, CATTUS, CAT-HOUSE, GATTUS, RAT. The cat was a long, low wooden gallery with a very steep roof strapped with iron. It was placed on rollers or wheels and moved up to the foot of a wall to be attacked after the ditch had been filled up. It permitted the miners to approach and work on the wall under cover. (Violet le Duc, Hist. 362). Some cats had crenelles and openings from which arrows could be discharged, these were called "crenelated cats." The besiegers sometimes operated a ram under cover of a cat. (Grose I, 386).

CATAPHRACTES. The Greek heavy cavalry. They wore casques that covered half of the face and protected the neck and ears, cuirasses of plate or of iron or horn scales, which covered the body front and back, while the thighs and right arm were also protected by armor. They wore boots and spurs, their weapons were the lance, long sword and sometimes the javelin. They were never very numerous. (Denison 30).

CATAPULT, CATAPULTA. An engine used from very early times for throwing heavy stones and other bulky missiles. The catapult consisted essentially of a heavy frame with a twisted skein of cord or sinew fixed between the longitudinal timbers. One end of a long lever was inserted in the twist and the other had a cup to contain the missile to be thrown. The beam was drawn back and caught under a hook, the stone was placed in the cup and a cord fastened to the hook was pulled; this released the beam which was thrown forward by the elasticity of the twisted skein, hurling the missile upwards and forwards with great force. Means were provided for tightening the skein and for arresting the forward motion of the beam after the force of the skein was nearly expended. There was also an arrangement of a windlass and tackles to draw down the beam. In some cases a sling was fastened to the end of the beam; this increased the range from thirty to fifty per cent. The sling had the additional advantage of allowing the range to be varied easily. Shortening it sent the missile higher and for a shorter distance, lengthening it threw the

police in Malaya to catch natives who have gone amok. (Guillemarde 267). Fig. 210.

CAT-FACED BURGONET. See Death's Head Burgonet.

CATRI. An Indian sacrificial axe. (Egerton p. 102).

FIGURE 209. *Catapult. From Payne-Gallwey, Projectile Throwing Engines, p. 12.*

stone at a lower angle but further. The old catapults could throw a stone weighing fifty to sixty pounds for four hundred or five hundred yards. Some of the Greek writers estimated that the engines in use about 200 B.C. shot from seven hundred to eight hundred yards. (Payne-Gallwey, Project. Eng. 11). Fig. 209.

CATCH-POLE, MAN-CATCHER. A pole with a fork on the end that had spring blades on the inside that prevented a man from withdrawing his neck once it was encircled by the fork. It was used in the early part of the 16th century—in war to pull men from their horses—and in peace to catch felons and escaping prisoners. The name was transferred to the officers who used it and survived long after the weapon had been abandoned. (Fairholt 288).

A modification of this weapon is still used by the

FIGURE 210. *Catch Poles. 1. Time of Henry VIII, now in the Tower of London. The middle V is made of two springs strengthened by the two flat sliding bars with trefoil ends. The staff is about 7 feet long, covered with crimson velvet studded with brass nails. 2. From Malaya (Guillemarde 267). The figure to the left shows the position when pushed against the neck of the man it is desired to secure. Not to scale.*

CAVALIER. An armed horseman.

A defensive work within a fortress that rises above the main walls. (Manucci 86).

An earth work raised in the inside of a bastion, or at some other point, to elevate the guns to a commanding position. In the 16th century besieging

CELT. A stone or bronze implement, either a chisel or an axe head, often found in prehistoric graves in Europe.

CERBOTANA. The Italian and Spanish name for the blowpipe. (Burton Sword 14).

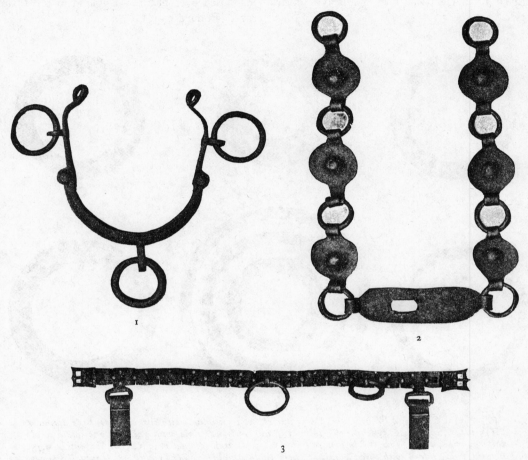

FIGURE 211. *Cavessons.* 1. *Spanish,* 18th *century.* 2. *Spanish,* 18th *century.* 3. *Italian,* 16th *century. Metropolitan Museum. Not to scale.*

armies often raised cavaliers as supports for their guns. (Violet le Duc, Hist. 362).

CAVATIONE, CAVAZIONE. In fencing, the disengagement, literally the "drawing away" of the sword. (Castle 101).

CAVESSON. A headstall with a nose band having rings for the attachment of a rein or cord by which the trainer on foot directs a horse in circles around him. Fig. 211.

CELATE. See Salade.

CERCLE. The 17th century name for the modern parry septime (half-circle). (Castle 141).

CERCLE LES ONGLES EN DESSOUS. A parry low outside, the modern septime, but with the hand kept high. (Castle 156).

CERCLE LES ONGLES EN DESSUS. A parry low inside, the modern septime. (Castle 156).

CERCLE MYSTERIEUX. The basis of a very artificial system of fencing described by Gerard Thibaust in 1628. (Castle 123).

CERCLE, PARADE DE. A guard made by "holding your hand in supination as high as your mouth, keeping the point low, and, by a swift movement of your wrist, cause your sword to describe the figure of a cone . . . having met your adversary's sword, send your riposte in carte." This is an old guard formerly used with the heavy rapier. (Castle 167).

CHACE. The part of a cannon extending from the trunnions to the muzzle. (Hoyt 379).

CHACHEKA. The French transliteration of the Russian *shashqa*, a sabre. See Shashqa.

CHACING STAVES. Iron shod clubs twelve feet long used by robbers in England in the 17th century. (Pollard 57).

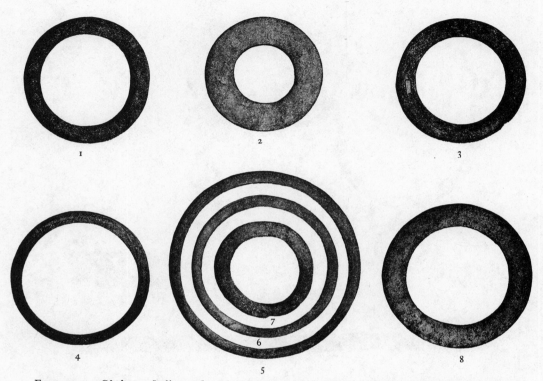

FIGURE 212. *Chakram, India, 18th-19th centuries. 1. Iron inlaid with silver. 2. Outside diameter 6.375 inches, inside 4.625. Unusually thin. 3. Plain steel. 4. Inlaid with gold, on one side a scroll pattern, and on the other a Sanskrit inscription. 5. Outside diameter 11.125 inches, inside 9.75. 6. Very finely inlaid with three Sandscrit inscriptions in gold. 7. Very rough. 8. Unusually heavy. Outside diameter 8.75 inches, inside 6.*

CERVELIERE. A steel skull cap worn under the coif of mail in the 13th century. It was often flat-topped. (Laking Armour I, 112). Similar head defenses were worn much later.

CESTUS. Heavy leather thongs, often weighted with lead or iron, wound around the hands and arms of Roman boxers to give additional weight to their blows.

CETRA. A round Roman shield about three feet in diameter. It was carried by light infantry. (Burton Sword 246).

CHACRA. See Chakram.

CHADO-KAKE. A stand for bows and arrows, Japan.

CHAGRDO. A flint Tibet. (Ramsay-Western).

CHAHAR-A'INA. See Char Aina.

CHAIN MAIL. See Mail.

CHAIN SHOT. Two balls joined by wire or chain. They were used from the 17th to the 19th century. At first they were used for both shoulder guns and cannon; those for the former having two

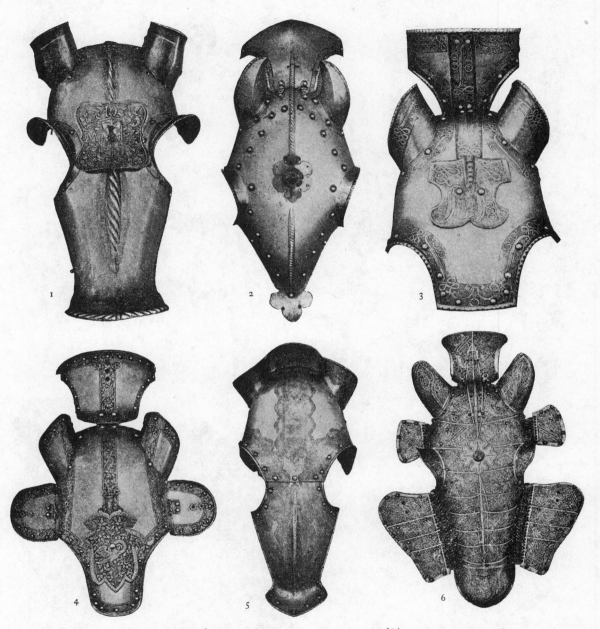

FIGURE 213. *European Chanfrons. 1. German, 1529. 2. Spanish(?), 16th century. 3. German, 1550. 4. German, 1545. 5. Italian or Spanish, 1560. 6. French, 1575. Metropolitan Museum. Not to scale.*

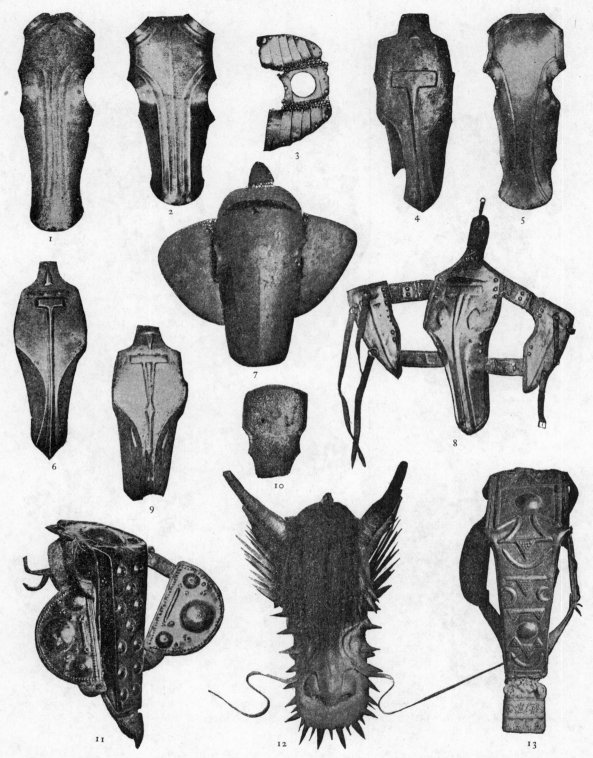

FIGURE 214. *Oriental Chanfrons.* 1. *Turkish, XV. Bright steel, engraved and fluted.* 2. *The same.* 3. *Cheek plates of a Turkish chanfron, XV.* 4. *Turkish, XV-XVI. Engraved and gilded copper.* 5. *Turkish, XVI-XVII. Bright steel with a shallow flute following the line of the flat front.* 6. *Turkish, late XV. Bright steel with an embossed rib.* 7. *Turkish, XV. Black steel with the cheek plates and the first plate of the crinet attached.* 8. *Turkish, XVI. Bright steel with the cheek plates and complete set of straps with padded leather linings.* 9. *Turkish. Bright steel with an embossed rib and ornaments.* 10. *Persian, XVI. Black steel inlaid with gold; the upper part only.* 11. *Sudan. Embossed copper with leather pads, straps and lining.* 12. *Japanese parade chanfron, XIX. Made of gilt paper and wood.* 13. *Sudan, XIX. Embossed brass plates on an embroidered leather head stall lined with figured cloth. Nos. 8, 11 and 13 are said to be for camels; each has a pronounced bend in the upper part of the front plate.*

balls joined by about six inches of wire; and those for the latter were either two balls connected by chain, or a single ball with a few links of chain fastened to opposite sides.

Chain shot were not considered legitimate for use against men but were mainly used to tear the sails and rigging of an enemy.

CHAKAR. See Chakram.

CHAKARANI. A steel quoit like the chakram of India, but used by the Jibba of Central Africa. (Burton Sword 39). This name is not African and was probably given by some Hindu working for the British there.

CHA KATTI. A chopper with a narrow, waved blade and straight handle. Non-Aryan tribes of Central India. (Egerton 60).

CHAKRA, CHACRA. A type of arrow with a head like the rowel of a spur. The head is very large and so far on one side of the shaft that it could not be used. It is one of the mythical types of arrow used by the Javan gods. (Raffles I, 295 and plate p. 296-297).

CHAKRAM, CHACRA, CHAKAR, CHAKRA. The steel quoit of the Sikhs, especially the Akalies. It is a flat steel ring from five to twelve inches in diameter and from half an inch to an inch and a half wide, the outer edge is sharp, fig. 212. It is usually plain but sometimes elaborately inlaid. Several of different sizes were often carried on a pointed turban, the *dastar bungga*.

Egerton says, p. 128, that it is whirled around the finger and thrown with great accuracy and force as much as sixty paces. A friend of mine who saw them thrown at the military games at Rawal Pindi gives quite a different description of how it is done. He says that the thrower stands squarely facing his objective, takes the chakram between the thumb and first finger of the right hand, holding it low down on his left side. He then turns his body so as to bring the right shoulder as far forward as possible and throws underhand with the full swing of his body. He also says that it is thrown with sufficient force and accuracy to cut off a green bamboo three-quarters of an inch in diameter at a distance of thirty yards.

CHAKU-I. A boomerang that swerves to the left when thrown, Lower Tully River, Queensland. (Roth, Aust. Mus. VII, 201).

CHALCOS. One of Homer's names for the sword. Actually it means copper or bronze. (Burton Sword 222).

CHALLA. The string of the *kampti*, or Bhil bow, Central India. Both bow and string are made of bamboo. (Egerton p. 75).

CHALLAWANG. See Tikara.

CHAMAR TASH. A flint in Salar, a Tibetan dialect. (Rockhill).

CHAMBER. The portion of a gun barrel that is enlarged to receive the cartridge. In mortars it is the recess in the breech to receive the powder, and is much smaller than the bore.

CHAMFRON, CHAMPFREIN. See Chanfron.

CHAMPONS. Foot armor of the 13th century. (Boutell 110).

CHANDONG. A kind of Malay knife. (Skeat & Blagden 643).

CHANDRA-HASA. A kind of Indian sacrificial axe. (Egerton 352 note).

CHANFRON, CHAMPFRON, CHAMPFREIN, CHANFREIN, SHAFRON, SHAFFEROON. The armor for a horse's head. It is usually a plate covering the front of the head, and often has side plates connected to it. Some authorities confine the name *chanfron* to those having side plates, and call the single plates *frontals*.

The earlier European chanfrons were of boiled leather, and the later of steel. They were used in classic times, but were abandoned and did not appear again in Europe until the end of the 12th century. They then continued in use until armor was finally given up. (ffoulkes 89). Fig. 213.

Chanfrons have been used in the East as long as in Europe. The Turkish, Persian and Indian chanfrons are much like the European, differing mainly in their decoration, fig. 214. The Japanese did not use horse armor until the 17th century, and then probably mainly for parade. A few of them are made of steel but most are of leather or even *papier-mache*. They are frequently grotesque, usually imitating some animal or fabulous monster,

FIGURE 215. *Japanese Chanfrons. 1. Steel, horse-faced type. 2. Wood, kirin-faced. 3. Wood, horse-faced. 4. Leather, dragon-faced. 5. Leather, horse-faced. 6. Leather, dragon-faced. All are of the 17th or 18th centuries. Metropolitan Museum. Not to scale.*

and are named for the resemblance—Horse-Face, Monkey-Face, Dragon-Face, etc. (Dean Jap. 62). Fig. 215.

belt or girdle. In heraldry it is called a crampet. (Planche 89).

FIGURE 216. *Chapels de Fer. 1. Swiss, 15th century. 2. Burgundian or Flemish, 1550. 3. Italian, 15th century. 4. Spanish, end of the 15th century. Metropolitan Museum.*

The Turks and Arabs had chanfrons for their camels which are quite similar to those for horses, except that they have a pronounced bend in the front plate at about the level of the eyes. 8, fig. 214.

The latest use of chanfrons, as of armor, was in the Sudan where they were worn at the battle of Omdurman. The Sudanese chanfrons are made of brass padded on the inside. 11 and 13, fig. 214.

CHANGI. The chief insignia of royalty in Mewar. It is a sun of gold in the center of a disk of black ostrich feathers, or felt, about three feet in diameter. It is elevated on a pole and carried close to the person of the Prince. (Tod I, 249).

CHAPAWE. See Chapel de Fer.

CHAPE, CRAMPET. A metal tip that strengthens the end of a scabbard, or the termination of a

CHAPEL DE FER, CHAPEL or CHAPEAU MONTEAUBAN, CHAPAWE. An open helmet worn from the 12th to the 15th century and, in its modified form of the pikeman's pot, until the 17th. As its name implies it is merely an iron hat. It varies considerably in shape but in all of its modifications it has a distinct crown and a rather wide brim turned down at the sides, fig. 216. In spite of its simplicity it is a dignified and thoroughly practical defense for serious and prolonged fighting.

FIGURE 217. *Chaqu, Persian clasp knife; all but the side plates are English.*

FIGURE 218. *Char Aina.* 1. *Indo-Persian, late XVII. Front and back plates only, height of both 13.5 inches, widths 8.25 and 9 inches. The decoration is chiseled in relief.* 2. *India, XVIII. Steel plates bound with brass; each has seven raised panels, four of which are higher than the others. Sizes, 6.25 x 8.75 and 8 x 10.75 inches.* 3. *Persia, XVII. Steel decorated with scrolls and borders in relief gilded. Sizes, 7 x 10.875 and 8.625 x 11.625 inches.* 4. *Mogul, XVII. Steel covered with an arabesque pattern in low relief; all are lined with red velvet with gold brocade borders. The upper right hand plate is inside out showing the lining.* 5. *India, XVII-XVIII. Plates of watered steel with gold inlaid borders and center ornaments. Sizes, 10.5 x 15 and 8 x 11 inches.*

Many of the helmets worn during the late war were chapels de fer.

CHAPPELINE. See Capeline.

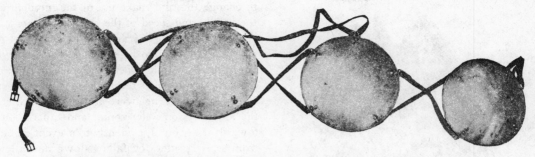

FIGURE 219. *Char Aina, Nepal. Four plates about 7 inches in diameter connected by crossed straps.*

CHAQU. Persian, a clasp knife. (Moser XII). The steel parts of practically all of the "Persian" clasp knives are English, though the bolsters are often Persian. The English were first known in Persia as makers of clasp knives and cotton goods. Fig. 217.

back plates are octagonal, 2, fig. 56. These plates are never large enough to meet around the body, and often leave as much mail exposed as covered.

They are hung from the shoulders by straps and are connected to each other by crossed straps from the top of one plate to the bottom of the next. Fig. 218.

In Nepal and the surrounding Hill States a modification consisting of round plates of equal size is used. Fig. 219.

FIGURE 220. *Chariot, Italian, about 550 B.C. Bronze plates on wood. Metropolitan Museum.*

CHAR AINA, CHAHAR-A'INA. Literally the four mirrors. Four plates worn over a shirt of mail in Persia and India. Usually they are rectangular and the two worn on the breast and back are considerably larger than those worn at the sides. The side plates are cut away at the top to allow free use of the arms; if the front plate is unusually large it is also cut away at the top. Sometimes the front and

CHARAL-JEGO. A fighting boomerang, i.e., one that flies low after striking the ground, Lower Tully River, Queensland. (Roth, Aust. Mus. 201).

CHARAY. See Khyber Knife.

CHARIN. A type of spear thrower used on the Lower Tully River, Queensland. It is a long, thin lath with two holes drilled in its extremity to which the peg is tied by lawyer cane. (Roth, Aust. Mus. VII, 200).

CHARIOT. Originally chariots were only used in war to bring the warriors quickly and without fa-

FIGURE 221. *Cha-Sen (Tea-Bag). A type of Japanese helmet. It is of red lacquer with a gilt maidate, the sun and moon.*

tigue to the place of battle. The warrior then dismounted and fought on foot, while the charioteer staid by to assist in the pursuit if he was victorious, or in retreat if he was defeated. Cyrus was the first to change this and make use of the momentum of the weight and speed of the chariot and horses. He invented a new sort of chariot with wheels of great strength so as not to be easily broken, and with a long axle to prevent its being overturned. The driver's seat was like a turret of strong timber. Scythes, about three feet long, were attached to each end of the axletree, some horizontal and others pointing towards the ground, evidently to prevent an enemy from seeking safety by falling down and allowing the chariot to pass over him. The horses and driver were clad in complete armor. Somewhat similar chariots continued in use for several centuries. Lighter and smaller chariots were also used. Fig. 220.

Herodotus mentions the Zavaces, a nation of Africa bordering on the Maxyan Libians, among whom it was customary to employ women to drive the chariots. (Denison 10).

FIGURE 222. *Chauves Souris, all Italian. 1, 2. About 1500. 3. About 1520. 4. Early 16th century. Metropolitan Museum. Not to scale.*

CHARONG. A field gun, Burma. (Egerton p. 94).

CHA-SEN. (Tea bag). A form of Japanese helmet. Fig. 221.

CHASTONS. Fastenings for crests worn by men and horses in tournaments in the 13th century. Possibly the same as the clavones, or rivets, used for the same purpose at the same period. (Hewitt I, 347).

CHATU KATU. Axe heads, non-Aryan tribes of Central India. (Egerton 59).

CHAUSSES, CHAUCES, CHAUCHES. Close fitting armor for the legs. They were only worn by nobles in the 13th century, but later by all classes. (ffoulkes 24).

Similar defenses were worn in India at a much later period.

CHEREB. The Hebrew sword, its character is unknown. (Burton Sword 180, 183, 184).

CHERKAJIS. A Persian word meaning "wheelers about." They were the skirmishers of Oriental armies and consisted of the best fighters and most expert horsemen. (Morier I, 148).

CHERN. (Black). Decorations in black on silver or other light metal. It is much used in the Caucasus. Here it is called niello.

CH'HURRA-KATI. A kind of Mahratta dagger. (Egerton 483).

CHICHAKI. Russian helmets rising in a long curve to a sharp point. The name is derived from the Russian *chiche*, a point. They are the same as the Turkish schischaks. (Rockstuhl LXXXIV).

FIGURE 223. *Chikuto. A Japanese fencing stick of bamboo with a leather covered guard. Length 3 feet 7.5 inches.*

CHAUSSONS. Towards the end of the 13th century the upper part of the leg was usually covered by chaussons of cuir bouilli or pourpointerie; in the 15th they were often of mail. (ffoulkes 24, Hewitt I, 242, III, 393, 409).

CHAUVES SOURIS. A pole arm of the korseke family, 15th century. It had a long, broad, triangular blade, with two similar but shorter blades projecting from the base. Fig. 222.

CHEE-A. A general name for spears on the Pennyfather River, Queensland. They are made of a butt portion mortised into a shaft tip which may consist of one or more points, sometimes of stingray spines, sometimes of bone barbed. (Roth, Aust. Mus. VII, 191).

CHEEKS. Pieces hung from the sides of an open helmet to protect the ears and sides of the face. (Hewitt III, 720).

CHEMISE. In fortification, a wall surrounding the donjon at a distance of a few yards. Back of the wall was a raised platform for the defenders which could be reached from the donjon by a postern and drawbridge. (Violet le Duc, Hist. 363).

CHICHI. The tabs on the edges of a sashimono through which the staff passes, Japan. (Garbutt 150). Fig. 696.

CHIGAKUSHI. The upper part of the Japanese breastplate. (Garbutt 159).

CHIKARA-GAWA. Crossed straps strengthening the cap used as a lining for a Japanese helmet. (Conder 263).

A stirrup leather, Japan.

CHIKUTO. A bamboo fencing sword, Japan. It is made of four strips of bamboo slightly separated but with enough spring to hit each other with a tremendous clatter when a blow lands. Fig. 223.

CHILANUM. An Indian dagger with a doubly curved, double-edged blade. The pommel and guard are of nearly the same shape and size and are usually forged in one piece with the blade. The shape of the blade is derived from that of the old horn knives, fig. 145. They are used by the Mahrattas, but a very similar knife was used in Nepal. Fig. 224.

CHIMAL. An Apache shield "of leopard(?) skin, ornamented with feathers, and with small mirrors, in the center, with which they succeed in dazzling the enemy." (Cubas 116).

CHIMALLI. A Mexican shield. The old shields were of two principal kinds, the *otlachimalli* (*otlatl* cane, *chimalli* shield), and the *quauhchimalli* or wooden shield. The former was the fighting shield and was described as "Of many kinds and made of strong, solid strips of bamboo-cane interwoven with thick, doubled, cotton thread. The faces were cov-

the lower end. In Tabasco and along the coast tortoise shells inlaid with gold, silver and copper were used as shields. Some shields were of an ordinary size; others were intended to cover the entire body, and were so constructed that when not in use they could be folded up and carried under the arm. (Hough 647).

CHIMBANE. A spear of the Tookrooris with barbs facing in opposite directions so that it could

FIGURE 224. *Chilanum.* 1. *All steel inlaid with silver. Length 15 inches.* 2. *Steel with finger guard.* 3. *Heavy forked blade with serrated edges.* 4. *All steel, length 13.25 inches.* 5. *Steel with a horn pommel riveted to the hilt.*

ered with feather work and circular plates of gold which so strengthened them "that only a hard crossbow shot could pierce them." The Spaniards found them so satisfactory that they adopted them and found that they had the additional advantage of not cracking or splitting. In Yucatan similar shields covered with deerskin were used. The feather decoration indicated the military rank of the bearer. They were usually round, though sometimes oval or rectangular. (Arc. f. Eth. V, 34). Fig. 225.

The Mexican shields were commonly made of flexible canes firmly bound together and covered with hide. They were round, oval or rounded on

neither be withdrawn nor pushed forward. From the borders of Abyssinia. (Baker Nile Trib. 528).

CHIMCHIR. See Shamshir.

CHI-NAGASHI. (Blood channels). The name given by the common people to the grooves in the blades of Japanese swords. (Gilbertson Dec. 78). These grooves were made to lighten the blades without impairing their stiffness.

CHINGONA. A curved throwing stick, Central Australia. It is a round stick with pointed ends and is about as much curved as many fighting boomerangs. (Vic. Mus. 25).

CHINNINIAP. See Apniniap.

CHINPIECE. The beavor of plate of the 15th century (buffe). (Dean, Hdbk. 49).

FIGURE 225. *Chimalli, from Archiv. für Ethnographie V, plate II.*

CHINZEI. The tassel of strips of leather, or paper, on the baton of a Japanese officer. See Sai Hai. Fig. 684.

CHIRIMEN. A surface like *crepe de Chine*. It is sometimes used as a background on Japanese sword fittings. (Joly Int. 35).

CHISA KATANA. A Japanese sword intermediate in length between the katana (long sword) and the wakizashi (short sword). (B. M. Hdbk. 52).

The blade is shorter and lighter than the usual fighting sword. It was worn with the *naga hakama* (very wide court trousers) and the court dress called *dai mon* (large crest). In the 17th century it was ordered that the daimio in attendance on the Shogun should wear only the chisa katana about eighteen inches long.

CHISEL-EDGED. A blade with one flat side and the other tapering towards it gradually until quite close to the edge, when the taper is much increased, fig. 226. In many parts of the world swords are edged in this way.

FIGURE 226. *Chisel edge.*

CHIU-KASA-JIRUCHI. Japan. A small flag with a crest, or other device, on it carried on the front of the helmet by a metal rod with three prongs; cords from the bottom were fastened to the helmet. It was intended for use in wet weather. (Conder 279). See Kasa Jiruchi.

CHIU-NIKU-BORI. Carving in medium relief, Japan.

CHODO-KAKE. A stand for bows and arrows, Japan.

CHOGAN. A spear, part of the regalia of the Malay state of Pelesu. "The great, broad chogan, shaped like a shovel, and fashioned of gold, blade, hasp and eight foot shaft." (Clifford, Since the Beginning, 143).

CHOJI. See Yakiba.

CHO-JU. A fowling piece, a shotgun, Japan.

CHOKU-TO. Prehistoric swords with straight, single-edged blades. Japan. (Weber I, 111).

FIGURE 227. *Choora. Heavy blade 8 inches long with a broad rib at the back. Hilt with bone grip plates and a horn pommel set in engraved brass. The edges of the tang are covered with engraved brass.*

CHOORA. The knife of the Mahsud, a tribe of the Khyber. It is like the Persian peshkabz; but made in the Khyber. Fig. 227.

CHOPE. The Nemal (Nepal) name for a dagger. (Kirkpatrick 240).

CHOPPER. A name given to many nondescript Oriental and savage weapons with broad heavy blades. Some are of the nature of cleavers and were made for smashing armor, while others are merely jungle knives. Fig. 228.

CHUL. A stratagem, Rajput. (Tod II, 294).

CHUNDRIK. A Javan sabre with an incurved blade and a straight carved hilt. (Raffles I, 296, and plate 296-297).

CHURA. The short, heavy, half sword, half knife, in vogue with the hill-tribes of Afganistan. (Gerard 256). Compare Choora.

Japanese war in 1894-5. (Horniman Museum). It is a well made and practical weapon. Fig. 229.

FIGURE 228. *Choppers. 1. Blade 10.25 inches long; bone handle 6 inches long. 2. Very heavy blade 8 inches long and 11/16 inch wide at the back. Steel handle in one piece with the blade, moulded and chased. 3. Blade 9.75 inches long; bone handle 8 inches long. All three Tanjore, 18th century.*

CHUJAK. The Mongol name for jazerant armor. See Jazerant.

CHUKAGI. A spear made of a single piece of wood, length five to nine feet. Lower Tully River, Queensland. (Roth, Aust. Mus. VII, 195).

CHU-KO-NU. A repeating crossbow, China. The bolts are contained in a box sliding on top of the stock, and moved by a lever pivoted to both. Throwing the lever forward and back draws the bow, places a bolt in position, and discharges the weapon. Some fired two bolts at once. (Jaehns 333). The Chinese used this weapon as late as the Chinese-

CHURI. Sinclair says (I. A. II, 216) that it is a very common Mahratta knife with a knucklebone hilt and a slight curve to the edge; and that it was introduced by the Mohammedans.

CICLATON. See Cyclas.

CINCTORIUM. The sword carried by Roman generals in the 4th century B.C. It was so called because it was carried at the girdle. (Burton Sword 257).

CINGHIARA PORTO DI FERRO. A fencing guard of the 16th century. "Then make thy scholer deliver a mandritto squalembrato, and cross over sideways, with the left leg a little in front of the right, and inform him that his sword is held in the guard of 'cinghiara porto di ferro!" (Castle 38).

CINGLATON. See Cyclas.

CINQUEDEA, ANELACE, ANELEC, SANGDEDE. A dagger of the 15th century of Italian origin. It has a straight, double-edged blade very wide at the hilt and tapering in straight lines to the point, the quillons are short and curve to-

CLAIDHEAMH-MOR. See Claymore.

CLASHIES. Native artillerymen in the Indian armies of the 18th century. (Compton 64).

CLAVONES. Rivets for fastening parchment crests on horse armor for tournaments in the 13th century. (ffoulkes 89). The name probably included all rivets at the time it was used.

CLAYMORE. Originally the Scotch two-handed sword of the 15th and 16th centuries. The claid-

FIGURE 229. *Chu-Ko-Nu. Chinese repeating crossbow. Light wood stock with a bamboo bow of two leaves like a carriage spring. Length 23.5 inches.*

wards the blade. The name is derived from the width of the blade, which was supposed to be five fingers wide at the hilt. It was carried horizontally at the back of the belt and placed so that it could be drawn readily by the left hand. Different examples differ very little in form but much in size and decoration. Some have blades not over eight inches long, while others are almost large enough to be called swords. In many the hilts and blades are exceedingly elaborate; the latter in particular, being often fluted and engraved. It continued in use from about 1450 to 1550. Fig. 230.

CIRCULAR PARRIES. In fencing, the parry that forcibly brings back the opposite weapon to the same line, which it closes again. (Castle 11).

CLADIBAS, CLADIAS, CLAIDAS. The long, heavy sword of the Celtic Gauls. (Burton Sword 266).

heamh-mor or claidhmhichean-mhora. It had a long, heavy blade with a straight grip with a small pommel and straight quillons slanting towards the blade. Usually the ends of the quillons have pierced ornaments of three or four circles. Fig. 231. (Drummond plate XV).

This name is usually used for the later Scotch broadsword which is actually the Venetian *schiavona*.

CLEMAL. An elk skin garment covering the whole body, with an opening on the right side to allow free action of the arm. It is nearly half an inch thick and arrow proof. It was used by the Chinooks. (Hough 646).

CLIPEUS. See Clupeus.

CLOTH-YARD ARROW. The old English arrow is often so called. The old rule was that the bow should be as long as the user, and the arrow

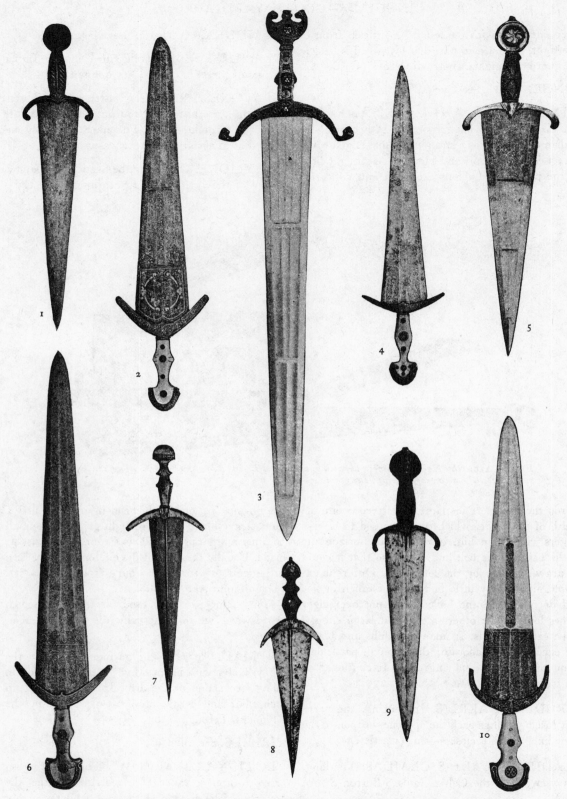

FIGURE 230. *Cinquedea.* 1. *Italian, 1535-50.* 2. *North Italian, 1525-50.* 3. *Venetian, 1525-50.* 4. *Italian, 1525-50.* 5. *Milanese, 1500-25.* 6. *Italian* 7. *Brescian(?), 1500.* 8. *Verona, 15th century.* 9. *Brescian(?), 1500-25.* 10. *Italian (Spanish?), 1550. Metropolitan Museum.*

half the length of the bow. Six feet being about the maximum length of bow the arrows issued by the commanders were made three feet long and cut off to suit those who used shorter bows.

Some recent books on archery have stated that "the old English cloth yard was twenty-eight inches." This is a mistake and the English cloth yard was never anything but thirty-six inches.

CLOUS PERDUE. False rivets, that is, those used solely for ornament, and not to hold the parts together. (ffoulkes 97).

CLUB. The club is undoubtedly the oldest, most widely distributed, most generally used and longest lived weapon. From it all of the cutting and thrusting weapons have been derived. Originally only a rough stick it has, in some cases, been elaborated until it is a work of art. It remains to this day the principal weapon of many savage races and those, like the Dinka, who rely on it almost entirely have devised ingenious defenses against it. (See Club Shields). In India it is still the usual weapon of the peasants and is a formidable staff several feet long, bound and shod with iron. With it the jungle people do not fear to attack the tiger, frequently driving it from its prey, if not killing it outright. (See Lohangi). In some cases the force of the blow from these clubs is increased by loose rings that slide towards the end when the blow is struck.

This is not the only means used to increase the force of the blow. Clubs are frequently weighted with metal or stone set in the striking end. In New Guinea, New Britain and some of the nearby islands, many of the clubs have stone rings on the ends. These are of two kinds, the one is of large diameter, thin, and with a sharp edge; the other is nearly spherical. Powell, p. 160, gives the following description of its manufacture:

"The stone club is the most formidable weapon of the kind that I have ever seen—it is formed of a large, round ball of stone on one end and with a long wooden handle through a hole in the centre.

"The way it is made is peculiar; first, the native takes a suitable piece of granite which he places in a slow fire of cocoanut shells, which gives an intense heat and allows it to become red hot. He then, by the aid of a split bamboo in place of tongs, removes it from the fire, and begins to drop water on it drop by drop, each falling in exactly the same place.

"The portion of the stone on which the water falls begins to fly and crack off, until the heat has gone out of the stone. He then repeats the operation until an irregular hole is formed through the centre; he then fixes a stick through it, and takes

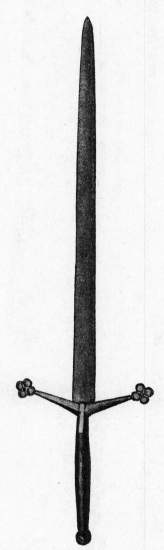

FIGURE 231. *Claymore from the Collection of Mr. A. McM. Welch.*

it off to a place where there is a large granite rock with a dent in it like a small basin.

"He then hits the stone on the rock until all of the rough corners are knocked off and it is fairly round; he then takes the end of the stick, and pressing the stone down into the hollow of the rock makes the stick revolve rapidly between his hands,

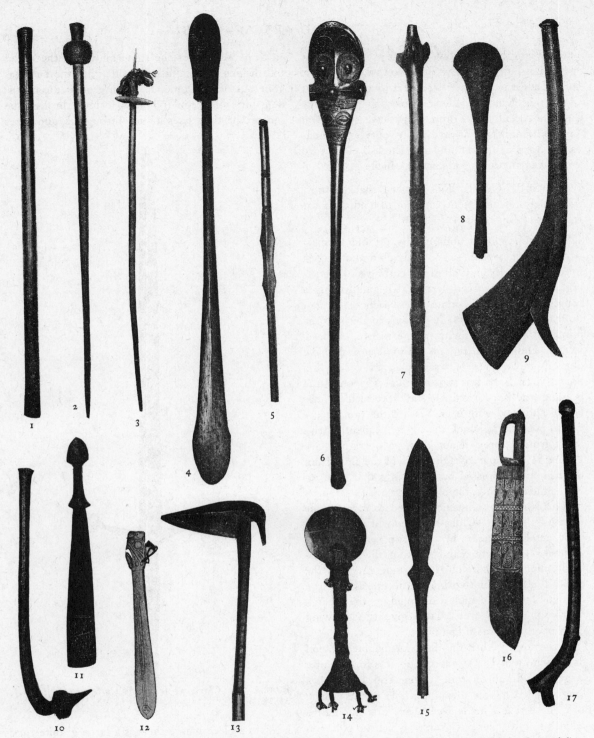

FIGURE 232. Clubs. 1. Fiji. Round club of dark wood with the handle carved. Length 3 feet 10.5 inches. 2. New Britain. A stone ball on a tapering wood handle 4 feet long. 3. New Guinea. Head a sharp-edged disk of dark stone 5 inches in diameter. Light handle 3 feet 8 inches long. 4. New Britain. Double-ended club of black wood 4 feet 9.5 inches long. It is flat on one side. 5. Central Africa. Ebony club with cylindrical ends. Length 2 feet 10 inches. 6. Marquesas. Brown wood with a carved head. Length 4 feet 5.25 inches. Head 6.75 x 4.375 inches. 7. Fiji. Dark wood 3 feet 8.5 inches long. The head is a number of branches, or roots, cut short. Handle bound with grass bands. 8. Samoa. Wide head with a rounded end. Carved with the "Polynesian" pattern filled in with white clay. Length 2 feet 2 inches. 9. Fiji. Well carved of dark polished wood 3 feet 6 inches long. Weight 7 pounds 3 ounces. 10. Fiji. Dark wood curved and carved at the end with a projecting point, handle bound with rushes. Length 3 feet 2 inches. 11. New Guinea. "Sword," the old shape before the coming of the whites. Ebony carved with lines filled in with white clay. Length 2 feet 4 inches. 12. British Columbia. Bone club 23 inches long carved and inlaid with ablona shell. 13. South Sea Islands. "Bird's head" of brown wood 2 feet 3.75 inches long. 14. New Caledonia. "Axe." Sharp-edged disk head of green stone 8 inches in diameter. Handle covered with woven cord. Length 22.5 inches. 15. South Seas. Dark wood with a short handle and a long spear-shaped head with a central rib. Length 2 feet 7.5 inches. 16. New Guinea, "sword," the later form after coming in contact with ship's cutlasses. It is shaped like a sword with a broad blade and a guard and finger guard all carved from one piece. Carved with a pattern of fine lines filled in with yellow ochre and white clay. Length 2 feet 5 inches. 17. Fiji. Dark wood curved at the end with a branch at the curve. Handle bound with rushes. Length 3 feet 2 inches.

weighting it with other stones fastened to the top of the stick until that side of the stone is worn perfectly smooth and round. He then shifts the other side of the stone downwards and works at that until both are smooth and even, choosing a handle of tough wood about four feet long, on which he fixes the stone with gum from the bread-fruit tree, leaving about four inches protruding beyond the stone."

The handles of these clubs are largest at the striking end, like those of pickaxes, so that the centrifugal force of the blow only tightens the head. The gum fastening that Powell speaks of is merely to keep the ball from sliding down the handle when not in use.

The ancient Peruvians used very similar clubs, but with rings or stars of copper on the ends instead of stone balls.

The variety of clubs is infinite but it was in Polynesia that they reached their highest artistic development. The club was as much an object of show and ceremony as a weapon, and it was carved and decorated with braids, bands and tassels of cane, grass and leaves, or with strings of small shells. The woods are hard and handsome and the carving is not only a monument of patient work, but the patterns and distribution of the ornament are truly artistic. Fig. 232.

Every island, and often every district, has its characteristic shapes and patterns, most of which are elaborate and graceful. In most of the islands of the Pacific the clubs are long, but in New Zealand the majority were short and heavy. They were made of wood, bone or stone, frequently of jade. They are usually of simple shapes, but are sometimes carved in very intricate patterns. The amount of work put on them was enormous, and it is said that it required three generations to make a jade club as the material is excessively hard and tough, and they had no metal tools to work with. See Patu.

Some savage clubs show the transition from the club to the axe very distinctly, having stone, or even metal blades inserted in the striking ends while still depending mainly on the weight of the club to make it effective. The Indians of both North and South America used clubs of this type. In many cases savages made clubs in the shape of the white man's weapons after coming in contact with him. Polynesian clubs shaped like guns, axes, and cutlasses are by no means uncommon.

The club was not only a weapon but was often carried as a symbol of authority. In the Polish and Russian armies the baton, a short decorated club, was the insignia of a colonel, and to throw it at the feet of a commander was to renounce allegiance. The Field Marshal's baton is still the sign of the highest military rank in many armies. Even the King's scepter is only a glorified club.

In its later and more elaborate forms, and when made wholly or partly of metal, it was called a mace, and was one of the most important weapons as long as armor was worn.

For the different varieties of clubs see: An-Gora, Baggoro, Barkal, Barkur, Baton, Beaked Boomerang, Bendi, Birra Jungee, Bi-Teran, Boomerang, Burrong, Chacing Staves, Chingone, Club Shields, Croc, Cudgel, Dabba, Dabus, Dangra, Danish Club, Denda, Furibo, Gada, Ganeugaodusha, Ganjing, Gargaz, Gibet, Gurz, Hani, Hercules Clubs, Hoeroa, Indan, Induku, Iruella, Iverapena, Iwatajinga, Jadagna, Japururunga, Jawati, Jitte, Kadumango, Kanabo, Kandri, Kasrulla, Katari, Katariya, Kauah, Keili, Kerrie, Kirasoo, Kirikobu, Knili, Knobkerrie, Knobstick, Kongozue, Konnung, Koombamalee, Kotiate, Kugerong, Kujerung, Kulluk, Kunnin, Langel, Leonile, Leowel, Lilil, Lisan, Lohangi, Lohangi Katti, Mabobo, Macana, Mace, Makana, Maquahuiti, Massue, Massuelle, Mattina, Mazule, Meeri, Merai, Miro, Morro, Mugdar, Muragugna, Naboot, Nilli, Nolla-Nolla, Nyaral, Pacho, Pagaya, Pahu, Patu, Periperiu, Pernat, Phalangae, Plombee, Pogamoggan, Potu, Pouwhenua, Purtanji, Quarter Staff, Quayre, Quirriang-An-Wun, Rabbit Stick, Rang-Kwan, Rungu, Sapakana, Schestopjor, Seki-Bo, Shakujo, Singa, Siwalapa, Suan-Tou-Fung, Taiaha, Tambara, Tanda, Tebutje, Te-Gi, Te-Ingkajana, Tetsu-Bo, Tewha-Tewha, Throwing Clubs, Tiglun, Tindil, Tombat, Trombash, Truncheon, Ulas, Uramanta, U'U, Waddy, Wadna, Wahaika, Wairbi, Wakerti, Wa-Ngal, Wanna, Warbi, Warra-Warra, Watillikiri, Weerba, Weet-Weet, Wirka, Wona, Wongala, Wonguim, Yachi, Yeamberren, Yaribo, Yu-Lun, Yural-Bara, Zai.

CLUB SHIELDS. The Dinka of Central Africa, whose favorite weapons are clubs, have developed two forms of shield for use with them. The first is a neatly carved stick about a yard long with an oval swell in the center which is hollowed out on one side to make a guard for the hand, this is called a *quayre*. The other, called *dang*, looks like a very heavy bow. The wooden part is held in the hand and the blow of the opponent's club is received on

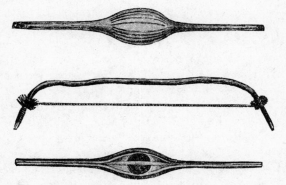

FIGURE 233. *Club Shields of the Dinka. The uppermost and lowest figures are the outside and inside of the* quayre. *The middle figure is the* dang. *From Schweinfurth, The Heart of Africa, I, p.* 155.

the string. It is hard to imagine a device better fitted for the purpose than the last. (Schweinfurth I, 230). Fig. 233.

CLUDEN. The Roman juggler's "shutting" sword, the blade of which ran back into the handle. (Burton Sword 258).

CLUPEUS, CLIPEUS, CLYPEUS. The large, round Greek shield. (Burton Sword 248).

COAT ARMOR. Any military garment with the armorial ensign of the wearer embroidered on it. 15th century and later. (Planche 117).

COAT OF DEFENSE. Body armor of as many as 30 to 40 thicknesses of linen. 15th century. (ffoulkes 34).

COAT OF MAIL. Commonly any mail garment that covers the body, strictly one that opens down the front.

COCK. The piece that holds the flint in the flint lock; or the one that strikes the cap in the percussion lock.

In the first the flint is held between a piece projecting from the body of the cock and a loose one that is pressed against it by a screw. The pieces that hold the flint are called jaws. In European locks the loose jaw is usually guided by a piece projecting from the body of the cock that fits in a slot in the back of the loose jaw. In Oriental locks the loose jaw has a projecting piece that passes through a mortise in the body of the cock; this holds the loose jaw much more steadily than the European form. Fig. 234.

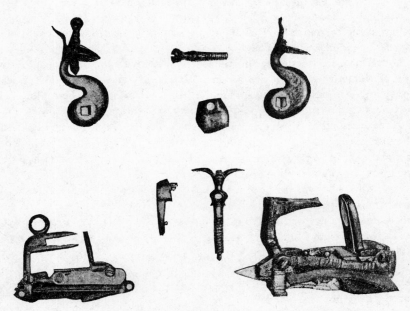

FIGURE 234. *Cock. The upper figures show an European cock assembled and its parts. The lower shows a lock from the Caucasus assembled, and the parts of a cock from the Balkans.*

At the present time what was called the cock is generally called the hammer. Formerly the hammer was the piece struck by the flint.

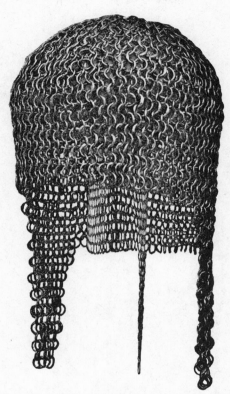

FIGURE 235. *Coif of mail, Italian or Swiss, 15th century. Metropolitan Museum.*

CODA LUNGA E ALTA. A fencing guard of the 16th century. (Castle 39).

CODA LUNGA E DISTESA. A 16th-century fencing guard. "Thou must cause thy pupil to remain with his left leg forward and lower his sword." (Castle 40).

CODA LUNGA E STRETTA. A 16th-century fencing guard. "Let thy scholar stand with his right leg foremost, with the sword and target well out, and see that his right hand is well outside his right knee with the thumb turned downwards." Castle 38).

CODPIECE. See Brayette.

COGNIZANCE, COGNOISSANCE. Strictly the badge of a gentleman entitled to wear arms, occasionally given to the surcoat, jupon or tabard embroidered with the whole armorial bearings of the wearer. The word first appears in the 11th century among the Normans. (Planche 119).

COIF DE FER. A steel cap, 13th century. (Planche 120). It is also sometimes used with a hood of mail.

COIFFETTE. A skull cap of iron worn in the 11th and 12th centuries. (Fairholt 280).

COIF OF MAIL. A mail hood. It usually covered the top, sides and back of the head and neck, fig. 235. It was worn by the lower classes as the sole defense of the head, and by the knights under the helmet. It was often worn over a cap of coiled rope. Fig. 236.

For the Oriental forms see Kulah Zira.

COIN. In gunnery, a wedge placed under the breech of a gun to raise or depress it. (Hoyt 381).

COINTOISE, COINTISE, CONTISE, QUINTISE, QUENTYSE. A scarf attached to the helmet in the middle ages. (Planche 121).

COLICHEMARDE, CONICHEMARDE, KONIGSMARK. A small sword which came in fashion between 1680 and 1690, and was said to have been invented by Count Konigsmark. The name *colichemarde* is supposed to be a very bad phonetic rendering of that of the inventor. It had a blade that exaggerated the difference between the fort and faible. It was quite wide (sometimes triangular) for about eight inches from the hilt, and then narrowed suddenly and was extremely light and flexible for the remainder of its length. Its

FIGURE 236. *A rope cap worn under a helmet or hood of mail, German, 15th century. Metropolitan Museum.*

1   2   3   4

FIGURE 237. *Combined Weapons, Europe.* 1. *Rapier and musquet rest. Italian, about* 1650. 2. *Halbard and linstock. The halbard is hollow and fits over the linstock. Italian, middle of the 17th century.* 3. *Flintlock pistol and hammer, German, 18th century.* 4. *Sword and wheel lock pistol. German, about* 1600. *Collection of Dr. Bashford Dean.*

lightness and the ease with which parries could be made with it made it a favorite until the middle of the 18th century. (Castle 239, Hutton 204).

Some of the old museum catalogues give this name to any sword with a triangular blade. In the colichemarde the forte is sometimes triangular, but the faible is always flat.

COLLERET. A kind of gorget of the 14th century. (Planche 120). Later it was synonymous with gorget.

COMB. A ridge on the top of a helmet. It is particularly characteristic of the burgonet and the morian. The former sometimes has three combs, fig. 200, and those of the latter are sometimes several inches high. Fig. 576.

COMBINED WEAPONS. In the 16th and 17th centuries they were particularly fond of combining guns with other weapons, such as swords, axes, hammers, maces and spears, figs. 237, 238, 239.

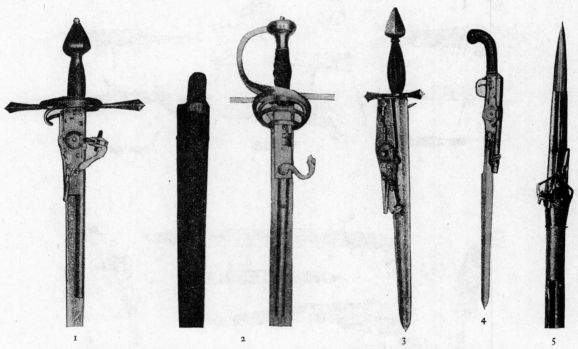

FIGURE 238. *Combined Weapons, Europe. 1. Sword and wheel lock pistol, Saxon, 1575. 2. Sword and matchlock pistol, Genoese Civic Guard, 1580. 3. Saxon, dagger and wheel lock pistol. 4. German, hunting sword and pistol, 17th century. 5. Pike and wheel lock pistol, German, 16th century. Metropolitan Museum. Not to scale.*

COLLERY, COLLARY. A long copper or brass horn used to call troops together in Mysore. (Egerton, p. 125, Mervin Smith 83).

A boomerang-like weapon of the Dravidian tribes of Madras. (Burton Sword 38).

COLLETIN. See Gorget.

COLMAN, COLOMAN, KOLMAN. Augsberg, 1476-1522. A celebrated maker of decorated armor who worked for Maximilian I and Charles V. Both his father, Lorenz, and his son, Desiderius, were also celebrated. (ffoulkes Armourer 133).

Such combinations were also made as late as the 19th century.

Similar combinations were also made in India where those of a gun and axe were fairly common; other combinations were also made. Fig. 240.

See also Whip-Pistol and Axe.

COMMANDING THE SWORD. Closing in and seizing the adversary's sword with the hand. (Castle 194). Gauntlets were made especially for this purpose. See Fencing Gauntlet.

COMPASSES. The length of the steps taken when

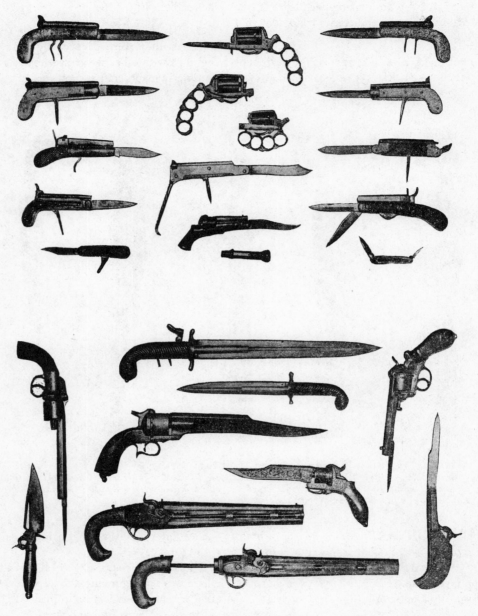

FIGURE 239. *Combined Weapons, late. Pistols and knives, 19th century. Collection of Mr. Charles Noe Daly.*

FIGURE 240. *Oriental Combined Weapons.* 1. *Axe and matchlock pistol. The handle of the axe is the barrel of the pistol, the head of the axe is its handle.* 2. *Indian mace (sonta) and hand gun. Length 28 inches.* 3. *Talwar with two percussion pistols on it. There are no triggers, the pistols were fired by snapping the cocks by hand. Broad, clumsy blade 32 inches long.* 4. *Axe and hand cannon, the latter with a covered pan. All one piece with the grip covered with wood.* 5. *A short barreled matchlock with an iron stock, the upper side of which is an axe blade, that can be protected by a hinged guard. Length 22 inches.* 6. *Axe and pistol. The guarded hilt screws into the end of the barrel and must be taken off before the pistol can be fired. The axe head is hollow and hinged to the stock, when closed it covers the flintlock.* 7. *Pistol and pike head. The spearhead slides in guides and fires the pistol if the point hits an obstruction.* 8. *Another, similar, except that the pistol can also be fired by pulling the trigger by hand.* 9. *Combined katar and talwar. The two blades are hinged together at the top and can be locked side by side by a bolt and nut. The katar hilt serves for both blades, but there is a loop handle on the side of the sword blade that can be held with the other hand when the knife blade is reversed.* 10. *Pistol with over and under barrels and a single flintlock which automatically fires the upper barrel first and then opens the lower pan and fires the under barrel. The hilt is the handle of a knife which fits between the barrels. Probably made in western Europe.*

fencing in the 16th century. They were: the *pasada,* a step of about twenty-four inches; *pasada simple,* one of about thirty inches, and the *pasada doble,* consisting of two pasadas stepped with alternate feet. (Castle 70).

CONISHMARDE. See Colichemarde.

CONNOILE. A cannon invented in 1346. When it was tried at Tournay it shot a quarrel through the walls of the town and killed a person on the other side. The inventor was tried for murder, but was acquitted on the ground that he had been ordered by the consuls to make the trial and could not see that the man was in the way.

We have no information regarding the design or construction of the gun.

FIGURE 241. *Contreplatine. Chiseled steel plate on a Turkish pistol, 18th century.*

CONTOISE. See Cointoise.

CONTRA CAVATIONE. A double disengagement in fencing. (Castle 101).

CONTRE GUARDIA. In fencing, this corresponds to the modern engagement. (Castle 106).

CONTREPLATINE, SIDE PLATE, NAIL PLATE. An ornamental plate or scroll, of metal on the stock of a gun or pistol opposite the lock. Usually it serves as a washer for the screws that hold the lock, sometimes it is purely ornamental. Fig. 241.

CONTRE POSTURA. Like the contra guardia. It is the beginning of the "guard" in its modern meaning. (Castle 98).

CONTRES. Circular parries. (Castle 144).

CONTRETEMPS. This formerly meant a double thrust, not a time thrust as at present. (Castle 193).

CONTUS. The Roman cavalry lance. Also wooden pikes sharpened by fire that were used by the Gaulish women. (Burton Sword 248, 269).

COOKRI. See Kukri.

COPE, COPING. Cutting off the tips of a hawk's talons and beak so as to blunt them slightly.

COPITA. A very early form of chanfron made of leather. It is first mentioned in the Windsor Roll of 1278. (Hewitt I, 348).

CORINTHIAN CASQUE. The Greek helmet made of a single piece of bronze, which protects not only the cranium but the nose, cheeks and chin. (Dean Hdbk. 28). Fig. 32.

CORNEL. See Coronal.

CORNEMUSE. Musical instruments, pipes of the 14th century. (Hewitt II, 308).

CORNET. In the 16th century a "Cornet" was a tactical subdivision of cavalry consisting of from one to three hundred men. (Denison 247).

In 1623 the English cavalry was divided into troops of one hundred men each commanded by a captain, lieutenant, cornet, quartermaster, three corporals and two trumpets. The infantry had no officer with this title. (Grose I, 181, 182).

CORONAL, CORONEL, CORNEL. A rounded head on a tilting lance with three blunt points projecting from it, 16th century and later. Fig. 242. It was adopted because it gave a sure hold on the armor with the least probability of injuring the wearer.

CORRIERS. See Curats.

CORS, CORSET. A breastplate, 14th century. (Hewitt II, 105, 136).

CORSELET, CORSLET. Originally it meant leather armor as its name indicates. Later its meaning was strictly plate armor for the body only, but it was generally used as meaning the entire suit under the terms of "corselet furnished" or "complete." It was the ordinary armor of a pikeman in the 16th century, fig. 43. A corselet differed from a cuirass in being only pistol proof whereas the latter was musquet proof. (Grose II, 251).

CORSEQUE, CORSESCA. See Korseke.

CORYTUS, CORYTO. A bow case. (Mosely 190).

COTE-ARMOR. A name applied to the tabard by Chaucer and others. (Fairholt 485).

COUPE. Cutting over the point. (Castle 144, 167).

COURSING HAT. An open headpiece with ear guards, worn in hastiludes in the 16th century. (Planche 139). Later an open headpiece with an umbril and a guard for the back of the neck.

COUSE. See Glaive and Couteau de Breche.

FIGURE 242. *Coronal and vamplate of a jousting lance, German, late 15th century. Metropolitan Museum.*

COUDES, COUDIERES, COUTES. See Elbow-Cop.

COULE. See Glizade.

COUNTER-CAVEATING. The circular parry. (Castle 195).

COUNTERING. Replying to an attack in fencing by a similar attack instead of parrying. (Castle 36, 57, 77).

COUP. In fencing, the action of an attack from its beginning to its conclusion.

COUSTIL A CROC. A short sword with a straight, double-edged blade, 15th century. (Castle 229).

COUSTILLIERS. Light infantry of the 15th century. (Hewitt I, 196, 204).

COUTAR. See Katar.

COUTEAU DE BRECHE. In its simplest form a sword blade fastened to the end of a staff. Generally the class of pole arm having a long, straight blade with a single edge and blunt back, 15th to

17th century, fig. 243. As the name indicates it was intended for the troops attacking a breach. It was sometimes called a couse.

FIGURE 243. *Couteaux de Breches. 1. French (?), 1475. 2. French, 1500. 3. Austrian, 1550. Arms of the Archduke Ferdinand of Tyrol. 4. German, 1528. Arms of John Theodore, Duke of Bavaria, Prince Archbishop of Freysig. 5. Savoyard, 1694. Metropolitan Museum. Not to scale.*

COUTEL, CULTEL. A knife carried by irregular troops in the 13th and 14th centuries.

COUTELACE, COUTELAS, COUTELAXE, COUTEL-HACHE. See Cutlas.

COUTES. See Elbow-Cop.

COVINUS. A Gaulish war chariot. (Burton Sword 269).

CRAB. Two hawks flown after the same quarry often fight in the air. This is called crabbing.

CRAKYS OF WAR. Believed to have been an early kind of cannon. (Hewitt II, 299).

CRAMPET. See Chape.

CRANEQUIN, CRIC. A rack and pinion turned by a crank by which crossbows of medium size were drawn. It was carried hung from the belt, and fixed to the stock, when needed, by claws fitting over a pin in the latter, or by a loop of cord going around the stock and prevented from sliding forward by a pin through the latter. Fig. 19.

CRAQUEMARTE. A heavy cutlas used at sea in the 17th century. (Jaehns 239).

CREANCE. A long line fastened to a hawk's jesses by a swivel and used when training her. A leash. (Phillott 38 note).

CREESE, CRIS. See Kris.

CRENEL. The peak of a helmet. The more common meaning is an embrasure.

CRENELATED PARAPET. One provided with battlements and loopholes.

CREST. The ornament surmounting a helmet. In classical times it meant a comb terminating in a peak in front on a casque, and was decorated with horse hair. Since the 13th century it has meant also a part of the insignia of the coat of arms of a gentleman.

From the 11th to the 16th century crests were worn very generally, especially for tournaments. Many were of huge size, made of paper or leather, painted and gilded, in the form of fabulous monsters or any strange form that the owner or maker happened to think of. They were not worn in war after the middle ages.

CRIC. See Cranequin.

CRINET, CRINIERE. The armor for the upper side of a horse's neck. It was made of narrow strips of steel articulated together, or of strips of steel alternating with broad bands of mail. Fig. 244. See Bardings.

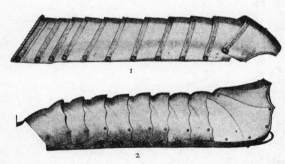

FIGURE 244. *Crinets. 1. Italian, 1480. 2. Italian, 1550. Metropolitan Museum. Not to scale.*

CRIS. See Kris.

CROC. A weapon of the 13th century. Planche calls it a "cornuted club." Hewitt says that it was probably a bill.

CROISSANTS. Small plates protecting the openings at the armpits. (Hewitt III, 377, ffoulkes 39, 68). See also Besagues.

CROSSBOW. The crossbow was used in classic times, but we have no definite information regarding the early forms. The European crossbows of the middle ages have been described under Arbalest.

In China crossbows were, and are, used largely. They are of all sizes from mere toys with bows a foot long to huge affairs mounted on carriages like field guns and used in defending, and attacking, fortified places. The bows were composite and made of horn, wood and sinew. The smallest were drawn by hand and the larger by goat's foot levers. We have no information regarding the working of the very large ones. Many of the lighter crossbows shoot clay balls, and are used for game. They also make and use repeating crossbows, some of which shoot two arrows at once. See Chu-Ko-Nu.

The Japanese also used a great variety of crossbows which differed as much in size as the Chinese. Some of those used in the old fortresses had bows twelve feet long and a foot in circumference. They also used smaller ones shot from the shoulder. See O-Yumi, Do-Kyu and Teppo-Yumi.

Several savage and semi-savage races used crossbows. In Africa the Mpangwe and some other tribes near the Gaboon River are almost the only ones that used them. See Nayin. In the Nicobar Islands crossbows, called foin, are used and they are occasionally found in other islands of the South Seas. In northern Burma amongst the Mishmis, Chalikata and Abors they are very common, in fact, they are characteristic weapons there. See Thami.

The crossbow is often used as a trap to kill wild animals by many races that never use it for fighting. When used for this purpose it is tied to a tree, or post, alongside a path that the desired animal is believed to frequent. Often poisoned arrows were used, and in any case, it is necessary to provide for the safety of human beings who might use the path. For this purpose three strings are fastened to the trigger; two cross the path at the height of a man's chest at some distance either side of the bow; the third string is considerably lower and opposite the bow. As this trap with poisoned arrows is mainly used for the larger carnivora, one of these going along the path will pass under the first string unharmed and discharge the bow by pressing against the middle one when in front of the trap. A man

going along the path will discharge the bow harmlessly by pressing one of the side strings before he reaches the bow.

CROSSES. Parries by crossing or countering. (Castle 91).

CROUPIERE. See Crupper.

CROWBILL. A weapon with a short, curved, pointed blade on a rather long handle. The blade is sometimes forked. It is usually a kind of axe with the blade at right angles to the handle; but sometimes it is in line with it as shown by Egerton (471, 472, 475, 718). See Bec de Corbin.

It is quite common in India. Compare Zaghnal.

CRUPELLARI. A kind of heavy cavalry mentioned by Tacitus. According to Roquefort they were soldiers and gladiators equipped in full armor from head to feet. (Denison 89).

CRUPPER, CROUPIERE BACUL. The armor for the hind quarters of a horse. The earliest was made of leather, mail was next used, and finally plate. Some are open frames of broad straps covered with steel scales. The most complete cruppers were made of several steel plates riveted, or hinged, together. (ffoulkes 90). Fig. 245. See Bardings.

CUBITIERE. An elbow cop, 16th century.

CUCHILLO. A Spanish clasp knife with a broad, leaf-shaped blade. It is thrown in two ways. The more common is to lay the blade flat on the hand and throw it point first underhand. Occasionally it is held by the handle and thrown overhand so as to reverse in the air and strike point first.

CUDGEL. A stout stick about the length of a sword, with a hilt of basketwork. It is used in practicing broadsword exercises. (Hutton 286).

CUELLO. Armor for the under side of a horse's neck. It is hung from the crinet. Sometimes it is entirely of articulated plates, sometimes of mail and sometimes of alternate bands of plate and mail. It is a very rare piece of armor and was, apparently, very little used. Fig. 123.

CUIRASS. The cuirass was originally a breastplate of leather as its name implies. Later it was made of bronze and finally of steel. Both back and breast are included in the term; they were fastened together by straps and buckles or other contrivances. (Grose II, 249). In the 16th century the cuirass was musquet proof, while the corselet was only pistol proof. See Breastplate.

CUIRASSINE. Hewitt (III, 588) quotes Rabutin (1552) regarding the armor of the arquebu-

CUIR BOUILLI, CUIRBULLY, CURBOULLY, QUIERBOYLE, QUIRBOILLY. Leather boiled and beaten until it could be moulded into the desired shape and then allowed to dry hard. It was very generally used for armor, not only in Europe but throughout the East.

FIGURE 245. *Crupper. German,* 1554. *Metropolitan Museum.*

sieres of Henry II, "Armez de jacques et manches de maille ou cuirassines." This leaves some doubt as to whether the cuirassine was a jack with mail sleeves or some substitute for it.

CUIRASSIERS. This name appears to have been first given to heavy cavalry in England about the middle of the 17th century. (Grose I, 106, 109).

Planche says that this name was applied to *light* cavalry at this time, p. 156. This is almost certainly a mistake.

CUIRIE, CUIRENA, QUIRET. A defense for the body originally made of leather as its name indicates, but also sometimes of cloth. It covered the body, only requiring the addition of arm guards to complete the suit, 13th century. (Hewitt I, 240).

CUISSES, CUISSARDS, CUISSARTS, CUISHES, GARDE DE CUISSES, QUISSHES, QUYSSHEWS. Defenses for the thighs first appeared in the middle of the 14th century. At first they were made of stuffed pourpointerie or boiled leather, both of which were gradually super-seded by plate. The first metal ones were made of two or three small plates overlapping each other and riveted to the knee cop and did not reach more

They continued in use until well into the 17th cen-tury. (Planche 156, ffoulkes 50, 58, 81). Fig. 246.

Cuisses are very rare with Oriental armor ex-cept the early Turkish. In the earlier ones the front

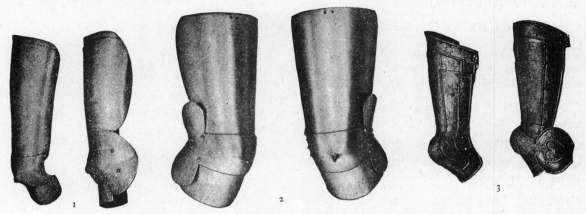

FIGURE 246. *European Cuisses.* 1. *Italian, about* 1400. 2. *Italian, about* 1400. 3. *English, about* 1600. *Metropolitan Museum. Not to scale.*

than half way up the thigh. Later they were made of one plate only, and finally a backplate was added enclosing the thigh entirely. About the end of the 16th century, when tassets were discarded, the cuisses were made of narrow plates connected by straps and sliding rivets so as to be quite flexible.

of the leg was guarded by two plates hinged in front, a large conical knee cop, and small plates and mail on the sides and back of the thigh. The later ones were entirely of small plates and mail, except for the knee cop which was a large elliptical plate. Fig. 247.

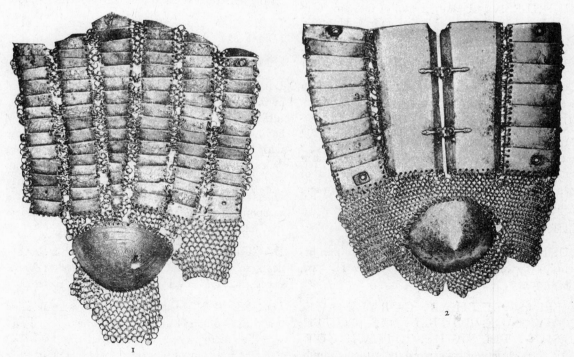

FIGURE 247. *Turkish Cuisses.* 1. *All plates engraved and inlaid with texts in silver,* 16th century. 2. *Plain steel,* 15th century.

CULET, CULESET, GARDE DE REINS. A skirt of articulated plates attached to the backplate to guard the loins. It was used from the middle of the 16th to the middle of the 17th century. (ffoulkes 62, Planche 157).

CULTEL, CULTELLUS. See Coutel.

CULTELLARII. Depredators of the 12th century, so named because they were armed with the knives called cultels or coutels. (Hewitt I, 155).

CULVERIN. A kind of large cannon. See Cannon.

CUMBER-JUNG. A quoit-flail, two heavy steel quoits hung by chains from a short handle, Central India. (Egerton 63T).

CURARE. The poison used on arrows and blowpipe darts in South America. It is an extract of *strychnos toxifera* or other South American species of *strychnos*. It acts only when introduced directly into the blood. When fresh it acts very rapidly.

CURAT. A back and breast.

CURB. See Bit.

CURBOULY. See Cuir Bouilli.

CURRIER. A 17th-century gun of the same bore as a caliver but with longer barrel. (Grose II, 296).

CURRUS FALCATUS. A scythed war chariot. (Burton Sword 177).

CURTAIN. In fortification, a flat wall joining two bastions or towers.

CURTANA. The name of the principal of the three swords which, in addition to the sword of state, are born before the sovereigns of England at their coronation. It is known as "the sword of mercy" and has a broad, straight blade without any point. (Planche 157).

CURTLE AXE. See Cutlas.

CUSTREL. An armed attendant of a man-at-arms, 15th and 16th centuries. (Hewitt II, 549, 584, 590).

CUTLAS, CUTILAX, CURTLE AXE, COUTELACE, COUTEL AXE, COUTELAS, COUTEL HACHE, CUTLASH, CUTLACE. A variety of backsword, or rather a family of backswords. The name has been used since the 15th century and has been applied to a considerable variety of weapons of the same general type. In the 18th and 19th centuries it has been practically confined to the sabres used on naval vessels.

CUTTY. A heavy chopper, Mysore. (Sanderson, 346).

CYCLAS, CICLATON, CINGLATON, SICLATOWN, SYNGLATON. A garment worn over armor in the 14th century. It differs from the surcoat in being shorter in front than behind. (ffoulkes 38).

D

DA-AAR. See Tirrar.

DA. An arrow, Western Tibet. (Ramsay-Western).

DABA-I-BARUT. Persian, a flask for charge powder; it is the same as the Indo-Persian Barutdan, which see.

DARBA. A practically straight, rough throwing stick with a piece of quartz fixed in a lump of resin on the handle, West Australia. (Vic. Mus. 28).

DABUS. A mace studded with nails, Arabia. (Blunt 42).

DADA. The middle line of kris blade, Java.

DAG, DAGG, TACK. Synonymous with pistol in the latter part of the 16th and early 17th centuries. Meyrick confines the name dag to pistols having stocks like those of musquets, and calls those with knob-like pommels pistols. There does not appear to be any good reason for this distinction, and most authorities agree in calling all early wheel-lock pistols dags. The dag was the main weapon of the cavalry of the early 17th century. Fig. 644.

DAGGER. A sheath knife. This name never appears to indicate any particular variety of knife, except that it is never applied to a clasp knife.

DAGNE. A Nias shield shaped like a Dyak kliau but with two handles. They are made of wood and weigh eight to twelve pounds; the length is about five feet and the width sixteen inches. The handles are one above the other crosswise of the shield. (Modigliani, Nias 232).

DAGUE A ROUELLE. A form of dagger introduced during the 15th century and continuing in favor until the middle of the 16th. In it the guard and pommel are disk-shaped or cylindrical, and the tang passes through their centers. In the earlier specimens the guard and pommel are fairly

DAIGORO TSUBA. See Gorobei.

DAIJIRI. The breech, or butt, of a gun, Japan.

DAIKYU. A large bow, Japan. An ordinary war bow as distinguished from the smaller kinds called yokyu and hankyu.

DAIMIO. A Japanese noble, the name means "great land owner." They constituted the feudal

FIGURE 248. *Dagues a Rouelles. 1. Italian, 14th century. 2. English(?), 14th century. 3. Origin unknown. 4. South German, 15th century. Metropolitan Museum. Not to scale.*

long cylinders which, in the development of the weapon, became gradually larger in diameter and thinner, while the blade was made narrower, thicker and longer. Fig. 248. The blades are much like those of Scotch dirks.

This type of hilt is still largely used in the East, especially in Nepal where it is always used with the national sword, the Kora.

DAI-BA. A fortification, Japan.

and military hierarchy. The district owner or controlled by one was called a *daimiat*, and was supported by a tax paid by the peasantry. This was calculated in kokus of rice. A koku was 5.13 bushels and varied in value from two and a half to five dollars.

They were of four classes. Those of the first class were usually named from the provinces they ruled. The members of this class were called *Sanke*, or exalted families, and were descendants, or representatives, of the younger sons of the Shogun Iyeyasu. They held the provinces of Owari, Ku and Mito. When a Shogun died without direct

The next class were *Tozama* (outside lords) of whom there were one hundred and fifteen in 1862, with incomes of from ten to three hundred and fifty thousand kokus.

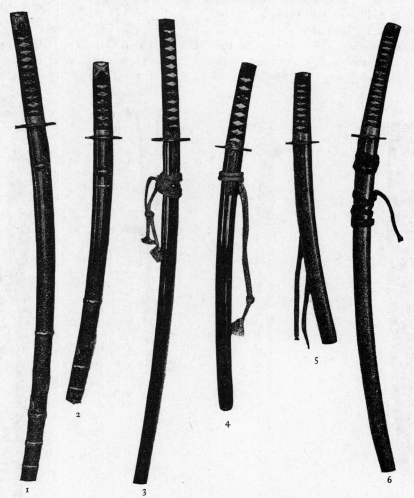

FIGURE 249. Daisho. 1, 2. *Katana, blade 26.25 inches long by Kanemitsu; wakizashi, blade 17.375 inches long, by Tadatsune. The mountings of both are alike; iron guards by Kanenori, other mounts of silver. 3, 4. Katana, blade 27.25 inches long. Signed Kasyn Kanekawa, Kaga province, 1680. Wakizashi, blade 17.25 inches long. Signed Osyn Sendaiju Kunikane, Mutsu province, 1672. Scabbards of fine black lacquer. Tsuba by Goto Tatsuzyo, Kyoto, 1790. Other mountings by Goto Zunjyo, Kyoto, 1670. All mountings of shakudo finely chased and inlaid with gold. 5, 6. Very light blades; katana 25.75 inches long, wakizashi 16 inches. Iron tsuba inlaid with gold scrolls, fuchi and kashira shibuichi. Scabbards with powdered ablona shell in the lacquer.*

heirs his successor was chosen from among the sons of the Sanke of Owari or Ku.

Of the second class, the *Kokushiu,* eighteen were called Kamon (Members of the family) and were related to the Tokugawa family. These were named Matsudaira, and had incomes of from ten to twenty thousand kokus.

This was the arrangement at the close of the Tokugawa period. Earlier the feudal arrangement was not nearly so complete.

DAIMIO NANAKO. Nanako in which the lines of grains are separated by spaces of equal width in which the original surface is left intact. (Joly Int.

34). A method of finishing the background, or as the entire decoration, of Japanese sword mountings.

Another finish sometimes called daimio nanako is to cut the surface diagonally with V grooves at right angles to each other so as to make a series of square pyramids.

DAI SEPPA. See Seppa.

Frequently both swords of a pair were mounted with fittings of the same, or closely related design. A pair of guards, or other mountings, if of similar design and one slightly larger than the other, were also called a daisho.

DAIYENZAN. "Great domed mountain." A type of Japanese helmet.

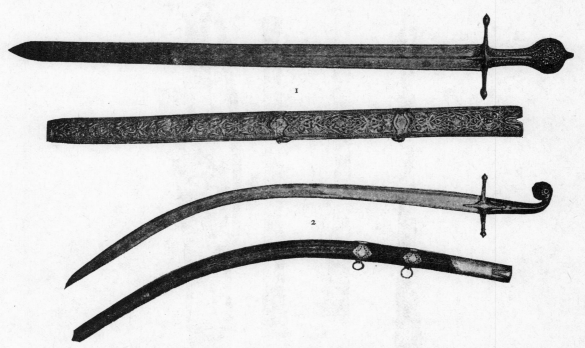

FIGURE 250. *Damascus Swords.* 1. *Broad, heavy, double-edged blade 36.5 inches long, with two inscriptions on each side for the entire length, inlaid in gold. Hilt and scabbard of heavily embossed and gilded metal; both of much later date than the blade.* 2. *Blade of the early Turkish shape; that is, it has a back edge but does not widen out near the point. Length in a straight line from hilt to point 33.5 inches. It shows the characteristic faint Damascus watering. The blade is covered with inscriptions. The older was engraved and the later inlaid in gold; both are much worn. Rhinoceros horn grip and gilded guard and scabbard mounts, both of much later date than the blade.*

DAISHO. Large and small, a pair. The long and short swords carried by all Japanese of the military class. The longer (dai) was the fighting sword, the *katana*, and the shorter (sho) the *wakizashi* which was used as a supplementary weapon; or to avert disgrace, for ceremonial suicide. On entering a house it was customary to leave the long sword in the vestibule and to lay the short sword on the mats at the owner's right. On account of this custom the mountings of the short sword were sometimes more elaborate than those of the long one. When the visitor desired to show great respect both swords were left in the vestibule. Fig. 249.

DALUDAG, LALAYU. Small flags mounted on trident-headed shafts with iron butts, Java. (Raffles plate I, p. 296/297).

DALWEL, DALWEY. A Burmese sword, "a nasty two-handed weapon with a blade about two feet long, and as sharp as a razor." (Burton Sword 219).

DAMAOQ. A Sumatran blowpipe dart. (Arc. f. Eth. IV, 279).

DAMARIAK. An Indian gun an ell and a quarter long. (Egerton p. 63).

DAMASCENING. Decorating a metal by inlaying, or attaching, another. See Inlaying.

DAMASCUS SWORDS. Much has been said and written about Damascus steel and swords, and it has had a very high reputation. It is very rare and, even in Damascus, is hard to find. The reason not after the 15th century. The ore is said to have come from the Lebanon. This was confirmed by finding ore and slag in the Museum of the College in Beiruth that was labeled as coming from an abandoned furnace in the Lebanon. None of those I saw there compared in quality with average Persian or Indian work. There was nothing distinctive

FIGURE 251. *Dao.* 1. *Darjeeling. Blade 22.5 inches long; ivory hilt.* 2. *Naga, blade 19.25 inches long. Carved ivory hilt set in silver.* 3. *Naga, blade 23.25 inches long. Finely carved ivory hilt.* 4. *Naga, blade 19 inches long. Wood hilt and open-sided scabbard with a rattan belt.*

for its reputation is probably that for centuries Damascus was the place where caravans from the East and West met and exchanged their products. Fine swords from the East were brought there and taken to the West where they were called "Damascus" although all of them were of Persian or Indian make. I have never seen a sword resembling those made in Damascus outside of it. Some swords were made in Damascus, though probably never many. Fig. 250.

The manufacture is said to have started in the 10th century, but there is no proof of this. All agreed that it did not continue for long, probably about their shape; most were like the Turkish kilij, a few were straight and double-edged.

DANG. In Burma, an oblong shield of wood or buffalo hide. (Egerton p. 94).

In Africa, a kind of shield used in fighting with clubs. See Club Shield.

DANGRA. A club used in religious dances in Northern India. (Egerton p. 150).

DANGWAN, JUGWAN, TAMA. A bullet, Japan.

DANISH CLUB. See Holy Water Sprinkle.

DANISKO, GOLO, GOLIYO, NJIGA. A hook-shaped knife used for throwing as well as cutting. It is used by the Baghirmi, Kamuri and Bornavi, Central African tribes. (Burton Sword 163, 237).

DANPIRA, DAMBIRA. A sword, Japan.

belt. It is almost the only tool the Naga has. With it he builds his house, clears the forest, makes the women's weaving tools and any wooden objects needed in his ordinary occupations. Fig. 251.

DAPOR BENER. A straight kris blade as dis-

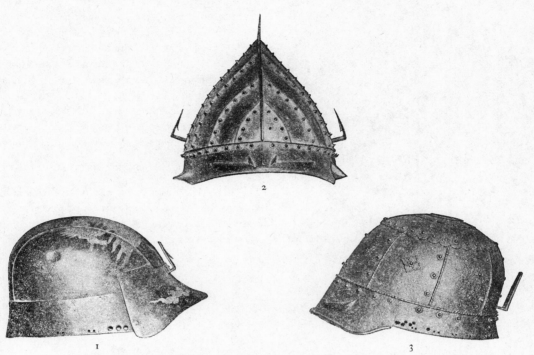

FIGURE 252. *Japanese helmets showing fastenings for different kinds of crests.* 1. *In front for the maidate.* 2. *At the sides for the waki-date.* 3. *At the back for the ushiro-date. No.* 1 *shows a dent made by a bullet when tested; the other plates show similar marks.*

DANSEN. A Japanese fan of the flat (not folding) type. It was carried by officers of the rank of Field Marshal, and was used mainly in directing operations, but also to ward off arrows and other missiles, and as a sun shade. See Uchiwa.

DANYAKU. Ammunition, powder and bullets, Japan.

DAO. The national sword of the Nagas of Assam. It has a straight, heavy, square-ended, chisel-edged blade narrowest at the hilt. The hilt is of a very simple shape, without a guard and with no distinct pommel. It is usually made of wood, bamboo root being considered the best, but sometimes of ivory, occasionally very well carved. It is often carried in an open-sided wooden scabbard fastened to a rattan

tinguished from a waved one, Java. (Arc. f. Eth. XIX, 93).

DA POR LOQ or ELOQ. A waved kris blade, Java. (Arc. f. Eth. XIX, 93).

DARAKSH. (Lightning). A name given by Tippoo to cannon. (Egerton p. 34).

DAS. A Burmese sword, see Dha. (Crawfurd Embassy to Ava, 149).

DASTANA. India, an arm guard. It is the same as the Persian Bazu Band. (Egerton p. 112). See Bazu Band.

DASTAR BUNGGA. The quoit turban of the Akali Sikhs. It is conical, about twenty inches high, and constructed of indigo blue cloth twisted around a framework of cane. Encircling it are quoits and, usually, a tiger's claw (bagh nakh) and other small steel weapons. (Egerton 613, 614).

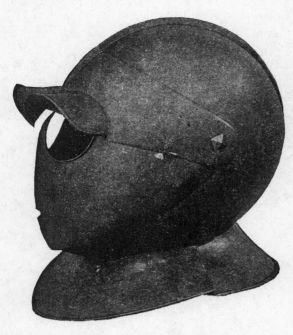

FIGURE 253. *Death's Head Burgonet, Savoyard, 17th century. Metropolitan Museum.*

DASTI. "Oriental falconers, instead of a glove, use a small square napkin of cotton, secured to the wrist by a noose, and twisted round the hand so that the bird sitting on the forefinger can clench it with its talons." (Burton Falconry 9).

This napkin is called a dasti and is used when a small hawk is thrown at its quarry, as is the custom in the East. Burton thus describes the operation: "Then jerking the wadded cotton napkin from its old position into the palm of the right hand, I placed the little savage (the hawk) flat upon it and secured her body within the grasp, her head and tail protruding at either extremity. . . . Then walking up to within twenty yards of the bush I motioned the assistant falconer to flush the partridge. It rose steadily and strongly. The moment I saw the quarry hastening away in the accustomed straight line, raising my right hand, with care, however, not to tighten the grasp I 'shied' my bird after it as Lilly does a cricket ball." (Burton Falconry 26).

Oriental falconers carry the hawk on the right hand, in Europe on the left.

DATE. Japanese, a helmet crest. There are four varieties, the name depending on the position on the helmet. If placed in front, the most usual position, it is called *maye-date*, or *maidate*; if on top in the hachimanza, *kashira-date*; if there are two, one on each side, *waki-date*; and if at the back, *ushiro-date*. (Weber I, 82). Occasionally it goes across the top of the helmet from side to side. Fig. 252.

Most of them are in the form of some animal or fabulous monster and all have some significance. They are generally made of some light material, wood, paper, leather, horn, whalebone, etc., but occasionally of metal. They are often very large and are gilded or painted in colors. See Maidate.

DATTO. Not wearing a sword, Japan.

DEAD ANGLES. Parts of the wall of a fortress that could not be seen from any other part when round towers were used. Polygonal towers were adopted to remedy this defect. (Grose II, 2).

DEATH'S HEAD BURGONET. A very heavy burgonet with round openings for the eyes, projecting hoods over them giving it somewhat the appearance of a skull. They were used by military engineers in the 17th century. Some weighed as much as twenty pounds. (Dean Hdbk. 97). Fig. 253.

DEDER, UKIRAN. A kris hilt, Java.

DEFAUT DE LA CUIRASSE. The openings at the armpits that were unprotected by plate in the 14th century. They were also called the "vif de l'harnois." Small plates called motons, besagues, croissants or gouchets were often hung in front of them. (ffoulkes 39, 68).

DEGAN. A Cymbrian dagger of cuneiform shape which caused it to be considered a symbol of the deity. (Burton Sword 274).

DEKARA, DE-KIR, TIKARA, TO-WARA. Spears with reed shafts and hardwood heads with several barbs of the spines of the stingray placed one behind the other, Northern Queensland. (Roth, Aust. Mus. VII, 193).

DEMI-BRASSARTS. Half armor for the arm; it is uncertain for what part. (Planche 169).

DEMI-CANNON. See Cannon.

DEMI-CONTRES. A parry intermediate between the simple and circular. This distinction is no longer recognized. (Castle 168).

FIGURE 254. *Deringer, rifled, percussion lock. Length 5.25 inches.*

DEMI-CULVERIN. See Cannon.

DEMI-HAG, DEMI-HACKE, DEMI-HAGUE. A small kind of hackbutt, 16th century.

DEMI-JAMBES. Armor for the front of the legs only. (Planche 169).

DEMI-LANCES. The light cavalry of the late 15th and early 16th centuries. (Hewitt III, 546, 584).

DEMI-LUNE. A low wall in front of the curtain connecting two bastions and separated from them by a ditch. It had two faces and two short flanks. (Violet le Duc, Hist. 365). See also Half-Moon.

DEMI-PLACCATE. An additional piece covering the lower part of the back or breast and rising to a point in the center. (Planche 401).

Usually the lower part of a Gothic breastplate.

DEMI-POULAINE SOLERETS. Foot guards of the 15th century with pointed toes of moderate length. (ffoulkes 70).

DENCHU-ZASHI. A palace sword, Japan. The name applies to special mounts, and not to any peculiarity of the sword itself.

DENDA. A club of the Javan gods. It was straight with three disk-like enlargements. The parts between were, apparently, padded. (Raffles plate I, p. 296/297).

DENGUN. The rear guard of an army, Japan.

DEPLUME. See Plume.

DERINGER. A type of pistol originally made by Henry Deringer of Philadelphia, but extensively copied by other makers. Deringer made pistols of all sizes as well as rifles and swords but the one that goes by his name is very small. The barrel was usually about an inch and a half long, though of 0.41 inch bore. It was carried in the pocket and, on occasions of emergency, fired through it. Deringers whether of the original make, or copies, were extremely popular in the South and in California in the middle of the last century. Fig. 254.

DE-RO. Long, heavy hunting spears with the butt portion at least five times the length of the head. The head consisted of three or four barbed points, North Queensland. (Roth, Aust. Mus. VII, 192).

DESTREZA. The complicated Spanish system of fencing taught in the 16th and 17th centuries, which is nominally based on the principles of geometry. (Castle 123).

FIGURE 255. *Detonators. 1. Pocket pistols by Forsyth & Co. The pills are contained in the small magazine connected to the cock by a link; it slides backwards and forwards placing a pill in the pan. 2. Pair of over and under pistols by D. Egg, London. The primer is a tube slipped into a transverse hole in the barrel. 3. Pepper box, J. R. Cooper, patentee. The primer is a very flat cap. 4. Pair by C. Moore, London. The pill is held on the nipple by a lever that automatically moves out of the way when the trigger is pulled. Collection of Mr. C. Schott.*

DESTRIER. The war horse of the middle ages, always a stallion. (ffoulkes 87).

DETONATORS, PILL LOCKS. A type of firearms intermediate in time between the flint lock and the percussion proper. The detonators were ignited by percussion, but the fulminate was either in the shape of a small ball or pill, or was contained in a tube, or was backed by paper, instead of being placed in a copper cap. Many systems were patented between 1812 and 1825. Westly Richards and

just room for the pill of fulminate. The hammer spring has been strengthened so that its blow forces the projection down and fires the gun. The whole arrangement is very simple and as effective as any of the more complicated European devices. This particular lock has a flat cocking lever back of the hammer; by pressing this down with the thumb the hammer is cocked. These guns were made in considerable numbers, probably for the army, as this one is numbered 1280.

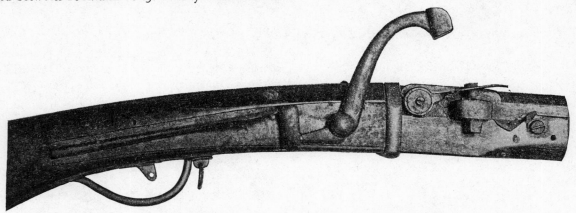

FIGURE 256. *Japanese Detonator. A matchlock has been converted into a detonator. The pan cover is raised to show the striker.*

Moore made the pill lock, in which the pill of fulminate was held on the pan by a lever which was moved out of the way by the falling hammer, 4, fig. 255. Forsyth placed pills of fulminate in a chamber that was connected to the hammer by a lever so that when it was cocked it drew the chamber back over the pan and primed it; when the trigger was pulled the falling hammer moved the chamber forward out of the way, 1 fig. 255. J. R. Cooper of London used a very flat copper cap which had to be held on the nipple by a lever, 3, fig. 255. Forsyth placed pills of fulminate in a by friction were invented they rapidly displaced the detonators.

Although the detonators were only in use for a few years some evidently found their way to Japan, and the Japanese showed their ingenuity by inventing a variety that could be applied to their matchlocks. Figure 256 shows one. The old pan cover has been removed and in its place there is a cover of spring steel hinged at the back of the pan; this cover has a projection on the lower side that reaches nearly to the bottom of the pan, leaving

DEVELOPMENT. A 17th century method of thrusting that is much like the modern lunge. (Castle 137).

DHA. The national sword of Burma, also used in several of the nearby countries. The dha has a guardless hilt and a slightly curved, single-edged blade. Both blade and hilt are frequently ornamented, the former with inlaying, and the latter with carving if of wood or ivory, or with a covering of chased or embossed metal. The scabbards are of wood, often partly or entirely covered with silver or gold. They usually have a heavy cord wound around them and fastened with a knot that leaves a loop that can be passed over the shoulder. The blades are of all lengths from a few inches to a couple of feet. As a rule they have long points, but occasionally they are square-ended. Fig. 257.

DHAL. The Indian shield, also used in Persia (*sipar*) and other countries between. It is nearly always round and varies in diameter from about eight inches to about twenty-four. Some are very nearly flat while others are strongly convex. The edges may be flat or rolled back in the reverse direction to that of the curvature of the shield. It is held by two handles fastened to ring bolts that pass through the shield and are riveted to bosses on the

FIGURE 257. *Dha. 1. Hilt covered with shark skin, brass pommel and ferule. Blade with an inlaid inscription. 2. Ivory hilt. Plain, broad blade 16.75 inches long. 3. Carved ivory hilt. Wooden scabbard with bands of cane. 4. Plain blade, ivory hilt. Hilt and scabbard mountings of silver. 5. Blade 24.625 inches long with silver figures and scrolls inlaid on a black ground on both sides and the back. Hilt chased and oxidized silver. Wood scabbard with heavy silver mountings. 6. Square-ended blade inlaid with copper and silver. Hilt shark skin, copper cap and ferule inlaid with brass. 7. Horn hilt and wood scabbard carved in the form of a conventional bird. 8. Blade inlaid with silver panels. Shark skin hilt. Scabbard mounts copper.*

outside. Between the handles there is a square cushion for the knuckles to rest against. The handles are so placed that, when tightly grasped, they force the backs of the fingers against the cushion giving a very firm and comfortable hold. Some Persian shields have three handles (fig. 729), two placed at the center as usual, and the third near the edge. The arm can be passed through the third loop and the center handles held in the hand; or it can be held by the center handles only. Some Scotch targets have similar handles. Fig. 258.

These shields are nearly always of steel or leather, the latter being often treated so as to render it translucent. Tod says (I, 512), "The shield of rhinoceros-hide offers the best resistance and is often ornamented with animals, beautifully paint-

ed, and enameled with gold and silver." Occasionally turtle shell and other materials are used for making these shields. The steel shields are usually inlaid with gold, silver and precious stones. The entire surface is sometimes covered with inscriptions. The hide shields are decorated with gilding and painting, the best with lac. The bosses are always ornamental, either by their shape alone, or through inlaying with gold, silver and jewels. The metal shields are lined generally with velvet, sometimes embroidered with colors, gold or silver.

Shields were formerly made in Persia of concentric rings of cane covered with silk threads woven on in patterns. Most of those we know were captured at Vienna after the siege by the Turks. No. 9, fig. 258, is of this construction but much smaller than most.

DHANU. The personification of the bow in Hindu mythology. "He has a small face, a broad neck, a slender waist and a strong back. He is four cubits high and is bent in three places; he has a long tongue, and his mouth has horrible tusks; his color is of blood, and he ever makes a gurgling noise; he is covered with garlands of entrails, and he licks continually with his tongue the two corners of his mouth." (Burton Sword 214).

DHANURVIDA. Bow science, a treatise containing the fullest description we possess of the ancient Indian arms and war implements. The date of its composition is very doubtful. (Burton Sword 213).

DHARA. A six-bladed mace, Mahratta. (Egerton 468).

DHARLL. A shield, Purbatti (Nepal). Evidently the Indian dhal. (Kirkpatrick 240).

DHAW. "A Burmese knife six inches long, equally fitted for domestic use or for stabbing." (Burton Sword 219). Compare Dha.

DHOUP. A straight-bladed Indian sword. It has a disk pommel with a spike and a broad finger guard. It is much used in the Deccan. (Egerton 527). Apparently the same as the khanda.

DILGE. See Knee Shield.

DIMARCHI. A species of dragoons formed by Alexander the Great. They were intended for fighting both on foot and horseback. (Denison 34).

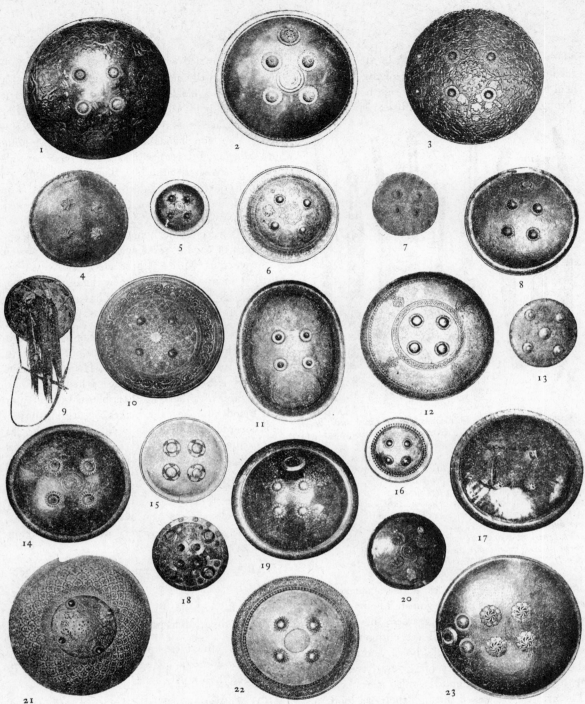

FIGURE 258. *Dhal.* 1. *Rajestan, XIX. Hide painted with flowers and hunting scenes in lac, partly in relief. Painted border round the inside. Diameter 20.75 inches. Silver bosses. 2. Unusually transparent hide. Border and center ornament painted in colored lac and gold. Four bosses and an ornament of chased and gilded brass set with colored stones. 3. Persia. The surface is covered with a flower pattern in low relief and colored green on a brown ground. Six bosses and handles so that it can be held in the hand or on the arm. 4. Kutch. Rhinoceros hide with gilt decoration. Four flower-shaped bosses of cast brass. 5. Translucent hide with four cast brass bosses. Diameter 8.5 inches. 6. Persia, XVII. Steel inlaid with gold and silver and with an elaborate chiseled border of animals and men. Diameter 15 inches. 7. Turtle shell with four metal bosses. 8. Elephant hide stained red, with a deep rolling edge. Four brass bosses and a crescent. 9. Afridi, probably Persian. Concentric circles of cane with colored silk woven over it in designs. Central iron boss with a spike, surrounded with red silk fringe. Diagonal iron reinforcing bars. Leather lining and braided handle. 10. Persia, modern. Steel with complicated etched designs and inlaid with gold and silver. 11. Leather decorated with designs in color inside and out. Oval 21.5 x 16.25 inches. 12. Very flat steel shield with etched designs and inlaid border. It has its original lining of red velvet embroidered with silver. 13. Roughly made of steel with five brass bosses. Diameter 10 inches. 14. Translucent yellow hide with a border and center ornament in gold lac. Highly decorative silver bosses. 15. Steel with a small rolled edge, four steel bosses with pierced borders. Diameter 12.5 inches. 16. Steel. The rim is a separate piece; it has a rolled edge and is pierced where it overlaps the center to which it is riveted. Decorated with a flower pattern in gold. 17. The inside of no. 14 showing the red velvet cushion and handles. 18. Beluchi. Hide with an iron rim set with 16 brass bosses. Four engraved brass bosses for the handles. The remainder of the front is almost covered with brass ornaments. 19. Very convex shield of black hide with a deeply rolled edge; four brass bosses and a crescent. Border and center painted with gold vines, four flower designs in gold and colors. Diameter 18 inches. 20. Kutch. Black leather with a very slightly rolled edge and four cast brass bosses. 21. Mogul, XVII. Leather, highly convex and with a deeply rolled edge. The entire surface is carved in high relief with a diaper pattern. It has a pierced brass plate 9 inches in diameter in the center. Diameter 21.5 inches. 22. Steel with an applied border of pierced and gilded copper. Four bosses and an inlaid ornament at the center. Lining of red velvet with patterns in gilt rivets. 23. Black hide with a slightly rolled edge. Six brass bosses and a crescent. The bosses for the handles are much more elaborate than the others. Diameter 21 inches.*

DIMARCHERII. Gladiators who carried two weapons. (Burton Sword 252).

DIRK. A dagger, especially that carried by the Scotch Highlanders. The Scotch dirk has a very heavy blade, thick at the back, single-edged and tapering uniformly from hilt to point. It has a barrel-shaped grip with a conical, flat-topped pommel,

DISPART. A wire foresight on a cannon, 17th century. (ffoulkes Armouries 85).

"A mark set on the muzzle ring of a cannon so that it is at the same distance from the center of the bore as the top of the base ring; hence a line drawn bewreen the two will be parallel to the axis of the gun. By this line the gun can be directed at its object." (Hoyt 393).

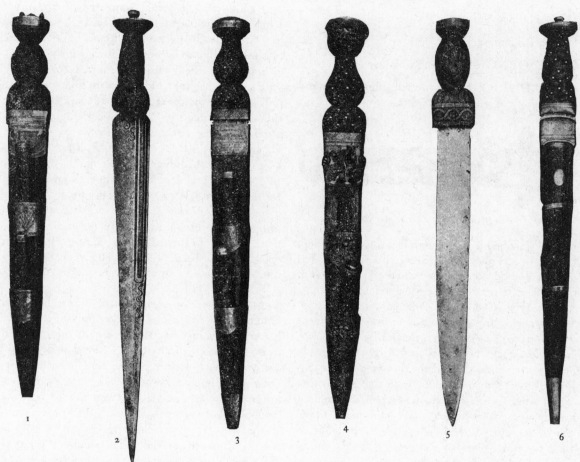

FIGURE 259. *Scotch Dirks*. 1. 1700-1720. 2. 1750-80. 3. 1850-70. 4. *Early 19th*. 5. 1690. 6. 1830-50. *All with wood hilts decorated with strap work. Collection of Mr. A. Mc. M. Welch.*

and no guard. The hilts are generally decorated with strap work. (Campbell 90, Drummond pl. XVII to XIX). Fig. 259.

The very short swords carried by midshipmen of the English navy in the latter part of the 18th and early 19th centuries were also called dirks.

DISARMING. In fencing, to deprive an adversary of his sword. This was done by a turn of one's own or by seizing his with the hand. (Castle 154, 155).

DISTANCE. Now called "measure" in fencing; namely to keep out of easy reach when on the defensive, and, conversely, never to deliver an attack without being within striking distance. (Castle 8).

DIWAL. An arrow of the Javan gods. It was small, with a diamond-shaped head and a double set of feathers. In Raffles' plate it is connected to a sort of club by a short cord. (Raffles I, plate p. 296/297).

DJABI. An Aru Island corselet made of two semi-cylindrical pieces woven of rattan and cocoanut fibre. Each has an opening near one end on the middle line; these openings are closed by flaps of the same material hanging from the top. The arms are put through the openings and the body and head are protected by the two curved baskets. (Arc. f. Eth. VI, 60).

DJERID. See Santie.

DJER-RER. See Tirrer.

DJOELOENG. A kind of Malay sword.

DJOEMBIJAQ. Malay, double-edged, a variety of jambiya. (Arc. f. Eth. V, 237). Fig. 396.

FIGURE 260. *Dogane. Silver engraved with kiri crests.*

DO. A Japanese corselet with its taces (Dean Jap. 5). There are two main classes, the *do-maru* that opens at the side and the *haramaki-do* that opens at the back. There are several subdivisions of each.

One type of do-maru, the *hatomune-do*, fig. 360, is copied from European forms or is even of European make. Another is made of a single piece front and back, both modeled to the form of a naked torso. This is called the *hotoke-do*, fig. 384. Both of these are stiff and uncomfortable and more complicated and flexible forms (*tatami-do*, folding breastplates) were much more common. These were made up of several plates; a breastplate, often with a separate plate riveted or laced to the top, a backplate of similar construction; a left side plate, *waki-ita* or *imuke* was hinged to both front and back plates; the right side plate was in halves, which were hinged to the front and back plates and overlapped each other when the do was worn. Most of the later corselets were of this form. In many cases a separate piece, the *wai-date* or *tsubo-ita*, was worn in place of, or in addition to, the hinged plates. This hung from the neck and was tied around the body before the rest of the armor was put on. It was then tied to the outer plates. In some of the later suits both of the side plates were in two pieces.

In many cases scales of metal, leather or whalebone were laced together with silk cords and used in place of plates. These were called *kebike* or *sugake do-maru* according to the style of lacing. The higher the rank of the wearer the closer together the lacing cords were placed. These varieties of do were also named according to the color of the cords. The laced armor was more elastic and was considered cooler in summer; on the other hand when the cords got wet they were very heavy and chafed badly and wore out quickly. They were also more liable to become infested with vermin.

Sometimes the plates of armor were covered with some other material and were given names to indicate what the covering was. If shark skin it was called *same-tsudzumi*, if tortoise shell *moji-tsudzumi*, if of cane work *anda-tsudzumi* or *ajiro-gake*, if of leather *kawa-tsudzumi*. The different colors of leather also had distinguishing names.

The haramaki-do is said to have been invented for the Empress Jingo who was pregnant when she made her expedition to Korea and therefore had to have an adjustable cuirass. Its general construction is similar to that of the do-maru except that it opened at the back. This opening was also sometimes protected by an extra plate. Figs. 358, 359, 838.

All of the forms except the solid hoteke-do and hatomune-do were hung from the shoulders by broad straps hinged to the back plate and fastened in front by loops and toggles. These shoulder straps were originally made of padded cloth as their name, *wata-gami*, implies. In nearly all existing suits they are made of steel, or leather, well padded. On the back plate between the shoulders there is an ornamental ring from which hangs a large bow and tassels. Cords from the *sode* (shoulder guards) were fastened to the loops of the bow to keep the sode from swinging forward when the wearer bent over. Many backplates also have sockets for the shaft of a small banner, the *sashimono*. The upper one is called the *sashimono-gane* and is shaped so as to carry the staff out clear of the neck guard of the helmet. The lower one is called the *uked-zutsu* and is close to the back.

The taces, *kusazuri*, were made of narrow overlapping plates, laced together and hung from the do by silk cords, which are called *yurigi-ito*. In the older armor the front and back plates had each a single set which was often split up part way to facilitate walking. The side plates had each a single set which slightly overlapped those of the front and back. In the later armor the number of taces is much greater; this makes movement easier, but gives less protection. (Conder 263).

DOG-FACED BASINET. A basinet with a pointed visor.

DOG'S HEAD. The cock of the Scotch flintlock. (Drummond pl. XXX).

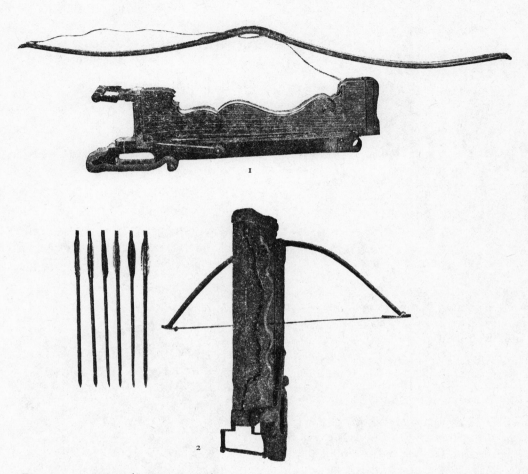

FIGURE 261. *Dokyu (frequently bow). A Japanese repeating crossbow.* 1. *The horn bow* 30.5 *inches long; below is the stock and magazine, length* 18 *inches. The extra bolts are held in the box in the upper part.* 2. *Another with its bolts. The second belongs to the Metropolitan Museum. Not to scale.*

DODHARA. (Double-edged). A double-edged sword, India. (Tod I, 540).

DOGANE. A broad collar of metal around the middle of the hilt of a Japanese sword or knife, most frequently the latter. Sometimes it has large openings in the sides in which the menuki are placed; sometimes they are fastened to it, in which case panels are usually formed for their reception. (Gilbertson, Dec. 80). Fig. 260.

DOG LATCH. The safety catch used with the dog lock, and on the Arab type of flintlock. See Dog Lock and Flintlock.

DOG LOCK. A variety of lock that is probably of Spanish or Moorish origin, but was also used in England and Scotland from about 1640 to 1690. It differs somewhat in construction from the ordinary lock, but its most noticeable peculiarity is the safety catch which is a hook pivoted on the rear end of the lock plate that engages with a similar hook on the back of the cock. (Pollard 63). See Flintlock, fig. 290.

DOGUSURI, ENSHO. Gunpowder, Japan.

DOGUSURI-IRO. A powder flask, Japan. They vary much in size and shape. See Hayago.

FIGURE 262. *Doloires. German, 16th century. Metropolitan Museum.* **Not to scale.**

DOHONG. A war sword, Dutch Borneo. This word is usually used in a figurative sense as implying bravery. The sword (weapon) is called mandau as in other parts of Borneo. (Peralaer 373).

DOHYO YARI. A very large quiver of the yadzutsu type, Japan.

DOJO. A fencing school, Japan.

DOKYU. A repeating crossbow, Japan. The name means a "frequently bow." It is copied from the Chinese Chu-Ko-Nu and is almost the only case in which the Japanese have not made at least as good a weapon as the one that they were copying. In the Japanese form the handles are awkwardly placed and it cannot be operated as rapidly or as smoothly as the Chinese. Fig. 261.

DOLOIRE. A battle-axe of the 15th century, the head of which is rounded below and pointed above. It is sometimes called a Wagoner's Axe. Fig. 262.

DOLPHINS. The handles cast on cannon. The early ones were in the form of dolphins. (Hoyt 393).

DO-MARU. A Japanese corselet opening under the right arm. See Do, fig. 263.

DOMBAY. A kind of gun used in the Caucasus. It is said to have been a favorite of the late Prince of Abkasia.

DO-MIO-BORI. The style of work done by the subsidiary lines of the Goto.

DONDAINE. A bolt for an espringald, a kind of engine. (Hewitt II, 326).

DONDORU. A percussion cap, Japan. A modern word.

DONJON. See Keep.

DOORGA. A fort, Rajput. (Tod I, 459).

DORGE. See Vajra.

DORGEY PHURBU. A Tibetan exercising dagger with a vajra hilt. See Phurbu.

DORNLACH, DORNLOCH. A quiver, Scotland. (Drummond 13).

DOUBLE BALTEUS. A Roman belt to carry sword and dagger. (Burton Sword 2,580).

DOWAK. A straight, flat throwing stick, West Australia. (Vic. Mus. 25).

FIGURE 263. *Do-Maru. Brigandine cuirass, 18th century. Metropolitan Museum.*

DO-WAR. A spear with a reed shaft and a head of black palm wood, North Queensland. (Roth, Aust. Mus. VII, 194).

DRACONNARIUS. The dragon, an ensign of the early Persians, and adopted by the Romans as a standard. (Macgeorge 25).

DRAGON. The gun carried by the dragoons in the 17th century. Dragoons were not regarded as cavalry but as mounted infantry. The gun is described "as a fair dragon, fitted with an iron works to be carried in a belt of leather, which is buckled over the right shoulder, having a turnmill of iron with a ring, through which the piece runs up and down. And these dragons are short pieces of sixteen inches the barrell, and of full musquet bore with firelocks or snaphaunces." It is uncertain whether the gun gave the name to the troops, or derived it from them; probably the latter, as the same kind of troops are called by the same name in France, but the gun is only so called in England, and rarely so even there. (Grose II, 297; Hewitt III, 720).

DRAGON. The dragon, Japanese *ryo*, is one of the most popular decorations of arms and armor in Japan. It represents either the powers of the air or the spirit. When shown with the tiger it means dominion over all things, except when the two are fighting, when it expresses the struggle between the flesh and the spirit.

DRAGOONS, DRAGON, DRAGOONERS. Mounted infantry. They were first employed in Europe in the 16th century. Pere Daniel says that they were created by the Marshal de Brissac, who is said to have used them in Piedmont. Duparcq, however, gives the credit of their introduction to Pierre Strozzi, who in 1543, that is to say seven years before the wars that de Brissac carried on in Piedmont, placed five hundred arquebusiers on horseback, in order to save them from fatigue, with the idea of their fighting on foot in case of need. (Denison 244). In the 17th century "the arms de-

fensive of the dragoons are an open headpiece with cheeks and a good buff coat with deep skirts." His offensive weapons were the dragon and a sword. (Hewitt III, 720).

DRUNMUNG. A very characteristic kind of shield from Victoria. It is made of hard wood and is about three feet long, one inch wide and four inches deep in the middle. The handle is cut from the solid and the front half is usually decorated with incised lines filled in with white clay. It is used in club fighting. (Vic. Mus. 14, 17). I, fig. 771.

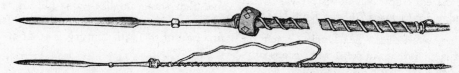

FIGURE 264. *Dung, Tibetan Spear. Shaft of cocoanut wood reinforced by a coil of iron. Rockhill Journal, p.* 170.

DUCK-BILLED SOLERETS. See Sabatons.

DUDGEON. A dagger with a wooden hilt. The derivation of the name is from that of the root of the box tree which was formerly used for making knife hilts.

DUEL, JUDICIAL. The judicial duel, or trial by combat, was general throughout Europe up to about the year 1500. Any person above a certain rank could claim trial by combat if accused of crime. The fight was either between the persons directly concerned, or by champions accepted by them.

DUELING GAUNTLET. See Fencing Gauntlet.

DUELING SWORD. After the carrying of swords had been abandoned a special sword was evolved for dueling. It had a simple hilt with a shell guard and triangular blade. It was much like the small sword of the 18th century, except that the hilt was simpler. (Hutton 323).

DUI TEMPI. Double time as contrasted with single in fencing. In the former the parry and riposte are separate actions, and in the latter they are combined in one. (Castle 99, 138).

DUKN, PARANG PEDANG. "The dukn, or parang pedang, is the scimetar so much used by the

Malays, and differs from it in being thicker and heavier. It is formed after the pattern of a German cavalry sabre, and has a cross handle of brass. The blade is two edged at the point, so that it can be used for thrusting as well as cutting. The sheath is of some light wood, and is stained crimson with dragon's blood. The Undups and Balaus (Bornean Dyaks) in particular have their sheaths covered with silver work, and the hilt with silver. The hollow of the hilt is decorated with human hair, and the edge of the sheath is adorned with a row of the wing feathers of the hornbill. The Malays wear the sword with the edge upwards but the Dyaks wear it with the edge downwards." (Ling Roth II, 135).

DUKU. The sword of the Sea Dyaks. It may be either of native or foreign make. (The accompanying illustrations show mandaus). (Gomes 78).

DUNG. The Tibetan spear. It varies in length from seven and a half to twelve feet, and has a long, narrow, two-edged head with a socket for the shaft. The butt has a heavy iron shoe. As good wood for shafts is scarce in Tibet it is frequently wound with a spiral band of iron to strengthen it. Rockhill gives a Tibetan use for the spear that is not common in other countries. "Wang-ma-bum, though past fifty, vaults on his horse's back by resting his left hand on the pommel of the saddle and grasping in his right his long lance, its butt resting on the ground. This is the usual way for an armed Tibetan to get into the saddle, and is a very graceful one." (Rockhill Jour. 130). Fig. 264.

DUNGEON. See Keep.

DUSACK, DUSSACK. The dusack is of Hungarian or Bohemian origin, but was soon adopted throughout Germany by the middle and lower classes as an excellent weapon, very simple and inexpensive. It consists of a single piece of iron, one part of which was fashioned into a cutlass blade, and the other curved into a loop which formed a grip and knuckle-bow combined. The double curve resulting from this arrangement was eminently favorable to cutting action. (Castle 77, 229).

DUTCHNA. A kind of Mogul dagger, apparently the same as the khanjar. (Wallace Orient).

DZU. A bow, Tibet. The bows used in Tibet are of the ordinary Chinese type, and are usually of Chinese make. (Rockhill Eth. 711).

DZU NARI, SAKU NARI. Japanese helmets that were more or less hemispherical. They were so called because they resembled the shape of the head. (Conder 257).

E

EARED DAGGER, ESTRADIOT. A dagger derived from Oriental models and first used by the Venetian Estradiots, for which reason they were often called "stradiots" or "estradiots." The usual name is derived from the disks fastened to the pommel that stand up like ears. (Dean Hdbk. 57). They were very popular, especially in Italy, in the first half of the 15th century. Fig. 265.

EAR-FLAPS, EAR-GUARDS. Ear-flaps first appeared on the helmets of the 11th century. During the 12th they were fixed, becoming an integral part of the defense, and gradually closed round until they joined the nasal, this arrangement at length forming the ventail or visor. In the 16th and 17th centuries they were hung from the helmet and called cheeks. (ffoulkes 26).

EBIRA, YEBIRA. A type of Japanese quiver carried hung from the left shoulder. (Garbutt 153). They vary considerably in size and design; but all consist essentially of an open box containing a series of bars to steady the arrow heads, and an open frame rising from the back with cords to hold the shafts. The box often has a small drawer in the lower part to carry extra bow strings, an ink slab or other small articles of equipment. Fig. 266.

ECAIO. A general name for spears, Engano. (Modigliani, Engano 243).

ECREVISSES. Armor made of overlapping plates or splints. (Skelton 30).

ECUYERS DE CORPS. The permanent royal guards of the 14th century. (Hewitt II, 36).

EFU NO TACHI. A form of tachi reserved for the princes and nobles of the Imperial retinue, Japan. (Joly, Hawkshaw xiv).

EGASHIRA. The end of a kozuka. Kozuka are sometimes signed on the egashira.

FGCHOS. The Greek bronze-headed spear. (Dean Europ. 15).

ELA(DA). The Nicobar harpoon-arrow. The head was formerly made of shell, but now iron is used. (Man, And. & Nic. 4).

became smaller and structurally simpler, though often elaborately embossed. The very large cops worn in the 15th century were necessary because

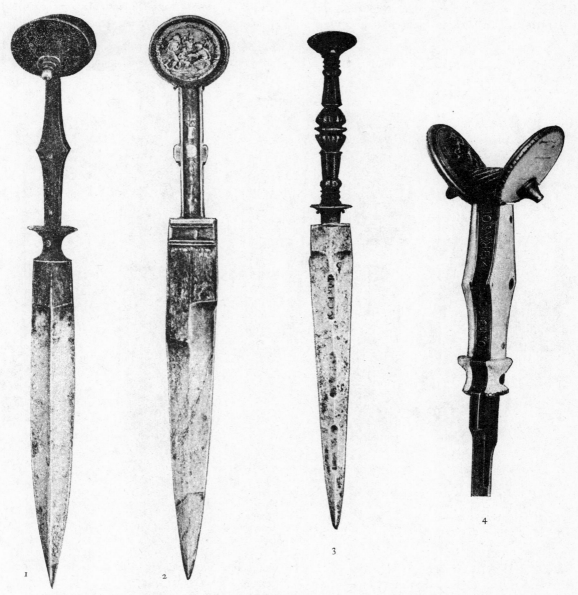

FIGURE 265. *Eared Daggers. 1. Italian, end of the 15th century. 2. Italian, about 1500. 2. Spanish, 16th century. 4. Italian, early 16th century. The first three are to scale. Metropolitan Museum.*

ELBOW COP, COUDE, COUDIERE, COUTE. Elbow guards of plate. They were first used in the latter part of the 14th century, and attained their greatest size and elaborateness in the second half of the 15th. Fig. 267. Later they again

the armorers had not learned how to articulate the arm plates so as to protect the joints; when they did the cops were reduced in size. Fig. 37.

ELBOW GAUNTLET. A long gauntlet of steel or leather reaching to the elbow and worn during the 16th century. It was copied from the Oriental Bazu Band. Fig. 268.

ELBOW GUARD. A large guard worn on the left arm over the regular armor in tournaments in the 15th and 16th centuries. (ffoulkes 77). Fig. 269.

ELBOW PIECE. See Elbow Cop.

EM. Gunpowder in Salar, a Tibetan dialect. (Rockhill Jour.).

EMBATTLED PARAPET. A parapet having in its upper line a range of indentations separated by solid parts, called merlons.

EMBOITMENT. A cuirass made of two or more plates, the lower overlapping the upper, and

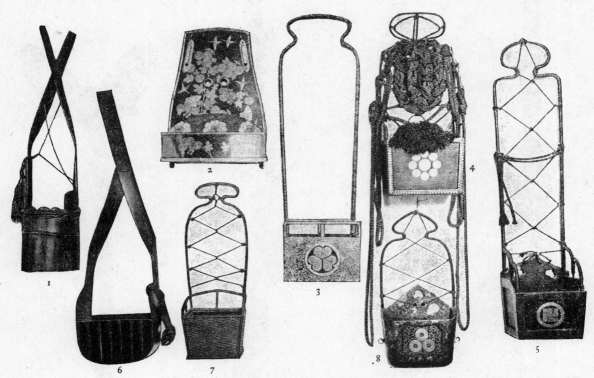

FIGURE 266. *Ebira.* 1. *The uprights and box, except the back, are made of a single piece of bamboo.* 2. *Hira Yanagui, low, wide form. Very fine gold lacquer, a gold vine on a powdered gold ground.* 3. *Square Box. Fine gold lacquer with a Tokugawa crest. It has a drawer, containing an ink slab, in the side.* 4. *Low, square box lacquered with a mon and dragon flies in gold.* 5. *Square box lacquered with a gold mon. Height 23 inches.* 6. *The front and back of the box are of bamboo and the sides, bottom and uprights of a single piece of whalebone.* 7. *Box woven of split bamboo.* 8. *Unusual form, a shallow box decorated with gold lacquer.*

EL-DARAKAH. Arabic, a shield. The origin of our word target. (Burton Sword 12).

ELEPHANT SWORD. Many of the early travelers in the East speak of elephant swords. Ludovici di Varthema (1501-1568) says that they were two fathoms long and attached to the trunk. More reasonable accounts describe them as blades projecting from sockets slipped over the tusks. (Burton Sword 216). Moser illustrates a pair of the latter description.

connected by straps or sliding rivets, making it flexible. (Hewitt III, 453). The ordinary form of the Gothic breastplate.

EMBOSSING. Embossing is changing the relative levels of different parts of a piece. It may be done by working from the inside to raise some parts above the rest, or from the outside to sink some parts below the others. In practice both are generally done; the main elevations being made by hammering the inside to force part up, then the work is turned over and the finer details are always put on from the outside. It may be done either hot or cold. Cold working strengthens and hardens the metal up to a certain point, but if carried beyond this makes it

shapes; if not they can be quickly made. If the relief is not too great and the work is done cold it leaves the metal stronger and harder than at first. The character of the hammer marks show clearly

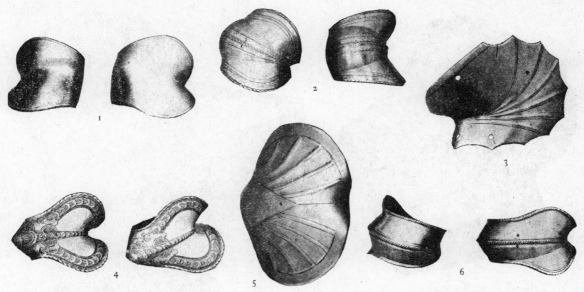

FIGURE 267. *Elbow Cops. 1. German, 1500. 2. German, 1535-45. 3. Probably German, early 16th century. 4. German, about 1535. Probably by Lochner. 5. German, early 16th century. 6. German, about 1570. Metropolitan Museum. Not to scale.*

brittle. To remove the brittleness it must be annealed, that is, heated to a particular critical temperature varying for each metal, and then allowed to cool slowly. Annealing iron and steel weakens the metal and if repeated too often leaves it much weaker than it was originally. When making fine details, or when working very soft metals, the work is usually backed with pitch which supports it and prevents it from cracking but yields enough to allow the design to show.

Forming the pieces of plate armor is embossing. The first step is to cause the metal to flow so as to thicken it at the points that will be in the highest relief. This is done to provide sufficient thickness of metal at these points after it has been stretched by the embossing. It is usually done hot as the subsequent cold work is sufficient to harden it as much as is required. Parts in very high relief like the combs of morians and burgonets are formed by hammering the outside over "stakes" held in holes in the anvil. The stakes are curved pieces of the shape of the inside of the part being formed. Most smiths have a large supply of stakes of different

whether the work was done hot or cold, the former leaving what the experts call "bad" marks, and the latter what they call "good" ones. The names bad and good correctly describe the effects but it would be better to call them the results of hot or cold working.

In Europe a great deal of embossing was done hot which is easier and does not take as much time, but necessitates frequent annealing which often left the pieces so weak that they had very little defensive value. In the East it was usually done cold and much more gradually which does not harden the metal as much so that annealing was seldom necessary. In much of the later and more elaborate ar-

FIGURE 268. *Elbow Gauntlet, Saxon, 1590. Metropolitan Museum.*

mor made in Europe the pieces have been seriously weakened by excessive embossing and annealing; this was not considered as serious as most of such armor was intended mainly for parade. There are

The mass was broken into small pieces and the smith selected those of the character he wanted and a bar was made for the particular purpose by welding those of similar character together. In

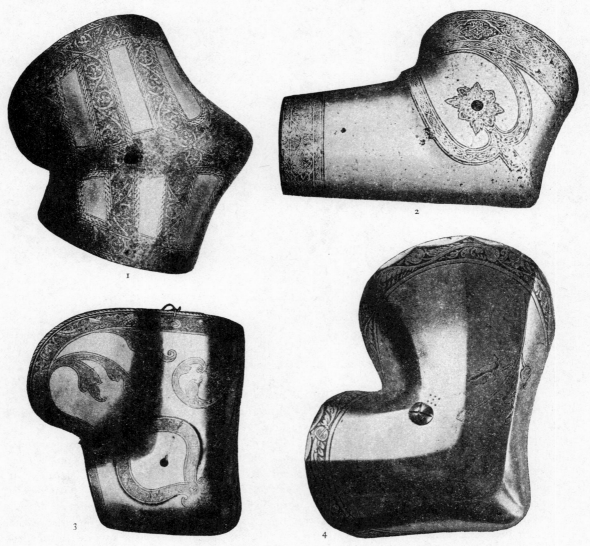

FIGURE 269. *Elbow Guards.* 1. *Italian, 1530.* 2. *German, 1550. Made by Wolf of Landshut for Spain.* 3. *German, 1570.* 4. *German, middle of the 16th century. Metropolitan Museum. Not to scale.*

two main causes for the different character of the work done in the East and West. In Europe the steel was made in large quantities and the most suitable pieces in the stock on hand were used for the work being done. In the East the steel was made by different methods which yielded metal of a great variety of qualities all partly fused together.

many cases the original bars were beaten out, doubled, and welded many times to give a homogeneous bar. In some Japanese sword blades less than a quarter of an inch thick there are over 4,000,000 layers giving a bar that is practically homogeneous. Also in the East great care was taken, and a tremendous amount of work was put on the bar to insure that it did not contain any inclusions of slag. In an old Japanese sword that we cut up no slag shows until it is magnified 500 diameters; even then the slag particles are barely visible. Professor Campbell of Columbia University, one of our leading authorities on the micro structure of metals, said it was the finest structure he had ever seen for a combination of hardness and toughness.

When the relief is not too great and the design intricate the work is often done entirely from the outside. The finer detail is always made from the outside; in fact it would not show unless it were. It is sometimes stated that the smaller details are made by pressing the metal between dies. This is a mistake as dies for such work are about the most troublesome and expensive tools made or used and are never employed unless a very large number of exactly similar pieces are to be made. For such work the two dies must be of different size and design and must leave sufficient space between for the desired thickness of metal.

In the East labor is cheap, the workmen are proud of the quality of the work they do, and no one is in a hurry. In consequence they put a quantity and quality of labor into a piece that has not been possible in the West for many centuries. The Japanese were the best metal workers the world has produced. The Persians come next and most of the best work done in the old Turkish Empire and in India was done by them. Their steel was excellent for swords used mainly for the draw cut, as theirs were, but it is hard and brittle and not as suitable for general use as some made elsewhere. Their decorative work is excellent. Most that we see is etched and it is frequently made solely for export. The finest is carved with chisels and is far better in every way. They did true inlaying as well as false damascening; the first being much finer than the last. The Persians rarely did elaborate embossed work.

In Malaya the embossing tool is a spring bar 20 to 30 inches long tapering towards both ends, each of which is turned up in a short blunt point. Between the two it passes through a mortise in a short stake firmly set in a heavy block of wood. The bar is held steady in the stake by a wedge through the upper part of the mortise. The scabbard covers to be embossed are from 14 to 20 inches long, of elliptical section, and often not more than $1.75 \times$

$1\frac{3}{8}$ inches at the mouth and $1\frac{3}{8} \times \frac{3}{8}$ at the closed end. The bar is set in the stake so that it can go inside the piece to be embossed to within an inch of the closed end. The work is held and moved by the left hand. It is held steadily so that it just touches the point on the end of the spring bar and moved as the design requires. The right hand holds a small hammer with which the spring bar is tapped and the spring of the bar brings it up with sufficient force to raise a small piece above the general surface. For fairly heavy, or hard, metal a very light iron hammer is used; but for softer or thinner metal one with a very light horn head. They make an elaborate pattern of dots and scrolls quite fast. When making covers for the finer kris scabbards they often use gold and make very elaborate patterns in high relief. See figs. 480-484. The whole apparatus is very simple and the workmen are very skilful and work much more rapidly than most Orientals.

The best Malay work in both metals and wood carving is of very high quality; but the best work is very rare. The krisses, fig. 480, are of the highest quality of Malay work.

EMPU. A kris maker, a smith, Java.

ENARMES. Loops on the back of a shield through which the arm was passed, middle ages. (ffoulkes 29).

ENCLOSING. In early fencing, closing in and seizing the sword of an adversary. (Castle 194).

ENDONG. A quiver, Java. It had a straight, narrow body with a wide scroll top. (Raffles plate I, p. 296/297).

ENGAGEMENT. A man is said to be engaged in a particular guard, in a given line, when the relative position of his weapon to that of his adversary is such as to defeat all attacks in that line, unless some means is taken to force an entrance. (Castle 10).

ENGINES, GYNS. Machines for throwing stones, arrows or other missiles. Those of classic time, the earliest of which we have definite knowledge, were apparently balistas and catapults, both of which depend on twisted skeins for their power. In the middle ages, on the contrary, neither of these was used, but only the trebuchet and crossbow types. Some of these were of great size: "Thus

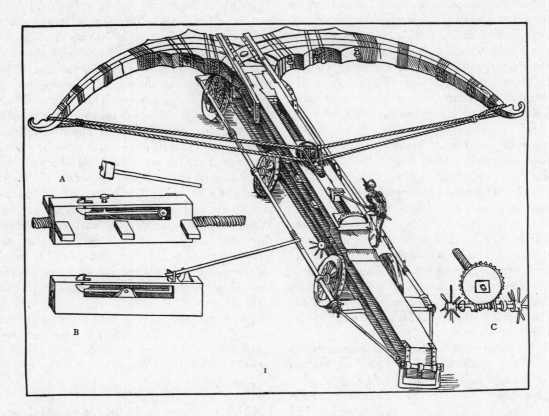

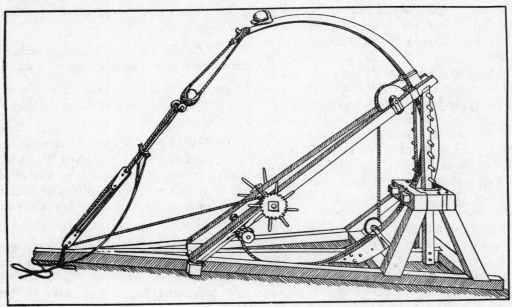

FIGURE 270. *Engines, Gyns.* 1. *A Balista in the form of a huge crossbow.* 2. *A spring engine with a sling attached that threw two stones at the same time. Both from Il Codice Atlantico, Leonardo da Vinci, 1445-1520. After Payne-Gallwey, Projectile Throwing Engines.*

Abulfeda speaks of one used at the final capture of Acre which was entrusted to the troops of Hamath, and which formed a load for one hundred carts, of which the historian was in charge of one himself. The romance of Richard Coeur de Lion tells how in the king's fleet an entire ship was taken up by one such machine and its gear:

'Another schyp was laden yet
With an engine hyght Robinet
(It was Richards o mangonel)
And all the takyl that thereto fel.'

ENSHO, DOGUSURI, GO-YAKU, KWA-YAKU, SHO-YAKU. Gunpowder, Japan.

ENSHO-IRE. A powder flask, Japan. See Hayago.

ENSIGN. The name originally included all flags, banners, standards, guidons, pennons, pencils and banderolls. Later it was confined to the colors of the infantry, and for a long time each company had its own stand of colors. The name was transferred to the man that carried them; this was the

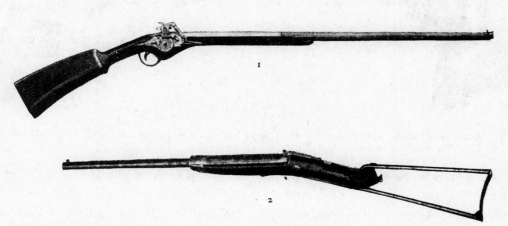

FIGURE 271. *Esclopettes.* 1. *French, wheel lock, 17th century.* 2. *French, about 1860. Metropolitan Museum. Not to scale.*

Twenty-four machines, captured from the Saracens by St. Louis in his first partial success on the Nile, afforded material for stockading his whole camp. A great machine which cumbered the tower of St. Paul at Orleans, and was dismantled previous to its defense against the English, furnished twenty-six cart loads of timber." (Marco Polo II, 165 note).

Before the days of cannon they were called artillery, the name later being transferred to the newer weapons. There were many varieties of these "gyns," but nearly all fall into one of three classes of which the catapult, balista and trebuchet are typical. Besides these machines the petrary, beugle or bible, matafunda and onager were used for throwing stones; and the scorpion, mategriffon, bricole and espringald for darts. The mangona, and its diminutive the mangonel, appear to have been class names rather than those of definite machines. Fig. 270.

junior commissioned officer, corresponding to the modern second lieutenant. The office of ensign was abolished early in the 19th century. At the present time the name signifies the national flag carried on a vessel.

EPAUL DE MOUTON, POLDER MITTON. A large curved guard worn over the regular armor to protect the *right* arm in tournaments, as the elbow guard protects the left. (ffoulkes 76).

EPAULIERES, EPAULETTES, EPAULETS, POLLETS. See Shoulder Cop.

EPHIPPARCHIE, EPITAGM, EPITARCHIE. See Ile.

EPIZYGIS. Iron bars holding the ends of the twisted skeins of catapults or similar engines. (Grose I, 370).

EPROUVETTE. See Powder Tester.

ERALILI. A curious cross-shaped shield of buffalo hide used by the natives of Wetter Island. (Arc. f. Eth. IV, 74).

ESCAUPILLES. Maya armor, a garment of quilted cotton covering the body down to the

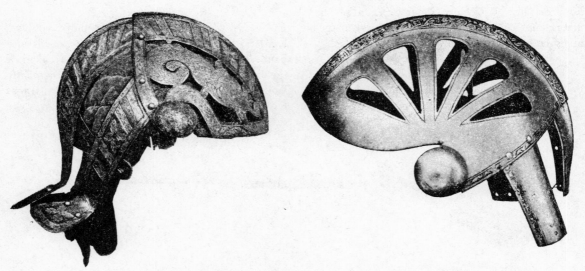

FIGURE 272. *Escuffa, both of German make in Spanish style, middle of the 16th century. Metropolitan Museum. Not to scale.*

ERIWA. A variety of Japanese gorgets. See Nodowa.

ERNANGNAK. A Greenland harpoon with two "feathers" of bone on the butt to increase the weight and guide the flight. (U. S. N. M. 1900, 240).

lower part of the thighs. It was considered arrow proof. (Hough 647).

ESCLOPETTE. Originally a short wheel-lock gun with a stock hinged so that it could be folded back on itself. It was carried in a holster like a long pistol, early 17th century. (Skelton 119).

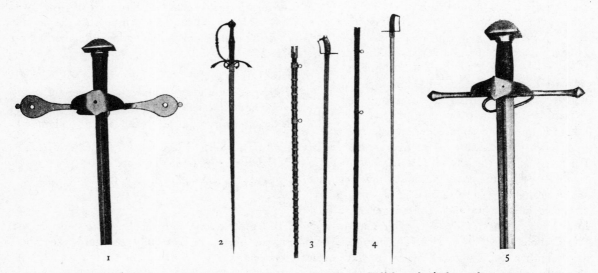

FIGURE 273. *Estocs. 1. Saxon, 1570. 2. Saxon, 1600. 3, 4. Polish, end of the 16th century. 5. Saxon, 1580. Metropolitan Museum. Not to scale.*

Similarly constructed guns, with other forms of ignition, were used as late as the 19th century. They were carried, mainly, by poachers who could fold them up and conceal them under their coats. Fig. 271.

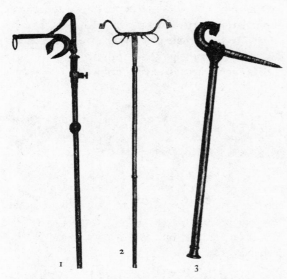

FIGURE 274. *Fakir's Crutches. 1. Brass, 24.75 inches long. The shaft is hollow and contains a stiletto. 2. All steel. 24.5 inches long. 3. The hand and tiger's head are of brass, the rest of steel. It contains a four-sided poniard.*

ESCRIME. Fencing, French.

ESCUFFA. An extra plate worn over the helmet in tilting; it covered the top and back of the head. (Laking Armour IV, 122). It was often pierced and highly decorated. Fig. 272. Compare Pate Plate.

ESPADON, SPADONE. A sword of the 15th century intermediate in size between the regular and two-handed; it is much like a hand-and-a-half sword. Meyrick gives this name especially to a two-handed sword with a straight blade about two feet long. (Planche 182).

ESPALLIERES. Shoulder guards formed of several lames flexibly connected and conforming closely to the shape of the shoulder, 16th century.

Some Japanese shoulder guards of much earlier date are the same. 1, fig. 358.

ESPINETTE. A variety of tournament of the 14th century. (Hewitt II, 340).

ESPRINGALD, ESPRINGAL, SPRINGAL, SPRINGALD. An engine for throwing large darts. (Grose I, 382). It was similar to the balista.

ESSEDUM. Latin, a war chariot. (Burton Sword 269).

ESTOC. A sword with a long, narrow, quadrangular blade intended solely for thrusting. The earlier ones were carried hung from the saddle when on horseback, or passed through rings on the belt when on foot. They had no scabbards. Later they were carried in scabbards like other swords. 13th to 17th centuries. Fig. 273.

ESTOCADE. In fencing, an exaggerated form of the modern lunge taught in the latter part of the 17th century. (Castle 140).

ESTRADIOT, STRADIOT. Originally Levantine soldiers in the Venetian service, later it meant light cavalry.

The eared dagger was sometimes called a stradiot because it was introduced in Western Europe by these troops.

ETCHEU. See Suneate.

EYESS. Strictly a hawk so young that it was unable to stand on its legs. In the ordinary language of hawking it meant a hawk that was taken from the nest before it was fully fledged, though it might be able to fly a little. Such hawks are called eyesses all their lives to distinguish them from haggards, which are caught after they have left the nest but have not made their first migration, and passage

FIGURE 275. *Fakir's Horns, India, 17th century. The animals' heads are of brass and the spear points of steel.*

hawks or passengers, hawks caught when full grown and after they have made at least one migration.

F

FABRI. The Roman sappers. (Burton Sword 249).

FACON. A Spanish knife about two feet long. It is thrown like the cuchillo. (Burton Sword 18).

FIGURE 276. *Falchion, German, 15th century. Metropolitan Museum.*

FAKIR'S CRUTCH. Indian fakirs (religious mendicants) are not allowed by their regulations to carry weapons. They evade this prohibition by having short crutches, to place under their arms when sitting, that are heavy enough to be very effective maces, or may contain concealed stilettos. Fig. 274.

FAKIR'S HORNS. As mentioned above, Indian fakirs are not allowed to carry arms; but could have a pair of black buck horns fastened together with their points in opposite directions, which makes an excellent substitute. Sometimes they stretched the permission far enough to have a pair of steel spear heads on the tips of the horns. Fig. 275. When a small circular shield is added this becomes a *madu*, a common parrying weapon. (Egerton 693, 694).

FALARICA. An engine for throwing darts to which burning substances were attached, middle ages. (Hewitt I, 89).

FALCASTRA, FALCASTRUM, FALK. A primitive weapon, supposed to have been a scythe fastened to a pole. (Planche 184).

FALCHION, FAUCHON. A sword of the middle ages. We have no very positive knowledge of it, but it is usually represented with a broad curved blade widest near the point, and in which the back joins the edge in a concave curve. (Planche 184). Fig. 276.

FALCON. See Cannon.

The bird. "It should be observed that although the term falcon has an established meaning among ornithologists as a name for the long-winged hawks (*falco*), it is used by falconers in quite a different acceptation. In hawking phraseology it is applied, in contradistinction to the term tiercel, to the female of the larger sorts of long-winged hawks, and especially to the female peregrine. Thus a falconer is described as being possessed of 'two falcons' or a hare is mentioned as having been taken by a 'fal-con;' the reader is expected to know that a female peregrine is referred to, and not a male peregrine, or a saker, lanner, or any other kind of a hawk." (Michell, 11 note).

FALCONER'S GAUNTLET. In the 16th century gauntlets were sometimes made with a small reel on the back of the hand; these have been called falconer's gauntlets; but it is very doubtful if this is correct. First because they offer no proper perch for a hawk, they are much too broad for her to grasp, and could not be padded, which is always done with a hawk's perch. Secondly the reels are not large enough to hold a leash, and would make it almost impossible to release a hawk for a flight. Fig. 277.

FALCONER'S GLOVE. For the larger hawks the glove was made of strong leather and had a gauntlet reaching half way to the elbow. For the small ones it was not larger or heavier than an ordinary walking glove.

FIGURE 277. *Falconer's Gauntlet. Saxon, late 16th century, probably made for the Emperor Christian II. Metropolitan Museum.*

FALCONET. A small cannon of about two inches bore. See Cannon.

FAL-FEG. An Igorot spear, Northern Luzon. It has a rather broad head with nearly parallel sides,

FALSE EDGE. In single-edged swords a few inches of the back near the point is frequently sharpened to make them more effective for thrusting. This portion is called the false edge.

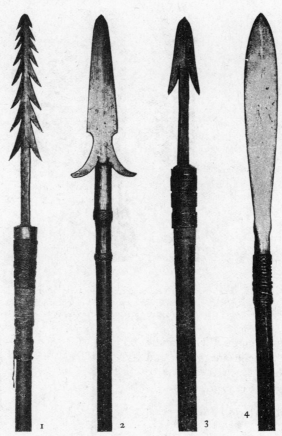

FIGURE 278. *Igorot Spears. 1. Sinalawatan. Spear carried as a protection against evil spirits. Head 11 inches, total length 5 feet 7.5 inches. 2. Kayyan. Spear carried as an ornament. Head 8.5 inches x 3.375. Total length 5 feet 3.5 inches. 3. Falfeg, the fighting spear. Head 8 inches, total length 4 feet 10 inches. 4. Fangkao, spear used mainly for hunting. Head with socket 12.5 inches, overall 5 feet.*

an ogival point and a single pair of rather large, blunt barbs. The shaft is heavy, about five feet long, and strengthened by an iron ferule, or a band of bajuco (cane) where the tang is inserted. The heads are from two to ten inches long, the lighter ones being preferred for war. The fal-feg is the type of spear most used by the Igorot in war and hunting and is carried most of the time by every man. The heavy staff is used as an alpenstock when climbing the steep mountain trails. (Jenks, 127). 3, fig. 278.

FALLING BEVOR. See Buffe.

FALX, FAUS, FALSO. A pole arm of the 14th century, probably a bill. Burton says "The falx is probably a large pruning knife, plain or toothed, with a coulter or bill, projecting from the back of the curved head. Besides this there are many other forms; one is a simple curve; another is a leaf-

FIGURE 279. *Fang. All iron, length 26 inches.*

shaped blade with an inner hook; while a third bears, besides the spike a crescent on the back." (Burton Sword 253; Hewitt II, 269). See Falcastra.

FAUCHON. See Falchion.

FAUCRE. A hook-shaped lance rest fastened to the breastplate, 15th century. (Demmin 51).

FIGURE 280. *Fauchards. 1. French, 15th century. 2. Venetian, about 1540. 3. Venetian, about 1500. 4, 5. Italian, early 17th century. 6. Venetian, 16th century. 7. Italian, about 1500. 8. German, 17th century, a peasant weapon. Metropolitan Museum. Not to scale.*

FANG. A Chinese weapon having an iron handle about two feet long with a blade in line with it and another at right angles to it. Each is about five inches long and double-edged. Fig. 279.

FANG-KAO. The Igorot barbless hunting spear, 4, fig. 278.

FARANG, FARANG KATTI. See Firangi.

FARARA. See Mkuki.

FARRAH. The ancient Irish war cry. (Grose II, 10).

FASCINES. Bundles of brushwood tied in several places. They were used in making temporary fortifications or in strengthening earthworks. (Hoyt 399).

FAUCHARD. A pole arm of the 16th century. It has a broad, single-edged blade curved on the cutting edge, and an ornamental prong, or prongs, on the back. (Dean Hdbk. 76). This name is applied to a variety of different weapons by different authorities. Fig. 280.

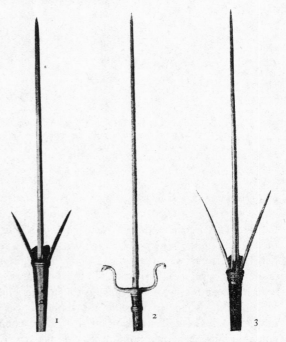

FIGURE 281. *Feather Staves. 1. Milanese, 1580. 2. Linstock feather staff, Italian, 1600. 3. Venetian, 1565. Metropolitan Museum. Not to scale.*

FAUS. See Falx.

FAUSSAR. A weapon of the 13th century. Apparently a very roughly-made falx. It was sometimes thrown. (Hewitt I, 324).

FEAK, FEAKE. For a hawk to wipe her beak on the perch after eating. (Harting 222).

FEATHER STAFF. A weapon of the 17th century carried by officers when not on duty. The body was of about the size and shape of a cane and had concealed in it one long and two short blades which could be ejected in position for use, by a jerk. (Tower 33, p. 104 and pl. 8). Fig. 281.

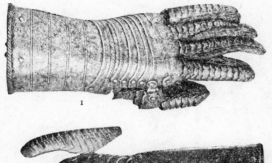

FIGURE 282. *Fencing Gauntlets. 1. French, 17th century. Metropolitan Museum. The mail lining can be seen on the thumb. 2. Collection of Mr. C. O. Kienbusch. Not to scale.*

FEINTS. In fencing, menacing in one line with the intention of attacking in another. (Castle II, 101).

FENCING GAUNTLET, DUELLING GAUNTLET. A gauntlet for the left hand especially designed for parrying a thrust or seizing an opponent's blade. The scales on the fingers lapped upwards, the reverse of the ordinary method, in order that a sword point could not catch under them. In addition the palms were often lined with mail so that a blade could be grasped with impunity. Late 16th and 17th centuries. Fig. 282.

FENDACE. According to Fairholt, a protection for the throat, afterwards replaced by the gorget. (Planche 190).

FERENTARII. Roman light infantry. (Burton Sword 245).

FERINGIHA. The large cannon used by the Moguls in the 16th century. The name is derived from Feringi, Frank. They were evidently regarded as European inventions. (Egerton p. 21).

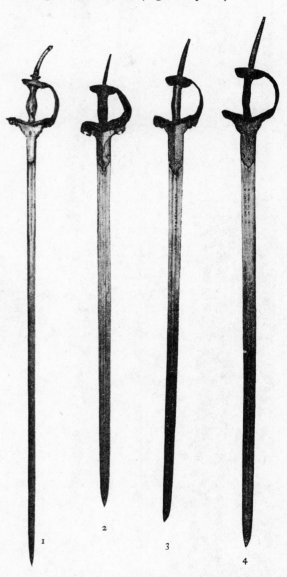

FIGURE 283. *Firangi. 1. Silver plated hilt. Solingen blade 42.25 inches long. 2. Hilt inlaid with gold, 17th century. European blade 35.5 inches long. 3. Hilt inlaid with gold scrolls and flowers. European blade 38 inches long, marked NOVAOE. 4. Hilt inlaid with gold figures and animals. European blade 41 inches long, marked OENVRC on one side, and SAN ROS OENRC on the other. The last two are from Tanjore.*

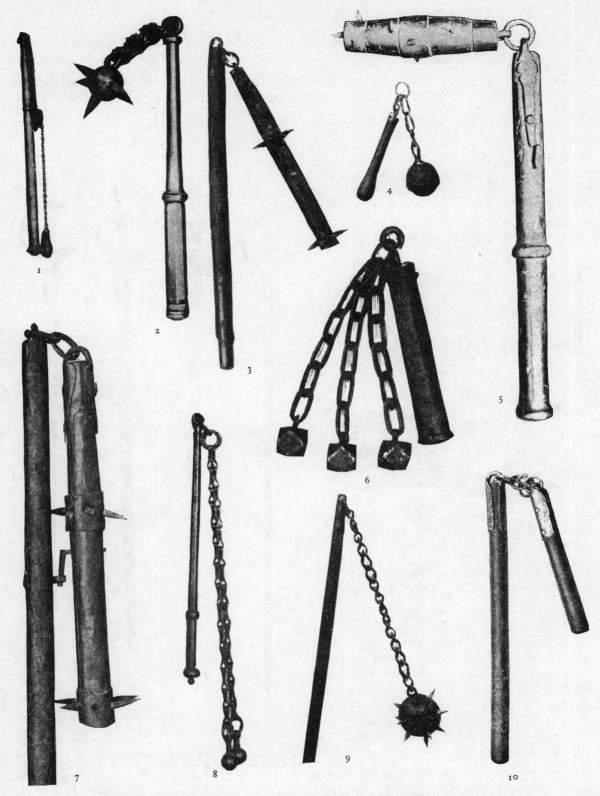

FIGURE 284. *Flails.* 1. *India, XVIII. Iron with a brass cap on the butt, length handle 16 inches.*
2. *German, XVI.* 3. *English, late XV.* 4. *French, XV.* 5. *German, XVII(?). Oak with iron mounts, length 20 inches.* 6. *German, XV.* 7. *German, XVII(?). It shows the hook to keep the swingle steady.* 8. *India, XIX. All iron, length handle 19.5 inches.* 9. *Swiss, about 1530.* 10. *Chinese, XVIII. 2, 3, 4, 6, 9, 10. Metropolitan Museum. 5 and 7. Collection of Mr. C. O. v. Kienbusch. Not to scale.*

FEU VOLANT. An early gunpowder. The receipt is: "Prenez j. li. de soufre vif, ij. li. de charbones de saux, vi. li. de salpetre, si les fetez bien et sotelment moudre sur un pierre de marbre, puis bultez le poudre; parmy un sotille coverchief, cest poudre vault a gettere pelottes de fer, ou de plom, ou d'areyne, ove un instrument qe l'on appelle Gonne." (Hewitt II, 292).

FIANCONATA. In fencing, the modern flanconade. (Castle 107).

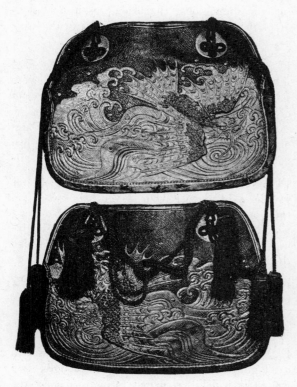

FIGURE 285. *Japanese Flanchards. Black leather with dragons and waves embossed and lacquered gold; red silk cords and tassels. Size 19.5 x 26.5 inches.*

FIEF DE HAUBERT. A definite estate in France in the 11th century. Only persons possessing this, or a greater estate, were allowed to wear hauberks. (Grose II, 246).

FIELD, of a flag. The upper quarter next the staff; where the stars are in our flag, or the crosses in the British.

FIL, FILO. The cutting edge of a sword. (Burton Sword 124).

FINGER GUARD, BOW, COUNTER GUARD, KNUCKLE BOW, WARD IRON. The portion of a sword hilt that protects the fingers from a cross cut. It is formed by recurving the quillons towards the pommel, or by connecting the quillons and pommel by a plate, a bar, or a system of bars. In its more elaborate forms it becomes the basket hilt. (Burton Sword 125).

FIRANGI, FARANG, PHIRANGI. Literally the Portuguese, or foreigner. A Mahratta cut-and-thrust, straight-bladed sword. The blades were either imported from Europe by the Portuguese, or made in imitation of them. Broadsword blades with either three or four shallow grooves were the most common, but rapier blades were also used. The hilts were of the khanda type, with broad guards and finger guards, and disk pommels with curved spikes on them. Most of the blades are of the 17th century, though some are of the 16th. Fig. 283.

FIREARMS. Firearms were first used in Europe in the 14th century, although gunpowder had probably been known earlier. The first gun was merely a tube with a handle and touchhole, to which a lighted match, held in the hand, was applied. This developed, on the one hand, into larger cannon, mortars, etc. — and, on the other, into the different kinds of mechanical matchlocks, flintlocks, detonators, percussion locks, and, finally, breech-loaders.

FIRE CARRIAGE. A number of flintlock muskets fixed on a wheeled carriage. All were loaded at once, a set of ramrods being fastened together and guided by a traveling brass plate. (R. U. S. M. 802, p. 80).

FIRELOCK. A name originally given to wheel lock musquets, but later transferred to those with flintlocks. Apparently it was synonymous with gun from shortly after the invention of the wheel lock to the disuse of the flintlock. Apparently it was never applied to percussion guns.

FIRE-POT. There were a number of ways in which fire was thrown at an enemy. The simplest was to throw a pot of clay, or some other fragile material, filled with burning substances, by hand. Larger ones filled with inflammable substances were used which, when broken, poured fire over the person attacked. These devices are said to have been introduced into Europe by the Arabs, who had, in turn, received them from the Chinese. (Hewitt I, 329).

FIRE-RAFTS. Rafts loaded with combustibles which were set on fire and allowed to drift against the ships of an enemy. They were often dangerous to their makers as, if the wind changed, they were liable to drift back to them.

FIRE ROCKETS. Rockets are a very old device and certainly antedate cannon. The early puranas and other records of the same period show that *agny astra*, fire-tipped darts, discharged from bamboo tubes, were used against cavalry. (Egerton p. 11, 151). Rockets were very commonly used in the wars of the 18th and 19th centuries.

FIRE-STICKS. Hand guns fired by a match held in the hand, 15th century. (Greener 20).

FIST SWORD. A stiletto only a span long, the Indian maushtika. (Burton Sword 215).

FLAG. Flags have been used from very early times to distinguish the troops of different leaders, and to serve as a rallying point for their troops. (Grose II, 51, 54).

A flag is hung directly from a vertical staff, while a banner is fastened to a crossbar hung from the staff. The part of a flag next the staff is called the *hoist*, the next part the *center*, and the outer portion the *fly*. The upper portion next the staff is often of a different color or design, and is then called the *field*.

FLAGELLUM. A three-thonged scourge used by Roman gladiators. (Burton Sword 253).

FLAIL, MILITARY FLAIL. The flail is a very ancient and widely distributed weapon. Originally it was probably the ordinary agricultural implement, but its effectiveness for military use was soon increased by adding weights or spikes to the short arm, or by substituting chains carrying weights for it. The flail was certainly used in Europe early in the 13th century and probably much earlier. It continued in more or less occasional use until the end of the 18th century. Flails were used in India, China and Japan. Some flails have a hook on the short arm (swingle) that could be slipped into a ring on the staff to keep the former from swinging about when marching, 7, fig. 284. Very short flails were sometimes used by horsemen. Fig. 284.

FLAMBERGE. In the early middle ages this name was applied to almost any large sword; but it became restricted to those with waved, or undulating, edges. From the latter part of the 16th century to the middle of the 17th it was used only for a special form of rapier. The peculiarities of this were the comparative simplicity of the hilt, which consisted only of quillons without knuckle bow or pas d'ane, covered by a very shallow cup of medium dimensions; the blade was usually slenderer than that of the ordinary rapier of the same period. (Castle 228, 237).

FLANCHARDS. Plate armor for a horse's sides. They hung from the saddle on each side and were sometimes curved upwards at the center to admit of using the spurs. (ffoulkes 90). See Bardings.

The Japanese flanchards were large oval plates of leather, highly decorated, and were often worn without other horse armor. Fig. 285.

FLANCONADE. An attack in fencing: "after you have overlapped your adversary's sword, in this you must go quite *under* his sword, turning your hand in Terce, and bring up his sword, giving him the thrust, as you give it when you play the *Single Feint at the head*." (Castle 194).

FLAON. A wedge between the shield and the breastplate, used in 15th century tournaments. It was usually made of wood, but occasionally of iron. (Calvert 53).

FLASK, POWDER FLASK. A case in which to carry gunpowder. One of the earliest, longest used and most widely distributed forms is a horn, the larger end being closed permanently, and the smaller temporarily, by wooden plugs. Horns are so generally used that the name powder horn is about as common as powder flask. Flasks are made of wood, leather, shell, or metal as well as horn. They frequently have a device for measuring the charge of powder attached to the outlet. The sizes and shapes vary infinitely. In general the older ones are larger than the later, as the old powder was very much less powerful than that used in recent times. Some of the old styles are distinctive of particular times and places but, as a rule, each type is very widely distributed. They were used wherever

FIGURE 286. *European Powder Flasks. 1. Spanish, 17th century. 2. French, early 19th century. 3. South German, early 17th century. 4. French, end of the 17th century. 5. Italian, early 17th century. 6. Italian, 17th century. 7. Saxon, 1690. 8. Venetian, 16th century. 9. South German, late 16th century. 10. German, 17th century. Bears Nuremberg mark and name of maker, Jeremias Ritter. 11. French, early 18th century. 12. Italian, late 16th century. 13. Italian, 1700. Metropolitan Museum.*

muzzle-loading guns were used. Figs. 286, 287, 288. For the Japanese flasks see Hayago.

The name flask is confined to those used for charge powder, the smaller ones used for priming powder are called primers.

FLETCHER. An arrow maker. They were a separate guild in England during the time that bows and arrows were used for military purposes, and there were many laws regulating their privileges and products.

FIGURE 287. *Flasks, Oriental and Savage.* 1. *Korea. Wood flask in the shape of a turtle, primer attached.* 2. *Japanese. Lacquered red with a gold mon.* 3. *The back of 2 showing the belt hook.* 4. *China. Lacquered black. Ivory cap and measure.* 5. *China. Carved wood.* 6. *China. Black lacquer.* 7. *Burma(?). Black wood flask with a grotesque beast carved on the stopper.* 8. *Kurdistan. Wood flask inlaid with bone and brass.* 9. *Central Asia. Inlaid leather with steel mounts.* 10. *Soudan. Flat flask of brown wood slightly carved and inlaid with shell.* 11. *China. Black lacquer.* 12. *Turkey, XVII. Body covered with brown leather set with silver studs and plaque. Neck covered with embossed silver.* 13. *India. Brown leather with a spring closure.* 14. *Cambodia. Horn with a carved wooden end. A small leather pouch is attached.* 15. *Cambodia. Silver mounted horn with a small leather pouch attached.* 16. *China. The end is carved with dragons and the body is lacquered red and black.* 17. *Morocco. Carved wood with brass nails.* 18. *Morocco. Horn with chased brass ends.* 19. *Morocco. Engraved brass inlaid with silver.* 20. *Cambodia. Large horn with a carved wood end.* 21. *Cambodia. Wood with a carved wood end.* 22. *Morocco. Leather covered with brass nails.* 23. *Africa. Covered with brown leather.* 24. *Morocco. Conical with a flat back, covered with brass nails.* 25. *Philippines. Limp leather with a wooden plug.* 26. *Soudan. Tin flask covered with colored leather, tassels attached.* 27. *Naga Assam. Large horn with a wooden cap that is also a measure. The cap and most of the horn are painted with red bands.*

FLEURET. A fencing foil, 18th century. (Castle 139).

FLINTLOCK. In the flintlock a piece of flint held in the jaws of the cock is struck violently

night, and the wheel locks were too expensive.

The Dutch lock was called a "snaphaan" (chicken thief) on account of the occupation of the inventors. The name is frequently spelled "schnapphahn," an obsolete German word mean-

FIGURE 288. *Moroccan Flasks.* 1. *Heavy flask covered with brown leather set with brass nails.* 2. *Very small steel primer.* 3. *Large flask covered with colored leather, ivory mouthpiece. Leather bullet pouches attached.* 4. *Carved wood flask.* 5. *Primer similar to 2.* 6. *Brass flask inlaid with silver.* 7. *Leather powder flask, Tunis.* 8. *Brass flask.*

against a piece of steel, the hammer or frizzen, sending a shower of sparks into the priming powder in the pan, and igniting the charge. Flintlocks were invented towards the close of the 16th century in Spain and Holland at about the same time. In both countries they were said to have been invented by robbers who found matchlocks unsatisfactory as the lighted matches betrayed their whereabouts at

ing either a thief or thief-catcher; not, as is often stated, a "pecking cock." In the snaphaan the hammer and pan cover are separate pieces which makes the closing of the pan rather complicated; it is, however, uncovered automatically by the act of cocking, or by a link from the cock. The moving parts of the lock are inside the lock plate and protected from dirt and injury. Fig. 289.

The Spanish lock is called "Miquelet," also from its inventors, the robber bands of the Pyrenees and Catalonia. In it the hammer and pan cover are in one piece, and the pan is uncovered by the flint striking the hammer and throwing it back, a simpler and better arrangement than the Dutch. On the other hand it is inferior in having a large part of the lock mechanism on the outside of the plate where it is liable to be injured. Furthermore the design of the lock is such that the cock is not held securely at half cock, and it is therefore necessary

that the cock is securely held and, when cocked, the spring throws the safety hook out of the way. I, fig. 290. With both the miquelet and the dog lock the cock is so securely held that a trigger guard is usually dispensed with. The dog lock is probably of Spanish or Moorish origin but was also used in England and Scotland as late as the end of the 19th century. The only flintlocks made in the far east were the snaphaans used in the Japanese firelighters called Hi Uchi Bukuro, fig. 368. They do not appear to have ever been used with guns.

FIGURE 289. *Early European flintlocks.* 1. *Snaphaan, dated* 1749. 2. *Miquelet lock, Italian, 17th century. Metropolitan Museum. Not to scale.*

to have a safety catch. This consists of a bolt that moves transversely through the lock plate, and a projection from the front of the cock that rests on it when at half cock. This bolt is withdrawn by the first motion of the trigger when firing, leaving the cock free to fall. Fig. 289. In the later Spanish form of this lock, which was used up to the middle of the 19th century, the mechanism was placed inside the lock plate, but the safety catch was retained.

Both of these forms of lock have survived until the present time. The snaphaan is used by the Kabyles and other North African tribes; and the miquelet was used in Turkey, the Balkans and as far east as Persia until displaced by breech loaders. Another early form of flintlock, the dog lock, is still used by the Arabs, and a similar one was used in Ceylon. In this the safety catch is quite different. It consists of a hook on the back of the cock and another pivoted on the rear end of the lock plate and normally held clear of the cock by a spring. When the safety is to be used — the cock is raised and the hook pushed forward until it engages with the one on the cock; the latter is then gently lowered until the two hooks bear. The angles are such

These forms of lock soon displaced both match and wheel locks, and were in turn, displaced by improved forms that combined the advantages of both types, having the mechanism inside the plate and the hammer and pan cover in one piece, and did not require a safety catch. The first flintlocks were not over reliable and, for some time, what were known as "musquet-fusils" were made. These had both match and flint locks. Similar combinations of match and wheel locks had been used earlier. Flintlocks continued in use in the British army until 1840.

FLO. A swift arrow. (Fairholt 500).

FLOTTERNEL. The quilted gambeson. (Hewitt II, 67, 129).

FLY. The portion of a flag furthest from the staff. (Macgeorge 68).

FLYSSA. The national sword of the Kabyles of Morocco. It has a long, single-edged blade, straight on the back and with a very long point. It is widest at about the center of percussion (roughly at a third of its length from the point) narrowing in an easy

FIGURE 290. *Oriental Flintlocks.* 1. *Arab lock with the safety catch that hooks into the back of the cock. Used in Turkey, Syria and Egypt.* 2. *Miquelet lock from the Caucasus. Some of the cocks have much longer and slimmer jaws. Used in the Caucasus and western Persia.* 3, 4. *Miquelet locks from the Balkans and Turkey.* 5. *Persian Miquelet lock. Similar locks were used throughout the Turkish Empire.* 6. *Kabyle snaphaan. Used by the Berber tribes of North Africa.*

curve to about half this width, and then widening again to nearly its maximum at the hilt. The blades are from twelve to thirty-nine inches long, and are frequently engraved and inlaid with brass. The

piece of leather between it and the blade to cover the openings; the other has short, straight quillons and a cup guard. Formerly foil meant any rebated weapon. (Castle 139).

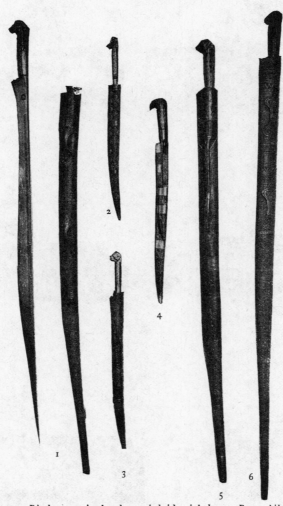

FIGURE 291. *Flyssa. 1. Blade 33.5 inches long, inlaid with brass. Brass hilt. Finely carved wood scabbard with four iron bands. 2. Slightly curved blade 19.75 inches long, brass hilt. Carved wood scabbard. 3. Knife similar to 2, slightly carved scabbard. 4. Plain blade 13.25 inches long, wood hilt inlaid with silver. Wood scabbard inlaid with silver, six brass bands. It has a pocket containing a small knife. 5. Similar to 1. Five leather bands on the scabbard. 6. Similar to 1, blade 38.5 inches long. Carved wood scabbard.*

hilts are small with one-sided pommels and no guards. The scabbards are of wood elaborately carved and have two sling hoops carved from the solid. Fig. 291.

FOIL. A fencing sword with a light square blade with a button on the end. Two types of hilt are common; one with a flat figure eight guard with a

FOIN. The crossbow of the Nicobar Islanders. It is used by the natives of the north group, and custom permits of its use only during the northeast monsoon. It has a very long stock shaped like that of a modern gun and a short wooden bow set far back. (Man, And. & Nic. 8).

FOINING WEAPONS. Thrusting weapons.

FONDES, FRONDES. Slings used by the Spanish troops in the 14th century. (Hewitt II, 281).

FORBIDDEN GAUNTLET. The locking gauntlet of the 16th century. In an action of arms, 1554, is a regulation — "He that shall have a close gauntlet or anything else to fasten his sword to his hand shall have no prize." (ffoulkes Armouries 107). See Locking Gauntlet, fig. 527.

a hook on one side with which to catch the bridle of an enemy. (Skelton 92).

FOWLING PIECE. A gun intended for shooting birds.

FRAMEA. The Frankish lance. (Boutell 91).

FIGURE 292. *Fuchi.* 1. *Iron, jar-neck shape. Bow and arrows associated with Hachiman's doves in gold and silver. (The dove is the messenger of Hachiman, god of war). Signed Umetada. 2. Copper, two children playing, gold and silver. Signed Joi. 3. Shibuichi, manzai dancer. Signed Masayoshi, at the age of seventy. 4. Shakudo, microscopically inlaid in gold with classical poems on shikishi (square poem paper). Signed Yoshu Matsuyama ju nin Shoami Moritomo. 5. Shakudo. Ground of gold inlay imitating lacquer. Rising sun, wave and flying crane. Signed Omori Teruhide. 6. Shibuichi, reaping hook and basket of millet in gold and copper. Goto School. 7. Shakudo, gold, copper and silver. The bell of Towara Toda being carried through the waves. Omori School. 8. Shakudo, nanako surface, dragon in high relief. Signed. 9. Shibuichi, nanako. Ear of rice in relief in gold. Signed Tsuji Masataka.*

FORE SHAFT. A supplementary part of an arrow, or spear, between the head and shaft.

FORK. See Military Fork.

FOUJDAR. A Rajput officer who commanded the troops of the State and the Royal Castles. (Tod II, 419).

FOURCH A CROCHET. A military fork with

FRANCISCA, FRANCISQUE. The battle axe, which was a favorite weapon with all of the northern nations of Europe, was called a "francisca" by the Romans because it was so much used by the Franks. (Hewitt I, 45).

FRIZZEN, HAMMER. The plate against which the flint strikes in the flint lock. In European locks it is usually smooth, in Oriental locks it is almost always ribbed vertically, a much more effective form.

FRONDES. See Fondes.

FRONT APPENDAGE. See Brayette.

FRONTAL. Armor for a horse's head. Some authorities distinguish between the chanfron and the frontal; limiting the former term to a complete covering for the head; and the latter to a plate covering the front only. (ffoulkes 90).

kashira. The fuchi has a plate on the bottom called the *tenjo kane* (ceiling) because it is above the head when the sword is being used in fighting. The tanjo kane is generally of a different metal from the body of the fuchi; and the signature, if there is one, is on the left when the blade is held edge up, the date or

FIGURE 293. *Fuchi Kashira. 1. Shakudo, Ho-O birds (the Japanese phœnix). Flat inlay of gold, silver and copper polished to imitate lacquer. Signed Shoyei, and Kakihan. 2. Shakudo nanako. A gourd vine in relief in gold and silver. 3. Copper, nanako, kinsunago-ji. Sparrows and grasses in gold. 4. Shibuichi, No-Kyogen (actor's masks). Inlay of gold, silver and shakudo. Signed Ganshoshi Nagatsune, and kakihan. 5. Shakudo, nanako. Pheasants and flowering trees in high relief in shakudo, shibuichi and gold. 6. Iron dragons and clouds in low relief. 7. Shakudo. Fuchi — Benten, kashira — Bishamon (two of the seven deities of luck), inlaid in relief in gold, shibuichi, silver and copper. Signed Joi suifu Katsukuni, and kakihan. 8. Iron. People seeking shelter from a shower in a tea house near a shrine. Inlay of gold, silver, shibuichi and copper. Signed Tetsugendo Shoraku. Seal inlaid in gold, Toshiyuki.*

FUCHI, TSUKA GUCHI. The first name means a border or margin, the second means the mouth of the hilt. The ornamental ring around the hilt of a Japanese sword or knife next the guard. The fuchi and kashira (pommel cap) were usually made to match by the same artist; but ornamental fuchi are sometimes used with plain horn

residence of the maker, and sometimes the name of a second artist, on the right. (Joly, Int. 13). Both fuchi and kashira are usually decorated like the other mountings. Figs. 292, 293.

The two most celebrated families of makers of sword mountings in Higo were the Nishi-gake and Kasu-ga. The former made fuchi of the jar-neck form, 1, fig. 292, and kashira of the cat's back type. The latter made their kashira in the form of "rings for a bull's nose." The Jingo, another Higo family, made fuchi in the form of a small drum. (Weber I, 270).

FUDAI. (Successful races). The fourth class of Japanese nobles in Tokugawa times. See Daimio.

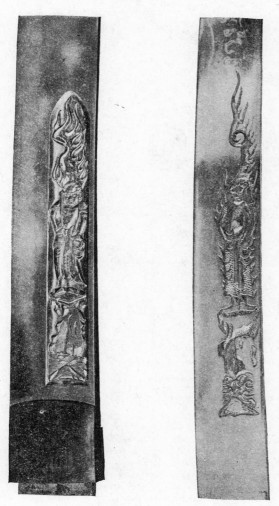

FIGURE 294. *Fudo, figures carved on sword blades.*

FUDO. A Buddhistic divinity identical with Achala, the immovable; he is also called Fudo Mio O, and is one of the Dai Nichi Nyorai; his other Sanskrit name is Akashobhya.

He is usually represented as seated on the brink of a precipice, or standing on a rock surrounded by flames, often under a waterfall. In his right hand he carries a vajra-hilted sword, or sometimes the

Amakurikara, and in his left a rope, which according to some, is intended to bind the wicked. His head is covered with black hair, with a long plait of eight strands extending to the left shoulder. (Joly Leg. 75). His figure is very frequently represented on blades and armor. Fig. 294.

FUETSU. Japanese battle axe, a weapon very seldom used in Japan. See Ono and Masakari.

FUJIHANASHI. A bow. An obsolete Japanese name.

FUJIWARA PERIOD. The primitive period in Japan, extending from A.D. 600 to 1100.

FUKIDAKE, FUKI-ZUTSU. A blowpipe, Japan. It is not likely that the blowpipe was ever used for fighting in Japan, though some of the older ones would have been effective weapons. The older form was made of two pieces of wood grooved on one side and fitted together to form the bore. This was wound with many layers of a heavy paper, called minogame, to make it air tight. It was fitted with a small mouthpiece and was over nine feet long and of about one-quarter inch bore. The arrows were slips of bamboo with paper feathers. Fig. 295.

The later, and more usual kind, was entirely different from any other blowpipe and was used by boys for shooting birds until driven out of use by airguns of European forms. The tube was a piece of cane about five feet long with a small trumpet-shaped mouthpiece projecting from the side a few inches from the end. The opening at the rear is closed by a wooden plug on the end of a crook handle. The plug is pulled out, the dart inserted and pushed forward by the plug until beyond the opening from the mouthpiece, and the dart blown. Fig. 295.

FUKIGAYESHI. The ear guards of a Japanese helmet. They are usually formed by rolling back one, or more, of the lames of the neck guard. (Dean Jap. 4). 3, 4, fig. 296. Sometimes they are a part of the brim, 2, fig. 206. Occasionally they are absent. 1, fig. 296.

In the early helmets the top lame of the neck guard was very wide making the fukigayeshi large. In some of the old helmets the one on the right was hinged so that it could be turned back out of the way shooting with the bow. (Conder 293). Fig. 412.

FUKI YA. A blowpipe dart, Japan. They are small slivers of wood with large paper cones on the end. Sometimes they had metal points. Fig. 295.

FUKURA. The curve of a Japanese blade, or of the yakiba, near the point. *Fukura-kaku*, sharply curved — *fukura-sugu*, nearly straight.

were worn as light armor or under ceremonial dress. The name means "bag-shaped." Fig. 297.

FUKUROKATA-KOJIRI. "A kojiri of a simple form and longer than it is wide." (Weber I, 441). A kojiri in the form of a bag or sack.

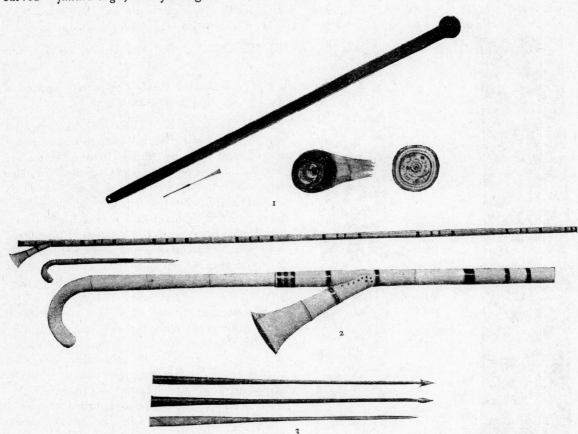

FIGURE 295. *Fukidake. 1. The old form. Made of two grooved pieces of wood fastened together and wound with several layers of paper. It is very light though 9 feet 2.5 inches long. From a Japanese drawing. 2. The later form, with the breech separate. Total length 6 feet 8.75 inches, of which the tube proper is 5 feet 11 inches. It is made of yellow cane with red and black painted bands. The total length of the breech plug is 15 inches of which 9.75 inches projects beyond the tube, and 5.25 inches at the opposite end is of whalebone and is simply to push the dart beyond the opening of the mouthpiece. The mouthpiece is 5 inches long. 3. The breech plug in place and three darts to a larger scale. Peabody Museum, Salem.*

FUKURIN. A tsuba decorated with the repetition of some object such as a crest.

An ornamental border, Japan.

FUKURO ABUMI. "Bag-shaped" stirrups, Japan. Stirrups with a sharp ridge across the front.

FUKURO-GOTE. Sleeves of silk or damask with a few small plates of iron near the wrist. They

FULMINATES. Fulminate of mercury, now universally used as a means of igniting gunpowder, was discovered by Howard in 1800. Loose percussion powder for priming was patented by the Rev. A. Forsyth in 1807. The percussion cap was invented by Colonel Peter Hawker in 1818, and the percussion musket appeared in 1848. (Hime 125).

FUMBARI. The part of a Japanese blade nearest the hilt.

FUNDA. The Etruscan sling. (Burton Sword 245).

FURIZUMBAI, BUNYARI. A sling, Japan.

FURSI. See Ancus.

FUSCINA. The trident of the Roman gladiators. (Burton Sword 253).

FIGURE 296. *Fukigayeshi. 1. Helmet without fukigayeshi, none of the lames of the neck guard being turned back. 2. The fukigayeshi are formed by prolonging the ends of the maye-zashi and turning them upwards. 3. The fukigayeshi are formed by turning back only the top lame of the neck guard. This is the most common form. 4. All five lames of the neck guard are turned back to make the fukigayeshi.*

FURIBO. A Japanese fighting club about four feet long and shod with iron. Fig. 298.

In the Peabody Museum, Salem, there is one with a long spiked head which is the scabbard of a straight-bladed sword. The handle is the hilt of the sword which is held in the scabbard by a spring catch.

FUSEE. See Grip.

FUSEES. Rockets of the 14th century which were used to set fire to besieged places. (Hewitt II, 280).

FUSHI-NAWA-ME-ODOSHI. Japanese armor laced with light green, white and dark blue cords in diagonal stripes. (Conder 271).

FUSIL, FUSEE. A flintlock gun. (Hewitt III, 271).

FUSILEERS. Infantry of the 17th century and later. They were probably so named because they carried fusils.

FUSTIBAL. A pole sling, that is, a sling mounted on the end of a pole. It was used by the Romans

as much as six and three feet in diameter. (Hoyt 409).

GADA. A mace, Rajput. (Tod II, 570).

A club of the Javan gods. It is straight, with four sets of three disks each, projecting from it. The parts between the disks are spherical. (Raffles I, plate p. 296/297).

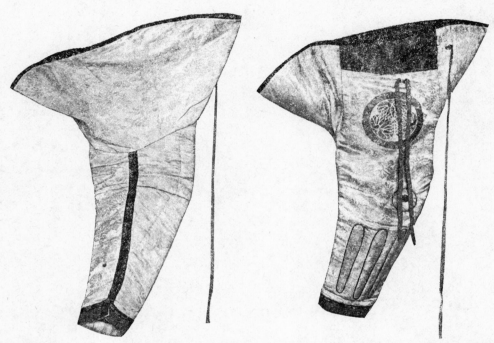

FIGURE 297. *Fukuro-Gote. Sleeves of light blue damask bound with printed leather and with a piece of velvet of a darker blue at the top. Each has a Tokugawa crest printed in gold. There are three iron splints and a round plate at the elbow quilted in.*

who called it *fustibulus*. This is undoubtedly the origin of the name, and it is not, as has been suggested, a compound of the Latin *fustis*, a staff, and the Greek *ballo*, to throw. (Burton Sword 19).

FUTA-SUJI-HI. A double groove in a Japanese blade.

FUTOMATA-YARI. A spear with a forked head, Japan.

G

GABION. A cylinder woven of twigs and filled with dirt to be used for making fortifications. Most of them were about three feet high, but some were

GADLINGS, GADS. Knobs and spikes on the backs and knuckles of gauntlets. They are characteristic of the armor worn in the last half of the 14th century. (ffoulkes 39). See Gauntlets.

GAGNAL. A cannon carried by an elephant, India. (Egerton p. 152).

GAGNE-PAIN, GAIN-PAIN, WIN-BREAD. A weapon, usually a sword, by which a soldier gained his bread, 14th and 15th century. (Hewitt II, 253).

Planche says that this name was sometimes applied to a small gauntlet in the 15th century, p. 195.

GAGONG. A skin jacket worn by the Sea Dyaks as a war coat. (Ling Roth II, 129).

GAKI, KENDO, KENJUTSU. Fencing, the art of fencing, Japan.

GAKIDO. Japan, a back and breast.

GALRAKI. An axe, Veddah, Ceylon. "The axe is the weapon with which they (the Veddahs) protect themselves against bears and other wild ani-

FIGURE 298. *Furibo. Club 3 feet 6.5 inches long, strapped and bound with iron.*

GAKU-NO-ITA. A plate, or collection of scales, on a Japanese kote to protect the muscles of the upper arm. (Conder 273).

GAKU-SODE. See Namban-Sode.

GALAH. The straight part of a kris scabbard, Java.

GALLOPER. A piece of ordnance of small caliber —one light enough to be galloped with. (Hoyt 410).

mals and they never travel without it. The head is of iron, and is not of their own manufacture." (Hiller & Furnace 35).

GAMA ISHIME. A method of decorating the metal of the background of Japanese sword mountings that is considered to resemble the skin of a toad. (Joly, Int. 35).

GAMBESON. See Aketon.

FIGURE 299. *Garuda kris hilts. The variation from purely conventional forms to those that are recognizably birdlike. Nos. 2, 3, 4 and 6 are of ivory, the others of wood.*

GANDJA. The top piece of a kris blade, Java.

GA-NE-U-GA-O-DUS-HA. The deer horn club of the Iroquois. It ended in a point about four inches long. (Burton Sword 28).

GANJING. A spindle-shaped iron club formerly used in Java. (Raffles I, 296 and plate p. 296/297).

GANTELOPE. A military punishment. It was carried out in two ways; in the first, called running

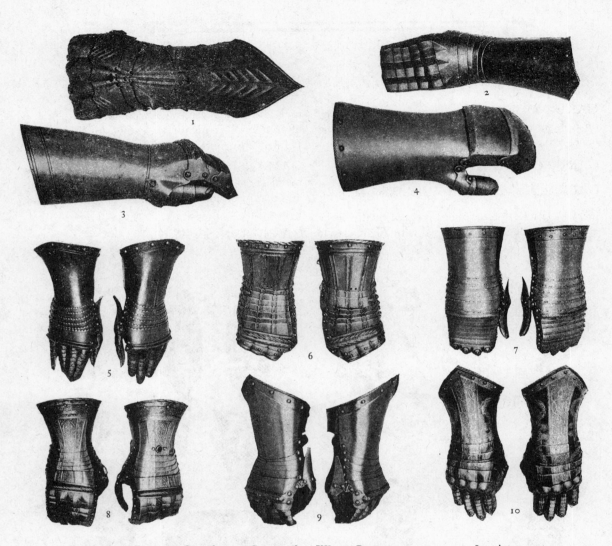

FIGURE 300. *European Gauntlets.* 1. *German, late XV.* 2. *German, 1530-1540.* 3. *Jousting gauntlet, late XVI.* 4. *German jousting gauntlet, early XVI.* 5. *French, late XVI.* 6. *German, 1530. Made for the Emperor Charles V.* 7. *German, middle of the XVI.* 8. *German, XVI. Made for Philip II of Spain by Wolf of Landshut.* 9. *German, second half of the XVI.* 10. *English, 1610. Made for Henry, Prince of Wales, by William Pickering. Metropolitan Museum. Not to scale.*

GANGA-JAMNI. Koft (false damascening) of the Punjab with both gold and silver. It is so called because the two metals are considered to resemble the mingling of the dark waters of the Jamna with the muddy stream of the Ganges. (Hendley 9).

the gantelope, the regiment formed up six deep, and the ranks opened and faced inwards, each man being furnished with a switch. The offender, naked to the waist, was led through the ranks, preceded by a sergeant, the point of whose reversed halbard was presented to his breast to prevent his running too fast. As he passed each soldier gave him a blow with his switch. In the other method the offender was tied to crossed halbards and the regiment marched past, each man giving him a blow with a cat. (Grose II, 107).

GANTSUBUSHI. See Metsubushi.

GARDANI. A crinet, armor for a horse's neck, India. It is much like the European. (Egerton p. 22).

GARDE DE BRAS. Armor for the arm. See Brassard.

GARDE DE CUISSES. Armor for the thighs. See Cuisses.

GARDE DE QUEUE. See Tail Guard.

GARDE DE REINS, GARDE REIN. A guard of plate for the loins. See Culet.

GARGAZ, GARS. A mace, India. Apparently a class name.

A mace with six to ten blades and usually a basket hilt. (Wallace Orient).

A mace with a spiked head and a guarded hilt. (Wallace Orient).

GARSOE KATAR. A katar with curved and elaborately moulded side and handlebars, Sind. (Egerton 727). 11, fig. 434.

GARUDA. The eagle, the doorkeeper of Vishnu. In some one of many conventional forms it is a common hilt on many Malayan krisses. In the majority of cases it would be difficult to recognize it as an eagle if an almost unbroken series of variations did not exist. The "kingfisher" hilts are Garudas. Fig. 299.

GARVO. A spear with a long, narrow, losenge-shaped head, India. (Tower 384, 385, 386, p. 4).

GASTRAPHETEN. A Roman engine on the principle of the crossbow. It received its name because "the bow was bent by the action of pushing with the belly." (Grose I, 389).

GATTUS. See Cat.

GAUDICHET. A kind of armor of uncertain character. (Fairholt 504).

GAUNTLETS. Armor for the hands. Gauntlets as separate pieces of armor first made their appearance about the beginning of the 14th century; previous to this the hands had either been bare or were covered by the long sleeves of the hauberk. The latter practice persisted in India as long as armor was worn. The first gauntlets were leather gloves covered with mail or leather scales. By the middle of the century the back of the hand and wrist were covered by a single plate, and the fingers by scales fastened to the glove. A little later the plates protecting the fingers were articulated to the hand plate and the gauntlet assumed essentially the form that persisted with slight modifications as long as they were worn. Frequently the upper edges of the cuffs were decorated with bands of brass embossed or engraved. In the latter part of the 14th century the knuckles were armed with points or knobs called gadlings. These sometimes took the form of animals, as on the gauntlets of the Black Prince. Towards the end of the century the finger plates were often modeled to represent the nails.

Early in the 15th century the fingers were covered with broad fluted plates articulated to the main plate, and the cuffs were long and more pointed. In the latter part of the century the gauntlets were elaborately fluted, with long pointed cuffs, separate fingers and gadlings. During the greater part of the 15th century mitten gauntlets were more used than those with separate fingers. Fig. 300.

For the tournament special gauntlets were worn. That for the left hand, the bridle gauntlet, was a very large and heavy mitten, while that for the right either had fingers or was made with very long finger plates that overlapped the wrist plate and could be fastened to it by a catch, thus securely locking the sword, or other weapon, in the hand. See Locking Gauntlet.

By the end of the 16th century gauntlets had practically been abandoned for war. In the early 17th century a special form of gauntlet was occasionally used for duelling. See Fencing Gauntlet.

In the near East and India the gauntlets were usually attached to the arm guards. See Bazu Band, fig. 140. They were of mail, padded cloth decorated with gilt studs or, more rarely, of overlapping scales. If separate gauntlets were worn they were almost always of mail, fig. 301. In Japan gauntlets of small plates of steel or leather were usually fastened to the arm guards. See Kote, fig.

475. They only covered the thumb and the back of the hand. Separate gauntlets of mail or articulated plates were occasionally, but very rarely, worn. Fig. 301.

GAUNTLET SWORD. The Mahratta pata, the hilt of which is a gauntlet. See Pata.

GENBET. A coarse cloth used as armor by the Subanuns of Mindanao. (Christie 97).

GENDAWA. A bow, Java. The bow was formerly much used in Java, but by the end of the 17th century it had been abandoned except for state occasions. The Javan bow is made of a single piece

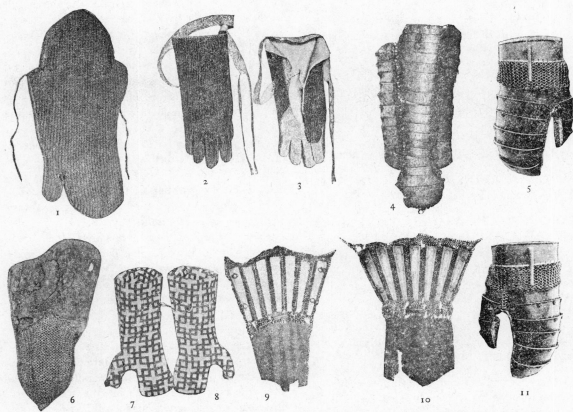

FIGURE 301. *Oriental Gauntlets.* 1. *India, late 18th century. Elbow gauntlet of bar-link mail on padded cloth.* 2, 3. *Japanese, 18th century. Mail lacquered a brilliant black on printed leather.* 4. *Turkish, 15th-16th century. Arm guard and gauntlet of small plates and mail.* 5, 11. *Japanese, 19th century. Very unusual form of plate and mail gauntlets.* 6. *Turkish, 17th century. Mail on leather.* 7, 8. *Japanese brigandine. Printed cloth lined with small pieces of hard leather.* 9, 10. *Indo-Persian, 18th century. Steel wrist plates inlaid with gold. Brass and iron mail gloves.*

GAVELOCK, GAVELOCE. A weapon of the 13th century variously described as a javelin and a double-bladed axe. (Planche 201).

GEE-JEE. See Gid-Jee.

GELDE, GELDON. Foot soldiers of the 12th century. (Hewitt I, 151).

GEMBI. The guard of a sword, basket guard, Japan. A modern term as none of the old swords had finger guards.

of wood with a very large handle in the middle and long horn tips. The length is usually about four feet. (Raffles I, 296, and II, p. 296/297). Fig. 302.

GENETAIRES. Hewitt says that they were light cavalry of the middle of the 16th century. Planche calls them javelins of Spanish origin. (Hewitt II, 28; III, 588; Planche 312).

GENOUILLIERE. See Knee Cop.

GENTLE. A peregrine falcon that has been caught

after it had left the nest but before it had begun to migrate.

GER, GYR, JER. At present this name is confined by ornithologists to the Norway falcon, *falco gerfalco*, but the old falconers used it for all of the larger species of the genus *falco*.

nalis) warped by heat so as to curve in both directions. The handle is a separate piece of wood inserted in holes in the shield while it is still green. It is roughly decorated with grooved lines, usually filled in with white and red. It is used as a protection against spears. (Vic. Mus. 15).

FIGURE 302. *Gendawa. Self bow 4 feet long with horn tips and a very large wooden handle. Arrows 27 inches long with conical heads and long nocks carved from the solid.*

GERRHES. Shields carried by the early Persians. They were rhomboidal and made of wicker work. (Boutell 51).

GESA. See Guisarme.

GHA. A saddle, Western Tibet. (Ramsay-Western).

GHASHIYA. A saddle cloth, Bokhara. It was of the usual Central Asian type, a square with openings for the horn and cantle of the saddle. Unlike the European saddle cloth it is put *over* the saddle. It is woven like the rugs of the country. (Moser XLI).

GHOLAIL. See Gulail.

GHOST DAGGER. See Phurbu.

G'HUG'HWAH. A mail coat and hood in one piece, India, 16th century. (Egerton p. 23).

GHULEL. See Gulail.

GHURCHARH'AS, GHURCHARKHAS. Armored cavalry carrying muskets in the Sikh army under Ranjit Singh in the early 19th century. (Egerton p. 128).

GIAM, KEREM, KARAGARM, BAMAROOK. A type of Australian shield. The third name is used on the Lower Murray River, and the fourth near Lake Tyers. It is from thirty-six to forty inches long and about ten wide in the middle, tapering in a curve to points at the ends. It is made of a light slab of gum tree bark (Eucalyptus Vimi-

GIANDONATO. An Italian sword maker of the 16th century. He is believed to have been a brother of Andrea Ferrara. (Campbell 44).

GIBET. Believed to have been a kind of mace of the 12th century. (Hewitt I, 153).

GID-JEE, GEE-JEE, BORRAL. A West Australian spear with a row of stone chips set in gum on one side of the head. (Brough Smyth I, 336).

GIG, GIGUE. A sling for a shield, middle ages.

GI-GHET. A bow string, Subanuns of Mindanao. (Christie 108).

GIN. Silver, Japan.

GIN-SAME. Silver plates covering the sides of a Japanese hilt instead of the usual shark skin. They are embossed to imitate the latter. Fig. 303.

FIGURE 303. *Gin Same. Two silver plates embossed to imitate shark skin.*

GIPON. See Jupon.

GIRTH. The band, or strap, holding a saddle in place.

 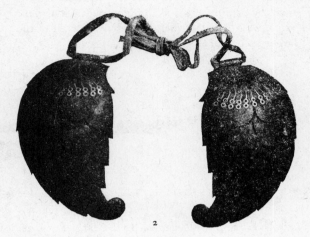

FIGURE 304. *Giyo-Yo-Ita.* 1. *Mail.* 2. *Scales, 18th century. Metropolitan Museum. Not to scale.*

GISARME. See Guisarme.

GIYO-YO-ITA. Small leaf-shaped plates worn as armpit guards with the later Japanese armor. The name is derived from a Chinese word meaning the leaf of the *icho* tree, which these plates resemble in shape. This form was worn by officers of inferior rank to those who wore the *sen-dan-no-ita* and *hato-wo-no-ita.* (Conder 269). Fig. 304.

GIZZIN. An Assyrian weapon of an unknown kind. (Burton Sword 204).

GLAIVE, COUSE. A broad-bladed pole arm in which the edge curves backwards near the point, 12th and 13th centuries. (ffoulkes 104). The couteau de breche is also sometimes called a couse. Similar weapons were common in China at a much later date.

GLANCING KNOBS, BOSSOIRS, PEZON-ERAS. Large bosses on the poitrel of a horse to deflect lance thrusts. In the 17th century, in the decadence of armor, they were often embossed with animal's heads, thus completely defeating their original purpose. (ffoulkes 90). 1, fig. 635.

GLIZADE, COULE. A movement in which the sword is thrust along that of an adversary with a sliding motion.

GOAT'S FOOT, HIND'S FOOT, PIED DE BICHE. A system of articulated levers by which

the lighter crossbows were drawn, fig. 305. Sometimes they were permanently fastened to the crossbows.

GODBERTUM. A hauberk, 13th century. (Hewitt I, 292).

GODDARA. A Perso-Turkish sabre. (Wallace Orient).

GODENDA, GODENDAG, GODENDAC. A Flemish halbard of the 12th century. (ffoulkes 103, Planche 212).

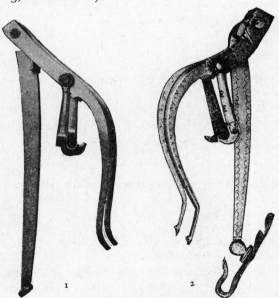

FIGURE 305. *Goat's Foot Levers.* 1. *Italian, first half of the 16th century.* 2. *German, early 16th century. Metropolitan Museum. Not to scale.*

GODHA. A leather bracer worn by Hindu bowmen. (Egerton p. 114).

GOKO. A vajra of three prongs. Fig. 831.

GOKYU. A strong bow, Japan.

GOLAIL. See Gulail.

on the back, nearly square next the hilt with a highly convex cutting edge. It is used in nearly all of the Malayan countries and there are great variations in size and in the shapes of the hilts and scabbards. The blades are from six inches to a couple of feet in length. Fig. 306.

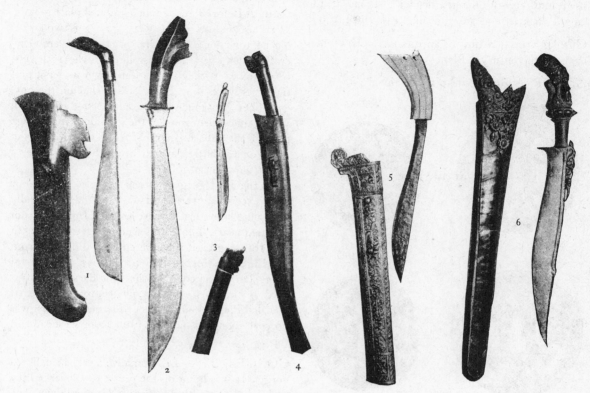

FIGURE 306. *Goloks. 1. Blade 12.75 inches long, horn hilt. Unusual wooden scabbard. 2. Bagobo, Mindanao. Wood hilt set in cast brass. 3. Blade 6.125 inches long, ivory hilt, wood scabbard. 4. Blade 12 inches long, rough wooden hilt and scabbard. 5. Sumatra. Blade 10.5 inches long, ivory hilt, embossed silver scabbard. 6. Bali. Blade 12.75 inches long with a brass ornament on the back. Hilt a bronze raksha set with white stones. The upper part of the scabbard is carved and painted red, the lower is covered with tortoise shell, and the back is covered with brass.*

GOLONG. See Golok.

GOLIAH. A heavy, slightly curved, Central Indian sword of the 18th century. It is said to have been used by men of rank. (Egerton p. 123).

GOLIO, GOLIYO. See Danisko.

GOLO. A Bongo spear having a barbed head with an additional pair of very long barbs below the head. (Schweinfurth I, 280).

GOLOK, GOLANG, BENDO. A favorite Malay jungle knife, or chopper, that is also used in war. The golok has a heavy, single-edged blade, straight

GOMOKU ZOGAN. (Dirt inlay). This name is given to the decoration of tsuba and other Japanese sword fittings, the whole surface of which is covered with scraps of copper and brass wire brazed on iron, apparently without definite arrangement. It is said to represent pine needles and branches floating on a mountain lake. Some have small crests of the Matsudaira family. These are usually from Kaga. Other crests are also used. (Joly, Hawkshaw 10; Weber I, 223). Fig. 307.

GONFANO, GUNFANTO. A very early form of standard borne near the person of the commander-in-chief. It was fixed in a frame made to turn like a ship's vane. That of William the Conqueror, as depicted in the Bayeux tapestry, has three tails, and was charged with a golden cross on a white ground with a blue border. (Macgeorge 28).

In the 12th century the name seems to have been used indifferently for the leader's standard, the knight's banner and the lance flag. (Hewitt I, 166).

GONJO. Body armor of an unknown kind worn in the 14th century. (Planche 213).

GONNE. A gun. See also Pistol Shield.

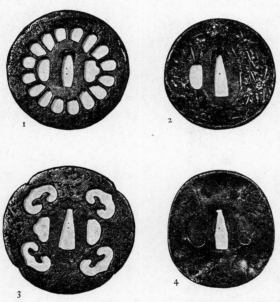

FIGURE 307. *Gomoku Zogan.* 1. *Tsuba decorated with brass wires and crests.* 2. *Decorated with a pattern called "leaves of the lacquer tree."* 3. *Pierced and decorated with wires only.* 4. *Solid, decorated with wires and crests.*

GONOME, GONOME NANAKO. Nanako in which the grains are arranged in diagonal lines to form lozenges, in the center of each of which there is a grain, or groups of five grains forming lozenges. It is said to have been invented by Muneta Matabei about 1560. (Joly Int. 34).

GO-NOME. See Yakiba.

GO-NOME ISHIME. A variety of ishime.

GOOLMARY. A long, heavy, oval shield with a convex front and a nearly flat back, with the handle carved from the solid. A typical one measures twenty inches long, seven inches wide and weighs

thirty-six ounces. The front is covered with patterns in incised lines, Queensland. (Brough Smyth I, 334). Fig. 771.

GORGET, COLLETIN. Armor for the neck. The earliest gorgets of which we have definite knowledge were made of mail and worn in the 15th century. Before these were abandoned plate gorgets were also in use. They were made of two pieces locked together around the neck, and were generally worn over the breastplate. In the 16th century, however, they were often worn under it and the arms were hung from locking pins on the gorget. They vary much in size, some being very small, while others cover most of the shoulders and a large part of the breast. In the 17th century a gorget worn over a buff coat was often the only piece of armor worn. Fig. 308.

In the East gorgets as separate pieces of armor were excessively rare, and when found are usually of mail. Plate gorgets were used in India, but not in recent years. The Turks wore gorgets in the 15th and 16th centuries that are entirely different from the European forms, fig. 309. They consisted of long plates that covered the shoulders and upper part of the back, with a projecting flange that guarded the back and sides of the neck. There was no corresponding piece in front as in western Europe.

GORGET PLATE. A small plate shaped like a gorget. It was hung on the breast by officers in the middle of the 18th century; and is still worn by Danish officers. It is the last remnant of the complete armor of earlier times. (Dean Hdbk. 99). Fig. 310.

GOROBEL. A celebrated Kioto tsuba maker of the middle of the 18th century. His family name is unknown, but he is commonly called Daimonjiya. He made pierced guards which were known as *Daigoro tsuba,* the name being a combination of the first syllables of each of his names. (Hara 12).

GOSENS. See Bishanswamis.

GOTO. The most celebrated family or guild of makers of sword mountings in Japan. The family name was Goto Shirobei, the latter being the *tsusho,* or *torino,* the name by which the artist family was known to the public, and which served as a trade name.

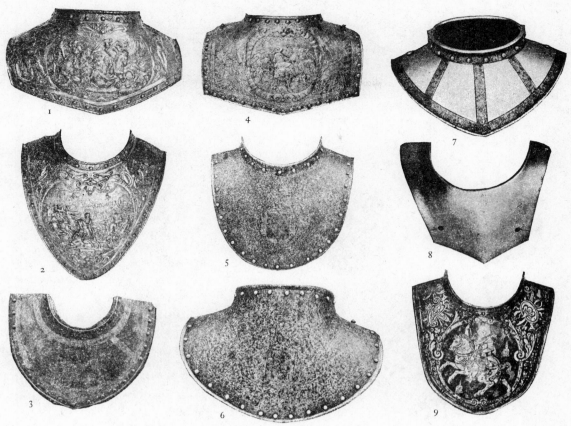

FIGURE 308. *European Gorgets. 1, 2. Back and front of a gorget of Italian workmanship with the arms of the Guiata family of Frankfort. 3. Venetian, 1650, front. 4. English, about 1610, back. 5, 6. Back and front of the gorget of the Guard of Louis XIII of France. Early 17th century. 7. French, early 17th century. 8. Jousting gorget, 16th century. 9. French, 1620. Metropolitan Museum. Not to scale.*

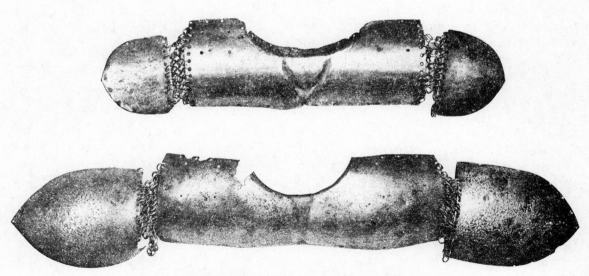

FIGURE 309. *Turkish Gorgets, 16th-17th century.*

The first of the line was called Yujo, 1450-1512. In all there were sixteen masters in the direct line and a very large number of pupils. The first eight masters rarely signed their work, but in the 17th century their successors began the process of identifying it and inscribing on it the maker's name followed by their own.

FIGURE 310. *Gorget Plate, English, 18th century. Metropolitan Museum.*

The last celebrated Goto, though not of the direct line, was Ichijo, 1791-1876. Throughout the more than four hundred years of its existence, the family preserved with recognizable accuracy the style and methods originated by the founder in the 15th century; for this reason it has received the name of *iyebori*, or "family chasing."

They worked mainly for the court and nobles and frequently made sets of mountings which were given as presents by the daimio to the Shogun and to each other. They had a wide range of subjects but were noted for their dragons, shishi and scenes from the civil wars. As a rule the figures are of gold in high relief on shakudo, usually with a nanako ground. In the 17th century much of the Goto work was entirely of gold. Jujo (Mitsutada), 1695-1742, occasionally inlaid his work with coral and semi-precious stones. The work of this family has always been very highly valued in Japan and very little of the best of it has been allowed to leave the country.

The following is a list of the Goto masters in the direct line:

1.	Yujo	1440-1512	(Masaoku)
2.	Sojo	1461-1538	(Takemitsu)
3.	Joshin	1512-1562	(Yoshihisa)
4.	Kojo	1529-1620	(Mitsuiye)
5.	Tokujo	1550-1631	(Mitsutsugu)
6.	Yeijo	1577-1617	(Masamitsu)
7.	Kenjo	1586-1663	(Masatsugu)
8.	Sokujo	1600-1631	(Mitsushige)
9.	Teijo	1603-1673	(Mitsumasa)
10.	Renjo	1627-1708	(Mitsutomo)
11.	Tsujo	1663-1721	(Mitsunaga)
12.	Jujo	1695-1742	(Mitsutada)
13.	Yenjo	1721-1784	(Mitsutaka)
14.	Keijo	1751-1804	(Mitsumori)
15.	Shinjo	1783-1834	(Mitsuyoshi)
16.	Hojo	1816-1856	(Mitsuaki)

While their work as a whole is uneven in design, their technique is always good and nearly all of the great makers of sword fittings were, at one time or another, pupils of some of the masters, or at least of someone taught by them. The influence of this family on the art of decorative metal working in Japan was probably the principal factor in shaping its course and determining its aim.

GOUSSETS, GAUCHETS. See Gussets.

GOWDALIE. Fishing spears with three sharp points of hard wood lashed to a shaft so that they would spread apart, Victoria. (Brough Smyth I, 306).

GO YAKU. Gunpowder, Japan.

GOZAME ISHIME. A surface resembling a straw mat. It is used as a background on Japanese sword mountings. (Joly Int. 35).

GOZUME. The reserve of an army, Japan.

GRADIS AL PERFIL. In the early, and very artificial, Spanish system of fencing "Ganados los grados al perfil" was to gain an advantage by successive steps around the adversary. (Castle 72).

GRAFFLE. A hook fastened to the belt by which some of the early crossbows were bent. (Laking Armour III, 140).

GRAISLE. A trumpet used in military signaling. (Hewitt I, 168; III, 311).

GRAND GUARD. A large plate worn over the regular armor in tournaments in the 16th century. It covered the lower part of the face, the left shoulder and sometimes came as low as the waist. In some of the earlier specimens it did not cover the face. (Hewitt III, 647). Fig. 311.

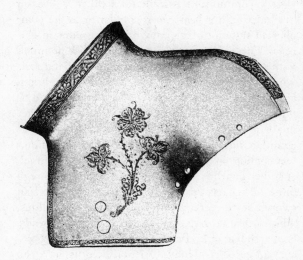

FIGURE 311. *Grand Guard, German, about 1550. Ex. Collection Stevenson and Tschille.*

Some authorities say that pieces of armor of this type should be called volant pieces if they do not cover the face.

GRANGGANG. A wooden spear with a straight, round point, Java. It is also used by the Dyaks for throwing. (Raffles I, plate p. 296/297).

GRAPESHOT. A number of small cast iron balls fitted in a case, or frame, so that it could be fired as a whole from a cannon. They were used until displaced by shrapnel in the middle of the 19th century.

GREAT BASINET. See Basinet.

GREAVES. Armor for the leg below the knee. The Greeks and Romans wore bronze greaves, many of which were beautifully modeled, fig. 31. In Europe they were worn from the 11th to the 17th century. The earliest ones, like the classic forms, covered the front of the leg only, later they usually covered both front and back. Fig. 312.

In the East greaves were rarely worn. In the 15th and 16th centuries the Turks wore greaves made up of a convex plate covering the front of the leg and mail covering the back and foot, fig. 51. In India and Persia greaves made of mixed plate and pourpointerie were used though rarely.

GREEK FIRE, WILD FIRE. This material was known to the Greeks as early as 673. It was probably a very slow burning gunpowder that would not detonate but threw showers of sparks for a considerable time. The terrors of these mixtures was enhanced by the belief that not only they, but the flames they kindled, could not be put out by water. (Hewitt I, 89).

GRENADE. An explosive shell thrown by hand.

GRENADIER. Originally a soldier trained to throw grenades. Later the name was given to picked troops composed of large men. In the early 18th century each infantry regiment had a grenadier company armed with grenades and hatchets. (Hewitt III, 741, 746, 747).

GRENENG. Notches in the end of a gandja (the top piece of a kris blade).

GRIP, FUSEE. The part of a weapon intended to be grasped by the hand.

GRUNEWALT, HANS. Nuremberg, 1440-1503. A celebrated armorer who worked for the emperor Maximilian I, and was the most serious competitor of the Missagalia of Milan. (ffoulkes Armourer 135).

GUADAGNARE DI SPADA. In the Spanish fencing, covering oneself by forcibly engaging the adversary's blade. (Castle 72).

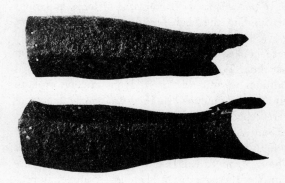

FIGURE 312. *Greaves, English, 14th century. Found in a cave near Bordeaux. They show traces of the original covering of stuff. Metropolitan Museum.*

GUARD. A man, or body of men, engaged in protecting a person or place.

A posture, attitude or condition of defense. In fencing, a position of person and sword and certain correlated motions calculated to prevent injury by an opponent.

The arrangement of parts on a weapon to protect the hand of the user. The three weapons usually so protected are—the lance, sword and knife. The lance guard was used only during the middle ages in Europe. It was a plate surrounding the lance in front of the grip, and was usually conical so as not only to guard the hand but to deflect the adversary's lance. See Vamplate. The guards of swords and knives are similar in design and character, but those of the latter are seldom as complicated as many used on the former. The simplest and earliest is the *cross guard*, composed of one or more bars, called quillons, projecting at right angles to the grip between it and the blade. A modification of this is the use of a plate instead of bars. This is the Japanese guard. See *Tsuba*. The quillons may be straight, curved towards the pommel, or towards the point (recurved). In the plane at right angles to the blade the quillons may be straight or curved in the shape of an S or 8. The *finger guard, knuckle guard, counter guard, bow* or *ward iron* is formed by curving back one, or more, of the quillons to meet the pommel, or by a system of bars connecting the quillons and pommel. In many Indian and some European swords it is a fairly broad plate connecting the plate guard to the pommel. In the case of many broadswords the counter guard completely surrounds the hand and wrist, forming the *basket hilt*. From the 11th to the 17th century the *pas d'ane* was used. It consisted of loops and rings surrounding the blade in advance of the quillons. It was designed to protect the fingers when they were hooked around the quillons as was usual at that time. To make the guard more effective it was common to add *side rings*, loops on one or both sides of the quillons. In the *shell guard* the loops were replaced by plates called shells. Often there was only one of these, which was sometimes large enough to cover and protect the back of the hand. The *cup guard*, as its name implies, was a cup surrounding the base of the blade and completely protecting the hand. It was very popular in the late 16th and early 17th centuries when it was generally used on rapiers. The cups of that time were hemi-spherical and often very large. They were frequently decorated by piercing in elaborate patterns. The *swept hilt* of the same period had a complicated system of bars that "swept" round in graceful curves from guard to pommel. Fig. 617.

In India a plate guard with a broad finger guard is very common; it is sometimes called a "basket hilt" although it bears no resemblance to the complicated system of bars known by that name in Europe. These swords often have large disk pommels with spikes on the top. These are used as hand rests when the weapon is sheathed, and, when fighting, as a supplementary grip to enable more force to be given to a blow. The inside of the guard and finger guard are often padded in these swords. A more common hilt in India has short, straight quillons terminating in knobs and a round, flat pommel. A finger guard is as often absent as present, though some hilts have three. Most Turkish and Persian swords have very light, long, straight quillons, which often terminate in acorns or animal's heads. Some Indian and Persian swords have short recurved quillons. Many Oriental swords have no guards. The guard of the Indian pata is a solid gauntlet that covers the hand and arm almost to the elbow; the grip is at right angles to the line of the blade. In Japan the disk guard is always used on the fighting swords; some of the court swords have different kinds of guards, see Tachi. In China and Central Asia the swords either have very short, heavy quillons or straight-sided cups with the open side towards the blade. The crutch hilt is used in India and Persia as a support. Some are simple crutches, others have combination guards and crutches.

In India maces and axes sometimes have guards exactly like those used on swords.

Almost all of the possible combinations of the different elements of guards have been used at one time or another on swords. The guards of knives are composed of the same elements, but, as already stated, are not usually as complicated. See Burton Sword 124, and Castle 230.

GUDDARA. An Indian sabre with straight quillons, a pistol hilt and a back edged blade that widens towards the point. (Wallace Orient).

GUDO, ORTA. The Tibetan sling. It is made of a square-braided cord with a loop at one end and a broad pocket of woven material in the middle. The end with the loop is shorter than the other. It is woven of a mixture of wool and hair, and is used as a whip when driving sheep or cattle. The Tibetan tent dwellers, both men and women, always carry one and are very expert in its use. Fig. 313.

FIGURE 313. *Gudo. Tibetan sling woven of hair and wool. Length 4 feet 11 inches.*

GUIDON. It was described as follows in the 17th century: "The guidon is the first colors that any commander of horse can flie in the field; this guidon is of damask fringed, and may be charged with a crest of him that is the owner thereof, or with other device at his pleasure. It is of proportion three foot at the least deepe in the top, next the staffe, and upon the staffe, and so down narrower and narrower to the bottom where the end is sharpe, but with a slit divided into two peaks a foot deepe; the whole guidon is six foot longe, and should be upon a lance staffe." At the present time it is a small forked guide flag carried by cavalry. The officer who carries this flag is also called a guidon. (Hewitt III, 730).

GUIGE. See Gig.

GUISARME, GESA, GISARME, GYSARME, JASARME. A very popular pole arm used from the 11th to the 15th century, but regarding which we have very little accurate information. It has variously been described as a partizan, a double axe and a glaive. "It was probably a variety of bill." (ffoulkes 103). Dr. Dean also calls it a bill. Laking confines the name to "a slender incurved sword blade from the back edge of which a sharp hook issues. This elongated hook runs parallel with the

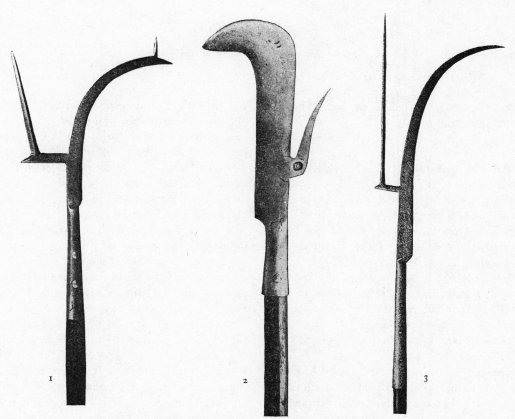

FIGURE 314. *Guisarmes. 1. English, 1450. 2. North Italian, 15th century. 3. English, 1450. Metropolitan Museum. Not to scale.*

back of the blade or diverges from it at an angle."
(Laking Armour III, 115). Sometimes there is an
additional spike near the end of the blade. Fig. 314.

Laking's description seems to be the most probable. It appears to have been a fairly common weapon and the name is not English, nor is the weapon,
while the bill was one of the commonest and most

**GUMBAI, GUNBAI, GUMBAI UCHIWA,
DANSEN.** Gumbai means the disposition of troops.
Uchiwa is a fan made of two pieces of wood or
leather fastened together on either side of a straight
handle. The gumbai uchiwa is a fan of this type used
by an officer when marshalling troops in old Japan.
See Uchiwa.

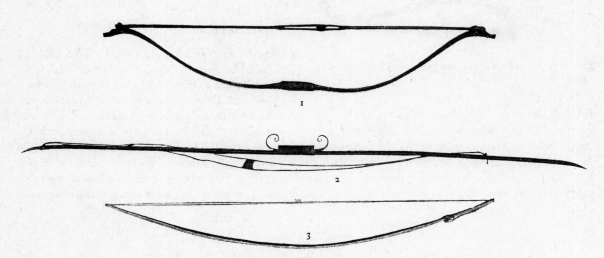

FIGURE 315. *Pellet Bows. 1. China. Painted bow 3 feet 5 inches long with a string of wood and cord.
2. Gulail, Central India. Bow of dark brown bamboo 5 feet 2 inches long. Steel tips and handle inlaid with silver. Sinew strings. 3. Gulail, Coorg. Bamboo bow 3 feet 7 inches long with one spreader.*

generally used weapons in England long before the
guisarme is mentioned.

GULABA. See Tikara.

GULAIL, GOLAIL, GHULEL, GULEL. The
Indian pellet bow. It is usually a self bow of bamboo with a double string held apart by a stretcher
at one end, and with a pocket in the middle for the
missile. The proper missile is a ball of baked clay,
but stones and other small objects are often used.
Forbes says, p. 26: "I have myself killed a squirrel
at eighty yards with one of these primitive weapons,
and in the hands of an expert marksman they are
indeed dangerous and even deadly." It is a favorite
weapon with most of the aboriginal tribes of India,
Burma and Nepal. (Egerton 304, 305, 386, 599,
600). Fig. 315.

At the instant of firing the bow must be moved
to the left or the missile will hit the thumb with
painful results. Those who have used them say that
each bow has its individual peculiarities which must
be learned before accurate shooting is possible.

GUN. The natural chronological classification of
guns is by the method of ignition — hand guns —
matchlocks — wheel locks — flintlocks — detonators —
percussion — and finally breechloaders. The entire
series has been used in Europe, but in the East
wheel locks were never used, and in many places
flintlocks were practically unknown. In Europe the
names given to different kinds of guns seldom had
any relation to the methods of ignition; in fact the
same name was often used after the method of ignition had been entirely changed.

In Europe arquebus or harquebus was one of the
earliest names. At first it meant gun, but later it
appears to have been confined to the lighter and
better guns used for sport by the wealthier classes.
The musquet became the military arm; originally
it was a smooth bored gun with a four foot barrel
and shooting round balls weighing twelve to the
pound. This name continued in use for whatever
type of gun was the standard military arm until the
adoption of rifles. The caliver was also used for certain kinds of troops; it was lighter than the mus-

quet but of larger bore. The currier is mentioned as a military arm but very little is known about it except that it was larger than the musquet. The haquebut was a very light gun, not much larger than some of the early pistols. The petronel was still smaller; it had a peculiarly curved stock and was fired from the breast. The dragon and carbine were short guns carried by cavalry. These guns have all been described under their proper names.

Along the south shore of the Mediterranean the

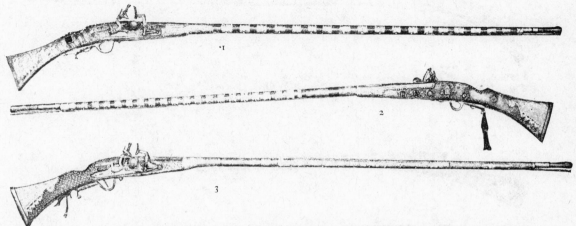

FIGURE 316. *Kabyle Guns.* 1. *Stock and barrel nearly covered with silver, partly decorated with niello and partly with enamel. Nineteen wire capucines. Length 5 feet 3.75 inches.* 2. *Stock and barrel almost covered with silver partly decorated in niello. Two brass, 2 silver and 19 wire capucines.* 3. *Stock and barrel nearly covered with silver decorated with niello. The stock is also ornamented with silver nails. Four silver and 2 iron capucines.*

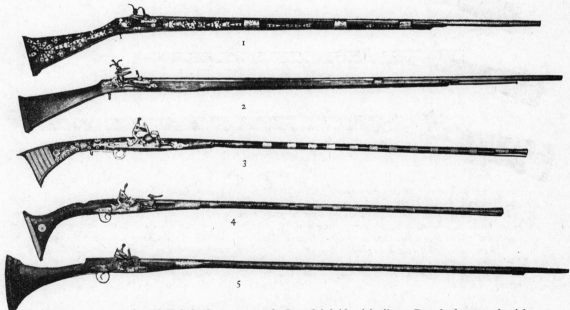

FIGURE 317. *Arab and Kabyle Guns.* 1. *Arab. Barrel inlaid with silver. Dog lock covered with embossed brass. Stock inlaid with colored bone, brass capucines. Length 5 feet 6 inches.* 2. *Arab. Plain stock and barrel, dog lock.* 3. *Kabyle. Plain barrel. Stock with ivory and silver inlaying. Three iron, 1 brass, and 12 silver capucines. Length 5 feet 6 inches.* 4. *Kabyle. Plain barrel, stock inlaid with ivory and silver. Two iron, 3 brass and 6 silver capucines. Length 5 feet 2 inches.* 5. *Kabyle. Plain stock and barrel. One iron, 28 engraved brass capucines. Length 6 feet 0.5 inches.*

Kabyles used very long guns with short, deep stocks and very large snaphaan locks. Three types of stock are used, figs. 316, 317. They differ considerably only make them in the cities in the interior of Sous. The workmen are very numerous. They also make gun-barrels, pistols, gun-locks, and all such things.

FIGURE 318. *Sardinian Gun. The stock is covered with pierced steel work. The lock is a typical Turkish miquelet, but has a trigger guard. Length 4 feet 7 inches.*

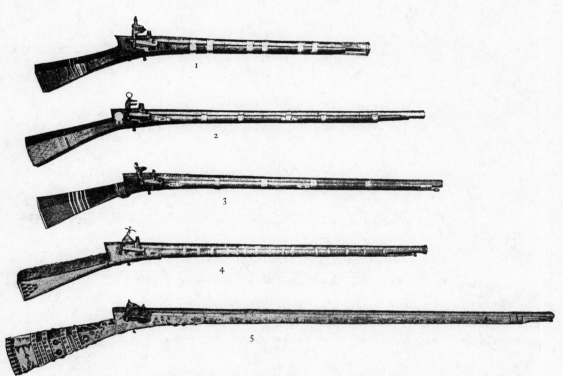

FIGURE 319. *Turkish and Persian Guns. 1. Persian rifle. Stock inlaid with brass and ivory. Barrel and lock inlaid with silver. Length 3 feet 1.75 inches. 2. Persian rifle. Damascus barrel inlaid with gold and silver. Miquelet lock inlaid like the barrel. Stock inlaid with ivory and brass. 3. Persian rifle. Lock and blued octagon barrel inlaid with chased silver. Stock of black wood inlaid with white and green ivory and brass. Length 3 feet 10.5 inches. 4. Turkish rifle. Damascus barrel inlaid with gold. Stock entirely covered with embossed silver set with coral. 5. Turkish, smooth bore. Very fine damascus barrel, round with a flat rib. Ivory stock inlaid with pearl and brass, and mounted with engraved silver set with colored stones. Miquelet lock inlaid with gold. Length 5 feet 7.5 inches.*

in shape but all are much decorated with ivory and bone inlays, and plates, straps and rosettes of silver and brass. Guns have been made in this region from quite early times—"More words about guns. They As for sabres and poniards, they are made by the Arab armorers. They make powder in every province, but only in small quantities." (Moorish Lit. 166).

The ordinary Arab gun with a triangular stock, long barrel, and the Arab variety of dog lock, is also used throughout this region as well as further east, 1, 2, fig. 317. Guns of the Turkish type are also used here.

to the greatest elaboration. This type of gun is used throughout the Turkish Empire, as far east as Persia and occasionally India. Many are of Persian make and these are generally decorated in better taste than the Turkish. Fig. 319.

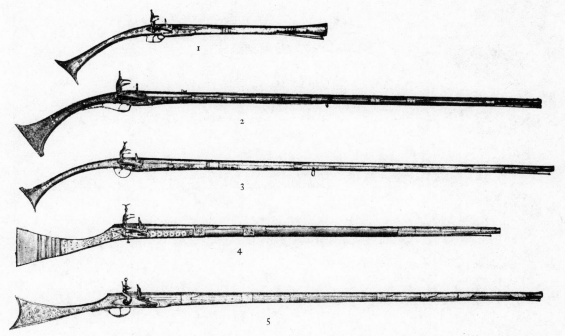

FIGURE 320. *Balkan Guns. 1. Albanian blunderbuss. Half octagon barrel inlaid with brass. Stock steel and brass, engraved. Length 2 feet 8 inches. 2. Albania or Montenegro. Chased brass capucines. Stock with engraved brass mountings and inlaid with pearl. 3. Albania or Montenegro. Chased brass capucines. Stock all iron inlaid with brass and pearl. Length 5 feet 2 inches. 4. Roumelia. The rear end of the stock is made of ivory separated by narrow plates of horn, the remainder is of wood inlaid with pearl. Two narrow, and one wide capucines of chased silver. 5. Said to be the gun of the Albanian palace guard. The entire stock is of a base silver alloy, partly gilded, and chased with a purely French design. Seven engraved silver capucines. Length 5 feet 1 inch.*

In Sardinia and Corsica a decidedly oriental type of gun was used until very recently. They usually had miquelet locks, though other types of flintlock and even wheel locks were used. The stocks were covered with pierced steel work. Fig. 318.

The typical Turkish gun has a thick stock of pentagonal section and a miquelet lock; the very early ones were matchlocks. The barrels vary greatly in size and thickness, some of the smooth bores being very light and thin, and some of the rifles very heavy. The rifles have heavy ogival backsights forged on the barrels, with several peepholes for use at different ranges. They vary in length from three and a half to five feet. They are decorated in many ways and degrees from extreme simplicity

In the Balkans a great variety of guns were used besides those of Turkish and Arab types. The stocks are generally short and light and vary much in shape. The barrels vary as much as the Turkish. Many of the types are confined to very small areas as they were made locally, every province and almost every town having its own gunsmith. Most of these guns have miquelet locks, also of local make, these often have cocks of characteristic shapes, though European locks were frequently used. Figs. 320, 321.

In the Caucasus and western Persia heavy rifles with straight, slim stocks, most frequently of elm root, were the commonest type. The barrels are generally Persian or old European, some being of

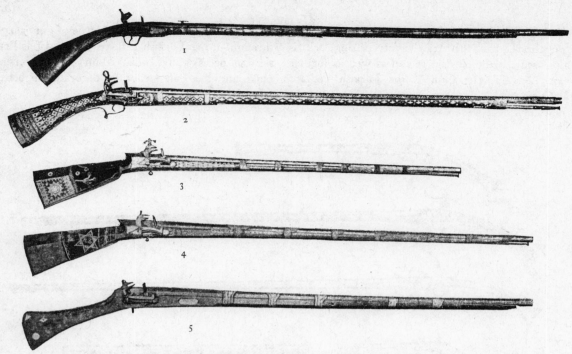

FIGURE 321. 1. *Herzegovinia. Stock entirely covered with engraved brass, seven capucines. Length 5 feet 2 inches. 2. Barrel chased and inlaid with silver and set with stones for its entire length. Miquelet lock with a trigger guard, both inlaid with silver. Stock inlaid with pearl and coral. 3. Turkish. Lock covered with engraved silver. Six silver capucines. Stock inlaid with brass and pearl. Length 4 feet 0.5 inch. 4. Similar to the last but larger. Both have embroidered bands of red velvet around the stock. 5. Italian barrel of the 17th century, inlaid with silver. The stock is of dark wood inlaid with pearl, ivory, colored stones and a vine pattern in wire. Five embossed capucines. Length 4 feet 10 inches.*

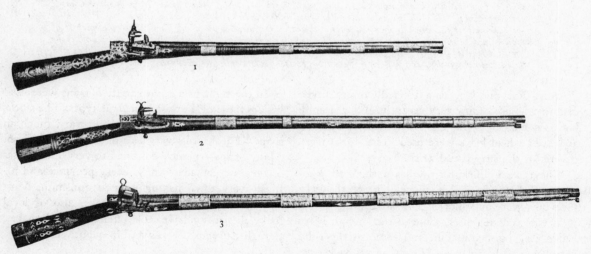

FIGURE 322. *Guns of the Caucasus. 1. Rifle, miquelet lock and damask barrel, both profusely inlaid with gold leaves and scrolls and an Arabic inscription. The bands and scrollwork on the stock are of white metal. Length 3 feet 5 inches. 2. Rifle, damask barrel inlaid with gold; plain miquelet lock. Mountings of white metal. 3. Rifle, plain octagon barrel. Miquelet lock inlaid with gold. Stock inlaid with ivory and brass, ivory butt. The capucines are of white metal decorated in chern.*

the 17th century or even earlier. The locks are of the miquelet type, either of Persian or native make. The latter have peculiar low cocks with very long jaws. The locks and barrels are generally inlaid— those of Persian make very well, the native ones not so well. The stocks are often inlaid with ivory and are almost always strapped with silver decorated in chern. It is not uncommon to find guns from fig. 323. These are sometimes very elaborately mounted. The other type is always plain but well made. They have very peculiar hooked stocks. Fig. 324.

Revolving matchlocks were used. Some are quite simple with short cylinders, 1, fig. 323. Others are much more elaborate with very long chambers, but firing fewer shots (Egerton 546). Guns were also

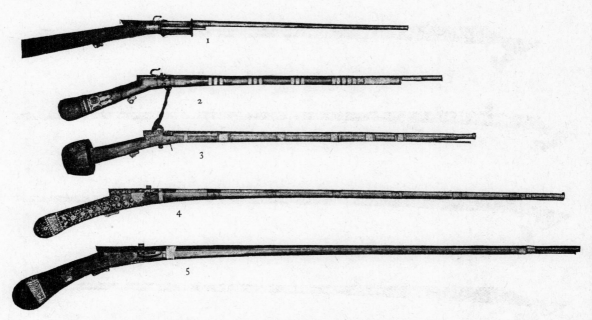

FIGURE 323. *Guns of India. 1. Revolving matchlock, six chambered. Plain stock. Barrel and chambers engraved and inlaid with silver. Length 4 feet 5 inches. 2. Hyderabad Arab. Fifteen silver capucines. Silver scrolls and straps on the stock. 3. Barrel inlaid with gold. One brass, 5 silver and 3 wire capucines. Plates of engraved brass on the stock. The unusual feature is the large block on the butt. Length 4 feet 8 inches. 4. Coorg. Barrel inlaid with gold for its entire length. Stock inlaid with ivory scrolls, gilded brass mounts. 5. Coorg. Plain barrel, two silver capucines and a broad band of embossed silver on the stock. Length 6 feet 5.75 inches.*

this region with beautifully inlaid Persian barrels and almost childish chern work on the stocks. In the Caucasus the stocks are always straight, but similar guns in Persia often have curved stocks like those of Afghan jezails. Figs. 322, 406.

The guns of India are mainly of two types which have been described under Banduk and Toradar. The Arabs of southern India have introduced a special type of matchlock with a rather clumsy, rounded butt, 2, fig. 323. These are generally decorated with many silver bands and ornaments, or even entirely covered with silver. In Coorg two types of gun were used; one with a thin, flat stock with a rounded butt and very long barrels, 4, 5,

made with square barrels and round bores, some even have square bores. See Toradar.

In Ceylon very characteristic guns were made. One type has a curious scroll-shaped stock and a modified form of dog lock, always on the left side of the stock. Some are elaborately decorated with panels of carved ivory or tortoise shell set in the stocks, and silver inlaying in the barrels. They are the only guns found east of Persia that have flint-locks apparently of native make. Fig. 325.

In the Museum of Colombo there are a couple of Sinhalese guns that are quite different. They have very clumsy stocks with a heavy backward projection from the top that looks as though it was intended to rest on top of the shoulder. The entire guns are very roughly made.

Several of the early travelers to Ceylon are very enthusiastic about the guns made there. "De Coute instances the remarkable fact, that whereas on the arrival of Almeyda in 1505, the Sinhalese were ignorant of the use of gunpowder, and as there was not a single firelock in the island, they soon excelled the

matchlocks of the Japanese type were used. The barrels are generally plain, but the locks and mountings are of elaborately chased brass, and the trigger guards are heavier and more ornamental than those used anywhere else. Frequently they have two brass objects, that look like seals, hanging from the lock by chains. These appear to be solely for ornament. Fig. 326.

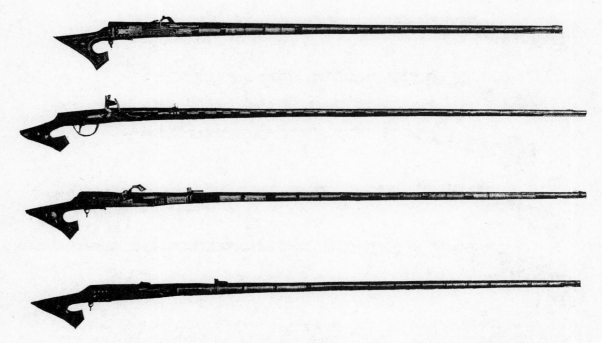

FIGURE 324. *Guns from Coorg. All have brass mountings. The second has been converted to a flintlock by putting on an English lock and trigger guard. South Kensington Museum.*

Portuguese in the manufacture of muskets and before the war was concluded they could bring twenty thousand stand of arms into the field." Faria y Souza says that at the close of the Portuguese dominion the Sinhalese "made the best firelocks in the East." Pyard, a French traveler (1605) expresses unqualified admiration for the Sinhalese workmanship in metal, especially the fabrication and ornamenting of arms, which, he says, were considered the finest in India, and even superior to those of France. Linshoten, the Dutch traveler who visited Ceylon in 1805, says, "the natural born people of *Chingalas*, make the fairest barrels for pieces that may be found in any place, which shine as bright as if they were silver." (Tennent II, 12).

Throughout Malaya short stocked guns with

In Sind and on the Afghan border matchlocks with deep, thin and exceedingly crooked stocks are used, figs. 5, 327. Some of them have very beautiful twist barrels and gold mountings finely enameled. The guns of Afghanistan are described under Jezail.

In Central Asia the guns have straight, slim stocks and match- or flintlocks. They usually have the A-shaped rests riveted to them, fig. 328. The guns of Tibet, which are similar to them, are described under Me-Da.

In Tonking, Annam and thereabouts the guns are intermediate in type between the Chinese and Malayan. Like the latter they have locks of the Japanese type, but the stocks are curved and pistol-shaped like most of the Chinese. They are, however,

FIGURE 325. *Gun, Ceylon. Half octagon barrel inlaid with silver. A panel of pierced ivory is set in each side of the stock in a frame of silver. The lock is of the Arab type and is on the* left *side of the stock. Length about 7 feet. Metropolitan Museum.*
Length about 7 feet. Metropolitan Museum.

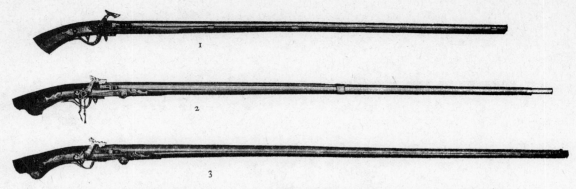

FIGURE 326. *Malayan Guns.* 1. *Plain octagon barrel. Polished black wood stock, lock and mount-ings of heavy chased brass. Length 4 feet 11 inches.* 2. *Similar to the last but with two brass orna-ments hanging from the lock.* 3. *Plain barrel, brass mountings. Length 5 feet 9.5 inches.*

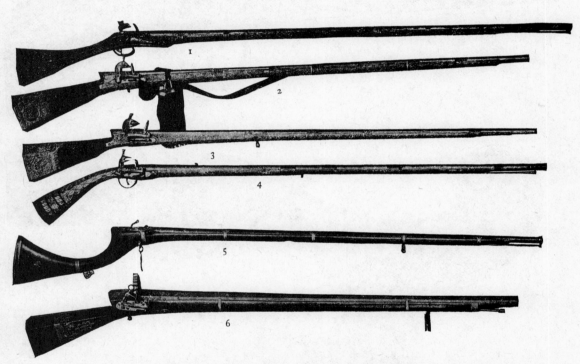

FIGURE 327. *Miscellaneous Guns.* 1. *Turkish, 17th-18th century. Gun of Albanian type. Made either for the Sultan or the commander of the Palace Guard. Smooth bore; barrel covered with worn engraving in high relief. French flintlock engraved and gilded. The flint has a jewel set in the edge. Stock completely covered with embossed and gilded metal covered with pearls except at the part grasped by the left hand when shooting. The rear end of the butt is also set with large pale sapphires and diamonds.* 2. *Turkish, 18th century. Barrel marked Angelo Pedretti. Flintlock partly covered with silver. The stock is completely covered with embossed silver, except where it is covered with red velvet. Red sling and tassels attached. Length 4 feet 10.75 inches.* 3. *Turkish, similar to the last except that the lock is inlaid with gold and the band is of green velvet. It has no sling.* 4. *Herzegovinia. Finely watered barrel. The entire fore end and a band around the rear of the stock of engraved and pierced steel. The rest of the stock back of the lock is inlaid with pearl shell.* 5. *Sind, 18th century. Barrel of finely watered steel, inlaid with gold. All stock mountings of plain silver.* 6. *Persian rifle. Barrel dated 921 A.H. (A.D. 1515) of finely watered steel, inlaid with silver at the breech. The stock of somewhat later date is mounted with finely engraved silver.*

much longer than many of the latter, being held under the arm when fired. They are also much better made than the Chinese. Fig. 329.

The Chinese guns are about the roughest and poorest made. They usually have short pistol stocks, and are often used like a pistol, but are held with both

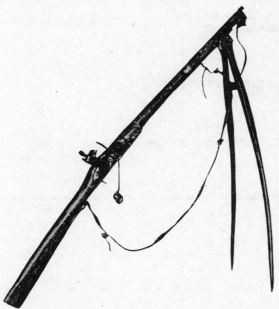

FIGURE 328. *Lamut (Siberia) Gun. Very rough stock and barrel, European flintlock. Two of the capucines are painted green. Typical Central Asian rest attached. Length 3 feet 1 inch.*

hands. In some cases they were fired from the hip. Most have matchlocks of the Indian type. Some have very simple locks, much like those used in the Burmese Hills. The Chinese guns seldom have sights, and when they do the two are not often in line with the barrel. Fig. 330.

In Assam and the Burmese Hills the guns are either Indian matchlocks or very rough copies of native make with a curious and complicated modification of the Japanese lock, fig. 331. See Matchlock.

The Japanese guns are well made and are often elaborately decorated. They are matchlocks with very short stocks intended for firing from the hip. They vary greatly in size, but most are about four feet long, fig. 332. Very heavy guns of the same pattern were made and used as wall pieces; some of them are of an inch and a quarter bore and weigh fifty pounds or more, fig. 844. The Japanese also made three-barreled revolving guns. They are quite short and the barrels are revolved by hand. 1, 2, fig. 332.

All of their guns were as much for display as use, though they used them when there was occasion. Most of the guns have two sights, and some have three, although the size and shape of the stocks made sights of no use. The locks have a serpentine that is held up by a catch and thrown down by a spring when the trigger is pulled and remain down until lifted. After the admission of Europeans some of these guns were altered to percussion locks by strengthening the spring and screwing a nipple into the pan cover; others were changed to detonators as already described (see Detonators). Some of the guns of the old type were fitted with European percussion locks.

A very rare type of gun is found in Formosa with the simplest form of matchlock known. The serpentine is pivoted in front of the pan and a piece of string is fastened to the top of it and to the middle of the trigger; pulling it drags the serpentine over and tips the match into the pan. These guns have long, light barrels and long, slim stocks with the rear end at right angles to the barrel. Fig. 333.

In the Philippines, parts of Siam and the surrounding countries very primitive hand guns were used within very recent times. In Siam they sometimes had three barrels which were very short and mounted on a short wooden handle, fig. 353. In the Philippines the stocks were roughly whittled to the shape of an ordinary gunstock. The barrels were

FIGURE 329. *Gun from Tonkin. Octagon barrel with raised ribs at the angles. Lock and trigger guard decorated with enamel. Stock mountings of chiseled brass, four very narrow capucines. Length 5 feet 4 inches.*

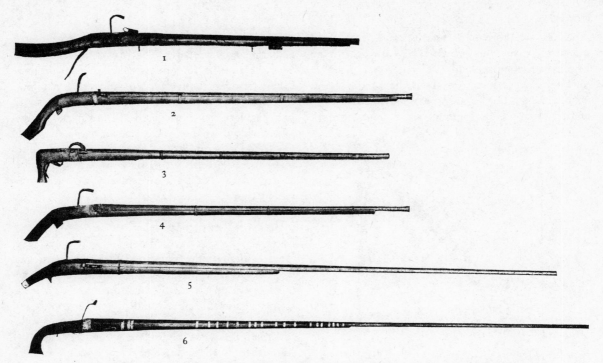

FIGURE 330. *Chinese Guns.* 1. *Stock painted red; two ringbolts for the slings. Length 3 feet 10.5 inches.* 2. *Barrel inlaid with flowers in gold and silver for its entire length; 4 capucines.* 3. *Black stock turned at a right angle. The trigger comes down to the end of the butt. Four cane capucines and one of iron.* 4. *Half octagon barrel, 4 bronze capucines. Length 4 feet 4 inches.* 5. *Tapering octagon barrel. Wooden stock with a bone butt.* 6. *Miao Chiang matchlock with a very peculiar lock. Light, tapering, octagonal barrel. Black stock and 21 flat silver capucines. Length 6 feet 5.25 inches.*

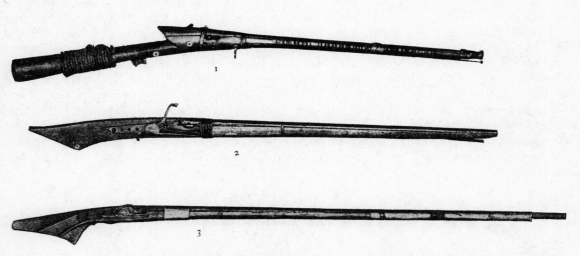

FIGURE 331. *Burmese guns.* 1. *Indian matchlock remounted in the Burmese Hills. The stock is roughly inlaid with ivory and the capucines are of leather and cane. The latter are tied in curious knots; only found in Burma and Japan. Length 3 feet 7.75 inches.* 2. *Khamti Assam. Matchlock. Length 3 feet 8 inches. The lock is the most peculiar feature and is shown in detail, 5, fig. 563.* 3. *Karen, Burma. Matchlock. Length 4 feet 4.25 inches. The lock is similar to the preceding. The butt is fan-shaped and fluted.*

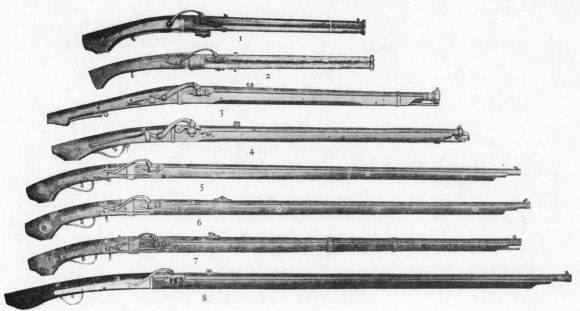

FIGURE 332. *Japanese Guns.* 1. *Three-barreled revolver. Barrels simply inlaid with silver, stock plain. Early type of lock. Length 2 feet 5.75 inches.* 2. *Three-barreled revolver. Barrels inlaid. In this and the preceding the barrels are revolved by hand and held in place by a catch.* 3. *Heavy octagonal barrel. The lock has been converted to a percussion by screwing a nipple into the pan cover and strengthening the spring.* 4. *Pill lock, see Detonators for details. The ramrod is fastened to the gun by a swivel. Length 3 feet 7 inches.* 5. *Barrel inlaid with silver, stock with brass. Two silver capucines.* 6. *Barrel decorated with dragons in gold and silver. Stock mountings of brass. Length 4 feet 5.5 inches.* 7. *Octagonal barrel inlaid with silver. Stock inlaid with brass and decorated with a flowering vine in colored lacquer.* 8. *Finely moulded octagonal barrel inlaid with silver. Plain stock. Length 4 feet 11 inches.*

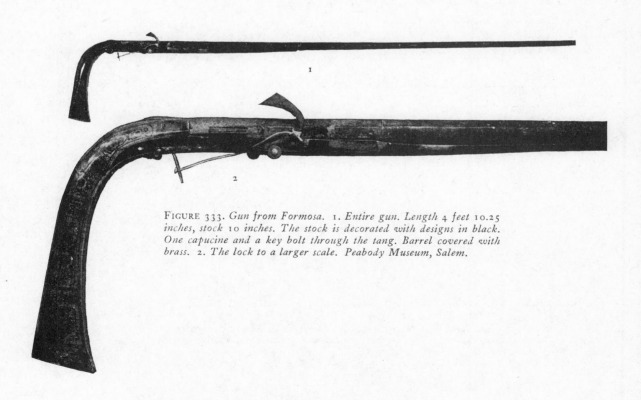

FIGURE 333. *Gun from Formosa.* 1. *Entire gun. Length 4 feet 10.25 inches, stock 10 inches. The stock is decorated with designs in black. One capucine and a key bolt through the tang. Barrel covered with brass.* 2. *The lock to a larger scale. Peabody Museum, Salem.*

made of gas pipe; and the pan was cut in the wood of the stock, fig. 334. They were known as cigarette guns, the ubiquitous cigarette being used as the match.

Arab type (dog lock) is used throughout the Turkish Empire, and a modified form in Ceylon. It is rather remarkable that only the earliest types of flintlock have survived in the East. Wherever later

FIGURE 334. *Gun from the Southern Philippines. Rough wooden stock, barrel a piece of ¾ inch gas pipe. The pan is whittled in the side of the stock. Length 2 feet 6 inches.*

In determining the country of origin of an Oriental gun the stock is generally the most valuable guide. The shapes are very numerous and can hardly be described in words. The most characteristic forms of butts are shown in fig. 335. The locks of most North African guns are snaphaans, which are used nowhere else. The miquelet lock is used in most Oriental countries as far east as Persia. The

types are found they are of European manufacture. In India, China and Central Asia the matchlocks are of the type in which the serpentine is held up by a spring until the trigger is pulled, and then returns automatically to its original position. In Japan, Malaya and Indo-China the match holder is held up by a catch, and remains down after the trigger is pulled.

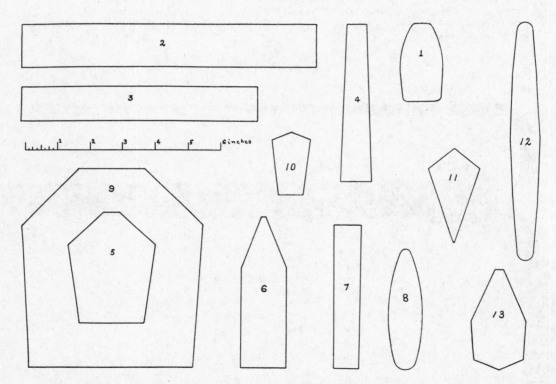

FIGURE 335. *Gun Butts. 1. Caucasus. 2, 3, 4. Kabyle. 5. Turkish and Persian. 6, 7, 8. Balkans. 9. Turkish wall gun. 10. India, the butt of the light barreled guns. 11. India, the butt of the guns with heavy barrels. 12. Sind, "Afghan Stock." 13. Malay.*

The barrels of most Turkish and Persian, and many Indian guns have heavy ogival peep sights forged on them. In many Indian guns the front sight is the nose of a man or animal chiseled on the muzzle; in others it is a long, slender pin, the great length being necessary to raise it above the heavy moulding at the muzzle. In some of the Balkan guns the back sight is on one of the capucines; a worse arrangement could hardly be imagined. The heavy Turkish and Persian wall guns have immense back sights pierced by a number of holes for different ranges.

Nearly all European guns have the barrels fastened on by pins or keys passing through the stock and loops on the underside of the barrel that fit in mortises in the stock. In the East the barrels are almost always held by bands (capucines). Both East and West there is frequently a tang at the breech that is fastened to the stock by a screw. In the West this usually passes through the tang and is screwed into the wood of the stock. In the East it generally passes entirely through the stock and is screwed into the tang. For the characteristic shapes of bands, see Capucines.

Slings for guns are very generally used by mountaineers, but rarely by horsemen. In the Balkans they are fastened to ringbolts on the side of the stock. In the Caucasus and Persia the sling is passed through mortises in the stock. In almost all countries the rear end of the sling is often fastened around the stock and the front to a ringbolt, clevis or mortise. In India the sling is apt to be fastened to clevises on the lower side of the stock.

For the different kinds and parts of guns see: Afghan Stock, Amusette, Arabas, Arquebus, Banduk, Banduk Dorahar, Banduk Jauhadar, Blunderbuss, Breech Loaders, Bridle of a Gun Lock, Bukmar, Butt, Butt Plate, Caliver, Camel Gun, Capucine, Carbine, Chamber, Cho-Ju, Combined Weapons, Contre Platine, Currier, Daijiri, Damariak, Demi-Hag, Detonator, Dog's Head, Dog Latch, Dog Lock, Dombay, Dragon, Esclopette, Firearms, Firelock, Fire-Stick, Flintlock, Fowling Piece, Frizzen, Fusil, Gonne, Gun, Gunda, Hackbutt, Hajigane, Hammer, Hand Gun, Harpoon Gun, Heel Plate, Hibasami, Hi-Buta, Higuchi, Hiki Gane, Hinawa, Hinawa Sashi, Hinawa Zutsu, Hi-Sao, Hizara, Jezail, Ju, Kanju, Karol, Kernali, Khang Prai, Khass Chut, Koombhe, Kunda, Lchkda, Limak, Lock, Lunt Cord, Lunt Work, Lunt Work Hagbut, Masha, Match, Match Box, Matchlock, Me-Da, Meynda, Meysha, Miquelet Lock, Mousqueton, Musketoon, Musket, Musquet, Musquet Arrow, Musquet-Fusil, Musquet Rest, Nail Plate, Niao-Chiang, Nu-Chiang, Ourousses, Pao, Patch, Patron, Percussion Lock, Petronel, Pill Lock, Pun Khas Sinla, Punt Gun, Pyrites Lock, Ramrod, Rest, Revolving Firearms, Rifling, Ryoju, Satengar, Scear, Schnapphan, Senapang, Serpentine, Seseri, Sher Bacha, Shingda, Shot, Side Plate, Sinapang, Singram, Snaphaan, Spanner, Spright, Suguchi, Tamagone, Teppo, Terkoel, Tesching, Toopin, Toradar, Trigger, Trigger Folding, Trigger Guard, Tschinke, Tubak, Tubak-I-Tikli, Tufanf-I-Chamaqui, Uchi Gane, Usted Kabir, Wall Gun, Whaling Gun, Wheel-Lock, Yerma Netchte.

GUNDA, KUNDA. A gunstock, Tibet. (Ramsay-Western).

GUNNAR'S BILL. The bill of the Icelandic hero Gunnar which was said to sing before battle. (Burton Sword 95).

GU-NOME. See Yakiba.

GUNPOWDER. An inflammable mixture of saltpeter, sulphur and charcoal has been known from very early times and was probably discovered in several places independently. Gunpowder as an explosive for the projection of missiles was almost certainly discovered in Europe early in the 13th century. Lieut.-Col. H. W. Hime, who has studied the subject exhaustively, is positive on this point. He states that similar mixtures of the same ingredients were used for rockets and incendiary bombs before this, but none of these mixtures were strong enough or rapid enough in their action to propel a missile. It was not until means were discovered for purifying nitre that it was possible to make an explosive powder. The first powder was a coarse meal, called serpentine powder, and it was not until the process of *corning* or forming grains of the powder, was discovered early in the 15th century that powder of any considerable strength could be made. For some time the corned powder was used only in small arms as the early cannon were not strong enough to stand its explosion. During the latter half of the 15th century it was noticed that the strength of the powder increased with the size of the grains; and it became the custom to vary the size of the grains to suit the purpose for which the powder was to be used. A coarser grained powder gives nearly the same muzzle velocity with much less pressure. From about 1250 to 1450 powders differed only in composition, all being simple mixtures of the ingredients not grained. From 1450 to 1700 powders differed in both composition and grain. Since 1700 the composition of all powders is substantially the same, but they differ greatly in grain size. (Hime 149).

GUNSEN, TESSEN, TETSUSEN. A folding war fan, Japan. It was like an ordinary folding fan except that the outer sticks, or all of the sticks were of iron. It was carried by the lower grades of officers for signalling, as a parrying weapon and also as a fan. It was often carried at night by all classes to guard with until a weapon could be drawn in case of an unexpected attack. See War Fan.

GUN TACKLES. The tackles by which cannon were moved and trained on board ship. Their principal use was to return the gun to its original position after firing; the recoil cylinder made them unnecessary.

GUPTI. An Indian sword cane. It is quite similar to those carried in Europe but the blades are often shorter and broader. It was fairly common in northern and central India. The blades were sometimes European; they often screwed into the scabbard which made them almost useless as weapons, as it took too long to get them out. The scabbards were sometimes of iron. (Egerton 516, 517, 641, 642). Fig. 336.

GUPTI AGA. A divan sword. See Zafar Takieh.

GURI, GURI BORI. A metallic imitation of guri lacquer sometimes used for sword fittings in Japan. Sheets of two or more metals, usually shakudo and copper were piled, sweated together, and then cut with deep V grooves in patterns. When pickled the two metals show as alternate layers of red and black in the grooves. Occasionally the grooves are round-bottomed which gives a totally different effect. The layers are very thin, as many as seventeen being in a guard but a little more than an eighth of an inch thick. This work was done mainly by a few members of the Ito and Shoami families. (Joly, Naunton xiii).

GUR-REEK. See Kur-Ruk.

GURRPAN. See Yirmba.

GURRUK. A spear thrower, Yarra tribe, Victoria.

GURZ. A mace, India. The head may be pear-shaped or flanged. (Wallace Orient).

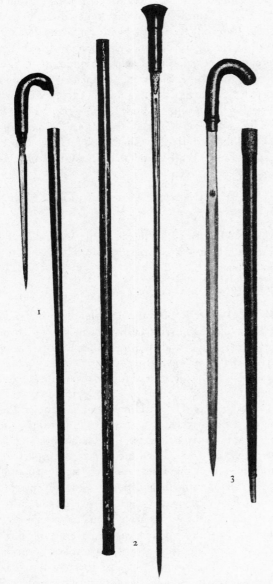

FIGURE 336. *Gupti. 1. Handle and body of iron inlaid with a diaper pattern in gold. Double-edged blade 12.375 inches long. The handle screws into the body. 2. Shaft painted wood. Hilt with a bone grip and a black horn top. European 17th-century rapier blade 41.5 inches long. 3. Iron handle with a flower pattern inlaid in silver and gold. Double-edged Indian blade 28.75 inches long. Body covered with dark green leather, chased silver caps on the ends.*

GUSBAR. See Ancus.

GUSOKU. A complete suit of armor, Japan.

GUSOKU BITSU. A box for armor, Japan. It was a light box made of wood or *papier mache*. If the suit was a light one the box had loops on the front through which the arms were passed, and the box was carried on the back. If it was heavy the box had iron handles on the ends with supplementary loops on them which stood up above the box

GWAE-FON. A very early form of British spearhead. It had two holes near the base by which to fasten it to the staff. (Skelton 47).

GYN. See Engine.

GYNOURS. Engineers, the men that operated the engines, or gyns.

GYR. See Ger.

GYSARME. See Guisarme.

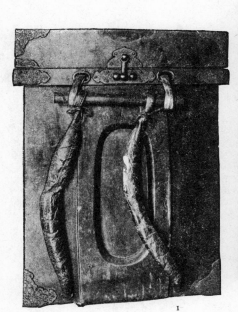

FIGURE 337. *Gusoku Bitsu. 1. For an early haramaki do. Lacquered box bound with bronze. Two sling loops for the arms. 2. Light wooden box bound with iron. The sling loops are square and come above the box when turned up. It is carried by two men slung from a pole passed through the loops. It belongs to an 18th-century Miochin suit.*

when the handles were turned up. When traveling two men carried the box by a pole passed through the loops. Fig. 337.

GUSOKU SHI. An armor maker, Japan.

GUSSET, GAUCHET, GOUCHET. Pieces of mail fastened to the arming doublet to protect the parts not covered by the plates at the joints in early armor. As armor was improved in design the plates were articulated, making the gussets unnecessary. (Planche 235, ffoulkes 62).

GUYDHOMME. See Guidon.

H

HA. The cutting edge of a blade, Japan.

HABAKI. A metal ferule surrounding a Japanese blade next the guard. It may be of one piece, *hitoye habaki*, in which case it fits closely to both blade and scabbard; or it may be of two pieces, *nijiu habaki*, the longer of the two fitting the blade, and the shorter, which fits over it, also fits the scabbard. The double form is the older. The older habaki that have survived, are either of gold or are heavily plated with it; the modern ones are usually only gilded; they are also made of silver and various bronzes. Generally they are plain or only covered with the cuts called cat scratches, or those imitating rain. A few are carved or inlaid elaborately. Fig. 338.

which the Emperor O-Jin was deified as the god of war. His messengers are doves. (Weber I, 241). His figure or name are frequent decorations on Japanese armor. Fig. 339.

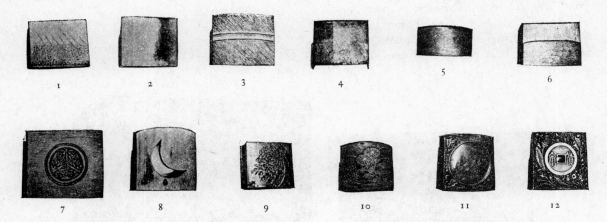

FIGURE 338. *Habaki.* 1. *Silver with "cat scratches" and raised grains.* 2. *Gold, plain.* 3. *Gold "cat scratches" and sunk lines.* 4. *Copper, the inner piece of a nijiu habaki.* 5. *The outer piece of no. 4.* 6. *The two pieces put together as used, gilded copper.* 7. *Gilded copper, Tokugawa crest in relief in a sunk panel.* 8. *Gilded copper, pierced with the moon on one side and the sun on the other.* 9. *Silver engraved with a flower design.* 10. *Iron inlaid with gold chrysanthemums.* 11. *Gold, elaborately carved and engraved.* 12. *Shakudo and gold, unusually elaborately carved and inlaid.*

The habaki not only makes a neat finish but holds the blade steady in the scabbard so that the edge cannot be injured. It also closes the opening tightly enough to practically prevent the entrance of moisture.

HABAKI MOTO, TE MOTO. The part of a Japanese blade covered by the habaki.

HABERGEON, HAUBERGEON. "A military defense of the 14th century, but whether of plate, mail or possibly both is uncertain." (Planche 236).

"A short hauberk of the 11th century." (ffoulkes 24).

HACHI. The bowl of a Japanese helmet.
A hanburi, which see.

HACHIMAKI. A cloth about five feet long and sixteen inches wide which was wound round the head like a turban to form a padding under the helmet. It was worn in early times in Japan and was later given up as the helmets were lined in such a manner as to make it unnecessary. (Garbutt 148).

HACHIMAN. The posthumous name under

FIGURE 339. *Hachiman. A breastplate embossed with the characters* hachi *and* man *and two doves, the messengers of the god of war. Signed Nike Miochin Munesuke, maker, and the name of the owner, Moriaki of the Fujiwara family, of the province of Soshu.*

HACHIMANZA, HACHIMAN'S OPENING, TEHEN, TENKU. An opening in the top of a Japanese helmet that is surrounded by an elaborate moulding, usually a conventional chrysanthemum. The above names are usually applied to both opening and ornament, but Weber (II, 504) says that the opening is the *tehen* and the ornamental ring the *hachimanza*. It was sometimes protected by a piece of silk tied over the top by cords attached to four knobs of metal called the *shi-ten-bio*.

HACHIWARA. Japanese helmet breaker. A slightly curved iron bar, usually about a foot long, with a hook near the handle. It was generally of square section, and was carried in a sheath like a knife. Fig. 340.

Although called a helmet breaker by both Japanese and Occidentals, Weber's statement (II, 504), that it is intended for parrying the blows of a sword and to break it, is undoubtedly correct. In fact it is a Japanese form of main gauche.

FIGURE 340. *Hachiwara. 1. Blade 11.5 inches long. Hilt and scabbard of carved horn. 2. Unusually long blade with a hilt like a sword. Shell lacquer scabbard that does not take in the hook. 3. Scabbard lacquered red and black. 4. Blade 12 inches long. Hilt and scabbard of carved wood lacquered a reddish brown and black. 5. Heavy elliptical blade mounted like a sword. In a gadrooned scabbard. 6. Blade without a hook, mounted like a sword. Scabbard fittings of brass.*

There are several explanations of the object of this opening in addition to the obvious one that it was intended for ventilation. Dr. Dean says (Jap. 31) that through it the brain of the wearer was believed to come in contact with heavenly influences. Garbutt says that it was to give room for a short, stiff pigtail in which the early Japanese tied up their hair. He points out the fact that, at the time these pigtails were worn, the openings were much larger than in the later helmets.

HACK. When hawks were taken from the nest before they were fully fledged they were usually manned, that is taught to stand on the hand, wear a hood and eat from the lure. When they had learned this much, sometimes before, they were turned loose for some days in order that they might learn to fly. During this time they were fed from the lure, or from a "hack board," that is, a board to which their food was fastened so that they could not carry it off bodily; they were also handled if they would allow it. They were often left out for three or four weeks; but, if they began to kill birds for themselves, they were taken up at once for fear that they would become totally wild again.

HACKAMORE. See Bridle.

HAGANE. Steel, Japan.

HAGE-RO. To fix an arrow to the bow, Japan.

HAGGARD. A wild hawk that has moulted for the first time. Hawks that are caught at this age are

FIGURE 341. *Hai-Date. 1, 2, 4. 17th to 19th centuries. 3. 1550. Metropolitan Museum. Not to scale.*

HACKBUTT, HAQUEBUT, HAGGEBUSH, HACKE, HAQUE. A kind of gun used in the 16th century. It was not more than twenty-seven inches long. (Grose I, 153).

HACKETON. See Aketon.

HADA. (Skin). The watering on a Japanese blade. The different varieties are: *Masama-hada*, straight grain. *Itama-hada*, curved grain. *Nachi-hada* (pear skin) in the shape of a halved pear. *Matsu-hada* (pine bark) ragged like the bark of a pine tree. (Lyman 9).

always called haggards to distinguish them from those caught younger, eyesses, or older, passage hawks.

HAGUNA. A white tassel on a spear, Japan.

HAI-DATE. The apron-like protection for the thighs worn under the tassets by the Japanese. The upper portion, which is covered by the tassets, is a divided apron of brocade or leather, and has two vertical slits like pocket holes in it. The lower part is covered with plates, lames or mail to protect the thighs and knees. (Conder 274). Fig. 341.

It was not used until the middle ages as the kusazuri (tassets) of the earlier suits were longer and larger.

FIGURE 342. *Syrian knife like the Indian haladie. Blades each 8.5 inches long. Bone grip.*

HAIL SHOT. Small bullets fired from cannon, 17th century.

HAJIGANE. The cock of a gun, Japan.

HAK. The southern Indian name for a Malay spear with a kris-like head. (Wallace Orient).

HAKASE. A sword, Japan.

HAKO-MUNE. Japanese, a square back to a blade.

HAKUBYO. A line drawing, Japan. A method of decorating sword mountings that imitated brush strokes.

HAKUJIN. A naked blade, Japan.

HAKUSHA. A spur, Japan. A modern word as the old Japanese did not use spurs.

HALAB, HALAT. A kind of Sikh, or Sind, sword with a grooved blade, finger guard and disk pommel. (Wallace Orient). A variety of talwar.

HALADIE. A Rajput double dagger with two short, curved blades fastened to the opposite ends of a straight handle. (Egerton 390). A similar weapon is still used in Syria. (Fig. 342).

HALBARD, HALBART, HALBERD. The halbard consists of an axe blade with a peak or point opposite it (sometimes another axe blade) and a long spike or blade on the end, the whole being mounted on a long shaft. It was used as early as the 13th century, and was carried by sergeants in the British army until the end of the 18th. It was apparently evolved from the voulge by the Swiss who appreciated it so highly that they substituted it for the pike in their armies in the 15th century. It rapidly spread all over Europe and became one of the most widely used weapons. The early forms were simple and heavy but gradually became lighter and more elaborate, fig. 343. The shafts had long iron straps on them to prevent their being cut.

Later they were covered with velvet (armins) and had large tassels just below the heads. In the 17th century they were used almost entirely to arm the guards of princes and were most elaborately decorated. Fig. 344.

HALDA. The broad hunting spear used by the thakurs (nobles) of the Sahydri Hills, India. (Sinclair, I. A. II, 216).

HALECRET. See Alecret.

FIGURE 343. *Italian halbard of about 1580. A parade arm of most exceptional quality. Collection of Mr. Edward H. Litchfield.*

HALF ARMOR. By the 17th century guns had become so effective and tactics had changed so much that mobility had become more important,

HALF MOON, DEMI LUNE. A pole arm with a crescent-shaped blade at right angles to the shaft, 16th and 17th centuries. Fig. 345.

FIGURE 344. *Halbards. 1. German, 1490. 2. Swiss, 1450. 3. Italian(?), 1500. 4. German(?), 1550. 5. German(?), 1550. 6. Swiss, 1400-1450. 7. Swiss, 1580. 8. Venetian, 1520. 9. German or French, 1550-1600. Metropolitan Museum.*

and armor was less used. The jambs, which were the first pieces of plate used, were the first to be given up.

The suits that covered the body and arms only were known as half armor. In some even the arms were not protected. Suits of this character, that were worn mainly by the officers, were much more apt to be highly decorated than the earlier ones that were worn more generally, and mainly for defense. Fig. 42. (ffoulkes 97).

HALF-CIRCLE. A 17th-century fencing guard like the modern septime. (Castle 138).

HALF-HANGERS. A guard for the sabre between the "medium" and "hanging" guards. (Castle 220).

FIGURE 345. *Half Moon, Spanish, 16th-17th century. Metropolitan Museum.*

HALSBAND. A contrivance of soft twisted silk placed like a collar round a hawk's neck and the end held in the hand. It was used by Indian falconers to steady a sparrowhawk when cast off. (Harting 224). This name is not Hindu but German.

HAMAYUMI. A bow for driving away evil spirits, Japan.

HAMIDASHI. A Japanese dagger with a guard scarcely larger than the grip. (Joly, S. & S. 45). Fig. 346. See Tanto.

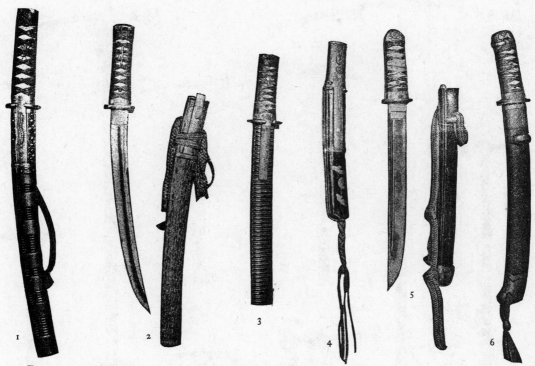

FIGURE 346. *Hamidashi.* 1. *Blade signed Akihiro. Mountings by Konkuan, shakudo ishime with insects in relief in colored metals. Scabbard of black lacquer in alternate plain and gadrooned bands, the upper part of chirimen same.* 2. *Blade 13.25 inches long by Kanesada. Scabbard lacquered to imitate wood. Mountings by Masaoki, toys in relief in colored metals.* 3. *Blade 8 inches long by Kaneyuki. Scabbard red lacquer gadrooned. Tsuba iron, pipe tree. Kozuka lacquered to imitate bamboo, with metal ants. Other mountings, shakudo with silver flowers. By Yoshinori, about 1820.* 4. *Blade 7 inches long. Mountings of silver and shibuichi. Scabbard of black lacquer with three men (gold) towing a boat which is on the other side of the scabbard.* 5. *Finely watered blade 12 inches long, signed Udifusa. Black lacquer scabbard decorated with birds in low relief. Silver mountings in bamboo designs.* 6. *Blade 9.375 inches long. Mounts iron, inlaid with a diaper pattern in gold.*

HAMANO SHOZUI. (Masayuki). A celebrated maker of tsuba, 1695-1769. He was a pupil of Nara Toshinaga and founded a school at Hamano that produced many famous artists. He not only made battle scenes and legendary subjects like his master, but treated with success others that he copied from nature or designed himself. Some of his work is not in high relief, but in *intaglio relievato.*

HAMATA. Roman armor made of hooked chains forming a kind of mail. (Burton Sword 248).

FIGURE 347. *Hamidashi Tsuba.* 1. *Silver with characters in relief.* 2. *Copper. A spider and a gourd vine in gold, both in relief.*

A tsuba so small that the openings for the kozuka and kogai cannot be made in it but become open notches. (Joly Int. 16). Fig. 347.

types of lock it is the piece that strikes, corresponding to the cock of the flintlock.

FIGURE 348. *War Hammers. 1. Italian, 16th century. 2. German, 16th century. 3. Venetian, first half of the 16th century. 4. German wheel lock pistol and hammer, 16th century. 5. Italian, dated 1591. 6. German, 16th century. 7. Venetian, 16th century. 8. Italian, 15th century. Metropolitan Museum.*

HAMMASTI. The "blade of the double sword," Egypt. (Burton Sword 204).

HAMMER, OF A GUN. In the flintlock the hammer is the piece struck by the flint; in the later

HAMMER, WAR. The war hammer was used wherever and whenever armor was used except in Japan. It was, however, never as popular in the East as in Europe, as the armor was generally lighter and more flexible and covered the body less completely, making a smashing weapon less essential. It usually had a long, sharp point on the back and a blunt pean, or a set of claws, in front. In some cases it had a narrow cutting edge and is difficult to classify, being as much axe as hammer. Fig. 348.

A heavy hammer, with a short spike on the end and a long handle with a round guard, was often used for fighting on foot in the lists in the 15th century. Fig. 349.

HAMPE. The shaft of a pole arm. (Laking Armour III, 121).

HAMPI. A Japanese surcoat without sleeves.

HANAGAWA. The nose strap of a bridle, Japan.

HANAIRO ODOSHI. Armor laced with light blue cords, Japan.

HANAMUSUBI. Flower knot. A knot used in fastening the Japanese corselet. (Garbutt 142).

HANBURI, HACHIGANE. A Japanese half helmet, or skull cap. It was made of metal or leather. Some were shallow and cup-shaped and only covered the crown of the head; others covered the forehead and temples. Some had a menpo attached. They were often made of several plates connected only by pins at the temples; these could be folded up for carriage. Holes were sometimes left for the ears and pigtail. Sometimes they were connected to a mail cap or hood. They vary more in shape and construction than any other form of Japanese head defense. Fig. 350.

FIGURE 349. *Hammer for fighting on foot in the lists. French(?), late 15th century. From a private collection. It is said to have been found in the moat at Carcassonne at the time the fortress was restored by Violet le Duc.*

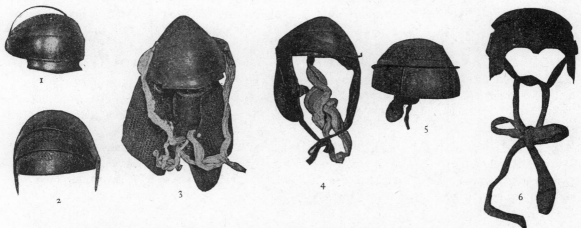

FIGURE 350. *Hanburi. 1. Three plates and an eye shade, also a narrow band to go round the back of the head. 2. Three plates decorated with applied scrolls. Ear guards. 3. Three plates and eye shade connected to a mail hood. 4. Three plates with a gilt mon. Very large ear guards. 5. Round plate for the top of the head, connected by mail to three hinged plates for the forehead. 6. Nearly flat plate covering the top of the head and laced to one covering the forehead down to the eyes.*

It is said that the hanburi was worn under the helmet. While this may have been done on occasions, it was generally used for night sorties, foraging parties, etc. (Conder 263).

FIGURE 351. *Hand-and-a-half Sword. Swiss, first half of the 16th century. Metropolitan Museum.*

HANDA. Tin, Japan.

HAN-DACHI. A Japanese sword, the mountings of which were partly those of a tachi and partly those of a katana, 1. 2, fig. 249. The name means "half a tachi." It was carried like a katana. (Weber II, 350).

HAND-AND-A-HALF SWORD, BASTARD SWORD. A long, straight-bladed sword of the 15th century, with a plain cross guard, long grip and rounded pommel. This type of sword was ordi-narily used with one hand, but the grip was long enough to allow it to be grasped with two or three fingers of the left hand if it was desired to give extra weight to the blow. Fig. 351.

HAND GRENADE. See Grenade. The smaller bombs were called "hand" grenades to distinguish them from the larger ones called "rampart grenades."

HAND GUN. The earliest form of gun consisted of a tube with a touchhole and a straight handle. It was held in the left hand and a match in the right. In Europe it was often hung from the neck by a cord which passed through a ring on the end of the handle. Fig. 352.

Similar weapons were also used in the East. Some had three barrels. Fig. 353.

HAND PALISADO, HOG'S BRISTLE, SWEYNE FEATHER. "It is a stake five or six foot long, and about four fingers thick, with a piece of sharp Iron nail'd to every end of it. By the one (end) it is made fast in the ground in such manner that one end lyeth out, so that it may meet the breast of a Horse, whereby a body of musketeers is defended with a palisado." (Hewitt III, 744).

HANDSCHAR. See Khanjar.

HAND-SEAX. A dagger worn by the Anglo-Saxons. (Planche 251).

HANGER, WHINGER, WHINYARD. Yule and Burnell (Hobson-Jobson 410) say that this name is derived from the Arabic *khanjar*, a knife.

It is a light sabre of the 17th and 18th centuries. (Castle 229).

A Scotch name for a dagger. (Planche 521).

HANI, TAIAHA. A New Zealand staff with a carved head and a long, round staff flattened towards the end. The head is a conventional face with an enormous tongue thrust out in the attitude of defiance; the tongue is usually much larger than the head and elaborately carved. The shaft is generally plain, always so in those intended for fighting. One was always carried by every Maori of po-

FIGURE 352. *Hand Gun, Europe, 15th century. Ex. Parham Collection. Metropolitan Museum.*

sition and was used to gesticulate with when speaking, as well as being one of the most popular weapons. The young men were taught a regular system of cuts and guards with it. Fig. 354.

HAN KYU. A small bow, Japan.

HANQUI. See Banqui.

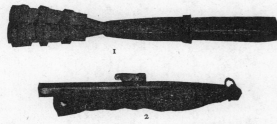

FIGURE 353. *Oriental Hand Guns.* 1. *Cambodian. Three barrels 3.5 inches long with a wooden handle.* 2. *Japanese. Bronze barrel 6 inches long with a swivel ring on the end. It has a swinging pan cover which protects the priming powder when it is carried. In this it is superior to any other.*

HANSHO-GOTE. A short kote of mail or three longitudinal plates connected by mail and lined with padded cloth. It was tied around the forearm. (Conder 349). Fig. 355.

HANZASHI KOZUKA. A kozuka of about half the ordinary size. It is said to have been invented by Tokujo. (Joly Int. 17). It is only used with very small knives. 2, fig. 356.

HAO SHI, MING TI. Chinese whistling arrows.

"Probably one is an arrow with openings in the iron head, and the other the ordinary whistling arrow with a large projection below, or in place of, the head with openings in it." (Laufer 225). See Whistling Arrow.

HAPPOJIRO. A Japanese helmet with four of its plates covered with silver. (Conder 259).

HAPPURI. Japanese armor for the head. See Hanburi.

HAQUETON. See Aketon.

HARA-ATE, HARA-ATE-GAWA. A leather corselet worn by the lower classes of retainers in Japan. It was similar in shape to the jackets worn by firemen. (Conder 280). The second name means made of leather.

Armor worn under ceremonial dress. It was made of laced lames and was hung from the shoulders. It covered only the front of the body from the neck to the knees. Fig. 357. Compare Renjaku-Do.

HARAI-DATE. The socket for the maye-zashi of a Japanese helmet in which the crest was placed. (Conder 260).

HARAMAKI. (Belly protector). A Japanese guard of silk interlined with mail or small plates. It is shaped like a modern vest but opens behind and is fastened with cords. (Garbutt 177).

The haramaki-do is often spoken of as a haramaki.

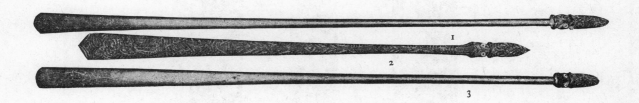

FIGURE 354. *Hani.* 1. *Carved and inlaid head, length 6 feet 6.75 inches.* 2. *Very dark polished wood finely carved for its entire length and inlaid with pearl shell. Length 4 feet 1.25 inches. A parade weapon.* 3. *Polished brown wood, well carved head inlaid with shell.* 4. *Detail of a head to a larger scale.*

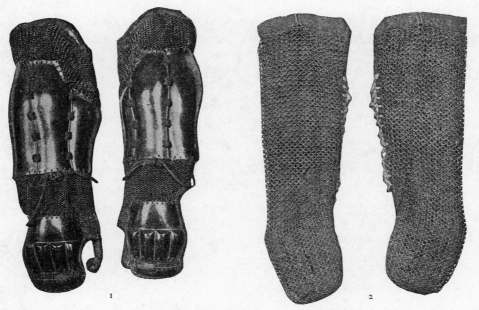

FIGURE 355. *Hansho Gote.* 1. *Lacquered leather plates and mail mounted on padded cloth.* 2. *All mail on padded cloth.*

FIGURE 356. *Hanzashi Kozuka. The three sizes of kozuka.* 1. *O-Kozuka. Silver, a tiger lily in relief in copper, gold, shakudo and shibuichi.* 2. *Hanzashi kozuka. Shibuichi, gold, silver and shakudo. A man and woman in relief.* 3. *Kozuka of the standard size. Shibuichi, silver, copper, gold and shakudo. A man carrying a giant forked radish, in high relief. All are of the actual size.*

HARAMAKI-DO. A Japanese cuirass lacing up the back. This is the earlier form, nearly all of the later ones open at the side. (Dean Jap. 27, 28). This form is said to have been invented for the Empress Jingo who was pregnant when she invaded Korea and therefore had to have a flexible and adjustable corselet. Figs. 358, 359. See Do.

to be better for this purpose than wood. (Garbutt 180). It is better because it neither splits nor warps.

HARNESS. This name was generally applied to armor, and occasionally to weapons during the middle ages. (Planche 253).

HARNOIS BLANC. Armor made of steel plate

FIGURE 357. *Hara-Ate. Armor for the front of the body only; it was worn under ceremonial dress. The top plate is covered with printed leather. The body and tassets are laced with silk cords of five colors; 4 tassets. Lining of red silk damask. Suspender straps of brocade.*

HARBER. Arabic, a dart. (Burton Sword 184).

HARETSU-GWAN. A bombshell, Japan.

HARI ISHIME. A surface decoration used as a background on Japanese sword fittings. It is covered with small openings as though it had been pricked with a needle. (Joly Int. 35).

HARINUKI. Papier mache. It was sometimes used for making armor cases in Japan, and is said

as distinguished from that made of cuir bouilli. (Hewitt III, 493).

HARPOON. A spear used for hunting large fish and marine mammals. The older European form had a head with a broad barb on each side. The later form is called a toggle iron, and has two short barbs on the same side of a short head that is pivoted on the end of a short iron shaft with a socket for the wooden shaft by which it is thrown. See

Toggle Iron. Harpoons of the latter pattern are used by the Eskimoes and nearly all of the American Indians living near the seashore.

FIGURE 358. *Haramaki-Do. 1. Do and sode, Kamakura period. The do is entirely covered with leather. The sode are curved to fit around the arms. 2. Ashikaga period. The lames of the do are individually covered with leather, except the top one, which is covered with same. 3. Small, early haramaki. Top plate covered with same.*

HARPOON GUN. A gun for shooting a harpoon. It is a small cannon usually mounted on a swivel on the bow of a boat.

HARQUEBUS. See Arquebus.

HARUAKI. One of the most celebrated makers of sword mountings of the 19th century in Japan. He was a pupil of Yanagawa Naoharu, and was awarded the title of Hogen, the highest art title given by the Emperor. He died in 1859 at the age of seventy-three. (Hara 14).

HARUBI. A saddle girth, Japan.

HASHI, WARI KOGAI. Chopsticks. The sword mounting called hashi is a kogai split lengthwise and usually has dowels and mortises to hold the two pieces in line. Dr. Dean says that it was not used to

HATO-WO-NO-ITA. The guard for the left armpit in old Japanese armor. It was smaller than that for the right side (sendan no-ita), and was made of a single plate of metal or thick lacquered

FIGURE 359. *Haramaki-Do. 1. Brigandine, about 1700. 2. Laced lames, 18th century. Metropolitan Museum. Not to scale.*

eat with but as ceremonial tweezers to handle incense and ashes. (Hdbk. 131). Other authorities believe, however, that both it and the kozuka were originally used for eating, a practice that would have obvious utility during a campaign. See Kogai.

HA-SODE, TAKA-NO-HA-SODE. Sode shaped like a bird's wing. (Conder 272). See Sode.

HASEGAI. See Assegai.

HASTARII. The Roman legionaries or spearmen. (Burton Sword 248).

HASTILUDES. Spear play, a general name for tournaments in which the lance was used. (Hewitt I, 181).

HATA JIRUSHI. A Japanese banner about two feet by twelve. Sometimes one short side was fastened to a swinging arm on the staff, at others one short side was fastened to a fixed arm, and one long side to the staff, this type was called *nobori*. It is said to have first been used between 1550 and 1600. (Weber I, 261).

HATOMOTO. A sub-daimio, a noble of the second class in old Japan. (Dean Jap. 53).

HATOMUNE-DO. A Japanese pigeon-breasted corselet. (Dean Jap. 37). It was copied from European forms, and was often of European make. Fig. 360.

leather with a metal border. At the top it spread out in the shape of a dove's tail. It was generally covered with ornamental leather. (Conder 268). Fig. 361. See Sendan-No-Ita.

FIGURE 360. *Hatomune Do, Pigeon-breasted corselet. Adapted from a European breastplate. Metropolitan Museum.*

HA-TSUYA. (Edge lustre). The light color of a Japanese blade near the edge as distinguished from the darker *ji-tsuya* (ground lustre) of the rest of the blade. (Lyman 13).

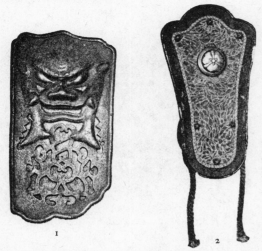

FIGURE 361. *Hata-Wo-No-Ita. Japanese guards for the left armpit. 1. Steel pierced and mounted over gilt leather. Gold eyes and border. 2. Iron plate covered and lined with printed leather, gilt mon.*

HAUBERGEON. A short hauberk of the 11th century. See Habergeon.

HAUBERK, BRUGNE. The long coat of mail that was the principal defense of the knights of the 11th, 12th and 13th centuries. It was worn over the quilted gambeson which prevented the body from being bruised when the mail was struck. It was split from the waist down, front and back, for convenience on horseback. The skirts reached to the knees, thus protecting the upper leg. The sleeves of the hauberk were sometimes short, at others they were long enough to cover the hands, sometimes ending in mail mittens. (ffoulkes 19, 23, 38).

HAVILDAR. Hindu, a sergeant.

HAUSSE-COL. A defense for the neck variously described as a combination of gorget and bevor worn with a salade, and as a standard of mail, or collar, worn under the plate gorget. (Planche 268).

HAWK'S BELLS. All trained hawks, except the very small ones, wear bells at all times. The long-winged hawks have the bells fastened to their legs by narrow strips of leather; the short-winged hawks are usually belled on the tail. In either case the leather straps are called bewits. The bells used in Europe are spherical with flat eyes, those of Indian manufacture are shaped like a small dumb-bell, very slightly constricted in the middle. Formerly they were made of silver for valuable hawks, now brass is chiefly used. Hawk bells are used, not only to give notice of where the hawk is, but as weights to handicap her when, at the end of her time of liberty, she begins to chase chance quarry. These are much larger than the bells used in the field, and are sometimes even weighted with lead.

HAWK'S HOOD. Before the crusades the hood was unknown in Europe; it was introduced by the Emperor Frederick II (died 1250), who adopted the use of it from the Syrian Arabs. The hood proper has a plume, the rufter hood is without one. (Harting 224).

A hawk's hood is made of stiffish leather, moulded on a wooden block to the size and shape of the head of the hawk for which it is intended, and stitched together. It has a plume on the top which is generally used as a handle when putting it on and taking it off. There are openings in the front and back that can be closed by pulling two straps, each fastened to one side and passing through slots in the other. It is opened by pulling two shorter and heavier straps fastened to the sides. (Michell 48). Fig. 362.

FIGURE 362. *Hawk's Hood, English, 16th-17th century. Metropolitan Museum.*

FIGURE 363. *Hayago. Japanese Primers and Flasks.* 1. *Boat-shaped ivory primer. The stop for the outlet is a bow and arrows.* 2. *Leather primer with a gilt mon.* 3. *Leather covered primer with an ivory neck.* 4. *Black wooden primer.* 5. *Ivory primer, ebony tinder box, leather bullet pouch and three bird calls.* 6. *Primer in the shape of a flattened eggplant.* 7. *Lacquer primer with ivory mounts.* 8. *Embossed leather primer with ivory mounts.* 9. *Lacquer primer inlaid with shell.* 10. *Black lacquer primer, an eggplant.* 11. *Flat wooden primer with ivory mounts.* 12. *Cow's horn primer with horn and ivory mounts.* 13. *Lacquer primer.* 14. *Flask, lacquer with a vine in black and gold lacquer, ivory netsuke.* 15. *Brown wood flask, ivory mounts.* 16. *Black lacquer flask with a gilt mon.* 17. *Bag-shaped black lacquer flask.* 18. *Cow's horn flask.* 19. *Metal lacquered with a vine and mon in gold. The discharge end is covered by a cap. Length 17.75 inches.* 20. *Flask, a turtle shell.* 21. *Flask. Black lacquer with a gilt mon.* 22. *Flask and tinder box. Black lacquer with gilt mon.* 23. *Flask. Red wood with horn mounts and raised gold lacquer mon.* 24. *Cylindrical wooden flask with ivory mounts.* 25. *Shell lacquer primer.* 26. *Flat round lacquer flask. Diameter 7.75 inches.* 27. *Brown lacquer flask with a gilt mon. Height 8.75 inches. Belt hook on back.* 28. *Wood flask.* 29. *Carved wooden flask and tinder box.* 30. *Shell lacquer flask with an octopus in raised red lacquer.* 31. *Round flask of black leather with a gilt mon.* 32. *Gold and black lacquer flask with a vine in relief. Lacquered ivory mounts.* 33. *Shell lacquer flask.*

The Indian hoods are of softer leather, and have a smaller and different plume. They are closed by braces (straps) which are laced through slots in the lower edge of the hood. (Michell 48). In a good Indian hood the beak aperture is cut away so that a hooded hawk can, with a little difficulty, both eat and cast, but in a Persian hood the hawk cannot open its beak sufficiently wide to give exit to the casting. (Phillot 102, note).

ened by straps at the back. (Phillott 126, note 102).

In his plate at page 212 Harting shows a Japanese falconer carrying a hooded hawk. The hood is much larger than the European and covers most of the hawk's neck.

HAYAGO, ENSHO-IRE. A powder flask, Japan. Japanese powder flasks are generally made of wood, or papier-mache, lacquered, and vary greatly

FIGURE 364. *Igorot Head Axes. 1. Kalinga. Engraved head 11 x 2.875 inches. Wood handle with a long iron ferule next the head and one of white metal on the other end. Length 24.5 inches. 2. Intermediate type, head 3.5 x 13.5 inches. Length 17.5 inches. 3. Bontoc. Head 3 x 8 inches. Very short handle with a long iron and short white metal ferule. 4. Balbelasan, a northern type. Head 3.625 x 15 inches. Length 21 inches.*

The Indian hood is a cap of soft, thick hog-deer hide, fitting the head closely but easily. About the neck it is provided with a string which runs easily in the holes, so that there is no difficulty in drawing or loosening it. Amongst the rich this part of a hawk's furniture is ornamented with embroidery, handsome silver aigrettes, tassels and other decorations. (Burton Falconry 47).

The hood used in Persia and the regions around Basrah and Baghdad is quite unlike the Indian hood. It is, in fact, little more than a bag of soft leather with two straps at the back to tighten it. The Persian, unlike the Indian hood, is opened and loosened by straps at the back.

in size and shape. Many of these flasks have an outlet tube at the mouth which is closed by a cap of bone or ivory which has an inner tube longer than itself that is used as a measure. This tube goes inside the neck of the flask. The primers are usually very similar to the flasks but smaller. They are closed by rather wide, flat caps with openings to fit over the tube at the neck of the flask, and smaller holes at the sides through which the ends of a very fine cord are passed and fastened to the primer. The cap can thus slide up and down the bight of the cord and still remain fastened to the primer. Fig. 363.

HAZU. The nock of an arrow, Japan. (Weber I, 177).

HEAD AXE. The most characteristic weapon of the Igorot of Northern Luzon. It has a broad head with the edge projecting in a point at the part furthest from the handle. This is balanced by a much longer and thinner point on the opposite side. The axes used by the northern tribes have decidedly concave cutting edges, while those used by the southern tribes are nearly straight. The northern handles are longer and usually have a projection on one side which is often made of brass. The axe is not only used as a weapon for fighting at close quarters but, in times of peace, as a knife. When used for this purpose the long point at the back is driven into the ground holding the axe steadily while the object to be cut is drawn along the edge. The northern axes are made in Balbelasan in old Abra Province, and the southern in Balawang. (Jenks 129). Fig. 364.

HEADSTALL. See Bridle.

HEAUME. The headpiece of the 13th century. It was evolved from the earlier helmet by fixing the earflaps which were made larger until they eventually joined the nasal, completely enclosing the face. This gave the barrel helm with a flat top and a slit, called the ocularium, in front through which to see. Later breathing holes were added. Later again the top was pointed, giving the sugarloaf helm. Notwithstanding the great weight of these helms they rested entirely on the head, which was protected by a padded cap. Not being fastened to the body they were liable to be struck off in battle and were sometimes chained to the breast. (ffoulkes 25).

HEEL PLATE, BUTT PLATE. The plate on the butt of a gun or pistol. In early times in Europe it was always made of metal; but at the present day for sporting guns it is made of horn or ebonite, glued and screwed to the stock. In the East it is generally made of horn or ivory.

HEICHOZAN. "Flat-Topped Mountain." A type of Japanese helmet.

HEITO. See Kashira.

HELM. See Heaume.

HELMET. Generically any headpiece, specifically the open headpiece of the time of the Norman conquest. In addition to the European forms, most of which have specific names, many Oriental and uncivilized peoples have characteristic helmets of which we do not know the names. Some of these are shown in fig. 365.

For the different kinds and parts of helmets, see: Akagane-Gasa, Akedama, Akurio, Armet, Armet a Rondelle, Asa-Gao, Asanodzukin, Ase Nagashi No Ana, Avantaille, Bacinet, Bacyn, Barbute, Barred Burgonet, Barrel Helm, Bascinet, Basinet, Basnet, Beavor, Beevor, Bellows Visor, Bourginet, Buffe, Bumbawe Tefao, Burgonet, Bycocket, Cabasset, Calote, Camail, Capeline, Carnet, Casque, Casque Normand, Casquetel, Cassis, Castle, Cat-Faced Burgonet, Celate, Cerveliere, Chapawe, Chapel de Fer, Cha-Sen, Chastons, Cheeks, Chichaki, Chikara-Gawa, Chinpiece, Chiu-Kasa-Jiruchi, Clavones, Cluden, Coif de Fer, Coiffette, Coif of Mail, Comb, Corinthian Casque, Coursing Hat, Crenel, Crest, Daiyenzan, Date, Death's Head Burgonet, Dog-Faced Basinet, Dzu Nari, Earflaps, Escuffa, Falling Beavor, Fukigayeshi, G'Hug'Hwah, Great Basinet, Hachi, Hachi-Gane, Hachimaki, Hachimanza, Hanburi, Happojiro, Happuri, Harai-Date, Heaume, Heichozan, Hineno, Hishi-Nui-No-Ita, Ho-Ate, Hood of Mail, Hoshi, Hoshi Kabuto, Hufken, Huvette, Icho-Gashira, Iron Hat, Itajikoro, Jerichonka, Jingasa, Kabuto, Kabuto Ji, Kahawat, Kalghi, Kan-Top, Kasa-Jiruchi-No-Kuwan, Kashira-Date, Kashira Zukuri, Kataitix, Katapu, Katapu Kaloi, Kawagasa, Kemili, Kettle Hat, Khod Chullumdar Gonjicri, Kikuza, Kimen, Kiyo, Korai-Bo, Koshi-Kumo, Kukehimo, Kulah Khud, Kulah Zirah, Kunee Chalkeres, Kusari Kabuto, Kusari-Zukin, Kuwagata, Lambrequin, Lavong, Lobster-Tail Helmet, Mabi-Sashi, Maidate, Maizashi, Manju, Maro Hashi, Mask Visor, Mayedate, Menpo, Mesail, Momidzukin, Momogata, Momonari, Morian, Morian-Cabasset, Moriyo, Moto-O, Mukashi Jikoro, Nai Shokpa, Namban Bo, Nasal, Nihojiro, Ocularium, Ogatame-No-Kane, O-Kina-Men, Onna-Men, Oreilletes, Orle, Palet, Panache, Parchment Crest, Pate Plate, Pig-Faced Basinet, Plume Holder, Pot, Sakugata, Salade, Saru-Bo, Schelom, Schischaks, Shaguma, Shida-No-Ana, Shihojiro, Shiigata, Shii Nari, Shikoro, Shinobi-No-O, Shira Hashi, Shiwazura, Skull, Sohatsu, Spider Helmet, Sugar-Loaf Helm, Tacula Tefao,

Tatami Jiku, Tatami Kabuto, Tengu, Tetanaulo, Tokage-Gashira, To-Kamuri, To-Kin, Tokwan, Top, Toppai, Tori-Kabuto, Tori-Tengu, Tosei Jikoro, Totosubai, Tsubame-Bo, Tsuyo-Otoshi No Hat, Wari Jikoro, Wreath, Yeboshi, Yodare-Kake, Zushozan, Zudate.

HENDOO. An ancus, Ceylon. (Tennent II, 382). See Ancus.

FIGURE 365. *Miscellaneous Helmets.* 1. *Turkish(?). Fluted steel cap, long neck guard of riveted mail.* 2. *Turkish(?). Steel cap with a border of engraved brass. Riveted mail neck guard.* 3. *Tibet. Gilded brass.* 4. *Tibet. Bronze with figures of Buddha in relief and a Sanscrit inscription. Nos. 3 and 4 are probably temple regalia.* 5, 10. *Top and front of a Korean parade helmet. Blackened copper with gold and silver ornaments at the intersections of the bars. The crown is an iron plate inlaid with silver.* 6. *Egyptian Arab. Steel inlaid with the names of the Caliphs in gold.* 7. *Caucasus(?). Steel bowl, apparently early Turkish, with a silver band of later date around the bottom. Riveted mail neck guard with steel ear plates.* 8. *Abor, Assam. Bamboo strips on a cane cap.* 9. *Singpho, Assam. Black leather ornamented with boar's tusks.* 10. *The front view of 5.* 11. *Central Asia. Conical helmet of steel plates riveted.* 12. *Korea. Officer's helmet. Black leather with gilded ornaments. A jade bird at the top. Neck guard of red cloth edged with fur and decorated with gilt ornaments.*

Kubo, Uchikabuto, Uke Bari, Umbril, Uniber, Ushiro Date, Ventail, Vervelles, Visor, Volet, Vue, Wage, Waki-Date, Wa-No-O, Warawazura, War

HENGOT. The hook by which a Dyak blowpipe quiver is hung from the belt. (Arc. f. Eth. IV, 269).

HEO. The leash of a falcon, Japan. It is usually of red silk cord; but if the hawk has distinguished herself, as by killing a crane, she is given one of purple silk. Compare O-O. Fig. 366.

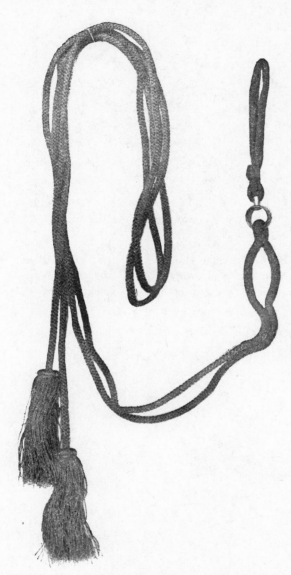

FIGURE 366. *Heo, a Hawk's Leash. Red silk cord with a leather loop and swivel on the end.*

HERCULES CLUBS. "Clubs which we called Hercules-Clubs, with heavy heads of wood with nails driven into the squares of them," used at sieges in the 17th century. (Hewitt III, 605).

HEREBRA. A Phoenician sword. (Burton Sword 180).

HEROLE. The vanguard of an Indian army. (Tod I, 122).

HERSE. The phalanx; later a portcullis.

HEYAZASHI. A very short sword, or knife, carried in the house, Japan.

HI, KESSO. The grooves in a Japanese blade.

HIA. A crossbow used by hand, China. (Jaehns 333).

HIBASAMI. The serpentine of a matchlock, Japan.

HIBU-JI. A tournament, Japan.

HI-BUTA. The pan cover of a matchlock, Japan.

HIDDAH. A horn-shaped wooden flask covered with velvet, Rajput. (Wallace Orient).

HIDE-TACE. Omaha, a target arrow used by boys when learning to shoot. It has a blunt conical head. (Dorsey 286).

HIGUCHI. A touchhole, Japan.

HIJI-GANE. A Japanese elbow cop. It is a round metal plate fastened to the kote. (Conder 273). Fig. 475.

HIKIAWASE. The edge of the opening in a Japanese corselet. (Garbutt 142).

HIKI GANE. A trigger, Japan.

HIKIHADA. A scabbard cover used in traveling in early times in Japan. (Joly S. & S. 30).
    A leather sword case. See Shirazaya.

HIKIME. An arrow with a perforated head, Japan.

HIKI-YA. A whistling arrow, Japan. See Whistling Arrow.

HIME KABURA. A grooved arrowhead, Japan.

HIMOGATANA. A stiletto, Japan. Fig. 367.

HIMO KOSHIATE. See Koshiate.

HIMO-TSUKI. Fastened with cords, a type of wakibiki.

HINA. A blowpipe, Sumatra. It consists of a tube, *anaqnao*, inside of a larger one. Both are made of the *Bambusa Longinodis*. (Arc. f. Eth. IV, 279).

HINAWA. A matchcord, Japan.

HINAWA SASHI. A reel for carrying match-cord, Japan.

FIGURE 367. *Himogatana. One piece of steel. Diamond section blade 6 inches long.*

HINAWA ZUTSU. A matchlock gun, Japan.

HIND'S FOOT. See Goat's Foot.

HINENO. A variety of shikoro, the neck guard of a Japanese helmet.

HINYUAN, HENYUAN. The spear used by the wild tribes, called Shon Pen, inhabiting the interior of Great Nicobar. It has a wooden head with a long, round point and several rows of barbs. (Man, And. & Nic. 10; Man, Nic. 366).

HIODOSHI. Flame color, scarlet and gold, the use of which in armor was restricted to the five great princely families until about 1600. (Dean Jap. 47).

Deep crimson cords for lacing Japanese armor.

HIOOGDO. A sling, Western Tibet. (Ramsay-Western). See Gudo.

HIPA. The Omaha arrow cement. It was a glue made from the skin of the head of an elk or buffalo, or from that of the big turtle. It was used for fas-

tening on the heads of hunting arrows. (Dorsey 287).

HIPPARCHIE. See Ile.

HIPPE. A form of halbard used in the 14th century. It had a rather short and very broad point. (Dean Europ. 62).

HIRA-MAKIYE. See Lacquer.

HIRATA DONIN, HIRATA HIKO-SHIRO. The inventor of a translucent enamel which he used to decorate tsuba in the latter part of the 16th century.

HIRATAHARUNARI. A celebrated maker of enameled tsuba, 17th century.

HIRA-TSUKURI. A Japanese blade with no shinogi; that is one that tapers uniformly from the back to the edge. (Weber I, 277).

HIRA YANAGUI. A flat quiver, Japan. A very wide, flat form with a low solid back, and narrower at the top than at the bottom. An early form. (M. M. S. II, 234). 2, fig. 266.

HIRA ZOGAN. Flat inlay, Japan.

HIRUMAKI. A ferule on a spear, Japan.

FIGURE 368. *Hi Uchi Bukuro (fire lighter).* 1. *Snaphaan lock and receptacle for tinder in an iron case.* 2. *Similar apparatus in on openwork case. Hanging from it is a leather tinder box.*

HI-SAKI-SHITA. A groove in a blade that does not reach the point, Japan.

HI-SAKI-UE. A groove in a Japanese blade that reaches the point.

HI-SAO. A ramrod, Japan.

HISHINUI. Cross stitches fastening together the scales of Japanese armor. (Conder 267).

HITOMATSU. The space between the inner and outer gates of a castle, Japan.

HITOYE HABAKI. An habaki made in one piece. (Joly Int. 20). Fig. 338.

HITSU. A side hole in a tsuba. There are frequently two, one oval for the kozuka, and one of three lobes for the kogai. Sometimes both are of the

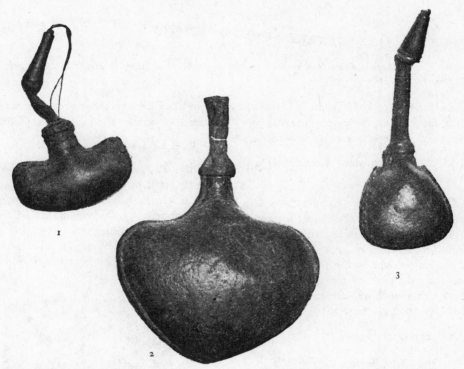

FIGURE 369. *Hman Skuk. Tibetan powder flasks. 1. Stiff leather flask with a flexible leather tube and a horn mouthpiece. 2. Very large flask for a reserve supply of powder. 3. Similar to 1 but the body is decorated with gilding and colors.*

HISHINUI-ITA. Cross-stitched plate. The lowest plate of the Japanese sode (shoulder guards).

The plate where the laces are fastened by cross stitches. (Conder 269).

HISHI-NUI-NO-ITA. The lowest plate of the neck guard of a Japanese helmet. (Dean Jap. 4). Where the cords are fastened by cross stitches.

HISHI-TOJI. The lowest plate of a piece of Japanese armor where the cords are fastened by cross stitches. (Conder 260).

HISHIU. A dagger, Japan.

HITA-TSURA. See Yakiba.

same shape. If either, or both, are not to be used the holes are often filled up, usually with a plain piece of metal. Occasionally they are decorated.

HI UCHI BUKURO. A brocade bag hung from the kurikata of a sword in early times in Japan. (Joly S. & S. 44, 48).

A fire lighter, a snaphaan lock in a small case with a chamber to hold the tinder to be lighted. (Weber I, 280). Fig. 368.

These fire lighters were sometimes carried hung from a primer, pepper blower or other small piece of equipment.

HI-YA. A fire arrow, a rocket, Japan.

HIYOTAN SODE. A sode shaped like the outline of a gourd. (Conder 272).

HIZARA. The pan of a gunlock, Japan.

It derived its name from the resemblance of the shape of the upper portion to that of the Hodo-Pata, a religious flag. The upper part is of scales

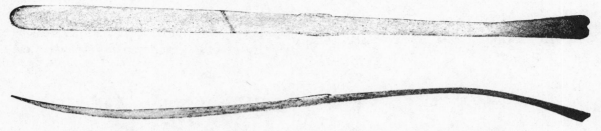

FIGURE 370. *Hoeroa. Maori club made from the jawbone of a sperm whale. The upper end is carved. Length 4 feet 6 inches.*

HIZA-YOROI. A knee cop, Japan. (Ogawa). It was usually fastened to, or was an integral part of, the suneate. In one type it is a separate piece.

HMAN, SMAN. Gunpowder, Western Tibet. (Ramsay-Western).

HMAN SKUK. The Tibetan powder flask. It is usually of stiff leather with a tube of soft leather at the mouth, which terminates in a horn tube that is closed by a plug of cloth. To use it the plug is removed, the opening closed by the finger, the flask inverted and the tube pinched together below the mouthpiece, which then holds a measured charge that is poured into the gun. Fig. 369.

HO. The head of a spear, Japan.

HO-ATE. A variety of menpo (Japanese buffe) that only covers the lower half of the face. (Dean Jap. 67). Fig. 567.
    Garbutt gives it as the general name for all kinds of face guards.

HOBBIES. Small horses used by light cavalry in the 14th century. (Grose I, 107).

HOBILERS. Light cavalry of the 14th century. The arms and equipment of a hobiler in the time of Edward III were: a horse, a haqueton, or armor of plate, a basinet, iron gauntlets, a sword, a knife and a lance. Mounted archers were also called hobiler archers. Later the same kind of troops were called demi-lances. (Grose I, 106).

HOBITZ. See Howitz.

HODO-HAI-DATE. A form of Japanese cuisse.

closely laced together; hanging considerably below this are four smaller separate pieces. (Conder 275).

HODO-ITA. A variety of haidate.

HOEROA. A doubly curved, flat bone weapon formerly used by the Maoris. It is cut from the lower jaw bone of a sperm whale, and is usually about four feet long by two and a half inches wide. It has a carved ornament on the handle which is narrower, thicker and more rounded than the striking end which has fairly sharp edges for about half its length. The curvature is in the narrower di-

FIGURE 371. *Hoguine and backplate, about 1520. Made for a member of the Radzivil family. Metropolitan Museum.*

mension, in the wider it is flat. The handbook to the Ethnological Collections of the British Museum says that it was used for throwing as well as striking. From its shape it would have been a very awkward and ineffective missile. Fig. 370.

HOGEN. The highest of the three titles conferred on artists by the Emperor of Japan. It means "Eye of the law."

HOKEN. A temple sword in the form of a ken, Japan. Fig. 438.

HOKKIO. The second of the three titles conferred on artists by the Emperor of Japan. It means "Bridge of the law."

HOKKU. A poem or epigram of seventeen syllables, Japan. They were often used as decorations on sword mountings.

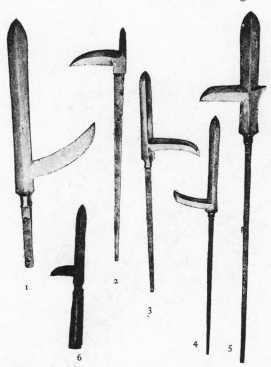

FIGURE 372. *Hoko. 1. Bright steel, 14.75 x 6.25 inches. 2. Flat on the back, 3.75 x 4.375 inches. 3. 7.5 x 4.25 inches, bright steel. 4. Bright steel, 7.875 x 3.6 inches. 5. Bright steel, 10 x 5 inches. 6. Black iron with a socket for the handle. Length 11.25 inches.*

HOG'S BRISTLE, SWINE FEATHER. See Hand Palisado and Sweyne's Feather.

HOGUINE. A protection for the buttocks made of narrow plates articulated together. It was only used for fighting on foot in the lists, 16th century. (ffoulkes Armouries 101). Fig. 371.

HOIN. The lowest of the three titles conferred on artists by the Emperor of Japan. It means "Sign of the law."

HOIST. The part of a flag next the staff. (Macgeorge 68).

HOJIU. See Ken.

HOKO. A Japanese spear with a long, straight point and one side blade at right angles to it. The side blade may be straight or curved towards, or away from, the point. Fig. 372.

HOKO-YUMI, OTOKANE. The tartar-shaped bow, Japan. In Japan these bows were built usually of three, or more, varieties of bamboo glued together. In some cases the ends and grip were of metal. The ends of the belly, where the string strikes, were made of metal and were called otokane. The string striking against them made a sound that was often used for signaling. (Gilbertson Archery 113).

HOLSTER. A case fastened to the belt or saddle in which to carry a pistol or other small weapon. It was usually made of leather and shaped, more or less, to fit the weapon. They were used in the East as well as in Europe and many are decorated with embroidery. Fig. 373.

HONJIN, HONYEI. The headquarters of a camp, Japan.

HO-NOKI. (Magnolia Hypoluca). The wood used in Japan for making scabbards.

HONORS OF WAR. When a fortress surren-

FIGURE 373. *Holsters.* 1. *Tunis. Covered with red velvet embroidered with gold. Length 16 inches, 18th century.* 2. *Japanese, 19th century. Black leather with a gilt mon. A copy of an American holster.* 3. *Central Africa, 19th century. Leather embroidered with colored wool.* 4. *Italian, 16th century. Stamped leather for a wheel lock pistol.*
The first three are to scale. The last is Metropolitan Museum.

HOLY WATER SPRINKLE, MORNING STAR. A shafted weapon with an enlarged head of wood or iron studded with spikes. (ffoulkes 107). It was a common peasant weapon for several hundred years in Europe. It was also used in the East though never as common there. Fig. 374.

HOMMERU. The citadel of a castle, Japan.

HOMYAHTA. A spear-like implement carried solely as an ornament by the people of the Nicobar Islands. (Man, And. & Nic. 7).

dered the garrison was sometimes allowed the "honors of war," which were that it could march out with "lighted match, bullet in mouth, drums beating and trumpets sounding." (Hewitt III, 697).

HON-TSUKURI. A Japanese blade with a shinogi; that is, one in which the sides are parallel near the back and then tapers to the edge.

HONZOGAN. True inlaying in which wires or plates are hammered, or pressed, into grooves cut in the ground, Japan. See Inlaying.

HO-O. The Japanese phoenix; it has a head like a rooster and a tail with very long flowing feathers. It was said not to eat live insects nor to tread upon grass. It is often used to decorate weapons and armor. Fig. 375.

By this means he this day drowned more than a dozen." 14th century. (Hewitt II, 244).

HOOLURGE. An axe with a thin, curved knife-like blade, Northern and Central India. (Egerton 472, 716).

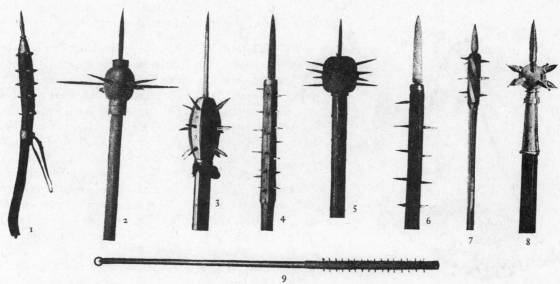

FIGURE 374. *Holy Water Sprinkles. 1. German, 17th century. 2. German, 16th century. 3. German, 17th century. 4. Swiss, 17th century. 5. English, 15th century. 6. German, 15th century. 7. German, 16th century. 8. Polish, 17th century. 9. Japanese, 17th century. All but no. 9 Metropolitan Museum. Not to scale.*

HOOD of Mail. See Coif of Mail.

HOOKED SPEAR. At the seige of Mortaigne the Sieur de Beaujeu was among the defenders, "and was provided with a stiff and strong spear, that had a long sharp blade; and beneath the blade there was a sharp and catching hook, so that when he made a thrust and could fix the hook into the plates or haubergeon of an enemy, the man was either drawn forward or overturned into the water.

A crowbill with a double point. (Wallace Orient). Compare Zaghnal.

HOPAK. See Shinpung.

HOPFER, DANIEL. Augsberg, circa 1495-1565. He was at first a designer and maker of stained glass and an engraver. He worked mainly with his brother George and much of their work was dec-

FIGURE 375. *Ho-O. 1. Tsuba. Iron with Ho-O birds in relief in brass, 17th century. 2. Sentoku tsuba with Ho-O birds in relief, 18th to 19th centuries.*

FIGURE 376. *Hora. Horn knuckle duster used by the Jettis, India. Length 5 inches.*

orating armor made by others, of whom Coloman Colman was the chief. It is said that the brothers Hopfer were ordered by the Emperor Maximilian to make one hundred and ten helmets for the Trabantian Guard. (ffoulkes 136).

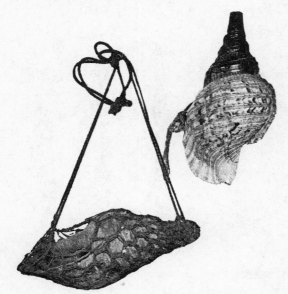

FIGURE 377. *Horagai. Japanese shell trumpets. The lower one is in a net of heavy cord in which it is carried.*

HOPLITES. The heavily armed infantry that formed the Greek phalanx. (Boutell 42).

HORA. A horn knuckle duster, oval with pointed ends and points along one side. It was used by the Jettis, India. They were a Telegu cast of performers and gymnasts. Fig. 376.

HORAGAI, HORA. A shell trumpet, Japan. Fig. 377.

HORIKI. A moat, Japan.

HORIMONO. Chiseled objects — kozuka, kogai, fuchi, kashira and menuki; either collectively or separately. (Joly Int. 14). Also the decoration on blades. (Weber I, 291).

HORIN. The Buddhist wheel of the law. The spokes are vajras of one prong. It was sometimes used as a guard on temple swords, Japan.

HORN ARMOR. Horn was used for making armor as late as the 15th century in Europe. Hewitt (II, 228) says that the shield of John of Gaunt was made of "wood, leather and plates of horn"

and (III, 443) mentions "vi jackes stuffed with horne." These were probably similar to the brigandines made of horn and cloth used in Tibet within a few years. Armor made of plates of horn connected by mail were used in the Philippines by the Moros at the time of the American occupation. At that time they also used helmets made of plates of horn on a leather foundation. Fig. 378.

HORN GROOVE. Flight shooting, that is shooting with a bow solely for distance without regard to a mark, has always been a favorite amusement of archers. The Turks excelled at this sport and used arrows considerably lighter and shorter than those ordinarily used. In order that the bow could be pulled to its full capacity a grooved piece of horn, or leather, was fastened to the left wrist to support and guide the arrow when it was pulled inside the bow. The grooved piece is curved crossways so as to keep the arrow in line; and lengthways from end to end, the middle being the highest part. This is done so that the arrow touches only at a single point giving the minimum of friction. The groove is fastened on an oval or palette-shaped shield of tortoise shell or shark's skin. The whole device is called "Sipar" by the Turks. This name is Persian and means "shield." Fig. 379.

One described by Payne-Gallwey (Orient. Bows 11) is a curved piece of horn with a ring on the back to fit the thumb, and a cord attached to the

FIGURE 378. *Horn Helmet, Moro. The shape is copied from a Spanish casque of the 17th century. The inside is a neatly made cap of hide which is covered with carefully fitted pieces of kabau horn sewed together and to the hide cap.*

front end to be held between the fingers to steady it. The ones illustrated in fig. 379 have loops and straps on the back by means of which they can be fastened on the hand. 3, fig. 379 shows the straps.

The Turks excelled in flight shooting and not only used very short and light arrows and the Turk-

fastened to the back of a mounted warrior so as to fill with wind and project from his back. Some say that it was stuffed with cotton, others that it was partially distended by a wicker frame. It was said to protect the wearer from arrows shot from behind. Figs. 380, 381.

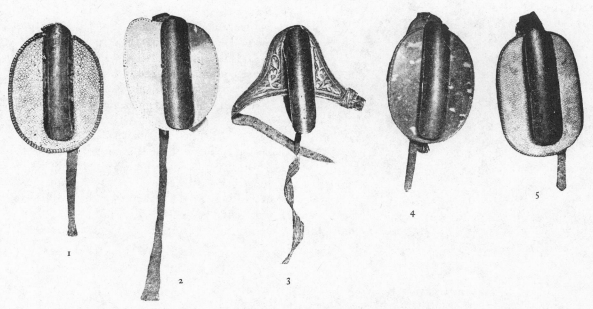

FIGURE 379. *Horn Grooves. 1. Oval hand guard 4 x 5 inches covered with white shark skin and edged with silver braid. 2. Palette-shaped of tortoise shell. 3. The wrist strap and groove only. Wrist strap of brown leather embroidered with gold. 4. Oval guard of tortoise shell on leather. 5. Oval guard of green shark skin on leather.*

ish form of archer's ring which is more effective than the usual forms of release as it bends the string at a point and allows the feathers to come close to the end of the arrow; but their archers are especially taught how to shoot. The Turks say that the important ones in obtaining good results are—the bow maker, the arrow maker, the ring maker and the shooting teacher. My old Turk in Constantinople said that there were many men who could pull a bow until the ends touched but could not send an arrow any distance until shown how to do it. See Bows.

HORN WORK. In fortification, two bastions connected by a curtain before a fortification. It was connected to the main works by wings.

HORO. A curious "defense" worn with Japanese armor in the 16th century. It was a cloth loosely

It was generally about six feet long and made of five strips of cloth sewed together and strengthened by plaits. The crest of the owner was placed at the top, middle and bottom, and both the upper and lower edges were fringed. The top was either fastened to the helmet or to the ring on the back plate; the lower end was held by cords tied around the waist. In some cases it was fastened to the helmet and to the forehead of the horse, being kept in position by cords to the stirrups. (Conder 277).

Garbutt, p. 171, says that there are many kinds of horo and that they differed considerably in size. He finds no mention of cotton stuffing, but describes several varieties of framework, called oikago, for supporting it. He also says that it was invented by Hatakeyama Masanaga in the Onin period (1467-1468). "Whether this refers to the horo or oikago is not clear."

The horo is not only a defense but had other virtues: "The horo is a very important 'overcloth'

FIGURE 380. *Horo. Metropolitan Museum.*

of military men and it is very wise to carry it always for it drives away all sorts of calamity and misfortune, and when you are killed on the battle field the enemy will understand, as they recognize the horo, that the dead was not a common person, and so your corpse will be well treated. When fighting the horo must be fastened to the ring called *horotsuke-no-kuan.*

"When you have killed an enemy who wears the horo, wrap his head which you cut off, in a piece of his horo.

"When anyone is exhausted and decides to die in the field, he must fasten the cord of his helmet to the *haigashira*, then cut it off to show that it will never be put on again. Also he must fasten the cord of the horo which is called *hino-o* (this is not explained in the book, but probably is the center fastening of the top of the horo), to the horo-fastening ring on the helmet and fasten the cord called *nami-tatsu-no-o* to the hole in the stirrup. This also means that he will fight no more.

"Further, one must cut off the ends of the obi and throw away the scabbard of the sword — this has the same significance."

When fighting at sea, or where there is not

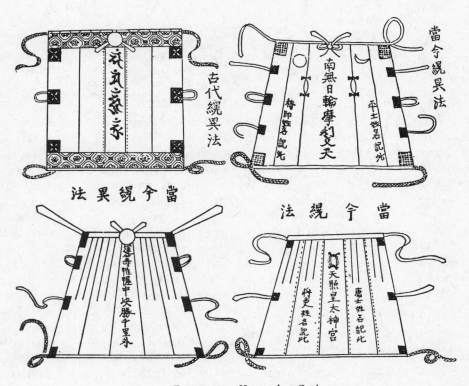

FIGURE 381. *Horo, after Garbutt.*

enough room to wear a horo, a small standard was said to have been carried in place of it, fig. 382. It was probably worn on the back like a sashimono.

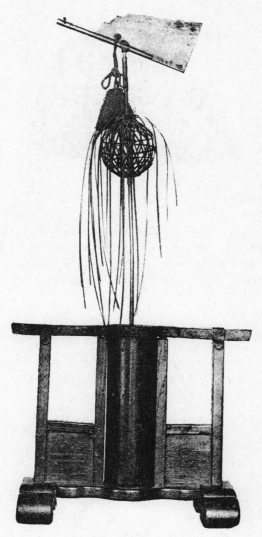

FIGURE 382. *Horo Substitute. A gilded rudder on top of a light shaft with an openwork ball and fringe of cane. The whole is on a wooden stand.*

HORSE ARMOR. See Bardings.

HORSE FURNITURE. The equipment of a horse, harness, trappings and armor.

HORSEMAN'S HAMMER. The war hammer with either a long or short handle, with plain or dentated head. It was a favorite weapon in the 15th century. (Hewitt III, 354). See Hammer, War.

HORSE PISTOL. Any large pistol carried by a horseman.

HORTUK. A small Battak axe; it is of the ordinary Malayan type. (Arc. f. Eth. VI, 120). See Biliong.

HORU. Carved, Japan.

HOSHI. Projecting rivets on a Japanese helmet. They are generally ornamental as well as affording extra strength. (Conder 258).

HOSHI KABUTO. A Japanese helmet having practically no ribs but many projecting rivets. Fig. 383.

HOSO TACHI. A variety of tachi.

HOSTING HARNESS. Armor for war as distinguished from that intended for tournaments. (ffoulkes 63).

HOTAI. A fort or fortification, Japan.

HOTOKE-DO. A breastplate that simulates the naked body. The name means "saint's breastplate," Japan. Fig. 384.

HOURD. A wooden gallery built outside the battlements in times of war to allow the defenders to see the foot of the walls and towers, and to throw stones and other missiles on any assailants that approached them. (Violet le Duc, Hist. 363). See Breteche.

HOURT. A crescent-shaped bag of linen stuffed with straw. It was worn on the horse's breast in tournaments in the 15th century. (Hewitt III, 537).

The only one known to be in existence is in the museum in Vienna.

HOWETT. The orthodox cry for encouraging a hawk when the quarry she chased into a hedge or bush has been routed out.

HOWITZ, HOBITZ. A kind of mortar mounted upon a field carriage like a gun. The trunnions of a howitz are in the middle, those of a mortar at the end. (Hoyt 419).

HOWITZER. A howitzer is a compromise between the mortar and the field gun, being intended for high angle fire like the former, and mounted on a movable carriage like the latter. It was invented about the end of the 16th century. (Grose I, 407).

HUATA. A long spear used by the Maoris in defending their fortified villages. It is a plain, pointed stick.

HUA-YAO. Gunpowder in San-Chuan Chinese.

the ends and drooping projections over the blade, a short grip and disk pommel (Wallace Orient).

HUNDWANI. Indian watered steel. (Marco Polo I, 93, note).

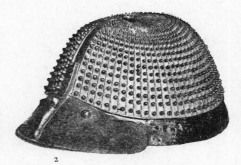

FIGURE 383. *Hoshi Kabuto.* 1. *Made of 62 plates with 1890 projecting rivets. Signed Nari Kunesada.* 2. *Made of 72 plates with 960 projecting rivets. Signed Miochin Munesuke. (22nd Miochin, 1688-1735).*

HUFKEN, HUSKIN. A light, open, close-fitting headpiece worn by archers in the 16th century. (Hewitt III, 597).

HOJIUR. Battak spears. The heads are usually of iron, but occasionally of bamboo. (Arc. f. Eth. VI, 120).

HUKIM KHANI. A type of sword hilt peculiar to Hyderabad. It has short quillons with seals on

HUNG. A small gourd carried by the Dyaks to hold pieces of pith for their blowpipe darts. The gourd is closed by a wooden stopper which is often carved with a monster's head. (Bock 194).

FIGURE 384. *Hotoke-Do, 18th century. Metropolitan Museum.*

FIGURE 385. *Hunga-Munga, throwing knife from the Lake Chad region. Length 23 inches. The handle is covered with rawhide.*

HUNGA-MUNGA. A heavy throwing knife with a hooked end. It is used by the natives south of Lake Chad. (Burton Sword 37). Fig. 385.

HUR! HUR! The Rajput battle cry.

HUSAIN. A celebrated Persian gunmaker of the time of Akbar. (Egerton, p. 64).

HU SIN KING. (Mirror guarding the heart). Circular plates of white metal with ornamental

the color of the company's uniform. Arm and leg guards made of wood and covered with leather or gold plates trimmed with feathers, and helmets of the same materials, shaped and painted to represent the head of some animal, snake or monster, completed the costume.

ICHIJO GOTO. The last celebrated tsuba maker of the Goto family who died in 1876 at the age of eighty-seven. Ichijo was not of the direct line, but

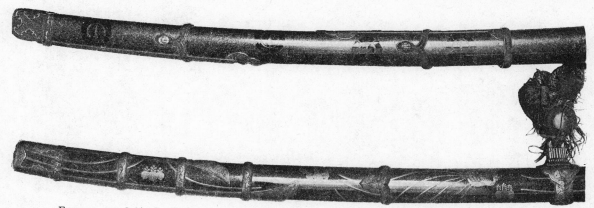

FIGURE 386. *Ichizuke. Tachi scabbard. Both show the long chapes with the bands that hold them.*

borders, worn on the breast and back of Chinese armor. (Laufer 286). Fig. 72, no. 2.

HUSKIN. See Hufkin.

HUISSIERS D'ARMES. Permanent guards of the French kings in the 14th century and later. (Hewitt II, 36).

HUVETTE. A kind of helmet. (Fairholt 550).

HYAGO. Cartridges, Japan. Probably charges in a bandolier. Compare Hayago.

HYOTO. The sound of an arrow, Japan.

I

I-AI. The art of drawing the long bow, Japan.

I-BA. A place for shooting with a bow, Japan.

ICHCAHUIPILLI. The body armor worn by the higher classes in ancient Mexico. It consisted of a breastplate of quilted cotton, one or two fingers in thickness. Over this was worn a cotton coat made in one piece and covering the arms and thighs; it fastened behind and was decorated with feathers of

was a son of Kenjo. His work is extremely delicate and shows much variety as he did not always adhere strictly to the family traditions. He was made Hokkio by the Emperor at the age of thirty-four, and Hogen, the highest art title, at the age of seventy-three.

ICHI-NO-ASHI. The upper band with a sling loop on the scabbard of a tachi. (Brinkley VII, 211). The lower band is called Ichi-No-Sei.

ICHIZUKE, ISHAZURI. The chape of a tachi; on the other types of sword it is called kojiri. (Joly, Hawkshaw xiv). It often has long projections that run up the edges of the scabbard. When it is comparatively short it is held by a single band called shibabiki; when it is long it is held by several called seme. (Gilbertson Dec. 95). Fig. 386.

ICHO-GASHIRA. (Icho leaf head). A form of ornament at the top of the silver plates sometimes found on Japanese helmets. (Conder 259). See Kato Jiro.

IGIMO. The loose piece between the head and shaft of the harpoons of the Eskimo of Point Barrow. (U. S. N. M. 1900, 280).

IGO-HAI-DATE. Japanese cuisses of very small plates sewn on silk or cloth. It was worn mostly by horsemen as being more flexible than the usual form. (Conder 275). Fig. 387.

IGURUMI. Shooting birds with an arrow having a cord attached to it, Japan.

ies an ephipparchie — two ephipparchies a telos — and two telos an epitagm of 4,096 horses.

ILI. An Indian sword of mythical times. It was two cubits long and five fingers broad; the front part curved; there was no hand guard, and four movements were peculiar to it. (Burton Sword 215).

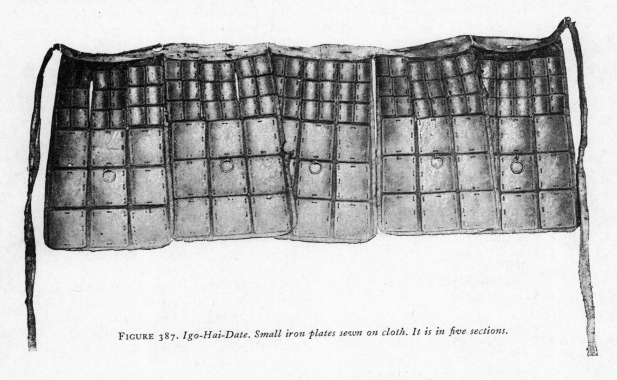

FIGURE 387. *Igo-Hai-Date. Small iron plates sewn on cloth. It is in five sections.*

IHORE-MUNE. See Mune.

I-IRO. To shoot with a bow, Japan.

IKA. The Ainu quiver. It is a flat box of willow with a tight fitting cover, both covered with cherry bark. They are usually well carved with conventional designs. Fig. 388.

A cuttle fish, Japan.

IKADA. A plate, or series of splints, connected by mail, which protects the forearm in Japanese armor. (Conder 273).

IKUBA. A mark for shooting at with a bow, a target. A tent for archery, Japan.

ILE. The tactical unit of Greek cavalry, a troop of sixty-four horses. Two iles formed an epitarchie — two epitarchies formed a tarentinarchie — two tarentinarchies a xenagie or hipparchie — two hipparch-

IMAKPUK. See Una.

IMBER. See Umbril.

IMBRICATE ARMOR. Armor formed of overlapping scales fastened to leather or cloth. It was worn in Europe in the 11th and 12th centuries and at some time in almost every country in which armor was worn. (ffoulkes 16). Fig. 29.

IMBROCATA. A thrust in the late 16th century fencing. It was made in a rather downward direction over the adversary's sword, hand or dagger. (Castle 83).

IMONO. A casting, Japan.

IMPING. Mending a broken feather of a hawk. It is done by pushing an imping needle into the pith of the undamaged part of the feather and into that of a similar feather that exactly matches the broken one. The imping needle is of triangular section and pointed at both ends. The needle rusts and sticks tightly in the pith, and the feather is about as good as ever if the operation has been skilfully performed. (Michell 227).

IMUKU. See Waki-Ita.

INAGI. A breastwork of rice straw, Japan.

engineer, Frederick Jambelli, in 1585. (Grose I, 410).

INLAYING. What follows is confined to the inlaying of metals with other metals or materials. There are several methods used in different parts of the world which produce quite different results. Very few of those who have written about it have

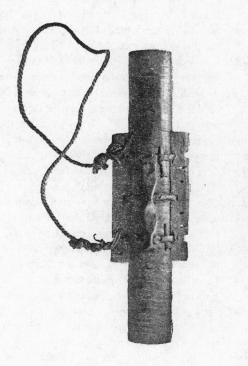

FIGURE 388. *Ika, Ainu quivers. Peabody Museum, Salem.*

INCARTATA. In the 16th and 17th century fencing—the volte, or half turn, either to escape a thrust or to get in a better position to riposte. (Castle 84).

INDAN. A club of the Javan gods. It is straight with a plain handle and spirally fluted body. (Raffles I, plate p. 296/297).

INDUKU. The Kaffir throwing club. (Ratzel I, 235). See Kerrie.

INEDI. The point of the spear thrower called palati by the Kakadu, Australia. (Spencer, North Ter. 378).

INFERNALS. Floating mines constructed in the bodies of boats. They were invented by an Italian

been familiar with the metals, tools, methods and appliances used and their descriptions are seldom technically correct. I know of no one place where all of the methods are described.

The simplest method called inlaying is to glue, or paste, one metal in patterns on another. It is not inlaying, and while the effect when first done is often quite good, it very soon wears off. Such work is mainly done on objects to be sold to tourists.

Another method often called inlaying is fire gilding and it produces very much the same effect. In it gold or silver is mixed with mercury to a thin paste (amalgam) and pressed on the base. It is then heated to drive off the mercury which leaves the precious metal firmly attached to the base. The result looks well and wears well if protected from abrasion. Unfortunately the layer of precious metal is necessarily very thin and soon wears off if much rubbed. This is the method almost always used for "inlaying" armor in Europe. It was sometimes, though rarely, used in the East.

The third method is called by the English false damascening, by Dr. Dean incrusting, in India koft, and in Japan nunome. In it the surface to be decorated is covered with cuts and scratches in various directions with the burrs left attached. The inlay is then pressed on in the lines of the pattern. If carefully done by a skillful workman the effect is good and fairly durable. Unfortunately it is seldom well done and usually wears off very soon.

The fourth, and best, method is called true damascening by the English, damaskening by Dr. Dean, tah i nishan in India and honzogan in Japan. In it the pattern is cut in fairly deep grooves, round bottomed for wire, and flat with straight sides for any other shaped pieces. The depth of the grooves should be about two-thirds of the diameter of the wires. The inlay should be of the softest metal procurable; usually pure metal if gold or silver, and carefully annealed in any case. It is pressed into the grooves and is sometimes hammered down flat, and sometimes allowed to stand up in relief.

Hendley says that if the inlay is to be kept in relief it is driven into the grooves with a hammer having a grooved face. In this I think that he is mistaken. I have watched inlayers at work in many parts of the world and have never seen such hammers used, nor among the tools. It would require not one hammer but dozens with different sized and shaped grooves, and it would be almost impossible always to strike at the exact angle necessary to set the wire in place and preserve the accuracy of the curves. The method I have always seen used is to press the wire into the groove and set up the edges of the latter against it with a blunt punch or chisel. This holds the inlay in position much more firmly than hitting it with a grooved hammer could possibly do.

If the surface of the inlay is flat and flush with the base the Japanese call the work hira-zogan; and if it is in relief, taka-zogan. There are very few other countries that have specific names for these varieties of work. When the inlay is left in relief it is usually carved. This method gives a much more brilliant and permanent effect than false damascening.

In Japan three other methods of inlaying are used, none of which are employed anywhere else as far as I have been able to ascertain. The first is called uttori zogan; in this the pieces to be inlaid are quite large and thick. If the piece to be set in is of one of the cheaper metals the recess for it is made of the full size of the piece, which is put in it and the edges set up by a punch. If it is of one of the expensive metals, gold or silver, a flange is made around the edge and a groove cut in the base to fit it. The flange is placed in the groove and the edges set up against it as before. The projecting part is then carved and often inlaid with other metals giving very elaborate colored effects when properly pickled. The whole of the carving and inlaying may be done before the piece is attached to the base; but it is better to attach it first, as it can then be more easily held steady when working on it. It also avoids the danger of injuring it while attaching it.

The next method is used for making the tiny dots that are the conventional Japanese representation of mist; also for very fine inscriptions in characters so small that most people require a magnifying glass to read them; and for other fine work. In this the hollows are cut in the background as usual and these are filled with gold amalgam. The object is then heated to drive off the mercury and the gold polished down flat. It is fire gilding, except that solid plugs of gold are left in the hollows instead of a thin layer over the surface. It is therefore much more durable than fire gilding.

The remaining method is very rarely used. It is to cut hollows for the design and cast sawari (speculum metal), a hard and very brittle variety of pewter, in them. The entire surface is then ground flat. This is done because the sawari is so brittle that it cannot be cut to shape. This alloy will take a very high polish of silvery whiteness and it is possible that it was originally finished in this way; in the few examples existing it is badly tarnished so that it is almost as dark as the background.

Both true and false damascening were used in Europe, though very rarely. Nearly all of the so-called inlaying used on arms and armor in Europe was fire gilding. Both true and false damascening were used in Persia and India, the former being almost always employed for the better work. In North Africa and Malaya only true damascening was used.

In North Africa quite broad surfaces are made by inlaying small wires close together and hammering the whole down flat. Little, if any, work is done in relief. Most of the work is done free-hand with no pattern before the worker. With very large pieces the main elements of the design are sometimes drawn on the work and inlaid. The details are then put in free-hand.

In Malaya the inlay is almost always in relief and the projecting parts are carved; even if flat it is generally decorated with carving. Gold is the only metal used as an inlay in Malaya and the carving is frequently very good. It misses the brilliant effects obtained by the Japanese who use metals of different colors, and the designs are purely conventional, otherwise it will stand comparison with Japanese work.

The finest and most complicated work is done in Japan. Not only are the designs and workmanship of the highest quality but a great variety of metals and alloys are used that give a diversity of colors when properly pickled. Ivory, amber and stones of various colors are also sometimes used as inlays.

In Europe if an artist had a surface to decorate he drew a special design to fit it. The East is more conservative, most of its designs are traditional, and the artist simply drew one from memory modifying it to fit the space available; and they often show wonderful cleverness in twisting a design to fit an irregular space. In Japan the better artists had very interesting sketch books. The decorations of tsuba and kozuka are frequently continued on the backs. This was not done haphazard. The artist made a sketch that included much more than the finished work. He often made three or four sketches, slightly modifying the design, until he had one that suited him. He then drew lines around the part, or parts, he intended to use. For a tsuba, for instance, he would have two ellipses the size of the guard spaced the thickness of the guard apart. What appeared on the different parts of the guard were parts of a whole and not separate designs. The making of the design was very complicated as no part of it should extend or appear on the seppa dai (the space in the middle covered by the hilt and seppa) or the riobitsu (the openings for the kozuka and kogai). In spite of what we are told I believe that the outlines of the guard were drawn on the paper before the design. In some of the very late guards these requirements were ignored and we find guards of the second half of the 19th century with the design covering a large part of the seppa dai. These, of course, were only made as ornaments and not for use.

We frequently complain of the grotesqueness of oriental designs, forgetting that they are simply following their traditions instead of ours. What seems to us the wildest imaginings of the oriental probably appear no more grotesque to us than some of the anatomically impossible monsters in poses that defy the law of gravitation that we admire in Italian paintings, would to him. The art of any country must be judged to a certain extent by its own standards and traditions.

In Turkey, Persia and India much good work was done, particularly in the inlaying of Arabic inscriptions which are very difficult as the letters are all formed of irregular curves, a slight variation in any of which may completely change the sense. Even much of the false damascening is quite durable as care is taken, in the better work, to confine its use to the parts that are not likely to be badly rubbed.

INOME. "Boar's eye," a heart-shaped opening, Japan. It is often used in the decoration of sword fittings.

INQUARTO. Time thrusts delivered on the adversary's attack by volting. (Castle 178).

INSTANCES. Methods of approaching an adversary in 17th century fencing. (Castle 125).

INTAGLIATA. Time thrusts delivered on an adversary's attack by passing. (Castle 178).

INUBASHIRI. A path between the walls and moat of a castle or fortress, Japan.

IOOROOM. The plate guard of a katar. (Tower 235, p. 29).

IPOH. The poison used for arrows and blowpipe darts by the Pagan Malayans. Its principal ingredients are the juices of the Ipoh, or Upas, tree (*antiaris*) and of the roots of the Ipoh creeper (*strychnos tieute*). These two are used separately or together, and are usually mixed with a variety of other substances such as tobacco, capsicum, onion, scorpion's stings, snake's fangs, pepper and, according to some, arsenic. The mixture is boiled to a thick syrup and spread on the heads of the darts or arrows, which are then dried in the sun. The proportions and ingredients varied in every locality, and with every individual, but one or both of the Ipoh were always present. The blowpipe darts were marked on the butt to show the strength of the poison on them. (Skeat & Blagden I, 261).

IPUA. A harpoon, Point Barrow. (U. S. N. M. 1900, 280).

FIGURE 389. *Iron Hat, English, about 1645. Metropolitan Museum.*

IPUDLIGADLIN. A variety of bear arrow used at Point Barrow. In it a short piece of barbed bone is placed between the flint head and the shaft and fastened to the former. Apparently the Eskimo were not able to make barbed flint heads and used this extra piece of bone to prevent the arrow from falling from the wound. (Murdoch 203).

IROIRO-ODOSHI. Japanese armor laced with cords of several colors.

IRON HAT. The chapel de fer. In the 17th century iron hats were occasionally made that were perfect copies of the hats of civil life. Fig. 389.

IROYE. Inlays of one, or several, alloys on a base of iron or some other metal or alloy. The name means colored picture from the fact that the several alloys developed their respective patina of different colors under the influence of the acid pickle in which the finished object was boiled. It was a favorite method of decorating Japanese sword mountings, especially in the 18th and 19th centuries. (Joly, Naunton xii).

IROYE MENUKI. Menuki decorated with inlays of several colors. (Joly Int. 15).

IRPULL. The ordinary barbed wooden spear of the Melville Islanders. (Spencer, North. Ter. 352).

IRUELLA, IRUWALLA. A name given by the Melville Islanders to a variety of clubs, some of which are straight and flat with distinct handles, and some of which have a variety of forked heads. (Spencer, North. Ter. 372, 374).

ISARI-BI. A torch used in fishing at night, Japan.

ISAU. A kind of sword used by the Balaus of Borneo. (Ling Roth II, 136).

ISHAZURI. See Ichizuke.

ISHIBIYA. A cannon, Japan. This name originally meant a cannon shooting stone balls.

ISHIHAJIKI. A ballista, Japan.

ISHILUNGA. The Kaffir shield. It is an oval piece of cowhide with the hair on, and strengthened by weaving two strips of similar hide about three inches wide through two lines of slits down

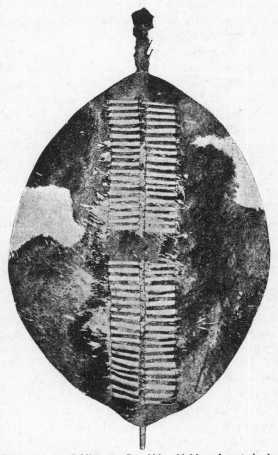

FIGURE 390. *Ishilunga. Cowhide shield 2 feet 8 inches long and 1 foot 11 inches wide.*

the middle of the shield, and also by a stick extending lengthwise of the back. This stick also serves as a handle. They are from two to four feet long, and the width is from one half to two thirds of the length. They are distinctive of South Africa. Fig. 390.

ISHIMATSU. A pattern of alternate squares of shakudo and silver or copper. Other metals are occasionally used but they are almost always of contrasting colors. Sometimes the squares are only a

FIGURE 391. *Ishimatsu. Kozuka of shibuichi decorated in ishimatsu of silver and shakudo.*

few hundredths of an inch across. The name is said to be derived from that of a very popular actor who dressed in a pattern of black and white squares. (Weber I, 318). The name means stone pavement. This pattern is sometimes used as a decoration on Japanese sword fittings. Fig. 391.

ISHIME. (Stone surface). The backgrounds of Japanese sword fittings are either polished, *jimigaki*; decorated with raised hemispheres, *nanako*; or *ishime*. Usually it is a roughened surface made by the pean of a hammer or with a blunt chisel or punch; but there are a great many varieties. *Wari ishime* is properly speaking a damasked surface; *zara ishime* and *tatsuta ishime* imitate stone; *hari ishime* is a surface covered with small holes as though pricked by a needle; *nashiji ishime* imitates the roughness of the skin of a pear; *gama ishime* is like the surface of a straw mat; other kinds imitate old leather, bark or crushed morocco.

ISHIYUMI. A stone bow, a pellet bow, Japan.

ISHIZUKI. A ferule on the end of a stick, the butt end of a spear, the chape of a tachi, Japan.

ISTENGARA. See Satengara.

ITA. A plate or lame, Japan. The name is used both for the borderings and for the lames of which Japanese armor is made. (Conder 266).

ITA-HAI-DATE. Japanese cuisses made of small square plates of metal sewn with leather cords to a lining of silk or leather. (Conder 274). Compare Igo-Hai-Date.

ITAJIKORO. A variety of shikoro.

ITA KOSHIATE. See Koshiate.

ITAMI. Mokume (wood grain) of iron. An iron surface in which imperfect welds show like the grain of wood; or a surface engraved or etched to give this effect.

ITAMI-HADA. See Hada. Curved line watering on sword blades, Japan.

ITE. An archer, Japan. In the middle ages in Japan the nobles were the archers.

ITO MAKI TACHI. A tachi with the upper part of the scabbard wound with braid or leather like the hilt. (Gilbertson, Dec. 96).

FIGURE 392. *I-Wata-Jinga. 1. Stone sewed in rawhide which also covers the handle. Length 20.5 inches. 2. Head a quartz pebble ground to a point at each end. The handle is covered with rawhide. Length 32 inches. 3. Dancing club. Stone head and wooden handle covered with horsehide stained red and brown. It is trimmed with two bands of buckskin, beaded, and with metal rattles. Length 22 inches.*

ITO ZUKASHI, ODAWARA ZUKASHI. Designs cut through metal with fine saws. It was used in Japan for decorating tsuba. The most celebrated masters of this style were some of the Ito family; the fineness and accuracy of their cuts is marvelous. (Joly, Hawkshaw 76).

IVERAPENA. A paddle-club of the Tupis of Brazil. It has a rounded shaft with a tabular, oval, slightly pointed blade. (Burton Sword 42).

IWA-SAKI YASUSADA. A Japanese armorer of the beginning of the 19th century celebrated for his repousse work. (Weber I, 324).

I-WATA-JINGA. An Omaha club consisting of a stone wrapped in hide and fastened to a wooden handle about two feet long. (Dorsey 284). It was used by most of the Plains Indians. Fig. 392.

IWO MUNE. See Mune.

IYEBORI. The style of work done by the direct line of the Goto family was called iyebori (family chasing) because its sixteen masters preserved for four hundred years, with more or less personal variation, the style originated in the 15th century by Goto Yujo, the founder of the line. (Joly, Hawkshaw 47).

The work of the subsidiary lines of the Goto was called do-mio-bori (chasing by the same family) to distinguish it.

J

JACK. Body armor worn by the rank and file in the 15th and 16th centuries. It was either a padded coat, or one interlined with mailplates or horn. (Hewitt II, 131). Canvas garments pierced with small, round holes close together worked round with the buttonhole stitch, were also called jacks. Fig. 393.

The male of *falco aesalon*, the female is called a merlin.

JACK, UNION JACK. The union is the upper part of a flag next the staff which carried the crosses in the British and the stars in our own. It is not proper to speak of it as a "jack" except when it is flown from the jack staff — a staff on the fore part of a vessel. (Macgeorge 64). The name is said to be derived from that of James I (Jacques), in whose reign it was first used. The proof of this is very slight. (Ibid. 66).

JACK BOOTS. Very large, heavy boots worn by horsemen from the 16th to the 18th century. They are said to have been so called because made of "jacked" leather. (Planche 48). Fig. 394.

JACOBE. A celebrated English armorer of the time of Elizabeth. He is usually identified as Jacob Topf; Laking (Armour IV, 12), however, believes that he was a different person.

JACULUM. A light Roman javelin. (Burton Sword 246).

JA-DAGNA. (Wood with a smooth head). An ironwood club, Omaha. It curved around at the end in which a ball was set. Sometimes the ball had a spike projecting from it. (Dorsey 283). Fig. 395.

JAGHEERDARS. Regular troops having lands set apart for their support, India. (Tod II, 343).

JAKUCHI. Kizayemon Jakuchi of Nagasaki worked in the middle of the 18th century. He was the founder of a school of tsuba makers who carved and inlaid Chinese landscapes, wind-blown bamboos, clouds, etc. He is said to have originally been a painter of "Chinese" pictures. (Hara 33).

JA-MANDEHI. Omaha lances of ash about six or eight feet long. The shafts are about an inch in diameter, and the heads are flat and of about the width of three fingers where they join the shaft. There is another variety called by the same name. (Dorsey 284).

JAMBEAUX. Leg armor, especially that made of leather in the 14th century. (ffoulkes 34).

JAMBIYA, JUMBEEA, JUMBIYAH. (Arabic Janbiya). The Arab knife which, in some modification is found in every country in which the Arabs have lived. The blade is always curved and double-edged, and generally has a rib down the middle. Each country has its own modification of the shape of blade, form of the hilt and scabbard, but all recognizable as belonging to the same family. The different forms of hilt and scabbard are more characteristic of the localities from which they come than the shapes of the blades. Fig. 396.

In Morocco the blades are straight and single-edged for about half their length from the hilt, and then curved and double-edged for the remainder. They seldom have ribs. The hilts and scabbards are usually of brass or silver, often the front is of silver and the back of brass. The scabbards frequently scabbard that is outward when the knife is carried is always elaborately, though crudely, decorated. The opposite side is much simpler, in fact, in many cases it is entirely plain.

FIGURE 393. *Button-Hole Jack, German, 17th century. Metropolitan Museum.*

curve so much that the ends point upwards. There are almost always large ornamental lugs on the sides that carry large rings to which a cord is fastened by which the knife is hung from the neck. The hilts are usually made entirely of metal and have large, flat pommels. The side of the hilt and

In Arabia the blades are shorter, broader, curved and double-edged for their entire length, and have pronounced ribs. The usual shape is formed of two smooth curves like half of a crescent; but some are made up of two curves that meet in quite an angle in the middle. The scabbards are much larger and decorated in better taste than the Moroccan. They curve much more, the tip sometimes being as high as the pommel when the knife is sheathed. The shapes of hilts and pommels vary in almost every part of Arabia. In general the pommels are moderately large and the grip very short. In the better

FIGURE 394. *Jack Boot, German, 16th-17th century. Metropolitan Museum.*

examples the hilts and scabbards are covered with silver, often filigreed, and sometimes gilded. The scabbards are fastened to the middle of the belt by a complicated arrangement of silver cords and rings so that they stand up well above it. The Wahabites use a distinct variety with much longer blades without ribs. Their scabbards do not turn up at the ends. 14, fig. 396.

In Turkey and the Balkans the blades are often longer, wider and not as much curved. They may, or may not, have ribs. The scabbards do not have the turned up ends, nor are they fastened to the belt but slipped inside it in the usual manner. They often have a small loop on the upper part of the scabbard, through which a cord can be passed to secure it to the belt, as is commonly done with

many oriental knives. The finer ones are wholly, or partly, covered with silver. The hilts are of ivory, or of wood bare or covered with silver. Some of the ivory hilts are much larger than those found anywhere else.

In Armenia the forms are intermediate between the Turkish and Persian; though pure Arab forms are also carried.

The finest and most beautiful of these knives come from Persia and India. In many the blade is of the Arab shape but of much finer steel and workmanship. The rib is a delicately modeled line instead of a lumpy ridge and the steel is frequently finely watered. One Indo-Persian form has the upper part of the blade straight, single-edged and with a wide rib at the back, while the curved point is double-edged. Some blades have sunk panels of watered steel on each side of the rib, while the edges and rib are bright. In this form there is frequently a panel next the hilt, that is, decorated with chasing and inlaying; not infrequently the borders of this panel are pierced. The hilts are often of ivory; and these, when of one particular shape, 34, 36, fig. 396, are always carved with quite Gothic figures. Similar figures are never used in decorat-

FIGURE 395. *Ja-Dagna. 1. Dance club, Ojibwa. 2. War club, Ojibwa. Museum of the American Indian, Heye Foundation.*

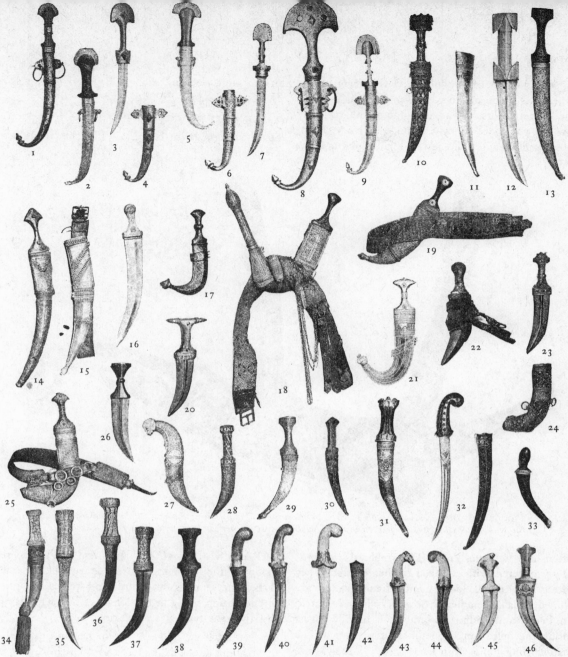

FIGURE 396. Jambiyas. 1. Morocco. Wood hilt, scabbard and mounts brass. 2. Morocco. Blade 9.375 inches long. Hilt of black wood with silver mounts. Scabbard of hexagonal section covered with silver. 3, 4. Morocco. The fronts of the hilt and scabbard are of silver, the backs of brass. 5. Morocco. Hilt of rhinoceros horn; scabbard and hilt mounts silver. 6, 7. Morocco. Gold inlaid blade 10.25 inches long. Scabbard and hilt mounts of silver decorated in niello. 8. Southern Morocco. Fronts of hilt and scabbard of silver, backs of brass inlaid with silver. 9. Morocco. Hilt and scabbard of brass and silver. 10. Turkey. Hilt and scabbard of gilt metal set with coral. There are several lines of small pendants which jingle when it is moved. 11, 12. Albania. Ribbed, watered blade 12.5 inches long inlaid with silver, ivory hilt. Scabbard covered with silver. 13. Balkans. Wood hilt carved with the same pattern as is embossed on the silver scabbard. 14. Arabia, Wahabite. Blade 16.375 inches long of a flat diamond section. Hilt and scabbard covered with brass. 15, 16. Arabia, Wahabite. Hilt and scabbard of silver, the latter is fastened to a leather belt. 17. Arab. Hilt and scabbard covered with embossed and gilded copper. 18. Hilt decorated with silver and a coin. Scabbard covered with black cloth and red and green leather with a very large chased silver locket and chape. Brocade belt with silver chains for fastening to the scabbard an amulet case and a small case containing a pair of tweezers. 19. Arab, Zanzibar. Blade inlaid with silver, wood hilt with silver ornaments. Scabbard covered with leather and cloth with a large filigree chape. Belt of red and silver brocade with silver gilt filigree ornaments. 20. Arab. Wood hilt covered with silver decorated with filigree. 21. Arab, Southern India. Ribbed blade 8.25 inches long. Hilt and scabbard of heavy silver gilt. 22. Arab, Southern India. Wood hilt and leather scabbard, both with silver ornaments. 23, 24. Arabia. Gold inlaid blade. Hilt and scabbard covered with gilded metal set with colored jewels. 25. Arab, Mecca(?). Hilt and scabbard of silver decorated with filigree. The scabbard of silver decorated with filigree. The scabbard is fastened to the belt by an elaborate arrangement of silver rings and cords. 26. South Indian Arab. Broad watered blade; hilt of polished black horn. 27. India. Rough blade 6 inches long. Hilt and most of scabbard covered with silver. Pommel of carved bone. 28. Syria. Hilt a mosaic of bone and horn, the latter inlaid with metal. Scabbard covered with stamped brass. 29. India. Hilt and scabbard of silver finely chased. 30. Malta. Hilt and scabbard set with gilded filigree set with transparent pink stones. 31. Armenia. Ribbed and grooved blade 10.125 inches long inlaid with brass, fluted ebony hilt with silver mounts. The pommel is set with a carnelian. Leather scabbard with silver locket and chape. 32. Egypt. Gold inlaid, watered blade 13.5 inches long. Hilt and scabbard mounts of black jade set with flowers of pink and green stones. 33. Borneo. Rough blade 6.25 inches long. Hilt and scabbard of ebony with bone mounts. 34. Indo-Persia. Watered blade. Ivory hilt with figures carved in very high relief. 35. Indo-Persia. Single-edged blade with a stiffening rib half way down the back, engraved and inlaid with gold. Bone hilt carved with figures. 36. Persia. Watered blade with an engraved panel. Ivory hilt carved with figures and an inscription. 37. Persia. Very fine black Khorassen blade, ivory hilt carved with figures. 38. Persia. Watered blade engraved and inlaid with gold. Steel hilt decorated with inscriptions, partly in relief and partly flat on a gold ground. 39. India. Watered blade. Hilt of soft stone with incised inscriptions in black and rosettes of gold set with jewels. 40. India. Watered blade engraved and inlaid with gold. Hilt of gray agate. 41, 42. India. Watered blade inlaid with gold. Marble hilt carved and colored blue and gold. Scabbard covered with a cloth woven of red silk and silver. 43. Northern India. Blade of yellow damask. Ivory hilt, a horse's head with a silver bridle. 44. India. Watered blade inlaid with gold. Crystal hilt inlaid with gold. 45. India. Iron hilt inlaid and partly covered with silver. It is hollow and the knob on the pommel is hinged, making a cover which can be fastened by a hook. 46. India. Watered blade paneled and inlaid with gold. Hilt of two plates of ivory riveted to the flat tang.

ing other forms of hilt, nor with this form except when it is made of ivory. Other forms of hilt are the "pistol," horse's head and others with variously scrolled pommels. They are made of ivory, horn, stone and metals. The jeweled jade hilts are not

of the same size and shape. (Egerton 244, 245; B. M. Hdbk. 47). Fig. 398.

JANETAIRES, GENETAIRES. Javelins of Spanish origin, 15th century. (Planche 312). See Genetaires.

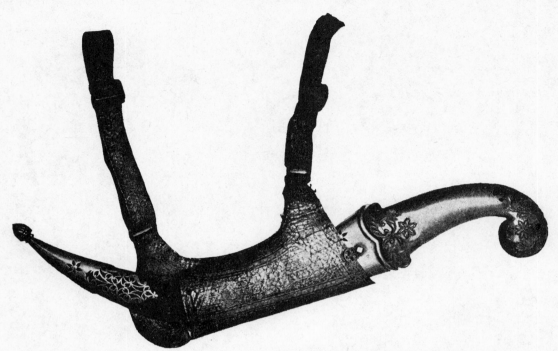

FIGURE 397. *Indo-Persian Jambiya, early 18th century. The hilt is of dark green jade, carved, and the scabbard mountings of pierced brass. The sling is of leather covered with vine patterns in gold.*

often used with this knife. The scabbards are generally covered with stamped leather or silk. They often have metal lockets and chapes which are chased, inlaid, enameled or otherwise decorated. In Persia and India the jambiya is usually thrust inside the belt; but, sometimes, it is carried in a leather sling hung from it, fig. 397. Jambiyas are used as far east as the Malay Archipelago where they are called "Arab knives." These are small and rough with no ribs on the blades. It is also found as far west as Malta, Spain and Morocco.

JAMBOYS. See Bases.

JAMBS. Armor for the legs from the knee down. See Bainbergs and Chausses.

JAMDHAR KATARI. Under this name Egerton figures the knives of the Kafirs of the Hindu Kush. They have straight, double-edged blades with broad, flat pommels and guards, both being

JAPANESE BLADES. Japanese blades were made by the same methods and are of the same shapes and sections for swords and knives, the difference being solely in the lengths. The lengths of the different types are approximately:

Jin Tachi	33 inches and over
Katana and Tachi	24 to 30 inches
Chisa Katana	18 to 24 inches
Wakizashi	16 to 20 inches
Tanto and Aikuchi	11 to 16 inches
Yoroi Toshi	9 to 12 inches
Kwaiken	3 to 6 inches

Those in existence today are always somewhat curved and generally single-edged, though a few are double-edged for at least a part of their length. Some have blunt back-edges.

The Japanese have names for many parts of the blade that we do not differentiate, as well as for the markings on it. These are shown in fig. 399.

Curvature. The curvature (*sori*) is measured by the greatest distance from the back of the blade to a straight line drawn from the point to the hilt excluding the tang. It may be *tsukuri-sugi*, nearly straight; or *tsukuri-sori*, having a noticeable curva-

FIGURE 398. *Jamdhar Katari, knife of the Hindu Kush. It is forged in one piece. Length 15.5 inches; guard and pommel 3.25 x 1.25 inches.*

ture but rarely greater than that of a modern cavalry sabre. It is often stated that tachi are more strongly curved than katana, but this is by no means always the case.

The extreme point is called *kisaki*, and the curve of the *yakiba* near the point the *boshi*. The point is formed by curving the edge round to meet the back. This curve may be *fukura-sugu*, nearly straight; or *fukura-kaku*, sharply curved. *U-no-kubi-tsukuri* (cormorant-neck shape) is a blade with a blunt, or sharp back-edge for at least a part of its length. *Kamuri-tsukuri* is similar to the last. *Shobu-tsukuri* (flag-leaf) is a blade back-edged for its entire length, or nearly to the hilt. The back (*mune, mine* or *sena*) may be *marumune*, rounded; *kaku-mune* or *ihoremune*, two planes meeting in an obtuse angle; or *mitsumune*, like the last but with a third plane cutting off the angle, fig. 580. The sides of the blade may each be a single surface so nearly flat that the curvature can only be detected by careful measurement, *hira-tsukuri*; by two par-

allel surfaces, *shinogi*, near the back, and two sloping to the edge, *jigane*. All are slightly rounded.

Many blades are grooved to lighten them without impairing their strength. The grooves (*hi* or *kesso*) are usually circular arcs. A groove that reaches the point is called *hi-saki-ue*; and one that does not reach it is called *hi-saki-shita*. A double groove is called *futa-suiji-hi*. Various sections are shown in fig. 400. Of these the three last are much the commonest.

The shapes of the tangs (*nakago*) and the file marks (*yasurime*) on them vary greatly, fig. 401. Both are characteristic of certain makers.

The steel formerly used in Japan was made mainly from an impure magnetite smelted in small blast furnaces. The smelting operation lasted four days; the furnace was then torn down and the

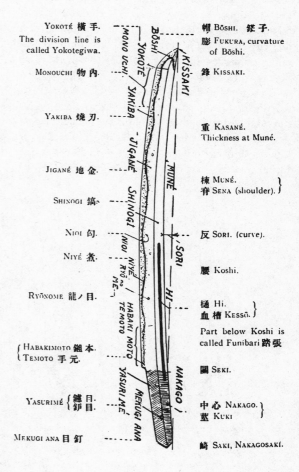

FIGURE 399. *Parts of a Japanese blade. From Joly Sword and Same.*

metal extracted. The upper sixth of the metal was burnt and useless; below this was a mass of steel varying from very hard to very soft. This was about one third of the metal produced; the remaining half was cast iron and was used for other purposes. The mass of steel was broken into small pieces, from which the smith selected those of the hardness he

FIGURE 400. *Sections of Japanese blades.*

desired and welded them into bars. As the metal varied from soft iron to hard steel much depended on the skill of the smith in selecting the proper ones for the purpose and in combining the first set of bars to make those which he finally used for his blades. It also explains the necessity for the extraordinarily complicated series of welding, doubling and piling employed for the bars from which the finest blades were made.

The first operation was to weld a flat strip of soft metal to a hard one, giving a bar hard on one side and soft on the other. This was called *kataha,* and was only used for the blades of kozuka, and for kitchen knives and similar articles. For very inferior swords a bar of iron was welded to the edge

of a wider bar of steel and forged so that the steel formed the edge of the blade. It was called *suyeha,* and was only used for the poorest swords. The next method was to split the edge of a bar of soft metal and weld one of hard in the cleft. It was called *wariha.* In the next, *kobushi,* a bar of iron with a wedge-shaped edge was inserted in a bar of steel doubled to a V section, and welded. In the *uchimaki,* or *awase ni mai,* method a *kataha* bar was doubled back on itself to bring the steel surfaces together and welded. In the *moroha,* a strip of iron was doubled around the edge of a bar of steel, leaving the edge of the steel bare, and welded. All of these were somewhat uncertain and did not always produce first class blades.

The *ori awase san mai* was more complicated. In it a bar of steel was placed between two bars of iron on an iron plate of the width of the three. It was welded and doubled so as to bring the steel to the steel, welded and forged. Another account says that the bar of steel was welded to the edge of a bar of iron, the resulting bar placed between two of iron and the whole welded. This appears more probable, as it would bring the steel where it would form the edge, while the first described method would cover the steel completely with iron.

Shihozume. Two plates were made by doubling and welding two *kataha* bars fifteen times. A narrow plate of hard steel was placed between them at

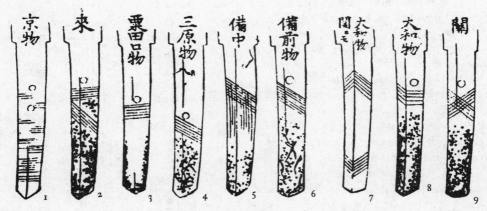

FIGURE 401. *Tangs and File Marks.* 1. *Katsura-Yasuri-Me, made in Kyoto.* 2. *Yoko-Sujikae, made by Rai.* 3. *The file marks made at Awataguchi, and sometimes found on swords made in the province of Etchiu.* 4. *Yoko-Yasuri, made at Mihara.* 5. *Sen-Moku, made in the province of Bitchiu.* 6. *Sujikae-Yasuri, made in the province of Bizen.* 7. *Taka-No-Ha, falcon's wing, made in the province of Yamato, by or at, Seki.* 8. *Kirisujikae-Yasuri, made in the province of Yamato.* 9. *Hijiki-Yasuri, made by Seki, a family name, or perhaps at a place called Seki. Lyman, p. 10.*
In the figures the file marks are shown on a part of the tangs; actually they cover them entirely.

one edge and the remainder of the space filled with an iron plate; the whole was then welded and forged.

A far better method than any of these was to take a *kataha* bar, double it on itself and weld, repeating these operations fifteen times. This gives 32,768 layers in the bar, making it practically homogeneous. If such a bar is forged by striking the edges of the layers it was called *masame*, and gave a watering of fine straight lines. If it was hammered on the diagonal it was called *nogi-hada* or *ko-masame*, and gave a different kind of watering.

The best method, and the one used by Masamune and others of the most celebrated makers, was to take four bars made as just described, pile them, weld and double and weld five times, giving 4,194,304 layers in the blade.

In all but the last two methods a piece of hard steel is welded in at a point that allows it to be made the edge when the blade is forged to shape; in the last two it is necessary to increase the carbon at the edge to make it possible to harden it. This is done by a process called cementation, which is to pack it in charcoal, or a mixture containing considerable carbon, and heat it to a high temperature for a considerable time. In some cases the Japanese smiths also largely increased the silicon in the steel, a thing that western metallurgists have never succeeded in doing in this way. Before cementing the blade is rough forged to shape and finished with a kind of drawing knife, called *sen*, which has the handles in line with the blade. As the heating and quenching changes the curvature of the blade considerably, allowance must be made for this when shaping it.

It was usually desired to produce "watering," that is, lines or cloudy patches on the surface of the blade. If the bar has been made by any of the methods in which the steel fixes the position of the edge the only kind of watering that can be produced is cloudy markings. To do this it is necessary to cut, or file depressions in the parts of the bar that are to form the sides of the blade and hammer them down flat before finally shaping the blade. In either of the methods in which the bar is doubled and welded many times, any one of four kinds of watering are possible. 1st. By cutting hollows in the sides of the bar: this makes cloudy markings, and is called *hidagitai*. 2nd. By filing grooves across the bar (usually making them deeper on one edge than on the other). This gives definite bands of watering

across the blade which often look like Roman letters. It is said that this was only done by one family of smiths; at any rate it is extremely rare. 3rd. By forging the blade so that the layers of the bar are parallel to the flat of the blade. This gives cloudy watering. 4th. By forging so that the layers of the bar are at right angles to the sides of the blade. If the work has been carefully done the lines will be nearly straight, usually they wave considerably. If the bar has been hammered on one corner while the diagonally opposite one rested on the anvil, the watering will be different on the two sides of the blade. See Watered Steel.

When the blade has been forged, scraped into shape and cemented it is painted over with a thin layer of clay and water. This must be very thin near the edge but must completely cover the metal. It is made thicker on the jigane, and very thick on the shinogi and mune. If it is desired to have a double yakiba the clay must be removed at the junction of the jigane and shinogi. The clay cover (*sabidoro*) is very carefully dried to prevent it from cracking or peeling off. The whole is then carefully heated to the desired temperature and the edge quenched in warm water. The Japanese are very careful that the temperatures of both blade and water are exactly as desired. This makes the edge extremely hard without making it brittle, and leaves the body soft and tough. The entire operation requires great skill as the blade is both hardened and tempered at one operation.

The blade is then ground and polished. The grinding is done on a series of fixed stones under a bath of oil. The first stone used is quite coarse; but, as the work proceeds, finer and finer stones are used. The final result is a beautiful polish and an accuracy of line and surface that leaves nothing to be desired. The work is slow, an expert grinder requiring as much as a month to finish a blade.

If the blade is to be decorated with carving this is next done, the parts to be carved having been given an extra coating of clay before hardening so that they will remain soft. The carving is the last operation as it was always possible that the grinding might disclose defects in the blade that would make it useless to put this extra work on it. It is also said that carving was sometimes done to cut out minor defects that would detract from the value of the blade.

The decoration was often a ken, or a dragon

wound around a ken; a dragon rising from the waves; a figure of Fudo; a branch of plum or other flowering plant; and very frequently bonji (Sanskrit) characters for the names of Buddhistic divinities. Sometimes it was an inscription in the ordinary hiragane characters.

If the blade was signed it was always on the tang; on the *ura*, the right side when the blade is held point up and edge away from the observer, if a tachi; and on the opposite side, the *omote*, for all other blades. In some cases additional information is inscribed on the side not used for the signature. The signing was usually done by professional signature engravers who visited the smiths and signed blades for them. Blades not signed at the time they were made were sometimes signed by the sword experts, signatures so added being usually inlaid in gold. Some of the best makers never signed their blades, saying that any one worthy of such a sword could tell the maker without a signature, and that any one too ignorant to do so did not deserve to know how valuable a blade he had.

When the blade is hardened the edge becomes lighter in color than the body of the blade and acquires a different lustre. The lighter color at the edge is called *ha-tsuya* (edge lustre) and that of the darker body *ji-tsuya* (ground lustre). There is sometimes a bright line at the junction of the two which is considered as an evidence of high quality.

The *yakiba* is the part of the blade that has been hardened and, as its contour can be controlled by varying the line of the clay cover, its shape and appearance are very characteristic of different makers and localities. Blades are sometimes made with two yakiba (*niuji yakiba*). Most of the early blades have straight and comparatively simple yakiba, on the later ones it is often very elaborate. In a good blade the yakiba should be narrow near the hilt where strength is required, and wider near the point where hardness is needed. Over one hundred varieties of yakiba are recognized and named; most of them, however, are combinations of a few simple forms.

Bright, cloudy and dark markings on the blade are also considered as evidences of its quality. *Niye* are darker spots on the yakiba, especially on the inner side, often running into bands. *Nioi* are brilliant spots on the *jigane* inside the yakiba. *Rio-no-me* are large scattered spots, *Yuha-shiri* and *tobi-yaki* are bright bands of hard metal. There are at least one hundred varieties of these marks recognized by the Japanese experts, but most of them can only be distinguished by those who have had long training.

The Japanese bladesmith was a person of importance and his occupation had an almost religious character. When making, or at least when finishing, a blade he wore ceremonial court costume and decorated his forge with gohei and other religious emblems. His blades were undoubtedly the finest that have ever been produced, and the best are as near perfect as any work of human hands. The two traditional tests of a fine blade were — first, it should be able to cut a common blade in two without having its edge nicked; second, if it was held in running water with the edge up stream and a lotus was allowed to float against it the stem should be cut. The first has been done many times; I know of no recorded case of the second, but the perfection of the edge and the ease of cutting with it makes it not improbable.

There is but one fitting that belongs to the blade, the *habaki*. It is a ferule about an inch long that fits tightly to both blade and scabbard, closing the latter practically hermetically so that air and moisture cannot enter and rust the blade. It also holds the latter steadily so that the edge cannot be injured. The blade is held to the hilt by a bamboo peg, the *mekugi*, which passes through holes in both. The holes are called *mekugi ana*.

The earliest swordsmith whose name is known is Amakuni who lived in the 7th century. Next comes O-haru Sanemori in the middle of the 9th. His blades are very fine. Munechika, who was born A.D. 938, was the greatest master of the 10th century. In the 11th, Yoshiiye of Kioto was celebrated both as a maker of swords and armor. The first blade signed by the maker was made by Shinsoku of Usanomia for the son of the Emperor Heisei Jenne in 806. In the 13th century Yoshi-mitsu, Kuni-yuki and Kuni-toshi were all great masters; and in the 14th Masa-mune, probably the greatest of all, Kane-uji, O-kane-mitsu and Muramasa. Sadamune, Masa-mune's son-in-law was also a very skilful maker. The son and grandson of Muramasa continued the celebrity of the family; but the tradition that their blades thirsted for blood and that ill fortune followed their possessors made them unpopular, although they are of the highest quality. In the 15th and 16th centuries the greatest names are Kane-sada, Kane-sane, Fujiwara, Uji-

Foussa and Umetada Miojiu who was called to Kioto by the Shogun Ashikaga Toshiharu in 1546. After the 16th century the city of Osafune in Bizen became the most important seat of sword manu-

(old), and those made later *Shinto* (new). The shinto smiths are not considered as good as a whole as the koto, although the best of them did better work than many of the older makers.

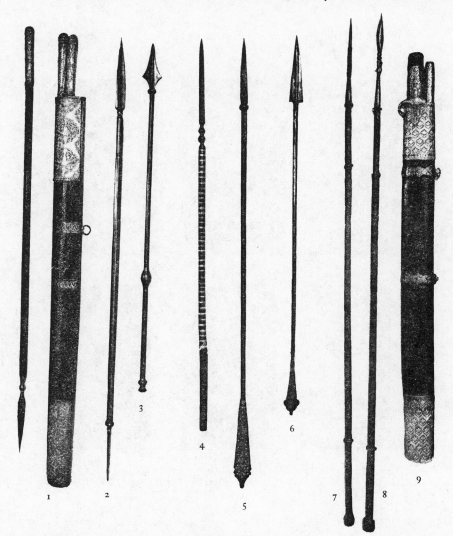

FIGURE 402. *Jarids.* 1. *Quiver and three javelins, Armenia. The javelins have steel heads, wood shafts and silver caps on the butts. The quiver is covered with red velvet with silver caps.* 2. *India. Steel inlaid with gold. Length 36.5 inches.* 3. *All steel, lozenge head with concave edges. Shaft slightly engraved.* 4. *Turkey. Triangular head with hollow sides. Shaft alternate disks of horn and bone strung on a steel shaft. Length 32.25 inches.* 5. *Turkey, 17th century. Round shaft, square head and flat butt. The ends are covered with silver and set with coral and turquoise.* 6. *Turkey, 18th century. All steel, four-sided head with hollow faces, square shaft with chamfered edges, flat butt. Shaft twisted half a turn at each end, inlaid with gold and silver.* 7. *Central Africa. Steel head, shaft covered with black leather and snake skin. Butt weighted with an iron coil.* 8. *The same as 7.* 9. *Persia. A hunting sword and javelin in a case with embossed silver mounts.*

facture. Among the principal Bizen smiths are — Haru-Mitsu, Suke-sada, Kiyo-mitsu and Yasu-tsugu. Blades made before 1600 are called *Koto*

JAPURURUNGA, TABURARUNGA. Melville Island clubs with double-pronged striking ends. The prongs may be short and thick or long and slender. They vary from a length of two and a half inches on a club nineteen inches long to seventeen inches on one thirty inches long. The width is from two to four inches. They are decorated in colors. (Spencer North. Ter. 374, 375).

JA-QUDE-HI. Gray wood, Juneberry. It was used for arrow shafts by the Ponkas. (Dorsey 286).

JARID BAZI. The "spear play" of the Biluchis. It is played by two men on horseback with a spear twelve feet long. They ride after each other, one throwing the jarid, or spear shaft, with full force, with the object of hitting and unhorsing his opponent, while the latter, by dexterous agility, endeavors not only to evade the blow, but to seize the

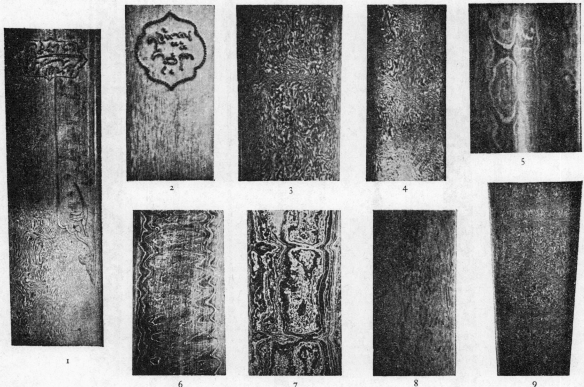

FIGURE 403. *Watered Steel.* 1. *Inscribed* Amelie Taban *("brilliant" work).* 2. *Turkish, inscribed* Baiaz Istamboul *(Constantinople white).* 3, 4, 8, 9. *Are of the pattern called* Kirk-Nerdeven *(forty steps). Catalogue of the Hermitage.*

JARID, JERED, DJERID. Oriental javelins. They have been used in the East from the earliest times both for war and hunting, especially the latter. In their later forms which probably do not differ materially from the earlier ones, they are light spears with shafts about three feet long and quadrangular steel heads about seven inches long; they often have ornamental caps on the butts. Sometimes they are made entirely of steel, often with flat heads. They are often carried in a flat quiver holding three, or a light hunting sword and one, or two, javelins. They are perfectly balanced and can be thrown with great accuracy. Fig. 402.

weapon in the air and attack in turn. (Egerton, p. 150).

JASARME. See Guisarme.

JAUHAR, JAUHARDAR. The grain or watering of Persian steel that we call "watering" or "damascus." The steel is made by welding together pieces of varying composition and hardness to form bars which are twisted and welded in various ways that have more to do with the patterns than the original material. After the desired object is forged it is polished and etched. For this *kasis*, ferric sulphate is used in India, Persia and Syria. Almost any acid will answer. The patterns can be controlled by varying the number of the rods used and the way they are twisted and welded. The most usual patterns are named from the country in which they are made, as Iran (Persia), or from the figure, as pigeon's eye, lover's knot, chain, etc. The

FIGURE 404. *Jazerant Armor, 15th century. Metropolitan Museum.*

ladder pattern is one of the most popular in Persia. In it there are well marked bands of transverse lines crossing the blade at fairly regular intervals. They are supposed to represent the rungs of the ladder on which the faithful ascend to Paradise. (Egerton, p. 56). Fig. 403. See Watered Steel.

JAVELIN. A throwing spear. See Assegai and Jarid.

JA-WETI. (Striking wood). A four-sided club about eighteen to twenty inches long, Omaha. (Dorsey 283).

JAYA. In Hindu mythology Jaya was the mother and creator of all weapons including missiles. They are divided into four great classes. The *Yantramukta*, thrown by machines; the *Panimukta*, thrown by hand; the *Muktasandharita*, thrown and drawn back and the *Mantramukta*, thrown by spells and numbering six species, form the *Mukta* or thrown class of twelve species. This is opposed

to the *Amukta*, or unthrown class of twenty pieces, to the *Muktamukta*, either thrown or not, of ninety-eight varieties, and to the *Bahuyuddha*, weapons which the body provides for personal struggles. All are personified. (Burton Sword 214).

JA'ZA'IRI. The palace guards of Abbas II. (Egerton, p. 141).

JAZERANT, JAZERAN, JAZERINE, JESSERAUNT. Armor made of strips or plates of horn, leather or metal fastened to cloth or leather. It is similar to brigandine, the distinction being that

FIGURE 405. *Jedburg Axe. Collection of Dr. Bashford Dean.*

in jazerant the scales are outside the cloth, and in brigandine inside. (Laking Armour II, 193). It is one of the earliest forms of armor and has been used in all parts of the world. It was particularly popular in Europe in the 14th century. Fig. 404.

JEDBURG AXE, JEDDART AXE. A kind of pole axe about nine feet long with a hook like a

JERKIN. The male gefalcon. In falconry the female only is called a falcon.

JESS, JESSES. Narrow strips of leather fastened around a hawk's legs to hold her by. They have knots on the ends and are long enough to twist around the fingers. In the East they are sometimes made of silk or cloth. Ordinarily the jesses are fast-

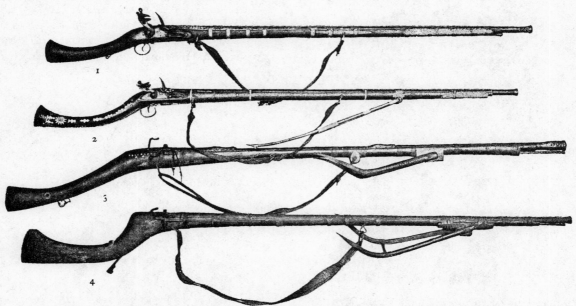

FIGURE 406. *Jezails. 1. Smooth bore, English flintlock. Round twist barrel inlaid with silver, 11 engraved brass capucines. Length 4 feet 11.5 inches. 2. Rifle, English flintlock, round damask barrel inlaid with gold. Four pierced silver capucines. Stock decorated with silver plates. Brass rest set with turquoises, attached by a clamp of silver and brass. 3. Very early Indian barrel carved with three monster's heads with jeweled eyes, and inlaid with gold and silver. Rough wooden stock with a horn rest. Matchlock. 4. Matchlock, plain rough barrel held by rawhide, brass and iron capucines. Forked rest with horn ends. Length 5 feet 7 inches.*

gaff, or one with a cutting edge, opposite the blade. (Campbell 96). A Scotch weapon used from the 15th to the 18th century. Fig. 405.

JEE-AOR. See Tirrer.

JEMPERING. Java, a blowpipe dart. It was made of bamboo single barbed and wrapped with a wad of raw cotton at the butt. (Arc. f. Eth. IV, 279).

JER. See Ger.

JEREED. See Jarid.

JERICHONKA. Arab helmets of the 16th and 17th centuries. They are bowl-shaped with the sides rising in an ogee curve to a sharp point. (Scheremetew 57, 58).

ened to a swivel and this, in turn, to a leash. The entire arrangement is for the purpose of controlling the hawk. The jesses are worn at all times, but the swivel and leash are removed when the hawk is flown.

JESSERAUNT. See Jazerant.

JEZAIL. The long-barreled, crooked stocked Afgan gun. Originally they were matchlocks, but many have been converted to flintlocks by fitting European locks to them. Many are well made and rifled and were of considerably greater range than the muskets carried by the British troops who first came in contact with the Afgans. Some are very large. I have seen one, in a private collection, that was about seven feet long and of one inch bore.

They are generally fitted with the A-shaped rests that are so much used in Central Asia. The stock of the jezail does not in the least resemble what is called the "Afgan" stock, being small and oval at the butt, while the latter is very narrow and deep. Fig. 406.

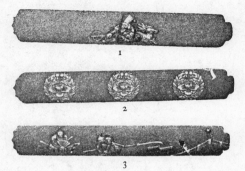

FIGURE 407. *Ji-Ita. All three are of shakudo, nanako with figures and mons in high relief in gold. Goto School.*

JIBORU. A spear used in northern Australia and on Melville Island. The shaft is nearly nine feet long and not over three-quarters of an inch in diameter. It has a piece of bamboo about a foot long fastened to the butt so that the point of the spear thrower can be fitted into it. The head has a bone point about an inch and a quarter long fastened to it by a hard gum, called kapei, from the root of the ironwood tree. (Spencer North. Ter. 358).

JIGAI. Ceremonial suicide by cutting the veins of the left side of the neck. It was formerly practiced by the Japanese women in cases where a man would have performed harikiri. The weapon employed was the kwaiken.

JIGANE. The part of a Japanese blade that slopes towards the edge.

JI-ITA. The decorated plate set in a kozuka or the handle of a kogai. Frequently this plate was the only part made by the master, the remainder being done by workmen or apprentices. Fig. 407.

JIM-BAORI, JIN-BAORI. A Japanese surcoat of cloth, silk, damask, brocade or leather worn over armor on ceremonial occasions. If it was without sleeves, the usual form, it was called *hampi*; if without sleeves but with frills around the armholes *karaka-baori*; and when it had flowing sleeves *sode-baori*. (Conder 277). It frequently has strips of brigandine on the shoulders. Fig. 408.

JIMIGAKI. Polished surfaces on Japanese metal work. (Joly Hawkshaw xxii).

JIN-DAI-KO. A war drum, Japan. (Weber I, 340).

JINDORI, JINYA, JINYEI. A military camp, Japan.

JINGASA. Open helmets worn by the retainers of Japanese nobles. They vary greatly in size and shape. They are frequently conical, sometimes almost flat, at others with distinct crowns. The brims are nearly always large and, in many cases curve up in front to give the wearer a better chance to see. They are usually made of steel, often of a

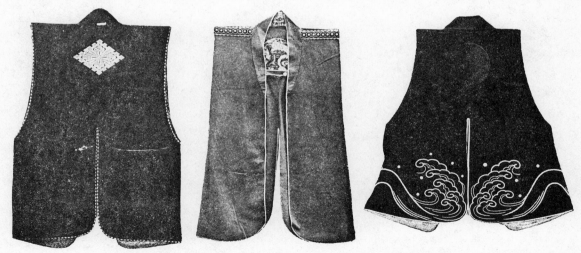

FIGURE 408. *Jim-Baori, 17th and 18th centuries. Metropolitan Museum.*

FIGURE 409. *Jingasa.* 1. *Iron with a square crown and sloping brim embossed with a demon's head. Signed Miochin Nobuharu. Width 18.375 inches, height 6.125.* 2. *Wood covered with lacquer containing pieces of pearl shell; bronze hachimanza. 14.5 x 13.875 inches, height 3.25.* 3. *Iron with a low, rounded crown and flat curved brim. Embossed with a dragon and clouds touched with gold. Width 17.75 inches, height 3.5.* 4. *Wood carved and lacquered to imitate iron. Width 14.5 inches, height 7.* 5. *Conical of 8 plates of iron; copper hachimanza. Embossed with a Chinese sage riding on a dragon with a peacock's tail. Width 14.75 inches, height 4.5.* 6. *Wood lacquered black with 3 mons and the sun in gold. Width 15.125 inches, height 3.* 7. *Iron with a rounded crown and curved brim embossed to imitate rivets. 15.875 x 15.5 inches, height 5. Shakudo hachimanza.* 8. *Iron of 16 plates riveted. Width 11.875 inches, height 6.* 9. *Wood elaborately carved with dragons and clouds and lacquered brown outside and red inside. Width 16.625 inches, height 2.375.* 10. *A cone of one plate with 3 shi-shi embossed in very high relief. Diameter 18.375 inches, height 7.25.* 11. *A single plate of iron embossed with a demon riding on a sea monster. Signed Miochin Munenobu, 20th. Miochin, 1616-1623. Width 18.25 inches, height 1.125.* 12. *Made of 20 iron plates riveted. Width 16.625 inches, height 3.25.* 13. *Iron, octagonal, of 8 plates riveted. Width 16.5 inches, height 5.*

single plate, but sometimes of as many as twenty riveted together. When more than one plate is used the front one overlaps those on each side of it so that all of the joints lap towards the back giving the best surface for causing a blow to glance. Many are made of wood lacquered; these were intended mainly for parade and ceremonial occasions and are frequently of very fine lacquer, often well decorat-

Many of the helmets worn during the late war were apparently modeled on Japanese jingasa.

JIN-GO YA. The tents, or huts, of a camp, Japan.

JINSEN. A folding war fan with iron ribs, Japan. It was used by officers of the lower ranks. See War Fan.

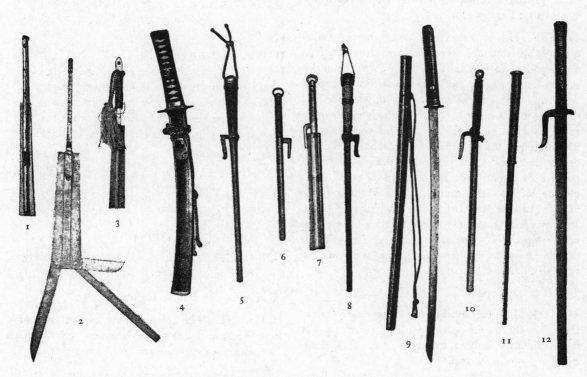

FIGURE 410. *Jitte. 1. Iron, fan-shaped club with a hook on one side. Length 12.5 inches. 2. Iron, fan-shaped club with three folding blades, two knives and a saw. Belt hook on one side. 3. Very heavy bronze, fan-shaped club 10.625 inches long. 4. All solid iron, shaped like a mounted sword with a broad belt hook on the back. 5. All steel with a moulded hook. Hilt wound with cord, silver cap on the pommel. 6. Brass, with a swivel ring on the handle. Length 10.5 inches. 7. Steel with an engraved brass handle. It has a bamboo sheath. 8. Steel rod, hilt covered with shark skin, iron mounts. 9. Made and mounted like a sword, but it has a curved iron bar 18.5 inches long in place of a blade. 10. Hexagonal bar with a hook and cord-wound hilt, all silver plated. Length 16 inches. 11. Three jointed iron club. The lower joints slide back into the handle end or can be thrown out by a jerk. Length closed 6.5 inches, open 18. 12. Plain iron with an hexagonal bar. Length 24.75 inches.*

ed. The steel ones may be plain, but are often embossed, sometimes very elaborately. There are usually two cylindrical pads in the crown that rest on the head, and padded loops on each side that hang down below the ears. A soft cord or folded cloth is passed through these loops and tied under the chin. Fig. 409.

JINSI. A park of guns, Rajput. (Tod II, 561).

JIN-TACHI. A very long, heavy two-handed sword, Japan. It was generally carried by an attendant.

JINTO. A war sword, Japan. (Gilbertson Dec. 96).

JINYA, JINYEI. See Jindori.

JIRAI-KWA. A mine of powder, Japan.

JI-TSUYA. The lustre of a Japanese blade outside the yakiba.

JITTE TEPPO. Japanese, a handgun. It is a short barrel with a swivel ring on the end of the handle. It is superior to all others in having a swinging pan cover so that it could be carried primed ready for instant use. Fig. 353.

JIT-TE, JITTEI. A weapon commonly called a fencer's baton, but formerly carried by the Japanese police. It is usually a rod with a hilt and a square hook on one side close to it. Sometimes it was hung from the belt by a ring on the handle; at others it was carried in a scabbard. A much rarer form is shaped like a mounted sword which has an iron club in place of a blade and scabbard; it has a broad hook on the side just below the guard. Obviously it is a parrying weapon, an oriental main gauche, with which a man could guard himself, but of very little use for offence, except when very large. In any case it was a very useful weapon for a police officer who was required to make arrests without injuring his prisoner, particularly if of much higher rank. Fig. 410.

JO. A castle, Japan.

JOHUR. The catalogue of the Zarkoe Sele collection gives this as the name of a kind of sword, but it is evidently only a different way of spelling "jauhar," watered steel.

JOHUR. The Rajput ceremony of sacrificing all of the women of a town or castle that was about to be captured. The women retired to an underground room and killed themselves; the place was then filled with combustibles and set on fire destroying the bodies and their jewels. The men then made a sortie and died attacking the enemy. (Tod I, 597).

JOI. Issander Joi, a pupil of Toshinaga, and one of the three most celebrated masters of the Nara school of makers of sword mountings. His work in engraving and relief could hardly be surpassed and his designs frequently show a keen sense of humor. He died in 1761 at the age of sixty-one. (Hara 35).

JO-MON. A mon (crest) registered by a daimio so that it could not be used by anyone else. It was used at ceremonies and important functions. See Mon.

JOOD-DAN. The "gift of battle." When a Rajput prince grew old and wished to die fighting, instead of by sickness, he asked some other prince for the "gift of battle," that is to meet and fight him at a specified time and place. He agreed not to take more than a specified number of men with him, and left the challenged free to bring as many more as he pleased. (Tod II, 207).

JOUST. A form of tournament in which a single horseman charged a single antagonist. (Hewitt I, 182).

JOWALA-MOOKHI, BALWA-NAL, MUG-UR-MOOKHAN. Cannon, India. The names mean respectively — mouth of flame — mighty tube — crocodile's mouth. They were consecrated before battle by sprinkling them plentifully with the blood of goats slain under their muzzles. (Tod II, 77, 80).

JOWING. The detachable head of a Dyak blowpipe dart. (Wood 1120).

JOWK. To sleep, spoken of a hawk.

JU. A gun or rifle, Japan.

JUBANGOTE. "Kote with shirt." A variety of connected kote. (Garbutt 161).

JUGWAN. A bullet, Japan.

JUHATSU. The thickest part of the ends of a Japanese bow which form shoulders against which the string bears. (Gilbertson Archery 113). See Yumi.

JUKEN. A sword bayonet, Japan. A modern word as bayonets were not known in old Japan.

JUMGHEERDHA. A sword with a long narrow, straight blade and a basket hilt. It was used by the Polygars of Nugger. (Egerton, p. 123). Probably the Firangi.

JUPON, JUPEL, GIPON. A garment worn over armor in the 14th and 15th centuries. It was tight fitting, sleeveless and usually embroidered with the armorial ensign of the wearer. ffoulkes uses the word as synonymous with surcoat—Planche says that it was a different garment and was worn at a later period. (ffoulkes 23, 40. Planche 317).

JUSO. A spear-shaped bayonet, Japan. A modern word as bayonets were not known in old Japan.

JUWO-GASHIRA. A variety of kakudzuri, a Japanese knee cop. (Conder 276).

K

KABJA, QABJA. A sword hilt, India. (Sinclair, I. A., 216).

KABURA-YA, HINIKI-YA. (Turnip head). The Japanese whistling arrow. It has a large spin-

made of, or covered with, silver thus giving decoration. In many cases the hashi has some fanciful form and is named for the object it is intended to represent as *momonari*, a peach — *toppai*, conical with the sides flattened to a blade shape at the top — *to kamurai*, in the shape of the ceremonial hat called kamuri — *kimen*, a demon's head, a favorite form — etc. The *tatami kabuto*, or folding helmet was made of horizontal rings laced together so that it could be shut down almost flat.

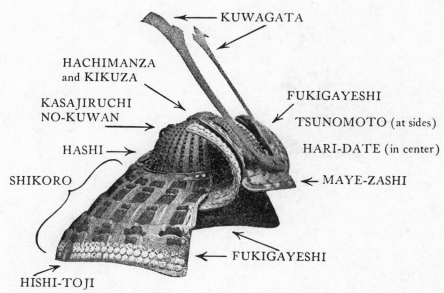

KUWAGATA

HACHIMANZA
and KIKUZA

KASAJIRUCHI
NO-KUWAN

HASHI →

SHIKORO

FUKIGAYESHI

TSUNOMOTO (at sides)

HARI-DATE (in center)

← MAYE-ZASHI

← FUKIGAYESHI

HISHI-TOJI

FIGURE 411. *Kabuto, a Japanese helmet and its parts.*

dle-shaped wooden head with openings in the sides through which the air rushes with a whistling sound. Sometimes it is mounted with a steel head projecting from the end. It is derived from the Chinese; and, as in China, was used for military signaling. One is preserved in the temple of Atsuta that is 8.25 inches long and 3.125 in diameter. (Gilbertson Archery 117). See Whistling Arrow.

KABUTO. A helmet, Japan, fig. 411. It consists of a bowl, *hashi*, sometimes made of a single piece of metal, but usually of a number strongly riveted together. Generally there is a raised rib at the front edge of each plate, of which there may be as many as one hundred. The outer heads of the rivets sometimes project greatly. If the ribs are very small and the rivets have large heads the helmet is called *hoshi-kabuto*. Occasionally some of the plates are

The hashi has a small peak, *maye-zashi*, in front, made of a plate riveted on. To it is affixed a socket, called *hari-date*, to receive the crest and other ornaments. In most helmets there is an opening in the crown, the *hachimanza, tehen* or *tenku*, which is surrounded by an elaborately moulded metal socket called the *kikuza*. This is generally a conventional chrysanthemum, hence the name. The opening is said to be intended to allow heavenly influences to reach the brain of the wearer. It is also stated that it was originally meant to allow room for the short pigtail formerly worn upright on the crown of the head.

This opening was sometimes closed by a piece of silk held in place by four strings tied to four metal knobs placed on the helmet for the purpose. These are called the *shi-ten-bio*, or Deva knobs. Individually their names are — *Bishamon Ten, Jikoku Ten, Komoku Ten* and *Zochu Ten*. On the lower edge of the sides of the helmet there are pairs of small holes fitted with metal eyelets, through which thin strips of leather, fastened to the lining, are passed and fastened on the outside.

The neck guard, *shikoro*, is made of from three to seven strips of metal, or stiff leather, laced together with silk cords. In some cases the strips are made of small metal scales, *kozane*, strongly laced

FIGURE 412. *Japanese Archer's Helmet. The right side of the neck guard can be turned back so as to be out of the way when shooting with the bow.*

together; as many as 100 to 138 are required for each strip. The top plate is riveted to the hashi, and the lowest plate is generally lined with leather to prevent its clattering against the armor. It is called *hishi-toji*, a name also given to the lowest plate of other portions of the armor, on account of the star shape in which the ends of the cords are fastened. The inside of the shikoro is often gilded, or lacquered bright red. The latter color is said to be used for the purpose of giving the wearer a fierce expression. At each side of the helmet there is usually a curved wing piece, called the *fuki-gayeshi*, which is often formed by turning back one, or more, of the lames of the shikoro, or by fastening curved plates to them or to the hachi. They are often covered with ornamental leather with a decorated border, and usually have the owner's crest in the center. Sometimes the one on the right side is hinged so that it can be turned back out of the way when shooting with the bow. Fig. 412.

At the back of the helmet there is an ornamental ring called the *kasa-jiruchi-no-kuwan* because it is used for the attachment of the badge called the kasa-jiruchi. Some of the older helmets have a sec-

ond ring higher up that was used for the attachment of the horo.

Three ornaments are fastened to the hari-date. Those at the sides are flat pieces of metal said to symbolize the leaves of the sagittaria, a water plant. The sockets are called *tsunomoto*, and the leaf-shaped ornaments *kuwagate*. They are usually broad, and sometimes very large; at others they are narrow and as much as twenty inches long. Between them is the *mayedate*, or crest. As early as the 11th century this began to take the form of some animal or mythical creature whose attributes were to be emulated by the wearer. The crest may be worn in any one of three other positions — in

FIGURE 413. *Japanese Helmet with three crests. Maidate in front. Kashiradate on top. Two at the sides, Wakidate.*

FIGURE 414. *Kabuto.* 1. *To-Kamuri (shaped like a ceremonial cap), crest of Tatsumo family, XVIII.* 2. *Momo-Nari (shape of a peach), XVII.* 3. *To-Kamuri, crest of Sakuri family, late XVIII.* 4. *Korean type, late XVI or early XVII.* 5. *XVII.* 6. *Korean type, about 1400.* 7. *Korean(?) type, late XVII.* 8. *Asagao (morning-glory, convolvulus), crest of Otawara family, XVIII.* 9. *The shape is copied from a European cabasset, XVIII. The first six are in the Metropolitan Museum. Not to scale.*

FIGURE 415. *Kabuto.* 1. *Made of a single piece, embossed as a mountain and trees.* 2. *Embossed in the form of a shi-shi. The entire hashi is of one piece, the tail only being separate. Early form of neck guard.* 3. *Rounded hashi and brim in one piece. The dragon ornaments on the front are riveted on.* 4. *Hashi of 62 plates signed* Tai ei roku nen ri gatsu kishi nichi. Miochin Nobuiye. *(Made on an auspicious day of the second month of 1526.) Nobuiye was the greatest of the later Miochins.* 5. *Unusual form. The bow-like projection rises 6 inches above the crown.* 6. *Hashi of 16 plates with elaborate projecting rivets. Signed Muneharu of Kaga (Late XVIII).* 7. *Very early hashi of 16 plates, mountings modern.* 8. *Momonari of 16 plates with ribbed vertical joints and projecting rivets.* 9. *Helmet of 4 plates in the shape of a European burgonet.* 10. *Hashi of 64 plates with ribs. Signed Yoshimichi, about 1530.* 11. *Hashi of 6 plates of which the 2 forming the crown project backwards beyond the others.* 12. *Momonari with eagles embossed in high relief on the sides. The crest is a tengu's head in the round with 4 long wings.* 13. *Hashi of 8 plates, top and brim. Scalloped butt straps.* 14. *Hashi of 6 plates and a flat brim. A silver character on each plate.* 15. *Very heavy hashi of 5 plates, 3 of which show deep dents from bullets where they were tested.* 16. *Embossed in the form of a shell from a single plate.* 17. *In the form of Fuku-Roku-Ju, one of the gods of good luck.* 18. *Helmet of very curious and unusual shape.*

the hachimanza, in which case it is called *kashira-date* — on a hook at the back, when it is called *ushiro-date*, or there may be two, called *waki-date*, carried on hooks on the lower part of the sides of the hashi. Occasionally as many as three crests are worn at once, fig. 413. If no crest is worn, or if it is not carried in the usual position on the front, the

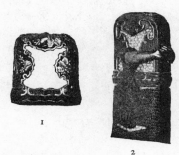

FIGURE 416. *Kabuto Gane. 1. Shakudo with gold kiri crests and ho-o birds. 2. Shakudo with gold Nabashima crests. It has the saru-te (monkey hands), the loop to which the udenuki cord is fastened.*

kuwagata are frequently joined and have a loop on the back that slips over a hook on the front of the helmet. See Date and Maidate.

The earliest helmets were made of a small number of plates and the neck guards were very large and projected greatly. Later the helmets were made of a much larger number of plates (as many as one hundred) and the neck guards were smaller and fitted close to the head. The helmets that were worn during the time that fighting was almost continuous were nearly always of simple forms. In the 15th century, after the Korean war, helmets of Korean and Manchurian shapes were in favor in Japan. Still later European cabassets and morians were fitted with Japanese neck guards, or copied, and worn. In the later Tokugawa period armor became largely a matter of decoration and many grotesque and almost useless forms of helmet were sometimes used. Figs. 414, 415.

The early helmets were not lined but the wearer wrapped up his head in a sort of turban or cushion. All of the later helmets had linings of cloth strengthened by crossed straps and a band around the lower edge. This lining was not as deep as the helmet and was firmly fastened to the lower edge of the latter so that the weight was carried by the lining and the helmet did not touch the top of the head. The elasticity of the lining thus made a spring

to protect the head from the shock of a blow. There are three, four or five loops or rings, fastened to the lower edge of the inside of the helmet, through which the cord that holds it in place is passed. This cord is called *shinobi-no-o*, and is made of cotton cloth, or silk crepe, folded and sewed up as a rope, or else a special kind of soft silk cord is used. Hard twisted cords are not suitable for the purpose. These cords are of three lengths depending upon the number of rings on the helmet. The three are called *mitzuchi, yetzuchi* and *atzuchi* — lengths seven, eight and nine feet. Each is tied in a different way. In all, loops are formed between the helmet rings and pins, hooks or rings on the menpo, and finally tied under the chin. When properly done the helmet is held firmly and comfortably, as the menpo distributes the pressure; but the wearer cannot open his mouth.

Garbutt quoting from an old Japanese book on wearing armor says: "Putting on a helmet in *ikubi* (wild boar neck) style means putting it on with the front part tilted upwards. This style is advantageous in fighting with sword or spear, and as it also looks better than others, its use is advised."

FIGURE 417. *Kagi-Nawa. White silk cord about a quarter of an inch in diameter and 17 feet 8 inches long with a four-pointed grapnel swiveled on the end.*

KABUTO GANE, TSUKA GASHIRA. The pommel of a tachi, a Japanese state sword. It comes down about an inch and a half on the hilt and has openings in the sides, fig. 416. The corresponding fitting on any other kind of sword or knife is called a kashira.

KABUTO JI. (Helmet letters). A form of writing used in ornamenting helmets in Japan. It belongs to the style of writing called *so-sho*, or cursive. (Weber I, 360).

KABUZUCHI. A knob or pommel, Japan.

KACCHA. Crude iron blooms made in Catalan forges in India and afterwards worked into wootz (steel). (Burton Sword 111).

KACHI-YUKI. A quiver, Japan. Obsolete.

KACHI YUMI. Shooting with a bow when on foot, Japan. In old Japan the nobles were the mounted archers.

KADIMANGO. See Wakerti.

KADJI. A stone-headed spear, Northern Australia. (Spencer, North. Ter. 328).

KADJO, KOD-JER. The East Australian stone axe. The handle is a stick pointed at one end and with a large lump of resin on the other. Two stones are set in the gum opposite each other, one blunt for use as a hammer, and the other chipped to a cutting edge making an axe. The stone usually employed is granite; the resin is that of the tough-topped xanthorrhea. The entire tool is usually colored with red ochre. (Brough Smyth I, 339).

KADUMANGO. An Australian club shaped somewhat like the "Indian clubs" used in gymnasiums. (Spencer, North. Ter. 433).

KANGAMA ITA. The cheek plate of a horse's bit, Japan.

KAGI NAWA. A thin rope about ten feet long with a multi-pointed grapling hook on the end. It was carried by Japanese soldiers and used in climbing walls, securing boats, hanging up armor, and other purposes. It was usually carried hung from the saddle. (Garbutt 153). Fig. 417.

KAGI-YARI. A hooked spear, Japan.

KAHAWAT. The fighting hat of the natives of Northern Nicobar. It is a round-pointed cap covered with coarse net, and with a hair fringe hanging over the sides and back of the head. (Man, And. 7 & Nic. 10).

KAHSITA. A barbed harpoon, Eskimoes of Nutka. (U. S. N. M. 1900, 230).

KAHUK. A blowpipe, Timor. It is a plain bamboo tube. (Arc. f. Eth. VIII, 6).

KAHUK ISIN. Blowpipe darts, Timor. They are made of bamboo with the butt covered with feathers. They are as much as three feet long, many times the length of any other blowpipe darts. (Arc. f. Eth. VIII, 6).

KAIDALIKI. An ancient type of Russian arrow. (Scheremetew 122).

KAIDATE. A breastwork of large wooden shields, Japan.

KAI-KUMI. To hold a spear close to the side in position for charging, Japan.

KAIRAGAI. A toy sword made of wood, Japan.

KAJOE PELET. (Kajo wood). A Malayan wood much valued for kris hilts and scabbards. It is a very hard, close-grained wood, nearly white but with broad, irregular black bands and patches. The tree is called Timongo (Kleinhovia Hospita). The wood does not always have these dark markings, which the Malays believe to be the result of disease. Finely marked pieces are much valued and formerly sold for tremendous prices. As much as $900 has been paid for an exceptionally good one.

KAKE. See Tsuyo no O.

KAKI-AGE. An earthwork, Japan. Obsolete.

KAKIHAN, KWAO. A written seal following a Japanese signature, or in place of it. Kwao means "stamped flower." Weapons and sword mountings were frequently signed in this way.

KAKI YOROI, KEIKO. A Japanese corselet of riveted scales, 4th century B.C. (M. M. S. II, 226).

KAKKO. A kind of drum, Japan.

KAKUDZURI, KOKUDZURI. A Japanese knee cop. It is usually a continuation of the greave, but sometimes is a separate plate. (Conder 276). The two principal varieties are called *yama-gata* and *juwo-gashira*.

KAKU UCHI. Target shooting, Japan.

KALAPU. See Katapu.

KALGHI. Black heron's feathers worn as plumes on the helmets by the Sikhs. They were much prized as only one suitable plume is found in each wing. The plumes are bound with gold wire. (Egerton, p. 69, 128).

the Buddhist king who had his chariot wheel lifted over a mantis.

KAMAKURA PERIOD. The period considered as ancient in Japan, from 1100 to 1336 A.D.

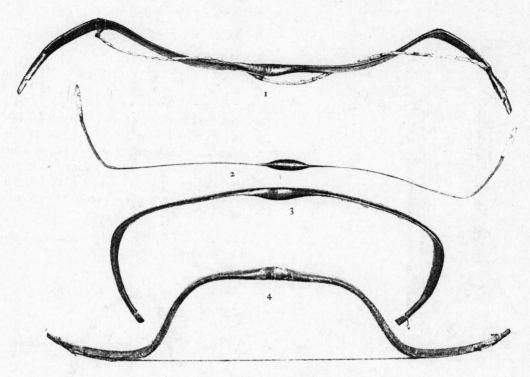

FIGURE 418. *Kaman. 1. Painted inside and out with black and yellow. Length from tip to tip, unstrung, 3 feet 8 inches. 2. Steel bow with the handle and borders lacquered in colors. Length from tip to tip, unstrung, 3 feet 4 inches. Punjab. 3. Lacquered with red and gold. 4. Lacquered in red, black and gold. Length from tip to tip, strung, 3 feet 6 inches.*

KALIHAN. The Kayan shield; it is of the usual Dyak type. See Kliau. (Arc. f. Eth. III, 239).

KALIS. A kris. (Arc. f. Eth. IV, 70).

KALKA, ALKIR. A general name for spears, Cape Bedford region, Queensland. (Roth, Aust. Mus. VII, 192).

KALLAK. See Kujerung.

KALLUM. A type of Australian spear thrower. See Wanmaiia.

KAMAKIRI. Japanese, a mantis, the emblem of courage. A not uncommon decoration of sword guards is a mantis and a wheel; it indicates that not even the courage of the mantis can overcome the wheel of fate. It may also refer to the old story of

KAMAN. The composite bow of India. It is built up, like the bows of most other Oriental countries, with a wood core, sinew back and horn belly. The ends do not curve back as much when unstrung as the Persian. The Indian bows are generally painted on both back and belly, or sometimes covered with brocade. (Egerton 366, 457, 459, 592, 598). Fig. 418.

KAMASHIMO ZASHI. A kind of sword given a Japanese boy when he first put on ceremonial dress. It was rather short, with a plain black lacquer scabbard and the cord of the hilt was plaited over the kashira of plain black horn; the other mountings were particularly fine. It was also worn by men with the court dress called *kama-shimo*, as it was short enough to wear in a litter and did not have to be left at the entrance of a house. (Weber I, 377).

FIGURE 419. *Kama Yari. 1. O-kama yari. Blade only. Length of cutting edge 8 inches. Inscriptions on blade and scabbard saying when and where it was used. 2. Kama Yari. Blade 6 inches long, handle partly lacquered.*

KAMA YARI. A Japanese pick. It has a straight shaft with a blade at right angles to it. The edge of the blade is straight and towards the handle, the back is curved. When it is unusually large it is called O Kama Yari. Fig. 419.

There is one in the Peabody Museum, Salem, in which the blade folds up like that of a pocket knife, with a slide on the handle that can be moved up against the blade to hold it open, or down so as to cover the end and hold it closed, and be fastened in either position by a pin through the handle.

KAMCHA. A whip, Turkish. It has a short, stiff handle with a long lash fastened to one side at the end. Fig. 420.

KAMI. A cartridge pouch, India. (Wallace Orient).

KAMI-KIRI. A kind of kozuka; this name means "paper cutter."

KAMJO. A whip in Salar, the Turkish kamcha. The Salar are a Turcoman tribe that migrated to Tibet in the latter part of the 14th century.

KAM-MA. See Uluwa.

KAMPILAN. See Campilan.

KAMR. India, belts carrying flasks, bullet pouches, and other loading implements. They are of the most varied forms and materials — wood, horn, ivory, paper, leather, cloth and metals are used. The decorations are of every sort known in India and Persia. Some are very simple and solely for use; others are extremely elaborate and decorative, quite as much for show as use. The combinations of articles carried also varies greatly, some not having more than two or three, while others have eight or ten. Fig. 421.

KAMURI OTOSHI. A Japanese blade similar to the u-no-kubi-tsukuri.

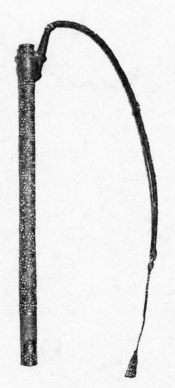

FIGURE 420. *Kamcha. Turkish or Persian whip. Handle 21 inches long of chased silver-gilt set with turquoise.*

KAMURI ITA, KAMURI-NO-ITA. The top plate of the Japanese shoulder guard. (Dean Jap. 5). Conder restricts this name to the top plate of the shoulder guard called *kusari sode*. (275).

KANABO. A long club, usually of iron, Japan. In many of the legends celebrated warriors are

guards with gold and silver. His guards are always of iron, usually decorated with simple landscapes, often with a few figures in the foreground, and slightly accentuated with inlays of the precious metals. The best work signed with his name is characterized by low relief, thin metal and very little

FIGURE 421. *Kamr.* 1. *Central India, 18th century. Belt and pouches of leather decorated with embroidery. Horn flask with ivory ends. One of the pouches contains one, and another four, wooden powder chargers. There is also a woven amulet case.* 2. *Central India, 18th century. A broad leather belt with a powder flask, two small pouches and one large one fastened to it. The flask is decorated with silver filigree and set with colored stones. All three of the pouches have silver fronts decorated in filigree and embossing and set with colored stones. The caps of the chargers in the large pouch are similar. All have tassels hanging from them with silver sockets.* 3. *Belt and two pouches of brown leather with pierced steel mountings. It also carries a flask. Afghan, 18th century.* 4. *Leather belt covered with velvet. The fronts of the bullet pouches and patch box are of silver. The flask is of iron, silver and brass. Hyderabad, 18th century.* 5. *The flask and the covers of the pouches are of watered steel with the borders inlaid with gold. The largest pouch contains ivory chargers, Persian, 17th century.* 6. *Belt, flask and two pouches covered with green velvet with patterns woven in silver wire. Punjab, 18th century.*

said to have used it. In art onis (imps) are often armed with it. (Weber I, 379). The later ones are made of wood bound with iron.

KANAGU. Collectively the mountings of a tachi, except the tsuba. For the other types of sword the corresponding term is kodogu.

KANAIYE. The first artist in Japan to inlay

inlay. The best of these guards suggest much more than they show and fairly hypnotize the observer.

According to Director Imamura of the Imperial Armory, Tokio, three generations of Kanaiye are alone known. The first Kanaiye Sho-dai, lived about 1550 and produced the most important guards of the family. His guards rarely bear contemporary signatures. The second Kanaiye Yoshimasa, about 1600, was the maker of the majority of the guards known as Sho-dai. The third Kanaiye San-dai, about 1650, prepared the guards whose decoration was in low relief, often decadent in treatment. The majority of the "Kanaiye" guards, however, are the work of copyists, 1650-1760. They are of interest only as simulating originals which have long since been lost. The most famous subjects of Kanaiye are derived from Chinese literature, Japanese poems, folklore and history. Undecorated guards by these artists are of extreme rarity.

KANA-MAKARI. See Sentan-Ita.

KANAMONO. Literally hardware, a term sometimes used as a name for unusual fittings that have no recognized names. It is also often given to poor forgeries of Japanese sword fittings.

KANDELAN. See Pendoq.

KANDRI. A slightly curved boomerang of round section, Detro tribe, Australia. (Hewitt 265).

KANDSCHAR, KANJAR. See Khanjar.

KANGRAS. Battlements, Rajput. (Tod I, 255).

KANJU. A gun, Salar. (Rockhill).

KANKWA. (Tate hoko). Shield and spear, Japan.

KANNAI. Rough spears made of tough saplings with the bark peeled off, the end pointed and the whole blackened by fire, the point, for about a foot, being afterwards scraped white. They were used for fighting, Brisbane, Queensland. (Roth, Aust. Mus. VII, 197).

KANO NATSUO. 1828-1898. He was one of the most celebrated makers of sword fittings of the 19th century, and the last. His work is of extraordinary delicacy and variety, and marvelous both in design and execution.

He was the head of the National Art School and Director of the Mint and designed the present Japanese coins.

KAN-SHOKA. A single-barbed harpoon with a loose head attached by a cord, Nicobar Islands. (Man, And. & Nic. 8).

KANT'HAH SOBHA. A gorget, India, 16th century. (Egerton, p. 23).

KAN-TOP. A close fitting Indian helmet with ear flaps. (Burton Sword 204).

KANTSCHAR. A Russian sword of the 17th century. It had a very narrow blade with short quillons curving towards the point. (Kaemmerer XXII). The name is derived from the Arabic khanjar, a knife.

KANURI OTOSHI. A small pointed stiletto, Japan.

KAPEE DHA. A sword with a short, broad blade and a leather scabbard, Assam. (Egerton 186).

KAPUN. A broad-bladed spear used for killing deer, Point Barrow. (Murdoch 243).

KARA-AYA-ODOSHI. Japanese armor laced with Chinese silk damask.

KARAKO BAORI. A Japanese surcoat without sleeves, but with frills around the armholes. (Conder 277).

KARAKUSA. A vine pattern, an arabesque, Japan.

KARANJA. See Yirmba.

KARASABI. See Ram Dao. (Rockstuhl LXVIII). A small sword, Japan.

KARASHISHI. See Shishi.

KARD. A straight-bladed Persian knife with a straight hilt and no guard. The point is often thickened to permit it to be forced through mail. They vary much in size and shape and are often of fine workmanship. (Moser XI). Fig. 422.

KARI-EBIRA. A variety of Japanese quiver. See Ebira.

KARIMATA. A forked arrowhead, Japan. They are sometimes very large; one is preserved at Itsukushima that is 6.375 inches long and nearly 5 across the points. (Gilbertson Archery 119).

KAROENKOENG. A suit of rattan armor, Dutch Borneo. (Peralaer 375).

KAROL. A heavy carbine used by Hyder Ali's cavalry. (Egerton 585).

KAROULA. An Indian knife with a hilt like that of a one-piece chilanum. The blade has a single instead of a double curve. (Rockstuhl CXLIII).

KAROULI. Tricks of horsemanship, high school riding, Rajput. (Tod II, 560).

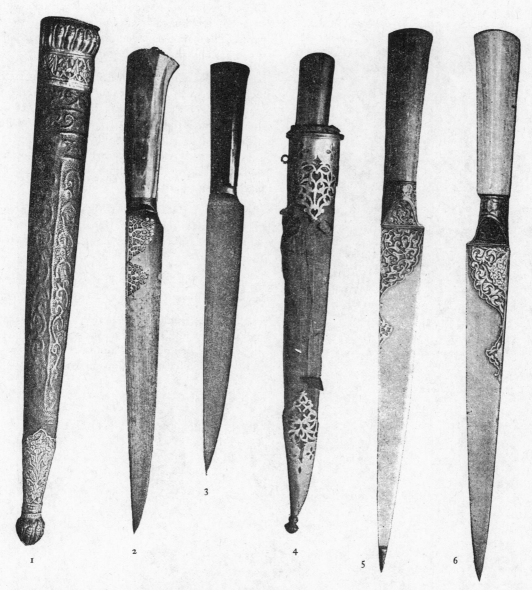

FIGURE 422. *Kard. 1. The scabbard of no. 2. Black stamped leather, embossed silver locket and chape. 2. Watered steel blade 9.125 inches long pierced with Arabic letters. Bone grips riveted to a flat tang, the edges of which are pierced like the blade. 3. Watered steel blade 8 inches long. Jasper grips on a flat tang covered with gold enameled in colors. 4. Watered blade 8.25, inlaid with gold. Bone grips. Scabbard covered with velvet with pierced silver locket and chape. 5. Very fine watered blade 10.875 inches long inlaid with a gold vine, Persia, 17th century. 6. Watered blade 9.5 inches long. It and the tang are heavily inlaid with gold. Ivory grips, Persia, 17th century.*

KARRAGARM. See Giam.

KARUD. Persia, a straight-bladed peshkabz. (Moser XII).

FIGURE 423. *Kasajiruchi-No-Kuwan. A gilt ring on the back of a helmet from which the kasajiruchi is hung. The helmet shown is of the type called Asa-Gao (Morning-glory).*

KARUKA, KUMIYA. A ramrod, Japan.

KA RYNTICH. The Khasi (Assam) bow. It is about five feet long, and made of bamboo with a string of the same. Its range is from 50 to 180 yards. The bamboos used for making it are called *u spit, u khen* and *u siej-lieh.* (Lyall 24).

KASA JIRUCHI. A piece of cloth about sixteen inches long, with a crest or other device on it, hung from a ring on the back of a helmet, or carried on a short rod fixed to the front, Japan. That of a commander was usually of brocade with the device in gold or silver thread; those carried by the common soldiers were of silk or cloth with the device in black. (Conder 261, 278).

KASA-JIRUCHI-NO-KUWAN. An ornamental ring on the back of a Japanese helmet from which the kasajiruchi was hung. (Conder 261). Fig. 423.

KASANE. The thickness of a Japanese blade at the back.

KASHIRA, HEITO. Literally, the uppermost part of anything. The cap on the pommel of a Japanese sword or knife. It is almost always of metal; but, occasionally, of horn, even when used with a

FIGURE 424. *Kashira. 1. Iron, an oni carved in relief. 2. Shibuichi, an old man's head in relief in copper and gold. 3. Iron, kiri crests in gold. 4. Shakudo, the three vinegar tasters in gold, silver and copper. 5. Shibuichi and gold. Shinno, the first physician. 6. Shibuichi, gold, silver and copper. A grotesque mask. 7. Shibuichi and silver. A helmet carved in the round. 8. Shibuichi and gold. A nio holding a shakudo vajra. 9. Iron, a dragon hiding under a bell. 10. Iron, with a skull and bone in relief in silver.*

highly decorated fuchi. The metal ones are chased, engraved and inlaid as elaborately as the other fittings. The design generally conforms to that on the fuchi on the opposite end of the hilt; frequently part

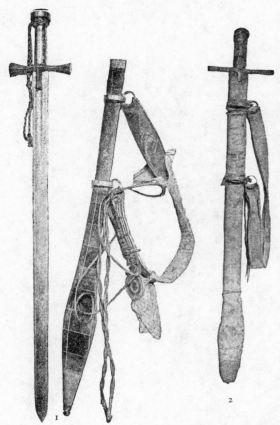

FIGURE 425. *Kaskara.* 1. *Double-edged Arab blade dated A.H. 357 (A.D. 967) covered with inscriptions. Length 35.5 inches. Straight cross guard gold plated; grip and pommel covered with gold plates, the former embossed and the latter carved with inscriptions in Arabic. Scabbard of leather partly covered with velvet with a gold chape.* 2. *Straight, double-edged blade 2 feet 8 inches long. Plain iron cross guard. Leather scabbard and belt.*

of a legend or story will be illustrated on one and the remainder on the other. Fig. 424. See also Fuchi.

On a tachi the corresponding fitting is called *kabuto gane.*

KASHIRA-DATE. A crest placed in the hachimanza of a Japanese helmet. (Weber I, 82).

A badge worn on the hachimanza of a helmet. (Garbutt 186). Fig. 413.

KASHIRA ZUKURI. A variety of Japanese helmet. (Garbutt 168):

KASKARA. The sword carried by the Baghirmi (Sahara). It is a straight-bladed sword with a plain cross guard such as is used in the Sudan. (Burton Sword 162). Some have fine old European or Oriental blades which are very highly valued. Occasionally the chapes and hilts are covered with gold. Fig. 425.

KASRULLAH. A knobbed stick carried by the Tripolitans, principally at night as a protection. (Furlong 72, 300).

KASTANE. The national sword of Ceylon. The blades are very frequently European and many bear the mark of the Dutch East India Company. Most are short, heavy, single-edged and curved. The hilts are of native make and the commonest form is very characteristic; it has two or four quillons which usually curve towards the blade, and frequently a rather broad counterguard. The pommel and the ends of the quillons and finger guards are monster's heads beautifully carved. The entire hilt is carved, inlaid and partly covered with silver; often it is made entirely of silver, or even gold, sometimes set with jewels. The scabbards are of carved wood or horn, or covered with embossed brass, silver or gold. Fig. 426.

The very short swords of this type are probably those given by the Dutch to native officials as a mark of office.

KASUN. A self bow, Burma. (Egerton, p. 94).

KATA-ATE. Pads worn on the shoulders to support the weight of the armor in Japan. (Conder 276).

KATA-HITSU. An opening for a kogai or kozuka in a tsuba. (Weber II, 507).

KATAITIX. A Greek helmet made of leather. (Skelton 44).

KATAKIRI-BORI. Cutting the lines of a design in channels of varying width and depth so as to suggest brush marks. It is often used in the decoration of Japanese sword fittings.

KATA KOSHIATE. See Koshiate.

KATANA. The oldest Japanese swords, those found in the dolmens of prior to A.D. 700 are straight and single-edged. Next come the straight two-edged ken, of which very few are in existence.

The first of the curved single-edged swords was the tachi, which was hung from the belt edge downwards. As a fighting sword it was abandoned centuries ago and its place was taken by the precisely similar katana which was carried edge up thrust through the belt. Fig. 427.

The Japanese treated his sword with great respect. When not in use it was placed in a rack with the edge up and hilt to the right. The scabbard was made of, or lined with, a soft wood and the sword was drawn and returned to it by sliding the back on the wood so that the edge did not get rubbed and

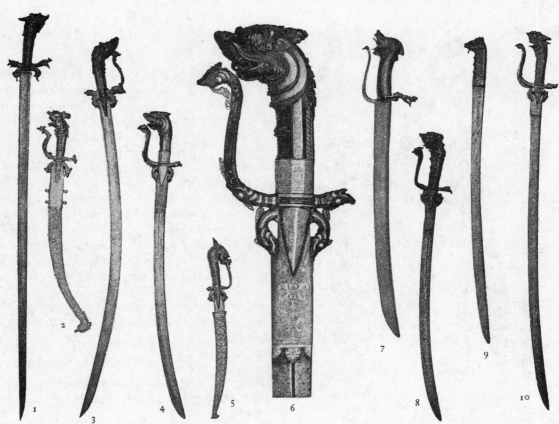

FIGURE 426. Kastane. 1. Straight blade 31.5 inches long, steel hilt. 2. A child's sword. Silver plated brass blade. Silver gilt hilt and scabbard, the former set with imitation jewels. 3. Hilt and guard of chased brass. 4. Blade 22 inches long with a panel of engraved brass next the hilt. Carved wood hilt and steel guard inlaid with silver. 5. Blade 10 inches long. Brass hilt and openwork scabbard. 6. The hilt of no. 4. 7. Brass hilt with a monster's head pommel, and a human figure seated in a chair for a guard. 8. Ivory hilt of the usual design, guard inlaid with brass and silver. 9. Blade with the mark of the Dutch East India Company, dated 1768. Horn hilt, no guard. 10. Blade 28 inches long. Hilt of the usual pattern except that it has a sharp ridge on the finger guard. The hilt is of a base silver alloy.

The mountings of the tachi and katana differ considerably but the blades are alike, except that they are signed on opposite sides of the tang, always on the side that is outward when the sword is carried. The blades of all Japanese swords and knives are similar, they differ much in length, but all are of the same form and construction. See Japanese Blades.

injured. In fencing he guarded with the flat of his sword; and if it was to be put away it was placed in a brocade bag. When traveling extra swords, in their bags, were put in locked cases. "In very ancient days warfare was a science. Artistic skill was always displayed in the use of weapons, and no soldier was proud of having wounded an enemy in any other manner than the one established by strict samurai rule. The long sword had for its goal only four points; the top of the head, the wrist, the side, and the leg below the knee." (Sugimoto 109).

The hilt of a katana is eight or ten inches long so that it can be used with one, or both, hands. It is usually covered with *same* (shark skin), some-

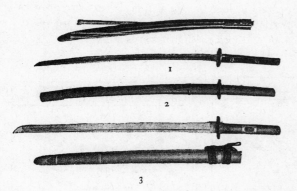

FIGURE 427. *Katana.* 1. *Light grooved blade* 25.125 *inches long,* 14*th century. Tsuba chickens by Ishiguro Koreyoshi; other mountings by Takeshiba Toshiteru. Black lacquer scabbard with a silver kojiri.* 2. *Hilt and scabbard covered with iron.* 3. *Heavy grooved blade* 27 *inches long. Signed Fujiwara Sadeyuki. Mountings of shakudo with kiri crests and dragons in gold. Red and black lacquer scabbard strapped and bound with silver in the style called nagafukurin.*

times by metal plates. In either case it is almost always wound with cord, flat braid or whalebone. The quality of the *same* is determined by the size and regularity of the grains and the whiteness of the whole. At each end the hilt is protected by a mounting; the one next the guard is called the fuchi, and the one on the pommel the kashira. The latter is sometimes made of horn; as a rule both are made of metal and decorated with similar or related designs. On each side of the hilt there is an ornament, menuki; these were originally used to cover the ends of the peg, mekuki, by which the hilt is fastened to the blade but for centuries they have been placed to one side of it. The cord winding of the hilt holds the menuki and kashira in place. There are several patterns in which the cord is arranged. The guard, tsuba, is the most important accessory of the sword and is described more fully under Tsuba. It is a flat plate of metal. Above and below the guard thin, flat, oval washers, called seppa, are generally placed. When more than one is used they have distinguishing names.

Below the guard the blade is surrounded by a ferule, the habaki, which fits tightly to both blade and scabbard preventing the edge from rubbing against the latter, and closing the opening so tightly that moisture cannot enter it and rust the blade. On the fine old swords the habaki was generally made of gold or silver; on the later ones it is apt to be of bronze gilded or plated. Most habaki are plain, many have diagonal cuts (neko gake, cat scratches) to keep it from slipping in the scabbard. A few are decorated with carving or inlaying.

The scabbard is nearly always made of honoki wood (Magnolia Hypoleuca), a fine grained light wood. It is lacquered and often decorated with its owner's crest or other ornaments. Sometimes the scabbard is covered with shark skin which has been lacquered either black or green and then ground to a flat surface, leaving circular patches of the ivory-like skin visible surrounded by the dark lacquer. It is then polished. This is sometimes called inlaid ivory.

Frequently one or two small sheaths are hollowed out in the sides of the scabbard for the kozuka, a small knife, and the kogai, or head pin. These are usual with the short sword, but much rarer with the long one, which only occasionally has the kozuka, and less often the kogai. The edge of the opening for the kozuka is guarded by a flat piece of metal, the uragawara; and that for the kogai by the kurikata. The latter is a projecting lug that keeps the scabbard from slipping through the belt. It is always used and is made of horn, wood lacquered or of metal. It has an opening in it through which a flat silk cord, the sageo, is passed. This cord is used to fasten the scabbard to the belt, or to tie back the flowing sleeves when fighting. Occasionally a hook, the soritsuno, is placed on the scabbard a few inches below the kurikata to prevent the scabbard from being pulled through the belt when the sword is drawn. This hook is seldom used on sword scabbards, and not very often on knife sheaths. The soritsuno is made of horn or metal. There is often a ring, kuchi-kane, around the mouth of the scabbard. The tip of the scabbard may be simply lacquered like the rest; or it may have a piece of horn glued on; or it may have a metal chape, the kojiri. All of the metal mounts are decorated with carving or inlaying; the entire set being, not infrequently, of the same or closely related designs.

In general the katana being the fighting sword and not carried indoors has not as many or as elaborate mounts as the short sword.

The blades brought, and still bring, very large prices in Japan. As much as 500 pounds sterling has been paid for one, so that few could afford to own many. It therefore became the custom to change the mountings for different occasions. This could readily be done by pushing out the peg (mekugi), removing the hilt and substituting another and a scabbard to match it. This habit of changing

fuse apologies. The owner held the blade with its back towards the visitor and drew it from the scabbard, inch by inch. It was never entirely drawn unless particularly requested. If it was put in the hands of a visitor he held it with the edge towards himself and drew it very slowly "making sounds expressive of admiration." To turn the scabbard in the girdle, or to allow the scabbard to strike that of another, was equivalent to a challenge. It was also provocative of mortal combat to lay one's sword on the floor and kick the hilt towards any one.

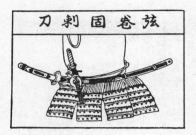 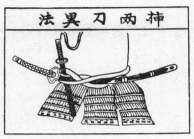 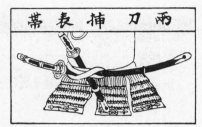

FIGURE 428. *Methods of carrying Japanese swords. Garbutt, Jr., Japan Society, Vol. XI.*

the mountings, and their intrinsic beauty, accounts for the much greater number of parts than of complete swords in existence. When not in use the blades were kept in plain wooden scabbards and had plain wooden grips, the only mounting being the habaki, and even this was often made of wood. The name of the maker, and sometimes a short account of the blade was usually written on the scabbard. This style of mounting is called shirasaya (white scabbard).

The sword was the object of an elaborate code of etiquette befitting the honor in which it was held. The katana-kake, or stand, on which it was placed when not in use, stood in a place of honor in the house and was always a piece of fine lacquer. A visitor, if accompanied by a servant, left his katana, with him on entering the house. If it was delivered to a servant of the house it was received on a piece of silk, and not on the bare hand. A stand was often placed at the entrance to receive the swords of visitors. On festive occasions, or prolonged visits, the short sword was also laid aside. It was a great breach of etiquette to touch another's sword unless invited to do so. No sword was ever exhibited except by special request, never made unless the blade was a rare one, and only complied with after pro-

The katana was usually simply thrust through the obi, sash, but was sometimes fastened to a koshiate (sword carrier) fastened to the belt. There were several varieties of these, some intended for a single sword, and others for a pair. An old method of carrying sword and dagger was called tsurumaki gatame no shi to. The sword was horizontal and the dagger vertical and passed through a tsurumaki, a ring shaped reel for carrying bow strings. Fig. 428.

The sword of a samurai should be capable of cutting off the head of a man at a single stroke; and tests were often made to see whether new blades would do it. Trying them on inanimate objects did not always satisfy their owners, and they were tried on the first peasant that happened to come along. This method of testing was common enough to acquire a name, tsujigiri. Swords were often tried on the bodies of criminals who had been executed. The test, tamashigiri, was made by the executioner in the presence of an expert who afterwards examined the blade and reported on its condition and performance. The bodies of murderers, persons with skin diseases, and tattooed men were not used for this purpose.

The corpse was sometimes hung up and cut

through either sideways or downwards. More often it was placed on a mound of sand (dodan) and cut across. On occasions two, or more, were piled on top of each other and as many as possible cut through at once. It is said that as many as seven bodies have been severed by one cut. The blades to

the top with a notch for the sword. The sword stood with the point upward. Vertical stands were also made for a pair of swords; they had two brackets with notches at different levels for the long and short swords. Most of the stands held the swords horizontally. They had uprights at the ends

1   2   3

FIGURE 429. *Katana Kake.* 1. *The base and top are aoi-shaped. Fine nashiji lacquer with a vine on the upright and Tokugawa crests on the base in raised gold lacquer. Height 25.75 inches.* 2. *Base in the shape of overlapping aoi leaves lacquered black. The stand proper is a dragon fly of gold lacquer except the eyes which are of green lacquer filled with powdered shell.* 3. *Stand for a pair of swords decorated in Chinese style, 18th century, no. 3. Metropolitan Museum and not to scale.*

be tested were wedged and keyed into a special handle.

Sixteen different cuts were recognized. Of these ten were crosswise of the body at different points. Through the wrist, through the elbow, the knee and the ankle. Through the shoulder cutting off the arm on the same, or on the opposite side. From the shoulder down through the chest; this was considered the easiest. Vertically through the center of the body. The most difficult was crosswise through the hips. (Joly S. & S. 117).

KATANA KAKE. Japan, a sword stand or rack. They are of several kinds. For a tachi the stand has a rather broad base and an upright with a piece on

with notches on one or both sides for the swords. Tachi were placed edge down, all other swords and knives with the edge upwards and the hilts to the right. In some cases the uprights were on the top of a small cabinet with drawers for extra mountings. Folding racks were also made that could be doubled up flat for convenience of carriage when traveling. Some of the very old racks were made of a pair of deer horns set in a block of wood. Most are of wood lacquered. Figs. 429, 430.

KATANA ZUTSU. A sword case, Japan. They are made of wood lacquered, and are generally decorated with the crests of their owners. They are in two parts of which one fits over the other and is held by a hasp and lock. Where the two lap the case is large enough to hold the guard and tapers and curves in both directions. Fig. 431.

times forked at the point, and katars with two, and even three blades occur. The Indian armorers occasionally made katars that were hollow and served

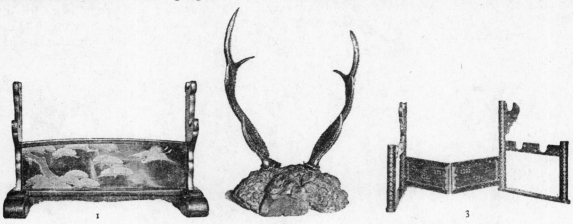

FIGURE 430. *Katana Kake.* 1. *Wooden stand for three swords. Black lacquer with trees and storks in gold and characters in red and gold.* 2. *Sword stand in the early style. A pair of deer horns mounted in a block of carved teak.* 3. *Folding rack for three swords. Wood lacquered black, gold and silver; panels of natural wood.*

KATAPU, KALAPU. A Sea Dyak war hat. It is a close fitting skull cap of rattan decorated with hornbill's feathers. (Ling Roth II, 128).

KATAPU KALOI. A Sea Dyak war cap made by sewing large fish scales on a cap of some soft bast-like material, plaited. (Ling Roth II, 101).

KATAR, COUTAR, KATAH, KOUTAH, KUTAH, KUTAR. The oldest and most characteristic of Indian knives. The peculiarity lies in the handle which is made up of two parallel bars connected by two, or more, crosspieces, one of which is at the end of the side bars and is fastened to the blade. The remainder form the handle which is at right angles to the blade. The blades are always double-edged and generally straight, but occasionally curved. They are of all lengths from a few inches to about three feet. The blades of South Indian make are often broad at the hilt and taper in straight lines to the point, and are elaborately ribbed by grooves parallel to the edges. European blades of the 16th and 17th centuries were often used, especially by the Mahrattas. Katars with native blades are often thickened at the point to strengthen them for use against mail. When European blades are used they are always riveted to projections from the hilt. The native blades are often forged in one piece with it. The blades are some-

FIGURE 431. *Katana Zutsu.* 1, 2. *Cases for a pair of swords. Aventurine lacquer with gold mon of the daimio of Tako in the province of Shimoza.* 3. *Black lacquer with three gold mons of Honda, daimio of Okazaki. All 18th century.*

as sheaths for smaller ones; or with three blades that folded together, appearing to be one, until the handle bars were pressed together, when they opened out. Fig. 432.

KATAR BANK. A Nepalese dagger with a slight double curve to the blade, straight grip and one-sided guard. (Egerton 335).

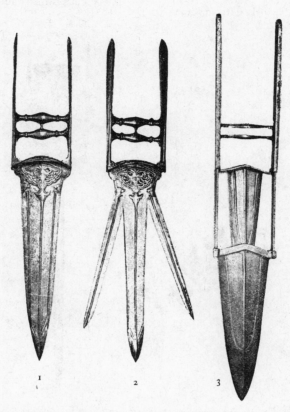

FIGURE 432. *Katars, Folding and Sliding.* 1. *Folding katar with the blades closed.* 2. *The same with the blades open.* 3. *Sliding katars. The smaller goes entirely inside of the larger.*

Among the Mahrattas the gauntlet sword, pata, was evolved from the katar. See Pata. Many katars have guards for the back of the hand. Most are solid plates but many are elaborately pierced, a form evidently suggested by the pierced shells and guards of the Portuguese rapiers. Some of the Tanjore katars have most complicated and beautiful hand guards, fig. 433. Many katars are perfectly plain, but they are often chiseled, inlaid, or both. There is no rule where the decoration shall be; it may be all on the blade, or all on the handle or divided between the two. Fig. 434.

The katar is a purely Hindu weapon and was rarely used by the Mohammedans, and is never found outside of India.

KATAR DORLICANEH. A katar with a forked blade. (Wallace Orient).

KATARI. A South Indian boomerang. (Egerton 68, 69).

KATARIYA. A boomerang made by the Kols of Guzerat. They are usually made of wood, but occasionally of iron or horn, flat and considerably curved. They have ball-shaped handles. (Egerton 1, 3). Fig. 435.

KATATA. A shield, Kaitish tribe, Central Australia. (Sp. & Gi.).

KATCHU. Armor, Japan.

KATOK, PANDAK. A kind of Malay knife. (Sk. & Bl.).

KATSUMI. The official tsuba maker of the last Shogun. 1829-1879.

KATTI TALWAR. A sword with a curved

KAWATSUDZUMI. A kind of Japanese corselet. (Garbutt 042). It is made of, or covered with, leather.

KAWAGASA. Japan, a leather helmet worn by the lower classes of retainers. The best were made

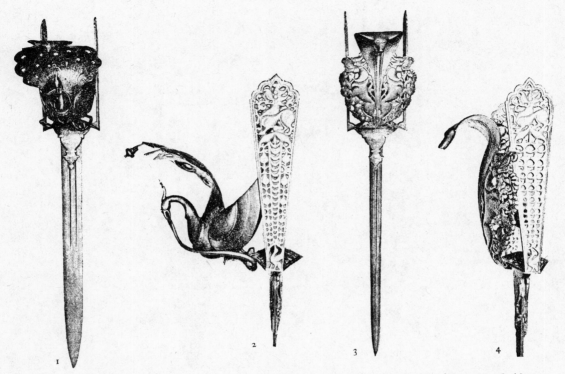

FIGURE 433. *Tanjore Katars, 17th century. 1. European blade 14.5 inches long. Pierced steel side bars. The hand guard is a peacock with its wings spread; it holds two cobra's tails in its beak. 2. The same side view to a larger scale. 3. European blade 15.5 inches long. Pierced steel side bars. The hand guard is a cobra with its hood spread between two griffons. 4. The side view of 3 to a larger scale. 1 and 3 are to the same scale. 2 and 4 are to a larger scale but the same for both.*

blade and a steel hilt with a spike projecting from the pommel, Nepal. (Egerton 334).

A sabre with an incurved blade. (Wallace Orient).

KATURIYEH. See Katuriya.

KAUAH, KAUAS. A cylindrical stone club fifteen inches long and two in diameter. It is thrown with great accuracy for distances up to twenty yards by the natives of Tanna, New Hebrides. (Arc. f. Eth. VII, 231).

KAU SIN KE. A Chinese whipping chain three or four feet long made of alternate ring and bar links. Fig. 436.

of a special kind of leather called *neri-gasa*. The leather was lacquered on both sides producing a hard, tough material. The crown was pointed and the brim was broad. The usual color was black with a gold crest in the center. The best of these were considered superior to the mail helmets. Fig. 437.

KAWA ODOSHI. Japanese armor laced with leather cords. (Conder 270).

KAWARA. Japanese armor made of leather scales sewed on cloth. It was used in very early times and only a few fragments of such armor are now in existence. (Dean Jap. 27).

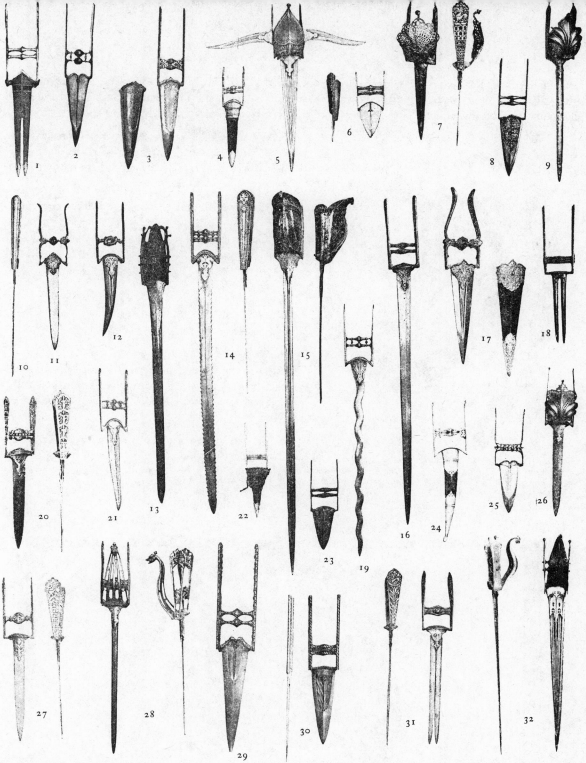

FIGURE 434. *Katars.* 1. *Heavy forked blade 8¾ inches long. Silver plated hilt. Scabbard covered with red brocade with a silver chape on each tip.* 2. *One piece. Blade 8¾ inches long.* 3. *Carved and paneled blade of black damask. Hilt pierced and inlaid with gold. Scabbard of brown leather with flowers on a gold ground.* 4. *Blade riveted to hilt. Hilt chased and silver plated. Chased silver scabbard mounts.* 5. *Triangular grooved blade. Guarded hilt with blades projecting from the side bars. Tanjore.* 6. *Very short, wide blade pierced and with a central rib. Hilt inlaid with gold.* 7. *Tanjore. Very open side bars and guard.* 8. *Plain gilded hilt. Blade carved with hunting scenes in relief; the animals have ruby eyes.* 9. *Tanjore. European blade. Guarded hilt with griffons.* 10. *Sind. European blade 14¼ inches long. Hilt covered with silver partly gilded, engraved with a flower design.* 11. *Blade 11½ inches long riveted to the hilt. Scroll side bars inlaid with silver.* 12. *Mahratta. Grip and side bars fish carved in the round.* 13. *Mahratta. Blade 26¾ inches long. Hilt with hand guard connected to the side bars by curved bars.* 14. *Blade 30¼ inches long with scalloped edges. Side bars chased to imitate pierced work.* 15. *Heavy ribbed blade 38 inches long. The hand guard joins the side bars completely enclosing the hand.* 16. *Roughly chased steel hilt. Blade 30¾ inches long.* 17. *Heavy blade set in a chased socket on the hilt. Hilt and scabbard mounts of silver gilt elaborately chased.* 18. *Two narrow, heavy blades and three handlebars; the whole forged in one piece.* 19. *Steel hilt riveted to a waved blade 23.125 inches long.* 20. *Rajput. Side bars with figures of Hindu gods carved in the round, silvered and gilded.* 21. *Pierced, watered, doubly curved blade. Silver plated hilt.* 22. *Plain blade 4½ inches long. Hilt engraved and gilded. Scabbard with a silver chape.* 23. *Very roughly made of soft iron. Blade 5 inches long.* 24. *Curved blade. Silver hilt and scabbard mounts.* 25. *Blade, scroll side bars and pierced grip all forged in one piece.* 26. *Tanjore. Watered blade; pierced side bars and hand guard.* 27. *European blade 12 inches long. Hilt of elaborately chased steel with traces of gilding.* 28. *European blade. Very open side bars and hand guard. The latter terminates in a dragon's head with a movable tongue.* 29. *Very heavy blade 10¾ inches long. Hilt and scabbard mounts with gold flowers on a black ground.* 30. *Round fluted side bars and handles gilded. Watered, paneled blade with a Sanskrit inscription that reads: "This kadarika katar in the hands of Bundeejaram Lord of Bundee is capable of piercing the temples of elephants, and hence is called the tongue of the god of death."* 31. *Tanjore. Two parallel blades, parts of a European rapier. Chased and pierced grip and side bars.* 32. *Southern India. Triangular fluted blade 20 inches long. Gilded hilt with hand guard.*

KAWARA SODE. Japanese shoulder guards consisting of large oblong plates with two movable plates at the bottom attached by leather cords. (Conder 272).

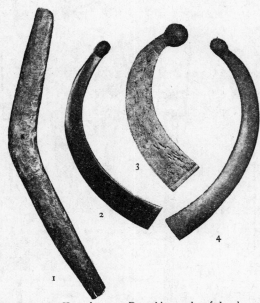

FIGURE 435. *Katariya.* 1. *Roughly made of hard wood, 26 inches long. Baroda.* 2. *Polished horn with a carved end.* 3. *Iron, roughly engraved. The ball is hollow. Length 14.5 inches, width at end 3 inches. Guzerat.* 4. *Dark polished wood 17.5 inches long. Guzerat.*

KAWA TSUCHUMI. Japanese armor in which the bands forming the cuirass are encased in leather. (Dean Jap. 27). Fig. 358.

KAWA TSUDZUMI. A Japanese corselet covered with leather. Many kinds of leather were used for this purpose, each giving its name to the corselet.

Kara-Kawa Tsudzumi		Chinese leather covering.		
Kin Kawa	"	Gilt	"	"
Ai-Gawa	"	Blue	"	"
Nuri-Kawa	"	Lacquered	"	"
Mon-Kawa	"	Diapered	"	"
Some-Gawa	"	Dyed	"	"
Aka-Gawa	"	Red	"	"
Kure-Kawa	"	Black	"	"
Hana-Gawa	"	Flowered	"	"

(Conder 284).

KAYE-MON. A registered crest used by the principal vassals on official occasions. It was generally derived from the Ju-mon. (Weber I, 35). See Mon.

KAY-YAN. An Igorot spear with a peculiarly shaped barbed head. It is not used in hunting, and seldom in war, but is made and carried for its graceful shape. (Jenks 128). Fig. 278.

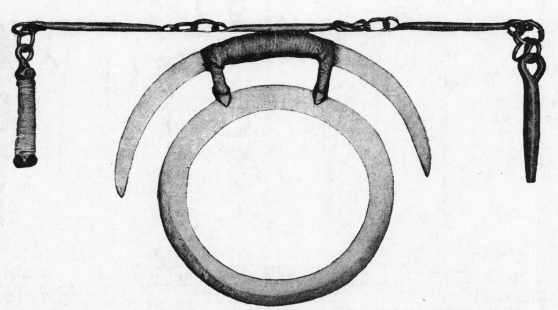

FIGURE 436. *Kau Sin Ke. Iron chain 3 feet 7 inches long. Below it is an unnamed Chinese weapon, all of the edges of which are sharp. The round blade is 12.5 inches in diameter.*

KAZILBASHES. "These were in addition to the military levies or 'Kazilbashes' (red caps)." (Egerton, p. 141). Persian soldiers. See Kissel Bash.

KEBIKI. Lacing the lames of Japanese armor with the cords very close together. This was only done for persons of importance. (Conder 270).

FIGURE 437. *Kawagasa. Helmet of black lacquered leather with a low, ribbed crown and a very large peak.*

KEBIKI DO-MARU, SUGAKE DO-MARU. Japanese armor made of metal scales laced with silk or leather cords. The two names indicate different ways of fastening the cords. This type of armor was very elastic, and was said to be cooler in hot weather and warmer in cold than that made of plates. (Conder 164). Some Japanese writers say that it was not as good because it was very heavy when wet, difficult to dry, and more apt to become infested with vermin when in camp. (Garbutt 143).

KEBORI. Hair line engraving, Japan. A method of decorating metal work.

KECHIL. A kind of Malay knife.

KEEP, DONJON, DUNGEON. The inner tower and citadel of a castle or fortress in the middle ages. (Grose II, 3).

KEERLI. A stone axe, Australia. (Spencer, North. Ter. 301).

KEGETSU. Fur shoes worn with armor, Japan. They were always worn at interviews with noblemen " as ordinary socks with sandals or bare feet are very vulgar." (Garbutt 160). See Kutsu.

KEIKO. See Kake Yoroi.

KEILI. A boomerang.

KELAU. Slingers who formed a corps d'elite in the Canaanite army. (Burton Sword 179).

KELAUITAUTIN. The Eskimo bird bolas. (Murdoch 248). See Bolas.

KEMILI. The fighting hat of the natives of Central and Southern Nicobar. It is a rectangular bag with half of one side cut away, the long side forming a flap to cover the back of the neck. (Man, And. & Nic. 10).

KEMPO. The rules of fencing, Japan.

KEN, HOJIU, TSURUGI. The oldest form of sword used in Japan in historic times. The older swords found in the burial mounds are single-edged. The ken has a straight, double-edged blade sometimes slightly widened close to the point. It only survives as a part of the temple regalia. Fig. 438.

KENDELAN, PENDOQ. The metal cover of a kris scabbard, Java.

KENDO, KENJUTSU. The art of fencing, Japan.

KENJO TSUBA. A type of guard given as presents to a superior in Japan. It was always of iron covered with geometrical patterns, or floral motives, in flat gold inlay. The edges were always gilded. They were made mainly in A-wa, also in Kyoto and in the province of Yamashiro, from the second half of the 17th century. (Weber I, 406). Fig. 439.

KEN-JU. A pistol, Japan. See Pistol.

KE-NON, BELAU. A blowpipe dart, sakai, Malay Peninsula.

KENUKI GATA TACHI. An old type of Japanese sword with the hilt and blade in one piece. The hilt is perforated with a slot enlarged at each end in the form of a pair of hair tweezers (Kenuki). This type of sword was carried as a sign of

FIGURE 438. *Ken. A Japanese temple sword, 16th century. Metropolitan Museum.*

mourning when visiting temples. (Weber II, 36). Fig. 440.

The knobs vary much in size and shape and are seldom decorated in any way; they are cut from

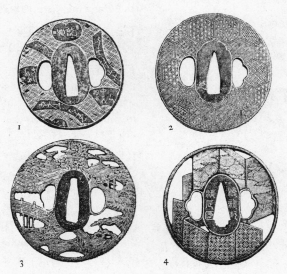

FIGURE 439. *Kenjo Tsuba. 1. Iron, with a diaper pattern in gold and inscriptions on panels. 2. Iron, with diaper patterns in gold in hexagons. Signed with kakihan. 3. Iron, pierced, a castle and trees, all inlaid with gold. 4. Iron. Screens in relief inlaid with gold. Signed.*

KENUKI GATA MENUKI. The openings in the hilt of a kenuki gata tachi, or menuki of the same shape. (Joly S. & S. 20). Fig. 440.

KENUKI KANAMONO. Strips of metal covering the joints between the two pieces of wood of which a Japanese hilt is made. They are decorated like the other fittings. (Joly S. & S. 22). Fig. 441.

KENYE. A bag in which to wrap a Japanese sword when it is to be put in a case. (Joly S. & S. 30).

KEPPAN. Attesting an oath by pricking the end of a finger with a kozuka and marking the print of the finger with the flowing blood. This had greater value than a seal in Japan. (Joly Int. 17).

KERRIE, KNOBKERRIE, TYINDUGO. The throwing stick of the Kaffirs of South Africa. It is a short stick with a large knob on one end.

the solid. The best are made of rhinoceros horn, most are made of wood. Fig. 442.

KESSO. Grooves in a Japanese blade. See Hi. (Joly S. & S. 109).

KETTLE DRUM. A drum with but one head and a hemispherical metal body. It is of Oriental origin and is used especially by cavalry bands.

KETTLE HAT, KETYL HAT. A headpiece of the 14th century of uncertain character. (Planche 320).

KEY. See Spanner.

KHADJA, AS, ASI. A sword introduced by Brahma according to Hindu mythology. It is sometimes described as a two-handed sword six feet long. (Burton Sword 214).

KHAMA. See Qama.

FIGURE 440. *Kenuki Gata Tachi. Early blade in an 18th-century scabbard. Collection of Dr. I. W. Drummond.*

KHANDA. The oldest and most typical of Indian swords. "In shape like the Andrea Ferrara, or long

FIGURE 441. *Kenuki Kanamono. All mountings of silver, chased and gilded in parts.*

cut-and-thrust." (Tod I, 453). It has a broad, straight blade, usually widening towards the point, which is generally quite blunt. Sometimes it is double-edged; but, it generally has a strengthening plate with ornamental borders on the back for a considerable part of its length. The hilt has a broad plate guard and wide finger guard which joins the large round, flat pommel. There is a spike on the pommel which acts as a guard for the

arm, and for a grip for the left hand when making a two-handed stroke. It is also used as a hand rest when the sword is sheathed. The inside of the guard and finger guard are padded. The khanda is the national sword of Orissa, but is very generally used by both Rajputs and Mahrattas. Fig. 443.

KHANDOO. A kind of Arab sword. (Tower 765, p. 13).

KHANG PRAI. A blunderbuss of Chinese make, Burma. (Egerton, p. 94).

KHANJAR, KANJAR, HANDSCHAR, KANTSCHAR. The name is Arab and means knife or dagger; it is used in many countries for many different weapons. In Turkey and the Balkans it is often applied to the yatagan. In Persia, according to Moser it is a double-edged dagger with a slight double-curve and, usually, a pistol hilt. In India Yule and Burnell say that it is "A large double-edged dagger with a very broad base and a slight curve." Egerton figures three different knives under this name, two of which correspond to the previous descriptions, while the third has a blade with a pronounced double curve and a lunette pommel. The first two are Mohammedan

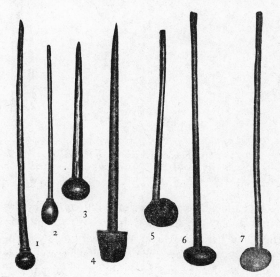

FIGURE 442. *Kerries. 1. Zulu, rhinoceros horn, plain round knob. Length 29.5 inches. 2. Masai type, rhinoceros horn. Oval knob with a bead below it. Length 21 inches. 3. Zulu, rhinoceros horn. Knob 3.5 inches in diameter. Length 18.5 inches. 4. Zulu, wood. Head of elliptical section, slightly carved. Length 28 inches. 5. Zulu, wood. Spherical head, faceted. 6. Zulu, wood. Rounded head. Length 29.5 inches. 7. Zulu, wood. Head roughly cylindrical with the flat sides parallel to the handle.*

types and are probably correctly named; the third is Hindu and is not likely to have been given an Arabic name by its makers. Egerton also gives this name to a two-handed sword. (577).

and a large lunette pommel. It is from Viziana-gram. (Egerton 500, 501). Fig. 445. He also calls a precisely similar knife a Khanjar.

FIGURE 443. *Khanda.* 1. *Etched blade 29.5 inches long. Hilt inlaid with a diaper pattern in silver.* 2. *Plain blade 31.5 inches long. Hilt of blued steel inlaid with gold, Sanskrit inscription on the finger guard.* 3. *The scabbard of 2 with an embossed silver chape.* 4. *Blade 25.75 inches long inlaid with gold on one side only. Hilt of blued steel inlaid with gold.*

The Indo-Persian knife generally known by this name is shown in fig. 444. It was very popular in India and Persia and is apt to be more highly decorated than any other form of knife from this region. The blades are generally fine forgings of watered steel, sometimes finely carved; and the hilts are of ivory, jade or some other hard stone, frequently set with jewels. The scabbards are often mounted to match the hilts.

KHANJARLI. Egerton gives this name to a Hindu dagger with a strongly double-curved blade

KHAPWAH. A knife with a curved double-edged blade with a strong rib. (Wallace Orient).

KHARGA. An Indian sacrificial axe. (Egerton 811 and p. 102).

KHARGA S'HAPNA. The Rajput worship of the sword, which takes place at the Noratri festival, sacred to the god of war and commencing on the first day of the month Asoj. The ceremony is very elaborate, requiring nine days for its completion. The sword worshiped is a khanda; it is supposed to

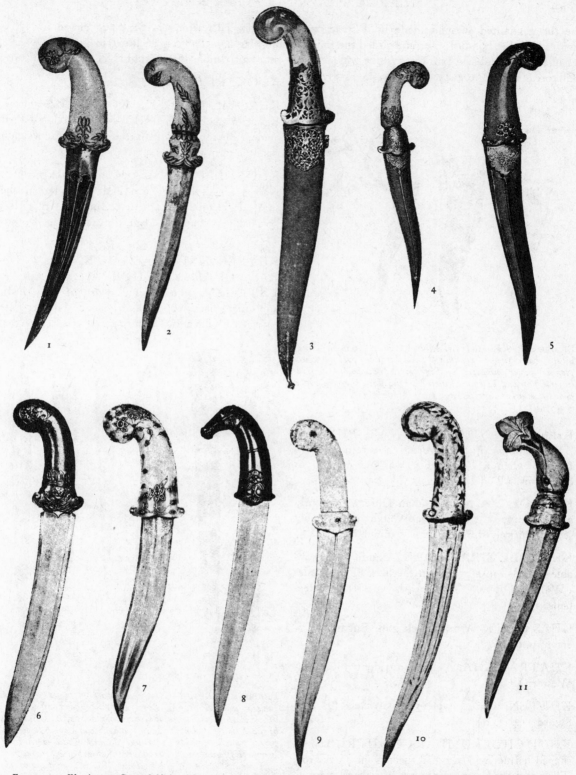

FIGURE 444. *Khanjar*. 1. *Grooved blade with a socket in the top into which a tang on the hilt fits. Carved hilt of light jade with a tang that fits into the blade.* 2. *Watered blade 8.125 inches long. Hilt of light carved jade.* 3. *Paneled blade of fine watered steel. Hilt of crystal set in an openwork gold ornament. Scabbard with locket and chape of pierced and chased gold.* 4. *Watered blade 7 inches long inlaid with gold. Hilt of carved jade inlaid with gold and set with red cabochon stones.* 5. *Finely watered blade 9.875 inches long, inlaid with gold vines and an inscription. Light jade hilt with colored stones set in gold.* 6. *Watered blade 11 inches long, inlaid with gold. Hilt of dark green jade carved.* 7. *Watered blade 9.25 inches long. Light green jade hilt set with jewels.* 8. *Hilt of black horn, pommel a horse's head with red stone eyes.* 9. *Blade 10.5 inches long. Hilt of white stone set with four rubies.* 10. *Fluted blade 11.375 inches long. Hilt of white agate inlaid with a vine in flat gold.* 11. *Black damask blade. Ivory hilt, a lotus set with four red stones.*

be the enchanted weapon made by Viswacarma, with which the Hindu Proserpine girded the founder of the race and sent him forth to the conquest of Chitore. (Tod I, 464-472).

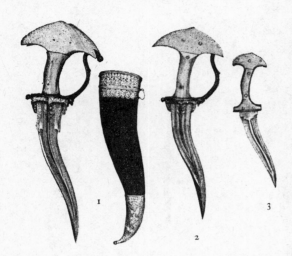

FIGURE 445. *Khanjarli. 1. Ribbed blade 8.75 inches long inlaid with silver. Scabbard covered with velvet with pierced silver mounts. 2. Fine ribbed blade; grip and lunette pommel of ivory riveted to the flat tang, the rivet heads are covered with rubies. 3. Blade 4.75 inches long, ivory hilt.*

KHARG BANDAI, YULWAR BUNDAI.

"The binding of the sword," a ceremony performed when a Rajput boy was old enough to bear arms. (Tod I, 129).

KHAROLL. A North Indian knife. Apparently a class name as the Wallace Catalogue describes several entirely different knives under it.

KHAROLL ZIRAH FORE. A knife with movable "pearls" in a groove in the back of the blade. (Wallace Orient). The "pearls" are usually steel balls.

KHAS CHUT. A matchlock gun, Burma. (Egerton, p. 94).

KHATRAMKHA. A Tibetan trident. (Ramsay-Western).

KHETEN. An Egyptian pole axe. (Burton Sword 154, 158).

KHOD CHULLUMDAR GONJICRI. A bowl-shaped helmet with a broad spear point on the top. The nasal has a very wide end, and there is a mail curtain that covers the entire face. The curtain has

a V-shaped opening in the front closed by a triangular flap that can be lifted to give the wearer more air, India. (Rockstuhl CXLIII).

KOOKERI. See Kukri.

KHROBI, KHOPSH, KOPIS. An ancient Egyptian sword with a sickle-shaped, double-edged blade. (Burton Sword 156). A very similar weapon is still used in the Congo.

KHUNDLI P'HANSI. A Mahratta fakir's crutch with a scroll-shaped head and a dagger in the shaft. Egerton calls it a mace, but says that it is "probably a crutch." (Egerton 470). See 3, fig. 274.

KHYBER KNIFE, AFGAN KNIFE, CHARAS, CHARAY, CHURRA, SALAWAR YATAGAN. The national sword of the Afridis and other tribes living in and near the Khyber Pass between India and Afganistan. It has a straight,

FIGURE 446. *Khyber Knives. 1. Watered blade 26 inches long inlaid with gold. Bone grip. Scabbard of stamped black leather with an embossed silver chape. 2. Unusually broad blade 14.5 inches long welded to a steel hilt with a finger guard. 3. Blade of rough damask inlaid with gold. Ivory grip, inlaid tang. Scabbard of stamped black leather. 4. Damask blade 23 inches long. The upper part of the hilt is of bone riveted to the flat tang, the lower part is of steel inlaid with gold.*

heavy, single-edged blade tapering gradually from the hilt to the point; and has a wide rib at the back. The hilt is without a guard and has a slight

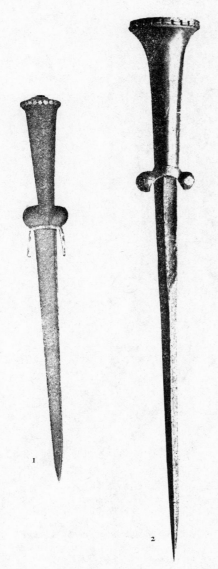

FIGURE 447. *Kidney Daggers.* 1. *French.* 2. *Burgundian, both 15th century. Metropolitan Museum. Not to scale.*

projection on one side by way of pommel. The hilt is usually formed of two flat pieces of horn, bone or ivory riveted to the flat tang. The scabbards are covered with leather and are long enough to take in the entire handle. They are worn thrust through the belt and are not fastened to it in any way. The blades are from 14 to 30 inches long. Fig. 446.

KIA. A leather cuirass, China archaic period. Laufer (175) says—"In order to accomplish a cuirass, first a form (dummy) is made, and then a hide is cut in accordance with it. The hide pieces are weighed; and two piles of equal weight are apportioned, the one for the upper, and the other for the lower part of the cuirass. The long strips into which the hide has been cut up, are laid around horizontally. In general when the hide has not been properly cured the cuirass is not strong; when the hide is worn out it will wrinkle. The method of inspecting the cuirass is as follows; the stitching, when examined, must be firm and close; the inner side of the hide must be smooth; the seams are required to be straight; the cuirass must perfectly fit into the case in which it is to be enclosed. Then it is taken up, and when it is examined, it must allow ample space (i.e., for the wearer)."

Rhinoceros hide was used; if of the two-horned variety, seven layers were required which would last for one hundred years; if of the single-horned, six layers would last two hundred years; and if of a combination of both, five layers would last for five hundred years!

KIDNEY DAGGER. A kind of dagger that had its origin in Northern Europe about the end of the 14th century, and was occasionally used as late as the early 17th. It has a heavy blade with a stout wooden handle with a carved guard of two rounded lobes, which suggested the name. Occasionally one is found with either one or three lobes. Fig. 447.

KIDNEY GUARD. The guard of the kidney dagger.

KIERO. A fighting spear, Chiangwa tribe, Western Australia.

KIGALEE. An Indian sacrificial axe, Meerut.

KIGOMI. A wadded garment worn under armor in winter, Japan.

KIGOTE. The general type of kote connected by shoulder pads. (Garbutt 161). Fig. 7.

KI-HOKO. A Japanese arrow with a pear-shaped wooden head; and, sometimes, a steel one in addition. They were used in dog hunts in the 12th century. (Gilbertson Archery 118).

KI KHNAM. Khasi (Assam), a general name for arrows. There are two kinds, both made of bamboo. The first is barbed and called *ki pliang*; it is used for hunting. The second is called *sop*, and is used only in archery matches. Both have iron heads which are of native make. The feathers used are

KIKUZA. The outer rim of the socket at the hachimanza of a Japanese helmet. It is so called because it represents a chrysanthemum (kiku). (Conder 259).

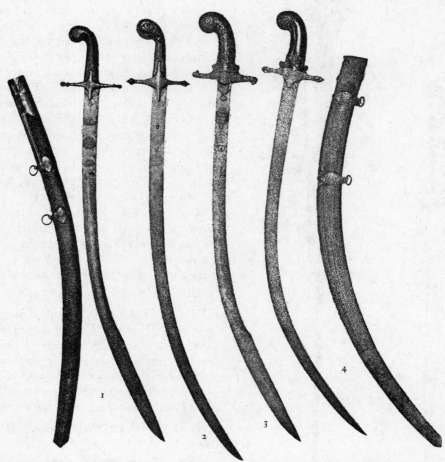

FIGURE 448. *Early Turkish Kilij. 1. Blade 30.5 inches long, of Turkish shape inlaid with cufic inscriptions in gold, 15th century. Hilt with horn grip. The guard and scabbard mounts are of steel inlaid in gold and are of the 18th century. 2. Blade of about the curve of the Turkish but without a back edge. Long cufic inscriptions on both sides. Dated A.H. 872, A.D. 1467. Horn grip and gold inlaid guard. 3. Watered blade of Turkish shape with a long cufic inscription in gold. Carved hilt of light green jade, chased, gilded guard. 4. Persian shaped blade with long cufic inscription in gold on one side and a short one on the other. Hilt of carved dark green jade, gilded guard with an inscription. Scabbard black stamped leather with gold inlaid sling loops.*

those of vultures, geese, cranes, cormorants and hornbills. (Lyall 24).

KIKUKI. The Warori (East Africa) javelin. It has a long, narrow blade of soft iron and is often barbed. The shaft is light, about four feet long, and tapers towards the butt. Occasionally it is made entirely of iron. (Burton Lakes 476). Compare Assegai.

KILIJ, KILIG, QILLIJ. The Turkish sabre. The blade is broader, shorter and less curved than the Persian shamshir, but the main difference from the latter is in the point. In the Persian the back is a fair curve nearly parallel to the edge, while in the Turkish the curve of the back stops eight or ten inches from the point; the blade then widens out abruptly and extends to the point nearly in a straight line with a sharp edge on the back. The Turkish sword can therefore be used for a thrust, though not very effectively, while the Persian cannot. This

are generally on opposite sides of the scabbard and it is hung in front of the wearer with the edge upwards, by a complicated harness of cords. Some-

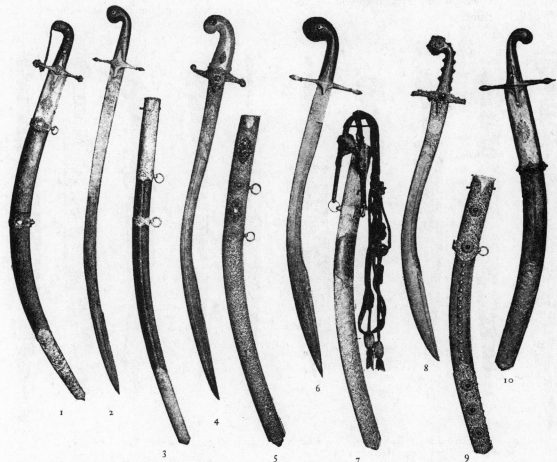

FIGURE 449. *Kilij.* 1. *Raised inscription on blade, silver hilt and scabbard mountings.* 2. *Persian blade with inlaid inscription, chased silver mounts.* 3. *Its silver mounted scabbard.* 4. *Watered blade inlaid with inscriptions in gold. White jade hilt with cartouches of jewels, guard incrusted with jewels.* 5. *Scabbard of silver gilt embossed and set with jewels.* 6. *Steel blade 28.5 inches long inlaid with gold.* 7. *Its silver mounted scabbard.* 8. *Watered blade 25.5 inches long, finely chased and inlaid with gold. Scabbard and hilt mountings covered with filigree silver and set with garnets and turquoise.* 9. *Its scabbard.* 10. *Steel blade, rhinoceros horn hilt, brass mounts.*

shape of blade was apparently adopted in the 15th century as some of the blades have it and others do not, fig. 448.

The hilt is usually pistol-shaped and made of two pieces of horn, bone, ivory or stone fastened to the flat tang. The guard is a straight, slim crossbar with balls or acorns on the ends. The curve of the blade is such that the back of the scabbard at the top must be open in order to admit it. The opening is often closed by a spring or a hinged plate. The sling loops

times it is hung edge down by two slings. Figs. 448, 449.

KILIS. Salar, a sword. Evidently a corruption of the Turkish name. (Rockhill).

KIMEN. A Japanese helmet in the shape of a demon's head. (Conder 257).

KIN. Gold, Japanese.

KINCHO. Confirming an oath or promise between samurai by striking their kozuka against each other. (Joly Int. 17).

KINCOB. An Indian brocade with gold or silver threads in it. It was sometimes used to cover scabbards or line armor.

paneled and marked with seals. The hilts are straight in the grip with broad pommels and an enlargement of nearly the same size and shape next the blade. The grips are often of two pieces of wood or horn riveted to the flat tang, sometimes they are

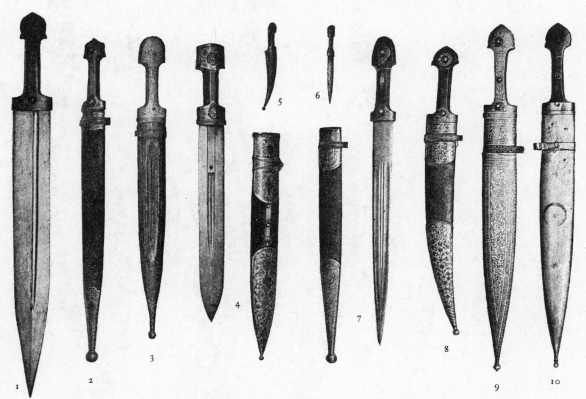

FIGURE 450. *Kindjal.* 1. *Black horn hilt, blade 18.25 inches long.* 2. *Narrow blade 14.625 inches long, horn and bone grips riveted to the tang. Leather scabbard, mounts of silver niello and gilt.* 3. *Ivory hilt with incised gilt scrolls. Leather scabbard with iron mounts inlaid with gold.* 4. *Unusual shaped blade. Hilt and scabbard mounts of silver niello, grip wound with silver wire cord. The middle of the scabbard is covered with purple velvet.* 5. *Blade 3.25 inches long, hilt and scabbard of niello silver.* 6. *Blade 3 inches long, niello silver hilt.* 7. *Blade 14 inches long, hilt of black horn. Scabbard mounts of silver niello and gilded.* 8. *Blade 12.5 inches long, hilt of black horn. Leather scabbard with niello silver mounts.* 9, 10. *Old Georgian blade 14.875 inches long. Hilt black horn with the front covered with niello silver. The scabbard is entirely covered with silver niello. Both the front and back are shown to illustrate the characteristic variation in the decoration.*

KINDACHI. A wooden fencing sword, Japan.

KINDJAL. The knife universally carried in the Caucasus. It is practically the same as the Georgian qama. The usual form has a broad, double-edged blade with nearly parallel sides for the greater part of its length, and a very long, sharp point. Occasionally the blades are curved, and a few straight ones have short points. The blades are frequently

of metal and cover the tang completely. The scabbards are covered with leather and have large silver chapes and lockets, or are entirely covered with silver. All of the silver parts are almost always decorated with chern (black). The decoration of the fronts of the scabbards is very well designed and executed, but that of the backs is very crudely done. The blades vary in length from about three to eighteen inches. Fig. 450.

The kindjal is the inseparable companion of every man in the Caucasus, and is used for the most varied purposes. "Decidedly dangerous in the hands of one who knows how to use it, more suitable for attack than for show, giving terrible, often mortal

geratedly long nose. There are three distinct types of this hilt. Fig. 451.

KING OF THE POPINJAY. The one who first hit the popinjay in the matches between crossbowmen from the 15th century on. (Hewitt III, 607).

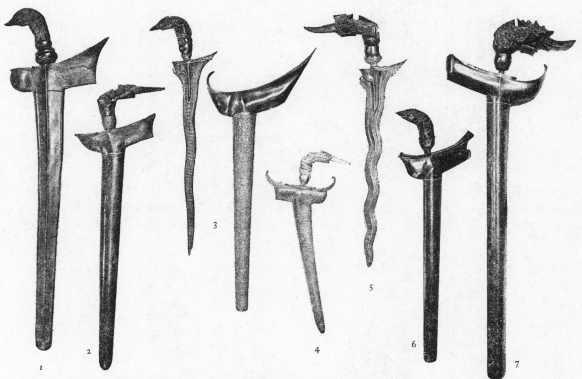

FIGURE 451. *Kingfisher Krisses.* 1. *Horn hilt, short nosed type. Scabbard made of a single piece of wood.* 2. *Horn hilt, long straight-nosed type.* 3. *Worn wooden hilt, short-nosed type. Finely Watered blade. Scabbard covered with embossed gold.* 4. *Silver hilt, long straight-nosed type.* 5. *Finely carved wood hilt, long curved-nose type. Watered blade inlaid with gold.* 6. *Horn hilt, short-nosed type.* 7. *Unusually large kris, simple blade, elaborately carved horn hilt of the long curved-nose type. The scabbard is much longer than the blade. Malay Peninsula.*

wounds, at once knife, hatchet, cork-screw, if necessary paper cutter, accessory of the dance, the kindjal is the offensive and defensive weapon *par excellence* of the Caucasus." When the owner wishes to show the steadiness of his hand he holds the points of two of these knives against his neck and performs an exceedingly acrobatic dance. The most expert are said to turn somersaults, keeping the points of the knives against their necks without cutting them.

KINGFISHER KRIS. The name given in England and this country to krisses, the hilts of which are the head of Avarta (Garuda) with an exag-

KINKAKU. Arms and armor, Japan.

KI-NO-HA-SODE. Sode shaped like a leaf. (Conder 272). See Sode.

KIN-SAME. Thin plates of gold covering the sides of a Japanese hilt, instead of the usual shark skin. They were often embossed to imitate shark skin, but sometimes chased and inlaid. (Weber II, 228).

KIN-SUNAJO-JI. (Gold sandy ground). A surface inlaid with gold and then nanako. It gives somewhat the effect of brocade. It is said to have been invented by Ichijo, and is occasionally used in decorating sword mountings. Fig. 452.

KI-PLIANG. See Ki Khnam.

KIPPA. The sharp edge of a sword, Japan.

FIGURE 452. *Kin-Sunajo-Ji. Tsuba, shakudo inlaid with butterflies of gold, copper and shibuichi and then nanako.*

KIRA. The stone knife of the Tjingilli tribe, Australia. The stone knives used by all of the Australian tribes are very similar. The blade is a flake of quartzite of triangular or trapezoidal section set in a handle of gum. Some of the tribes flatten the lump of resin and insert a flat piece of wood in the end. This is always decorated with a pattern in yellow, black and white, while the resin is always colored with red ochre. To protect the blade it is encased in a sheath of paper bark derived from the acacia or, in the far north from the tea tree (Melaleuca Leucodendron). The thin bark is cut in strips which are laid lengthwise of the blade, and then wound closely with fur, vegetable fibre, or human hair cord. The whole is then frequently covered with pipeclay, and a small bunch of emu or cockatoo feathers, usually the former, is inserted in the end. When emu feathers are used, some twenty or thirty of them are attached, always by their free tips, to a short stick, so that when placed in position their quills form a radiating bunch which projects from the end of the sheath. (Sp. & Gi. 640). Fig. 453.

KIRASOO. An Indian throwing stick, Mysore. "It is a spiral stick about three feet long ending in

FIGURE 453. *Kira. 1, 2. Trapezoidal section quartzite blade 6.25 inches long set in gum with a flat piece of wood colored yellow with white spots. Bark sheath wound with cord and covered with pipe clay, emu feathers in the end. 3, 4. Quartzite blade of triangular section, 3.5 inches long set in gum colored with red ochre. Bark sheath wound with human hair cord and colored black, red and white with clay. 5. Similar to 4.*

a knob. It is made from the common ironwood shrub; its weight varies from eight to twelve ounces. There are two methods of throwing the kirasoo, and in both the narrow end is held in the hand, the knob being forward. If an object on the ground is aimed at, the kirasoo is thrown under-arm by a jerk, its flight being straight with a screw motion.

FIGURE 454. *Kirin. Ivory kirin on a kozuka.*

Immediately the knob strikes the ground the curled portion swings over describing a circle. The knob now jerks away a few feet and another circle is described, and so on a series of loops and circles are made with the stick until it finally falls to rest. The other method of throwing the kirasoo is far more difficult and requires considerable skill. The stick is swung round the head several times, and then launched forward. After a straight flight of about twenty yards it makes a series of zigzags upwards and then drops. Among a flock of pigeons in flight this does great execution, killing and maiming many." (Mervin Smith 80).

KIRI. The circles of a target, Japan.

KIRIKOBU. A wooden club formerly carried by palace watchmen, Japan.

KIRIN. A mythical monster, K'ilin, combining the male animal K'i, and the female, Lin, into one compound name. Its body is that of a deer, its legs and hoofs those of a horse, its head like that of a horse or dragon, and its tail like that of an ox or lion. It has one horn on its head, the end of which is fleshy, its color is yellow. Some representations endow it with scales or protuberences, perhaps to make it appear like a piebald horse, often surrounded by flames. (Joly Leg. 175). Its footsteps were said to be so light that it left no track, even on new fallen snow. Fig. 454.

KIRO. Carved, Japan.

KIROMONO. Grooves or hollows in a Japanese blade filled with crimson lacquer. They are sometimes carved with Fudo. Marishiten, dragons or bonji (Sanskrit) letters or Chinese characters such as kimi-ban-zei, will cut for a thousand years; ten-ka-tai-hei, peace under heaven, etc.

KISSAKI. The extreme point of a blade, Japan.

KISSEL BASH. A nickname given to the Persians by themselves. It means red head, and refers to their common practice of dying their hair henna. (Morier I, 167). This is probably the origin of the practice of calling the ordinary levies of the Persian army "Kazilbashes."

KITE TASH. A flint in San Ch'uan Chinese. (Rockhill Jour.).

KITSUKE, KURA-OI. A saddle cloth, Japan.

KIXODWAIN. The arrow used for small birds by the Eskimo of Point Barrow. It has a blunt, wedge-shaped head two or three inches long inserted in the end of the shaft. (Murdoch 206).

KIYAHAN-SUNE-ATE. Japanese greaves of mail sewed on a padded lining. The lower portion of the pad, not the mail, partly covered the foot. It had no knee cop. (Conder 279).

KIYO. A female demon, a type of menpo.

KLAHULON. The sight of a Dyak blowpipe. (Arc. f. Eth. IV, 269).

KLAMBI TAIAH. See Baju Tilam.

KLAU. See Kliau.

KLEDYV. The ancient Welsh sword. (Burton Sword 279).

KLEWANG, LAMANG. One of the common-

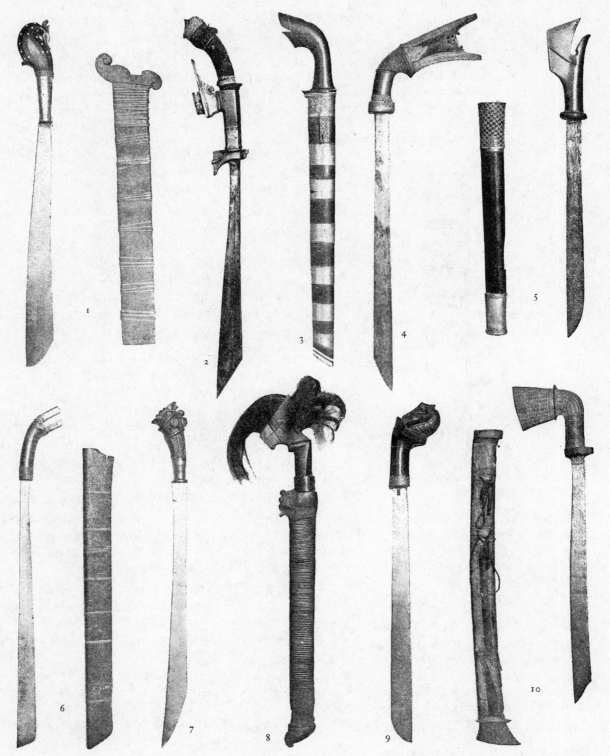

FIGURE 455. *Klewang.* 1. *Moro. Blade 18 inches long, black hilt inlaid with white bone, long silver ferule.* 2. *Adenara, blade 18.625 inches long. Hilt of bone, horn and lead.* 3. *Probably Sumatra. Finely watered blade, horn hilt. Silver band on scabbard.* 4. *Gorontalo. Blade 20.75 inches long, horn hilt partly covered with tin foil.* 5. *Rough, curiously marked blade, horn hilt. Silver mounted black scabbard.* 6. *Straight blade, horn hilt. Sumatra.* 7. *Nias. Blade 20 inches long, carved wood hilt.* 8. *Black horn hilt decorated with hair. Scabbard wound with rattan.* 9. *Celebes, carved wood hilt set in hard lead.* 10. *Gorontalo, Celebes. Fluted wooden hilt and carved scabbard entirely covered with tin.*

est forms of Malay sabre. It has a straight, single-edged blade widening towards the point which is rounded towards the back, or makes an obtuse angle with it. It is used in many places in the Archi-

single piece of wood three or four feet long and eighteen to twenty inches wide. The ends are pointed and the shield curves in both directions with a ridge down the center. It is usually laced across

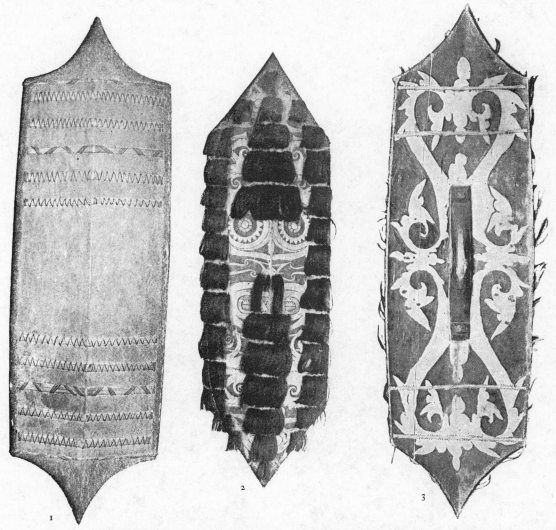

FIGURE 456. *Kliau.* 1. *Dutch Borneo. Ends and edges stained bluish black; 12 cane bands. Length 4 feet 4 inches, width 14.25 inches. 2. Kayan. Decorated with scrolls of bluish stain and with tufts of human hair. Length 3 feet 11 inches, width 13 inches. 3. The inside of another shield. It is decorated with elaborate designs in red and white and with tufts of hair. Four cane bands.*

pelago and the forms of hilts and scabbards vary in each locality. Fig. 455.

KLEWANG TJARA ATJEH. A variety of klewang used in Acheen. (Arc. f. Eth. V, 234).

KLIAU, KLAU. The commonest and most typical Dyak shield. It is carved, handle and all, from a

the ends to prevent its splitting. The decoration is sometimes confined to staining the ends and borders, at others the whole surface is painted with grotesque or geometrical figures. With some tribes it is almost covered with tufts of human hair. Fig. 456.

KLINKETS. Small gates in the palisades for the purpose of sallying. (Hoyt 424).

KNEE COP, KNEE PIECE, GENOUIL-LIERE. Knee cops first appeared in Europe in the

FIGURE 457. *Knee Cops (poleynes). Italian, 1460. Metropolitan Museum.*

13th century. The earliest were made of leather, the later of plate. At first these pieces only covered the knee and were fastened to mail, or leather, thigh pieces. They were then called poleynes, fig.

457. In the 15th century the knee cops were merged in the plate cuisses.

In the East, except in Japan, knee cops as separate pieces of armor were seldom used east of Turkey. For the Turkish knee cops, see Cuisse. In Japan separate knee cops were worn with one form of cuisse. See Sune Ate.

KNEE GUARD, DILGE, LEG SHIELD, TILTING CUISSE. A large plate guard of steel curved in the middle to cover the outside of the leg, and with the ends projecting, front and back, so as to cover a good part of the horse's sides. It was worn in tournaments in the 15th century as an extra protection. Fig. 458. (ffoulkes 77).

KNEMIDES. The Greek greaves. (Dean Europ. 15). Fig. 31.

KNIFE. The knife is the most generally used weapon there is. It is found in all countries and all ages, and the varieties are infinite. At first in Europe, and always in many countries, it was carried more as a convenience than as a weapon. During the middle ages, when men fought in complete armor the knife was useless for fighting. It was neces-

FIGURE 458. *Tilting Cuisses. South Kensington Museum.*

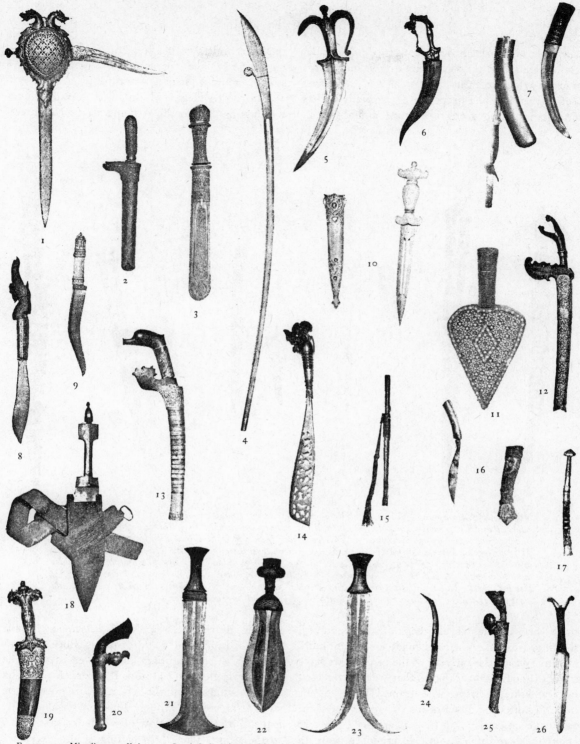

FIGURE 459. *Miscellaneous Knives.* 1. *South Indian katar with a bichwa blade at right angles to the main one.* 2. *Malay knife. Straight Persian blade. Hilt and scabbard of gold decorated with embossing and filigree set with jewels.* 3. *Bhutan knife. Straight, double-edged blade 8 inches long. Hilt and scabbard of elaborately chased and pierced silver set with turquoises.* 4. *Siam. Knife for trimming rattan. Blade 8.5 inches long. Horn handle 24 inches long.* 5. *Nepal. Knife made of a single piece of steel.* 6. *Mahratta dagger; plain curved blade. Hilt and finger guard of silver with a monster's head on the pommel.* 7. *Japanese knife with a strongly curved blade, sharp on the convex side. Simple scabbard with a very short kozuka with a gold kiri mon.* 8. *Siam. Broad blade; bidri work grip; pommel a monster's head of carved and gilded wood.* 9. *Nepal. Incurved, single-edged blade. Engraved silver hilt.* 10. *Turkish woman's knife. Straight, slotted blade inlaid with gold. Scabbard covered with green shark's skin. Hilt carved white jade. Locket and chape of chased gold set with jewels.* 11. *Trowel-shaped Sudanese knife. Hilt wound with leather. Wood scabbard inlaid with wood and ivory in geometrical patterns.* 12. *Menangkabau (Sumatra) knife. Hilt of dark wood set in brass. Scabbard covered with embossed gold plated metal, scroll top of black horn.* 13. *Sumatra. Incurved, fluted blade. Polished wood hilt and scabbard with many silver bands, some embossed.* 14. *Javan knife with a pierced blade. Hilt of carved horn with a band of chased gold on the lower end.* 15. *Chinese knife, straight, single-edged blade, jade hilt. Scabbard covered with shark skin, chased and gilded mounts.* 16. *Moro knife for cutting betel nut. Blade with convex edge and bone hilt. Carved wood sheath.* 17. *Siam. Engraved blade. Hilt and scabbard of silver, the latter partly lacquered red.* 18. *Central Africa. Irregular, leaf-shaped blade. Hilt of ivory with a black ring at the lower end of the grip and a silver ornament on the top.* 19. *Ceylon. Broad, fluted, double-edged blade. Hilt and scabbard mounts of finely chased silver.* 20. *Celebes. Hilt and scabbard of carved yellow wood.* 21. *Upper Congo. Blade with parallel sides widening out to a convex crescent at the end.* 22. *Upper Congo. Broad, leaf-shaped blade. Hilt inlaid with white metal.* 23. *Upper Congo. Double-edged blade forked at the end with widely spreading points. Hilt of black wood.* 24. *Siam. Knife for trimming rattan. Blunt ended blade 4 inches long. Hilt of shell.* 25. *Sumatra. Plain blade set in silver. Hilt and top of scabbard of ivory with embossed and filigree silver mounts.* 26. *British Columbia. Made of a single piece of steel with a forked pommel. Grip wound with leather.*

sary first to knock an opponent senseless with an axe, or club, and the victor could then hunt for a crack in which to thrust a knife. All of the knives used at this time in Europe were practically useless for actual fighting. Later in Europe, and always in

the heart unless he is asleep, uncovered and lying on his back. The ribs are close together and are strong enough to spoil a thrust if hit.

The most widely used knife is the Arab jambiya which is used from the Atlantic across North Af-

FIGURE 460. *Compound Knives.* 1. *Hilt of white jade with rubies set in gold. Watered steel blade pierced and inlaid with gold. It has six balls of ruby and emerald that slide up and down in the short groove just below the hilt.* 2. *Watered steel blade and gold inlaid hilt forged in one piece. It is hollow and has a hinged cover.* 3. *Similar to no. 2 into which it fits.* 4. *Steel blade and ivory hilt. It fits into no. 3.* 5, 6. *Watered steel blades and bone hilts. They are flat on the inner sides and have bayonet catches by which they can be locked together.* 7. *Steel blade and ivory hilt. It fits into no. 8 which is of steel with a gilded metal hilt.* 9. *Set of three knives with steel blades and ivory hilts which fit into each other. Sheath of pierced and engraved silver.*

most parts of the world, the knife was a useful fighting weapon as it was made of much more effective designs. Nearly all of the pictures we have show the combatants in poses that were never used by real knife fighters. The trained knife fighter held his knife low down at his right with the point and edge upwards; and his left arm crossways at about the level of his chin. He crouched with his knees bent and moved all the time. If he could catch his opponent's arm he thrust upwards. It is only in picture books and the stories of reporters that a man is "stabbed through the heart." The Malays say that it is useless to try to stab a man in

rica, in Turkey, Syria, Arabia, Armenia, Persia through India and as far east as Borneo. It is one of the best fighting knives ever made. The best purely thrusting knife is the Persian peshkabz (which is the same as the Afgan choora), either the straight or curved variety. The best slashing knife is the Gurka kukri, a blow of which can split a man to the waist. The Moro barong is also excellent, especially if back-edged, as it is then effective for both thrusting and cutting. The Japanese knives are among the best, largely because they are made of better steel and extraordinarily well ground.

The more typical and better known ones have

been described under their names; but many either do not have specific names or we do not know them. A few characteristic ones are shown in Fig. 459.

In the East some knives were made simply to show the skill of their makers. Some are hollow and contain a smaller knife. Often there are three, two hollow and the smallest solid. In other cases two knives were made each with one flat side so that they could be locked together with bayonet catches and appear as one; or be separated and used as two. Knives and swords were made with grooves in the blade containing movable "Rolling pearls," usually steel balls, but sometimes jewels that moved when the weapon was tipped. Fig. 460.

The names and parts of those described in the text are: Acinace, Aikuchi, Alfange, Ali-Ali, Ane-lec, Anneau, Anlas, Arm Knife, Axe Knife, Bade-Bade, Badiq-Loktiga, Balembeng, Ballok Knife, Bank, Banuwayu, Bara Jamdadu, Barong, Base-lard, Baswa Knife, Batardeau, Battig, Bayu, Bel-enda, Bendo, Bhuj, Bichaq, Bich'hwa, Bidag, Bodkin, Boku-To, Bolo, Boshi, Buckie, Bundi Katari, Buyo Knife, Capulus, Chandong, Chape, Chaqu, Charay, Ch'hurra-Kati, Chilanum, Chisel-Edge, Choora, Chope, Chura, Churi, Cinquedea, Coutar, Coutel, Creese, Cuchillo, Cultel, Dada, Dagger, Dague a Rouelles, Danisko, Dapor Bener, Dapor Loq, Deder, Degan, Dhaw, Dirk, Djoem-bijaq, Dogane, Dorgey Phurbu, Dudgeon, Dutch-na, Eared Dagger, Egashira, Facon, False Edge, Finger Guard, Fist Sword, Fuchi, Fusee, Galar, Gandja, Garsoe Katar, Garuda, Ghost Dagger, Gin-Same, Goko, Golang, Golok, Greneng, Grip, Guard, Ha, Habaki Moto, Haladie, Hamidachi, Handschar, Hand-Seax, Hanger, Hanzashi Kozu-ka, Hashi, Ha-Tsuya, Hayezashi, Hi, Himogatana, Hishiu, Hunga-Munga, Iooroom, Jambiya, Jamd-har Katari, Japanese Blades, Kajoe Pelet, Kalis, Kami-Kiri, Kanuri Otoshi, Kard, Karoula, Karud, Kashira, Katar, Katar Bank, Katar Dorlichaneh, Katok, Kechil, Kendelan, Keris, Kesso, Khanjar, Khanjarli, Khapwah, Kharoll, Kharoll Zirah Fore, Khyber Knife, Kidney Dagger, Kidney Guard, Kincho, Kindjal, Kingfisher Kris, Kin-Same, Kira, Kiromono, Kissaki, Kodogu, Koedi, Kogai, Koi-Guchi, Koi Guchi Kanagu, Kojiri, Ko-Katana, Korambi, Koshigatana, Koutar, Kozuka, Kris, Kris Cherita, Kubikiri, Kukri, Kurikata, Kurtu, Kusungobu, Kwaiken, Lading, Lamang, Landep, Leilira, Lidah Ayam Lipet, Locket, Lodgo, Main Gauche, Mandaya Knife, Matana Seleka, Mattu-cashlass, Maushtika, Mekugi, Mekugi-Ana, Men-daq, Menuki, Metazashi, Midliu, Mihili Mezzir, Mijiki Katana, Misericorde, Mit, Mitokoro Mono, Mongwanga, Moplah Knife, Motagi, Mulu Chito-ho, Mune, Nakago, Nakago Ana, Nata, Ndziga, Ne, Netaba, O Kozuka, Omote, O-Shitodome, Padja, Pahua, Paiscush, Palati, Pangulu, Panji Sekar, Paps-I-Tuti, Parang Kajoeli, Parazonium, Patra, Pattani Jamdadu, Pavade, Pechak, Pedang, Pendoq, Peqsi, Pesh-Kabz, Phurbu, Pichangatti, Pichaw, Piha-Kaetta, Pija, Pinabolan, Pincha, Pisau Raut, Piso Tongkeng, Poignard, Pokwe, Pugio, Pu'tjor, Qama, Raut, Roentjau, Sabiet Mata Dora, Sadoep, Saffdara, Saki, Same, Sarong, Sar-ongan, Savigron, Savik, Saya, Sclepista, Scramasax, Sekin, Sele, Seli-Besi, Seppa, Seppa Dai, Seyeva, Sgian Dubh, Shinto, Shirasaya, Shito, Shitodome, Shuri-ken, Sibak, Siterampuri Katari, Siwar, Skain, Sode Kozuka, Soedoek, Soritsuno, Soroimono, Stiletto Stradiot, Tang, Tanto, Tayu-Kogai, Telek, Ten-jo Gane, Tetsu Same, Throwing Knives, Tjoen-dre, Tjombong, Tooroom, To-Su, Tsuba, Tsuka, Tsuka Gashira Tsuka-Ito, Tsuka-No-Kanemono, Tsuruimaki Gatami No Shi To, Tuba Knife, Tula, Tumbok, Turup, Ukiran, Ulu, Uragawara, Ura-hokin, Vajra Hilt, Vinchu, Wari Kogai, Wedong, Whinyard, Whittle, Yakiba, Yamagatana, Yasu-rime, Yoroi Toshi, Zirah Bouk.

KNILI. A boomerang, Australia.

KNOBSTICK, KNOBKERRIE. See Kerrie.

KNOPSH. See Khrobi.

KNUCKLE-BOW. The finger guard of a sword. (ffoulkes Armourer 162).

KNUCKLE DUSTER, BRASS KNUCKLES. Objects held in the hand to give additional weight to the blow and to give a better striking surface. They are survivals of the Roman cestus. In mod-ern Europe and America they are pieces of metal with holes for the fingers. They were never re-garded as legitimate weapons here and were only used by criminals. In other parts of the world they were used in fair fighting. In Samoa and the Gil-bert Islands they consisted of cords with shark's teeth fastened to them, that were wound round the hand. Pieces of wood with shark's teeth, or a single large tooth, were used in Hawaii, also curved sticks with shark's teeth on the ends. (Horniman Mus.). In Central Africa spiked rings were used or curved knives were worn on the fingers. In Japan knuckle dusters were made of steel and shaped so that a blow could be struck either forward or downward. Fig. 461. See also Hora.

of India. The surface of the metal to be decorated is roughened by scratching and picking, and a thin coat of gold or silver is pressed into the lines of the pattern and is held by the burrs of the roughened surface. Hendley describes the operation as follows. "The more common process is superficial only. For this the metal is heated to a blue colour; and

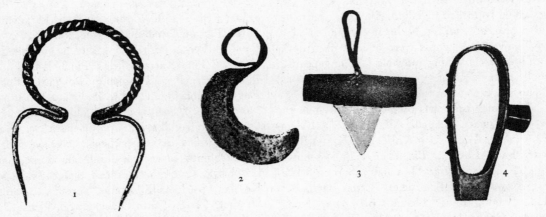

FIGURE 461. *Knuckle Dusters. 1. All iron, two spikes, Jur, Upper Nile. 2. Turkana or Irenga, Upper Nile. Knife worn on the second finger of the left hand. 3. Honolulu. Cast of a knuckle duster. A large triangular shark's tooth set in a piece of wood with a loop of cord to go around the finger. Bishop Museum, Honolulu. 4. Japan, steel with teeth on one side and a knob opposite, a third striking surface on the end.*

KNUCKLE GUARD. See Finger Guard.

KOANIE. A fish spear with a bone point and a single barb, Victoria. The bone point is called *kulkie* and the barb *tilloo*. (Brough Smyth I, 306).

KOBUSHIGATA TSUBA. A Japanese sword guard "of ovate shape with the contour of the closed fist." A style of tsuba introduced by Kanaiye I, in the 16th century.

It is also said to be the same as the shitogi tsuba.

KODELLY. A light axe carried by the Sinhalese as a protection against wild animals. (Tennent I, 138).

KODOGU. Collectively all of the fittings of a Japanese sword or dagger, except the tsuba. This name is not used for the fittings of a tachi, which are called *kanagu*. (Joly Int. 5).

KODZUKA. See Kozuka.

KOEDI. A Malayan knife. See Kudi Tranchang.

KOFT, KOFTGARI. The false damascening

then hatched with a knife, and the design is drawn upon the hatching with a fine bodkin. This done, a gold wire is conducted according to the pattern which has been drawn, and sunk carefully into the metal with a copper tool. In some instances cheap specimens are made by merely applying gold or silver leaf with some adhesive substance."

When well done the effect is good and the result fairly durable; but much is so light that it soon wears off. See Inlaying.

KOGAI. The skewer or "Head-Pin" often carried in a pocket in the scabbard of a Japanese sword or knife. It is generally carried with the short sword, frequently with the dagger, and rather seldom with the long sword. It has been used longer than most of the fittings but there is no definite and generally accepted explanation of its purpose. Old Japanese stories show that it was sometimes used to arrange the hair and put it in order; but it is not well adapted for this purpose, and there is almost certainly some other reason for its having been so generally carried. Kogai decorated with the crest

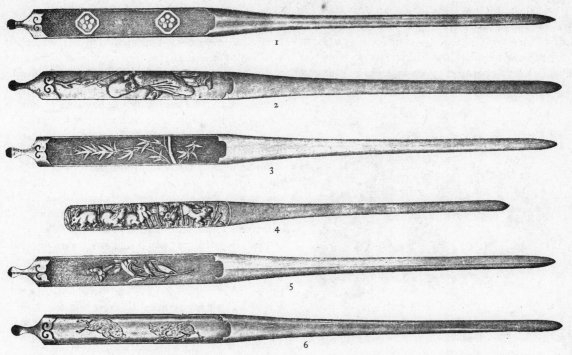

FIGURE 462. *Kogai.* 1. *Shakudo, nanako. Two crests in silver in relief in a sunk panel.* 2. *Copper. Fukurokuju in low relief.* 3. *Shakudo, nanako. Bamboo in relief in gold. Signed Omori Mitsuoki.* 4. *Iron, gold, silver, shibuichi and copper, rabbits in grass. Signed Masamitsu of the East (Hiyashi).* 5. *Shakudo, nanako. The blade is half gold and half shakudo. A lily in relief in gold and silver.* 6. *Shibuichi. Engraved with two wild boars fighting. Signed Riusensai Yukinaga.*

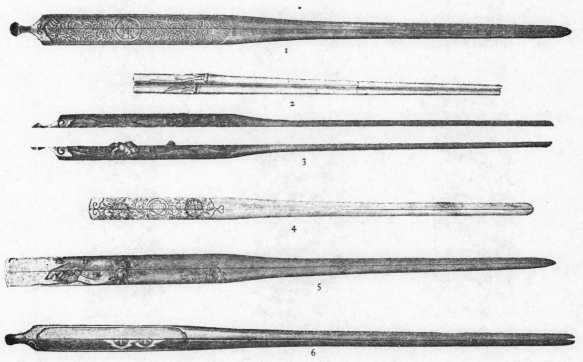

FIGURE 463. *Split Kogai.* 1. *Copper. Carved with a crest and an arabesque design.* 2. *Silver. Two twigs of bamboo. The ends pull out, reverse, and fit in the sockets when they provide a writing brush and stylus.* 3. *Shakudo. A hare running on waves.* 4. *Silver, engraved, and with gold flowers in relief.* 5. *Shibuichi with the end of silver. A scarecrow in a rice field; gold, silver, copper and brass. Signed Yoshikawa Nampo ju ye, and kakihan.* 6. *Shakudo. Three crests in flat inlay of gold, silver and copper.*

of their owner are said to have been left in the body of an enemy killed in a clan feud, as a mark of identification to let his friends know who had killed him. Comparatively few kogai are decorated

FIGURE 464. *Kohong Kalunan. From Furness, Home Life of the Borneo Head Hunters.*

with mon; and it is not likely that a number would have been carried for possible use in this way. It is also said to have been used to carry the severed head of an enemy, either thrust in his ear or hair. On the other hand we are told that the proper way to carry a head is to take it by the hair and to hold a piece of oiled paper against the neck to keep the blood from dripping. Mrs. Sugimoto who comes from an old samurai family and who is thoroughly familiar with samurai traditions says (109): "But the blunt little kogai had many uses. It was the key that locked the sword in the scabbard; when double it could be used as chopsticks by the marching soldier; and it has been used on the battlefield, or in retreat, mercifully to pierce the ankle vein of a suffering and dying comrade, and it had the unique use in a clan feud, when found sticking upright in the ankle of a dead foe, of bearing the silent challenge 'I await thy return.' Its crest told to whom it belonged and, in time, it generally returned — to its owner's ankle."

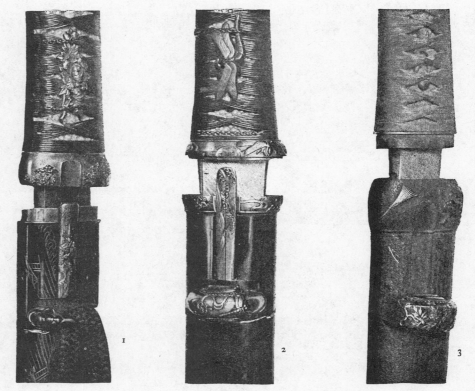

FIGURE 465. *Koi-guchi.* 1. *In this the fuchi covers the koi-guchi. Gold with trees in high relief in shakudo and silver.* 2. *When the knife is sheathed the koi-guchi and fuchi form a complete ornament, half of the design being on each. Silver dragon flies in relief in gold.* 3. *In this the fuchi fits inside the koi-guchi. Iron, chased and inlaid with gold.*

Sometimes the kogai was split lengthwise forming a pair of chopsticks, hashi. It was then called hashi, wari-kogai or tayu-kogai. Dr. Dean (Hdbk.

anese. The fitting between the hilt and scabbard of a knife without a guard (aikuchi) is also called a koi-guchi.

FIGURE 466. *Koi-Guchi Kanagu.* 1. *Shakudo with a vine and wheel in relief in gold and silver.* 2. *Shakudo with beaded edges and ishime surface.* 3. *Copper with a vine and flowers in relief in gold and shakudo.*

131) says that the kogai was not used for eating, but as ceremonial tweezers to handle ashes and incense. Joly points out the obvious convenience to a soldier of having his knife and chopsticks in the scabbard of his knife, and believes that it was used for eating. Mrs. Sugimoto's statement apparently settles the question. Figs. 462, 463.

KOGAI JI-ITA. A decorated plate set in the handle of a kogai. (Weber I, 381). Fig. 407.

KOGAI NAOSHI. A kogai of which the decorated part is a separate piece (ji-ita) which is set in the kogai. Particularly with the older kogai these plates were frequently the only part made by the masters, and were set in the kogai by assistants. They were sometimes later taken from the kogai and set in kozuka. See Sode Kozuka.

KOGANE-MAJIRI NO-YOROI. Armor made of a mixture of leather and iron, Japan 9th century. (Conder 256).

KOGUSOKU-KOTE. (Little armor-like kote). Connected kote, so called because so complete. The one shown in fig. 7 is probably one of these.

KOHAZE-GAKE. "Fastened with hooks," a type of wakibiki.

KOHEI. A soldier in armor, Japan.

KOHI. See Obitori.

KOHIRE. Epaulettes, Japan. (Garbutt 143).

KOHONG KALUNAN. A pattern of several grotesque faces that is frequently used on the hilts of Dyak mandaus. (Furness 20). Fig. 464.

KOHRA. See Kora.

KOI-GUCHI. (Koi-carp, guchi [kuchi]-mouth). The open end of a Japanese scabbard. It is considered to look like the mouth of a carp by the Jap-

The mount on the top of the scabbard of an aikuchi into which a projection from the fuchi fits. It was often several inches long and very elaborate. (Gilbertson Dec. 83).

There are three types. It may be a perfectly plain ring on the scabbard which fits into a decorated projection from the fuchi on the hilt, 1, fig.

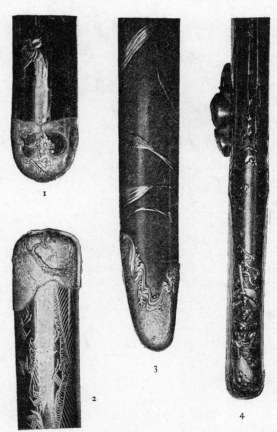

FIGURE 467. *Kojiri, mounted.* 1. *Silver inlaid with gold flowers.* 2. *Gold with a tree in relief in shakudo and silver.* 3. *Gold, wave design by Hitikgi Hidemune, date 1868.* 4. *Shakudo with Marashiten riding on a boar, shakudo and gold. Signed Jafudo Shinzui.*

465. It may be a decorated piece with a shoulder that fits into the fuchi, the decoration being half on each, 2, fig. 465. It may be a decorated piece on the scabbard into which a perfectly plain fuchi fits, 3, fig. 465.

or simply a piece of horn glued on the end. On the katana it is usually quite short, seldom over four or five inches long. On the wakizashi and knives it is often much longer and more elaborate, though on

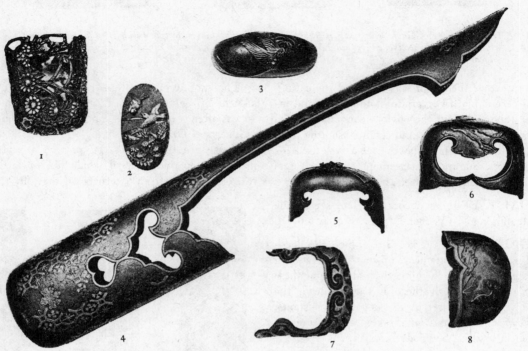

FIGURE 468. *Kojiri, unmounted. 1. Copper, silver and gold, flowers carved and pierced. 2. Shakudo, gold and silver. Birds and spring flowers. Signed Koreyoshi. 3. Iron, a dragon fly in low relief in gold and shibuichi. 4. Iron, a diaper pattern and kiri crests in gold. Kaga style. 5. Shibuichi. A mask, fan and spray of plum in gold, silver, shakudo and copper. 6. Iron, a white heron under a willow tree. 7. Guri bori with a surface of silver. 8. Deer under a maple tree. Gold, shakudo and copper.*

KOI-GUCHI KANAGU, KUCHI-KANE, KUCHI-GANE. The ring or cap at the mouth of a Japanese scabbard. In early times it was generally made of buffalo horn and was only used by the lower classes, the samurai considering it beneath their dignity to use it. Later it was often made of metal, frequently decorated like the other fittings. Fig. 466.

KOI-GUCHI WO KIRU. (Cut the koi-guchi). To prepare to draw the sword. It is exactly equivalent to the English "loosen the sword in the scabbard."

KOJIRI, SAYA-JIRI. The chape of a Japanese scabbard. They vary more in size and shape than any of the other fittings. Many swords have none,

some it is of the same size and shape as the kashira. Figs. 467, 468.

The corresponding fitting on a tachi is called *ishizuke.*

KOJJER. See Kadjo.

KO-KATANA, KOGATANA. Some authorities give this as the name of the complete knife carried in the scabbard of a Japanese sword; restricting the name kozuka to the handle.

Brinkley (VII, 210) says that it is "any kind of a knife, such as is used by a wood carver" and that the knife carried in a sword scabbard is a kozuka.

Weber (I, 438) says — originally the blade of the kozuka, also called sahi. Later the name kozuka was applied to the entire knife.

Kozuka appears to be the correct name for both the handle and the entire knife.

KOKUSHIU. The second class of Japanese nobles.

KOLTSCHAN. A quiver, Russian. It is of the oriental type. The quiver was carried hung on the

long wooden handle with brass or iron mounts. Non-Aryan Central India. (Egerton 61).

KONGO-ZUE. (Diamond scepter). A staff with iron rings at the end, used by Yamabushi.

KONIGSMARK. See Colichemarde.

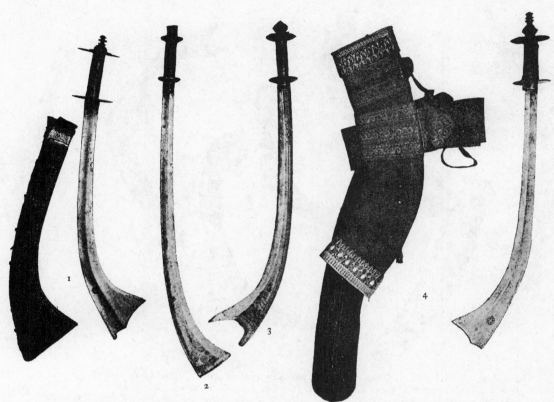

FIGURE 469. *Kora. 1. Nepal. Heavy blade 19.5 inches long. Red leather scabbard with silver mountings; it is closed down the back by loops and buttons. 2. Tibet. Blade 24 inches long, engraved and inlaid with red and gold lines. Brass pommel and guard, grip wound with brass wire. 3. Tibet. Blade similar to the preceding, engraved steel hilt. 4. Nepal. Light blade 22 inches long, plain steel hilt. Black leather belt and scabbard embroidered with silk. Pierced silver caps on both ends of the scabbard.*

right side of the belt, and the bow case on the left. (Scheremetew 119). See Bow Case.

KOMAGAKI. The battlements of a castle, Japan.

KOMI. See Nakago.

KOMIDARI. See Yakiba.

KOMIYA. See Karuka.

KONGAVAL. One of the nondescript weapons classed as choppers. It has a curved blade with a

KONKUAN. Iwamoto Konkuan of Yedo, the celebrated pupil of Riokwan I, and adopted son of Riokwan II, died in 1801 at the age of fifty-eight. He was one of the most skillful makers of tsuba of the latter part of the 18th century. (Hara 56). He was particularly celebrated for his minute monkeys. He also carved fish remarkably well.

KONNUNG. A straight, round club about two and a half to three feet long with sharply pointed ends. It is held in the middle and used for stabbing. Victoria. (Brough Smyth I, 302).

KON ODOSHI. Japanese armor laced with navy blue cords.

KOOKERI, KOOKHERI. See Kukri.

KOOM-BAH-MALEE. See Kujerung.

A variety of kora with a longer, and much lighter blade is sometimes found in Tibet. Fig. 469.

KORAI-BO. (Korean face). A variety of Japanese menpo.

KORAMBI. A Sumatran knife with a sickle-

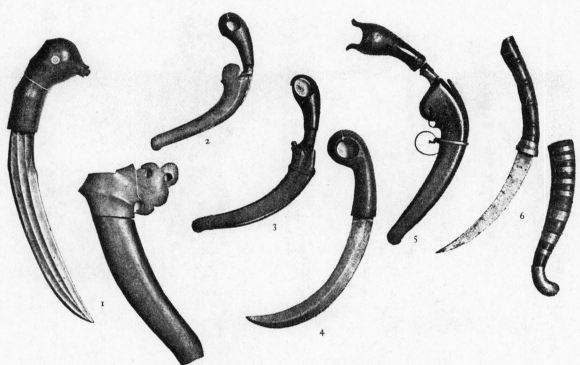

FIGURE 470: *Korambi. 1. Celebes. Hilt and scabbard of light wood. Fluted blade 8 inches long. 2. Wood hilt and scabbard. Blade 4.25 inches. 3. Wood hilt, black horn scabbard, Sumatra. 4. Hilt, wood and horn, 6 inch blade. 5. Horn hilt. Wooden scabbard with a horn spring back. 6. Wooden hilt. Silver bands on scabbard.*

KOOMBHE. A tree of northern India with a tough and stringy bark, that is used for making match cord for guns. (Inglis 462).

KOPIS. See Khrobi.

KORA, CORA, KHORA. The national sword of Nepal. It has a very heavy, single-edged blade much incurved and widening greatly at the end, which usually terminates in two concave curves. There is always an eye, or other Buddhistic symbol, inlaid on each side. The scabbards are of two kinds. The commoner is a wide sheath into which the blade can be slipped; the other is shaped to fit the blade and buttons down the back. Fig. 469. It is sharp on the concave side.

shaped blade four to six inches from point to hilt. The hilts and scabbards are often of horn. Fig. 470.

KORAZIN. See Jazerant.

KORSEKE. A pole arm of the 15th century. (Dean Hdbk. 56). It has three rather broad points with the middle one much longer than the others. It is very closely related to the chauve-souris and the runka. Fig. 471.

KO SEPPA. See Seppa.

KOSHIATE. Japan, a sword carrier. It is a device for holding the sword firmly in the belt. There are several kinds, *rio-koshiate*, a double holder, that is one for a pair of swords. *Kata-koshiate* for a single sword; *himo-koshiate*, "lord" holder, of which there does not appear to be any definite description; *tsutsu-kosjiate*, tube holder, in which the scabbard is passed through a tube that is fastened to the belt;

ita-koshiate, board holder, in which the sword, or swords, are fastened to a board attached to the belt. Figs. 472, 473.

A kind of shield over the loins to protect them from the quiver.

KOSHIGATANA. A short dagger used in Japan in very early times. Being very short it could be hidden in the folds of the kimono, thus it became the *kwaiken* or *Kwaito* used by women in committing *jigai*, ceremonial suicide by cutting the veins of the neck. (Joly, Naunton xviii).

Kwai signifies something carried inside of the clothes.

KOSHI-KUMO. Ornamental bands around the bowl of a Japanese helmet near, and parallel to, the brim. (Dean Notes 7).

KOSHINAWA. A rope about five feet long with a ring, or loop, at one end. It was carried by warriors in Japan either fastened to the saddle or tucked under the belt, and was used largely as a spare girth, for binding a prisoner, tethering a horse, or even as a helmet cord. (Garbutt 152).

KOSHI-SASHI. The badge of a Japanese cavalryman. It was a device on a piece of leather or thick paper, about three and a half inches square, attached by a cord at one corner to a short stick. It was carried stuck in the belt at the back. (Garbutt 156). Fig. 474.

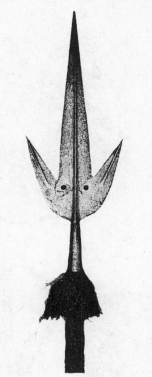

FIGURE 471. *Korseke, Italian, about 1550. Metropolitan Museum.*

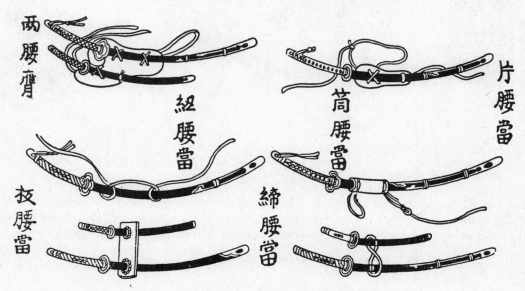

FIGURE 472. *Koshiate. After Garbutt, Jr., Japan Society, Vol. XI.*

KOSHI-TSUKE-NO-O. The upper part of the Japanese cuisses. It is always made of silk or damask with the crest of the owner woven or embroidered

"it consists of a cord attached to a wooden rod. The spears were thrown underhand, being first stuck lightly into the ground. It was used for throwing

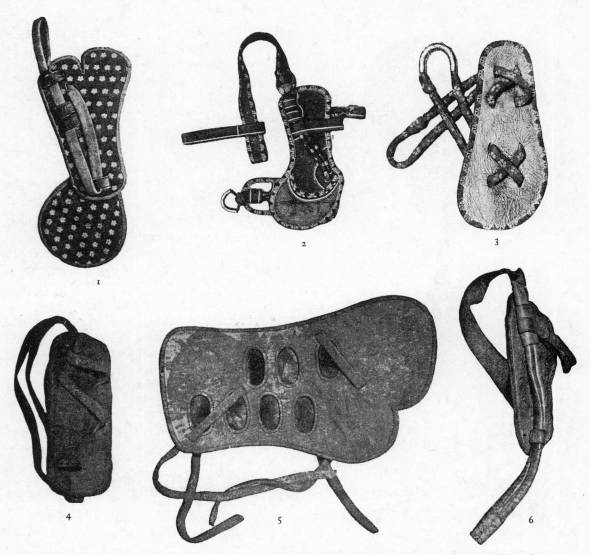

FIGURE 473. *Koshiate. All but no. 5 are single hangers. No. 5 is for a pair of swords. 1, 2. Figured leather. 3. Gilded and figured leather. 4, 5, 6. Plain buff leather. 1, 2. Metropolitan Museum. The last four are to scale.*

on it, and in all respects treated like the hakama, having slits at the sides like pocket holes, and called muchi-gashi-no-ana. (Conder 275). See Hai-Date.

KO-SHU TSUBA. Mukade tsuba made in Koshu. (Weber I, 457).

KOTANA, KOTAHA. A Maori spear thrower;

spears into besieged camps, in some cases for the purpose of carrying lighted leaves to set fire to the camp." (Horniman Mus. 34, Cowper 238).

It was quite a common toy when I was a boy. The missile is stuck lightly in the ground, the string wrapped around it three or four times with the turns covering the end of the string. The stick is swung back and brought sharply forward, which sends the missile a surprising distance. The cord must be long enough to give considerable slack between the stick and the missile.

FIGURE 474. *Koshi-Sashi. Gilt card pierced with a mon. On top of the handle are three rings which can be placed so as to form a ball or turned so as to fit inside of one another.*

KOTE. A fortress, sometimes a bastion, India. (Tod II, 283).

KOTE. A Japanese armored sleeve. "It consists of a close fitting sleeve of padded cloth, silk or leather, widening at the mouth where it fits over the shoulder, and is tied by strings around the chest. The kote is covered in parts by mail and additional metal plates, and terminates in a hand guard or semigauntlet called *tetsu-gai*. These metal defences are applied only to the outside of the arm, the inside, towards the body, not requiring protection. It is upon the inside that the cloth or leather which forms the body of the sleeve is laced up tightly with silk or leather cord to within a few inches of the mouthpiece. The uppermost plate of the kote covering the shoulder below the sode is called the *kamura-ita*, and to this are attached three cords, two of which are tied around the chest, while one connects with the cord from the opposite kote. Immediately below this for the protection of the principal muscles of the upper arm, is a large metal plate or collection of scales connected by mail, and called *gaku-no-ita*. At the point of the elbow is a circular plate of metal forming the elbow cop and called the *hijigane*. The lower part of the forearm is protected by a plate called *ikada*, which sometimes consists of parallel splints of metal connected by mail, and sometimes is in one piece of embossed and pierced metal. Attached to the bottom of the same piece is the *tetsu-gai*, which generally consists of a rounded plate following the shape of the back of the hand above the fingers. It is lined with leather and has loops on the inside through which to pass the fingers. In addition to these leather gloves were worn. In some of the older, and more complete, suits separate finger pieces were attached by chains to the body of the gauntlet." Fig. 475.

In most of the later armor the kote are hung from the shoulder straps by loops of cord fastened to the kamuri-ita.

There are many kinds of kote, of which the following are the principal; *tetsu-gote*, in which the whole is covered with mail and the upper and lower arm are further protected by metal plates or splints. *Tsugi-gote*, in which the upper arm is protected by a wide plate loosely attached to the shoulder in addition to the usual mail and plate for the forearm. This extra piece is precisely like a sode but smaller. *Shino-gote, yetchiu-gote* and *awase-gote* differ only in the way they are tied. They are entirely covered with mail with plates of about two and a half by half an inch spaced regularly. The *oshi-no-gote* has the outside of the forearm covered with splints and mail alternating. The *hansho gote* covers only the forearm; it is sometimes made up of three long plates connected by mail and lined with padded cloth, silk or leather. See Hansho-Gote. The *tominaga gote* is two kote connected by a brocade or leather collar instead of being tied separately. The

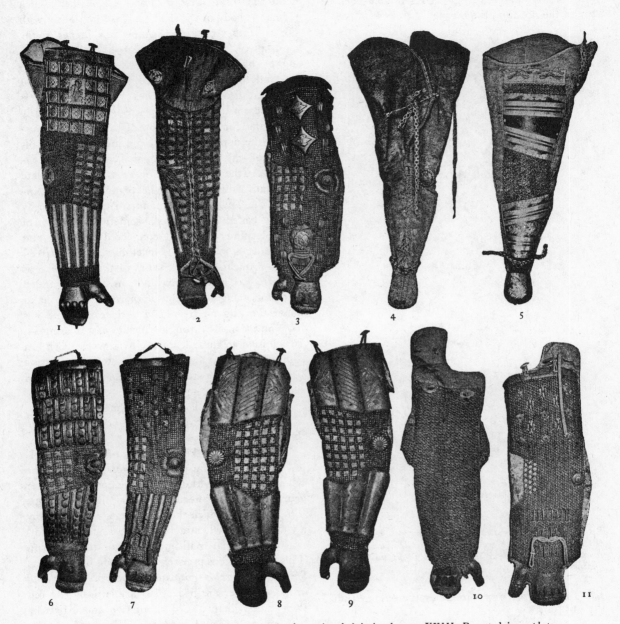

FIGURE 475. *Kote.* 1, 2. *Front and back of a pair of daimio sleeves, XVIII. Russeted iron plates pierced with the owner's mon, except the largest which is finely carved with a figure in high relief with gold eyes. Linings of green cloth stamped with gold mons. 3. Mail and iron plates decorated with silver Ogawa mon. 4, 5. So-called Yoshitsune sleeves. Large plates lacquered black with broad, diagonal gilded bands cover the fore and upper arms. The mail is of broad circular links each connected to six long fine links. Brocade sleeves; printed leather linings to the gauntlets. 6. Mail and leather scales on brocade. 7. Mail with iron plates and ornaments. The bars and gauntlet plates are decorated with silver imitating snow. 8, 9. Pair of sleeves with pierced iron plates and mail, brocade linings. 10. Riveted mail of the international type of broad, flat links. Armpit guards of the same type of mail. 11. Small iron plates decorated with scrolls in relief, connected by very fine, hexagonal bronze mail. Lining of brocade; toggles of carved ivory, XVII.*

yu-gote is made of silk or brocade usually without metal parts. It is used when shooting with the bow. (Conder 272). See Hansho-Gote, Tsugi-Gote and Yu-Gote.

KOTE HARAMAKI. A pair of kote that "cover even the belly." Kote connected by a garment that covers the entire body. (Garbutt 161).

KOTETSUKE. The space left unprotected between the upper end of the kote and the watagami in Japanese armor. (Garbutt 145).

KOTIATE. (Liver cutter). A Maori club shaped something like a violin. It is made of wood or whale's bone. The handle is usually carved and the blade left plain. Fig. 476.

KOTO. The "old" swords and their makers in Japan, that is those prior to the 17th century. The makers are further divided into those earlier than the 10th century and those of later date.

The most celebrated artists of the first group are, in chronological order:

Amakuni	of Yamato	A.D. 700
Amasa	of Yamato	700
Shinosuke	of Bizen	720
Jiniki	of Mutsu	750
Yasutsune	of Hoki	800
Sanemori	of Hoki	820
Sanetsugu	of Chikuzen	850

The most celebrated of the second group, arranged in order of merit are:

Masamune	Sagami, Kamakura	1290
Yoshimitsu	Yamashiro	1275
Yoshihiro	Echizen	1320
Hisakuni	Yamashiro (Kioto)	1190
Kuniyoshi	Yamashiro (Kioto)	1325
Kuniyasu	Yamashiro (Kioto)	1236
Yukihira	Bungo	1200

Masamune is the most renowned of all the sword makers of Japan. Muramasa, 1340, whose blades are considered by many as equals of Masamune's is not generally included in the lists as his blades were considered "as ignoble, bloodthirsty and of evil spirit." It is frequently stated that if a Muramasa blade is drawn it cannot be returned to the scabbard until it has tasted blood; and that if it is not frequently allowed blood it brings bad luck to its owner. Certain it is that they were prohibited for court wear, the reason apparently being that one or two members of the Tokugawa family had been accidentally wounded by them.

Other lists have been made in which the makers were put in a different order. In the appendix to his paper on blades Gilbertson gives one made in 1702, in which the makers are grouped according to the value of their blades. The values are given in

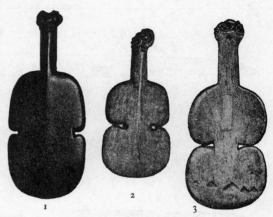

FIGURE 476. *Kotiate. 1. Brown wood 14 inches long. The end of the handle is carved. 2. Made of the bone of the sperm whale, well carved end of handle. 3. Whale bone, unusually light. 2. Peabody Museum, Salem.*

gold mai, pieces which then had a value of about sixty dollars of our money. The first class comprises those whose blades are beyond price; and consists of:

Kunihide (Rai)	of Yamashiro	
Kuniyoshi	of Awataguchi	about 1288
Masamune		
called Goro Niudo	of Sagami	about 1288
Masatsune	of Bungo	about 1331
Yoshihiro	of Yetchu	about 1288
Yoshimitsu	of Awataguchi	about 1275

The next class whose blades are valued at 25 mai includes:

Tayema	of Yamato	about 1288
Nagamitsu	of Osafune,	
	Bizen	about 1288

In all there are nineteen classes given with the value dropping gradually to one mai.

KOUTAR. See Katar.

KOVEH. A Bechuana spear "the assegai of torture." It has a long barbed head on the end of a long shank the angles of which are lined with small barbs, of which those on two diagonally opposite angles point towards the head, and those on the two other angles towards the shaft. The construction thus being such that it could neither be withdrawn nor pushed through. (Wood 283).

Japanese armor laced with cords of light blue leather stamped with conventional cherry blossoms in white. There are several varieties. (Conder 271).

FIGURE 477. *Kozuka Knives.* 1. *Handle shakudo inlaid with gold to imitate togidashi lacquer. Blade signed Kunimasa, and engraved with three lines of microscopic writing.* 2. *Handle iron with an arrow in relief; on it is a paper reading "At eventide I lie beneath the (cherry) tree. Will its blossoms be my host tonight?" Blade signed Tamba no Kami, Yoshimichi.* 3. *Handle dark shibuichi engraved with Hotei. Blade carved with a blossoming plum branch.* 4. *Handle lacquered, with a bronze dragon in relief. Blade signed Kinkazan no shu Gifu Fujiwara Kionaga.* 5. *Handle shakudo, nanako. Two shi-shi in high relief in gold. Blade signed and engraved with figures and inscriptions.*

KOWAI LOKO DUTNGA. The Nicobar harpoon. (Man And. & Nic. 4).

KOWAT. See Uluwa.

KOYUN. A wooden spear with a single barb cut from the solid, Victoria. (Vic. Mus. 31).

KOYUNG. An unbarbed and unhafted spear used in Victoria. (Vic. Mus. 31).

KOY-YUN. A spear with a very long, sharp, carefully finished point, the whole well balanced and well made. It is from nine to eleven feet long and a little larger in the middle than at the butt, Victoria. (Brough Smyth I, 307).

KOZANE. Small scales of metal which were bound together with silk cords and used for making armor in Japan. (Conder 260).

The small scales from which early armor was made in Japan. (Dean Notes 22).

KOZUKA, KODZUKA. The small knife carried in a pocket in the scabbard of a Japanese sword or dagger, also its handle when separate. The blades are straight and chisel-edged; they are made of kataha plates, that is plates made by welding together a plate of iron and one of steel. The steel side is flat and highly polished, while the iron one is usually left rough and tapers towards the edge. Sometimes the iron side is engraved or inlaid. Many

FIGURE 478. *Kozuka.* 1. *The foxes' wedding. Sumizogan of shakudo, copper and dark shibuichi on light shibuichi. Signed Morisada.* 2. *Shibuichi. A moonlit landscape. Flat inlay of gold, silver, shakudo and copper. Signed Hosono Sozayemon Masamori.* 3. *Shakudo, nanako. Butterflies and a stream; gold, silver and copper. Back shibuichi engraved with autumn grasses. Signed Goto Hokkio Ichijo, and kakihan.* 4. *Iron. Fuji and Matsubara in low relief and gold inlay. Signed Kikugawa Hisahide.* 5. *Copper, ishime. Flying storks and reeds in relief in gold, silver and shakudo. Signed Mitsuhiro, and kakihan.* 6. *Iron. A dragon fly in relief in silver.* 7. *Copper, nanako. Fuji and grasses in gold, silver and shakudo.* 8. *Iron. A crab in relief in copper. Signed with a tripod in gold. The tripod was the seal of Mitsuoki (Otsuki).* 9. *Shibuichi, the cap of iron. A bridge post, in front of which a white heron is perched on an oar handle.* 10. *Pewter inlaid with a lighter colored variety. Heron and reeds.* 11. *Silver engraved with a tiger; the engraving includes the front, back and one edge. Signed Soyo.* 12. *Shibuichi, shakudo and silver. Hotei shaking Karako from an embroidered bag. Signed Kano Natsuo.* 13. *Shakudo. Millet in high relief in gold. Signed Tomei, and kakihan.* 14. *Shakudo, nanako. Bamboo, snail and sparrow, slight inlay of gold.* 15. *Shakudo, nanako. A flower in a hanging vase in relief in gold and silver. Signed Goto Sekijo.* 16. *Shakudo, ishime. A shishi in high relief in gold continued on the back (gold) in engraving. Signed Somin.* 17. *Shibuichi, copper, shakudo and gold. Bust of a Nio in high relief. Signed Hitotsuyanagi Tomonaga.* 18. *Shibuichi. A gold carp ascending a waterfall. Signed Omori Tokunobu, and kakihan.* 19. *Iron. Takaramono (the contents of the mythical treasure ship) in relief and inlaid with gold.* 20. *Shakudo, nanako. A battle across a stream; carved and inlaid with gold, silver and shibuichi. Signed Goto Kenjo, and kakihan. (The 7th Goto master).* 21. *Shakudo, nanako. Three rats keeping accounts, in relief and inlay of gold and silver. Signed Ito Masanaga zo, and kakihan.* 22. *Shakudo Center — chrysanthemums in relief on a reserve; ends — diaper patterns in flat inlay on gadroons.* 23. *Copper. Gomane (a dried sardine). Tail and fins of silver, gills of gold. Signed Hamano Masayuki.* 24. *Shibuichi, jimigaki. An inro and pouch with ojime and netsuke. In relief in gold, copper, malachite and coral.* 25. *Ivory and shitan (red sandalwood). Utensils for the tea ceremony in lacquer, ivory and tortoise shell. Signed Dosho (an ivory carver).* 26. *Shakudo, ishime. A number of small panels of cloisonne enamel and two "Hirata curls," with some dots of gold.* 27. *Staghorn. Daruma. Signed Haruhide, and kakihan. (A netsuke maker).*

of the blades were made and signed by celebrated swordsmiths. The steel side is always inward when the knife is sheathed. Fig. 477.

The handles are made of three sizes: the standard, which includes nearly all, is about nine-sixteenths of an inch wide by three and three-quarters long; occasional ones vary slightly from this. The

FIGURE 479. *Kris Scabbard Parts. 1. The top piece of a scabbard, finished except the opening for the blade. 2. A hilt finished. 3. The top piece of a scabbard of a different shape roughed out with an adze. 4. Straight part of a scabbard in the rough. 5. Metal cover of embossed white metal.*

o-kozuka is considerably larger, about four and a quarter by three-quarters of an inch; and the *hanzashi-kozuka* is much smaller, about an inch and a half by half an inch. Fig. 356.

Kozuka are generally of metal, and the backs and fronts are frequently of different metals. They are also made of wood, bone, ivory or staghorn. Next to the tsuba the Japanese consider the kozuka the most important fitting of the sword and decorate it by carving, engraving, inlaying, and enameling, usually by combinations of two, or more, of these methods, fig. 478. Generally the decoration is confined to the front; but, not infrequently, it extends to the back. A very common decoration for the back is a poem, proverb or sentiment. Some of these are very amusing as—"Drinking sake makes the mind like a day in spring, and the voice of a creditor like a nightingale's song," on the back of a kozuka showing men drinking, and signed "playfully made Mitsuoki." Often the face is decorated with figures in high relief, which are continued on the back by engraving. The back is very rarely decorated in relief. Sometimes the ornament is entirely on a separate plate, *ji-ita*, made by the master and set in the handle by an apprentice. In some cases the ji-ita is

taken from a kogai and set in a kozuka. As the handles are shorter than kozuka this leaves a blank space at each end. These spaces are called *sode* and such kozuka *sode-kozuka*; they are considered of inferior value.

If kozuka are signed it is usually on the back, sometimes on the edge and rarely on the end, *egashira*. The kozuka is always carried in the side of the scabbard next the wearer.

It is said that every samurai boy was expected to learn to throw a kozuka accurately before he was old enough to wear a pair of swords. For short distances it was laid flat on the hand and thrown underhand, point first. For longer distances it was held by one end and thrown overhand; for very long throws the handle was removed. The thrower should be able to hit a man in the eye at twenty feet. "The throwing dagger (kozuka) must speed on its way, true as an arrow, direct to forehead, throat or wrist." (Sugimoto 109). It was not considered creditable to hit a man by a thrown knife in any other part.

KRIS, CRIS, CREESE, KERIS. The typical Malay knife. It is a very old weapon and is said to have originated in Java, but has long since been adopted in all parts of the Archipelago. The Javans ascribe the invention of the kris to Inakto Pali, King of Janggolo in the 14th century. It is first shown in the sculptures of the 15th century. (Egerton, p. 97).

Every island, and often every district has its own particular forms of blade, hilt and scabbard. To make the confusion worse, different typical forms are often found on the same kris — it may have, for instance, a Bali blade, a Javan hilt and a Sumatran scabbard. In the market at Djockjakarta (the only place where kris mounting is done on a large scale at present) there are at least twenty stalls where mounts are sold in the rough and fitted to blades brought there to be mounted. Figure 479 shows a number of parts bought there in May, 1930. The wooden parts are roughed out with a small adze and finished with a knife made of a half-round file. The carvers are very expert and work much more rapidly than most Orientals.

The finest blades are made in Java and Bali; and Java has produced more shapes of blade than any other place. More than forty named shapes, besides many varieties with no specific names, are recognized. (See Raffles I, 296). In all of its changes the blade has one characteristic not found in any other knife — it widens out in a sharp point next the hilt on one side only, excepting in one rather rare form which widens out on both sides.

They vary in size from some of the krisses of the Javan women with blades five or six inches long that weigh a couple of ounces to the Moro weapons with blades two feet long that weigh as much as two pounds. Excepting for the Moro kris-

FIGURE 480. *Bali Krisses.* 1. *Hilt an ivory Raksha mounted in a gold cup set with diamonds. Fine pamir blade inlaid with a vine pattern of chased gold.* 2. *Its scabbard of wood, the lower part covered with finely embossed and chased gold.* 3. *Hilt a conventional Garuda of gold set with jewels of different colors. Blade carved with a snake with a dragon's head inlaid with gold. It is also inlaid with flowers and leaves of chased gold.* 4. *Its scabbard of wood painted with small figures of Buddha in gold and colors, the back and sides of the lower part are covered with chased gold. These two krisses are of the highest class of Malayan work.*

This point serves as a species of guard and is frequently notched to catch an opponent's blade. The blade may be straight, half waved and half straight, with the waves either next the hilt or next the point; or they may be waved for their entire length, and have from five to fifteen waves. The kris cherita is said to have "many tens of waves in the blade" but this is figurative, and there are seldom more than fourteen. Contrary to the general impression, straight blades are much more numerous than waved ones.

ses, which are much larger than those found anywhere else, the size of the blade is not characteristic of locality. The kris malala (one with raised ribs on the blade) is more often found in Bali than anywhere else, but is also used in many other places. The hilts are slightly more characteristic in some cases, particularly for some Bali and Javan forms; other Javan types are very widely distributed. The scabbards are slightly more distinctive but most of the shapes are found in many places. Except in the rather rare cases where blade, hilt and scabbard are all typical of the same locality it is almost impossible to say where a kris comes from. In the Museum in Batavia, which probably has the finest collection of krisses in existence, the krisses are classed by the shapes of the blades. The blade is, of course, the most important part, but the shapes are so many and differ from each other so slightly, that but few people can discriminate.

In Malaya the kris was a regular part of the dress and was carried at all times. Every man had a number and, in war, carried three — one a family heirloom that had been given him by his father, one that had been given him by his father-in-law on his marriage, and one that he considered particularly his own. The last was worn at the left side ready for immediate use, the two others, respectively, at the right and back. In peace the kris was worn at the right side, and to wear it in any other position was considered rude, and even insulting.

Prince Pakoet Alam at Djockjakarta showed me the old methods of fencing with the kris. He said that if a man had only one kris with him he held the scabbard in his left hand with the straight part extending along his forearm and guarded with it. If he had two krisses, he took his favorite in his right hand and the other in his left to guard with. The left-hand kris was held against his forearm with the edge and point at the top outward. In this position it was not only useful as a guard, but if his opponent tried to catch his arm a slight motion would cut his hand severely.

In the Malay Peninsula to appear at court without covering the kris hilt with a fold of the sarong (skirt) was treason, and likely to cost the offender his life. The krisses of well known fighters were frequently named and were as well known as the faces of their owners. There was a fairly definite relationship between the quality of the kris and the rank of the wearer; and it was a serious offense to carry a kris of much better quality than a man's rank entitled him to. When a young noble acquired a new kris it was quite usual for him to try it on the first Chinaman or low class Malay that he met. Such assaults were rather encouraged by the Rajas as their rule depended more on the fear inspired by their immediate followers than on moral right.

The blades are almost always beautiful forgings and many are finely finished. The top of the blade next the hilt is nearly always a separate piece, called the ganja or gandja in Java. The top of it which shows when the kris is sheathed is more often inlaid than any other part of the blade.

The fine old blades were made by piling three layers of iron, or soft steel, separated by thinner ones of meteoric iron called pamir. The meteoric iron contains about three per cent of nickel and remained bright when the blade was etched, while the steel was blackened by the etching solution. In the few fine krisses made recently Krupp nickel steel, or even pure nickel, is used in place of the meteoric iron. The bar is welded, beaten out and doubled and twisted in various ways depending on the pattern it is desired to produce. See fig. 848, watered steel. The bar is next cut in three pieces, a small one for the ganga, and two larger ones for the blade. The latter are then forged to the desired shape and welded to opposite sides of a piece of hard steel of the same shape but a little longer and wider; the projecting parts of the steel thus form the point and edges of the blade. The forging is then finished, the ganga fitted and the blade decorated by carving and inlaying. It is then etched with a mixture of arsenious acid and lime juice which brings out the watering.

This is due to the fact that the arsenic blackens the iron and leaves the meteoric iron or nickel bright. In a well finished blade the result appears like a polished black metal inlaid with silver. This etching is a dangerous process as the gas given off will cause death with horrible suffering. In Malaya it is done out of doors with a strong trade wind blowing. The blades are occasionally cleaned with lime juice. This continual etching somewhat dims the brightness of the watering and gradually wears away the blade. It is the reason for the rough surface of most blades and the extreme lightness of the very old ones.

Many patterns of watering are recognized and can be reproduced at will, although no two specimens are absolutely alike. A favorite design for the decoration of blades is to carve a snake following the undulations of the blade and having a dragon's head on the side opposite the guard-like point. The eyes of the snake are frequently jewels. In rare cases the snake has two heads, one on each edge of the blade. In many krisses there is a hook-shaped projection from the blade opposite the guard; this is said to be a conventional representation of an ele-

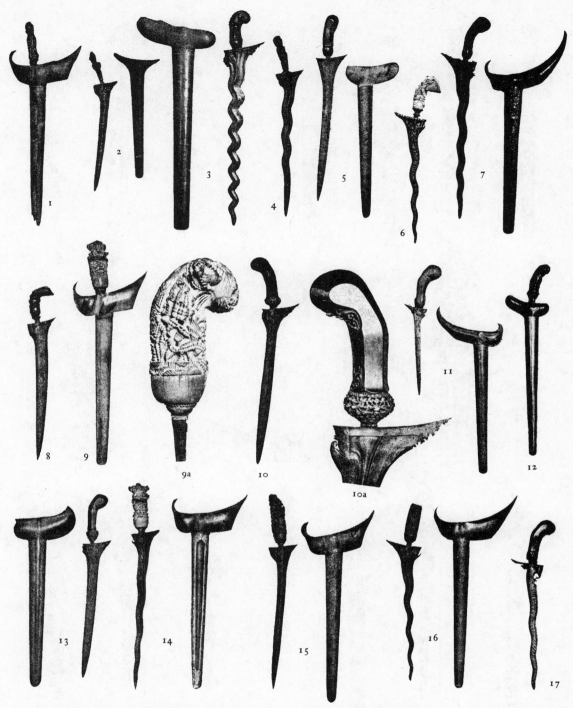

FIGURE 481. *Javan and Madura Krisses.* 1. *Java. Hilt a figure roughly carved of staghorn. Scabbard of kajoe pelet.* 2. *Madjepahit kris. The oldest form of kris. Hilt a human figure forged in one piece with the blade. Blade 10 inches long.* 3. *Java (?). Blade 16 inches long with many sharp waves (kris cherita). Hilt of redwood carved with strapwork. Scabbard painted red on one side.* 4. *Madjepahit kris, modern form. Blade carved with a snake.* 5. *Java. Blade with a hook projecting from the back.* 6. *Java. Watered blade inlaid with a chased gold vine and an inscription. Ivory hilt, a conventional garuda.* 7. *Java. Blade carved and inlaid with gold, gold figures on the top. Scabbard covered with embossed gold.* 8. *Pamir blade. Gold hilt set with many small diamonds.* 9. *Madura. Pamir blade 14.25 inches long. Old carved ivory hilt. Scabbard kajoe pelet.* 9a. *The side view of the hilt of 9.* 10. *Blade of exceedingly fine pamir; wood hilt mounted in a white metal fitting set with diamonds.* 10a. *The hilt of 10, the most typical Javan form.* 11. *Java. Blade 8 inches long.* 12. *Gold hilt set with white stones. Old blade almost worn away from continual etching. Scabbard modern.* 13. *Blade watered in nearly straight lines. Wood hilt set in a chased silver cup above one set with two rows of clear white stones. Scabbard covered with engraved brass. Java.* 14. *Madura. Pamir blade; very finely carved ivory hilt. Scabbard of kajoe pelet, partly covered with metal.* 15. *Java. Hilt of elaborately carved staghorn. Scabbard of kajoe pelet.* 16. *Java. Very light blade 12.375 inches long. Bone hilt, a conventional owl. Scabbard covered with engraved brass.* 17. *Java. Unusual shaped watered blade, wood hilt.*

FIGURE 482. *Krisses, Bali and Lombok.* 1. *Waved, watered blade* 15 *inches long. Hilt a silver garuda. Kajoe pelet scabbard with a silver head of Bonaspati.* 2. *Straight pamir blade. Hilt a silver garuda. Scabbard, top of carved bone, lower part covered with embossed silver.* 3. *Pamir blade. Notched hilt and scabbard of kajoe pelet.* 4. *Blade* 17.375 *inches long, inlaid with gold. Kajoe pelet hilt.* 5. *Lombok. Straight, pamir blade. Hilt of dark brown wood wound with fine cord. Scabbard of kajoe pelet.* 6. *Pamir blade, notched ivory hilt.* 6a. *The hilt of 6.* 7. *Watered blade* 13.25 *inches long. Hilt a finely carved figure of Krishna set in silver.* 7a. *The hilt of 7.* 8. *Bali. Heavy ribbed blade with very brilliant pamir. Wood hilt carved and colored red and gold.* 8a. *The hilt of 8.* 9. *Bali. Waved pamir blade. Hilt and upper part of scabbard kajoe pelet; lower part of scabbard covered with brass and tortoise shell.* 10. *Bali. Straight plain blade. Plain wood hilt.* 11. *Very sharply waved blade (kris cherita). Hilt kajoe pelet. Scabbard covered with chased gold.* 12. *Brilliant pamir blade* 13 *inches long. Wood hilt.* 13. *Pamir blade. Kajoe pelet hilt. Scabbard painted with vines, scrolls and a dog in red, black and gold.*

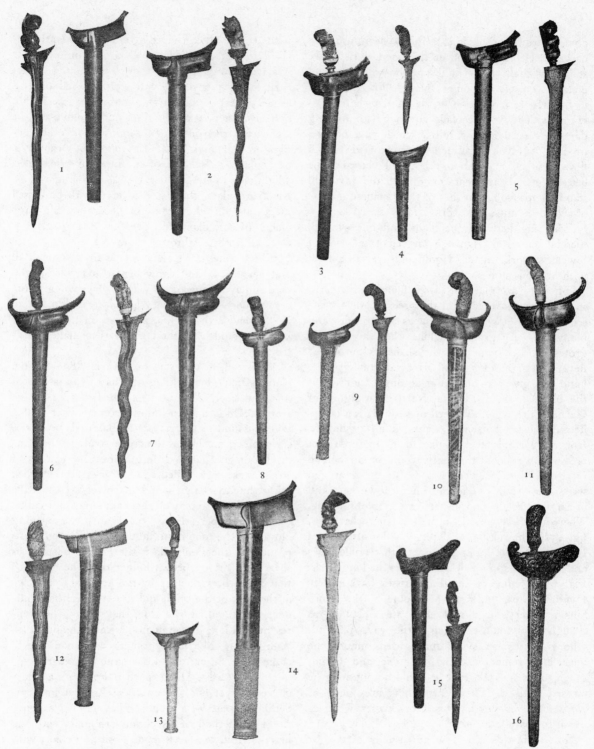

FIGURE 483. *Krisses. Sumatra.* 1. *South Sumatra. Polished black, ribbed blade 14.5 inches long. Wood pistol hilt, garuda(?). Horn tip on scabbard.* 2. *South Sumatra. Blade with a chevron pattern. Garuda hilt of white stone.* 3. *South Sumatra. Pamir blade. Well carved ivory garuda hilt. Scabbard of mottled wood.* 4. *Sumatra(?). A woman's kris. Blade 6.25 inches long, weight two ounces. Ivory garuda hilt. Scabbard covered with tortoise shell.* 5. *South Sumatra. Blade 15 inches long with watering in relief. Ivory garuda hilt set in copper and silver set with white stones.* 6. *Sumatra(?). Narrow, straight blade 12 inches long. Hilt a raksha of wood. Sheath of polished black wood.* 7. *Java. Black blade inlaid with a gold vine. Hilt a raksha finely carved of ivory. One piece scabbard of yellow and brown wood.* 8. *Unusually heavy, straight blade 10.5 inches long. Ivory garuda hilt. Scabbard of light wood.* 9. *Watered blade 9 inches long, carved wood hilt. Scabbard covered with silver, plain on the back, carved and pierced on the front.* 10. *Straight pamir blade 14.25 inches long; hilt carved of vegetable ivory. Body of scabbard covered with tortoise shell and metal.* 11. *Straight pamir blade; hilt a figure of vegetable ivory. Lower part of scabbard covered with brass.* 12. *Sumatra(?). Pointed hilt made of a piece of an elephant's tooth. Dark wood scabbard wound with cane at the lower end.* 13. *South Sumatra. Watered blade 5.5 inches long; black horn hilt set in silver. Lower part of scabbard covered with engraved silver. A woman's kris.* 14. *Central Sumatra. Watered blade 15.875 inches long. Top of scabbard of light wood, middle of black, and a long chape of finely chased gold with a diamond set in the end.* 15. *Sumatra. Blade 9.25 inches long. Wood scabbard and hilt well carved. The hilt is set in a cup of silver filigree.* 16. *Sumatra. Straight pamir blade. Very finely carved hilt and scabbard of yellow wood.*

phant's trunk, it having formerly been usual to carve an elephant's head at this point. Krisses are still occasionally found with one, or even two, elephant's heads carved on the blades. There is a kris in the Moore Collection in the Metropolitan Museum, with the entire blade covered with wayang dancers carved in low relief, which is, I believe, unique. A favorite pattern consists of vines and flowers inlaid in gold in relief and chased. The better work of the decorators of Bali and Java will stand comparison with that of the Japanese makers of sword mounts. Fig. 480.

The ring between the blade and hilt (Javan, mendak or uwar) is often an elaborate piece of jeweler's work, made of gold or silver, often set with precious stones.

The hilts are made of wood, bone, ivory, horn, stone, or are covered with the precious metals, often set with jewels. The shapes are infinite and many are very graceful while others are merely grotesque. But whatever the shape its purpose is never lost sight of and all fit comfortably in the hand and give a firm grip at an angle that allows the blade to be used effectively. The figure of Garuda (the eagle, the steed of Vishnu) is a favorite subject for hilts and occurs in all gradations from very elaborate bird-like forms to those that are so conventional that they would be difficult to recognize if there were not an almost unbroken series. Fig. 299. The form of hilt known here and in England as the "kingfisher" is a form of Garuda. There are three varieties of it; see Kingfisher Kris, fig. 451. The raksha, or demon, is also often used. It is a grotesque human figure with terrible tusks and his hair hanging down his back in long curls. Fig. 670. Some of the Bali krisses have purely Hindu figures, 7a, fig. 482. Some of the Moro hilts are very large and elaborate and look as though they would be much in the way. A friend, who is an expert swordsman, tried one of the most inconvenient looking of mine and found, much to his surprise, that he could do anything he pleased with it. These large hilts are made of ivory or silver and are used on krisses worn as much for parade as use.

The scabbards are of wood, usually of two or three pieces, but occasionally of one. In most cases their decorative value depends solely on the graining of the wood, and the shape, which is frequently extremely graceful, especially in Java. The scab-

bards called "boat-shaped" here are evidently derived from the orchids which are common in the Malayan jungles. The straight part of the scabbard is often covered with tortoise shell or embossed metal, brass on the commoner specimens, and silver or gold on the finer ones. Sometimes the scabbards are painted with figures and other designs in Bali and Java. The hilts and scabbards, particularly in Bali, are often carved of kajoe pelet, a light wood with peculiar irregular dark markings. Most are plain, some are covered with embossed metal, and on others the only decoration is a large plaque of rose diamonds. See figs. 481, 482, 483, 484, 485, 486. All to the same scale.

The kris has one serious defect, the tang is small and very weak and easily bent. Our sailors, who used to have many fights with Malays when in the eastern ports said that they had no fear of a Malay if they had a short club, as a rap on the blade of his kris would bend the tang so as to make it useless.

Winstead, p. 114, says of the kris: "Shortly, the blade is made by welding alternate laminations of iron and steel. The most esteemed weapons come from Celebes, and the most artistic workmanship will be found in the creeses of Bali and Java. Besides these finer blades the creese made in the Peninsula is a cheap and clumsy knife. One pattern of straight creese is called 'The black fighting cock with white markings,' another trowel-like the 'cake spoon.' The patterns of the damasking are called 'the grasshopper's legs,' 'the bean,' 'the opening blossom,' 'the mountain,' and so on. The only kris peculiar to the Peninsula is the Patani weapon, its sheath of Javan type but longer than the blade, so that it can be kicked up by the heel from its place at the back of the thigh and drawn over the shoulder; its hilt called 'the kingfisher's head,' but representing a long-nosed demon with teeth and tusks. 7, fig. 451. The long straight 'execution' creese comes from Sumatra and is common in Negri Sembilan, fig. 487. The 'pepper crusher' a short curved dagger, is also Sumatran; Rembau in Negri Sembilan boasts of a peculiar hilt for this weapon."

"The method of executing criminals with the kris is as follows: He is made to sit in a chair, with his arms extended horizontally, and held in that position by two men. The executioner, who stands behind him, inserts his kris above the collar bone, in a perpendicular manner, which causes instant

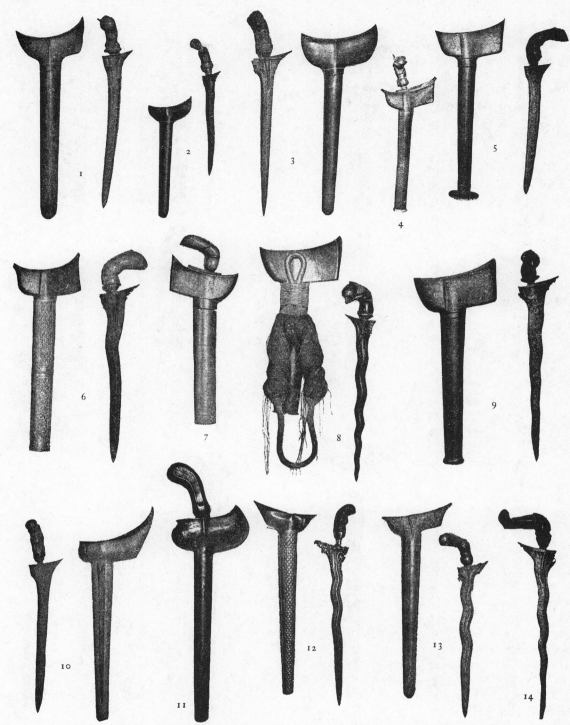

FIGURE 484. *Krisses.* 1. *Sumbawa. Hilt a contorted figure of carved bone set in braided silver wire above an engraved brass cup. Scabbard of light, polished wood with a horn tip.* 2. *Sumbawa. Blade of diamond section 8.5 inches long; hilt wood, a highly conventionalized garuda set in a large and elaborate silver cup.* 3. *Sumbawa. Watered blade 13.25 inches long. Ivory garuda hilt elaborately carved. Polished wood scabbard.* 4. *Sumbawa(?). Waved blade 10 inches long. Hilt, wood, a conventional garuda. Scabbard of light wood with a bone tip.* 5. *Central Sumatra. Watered blade, ivory pistol hilt set in brass. Wood sheath with a large silver chape.* 6. *Central Sumatra. Half-waved blade 14.75 inches long. Ivory pistol hilt set in silver. Scabbard covered with heavy embossed silver.* 7. *Central Sumatra. Straight, watered blade. Ivory pistol hilt.* 8. *Wood pistol hilt with applied brass ornaments. Scabbard of mottled wood. A large loop of red silk cord is fastened to the scabbard by a band of red silk and silver.* 9. *Central Sumatra. Pamir blade, pistol hilt of dark wood. Scabbard of dark wood.* 10. *Wood garuda hilt. Unusual shaped scabbard, the lower part covered with brass open on one side over red velvet.* 11. *Chinese. Straight brass blade 16 inches long. Hilt and scabbard of typical Javan form but of Chinese workmanship and covered with red-gold Chinese lacquer.* 12. *Blade carved with a snake and inlaid with gold. Garuda hilt of wood. Scabbard covered with brass embossed in a lozenge pattern.* 13. *Borneo(?). Blade similar to the last with moulded gnanja, and inlaid with gold. Scabbard carved and lacquered in brown and gold.* 14. *Plain waved blade 14 inches long. Carved wood hilt ending in a bird's head.*

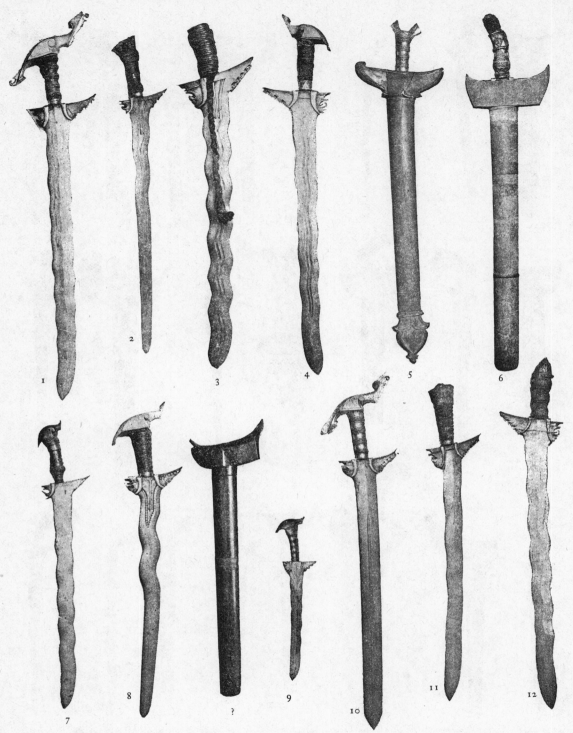

FIGURE 485. *Moro Krisses.* 1. *Parade kris, Buan. Blade 24 inches long; ivory pommel 8 inches long; grip wound with black cord.* 2. *Mindanao. Black horn hilt, grip wound with cord.* 3. *Mindanao. Blade 25.625 inches long and 2.625 wide, weight 2 lbs. Grip wound with cane.* 4. *Mindanao. Blade etched and inlaid with a silver line. Ivory pommel 5.25 inches long, grip wound with cord.* 5. *Silver hilt with an octagonal pommel. Sheath with a carved end.* 6. *Illana Moro, Tucuran Bay, Mindanao. Hilt a conventional garuda of native gold.* 7. *Tawi-Tawi. Blade 19.5 inches long. Ivory pommel, grip with chased bands of gold and silver.* 8. *Blade inlaid with silver and a white metal for its entire length. Ivory pommel, cord grip. Horn tip on scabbard.* 9. *Magindanao Moro, Mindanao. A boy's kris. Horn hilt, engraved silver panel in blade.* 10. *Sulu. Silver pommel and grip.* 11. *Sulu. Octagonal pommel of two pieces of ivory separated by one of black horn, a silver ornament on the end.* 12. *Tapiantana Moro, Mindanao. Cord wound hilt, pommel of engraved native gold.*

FIGURE 486. *Miscellaneous Krisses.* 1. *Sumatra(?). Kingfisher hilt. Scabbard covered with silver.* 2. *Similar to no.* 1. 3. *Java. An embossed silver ornament across the top of the scabbard.* 4. *Black wood hilt and scabbard. A shell on the pommel and the scabbard covered with embossed silver.* 5. *Waved pamir blade 12.75 inches long. Hilt of black wood, an elephant(?) set in embossed brass. One piece scabbard.* 6. *Straight pamir blade.* 7. *Very heavy blade of unusual shape carved with a snake. Narrow topped, one piece scabbard.* 8. *Very old waved blade 11 inches long, wood hilt.* 9. *Java. Hilt, a bird painted red, green and brown.* 10. *Java. Scabbard painted in a diaper pattern in red and green.* 11. *The hilt of no.* 5. 12. *The hilt of no.* 1. *Black wood set in silver.* 13. *Celebes. Much waved blade finely inlaid with gold. Very heavy plain scabbard.* 14. *The hilt of no.* 8. *A much worn figure of a warrior with a sword and round shield.* 15. *Java. Blade inlaid with pamir in rectangular patches.* 16. *Java. Painted scabbard.* 17. *Bali. Painted scabbard with a procession of warriors on the top.* 18. *Bali. Painted scabbard, a fight between a dragon-headed snake and two men.* 19. *Madura. Blade watered with pamir in unusually large patches.* 20. *The hilt of no.* 9. 21. *Java. Waved blade inlaid with gold, crystal hilt. Scabbard covered with silver embossed and filigree.* 22. *Bali. Waved blade with very brilliant pamir. Hilt a gilded figure set with pink stones.* 23. *Straight pamir blade, wood hilt. Scabbard covered with embossed silver plated copper.* 24. *Java. Blade carved with a serpent and an elephant's head on each edge.*

death, as the weapon enters the heart." (Marryat 101). The executioner's krisses have very long, straight, narrow blades and straight hilts with rounded pommels. Fig. 487.

of the thumb. These pieces laid on the blade alternately lengthwise and crosswise would reveal the suitability of the weapon for my use by the direction of the last piece — crosswise it would indicate a

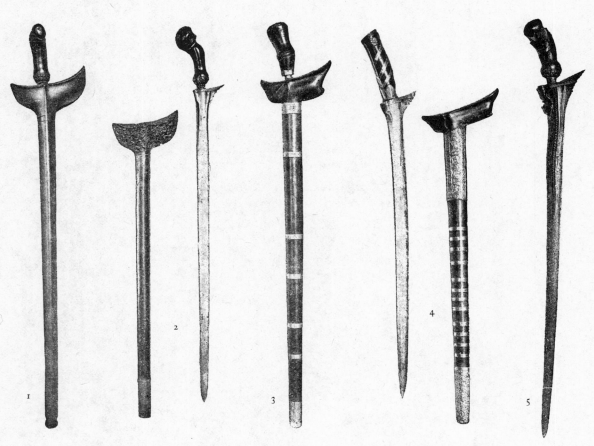

FIGURE 487. *Executioner's Krisses.* 1. *Sumbawa(?). Plain hilt of black wood. Wood scabbard with a horn tip.* 2. *Horn hilt set in a gold mount and carved at the pommel. Wood scabbard with a carved and pierced horn top; tip missing.* 3. *Sumatra. Hilt and scabbard of dark wood with silver mounts.* 4. *Blade 19.25 inches long. Wood hilt with silver cap, bands and ornaments. Scabbard with chased silver caps and plain, narrow bands of silver.* 5. *Blade 23 inches long carved with a snake in relief. Hilt a conventional garuda of wood.*

Forbes in *A Naturalist's Wanderings* (p. 116) describes the proper method of selecting a kris: "To be a trusty weapon for me it ought to be especially made to some measure of my own body — of hand, arm or thigh, or of the breadth of my two thumbs or of my span; but to discover the same potency in a ready made blade, I ought to divide a straw or grass-stem, of equal length with the blade into as many lengths as it contains its own breadth at a distance from the hilt of twice the measure of the first joint

fence — a 'bar sinister'; lengthwise, no obstruction — a favorable omen. Another test was to measure the length by the breadth of my right and left thumbs alternately, repeating at each alternation one of the words, Sri, Dungu, Dinia, Rara, Pati, Sri, &c. According to which of these words fall to the last thumb-breadth would the blade be a wise choice or not. Sri being a designation of honor, and Dinia, signifying the world, would be considered good ones, whereas Rara meaning sickness, and

Pata, death, would indicate misfortune, and the purchase of the kris would bring disaster."

The Javan names for the parts of a kris are:

Keris: a kris.

Ukiran, Deder: hilt.

Pandji Sekar: the top piece of the blade when it is bowed.

Greneng: notches in the end of the gandja.

Sarongan, Wrangka: the wide top of the scabbard.

FIGURE 488. *Kris Stands. 1 and 3. A pair. Grotesque figures carved of wood and painted in bright colors. Heights — no. 1, 18 inches; no. 3, 18.5 inches. Each is holding a typical Bali kris with notched hilt and scabbard of kajoe pelet. 2. A wayang dancer finely carved of brown wood. Height 23.75 inches. He is holding a Bali kris with a typical gold hilt and a beautifully marked kajoe pelet scabbard.*

Wilah: blade.

Sarong: scabbard.

Patra: carvings on the hilt.

Mendaq, Uwar: metal fitting between the hilt and blade.

Dapor Loq, or Eloq: a waved blade.

Dapor Bener: a straight blade.

Landep: the cutting edge of the blade.

Putjor: the point of the blade.

Paksi: the tang.

Dada: the middle line of the blade.

Gandja, Ganja: the top piece of the blade.

Galar: the straight part of the scabbard.

Kendelan, Pendoq: the metal cover of the scabbard.

In some cases different names are given in Celebes. A kris is called Sele; the hilt Pangulu; the blade Matana Seleka; the scabbard Banuwaya; the enlarged top of the scabbard Belembeng; and the enlarged lower end of the scabbard Padja.

In Bali most of the houses of the higher classes had kris stands, grotesquely carved human figures about two feet high, in the open hands of which a visitor left his kris while visiting the house. Most of them held only one kris, but some could hold two. Fig. 488.

KRIS CHERITA. A long kris with "many tens of waves to its blade." (Clifford, Brown Humanity 79). The "many tens" is figurative as there were seldom more than fourteen.

KRUG. The Russian name for the round Turkish breastplate, commonly called "pot lids." (Scheremetew 88). Fig. 489.

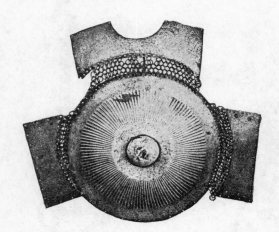

FIGURE 489. *Krug. The round Turkish breastplate of the 15th and 16th centuries.*

KUBIBUKURO. (Head bag). A net bag with slings and broad shoulder straps in which to carry the severed head of an enemy. It was hung from the waist when on foot, and from the saddle when mounted. Japan. (Garbutt 153). Fig. 490.

KUBIKIRI. A Japanese knife, or short sword, with an incurved, chisel-edged blade. It was used to cut off the head of a dead enemy. The name means head cutter. Fig. 491.

KUBI OKI. A shallow bucket of white wood with a tall cover, and a short, heavy, strong spike of hard wood in the center. One was kept in every samurai house and was used if it was necessary to send the head of any member of the family who had committed harikiri to the governor for identification. When the head had been identified, it, and the bucket, were returned to the family and were burned, or buried, with the body.

KUCHAKU. A Japanese scabbard mounting of an unknown kind.

KUCHI-GANE, KUCHI-KANE. See Koi-Guchi Kanagu.

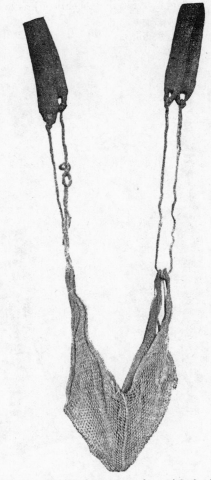

FIGURE 490. *Kubi Bukuro. A net bag with shoulder slings for carrying a severed head.*

KUCHI GUSURI. Priming powder, Japan.

KUCHI-GUSURI-IRE. A priming flask, Japan. See Hayago.

FIGURE 491. *Kubikiri. Blade 12.375 inches long, carved with Fudo. All iron mounts. Fudo on the kashira, a peacock on the kozuka.*

KUCHIKAGO. A horse muzzle, Japan. See Muzzle.

FIGURE 492. *Kuda Yari. 1. Bronze with the guard a 16-petaled chrysanthemum 3 inches in diameter. The handle is fluted in rings and lacquered black. Length 5 inches. It is wound with a long silk cord which is said to be used to fasten it to the arm. 2. Iron. The guard is round and 3.375 inches in diameter. Height 3.5 inches. 3. Iron. The guard is 3.375 inches in diameter and the height is 4 inches.*

KUDA YARI. (Spear pipe). A short iron tube with a wide, round flange on one end. The tube was held in the left hand with the flange forward, and placed over the shaft of a spear to steady and guide it when fencing. When a thrust was made the spear slid through the tube and the flange guarded the hand. It is said that a thrust could be made more quickly with it, fig. 492. In the Peabody Museum, Salem, there is a spear with a kuda yari permanently attached to it. On the flange it has two hooks normally thrown outward by springs. By sliding it up close to the head and pressing in the hooks they can be made to engage with two holes in a small flange close to the head, from which it then hangs. To free it, it is pushed up close to the head when the springs throw the hooks out and free it so that it can slide up and down the shaft.

KUDI TRANCHANG. A very peculiar sword formerly used in Java and other Malayan countries. Raffles says that it was given up in Java in the 18th century. Fig. 493.

Similar arms were used quite recently in Madura. They vary so much in shape that it is difficult to see their relationship. (Tidsschrift, Taal Landen Volkerkunde LI, 471). Fig. 494.

KUGE-NO-TACHI. A form of tachi reserved for the princes and nobles of the Imperial retinue, Japan. (Joly, Hawkshaw xiv).

KUGERONG, KOOM-BA-MALEE. A club swelling from the handle to a round head ending in a long point. (Vic. Mus. 27). Compare Kujerung.

KUJAKI. The Russian name for jazerant armor.

KUJERUNG, KALLAK. A throwing club with a heavy, spindle-shaped end and a roughly carved handle. Kurnai tribe, Australia. (Hewitt 265). Fig. 495.

KUJORU, KUMBATA. A spear peculiar to the Melville Islands. "It consists essentially of four prongs of hard wood, and a short length of bamboo into which they are inserted. The prongs are free for just three feet. From this point down towards the handle they are arranged around a central stick, immediately above which a pad of paper bark is inserted between the prongs which are then tightly bound round outside for four inches first with banyan string and then with split cane. . . . Beyond the split cane the four prongs and central stick are uncovered, then comes a length of bamboo measur-

FIGURE 493. *Kudi Tranchang. Blade 17.25 inches long inlaid with round pieces of brass. Handle missing.*

ing twelve inches, into which they are inserted, fitting tightly. For some six inches the upper end of

FIGURE 494. *Kudi Trąnchang.* 1. *A carpenter's tool, Madura.* 2. *Madura.* 3. *Called "bird form."* 4. *A variety of the bird form.* 5. *Pamerkasan.* 6. *The sheath of no. 5 made of kajoe pelet. Tidschrift voor Indische Taal-Landen Volkenkunde. Deel LI, p. 472.*

the bamboo is wound with banyan string, evidently to prevent it from splitting, as the pressure is considerable. Each ends in a sharp pointed bone, an inch long, projecting from a rounded mass of Kapei resin. The total length is only five feet three inches. This special form of spear is mainly used for catching fish and the large fresh-water snake called

FIGURE 496. *Kukigu. Wooden shafts with heavy ivory heads in which small barbed ivory heads are placed loosely, the latter are attached to the shafts by a long cord and martingale. Length 4 feet to 4 feet 3 inches.*

Tiradjune, of which the natives are very fond." (Spencer, North. Ter. 358).

KUKEHIMO. A cotton cloth folded and sewed up as a rope. It is used for fastening on a Japanese helmet. (Garbutt 170).

KUKI. See Nakago.

KUKIGU. Light darts used in taking very small seals. They have shafts of cedar or some light wood about fifty-five inches long, with a heavy head of walrus ivory into which the barbed point fits loosely. The point is fastened to the shaft by a cord and martingale so that it drags at right angles to the line. (Murdoch 218). Fig. 496.

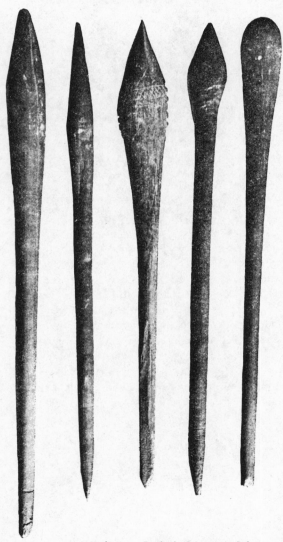

FIGURE 495. *Kujerung. Peabody Museum, Salem.*

KUKIKSADLIN. A kind of bear arrow, Point Barrow. It has a flint head about two inches long inserted and lashed in the split end of the shaft. The entire arrow is from twenty-five to thirty inches long. (Murdoch 202).

region. It is carried in a leather sheath with two small knives and a leather pouch. The small knives are shaped like the kukri, though one is often without an edge and is said to have been used for a

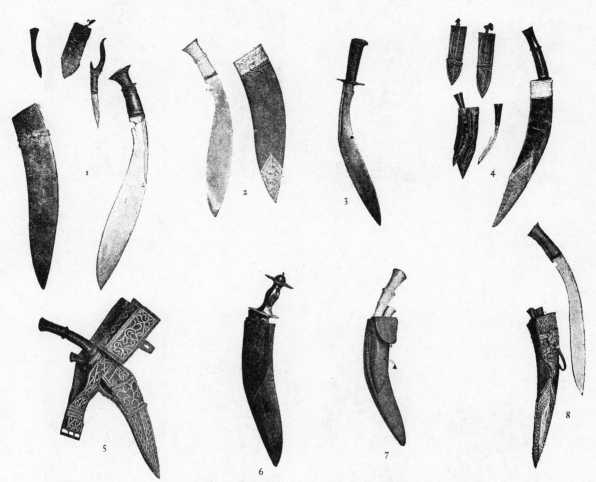

FIGURE 497. *Kukri. 1. Blade 17.5 inches long, wooden hilt. Black leather scabbard with pockets for the pouch, small knife with a staghorn handle and one for use as a sharpener. 2. Ivory hilt, blade 14.5 inches long. Scabbard mounts of chased, pierced and embossed gold. 3. Hilt with a cross guard, probably made for an Englishman to use as a hunting knife. 4. Dark wood hilt, blade 14 inches long. Two small knives with horn handles and two pouches. Scabbard with pierced gold mounts. 5. Light blade, wood hilt. The scabbard belt and pouch are of leather embroidered with quills. 6. Hilt with disk guard and pommel like a kora. 7. Narrow blade 12.5 inches long. The hilts of the kukri and small knives are of ivory. 8. Blade 14 inches long. Hilt and scabbard mountings of chased silver. The hilts of the small knives are of wood.*

KUKRI, COOKRI, KOOKERI. The national knife and principal weapon of the Gurkas of Nepal. It has a heavy, curved, single-edged blade sharp on the concave side. The hilt is usually straight and without a guard; occasionally it has a disk guard and pommel like the sword (kora) from the same

sharpener. Quite often one, or both, of these knives have hilts of branching staghorn. The weight of the blade of the kukri is well towards the point and a tremendous blow can be struck with it with very little muscular exertion. There are well authenticated instances of a Gurka having split the head of

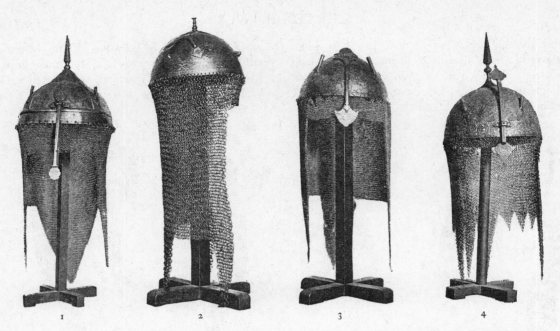

FIGURE 498. *Kulah Khud.* 1. *Plain 17th-century bowl with applied decorative ribs and border inlaid with gold. Neck guard of open iron and brass links in patterns.* 2. *Bowl inlaid with patterns and inscriptions in gold. Neck guard all steel riveted, 17th century.* 3. *Etched band around the bowl inlaid with gold in a floral pattern. Neck guard of iron and brass.* 4. *Elaborately etched and inlaid with gold and silver, Persia, 19th century. The first three are Indian.*

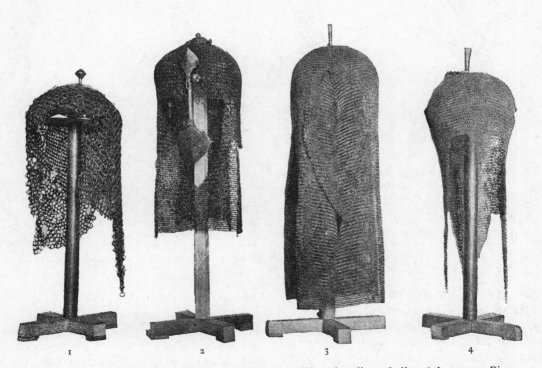

FIGURE 499. *Kulah Zirah.* 1. *Mahratta, 18th century. Riveted mail.* 2. *India, 18th century. Riveted mail with a movable nasal.* 3. *India, 18th century. Unriveted mail with a pattern worked in brass and copper links. The sides are cut away with square-headed openings over the shoulders. It has a triangular flap covering the face.* 4. *Very fine butted mail with a plate and plume holder at the crown.*

a man and cut well down into his chest with a single blow. It is carried by the Gurkas at all times and is used as a jungle and hunting knife as well as for war. The scabbards are often embroidered with quills or decorated with silver or gold chapes. Fig. 497.

FIGURE 500. *Kumade (Rake).* 1. *Three claws and a short spike. Length 5 feet 4 inches, iron ferule on butt.* 2. *Two claws and a pick blade 3.5 inches long opposite it. Wooden sheath for the pick. The shaft has been cut off.*

KUKUMI, KUTSUBUMI, KUTSUWA. A bit, Japan. See Bit.

KULAH KHUD. A Persian bowl-shaped helmet with a movable nasal and a mail neck guard. It is the usual type of helmet worn in Persia and India where it is called *top.* It generally has a spike on the top and two sockets for plumes on the front. There may be a plume holder on the top instead of the spike. In rare cases there may be three "nasals," one on the front, and one on each temple, fig. 62. The bowl is usually engraved or inlaid with gold and silver. The mail neck guard is cut away in front leaving the face uncovered, and at the sides

to clear the shoulders, front and back it hangs down in long points. The mail is generally of open links, though the best of the older ones are of riveted mail. The open mail generally has patterns woven in it with brass or copper links. Fig. 498.

KULAH ZIRAH. Persian and Indian helmets of mail or small plates connected by mail; those of mail are generally open hoods with a small, round plate at the crown carrying a plume holder, or a spike. Some have movable bar nasals, others have a triangular flap of mail to cover the face. Fig. 499.

Those of plate and mail vary much in design and construction. Some have very large nasals that cover most of the lower part of the face. 1, fig. 56.

KULBEDA. An iron boomerang used by the Dinka. Similar weapons, but generally made of wood, are used by several other African tribes. It is also called trombash or trumbash. (Schweinfurth II, 9). Burton says (Sword 37) that it is the boomerang of the Nyam-Nyam.

KULERU. The knob of resin forming the handle of a kind of Australian spear thrower called palatai. (Spencer, North. Ter. 377).

KULKIE. The spike of bone forming the point of the fishing spear called koanie in Victoria. (Brough Smyth 306).

KUL-LUK, BIR-BEN. A curved fighting club of some dark, heavy wood. It has a distinct handle. It is called kul-luk in Gypsland, and bir-ben on the Murray River. (Vic. Mus. 26).

KUMADE. (A rake). A grappling hook of two or three prongs, usually with a spike on the end or a pick blade opposite it. Japan. Fig. 500.

KUMPTAS. The bows and bowmen of the Meenas, aboriginal tribe of Rajestan. (Tod II, 239, 541).

KUNDA, GUNDA. A gunstock, Tibet. (Ramsay-Western).

KUNEE CHALKERES. The Greek helmet, see Corinthian Casque.

KUNI-KUZUSHI. A battering ram, Japan.

KUNJOLIO. A light spear used by the Kakadu, Northern Australia. The shaft is of bamboo colored with red ochre. The head is called *mageriyu,* and is made of a hard wood called *ainya,* a species of acacia. The head is tapered and ends in a very sharp point. The butt of the shaft has a hole, *munjan jil*, into which the tip of the spear thrower fits. It is only about five feet long and weighs but a few ounces. Nevertheless it is the most effective weapon

often measuring three and a half by one and a half feet. (Roth, Aust. Mus. 205).

KUNNIN. A spindle-shaped throwing stick, Kurnai tribe, Australia. (Howitt 265).

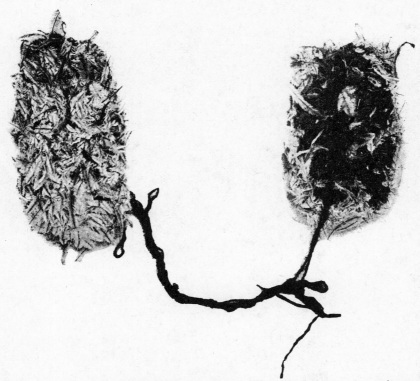

FIGURE 501. *Kurdaitcha Shoes. They are woven of human hair cord and emu feathers.*

the Kakadu possess. It can be thrown with great speed and accuracy of aim, and possesses great penetrating power.

The same name is often used for the spear thrower used with this type of spear. The thrower is a straight, round stick about half an inch in diameter and forty to fifty inches long. At the handle end it is coated with kapei resin, with a raised ring about five inches from the end, which makes a very efficient handle. The point is either of kapei, or of wood fastened on with the resin.(Spencer, North.Ter. 359, 377). See Spear Thrower, 15, 16 fig. 744.

KUNJUKDAN. A bill-like weapon with a hand guard, Southern India. (Tower 809, p. 32).

KUNJURI. A shield of the Bloomfield natives, Queensland. It is similar to the pi-kan, but larger,

KUNTAN. The shield of the Brisbane natives, Queensland. There are two kinds, both called by the same name. The first is a thin, broad one for warding off spears in the big fights; the second is narrow and is used for guarding against club blows in single combat. Both are made of cork wood with sharply rounded ends and slightly curved sides; the fronts are strongly convex and the backs concave or flat. The hand holes are cut, or burned out, as usual. The fronts are covered with beeswax and painted with pipe clay. (Roth, Aus. Mus. VII, 206).

KURA. A saddle, Japan. See Saddle.

KURABIT. The shield of the Mentawei Islanders. (Arc. f. Eth. xviii, 134).

KURABONE. A saddletree, Japan.

KURADAN. The barbed head of a harpoon, Cape Bedford, Queensland. It is a piece of wood eight to fourteen inches long, of semi-circular section. The barb, or barbs if two, are set in grooves and lashed

KURA-OI. See Kitsuke.

KURA TSUBO. The seat of a saddle, Japan.

KURDAITCHA SHOES. The Australian native only understands death by accident or injury. Death

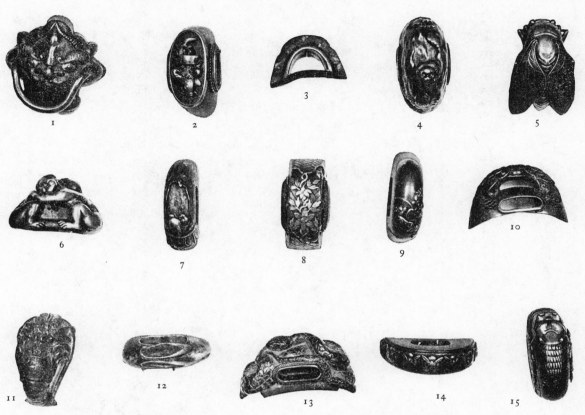

FIGURE 502. *Kurikata.* 1. *A grotesque face carved in wood with gold eyes. A metal loop for the sage-o.* 2. *Shibuichi, gold, silver, shakudo and copper. Kuiko sennin riding on a carp.* 3. *Saddle bow of iron inlaid with gold.* 4. *A hollow tree of sentoku with a monkey (shakudo and copper) leaning out and catching a crab that has also caught him.* 5. *A large fly of shibuichi and gold.* 6. *Wrestlers; shakudo, copper and gold.* 7. *Two doves in a hollow tree, iron and silver. The story of Yoritomo.* 8. *Shakudo and gold, a flowering vine on basketwork.* 9. *Shibuichi, gold, silver, shakudo and copper. Two deer in the woods.* 10. *Copper with gold inlay. The handle of a mokugyo (wooden temple bell).* 11. *Shibuichi and gold. A crawfish.* 12. *Ivory, a crouching rabbit. Signed Mitsuhiro.* 13. *Wood, a coiled snake.* 14. *Shibuichi, rabbits in gold, silver and copper.* 15. *Shibuichi, gold and silver. A monster.*

in place with tendon and cemented with resin. (W. E. Roth, no. 7, p. 31).

KURA NO BAJU. A saddle with its trappings, Japan. The saddle usually has a lacquered tree much like that used in the U. S. army. The saddle cloths are of leather elaborately lacquered and embossed. The finer harnesses are of silk with large tassels. See Saddle.

from any other cause he regards as the result of witchcraft which must be avenged. When the witch doctor has decided who is the guilty party, generally a member of a tribe with whom his own are on bad terms, he makes a pair of kurdaitcha shoes for the avenger. These shoes, fig. 501, are woven of human hair cord and emu feathers, and are believed to make the wearer invulnerable while engaged in the pursuit of the person who has be-witched the deceased. They are probably the most effective armor ever made, as not only the wearer, but all who would be liable to attack him have implicit faith in their efficiency.

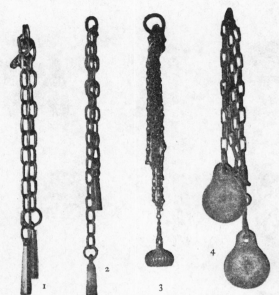

FIGURE 503. *Kusari Gama.* 1. *Two hexagonal weights connected by a chain 36 inches long. Signed on weights.* 2. *Rectangular weights connected by a chain 23.5 inches long.* 3. *One fluted bronze weight on a chain 50 inches long.* 4. *Two heavy cast weights connected by a chain 36 inches long.*

KURDIGI. A type of West Australian shield. It is long and narrow with ogival ends and is decorated with incised lines covered with pipe clay and red ochre. It is used in club fighting. (Vic. Mus. 17).

KURIJIMI-NO-O. The cords for closing the opening in the Japanese corslet. (Garbutt 175).

KURI-JIRI. (Chestnut-shaped). A rounded end on the tang of a Japanese blade. (Gilbertson Blades 193).

KURIKATA. A projecting knob on the side of a Japanese scabbard to prevent it from slipping through the sash. It is frequently of horn or wood lacquered like the rest of the scabbard; but, more often, it is made of or covered with metal decorated like the other fittings. It is fastened to the scabbard by two strong dowels. It has a hole through it with ornamental thimbles called *o-shitodome* on

each side. A cord, the *sageo*, is passed through them and is used either to fasten the scabbard to the belt, or to tie back the flowing sleeves when fighting. The kurikata is usually quite simple in shape, but sometimes varies so much from the usual form that it would hardly be recognized for what it is if seen away from the scabbard. Fig. 502.

The kurikata also serves as a guard for the opening in the scabbard for the kogai, as the uragawara does for the kozuka.

KURISAGE-NO-O. The cords for fastening a Japanese breastplate around the body. (Garbutt 142).

KURI-YA. A kind of arrow made of a peculiar species of bamboo from Mount Kayasan. It has a wooden head and is fletched with duck's feathers. It was used for shooting at a mark at distances of over one hundred yards. (Gilbertson, Archery 122).

KURO-BOSHI. The bull's-eye of a target, Japan. It is always black.

KURO TACHI. A tachi with mountings of black shakudo, or lacquered material, with gilt menuki

FIGURE 504. *Kusari Kabuto. Steel plates connected by mail of three or four long links connected to a round one; neck guard of international mail.*

bearing the crest of the owner. Such tachi were carried by young retainers following the nobles of the

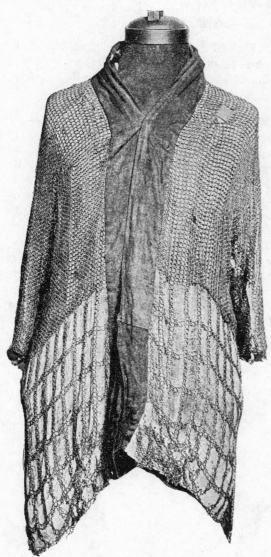

FIGURE 505. *Kusari Katabira. Fine mail, 17th century. The small plate on the left shoulder is inscribed: (Made by) Kojima Yamashiro-no-Kami (for) Hata Iyeshige (this mail is) best under heaven.*

first four ranks during the Ashikaga period. (Joly, Hawkshaw xiv).

KUR-RUK, GUR-REEK, MOOR-OONA, MURRI-WUN, MEERGA, WOMERAH. Various names given by the natives of Victoria to a special type of spear thrower. The last name is the one generally used by the white people of Australia

for *all* spear throwers. This thrower has a straight, round handle, the middle of which is the widest part and is semi-circular in section. It narrows towards the ends. The width of the main part varies greatly in different specimens, some being very little wider in the middle than at the ends, while others are five times as wide. The broad part is usually carved with figures and patterns in incised lines. (Brough Smyth I, 309). See Spear Thrower. Fig. 744.

KURTANI. A coat of mail, India. (Wallace Orient, Egerton 591T).

KURTU. A stone knife, Binbinga tribe, Central Australia. See Kira.

KURUPATU. A boomerang, Tijingilli tribe, Central Australia.

KURURI. A flail, Japan.

KUSARI. Mail, Japan, literally a chain. When used with another word it usually means that the object is made of mail. Many varieties of mail were made in Japan; for these see Mail.

KUSARI GAMA, KUSARI FUNDO. A slung shot, Japan. There are two varieties. The first consists of two weights connected by a chain. It was used to strike with, and also as a guard against a sword cut, a weight being held in each hand. The second has but one weight and is much longer; it was often attached to a kama yari. Either the hook or the weight was thrown from a wall at besiegers

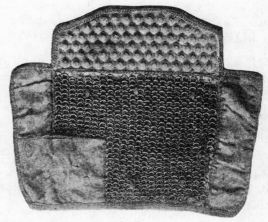

FIGURE 506. *Kusari Kiahan. Very heavy mail of the international type on brocade. The knee cop is of brigandine.*

and retrieved by the chain. It is also said to have been used by women. Fig. 503.

KUSARI GOTE. Kote made of mail. (Garbutt 177). See Kote.

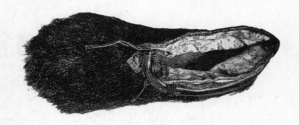

FIGURE 507. *Kutsu. Shoes with lacquered leather soles and bearskin uppers. Brocade lining projecting above the uppers.*

KUSARI KABUTO, TATAMI KABUTO. Japanese helmets made of small plates connected by mail and sewed on padded cloth. Such helmets were carried when traveling, and were worn by the lower class of retainers. (Conder 279). Fig. 504.

Properly "kusari kabuto" is a hood of mail, and "tatami kabuto" is a folding helmet, and not made of mail. See Tatami Kabuto.

KUSARI KATABIRA. An under garment of fine mail, Japan. It was worn under the ordinary clothes like the "secret" of Europe. Fig. 505.

KUSARI-KIAHAN. Mail leggings, Japan. (Garbutt 177). Fig. 506.

KUSARI SODE. Sode made of an oblong piece of leather, or padded cloth, covered with mail and having a narrow plate (kamuri-ita) at the top to stiffen it. (Conder 272).

KUSARI TACHI. A tachi hung from the belt by chains. (Gilbertson Dec. 95).

KUSARI TOJI. A variety of mail body armor, Japan. (Garbutt 142).

KUSARI WAKIBIKI. Japanese armpit protectors made of mail. (Garbutt 142).

KUSARI-ZUKIN. Japan, a mail cap. It was fastened under the chin by a cord and there was a hole in the top to allow the passage of the motodori (pigtail). (Garbutt 177).

KUSAZURI, KUZADZURI. The Japanese taces. They are made of overlapping strips of metal laced together by a continuation of the cords by which they are hung from the corslet. In the older armor the taces of the front and back plates were each made up of one set, widening considerably towards the bottom and slit up part way in the middle to facilitate movement. The taces of the side plates were entirely separate and overlapped the front and back ones slightly. In the later armor the taces were made narrower and there were a greater number, sometimes as many as eight or nine. (Conder 267).

The later kusazuri were more convenient for walking or riding, but did not give as much protection as the earlier form. The hai-date was not worn until the kusazuri was divided into more than four parts.

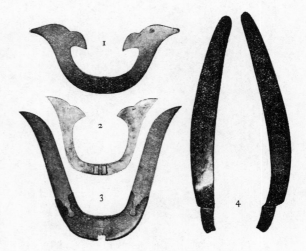

FIGURE 508. *Kuwagata. 1. A pair in one piece, whalebone gilded. A mon in relief on the front. 2. Silver, 9.25 inches across the points. It shows the double socket to go over the hooks on the helmet. 3. Gilded whalebone. It is reinforced in the middle by an extra piece of black whalebone, 13.75 inches across the points. 4. Unusual form, long narrow strips of gilded whalebone. Length 19.25 inches.*

KUSHI-GATA. The top plate of a sode (Conder 269).

KUSUNE. A special kind of Japanese bowstring softer than the ordinary sort. (Garbutt 153).

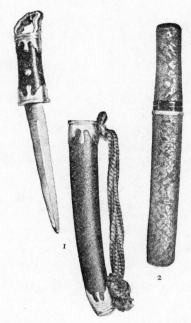

FIGURE 509. *Kwaiken. 1. Double-edged blade 5 inches long. Scabbard of nashiji lacquer; all mounts of plain silver. 2. Single-edged blade 5 inches long. Signed Michi Yoshi. Scabbard covered with gold brocade; mounts of black horn.*

KUSUNGOBU. (Nine sun, five bu, nine and a half Japanese inches, equal to 10.45 inches English measure). The aikuchi was sometimes called "kusungobu" because, at one time, its blade was of this length.

KUTAH, KUTAR. See Katar.

KUTSU. The shoes worn with Japanese armor. The soles were of stiff leather and the uppers of bearskin lined with brocade. (Conder 276). Fig. 507.

KUTSUMAKI. The wrappings of an arrow next the head, Japan. They were to prevent the pressure of the tang from splitting the shaft.

KUTSUWA. A bridle bit, Japan.

KUTSUWAZURA. Reins, Japan.

KUTTI. See Bhuj.

KUWAGATA. The horn-like pieces that project above the front of a Japanese helmet on each side of the crest. When the crest is not worn on the front the kuwagata are often made in one piece. They are said to symbolize the leaves of the water plant *sagittarius*. About the beginning of the 16th century they were sometimes of enormous size. Fig. 508.

KUYAN, TORIL, TURAL, WAR-PA. A spear with a long butt, short shaft and a long wooden head with quartz chips set in each side. The small flakes of quartz are set in grooves in the sides of the head and fastened with gum cement. Their axes are not at right angles to that of the spear but project forward, and they become smaller towards the point. (Roth, Aust. Mus. VII, 193).

KWAIKEN, KWAITO. A very old style of Japanese dagger carried by women and used for committing ceremonial suicide by cutting the veins of the left side of the neck. It has a slightly curved single, or double-edged blade. The scabbards do not have the fittings usually found on those carried by men. Fig. 509.

FIGURE 510. *Kwanyu. 1. Kozuka with Kwanyu in front and his attendant standing behind carrying his spear; in relief an inlay of gold, silver and copper on shakudo. 2. His spear, sei-ryo-ken, in relief of copper, gold and colored enamels on shakudo.*

KWANYU. A celebrated Chinese general of the 2nd century, deified in 1594 as the god of war. He is frequently used as a decoration on Japanese sword fittings, and is represented with a large spear (*sei-ryo ken*) generally carried by an attendant. Fig. 510.

KWAO. (Stamped flower). A kakihan or written seal. Kakihan were often used as signatures by artists in Japan. Sometimes they follow the written name.

KWA-YAKU. Gunpowder, Japan.

KYLIE. The West Australian boomerang. It is very thin and light. The length is from twenty to twenty-three inches, width from one and three-quarters to two inches, and the thickness about three-tenths of an inch. It weighs from four to five ounces. While the general curve is similar to that of the boomerang from further east, one end has a slight reverse curve. It has a slight twist and can be thrown further than the eastern type. It is never carved or colored. (Brough Smyth I, 335).

The Catalogue of the Victoria Museum says that the kylie is a returning boomerang from West Australia, which agrees with the above description.

KYU. A bow, Japan.

KYUBI NO ITA. A variety of Hata-Wo-No-Ita.

KYU-DO. Japan. The art and practice of archery.

KYUJUTSU. Archery, Japan.

KYUSEN. A bow and arrows, Japan.

L

LAANGE. A spear with a four-sided head and hollow shaft. It was used by both horse and foot soldiers at the siege of Seringapatam. (Egerton, p. 123).

A spear with a knife-like head or one of diamond section. (Wallace Orient.).

LABARUM. A Roman standard of silk much like the vexillum. The head of the reigning Emperor was represented upon it. (Macgeorge 24).

LACQUER. Lacquer was used in Japan as early as the 4th century, but does not appear to have been in general use until the 7th. The varnish is made from the sap of the *Rhus Vernicifera*. The principal kinds are: *hira makiye*, or flat gold; *taki-makiye*, or raised gold; *togi-dashi*, or black and gold; *ro-iro*, pure black; *shu-nuri*, red lacquer; and *nashiji*, or lacquer sprinkled with gold in imitation of the skin of a pear. This last is often called aventurine in Europe, from its resemblance to that variety of Venetian glass. (Bowes 273). *Guri* is alternate layers of red and black lacquer with a pattern cut in deep V grooves to show the two colors.

In Ceylon lacquer is made from the resinous exudations from a shrub called *Wael-Koeoppetya* (*Croton Lacciferum*). It is mixed with pigments and is formed into fine threads and films chiefly by the thumb-nail of the left hand, which is kept long for the purpose. It is applied by heat and polishing. It is used for the decoration of bows, spear shafts, etc. (Tennent I, 491).

LADING. Dyak, a knife; the name is generally qualified to express the variety by a suffix, as— L-tjara, Arab art—L.djawa, Javan art, etc. (Arc. f. Eth. III, 242).

LADING BELAJOENG LAMAH. A sabre with a short, heavy blade widening towards the point, a pistol hilt and no guard, Borneo. (Arc. f. Eth. V, 232).

LADJAU. A blowpipe dart with a brass point, Borneo. (Arc. f. Eth. IV, 279).

LAINGEL. See Leonile.

LAKAR KOTI. Wooden or stockaded forts, India. (Egerton, p. 33).

LALAYU. See Daludag.

LALL-I-WALL. A narrow, curved sword with a very broad back, Mysore. (Egerton, p. 123).

LAMANG. See Klewang.

LAMBOYS. See Bases.

LAMBREQUIN. The mantling of a helmet in the 15th century. It had scalloped edges and terminated in two tails. It was generally of the colors of the armorial bearings, and was sometimes embroidered with the badge of the family. (Planche 335).

LAMES. Strips of metal which overlapped to form portions of the armor, such as shoulder cops, solerets or gauntlets. (ffoulkes 50).

LANCE. The horseman's spear. In the middle ages the lance consisted of four parts—the truncheon, shaft or staff—the head—the vamplate—and the grate or grapper. In the earlier war lance the shaft was cylindrical for almost the entire length, and they were leaf-shaped, fig. 512. For jousting, lance heads were blunted but this not being sufficient to prevent injury, heads with three blunt points were adopted by the end of the 13th century. These were called coronals, cornels or crownackles. They were

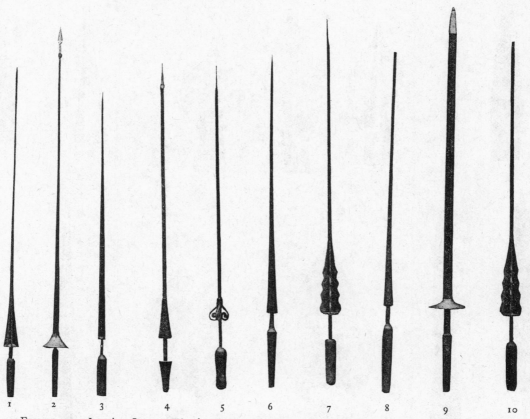

FIGURE 511. *Jousting Lances. The first is French, the others are German. 1, 2, 3, 4 and 9 are of the 16th century. 6, 7, 8 and 10 are of the 17th. 5 is of the 18th century. Metropolitan Museum.*

about two inches in diameter. In the early 15th century it had two cone-shaped swellings, one on each side of the grip. Back of the grip it was enlarged again and was cylindrical or conical, to the butt. Some tilting lances were of enormous size and weight, as much as five inches in diameter, others were much lighter and ribbed to give stiffness without excessive weight. At first the shafts were made of ash; in the latter part of the 15th century cypress was also used; still later aspen, pine and sycamore were employed. The length was from ten to fourteen feet, usually about thirteen. Fig. 511.

The heads of the lances were called sockets, from their resemblance to plowshares; but, as a rule,

very satisfactory for the purpose as they gave the maximum of bite with the least liability of penetration. Fig. 242.

The vamplate was the guard for the hand and was adopted early in the 14th century. It was usually conical and from five to twelve inches in diameter; but for jousting much larger and more elaborately shaped ones were sometimes used. In the 15th century the war vamplate was still nearly flat and that for jousting more conical. The vamplate was fastened to the shaft immediately in front of the grip or hanste. Fig. 833.

The grate or grapper, later called the burr, was a heavy ring of metal fastened to the shaft just behind the hanste. It was adopted for jousting about 1325 to distribute the shock over the entire body by bearing against the lance rest which was lined with felt. It continued in this form until the end of the

light cylindrical shafts with fairly broad, flat heads. In India and Persia the shafts were usually of wood but sometimes of bamboo. The heads were small and the weight of the lance was counterbalanced

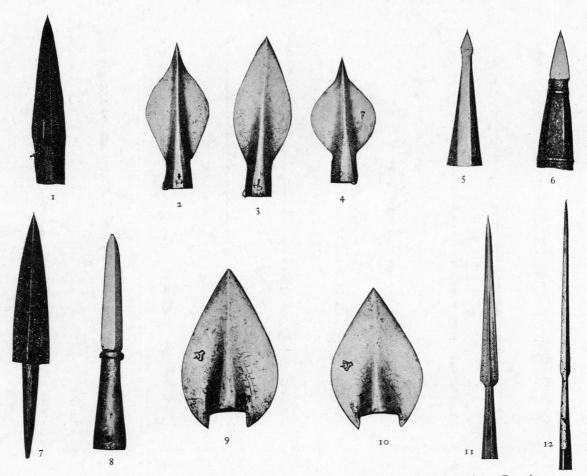

FIGURE 512. *Lance Heads. 1. English, 15th century or earlier. 2, 3, 4. Spanish, 15th. 5. French, 15th. 6. Italian, 16th. 7. French, 16th. 8. German, 17th. 9, 10. Spanish, 15th. 11. Italian, 15th. 12. Probably Hispano-Arab, 15th. Metropolitan Museum. Not to scale.*

century, by which time the lance rest had become a regular part of the war harness. It then became wider and had blunt spikes on the back which were forced into the lining of wood or lead in the rest. See Lance Rest.

The lances were often fancifully painted with the colors of their owners. For a full account see Laking Armour III, 81.

In the East the lances have always been much lighter than in Europe and much shorter, rarely exceeding ten feet in length. In Turkey they had

by an ornamental ball and spike on the butt. This spike was thrust into the ground when in camp. This not only kept the lance upright, but prevented it from getting bent as it would if allowed to lean against any solid object. Some of the parade lances were made of ivory cylinders strung on a steel rod, and were very decorative. Some lances were made entirely of steel, a number of small pieces being locked together to make a light, stiff, strong shaft. Fig. 513.

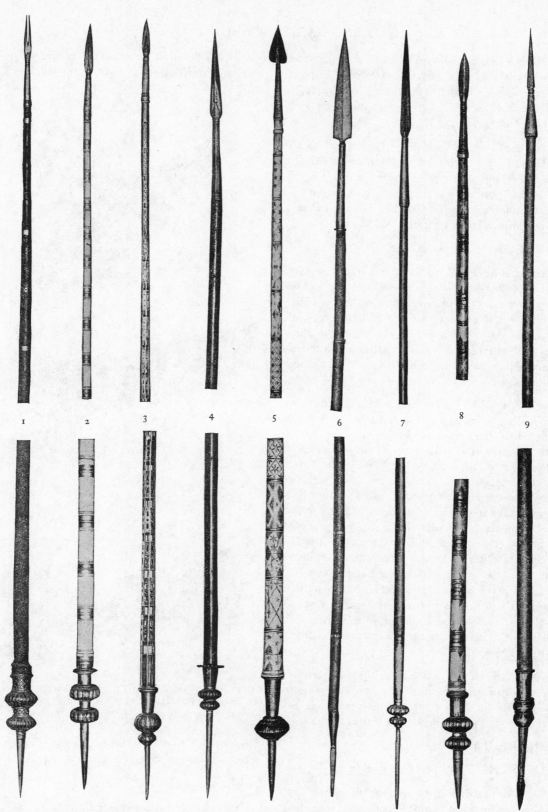

FIGURE 513. *Oriental Lances.* 1. *Bamboo shaft with the lower part covered with red and gold brocade and the upper banded with silver. Very small forked head inlaid with gold. Elaborate butt inlaid with gold. Length 10 feet 4 inches.* 2. *Parade lance. Shaft of short ivory cylinders joined by gilded metal bands and strung on a steel rod. Steel head and gilded butt. Length 10 feet 6.5 inches.* 3. *Mahratta. All steel. The shaft is hexagonal and built up of six strips and a large number of small pierced plates. Length 8 feet 7.75 inches.* 4. *Wooden shaft lacquered red. Head inlaid with gold and the butt with silver.* 5. *Parade lance. Shaft of pieces of ivory with incised patterns in colors, the whole strung on a steel rod. Head and butt chased and inlaid with silver.* 6. *Turkish, 17th century. Cylindrical shaft covered with shark skin, with narrow silver bands. Plain butt, head with inscriptions. Length 7 feet 11 inches.* 7. *Modern trooper's lance. Bamboo shaft, triangular grooved head, simple steel butt. Length 6 feet 10 inches.* 8. *Parade lance. Ivory similar to the others but with wider metal bands joining the sections. Leaf-shaped head issuing from an animal's mouth, gilded butt.* 9. *Bamboo shaft painted with figures and medallions in gold, silver and colors. Plain steel head and butt. Length 12 feet 3.5 inches.*

LANCE-AGUE, LANCEGAYE. A light lance, occasionally used as a dart. It was carried in place of the war lance in the 14th century; the latter, at that time, was about fourteen feet long and very heavy. (Hewitt II, 242).

LANCE FOURNIE. A man-at-arms and his attendants. In the 14th century the number of men included in this term varied from three to ten; in the 15th the number was reduced to four, and in the 16th increased to six, and then disappeared as a military unit. (Hewitt II, 26, III, 584).

LANCEGAYE. See Lance Ague.

LANCEPESATA. Originally a man-at-arms who, having broken his lance on the enemy and lost his horse, was entertained as a volunteer assistant by a captain of foot, receiving the pay of a trooper, until he could remount himself. From being the companion of a captain he was soon degraded to the assistant of a corporal, and did the duty of that officer on the pay of a private. (Grose I, 261).

LANCE REST, LANCE ARREST. The lance rest first appeared as a simple hook fastened to the right side of the breastplate in the early part of the 14th century. It did not support the lance, as its name indicates, but acted to distribute the shock over the entire breastplate. At first it was lined with felt to cushion the blow that was transmitted to it by a ring fastened to the shaft of the lance. Later it was lined with wood, or lead, and the ring was provided with projecting points which were driven into the lining. Still later it became much more elaborate and did support the lance. In the latter part of the 16th century it had an extra piece, the queue, that projected a foot or more from the back with a hook on the end to hold down the butt of the lance, thus relieving the user from the necessity of balancing it. Figs. 48, 514.

LANCERS. In the first half of the 16th century the men-at-arms were formed into regiments called lancers. At the present time it merely means any cavalry armed with lances. (Hewitt III, 584).

LANDEP. The cutting edge of a kris, Java.

LANDSKNECHT. See Lansquinet.

LANGA. The darts for the Dyak blowpipe. They are light splinters of bamboo about ten inches long with pith cones on the butts to fit the bore of the

blowpipe. The heads are usually simple straight points, and are covered with poison, ipoh. They are

FIGURE 514. *Lance Rests. 1. German, 1530. 2. German, 1554. From the harness of Philip II, by Wilhelm of Worms. 3. German, 1560. Metropolitan Museum.*

often notched just below the head so as to break off in the wound and be difficult to extract. Fig. 515.

LANGEL. See Leonile.

LANGKAP. A strong bow, Bali. (Arc. f. Eth. IV, 280).

LANGUE DE BOEUF, OX TONGUE. A pole arm of the 16th century with a broad, straight, double-edged blade. Fig. 516.

LANIERS. Leather straps for fastening together the different parts of the armor, 14th century and later. (Planche 338).

That they frequently did wear armor is indicated by the fact that a particular type of armor worn at that time is commonly called "Lansquinet's armor."

LANTAKA. The Malay cannon. They are brass guns from twenty inches to seven feet long, with a

FIGURE 515. *Langa. 1, 2. North Borneo. Black, solid cones on the butts. Some with barbed heads. 3, 4. Dutch Borneo. Instruments for punching holes in the pith cones, and for holding them while they are being cut to shape. 5. Dutch Borneo. Some of the cones are hollow and some solid. 6. A dart in a bamboo tube that fits in the quiver. 7. Darts with barbed heads. 8. Dutch Borneo. The cones are hollow. Length 10.625 inches. 9. Sakai darts, solid cones.*

LANISTA. The Roman maître d'armes, who conducted schools of military exercises. (Burton Sword 249).

LANKH. War shells, conch shells used as trumpets by the Rajputs. (Tod I, 492). Fig. 517.

LANNER. A hawk, the female of *falco lanarius.*

LANNERET. A hawk, the male of *falco lanarius.*

LANSQUINET, LANDSKNECHT. German mercenaries of the first half of the 16th century. As a rule they did not wear armor; their weapons were the halbard, pike and sword. (Hewitt III, 592, 607, 656).

swivel and pin for mounting attached to the trunnions. There is a tube at the breech by which to train the gun. Sometimes they are double, that is, two guns cast side by side in one piece. Very small ones are often found; these are not toys though only a few inches long. They are intended for saluting. Salutes are obligatory on many occasions and one fired from one of these miniature guns is as effective, and much more economical of powder. Figs. 518, 519.

These guns are very popular with all of the Malayans and are used both ashore and afloat. In Borneo they are one of the principal forms of wealth, and are even used as currency, fines usually being levied of a certain number, or weight, of guns. They are generally decorated, the patterns often showing Chinese or Spanish influence.

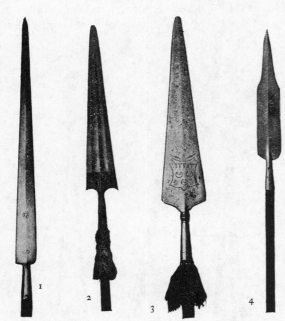

FIGURE 516. *Langues de Boeufs. 1. Italian, late 15th century. 2. Italian, 1510. 3. Dutch, 1510. Arms of Duivenoorde. 4. French, late 18th century. Metropolitan Museum. Not to scale.*

LAQUEATORS. Roman gladiators who used the lasso. (Burton Sword 210).

LARKAN. A long-handled chopper from Madura. The blade is usually narrow, single-edged and bends forward. The handle is quite long and decorated. (Arc. f. Eth. XVI, 52, 247).

FIGURE 517. *Lankh. Rajput shell trumpet, ivory mouthpiece fastened on with black gum. Length 9 inches.*

LARNA-PE. Long, heavy fighting spears with sting ray spine heads. The name means "sting ray spine." They are common in Northern Queensland. (Roth, Aust. Mus. VII, 192).

LARWA. See Yirmba.

LASAG. A shield, general name, Subanun of Mindanao. A round shield is called ta-ming. (Christie 111).

LATCH. The English name for the crossbow in the 16th century. (Planche 338).

LATCHEN BLADE. The workmen's name for

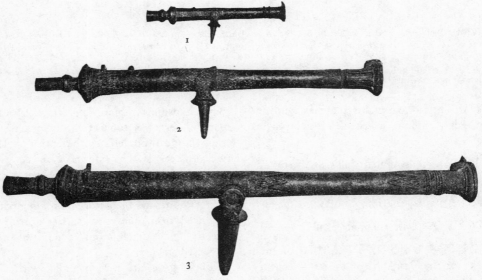

FIGURE 518. *Lantakas. 1. Mindanao, saluting gun. Length 10.5 inches. 2. North Borneo. Length 25.75 inches. 3. North Borneo. Length 34.5 inches. Bore 1.125 inches.*

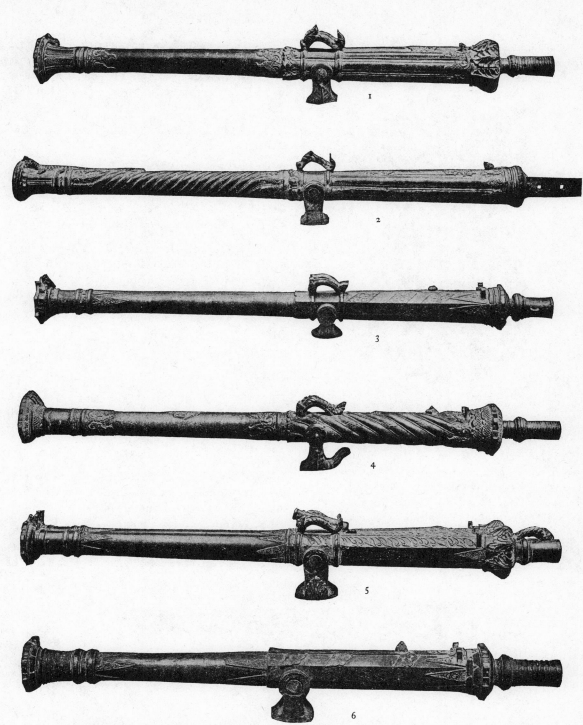

FIGURE 519. *Lantakas. Bronze guns from five to seven feet long. No. 5 is double, two guns cast in one piece, and has a small saluting gun mounted between the dolphins. Collection of Mr. Theodore Offerman. Not to scale.*

a sword blade of nearly square lozenge section. (Burton Sword 135).

FIGURE 520. *Lave. Rough wood shield 2 feet 10 inches long. The middle is covered with neatly woven cane and the ends are decorated in black. The fringe is of colored feathers. It has a single U-shaped handle of cane.*

LAVE. Shields, New Guinea. They are usually of wood, but sometimes of basket work. The most common shape is with straight sides and rounded ends, one being considerably wider than the other. Near Port Moresby the shields are shaped like a figure 8, and the middle is covered with very neatly woven cane. (Brown, Mel. & Pol. 163). Fig. 520.

LAVONG. A Kyan, Borneo, war cap. It is round and covered with hair of various colors, and has two eyes to represent a face. The long tail feathers of the hornbill are stuck in the top. (Ling Roth II, 128).

LCHAKDA. An iron ramrod, Tibet. (Ramsay-Western).

LCHAKS-I-KHORLO. A quoit, Tibet. (Ramsay-Western).

LCHAKS-I-TSCHERMANG, LCHAKS-I-ZEYMA. A spur, Tibet. (Ramsay-Western).

LEASH. A leather strap fastened to a hawk's jesses by which she is secured when not flying. In Japan it is made of silk cord, see He O. Fig. 366.

A strap to restrain a hound until it is "slipped" at game.

LEG SHIELD. See Knee Shield.

LEILIRA. A stone knife, Central Australia. See Kira.

LELAH, LELAS. The Malay lantaka. A brass swivel gun carrying a ball of from half a pound to three pounds. (Kepple II, 195).

LEMBING. A spear, Malay.

LENI CROICH. (Yellow shirt). Scotch Armor, a padded or quilted garment made of twenty-four ells of yellow cloth. (Drummond 8).

LEONILE, BENDI, LIANGEL, LANGEL, LANGEEL. A club used by the natives of Victoria. It is a favorite for single combat because of

FIGURE 521. *Leonile. Peabody Museum, Salem.*

the ease with which the point can be turned in any direction at the moment of striking, making it dif-

the purpose of letting the officer in charge of the exercises know when the men stopped. Fig. 522.

FIGURE 522. *Lezam. Bow made of three strips of whalebone 1.125 x 1.3125 inches, bolted together. Length 4 feet 8 inches. String a heavy chain.*

ficult to avoid. It is made of any hard, tough wood, preferably a sapling of which a part of the root forms the head. (Brough Smyth I, 302). Fig. 521.

LEOWEL. A boomerang-like weapon of the Malga. (Burton Sword 37).

LEPA. A bow, in Neman, a Nepalese dialect. (Kirkpatrick 240).

LEZAM. A stiff bow of bamboo, or whalebone, bent by a heavy chain on which a number of small plates of iron are loosely fastened to increase the weight and to make a jingling noise. It was used by the native troops in India as a training for drawing the bow. The jingles are said to have been for

LICE. The space between the exterior defense and the main body of a fortress. (Violet le Duc, Hist.

FIGURE 523. *Lil-Lil. Brown wood carved on both sides, length 25.125 inches.*

364). It was often used as a tilt yard and our name lists is derived from it.

LIDAH AYAM LIPET. A kind of Malay knife.

FIGURE 524. *Linstocks. 1. Italian, 1625. 2. French, 17th century. 3. Swiss, 1590. 4. Italian, 1650. 5. Saxon, 16th century. 6. 17th century. 7. Italian, after 1600. 8. Italian, 1590. 9. Italian, 1600. 10. German, 16th–17th century. Metropolitan Museum. Not to scale.*

LIGHT DRAGOONS. The light dragoons of the beginning of the 19th century wore helmets with bearskin crests, while the heavy dragoons wore cocked hats with feathers. (Hewitt III, 721). This is almost certainly a misprint and the descriptions should be reversed.

with incised lines representing a lagoon. (Brough Smyth I, 314). Fig. 523.

LIMAK. The curved stock of the Afgan jezail. (Egerton, p. 140). Fig. 406.

LIME POTS. Earthen pots filled with quicklime

FIGURE 525. *Lobster-Tail Helmets.* 1. *Hungarian, 17th century.* 2. *Polish, 17th century. Guard of Augustus the Strong.* 3. *French, end of the 17th century.* 4. *Hungarian, 17th century. Metropolitan Museum. Not to scale.*

LI-LIL, LIL-LIL, BUNJ-JUL, BOL-LAIR. A fighting club used by a few of the tribes of Victoria. It looks like a boomerang with one end widened out on the concave side; it is also curved in two waves in the opposite direction. The edges of the wide end are sharp, and it is thickest in the middle of this end. It was used mainly for striking, but was also thrown. The measurements of a typical one are—length 27 inches, width of blade 5.5 inches, width of handle 2 inches, greatest thickness 0.5 inch, weight 14 ounces. The enlarged part is carved

to be thrown in the faces of attacking parties. (Hewitt II, 329).

LINEA PERFETTA E LINEA RETTA. Keeping the line with the sword's point always directly menacing the adversary. (Castle 133).

LINEAS INFINITAS. Two parallel lines on which two antagonists stood and along which they could move indefinitely without coming in reach of each other. It was a term of the early, and very artificial, Spanish system of fencing. (Castle 9).

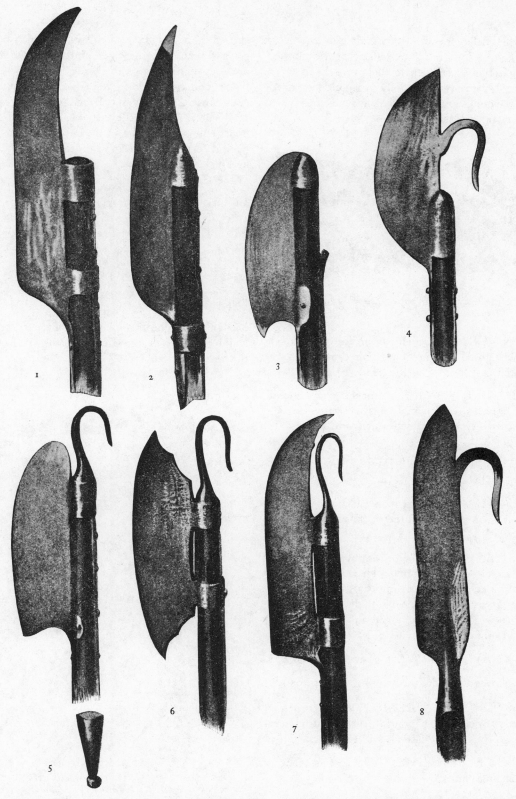

FIGURE 526. *Lochaber Axes.* 1. *Old City Guard, Edinburgh. It shows the transition from the glaive to the Lochaber axe.* 5. *From the National Museum of Antiques, Edinburgh.* 7. *Axe of the Old City Guard, Edinburgh. From Drummond, Ancient Scottish Weapons.*

LINES. In fencing, an attack is described as being in a high or low, inside or outside line, according to its position in relation to the sword hand when on guard, in front of the body in a position approximately equidistant from all points which have to be protected. (Castle 9).

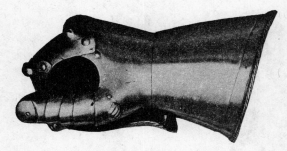

FIGURE 527. *Locking Gauntlet, German, 16th century. Metropolitan Museum.*

LINSTOCK. A pike with branches on each side to hold lighted matches for firing cannon. It was invented in 1550. (Planche 341). Fig. 524.

LIONOIS, LYONORS. A machine for defending a breach invented in Lyons. It was a carriage with curiously curved blades in front. (Grose II, plate p. 5).

LI-PUN, PA-NA. An arrow, Subanun of Mindanao. (Christie 108).

LISAN. An ancient Egyptian club with a curved end; it is of uniform diameter throughout. (Burton Sword 32).

LIVERY. A coat or hood given by a sovereign or noble to one of his servants, soldiers or retainers. It was of his colors and sometimes carried his badge or collar. It served as a means of distinguishing the party to which a man belonged and was the beginning of uniforms. (Planche 342).

LLAVNAWR. The Welch glaive. (Skelton 47).

LO. A round shield, Burma. (Egerton, p. 94).

LOBSTER-TAIL HELMET. An open helmet of the 17th century having a neck guard of overlapping plates like a lobster's tail. Fig. 525.

LOBSTER-TAIL TASSETS. Tassets made of overlapping plates.

LOCHABER AXE. "The blade long and thin, carried on a shaft by two collars, of which the upper is forged with the blade and the lower riveted on; the upper end of the blade waved while the lower is merely curved; the edge curved with the ends considerably beyond the length of the back of the blade. A stout recurved hook is inserted in the upper end of the shaft and the butt is protected by a conical ferule, with a knob on the end." (Campbell 98). It was a favorite weapon with the Scotch in the 16th century. Fig. 526.

LOCHNER, CONRAD. Nuremberg, 1510-1567. He was for a time court armorer of Maximilian II. He frequently used tritons and sea-monsters in his decorations. (ffoulkes 136).

LOCK. The mechanism by which a gun or pistol is fired. See Matchlock, Wheel Lock, Flintlock and Detonator.

LOCKET. The band on a scabbard carrying a ring by which it is suspended, also the band around the top of the scabbard.

FIGURE 528. *Lohar, Bannochie tribe. All steel but the handle which is covered with brass. The handle and back of the blade are inlaid with silver. Total length 16 inches.*

LOCKING GAUNTLET. A gauntlet of the 16th century with extra long fingers so that they could be locked to the wrist, fastening the sword or mace in the hand so that the user could not be disarmed. It was sometimes called the forbidden gauntlet because, at one time, its use was not allowed in tournaments. Fig. 527.

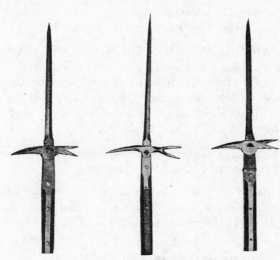

FIGURE 529. *Lucerne Hammers. Swiss, about 1520. Metropolitan Museum. Not to scale.*

LOCKING PINS. Revolving pins with eccentric heads, used to fasten together parts of armor.

LODGO. A stone knife, Central Australia. See Kira.

LOHANGI, LOHANGI KATTI. A long bamboo shaft bound with iron and with an iron mace head. Aboriginal tribes of Central India. (Egerton 8, 9; Sinclair I. A. 128).

LOHAR. A small pick used in place of a sword by the Banochie, a Khyber tribe. Each man makes his own and decorates the handle with inlays of silver and brass. Each individual has his own patterns which differ from those used by others, though all are similar. Fig. 528.

LOK FAI. A fireball thrown from a tower to fire a town, Burma. (Egerton, p. 94).

LOMBU LOMBU. A Battak shield made of a heavy rectangular piece of buffalo hide. (Arc. f. Eth. VI, 121).

LONG BOW. The weapon with which the English won their victories at Senlis, Crecy and Agincourt. It was a self bow as long as the user and was preferably made of yew, or when that wood was scarce, of witch-hazel. The tips were made of horn, and the string of hemp or silk. None are in existence and we have no definite information about its shape or proportions. See Bow.

Wonderful tales are told of its power and accuracy. It was constantly used by all classes in England and there were many laws relating to its manufacture, prices and uses. See Grose I, 134, and II, 272. It was called the "long" bow to distinguish it from the arbalest, the bow of which was much shorter.

LORICA CATENATA. Roman mail which was similar to that made and worn at other times and places.

LUCERNE HAMMER. A species of pole axe of the 15th century with a hammer head of four points opposite a single point, and having a long, straight spike on the end. (Dean Europ. 62). Fig. 529.

LU KIO. (Stag horns). An abattis, China. (Laufer 233).

LUMO. A bow in San Ch'uan Chinese. (Rockhill).

LUNGE. A thrust in fencing in which the reach is increased by stepping forward with the leading foot at the same time that the sword is extended. It began in a very imperfect way in the 16th century, but did not reach its full development until the 18th.

LUNT CORD. The match with which a cannon was fired. (Hoyt 430).

LUNT WORK. A Scotch variety of matchlock.

LUNT WORK HAGBUT. A matchlock gun, Scotland. (Drummond 13).

LURE. A rough imitation of some bird, or beast, to which a hawk's food is fastened and given her to eat from; it thus becomes a bait to which the hawk comes. It is fastened to a strong cord or strap about a yard long, sometimes by a swivel. The food should be fastened to the lure so securely that the hawk cannot pull it off, but must eat it where it is. The lure is weighted so that the hawk cannot carry it off. It is not only used in training, but is always carried in the field, but out of sight, and is only exhibited when it is desired to recall the hawk.

The Japanese carry the lure in a basket made of split bamboo. One end is conical and the other a frustrum of a cone with a larger end joined to the base of the conical part, and the other open.

LU-YU. See Yirmba.

FIGURE 530. *Mabishaku. 1. The bowl is a cocoanut shell and it and the handle are decorated with a gold lacquer vine. Length 26 inches. 2. Very small dipper lacquered black. 3. Wooden dipper lacquered black with a gold mon. Length 23.75 inches.*

M

MA. An arrow, Omaha. The shafts were about two feet long, and the feathers employed are those of the eagle, buzzard, wild turkey, great owl and goose; sometimes hawk's and crow's feathers were used. The heads were originally of flint, later of iron. The heads of the hunting arrows were without barbs and were firmly fastened to the shafts by cement and lashings of sinew. The war arrows had barbed heads loosely attached to the shafts so that they would remain in the wound when the arrow was withdrawn. The shafts were generally made of *masaqtihi*, or "real arrow wood" (*Viburnum*); sometimes of chokeberry; and occasionally of ash or hickory. The Ponka used *ja-qude-hi*, "gray wood" (juneberry) which does not grow in the Omaha country. (Dorsey 288).

MABI-SASHI. The brim of a Japanese helmet.

MABISHAKU. A long-handled dipper used by the early Japanese to give water to their horses. They are all very small for the purpose. Fig. 530.

MABOBO, WAKIDI, MAPUPU. A club used by the Iwadji and some other tribes near Port Essington, Australia. It is nearly straight, four feet long, and has a rounded point and square-ended handle. It is decorated in red and white. (Spencer, North. Ter. 367, Vic. Mus. 26).

MABUSASHI. An eyeshade on a Japanese helmet. (Garbutt 168). Compare Mabisashi.

MACANA. A South American club of rectangular section, largest at one end and smallest near the middle. It is sometimes used as a missile. (Wood

FIGURE 531. *Macana. All British Guiana. These show about the range of sizes; the longest is 22.25 inches. Museum of the American Indian, Heye Foundation.*

1212). It frequently has the handle covered with woven cane, and often has a stone blade set in one end. Fig. 531.

"A Brazilian club. In some cases it is paddle-shaped with sharp edges, in others it is rounded." (Burton Sword 42).

also common. Some of the Indian maces are simply curved bars (see Sonta). They often have guarded hilts like khanda. The Japanese rarely used maces; the few I have seen were straight iron bars with spherical heads. Many Chinese maces were straight iron bars with sword-like hilts; others have ball-

FIGURE 532. *European Maces. 1. Italian(?), 15th century. 2. Venetian, 16th century. 3. Italian (French?), 16th century. 4. German, 16th century. 5. Italian, 16th century. 6. Venetian, 17th century. 7. Polish, 17th century. 8. German, late 16th century. 9. French(?), late 15th century. Metropolitan Museum.*

MACE, MASSUE, MAZULE, MAZZUELLE.

A club-like weapon made entirely of metal or with a metal head. It was one of the principal weapons used for hand-to-hand fighting in Europe as long as complete armor was worn, but mainly from the 11th to the 16th century. The commonest European forms were pear-shaped or had six or eight radiating flanges, and a short, straight handle. Fig. 532. It was commonly hung from the saddle.

Oriental maces varied much more in shape, although the European forms were used throughout the East. The typical Persian form was a bull's or devil's head which had openings at the nostrils and ears which gave a whistling sound when a blow was struck. Other Persian and Turkish maces have globular, or spindle-shaped heads. Flanged maces were

shaped heads. One Chinese form is quite characteristic. It has the "long life" character in quite high relief repeated six times around the head. It would not only smash a man's head but stamp it with the character meaning long life. Fig. 533.

MACHERA.

A Greek sword with a long, straight blade. (Burton Sword 224).

MACHICOULIS, MACHICOLATIONS.

Openings between the wall and parapet formed by building the latter out on corbels. Through these openings missiles, boiling water, melted lead and other objects were thrown on besiegers. (Hewitt I, 357).

Stone machicoulis were adopted in France to-wards the end of the 13th century to replace the

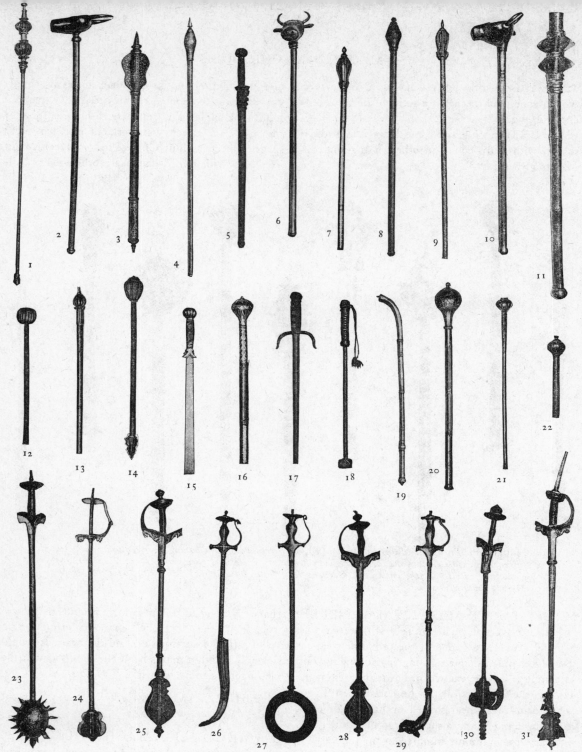

FIGURE 533. *Oriental Maces.* 1. Mahratta, XVIII. All steel; very slim shaft and two sets of flanges. Length 31.25 inches. 2. Persia, XVIII. Bull's head, steel engraved. 3. Persia, XVIII. Shishpar (six bladed). Black iron inlaid with engraved silver. The middle of the shaft is covered with leather. 4. Persia, XVII. All steel with spindle head. The whole inlaid with silver and set with turquoises. 5. China, XIX. Brass cast around a steel rod. Below the handle is a dragon's head. Length 23.5 inches. 6. Persia, XIX. Bull's head of steel inlaid with silver. 7. Persia, XVII-XVIII. All steel; six small, heavy blades. Length 24 inches. 8. Persia, XVII. All steel inlaid with silver. 9. Persia, XVII. All steel; small, rough head of six wings, inlaid with silver. 10. Persia, XVII. Steel inlaid with gold. Bull's head, heavy and finely worked, the shaft fluted in relief. 11. Northern India, XVI. Bamboo shaft with iron ends. Double set of steel wings held by iron bands. Length 31 inches. 12. China, XVIII. Melon-shaped brass head, iron handles. Length 16.25 inches. 13. Persia, XVII. Small and well finished head of 13 flanges, wood shaft. Length 20 inches. 14. China, XVIII. Iron shaft with a brass ornament at the butt and a brass head. 15. China, XVIII. Straight steel bar of rectangular section, ebony hilt with brass mountings. Length 20 inches. 16. Asiatic Turkey, XVIII. Ball head with a long socket and chape. All metal parts are chiseled in low relief and inlaid with silver. 17. China, XIX. Tapered octagonal brass rod with a curved guard. Hilt wound with red cord. 18. China, XVIII. All iron, head a cube and octahedron, handle wound with rattan. Length 20 inches. 19. India, XVIII. Sonta. Steel rod with a curved end and moulded rings, entirely silver gilt. Length 23 inches. 20. Persia, XVI. Pear-shaped head and paneled shaft decorated with a palmette pattern in relief overlaid with gold. Length 25 inches. 21. Persia, XVII. All steel; head a grooved ball, shaft engraved for about half its length. 22. Persia, XVI. Head a ball made up of separate strips welded together, socket for shaft. Length 10 inches. 23. Southern India, late XVIII. Spherical head with triangular spikes, guard and disk pommel. The whole inlaid with gold. Length 32.75 inches. 24. Rajput, XVII. All steel, winged head and guarded hilt. 25. Tanjore, XVII. Ten wings guarded hilt with monster's heads supporting the broad guard. Length 30 inches. 26. Mahratta. Guarded hilt and a single curved blade. The shaft is elaborately chased. Length 26 inches. 27. Guarded hilt and the head a quoit 6 inches in diameter. The shaft is chased in high relief. 28. Tanjore, XVII. Eight blades, shaft silvered, guarded hilt chased and gilded. 29. Tanjore, XVIII. Guarded steel hilt and shaft. Head a griffon's head of chiseled brass. 30. Malabar, XVII-XVIII. The head consists of seven blades of the ordinary shape and one axe, scalloped spike on the end. Length 28 inches. 31. Madras, XVIII. Two sets of eight flanges each (some of the upper set have been broken off), fluted shaft, guarded and spiked hilt. Length 31.5 inches.

wooden hourds previously used for the same purpose, as the latter were easily burned. In Syria the
Christians adopted machicoulis as early as the 13th
century. (Violet le Duc, Hist. 364).

MAGARI KANE. A ring carrying bells on the
hilt of an early kind of Japanese sword called *tama-maki no tachi*. (Joly, S. & S. 15).

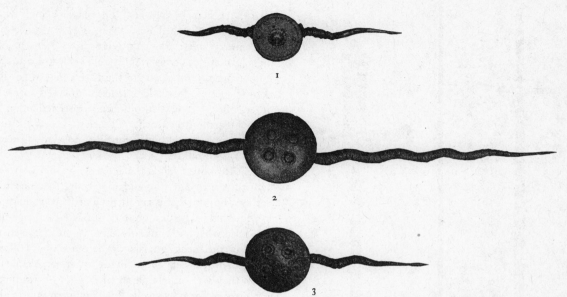

FIGURE 534. *Madu. 1. Steel shield 5.5 inches in diameter with a brass boss and a knife-like spike. Lapped horns with steel tips. 2. Steel shield 8.75 inches in diameter, chiseled border inlaid with gold. Very long horns placed end to end and separated by an ivory handle. Length 5 feet 2 inches. 3. Leather shield with brass bosses and ornaments. Lapped horns with steel tips.*

MA-CIQADE. Arrow polishers, Omaha. Two
pieces of sandstone with grooves in them. They were
placed around the arrow which was drawn backwards and forwards between them to smooth and
polish the shaft.

MADRIER. A strong plank to which the mouth
of a petard was fastened. (Grose I, 409). See Petard.

MADU, MARU, SINGAUTA. An Indian parrying and thrusting weapon consisting of a pair of
black buck horns fastened together with their points
in opposite directions. Usually the horns overlap,
but sometimes they are fastened to the opposite ends
of a short handle. In either case the hand is protected by a small circular shield of leather or iron.
The horns usually have steel points on the ends. It
was used by the Bhils and other wild tribes and was
a favorite with Hindu religious beggars. It was also
used by swordsmen for guarding, being held in the
left hand. (Egerton 434, 436, 630, 694; Sinclair
I. A. II, 216). Fig. 534.

MAGARI YARI. A Japanese trident. The side
blades project at right angles to the center one and
only turn forward for a short distance close to the
points. (B. M. Hdbk. 54). Fig. 535.

MAGARIYU. The point of the Australian spear
called *kunjolio* by the Kakadu.

MAGHRIBIS. An engine similar to the mangonel.
India, 13th century. (Egerton, p. 16). Most authorities say that mangonel is a class name.

MAHEE. The ordinary spear of the Bongo (Central Africa). It has a plain lancet-shaped head.
(Schweinfurth I, 280).

MAHI-SI. An arrowhead, Omaha. (Dorsey 287).

MAIDATE, MAYEDATE. An ornament worn
on a Japanese helmet. It is usually an animal, or
any mythical creature, whose characteristics the
wearer is supposed to copy. It corresponds to the
crest worn on European helmets. (Dean Jap. 4).
   Maidate vary greatly in subject and size, and fre-

quently have no visible connection with the behavior or characteristics of the wearers. Fig. 536.

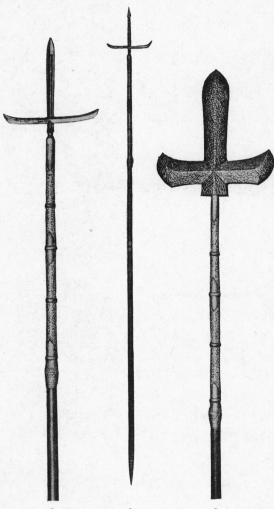

FIGURE 535. *Magari Yari. Head 9.5 inches long and 8.75 wide. The shaft is of kashi wood partly covered with same and banded with metal. Length overall 8 feet 7 inches. The sheath is lacquered red. 1. The head unsheathed. 2. The entire trident. 3. The head sheathed.*

Maidate is used as a general name for all kinds of crest-like objects worn on the helmet; specifically it means only one worn in front. If worn at the back it is called *ushiro-date*; if on top *kashira-date*; if there are two, one on each side, *waki-date*. Occasionally one is worn reaching from side to side across the top. 2, fig. 536.

MAIL. The breast feathers of a hawk.

To mail a hawk is to wrap it in a sock or piece of cloth, so that it is in a kind of straight jacket. This is done when the hawk's claws or beak are to be trimmed (coped) or when a surgical operation is necessary. (Phillott 59 note).

MAIL, CHAIN MAIL. The earliest mail was made of rings sewed on leather, fig. 29, and was extremely heavy as the links were large. "The heaviness of mail was considerably relieved by the adoption, about the early part of the 12th century, of the Asiatic species, formed of rings connected to each other, and so held without being fastened upon a leather garment beneath." (Fairholt 162). At the present time the name is confined to armor made of interlaced links.

In the poorest kinds the links are made of wires bent to form rings, the ends not being fastened together. This kind was rarely used in Europe, except in some very late armor, but is fairly common in the East where it is mainly used for minor pieces, such as the neck guards of helmets and collars though entire suits were made of it, particularly when they were made partly of iron and brass links arranged to form patterns. The Japanese mail is always made of unriveted links, but the wire is very hard and highly tempered so that the mail is as strong as the riveted. The links are frequently made of coils of two or three turns, giving the effect of two or three links side by side, nos. 1, 2, 3, fig. 537. Such mail is quite as strong as any riveted. Most of the wire used in the East is harder and stronger than that used in Europe.

Sometimes the ends of the links are apparently welded, but usually they are riveted. In rare cases two, and even three, rivets are used to make the joint. Triangular rivets are said to have been used in Europe in early times. I have not been able to find any evidence of this. In pieces of early mail examined at the Metropolitan Museum the holes were round and it is not likely that triangular rivets were used in them. The early European double riveted mail was sometimes made of a U-shaped rivet bringing both of the heads on one side of the link with a straight bar connecting them on the other. In the East the rivets were always round; and if more than one was used they were entirely separate. In some of the mail made in the Caucasus the ends of the links were apparently welded and stamped to imitate rivet heads. In the Museum of Lucerne

FIGURE 536. Maidate. 1. An arrow. All metal. 2. Wood. Black flowers on a gold ground. To go across the top of the head. 3. Wood. A monster's head with teeth and horns, gilded. 4. Iron with gilded border. 5. A monster's head with very long engraved kuwagata. All gilded metal. 6. A large bee of wood with leather wings and metal legs. 7. A gilded wooden gourd 10 inches long. 8. Flat flying dragon of engraved and gilded metal. 9. A crouching rabbit of wood. 10. A kirin of brass, gilded, with metal hair. 11. Gohei (Shinto papers) of silver fastened on a stick. 12. A pair, waki-date, of myoga of gilded wood. 13. A crescent and a barred disk of gilded metal. 14. A dolphin of wood lacquered black. 15. Strips of whalebone gilded; to go over the top of the head. 16. A vajra-hilted ken of metal. 17. A fly, carved and colored of wood and metal. 18. A monster's head of wood with large ears and horns. 19. A long-eared rabbit with a gilt sun between its ears. 20. A pair of flat, gilded whalebone horns 19.5 inches across. 21. An iron dragon fly. 22. A war fan of wood lacquered black with a silver sun and moon. 23. A butterfly of different colored metals. 24. A monster's head of gold lacquer. Large ears and horns. 25. A flat gilt circle with the name Hachiman across it. 26. A fox. 27. A tiger. 28. A dragon. All of carved wood lacquered. 29. A nut in a burr, metal.

there is a shirt of mail (no. 27 marked 17th century), each link of which is made of a coil of two
turns, the ends being slightly overlapped and sol-

Except for certain varieties of Japanese mail to
be described hereafter, in all of the mail that I have
examined each link passes through four others in a

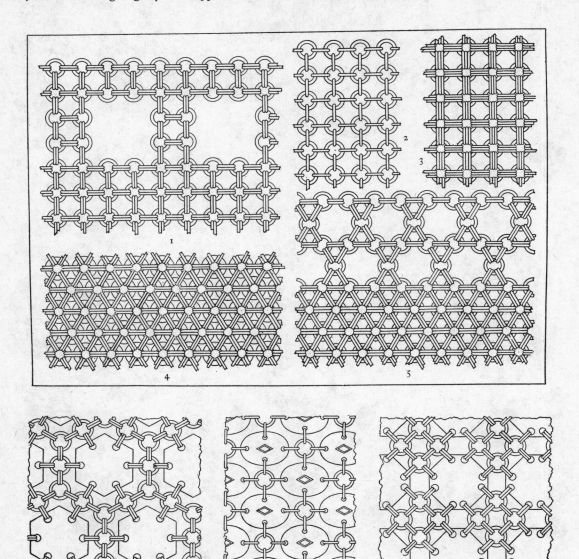

FIGURE 537. *Japanese Mail.* 1. *Square pattern, links of two turns.* 2. *Square pattern, links of one
turn.* 3. *Square pattern, links of three turns.* 4. *Hexagonal pattern, wide center links.* 5. *Hexagonal pattern, narrow center links.* 6. *Hexagonal plates connected by mail.* 7. *Elliptical plates
connected by mail.* 8. *Octagonal plates connected by mail.*

dered. It has the appearance of two links side by
side. In the Field Museum, Chicago, there is a suit
of late mail that is made of short bars with an eye
at each end, the eyes being interlocked. Fig. 538.

regular pattern so that the links lie flat, 1, 2, 3, 4,
fig. 539. Baron de Cosson says (Helmets and Mail
110):"Thus in the British Museum there is a standard of mail of which the rings of the top edge are

exceedingly close and stiff, and the usual arrangement being altered, so that six rings go through the seventh, not four into the fifth." Others who have carefully examined this piece disagree with him, and

I believe that he is mistaken as I have been unable to arrange combinations of seven links that would lie flat, as well made mail must do. The question is rather important as the very close mail he speaks of is known as "double mail" which is so closely woven that there are no visible openings between the links. All of the examples of double mail that I have examined are made in the ordinary manner, each link passing through four others, but the links are much wider than usual. It is obvious that if the

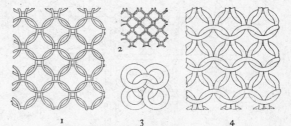

FIGURE 539. *Ordinary, or International Mail.* 1. *Light links separated to show how they interlock.* 2. *Small links.* 3. *Group of five links only.* 4. *Mail of heavier links touching each other as they would when worn.*

width of the link is more than half of the internal diameter there can be no opening. Fig. 540 illustrates the gradual disappearance of the opening between the links as the internal diameter of the links decreases. The outside diameter of the links in all four drawings is the same.

Mail has been made and used from very early times by almost every race that used armor. The Chinese are about the only exceptions as they, apparently, never made it, although they occasionally wore mail procured from the Persians. The type of mail described above was used everywhere. In addition to it other types have been used in more or less restricted areas. In the Musee de l'Armee in Paris there is a fragment of Etruscan mail, fig. 541,

FIGURE 538. *Late mail gauntlet, 17th century. Field Museum, Chicago.*

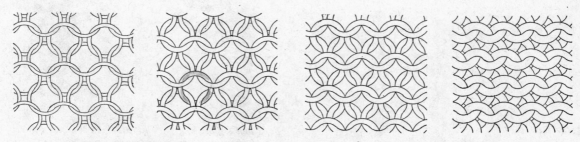

FIGURE 540. *The transition from ordinary to double mail. In all four drawings the outside diameter of the links is the same but the inside diameter gets progressively smaller, closing the openings.*

that is illustrated in de Cosson and Burgess, Helmets and Mail, that is quite different in character, and looks much like some of the Japanese. During the middle ages but one species of mail was used in

ments, inlaid or stamped on each link. Especially in India and Persia the collars and capes of helmets, and sometimes entire suits, are decorated with patterns in brass and copper links, 1, fig. 64. Usually

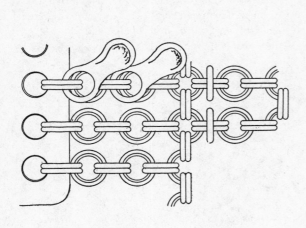

FIGURE 541. *Etruscan Mail. From de Cosson and Burgess, Helmets and Mail.*

Europe, fig. 539. In the 17th century occasional specimens are found of different construction. In addition to the two already described, Dr. Dean had a shirt of Italian mail that closely resembles the Japanese type, 1, fig. 537, but differs from it in having all of the links circular. In Persia and India mail was often made of alternate rows of links cut from a plate each with a bar across it, and ordinary round links. Each link is connected to four of the other kind but not to any of its own. It is known as "bar link" or "theta" mail, from the resemblance of the barred link to the Greek theta. Fig. 542.

European mail is rarely, if ever, decorated, but Eastern mail sometimes has inscriptions, or orna-

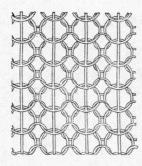

FIGURE 542. *Indian Bar-Link, or Theta mail.*

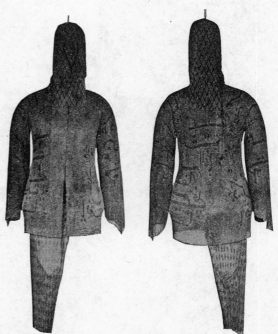

FIGURE 543. *Persian Suit of Mail. The patterns on the hood and leg are made with brass links. Those on the coat are of copper and brass, and form an Arabic inscription. There is a broad strip of double mail on each side of the front.*

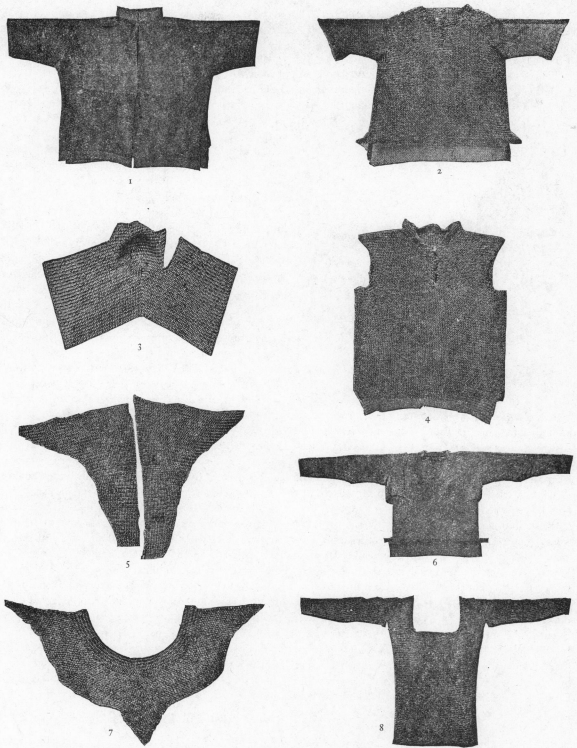

FIGURE 544. *European Mail.* 1. *Coat of mail, German, 15th century. The collar and chest are of double mail.* 2. *Shirt of mail, 15th century.* 3. *Brayette, German, 15th century.* 4. *Shirt of mail, German, 16th century.* 5. *Gussets of mail, 16th century.* 6. *Shirt of mail with extra pieces guarding the shoulders and armpits, 16th century.* 7. *Gorget, German, 15th and 16th centuries.* 8. *French, 19th century. Probably made for export to the colonies. Metropolitan Museum. Not to scale.*

the patterns are geometrical but in rare cases they take the form of inscriptions as shown in the coat of fig. 543.

There is a much greater variation in the sizes of the links and wires used in Oriental mail than in European; and wire of elliptical or rectangular section is not uncommon. In one respect the Oriental

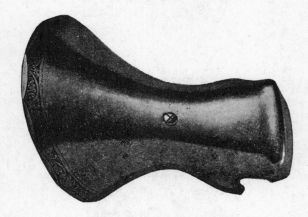

FIGURE 545. *Mainfaire, German, middle of the 16th century. Metropolitan Museum.*

mail is superior to the European. In Europe all of the links of a piece, or suit, are nearly always of the same size and weight (occasionally there is a section of double mail at some exposed part, fig. 544). In most of the Eastern suits the size and section of the links varies considerably in different parts, the mail being much heavier on the more exposed portions, such as shoulders and chest, than on those it is less important to protect. The result is that adequate protection is given with less weight. In some suits the links at the bottom of the skirts are of less than half the diameter and not over one-sixth of the weight of those on the shoulders and grade evenly between. For European Mail, see fig. 544.

In Japan the mail is rarely of the pattern used everywhere else, though such mail is sometimes used there. Generally Japanese mail is made of circular links and of links having semi-circular ends and parallel sides. The latter are usually made of coils of wire of two or three turns. As the wire is of very high temper this gives a very strong construction although the ends of the links are not fastened together. Usually each round link is connected to four of the long ones, giving a pattern of squares, 1, 2, 3, fig. 537. Sometimes the round link is joined

to six long ones, giving a pattern of hexagons, 4, 5, fig. 537. The round links may be wide and flat, 4, giving very small openings between the links; or of round wire making the mail much lighter and more open. Other types of Japanese mail are made of small plates of regular forms connected by mail. The plates may be round, square, elliptical, hexagonal or octagonal. 6, 7, 8, fig. 537.

In most parts of the East armor was often made of mixtures of small plates and mail; sometimes to such an extent that it is difficult to know whether to call it plate or mail. Fig. 58.

In comparing the armor of the East and West the differences in climate and the methods of fighting must be kept in mind. Anyone who has tried wearing European armor will say that the greater part of the inconvenience came from the heat and lack of ventilation. The weight was not more than a man in decent training could bear; but, especially in hot weather, the lack of ventilation sometimes incapacitated as many as wounds. Plate armor was made in the East but the lighter and cooler mail was preferred. The tactics of West and East were also different. In the West dependence was placed on weight and crushing power. The knights and their horses were covered with heavy armor and struck with the full weight and momentum of all three. The lances were frequently broken by the shock, and even if not broken they were useless at close quarters. Swords were practically useless against men in complete armor, and the weapons used were maces and axes, purely smashing ones. The infantry were only meant to check the impetus of the charge; they were mainly serfs and were only meant to be killed. In the East the climate forbade very heavy armor and mobility was considered of much more advantage. All of the weapons used were much lighter and more manageable, the lances were shorter, lighter and better balanced, the swords were of better quality and better adapted for use at close quarters. Both swords and spears were meant for cutting and piercing, and the smashing weapons, maces and axes, were much lighter and not as much used.

MAILLET DE FER. See Hammer, War.

MAINFAIRE, MAINFER. The large gauntlet worn on the bridle hand in tournaments in the 16th century. The name is an obvious contraction of *main de fer*. (ffoulkes 76). Fig. 545.

MAIN GAUCHE. A left-handed dagger used to guard with when fencing in the 17th century. The blade is straight and double-edged, and frequently plaiting the braid of a Japanese hilt so that it crossed over the kashira which was of plain black horn. The fuchi and other fittings were of shakudo with gold

FIGURE 546. *Mains Gauches. 1, 4, 5. Spanish. 2, 3. Italian, All 17th century. Metropolitan Museum. Not to scale.*

has prongs next the hilt to catch the blade of an adversary's sword. The grip is very short as the thumb was extended on the blade. The quillons are long and straight, and the counter guard is triangular, broad at the quillons and tapering to a point where it joins the pommel. The counter guard is of plate and was frequently elaborately chased and pierced to match the cup of the rapier with which it was used. Fig. 546.

MAIN GUARD. An extra piece of armor of uncertain description worn in tournaments in the 16th and 17th centuries. (ffoulkes 52). Probably the Grand Guard.

MAIZASHI, MABI-ZASHI. The peak of a Japanese helmet. (Dean Jap. 4). See Kabuto.

MAJIHA. Omaha, a quiver. Those of the men were of buffalo hide and those of the boys of otter or cougar skin with the tail hanging from the end of the quiver. (Dorsey 287).

MAKAGOYA. A hunting arrow, Japan.

MAKANA, MAQUAHUITL. An Aztec club with sharp-edged stones set in the sides. (Jaehns 207).

MAKIKAKE-NO-KASHIRA. The method of

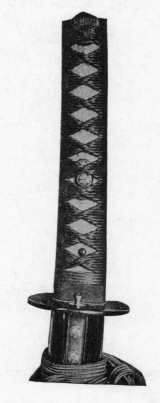

FIGURE 547. *Makikake-No-Kashira. Blue silk braid over a kashira of plain black horn.*

ornaments in relief on a nanako ground. The only ornaments were generally the crest of the owner. The guard was sometimes a perfectly plain piece of metal, steel or shakudo, by a celebrated maker. Such swords were carried at court. Fig. 547.

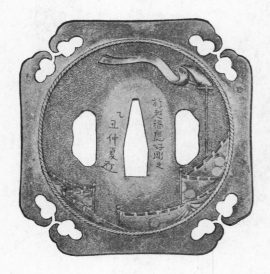

FIGURE 548. *Maku. Tsuba of shibuichi showing the curtains called maku. They bear the crest of the Toda family.*

MAKIWARA. A bundle of straw used as a target, Japan.

MAKRIGGA. A Bongo (Central Africa) spear having a plain barbed head below which the shaft is covered with teeth symmetrically arranged, some of which point forward and some backward. (Schweinfurth I, 280).

MAKTAH. An Indian self bow, that is, one made from a single piece of wood. These bows are used by the aboriginal tribes.

MAKU. Curtains surrounding the tents of warriors of the higher classes in Japan. They were generally decorated with the mon of their owners. (Weber II, 10). Fig. 548.

MAKURA DASHI. A pillow sword, Japan.

MAKURA YARI. A javelin placed by the pillow, Japan. It is a very light spear with a small, straight head. Fig. 549.

MALAB, MALAT. The Kayan name for the Dyak sword, mandau. (Ling Roth II, 136; Hose I, 159).

MALALI. The Veddah bow, Ceylon. It is of ovoid section and from five feet to five feet three inches long. The string is of twisted bark. The arrows (*moriankatu*) are of wood thirty to thirty-six inches long, and have three feathers. Some have simple sharpened points; others have large leaf-shaped iron heads. "In shooting, they draw the hand back to the ear, holding the fingers to the string as we do. The bow is fairly stiff, they string it by placing one foot on it, while both hands are occupied in putting the string in the notch at the end. They have no quiver, but carry their extra arrows in their hand, and while shooting, they hold the arrows between their knees or thighs. . . . A leaf two and a half inches broad was placed against a tree for a target, and at a distance of eleven yards, five Rock Veddahs took two shots each at it; not an arrow touched the leaf, and one missed the tree." (Hiller & Furness 35).

Dr. Hoffmeister who wrote of the Veddahs some sixty years earlier does not agree with the above. He says: "They were carrying bows and arrows—the former handsome ones of red wood—and were shooting in capital style. Mr. Layard promised sixpence to any of them that could shoot his hat. It was forthwith suspended from a pole at a distance of sixty paces; yet notwithstanding the evening twilight, it fell pierced through and through at the first shot." (Hoffmeister 165).

MALLEOLUS. A fire arrow made "of cane, or reed, and at the part where the head joins the body, there is a piece of iron open-work communicating with the middle of the arrow, which was made hollow, and the cavity filled with combustible mate-

FIGURE 549. *Makura Yari. Head 2 inches long, shaft 4 feet 3 inches long. The upper 12 inches is wound with red and black cane.*

rials. When these arrows were used, the substance within was enflamed, and, after being shot, sticking to the object, burned with great rapidity whatever came in its way." (Mosely 178).

MAMELIERES. Circular plates of metal fastened to the breast of a knight's surcoat in the 14th century. They had rings at the center for the attachment of chains leading to the sword hilt and heaume. (Planche 353).

Later the name was used for any circular plates fastened to the breast. Fig. 550.

is from New Guinea, and is a spike on the end of a pole with a stiff loop of rattan around it. The loop was put over the head of a fleeing enemy and he was thrown back against the spike by a sudden sharp jerk.

MANCHETTE. An attack with the broadsword consisting in cutting at the hand, wrist and forearm with the inner edge. (Burton Sword 12).

MANDAU. The Dyak sword. The name means "head hunter," but it is used as a jungle knife and

FIGURE 550. *Mamelieres, Venetian, Palazzo Tiepolo, early 16th century. Metropolitan Museum.*

MAMORI KATANA. The first sword worn by a samurai boy. It was a charm sword with the hilt and scabbard covered with brocade to which was attached a *kinchaku* (purse or wallet). It was worn by boys under five years of age. (Joly, Naunton xvi).

This name is also said to mean a dagger with a blade a foot or less long which was carried in place of the wakizashi.

MAN-AT-ARMS. During the existence of the feudal system the holders of estates of a certain size were obliged to render military service. The holder of the estate wore complete armor and his horse likewise, hence the name. A man-at-arms had a specified number of attendants who were also armed, but less completely than their master, and the entire party was included in the term. Thus a force of fifty men-at-arms might contain from 150 to 300 persons.

MAN-CATCHER. See Catch Pole. No. 1 of the fig. 551 was probably used mainly by the police, but also to pull men from their horses in war. No. 2

tool as well as for head hunting. The Malay name for it is *parang ihlang*, and much confusion has arisen from some writers using one name for it and some the other, while some insist that they refer to different weapons.

It has a short, straight, single-edged blade of most unusual outline and section. The latter is strongly convex on one side and slightly concave on the other. The result of this is said to be that only two effective cuts can be made with it, from the right downward and from the left upward, or the reverse, depending on which side is convex. Notwithstanding this disadvantage it is a very effective weapon in the hands of a man accustomed to its use, and the Dyaks are said to give blows of a power one would hardly believe possible considering the lightness of the weapon. The hilt is of wood or staghorn, without a guard, and with a long, one-sided pommel. The pommel is generally carved with grotesque faces or other ornaments, and is decorated with tufts of hair. The scabbard is made of two pieces of wood, well carved in high relief, and bound together with bands of braided cane. Occasionally a piece of rattan is used to cover the joint, being put under the cane bands. These scabbards are frequently decorated with tassels of colored hair and beadwork. On the back of the scabbard there is al-

and forged their own blades which they frequently inlaid with brass dots. At present most of them use European or Chinese iron. Fig. 552.

There is a variation of this sword with a curved

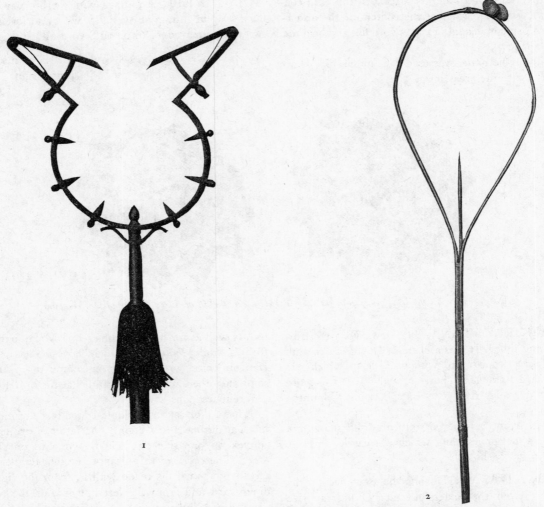

FIGURE 551. *Man Catchers. 1. German, 16th-17th century. Metropolitan Museum. 2. New Guinea. Not to scale.*

ways a pocket of bark, or cloth, to hold a knife with a short blade and a very long handle. It is exactly like the Malay pisau raut, which is used for trimming rattan. This knife is often missing from the mandaus brought here as the Dyaks are said to be more unwilling to part with it than with the sword itself, possibly because they use it for cleaning up the heads they have taken from their enemies. Formerly many of the tribes smelted their own iron

blade of symmetrical cross section, and widening towards the point, but otherwise as described, 6, 7, fig. 552. It is sometimes called a jimpul. (B. M.).

MANDAU PASIR. A mandau with a very wide blade. (Arc. f. Eth.).

MANDAYA KNIFE. A knife used by the Mandaya, a Philippine tribe. It has a leaf-shaped, double-edged blade and a wooden hilt with a very deep crescent-shaped pommel. The tang is very long and projects through the hilt between the horns of the pommel. It, and its scabbard, are generally pro-

the belly and convex on the back, and with a double curve. It was sometimes strengthened by gluing sinews on the back.

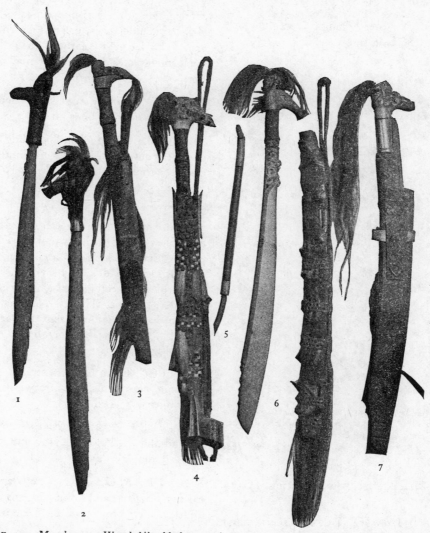

FIGURE 552. *Mandau. 1. Wood hilt, blade 20.5 inches long, inlaid with brass dots. 2. Carved staghorn hilt, blade 22 inches long, inlaid with brass. 3. Staghorn hilt, carved wood sheath. 4. Plain blade, staghorn hilt. Sheath of carved wood decorated with tufts of red, white and black hair, woven bands and beads. 5. Small knife carried in the sheath. 6. Blade 2 feet long, engraved near the hilt. Carved wood sheath decorated with colored hair. 7. Staghorn with a wide silver ferule. Plain blade 22.5 inches long; carved wood sheath. Nos. 1 to 4 have blades that are convex on one side and concave on the other. Nos. 6 and 7 have blades of symmetrical section.*

fusely decorated with silver and cane work. Fig. 552.

MANDE. A bow, Omaha. The string is of twisted elk or buffalo sinews. (Dorsey 285, 286). This bow is only about three feet and a half long, flat on

MANDEHI. Omaha, a general name for spears and darts. (Dorsey 284).

MANDEHI CIGUJE. The "bent spear" of the Omaha, called *wahukeza* by the Dakotas. It is ornamented with eagle feathers, one being at the end of the curved part. It usually has an iron point on the butt. (Dorsey 285).

MANDOBLE. In fencing, a cut from the wrist, a flip of the point. (Castle 71).

MANDOBOLO. An ascending cut with the false edge of a sabre. (Castle 135).

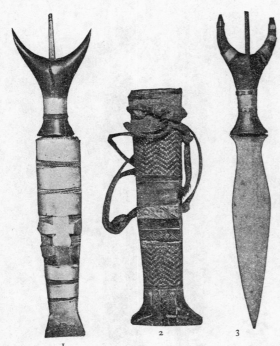

FIGURE 553. *Mandaya Knives. 1. Wooden hilt and scabbard with silver bands. 2. Wooden hilt with silver bands. Scabbard covered with cloth and wide bands woven of yellow and black cane, embossed brass mountings. 3. Blade 7.5 inches long.*

MANDRITTA. A cross blow in fencing. (Castle 81).

MANGONA, MANGONEL. A generic name for all engines throwing large stones and darts. Its diminutive, mangonel, was applied to the smaller engines. 11th and 12th centuries. (Grose I, 381).

MANIFER. See Mainfaire.

MANIPLE. One-third of a Roman cohort. (Burton Sword 246).

MANIPULUS. A Roman standard consisting of a wisp of hay on the end of a pole. (Macgeorge 22).

MANJANIK, MAGHRIBIHA. An engine for throwing large stones, used by the Mahommedan invaders of Sind in the 8th century. (Egerton, p. 151). The name means "western," showing its origin. (Hime 83).

MANJIYUWA, MANJU-NO-WA. Japan, a combination of the yeri-mawari, kate-ate and waki-biki, or shoulder pads, collar and armpit guards in one. (Conder 277, Garbutt 461). It is made of mail, small plates connected by mail or brigandine. Fig. 554.

MANJU. A variety of shikoro (neck guard of a Japanese helmet). (Garbutt 68).

MANOPLE. A Moorish "boarding sword," 14th and 15th centuries. A species of gauntlet sword with a rather short blade with two very short curved side blades. (Calvert pl. 207). Fig. 555.

MANTEAU D'ARMES. A fixed shield worn in tournaments in the 16th century. Its object is to catch the point of the lance and prevent it from slipping so that either it was broken or the rider unhorsed. Dean (Hdbk. 67) says that it was made of steel with a projecting lattice and was worn on the shoulder. (Hewitt III, 648) says that it was a thick piece of wood extending from the neck of the horse to that of the rider. Probably the latter is the earlier form. Fig. 556.

MANTLE. For a hawk to stretch out a leg sideways and backwards, and afterwards to stretch the wing over it. (Michell 19).

MANTLET. A large shield supported from the ground and used as a defense in attacking fortified places. Compare Pavis.

MANTRAMUKTA. The class of weapons thrown by spells, and numbering six species, ancient India. (Burton Sword 214). See Amukta.

MANUBALISTA. The Latin name for the crossbow. See Arbalest.

MAPUPU. See Maboku.

MAQUAHUITL. See Makana.

MARA MUNE. See Mune.

MAREK. The Ainu salmon spear. It has a hook about eighteen inches long fixed to a pole eight feet long in such a way that when a fish is struck the point enters its flesh and is drawn over so as to keep the fish between it and the pole, hence the more the

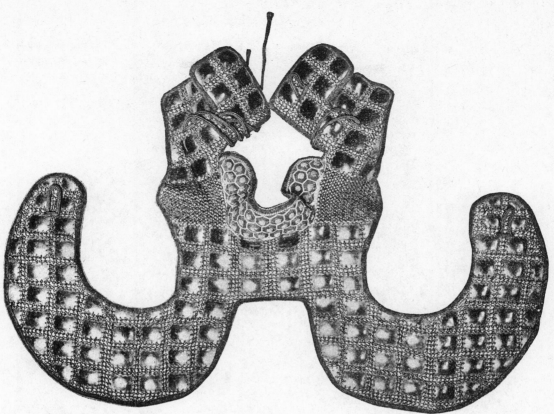

FIGURE 554. *Manjiyuwa. Collar of brigandine of hexagonal plates quilted and tied in. Body of rectangular lacquered plates connected by mail.*

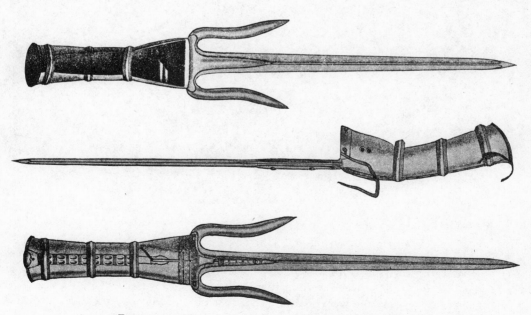

FIGURE 555. *Manople, Armeria Real, Madrid. After Jubinal.*

fish struggles the tighter the hook holds it. (Batchelor 152). It is precisely like the lumberman's cant
hook. Fig. 557.

MARISHITEN. A deity of Brahminic origin, also
called the queen of heaven. In Japan she became
the goddess of war, and particularly of archers. She

FIGURE 556. *Manteau d'Armes, German, first half of the 16th century. Metropolitan Museum.*

MARINES. Men trained and equipped as soldiers
and serving on vessels of war. The corps was established in England in 1684. The marines were then
considered as a part of the army and were the third
regiment on the list. (Grose I, 167).

is represented with three faces and eight arms holding the sun, moon, a war fan, a bow and arrow.
She is usually shown standing on a boar. (Weber
II, 14). She is frequently used as a decoration on
sword mountings in Japan.

MARO. See Morro.

MARO HASHI. A kind of helmet worn between 300 and 400 A.D. in Japan.

MARTEL DE FER. See Hammer, War.

FIGURE 557. *Marek, an Ainu fish spear used for catching salmon. U. S. N. M.* 1890, *p.* 470.

MARTINET. An engine for throwing large stones, 14th century. (Hewitt II, 327).

MARU. See Madu.

MARU-AGA. See Mulga.

MARU-BORI. Japanese carving in the round.

MARU-KI. A round wooden bow, Japan. (Gilbertson Archery 113).

MARU-MIMI. A rounded edge, as of a tsuba. (Weber I, 203).

MARU-SODE. A sode made of a single oval plate. It was usually decorated with some pattern or crest. (Conder 272).

MASAME-HADA. Japan, straight-grain watering on a blade. See Hada.

MASA-KARI. A battle-axe, Japan. The battle-axe was rarely used in Japan, and mainly by the Yamabushi. This axe is of a different type, with a narrower blade, longer point and shorter handle. Fig. 558.

MASAMUNE. Okazaki Goro Niudo Masamune was the most celebrated Japanese swordsmith. He was the son of Tozaburo Yukimitsu, a native of Soshu, and was born in Imakoji, Kamakura, in Bunyei 1 (1265). He left home when seventeen and studied under Kunitsuna. Later he traveled extensively and studied under many famous smiths. He had no son but, following the Japanese custom, adopted successively Samonji and Sadamune. It is said that when Samonji was working at the forge he tested the temperature of the water to be used for quenching a blade by putting his hand in it. Masamune resented this attempt to learn one of his

secrets by immediately cutting off the hand; Samonji died not long afterwards. Whether his death was the result of his wound we are not told. Samonji was succeeded in 1336 by Sadamune, who later married Masamune's daughter to whom Samonji had been betrothed. Sadamune died in 1351 at the age of fifty-one. Masamune lived until 1358 and died at the age of ninety-three. Besides being a most remarkable sword maker he was a man of the highest character and was universally loved and respected. He rarely signed or decorated his blades.

MASAQTIHI. "Real arrow wood" (viburnum) used for arrow shafts by the Omaha. (Dorsey 286).

MASCLE. Mail. Meyrick considered that it meant a special variety, but this is not generally considered to be the case. Both mascle and mail are derived from the same Latin root (macula) from their resemblance to the meshes of a net.

MASHA, MEYSHA. A trigger, Tibet. (Ramsay-Western).

MASK VISOR. A visor in the form of the face of a man, beast or monster. Such visors were quite common in the latter part of the 16th century. (Hewitt III, 574). Fig. 41.

MASNAD, MUSNUD. Literally a cushion, but generally used as meaning a throne. India and Persia. (Egerton, p. 30).

MASSUE. See Mace.

MASSUELLE. A small mace. (Planche 345).

MASUGATA. The courts of a castle, Japan.

MATAFUNDA. An engine for throwing large stones, probably by means of a sling. (Grose I, 382).

FIGURE 558. *Masa Kari, Japanese Axe. Heavy head* 15 *inches long with a heavy point opposite the edge. Total length* 30.5 *inches.*

MATANA SELEKA. A kris blade, Celebes. (Arc. f. Eth. XVIII, 64).

MATCH, MATCH CORD, SLOW MATCH.

A cord that would burn slowly but steadily that was used for lighting the powder in the pan of a matchlock or cannon. It was often carried wound around the hat, but more often hung from the belt. Walhausen (L'Art pour l'Infanterie, 1615) says: "It is necessary that every musketeer knows how to carry his match dry in moist and rainy weather, that is, in his pocket, or in his hat; or by some means guard it from the weather. The English law of 1662 required each musketeer be provided with half a pound of powder, half a pound of Bullets, and three yards of Match." (Grose II, 294; Hewitt III, 734). The match was often carried in a metal tube.

In the East match cord was often made of twisted bark. "The Mogiahs (a criminal tribe of Central India) . . . habitually carried long barreled, ricketty looking matchlocks, and a fid of cow dung to ignite the match withal." (Gerard 348).

MATCH BOX, MATCH PIPE.

A small tube of copper or tin about a foot long, pierced with holes, in which to carry a lighted match. It was used at night so that the lighted matches could not be seen and betray the whereabouts of the carriers. (Grose II, 294).

In India extra match cord is generally carried wound around the stock of the gun or carried in one of the pouches of the kamr. In Tibet there is generally a leather pouch for match cord on the side of the stock. In China it was carried in a leather pouch; and in Assam it was wound on a basketwork reel much like a Japanese bowstring carrier, but larger. In Japan it was carried in a metal tube with a flat cylindrical end, the cover of which is

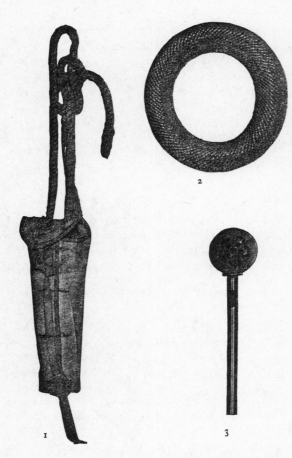

FIGURE 559. *Match Carriers.* 1. *Chinese. Pouch of white leather bound with green.* 2. *Shan, Assam. A reel of basketwork 6 inches wide and 6.5 high.* 3. *Japan. A bronze box 2.375 inches in diameter and 1.125 high, connected to a tube 0.5 inches in diameter by 7.5 long. The box cover is pierced.*

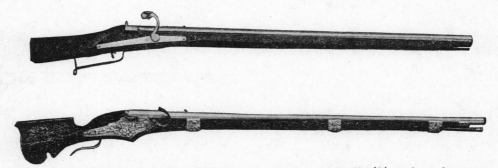

FIGURE 560. *Matchlock Arquebuses.* 1. *German, dated 1529.* 2. *English(?), early 17th century. Metropolitan Museum. Not to scale.*

pierced with holes, fig. 559. The Director of the Armor Museum in Tokyo says that this implement could hardly be said to have a name as it was called by a different one in every province.

MATCHLOCK. The earliest mechanism for discharging a gun. The first form consisted of an S-shaped lever (the serpentine) pivoted to the stock near its center and forked at its upper end to hold

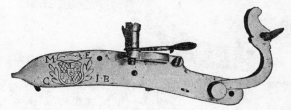

FIGURE 561. *Matchlock, Bavarian, 17th century. From an arquebus of Maximilian II, Elector of Bavaria (1697-1726). Metropolitan Museum.*

the match. By pressing the lower end of the lever the match was forced down into the flashpan and ignited the priming. In some cases the serpentine also had a side movement and the match in it was not kept lighted, but was ignited when moved over a slow match burning in a holder on top of the barrel, and then swung back and pressed down into the pan. The serpentine in this arrangement was back of the pan. The next improvement was to place it in front of the pan and hold it up by a catch which was released by a pull on the trigger, when the serpentine was thrown down by a spring, figs. 560, 561. Both types of matchlock are still in use: the former in India, China and Central Asia; and the latter in the Indo-Chinese countries, Malaya, in parts of China, and, in comparatively recent times, in Japan. Some of the Chinese locks are merely the oldest form of serpentine, but are more apt to be the Indian modification in which there are three pieces—the serpentine—a long trigger—a link connecting the two. The trigger is pivoted far back and the front end is split, the upper part forming a spring that holds the trigger down, and, consequently, the serpentine up, fig. 562. The Japanese, and other locks, work like the later European matchlocks, except that the serpentine is placed back of the pan. One of the simplest forms of lock is sometimes found in Formosa and China. In it the serpentine is pivoted in front of the pan and the top of it is connected by a string to the middle of the trigger, which is loosely hung from the stock, fig. 333. Several curious forms of matchlock are used in China and the hill states south of it. Fig. 563.

In the 18th century many European adventurers commanded armies for the Indian princes. The ablest of these was de Boigne, a Savoyard, who organized and equipped an army for Scindia. He had his own arsenal at Agra in charge of a Scotchman named Sangster, where he made both cannon and small arms for his troops. At Agra he made matchlocks with bayonets and locks of an improved de-

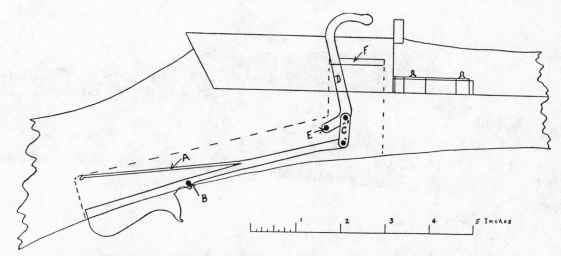

FIGURE 562. *Indian Matchlock. A. The spring on the back of the trigger. B. The pivot for the trigger. C. The link. D. The match holder. E. The pivot for the match holder. F. The slot in the stock in which the match holder works; it is curved so that it moves the match over the pan. Central India.*

FIGURE 563. *Oriental Matchlocks. 1, 2. Japanese. 3. Malay. Chased brass. 4. Tonkin. Brass engraved and decorated with enamel. 5. Khamti, Assam. Plain iron. These five are of the Japanese type. 6. Central India. It has a removable clip hung by a string instead of the usual removable pan cover. 7. Hyderabad. 8. Sind. 9, 10. China. These five are of the Indian type. Not to scale.*

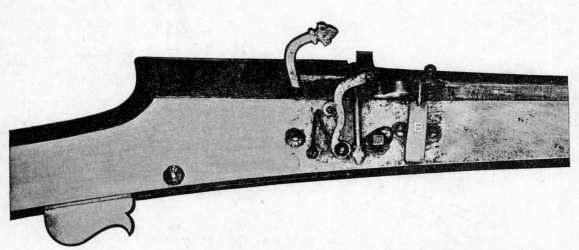

FIGURE 564. *Indian matchlock with an automatic pan opener. The cover is held shut by the catch A which fits in a slot in the rear end of the pan cover. When the trigger is pulled this catch is drawn back just before the match reaches the pan. The cover is thrown open by the spring B.*

sign (Compton 47). The lock shown in fig. 564, is probably one of those made by Sangster. The pan is automatically uncovered by a spring which is released when the trigger is pulled. This gun also has a bayonet, fig. 139, evidently made under European influence.

MATE-GRIFFON. An engine for throwing either darts or stones. (Grose I, 382).

MATO. A target, Japan. The bull's-eye was always black.

MATO-BA. A place for target shooting, Japan.

MATO-YA, SASO-YA. Blunt arrows with wooden heads for target practice, Japan. (Gilbertson Archery 121).

MATRAS. A crossbow bolt with a round disk head. It was used in hunting so as not to injure the skin of the game. (Demmin 59).

MATSUDAIRA. Japanese nobles having incomes of from 10,000 to 20,000 kokus of rice. See Daimio.

MATSU-HADA. Watering like the bark of a tree, Japan.

MATTINA. A double-pointed club with teeth on two sides of the head, Queensland. (Vic. Mus. 30).

MATTUCASHLASS. A Scotch dagger carried under the armpit. (ffoulkes Armourer 165).

MAUSHTIKA. An ancient Indian stiletto only a span long. (Burton Sword 215).

MAWIDA. Omaha, a set of arrows. A set usually was ten, but the number varied; sometimes there were two, four, or even twenty. (Dorsey 287).

MAXIMILIAN ARMOR. A style of armor made originally for the Emperor Maximilian and used extensively between 1500 and 1540. "It is distinguished by radiating fluted channels that spread from a central point in the breastplate, closely resembling the flutings of a scallop shell. The main lines of the suit are heavier and more clumsy than those of the Gothic variety. The breastplate is shorter, globose in form, and made in one piece as distinguished from the Gothic breastplate, which was generally composed of an upper and a lower portion. The pauldrons are larger and the upstanding neck guards are pronounced. The coude and genou-illieres are both smaller than in the Gothic suit, and fit more closely to the limbs. In imitation of the civil dress the solleret became shorter and broader at the toes. . . . The pauldrons of the Maximilian suit are generally of unequal size; that for the right arm being smaller to admit of couching the lance under the armpit. The tassets are made in two or more pieces, connected by a strap and sliding rivets." (ffoulkes 73). Fig. 38.

MAYEDATE. See Maidate.

MAYEWARI-GUSOKU. A Japanese corselet opening in front. The right side of the opening should be over the left. (Garbutt 161).

MAZULE, MAZUELLE. See Mace.

MEASURE. In fencing, distance. To keep the proper measure is to keep out of easy reach when on the defensive, and not to deliver an attack without being within striking distance. (Castle 8).

ME-DA. One of several Tibetan names for a gun. (Rockhill Eth. 712). The Tibetan guns are matchlocks, and all of the iron parts are usually of Chinese make and very rough. The gun is the Tibetan's most valued possession and he is very proud of his marksmanship, though never able to hit a moving object according to Rockhill. The stocks are straight and much like the Indian; they are often covered with wild ass's skin stretched tightly and sewed on. The pan cover is a flap of leather fastened to the left side of the stock and held down by a tag hooked over a pin on the right. The spare match cord is carried in a long, narrow pouch on the right side of the stock. It is usually decorated with inlays of colored leather and silver studs. These guns are always fitted with the Central Asian forked rest which is pivoted to a projection on the lower side of the stock. These rests are tipped, either with iron, or antelope horns, those of the orongo being the most valued for this purpose. These guns vary considerably in size, being from three to five feet long. Fig. 565.

There are two extraordinarily good specimens of these guns in the Art Museum in Honolulu.

MEERA. See Kur-Ruk.

MEERI. A Queensland club with two small points on the end and an enlargement below them. (Brough Smyth 302).

MEGURIWA. A variety of nodowa, a Japanese neck guard. See Nodowa.

MEI. The name of the maker inscribed on a sword, Japan.

called *motagi*. They served to disguise this necessary, but not ornamental fitting. In the later swords the ends of the pin are left uncovered and ornaments called *menugi* are placed to one side of them.

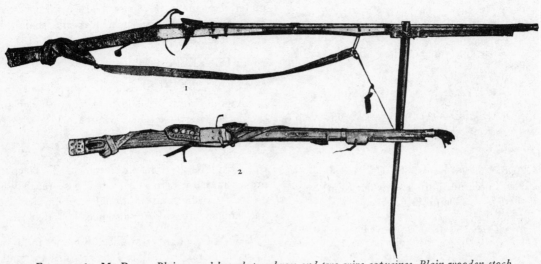

FIGURE 565. *Me-Da.* 1. *Plain round barrel, two brass and two wire capucines. Plain wooden stock. Forked rest of wood and iron attached. Length 4 feet 10.75 inches. 2. Plain barrel 22.5 inches long. Capucines three coils of brass wire. Stock covered with wild ass's skin, strapped with iron and decorated with silver studs. The pan cover and pouch for match cord are made of leather of several colors and decorated with silver studs. Length 3 feet 4 inches.*

MEIGEN. Twanging a bow to keep off evil spirits, Japan.

MEITEKI. "An arrow that hums in its flight." A whistling arrow, Japan. See Whistling Arrow.

MEKIKE. The official Japanese expert who judges and values blades and teaches others how to do so. The Honami family have held this office since the first was appointed in 1334. (Gilbertson Blades 199).

MEKUGI. The peg that holds the hilt of a Japanese sword to the blade. Originally it was double, one part fitting, or screwing, into the other; in practically all of the later swords it is merely a peg of bamboo. In some of the earlier swords the heads of the double pin were ornamented, and were then

MEKUGI ANA. The holes in the hilt and tang of a Japanese sword or knife for the mekugi.

MEL PUTTAH BEMOH. A two-handed sword with a long rapier blade, and two guards, the lower round and the upper shaped like a broad figure eight; and a large pommel, Southern India. (Egerton 134). Fig. 566. The specimen in the India Museum, South Kensington, has the hilt profusely decorated with long silk fringe.

MEMPO. See Menpo.

MENDAQ, UWER. The ornamental ring between the hilt and blade of a kris, Java. (Arc. f. Eth.). In the finer krisses it is usually made of gold, often set with precious stones, and is a beautiful example of jeweler's work.

FIGURE 566. *Mel Puttah Bemoh, Southern India, 18th century. Two guards; the upper is rectangular with rounded corners, the lower is round. Length blade 3 feet 10 inches, total 5 feet 4 inches.*

MENPO, MEMPO, MENKO, SAKU-BO. The Japanese face guard. It is commonly spoken of as a visor but is actually a buffe as it is never fastened to the helmet and cannot be raised. Conder says (261): "The menko is a metal mask either covering the whole features, having holes for the eyes and nostrils, in which case it is called *Menpo*, or

more than one meaning. The complete mask is sometimes made of a single plate; but is more often built up of several riveted, hinged or locked together by turning pins. It is frequently divided horizontally at the level of the eyes, so that the upper part can be removed and the lower worn alone. The nose is also often removable.

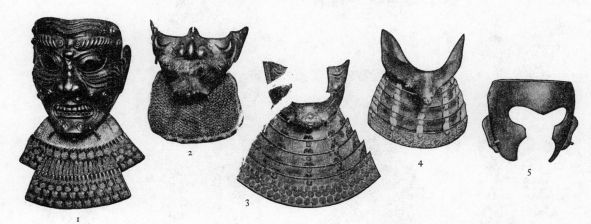

FIGURE 567. *Five kinds of Menpo. 1. So Menpo, embossed from a single piece. Signed Miochin Munemitsu. 2. Ho-Ate. Removable nose; mail neck guard. 3. Saru-Bo. No ear guards. Very wide neck guard of five steel plates. 4. Tsubame-Bo. Chin projects greatly. Lower plate of neck guard of gold lacquer. 5. Forehead and cheeks only. Made of a single plate lined with printed leather.*

smaller, covering only the cheeks and the portion of the face below the nose, in which case it is called *Ho-Ate.*"

"There are four varieties; *membo* which covers the whole face; *hoate* which covers all below the level of the eyes; *saru-bo* which covers the cheeks and chin only; and the *tsubamegata* which covers the chin alone. The first and last are not good, because the one is over complete and the other too much abridged.

"There are about six different styles (of *ho-ate*, *menpo*), and they are all to cover the cheeks and chin. A movable nose piece is recommended. Whiskers on the mask are not particularly necessary, but it is desirable to have moustaches. Before putting on the mask you must put a *fukusa* (a kind of handkerchief) between the mask and chin, and then fasten the ends of the cords on the top of the head slightly towards the back." (Garbutt 146).

Actually there are five kinds. Fig. 567.

1. Covers the entire face. Conder calls it a *menpo*, Garbutt *menbo*, and it is also called *so-menpo*. The last name seems the best as it is not used with

2. The half mask covering the face below the eyes. It is called *hoate* or *menpo*. It is also sometimes made of a single plate, but more often of several. The nose is almost always removable, and is often fastened on with hinges with loose pins, so that it can either be turned back or taken off altogether. The half mask is much the most popular form.

3. A mask that covers the cheeks and chin up to the eyes, but not the nose and mouth. It is called *saru-bo* (monkey face). It is frequently made of a single plate; but the under side of the chin is often a separate piece. It is like the hoate with the nosepiece removed.

4. This is much like the last but only covers the lower part of the cheeks and chin; sometimes the chin only. It is called *tsubame-bo* or *tsubame-gata* (swallow face). It is a rather rare form.

5. This covers the forehead and cheeks only. It is the rarest form because it is the least useful as it only guards the parts that are already well protected by the helmet, leaving the lower part of the face without defense, and it gives no place for attaching the helmet cord.

FIGURE 568. *Menpo. 1. Saru-bo. No ear guards. Neck guard of three wide lacquered lames. 2. Ho-ate. Nose in one piece with mask. Hooks on cheeks. Surface lacquered and grooved; inside gilded. 3. So menpo. The forehead is a separate piece that can be removed, making an ho-ate; the nose is also removable. Ring bolts on cheeks. 4. Ho-ate. Removable nose. Hooks on cheeks. Neck guard laced with yellow cords. 5. Ho-ate. Sharp-nosed tengu. Removable nose; hooks and swastika on cheeks. Stiff moustache and goatee, teeth and red lips. 6. Ho-ate. Removable nose. Flanges on cheeks; two pins on chin. Black surface. 7. Ho-ate. Very heavy with a rough lacquered surface. Fixed nose, teeth and thin red lips. 8. So menpo. Sharp-nosed tengu. Of two pieces riveted together with a removable nose. Neck guard of two wide lames hung from figured leather. 9. Ho-ate. Old man's face. Removable nose. Very long moustache. 10. So menpo. Early type of two pieces riveted together. 11. Ho-ate. Removable nose. Very large neck guard of two plates hung from figured leather. 12. Ho-ate. Hinged nosepiece; hooks on cheeks and three pins on chin. Neck guard of 4 wide iron plates. Signed. 13. So menpo. Long-nosed tengu. In two pieces with a removable nose. A mon in relief on the chin, hooks and cheeks. 14. Ho-ate. Removable nose, hooks on cheeks. 15. So menpo. Sharp-nosed tengu of one plate lacquered red. It is attached to a mail hood. 16. Saru-bo. Lacquered black. Hooks on cheeks. Neck guard of five laced lames. 17. Ho-ate. Removable nose. Moustache indicated by lacquer lines. Small neck guard of four plates.*

All of these masks were generally made of steel; but occasionally of leather moulded to shape.

In all of the forms that cover the chin there is an opening under it called *asa nagashi no ana* (sweat running hole); or a short pipe, *tsuyo otoshi no kubo* (dew dropping tube) to allow the perspiration to run out. Usually a neck guard of plates, mail or scales, is hung from the menpo. In some cases these lames have pieces hinged to them that reach around the neck forming a nodowa.

In addition to the usual strings for fastening it on, some of the later menpo have skull caps of silk or mail fastened to the top of the forehead. When signed it is usually under the chin; sometimes on the cheeks high up. The modeling of the finer specimens is superb and the relief obtained by embossing is a testimonial, both to the skill of the makers, and the excellence of the material. Fig. 568.

There are many patterns recognized; the names of some of them are: *Korai-Bo*, Korean face; *Moriyo*, ghost; *O Kina Men*, old man's face; *Onna-Men*, woman's face; *Warawazura*, young boy's face; *Tengu*, mountain demon, of which there are two varieties, the long-nosed and the bird tengu, etc. Fig. 568.

In addition to being a guard for the face the menpo is important as providing a means of fastening on the helmet without too great discomfort to the wearer. A Japanese helmet is not only heavy, but top-heavy, and the brim comes so low that it must be tipped back to allow the wearer to see effectively. The neck guard is very wide and deep and a blow on the side would knock the helmet entirely out of place if it were not well secured. The means provided for this purpose were rings, or loops, at the lower edge of the helmet; and hooks, pins or rings on the menpo. The middle of a soft, heavy cord was fastened to the ring at the back of the helmet and the cord was laced up and down from the rings on the helmet to the fastenings on the menpo and finally tied under the chin of the latter. This held the helmet securely and the menpo distributed the pressure. A cushion was fastened in the chin or a handkerchief was used as padding as mentioned by Garbutt; and the inside of the menpo was smoothly lacquered to prevent it from chafing the face. When the helmet was properly laced in place it was perfectly secure but the wearer could not open his mouth.

MENTOK. A Javan sword with a slightly curved blade widest near the point. (Raffles plate p. 296/297).

MENTONIERE. The tilting breastplate which also protected the lower part of the face. It was an extra piece worn over the regular armor in tournaments. (ffoulkes 82).

MENUKI, MENUGI. Ornaments on the sides of the hilt of a Japanese sword or knife. They were originally intended to conceal the peg that fastens the hilt to the blade; but in practically all existing specimens they are placed to one side of it so that the hilts can be easily removed. They are held in place by a projecting lug, *ne* (root) on the back that fits into the side of the hilt, and by the braid with which it is usually wound. On a tachi they are called tsuka-ai (hilt companions). They frequently match the design of the other mountings, but often have no relation to it as many of the artists did not make both mountings and menuki. The best of them are beautiful pieces of jewelry. Fig. 569.

MERAI, MERE, PATU PONAMU. A Maori war club made of jade. See Patu.

MERLIN. A hawk, the female of *falco aesalon*. The male is called a jack.

MERATE, FRANCISCO and GABRIELLE. Two celebrated Italian armorers of the end of the 15th century. The Emperor Maximilian I brought them from Milan to Artois in Burgundy in 1494 under a three year contract. They are mentioned in a letter from Maximilian to Ludovico il Moro in 1495 as excellent armorers. (ffoulkes 136).

MERLON. A stone pier separating the openings in the battlements. During the middle ages the merlons always had openings in the middle through which the archers could shoot. The openings between the merlons could be closed by wooden shutters that could be raised and lowered by means of windlasses turning in collars fastened to the upper part of the merlons. (Violet le Duc, Hist. 364).

MESAIL, MURSAIL. The movable visor of the "pig-faced" basinet. (Boutell 127). Fig. 132.

MESANKULE. See Amentum.

METAZASHI. See Yoroi Toshi.

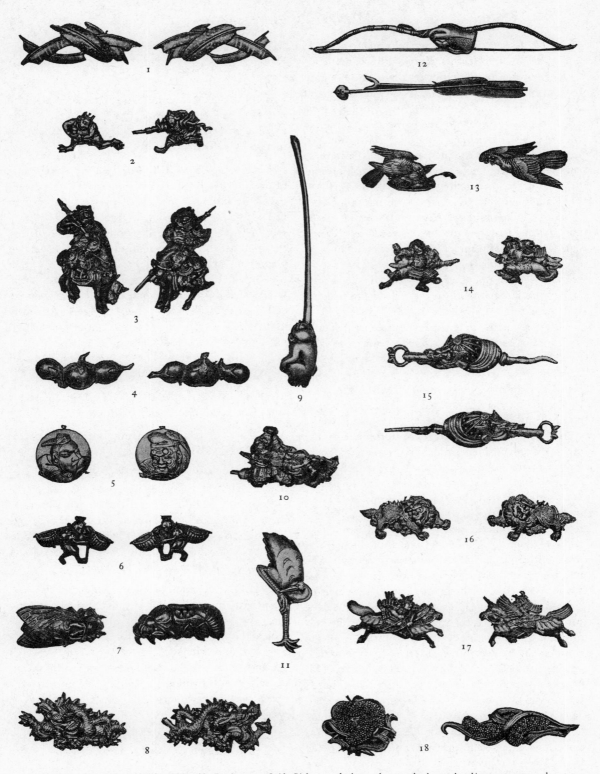

FIGURE 569. *Menuki.* 1. *Shakudo and gold. Feathers.* 2. *Gold. Bishamon chasing a demon who has stolen his stupa, or pagoda.* 3. *Shakudo, gold and copper. Kwanyu and Chohi. Chinese heroes of the 3rd century. Signed Hamano Noriyuki.* 4. *Copper, shakudo and shibuichi. Eggplants.* 5. *Gold, button-shaped. Heads of sambaso dancers.* 6. *Shakudo. Peasants carrying baskets.* 7. *Cicadas. Right, a pupa of copper; left, the winged insect, shakudo, shibuichi and gold.* 8. *Gold. Dragons. Goto School.* 9. *Silver. A monkey stretching his arm upwards, reaching for the moon. Symbolical of man striving for the unattainable.* 10. *Gold. Tadamori and the oil thief. Signed Mingioku.* 11. *Silver, shakudo and gold. A stork standing on one leg.* 12. *Shakudo and silver. A bow and archer's glove; arrows. Signed Shokatei Motohiro.* 13. *Gold, silver and shakudo. Hawks, one flying, the other eating a crane. Signed Ishiguro Masaaki.* 14. *Gold, shakudo and shibuichi. Asahina pulling off a piece of Goro's armor. (A favorite subject known as the Kusazuri episode). Signed Noriyuki.* 15. *Shakudo and gold. Helmets and whips.* 16. *Gold. Shi-shi. Goto School.* 17. *Shakudo and gold. Shigemori and Yoshihiro, two famous warriors of the 12th century.* 18. *Gold. Millet. Signed Tomei.*

METSUBUSHI, GANTSUBUSHI, PEPPER-BLOWER. An instrument formerly carried by the Japanese police for blowing pepper, or dust, in the eyes of a person they desired to capture, so as to

MEYSHA, MASHA. A trigger, Western Tibet. (Ramsay-Western).

MEZZA CAVAZIONE. The passage from a high line to a low one in Italian fencing. (Castle 101).

FIGURE 570. *Metsubushi.* 1. *Box of plain black lacquer, the outlet end.* 2. *Made of one piece of brass. Signed.* 3. *Black lacquer box with an engraved metal mouthpiece, the mouthpiece end.* 4. *Fine nashiji lacquer with a gold lacquer mon.* 5. *Fine black lacquer with a dragon in silver lacquer. Engraved metal mouthpiece. It has the square rod to close the outlet which is usually missing.*

blind him. It is a lacquer, or brass, box with a wide mouthpiece on one side and a hole, or pipe, on the other through which to blow the pepper. The mouthpiece has a wire screen on the inner side; and the outlet should have a plug to close the opening when not in use. This plug is frequently missing. Fig. 570.

Many are so well made and of such fine lacquer that it is probable that they were sometimes used by persons of higher rank than the police.

MEWS, MEW. The place where hawks were kept when moulting. (Phillott 38 note).

MEYNDA. The name for a matchlock gun in Western Tibet. (Ramsay-Western).

MEZZO CERCHIO. The Italian parry for an attack in the low inside line. (Castle 178).

MEZZO DRITTO. A time thrust on the wrist. (Castle 130).

MEZZO TEMPO. It is described by Doccolini, 1601, as "when thine enemy thrusts at thee break thou his thrust, striking him at the same time." (Castle 96).

MI. A blade, Japan.

MIAN. A spear with prongs, Nicobar Islands. The number of prongs was indicated by a second word: *Mian mom-anya,* two pronged; *M. loe,* three pronged; *M. foan,* four pronged; *M. tannin,* five pronged. They are used for spearing fish. (Man, And. & Nic. 8).

MIDLAH. An Australian spear thrower. (Wood 730).

MIDLIU. A throwing knife, Toda, Africa. (Jaehns 258).

varies considerably. Originally it was the type of fork used by the peasants in the fields, but it was soon modified to make it more serviceable as a weapon. In some cases it is a straight fork with one, or both, tines widened out to form cutting blades; in others it is a fork with a hook on the back; in

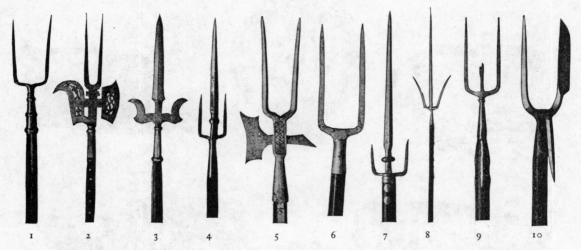

FIGURE 571. *Military Forks. 1. French, 1675. 2. Savoyard, 1579. 3. Italian, 1580. 4. French, 16th century. 5. English(?), 16th century. 6. Swiss, end of the 17th century. 7. French, 1590. 8. Italian, 1500. 9. French, 1560. 10. English(?), 1550. Metropolitan Museum. Not to scale.*

MIHILI MEZZIR. A large cultellus, a kind of knife. (Burton Sword 272).

MIJIKI KATANA. A Japanese dagger. See Tanto.

MIKA-DZUKI-NO-ITA. See Mune-Ita.

MIKUL. See Yeripul.

MILBIR. The spear thrower used near Cape Bedford, Queensland. It has a long blade of ironwood of even width throughout, and a short peg with a slight nick. The peg is set in the plane of the blade and is fastened to it by cords passing around the peg and through holes in the blade. The end of the blade and back of the peg are covered with resin. It is either haftless or has two oval plates of melo shell fixed on with beeswax or else a thin lath bent on itself. (Roth, Aust. Mus. VII, 190).

MI-LI-LANG. Gunpowder, Subanun of Mindanao. (Christie 159).

MILITARY FORK. The shape of this weapon

others again it had a double prong for thrusting on the back of a bill-hook blade. It was mainly used in the 14th century. (Hewitt II, 269). It was used as an improvised weapon by peasants up to the end of the 18th century. Fig. 571.

MILLED ARMOR. Bright and burnished armor, or glazed armor, 17th century. (Hewitt III, 702).

MIMI. An edge, Japan. The edge of a tsuba. Each form of edge had its distinguishing name.

MINE. See Mune.

MINE. Military mines are of two kinds. One was merely a subterranean passage to give access to a besieged place; the other was to throw down and destroy walls and towers. Before the invention of gunpowder the latter were often very large, the ground being supported by wooden props until the work was completed, when they were drawn or burned away, allowing the mine to cave in. (Grose II, 5).

MING-TI. See Whistling Arrow.

MINIE BALL. A rifle ball with a hollow base, the pressure of the powder gases in which forced the bullet into the grooves of the rifling. At first an iron cup was placed in the hollow, but this was found to be unnecessary.

MINION. See Cannon.

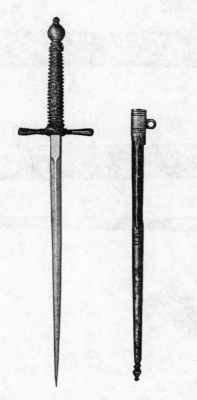

FIGURE 572. *Misericorde, French, 16th century. Metropolitan Museum.*

MIOCHIN. The most celebrated school, or guild, of Japanese armorers. It was founded by Miochin Munesuke in the 12th century. The family name was Masuda until the Emperor Konohe (1142-1155) gave them that of Miochin. Miochin Munesuke worked at Kyoto from 1154 to 1185, and the family reputation was maintained by his successors until 1756. Nobuiye, whose tsuba are so rare and so celebrated, was the 17th Miochin. Nobuiye, Yoshimichi and Takayoshi are the most celebrated masters of the family, except the founder. They are known as *Nochi-no-San-Saku*, the "three later renowned artists." The Miochin family not only made armor and tsuba but many other kinds of artistic iron work.

The first ten generations form a separate group, the Miochin Judai. Their work is never signed. They were called the *Sorui*, as all of their names begin with the character So (Mune). The next six ending with Yoshiyasu, are called Girui, their names beginning with the character Gi (Yoshi). It was not until the time of the twenty-first Miochin, Kunimichi (1624-1643), that they examined and certified the work attributed to their predecessors. There were twenty-four masters in the direct line, the last being Mune-Masa, 1688-1740. Including pupils who were considered as members of the family there were one hundred and fifty-one. (Gilbertson Genealogy).

MIOLNER. The hammer of Thor which flew back to his hand when thrown. (Burton Sword 35).

MIQUELET LOCK. One of the earliest forms of flintlock which continued in use in Turkey and the neighboring countries until very recently. See Flintlock.

MIRO. A double-pointed club, Queensland. (Vic. Mus. 29).

MIRO. See Periperiu.

MISERICORDE. The "dagger of mercy" intended to be thrust between the plates of a fallen foe and give him the "*coup de grace*." The sight of the uplifted dagger often caused him to surrender, hence the name. It had a long, narrow blade intended solely for thrusting. (Hewitt I, 319). Fig. 572.

MISSAGLIA. The Missaglia family of Milan were the most celebrated of the early armorers. The family name was Negroni, and the first of whom we have knowledge was Petrojolo Negroni of Missaglia who worked about 1390. His son Thomaso (about 1418-1468) and grandson Antonio Missaglia (about 1430-1492) were the most celebrated members of the family. Later they resumed the family name of Negroni, or Negroli; and in the next century Philippo, Jacomo and Francesco Negroli were celebrated for their decorative work, which was wonderfully elaborate, but not generally so much so as to destroy its usefulness. The casque, fig. 201, no. 6, was the work of Philippo.

In the 15th century the house and workshop of the Missaglia was in the Via degli Spadari. The heavy work was done at their mill near Porta Ro-

MISURA STRETTA. A measure (distance) in fencing so close that a thrust can only be made by moving the hand alone. (Castle 99, 107).

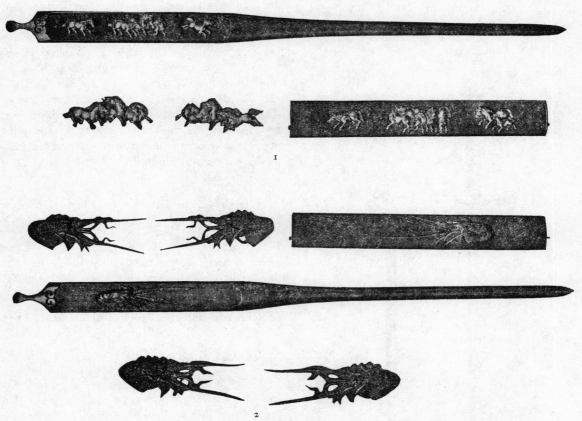

FIGURE 573. *Mitokoro Mono. 1. Shakudo, nanako. Horses in high relief in gold. Goto School. 2. Daisho set. Kozuka and kogai of shakudo, nanako, with copper crawfish in relief. Signed Nomura Masahide, and kakihan. Menuki copper crawfish. Signed Masayuki.*

magna, and later near the S. Angelo canal. They leased and afterwards bought the iron mines near Lago del Segrino. Both Thomaso and Antonio were ennobled by the State and did much to make Milan famous for its armor.

They not only made suits for the nobles, fig. 37, but took government contracts for equipping large bodies of troops, and did it in the most modern manner—mining their own ore, smelting it, converting the steel into plate at their own mills and then fabricating the armor from it. (ffoulkes Armourer 137).

MISURA LARGA. A measure (distance) in fencing in which it is only possible to deliver an attack by stepping forward or by lunging. (Castle 99, 107).

MIT. A Siamese dagger with a melon-shaped pommel. (South Kensington Museum).

MITOKORO MONO. "Objects for three places"—kogai, kozuka and menuki. Such sets made by famous artists, were very highly valued by the Japanese and were frequently given by the Shogun to nobles that he desired to honor; and by the latter to each other. Fig. 573.

MITSUKI. The guardhouse at the entrance of a castle, Japan.

MKUKI, FARARA. The East African spear which is used almost entirely for stabbing. "It has a long, narrow blade of untempered iron so soft that it can be bent with the fingers, but capable of receiving a fine edge. The shoulders are rounded, and one or two lines extend over the entire center. At the socket, where the shaft is introduced, it is covered with the skin from the tail of an animal

piece of buckskin; the Western Indians usually made their moccasins with stiff soles. Some of the Southwestern tribes are said to have used a special war shoe with a round, stiff sole so that it was diffi-

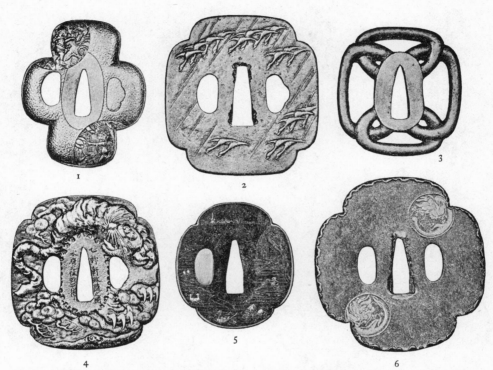

FIGURE 574. *Mokko Tsuba.* 1. *Sentoku with a gold rim. Designs in low relief copied from Spanish stamped leather.* 2. *Iron, slight gold inlay. Geese flying in the rain.* 3. *Iron, plain.* 4. *Iron, a tiger and pine tree in low relief, inlaid with shakudo, gold and silver.* 5. *Shakudo, engraved landscape with inlays of gold and silver.* 6. *Iron with coiled dragons in low relief in gold.*

drawn on like a stocking, but sometimes the iron is forced on when heated so as to adhere by the contraction of the metal. The shaft, which is five or six feet long, is made from the dark brown *mkole* or the light yellow *mtate* tree, chosen because they are close grained, tough, pliable and free from knots. It is peeled, straightened in hot ashes, pared down smoothly to the heart and carefully oiled or greased, without which it soon becomes brittle. The shaft is usually ornamented with coils of brass or copper wire, and sometimes tin or zinc. It generally has an iron heel for planting in the ground. The best are made at Karagwah." (Burton Sword 475).

MOCCASIN. The shoe of the North American Indian. The moccasin of the Indians of the Eastern woodlands was a soft slipper made of a single

cult to ascertain from the tracks in which direction the wearer had gone.

MOCHIDATE. A shield carried on the arm. A target, Japan.

MODORI. A barb, Japan.

MOFUTAGI. See Motagi.

MOJIRI. See Sode Garami.

MOJI TSUDZUMI. A Japanese corselet covered with silk. (Conder 263).

MOKKO. A Japanese tsuba of four lobes, a quite common form. Fig. 574.

The name is derived from the shape which is that of a section of the four-lobed tree melon, *mokko*. (Weber II, 59).

MOKO-ITA. The top plate of the back of a Japanese corselet. It is like the muna-ita at the top of the breastplate. It often carried a fastening for the socket, sashimono-gane, for the shaft of a small flag

together, and then twisting and beating them out of shape in various ways, and finally planing the slab down to thin sheets. These were then pickled to obtain the varied colors of the different constit-

FIGURE 575. *Moplah Knives. 1. Wood hilt with engraved steel mounts. 2. Blade 14 inches long, wood hilt with engraved and pierced brass mountings. 3. Ebony hilt mounted with chased brass. 4. Blade 12.5 inches long. Pierced and chased brass mounts.*

carried on the back. A second socket, uke-mochi, on the lower part of the backplate held the lower end of the shaft. (Conder 266). The upper socket projected much further from the back than the lower in order to carry the staff out clear of the neck guard of the helmet.

MOKUME. Japanese "wood grain." The word is used in three meanings. First for a special kind of watering on blades that resembles the grain of wood. Second, for a decoration of engraved, or etched, lines on iron imitating the grain of wood. This is often found on Miochin guards. It is called mokume hada and is, or should be, the lines of the welds of the metal.

Third, a material made by piling on one another sheets of different metals and alloys, soldering them

uents. It was used for tsuba and other sword mountings. The Takahashi family was celebrated for this kind of work.

MOKUMA HADA. Iron mokume with a surface like the grain of wood.

MOMIDZUKIN. A kind of skull cap worn under a Japanese helmet. (Garbutt 169).

MOMOGATA. A type of Japanese helmet. (Garbutt 168).

MOMONARI. A Japanese helmet that is considered to resemble a peach in shape. (Conder 257).

MON. A crest, Japan. The Japanese had an elaborate system of heraldry and the mon were often used as decorations on arms and armor. The mon

FIGURE 576. *Morians.* 1. *Italian,* 1570. 2. *German, Munich Civil Guard, end of the 16th century.* 3. *Saxon,* 1560. 4. *French,* 1570. 5. *Saxon,* 1575. *Guard of Christian I.* 6. *Italian,* 1570. *Metropolitan Museum. Not to scale.*

FIGURE 577. *Morion-Cabassets.* 1. *Italian,* 1585. 2. *Italian,* 1570. *Metropolitan Museum. Not to scale.*

was hardly the equivalent of the European crest as it did not originally belong to any particular family. Later, 1642, the daimios were required to register their mon which could not then be used by anyone else. The registered mon was called a *jo-mon* and could only be used on the occasion of solemn ceremonies, or when performing some important function. Another form of registered mon, the *kaye-mon*, usually derived from the jo-mon, was used by the principal retainers and by the family on unofficial occasions. (Weber I, 35).

MON-GIL MON-GIL. A Cape Bedford spear with a long reed shaft and a short hard wood head with wooden barbs placed in pairs alternately on opposite sides. (Roth, Aust. Mus. VII, 194).

MONGILE, WAL. Mongile is apparently a general name for a spear in Victoria; and wal was only used near Lake Tyers. Brough Smyth (I, 304) describes two entirely different spears under these names. The first has jagged chips of stone set in grooves on opposite sides; the second is made entirely of wood and has long, slim, curved barbs in pairs; it is very light and is thrown by hand.

MONGOLI. A fighting spear with a flattened head barbed on both sides, Victoria. (Vic. Mus. 33).

MONGWANGA. A throwing knife, Congo. (Jaehns 258). See Throwing Knife.

MONOKIRI. The edge of a sword, Japan.

MONONOGU. Arms and armor, Japan.

MONS MEG. A celebrated cannon made at Mons in Belgium and now in Edinburgh castle. It weighs four tons, is of about twenty inches bore and its stone shot is estimated to have weighed 350 pounds. (Greener 27).

MONTANTE. An ascending cut with the false edge of a sabre. (Castle 135).

MONTEAUBAN, CHAPEL DE. See Chapel de Monteauban.

MOONOE. See Yeamberan.

MOORISH PIKE. See Morris Pike.

MOOR-OONA. See Kur-Ruk.

MOPLAH KNIVES. The Moplah. Indigenous Mohammedans of Malabar have a curious sword,

or knife, of their own. It has a light, broad, double-edged blade curved at the end. The hilt is straight and without a guard. The hilt mounts and rein-

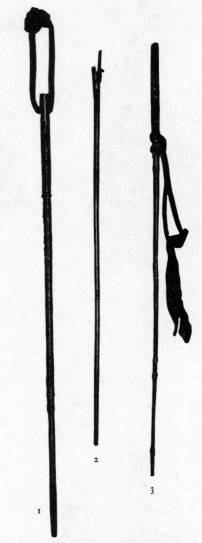

FIGURE 578. *Muchi, Riding Whips. 1. Ringed red stick wound with coils of yellow cane. Leather covered handle, bronze caps on both ends. Length 30.875 inches. 2. Stick of black whalebone with a brass whistle on the handle. 3. Black whalebone with coils of yellow cane. Handle covered with red cloth. Length 30.5 inches.*

forcing pieces on the blade are of brass or silver and are elaborately pierced and engraved. The sword is carried without a scabbard, blade up, with the handle thrust inside the belt at the back. Fig. 575.

Egerton calls this weapon an ayda katti.

MORI. A harpoon, Japan.

MORIAN, MORION. A light, open headpiece with a high comb and a brim forming high peaks front and back, and turned down at the sides. The finer ones are marvelous forgings. The best are made of a single piece of steel with a hollow comb

lance having the point rebated, or turned back, to prevent injury to the opponent. (Planche 372).

MORNING STAR. See Holy Water Sprinkle.

MOROHA. A double-edged blade, Japan.

MORRIS PIKE, MOORISH PIKE. A kind of

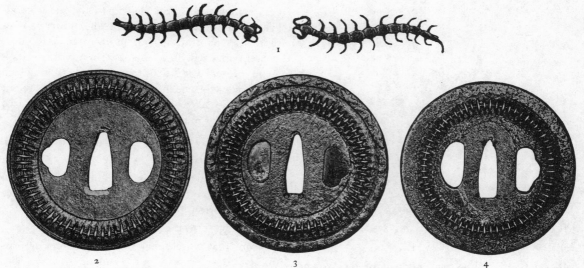

FIGURE 579. *Mukade. 1. A pair of menuki, shakudo and copper. Realistic centipedes. 2, 3, 4. Mukade tsuba, the conventional centipedes. 2. Iron, the ring of copper and the cross wires, alternately, of shakudo and sentoku. Collection of Mr. R. H. Rucker. 3. Iron, the mukade is of shakudo and sentoku, the conventional pine trees around the edge are of brass. 4. Iron, the mukade is like the others. The surface is of gomoku zogan.*

as much as four inches high. Many are made of two pieces joined on the center line of the top. It was very popular from the middle of the 16th century until the abandonment of armor. At first it was worn mainly by pikemen, later it was used by the guards of princes. Fig. 576.

MORIAN-CABASSET. An open helmet with a crown like that of a cabasset and a brim like that of a morian. Fig. 577.

MORIANKATU. Arrows of the Veddah of Ceylon. They are of wood thirty to thirty-six inches long and have three feathers. Some have simple wood points, others have large leaf-shaped heads. See Malali. (Hiller & Furness 35).

Cowper says, p. 189, that they have five feathers.

MORIYO. Ghost, a type of Japanese menpo. (Conder 262).

MORNE, MORNETTE. The head of a tilting

pike much used during the 16th century. It is uncertain in what respect it differed from the ordinary pike. (Grose I, 129, II, 280).

MORRO, MARO, KUNBAI-IL, PA-UL. A throwing stick of Northern Queensland. It is a straight, round stick enlarging towards the handle which is pointed. It is sometimes made of *gidyea* (*Acacia Hamalophylla*) colored black with charcoal and grease. It is as much as thirty-two inches long. (W. E. Roth, No. 7, p. 34).

MORTAR. A variety of cannon designed for high angle fire, and having a powder chamber of smaller diameter than the bore. The earliest large cannon were mortars.

MOSHA-KINA. A plant from the fibres of which the Ainu make their bowstrings. (Greey 61, 109).

MOTAGI, MOFUTAGI. Decorated heads on the mekugi when it is made of metal and in two pieces. With the later swords a wooden peg is generally used and the menuki placed beside it to take the place of the motagi. (Joly, Int. 530).

MOTODORI. The short pigtail formerly worn by the Japanese. (Garbutt 149).

MOTOHAZU. The ends of a bow, Japan.

MOTON. See Besague.

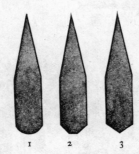

FIGURE 580. *Mune.* 1. *Maramune.* 2. *Mitsumune.* 3. *Ihoremune.*

MOTO-O. The main cord for fastening on the Japanese helmet. (Garbutt 147).

MOULINET. The arrangement of tackles and windlass by which the larger crossbows were drawn. Fig. 19.

MOUSQUETON. A smooth bore gun with a flintlock and a barrel about four feet long, 17th century. (Hewitt III, 749).

MOUTON. A huge engine forty feet long, twenty wide and twenty high used for throwing stones at the siege of Ghent in 1382. (Hewitt II, 327).

MOVABLE TOWERS. See Belfry.

MOYEGI-NIOI-ODOSHI. Japanese armor laced with green cords of several shades. (Conder 271).

MUCHI. A riding whip, Japan. A flexible stick, or switch, without a lash. Fig. 578.

MUCHI-GASHI-NO-ANA. The slits in the upper part of the Japanese cuisses. (Conder 275).

MUGDAR. A heavy wooden club, two feet or more long, and weighing fourteen to twenty pounds. It was sometimes weighted with lead. It was used for exercise by the sepoys in India. (Egerton, p. 147).

MUGUR-MOOKHAN. See Jowala Mookhi.

MUKABAKI. A guard worn on the front of the leg when hunting, Japan.

MUKABIKI. Armor for the legs, leggings, Japan. Compare Mukabaki.

MUKADE. A centipede, Japan. It is often used in the decoration of sword fittings and armor in commemoration of the slaying of the giant centipede by Tawara Toda in the 10th century. Sometimes it is naturalistic, but more often it is much conventionalized. One of the commonest forms is a ring of wire parallel to the edge of a tsuba which is crossed at frequent intervals by shorter wires. The guards called shingen are, by some, considered as a variety of mukade. (Weber II, 68). Fig. 579.

MUKASHI JIKORO. A variety of Shikoro. (Garbutt 168).

MUKTA. In the ancient Hindu classification of weapons—those that are thrown, it includes twelve species. (Burton Sword 214). See Amukta.

MUKTAMUKTA. The ancient Hindu class of weapons that were either thrown or not, comprising twenty-nine varieties. (Burton Sword). See Amukta.

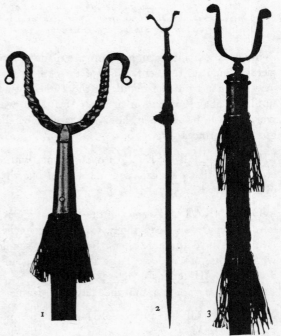

FIGURE 581. *Musket Rests.* 1, 3. *German.* 2. *Italian. All 17th century. Metropolitan Museum.*

MUKTA SANDHARITA. The ancient Hindu class of weapons that were thrown and drawn back. (Burton Sword 214). See Amukta.

land natives, and the others by those of the lower Murray. It is relatively narrow, with the front more or less convex and the cross section triangular,

FIGURE 582. *European Horse Muzzles. 1. Probably German, 1552. 2. Italian, 1567. 3. Italian, 1575. 4. German, 1575. Metropolitan Museum. Not to scale.*

MUKU GITAI. Japanese blades made entirely of steel (cemented). These show good wood grain. (Weber II, 69).

MULAMA. Fire gilding, that is, covering the parts to be gilded with gold amalgam and driving off the mercury by heat. India and Persia.

MULGA, MULGON, MARU-AGA. A type of shield, Australia. The last name is used by the Gyps-

the handle being cut from the solid. The front is always ornamented with incised lines in herring-bone, chevron or lozenge patterns. The grooves are usually filled in with white, red or yellow pigments. The length is about two feet and the width rarely more than five inches. It is made of some hard, heavy wood such as ironbark or acacia and weighs two and a half to three and a half pounds. (Vic. Mus. 13). It is used in parrying club blows.

MULON, MURGON, MURR-AGA, RI-ANGAPA, RI-ANG-PAL, TA-CHAL. Cape Bedford spears with bamboo or reed shafts and

FIGURE 583. *Japanese Horse Muzzle, 17th century. Iron.*

hardwood heads with pieces of bone fastened diagonally to the tips so as to form both point and barb. (Roth, Aust. Mus. VII, 192).

MULO CHITOHO. A dagger in San Ch'uan Chinese. (Rockhill).

MUNA-ITA, MIKI-DZUKI-NO-ITA, MU-NA-KANA-MONO. A narrow plate at the top of a Japanese breastplate. The first is the general name; the second refers to the crescent shape of the upper edge; and the third means "made of metal." It is usually covered with ornamental leather and carries rings for attaching the shoulder pieces. (Conder 265).

MUNE, MINE, SENA. The back of a blade, Japan. Mine is an obsolete name. There are three shapes: *Maramune*, rounded; *Mitsumune*, three-sided; and *Ihore-Mune* or *Kakumune*, shaped like the roof of a small temple, i.e., two planes meeting at a slightly obtuse angle. Fig. 580.

MUNE-UCHI. Striking with the back of the blade, Japan.

MUNJANEKA. Balistas used by the Tartar Ali at the siege of Chitore at the end of the 13th century. (Tod II, 606).

MUNJAN JIL. The hole for the spear thrower in the butt of the Kakadu spear called Kunjolio.

MUN-UP. See Yeamberen.

MURAGUGNA. A Melville Island club. "A straight stick with a very marked swollen head and a more or less rapidly tapering point. The surface is strongly grooved. In the widest part the diameter is two inches or slightly more." (Spencer, North. Ter. 369).

MURAMASA. Next to Masamune the most celebrated Japanese sword maker. There is a superstition that his blades thirsted for blood and would not rest in their scabbards but impelled their owners to kill others, or to commit suicide. They were supposed to be particularly unlucky for the Tokugawa family; and at one time their use was forbidden at the Shogun's court. Though Muramasa's work is of the highest quality his name is often left out of the lists of celebrated makers because of the reputation of his blades for bloodthirstiness and for bringing bad luck to their owners.

MURASAKI ODOSHI. Japanese armor laced with purple cords.

MURDERER. A small mortar. (ffoulkes Armouries 84).

MURGON. See Mulga.

MURIWUN, MURRI-WUN. See Kur-Ruk.

MU-RONGAL. A spear with a short grass-tree shaft and a long barbed head of hardwood, North Queensland. (Roth, Aust. Mus. VII, 194).

MURR-AGA. See Mulga.

MURSAIL. See Mesail.

MUSCHETTAE. A kind of crossbow bolt feathered with cardboard, 14th century. (Hewitt II, 279).

MUSCULUS. A movable contrivance for sheltering besiegers while at work, 9th century. (Hewitt I, 88).

MUSKET. A male sparrow hawk. Also see Musquet, a gun.

MUSKETOON. A gun lighter and shorter than a musquet. It was carried by cavalry. A short musquet with the bore the thirty-eighth part of the length. (Hoyt 441).

MUSQUET, MUSKET. Originally a matchlock gun too heavy to be fired without a rest, therefore the smallest of cannon. As many cannon were given the names of birds and animals, this was called a musket, the falconer's name for the male sparrow hawk, the smallest of hawks. (Pollard 7).

The musquet was the largest gun carried and used by a single man; some of the very early ones are said to have been of one inch bore. In 1691 "the barrel of a musquet should be four feet in length, the bore capable of receiving bullets, twelve whereof weigh a pound." The early musquets were always fired from a rest. They were heavier than arquebuses which usually had wheel locks, while the musquets had matchlocks. Later the name came to signify any kind of a gun used by regular infantry. (Grose II, 292).

MUSQUET ARROW, SPRIGHT. In the early days of firearms wooden arrows were often used as missiles for them and were said to pierce objects that would resist lead bullets. (Grose I, 157).

MUSQUET-FUSIL. A gun having both match- and flintlocks. It was sometimes used in the early days of flintlocks before they became sufficiently developed to be reliable.

MUSQUET REST. The simplest form of rest was a staff with a fork at the end in which to rest the barrel when the gun was fired. Later one of the prongs of the fork was often lengthened and pointed at the top so that it could be used as a defense against cavalry. Some had long spikes concealed in the shaft which sprang out on opening a small cover on the end; these were called swine's, or Swedish, feathers and were planted in the ground to protect the musqueteers when reloading. (Grose I, 156). Fig. 581.

In Northern and Central Asia a very common form of rest is an A-shaped frame pivoted to a lug on the stock, fig. 328. It is short as the users sat or squatted when they shot.

The Plains Indians used two short sticks, held crossed in the left hand, as a rest for their guns. They also kneeled or squatted to shoot.

MUSUBI GANE. (Knot metal). A ring attached to the pommel of a tachi to which the udenuki cord (sword knot) was fastened. It is uncertain whether the saru-te was considered a variety of musubi gane, or a substitute for it.

MUTE. To defecate, spoken of a hawk, except the sparrow hawk and goshawk which "sliced."

MUTU GITAI. The best method of making Japanese blades. A soft steel bar was doubled, welded and forged to the original section, and these operations were repeated many times. It was then forged to shape, cemented, hardened and tempered. See Japanese Blades. Gilbertson mentions one in which the final bar was composed of 4,194,304 layers. (Gilbertson Blades 191).

MUZZLE. Elaborately pierced and chased steel muzzles for horses were used in the 16th century. They were probably used in tournaments to prevent the horses from biting. The heavy chargers of the time were invariably stallions, and usually vicious, and some protection from them was needed. Fig. 582.

The Japanese used very similar muzzles, their ponies being notoriously bad tempered. Fig. 583.

FIGURE 584. *Nagafukurin. The binding strips are of silver engraved with kiri crests. The scabbard is of red and black lacquer.*

MYSTERIOUS CIRCLE. A circle, the radius of which was the length of the sword blade, was the basis of a system of fencing described by Girard

FIGURE 585. *Nagegama. Blade 2 inches long forged in one piece with the shaft. Total length 12.25 inches.*

Thibault in 1628. Though published in Antwerp it appeared to be based on the elaborate Spanish treatises of the period. (Castle 124, 125).

N

NABOOT. A quarterstaff of palm wood, Egypt.

NACAIRE, NAKERE. A kind of drum. Both name and instrument are of Eastern origin. It is believed to have been a kettledrum, 14th century. (Hewitt II, 309).

NAGAFUKURIN. A Japanese scabbard with two long strips of metal on the edges, held in place by rings. This form is derived from the style of the *kazuchi no tachi*. The pieces of metal covered the joints between the two pieces of wood of which the scabbard was made and, with the rings, held them firmly together. (Joly S. & S. 22). Fig. 584.

The literal meaning of the name is "a long ornamental border."

NAGAMAKI. A Japanese spear with a long, and almost straight, blade. It is much like a naginata. (Ogawa).

NAGATACHI. A long sword, Japan.

NAGAYE. The shaft of a spear, Japan.

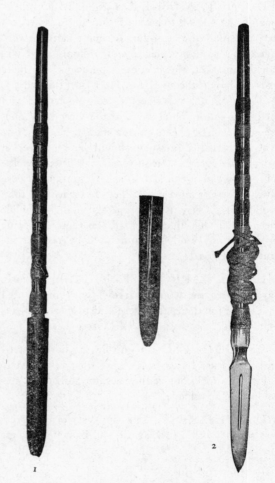

FIGURE 586. *Nageyari. 1. Head of quadrangular section 4.5 inches long. Shaft wound with bands of red and yellow cane. Total length 17 inches. Black lacquer sheath. 2. Head 5 inches long, of triangular section, set in a silver socket. Red shaft wound with bands of red and black cane. Total length 17.75 inches. Black lacquer sheath.*

NAGEGAMA. A Japanese weapon with a short, sickle-like blade at right angles to a short handle with a chain attached. It was used particularly by and decorated with metal mountings. Like all Japanese spears it was always carried sheathed. (Dean Hdbk. 133). Fig. 587.

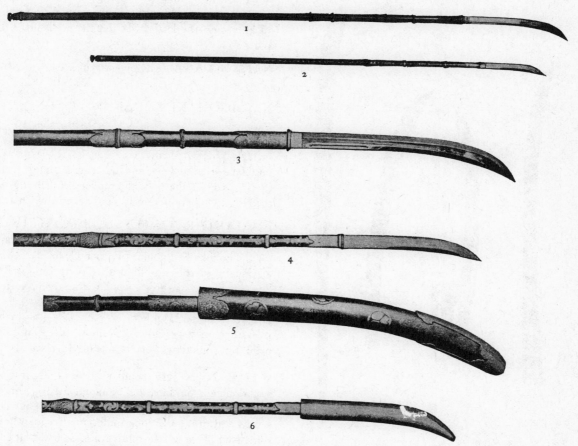

FIGURE 587. Naginata. 1, 3, 5. Length blade 18.25 inches. The shaft and sheath are of nashiji lacquer with gold lacquer Tokugawa crests. The mountings are of engraved bronze. A parade weapon. Length overall 8 feet 4.5 inches. 2, 4, 6. Length blade 10.75 inches. Shaft of black lacquer decorated with a vine and Arima crests in gold, mountings of silver. The scabbard is of gold lacquer.

the defenders of castles. It was thrown down from the wall and drawn back by the chain. Fig. 585.

NAGEYARI, NAGARI, NAGUYA. A javelin, Japan. It has a short, heavy head and a short shaft that tapers towards the butt. Fig. 586.

NAGINATA. A Japanese spear with a head like a sword blade curving back very much near the point. It is sometimes called the "woman's spear," because women were taught to use it, mainly for exercise, but partly so that they were prepared to use it in case of necessity. The shafts are lacquered

There are three varieties; the most usual one has a tang that fits into the shaft; the naginata-no-saki has a socket on the end of the blade into which the shaft fits. It is the rarest form. The oldest form is the tsukushi naginata which has a loop, or loops, on the back of the blade into which the handle fits. Fig. 588.

The naginata was very generally used for the guards of princes and sometimes has a banner-like cover of brocade or plain cloth, usually with the owner's mon embroidered on it. Fig. 589.

NAGINATA-NO-SAKI. A naginata with a socket for the shaft on the end of the blade. 1, fig. 588.

FIGURE 588. *Naginata Blades. 1. Naginata-No-Saki, with a socket on the end of the blade. 2, 3. Tsukushi Naginata. Sockets for the shafts on the backs of the blades. 4. Usual form with a tang.*

NAGPHANI DHAL. A Nepalese shield with a border of interlaced cobras, usually in high relief. The name means "snake hood shield." (Egerton 365).

NAHAR-NUK. See Bagh Nakh.

NAIL PLATE. See Contreplatine.

NAI SHOKPA, NAI SHROKPA. A helmet, Western Tibet. (Ramsay-Western).

NAKAGO, KOMI, KUKI. The tang of a Japanese blade. The shapes of most of the tangs and the file marks on them are characteristic of the makers. Some are of the shape of memorial tablets in order that when the owner fought he might have something holy in his hand. The left side, when held point up and edge away from the holder, was called the *ura*, and the opposite side the *omote*. Tachi were signed on the former and katana and all knives on the latter. See Japanese Blades. Fig. 401.

NAKAGO ANA. The opening in a tsuba for the tang.

NAKAGO SAKI. See Saki.

NAKHUNA. An archer's ring. Central India.

NALUTSCH. A bow case, Russia. It was of the familiar Oriental type, and was carried hung from the left side of the belt, the quiver being hung on the right. (Scheremetew I, 249). See Bow Case.

NAMAKO RYO-HITSU, RYO-HITSU. Openings in a tsuba shaped like kidneys. They are for the kozuka and kogai. (Weber II, 84).

Usually there is an elliptical opening for the kozuka, and one of three lobes for the kogai. Often both are of the same shape; sometimes they are of fanciful shapes. If either, or both, are not to be used they may be closed by metal plugs, usually plain, but sometimes very beautifully decorated.

NAMBAN. A very popular style of decorating sword fittings in Japan. The metal used is almost always iron which is pierced in very open designs of scrolls and dragons, much undercut. Frequently in some part of the guard there is a loose ball that can be seen and moved through openings smaller than its diameter. This ball represents the pearl the dragon is guarding. In some the dragons are movable. Unlike most tsuba the seppa dai is usually decorated in nambans. This name also includes the thousand monkey design. Fig. 590.

The namban is also called the "Chinese" or "Canton" style, as it is very similar to many of the Chinese guards. Both are probably derived from the Portuguese, the Chinese cup guards certainly are. In fig. 590, no. 2 shows a Chinese cup, and no. 5 one of Japanese make. The Japanese work is much finer, otherwise they are very similar.

NAMBAN-BO. "Southern barbarian's face," a type of menpo.

NAMBAN SODE, GAKU-SODE. Japanese shoulder guards shaped like the framed tablets hung in front of temples. The central portion was of one

NANAKO. "Fish roe surface," a surface decoration produced by forming very small raised bosses by a sharply struck cupped punch. Shakudo is the

FIGURE 589. *Naginata Covers. 1. Red cloth with a mon embroidered in white. 2. Brocade with a mon embroidered in black and white. 3. Black cloth with a white embroidered mon applique.*

plate of metal lacquered with a dragon or some other device; and the border, which resembled the frame of a tablet, was of some bright ornamental metal. (Conder 272).

NAMBAN SEKI BORI. Pierced in namban style.

NAMBAN TETSU. "Foreign iron," or "iron of the southern Barbarians." European iron which was very highly valued in Japan for making armor in the 16th and 17th centuries. (Dean Hdbk. 127).

The Japanese considered all foreigners, with the exception of the Chinese, as barbarians; and as all foreigners arrive in Japan from the south, they were called "southern barbarians."

NAME. A pad under a saddle, Japan.

NAMRAL, RAGEE. A sword, Western Tibet. (Ramsay-Western).

metal most often used, though copper and gold are quite often employed. The harder metals, shibuichi, silver and iron are rarely decorated in this way. The size of the dots varies from about 0.04 to 0.008 inches in diameter (25 to 125 to an inch) and the regularity of the work is marvelous as the dots must be spaced entirely by touch. The dots are generally arranged in straight lines, or in lines parallel to the edges of the piece being decorated; but sometimes in more elaborate patterns. It is sometimes in diagonal lines forming lozenges. This is called *gonome* or *gunome* nanako, and its invention is ascribed to Muneta Matabei, about 1560. The *daimio* nanako was introduced by Muneta Norinao about 1740. In it the grains are separated by spaces of equal size. It is very rare. In some the background has flowered figures on it so small that they can only be seen with a fairly strong magnifying glass. In some cases there are three grains, one on top of the other. In the style of decoration called *kin-sunago-ji* the design is in flat inlay of various metals and then gone over with nanako. The uniformity and regularity

of stone attached by gum. Victoria and Central Australia. (Brough Smyth I, 305).

NARNAL. A cannon small enough to be carried by a single man, India. (Egerton, p. 152).

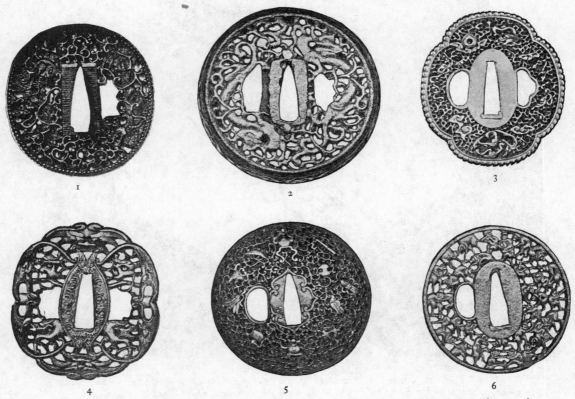

FIGURE 590. *Namban Tsuba.* 1. *Iron, pierced with dragons and scrolls.* 2. *Iron, Chinese form and workmanship.* 3. *Shakudo, pierced with dragons and scrolls and a movable ball.* 4. *Iron and gold, dragons and scrolls.* 5. *Iron, cup-shaped, pierced scrolls with a takaramono in gold. The takaramono is the contents of the mythical treasure ship.* 6. *Iron, the thousand monkeys.*

of the dots when changing from a hard to a very soft metal, or the reverse, is wonderful. Fig. 452.

Nanako is very generally used as a background on sword fittings; in fact at one time it was considered as the only one permissible for use on court swords.

It is said that the nanako workers were always women. This is very probable as their sense of touch is much more sensitive than that of men.

NANIYE KITAE. "Beaten seven times" is often inscribed on iron tsuba, chiefly on those of Miochin work.

NANDUM. Heavy wooden spears with a line of barbs on one side only. Sometimes the barbs are chips

NASAL. A piece depending from the front of a helmet to protect the nose of the wearer. Fixed nasals were characteristic of the European helmets of the 11th century, and nasals were used with some kinds of open helmets until the abandonment of armor. They have always been used with Persian, Turkish and Indian helmets. In the East they are always movable, passing through a loop on the front of the helmet and being held up out of the way by a setscrew or a link and hook. They were used even on mail hoods. This form of nasal was lowered to protect the face, or was hung up out of the way when not required. Occasionally Indian helmets have three "nasals," one in front of the nose and the other two on the temples, fig. 62. The Oriental nasals usually have a plate on each end which is usually decorated; in some cases the lower one is large enough to cover most of the face below the eyes. Fig. 365.

swords, spears, javelins and bows. (Tennent I, 499).

NAWAMIMI. A roped edge of a tsuba. (Weber I, 203).

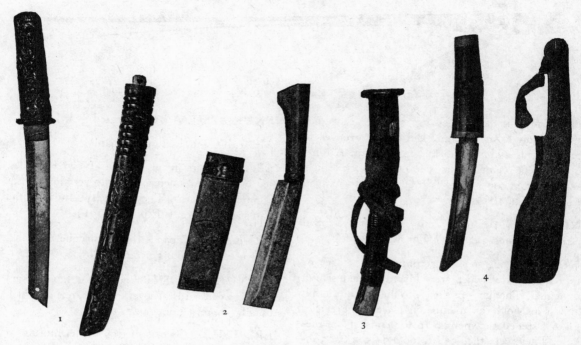

FIGURE 591. *Nata.* 1. *Scroll-ended blade 8.5 inches long. All mounts of wood, the animals of the Zodiac. The kashira is the cock; the fuchi the dog and monkey; the edge of the tsuba the snake; the kurikata the rat; the soritsuno the pig; the kojiri the rabbit; the kozuka the ox; and the rest of the animals are carved in low relief on the hilt and scabbard. 2. Plain handle; blade 6 inches long, chisel-edged with a square chisel end. Scabbard inlaid with birch bark. Probably Ainu. 3. Chisel-edged blade 6.375 inches long. Rough wooden scabbard with cane bands and staghorn mounts. 4. Very rough, heavy blade engraved with a dragon. Possibly Chinese.*

NASHI-HADA. See Hada.

NASHIJI. See Lacquer.

NASHIJI ISHIME. A metal surface so treated as to resemble the skin of a pear. It is used as a background on Japanese sword fittings. (Joly Int. 35). The name is due to its resemblance to nashiji lacquer.

NATA. A hatchet. A Japanese knife with a curved, chisel-edged blade with a scroll end. It is usually called a gardener's knife, or a hunting knife. Fig. 591.

NATA. A hatchet. A Japanese knife with a metal ring on the end. It was included in Ceylon in the "five weapons of war," the others being

NAWAZ KHANI. A sword with a hilt like that of a firangi, and a blade back edged and slightly incurved, Deccan. (Wallace Orient).

NAYIN. The crossbow of the Mpangwe of the Gaboon River. To bend it they sit on their haunches and apply both feet to the middle of the bow, while they pull with all of their strength on the string. The stock is a straight piece of wood, considerably wider at the end containing the mortise for the bow. There is a vertical opening through the stock at the middle of the notch for the string. A thin piece is split from the under side of the stock in such a way that it remains firmly attached at the front end. Where it passes under the notch a block is fastened to it which pushes the string out of the notch when the split piece is pressed upwards. Two kinds of arrows are used with it; the larger ones are about two feet long, have iron heads and are used for game. The smaller are slips of bamboo about a foot

It is believed that they were intended to keep the pieces from slipping from the scabbard. (Joly, Naunton xii).

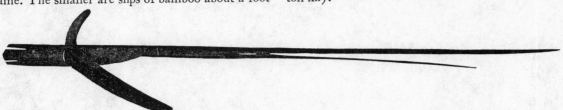

FIGURE 592. *Nayin. Stock 3 feet 9.5 inches long. Wood bow 2 feet 1 inch long.*

long and poisoned. They are so light that they would blow away if simply laid on the groove; to prevent this a kind of sticky gum is used. A lump of it is kept on the under side of the stock, and a small spot in the groove is rubbed lightly with it. (Du Chaillu, 107). Fig. 592.

NDZIGA. A throwing knife, Baghirmi, Central Africa. (Jaehns 258). See Throwing Knife.

NE. (Root). A short lug connected to three or four small plates which are soldered to the inside of a menuki. The lug is pressed into the side of the hilt and helps hold the menuki in place. The earlier Goto fastened the menuki to the ends of the mekugi. They were then called motagi. Kenjo, 1585-1663, was the first to separate the two. (Joly, Int. 14).

NECK GUARD, SHOULDER GUARD. Upright plates on the shoulder cops, 15th and 16th centuries. Fig. 38.

NEGROLI. The original and final name of the family usually called the Missaglia. Phillip was the most celebrated and skillful of them after they resumed the original name. He was born about 1500 and died in 1561. His principal work was done for the Duke of Urbino and the Emperor Charles V. His embossing was remarkably fine. Fig. 201. See Missaglia.

NEKO GAKE. "Cat scratches." They are peculiar cuts on the habaki, or backs of kozuka and kogai, with the chisel burrs left in place and flattened.

NENUKI TSUBA. A perforated guard, Japan.

NERAI. To aim, as a gun, Japan.

NERAU. Spears from Tanna, New Hebrides. They are heavy wooden spears with very long heads and numerous barbs. They are very similar to the Fijian spears. (Arc. f. Eth. VII, 231).

NERI-KAWA. Japanese leather lacquered black. It was used for making armor. (Conder 280).

NERINUKI-ODOSHI. Lacings for Japanese armor of braided cords of several colors, one of which is usually white. (Conder 271).

NERI TSUBA. Sword guards made entirely of lacquered hide. During the Gempei period guards were made of leather, or rawhide, clamped between iron plates, or covering a single plate, the whole being covered with black lacquer to make it waterproof. (Joly, Naunton xix).

NESHAN. A company of one hundred men, armed with guns, Rajput. Literally it means a standard. (Tod I, 422).

NETABA. The edge of a sword or knife, Japan.

NEZA. Lances with long, slender heads, Punjab. (Egerton 611).

NEZUO. A cord for fastening a bell to a hawk's neck, Japan.

NIAO-CHIANG. The Chinese matchlock used in Miaotzu. It had a pistol stock and a very long bar-

FIGURE 593. *Nil-Li. North Queensland Club, Peabody Museum, Salem.*

rel. The barrels are usually round, except in Kwei-chow, where they are octagonal. These guns were not put to the shoulder but were held like a pistol,

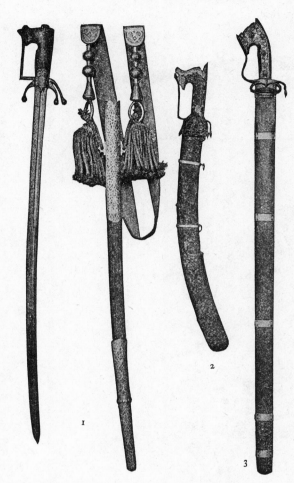

FIGURE 594. *Nimcha. 1. Morocco. Gold inlaid blade 34 inches long; horn hilt, guard inlaid with gold, engraved silver band. Scabbard covered with blue velvet with an engraved silver locket and chape. Bandolier of gold brocade with silver ends and large tassels. 2. Arab. Grooved blade 21 inches long. Hilt covered with tortoise shell and inlaid with pearl, engraved silver mounts and brass guard. 3. Straight, double-edged, 16th century German blade. Wood hilt covered with silver plates decorated with filigree and set with red and green stones. Very finely forged guard. Plain wooden scabbard with silver bands.*

but in both hands. The barrels are from three to seven feet long. (Greener 124).

NIELLO. A method of decorating metal first used in Persia. Egerton says: "The desired pattern is cut rather deeply into the object to be ornamented and the hollow filled with a molten alloy of silver, copper and lead. It is then heated, rubbed with borax, again heated, allowed to cool, rubbed smooth and burnished." The Russian work, *chern*, is often called niello but is said to be made by a different process.

NIFO OTI. Literally "death tooth." A bill-hook knife of European make used as a weapon in Samoa. (Brown, Mel. & Pol. 168).

NIJIRI. The handle of a bow, Japan.

NIHOJIRO. A Japanese helmet having two of its plates covered with silver, one in front and one at the back.

NIJIU HABAKI. An habaki made of two pieces. The inner one is the longer and fits the blade, the outer is shorter and fits the scabbard. (Joly Int. 20). See Habaki.

NIJIU YAKIBA. A double yakiba.

NIKU-BORI, TAKA-BORI. Carving in relief, Japan. Low relief, *usu-niku-bori*; medium relief, *chiu-niku-bori*; high relief, *atsu-niku-bori*.

NIL-LI. A North Queensland club with a pointed head, below which there is an enlarged cylindrical portion divided into squares by deep grooves. (Roth, Aust. Mus. VII, 208). Fig. 593.

NIMAI KANA NO DO. A Japanese folding corselet made of two plates.

NIMCHA. An Arab sabre with a knuckle guard rectangular at the base with drooping quillons on the opposite side. (Wallace Orient). It is also used in Morocco. Fig. 594.
    A Mahratta sabre. (Egerton 534T, 535).

NI-NO-ASHI. The lower band with a sling loop on a tachi scabbard. (Brinkley VII, 211).

NI-NO-MARU. The inner wall of a castle, Japan.

NIOI. Bright spots on a Japanese blade inside the yakiba. They are considered as evidences of good quality.

NIS-SHO. The Japanese national emblem, the sun.

NIWO-SUNE-ATE. Japanese greaves of two curved plates hinged together and lined with pads. The knee cop is separate. (Conder 276).

NIYE. Darker spots on the yakiba of a Japanese blade, especially near the inner edge. They often run into bands.

NJIGA. See Danisko.

1485-1564. He used very hard, dense iron and is distinguished for his forcible style. His guards are simple in decoration, rarely have raised edges, and are typical fighting guards. They are rare but forgeries of them are common.

FIGURE 595. No-Dachi. 1. Long, heavy, signed blade. Plain wooden scabbard and mounts. Tsuba, a plain iron wheel. Length 6 feet 3 inches. 2. After Garbutt, Journal Japan Society, Vol. XI.

NO. An arrow shaft, Japan.

NOBORI. A kind of standard, Japan. See Hata Jirushi.

NOBUIYE. The most celebrated maker of iron tsuba. He was the seventeenth Miochin and lived

He was also especially distinguished for his armor, particularly helmets.

NOBUT. A kettledrum, India. (Tod II, 30).

NOCK. The notch in the end of an arrow for the string.

FIGURE 596. Nodowa. 1. Variety meguriwa, 17th century. 2. From an O-Yoroi of the late 18th century. 3. Laced plates, probably a meguriwa. 4. Laced plates and complete throat ring. 5. Mail on brocade. 6. The inside of a nodowa. 7. Brigandine collar and two pads. 8, 8a. Eriwa. Three lacquered plates hinged together forming a throat ring and two extra plates hanging from the front. 9. Brigandine collar of three pieces. 10, 10a. Brigandine collar of hexagonal plates quilted and tied in. 1, 3 and 6. Metropolitan Museum.

NO-DACHI. Literally a field sword, Japan. A very long and heavy sword used in early times by very strong men. It was twenty-five per cent longer than the ordinary sword and was carried in addition to it, hung over the shoulder by a narrow belt passing over the shoulder and fastened to the right side of the waist, so that the hilt was above the shoulder and the edge of the blade to the left. (Garbutt 165). Fig. 595.

NODOWA, MEGURIWA. Japanese, a gorget, literally a throat ring. The nodowa proper is fastened at the back of the neck by cords, the meguriwa by hooks and the eriwa by a buckle. The manjiuwa, another variety, is fastened to the menpo and to the upper part of the corselet. It was said not to be satisfactory for actual fighting. (This seems doubtful as none of the nodowa I have seen that were a part of the neck guard of the menpo had any means of fastening them to the corselet.) The tentsuki style is said to have been the most popular, but no description of it is available. Possibly it is similar to the one illustrated as nodowa. Fig. 596.

Its usefulness is attested by the following taken from the *Chuko Kachu Seisakuben*: "In 1564 (Yeiroku V), on the 7th day of the first month, two battles took place at Konodai, in Shimoza, between Hojo Ujiyasu and Satomi Yoshihiro, assisted by Ota Sukemasa Niudo Sanrakusai, in which the Hojo forces were victorious. Ota fought desperately and had received two wounds, when Shimazu Tarozayemon, a man noted for his strength, threw down the now weary Ota, and tried in vain to cut off his head. At this Ota cried out 'Are you flurried, sir? My neck is protected by a *nodowa*. Remove it and cut off my head.' Shimazu replied with a bow, 'How kind of you to tell me! You die a noble death! You have my admiration!' But just then as he was about to remove the *nodowa*, two young squires of Ota rushed up, and throwing down Shimazu enabled their master to decapitate *him*." (Garbutt 145).

NOIRS HARNOIS. The German Reiters of the 16th century were so called on account of their black armor. (Hewitt III, 589).

NOLLA-NOLLA. A throwing club of the natives of Queensland. "It is a piece of hard and heavy wood sharpened to a point at both ends. One end is thick and tapers gradually to the other end, which is made rough to give the hand a more secure hold; in using the weapon the heavy end is thrown back before being hurled. No great pains are taken in the making of these clubs. The majority of them are about two feet long." (Lumholtz 72).

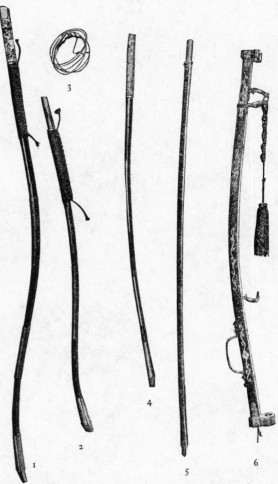

FIGURE 597. *Nukigomedo.* 1, 2. *Lacquered bow in two sections joined by a metal sleeve. Bronze ends and red cord bands. Length 5 feet 11.5 inches. 3. Its string of colored silks. 4, 5. Lacquered bow similar to 1, 2. 6. Its carrying frame lacquered red, black and gold.*

NO NOTARI. See Yakiba.

NORATRI FESTIVAL. A Rajput festival sacred to the god of war. See Karga S'hapna.

NOVACULA. A Cypriot sickle-shaped implement which may be a razor, sickle, pruning hook or weapon. (Burton Sword 189).

NU. A crossbow, China. (Jaehns 333).

NU-CHIANG. A gun in San Ch'uan Chinese.

NUIAKPAI. A bird spear with a straight, barbed head and three or more curved, barbed points projecting from the shaft a little back of the center, Point Barrow. (Murdoch 211).

NUKIGOMEDO, NURIGOMEDO. A ceremonial, or parade, bow, Japan. It is lacquered and made in two pieces which fit into the ends of a short metal handle. Fig. 597.

NUKO, BAN-GUSOKU. The armor worn by the lower classes of retainers in Japan. (Conder 279).

NULLIGA. The tasseled spear thrower, Worgai tribe, Australia. See Spear Thrower.

NUMINA LEGIONUM. A Roman standard; a spear with a crosspiece at the top with a hand above it, below a small, round shield. The shield originally had the figure of one of the warlike deities (Mars or Minerva) on it. Later the heads of the emperors, or their favorites, were used. The name was derived from the coin-like appearance of the shield. (Macgeorge 22).

NUNOME. False damascening, or inlaying, in which thin sheets of metal are pressed on a surface previously roughened by cuts or scratches, Japan. (Joly, Naunton xii).

NURIGOMEDO. See Nukigomedo.

NUT. The catch for the string of a crossbow.

NUTKODLIN. A deer arrow, Point Barrow. It has a three-cornered head four to eight inches long, with a sharp three-edged point, slightly concave on the faces. Two of the edges are rounded, and the third is sharp and has one or two barbs. A short tang on the head fits into the shaft. (Murdoch 205).

NYARAL. A toy boomerang, that is, one that flies high after striking the ground. If it is thrown wrong end to the ground it will rise but little, Lower Tully River, Queensland. (Roth, Aust. Mus. VII, 201).

O

OARAME. Lacing the lames of Japanese armor with the cords far apart. The higher the rank of the owner the closer together the cords were placed. (Conder 270).

OBCHEN, OPCHEN. A stirrup, Western Tibet. (Ramsay-Western).

OBIKANE, OBIGANE. See Soritsuno.

OBI-TORI, KOHI. The rings on the sling bands of a tachi through which the suspension cords pass. (Joly Int. 8). Fig. 95.

The Japanese usually call the kurikata "obi-tori," though no one who has written on the subject does so.

OCREA. The Roman greaves. (Burton Sword 247).

OCTAVE. A low thrust towards the opponent's right side or the corresponding parry.

OCULARIUM. The opening in the front of a closed helmet through which the wearer looks. (ffoulkes 26).

ODACHI. A long sword invented in Japan in the 14th century. The blade was four or five feet long. It was often carried slung from the shoulder. Compare No-Dashi.

ODATE-AGAYEMON. See Sune-Ate.

ODAWARA-INARI. A variety of kote. (Garbutt 140).

ODAWARA SUKASHI. See Ito Zukashi.

ODOSHI. The style in which the lames of Japanese armor are laced together by silk or leather cords, as hi-odoshi, red lacing. It is said that at the time of the Emperor Seiwa (859-876) the great families adopted special colors; the Taira taking purple, the Fujiwara light green, the Tachibana yellow, etc.

ODOSHI-GE. Colored silk cords for lacing together the parts of Japanese armor.

ODOSHI-TOSEI. A laminated variety of hai date. (Garbutt 140).

OGATAME-NO-KANE. Metal rings inside of a Japanese helmet through which the cords that fasten it on are passed. (Garbutt 147).

OGISAKI. A round-pointed blade, Japan.

OIKAGO. The frame for distending the Japanese

horo. It is said to have been invented by Hatake-yama Masanaga in the Onin period, 1467-1468.

There are three kinds of oikago. The first has whalebone ribs, usually fifteen or sixteen, arranged something like the ribs of a fan and secured to a

①鳶月
②串
繩骨
③緊緒
④筒入
⑤要
⑥編糸
⑦骨
⑧肱金

竪骨　山頂
小骨
骨尺一尺七寸
繩骨
串尺二尺八寸
横骨　筒入
一尺廣狸　一尺

口竪一尺五寸
籠二尺八寸
串二尺八寸
口横一尺八寸
筒入一尺三寸
籠　繩

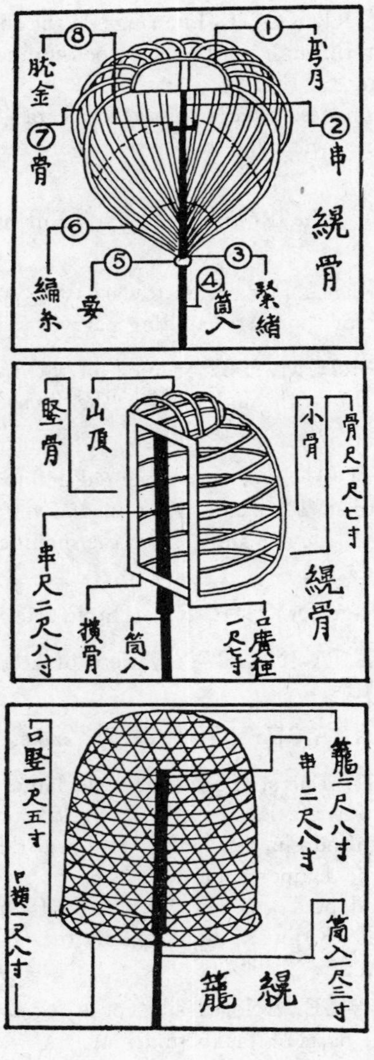

FIGURE 598. *Oikago. Frames for distending the horo. After Garbutt, Jr. Japan Soc., Vol. XI.*

short staff which was carried in sockets on the back of the corselet. The second had a whalebone framework like a lantern with three ribs at the top and ten in the body. It was carried on a staff like the first. The third was a staff with a basket of whalebone made of 12 vertical and 18 horizontal frames.

It was 18 inches in diameter and 21.5 high. (Garbutt 173). Figs. 598, 599.

OIKANE. See Soritsuno.

OKEGAWA, OKE-GAWA-DO. A Japanese corselet made of scales of leather, or metal, overlapping and riveted or fastened together by mail. (Conder 264, Garbutt 161).

O-KINA-MEN. "Old man's face." A very common type of menpo. It has a long gray moustache. (Dean Jap. 67). 9, fig. 568.

O-KOZUKA. A kozuka considerably larger than usual. See Hanzashi Kozuka. Fig. 356.

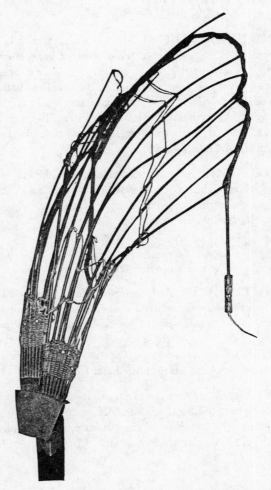

FIGURE 599. *Oikago. Sixteen whalebone ribs from 22 to 43 inches long set in a gilt metal socket and connected by stays so that it can be stretched out in an ellipsoid to support the horo.*

OLIPHANT, OLIFANT. A signalling horn used in war and hunting from the 12th century on. They were sometimes made of ivory and finely carved. (Dean Hdbk. 40). Fig. 600.

OMAYARI, OMIYARI, SU YARI. A kind of Japanese spear with a straight blade. (B. M. Hdbk. 54).

FIGURE 600. *Oliphant, 13th century. Metropolitan Museum.*

OMODAKE. An arrowhead, Japan.

OMOGAI. The headstall of a bridle, Japan.

OMOTE. The side of the tang of a Japanese blade that is inward when it is carried edge up in the belt. Katana are signed on this side.

ONAGRE. An engine of classic times for throwing stones. It was so called because the fabulous monster, onagre, was said to throw stones at its pursuers with its feet. (Grose I, 380).

ONCIN, UNCIN. A one-sided pick used in the 12th century.

ONDANIQUE, ANDANICUM, ANDAINE. These three names are given in different texts of Marco Polo to a special steel. He frequently speaks of "steel and ondanique" much as in India they speak of a blade of steel, meaning ordinary steel, or of "jauhar" (watered steel) meaning what is ordinarily called Damascus steel. By ondanique Marco Polo undoubtedly means watered steel, the Indian *hundwan.* (Marco Polo I, 93, note).

ONNA-MEN. "Woman's face," a type of menpo. (Dean Jap. 67). See Menpo.

O-NO. A Japanese pole axe used by the Yamabushi. It has a very large head with a very convex cutting edge and a large scroll-shaped pean opposite it. It has a sheath covering only the edge of the blade. The entire length is nearly six feet. Fig. 601.

O NOTARI. See Yakiba.

O-O. Japanese, a hawk's leash. It is made of eight strands of silk, red for ordinary hawks, and purple for those that have distinguished themselves by killing cranes, etc. (Harting 214). See He-O. Fig. 366.

OOLOO. See Ulu.

OONAK. See Unak.

OOOLOOBALLONG. See Ulubalang.

OPCHEN. See Obchen.

FIGURE 601. *O-No, Yamabushi Axe. Large head with a convex semi-circular edge pierced by a heart-shaped opening and an elaborate pean on the back. Total length of shaft 5 feet 9.5 inches. There is a sheath for the edge.*

OPI. A Malayan sword, a variety of klewang. The hilt is usually of horn with a very large pommel decorated with long locks of hair. It is used on Wetter Island. (Arc. f. Eth. IV, 74). Fig. 602.

OPI KARBAN. The sheath of the preceding. Fig. 602.

FIGURE 602. *Opi, knife and opi karban, scabbard. Blade 14.5 inches long, black horn hilt decorated with hair. Wood scabbard wound with rattan.*

OREILLETTES. Ear guards attached to the open helmets of the 15th and 16th centuries. They were often hinged so that they could be turned up out of the way. (Planche 381).

They were also used on some Turkish helmets of the same period. Fig. 55.

ORGUE, ORGAN. A group of gun barrels fixed in a frame so that all could be fired at once. In the 17th century as many as 160 barrels were sometimes arranged in this way. (Hewitt III, 698).

ORI-AWASE-NI-MAI. (Two plates folded and forged). A method of making Japanese blades in which two plates are made by welding an iron plate to a wider one of steel, and then welding the two together, steel face to steel face. (Gilbertson Blades 129).

ORI-AWASE-SAN-MAI. (Three plates folded and forged). A method of making Japanese blades in which a plate of iron is welded edge to edge, to one of steel; the resulting bar is then placed between two plates of iron, and the whole welded. (Gilbertson Blades 129). This method can only produce an inferior blade.

ORIFLAMME. Originally an ecclesiastical banner; it was red with a green fringe. By the end of the 10th century it had become the royal standard of France. In one of the windows of the cathedral of Chartres (13th century) there is the representation of a banner believed to be the Oriflamme. It has five points (other examples have three) each having attached a tassel of green silk. (Macgeorge 103).

ORIKAMI. A certificate of a sword expert giving the name of the maker, description and value of a Japanese blade or mounting. It was signed by a *Mekike* (sword expert) and marked with his seal on the opposite side. It was written on a peculiar kind of soft, thick paper called *Kaga-Bosho*, which was made for the Shogun in the province of Kaga. (Gilbertson Blades 199). Fig. 603.

ORIKANE. See Soritsuno.

ORLE. A wreath worn like a turban around a helmet. It was highly decorated and often jeweled. (ffoulkes 45).

ORTA. See Gudo.

O SEPPA. See Seppa.

OSHI-NO-GOTE. A kote in which the outer part of the forearm is covered with metal splints separated by strips of mail. (Conder 274).

O-SHITODOME. Ornamental thimbles placed in the openings in a kurikata, and through which the sageo is passed.

OSHITSUKE. The backplate of a Japanese corselet. It is finished at the top by a separate plate, the *moko-ita*, corresponding to the *muna-ita* in front. (Conder 266).

OSTRINGER. A falconer, India and Persia.

OTE. The first gate of a castle, Japan.

OTOGANE. Metal tips on a bow, Japan. They make a sound when the arrow is shot.

OTOKANE. See Hoko-Yumi.

OTOSHIZASHI. The fashion of wearing the tachi slipped through the belt instead of hung from it.

OURUMA. The wood from which the Ainu make their bows. It is a species of yew. (Greey 109).

OX TONGUE. See Langue de Boeuf.

FIGURE 603. *Orikami. First column (right). Sagami no kuni Kamakura ju Fuji genji Sukesane — Sukesane of the Fujigenji family of the city of Kamakura in the province of Sagami. Second column. Sho shin — genuine Zei mei inscription. Nagasa nishaku sanzun nibu — length two feet three and one-fifth inches. Hio renpi kore aru nari. Front and back have grooves. Third column. Dai kin go hiyaku mai — price five hundred and fifty pieces of gold. Fourth column. Shiwatsu Mikka — December 3rd. Hon ami Eiji ro Sei o. Signed by Honami Eijiro Seio.*

OTSUBA. The feathered end of an Ainu arrow (Greey 109).

OUNEP. A kind of spear thrower used in New Caledonia and the vicinity. It is plaited of cocoanut fibres and fishskin, with a knob on one end and a loop on the other. The length varies from a few inches to a foot. In using it the loop is slipped over the forefinger and the other end is fastened around the spear by a half hitch. As long as the cord is stretched by the pull of the forefinger it holds the shaft. As soon as the latter is relaxed the elasticity of the cord throws the spear forward, at the same time releasing itself from the shaft. (Wood 885). Fig. 604.

It is similar in its action to the Greek ankule, but is superior to it in remaining in the hand when the spear is thrown instead of going with it.

OUROUSSES. A kind of gun much valued in the Caucasus. It is said to have been brought to the Crimea in the time of the Golden Horde.

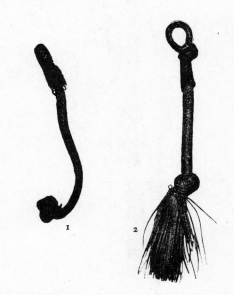

FIGURE 604. *Ounep. 1. New Caledonia, length 8 inches. 2. A similar spear thrower from the Legality Islands, called Lifu. Length including tassel 10.25 inches.*

O-YOROI. Japanese ceremonial armor. It was usually of a type much earlier than the time at which it was worn. (Dean Hdbk. 121).

The o-yoroi was the type of armor worn by the daimio on their annual visits to the Shogun's court

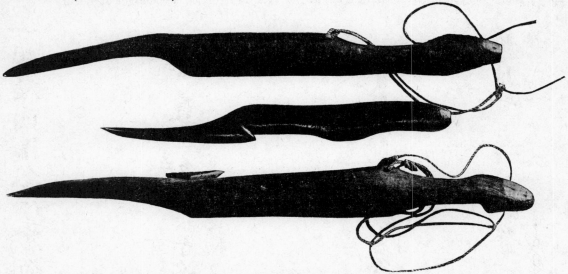

FIGURE 605. *Pahua. Sandwich Island wooden knives. Bishop Museum, Honolulu.*

FIGURE 606. *Pakayun. Murut (Borneo) sabre. Blade 27 inches long, brass guard, forked wooden pommel stained red. Wood scabbard carved and decorated in red and white.*

during the Tokugawa period. At these visits they tried to outdo each other in the elaborateness of their equipment. The armor was the most complete and elaborate ever worn in Japan; much of it was copied from celebrated suits of the 12th and 13th centuries that are kept in the temples. A good suit of it gives a much more accurate idea of how the old armor looked than the faded and ragged suits of early times in the temples and museums.

O-YUMI. (A large bow). A crossbow, Japan. The crossbow was called o-yumi because many of those used in the castles were very large. Some had bows as much as twelve feet long and over a foot in circumference.

Lighter crossbows called teppo-yumi were also used as well as repeating crossbows, copied from the Chinese. See Teppo-Yumi, Chu-Ko-Nu, and Dokyu.

OZONAKAMA. The body of organized soldiers attached to a Japanese temple. (M. S. S. II, 226).

O-ZUTSU. A cannon, Japan.

P

PACHO. A South Sea Island club edged with shark's teeth. (Burton Sword 48). See Tebutje.

PADJA. The enlarged lower end of a kris scabbard, Celebes. (Arc. f. Eth. XVIII, 65).

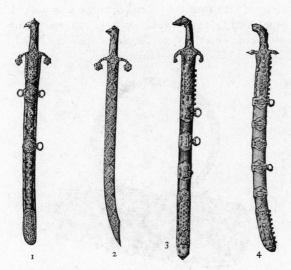

FIGURE 607. *Palache.* 1. *Scabbard covered with blue silk with mountings of silver gilt set with turquoise and other stones.* 2. *The blade of the same; it is damascened in gold and set with coral and turquoise.* 3. *Scabbard covered with red velvet; mountings of silver gilt set with turquoise and plaques of jade set with gold and rubies.* 4. *Silver scabbard mounted and decorated like the preceding; guard of silver gilt. After Rockstuhl.*

PAGAYA. A Brazilian paddle-shaped club. (Burton Sword 42).

PAHU. A spindle-shaped New Zealand club(?). (Jaehns 162).

PAHUA. A wooden dagger of the Sandwich Islands. It is straight, double-edged and about two feet long. Occasionally it is double-ended with the handle in the middle. It is fastened to the wrist by a cord passing through a hole in the handle. (Wood 1088). Fig. 605.

PAIAHA. See Tewha-Tewha.

PAIR OF PLATES. The breast and back plates were often so-called in the 14th century and later. (ffoulkes 33).

PAIR OF SPLINTS. Short taces worn with light armor in the 16th century. (ffoulkes 63).

PAISCUSH. A guarded katar, that is, one with a plate guard protecting the back of the hand. (Skelton 139, 141).

PAKAYUN. A Murut, Borneo, sabre with a light curved blade and a curious forked wooden pommel. Fig. 606.

PALACHE. A Polish sabre of the 17th century. The blades are straight or very slightly curved; the hilt has a short pommel, somewhat like the Persian, but heavier. The quillons are short and usually curve towards the blade. (Rockstuhl CVIII, CLXX). Fig. 607.

PALATI. A type of spear thrower used by the Kakadu of Northern Australia. It is a strip of hard, dense wood about four feet long, two and five-eighths inches wide and three-sixteenths of an inch thick. It is sometimes straight, but generally has a decided curve. The handle is made of a knob of *kapei,* or ironwood resin, about an inch and three-quarters in diameter and two and three-quarters

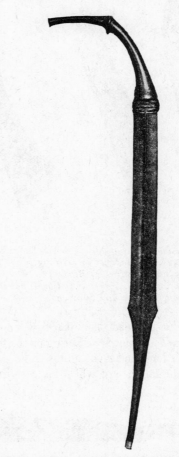

FIGURE 608. *Palitai, Mentawi Island. Straight, double-edged blade 12.625 inches long. Carved wood hilt and scabbard, the latter with a bone tip.*

long. It is fixed on one end which is cut away on each side to give a better grip. The knob is called *kuleryu*. The other end is narrowed down and has

jection where it bears on the blade. The point is called *inedi*. This form of spear thrower requires considerable experience in its use as the spear is held alongside the thrower instead of above it as with all other forms. It is, however, very effective, offering very little resistance to the air. (Spencer, North. Ter. 377). See Spear Thrower.

FIGURE 609. *Panabas. 1. Blade 15 inches long, wooden handle, Malabang. 2. Blade 21 inches long, wood handle with brass bands, Cotobatto. 3. Blade 18.5 inches long, carved wooden handle with copper and brass bands, Rancheria of Labuan, Sibugny Bay, Mindanao.*

FIGURE 610. *Panji, Burma. Pointed pieces of bamboo about 7 inches long, wrapped in cocoanut fibre with an arm band of braided cane.*

PALET. A kind of helmet originally made of leather, but later sometimes of steel. It is not known what kind of a headpiece it was, 14th and 15th centuries. (ffoulkes 34, Hewitt II, 221).

PALIARTI. A flat spear thrower, Australia. (Spencer, North. Ter. 311).

PALITAI, PALITE. A knife, Mentawi and Siberut. They have straight, double-edged blades and long, slim and curiously curved handles. Fig. 608.

PALTA. An axe in Salar, a Tibetan dialect. The name is obviously derived from the Turkish *balta*, an axe. (Rockhill, Jr.).

PANABAS. A kind of Moro jungle knife said to be used for executions. It has a long, straight hilt without any guard. The blade is widest near the point and bends sharply backward close to the handle. Fig. 609.

a wooden point fastened on by kapei wound with banyan string. The point is a tapering piece of wood about an inch long and five-eighths of an inch in diameter at the larger end which has a short pro-

FIGURE 611. *Panji Sekar, a ganga that bows upwards. It is on a Javan kris.*

PANACHE. A plume, or according to some, a plume holder on a helmet. (Planche 386, ffoulkes 83).

PANAH. A bow, Malay.

PANSIERE. The lower piece of a Gothic breast-plate. (Dean Hdbk. 60).

PAO. A Chinese name for a gun; it is also used in Eastern Tibet. (Rockhill, Eth. 712).

FIGURE 612. *Parang Ginah. Length 23 inches.*

PANCHANGRA. The five-colored flag of the Rajputs of Amber. (Tod I, 114).

PANDI BALLAM. A hog spear, India. (Egerton 29).

PANDOO. A squire, a shield bearer, India.

PANGALLA. A powder horn, Central Sumatra. (Leiden X, 148).

PANGULU. A kris hilt, Celebes. (Arc. f. Eth. XVIII, 65).

PANIMUKTA. One of the ancient classes of weapons, India. It comprises those thrown by hand. (Burton Sword 214). See Amukta.

PANJI. Sharpened stakes planted in the paths near villages expecting an attack, or in those followed by a retreating party in Assam, fig. 610. The Mao and Maram Nagas wear a curious tail as part of their war dress that contains a pocket in which to carry panjies. (Hodson 37). Similar spikes are used in most Malayan countries.

PANJI SEKAR. A gandja that bows upwards, Java. Fig. 611.

PAPEGAY. See Popinjay.

PAPS-I-TUTTI. A kind of Mogul knife. (Wallace Orient.).

PARABAS. A Dyak stratagem. A tree is cut nearly through and held upright by rattan cables. As an enemy approaches these are cut allowing the tree to fall on him. (Peralaer 374).

PARA-I-TUTTI. A Mogul knife with a double curved blade and a flat tang with grip plates riveted on. (Wallace Orient.).

PARALYSER. A Malay spear with two barbed blades of unequal length. When stabbed with the longer blade a man is powerless as he cannot withdraw on account of the barbed tip, and the sharp point of the shorter blade prevents his running up the spear and killing his antagonist, as has frequently been done in the Peninsula by one mortally wounded. (Clifford Brown Humanity 208).

PARANG. Malay, a chopper or jungle knife. Class name.

PARANG BEDAK. A short Bornean sword with a heavy, single-edged blade convex on the edge and

FIGURE 613. *Parang Latok. Length blade 2 feet 5 inches, carved horn hilt. Wood scabbard carved and painted with bands of red and black.*

with the back straight to within a few inches of the point, when it becomes concave. (Arc. f. Eth. V, 236).

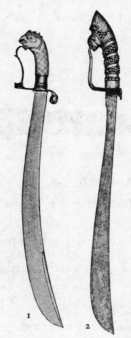

FIGURE 614. *Parang Nabur.* 1. *Blade 20 inches long. Brass guard and counter guard, ivory hilt pommel a parrot's head with red stone eyes.* 2. *Iron guard and counterguard; wood hilt ornamented with silver plates and knobs which outline a face on the pommel.*

PARANG GINAH. A sickle-shaped Malay implement, whether a sword or sickle is uncertain, probably the latter. Fig. 612.

PARANG IHLANG. The Malay name for the Dyak mandau.

PARANG JENGOK. A sword used by thieves among the Kalentan Malays. "Their favorite instrument is called parang jengok — or 'peeping knife' — which is armed with a sharp peak at the tip standing out almost at right angles to the rest of the blade. Armed with this, on a dark night the robber walks down the street, and just as he passes a man, he strikes back over his left shoulder, so that the peak catches his victim in the back of the head and knocks him endways. He can then be robbed with ease and comfort, and whether he recovers from the blow or dies from its effects is his own affair, and concerns the thief not at all." (Clifford, Court and Kampong, 26).

PARANG KAJOELIE. A knife with a blade like a barong, Borneo. (Arc. f. Eth. V, 238).

PARANG LATOK. A Dyak jungle knife, also used as a sword. It has a heavy, single-edged blade widest near the point. The blade makes an obtuse angle with a square shank on which there is a wooden handle without a guard. It is carried in a carved wood sheath that is only long enough to hold the blade proper. Fig. 613.

PARANG NABUR. A Malayan sword also used by the Dyaks. It has a short blade curved towards the point, and widest at the point of curvature. The hilt is generally of bone and has a guard and finger guard of brass or iron. (Ling Roth II, 135). Fig. 614. See also Dukn.

PARANG NEGARA. The Malay name for a variety of mandau with a grooved blade. (Arc. f. Eth. V, 234, 236).

PARANG PANDIT. A Sea Dyak sword much like the parang latok, but with an iron hilt with a short cross guard. Fig. 615.

PARANG PARAMPOEAN. A variety of klewang, Borneo. (Arc. f. Eth. V, 236).

PARANG PEDANG. See Dukn.

PARAZONIUM. A broad-bladed dagger almost

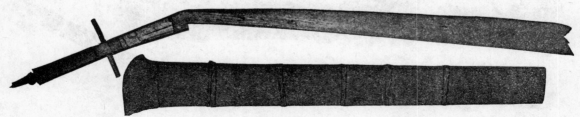

FIGURE 615. *Parang Pandit. Blade 19.75 inches long, steel hilt partly covered with silver and brass. Wooden scabbard with cane bands.*

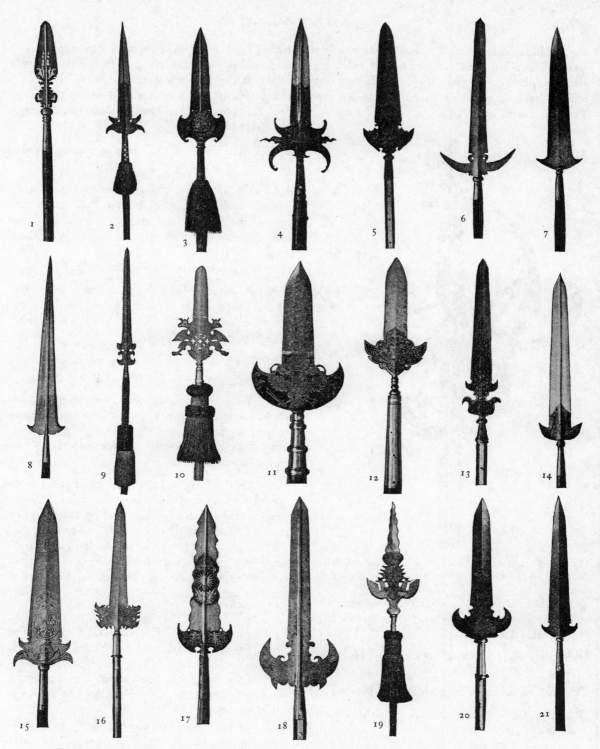

FIGURE 616. *Partizans.* 1. *Italian, 1700.* 2. *French, 1570.* 3. *Spanish, 1715.* 4. *French, 1700.*
5. *German, 1642.* 6. *Flemish, 1535.* 7. *German, 1550.* 8. *Italian. late XV.* 9. *Saxon, 1680.*
10. *Polish-Saxon, 1720. Guard of Augustus the Strong.* 11. *Austrian, 1740. Imperial cypher of
Charles VI.* 12. *Arms of Austria, Maria Theresa and Francis I, 1750.* 13. *Saxon, 1616. Arms of
Johann Georg III.* 14. *Italian, 1550.* 15. *Italian, 1600.* 16. *French(?), 1660.* 17. *French, 1690.*
18. *Flemish, XVII.* 19. *Polish, 1680. Arms of Augustus the Strong.* 20. *German, 1625.* 21.
French(?), 1600. Metropolitan Museum. Not to scale.

exactly like a cinquedea. The blade was twelve to sixteen inches long and made of bronze in the earlier specimens and iron in the later. It was originally Greek, but was also used by the Romans. (Burton Sword 239).

FIGURE 617. *Swept hilt with pas d'ane. The latter is the series of loops below the quillons.*

PARCHMENT CRESTS. Crests made of parchment were worn by knights and their horses in the 13th century.

PAREH. An Australian stone axe. (Ratzel I, 355).

PARKAN. A boomerang, Australia. (Jaehns 203).

PARMA. A small, round Roman shield. (Burton Sword 248).

PAROOM. See Burrong.

PARRYING SHIELD. See Adaga and Madu.

PARTIZAN. A broad-bladed pole arm usually having short, curved branches at the base of the

blade; but the shapes of the blades vary greatly. It was, and is, particularly the weapon of the guards of dignitaries and many specimens are elaborately decorated. It was used throughout the 16th and 17th centuries and is still used as a ceremonial weapon. Fig. 616.

PARUSA. The battle-axe of a legendary invader of India. (Egerton, p. 7).

PAS D'ANE. A guard formed of loops surrounding the blade of a sword. It first made its appearance in the 14th century but did not come into general use until the 16th when it became customary to put the fingers around the quillons of a rapier; the pas d'ane then protected them. Fig. 617.

PASER. Java, a blowpipe dart. They were similar to those used by the Dyaks. The blowpipe has not been used as a weapon of war in Java for centuries. (Raffles 296). See Langa.

PASPATI. An arrow of the Javan gods. It had a crescent-shaped head. (Raffles plate p. 296/297).

PASSAGE HAWK, PASSAGER. A hawk that is old enough to make its first migration about the middle of September of the year it is hatched. Hawks caught at about this age are afterwards called "passage hawks."

PASSES, PASSING. In fencing, before the invention of the lunge, the only way of coming in measure (reach) of an adversary was by taking a step forward, that is, bringing the rear foot to the front. "'Passing' in contradistinction to 'lunging,' consists in the action of carrying one leg in front of the other instead of preserving the relative positions of the feet and merely increasing their separation." (Castle 48).

PASSGUARD, PASSE-GUARD. Formerly this was believed to be the projecting plates, like wings, on the shoulder cops of the 16th century, later investigations make it appear probable that it was a reinforcing piece for the right elbow in jousting. (ffoulkes 50, 52).

An extra defense for the *left* elbow in tournaments in the 16th century. (Tower 10, p. 141, and plate 14).

PATA. The Indian gauntlet sword, which is an evolution from the katar. The katar has side bars that protect the sides of the hand. First a plate guard was added to protect the back, next the side bars and hand guard were connected by bars, and later by plates making a short gauntlet, then a single plate was used to protect both, next this was given

the Bombay Museum decorated with Fatima's hand.

In Southern India a different form is used which was evolved from a knife used there which has a cross-loop handle and a plate guard for the back of

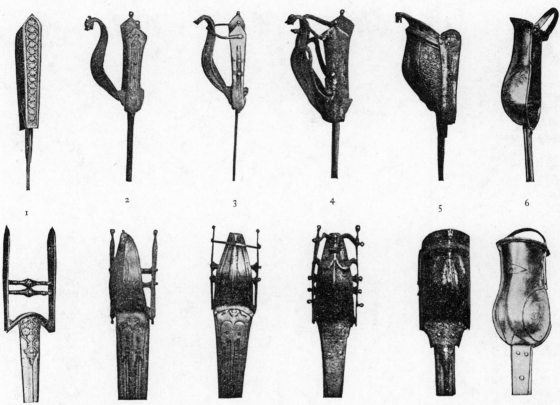

FIGURE 618. *Evolution of the Pata.* 1. *The ordinary katar.* 2. *The katar with a guard to protect the back of the hand.* 3. *The same with a light stay to keep the hand guard from being bent.* 4. *The single stay replaced by two wider ones, making the guard more complete.* 5. *The side bars and hand guard connected by plates enclosing the hand. In all of these the katar form with independent hand and side guards is maintained.* 6. *A short gauntlet made of a single plate is used.*

the shape of a short gauntlet which was finally extended to the elbow. Fig. 618.

The pata has a long, straight blade, almost always double-edged, and frequently of European make. The gauntlet covers the arm almost to the elbow, and has an iron strap hinged to the upper end that goes around the arm. The grip is at right angles to the blade as with the katar. The gauntlets are generally embossed, inlaid or otherwise decorated, fig. 619. It was a favorite weapon with the Mahrattas, but was also used by most of the Indian nations. It has been said that it was not used by the Mohammedans but this is not the case. No. 4 of fig. 619 has Arabic inscriptions and there is one in

the hand. In place of the full gauntlet the southern form has a nearly flat plate that covers the back of the hand and the outside of the arm. Fig. 620.

The gauntlet sword deprives a man of the use of his wrist and would be a very awkward weapon for fencing, and it was only used by cavalry; it therefore seems probable that it was used as a lance, for which purpose its great length would make it available. This seems quite probable when we consider the Mahratta method of fighting. This was to make a charge and, if successful, start looting; if driven back, to run away.

PATATI. See Toki Poto.

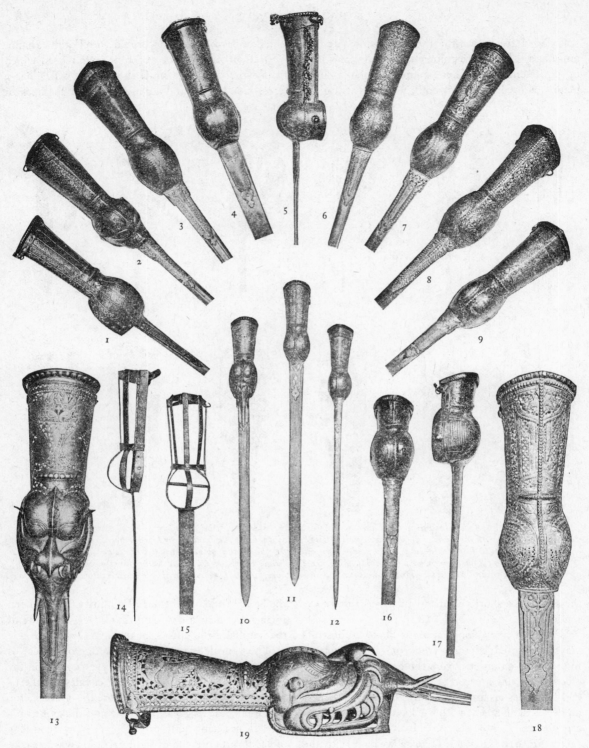

FIGURE 619. *Pata.* 1. *Double-edged blade 34.5 inches long. Iron gauntlet chased, inlaid with gold and set with rubies and diamonds. 17th century.* 2. *A tiger's head inlaid with silver vines.* 3. *Blackened steel inlaid with gold.* 4. *Northern India. Broad blade 40.75 inches long. Gauntlet with a vine pattern and inscriptions in gold.* 5. *Southern India, 17th century. Iron gauntlet with brass borders and a monster's head in the round at the top. It has a line of swinging ornaments on each side.* 6. *Foliage and acrobats inlaid with gold and silver.* 7. *Tracery in relief inlaid with gold on a black ground.* 8. *All steel, tracery in relief.* 9. *Trooper's sword, slightly engraved.* 10. *Tanjore, 17th century. Blade 35 inches long and 1.75 wide. Hilt magnificently embossed with the head of a monster swallowing an elephant. The trunk of the latter extends down the blade.* 11. *Tanjore, 17th century. Blade 38 inches long and 2 wide. Chased and pierced gauntlet covered with gold lacquer.* 12. *Trooper's sword. The same as no. 9.* 13. *Enlarged view of the hilt of no. 10.* 14, 15. *Skeleton gauntlet, to be covered, or lined, with leather.* 16, 17. *Short gauntlet sword, an early type.* 18. *An enlarged view of the hilt of no. 11.* 19. *Side view of the gauntlet of no. 10.*

PATCH. In the early rifles it was customary to use bullets considerably smaller than the bore of the rifle and to wrap them in pieces of greased leather, called patches, to make them fit the bore. A bullet

smaller. The lower part of the head usually carved in relief and covered with silver. The shafts are generally painted with bands of lac of different colors. They vary greatly in size. Fig. 623.

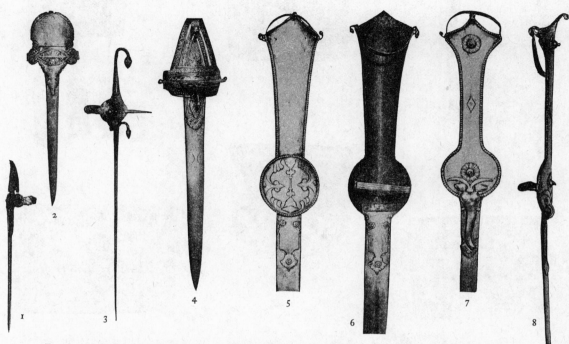

FIGURE 620. *South Indian Pata. 1, 2. Knife with loop grip and flat hand guard from which this form of pata is derived. 3, 4. Another variety of this knife. 5, 6. Front and back of a sword. Blade 3 feet long and 1.75 inches wide. Hilt all steel, with beaded edges. 7, 8. Front and side of a similar but lighter sword. Steel hilt with roped edges and brass ornaments.*

that fitted accurately could not be used as it required too much force to push it home. (Greener 632).

PATCH BOX. A box in which to carry patches. It was carried on the belt or slung from the shoulder. Such boxes were often used to carry cleaning rags, spare flints, caps and other small accessories, particularly in eastern countries. They are frequently quite elaborate. Fig. 621.

PATE PLATE. An iron cap, or cage, worn inside of the hat, 17th and 18th centuries. Fig. 622.

PATERNOSTER BLADE. A sword blade pierced with openings so as to answer the purpose of a rosary, and enable the pious owner to count his prayers even in the dark. (Burton Sword 136).

PATISTHANAYA. A Sinhalese spear with a head much like that of a European partizan but

PATOBONG. A covered pitfall about three feet deep filled with sharp spikes. It was used by the Dyaks in defending their forts and villages. (Kepple I, 153).

PATRA. The carving on the typical Javan kris hilts.

PATRARY. See Perrier.

PATRIDGE MORTAR, PARTRIDGE MORTAR. A common mortar surrounded by thirteen smaller mortars, bored around the circumference, in the body of the metal. The large center one was loaded with a shell and the smaller ones with grenades. (Hoyt 440).

PATRON. A paper cartridge first used for pistols and later for musquets. The boxes in which they were carried were also called patrons, 17th century. (Hewitt III, 743). Fig. 624.

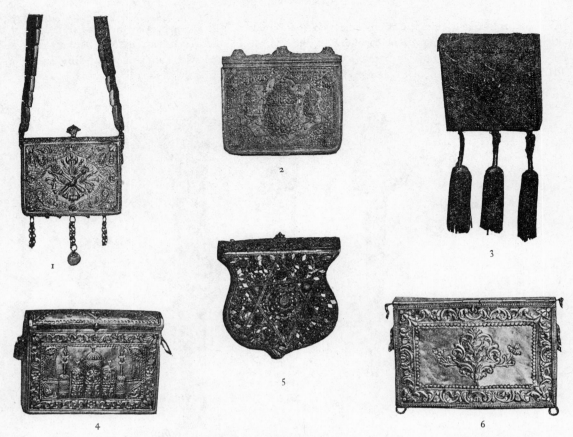

FIGURE 621. *Patch Boxes.* 1. *Silver box with a sliding top.* 2. *Heavy box 4.5 x 3.5 inches of silver gilt. Belt loop on the back.* 3. *Silver plated box covered with silver filigree with a piece of coral in the center. The tassels are of brown silk.* 4. *Silver box 5 x 4 x 1 inch. Rounded hinged cover.* 5. *Silver box covered with silver gilt filigree and set with red and blue stones. Two narrow belt loops on the back.* 6. *Silver box 6 x 4.375 x 1 inch. Flat hinged top fastened by a sliding pin. The back was of leather but is now missing.*

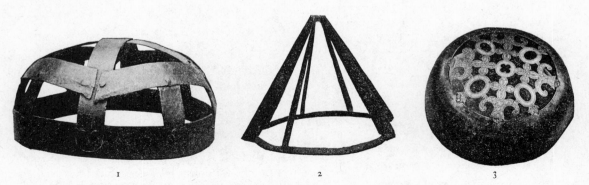

FIGURE 622. *Pate Plates.* 1. *German hat lining, 17th century.* 2. *French, 17th century.* 3. *Italian, 17th-18th century. Metropolitan Museum. Not to scale.*

FIGURE 623. *Patisthanaya.* 1. *Head 8.5 inches long, deeply engraved and covered with silver plates forced into the engraving. Shaft lacquered in bands of several colors. Length 4 feet 11 inches.* 2. *Head 11.5 inches long with engraved brass panels on each side. Shaft strapped and banded with steel and painted like the preceding. The butt has been cut off. Present length 6 feet 4.5 inches.*

FIGURE 624. *Patrons.* 1. *Dutch, 16th century.* 2. *German, 16th century.* 3. *German, 17th century. Metropolitan Museum. Not to scale.*

PASHKOHU. See Rabbit Stick. This is the Hopi name.

PATTANI JAMDADU. A long-bladed katar, Mahratta. The name means "Death-giver," according to Egerton (512). Fig. 434.

PATTISA. A two-handed axe, India. (Burton Sword 215).

PATU. A short fighting club that was the Maori's principal weapon. They were made of stone, wood or bone. The stone clubs are of a simple spatulate

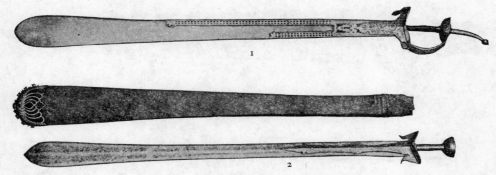

FIGURE 625. *Pattisa.* 1. *Central India, 18th century. Very broad, heavy blade 3 feet 1.25 inches long with reinforcing pieces on both edges. Hilt inlaid with silver. Scabbard buttons down the back; it is covered with yellow velvet and has a pierced iron chape inlaid with silver. 2. Malabar, 18th century. Blade 3 feet 1 inch long. Engraved steel hilt with projections riveted to the blade.*

PATTISA. South Indian sword with a straight broad blade, double-edged and widest near the point. The hilt usually has a round pommel, broad guard and a heavy piece extending on each side of the blade to which it is riveted. (Egerton 526). Fig. 625.

shape and quite sharp on the edges, 2, 3, and 6, fig. 626. The name is qualified by the addition of another word to indicate the material from which it is made, as *patu onewa*, one made of basalt — *patu paraoa*, one made from the jawbone of the sperm whale — *patu pounamou*, one made of jade; the last

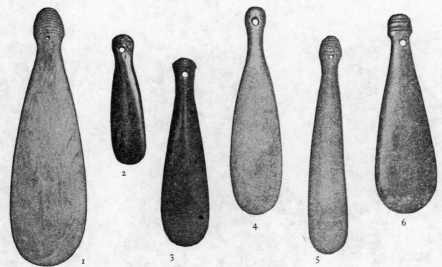

FIGURE 626. *Patu.* 1. *Patu paraoa, 20 inches long and 5.875 wide, carved rings on the handle. 2. Patu pounamou or mere. Jade club 10.25 inches long, slightly carved at the handle. 3. Patu onewa, dark green basalt, handle carved with rings. Length 14.5 inches. 4. Patu paraoa. Length 16.25 inches. 5. Patu paraoa. Bone club flat on one side and convex on the other. Length 16.875 inches. 6. Patu pounamou. Translucent jade. Length 15.25 inches.*

is also called *mere*. A mere is always a jade club and it is not proper to call a club of any other material by this name. All of the stone clubs are almost always without ornament other than some fluting on the end of the handle.

FIGURE 627. *Pavis. Both German, about* 1400. *Metropolitan Museum.*

The *kotiate* (liver cutter) was made of bone or wood and was broad, flat and symmetrical with an indentation on each side that gives it somewhat the shape of a violin. It usually has a head carved on the end of the handle as the only ornament.

The third form, the *wahaika*, is almost always made of wood and is often covered with carving. Sometimes it is made of bone and is then not apt to be elaborately carved. The shapes and decoration of wahaika vary more than those of either of the other forms, fig. 626 and Kotiate and Wahaika.

PA-UL. See Morro.

PAULDRON. See Shoulder Cop.

PAVADE. A long dagger. (Planche 391).

PAVIS, PAVOISE, PAVAS, PAVISE, PAVAIS, PAVACKE, TALLEVAS, TALVAS, TALOCHE. A large shield of the 15th century and later, used as a protection for archers and crossbowmen at sieges. It was large enough to cover two men completely; the lower end rested on the ground and the upper was supported by a prop or an attendant. (Grose II, 257). Fig. 627.

Other more or less similar forms of shield are called by the same name.

PAVISER. One who carried and supported a pavis for an archer. This was a position of responsibility and danger, and men were regularly employed for this purpose. (Grose II, 257).

PEACOCK ARROWS. Arrows winged with peacock's feathers are frequently mentioned in the old inventories of the 14th and following centuries. The solid feathers of the wing were undoubtedly used, not the highly colored tail feathers which would have been useless.

PEASCOD BREASTPLATE. A form of breastplate worn in the latter part of the 16th century, the lower part of which projected outward and downward like the civilian doublet of the period. This form is preserved in the familiar costume of Punch. (ffoulkes 97).

PECHAK. A dagger, Western Tibet. (Ramsay-Western).

FIGURE 628. *Pedang, Sumatra. Plain blade* 10.5 *inches long. Ivory hilt, scabbard covered with embossed silver.*

PECTORAL. A covering for the breast, either defensive or ornamental. (Planche 391).

PEDANG. A variety of Javan knife. The edge is shaped much like that of a flyssa, the back is straight next the hilt and curves in to meet the point. The hilt is usually straighter than that of the Javan go-lok. (Raffles 296 and plate p. 296/297). Fig. 628.

PEDANG DJAWIE BESAR. A Bornean sword with a straight, double-edged blade widening towards the point, and a straight hilt with recurved quillons. (Arc. f. Eth. V, 233).

PEFFENHAUSER, ANTON. Augsburg, 1525-1603. A well-known maker of elaborately decorated armor, in fact it was often so over decorated as to be practically useless. The suit made for King Sebastian of Portugal is one of the most ornate known. (ffoulkes Armourer 140).

PEL or POST QUINTAIN. A stout post six feet high, securely planted in the ground, on which the young aspirant practised with sword, mace or axe. He was required to keep himself covered with his shield while so doing, and the arms employed were heavier than usual so as to give as much exercise as possible. (Hewitt II, 337).

PELL. See Pill.

PELLET BOW, STONE BOW. A bow for shooting clay balls, stones, lead bullets and similar missiles. It is an ordinary bow with two strings connected by a pocket in the middle for the missile. The strings are usually held apart by stretchers at one or both ends. In Europe they were used entirely for game and in China also. In many parts of the East they were also used for serious fighting. The guards at the Siamese royal palace, who were stationed on the walls, were armed with pellet bows with which they fired at all passers-by who did not properly salute the royal residence. (Mouhot 10).

When shooting a pellet bow it is necessary to move the bow hand sharply to the left at the moment of releasing the string or the missile will hit the thumb with results that may be serious.

For the Indian pellet bow see Gulail. A Chinese pellet bow and its string have been described under Bow and Bow String. Figs. 176, 315.

PELLET CROSSBOW. See Arbalete a Jalet.

PELT. The dead quarry of a hawk.

PELTA. The Greek javelin. It had a leather strap, the *amentum*, fastened to the middle of the shaft to assist in throwing it. (Boutell 48).

Cowper, p. 229, calls attention to the fact that the name *amentum* is Latin and says that the proper Greek name is *ankule* or *mesankule*.

PELTASTE. Greek light infantry, javelin men. (Boutell 48).

PEN CASE, LAMA'S. The Tibetan lamas, like most priests, are not ordinarily allowed to carry weapons, but are said to fight with their pen cases. These are fairly effective weapons, many being over a foot long, made of iron and quite heavy. Many of the older ones are beautifully chiseled and pierced in designs of dragons and clouds, or else inlaid with silver. Fig. 629.

PENCIL. A small streamer fixed to the end of a lance. It was decorated with the coat of arms of the bearer and served to identify him in battle. (Grose II, 51).

PENDANT, PENNANT. A flag used on ships of war. It is of two kinds, the long and the broad. The first is a very long, narrow, tapering flag—the usual length being sixty feet and the breadth at the head only four inches. It is believed to have been first used in 1653 by an English admiral to represent the lash of a whip, signifying that he had whipped his enemies (the Dutch) off the seas. The broad pennant, or burgee, tapers slightly and is forked at the fly. (Macgeorge 72).

PENDEWAN. A Dyak fish spear with a barbed head and slender iron foreshaft. (Ling Roth I, 462).

PENDOQ. See Kendelan.

PENICHUL. A blowpipe, Semang, Malay Peninsula.

PENJUKIR. A maker of kris hilts, Java.

PENNON. A flag, the sign of a knight bachelor. It had a square body ending in a triangular point, and was charged with the armorial bearings of the owner. The pennon was converted into a banner by the king, or commander-in-chief, cutting off the point—whereby the knight was raised to the rank of banneret. (Grose II, 52).

PENONCEL. The diminutive of pennon, being half its length. It was carried by a squire and usually bore his cognizance. (Macgeorge 29).

FIGURE 629. *Lama's Pen Cases.* 1. *Iron pierced and gilded, 17th century. Length 16 inches.* 2. *Octagonal, iron inlaid with silver. Length 13.5 inches, 18th century.*

PEPPER BOX. A kind of revolver popular in the middle of the 19th century. It has no separate barrel but the chambers are much longer than in the other types. It was usually constructed so that when the trigger was pulled the barrels revolved and the hammer was raised. Some had the hammer above the chambers, and others had it below. A few of them were double acting, that is, they were cocked by hand and not by the pull of the trigger. They vary greatly in size, design and number of barrels. Fig. 630.

PEQSI. The tang of a kris.

PERCUSSION LOCK. The percussion lock, both for muzzle- and breechloaders is the latest form of ignition. It was introduced early in the 19th century and soon displaced all other forms wherever it could be made and caps procured. In the percussion lock a cap loaded with a detonating mixture is placed on a hollow nipple and exploded by the blow of a falling hammer. Its advantages are great rapidity of action and the ease with which the cap can be waterproofed and protected from dampness.

PERFORATED SHIELDS. Shields often had openings in them. These were of two kinds: first, notches (bouches) at the top for the lance; second, openings at the center for sight, so that the user could cover himself and see the movements of his adversary at the same time. (Grose II, 261).

PERIPERIU, MIRO. The first is the Kakudo and the second the Iwadji name. Both are tribes of the extreme north of Australia. It is a heavy club about five feet long with an extreme width of about three and a half inches. It is somewhat flattened and widened towards one end which is bluntly pointed. The other end is much narrower and is always marked with a distinct concavity. It is very characteristically decorated in red and white. (Spencer, North. Ter. 367).

PERNAT. A mace, Russia. (Scheremetew 107, 108, 109).

PERRIER, PIERRIER, PATRARY, PATE-RARA. An engine for throwing large stones. The name frequently does not signify any particular mechanism. (Hewitt I, 349, 356; Grose 382).

PESH-KABZ, PESHCUBZ, PESHQABZ. A form of dagger used in Persia and Northern India.

FIGURE 630. *Pepper Boxes.* 1. *Single action, top hammer.* 2. *Double action, under hammer.*

The name is Persian and means "foregrip." The blade is of T section and is quite wide at the hilt, narrowing suddenly just below it, and then tapering regularly to a very slender point. As a rule the blade is straight, but not infrequently has a pro-

cated cone with a touchhole in the center of the breech, and four handles for fastening it to a heavy plank, called a madrier. Petards varied considerably in size, but were usually about five inches in diameter at the breech, eight or nine at the mouth, and

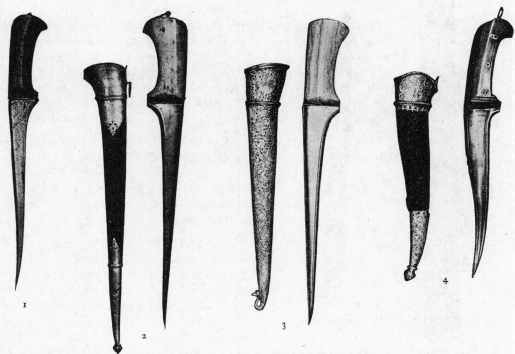

FIGURE 631. *Pesh-Kabz. 1. Steel blade 10 inches long engraved with flowers, horn grip. 2. Watered blade 12.5 inches long, ivory hilt. Scabbard mounts of engraved copper, probably originally gilded. 3. Blade 11.5 inches long of black Khorassan damask, slightly inlaid with gold. Solid hilt of walrus ivory. Scabbard covered with pierced and engraved silver in patterns of flowers and birds. The tip is a peacock's head. 4. Steel blade 8.875 inches long, very thick tang inlaid with gold flowers and inscriptions. The grip is of ivory riveted to the flat tang. The burrs under the rivet heads are silver flowers. Scabbard green velvet and silver.*

nounced reverse curve. The hilt is often of walrus ivory (Persian, shirmani), and is heavy and has neither guard nor pommel. This knife is obviously intended for forcing an opening in mail; and as a piece of engineering design could hardly be improved upon for the purpose. (Hobson-Jobson 701; Egerton 346, 381, 382, 484, 485, 581, 617 to 625, 717 to 724, 760). Fig. 631.

PESO. In old fencing, balance, supposed to be perfect if the weight of the body bore on the left leg when on guard, and on the right when attacking. (Castle 132).

PETARD. A device for bursting open gates and doors. It is a kind of mortar of the form of a trun-

ten or twelve long. They weighed about sixty pounds.

The petard was nearly filled with powder, which was covered by a wad, and then by a tightly fitting piece of wood driven into place, and the remainder of the open space filled with wax or pitch. The whole was then covered with waxed cloth. The mouth of the petard was then placed in a hollow in the madrier and securely fastened by cords from the handles to staples on the latter. The madrier was about eighteen inches square and was strengthened by crossed bands of iron on the back. It was provided with a hook at the top by which it could be hung against the gate to be forced, and the fuse lighted. If the petard was strong enough the gate was blown in, but frequently it did more damage to the users than to the gate. It is said to have been invented in 1579. (Grose I, 408). Figs. 632, 633.

FIGURE 632. *Petards. The figure shows two ways of using the petard; and also the petard, its wooden wad, the madrier, and the hooks and staples for hanging it. From Grose I, p. 408.*

PETARDIER. One who uses a petard.

PETERARA. See Perrier.

PETI. An Indian cuirass of brigandine. It is rectangular with a neck guard and shoulder straps. (Egerton 573).

PETRARY. An engine for throwing stones, apparently any kind of engine.

PETRONEL, PETRINAL, POITRINAL. A firearm of the 16th century intermediate in size between the pistol and the arquebus. It was short but of large caliber and heavy. It had a peculiarly curved

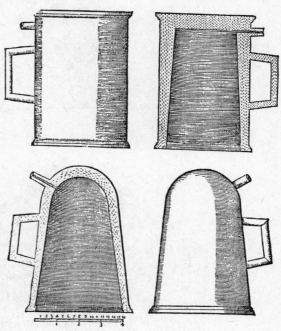

FIGURE 633. *Petards. Two Spanish petards of the early 17th century. From Lechunga, Discurso de le Artilleria.*

stock and was fired with the butt against the chest, from which practice it derives its name. (Grose I, 105, Planche 394). Fig. 634.

PETTY SINGLES. The toes of a hawk.

PEYTRAL, PECTORAL, POITRAL, POITRINAL. The armor for a horse's chest, sometimes the breaststrap. It covered the front of the chest and the sides as far back as the saddle. The earlier ones were made of boiled leather and the

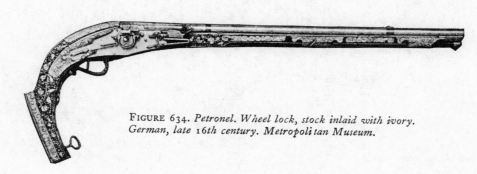

FIGURE 634. *Petronel. Wheel lock, stock inlaid with ivory. German, late 16th century. Metropolitan Museum.*

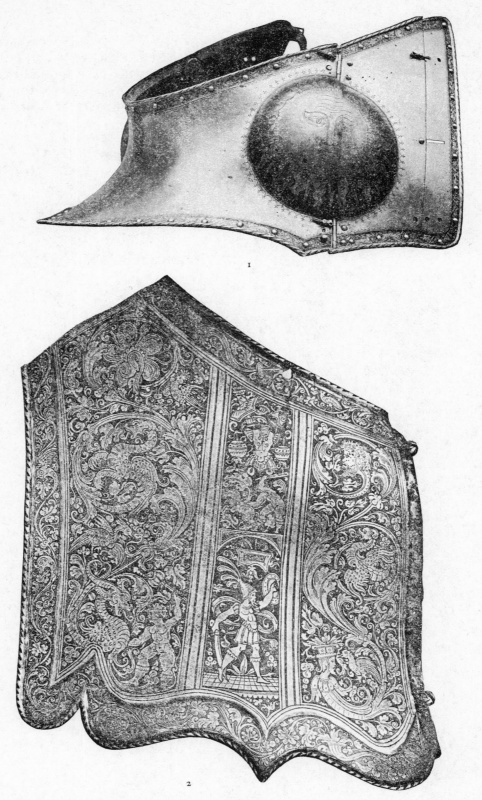

FIGURE 635. *Peytral.* 1. *German,* 1553. *It has the large glancing knobs.* 2. *Italian,* 1560. *Metro-politan Museum. Not to scale.*

later of steel. (ffoulkes 89). Fig. 635. See Bardings.

PEZONERAS. See Glancing Knobs.

PHALANGAE. Clubs used by the African negroes against the Egyptians. (Burton Sword 32).

PHALARICA. A fire missile used by the Romans. (Burton Sword 248).

PHALEE, PHUK. A shield, Western Tibet. (Ramsay-Western).

PHARI. A cane shield, India, 16th century. (Egerton, p. 23).

PHARSI. A sort of brown bill used by watchmen in Khandish. (Sinclair I. A. II, 216).

PHASGANON. One of the Homeric names for the sword. (Burton Sword 222).

PHEON. "A barbed javelin carried by sergeant-at-arms in the king's presence as early as the reign of Richard I." (Planche 296).

PHIRANGI. See Firangi.

PHLO. A small fireball, Burma. (Egerton, p. 94).

PHUK. See Phalee.

PHURBU. The Tibetan exorcising knife, or "ghost dagger," used by the lamas in driving out evil spirits. It has a three-winged blade and a hilt made up of lamaistic symbols. The pommel is usually a head with three faces crowned, with an animal's head and neck projecting from the top. Thunderbolts (vajras), dragons and dragon's heads are frequently present. Usually the blades are made of iron and the hilts of brass; sometimes the entire knife is of brass, and occasionally of wood. Fig. 636.

PICCININO, LUCIO. It is uncertain whether he made armor or only decorated it. His work was over elaborate but extremely minute and shows great technical skill. He was the son of Antonio Piccinino and lived in Milan about 1590. (ffoulkes Armourer 140).

PICHANGATTI. The Coorg knife. The name is Tamil and means "hand knife." It has a broad, heavy, single-edged blade about seven inches long, and a plain hilt ending in a round pommel. The hilt and scabbard are profusely decorated with brass,

silver or gold or of some two or three of these metals in very good style. Attached to the sheath is a brass, or silver chain carrying tweezers, nail and

FIGURE 636. *Phurbu.* 1. *Steel blade 2.5 inches long. The figure forming the hilt is of brass and has a vajra in one hand and a snake or sling in the other. There is a wax seal in a recess in the back.* 2. *Carved wood 23.25 inches long. Lacquered a dark coppery red.* 3. *Made entirely of brass. Length 9 inches. The grip is a vajra, and the pommel a crowned head with three faces.* 4. *All brass, three faces at the top. Length 8.25 inches.* 5. *All brass, a winged figure on the top. Length 6 inches.*

ear cleaners, etc. The knife is always carried in the front of the belt that carries the ayda katti. It is not a weapon but is used much as we use a pocket knife. (Egerton 102 to 105). Fig. 637.

PICHAW. The Khiva dagger of honor, presented to heroes. A typical one has a straight, single-edged blade and a hilt made of two grip pieces of ivory or jade riveted to the flat tang. The pommel is a cylindrical cap, usually set on a ring of jewels. The scabbard is nearly cylindrical and covered with decorated metal. (Moser XVIII).

PIED DE BICHE. See Goat's Foot.

PIERRIER. See Perrier.

PIG-FACED BASINET. The basinet with a projecting visor. See Basinet.

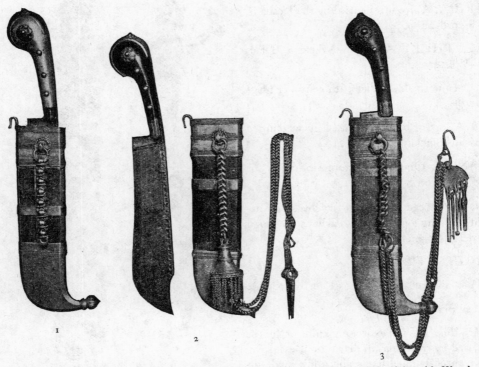

FIGURE 637. *Pichangatti. 1. Plain blade 7 inches long. Silver hilt decorated with gold. Wooden scabbard with silver mountings and chain. 2. Blade 7.5 inches long. Chain, manicure set and mountings of silver. 3. Horn hilt, wooden scabbard, brass mountings.*

PICKERING. William Pickering was a celebrated English armorer of the early part of the 17th century. In 1614 he was made Master of the Armoury at Greenwich, and he received £240 for a suit of armor for Prince Henry who died in Nov., 1612. (ffoulkes Armourer 122).

PICKET. A military punishment used in the English army as late as the 18th century. The offender was hung by the right waist from a high post, with his bare heel resting on a blunt pointed stake driven into the ground. It was finally abandoned as causing too much injury. (Grose II, 107).

PIECES OF ADVANTAGE. Reinforcing pieces worn over the regular armor for the joust. (ffoulkes 164).

PIG'S FEATHER. See Sweyn's Feather.

PIHA-KAETTA. The Sinhalese knife. These knives have rather rough, heavy blades from half an inch to two inches wide and from five to eight long. They are usually decorated with a panel near the back and close to the hilt. These panels are either inlaid with silver, brass, or both; or deeply engraved and covered with thin plates of silver pressed into the hollows of the engraving. The hilts are decorated with chased silver or brass. Sometimes they are made of silver or crystal. The scabbards are made of wood, usually fluted, and often covered with silver. Frequently a stylus is carried in the sheath with the knife. Fig. 638.

PIJA. A dagger, Salar. (Rockhill).

PI-KAN. A type of shield used on the Lower Tully River, Queensland. In making it a piece is split from one of the flange-like roots of the *ficus chretioides* or similar tree. "A curved incision is

faces of the piece are chipped away leaving a boss on each face at the center and a hand hole is cut in the one at the back. The front is decorated with painted designs. The front of this shield is called

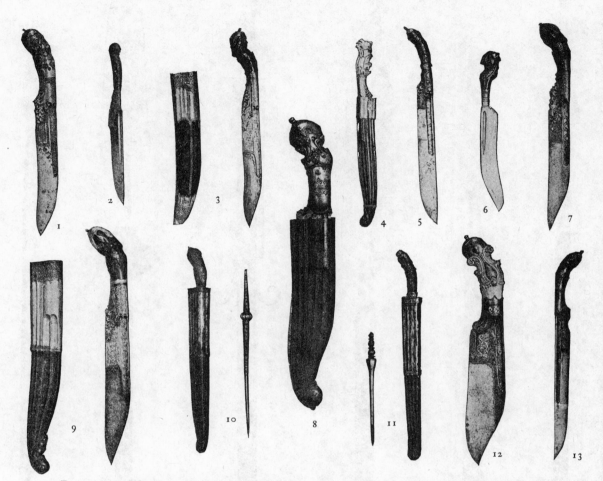

FIGURE 638. *Piha-Kaetta.* 1. *Ivory hilt, blade 7.25 inches long.* 2. *Horn hilt, silver inlaid blade. Length 9 inches.* 3. *Blade 7.25 inches long, set in brass and inlaid with silver, horn hilt. Hilt and scabbard mountings of silver gilt.* 4. *Crystal hilt, blade 5.75 inches long. Silver top to scabbard.* 5. *Hilt, carved horn set in silver and brass which extend down the blade for some distance. Length 10.75 inches.* 6. *Ivory hilt a monster's head.* 7. *Blade set in brass inlaid with silver. Wood hilt with silver mountings.* 8. *Heavy blade 8.25 inches long. Ivory hilt with silver and brass mountings.* 9. *Heavy blade 8 inches long inlaid with silver and brass. Horn hilt with a silver panel. Wooden scabbard partly covered with silver.* 10. *Knife similar to 5. The scabbard also contains a stylus 9 inches long inlaid with silver.* 11. *Similar to 10 but with a short silver handled stylus.* 12. *Very heavy blade 8.25 inches long inlaid with brass and silver. Ivory hilt with silver inlays.* 13. *Similar to 5 but with the hilt covered with silver.*

made in the flange both above and below, and the spur chipped about half way through along the lines required, and the piece hammered or pushed out." This gives a piece with rounded ends and with one long side convex and the other concave. Both sur-

kananja, a word meaning "inside" in reference to the bark having been removed. The central portion is called *namma,* the back the *chu-cha,* and the handle the *dumbul.* (Roth, Aus. Mus. VII, 204).

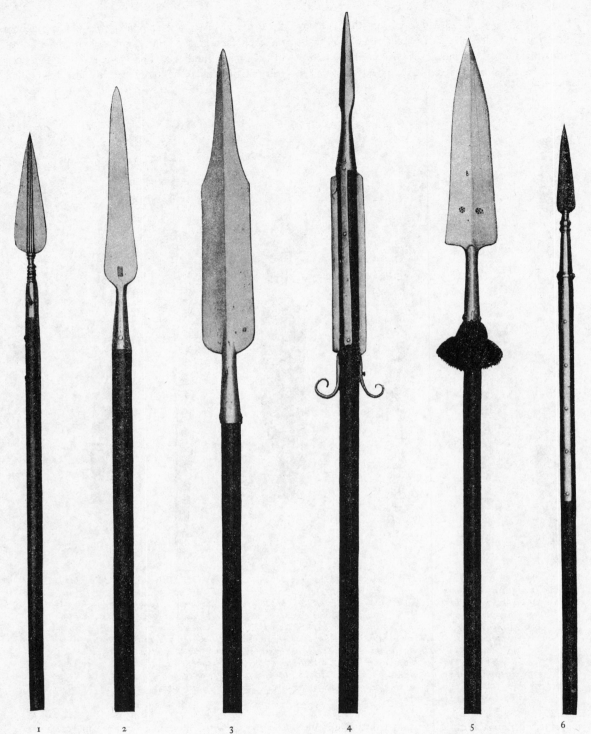

FIGURE 639. *Pikes.* 1. *French(?)*, 1725. 2. *Swiss*, 1600. 3. *French, late 18th century.* 4. *Polish*, 1600. 5. *Italian*, 1500. 6. ——, 1700. *Metropolitan Museum.*

PIKE. The spear of the heavy infantry in early times. The head was comparatively small, usually leaf or diamond-shaped, and mounted on a very long shaft. The shafts were protected for three or four feet from the head to prevent their being cut by the swords of opposing cavalry. Those used by the Greek phalanx were very long, those of the Romans considerably shorter. They gradually decreased in length until in the latter part of the 15th century they were eighteen feet long. They were a favorite weapon of the Swiss for some time, and in 1425, thirty-eight per cent. of the men of Lucerne were armed with them. Pikes were used mainly as a defense against cavalry, the butts being braced against the ground. The infantry were composed of musketeers and pikemen, the latter protecting the former while they were reloading their guns. Fig. 639.

PIKE-FORK. See Military Fork.

PI-LAK. A squire or fighting companion, Subanuns of Mindanao. (Christie 97).

PILANI. The Roman javelineers. They were veterans and formed the reserve. (Burton Sword 248).

PILE. The head of an arrow.

PILETE. A pike. (Hewitt I, 207).

PILL, PELL. A sharpened stake used as a weapon by peasants in the Norman armies. (Planche 329).

PILLARA. A West Australian spear with two parallel heads placed close together, each with a single row of barbs cut from the solid. It was about nine feet long and was mainly used for thrusting, but was also thrown with a thrower. (Brough Smyth 337).

PILL LOCK. A form of lock that fired a detonating mixture made into the form of a ball or pill. See Detonator.

PILLOW SWORD. The name is derived from its being hung by the pillow of the master of the house, ready for use in case of emergency. First quarter of the 17th century. (Windsor, p. 206, no. 689). It was a straight-bladed sword with a straight cross guard. (Fig. 640).

The Japanese used a particular sword for the same purpose, and called by the same name.

PILUM. The Roman spear which was the principal weapon of the legionaries. It appears to have had a long neck between the head and the socket for the shaft, but its exact form is uncertain.

FIGURE 640. *Pillow Sword, German, 17th century. Blade memorial with busts of Adolphus and Frederic of Nassau. Metropolitan Museum.*

PILUS. The first division of the section of the Roman army that carried the standards. (Burton Sword 247).

PINABOLAN. A "bolo-shaped knife." Subanuns of Mindanao. (Christie 95).

PINCHA. A throwing knife, Luhr, Africa. (Jaehns 258).

PINDARRY. Irregular troops of India who are believed to have originally come from Pandhar. They formed a part of the Màhratta army in the 17th and 18th centuries. After the final defeat of the Mahrattas by the English the bands of outlaws who ravaged the country were composed so largely of Pindaries that the name was given to the whole.

armies as early as the 14th century and continued as a separate force until some time in the 19th. (Hewitt II, 37, 94, 95).

PIPES. Bagpipes were used for military music as early as the 16th century and are still used by the Scotch regiments and by some of the Indian troops in the English service.

PIQUENAIRES. Pikemen of the 15th century. (Hewitt II, 37).

PIRA. A kind of Malayan sword with a blade like the old falchion. It has a long projection from the pommel, Philippines. Fig. 641.

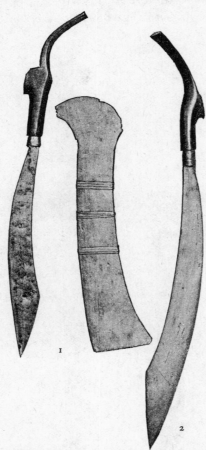

FIGURE 641. *Pira.* 1. *Blade 16.125 inches long, black horn hilt. Flat wooden scabbard.* 2. *Basilian. Blade 21.5 inches long, horn hilt.*

They were finally completely crushed by the Marquis of Hastings in 1817. (Hobson-Jobson 711).

PI-NU-TI. A bolo of good workmanship used only as a weapon, and not for field work, Mindanao. (Christie 115).

PIONEERS. Men attached to an army whose duty it was to clear forests, make roads, dig trenches, etc. They were employed in both the English and French

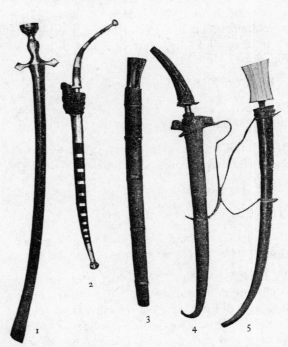

FIGURE 643. *Battak Swords.* 1. *Piso Podang. Steel hilt with a cross guard and cup pommel. Length blade 24.25 inches. Wood scabbard.* 2. *Small flyssa-shaped blade, curved wood hilt. Wood scabbard with a carved top. Silver bands on hilt and scabbard.* 3. *Piso Gading. Fluted hilt of old ivory. Plain wooden scabbard.* 4. *Piso Eccat. Staghorn hilt set in brass. Leather sheath. Blade 20 inches long.* 5. *Piso Gading. Fluted ivory hilt. Blade 18.25 inches long. Dark wood scabbard partly covered with leather. All but no. 1 have flyssa-shaped blades.*

FIGURE 642. *Pisau Raut. Dyak knife for trimming rattan. Blade 4.375 inches long inlaid with brass. Wooden handle with inlaid rings of buffalo and staghorn, two of the latter are carved. The end is of carved staghorn. This is an unusually elaborate specimen.*

PIRR-BEN. See Kul-Luk.

PISAU RAUT. A Malay knife, also used by the Dyaks. It has a blade about four inches long with a straight handle about a foot long. It is the same as the knives carried by the Dyaks in their mandau sheaths. It is used by the Malays in preparing rattan; the name means "rattan knife." (Arc. f. Eth. III, 242; Clifford Malay Mono. 114). Fig. 642.

PISO ECCAT. The type of Battak sword with a deer horn hilt. The blade is like a short flyssa. (Modigliani, Battachi 128 plate XXII). No. 4, fig. 643.

PISO GADING. The type of Battak sword with a fluted ivory hilt. The blade is similar to the preceding. (Modigliani, Battachi 128 plate XXII). 3, 5, fig. 643.

PISO HALASAN. A Battak sword with a curved blade and a hilt made of a thick cylindrical piece of staghorn. (Arc. f. Eth. VI, 121).

PISO PODANG. A Battak sabre with a cross guard and a large pommel. (Modigliani, Battachi, plate XXII, p. 128). No. 1, fig. 643.

PISO TONKENG. A Dyak knife with a straight, square blade, and a wire wound grip set at a sharp angle. (Arc. f. Eth. IX, 75).

PISTOL. A hand firearm used with one hand. There is considerable uncertainty as to where and when they were invented. They are said to have been first used in England in 1521, and in France in 1531. They were certainly used by the French infantry at Cerisoles in 1544, the infantry being protected by pikemen. The German Reiters used pistols at the battle of St. Quentin in 1557. (Denison 235). The earliest pistols were undoubtedly the wheel lock daggs of the 16th century, fig. 644. The dagg was the weapon of the cavalry of the 16th and 17th centuries. The drill for its use is shown in an excellent series of plates in Grose, p. 364 et seq.

Matchlock pistols were rarely used in Europe, although they are not unknown in certain parts of the East. Pistols have continued in favor in all countries using firearms, and have been made for all of the systems of ignition used for guns as well as several others. They are of all sizes from pocket pistols three or four inches long, to cavalry weapons of a couple of feet. They have been made with any number of barrels up to twenty-four and with all imaginable groupings of barrels. For some of the later pistols, see fig. 645.

Combinations of pistols with swords, knives, axes, spears, maces, whips and even stirrups have been made and used in many parts of the world. See Combined Weapons.

In Turkey and the Balkans the commonest pistols were of western European manufacture or copied from them. In most cases the locks were from western Europe, though miquelet locks of local make were almost as common. They were generally very large, about eighteen inches long, with rounded pommels and frequently no place for a ramrod. For these a separate ramrod, the suma, was carried hung from the belt, figs. 646, 647. A special style of pistol with a very long, slim stock and a long, pointed pommel, was used in Albania and Montenegro. It is often called "rat-tailed" by collectors, nos. 1, 2, 3, fig. 646. Throughout the Turkish Empire blunderbuss pistols shaped like guns were quite common, fig. 648. The smallest were about a foot long, the largest were full-sized guns.

In Morocco and North Africa most of the pistols were European, or like the Turkish, except for the decoration. The stocks were often inlaid with wire scrolls or with rather large pieces of brass or steel. Pistols apparently of native make were also used. These had snaphaan locks, like those of the Berber guns, and peculiar oval pommels. Fig. 649.

In Persia the pistols were generally similar to the Turkish or like very short guns, fig. 648. Both kinds have miquelet locks. In the Caucasus the usual pistols have very light, slim barrels, miquelet locks and very large globular pommels with a ring on the butt. They were generally carried in a small holster fastened to the back of the belt a little to the right so as to be drawn easily when needed. After firing, if in a melee, the pistol was dropped and remained hanging by the ring from a cord worn like a baldric for the purpose. Usually the pommel is of ivory or silver decorated with gilding or chern. The stocks are made of elm root or are covered with black leather. The mountings are much decorated with chern like all of the other weapons from this region. The stocks and locks are generally of native make but the barrels are frequently European, and often bear the marks of celebrated makers of the 17th and 18th centuries. Fig. 650.

In the remainder of continental Asia pistols were never generally used, and when found are either of

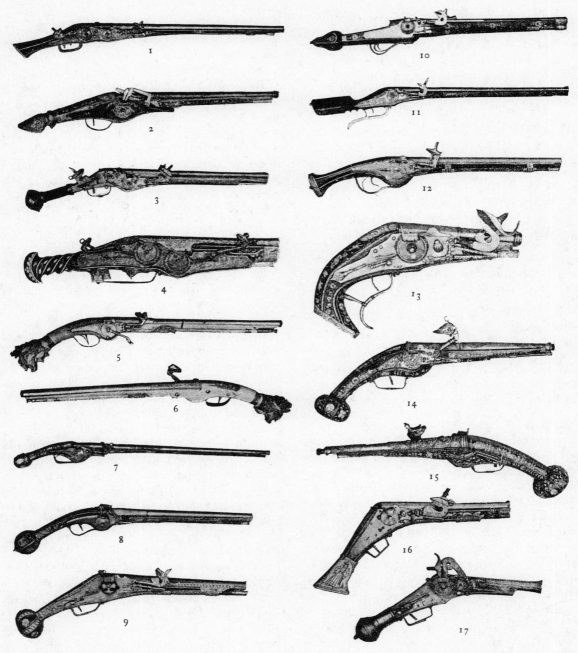

FIGURE 644. *Wheel Lock Pistols. 1. Saxon, dated 1561. It has a double lock. 2. French, XVI. 3. German, 1550-1600. Double-barreled. 4. German, about 1550. Double-barreled. Made for the Emperor Charles V. 5 and 6. Pair, Dutch, XVII. Signed Maesbricht. 7. French, 1575-1580. 8. French, early XVII. 9. Saxon, about 1590. 10. German, XVI. 11. French, XVII. 12. Austrian or Swiss, about 1620. 13. Swiss dagg, about 1590. 14 and 15. Pair, French, about 1500. 16. Nuremberg, about 1550. 17. German, late XVI. Metropolitan Museum. Not to scale.*

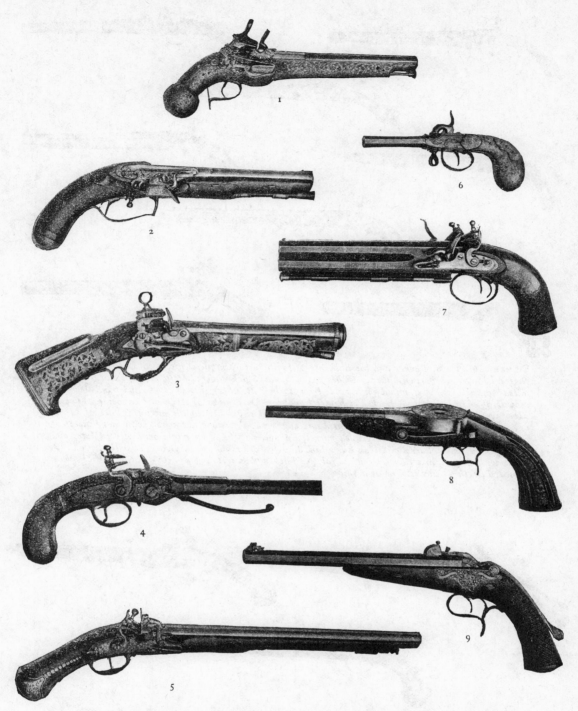

FIGURE 645. *Late Pistols from Western Europe.* 1. *Miquelet lock, Spanish, by Alexis du Four, dated* 1687. 2. *Flintlock inverted. By Tatham & Egg, London, end of the 18th century.* 3. *Blunderbuss pistol, miquelet lock, Spanish, 18th century.* 4. *Flintlock repeating pistol. Made by H. W. Mortimer, London, about* 1805. 5. *Snaphaan pistol, Italian, end of the 17th century. Barrel inscribed Pietro Moretta.* 6. *Detonator, Belgian, about* 1810. 7. *Over and under, flintlock pistol. G. Sturman, London, early 19th century.* 8. *"Monitor" pistol, Belgian(?), 19th century. Inscribed H. Genhart.* 9. *Target pistol, Viennese, middle of the 19th century. By Joseph Springer, Erben. All from the Schott Collection.*

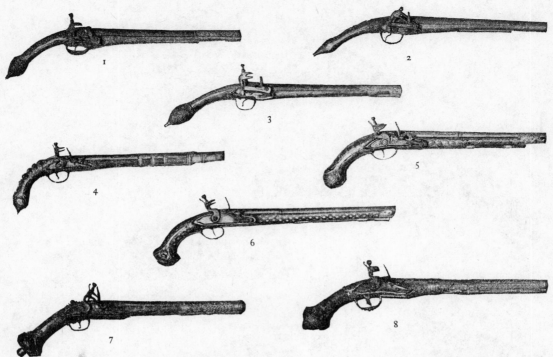

FIGURE 646. *Pistols, Turkey and the Balkans.* 1. *Plain barrel, miquelet lock. Stock of a silver alloy chased in high relief. Length 20.5 inches.* 2. *Albania. Stock covered with engraved brass. "Rat-tailed" pistol.* 3. *Barrel inlaid with gold. Iron stock, butt, upper side of stock, and band near the muzzle of chased silver.* 4. *Lock and barrel European. Decoration of stock and capucines Turkish silver work set with coral.* 5. *Barrel inlaid with chased silver. All of the mountings are of silver, or of iron covered with silver plates chased and engraved. The stock is covered with large pieces of coral set in chased silver.* 6. *Engraved barrel, European lock. Stock inlaid with silver plates and wire, butt silver.* 7. *Barrel and lock European. Stock carved wood, mainly covered with silver decorated with filigree and tula set with coral.* 8. *Lock and barrel inlaid with gold. Stock of silver chased. Length 21 inches. One of a pair.*

FIGURE 647. *Pistols made in western Europe and decorated in the East.* 1, 2. *Stocks carved. Barrels, locks and mounts inlaid with gold in Turkey.* 3. *English pistol decorated in Egypt with chasing, gilding and heavy inlaying in gold. Signed and dated 1829.* 4, 5. *Barrels and all mounts carved and largely covered with silver. Stocks inlaid with vines and scrolls of silver. Turkish work.*

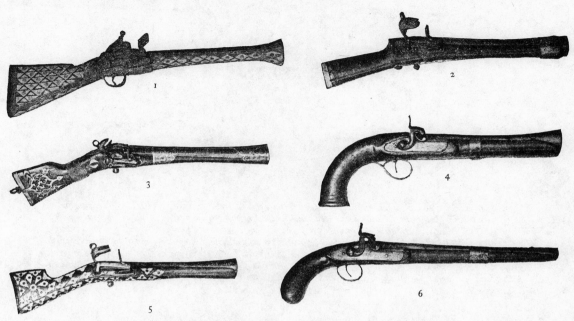

FIGURE 648. *Blunderbuss Pistols, etc.* 1. *Turkey. Roughly made pistol with the stock inlaid with bone.* 2. *Persia. Engraved barrel. Stock inlaid with bone, turquoise and brass, ivory butt.* 3. *Plain barrel with the tang inlaid with silver. Miquelet lock inlaid with silver. Stock inlaid with bone, pearl and brass; silver scrolls on each side; grip wound with silver wire.* 4. *Persian barrel of very finely watered steel; remounted on a European stock of much later date.* 5. *Engraved twist barrel. Stock inlaid with bone and brass, Turkey.* 6. *Persian barrel of watered steel chiseled with ornaments in relief. Remounted on an English stock of much later date.*

FIGURE 649. *Moroccan Pistols.* 1. *Snaphaan lock nearly covered with plates of engraved silver. Barrel inlaid with gold. Stock inlaid with scrolls of silver wire. Length 18 inches. From the Collection of Mr. Charles Noe Daly.* 2. *Flintlock, barrel and mountings inlaid with brass. Stock inlaid with scrolls of silver wire. It has a silver cap on the fore end.* 3. *Lock, barrel and mountings inlaid with brass. Fore end of ivory. Length 19.5 inches.* 4. *Spanish pistol roughly repaired in Fez. Engraved steel lock and butt; very rough capucines. Length 14.5 inches.*

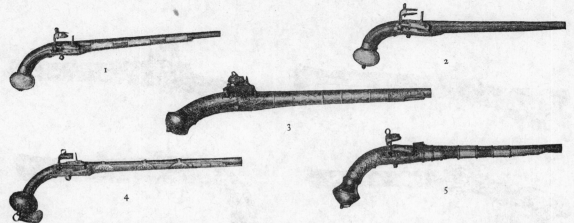

FIGURE 650. *Pistols, Caucasus.* 1. *Octagon damask barrel. Stock covered with black leather over which are silver plates chased and decorated with tula. Length 19 inches.* 2. *Damask barrel carved in relief and inlaid with gold. Miquelet lock. Stock covered with black leather, ivory pommel. Decorated with bands and scrolls of silver with tula patterns.* 3. *Round barrel entirely covered with black leather, ivory butt, silver mounts decorated with tula. Length 17.375 inches.* 4. *Round barrel. Miquelet lock. Stock covered with black leather, mounts silver, partly gilded and partly decorated with tula.* 5. *Barrel and lock covered with gold inlaying. Stock covered with silver decorated with tula. Length 21 inches.*

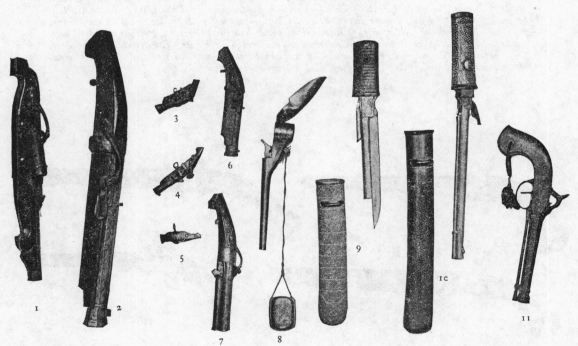

FIGURE 651. *Japanese Pistols.* 1. *Two shot matchlock pistol with swinging chambers.* 2. *Matchlock pistol. Stock inlaid with brass flowers. Barrel inlaid with silver dragons, silver band at muzzle. Length 17.5 inches.* 3, 4, 5. *Netsuke pistols. Lengths 3, 4 and 2.375 inches. No. 3 is inlaid with a gold dragon.* 6. *Round barrel inlaid with gold and silver, ebony stock. Length 6.5 inches.* 7. *Three barreled revolver. Barrels inlaid with silver and gold, brass lock. Length 8 inches.* 8. *Combination of pistol and pen case. Attached is a small bronze inro, apparently a cap box.* 9. *Combination of pistol and knife. Percussion lock. Knife blade 6.5 inches long. Leather covered hilt and scabbard. Length 11.25 inches.* 10. *Plain round barrel, percussion lock. Mounted like a knife with a same hilt and leather scabbard.* 11. *Small percussion pistol with a swiveled ramrod, copied from an American model.*

European make or copied from them. An exception must be made for the very rare matchlock pistols of India.

Japan alone of Asiatic nations made distinctive styles of pistols. The idea of the pistol was derived from Europe as is shown by the original Japanese names, *tanegashima* and *pistoru*, the first being the name of the island on which the first European traders had their station, and the second being obviously derived from the English name. Though they adopted the idea they made the weapons of purely Japanese form, in fact the early Japanese pistols are simply very small guns. Occasionally they made three-barreled revolvers, which, however, were sometimes purely for show as many could not be fired, not having any touchholes. Two-shot pistols with two chambers, either of which could be swung into line with the barrel, were also made. Very small pistols of the usual form were made and used as netsuke. They were too small to be of any use as pistols but were complete in all respects. Fig. 651.

In the middle of the 19th century, after Japan had been opened to foreigners, the ordinary European types of pistol were made there as well as several very curious types of percussion pistol. Some had very small locks and straight stocks like dagger hilts and were carried in scabbards like those of knives. Others had a barrel mounted on the back of a knife blade, with a hilt and scabbard like those of a knife. Neither could be distinguished from daggers when sheathed. Others again were a combination of pen case and pistol. The tube for the writing brush formed the barrel of the pistol and the lock was enclosed in the larger end with the inkwell. When closed it appeared like an ordinary pen case. It must have been very inconvenient to use as the writing brush screwed into the nozzle of the pistol and it required considerable time to remove it before the pistol could be fired. None of these odd forms were in general use and were probably made to find out whether they would prove to be useful. Possibly some of the samurai desired some weapon that would not be obvious enough to get them in trouble with the police, and would take the place of the swords that they were no longer permitted to carry. Fig. 651.

PISTOL SHIELD, GONNE. A shield with a pistol barrel fixed in the center. They were not very uncommon in the 16th century. (Hewitt III, 684). Fig. 652.

PITCH. The height at which a hawk flies when waiting for game. The higher the pitch the better.

FIGURE 652. *Pistol Shield, English, 16th century. From a guard of Henry VIII and the Tower of London. Metropolitan Museum.*

PIZAINE, PUZANE. A species of gorget or breastplate worn in the 13th and 14th centuries. It was sometimes made of steel and sometimes of jazerant work. (Hewitt II, 141).

PIZIKSE. A bow, Point Barrow. Similar bows are used by many of the Eskimo. Murdoch, p. 195, describes a typical one as follows: "They are made of spruce, forty-five to fifty inches long, three quarters of an inch wide at the handle, widening to an inch and a quarter. They are backed by a continuous cord of three braided sinews, which may be forty to fifty yards long on a large bow. This is looped around the nocks and stretched along the back. When enough strands have been laid on they are divided into two equal portions and twisted into tight cables, thus greatly increasing their tension. The cables are secured to the handle of the bow so that they cannot untwist.

PIZIKSIZAX. A bow case, Point Barrow. It is made of sealskin and is of such a size and shape that a bow can be carried in it strung. It is fastened to the quiver and is carried on the back. The quiver is a cylindrical or conical bag of skin with a cap on the lower end. It has a wooden or bone rod in the seam to keep it straight when empty. (Murdoch 207). Fig. 653.

FIGURE 653. *Piziksizax. Sealskin bow case, Canadian Eskimo. Museum of the American Indian, Heye Foundation.*

PLACARD, PLACATE, PLAQUET. The lower part of the Gothic breastplate, or an extra piece covering the lower part of the breast and worn in tournaments. (Planche 401, Grose II, 252).

PLASTRON. An iron breastplate worn between the hauberk and gambeson. (Grose I, 101).

At the present time it is a pad worn on the breast when fencing. (Castle).

PLATE, PLATE ARMOR. Armor made of steel plates as distinguished from mail, scale, brigandine or jazerant armor.

PLOMBEE, PLOMMEE. A mace made of, or weighted with, lead, 14th century. (Hewitt II, 267).

PLUME, DEPLUME. For a hawk to pluck the feathers from a bird she has killed.

PLUME HOLDER. A tube fixed to a helmet to hold a plume. In some of the 17th-century helmets from Turkey and eastern Europe they were very large and placed on one side of the front. Most Persian and Indian helmets have two and sometimes three plume holders.

PLUTEUS. A movable contrivance for sheltering besiegers when attacking a fortified place, 9th century. (Hewitt I, 88).

POEOT. The Poonan blowpipe, Borneo. It is a polished wood tube with a horn ring at the mouthpiece and may or may not have a spearhead attached. (Leiden II, 86, 87).

POGAMOGGAN. A war club consisting of a stone fastened to the end of an elastic wooden handle. Both stone and handle are often covered with rawhide, Plains Indians. Compare I-Wata-Jinga. Fig. 392.

POIGNARD, PONIARD. A small dagger having a blade of square or triangular section, and therefore only useful for thrusting.

POINCON. An armorer's mark stamped or inlaid on his work.

PO-INI. Small, light spears used as toys in North Queensland. (Roth, Aust. Mus. VII, 191).

POINTS. See Aiguilettes.

POITRAL, POITREL, POITRINAL, PECTORAL. See Peytral and Petronel.

POKWE, POUCUE. A knife of the Lunda, Central Africa. It has a broad double-edged blade with waved edges, and a straight, guardless hilt. (Burton Sword 189).

POLDER MITTON. An extra guard worn over the bend of the right arm in tournaments in the 15th century. (ffoulkes 78). See Epaul de Mouton.

FIGURE 654. *Pole Arms.* 1. *Military fork, Swiss or German, first half of the 16th century.* 2. *Partizan, German (Austrian), 16th-17th century.* 3. *Fauchard, Italian, 16th century. Guard of the Duke of Gonzaga.* 4. *Halbard, German, 16th century.* 5. *Awl pike, German or Swiss, 15th century.* 6. *Halbard, German (Austrian), 16th century. Guard of the Emperor Maximilian II.* 7. *Axe, French, middle of the 14th century.* 8. *Berdiche, German or Swiss, 14th-16th century.* 9. *Berdiche, Turkish, 14th or 15th century. Metropolitan Museum.*

POLE ARMS, SHAFTED WEAPONS, STAVES. Any form of cutting or thrusting weapon mounted on a long handle. The handle is variously called the pole, shaft, haft or hampe. In Europe the handle was often covered with cloth or

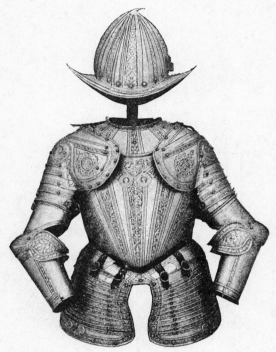

FIGURE 655. *Pots and Mops, Pisan Armor, 1570. Metropolitan Museum.*

velvet, originally to give the hand a firmer hold, later mainly for decoration. It was usually strapped with iron for several feet from the head to prevent its being cut by the enemy.

There is no class of weapons regarding the nomenclature of which there is so much confusion. There are a great many varieties, some of which are quite distinctive in form, but there are many intermediate forms that are very difficult to classify. To add to the confusion certain specialized forms are called by different names by those who have studied the subject carefully, and totally different types are called by the same name by those who should know the most about them. Fig. 654.

In Europe pole arms may be grouped in four classes: those meant solely for thrusting — those meant mainly for cutting — those meant for both cutting and thrusting — those meant for special purposes. The first group includes the Awl Pike, Boar

Spear, Bohemian Ear-Spoon, Chauve-Souris, Feather Staff, Fork, Fourche a Crochet, Korseke, Langue de Boeuf, Linstock, Partizan, Pike, Pike-Fork, Spontoon, and Runca. Of these the Bohemian Ear-Spoon, Chauve-Souris, Korseke and Runca are slight modifications of the same type. Second group: Berdiche, Fauchard, Glaive, Jedburg Axe, Lochaber Axe, Pole Axe, Scythe, and Voulge. Third group: Bill, Brandestoc, Couteau de Breche, Godenda, Guisarme, Halbard, Half Moon, Hippe, Lucerne Hammer, and Scorpion. Of these the Bill and Guisarme are closely related, and the Godenda, Hippe, Halbard and Scorpion are mere variations. Fourth group: Bec de Corbin, Catch Pole, Flail, Holy Water Sprinkle, Quarter Staff and Scaling Fork.

POLE AXE. A long handled weapon with an axe blade on one side and a spike or hammer opposite, and no spike on the end, Middle Ages.

POLEYNES. Knee cops of plate. They were the first pieces of plate to be added to mail in the 14th century, and at first were worn over mail chausses. (ffoulkes 34). Fig. 457.

POLLET. See Shoulder Guard.

POMMEL, PUMMEL. The knob on the end of a sword, or knife, hilt, or on the butt of a pistol. It was named from the resemblance of many to an apple.

The front peak of a saddle.

POMPEO della CESA (or CHIESA). An Italian armorer who worked in the latter part of the 16th century. He was one of the first makers of the so-called Pisan armor; simple in form but much over-decorated with etched work. (Laking Armour IV, 77). The Pisan armor is often called "Pots and Mops" or "Mops and Brooms" on account of its commonplace decoration. Fig. 655.

PONIARD. See Poignard.

POPINJAY, PAPEGAY. The figure of a bird, usually hung loosely from a pole and used as a mark by archers and crossbowmen. The various companies of archers had annual contests in shooting at the popinjay, the winner being the king for the ensuing year. The custom was kept up by various societies until very recently.

PORT. See Bit.

FIGURE 656. *Pourpoint of padded and embroidered leather. French, about 1580. Metropolitan Museum.*

POTS AND MOPS. A name given to the type of armor called Pisan, because it is so much over-decorated with commonplace designs. Fig. 655.

POTU. A straight Guianian club. The handle is usually wound with cotton cord. (Wood 1239).

was adopted by the French, and on Sept. 18, 1686, an ordinance was passed rejecting all powder three ounces of which would not throw a sixty pound ball from a government mortar at least fifty toises (320 feet). (Hime 163).

FIGURE 657. *Pouwhenua. Dark brown wood 4 feet 4 inches long. One end pointed, the other spatulate. One roughly carved band.*

POUCUE. See Pokwe.

POUNCES. The claws of the short-winged hawks; those of the falcons are called talons.

POURPOINT. A close fitting garment of leather, padded and decorated with needlework, worn under armor in the 16th and 17th centuries. Occasionally when heavily padded it was worn alone as light armor. (Dean Hdbk. 100). Fig. 656.

POUWHENUA. A Maori weapon like a hani but having a pointed end instead of the conventional face. Fig. 657.

POWDERHORN. A powderflask made of horn. The hollow horns of the ruminant animals being admirably adapted for the purpose have been used very generally in all parts of the world. Occasionally the horns of various species of deer are hollowed out and used to contain powder. See Flask.

POWDER TESTER, EPROUVETTE. An apparatus for testing the strength of gunpowder. The earliest of which we have record was invented by Bourne in 1578. It was a small cylinder with a heavy hinged lid which could not shut itself when raised. The powder was exploded in it, and the angle to which the cover was raised was supposed to indicate its strength. This device was very inaccurate. Fortenbach, 1627, invented a similar instrument in which the cover was loose but was guided in its upward movement by two wires with teeth on their inner sides that prevented its falling back. Fig. 658.

Many others were proposed and used, but none gave very useful information until Nye in 1647 introduced the mortar eprouvette. This was a small mortar from which a standard ball was fired with a definite charge of the powder to be tested. This

PRAAH-BA-WITTOO-AH. A kind of boomerang. See Barngeet.

PRASA. "An ancient Indian spear, sometimes a broadsword." (Burton Sword 213).

PRICEI. The round shield of the Sea Dyaks. (Ling Roth II, 139).

PRICK SPUR. A spur with a single point instead of a rowel, or toothed wheel, used later. It was used in Europe in the 11th and 12th centuries and has continued in use among the Arabs until the present day. See Spur.

FIGURE 658. *Powder Tester, Spanish, 17th century Metropolitan Museum.*

PRIME. The first mention of a thrust in prime is by Charles Besnard, 1653, in his book on fencing. He says: "It is given from above downwards, the wrist being held higher than the head." (Castle 137).

PRINCIPES, PROCEI. The Roman heavy infantry. (Burton Sword 247).

PRINSE. In fencing, the seizing of an opponent's sword. (Castle 59).

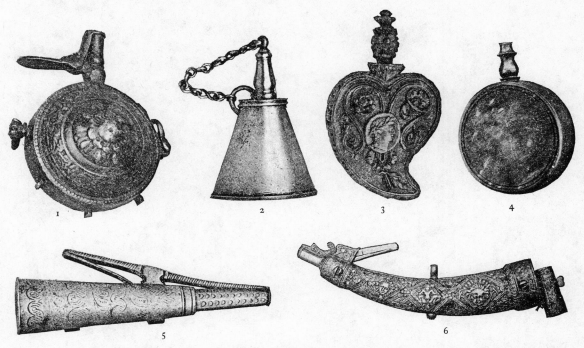

FIGURE 659. *European Primers. 1. Russian, 17th century. 2. Italian, 17th century. 3. French, stamped leather, 18th century. 4. American, about 1750. 5. Italian, 17th century. 6. Primer and spanner, French, 1550. Henry II of France. Metropolitan Museum. Not to scale.*

PRIMER, PRIMING FLASK. With matchlocks, wheel locks and flintlocks it was necessary to use finer powder in the pan than in the charge. The act of filling the pan was called priming, and the flask to hold the fine powder the primer. In Europe it was frequently a small counterpart of the flask used for charge powder; but in the East a great variety of special shapes have been used for the purpose. In Europe the primer was often combined with the spanner for wheel locks, or with a bullet pouch for any kind of gun.

Flasks of all kinds have been favorite objects for decoration in all times and countries but the primer being small and constantly carried, has been particularly chosen for this purpose. Primers were made of all kinds of materials and decorated in every way that human ingenuity has devised, figs. 659, 660. For the Japanese, see Hayago, fig. 363.

PRODD. See Arbalete a Jalet.

PROMACHOI. The Greek troops forming the front line. (Burton Sword 248).

PRONATION. In fencing, the position of the hand in which the nails are turned towards the ground. (Castle 10).

PROOF, ARMOR OF. Armor that had been tested. In the earlier times this was done by firing a bolt from a crossbow at short range, later a musquet was used and the piece so tested was stamped with the maker's mark.

PUBU. A bamboo blowpipe, Wetter Island. (Arc. f. Eth. IV, 78).

PUBU ISI. Blowpipe darts, Wetter Island. They are bamboo splinters with one-sided barbed heads

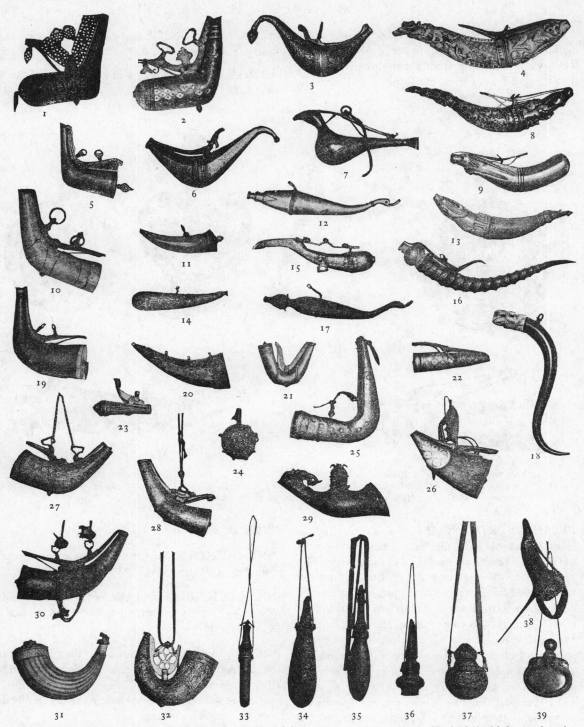

FIGURE 660. Oriental Primers. 1. Persia. Pierced and engraved bronze over red velvet. 2. Persia. Wood inlaid with brass and pearl shell. 3. Persia. Brass with applied silver ornaments. 4. India. Carved ivory. 5. Persia. Watered steel inlaid with gold. 6. Persia. Engraved brass. 7. Persia. Engraved bronze. 8. India. Carved ivory; it is dark brown in the hollows. 9. India. Carved ivory. 10. Persia. Ivory with steel mounts. 11. India or Persia. Carved jade with a ring of small diamonds around the knob on the end. 12. Persia or India. A silver fish with a bird's head on the tail. 13. India. Ivory carved so that the gazelle's head on the end appears complete from any direction. 14. India. Carved jade. 15. India or Persia. Engraved brass. 16. India. Chinkarra horn with a bone end. 17. Similar to 12 but made of bronze. 18. India. Black horn with a carved bone mouthpiece. 19. Persia. Black horn with a bone end. 20. Ceylon. Wood with filigree brass caps. 21. India. Silver plated. 22. Caucasus. Long silver caps decorated with chern. 23. Morocco. Silver set with coral. 24. Brass chased and enameled. 25. Soudan. Horn with flat sides crudely decorated with carved rings. 26. Caucasus. Flat horn with a large silver cap decorated with chern. 27. Greek. Embossed silver. 28. Turkey. Wood with embossed silver mounts. 29. Battak, Sumatra. Carved horn. 30. Turkey. The body is covered with shark skin, silver caps. 31. Turkey. Carved ivory. 32. Turkey. Embossed silver. 33. Battak, Sumatra. Wood and cane. 34, 35, 36. Battak, Sumatra. Black wood. 37. China. Orange peel moulded and dried. 38. Tibet. Black horn with a horn spring to close the opening. 39. China. Black lacquer.

and bunches of cock's feathers on the butts. (Arc. f. Eth. IV, 76).

PUCUNA. A variety of blowpipe used in parts of Guiana. It has an inner tube of reed (the *Arundinaria Schomburgkii*) which is about half an inch in diameter and fourteen to sixteen feet long. The outer tube is made of a palm (the *Ireartia Setigera*) the pith of which is pushed out and the reed fitted in and held by gum. The mouthpiece is wound with

PUNKHA NOK YANG. A short wall piece, Burma. (Egerton, p. 94).

PUN KHAS SINLA. A flintlock musket, Burma. (Egerton, p. 94).

PUN LANG CHAN. A swivel gun carried by an elephant, Burma. (Egerton, p. 94).

PUN LANGMAA. A pistol, Burma. (Egerton, p. 94).

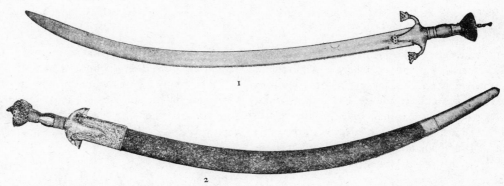

FIGURE 661. *Pulouar.* 1. *Watered steel blade 29 inches long. Steel hilt with a silver loop on the pommel.* 2. *Plain Persian blade. Steel hilt wound with silver cord. Scabbard covered with velvet, steel chape, silver locket.*

cord made of silk grass, and the other end is tipped with half an acquero nut to preserve it from accidental injury. A sight made of the incisors of the acouti is fastened on about eighteen inches from the mouthpiece. It makes a very light weapon. (Wood 1223).

PUFFED ARMOR. Armor decorated with puffs and slashes in imitation of the civil dress of the 17th century. (ffoulkes 74).

Armor of this character was also made in the previous century. Fig. 41.

PUGIO. The straight, two-edged Roman dagger. (Burton Sword 256).

PULOUAR. An Indian sword. The hilt has short quillons curving towards the blade, a hemispherical pommel and no counter guard. (Egerton 392 and p. 5). Fig. 661.

It is a variety of talwar.

PUMMEL. See Pommel.

PUNGLU. A blowpipe dart, Bali. It has a plain poisoned point and a cone of pith on the butt. (Arc. f. Eth. IV, 270).

PUNTA DRITTA. A thrust delivered from the right with the hand in pronation. (Castle 64).

PUNTA SOPRAMANO. The earliest description of the lunge is given under this name by Angelo Viggiani in 1575. He says: "When thou shalt have a mind to deliver a 'punta sopramano,' see that thy right foot advance one great step and immediately let thy left arm fall, and let thy right shoulder at the same time press the arm forwards, dropping the point slightly downwards from above, and aiming the while at my chest, without in any way turning the hand. Push thy point as far as ever thou canst." (Castle 66).

PUNT GUN. A heavy, single-barreled gun mounted on a swivel in a boat, and formerly used in England for shooting wild fowl. The bore was from an inch and a quarter to an inch and a half, the weight about one hundred pounds. (Greener 404).

PUNYEI. A cannon, Burma. (Egerton, p. 94).

PURDESI. A foreign soldier of the state, Rajput. (Tod I, 498).

PURTA. See Yirmba.

PURTANJI. A type of spear thrower found among the tribes near the Gulf of Carpentaria, the Warramunga. This type consists of a rounded stick

the pan. At the end of the stroke the hammer lies with its jaws parallel to the axis of the barrel rather than at the usual sharp flintlock angle with the jaws

FIGURE 662. *Purtanji. Tasseled spear thrower, Australia. Wood point fastened on with gum, tassel of human hair cord. Length 33 inches.*

made of some dark wood, such as acacia, and tapers slightly towards one end, at which a small round knob of wood is attached by means of a lump of resin. There is no direct handle, but a tassel which is always made of human hair string, is attached to the wider end. It is the most effective thrower in Australia. It is made and mainly used by the Umbaia and Gnanji tribes. (Spencer & Gillen 669). Fig. 662.

PURTJIMALA. A fighting club, Mara tribe, Australia.

PUSANE. See Pizaine.

PUTJOR. The point of a kris, Java.

PYRITES LOCK. A lock similar to the flintlock in principle and action but using a piece of pyrites in place of flint. The greater friability of the pyrites causes certain difference. "The typical pyrites lock has a curiously long hammer set relatively far back towards the tail of the lock plate. The hammer is curved or bent almost to a true right angle and carries at the extremity of the long arm a pair of jaws clamping together with a screw. The pan is attached to the lock plate and covered by a pivoted arm working against a light spring and bearing on its upper surface a removable steel or frizzin. . . . a relatively light spring is used. It is hardly more powerful than those fitted to matchlocks and generally weaker than those applied to flint arms, . . .

"The angle of the fall of the hammer is totally distinct from that of a true snaphance of flintlock, for in the pyrites lock the arc of movement is such that a properly set piece of pyrites strikes relatively lightly and at a descending angle on the top of the curved steel and wipes against it for a full inch before the thrust forces back the steel and uncovers

pointing down into the pan. Some pyrites locks appear to be conversions from matchlocks.

"The simplicity of the mechanism and the very clear resemblance of the very long hammer to the cock or serpentine of a matchlock suggests that the type was first evolved by adapting a matchlock. It

FIGURE 663. *Qama. 1. The blade and the back of the hilt. Blade 15.5 inches long. 2. The same in the scabbard, front of hilt and scabbard covered with embossed silver set with coral. 3. Front of hilt and scabbard covered with embossed silver set with coral on the front only. 4. The blade and back of the hilt of no. 3. Blade 15.5 inches long.*

is to all intents and purposes a matchlock in which the jaws of the serpentine have been adapted to take a piece of pyrites; a steel for this to strike on has been adapted to the cover of the pan." (Pollard 33). It was used in the latter part of the 16th century.

Q

QAMA, KHAMA. The national weapon of Georgia. It is the original of the Cossack kindjal, and one of the principal grievances of the Georgians was that their hereditary enemies, the Cossacks, were allowed to carry the Georgian national knife. Qamas vary less in size than kindjals and are more uniformly of good workmanship. The better ones have fine paneled blades and the hilts and scabbards are covered with embossed silver, frequently set with coral. They are seldom, if ever, decorated with chern. Fig. 663.

QATIRN. The foreshaft of a harpoon, Eskimo of Cumberland Sound. (U.S.N.M. 1900, p. 261).

QIJUGTENGA. The shaft of a harpoon, Eskimoes of Cumberland Sound. (U.S.N.M. 1900, p. 261).

QILIJ. See Kilig.

QUADDARA. A Persian broadsword that is precisely like a very long kindjal. (Moser IX). Fig. 664.

QUADRELLE. A small mace with four flanges. (Planche 345).

QUADRIGA. The four-horse chariot of ancient Rome.

QUARREL. See Bolt.

QUARRY. The game sought, or killed, by a hawk.

QUARTE. See Carte.

QUARTER SHOT. A kind of cannon ball used in the 17th century but not considered altogether desirable. "Some, contrary to the laws of the field, use chaine-shot, and quarter-shot, which is good in the defense of a breach, to keep the forteresse, or upon ship-board; but being daily used, it will gaule a peece within and put it to hazard to breake." (Hewitt III, 697).

QUARTER STAFF. A long, straight club used as a staff when walking, and as a club when fighting. It was long enough to require the use of both hands.

QUARTING. The modern quarto, a fencing term. (Castle 193).

QUASHQAH. A chanfron, India. They were quite similar in shape to the European. (Egerton, p. 23). Horse armor was seldom used in India.

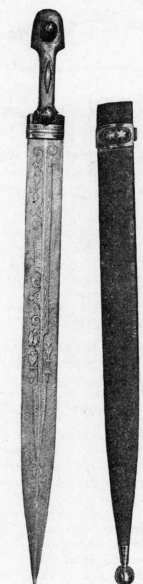

FIGURE 664. *Quaddara. Straight, double-edged blade 28.75 inches long, etched in patterns inlaid with gold figures and inscriptions. Black horn hilt. Mounts of hilt and scabbard of silver decorated with chern.*

QUATRIANGLE. A four-sided figure on which a system of fencing was based in the 16th century. (Castle 57).

QUAYRE. See Club Shield.

QUERQUER. See Quiver.

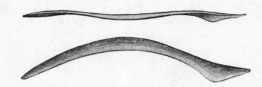

FIGURE 665. *Quirriang-An-Wun., Brough Smyth, p. 315.*

QUEUE. A long bracket projecting from the back plate of some 16th-century tilting suits to hold down the butt of the lance. (ffoulkes 77). Fig. 48.

QUIA-MARA. The tasseled spear thrower, Marra tribe, Australia. (Sp. & Gi.). See Purtanji.

QUIERBOYLLE, QUIR BOILLY. See Cuir Bouilli.

QUILLON. A sword guard composed of one or more bars between the hilt and blade. In most cases it is a single straight bar, sometimes it is curved towards the blade (recurved), at others it curves towards the pommel. Frequently there is one straight bar, and one curved back to the pommel and forming the counterguard.

QUILTED ARMOR. Armor made of several thicknesses of linen, or other cloth, quilted or pourpointed together, was common in Europe in the 14th century. Similar armor was worn in China and Central Asia until very recently. Fig. 30.

QUINTAIN. "The more ancient quintain was merely a post, or shield, fixed on a pole, which the tyro attacked in lieu of a living antagonist. But a new element was given to the quintain, which at once brought it into favour with the populace; it was so contrived as to inflict summary punishment on the inexpert. To one kind, a bag of sand was fastened, which whirled round from the blow struck on the opposite end, buffeting the tilter who was not expeditious enough to get out of the way. Others were made in the form of a Turk, armed with sword and shield; these moving on a pivot as before inflicted a smart blow on the lagging assailant. In another variety, a large tub of water was fixed to a post, which discharged its contents on the person of the clumsy jouster." (Hewitt I, 187). See also Pell.

QUINTE. The old fencing term for the modern octave. (Castle 156).

QUINTISE. See Cointoise.

QUIRET. See Cuirie.

QUIRRIANG-AN-WUN. A weapon generally used as a club, but occasionally as a missile, by the natives of Victoria. It is curved like a boomerang, but is widened and pointed at one end and twisted in a peculiar and complicated manner. A typical one measures three feet long, greatest breadth three and a quarter inches, width of handle two and a half, greatest thickness of blade four-tenths of an inch, and weight ten ounces. (Brough Smyth 315). Fig. 665.

QUISSHES. See Cuisses.

QUIVER, QUERQUER. A case in which to carry arrows. Quivers have been used in all times and by all peoples who used bows. The commonest

FIGURE 666. *Italian Quiver, early 16th century. Metropolitan Museum.*

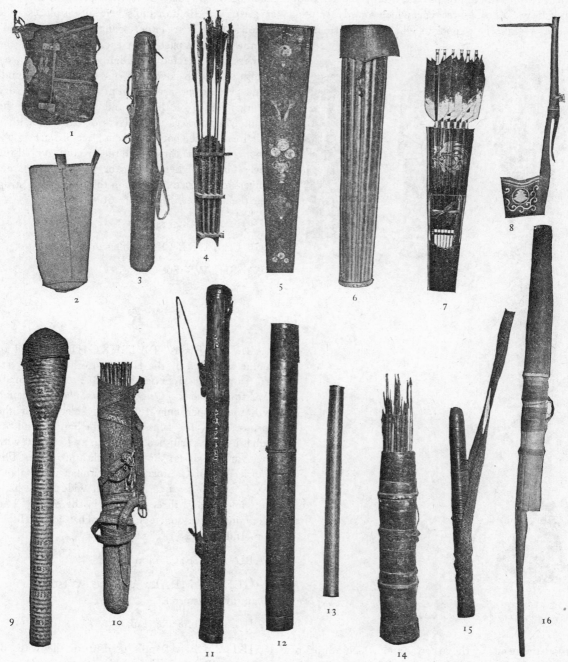

FIGURE 667. *Oriental Quivers.* 1. *China. Showing the extra pocket on the back for the heads of special arrows.* 2. *China. Bucket-shaped, of white leather.* 3. *Indo-China. Round wooden quiver painted red with patterns in yellow and green, leather cover. Length 22.5 inches.* 4. *Java. Wood back with three shelves with holes in them for the arrows.* 5. *Turkey. For flight arrows. Painted wooden box with a hinged cover. Inside near the top is a shelf with holes to keep the arrows apart.* 6. *Turkey. Of elliptical section and fluted. Black leather with cover. Length 28 inches.* 7. *Japan. Case of nashiji lacquer with raised gold decorations. Arrows with crystal nocks and long gilded heads. Probably a New Year present.* 8. *Japan. A leather pocket for the heads and an arm at the top with holes for the shafts.* 9. *Sikkim. Woven of red and white cane with a cover of the same.* 10. *India. 18th century. Covered with red velvet embroidered with silver. Belt with silver buckle, chape and tags.* 11. *Korea. Bamboo carved with an inscription in relief. Cover a wooden monster's head, catch a brass turtle. Sling loops wooden beavera.* 12. *Korea. Paper box with a cap. It is decorated with a vine pattern in dull colors.* 13. *South Sea Islands. A length of bamboo carved with an incised design.* 14. *Central Africa. Heavy bucket of brown leather.* 15. *Abor, Assam. Bamboo quiver wound with red cane, wooden cover.* 16. *Tiruray, Mindanao. Bamboo quiver with a node forming the bottom, and a piece projecting below it that can be thrust into the ground to hold the quiver upright while waiting for game.*

form is an open bag, or bucket, a little shorter than the arrows. The Chinese type, which is used throughout Asia, is a series of pockets which holds little more

made of wood, paper or leather. Basketwork quivers are used in Bhutan and several other places. The Japanese quivers are either open racks (ebira) holding the arrows apart from each other so that the feathers are protected from damage, or closed boxes (yadzutsu) with covers on one side near the end. They protect the arrows from rain, but are very inconvenient to get them in and out of. Some of the pagan Malay races use quivers of bamboo with a node forming the bottom, and a piece projecting below it that can be thrust into the ground to hold the quiver upright when resting or waiting for game. Quivers are carried hung from the belt or by a strap over the shoulder. Figs. 666, 667, 668.

QUOIT. See Chakram.

QUOIT TURBAN. See Dastar Bungga.

QUYSSHEWS. See Cuisses.

R

RABBIT STICK, PATSHKOHU. A kind of boomerang used by the Hopi and other southwestern tribes. The Hopi name is *patshkohu*. It is made of Gambell's oak (*Quercus Gambelli*), a branch with the proper curvature being selected for the purpose. One end is cut to form the handle, and the club is usually varnished with resin and painted with an invariable design in red, black and green. The Gabrielenos of California used similar sticks about two feet long, an inch and a half wide at the handle, and one and three-quarters in the middle, and averaging three-quarters of an inch thick. (Hdbk. Am. Ind. II, 348). Fig. 669.

RABINET. See Cannon.

RAGEE, NAMRAL. A sword, Western Tibet. (Ramsay-Western).

RAIFU. A stone axe, Japan.

RAIKLAS. Swivel guns used from the walls of fortresses, Rajput. (Tod I, 559).

RAKING. For a hawk to wander off, when she should be over the falconer's head, while waiting for game.

RAKSHA. A Malayan demon. "It has eyes set obliquely in its head; it is ugly, broad, bulky, mis-

FIGURE 668. *Quivers of the Lolo, Szechuan, China. Field Museum, Chicago. Not to scale.*

than the heads of the arrows, and which admits of keeping different kinds separate. It also holds the arrows apart so that the feathers cannot be damaged. (See Bow Case, fig. 174). The Ainu use flat willow boxes, with tight fitting covers of the same, see Ika, fig. 388. The Korean quivers are long cylindrical, or elliptical, boxes which take in the entire arrow and have caps to keep out the wet. They are

shapen, and has terrible teeth." (Cabaton 4). It is frequently represented on kris hilts as a monster in semi-human form, with huge tusks and long curls. Fig. 670.

RAMRODS. Ramrods are a necessity with muzzle-loading firearms. They are generally perfectly plain rods of wood, or metal, somewhat enlarged at one end. The wooden ramrods usually have a metal

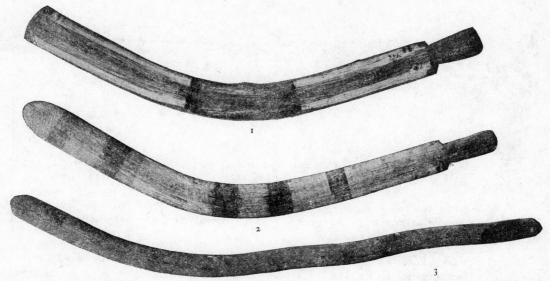

FIG. 669. *Rabbit Sticks.* 1, 2. *Hopi, Arizona.* 3. *Ceremonial throwing stick, used by the Sun Man in Tata Huila dance, Mesa Grande, San Diego County, California. Museum of the American Indian, Heye Foundation.*

RAM. See Battering Ram.

RAMA INA. A bow, Wetter Island. It is made of bamboo and is about forty-two inches long and a little over an inch wide. It has two notches for the string at one end and one at the other. (Arc. f. Eth. IV, 75).

RAMA ISIHN. Wetter Island arrows. The shafts are of bamboo and the heads of wood. They are often barbed. (Arc. f. Eth. IV, 75).

RAM DA'O. A kind of sacrificial sword, Nepal. It has a very broad, heavy blade much incurved at the end, with an eye carved or inlaid on each side. The handle is straight and usually mounted with brass. (Egerton 350, 351). In making the sacrifice the head of the animal should be cut off with a single blow and these weapons are admirably adapted for the purpose, the greater part of the weight being close to the end. Fig. 671.

RAMPART GRENADE. A large grenade thrown from the ramparts at attacking troops. It was given this name to distinguish it from the smaller hand grenades.

cap on the large end; and often a covered screw on the opposite end for drawing the charge. The screw is covered by a cap. In a few cases in Europe and many in the East, they have mountings of silver or other metal to match the gun to which they belong. In Turkey and the surrounding countries orna-

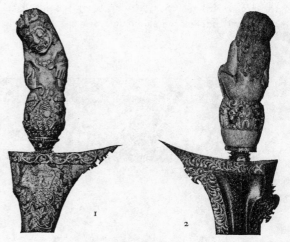

FIGURE 670. *Rakśha. Ivory kris hilts.* 1. *Front of a hilt from Bali.* 2. *Back of a Sumatran hilt.*

mental pistol ramrods were frequently carried hung from the belt. See Sumo. The later muzzle-loading cavalry pistols had ramrods attached by swivels so that they could be drawn, used, and returned while

RANJAKDAN. Hindu, a primer. The Indian and Persian primers cover the same range of types and are made of the same materials, wood, horn, ivory, jade and various metals. They are usually decorated

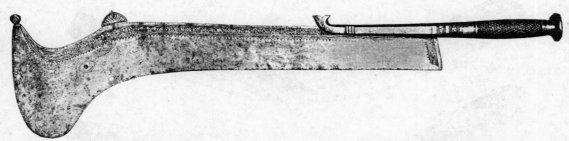

FIGURE 671. *Ram Da'o. Blade 27.5 inches long, thickest in the middle of the widest part. The eye is inlaid with gold and the incised lines are filled with red paint. Wood hilt with brass pommel.*

still fastened to the pistol. After Japan was opened to Europeans a similar arrangement was used on some Japanese guns and pistols. Fig. 672.

RAMROD-BACK SWORD. A sword with a very thin, flat blade fastened to a rod at the back. It was experimented with by the English, but was a failure and was abandoned. (Burton Sword 133).

RANG-KWAN. A woman's fighting club, Rockhampton District, Queensland. It is about six feet long and tapers throughout its length, the handle end being the smaller. Both ends are pointed. (Roth, Aust. Mus. VII, 209).

RANGLE. Stones or pebbles given hawks with their food; they are afterwards vomited and appear to remove mucus from the crop. It is said that a hawk will not keep in good health without rangle.

with carving, inlaying, or applied ornaments of a different material from the body of the flask. See Primer.

RANJAU, SUDAS. Bamboo spikes planted in the paths to delay an attacking party or pursuing enemy. They are usually about six inches long and are said to be occasionally poisoned. They are used throughout the Malayan countries and are precisely like the panjies of Assam. See Panji. Fig. 610.

RANKLING ARROW. One with a loose barbed head that remains in the wound when the arrow is extracted. (U. S. N. M. 1900, p. 200).

RANSEUR, RANSON. See Runka.

RAPIER, TOCK, TUCK. A sword especially designed for thrusting and provided with a more or

FIGURE 672. *Japanese ramrod connected to the gun by a jointed swivel so that it could be drawn, used and replaced while fastened to the gun. The end is bent around and covered with wood to form a tompion.*

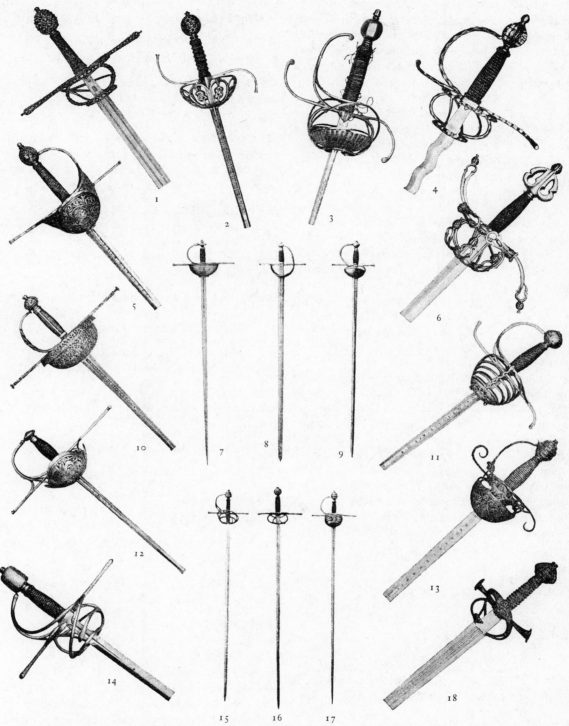

FIGURE 673. *Rapiers.* 1. *Italian, 1525-50.* 2. *Savoyard, 17th century.* 3. *Pistoyan, about 1600.* 4. *French, late 16th century.* 5. *Italian, early 17th century.* 6. *Spanish, 17th century.* 7. *Spanish, 17th century.* 8. *Spanish, 18th century.* 9. *Spanish, 17th century.* 10. *Spanish, 1620.* 11. *Italian, late 16th century.* 12. *Spanish, about 1630.* 13. *Italian, early 17th century.* 14. *Italian, late 16th century. The swept hilt.* 15. *The same. The entire sword.* 16. *French, end of the 16th century.* 17. *Italian, end of the 16th century.* 18. *French, 16th century. Metropolitan Museum. Not to scale.*

less elaborate guard. The name first appears in England about 1560, although this type of sword was brought there much earlier by the Spaniards. The early rapiers had double-edged blades and could be used for cutting as well as thrusting, though better adapted for the latter. As the art of fencing was developed rapiers were made solely for thrusting. The usual guard was a hemispherical cup and long, slim, straight quillons; the grip was very short as the thumb and first finger were passed around the quillons. In the 16th century the blades became so long that they were a nuisance — "Shortly after the thirteenth year of Elizabeth (1571) began long ruffs and long rapiers, and he was held the greatest gallant who had the deepest ruff and longest rapier. The offense to the eye of the one, and the hurt to the life of the subject that came by the other, caused her Majesty to make proclamation against both, and to place selected grave citizens at every gate to cut off the ruffs and break the rapier's points of all passengers that exceeded a yard in length of their rapiers and a nayle of a yard in depth of their ruffes."

The rapiers of the 16th and 17th centuries had very long, heavy blades and very elaborate guards made up of all sorts of combinations of cups, shells and loops. The typical ones had a squared piece between the blade and tang, called the *ricasso*. At first in fencing with the rapier it was used solely for the attack, and the guarding was done with a cloak wound around the arm, or with a dagger, or buckler, held in the left hand. As the capabilities of the rapier became better appreciated a system of guarding with it was gradually developed and the other defenses abandoned. This change in the method of using the sword caused changes to be made in it — the hilt was made simpler and the blade lighter and adapted only for thrusting. Thus by a slow evolution the rapier was transformed into the small sword. (Planche 414, Castle 234). Fig. 673.

RAT. See Cat.

RAUT. A knife, class name, Malay.

RAVELIN. The old name for the demi-lune. It consists of two faces open at the back and is intended to protect the space between two bastions. (Violet le Duc, Hist. 365).

RAVEN'S BEAK. Egerton, p. 115, illustrates a weapon which he calls a raven's beak. It is a broad-bladed, doubly curved knife on the end of a long, straight handle, Mahratta.

REBATED SWORDS. Blunt swords with protected points used for practice. (Castle 246).

REDAN. A fortification consisting of lines and faces that form sallying and reëntrant angles flanking one another. (Hoyt 406).

REIN GUARD. Hinged plates fastened to the reins of a war bridle to prevent their being cut, 16th century. (ffoulkes 91). Sometimes the entire reins were made of iron. Fig. 123.

REITERS, ROUTERS. Cavalry of the first half of the 16th century armed with pistols. They were also called *noirs harnois* or *schwartz reiters* on account of the black armor they wore. (Hewitt III, 584, 589, 655).

RENJAKU-DO. A Japanese corselet hung from the shoulders by suspenders (*renjaku*) inside it. (Garbutt 161). Compare Hara Ate.

REPRISE. Redoubling an attack which the adversary has parried without riposting. (Castle 138).

REREBRACE. Plate armor for the arm above the elbow. It was first worn in England in the early part of the 14th century. (ffoulkes 36).

REST. (For a gun). See Musquet Rest.

REST. (For a lance). See Lance Rest.

RETIARII. Roman gladiators armed with nets in which to entangle their adversaries, and tridents with which to dispatch them. They were opposed by men in armor carrying swords and shields, and called scutors.

REVERENCE. The salute with the sword before fencing. (Castle 139).

REVOLVING FIREARMS. Revolving firearms were invented in the 16th century and there is a revolving matchlock in the Tower of London said to have belonged to Henry VIII. The early revolvers, however, did not have much practical value. The first workable revolver was a flintlock with a single pan and a magazine for priming powder in the frizzen which acted automatically. The first revolver to come into general use was invented by Colonel Colt in 1835. Revolvers have since been made in an immense variety of forms and for from four to twenty-four shots. Fig. 674.

FIGURE 674. *Revolver. An early Colt that was carried in California in* 1849.

The Japanese made three-barrelled revolving matchlocks, both guns and pistols, but more for show than use, figs. 332, 651. In India revolving matchlock guns much like the early European forms, were occasionally made, but probably not earlier than the 18th century. Fig. 323.

RHONCA. See Runca.

RI-ANG-PAL, RI-ANGAPA. See Mu-Lon.

RIBEAUDIQUIN, RIBEAUDEAU. A kind of cart armed with spikes forming a movable fortification, 14th century; later a cannon was added. (Hewitt II, 97).

An engine on the principle of the crossbow, the bow of which was as much as eight feet long. (Laking Armour III, 131).

RICASSO. The squared part of a rapier blade next the hilt.

RICAVATIONE. The modern contre, making a second disengagement so as to deceive the adversary's action. (Castle 101).

RIDING THE CITY. In Italy in the 14th century this meant to charge the cavalry through the streets of a captured city to prevent the inhabitants from erecting barricades. (Denison 196).

RIDING THE WOODEN HORSE. A military punishment used in the English army in the 18th century. The wooden horse was made of planks nailed together so as to form a sharp ridge about eight feet long. This ridge represented the back of the horse. It was supported by four posts about six or seven feet high, and a head and tail were added to complete the resemblance. The of-

fender was placed on the horse with his hands tied to his legs and frequently, to increase the punishment, musquets were tied to his feet. It was found to injure the men so seriously that it was abandoned about the middle of the century. (Grose II, 106). Fig. 675.

RIFLING. Cutting spiral grooves in the barrel of a firearm to cause the ball to rotate on its own axis, which gives the flight greater accuracy. Rifling is generally believed to have been invented in the 16th century, but it is not certain that spiral grooves were used at that time. Straight grooves, to lessen the fouling, were certainly used in cannon. The grooves are from two to twelve in number, and of many different profiles; the spaces between the grooves are called lands. The amount of twist in the older rifles was one turn in two or three feet, later it was often made much sharper. In most cases the grooves are now made with an increasing twist towards the muzzle.

RIKISHA. An armor-bearer or inferior attendant, Japan.

RIMANKYU. A frame for carrying a small bow and its arrows, Japan. Fig. 676.

RINDI. A bullet, Western Tibet. (Ramsay-Western).

RINGED ARMOR. Armor made by fastening metal rings on cloth or leather. It was used in Europe in the middle ages, and is still used in the East. Fig. 29.

RINGS TO CARRY ARMS. In the 14th cen-

FIGURE 675. *Wooden Horse, Grose II, 106.*

tury rings were often fastened to the belt or saddle in which to carry maces, axes or estocs. The weap-

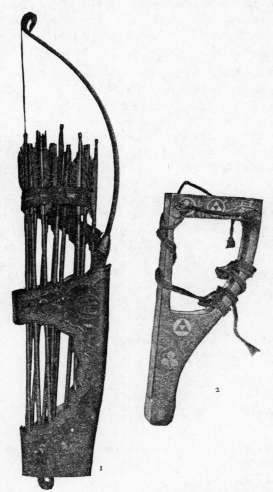

FIGURE 676. *Rimankyu.* 1. *Case of fine lacquer with crests and other ornaments in colors. It contains a short whalebone bow and its arrows.* 2. *Case only. Black leather with gilded mons of Hirano, daimio of Tawara. There is a silver cap on the end engraved with the same crest.*

ons were held securely and at the same time could be drawn more quickly than from a scabbard. (Hewitt II, 264).

RIN SANKH. A war shell, a shell used as a trumpet, Rajput. (Tod II, 413). See Lankh. Fig. 517.

RIOBITSU. The openings in a tsuba for the kozuka and kogai.

RIPOSTE. A return attack in fencing.

ROBINET. An engine for throwing either stones or darts.

ROCHETTES. Fire arrows thrown from balistas, 14th century. (Hewitt II, 280).

ROCKETS. Rockets have been used in war in all parts of the world since the invention of gunpowder. They undoubtedly preceded firearms as the earliest powder had force enough to propel them, but was not rapid enough in its action for use in guns. They were used up to the middle of the 19th century.

RODA-DEDALI. An arrow of the Javan gods. The head is very large and entirely on one side of the shaft. It is in the form of a bird with extended wings. (Raffles I, 295, plate p. 296/297).

ROENTJAU. See Bade-Bade.

RO-GIN. (Misty silver). A variety of shibuichi, an alloy much used in making Japanese sword fittings.

ROGOROUK. A variety of Australian spear thrower. (Earl 205).

RO-IRO. See Lacquer.

ROKOGU. "A complete armor consisting of six pieces," Japan.

RONCIE. See Runka.

RONCIN. A war horse lighter than the destrier and heavier than the hackney, 14th century.

RONDACHE. A round shield carried on the arm, 17th century. (Hewitt III, 687).

RONDELLE. A round plate to guard the openings at the joints of the armor. See also Lance Guard.

RONDELLE A POIGN. A very small, round buckler used in fencing. (Hewitt III, 662).

RONGA. An East African quiver. "It is a bark case, neatly cut and stained. It is of two forms, full length, and provided with a cover for poisoned, and half length for unpoisoned arrows." (Burton Lakes 478).

RORARII. Roman light infantry. (Burton Sword 245).

ROTELLA. A target, or shield, carried on the arm by two straps, 16th century. (Hewitt III, 687).

ROUSE. To shake herself, spoken of a hawk.

ROUTERS. See Reiters.

ROVERSI. A cut delivered from the left, consequently on the adversary's right side. (Castle 36).

ROVESCIA. A thrust delivered from the left with the hand in supination. (Castle 64).

RUNGU. "The rungu or knobkerrie is the African club or mace; it extends from the Cape to the negroid and the Somal tribes north of the equator. The shape varies in almost every district; the head is long or round, oval or irregular, and sometimes provided on one side with an edge; it is cut from the

FIGURE 677. *Runkas. 1, 2. About 1520. 3. About 1525. 4. About 1540. 5. 16th century. All Italian. Metropolitan Museum. Not to scale.*

ROWEL, ROUELLE. The toothed wheel of a spur.

RUDIS. A rod or wooden sword used by Roman gladiators in practice. (Burton Sword 250).

RUFTER HOOD. A hood used in training hawks. It is made of softer leather than the regular hood and has simpler fastenings and no plume.

RUMMH. The lance of Northern Arabia. It has a diamond-shaped head with the edges towards the point much longer than the others; the shaft is fifteen to eighteen feet long. In camp it is kept upright, the butt being thrust into the ground. On the march it is carried horizontally with the middle of the shaft resting on the shoulder. Until recently it was the main weapon of the Bedouins but has been displaced by firearms. (Blunt 342).

hardest wood, and generally from one piece. In some cases the knob is added to the handle, and in others it is supplied with a spearhead. The handle is generally about two feet long, and is cut thin enough to make the weapon top-heavy. The Mnyamezi is rarely seen abroad without this weapon; he uses it in the chase, and in battle against the archer; he trusts it in close quarters rather than the featherweight arrow or the spear that bends like guttapercha, and most murders are committed with it. The East people do not, like the Kafirs, use the handle of the knobkerrie as a dibble." (Burton Lakes 478). See Kerrie. Fig. 442.

RUNKA, RANSON, RANSEUR, RHONCA, RONCIE. A pole arm of the 15th and 16th centuries. It has a long, sharp, rather narrow blade with two short lateral blades at the base; the short blades may be either straight or curved, fig. 677. It is very closely related to the korseke and chauve souris.

RUNNING THE GANTELOPE. See Gantelope.

FIGURE 678. *Sabre Halbard. Swiss or German, 1650. Metropolitan Museum.*

RUPTARII, ROUTERS, REITERS. Mercenary troops employed in all European armies during the middle ages. See Reiters.

RYO. Japanese, a dragon. The dragon typifies the spirit as opposed to the flesh typified by the tiger. If the two are at peace and not fighting it means dominion over all things. If they are fighting it means the struggle between the flesh and the spirit. In China and Japan only the Emperor and the heir apparent were allowed to use five clawed dragons; younger sons of the Emperor, and sometimes some of the higher nobility, could have them with four claws; ordinary people could only have a three-clawed dragon. The dragon is frequently used in the decoration of arms and armor in Japan. See Dragon.

RYO-GOSHIATE, RIO-GOSHIATE. Japan, a double sword hanger, a single hanger for a pair of swords. (Garbutt 167). See Koshiate.

RYOJU. A shotgun, Japan.

RYONOME. Large scattered spots on a Japanese blade.

RYUSHA. A war chariot, Japan.

RYUYEI. The headquarters of a camp, Japan.

S

SA. An arrow, Japan. See Ya.

SABAR. A crowbill axe, India. See Hoolurge.

SABARCANE. A blowpipe. The name is European like the French *sabarcane*, Italian and Spanish *cerbotana*, and the Portuguese *gravatana*, none of which names are known to the people who use the blowpipe.

SABATONS, SABATAYNES. The broad-toed foot armor of the middle of the 16th century. They only covered the upper side of the foot and were held down by straps passing under the soles. They were sometimes called "Bear-Paw" or "Duck-Billed" solerets. (ffoulkes 62, 73). Fig. 38.

SABIDORO. The protective covering of clay put over all but the edge of a Japanese blade when it is heated and quenched to harden it. The line of the yakiba is determined by the shape of the edge of this clay cover. (Joly S. & S. 89). See Japanese Blades.

SABIET. A Sumatran knife with a greatly curved blade sharp on the concave side for its entire length, and on the convex for half its length. Two horns on the pommel form a ring. (Arc. f. Eth. V, 237). Compare Korambi.

SABIET MATA DORA. Two small curved knives, flat on one side and connected at the top by a pin. The two can be turned so that when both handles are grasped a blow can be struck in either direction, Borneo. (Arc. f. Eth. V, 237).

SABRE. A sword with a single-edged, slightly curved blade, usually with a short back edge. It is intended mainly for cutting, but is also effective for thrusting.

SABRE HALBARD, BAVARIAN WAR-SICKLE. A German pole arm of the 16th century. It is a halbard with a sabre blade instead of the usual spike. Fig. 678.

SACAR. See Cannon.

SADAK, SAGHDACH. The equipment of an archer, Russia. (Scheremetew 119).

SADDLE. Saddles were not used by cavalry until about the year 340 A.D. and were not perfected until some fifty years later. Under Theodosius the ages the war saddles were huge affairs with high pommels and cantles covered with steel plates which were frequently chased and decorated. In peace the so-called "ivory" saddles (made of carved bone) were often used as a matter of display. With the abandonment of armor saddles became simpler and were usually covered with leather. Fig. 679.

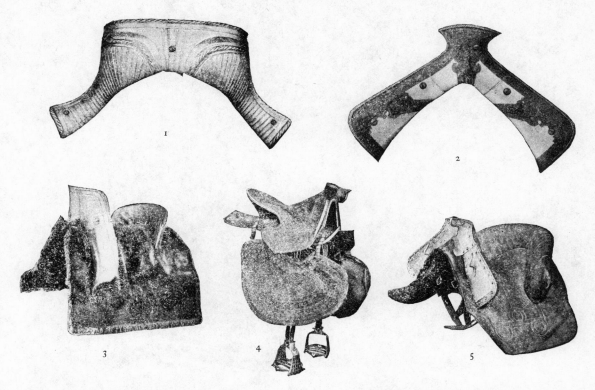

FIGURE 679. *European Saddles.* 1. *Back plate of a German war saddle, about* 1520. 2. *Front plate of a French war saddle of about* 1565. 3. *Bavarian,* 1550. 4. *Spanish,* 16th century. 5. *German,* 1540. *Metropolitan Museum. Not to scale.*

Great the Roman cavalry used a double covering, or pad, of cloth, hide or skin; the lower piece was larger than the upper and was sometimes plain and sometimes bordered by a fringe. It was held in place by a girth, crupper and breaststrap. Over it a smaller pad was placed, the lower edge of which was sometimes ornamented. The two pads were fastened together by buttons and straps or else by ribbons. No stirrups were used until nearly two hundred years later, about the middle of the 6th century. (Denison 70).

The frame of a saddle is called the *tree,* the front the *pommel* and the back the *cantle.* In the middle

In the East saddles varied greatly in size and shape. In Morocco and North Africa generally the saddles are large with very high pommels and cantles. The better ones have elaborate covers of velvet embroidered with gold; with large saddle cloths and breaststraps to match. In the desert camels are used more than horses, and quite different saddles are used for them. The most characteristic is the one used by the Tuaregs. Like all camel saddles it goes on top of the hump and has a round, flat seat with an enormously high pommel and cantle; the latter is as high as the rider's shoulders and is pointed at the top. The former is the inevitable Tuareg

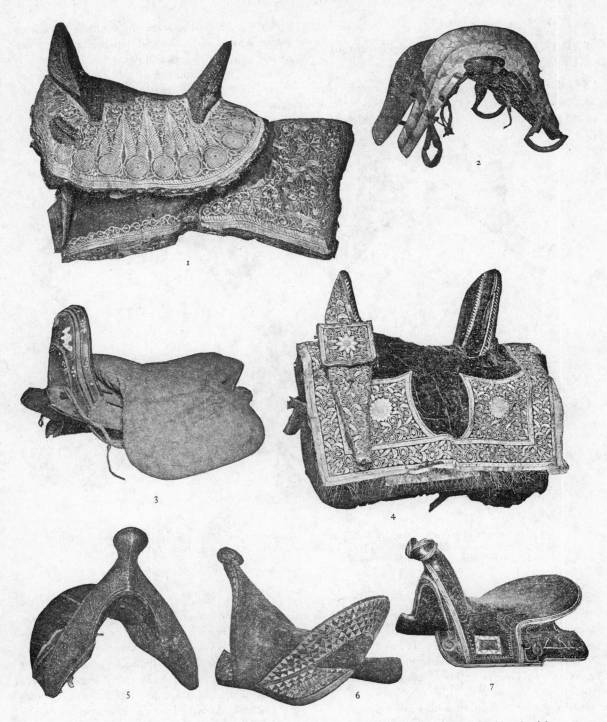

FIGURE 680. *Oriental Saddles.* 1. *Moroccan saddle and saddlecloth of red cloth embroidered with gold. Late 18th century.* 2. *Japanese, 18th century. Wood lacquered black with decorations in raised gold lacquer.* 3. *Chinese, 17th century. Lacquered black with inlaid ornaments in ivory.* 4. *Tunis, 17th century. Saddle cover and holsters of red velvet embroidered in gold. Said to have belonged to a former Bey.* 5. *India, 18th century. Bows covered with embossed silver. Seat covered with velvet.* 6. *India, 18th century. Bows inlaid with pearl shell. Seat covered with leather.* 7. *Persia, 18th century. All wood lacquered in brilliant colors.*

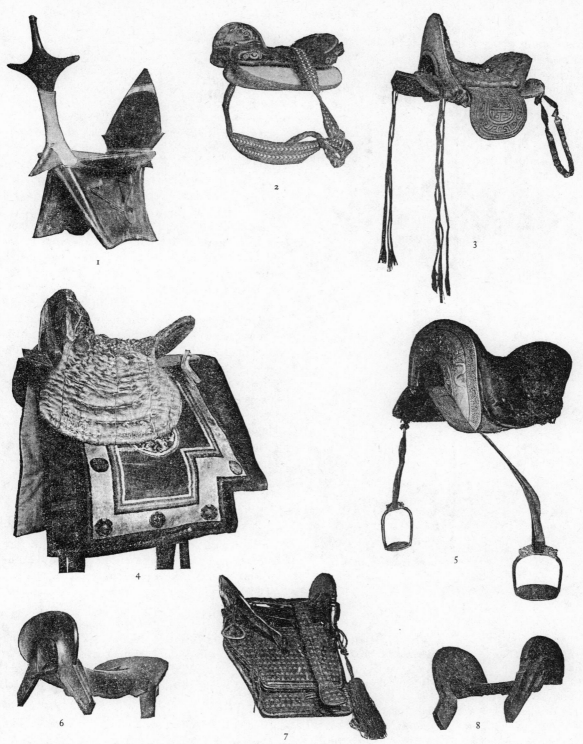

FIGURE 681. *Oriental Saddles.* 1. *Tuareg camel saddle. Wood partly covered with leather, 19th century.* 2. *Burma, 19th century. Nearly flat pad covered with cloth and embroidered in colors.* 3. *Korea, 17th-18th century. The frame is of wood covered with shark skin and bound with silver enameled in colors. The seat cover is of embroidered deerskin with the hair on. It is decorated with enameled silver plaques. The flaps are of embossed leather. The crupper is of leather with enameled silver plates.* 4. *China, 17th century. The frame is of wood inlaid with bone. The pad is of silk embroidered in colors. The saddlecloth is a rug mainly in blue and white.* 5. *Tibet, 17th century. The wood frame is covered with carved, pierced and gilded steel set with semi-precious stones. Plain silk pad and Chinese type stirrups.* 6. *Japanese, 17th-18th century. Plain wood frame which has been lacquered gold and has a mon on the lower part of the pommel.* 7. *Japanese, 19th century. Elaborately lacquered with hawks in relief.* 8. *Japanese, 17th century. Wood lacquered black and inlaid with copper mon on the outer sides of the bows and pewter ones on the inner ones.*

cross and is nearly as high as the cantle. The saddle is made of wood covered with leather. When on a raid the Tuareg sleeps in the saddle resting his arms on the cross and putting his head down on them. In

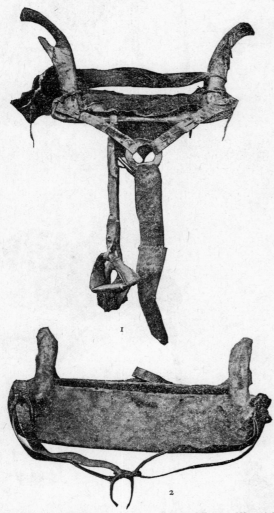

FIGURE 682. *North American Indian Saddles.* 1. *Woman's saddle.* 2. *Man's saddle. Both Arapharoe, Wind River, Wyoming. Museum of the American Indian, Heye Foundation.*

this way he can make marches of three or four hundred miles. They are the greatest thieves and raise the best camels in the desert, and they never sell a sound camel. The French made very little headway against their raiding until they captured some camels from them and raised some for themselves. At present there are radio stations scattered over the desert and raids are reported as soon as they start

and as they proceed and raiding is becoming unprofitable.

In Turkey and Persia the saddles are quite small, with fairly high pommels usually with a double spiral at the top. The cantle is nearly flat. These saddles are generally painted and quite elaborately decorated. In India the saddles vary considerably. Many are quite small with rather narrow pommels, and distinct, but low, cantles. The seats are covered with leather or velvet and the trees are decorated by inlaying or are covered with silver. In China, Tibet and Central Asia the saddles are larger and have high, wide pommels and may or may not have cantles. Many are decorated with inlays of bone or ivory and sometimes covered with metal plates. In Korea the saddles are similar in shape but much smaller. The trees are sometimes covered with shark skin and strapped with silver with enameled ornaments. In Japan the saddles are made of four pieces of wood laced together, very much in the shape of our army saddles. A few are of plain wood, some are inlaid with metal, but most are lacquered with stirrups to match. The North American Indian has reduced his saddle to its simplest form, a very simple tree with a blanket or piece of skin over it. Figs. 680, 681, 682.

SADOEP. A knife with a long, straight, tapering, single-edged blade, Borneo. (Arc. f. Eth. V, 237).

SAFFDARA. An Indian knife with a narrow, two-edged blade, Mysore. (Egerton 561).

SAFFRON ROBE. To wear a saffron robe or to dye the hair and beard with saffron was the sign that a Rajput or Mahratta meant to fight to a finish and would neither give nor receive quarter. (Tod I, 491).

SAGEDACH. See Sadak.

SAGE-O, TUSAKI. A flat silk cord passing through a fitting (the kurikata) on the scabbard of a Japanese sword. It was used either to fasten the scabbard to the belt, or, when fighting, to tie back the flowing sleeves. (Joly, Naunton xvii).

SAGE-OBI. A belt with slings for a tachi. Fig. 717.

SAGHDAK. A quiver, Western Tibet. (Ramsay-Western). Compare Sadak.

SAGHRI. Wild ass's skin. It was often used for

covering scabbards in Persia and gunstocks in Tibet. The word is Persian.

SAGURI. See Soritsuno.

FIGURE 683. *Saif.* 1. *Plain blade 26.75 inches long. Silver hilt and guard. Scabbard covered with pierced and chased silver over green tinsel. 2. Southern India. Silver hilt and scabbard mounts. 3. Java. Heavy grooved blade; horn hilt inlaid with brass. Wood scabbard with silver bands and chape. 4. Plain blade 28.5 inches long. Silver hilt and scabbard mounts. Scabbard covered with embossed black leather.*

SAHARI, SAWARI. Pewter, speculum metal. It is used in Japan for decorating sword fittings. Being very brittle it is cast in grooves in the object to be ornamented, giving the effect of inlaying. Most of the objects treated in this way are very old and much tarnished. As this material is susceptible of a high polish it is probable that they were originally polished.

SAIF, SAYF. An Arab sword, a rather broad-bladed sabre with a peculiarly hooked pommel. The sizes vary greatly. It is carried in front slung from two rings fastened to opposite sides of a broad band around the scabbard, fig. 683. It is found in all countries in which the Arabs have lived, and each has its own variety.

SAIGAI BACHI. A very early form of Japanese helmet.

SAI-HAI. A peculiar baton consisting of a short staff with a tassel of leather or paper on the end. It was the recognized implement used for signaling in Japan, not only by officers, but by master carpenters and the head men of whaling expeditions. (Garbutt 158). Fig. 684.

The similar baton with a yak's tail forming the tassel is a religious emblem.

SAINTIE. An Indian parrying weapon. It is a straight bar of steel with a loop guard in the middle and a spear point on the end. Sometimes a second spear point is placed on the hand guard or a concealed dagger in the shaft. (Egerton 557). Fig. 685.

The Chinese used a very similar weapon. Fig. 686.

SAKA-ASHI. See Yakiba.

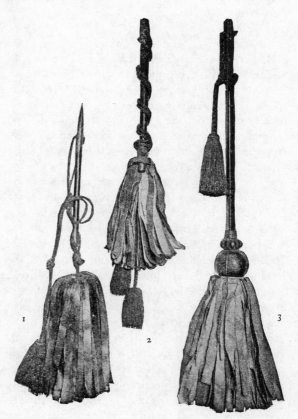

FIGURE 684. *Sai-Hai.* 1. *Lacquered handle with silver caps. Gilt paper tassel hung by a cord. 2. Lacquered handle 14.5 inches long. Tassel of red and white paper hung by a cord. 3. Lacquered handle 23 inches long with copper fittings and bands of red cord. Paper tassel which is held in a fitting that locks around it.*

SAKA-TE. Holding a sword or knife with the point downwards, Japan.

SAKI-NAKAGOSAKI. The end of the tang, Japan.

hand rest. (Wallace Orient.). Fig. 688. See also Zafar Takieh.

SALAPANG. A fishing spear, Subanun of Mindanao. (Christie 111).

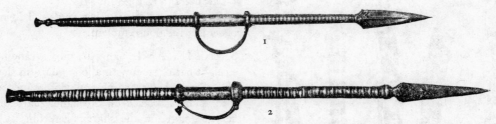

FIGURE 685. *Saintie.* 1. *Ringed steel shaft 26.75 inches long with a spearhead on one end, and a fluted loop hand guard.* 2. *Similar to the last but more roughly made. Length 2 feet 8.25 inches.*

SAKU-BO. See Menpo.

SAKUGATA. A variety of Japanese helmet. (Garbutt 168).

SAKU NARI. See Dzu Nari.

SALADE, CELATE, CELATA, SALET, SALETT. Very popular headpieces of the 15th century which were apparently evolved from the war hat. Two entirely different types of helmet are usually included when these names are used. The German type (salade) comes close to the head in front and at the sides and extends backwards in a broad tail that is often very long. It covers the entire face of the wearer, and sometimes has a movable visor. In others there is merely a slit across the front through which the wearer could see. The French and English salades were similar but did not have such long projections at the back. The Italian form is quite different, fitting closely to the head and neck, being almost exactly like the Greek casque. Sometimes it leaves the entire face uncovered, but usually it has a T-shaped opening that guards the face and allows the wearer plenty of room to see and breathe. It never had a movable visor. It is generally called barbute or celata. Both types were very popular for both war and the tournament, the main objection being that the entire weight rested on the head. As the Italian form is much more compact and lighter it must have been more comfortable to wear. Many of them are very fine forgings, fig. 687. See Barbute, fig. 121.

SALAPA. An Indian sword with a crutch hilt or a disk pommel with a projecting arm to serve as a

SALAWAR YATAGAN. See Khyber Knife.

SALET, SALETT. See Salade.

SALUTE. A conventional series of movements with the sword performed as a prelude to a fencing match or as an exercise. Compare Reverence.

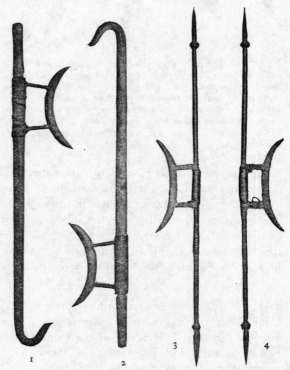

FIGURE 686. *Chinese Parrying Weapons.* 1, 2. *Length* 37.5 *inches. The edges are sharp everywhere except at the cord wound handles.* 3, 4. *Round iron shafts* 41 *inches long, with blunt spearheads on the ends, crescent side blades and rattan wound handles.*

SAMA. A loophole, Japan.

SAMBON SUGE. See Yakiba.

SAME. Same is the skin of a small species of shark and is much used in Japan for covering the hilts

network of green or black. This sort of work is often called "Inlaid Ivory."

Particularly good skins were sometimes mounted for sale on wood framed in brocade. Such mounted specimens were often given as presents. Fig. 689.

FIGURE 687. Salades. 1. German, second half of the 15th century. 2. German, late 15th century. 3. German, 1480. 4. Nuremberg, end of the 15th century. 5. French or Burgundian, about 1480. 6. German, end of the 15th century. Metropolitan Museum.

and scabbards of swords and other weapons. Many different varieties are recognized depending on the color and arrangement of the knobs, or protuberances, on the skin. Apparently the skins of a number of species of sharks and rays were used for scabbards but the only one used for hilts was that of *Urogymnus Asperrimus* according to Joly (S. & S. 3).

The skins were scrubbed with a bamboo brush until made as white as possible, as whiteness is one of the most desired qualities. The skins of old and large fish are more difficult to clean than small ones, but are more valuable when cleaned as the knobs are larger and of better shape. As the valuable knobs occur only at one place on the back of the fish, but one first-class handle is obtained from each. As large knobs add to the value of a skin, large knobs from otherwise poor skins, or artificial knobs, were often cemented on skins of good color but without large knobs.

For covering scabbards the skins were often lacquered black or green and the tops of the knobs ground off, giving the appearance of ivory set in a

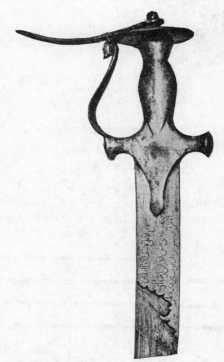

FIGURE 688. *Salapa. Silver plated steel hilt.*

SAME TSUDZUMI. A Japanese corselet covered with shark skin. (Conder 263).

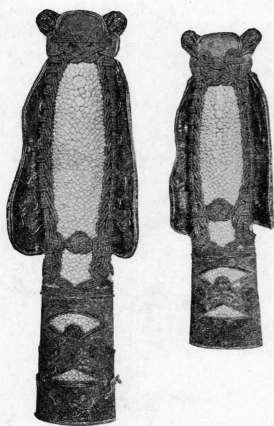

FIGURE 689. *Presentation Same. Two pieces for a pair of sword hilts. They are covered and framed in brocade ready for sale or to be given as New Year's presents.*

SAMEZAYA. A Japanese scabbard covered with shark skin.

SAMPEI. Skirmishers, Japan.

SAMURAI. Minor nobles, Japan. Properly it included all who were entitled to wear two swords, including the daimio, but was usually understood to include only those of the lower rank. Next to the daimio came the hatomoto, or flag supporters, who were vassals of the Shogun. The gokanin were inferior in rank and wealth to the hatomoto but with them constituted the Tokugawa clan. All of the above with their military retainers were samurai, and received incomes of rice from the government. A samurai unattached was called a ronin, and was generally a vagabond and a criminal.

SAMVAT. See Sumbut.

SANE. The scales of which armor was composed, Japan.

SANG. The Rajput lance. It was made wholly of iron or had iron straps on the shaft for some feet from the head. These weapons were used when fighting from camels in the desert. (Tod I, 541, II, 91). Fig. 690.

SANG: SANGER. A Sinhalese processional spear, also used in southern India. They have very heavy heads with curved, double-edged blades and elaborately moulded and engraved sockets for the shafts. (Clarke). Fig. 691.

SANGDEDE. See Cinquedea.

SANGIN. A sword bayonet, Nepal. (Egerton 383).

SANGKOH. A Sea Dyak spear with a steel head and a long wooden shaft. The head is about a foot long and broadest near the point. The tang is not inserted in the shaft but is lashed to it with wrappings of cane or brass wire. The shaft is usually of ironwood with a bone spud at the butt. If it has no spud it is pointed so that it can be stuck into the ground. (Ling Roth II, 132). Fig. 692.

SANGU. A Central Indian spear made entirely of steel. It has a long triangular or quadrangular head. (Egerton 72, 461). Compare Sang.

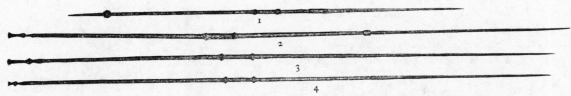

FIGURE 690. *Sang.* 1. *Square head 23 inches long, moulded, engraved and inlaid with brass. Length 5 feet 7 inches.* 2. *Moulded and fluted head 2 feet 8.5 inches long. Moulded shaft inlaid with gold and silver. Length 8 feet.* 3. *Square head, ringed and fluted with a moulded butt.* 4. *Similar to no. 3.*

SANKE. The highest class of Japanese nobles. See Daimio.

SANKO. A vajra of three points.

FIGURE 691. *Sang: Sanger. 1. The socket and ornaments on the blade are covered with silver parcel gilt. 2. Chiseled head and socket. Length blade 12 inches, overall 16.5 inches. 3. Finely engraved socket. Length blade 12 inches, overall 19.25 inches.*

SAN-MAI. (Three plate method). A method of making blades formerly used in Japan, particularly by the smiths of Bizen, in which a plate of steel was welded between two of iron. (Gilbertson, Blades 192). It did not produce first-class blades.

SAN-NO-SAI. A ring on the scabbard of a tachi. (Weber II, 251).

SANTIE. A javelin with a square or "bayonet-shaped" head. (Wallace Orient).

SAPAKANA. A Guianian club with a decorated handle and a broad, paddle-shaped head. (Wood 1239). Fig. 693.

SAPARA. An ancient type of Assyrian sword. It has a very peculiarly curved blade and no guard. (Burton Sword 207). Fig. 694.

SAPOLA, SAPOLA TALWAR. A sabre with a bifurcated point, and a hilt with straight quillons, a finger guard and griffon pommel. (Wallace Orient).

SARAMPANG. A Dyak fish spear with a loose head attached by a cord to a bamboo shaft. (Ling Roth I, 462).

SAREN-DAN. Chain shot, Japan.

SARISSA, SARISSE. The pike used by the Greek foot soldiers. It had a shaft sixteen to twenty-four feet long. (Burton Sword 182, Boutell 43).

FIGURE 692. *Sangkoh. Dyak spear with the head lashed to the side of the shaft. Head 9.25 x 2 inches.*

SARONG. (A skirt). A kris scabbard, Java.

SARONGAN, WRANGKA. A wooden kris sheath, Java. (Arc. f. Eth. XIX, 93).

The wide top of a kris scabbard, Java.

FIGURE 693. *Sapakana. Brazilian club of dark brown wood. Length 2 feet 5.5 inches.*

SARU-BO. (Monkey face). A type of Japanese menpo that covered only the cheeks and chin. (Weber II, 20). See Menpo.

SARUMATSUBUYE. A hunting horn, Japan.

SARU-TE. (Monkey hands). A loop of metal fastened to the kabuto gane (pommel) of a tachi that reaches half way around the hilt. Frequently it has the shape of two hands clasped monkey fashion (with the thumbs and fingers together). The sword knot is fastened to it. The latter is often made of leather with metal chapes. (Gilbertson, Dec. 80). Fig. 416.

SASH HOOK. See Belt Hook.

SASHIMONO, SHIRUSHI. A small banner marked with a mon, or other device. Sometimes a group of streamers was substituted for the banner. It was fastened to a rod that raised the banner above

FIGURE 694. *Sapara. Assyrian sword of bronze. Metropolitan Museum.*

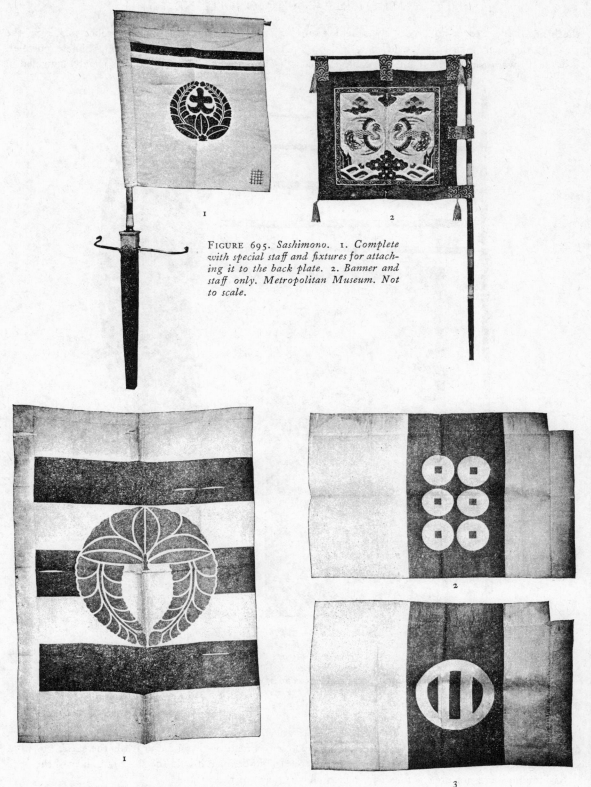

FIGURE 695. *Sashimono.* 1. *Complete with special staff and fixtures for attaching it to the back plate.* 2. *Banner and staff only. Metropolitan Museum. Not to scale.*

FIGURE 696. *Sashimono.* 1. *White silk with three black bars and a Fujiwara mon in red. Length 40 inches, width 28.25.* 2. *White silk 29.5 x 20 inches, with the mon of Abi daimio of Okabe in red.* 3. *White silk 29.75 x 19.25 inches with an Ashikaga mon in red.*

the head of the wearer and the sockets held it out clear of the neck guard of the helmet, fig. 695. The shaft was usually made in three pieces that

SASHIMONO GANE. The upper socket for the banner staff on the back of a Japanese corselet. (Conder 267). The socket was usually swiveled in

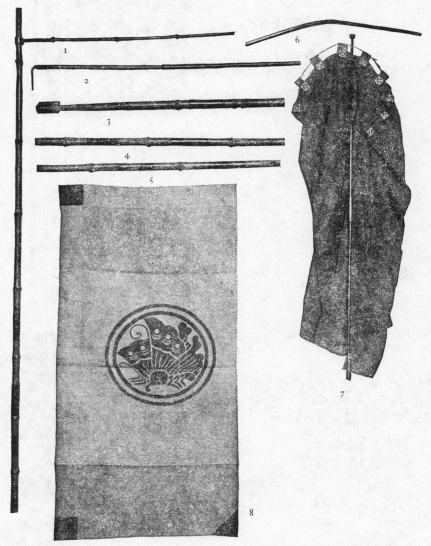

FIGURE 697. *Sashimono and Supports. 1. Support of three pieces locking together with brass ferules. The arm swings from a sleeve going around the upright. 2. The arm of another set. It swings from a pin fitting in a sleeve on the upper section of the upright. 3, 4, 5. The jointed upright. The three pieces are joined by brass ferules with spring locks. 6. The lower joint of no. 7. It is bent to throw the sashimono out clear of the helmet. 7. Sashimono of a number of strips of red silk hung from a wire ring. Attached are the two upper pieces of the upright. 8. Sashimono. White silk with a Taira mon in red.*

locked together with ferules, like a fishing pole. The arm either had a hook that fitted in a socket on the shaft or a sleeve that fitted over it. Fig. 696, 697.

Sashimono were not used before 1573. (Conder 279).

a wire bow fastened to the shoulders. Sometimes it was a plate with a hole in it for the staff, fig. 698. In either form it held the shaft out clear of the neck guard of the helmet.

SASHI-ZOE. A wakizashi, the short sword of the Japanese daisho.

SASI-YA. See Mate-Ya.

SASSARA SEPPA. See Seppa.

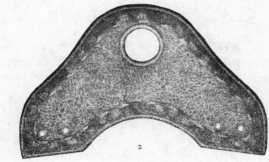

FIGURE 698. *Sashimono Gane. 1. Wood lacquered black. 2. Metal covered with figured leather. Edges and opening for the staff of engraved bronze. The opening for the staff inlaid with gold.*

SASU-MATA. A spear with a forked head and spikes on the shaft below it. It was formerly used by the Japanese police and firemen.

SATA-ITA. The second plate from the top of the back of a Japanese corselet. It was formed of one or two rows of scales firmly bound together by cross-stitches, *hishinui*. In the center was fixed a large ornamental ring from which hung a large silk cord and tassel, the *age-maki*. Cords from the sode were fastened to the loops of this bow to hold the sode in place when the wearer bent forward. (Conder 270). See Age-Maki.

SATELLITES. Inferior troops in the French armies of the 13th century. (Hewitt I, 196, 209).

SATENGAR, ISTENGARA. A Malay matchlock gun, Padang Sumatra. (Raffles Museum, Singapore).

SATSU YA. A hunting arrow, Japan.

SATSU YUMI. A hunting bow, Japan.

SAUNION. A light javelin of the Samnites. The shaft was about three feet and a half long, and the head five inches. (Burton Sword 287).

SAUVETERRE. A scimeter. (Jaehns 239). See Shamshir.

SAVIDLIN. A form of bear arrow, Point Barrow. It has a head of metal, iron or copper, which is generally broad and flat, and either rhomboidal with the base cut into numerous teeth or else triangular with a shank. The barbs are usually bilateral. (Murdoch 203).

SAVIGRON. A small curved knife used for carving bone and ivory by the Eskimo of Point Barrow. (Murdoch 157).

SAVIK. A knife, literally iron, Eskimo. (U. S. N. M. 1897, p. 731).

SAWARI. Hyder Ali's standards; one represented the sun and the other the moon and stars embroidered in gold on a blue ground. They were carried by elephants. (Egerton, p. 121).

Speculum metal, Japan.

SAYA, SCIA. A scabbard, Japan. Japanese scabbards are almost always made of wood, and are lined with it even if the outside is made of metal. *Honoki* wood (*Magnolia hypolouca*) is generally used for this purpose; it is a fine grained light wood. The scabbards are generally lacquered and the mountings correspond with those of the hilt. The only essential mounting is the *kurikata*, a knob on the side of the scabbard that keeps it from slipping through the belt. It is found on all Japanese scabbards except those of tachi and some small knives. The other fittings are the *koiguchi kanagu*, a ring or cap at the top; the *uragawara*, a strip of horn or metal that guards the opening for the kozuka; the *soritsuno*, a hook below the kurikata to keep the scabbard from being pulled through the belt when the blade is drawn; the *kojiri* or chape. Sometimes ornaments, called *menuki*, are fastened on the scabbard but they are simply for decoration. All scabbards but those of tachi, usually have pockets for the kozuka and kogai.

Tachi scabbards have different mountings, or if they are not different they have different names except the koi-guchi kanagu. They are hung by the *ichi-no-ashi* and *ni-no-ashi*, each carrying a loop, *obi-tori*, for the slings. The chape is called *ishi-zuke* and is often very long. Sometimes it was extended along the edges of the scabbard by pieces called *ama-oi*. These are held in place by a band called *shiba-biki*, or if there are more than one, the others are called *sei*.

It was not uncommon to have four scabbards for one sword—one perfectly plain case of natural wood in which to keep the blade when not in use; one with quite simple mountings for everyday wear; a plain one covered with iron for war; and an elaborate one for occasions of ceremony. Each had a corresponding hilt. Sometimes the scabbards were double, one fitting inside the other, the idea being that if a blade had to be reground a new inner scabbard could be made to fit it and the expensive outer scabbard used again. They were not found satisfactory and are rarely seen. See Aikuchi, Hamidashi, Katana, Kwaiken, Tachi, Tanto and Wakizashi.

SAYA-ATE. To strike one's scabbard against that of another; it was equivalent to a challenge in old Japan. (Weber II, 262).

SAYAJIRI. An old name for the chapes of all kinds of Japanese swords. See Kojiri.

SAYAMAKI. A scabbard wound with colored cord like a hilt, Japan.

SAYAMAKI TACHI. A tachi with the entire scabbard and hilt wound with cord or leather. (Gilbertson, Dec. 96).

SAYF. See Saif.

SAYO. An ancient Mexican corselet of hide with the hair on. (Cubas 522).

SAZ. The Bokhara bridle with the neck and breast-straps. (Moser XLI).

Pouches for bullets, wadding, etc. Mahratta. (Tower 201, p. 25).

SBASSO. A time thrust delivered on the adversary's attack by lowering the body. (Castle 178).

SCALE ARMOR. Armor made by fastening scales of horn, leather, metal or any hard substance on cloth or leather. Such armor was used by the Romans during the middle ages in Europe and in many other parts of the world. Fig. 29.

SCALING FORK. A military fork with a hook attached so that it could be used in scaling walls.

SCALING LADDER. A light ladder used in attacking walled towns and fortresses.

SCEAR. The piece of a gunlock that engages with the trigger and releases the hammer so that it is thrown down by the spring.

SCHARFRENNEN. A form of tournament in which the mounted contestants were armed with sharp lances and in which there were no barriers. (Hewitt III, 647, Dean Hdbk. 64).

SCHELOM. Russian helmets of the 17th century. The body is a bowl with a slight point at the crown; it has pendant ear and neck guards. (Scheremetew 60).

SCHESTOPJOR. Russian, a mace. (Scheremetew 107, 108).

SCHIAVONA. The Venetian broadsword of the 16th century. It has a broad, straight blade with a very heavy and elaborate basket hilt that covers the entire hand. The name is derived from *schiavoni*—hired soldiers. The Scotch broadsword of the 17th century and later is copied from it. In Scotland it is commonly called a "claymore," although it does not resemble the true claymore in the least. See Broadsword, fig. 192.

SCHISCHAKS. Russian and Mongol helmets used from the 13th to the 17th century. They are round helmets of ogee section rising to a sharp point. They have small brims, hinged ear and neck guards, and some have movable nasals. (Kaemmerer XXV, Scheremetew 54, 55, 56, 57).

SCHLEGER, SCHLEGER PLAY. The schleger is the sword used by the German students in their duels. It has a huge basket cup hilt and a long, straight blade sharpened for only a few inches near the point. The system of fencing with it is purely artificial and useless as a means of defense except under the conditions in which it is used by the students. (Castle 185).

SCHNAPPHAHN. One of the earliest forms of flintlock. See Flintlock.

SCIA. See Saya.

SCIMETER. See Shamshir.

SCJAN. See Skain.

SCLEPISTA. The Roman sacrificial knife. It was

made of copper even after iron was in universal use for weapons. (Burton Sword 56).

SCORPION. This name was used for a great variety of weapons in different times and places. Bur-

FIGURE 699. *Scorpion, Italian, 15th century. Metropolitan Museum.*

ton (Sword 157) gives it to the Egyptian whip-goad, apparently a short flail with two weighted lashes. Grose (I, 367) describes an engine on the principle of the crossbow under this name. In India a knife, the bich'hwa (scorpion) is, or was, quite common. In Europe it is a variety of halbard with a very deep and narrow blade. Fig. 699.

SCOT'S PLAY. A system of fencing taught by Sir William Hope about 1687. He says of his method: "It runneth all upon binding and securing your adversaries' sword before you offer to thrust, which maketh your thrust sure and your adversaries incapable of giving you a contretemps." (Castle 191).

SCOURGE. The scourge was the emblem of official rank in the Assyrian army. (Burton Sword 206).

SCRAMASAX. A Frankish dagger. It had a broad, long blade grooved on both sides. (Boutell 93).

SCROO, FRANZ. An armorer of the early 16th century who lived in Brussels. Boeheim attributed the suit, fig. 41, to him. (Laking Armour III, 257).

SCULL. See Skull.

SCUTAGE. A money payment in place of military service, 15th century. (Hewitt I, 99).

SCUTEM. A shield, that of the Roman legionary. It was rectangular, about four feet long and two and a half wide, and curved. The framework was of wood, covered probably with leather, with a metal boss and platings. (Burton Sword 247).

SCUTIFER. Latin, a shield bearer. In the middle ages the attendant who carried and supported the pavis for crossbowmen at sieges. (Grose II, 257).

SCYMITER, SCIMETER. The strongly curved Oriental sabre. This name is said to be derived from the Persian shamshir.

SCYTHE. In the middle ages the scythe was frequently used as a weapon, the blade being mounted in line with a long, straight shaft. It does not appear to have given rise to any important modification, especially adapted for fighting. It was used as

FIGURE 700. *Scythes. 1. German, 17th century. 2. French, 1580. 3. Seventeenth century. Metropolitan Museum. Not to scale.*

an improvised weapon by peasants as late as the end of the 18th century. Fig. 700.

SEAX. The curved Anglo-Saxon sword. (Hewitt I, 35).

FIGURE 701. *Sei-Ita. Back plate of a harimaki-do, Ashikaga period. Laced lames with a large age-maki knot.*

SECONDE. A thrust, parry or other movement of the sword downwards towards the left.

SECONDE, QUARTE EN. A thrust in seconde with the palm up. (Castle 137).

SECONDE, TIERCE EN. A thrust in seconde with the palm down. (Castle 137).

SEEL. To sew up the eyes of a hawk. It was formerly done to newly caught hawks as they were more easily handled and "manned" when blinded in this way. The stitches were taken through the eyelids and did no permanent injury.

SEFIN. Turkish, an archer's ring. See Archer's Ring.

SEI. Bands, when more than one, holding the longitudinal straps and the prolongations of the ishizuke of a tachi scabbard in place. (Joly Int.).

SEI-ITA, SEI-ITA-NO-YOROI. An extra plate closing the opening in the better specimens of Japanese armor that opened down the back. This type of corselet should not be confused with the *shiwara-gusoku,* which also opened down the back and was closed by clasps and cords. The latter was worn only by common soldiers. (Conder 268). Fig. 701.

SEIRO. A blockhouse, Japan.

SEI-RYO-KEN. Kwanyu's spear. The type commonly called a "temple spear." The broad blade issues from a dragon's mouth. (Weber II, 82). Fig. 510.

SEKI-BO. Stone clubs used in pre-Yamato times in Japan. (Joly S. & S. 139).

SEKIN. A Sumatran knife with an incurved, single-edged blade with a peculiar projection next the hilt. (DeWit 25). Fig. 702.

SEKO. An axe in San Chuan Chinese.

SELE. A kris, Celebes. (Arc. f. Eth. XVIII, 64).

SELF BOW. One made from a single piece of wood.

SELI-BESI. "Iron kris," probably the Majapahit kris with an iron hilt forged in one piece with the blade. (Walcott 110). No. 2. Fig. 481.

SEMBO. The advance guard of an army, Japan.

FIGURE 702. *Sekin, Sumatra. Blade 10.75 inches long with an openwork projection near the hilt. Hilt of dark brown wood set in silver. Wooden scabbard with silver mounts.*

SEME. An attack, assault, charge, Japan.

The sword of the Masai of East Africa. It has a well forged, heavy, double-edged blade widening towards the point, and with a strong central rib. The hilt is small, ringed and without a guard. It is usually about twenty inches long, though sometimes

SEME GUTSUWA. A curb bit, Japan. A foreign innovation.

SENA-ATE. Armor for the back, a backplate, Japan.

SENA. See Mune.

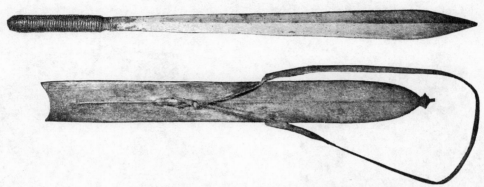

FIGURE 703. *Seme, Masai Sword. Blade 19 inches long, hilt and scabbard covered with rawhide.*

much longer, and is carried in a rawhide scabbard hung from a cord around the neck. (Sheldon 292). Fig. 703.

Bands on the scabbard of a tachi holding the long projections from the chape in place. Sometimes these pieces extend almost the entire length of the scabbard. (Gilbertson, Dec. 95).

SEMEGUCHI. A breach, the point of attack on a fortress, Japan.

SENANGKAS BEDOK. A Malay sabre with a heavy, slightly curved blade with wide, flat grooves. It has a scroll pommel and no guard. (Arc. f. Eth. V, 234).

SENAPANG. A gun, Malay. (Leiden II, 113). See Gun.

SENDAN-NO-ITA. The guard for the right armpit in old Japanese armor. It is generally about three inches by nine and is made of three plates, or rows of scales, connected by cords and lined with leather. (Conder 268). Fig. 704. See also Hato-Wo-No-Ita, the guard for the left armpit.

SEN-NARI HISAGO. "At a fight between Toyotomi Hideyoshi and another of the Kuge, or retainers, of Ota Nobunaga, Hideyoshi having no standard to carry before him, improvised one by plucking a gourd plant by the roots and used it as

FIGURE 704. *Sendan-No-Ita. Guards for the right armpit in old Japanese armor.* 1. *Top plate lacquered with a mon and other decorations; three lines of laced lames.* 2. *Top plate covered with printed leather, gilded mon. Three rows of laced lames. Compare Hato-Wo-No-Ita, fig. 361.*

FIGURE 705. *Seppa.* 1. *Sasara Seppa, shakudo with a silver rim.* 2. *Ko Seppa, brass covered with silver.* 3. *Dai Seppa or O Seppa, shakudo. This set is from a tachi.*

a standard, vowing that he would add to his banner, *umajirushi*, one gourd for each victory he won thereafter." This incident is said to date from about 1550. (Joly Leg.).

SEN-SHA. A war chariot, Japan.

SENTAN-ITA, KANA-MAKARI. The curved plates at the tops of the side plates of a Japanese

moulded edges. The later ones are made of brass, gold-plated brass, brass covered with sheet gold or solid gold, depending on the quality of the sword. Fig. 705.

On tachi the *dai seppa* is sometimes used. It is almost as large as the guard and is highly decorated; often it is intricately pierced while the guard below it is plain. (Weber II, 273). Fig. 706.

1   2

FIGURE 706. *Dai Seppa.* 1. *Seppa of shakudo pierced and decorated with gold crests.* 2. *The silver tachi guard to which it belongs. The silver is somewhat tarnished opposite the openings in the seppa.*

corselet. They never fitted closely under the arms. (Conder 266).

SENTOKU, SENTOKUDO. An alloy imitating, and named for, the Chinese bronze of the period SuenT'ieh (1426-1436). It contains about seventy-three per cent. of copper, eight of tin and six of lead. When pickled with sulphate of copper or nitre the surface shows bright spots like aventurine lacquer. (Weber II, 273). It was often used for sword fittings in Japan.

SEPPA, ZAKANE. Washers placed each side of the guard of a Japanese sword. Originally they were used to support and strengthen the guard which was then made thin in the center. They were graduated in size; the largest, the *o-seppa*, being next the guard; over this the smaller *ko-seppa* was placed. Sometimes still smaller ones, the *sasara-seppa* and *kowari-seppa*, were also used. On the later swords only two are used, which are just enough larger than the fuchi and koiguchi to show their

SEPPA DAI. An oval space in the center of a tsuba around the opening for the tang. It is usually plain, and if the guard is signed, it is on the seppa dai, the name of the maker being on the left of the opening and his residence, the date, or other information on the right.

On namban guards the seppa dai is decorated by carving in relief, but rarely on others. On all guards it is covered by the seppa when mounted.

SEPTIME. The seventh parry in fencing. The hand is held, nails up, opposite the right breast, the blade slightly depressed and moved in a curve towards the left.

SEREPANG. A Dyak fish spear with a long bamboo shaft and two, three or four parallel prongs. (Ling Roth I, 462).

SERPENTINE. The match holder of a matchlock.

A kind of cannon. See Cannon.

SERPENTINE ORGAN. A number of small cannon (serpentines) mounted together on one carriage, 16th and 17th centuries. (Demmin 500).

SERYE. See Sirohi.

SERZALA. See Char Aina. The name *serzala* is used in the oldest Slavish chronicles. This form of breastplate was worn in Russia in the 16th and 17th centuries. (Scheremetew 27).

FIGURE 707. *Sgain Dubh, Scotch, 18th century. Collection of Mr. A. McM. Welch.*

SESERI. A bamboo cleaning rod for a gun, Japan. (Garbutt 153).

SETSUBO. A yak's tail mounted on a handle. In early times it was one of the insignia of command in China and Japan. (Joly S. & S. 65). Later it appears to have been purely a religious emblem.

SETTO. A sword formerly given by the Emperor of Japan to the commander-in-chief as a commission.

SEUSENHOFER. There were three brothers, Conrad, Hans and Jorg. All three were at different times court armorer to Maximilian I. Conrad working under the orders of the Emperor evolved the type of fluted armor known as Maximilian. The celebrated "engraved" suit in the Tower of London was made under his direction. He preferred to make elaborately ornamented armor that was not satisfactory to the officers responsible for the equipment of the troops. (ffoulkes 141).

SEVERGI. An ancient type of Russian arrow. (Scheremetew 122).

SEWARI GOSOKU. A leather corselet made of large pieces of *neri-kawa* (black leather) lacquered black. It was fitted and laced together to form one piece opening at the back, which was closed by clasps or lacings. There are several shapes, of which the "pigeon-breasted" was considered the best. It had five short taces hung from it. It was worn only by the lower classes of Japanese retainers. (Conder 280).

SEYEVA. A curved dagger, Bencoolen, Sumatra. (Tower 602, p. 23).

SGAIN DUBH. The Scotch stocking knife, a small, straight-bladed dagger without a guard. (Campbell 93). Fig. 707.

SHA, SHAGAI. Archery, Japan.

SHABRACK. A housing or saddle cloth for a cavalry horse.

SHAFRON, SHAFFEROON. See Chanfron.

SHAFT. The staff of a spear, halbard or pole arm.
    The staff of a lance.
    The body of an arrow, sometimes the entire arrow.

SHAFTED WEAPONS. See Pole Arms.

SHAGEI. Archery, Japan.

SHAGUMA. "The hairy end of a red ox's tail" —used as a plume on a Japanese helmet.

SHAH NAWAZ KHANI. A sabre with a slightly curved blade with a reinforced back. It has a disk pommel. (Wallace Orient.). Egerton, p. 123, also mentions it but gives no description of it.

SHA-HO. The rules of archery, Japan.

SHAIL. Rajput, a lance with a bamboo shaft as distinguished from one (sang) which has an iron shaft or a wooden one plated with iron. (Tod II, 260).

SHAKH-DAHANA. Persian, a priming flask. The Persian primers are practically the same as the Indian. See Ranjakdan and Primer.

SHAKU. A Japanese measure of 11.9275 inches, commonly called a foot. It is divided into ten *sun* of ten *bu* each.

SHAKUDO. A Japanese bronze much used for sword mountings and other decorative metalwork.

movable head which formed the sheath for an ordinary straight-headed spear. It was carried by samurai when they were on secret missions and did not wish to be noticed.

SHAMSHIR, SHAMSHEER, CHIMCHIR.

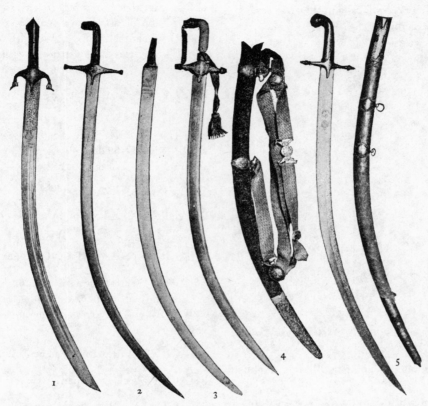

FIGURE 708. *Persian Shamshir. 1. Fine watered blade with an inscription in relief inlaid with gold. Gold inlaid steel mountings, black horn grip. 2. Very fine ladder pattern blade. Engraved steel mountings, staghorn grip. 3. Blade of yellow damask. 4. Extremely fine blade of "kara Khorassan" (black damask); ivory grip. All of the mountings are of silver enameled in blue and green. 5. Damask blade beautifully inlaid with long passages from the Koran in gold. Leather covered scabbard. Hilt and scabbard mountings of steel inlaid with gold.*

When properly pickled it assumes a bluish black or a deep velvety black. It is said to be made of thirty parts of antimony, seven of gold and one hundred of copper; but it undoubtedly varies much in composition. It sometimes contains as much as twenty per cent of gold, and it is said that it must contain as much as four per cent to give the desired color.

SHAKUJO. A staff armed at the end with metal rings. It was carried by begging priests in Japan.

SHAKUJO YARI. A pilgrim's staff with a re-

The curved Persian sabre. Our word scimeter is supposed to be derived from the Persian name.

The Persian sabre is purely a cutting weapon, the point being practically useless owing to the extreme curvature. The curve is, however, perfect for the drawcut, so much used by Asiatics, for which it is intended. The blades are narrow but rather thick, and are not usually decorated except with the name of the maker or owner, and perhaps the date. The hilts are simple and light with a single cross guard and a pommel projecting at one side. Occasionally a different style of hilt is used; it has short recurved quillons and an ogival pommel. The scabbards are usually covered with leather, often embossed, and ways of watered steel, and the finest are of great beauty. As the blade has an even curve it is not necessary to split the back of the scabbard to admit it

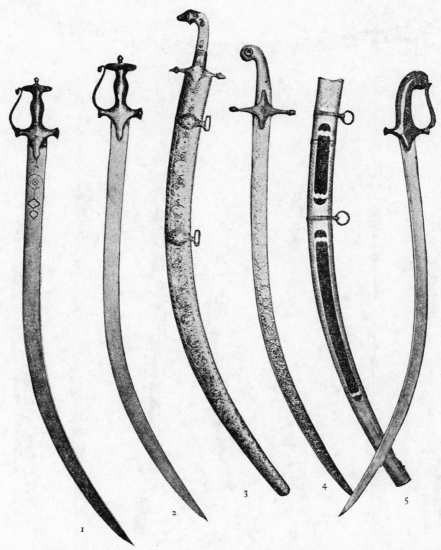

FIGURE 709. *Indian and Turkish Shamshir. 1. Blade of yellow damask inlaid with gold. Steel hilt inlaid with gold flowers. 2. Watered blade 32 inches long. Both hilt and blade inlaid with gold. 3. Blade of rough damask, ivory grip. The scabbard, guard and pommel are of engraved silver enameled in colors. 4. Steel blade entirely covered with champ levee hunting scenes very well drawn. A hunting sword. The hilt and scabbard are Turkish and of later date. 5. Plain steel blade 29.75 inches long. The hilt, guard and finger guard are carved from a single piece of agate.*

the steel mountings are chiseled, or, more rarely, inlaid. The hilts and mountings are sometimes decorated with carving, inlaying or enamel, but are more often quite simple. The better blades are always of watered steel, and the finest are of great beauty. As the blade has an even curve it is not necessary to split the back of the scabbard to admit it as with the Turkish form. It is carried, edge down, hung from the left side of the belt by two slings. Fig. 708.

Persian shamshir blades are frequently used in

FIGURE 710. *Shamshir Shikargar. Watered blade 22.25 inches long carved with animals in low relief outlined in gold. Blued steel hilt with gold borders, India.*

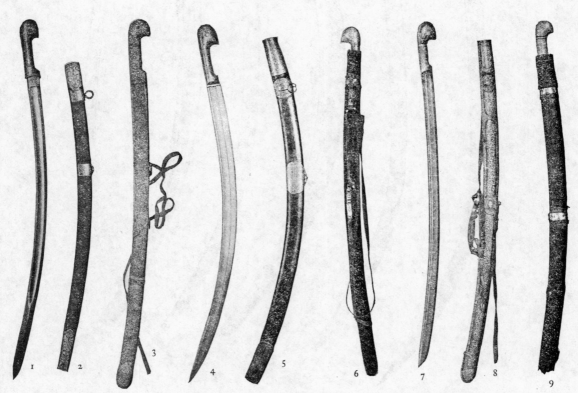

FIGURE 711. *Shashqa. 1. Blade 32 inches long, marked Wh. Walscheid, Solingen. Scabbard covered with black leather. Hilt and scabbard mounts of silver decorated with chern. The scabbard does not take in the hilt. 2. Its scabbard. 3. Blade etched with scrolls and a horse battery. Hilt and scabbard silver, carved with vines in low relief. Back of scabbard and belt mountings decorated with chern. 4. Persian blade 32 inches long with fine and unusual watering in the broad groove. It is marked with the name of the original owner, Achmet Beg, and the date 1235 A.H. — 1819 A.D. All of the silver mounts are stamped 84 (84/96 silver) and dated 1879. On the back of the upper scabbard mount are the initials of the owner P. A. V., and a Russian inscription reading "The reward of bravery." 5. Its scabbard. 6. Plain blade. Silver hilt, partly gilded and wound with silver cord. Scabbard covered with green velvet. Narrow leather belt with silver mounts decorated with chern. 7. Watered blade 30¾ inches long. Hilt and scabbard with gilded metal borders and panels of silver inlay on a black ground. 8. Its scabbard. 9. Blade 31 inches long, marked with the running wolf and M. N. ivory hilt. Silver mounted scabbard of red leather over which there is an outer cover of black. This scabbard takes in the entire hilt but the pommel.*

both Turkey and India where they are generally remounted in the styles characteristic of these countries. Fig. 709.

SHAMSHIR SHIKARGAR. Persian, a hunting sword. It is the ordinary shamshir of India and Persia except that the blades are engraved with hunting scenes. Fig. 710.

each other by loops and buttons of niello silver. . . . Unlike their neighbors the Turks and Persians they slash and use the point but not the drawcut."

Another form of scabbard is also quite common. It is made of wood, not covered with leather, and does not take in the hilt. It usually has a locket, chape and sling bands of silver decorated with chern.

FIGURE 712. *Sher Bacha, Turkish wall gun: Octagon damask barrel inlaid with gold; very large back sight pierced with a number of holes for different ranges. Heavy wood stock inlaid with silver. Length 4 feet 10.5 inches; weight 32 pounds.*

SHANEN KOPATON and SHANEN YANOMA. War spears of the Nicobar Islanders. The first has a broad, barbed blade with a tang set in the shaft. *Shanen* signifies a bladed spear. (Man, And. & Nic. 7).

SHANEN MONG-HEANG and SHANEN HOPLOAP. Hunting spears of the Nicobar Islanders. (Man, And. & Nic. 7).

SHASHPAR. A six bladed mace, India. (Egerton, p. 21).

SHASHQA, CHACHEKA. (The last name is the French transliteration of the Russian). It is the national sword of the Circassians but has been adopted by most of the races of the Caucasus. Rockstuhl, plate CX, describes it as follows: "The chacheka ordinarily has a straight blade, or one very slightly curved towards the point, and a hilt without any guard whatsoever, nearly always of silver niello and sometimes gilded. When the arm is sheathed the hilt enters the wooden scabbard covered with leather, if desired, as far as the pommel. The latter is divided into two straight wings like a Trepizond yatagan. The scabbard is nearly always covered with red morocco, over which a second cover of black morocco is drawn like a stocking. The black morocco is ornamented with silver lace, and is often divided into several parts fastened to

Many of these swords have fine old blades from Persia and all parts of Europe. Fig. 711.

SHATAGNI. The name means "hundred killer," and has been said to signify cannon. Hime says, p. 7: "There is nothing to connect '*shatagni*' with fire. It seems to have been a mace, for in the *Raghuvansa* the demon is said to have laid his ironheaded *shataghni* upon Rama, just as Kuvera laid his club on Jamraj."

SHATEKI. An archer, Japan.

SHAWADZURA. See Shiwazura.

SHEAF OF ARROWS. A sheaf of arrows consisted of twenty-four. (Grose II, 269).

SHEARING SWORD. A sword with a light and flexible, double-edged blade, 16th and 17th centuries. (Castle 243).

SHELLS. Large projecting plates to guard the joints at the elbow and knee in the armor of the 16th century. (Dean Hdbk. 61).

Plates shaped like a scallop shell used as guards on swords and knives.

SHER BACHA. Egerton defines it in several places as a musquetoon, a wall piece, and as a mountain gun. (410, 663, 761, 762).

Moser says it is a heavy Persian wall gun with a

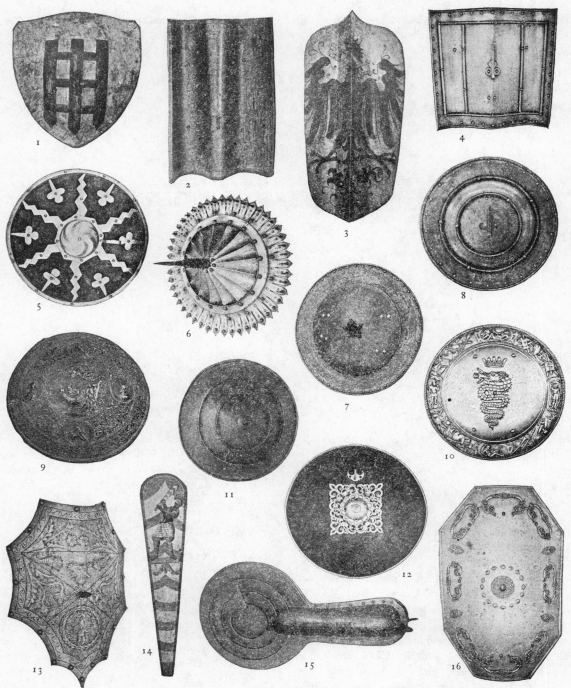

FIGURE 713. *European Shields. 1. Spanish, XIV. 2. Italian, XV. 3. German, XV. 4. Italian (Spanish), XVI. Steel with a hook from which to hang a lantern. 5. Italian buckler, early XVI. 6. Italian buckler with an elaborate serrated border with hooks and spikes to catch the adversary's sword, XVI. 7. Italian target with elaborately engraved surface, XVI. 8. Italian buckler with a hook for a lantern, XVI. 9. Italian shield of tooled leather, about 1560. 10. Italian, about 1550. Arms of Visconti of Milan. 11. Italian buckler, XVI. 12. Spanish buckler with a hook for a lantern and a raised ornament to catch the adversary's sword, XVI. 13. Italian pageant shield, first half XIX. 14. Pisan wooden shield for the Giuoco del Ponte, XVII. 15. Italian fencing shield with a hook for a lantern and raised rings to catch the adversary's sword, XVI. 16. Italian pageant shield, early XIX. Metropolitan Museum. Note to scale.*

pentagonal stock and a huge back sight with several peepholes for different ranges.

Exactly similar guns to that described by Moser were used in the Turkish Empire. Fig. 712.

SHIBABIKI. A single band holding the projections from the chape of a tachi when they are short. (Gilbertson, Dec. 95).

The lowest band on a tachi scabbard. (Brinkley VII, 211).

SHIBUICHI. A Japanese alloy much used for ornamental work. The name means "four parts," one being silver and the others copper, lead, tin and zinc. The proportions vary greatly, the silver being sometimes over ninety per cent. in which case it looks and acts like silver. The alloys of lower percentages of silver assume beautiful patines when properly pickled. The appearance and color can be greatly modified by changing the composition and treatment.

SHIDA-KAWA-ODOSHI. Japanese armor laced with cords of light blue leather decorated with a diaper pattern of white fern leaves. (Conder 271).

SHIDA-NO-ANA. Small holes in pairs around the lower edge of a Japanese helmet. Strips of leather fastened to the lining cap are passed through these and tied firmly on the outside. This cushions the weight of the helmet, or the force of a blow on it, by the elasticity of the cap which is not as deep as the helmet.

SHIELD. Shields are probably the earliest means of defense and have been used longer than history records. They have been made of all sorts of materials—wood, leather, wickerwork, metals, cloth and even turtle shells. The shields of classic times were mainly circular, though many were elliptical, and the Roman shields were often a section of a cylinder. The Franks, Danes and other northern nations of Europe used round, elliptical or rectangular shields of basketwork, leather or wood with umbos (central bosses) of metal.

In the 11th and 12th centuries the shields usually had straight, or slightly curved tops, and two curved sides meeting in a point at the bottom. This type of shield is usually called "heater-shaped." A little later shields assumed the most fantastic shapes both in outline and profile; the object of some of these forms is difficult to imagine, fig. 169. Still later

round shields were again used. In Europe shields were of two classes—bucklers and targets. The distinction is in the way they were held, bucklers having the handles in the middle which were grasped with the hand and held at arm's length, while targets had two widely separated handles through one of which the arm was passed while the other was held in the hand. Some Scotch and Persian shields had three loops placed so that they could be used either as targets or bucklers. In Europe the handles were called *enarmes*, and the sling by which the shield could be hung from the neck the *guige*. Fig. 713.

In Oriental countries the round buckler is, and always has been, the rule, see Dhal. The shields of the Malayan peoples are also frequently round and are generally made of woven cane or of wood. Some are targets, but most are bucklers. The Dyaks use wooden shields (kliau) mainly but, occasionally small shields of bark, rounded at the top and pointed below. See Utap, fig. 828.

The Papuans use very rough rectangular or oval wooden shields, usually grotesquely carved, and often decorated in colors. In the Philippines the native tribes use a great variety of shields, almost every tribe having a characteristic type. The Moros use round wooden targets made of a very light wood of considerable thickness. In Mindanao the shields are also of wood, carved and inlaid with shell and decorated with tufts of hair. Many have peculiar shapes. The Igorot of Luzon use wooden shields with three prongs projecting from the top and two from the bottom, the whole well carved from a single piece of wood. Those of the northern tribes are the most elaborate and of the most graceful shapes. They become rougher and heavier towards the south and the prongs are shorter and broader, until with the southernmost tribes, they are rectangular with pointed tops.

In Africa shields are general and of infinite variety. They are round, elliptical and rectangular and made of hide or basketwork. The Kaffir races of the south use elliptical shields of cowhide strengthened by strips of hide about four inches wide laced through slits each side of the center line and further stiffened by a stick up the back. See Ishilinga, fig. 390.

In tropical Africa the shields are of hide or basketwork; and towards the north, almost entirely of hide. The skin of the rhinoceros is the most high-

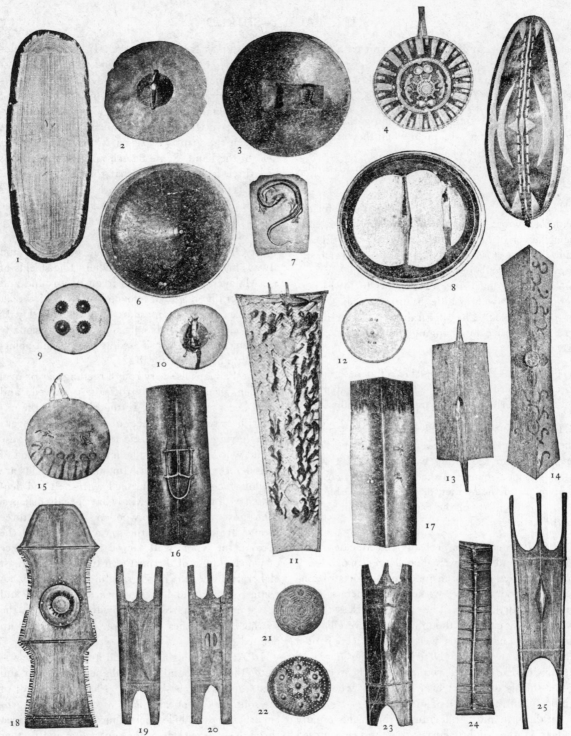

FIGURE 714. *Miscellaneous Shields. 1. Central Africa. Basketwork edged with fur; wooden handle lashed to the center. 2. Sudan. Buckler of hippopotamus hide with a high, conical umbo guarded by iron straps. 3. Chinese, XVII. Wood 26.5 inches in diameter, painted with ships, fish and islands in colored lac. The inside showing the handle which has a shelf at top and bottom which distributes the weight over the entire forearm. 4. Abyssinian chief's shield. Hide lined with red leather and covered with purple velvet decorated with silver gilt plates pierced, embossed, filigreed and tooled. 5. Masai (East Africa). Buckler of hide with painted decorations in red and black. It is highly convex lengthwise. 6 and 8. Outside and inside of a Moro shield 29 inches in diameter. It is made of a single piece of very light wood painted black on the outside. The edge is bound with heavy cane. 7. Japanese. Bronze decorated with a dragon in high relief. 9. Afghan. Basketwork covered with woven cotton cord with leather at the edges, four iron bosses. Diameter 14.5 inches. 10 and 12. Inside and outside of a Somali rawhide buckler stamped with a pattern of concentric rings. 11. Naga, Assam. Woven of heavy split cane decorated with tufts of red hair. Length 4 feet 11 inches, width 1 foot 8 inches. 13. Tinguian (Luzon). Wood stained a grayish black. The body is 13 by 22.5 inches. 14. Celebes. Made of two pieces of wood joined in a V section. It is decorated with painted scrolls. 15. North American Indian. Hide shield decorated in colors. 16 and 17. Inside and outside of a Naga, Assam, shield. Buffalo hide with a folded ridge down the center; decorated with tassels and a fringe of hair. 3 feet by 13.5 inches. 18. Bagobo, Mindanao. Wood 3 feet 11 inches long; carved and inlaid with shell. 19. Igorot. Wood carved and decorated in yellow and black. Length 2 feet 11 inches, width 9 inches. 20. The inside of 19. 21. Batak, Sumatra. Woven cane decorated with seven openwork brass bosses. Diameter 10.25 inches. 22. Batak, Sumatra. Woven cane covered with cloth and ornamented with brass plates and nails. 23. Bontoc Igorot. Wood carved and painted black. 24. Ysabel, Solomon Islands. Wood 7 by 42 inches, strongly convex from end to end, the outside is covered with a black varnish. The inside is shown with the transverse trusses and longitudinal handle. 25. Kalinga Igorot. Wood carved and decorated in yellow and black. Length 4 feet 1.5 inches.*

ly valued for this purpose, and that of the giraffe comes next.

In Australia the shields are of two radically different types. Either they are broad and flat and much longer than they are wide, or very narrow and thick, sometimes not more than an inch wide and four or five inches thick in the middle. The first are used in the general fights and the second in duels with clubs or throwing spears. Their thickness and weight make them effective guards against club blows, and their length and narrowness enable them to be used to knock aside a spear by a turn of the wrist.

The North American Indians used shields of various kinds and sizes. Those of the wooded regions of the East rarely used any; those they had were made of hide or wickerwork, sometimes covered with hide. The Ntlakyapanuk used oblong shields of elk hide four or five feet long. Practically all of the other shields used on this continent were round. The shields of the Indians of the Plains were from twelve to twenty-six inches in diameter, averaging about seventeen. They were usually of buffalo hide with one or more covers of buffalo, elk or deerskin. The covers were painted with totemic designs, that of the inner cover being different from the others, and only exposed on going into a fight. Occasionally the shields were made of woven rods covered with dressed deerskins. These were supposed to possess protective power due to "medicine." Catlin (I, 241), gives a description of "smoking the shield," that is, shrinking and thickening the green hide by heating it over a slow fire. The process is quite elaborate, requiring the assistance of several men. In the southwest the shields were sometimes made by sewing together two thicknesses of hide. The Mexicans made a variety of shields, some of which were very elaborate. See Chimalli.

In Japan shields were seldom used and the few that we know are made of metal. In China large, round, convex shields were very general. Some are of wood lacquered and painted, and others are of cane covered with cloth. A favorite design is a tiger's or monster's head that covers the entire shield.

Some of the shields that appear light and weak were much more effective at the time they were made than they appear to us with our knowledge of present-day weapons. Wallace, p. 360, speaking of the Aru Islander's shields says: "One of the war shields was brought to us to look at. It was made of rattan and covered with cotton twist, so as to be both light, strong and very tough. *I should think it would resist any ordinary bullet.* About the middle there was an armhole with a shutter or flap over it. This enables the arm to be put through and the bow drawn, while the body and face, up to the eyes, remain protected, which cannot be done if the shield is carried on the arm by loops attached to the back in the ordinary way. Miscellaneous Shields. Fig. 714.

For the various kinds and parts of shields see: Adaga, Antia, Aspis, Baluse, Bemaruk, Boce, Bord, Boss, Bouche, Brochiero, Broquel, Buckler, Cetra, Chimal, Chimalli, Club Shield, Clupeus, Dagne, Dang, Dhal, Dharll, Dilge, Drunmung, El-Darakah, Enarmes, Eralili, Gerrhes, Giam, Gig, Gonne, Goolmary, Guige, Ishilunga, Kaidate, Kalihan, Katate, Kliau, Knee Guard, Kunjuri, Kuntan, Kurabit, Kurdigi, Lasag, Lave, Leg Shield, Lo, Lombu Lombu, Madu, Manteau d'Armes, Mantlet, Mochidate, Mulga, Nagphani Dhal, Parma, Pavis, Paviser, Perforated Shield, Phalee, Phari, Pi-Kan, Pistol Shield, Pricei, Quayre, Rondache, Rondelle a Poign, Rotella, Saintie, Scutem, Scutifer, Shoulder Shield, Sipar, Socket, Talawang, Talvas, Tamarang, Tameng, Taming, Tamua, Target, Tarian, Tate, Tate-Mochi, Tatenui, Te-Date, Tharuma, Totochimalli, Trabei Klit Klau, Tun, Turnmung, Ulquita, Umbo, Utap, Woonda, Yaochimalli, Ysgwyd.

SHIGETO-YUMI. A large bow wound with rattan, Japan. (Gilbertson Archery 113).

SHIGURE. Literally "a drizzling shower." File marks to imitate rain as a decoration on Japanese sword mountings.

File marks on the tangs of Japanese blades which are usually so made as to be an indication of the makers or localities where made. See Japanese Blades, fig. 401.

SHIHAB. "Falling star," a rocket, India. (Egerton, p. 34).

SHIHOJIRO. A Japanese helmet having four of its plates made of, or covered with silver, front, back and at each side. These silver plates reached from the base to the apex and sometimes covered more than one gore, and were highly ornamented. When silver plates were used the helmet was called *nihojiro* if two; *shihojiro*, if four; and *happojiro*, if eight. These names mean two, four and eight white.

SHIIGATA. A variety of Japanese helmet. (Garbutt 168).

SHII NARI. "Nut-shaped," a Japanese helmet of a more or less conical shape. (Conder 257).

SHIKO. A Japanese quiver carried at the right side of the waist.

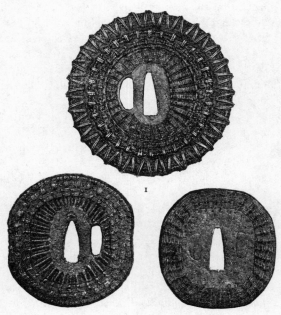

FIGURE 715. *Shingen Tsuba. 1. Iron and silver, 17th century. Diameter 4.375 inches. 2. Iron core wound with silver and brass wire, 17th century. 3. Sentoku surface and rim with an iron core.*

SHIKOME-ZUE. A sword case, Japan. See Katana Zutsu.

SHIKORO. The neck guard of a Japanese helmet. There are several varieties. (Dean Jap. 4). See Kabuto.

SHIMAI-KANE-NO-DO. A Japanese folding breastplate made of four plates. (Conder 264).

SHINAI-UCHI. Fencing, Japan.

SHINCHIU. A kind of brass used in making sword fittings in Japan. (Joly, Hawkshaw xxii).

SHINGDA. A wooden ramrod, Western Tibet. (Ramsay-Western).

SHINGEN. A type of tsuba made of a plate of iron, or brass, with silver and copper wires woven through and over it. It is named from Takada Shin-

gen, who is said to have greatly favored this type. He was the most powerful noble in Japan in the middle of the 16th century. By some it is considered a variation of the mukade (centipede) design; others say that it represents the mat used in the tea ceremony. They vary much in size and weight, some being very large and heavy while others are very light. Fig. 715.

SHINGETO. A Japanese bow wound with coils of red cane on a black ground.

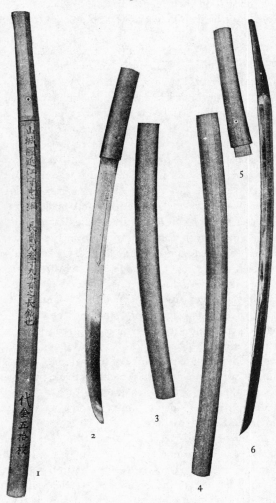

FIGURE 716. *Shirasaya. 1. Blade 28.5 inches long, signed Tadatsuna, about 1675. The inscription written on the scabbard is by the honami who examined it. 2. Finely watered blade 21.75 inches long with Fudo on one side and a ken on the other. Signed Taikei Masanao, Third Year of Koka. The plain hilt is in place. 3. The scabbard of 2. 4. The scabbard of 6. 5. The hilt of 6, the wooden habaki, is in one piece with the hilt. 6. The blade 28 inches long, signed Muramasa.*

SHINKEN. A real sword as distinguished from a wooden one, Japan.

SHINOME-ZUE. A sword case, Japan. See Katana Zutsu.

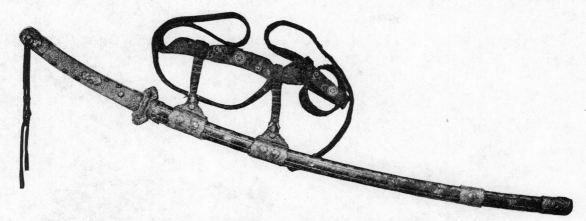

FIGURE 717. *Shira Tachi, with Sage-Obi and Tsuyo-No-O. Sword with an unsigned blade of good quality. Scabbard with a wood panel down each side and the edges lacquered; decorated with Taira mon in lacquer and shell inlay. Hilt with tsuka-ai of transparent green material resembling emeralds. All mounts of very finely worked silver with gold Taira and Sakai mon. Sage Obi of brown leather embroidered with colored silk. Tsuyo-No-O of leather cord with tsuyo (chapes) and kohaze (clamp) of very finely chased silver.*

SHIN-NO-TACHI. A tachi with a shagren hilt which should have seventy-five examples of the owner's crest on the mountings.

SHINOBI-NO-O. Helmet cords, Japan. They were of three lengths depending on whether the helmet had three, four or five loops, or rings through which it was passed and laced to the pins, hooks or rings on the menpo. The *mitsuchi* was seven feet long, the *yotsuchi* about eight, and the *itsuchi* nine. They were made of cotton cloth, silk crepe, soft silk cord or untwisted silk cord. Hard twisted cord was not suitable for this purpose. (Garbutt 170).

SHINODARI. Symbolized swords of Fudo, god of wisdom and mercy. They are frequently used as ornaments in Japan, particularly on sword blades. (Dean Notes 8).

SHINO DZUTSU. See Suneate.

SHINOGI. The flat part of some Japanese blades near the back where the sides are parallel.

SHINO-GOTE, AWASE-GOTE, YETCHIU-GOTE. Japanese mail sleeves with metal plates about two inches long and half an inch wide at regular intervals. (Conder 273). See Kote.

FIGURE 718. *Shirazaya, Scabbard Covers. 1. Scabbard of bands of red and black lacquer. Black leather cover with a spiral red stripe. Gilt mon on end. 2. Black leather cover with gilt mon. 3. Leopard skin cover 22 inches long.*

SHINO-ODATSUGI. A variety of kote. (Garbutt 140).

SHINOTATE-SUNE-ATE. See Sudare Sune-Ate.

SHI-NO-ZUMI. A method of making Japanese blades in which bars of very soft iron or steel are

SHIPPO. Enamel, Japan. It was sometimes used for decorating sword mountings.

SHIRA HASHI. A Japanese helmet with silver stars on the plates.

SHIRA HATA. A white flag, a flag of truce, Japan.

FIGURE 719. *Shishi. Two Japanese breastplates embossed with shishi, 18th century.*

welded to the opposite sides of a bar of hard iron and the resulting bar placed between two of mixed iron and steel and the whole welded. (Gilbertson, Blades 192). This method did not produce first-class blades.

SHINPUNG and **HOKPAK.** Nicobar fishing spears, the first is the smaller. (Man, And. & Nic. 10).

SHINTO. (New). Japanese blades made later than 1603, as distinguished from those made earlier, which are called *koto* (old). (B. M. Hdbk. 52). Most of those who have written on the subject give the date as 1596.

SHIODE. Straps or cords on the side of a Japanese saddle for holding the flaps, etc.

SHIRASAYA. (White scabbard). The plain wooden handle and scabbard in which fine blades were kept in Japan when not in use, sometimes the blade itself when so mounted. They are made of honoki wood, perfectly plain but beautifully fitted and finished. Usually an inscription on the scabbard gives the name of the maker and other information about the blade. Fig. 716.

SHIRA TACHI. White tachi; that is, one with silver mountings. It was carried by nobles of the first four ranks in the Ashikaga period in Japan. (Joly, Hawkshaw xiv). Fig. 717.

SHIRAZAYA. A Japanese sword, the scabbard of which broadens out greatly near the end. Those of the higher officials were covered with bear, leopard and tiger skins. (Gilbertson, Dec. 96).

A scabbard cover of tiger, bear- or deerskin. In very early times it was carried by all classes, later only by the higher grades of officers. (Garbutt 168). Fig. 718.

SHIRIGI. The crupper of a saddle, Japan.

SHIRIMONO. Hardware, a name given to poor

Bishamon Ten, Jinkoku Ten, Komoku Ten and Zoochu Ten, Buddhistic divinities. They are four knobs on a Japanese helmet to which cords could be fastened to hold a silk cover over the hachimanza.

SHITO. An old name for the Japanese tanto. (Joly S. & S. 34).

FIGURE 720. *Shitogi Tsuba.* 1. *Sentoku, engraved and gilded.* 2. *Plain red bronze.* 3. *Plain, gilded.* 4. *Sentoku, engraved and gilded. The first three are of the 17th century or earlier; the last is of the 19th.*

copies of old sword mountings made for sale to tourists or for export, Japan.

SHIRMANI. Walrus ivory, Persia. It is highly valued for sword and knife hilts as it is not considered as liable to split as elephant ivory.

SHIRO. The fortified castle of a Japanese noble.

SHIROGAKE. A variety of Japanese corselet. (Garbutt 142).

SHIRUSHI. See Sashimono.

SHISHI, KARA-SHISHI. The Chinese lion, often used in the decoration of Japanese arms and armor. (Dean Jap. 57). It is also called the "Dog of Fo." Fig. 719.

SHI-SHI-AI-BORI. Recessed carving, a design in a sunk panel, Japan.

SHISHI-YA. (Lion arrow). A hunting arrow, Japan.

SHITAGI. (Groundwork, foundation). The metal of which the body of a sword mounting was made in Japan.

SHITAGURA. A pad placed under a saddle, Japan.

SHI-TEN-BIO, SHI-TEN-NO. The four Deva knobs which are named for the four Deva kings—

SHITODOME. The thimbles in the openings in the kashira through which the cord windings of the hilt pass. (Joly Int. 12). The precisely similar thimbles in the kurikata being larger are called o-shitodome. The name "May be derived from the name of a bird, as its shape is like that of a bird's eye." (Joly S. & S. 51). The outer flange of the shitodome, which is the only part that shows, is frequently decorated.

SHITODOME-ANA. The openings in the kashira and kurikata for the shitodome. (Joly Int. 12).

SHITOGI TSUBA. An early form of guard which was used on ceremonial tachi long after its use was discontinued on fighting swords. The original shape is said to be derived from the ritual rice cake, called *shitogi*, which was made by squeezing

FIGURE 721. *Tsuba like sections of a shitogi.* 1. *Shakudo and gold, plants in relief.* 2. *Sentoku. The loops are dragon's heads in the round. Signed Denriusai.*

a handful of cooked rice so as to leave the impression of the fingers in it. Although this guard is of considerable thickness it is narrow and afforded little protection for the hand. It was therefore supplemented by a loop of metal on each side. Fig. 720.

opening up the back and closed by clasps or cords. It was worn by common soldiers. (Conder 265).

SHIWAZURA, SHIWADZURA. "Wrinkled face," a type of menpo. (Dean Jap. 67).

FIGURE 722. *Shoka. Head 7.5 x 3.5 inches.*

Occasionally flat guards are made like a section of a shitogi tsuba. It is a plate like a section of the body of the guard with an opening for the tang in it, and a loop on each side like those of a shitogi tsuba. Fig. 721.

SHIWARI-GUSOKU. Japanese body armor

SHI-ZU. The cantle of a Japanese saddle.

SHO. A saddle flap, Japan.

SHOBU-KAWA. Printed leather, so called because it had printed on it a pattern of iris (shobu) leaves. It was often used in Japan for sword slings and armor fittings. (Joly S. & S. 23).

SHOKA. The battle-axe used by the tribes around Lake Tanganyika. It has a triangular blade somewhat longer and thinner than that used as a working tool. The short tang passes through the bulging end of a short handle made of the wood of the *bauhinia*, or some other equally hard. (Burton Lakes 478). Fig. 722.

SHOT. The old chronicles use the name shot, not only for missiles, but for guns, and not infrequently for men armed with guns. (Hewitt III, 592, 698).

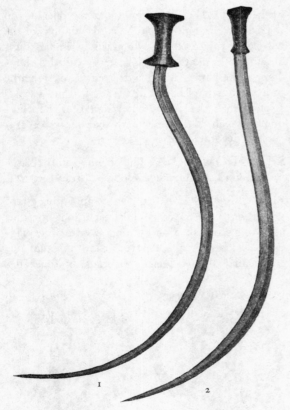

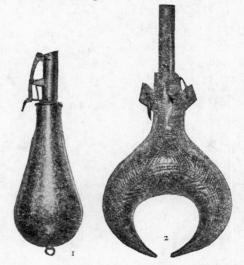

FIGURE 723. *Shotel. 1. Wood hilt. Blade 2 feet 6 inches from hilt to point and 3 feet 4.5 inches around the curve. 2. Wood hilt. Blade 2 feet 8 inches from hilt to point in a straight line.*

FIGURE 724. *Shot Pouches. 1. Persian. Steel inlaid with gold, 18th century. 2. Tunis. Embossed, crescent-shaped leather pouch, brass mouthpiece. Length 11 inches.*

SHOTEL. The Abyssinian sword. It has a double-edged blade of diamond section curved almost in a half circle. The blade is about thirty inches in a straight line from hilt to point and about forty around the curve. It has a simple wooden hilt without a guard. The scabbards are of leather and are made to fit the blade closely, fig. 723. The Abys-

lapping each other and riveted to the arm piece. Still later the shoulders were covered by single large plates called the pauldron. (Planche 180). Fig. 725.

SHOULDER SHIELD. An extra guard worn on the left shoulder in tournaments in the 16th century. See also Manteau d'Armes.

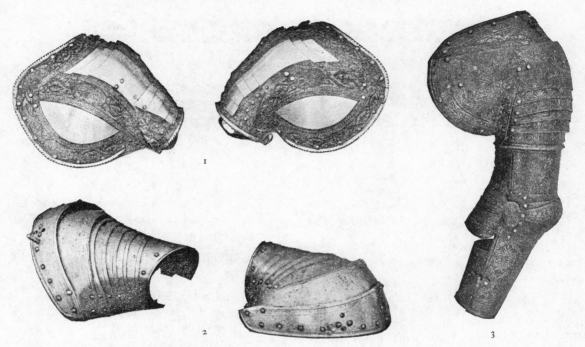

FIGURE 725. *Shoulder Cops.* 1. *Italian,* 1560. 2. *Probably German,* 17th century. 3. *Savoyard,* 1590. *Metropolitan Museum. Not to scale.*

sinians have no idea of fencing and use this extremely awkward weapon to strike over, or around, the shield of an opponent.

SHOT POUCH. Occasionally shot pouches with chargers like the European are found in the East. It is probable that the chargers are of European make and have been put on native powder flasks. Fig. 724.

SHOULDER COP, SHOULDER GUARD, SHOULDER PIECE, EPAULIERE, EPAULETTE, EPAULET, PAULDRON. Shoulder plates either of one piece or articulated. They were first worn about 1300. They were then small plates, plain or ornamented, covering the point, or front, of the shoulder and fastened to the hauberk by points or laces. These were succeeded by plates covering the shoulder and upper part of the arm, over-

SHRAPNEL. In 1784 Lieut. Henry Shrapnel, R.A., invented a projectile which he called "spherical case." It was designed for use against troops in open order beyond the range of ordinary case shot. In it a very light bursting charge was used and the fragments were projected by the charge of the gun from which it was fired. It was not until 1803 that his invention was formally adopted by the British government. The original shell had very light walls and was filled with bullets and scrap iron, with just enough powder to burst it. It did not attain its maximum value until long after its invention as no accurate time fuse was available. The modern shrapnel is a short, chokebored gun filled with bullets, and with both a very accurate time fuse and one for impact. (Hime 182).

SHUJU. A pistol, Japan.

SHU-NURI. See Lacquer.

SHURI. The shaft of an Ainu arrow. (Greey 109).

SHURIKEN. A knife made for throwing, Japan. The hilt and blade are forged in one piece. As it was usually lost when thrown it was plain. Fig. 726.

SILIGIS. Wooden javelins, Borneo. They were thrown and the more valuable iron-headed spears were only used at close quarters where there was no danger of their being lost. Compare Sligi.

SILLAH-KHANA, SILLEH-KHANEH. An armory, Rajput. Every Rajput lord had his armory

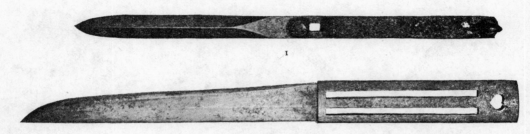

FIGURE 726. *Shuriken.* 1. *Triangular blade and hilt forged in one piece. Length 9 inches. The handle was originally covered with wood or leather.* 2. *Handle and blade forged in one piece. Length, blade 8.375 inches, total 10.625 inches.*

SHUSHBAR. An Indian mace with a straight handle and six wings in the head. (B. M. Hdbk. 48).

SHUTRNALS. Swivel guns carried by camels, India, 18th century. (Egerton, p. 29).

SIBAK. A kind of Malay knife or sword.

SICA. A short Roman sword. It was either straight or curved, the main object being to have it fit closely to the body under the armpit, hence it was a favorite with assassins. (Burton Sword 252).

SICARII. Hired assassins who used the knife. They are mentioned by both Josephus and Tacitus. (Burton Sword 185).

SICLATOWN. See Cyclas.

SIDE DRUM. The ordinary snare drum, so called because it was hung at the side. (Grose II, 42).

SIDE PLATE. See Contreplatine.

SIDE RING. A ring-shaped guard projecting from the side of a sword hilt. It was first used in the 16th century. (Castle 231).

SIGAGUT. The great Greenland and Hudson Bay harpoon thrown with a spear thrower. (U. S. N. M. 1900, 240).

SILEPE. The Basuto axe. The blade has a wide edge but not much depth. It is connected to the handle by a wide, flat tang. (Burton Sword 93). Fig. 727.

and collection of arms and armor. The keeper of the armory was one of the most confidential officers about the person of the prince. (Tod I, 512).

SILLAHPOSH. Rajput, wearing armor. (Tod I, 591).

SIMBILAN, BAGSACAY. A wooden javelin about half an inch in diameter, used by the Sulu Moros. It is said that they could throw as many as four at once. (Foreman 147).

SIME. The East African sword. The form of this weapon appears to differ in almost every tribe. The Wahumba, or Wamesi, use blades about four feet long by two fingers in breadth; the long, round, guardless hilt is ribbed for security of grasp and covered with leather. Their iron is of excellent quality, and the shape of the weapon has given rise to the report "that they make swords on the model of those of the Knights Templars." (Burton Lakes 478).

Apparently it is the same as the Masai Seme. Fig. 703.

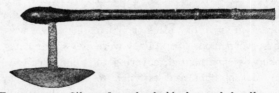

FIGURE 727. *Silepe. Iron head, black wood handle 21 inches long, strengthened by coils of brass wire.*

SIMONG. The Kyan, Borneo, war jacket. It is merely a strip of goatskin with an opening for the head at the center, and covers the front and back of the body. It is decorated with hornbill's feathers

1   2

FIGURE 728. *Sinan. 1. Persian, 16th century. Steel head and socket inlaid with gold. Dated 1592. 2. Persian. Fine watered steel 9.5 inches long, paneled and inlaid with gold. The socket is divided into eight panels by raised ribs with ornaments at the ends inlaid with gold. Total length 16 inches.*

and has a large, thick shell (Blasung) hanging on the breast. (Ling Roth II, 128).

SINALAWITAN. An Igorot spear similar to the falfeg, or ordinary war spear, except that it has several barbs in place of a single pair. It is not used in war or hunting but is valued solely as a protection from *anito*, or evil spirits. When a man goes alone into the mountains the anito are very apt to trouble him; if, however, he carries one of these spears they will not molest him as they are afraid of the formidable array of barbs. The more barbs the more effective the spear. (Jenks 128). Fig. 278.

There is one in the American Museum of Natural History with sixteen pairs of barbs. The original owner must have been a most timid person.

SINAN. A Persian spear with a long, straight blade tapering evenly from the socket to the point. (Moser XXXV). Fig. 728.

SINAPANG. A gun, Subanun of Mindanao. (Christie 109).

SINEGAGLIA. A globular breastplate worn under the hauberk in the 14th century. (Skelton 14).

SINGA. A boomerang, southern India. They were made of steel and were from eighteen to twenty inches long. (Egerton 70).

SINGAT. Literally hornets. A party of left-handed men chosen by the Dyaks to ambush an enemy. (Hose 171).

SINGAUTA. See Maau.

SINGRA. Sikh, a priming horn. (Egerton 683).

SINGRAM. The name given to the matchlock with which Akbar shot Jeimul when Chitore was taken in 1568. (Tod I, 262).

SINNOCK. A spear with a light shaft and a fixed head, used by hand, Mosquito Coast. (U. S. N. M. 1900, 220).

SI OR. The pellet bow of the Toba Battaks. The pocket for the missile is quite close to one end. (Arc. f. Eth. VI, 121 [?]).

SIPAR. Persian, a shield. It is the same as the Indian Dhal. Occasionally the Persian shields have

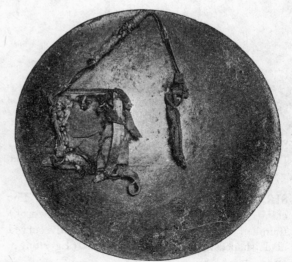

FIGURE 729. *Sipar. The inside of a Persian shield showing the three handles, so that it can be used either as a target or buckler.*

three handles so that they can either be held in the hand or carried on the arm, fig. 729. Some Scotch targets have similar handles.

SIPET. A blowpipe, Dutch Borneo. (Peralaer 375).

SISILI MILAK. Roti, a wooden hunting spear with a sheath woven of palm leaves with long streamers on each side. (Arc. f. Eth. VIII, 7).

SITERAMPURI KATARI. A variety of katar from Vizianagram. (Egerton 511).

FIGURE 730. *Small Swords.* 1. *French, end of the 17th century.* 2. *French, end of the 18th century.* 3. *English(?), early 18th century.* 4. *Hilt probably German, of the middle of the 18th century. Blade, Toledo, dated 1788. Metropolitan Museum.*

SIREN. The poison used on blowpipe darts in Dutch Borneo. It is the same as the ipoh. (Peralaer 375).

SIROHI, SERYE. A kind of Rajput sword. "The chief favorite of all the various kinds (of swords) found in Rajputana is the Sirohi, a slightly curved blade shaped like that of Damascus." (Egerton, p. 105).

Swords made in the city of Sirohi which were famous for their temper. (Tod II, 91).

SIWALAPA. A Surinam club of hard wood with a small cylindrical handle widening out in concave curves to a square end. (Arc. f. Eth. XVII, Sup. 115).

SIWAR. A variety of bade-bade.

SIXTE. A parry in which the hand is opposite the right breast and the sword is carried slightly to the right.

SKAIN, SKEIN, SKEYN, SCJAN. The dagger

of the ancient Irish. It had a short, straight, double-edged blade. (Burton Sword 26).

SKULL, SCULL. A close fitting open headpiece worn from the 15th to the 16th century. Also the fixed part of a closed helmet as distinguished from

SLING. The sling is one of the oldest and most widely distributed of weapons, and its construction and use are practically the same everywhere. It is merely a strip of some flexible material with a pocket at or near the middle. The object to be thrown

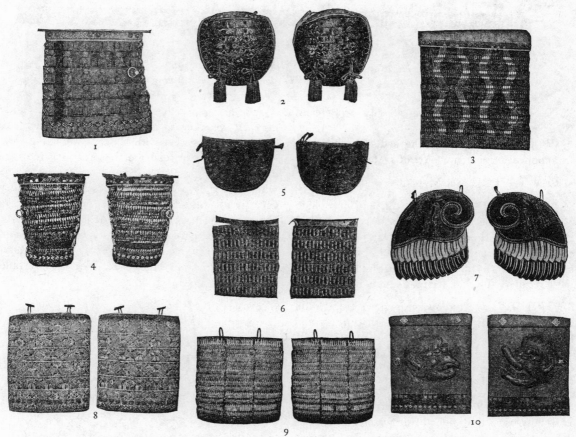

FIGURE 731. Sode. 1. Steel plates laced together, XVI. 2. Maru Sode. Named for their shape. This type is usually made of a single plate, XVIII. 3. Laced lames built up of scales, XVI. 4. Laced lames built up of scales, XVI. Possibly remodeled in the XVIII. 5. Single plates, XVIII. 6. Small plates connected by mail, XIX. 7. Ha Sode or Taka-no-ha-sode, about 1825. 8. XVIII. 9. Laced lames built up of scales, XVII-XVIII. 10. Iron plates embossed with tengu heads, XVIII. Kawara Sode. All but 10 are in the Metropolitan Museum. Not to scale.

the movable parts covering the face and ears. (ffoulkes 49).

SLICE. To evacuate, spoken of the goshawk and sparrow hawk; the other kinds "mute."

SLIGI. The Sea Dyak wooden spear, the point is hardened by fire. It is used as a missile, the more valuable spears with iron heads being used only for thrusting. (Ling Roth II, 133). Compare Siligis.

is placed in the pocket and the ends taken in the hand, one being wrapped securely around it, and the other held loosely. The sling is whirled round the head and, when it has acquired sufficient momentum, the loose end is released and the missile flies forward. It is still a common weapon in many savage countries and numerous travelers have testified to its accuracy. "I have seen a native (of New Britain) knock a bird off a tree at about a hundred yards distance; they seldom pitch a stone further from the object aimed at than three or four yards." (Powell 162). See Gudo, fig. 313.

SLING HAFTED. Mounted on a cord or chain fastened to a handle. (Horniman Museum 20).

FIGURE 732. *Sode Garami.* *(Sleeve tangler). A pole 6 feet 5 inches long with three lines of blunt spikes for 20 inches from the head. Six double barbed hooks on the end pointing in opposite directions.*

SLIP, SLIPPING. Deceiving, an old fencing term. (Castle 192).

Withdrawing a part of the body at which the antagonist directs a cut. (Art of Defense 46).

SLOW MATCH. See Match.

SLUNG SHOT. A weight on the end of a chain or flexible handle. It has never been recognized in Europe as a legitimate weapon of war, but was often carried in the early days in the West, and is often used by robbers at the present time. Similar weapons were regularly used in Japan. See Kusari Gama.

SLUR BOW. A crossbow with a barrel slotted on both sides for the string. Early 16th century and later. (Payne-Gallwey, The Crossbow 129).

Slur bows have been used and are still made in China. They are of all sizes from mere toys to serious weapons. Fig. 170.

SMALL SWORD. The last form of the rapier. It usually has a triangular blade which can only be used for thrusting, and the advantage of which consists in its lightness. The hilt is simple, the guard consisting of an elliptical plate, or two shells, and a light finger guard. The small sword first appeared in the end of the 17th century and continued in use as long as swords were worn as a part of the civilian dress. (Castle 239). Fig. 730.

SMAN, HMAN. Gunpowder, Western Tibet. (Ramsay-Western).

SNAFFLE. See Bit.

SNAPHAAN, SNAPHAUNCE. One of the earliest forms of flintlock. See Flintlock.

SOAR HAWK. A hawk that has left the nest but whose feathers are not yet fully grown.

SOCKET. See Knee Shield. (Skelton 129).

SODE. Japanese shoulder guards which are, by some, considered to resemble the ailettes of European armor.

Sode are generally made of small scales firmly fastened together to form long strips which are loosely laced together with silk cords. The top piece is always a strip of solid metal. Sometimes they are made of a single plate of metal or of a large one with one or two narrower ones below it. They vary greatly in size and shape; most are nearly square and from six to fourteen inches across. Three classes are recognized—O-Sode, Chu Sode, and Ko-Sode—large, medium and small sode. The Oki-Sode is a variety of small sode. The medium and

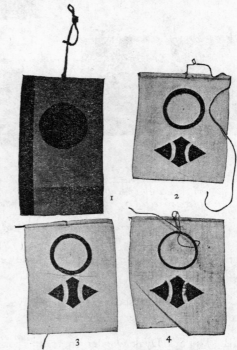

FIGURE 733. *Sode Jiruchi. Identification badges worn on the sode when in action; printed cotton. 1. 9.75 x 5.25 inches. Red edge and black sun. 2, 3, 4. All 6 x 7.5 inches; designs in black on white.*

large sode were worn by important officers. (Garbutt 143). In general the older ones are apt to be the larger. Fig. 731.

For some of the varieties see: Gaku-Sode, Ha-Sode, Hiyotan-Sode, Kawa-Sode, Kawara-Sode, Ki-No-Ha-Sode, Kusari-Sode, Maru-Sode, Namban-Sode, Taka-No-Ha-Sode.

FIGURE 734. *Sode Kozuka. The body is of copper and the ji-ita of shakudo carved with waves in relief.*

SODE BAORI. A Japanese surcoat with sleeves. (Conder 277).

SODE GARAMI. (Sleeve tangler). A pole with barbed hooks on the end used to catch thieves in Japan. Fig. 732.

SODE JIRUCHI. A piece of silk or cotton about the size of a sode with a crest or other device on it. It was fastened to the rings at the top of the sode, the lower end being left loose. The device on the badge was determined by the commander and it was put on only on the eve of battle. (Conder 278). Fig. 733.

Garbutt says that it was only worn on the right sode.

SODE KOZUKA. The decorated surface plate (ji-ita) of a kogai was sometimes mounted on a kozuka. As kogai are much shorter than kozuka this left blank spaces at the ends; these were called sode (shoulder) and the whole a sode kozuka. Being an obvious patchwork it was considered as of less value than a kozuka of the usual form. (Weber II, 324). Fig. 734.

SOEDOEK. A kind of Malay knife.

SOHATSU. A variety of Japanese helmet. (Garbutt 168).

SOHEI. Soldier monks of the temples of Hai, Kasuga, Kitano, etc. They were similar to the Yamabushi. (Joly Leg. 392).

SO-JUTSU. The art of using the spear, Japan.

SO-KAN. A spear shaft, Japan.

SOKET. A head for a tilting lance shaped like a small plowshare, 13th century. (Hewitt I, 306).

SOKI. A pennon on a spear, Japan.

SOKO. Ramparts, trenches, fortifications, Japan.

SOLERETS, SOLARETS. Plate armor for the feet. They appeared in the 13th century as strips of metal riveted to leather, later the plates were riveted to each other in such a way as to give the required flexibility. This was accomplished by lapping those nearest the leg so that the open joints were towards the front, while those covering the front of the foot lapped in the opposite direction. The soleret had no sole but the sides were connected by straps passing under the foot. In the 15th century the toepieces became excessively long, the longest being known as "a la poulaine," and those of intermediate length as "demi poulaine." These very long toepieces were detachable as a man could hardly have walked with them in place. In the 16th century the foot guards were shortened and the toes became very broad. They were then called sabatons or bear-paw or duck-billed solerets. Figs. 11, 38.

SOMAI. A bolas with two balls. (Wood 1174). See Bolas.

SOMIN 1st. (Yokoya). He was considered next to Yujo (Goto) the most skillful maker of sword mountings in Japan. He lived 1669 to 1733.

SOMON. The principal gate of a castle, Japan.

FIGURE 735. *Soritsuno.* 1. *Black lacquer.* 2. *Iron inlaid with a very fine geometrical pattern in gold.*

SONDANG, SUNDANG. The Malayan broadsword. (Clifford, Malayan Mono. 28).

SOP. See Ki Khnam.

SOPOK. The Dusun, Borneo, name for both spear and blowpipe. Most Bornean blowpipes have spearheads attached. (Ling Roth II, 185).

It is very rarely found on the scabbards of long swords, and not often on those of short, though fairly common on knife scabbards.

SOROIMONO, SORIMONO. A set of uniform objects, Japan; frequently the fittings for a sword. It may consist of almost any combination of fittings

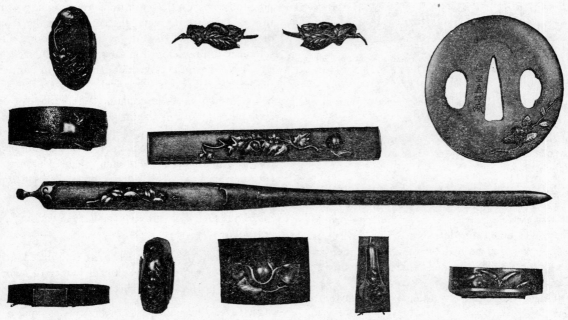

FIGURE 736. *Soroimono. Shibuichi with flowers and vegetables in relief and inlaid with gold, coral, pearl and malachite. Signed Naoyoshi, second half of the 18th century. This set is unusually complete.*

SORAK. The Malay war cry. It was also shouted when dancing or on any occasion of excitement.

SORI. The curve of a Japanese blade. It was measured by the greatest distance from the back of the blade to a straight line drawn from end to end of the blade excluding the tang. (Gilbertson, Blades 196).

SORIKIN. See Soritsuno.

SORITSUNO, OBIGANE, OIKANE, ORIGANE, SAGURI, SORIKIN. A small hook on the side of a Japanese scabbard below the kurikata to prevent the scabbard from being pulled through the belt when the blade was drawn. (Joly Int. 9).

It was usually made of wood or horn and lacquered like the rest of the scabbard, but often made of metal decorated like the rest of the fittings. Fig. 735.

except that of kozuka, kogai and pair of menuki, which is called a *midokoro mono*. The most complete is the entire fittings for a pair of swords which is called a *daisho-no-soroimono*. This may consist of as many as twenty-four pieces, though such complete sets are practically unknown. Sets of fittings were highly valued in Japan and were often given as presents. Fig. 736.

SOSUN. A straight Indian sword with reinforcements on the blade and a hilt with a cup pommel with a spike on it. (Wallace Orient).

SOSUNPATTAH. An Indian sword with a broad, yatagan-like blade with a padded hilt with a spike on the pommel. (Egerton 578T).

A sword with a straight blade and a spike on the pommel. (Wallace Orient).

SOTA. India, a ceremonial mace, a mace of office. (Wallace Orient).

SOTEN. A tsuba maker of the 17th century celebrated for his elaborately pierced guards minutely inlaid with gold, silver and bronzes. Usually they represent scenes from the civil wars. He founded a school that was very popular but much of the work of which was not of a high class though his own is excellent. I, fig. 808.

the broadsword, and made both to cut and thrust, is therefore a weapon well adapted to those gentlemen who are masters of both small and broadsword, and unite according to circumstances the defensive and offensive movements of the two. In thrusting the spadroon has an advantage over the broadsword, on account of the celerity with which the fatal movement can be executed, but in cutting it is much weaker in its effect." (Art of Defense 91).

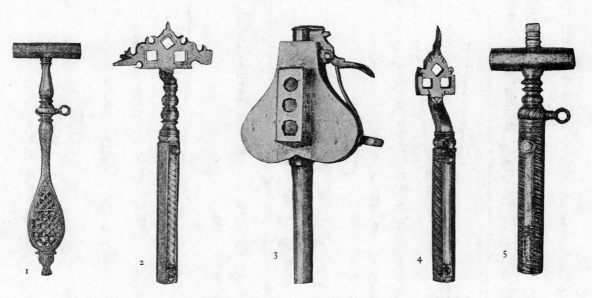

FIGURE 737. Spanners. 1. Italian, end of the 16th century. 2. Spanner and powder measure, French, early 17th century. 3. Spanner, primer and ramrod, German, 17th century. 4. Spanner and primer, French, 17th century. 5. Italian, 17th century. Metropolitan Museum. Not to scale.

SOW. A movable protection made of a light wooden framework covered with undressed hides. It was used to shelter men undermining the walls of fortresses in the 11th century. (Hewitt I, 173).

SO-YA. A plain arrow such as was used in war, Japan.

SOYO 1st. The founder of the Yokoya school of tsuba makers. He lived in the latter part of the 17th century and was the Shogun's chiseler.

SPADONE, ESPADON. A two-handed sword, 16th century.

SPADROON. The English "cut and thrust" play with the back sword. The name is probably derived from the German spadroon, a very light sword adapted for both cutting and thrusting. (Castle 207, 243). "The spadroon being much lighter than

SPADROON GUARD. The spadroon guard "is formed by dropping the point to the right from the outside guard, till it comes under the adversary's blade, turning the edge upwards at the same time raising the wrist." . . . "Although this is denominated the *spadroon* guard, yet it is not to be considered as the chief posture of defense with that weapon. It is indeed the weakest guard of any, and should never be had recourse to, but in such circumstances as will not admit of immediately changing to another without danger of a time thrust or cut." (Art of Defense 60).

SPANDREL. The shoulder guard of the ancient Romans. (Dean Hdbk. 29).

SPANNER. The wrench with which wheel locks were wound. Spanners were frequently highly ornamented and sometimes the handles were hollow forming primers. Fig. 737.

SPARTE. An Anglo-Saxon battle-axe. (Planche 474).

SPATHA, SPATA. The long sword of the Roman cavalry. (Burton Sword 142).

of wood, but often have barbs of stone or shell. Fig. 738.

Dodge thus describes the spear of the Indians of the Southwest: "It consists of a short shaft from eight to twelve feet long, terminated by a head of stone or steel. . . . the Indian wants no tough, stiff ash poles, but selects light and rather pliable wands."

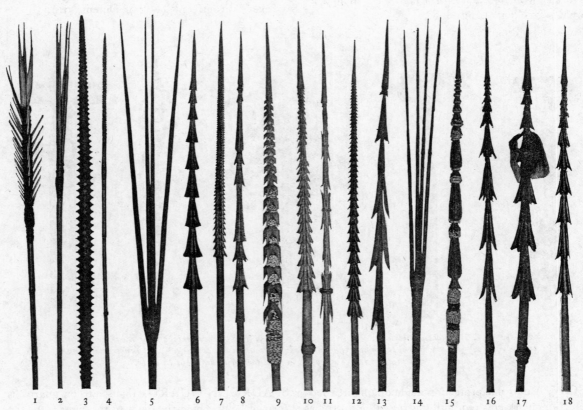

FIGURE 738. *South Sea Island Spears. 1, 2. New Hebrides. 3. Mangaia Island, Hervey Group. 4. Australia. 5 to 18. Fiji. Peabody Museum, Salem. Not to scale.*

SPEAR. Any long shafted weapon intended solely for thrusting. It is a class name and includes many named as well as nameless weapons. Wooden spears have been used from the earliest times and are still used by many savages. Stone, bone, horn, ivory and shell have been used for spearheads, but iron is, of course, the commonest material.

The most elaborate of the wooden spears come from the South Sea Islands, where they are often beautifully carved, the most highly decorated being more for show and as accessories to the dance than for war. They are carved, painted and decorated with bands of colored grass; the heads are generally

The Comanches and Apaches not infrequently used long, dry stalks of the soap-plant (*Phalangium pomaridranum*). The favorite point was a long, straight sword blade which they procured from the Mexicans."

In Central Africa the spear is not only the commonest weapon but is used as currency. The tribes that smelt their own iron trade spearheads to their less skillful neighbors. Among the Masai the best spear maker is usually the chief. African spears are almost universally well made; those of Central Africa have sockets that fit on the shafts while those of the south have tangs that fit in them. Fig. 739.

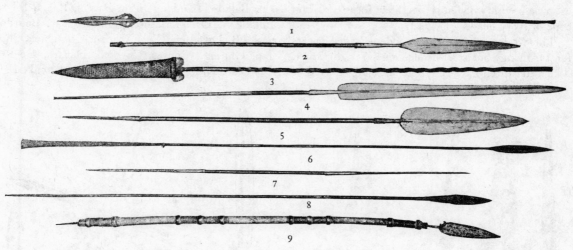

FIGURE 739. *African Spears. 1. Upper Congo. Iron head and butt. 2. Upper Congo. Socketed head 18.5 inches long; shaft wound with iron, brass and copper. 3. Upper Congo. Head 19 inches long. Length overall 6 feet 2 inches. The shaft is carved in a spiral for its entire length. Woven cane sheath. 4. Masai. Head 3 feet 10 inches long; butt piece nearly as long. 5. Rhombo, or old Masai style. 6. Tuareg. All iron inlaid with brass. Length 6 feet 7 inches. 7. Arab. Diamond section, socketed head 17 inches long; long steel butt. Both head and butt are inlaid with brass. 8. Australian. Obsidian head. 9. Ashanti. Iron head 2 x 12 inches. Shaft covered with decorative leather work.*

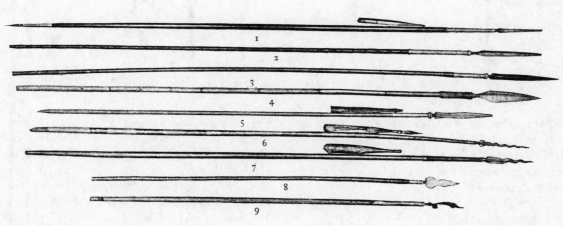

FIGURE 740. *Malayan Spears. 1. Java. Watered blade 8 inches long, silver gilt mounts. Length 7 feet 11.75 inches. 2. Malay. Silver ferule, dark wood shaft. 3. Moro, Lake Lanao. Silver ferule. Shaft carved to imitate bamboo. 4. Moro. Bamboo shaft wound with braided brass wire near the head. 5. Malay. Kris-like head, silver ferule. Wood scabbard with horn ends. 6. Bali. Head 9.5 inches long. Length overall 7 feet 5 inches. Wood sheath carved, painted black and decorated with red and gold. 7. Bali. Shaft painted red. Wood sheath similar to the last. 8. Java. The head is the figure of a seated man. 9. Java. The head is a conventionalized bird.*

The Eskimo and other races of the extreme north use spears with wooden shafts, bone foreshafts, and bone or ivory heads. Fig. 742.

The Malayan races use wooden-headed spears for throwing, but steel-headed ones for thrusting. The latter often have rough heads, either waved or rest, Assegai, Aunurgitch, Awl Pike, Azagai, Bakin, Ballam, Bandang Barb, Barchi, Bhala, Bilari, Binaukan, Birch'ha, Birchi, Boar Spear, Bourdonasse, Budiak, Burr, Butt, Chee-a, Chimbane, Chogan, Chujagi, Contus, Coronal, Dekara, De-Ro, Do-War, Dung, Ecaio, Egchos, Ernangnak, Fal-

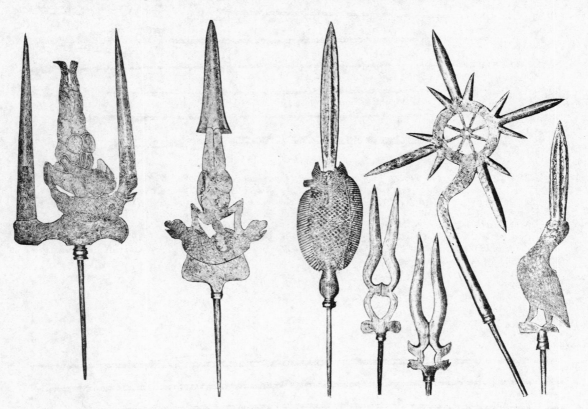

FIGURE 741. *Old Javan spearheads from Meyer and Uhle, Seltene Waffen.*

straight, quite like kris blades. The best are beautifully made and inlaid, fig. 740. Some of the old Javan spearheads were very elaborate, being like birds or men in grotesque attitudes, sometimes inlaid with gold. Fig. 741.

In parts of Malay and in Assam the spears are very large and of unusual shapes. Fig. 742.

The Japanese and Malayans always used sheaths for their spears, in fact the law required their use in Japan. The Malaya sheaths are carved and sometimes colored, fig. 743. Those of the Japanese were lacquered. Figs. 549, 587, 760.

For the different kinds and parts of spears, lances and javelins (except pole arms) see: Aclys, Agligak, Angon, Anguvigang, Apniniap, Armins, Ar-

Feg, Fang-Kao, Faucre, Fore Shaft, Framea, Fuscina, Futomata-Yari, Garvo, Gid-Jee, Golo, Gowdalie, Granggang, Gwae-Fon, Haguma, Hak, Halda, Harber, Harpoon, Hastilude, Hinyuan, Hirumaki, Ho, Hoko, Homyata, Hooked Spear, Huata, Hujiur, Igimu, Ipua, Irpull, Ishizuki, Jaculum, Ja-Mandehi, Janetaire, Jarid, Jarid Bazi, Javelin, Jiboru, Joust, Kadji, Kagi-Yari, Kahsita, Kai-Komi, Kalka, Kannai, Kan-Shoka, Kapun, Kay-Yan, Khatramkha, Kiero, Kikuki, Koanie, Koveh, Kowai Loko Dutna, Koyun, Koyung, Koy-Yun, Kuda-Yari, Kujoru, Kukigu, Kulkie, Kunjolio, Kuradan, Kuyan, Laange, Lance, Lance-Ague, Lance Rest, Larna-Pe, Lembing, Magari Yari, Magaroyu, Mahee, Makrigga, Ma-

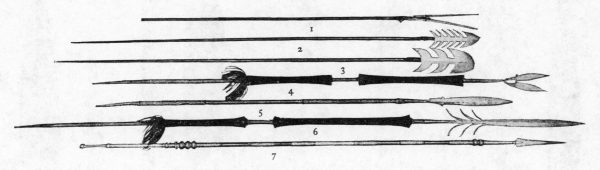

FIGURE 742. *Miscellaneous Spears. 1. Eskimo bird spear with three barbed bone points. 2. Engano. Head 8.25 x 3.5 inches. 3. Engano. Head 10 x 4.75 inches. 4. Assam. Double bladed head 12.5 inches long. Shaft covered with cut red hair. 5. Assam. Head, including socket, 19.5 inches long. Shaft covered with woven red and yellow grass. 6. Assam. Head 29 inches long. Shaft covered with cut red hair. Total length 9 feet 2 inches. 7. Sind. Black wood shaft almost covered with gilded copper and silver engraved in a diaper pattern.*

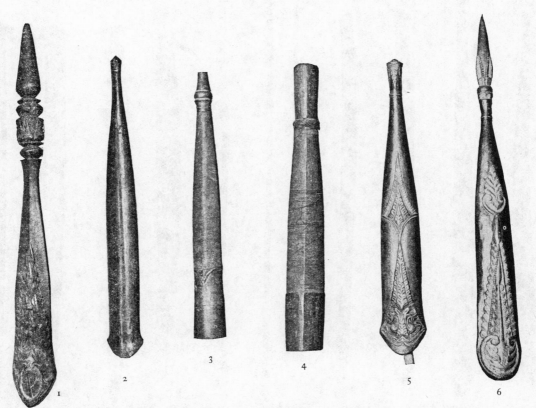

FIGURE 743. *Malayan Spear Scabbards. 1. Java. Well carved brown wood. 2. Java. Plain kajoe pelet. 3. Moro. Wood slightly carved. 4. Moro. Wood wound with thread. 5. Bali. Carved and painted with gold and red on a black ground. 6. Bali. Carved and gilded on a black ground.*

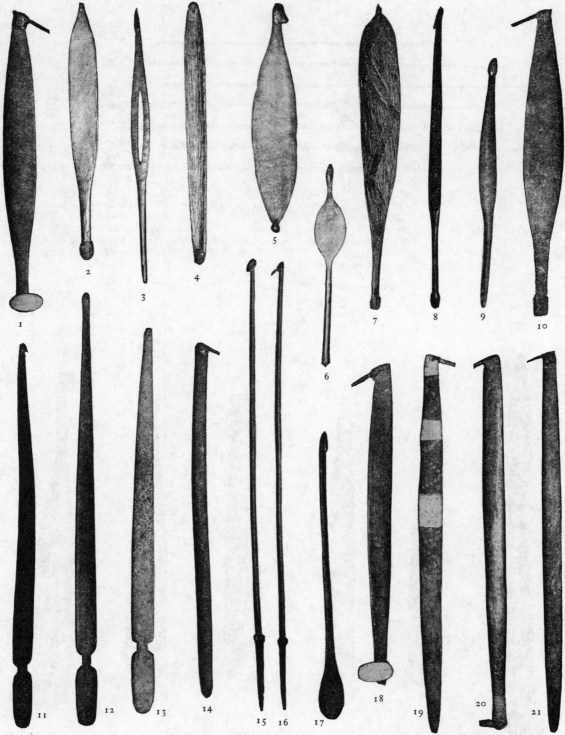

FIGURE 744. *Australian Spear Throwers.* 1. Borna, North Queensland. Flat blade 2 feet 5.625 inches long. Shell handle. 2. Amera, Central Australia. Concave surface carved with grooves. Gum handle with a quartzite blade set in it. 3. Probably New Guinea. Finely carved from one piece. There is a hook on the back at each end of the central opening. Length 28 inches, width 2 inches. 4. Australia. Semi-circular section, carved back and front. Gum handle, wood hook set in gum. 5. Flat blade 23 x 4.5 inches. Handle wound with cord and covered with gum. Wood point set in gum. 6. Kurruk, Australia. Slightly carved. Length 20.5 inches. The most widely distributed of Australian types. 7. West Australia. Broad carved blade 3.875 inches by 2 feet 5.75 inches. 8. Kurruk, Victoria. Brown wood carved with lines and figures. Length 2 feet 5.5 inches. 9. Kurruk. Victoria. Plain, 25 inches long. Bone point set in gum. 10. Northern Queensland. All wood. 11. Australia, probably the most widely distributed type. Length 3 feet 0.5 inch. Wanmaiia. 12. Wanmaiia similar to no. 11. 13. Wanmaiia, Kimberley region, West Australia. It is decorated with white dots and yellow figures on a red ground. 14. New South Wales. A straight, flat stick 2 feet 11.75 inches long by 1.375 wide. Long point fastened on with gum. 15. Kunjolio, Northern Territory. A round stick about half an inch in diameter and 3 feet 8.25 inches long. Gum handle and point. It is used with the reed spear called by the same name. 16. Kunjolio, similar to the last except that it has a bone point fastened on with gum. 17. Probably New Guinea. Black wood 2 feet 4 inches long, with a spatulate handle and a very heavy hook cut from the solid. 18. Arai-I, Queensland. A type of which there are many small modifications. 19. A variation of the same type without the shell handles. It is decorated with white bands and dots on a red ground. 20. Milbir, North Queensland. Similar to the last but with a short wooden handle. 21. The same type but perfectly plain.

kura Yari, Mandehi, Mandehi Ciguje, Marek, Mian, Mkuki, Mon-Gil Mon-Gil, Mongile, Mongoli, Mori, Morne, Mulon, Munjan Jil, Mu-Rongal, Nagamaki, Nagaye, Nageyari, Naginata, Na- So-kan, Soket, Soki, Sopok, Spear Thrower, Spiculum, Sudis, Suji-Gane, Su-Yari, Tahr Ladok, Tahr Ruan, Take-Yari, Tampo, Tao, Tarronie, Taru, Tawok, Te-Boko, Telempang, Te-Yari,

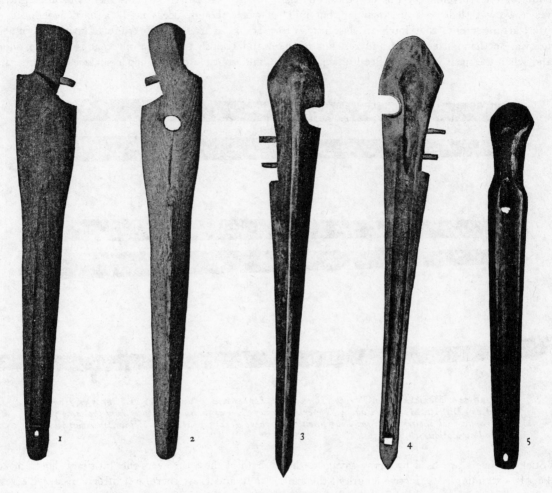

FIGURE 745. *Eskimo Spear Throwers.* 1, 2. *Front and back of thrower with one peg and finger hole. Length 19.5 inches.* 3, 4. *Front and back of two peg thrower. Length 19.5 inches.* 5. *Eskimo type of thrower, Vancouver. The first two are from Alaska.*

ginata-No-Saki, Nandum, Nerau, Neza, Nuikpai, Omayari, Pandi Ballam, Paralyser, Patisthanaya, Pelta, Pencil, Pendewan, Penoncel, Pheon, Pike, Pilani, Pilete, Pillara, Pilum, Po-Ini, Prasa, Qatirn, Qijugtenga, Queue, Rummh, Salapang, Sang, Sang: Sanger, Sangkoh, Sangu, Santie, Sarapang, Sarissa, Sasu-Mata, Saunion, Sei-Ryo-Ken, Serepang, Shaft, Shail, Shanen Kopaton, Shanen Mong-Heang, Shinpung, Sigagut, Siligis, Simbilan, Sinalawitan, Sinan, Sinnock, Sisili Milak, Sligi, So-Jutsu, Tika, Tilloo, Torok, Tirrer, Tjunkuletti, Toemba, Toemba Djangat, Toembak, Toggle Iron, Toho, Tokang, To-Ono, Toyle, Trident, Trisul, Tsukushi-Boko, Tsukushi Naginata, Tumba, Tumbak, Tumpuling, Tuu, Uchi-Ne, Ukumalita, Uluwa, Um Konto, Una, Vamplate, Vericulum, Wainian, Waisko-Dusa, Wallunka, Werranee, Wi-Valli, Wormegoram, Wor-Poi, Yari, Yari-Ate, Yari-Saki, Yeripul, Yirmba, Yugo, Yumi Yari, Zagaye.

SPEAR THROWER. Some means of assisting the human hand in throwing a spear has been used in many widely separated places. The Greeks used a strap, the *ankule*, fastened permanently to the middle of their javelins for this purpose. The natives of New Caledonia have a similar, but much better, arrangement; they hitch an elastic strap to the spear so that it frees itself and remains in the hand when the spear is thrown. See Ounep.

straight, flattened piece of wood with a point of wood or bone fastened to one end by means of resin or beeswax. At the opposite end the thrower is cut away on both sides to form a handle that can be easily grasped. It is usually made of some light, soft wood though occasionally a hard wood, such as acacia, is used. The Arunta, Luritja, Unmatjera and Kaitish tribes use one that is broader, shorter and concave on the upper surface, see Amera. In

FIGURE 746. *Mexican Spear Throwers, Atlatl.* 1. *Upper and* 3 *lower sides of a thrower from the Mixtecan District, Mexico.* 2 *and* 4. *Upper and lower sides of another thrower from the same place.* 5. *From a rock shelter at Allied Bluff, Benten County, Arkansas. Museum of the American Indian, Heye Foundation.*

Stick throwers are used by many savages; they all act by extending the effective length of the arm. A description of using one type of Australian thrower will illustrate the method. "When in use the native first holds the thrower with his right arm well back and low down. With his left he supports the spear as far along its length as he can reach. The right arm is raised, and the left hand removed from the spear, which is then poised on the thrower, supported only by the man's thumb and forefinger. As the thrower is brought into play and used as a lever, the finger and thumb let go of the spear, which is then propelled forward by the thrower." (Spencer & Gillen 668).

There are five general forms of spear thrower used by the Australian tribes. The commonest is a

both of these throwers the flat side is held horizontally and they, therefore, offer considerable resistance to the air. In the north the throwers are held with the flat side vertical so that the edge is opposed to the air and they are much more effective. They are straight, or slightly curved, sticks about two inches wide, a quarter of an inch thick and thirty to forty inches long. The peg is lashed, cemented, or both, to the end of the stick and projects above it. The other end may be plain or have a handle of two oval pieces of shell fastened to it at any angle. In the east the thrower is a stick with a large tassel of human hair string for a handle, see Purtanji. Among the tribes near the Daly River a still simpler type is used. The shaft is round and tapers to a point at the handle end. At the other end there is a lump of resin worked into a point that fits into a hollow in the butt of the spear. About six inches from the pointed end there is a raised ring of resin, and from this to the end is wound a flat strip of resin which offers a good grip for the hand. Fig. 744.

The Eskimo spear throwers are considerably more elaborate. They have ivory points to fit in the notch at the end of the spear, or projecting points,

The Australian blacks have some curious superstitions regarding throwers: "In case of spear throwing among the Ducie blacks, if a small piece of human flesh be fixed to the womera (thrower), between the two shells forming the handle, the spear will never err in its flight. In the same way the Olkulo blacks, on the northern extremity of Princess Charlotte Bay, will fix a piece of human bone on the spear thrower for luck when after kangaroo

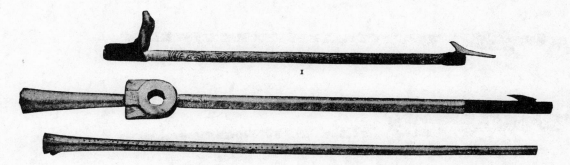

FIGURE 747. *Peruvian Spear Throwers.* 1. *Length about 17 inches. The bird on the end is of gold. The mountings of the others are of copper or bronze. Museum of the American Indian, Heye Foundation.*

to fit in holes in it. The handle ends are quite complicated, being carved to fit the fingers and often have a hole for the thumb. The Eskimo requires a good and secure hold as he, and all of his belongings, are usually greasy, and his hands and spear thrower are generally wet and slippery. The carved handle gives an excellent hold. Fig. 745. See U. S. N. M. 1884, 279.

The ancient Mexicans used very elaborate throwers, and similar but much simpler ones are still in use in some places, 2, fig. 746, 748. They are straight and have an enlargement close to the handle with two finger holes in it, or else have cord loops for the fingers. See Atlatl and Arc. f. Eth. III, 234.

The New Guinea throwers are pieces of bamboo cut away on one side and having large carved ornaments projecting from the top. Fig. 748.

Some of the early Peruvian throwers are about the finest used anywhere, having very beautiful mountings of bronze or sometimes of gold, fig. 747. K. Bahnson (Arc. f. Eth. II, 217) describes some as semi-cylindrical, tapering pieces of wood about twenty-eight inches long and grooved on one side. The groove is closed at the narrow end to bear against the end of the spear.

or emu. At Cape York the flight of the spear will be absolutely true if the thrower (man) swallows some ground quartz crystals." (W. E. Roth, No. 5, p. 27).

There is an excellent and fully illustrated article on Spear Throwers by F. Krause in the Archiv. fur Ethnographie XV, p. 121.

SPETUM. A pole arm of the 16th century. It has a long, narrow blade with curved lateral projections at the base. It is often confused with other members of the korseke family to which it belongs. The name is said to be derived from the Italian *spido*, a spit. (Hewitt III, 603).

SPICULUM. A light Roman javelin. (Burton Sword 246).

SPIDER HELMET. An open helmet of the 17th century surrounded by hinged bars that can be turned up to rest against the crown or down to protect the face and sides of the head. Fig. 749.

SPINGARDA, SPINGARDELLA. A large crossbow mounted on wheels much as field guns are today, 14th century. (Hewitt I, 363).

SPLINTS, SPLINTED ARMOR. Armor made of narrow plates or splints riveted together, or to a backing of cloth or leather, so as to be flexible. (ffoulkes 33, 41). Similarly constructed armor was worn in Turkey and China.

rowel, or toothed wheel, was not developed until the 14th century. (Denison 153). The prick spur changed but little from B.C. 700 to B.C. 200, when

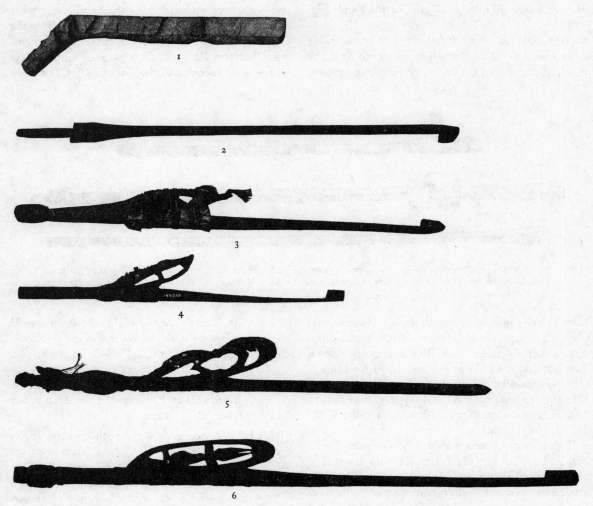

FIGURE 748. *Miscellaneous Spear Throwers. 1. Siberia, Eskimo. 2. Terescan, Mexico. (From Janicho, Michoacan.) 3, 4, 5, 6. North Coast of New Guinea. Field Museum, Chicago.*

SPONTOON. A half pike. Many look like small partizans. The spontoon was carried by color sergeants in the British army until the end of the 18th century. (ffoulkes 106). Fig. 750.

SPRIGHTS. See Musquet Arrow.

SPRINGALD, ESPRINGALD. An engine for throwing stones and bolts. It was used on both sea and land in the 14th century. (Hewitt II, 275).

SPUR. The earliest form was the "pryck spur," or one with a single straight point. The spur with a

in one line of development the heel plates became longer and fitted the foot better. In another line the spike became much longer, so much so as to become dangerous to the horse, and was modified by making it more blunt, or by putting a stop on it to prevent it from going too deeply into the horse's body. (About 1100 A.D.). Similar spurs with stops are still used in Morocco. In the middle ages spurs developed on several lines. While horse armor was used the necks became greatly elongated to enable the rider to reach his mount under the bardings.

The rowels of some attained enormous size about the year 1600. Later they again became smaller until at the present day some are almost microscopic.

FIGURE 749. *Spider Helmet, French, 17th century. The hanging bars are hinged and can be folded back over the crown. Metropolitan Museum.*

In some cases the number of rowels was increased to two, three, five or even more. Fig. 751.

The South American and Mexican spurs are of the Spanish type and have very large rowels with jingles. Some of the South American rowels are six inches in diameter and very sharp. Nearly all of the Eastern nations use some variation of the Arab spur, a single long point with or without a stop. Fig. 752.

The parts of the spur are: the rowel, or toothed wheel, that goads the horse. This is supported by a fork called the rowel box. This in turn is carried on the end of the neck or piece projecting from the heel. The ridge is an ornament on the upper side of the neck. The heel plate covers the heel and is connected to the sides. The latter terminate in the strap plates and studs to which the straps are fastened. The top of the heel plate is called the crest. Some spurs have two pieces on the rowel box that swing loosely and are called jingles. They are characteristic of the Spanish and Mexican spurs. (Dean, Bul. M. M., vol. XI, 217).

SQUAMATA. Roman armor of scales sewed on cloth or leather. (Burton Sword 248). Precisely similar armor was worn in China within the last century. Fig. 29.

SRESNI. An ancient type of Russian arrow with a broad, shovel-shaped head. (Scheremetew 122).

STAFF SLING. A sling mounted on a pole. See Fustibal.

STAKE, ARCHER'S. Pointed stakes about six feet long that were carried by archers in the 15th century to plant in the ground as a defense against cavalry. (Hewitt II, 528).

FIGURE 750. *Spontoons. 1. Russian, about 1700. 2. Maltese, 18th century. 3. German, Brunswick, 18th century. 4. French, about 1725. 5. Italian, 17th century. 6. Italian, about 1590. 7. German. Arms of the Landgraf von Fuerstenberg. Metropolitan Museum. Not to scale.*

FIGURE 751. *European Spurs.* 1. *Italian or French, 15th century.* 2. *French, end of the 16th century.* 3. *Spanish, 17th century. It has one very large and two small rowels.* 4. *Spanish, 17th century. It has an enormous rowel with six very long spikes.* 5. *French, 15th century.* 6. *French, 16th century. It has two rowels side by side.* 7. *Tilting spur (right). German, early 16th century.* 8. *French, 14th century. It bears the arms of de Dreux.* 9. *French, 17th century. Metropolitan Museum. In nearly all cases the Museum possesses the pair, although but one is shown here.*

STANDARDS. Standards have been used from the time of the Assyrians and Egyptians. The earliest were representations of some animal or other object carried on a pole. The earliest Persian standard was a blacksmith's apron. In the 15th century the royal standard was square while those of the subjects were forked. The size of the standard in the time of Henry VII varied with the rank of the owner. The royal standard was from eight to eleven yards long, that of a duke seven yards, of a banneret four and a half, and that of a knight bachelor four yards. All tapered towards the fly. (Macgeorge 36).

In the middle ages standards at first were large flags fixed on the tops of towers or other elevated positions; later they were made movable but still retained the same name. Among the Turks and Tartars the *bunchuk*, or horse-tailed standard, was the mark of high authority; the higher the rank the greater the number of tails. It was sometimes sent as a symbol to compel obedience. The Poles copied this standard from their eastern neighbors.

STANDARD OF MAIL. A collaret of mail worn

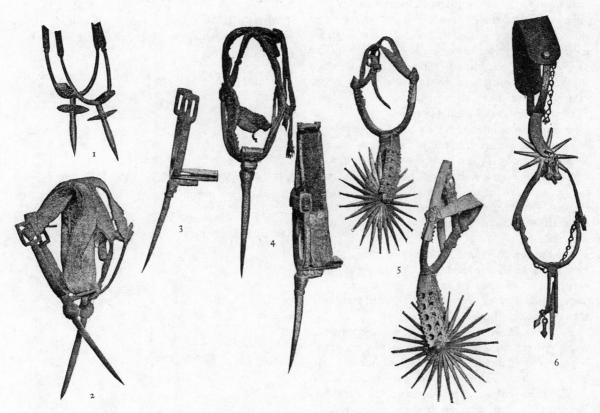

FIGURE 752. *Miscellaneous Spurs.* 1. *Morocco. Arab spurs with round stops.* 2. *Morocco. Very rough, heavy spurs.* 3. *Arab spur decorated with a chased silver plate set with coral.* 4. *A pair of Arab spurs. The straps are covered with velvet and the spurs are set with diamonds.* 5. *Chili. The rowels are six inches in diameter and have twenty-four points. The frames inlaid, and partly covered with white metal.* 6. *Mexican. Plain steel with jingles and broad leathers.*

under a plate gorget in the early 15th century. (ffoulkes 68).

STARI. An axe, Western Tibet. (Ramsay-Western).

STAVES. Pole arms, the *"armes d'haste"* of the French. They are also called shafted weapons.

STESSO TEMPO. Single time in fencing, that is, parrying and returning with a single action. (Castle 99).

ST. GEORGE'S GUARD. The head parry, so

called because St. George is usually represented in this position when slaying the dragon. (Castle 220).

STILETTO. A small dagger with a slender blade intended solely for thrusting. Fig. 753.

STIRRUPS. Stirrups were not used by cavalry until the end of the 6th century. (Denison 70). When once introduced their advantage was so obvious that their use spread very rapidly and they have been almost universally used by horsemen everywhere. The simplest stirrup is a knot on the end of a rope which is held between the toes. It was used by the North American Indians and in several parts of the East. It was used in Java within a very few years. In Europe and throughout the East stirrups are almost always made of metal, but in parts of South America and Mexico they were frequently made of wood and are large and elaborately carved. In Europe the general style of the stirrups followed the development of armor very closely, and since its abandonment they have become very simple and purely utilitarian.

In Turkey and the Near East the stirrups were very large with huge treads with sharp corners that were sometimes used as spurs. In general the later ones are the smaller. Very similar stirrups were used throughout the Turkish Empire.

In China, Korea and Tibet the stirrups have the same general shape as the European but are much heavier and frequently have dragons' heads on the top of the bows. The foot plates are much larger, usually oval with a raised edge and are sometimes lined with cork to keep the feet from slipping.

For the Japanese stirrups, see Abumi.

The stirrups of Central India have low, wide bows and rectangular treads that are often pierced. The Javan stirrups are quite similar to the Indian but have oval foot plates. Figs. 754, 755.

The most curious of the European forms are the "conquistador" stirrups with large, pierced projections downward and sideways. They are said to have been used by the early Spanish invaders as weapons to strike with when riding down the natives. Fig. 756.

STIRRUP CROSSBOW. The large crossbows had stirrups on the ends in which to put the foot to steady the weapon while winding it up with a winch the management of which required the use of both hands. Fig. 19.

STOCCATA. In the 16th century a thrust reaching the enemy under the sword, dagger or hand, delivered with the hand in any position. (Castle 84).

STOCCATA LUNGA. The modern lunge. (Castle 113).

STOCK, STUCK. See Estoc.

STONE BOW. This name was applied to both long and crossbows used for shooting stones, pellets or balls.

STONE SHOT. In the early days of cannon the balls were always made of stone. Some weighed as much as twelve hundred pounds.

STOOP. Making a dash at a quarry by a hawk.

STRADIOT. See Estradiot and Eared Dagger.

STRAMAZONE, TRAMAZONE. A tearing cut with the extreme point. (Castle 135).

STRIKE. Hawks of the genus *falco* make a rapid dash at their quarry from above and strike it with

FIGURE 753. *Stiletto, Spanish or Italian, 17th century. Metropolitan Museum.*

their feet and hind talons, killing or knocking the wind out of it. This is to "strike" as distinguished from "binding" or seizing with the claws as the other varieties of hawks do.

SUBLIGALLICUM. The apron worn by Roman gladiators who, armed with a shield and three-thonged scourge, fought with one armed with sword and shield but otherwise naked. (Burton Sword 253).

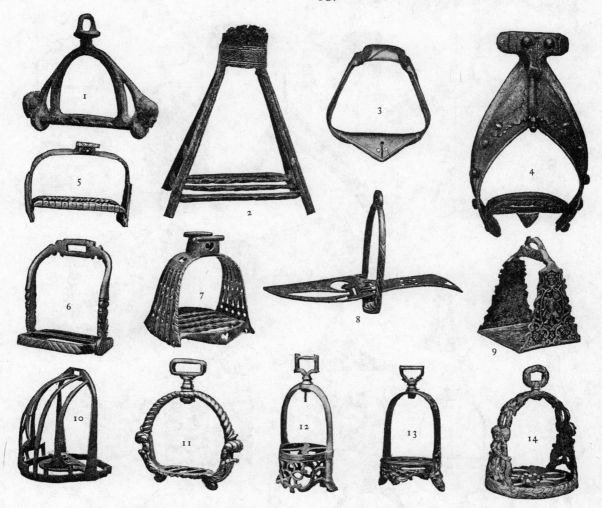

FIGURE 754. *European Stirrups.* 1. *Classical.* 2. *Italian, 14th century.* 3. *French, early 15th century.* 4. *Italian(?), 15th century.* 5. *German, 1510.* 6. *Italian, 17th century.* 7. *Spanish, first half of the 16th century.* 8. *French, 16th century.* 9. *French, 17th century.* 10. *German(?), 17th century.* 11. *French, end of the 17th century.* 12. *Spanish, 17th-18th century.* 13. *French, 1700.* 14. *French, 18th century. Metropolitan Museum.*

STEELY. An arrow, Russian, class name. (Scheremetew 119).

SUAN-TOU-FUNG. A Chinese mace consisting of a straight bar with a globular or polygonal head. See Mace.

SUBEKI, KU. To test a bow by drawing it without an arrow, Japan.

SUDARE-SUNE-ATE, SHINODATE-SUNE-ATE. Japanese greaves composed of alternate strips of mail and plates, usually about eight. (Conder 276).

SUDAS. See Ranjau. (Kepple I, 172).

SUDIS. A pike of the 12th century. (Hewitt I, 155).

FIGURE 755. *Miscellaneous Stirrups.* 1. *Turkish, 16th and 17th centuries. Foot plates 14.25 inches long, 5 inches wide in the middle and 8.5 at the ends. Iron inlaid with gold.* 2. *Turkey, 18th century. Chased, pierced and gilded brass.* 3. *Java, 18th century. Brass stirrups with oval foot plates and braced bows.* 4. *Central India, 19th century. Very light stirrups of native make copied from the European.* 5. *Central India, 17th and 18th centuries. Brass moulded.* 6. *South America, west coast. Carved wood.* 7. *Haussa, Africa. Cast brass with a loop for the lance on one.* 8. *Spanish mule stirrups. Wood with pierced brass plates.* 9. *Central India, 17th and 18th centuries. Cast brass, much decorated.* 10. *Tunis, 18th century. Pair of light brass stirrups with projections on one side to be used as spurs.* 11. *South America. Carved wood.* 12. *Tibet, 18th century. Chinese type. Iron with dragon's heads on the bows.* 13. *Morocco. Brass with coils of silver wire in relief.* 14. *Morocco. Silver plated iron.* 15. *Mexico. Carved and colored wood.* 16. *China. Cloisonné, 19th century.* 17. *China, 17th century. Iron heavily gilded. Dragon's heads on the bows. Cork linings in the footplates.* 18. *India, 19th century. Troopers' stirrups with rings for the lance butt on the side.* 19. *India. Troopers' stirrup. Two loops to which to fasten a lance bucket on the side.*

SUGAKE-DO-MARU. See Kebike-Do-Maru.

SUGAR-LOAF HELM. The pointed helmet that replaced the flat-topped one of the 12th century. (ffoulkes 27).

FIGURE 756. *Conquistador stirrup, 17th century. Probably Mexican. Metropolitan Museum.*

SUGUCHI. The muzzle of a gun, Japan.

SUGUHA. See Yakiba.

SUIBA ABUMI. Literally "crossing a river on horseback stirrups." Stirrups with openings in the foot plates to let the water out after riding through a stream, Japan. (M. M. S. II, 228). 5, fig. 1.

SUITO. A canteen, Japan. It was shaped much like the European form, being round and flat. It was usually lacquered and often inlaid with shell.

SUJI-GANE. Strips of metal on the shaft of a pole arm to keep it from being cut, Japan.

SUKASHI. Ornamental openwork, pierced work, Japan.

SUKE-HIRO. A celebrated Japanese sword maker of the latter part of the 17th century. He also made arrowheads.

SULTANI. A heavy, clumsy sword with a slightly curved blade, southern India, 18th century. (Egerton, p. 123).

SUMA. The Turkish pistol ramrod carried hung from the belt and not in loops on the pistol. They were usually ornamental as well as useful, the handles, if not the entire ramrod, being generally decorated. The body was often the sheath for a three, or four, sided poniard, or a pair of tongs for lighting the pipe. Fig. 757.

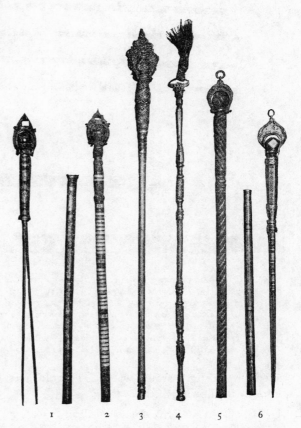

FIGURE 757. *Suma. 1. Steel body and brass handle inlaid with horn. A cap on the lower end covers a screw for drawing charges. The body is hollow and contains a pair of tongs. 2. Bronze ends connected by a rod covered with disks of green and white ivory separated by thinner disks of black horn. Length 14 inches. 3. Body of plain steel, handle of chased silver partly gilded. Length 19 inches. 4. All steel. At two points it is pierced by slots, probably for use as a cleaning rod. 5. Silver gilt decorated with a spiral moulding. The body is hollow and is the sheath for a four-sided poniard. 6. Hollow steel body forming the sheath of a triangular poniard, the upper part is round and inlaid with brass. The handle and sling loop are of silver decorated with chern. From the Caucasus.*

SUMBUT, SAMVAT. The era of Bikramajet (Vicramaditya) beginning B.C. 56. It is the common basis of Hindu chronology. The year is of 365 days.

SUMI-NAGASHI. "Ink on the water." A mokume of copper and shakudo with waving incised lines of gold. It is said to represent paint floating on

chosen and felled the tree, often one of large size, the craftsman splits from it pieces about eight feet in length. Such a piece is shaved with an adze until it is roughly cylindrical and three or four inches in diameter. The piece may be carried home to be worked at leisure, or the boring may be done on the spot. A platform is erected about seven feet from

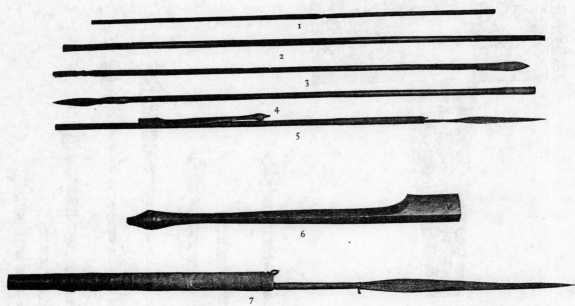

FIGURE 758. *Sumpitan. 1. Light blowpipe made of two joints of cane connected by a sleeve of the same. 2. Blowpipe of dark, polished wood. 3. Black wood 5 feet 1 inch long, with a spearhead 7.25 inches long lashed to it with brass wire, sight of brass wire. The mouthpiece is missing. 4. Similar to the last except that the lashing is of cane and it has a bamboo mouthpiece decorated with incised patterns in black. 5. Dark wood blowpipe 4 feet 5 inches long with a wire sight and a brass ferule at the mouthpiece. Spearhead 17 inches long attached; wooden sheath stained black. 6. The sheath of no. 5. 7. Detail of sight and spearhead of no. 5.*

water for making marbled water. The gold lines represent the flowing of the water.

SUMI ZOGAN. (Ink inlay). Inlaying with a dark metal in a lighter one. Its invention is attributed to Mura-Kami Jo-Chiku, second half of the 18th century. (Weber II, 343). See 1, fig. 478.

SUMMED, FULL SUMMED. Said of a hawk when she has grown all of her new feathers after moulting. (Phillott 40, note).

SUMPITAN, SUMPIT. The blowpipe of the Dyaks of Borneo. It is a wooden tube five to eight feet long with a bore of about three-eighths of an inch. "The best sumpitans are made of the hard, straight-grained wood of the *Jagang* tree. Having

the ground, and the prepared rod is fixed vertically with the upper end projecting through the platform and the lower resting on the ground. Its upper end is lashed to the platform, its lower end to a pair of stout poles lashed horizontally to trees, and its middle to another pair of poles similarly fixed. The next operation, the boring of the wood, is accomplished by the aid of a straight rod of iron about nine feet long, of slightly smaller diameter than the bore desired for the pipe and having one end chisel-shaped and sharpened. One man standing on the platform holds the iron rod vertically above the end of the wood, and brings its sharp chisel edge down upon the center of the flat surface, lifting the rod with both hands, he repeats the blow again and again, slightly turning the rod at each blow. He is aided in keeping the rod truly vertical by two or three forked sticks fixed horizontally at different levels above the platform in such a way that the vertical rod slips up and down in the forks which thus serve as guides. The rod soon bites its way into the wood. An assistant, squatting on the platform with a bark bucket of water beside him, ladles the water into the hole after every two or three strokes, and thus causes the chips to float out. This operation steadily pursued for about six hours completes the boring. In boring the lower part the craftsman aims at producing a slight curvature of the tube by slightly bending the pole and lashing it in the bent position; the pole, being released, then straightens itself, and at the same time produces the desired slight curvature of the bore. This curvature is necessary in order to allow for the bending of the blowpipe when in use, by the weight of the spear blade which is lashed on bayonet fashion. . . . It only remains to whittle down the rough surface to a smooth cylinder slightly tapering towards the muzzle, to polish the pipe inside and out, to lash the spear blade to the muzzle end with a strip of rattan, and to attach a small wooden sight to the muzzle opposite the spear blade." (Hose 216). Fig. 758.

The darts are made of the wood of the *nibong* or wild sago palm. They are about nine inches long, and from an eighth to a sixteenth of an inch in diameter, and have a pith cone on the end that accurately fits the bore of the blowpipe. The darts are poisoned with *ipoh* (Q.V.). They are carried in cases made of a section of bamboo with a tight fitting cover of the same or of wood. It is neatly covered with braids of rattan which hold the wooden hook by which it is hung from the belt. The darts are called *langa*, and the case *tolor*.

The Sakai, a pagan tribe of the Malay Peninsula, make excellent built-up blowpipes. The inner tube is made of the long-jointed bamboo (*Bambusa Wrayi*). At a few places this is found with long enough joints to form the tube of a single one; usually, however, they are shorter and it is necessary to use two, one of which is always longer than the other. The ends of the two pieces are tapered and a short piece tapered in the opposite direction is fitted between them. The outer tube is made of the same material, but is in one piece, a node being punched out and the inside smoothed by drawing prickly rattan backwards and forwards through it until it is just large enough to fit snugly over the inner tube. It is fitted with a wooden mouthpiece. The Samang, another pagan tribe of the same region, make similar blowpipes but do not finish them as well. The Jakun, an aboriginal Malayan tribe, make two quite different types of blowpipe. The first is made of two joints of the *semeliang* bamboo, the nodes of which are much shorter than those of the *wrayi*. The two pieces are butted together and the joint wrapped with a rag smeared with resin and then coated with gutta-percha; an outer casing is made of the mid-rib of the leaf of the *langkap* palm and is drawn over the built-up inner tube. The mouthpiece is of gutta-percha or of wood covered with it. They are said to be the poorest blowpipes made in the Peninsula. The second type is made from a cylinder of hard wood which is split lengthwise, and the halves grooved so that when placed together they make a straight tube. They are bound tightly from end to end with a long strip of cane which is thickly covered with some gutta-percha-like substance to protect it and prevent its getting loose, as well as to close any cracks that would otherwise leak air. In some cases an outer casing of bamboo is used over the lashings.

The bore of a well made blowpipe is always slightly smaller at the muzzle than at the mouthpiece. In the bamboo tubes the natural taper insures this as the root end is always the mouthpiece; in the wooden tubes the same result is obtained by care in cutting the grooves. Unlike the Dyak weapon the blowpipes of the Peninsula do not have sights, nor are they fitted with spearheads.

In shooting the tube is held with both hands close together and close to the end. The entire mouthpiece is sometimes placed in the mouth. It is said that a dart can be propelled for eighty yards, but the usual working range is only about fifteen or twenty.

Both blowpipes and quivers are usually decorated with elaborate patterns of incised lines. These patterns are quite characteristic and have definite meanings for their makers. A cleaning rod of palm wood, with strips of leaves threaded through perforations near the end, is regularly used by some tribes. It is usual to keep the muzzle stopped with leaves to keep out white ants and the small wild bees, called *kekulut*, a very necessary precaution in the Malay Peninsula.

SUNDANG. See Sondang.

SUNE-ATE, SHINO-DZUTSU. Japanese shin guards. The front is usually made of pieces of leather or metal hinged together, and the back of pad-

the inner side of the leg where it comes against the stirrup. (Garbutt 139). Fig. 759.

SUPERNUMERARII. Light-armed Roman troops. (Burton Sword 256).

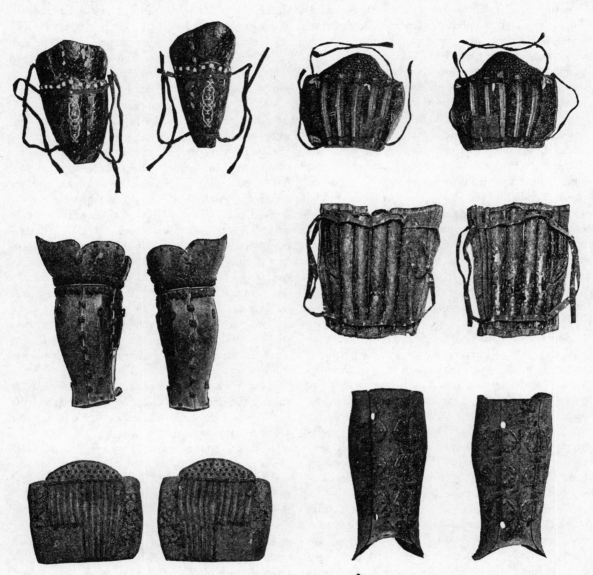

FIGURE 759. *Sune-Ate. Seventeenth to nineteenth centuries. Metropolitan Museum. Not to scale.*

ded cloth. In a few cases it is entirely of metal. In some of the earlier ones there was a broad plate projecting upwards and backwards from the knee to protect the thigh when on horseback. Fig. 79.

There are a number of kinds: Shino-Dzutsu, Odate-Agayemon, etc. All have leather guards on

SUPINATION. In fencing the position of the hand with the nails turned upwards. (Castle 10).

SURAI. A Mahratta sword, straight for two-thirds of its length and curved for the remainder. (Sinclair, I. A. II, 216).

SURALOCA. The Rajput warrior's heaven. (Tod II, 421).

SURCOAT. A military garment worn over armor in the 13th and 14th centuries. It was a loose tunic and, like the hauberk, was split up to the waist, front and back, for convenience on horseback. It was frequently decorated with the armorial bearings of the wearer. (ffoulkes 23, 25).

The Japanese wore a similar garment. See Jimbaori.

does of four and one-half feet in length, headed with sharp forked heads of six inches length, and a sharp iron foot to stick into the ground for their defense against horse." In some cases they were made entirely of iron. These were occasionally carried inside the musket rest. (Hewitt III, 720, 744).

SWORD. The effectiveness of the sword as a weapon, both of offense and defense, the ease with which it could be carried, and the opportunities that

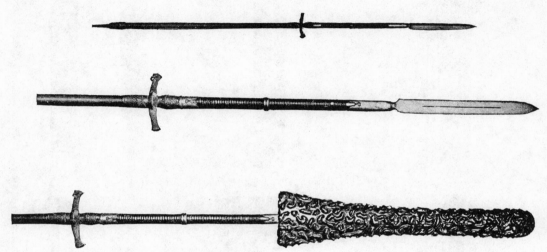

FIGURE 760. *Su Yari. Triangular head 6.75 inches long, wooden shaft with silver mountings. Length over all 5 feet 5.5 inches. Sheath 20.5 inches long, carved and lacquered red.*

SU YARI and OMI YARI. Japanese spears with straight blades. (B. M. Hdbk. 54). Fig. 760.

SUYE-HA. A Japanese method of making blades.

SUZU. Hawk's bells, Japan.
    Tin, Japan.

SUZUKAKE. A coat worn by Yamabushi.

SUZUME YUMI. A small bow used for amusement, Japan.

SWEPT HILT. A form of hilt often used with 17th-century rapiers in which a number of slender, intertwined guards formed a basket that "swept" around the hand. (Dean Hdbk. 74). Fig. 617.

SWEYNE'S FEATHERS, SWEDISH FEATHERS, PIG'S FEATHERS. Long iron spikes carried by musketeers in the 17th century as a defense against cavalry. "Each dragoonier should carry at his girdle two swyn feathers or foot palisa-

it presents for display in the ornamentation of blade, hilt, scabbard and belt, long made it a favorite with all metal-using nations. This is amply proved by the numerous references to it in literature where it typifies arms, power and bravery. In spite of this there is no definition of the sword, that is, none that differentiates it from all other weapons. The reason is simple—the series of knife, sword, espadon and glaive is an unbroken one, and there is no point that can be agreed upon as that at which a division should always be made. Neither length of blade, kind of hilt nor method of use define it—all overlap. In the majority of cases it is easy to classify a given weapon, but many are on the border line.

Swords may be divided into three classes: those for cutting only, those for thrusting only, and those for both cutting and thrusting. The cutting sword is undoubtedly the oldest, being an evolution from the club. Later, when it had been learned that a thrust was more effective and required less exer-

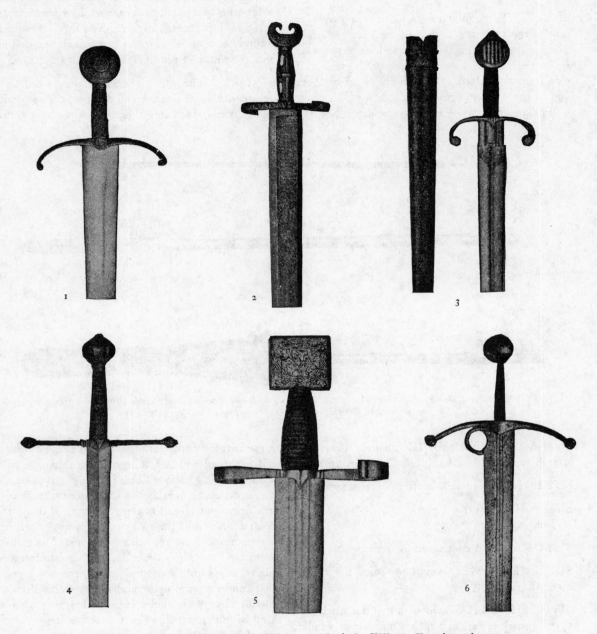

FIGURE 761. *Early European Swords.* 1. *German, end of the XIV.* 2. *Venetian, about 1500.* 3. *French, 1510.* 4. *Italian, 1520.* 5. *Spanish, end of the XV.* 6. *French, XV. Metropolitan Museum. Not to scale.*

tion than a cut, the design was modified to make it available for both. When the development of fencing made skill superior to brute force, swords were made solely for thrusting.

A sword broadly consists of two parts, the blade and the hilt. The former is subdivided into the tang, or portion of the blade that fits into the hilt, and the blade proper. The latter is again subdivided (starting at the hilt) into the strong, half strong, half weak and weak. The lengths of these parts being, respectively, about 22, 22, 37 and 19 per cent of the length of the blade. Sometimes the division is simpler being into forte and faible, or strong and weak. The blade is also divided into the edge, point, back and false edge. The latter is the sharpened portion of the back near the point in many single-edged swords. Most of the early rapiers have also the ricasso or squared portion between the tang and blade. Various forms of guard have names of their own. See Guard.

There are five methods in common use for attaching the hilt to the blade. In the first the tang, which is quite small, passes entirely through the solid hilt and is riveted over the outside of the pommel. This gives a very secure attachment and is the method generally employed in Europe. The next is to rivet pieces forming the grip to each side of the flat tang. This is fully as strong as the first and is very common on the swords of the Near East. The Japanese method is to attach the hilt by a single removable wooden peg through both tang and hilt. This gives a much stronger and more rigid attachment than would seem probable, but requires first-class materials and workmanship. The fourth method is to rivet the blade to projections from the hilt; it is used mainly in India, particularly in the south. It is secure but clumsy. The last method is to cement the tang into the hollow hilt. It is used mainly, but very generally, in the Far East. It gives a good and secure hold provided the right kind of cement is properly applied. Occasionally swords are made with the hilt and blade forged in one piece.

Swords intended solely for cutting nearly always have curved blades. They are very rarely double-edged, but often have a false edge. They may be sharp on either the convex or concave side. Those intended for the drawcut are always sharp on the convex side. The extreme example of this form is the Persian shamshir, the curve of which corresponds so accurately to the motion of the arm that the longest possible cut can be made with it. It is very rarely used for slashing. Straight swords without points are used in many parts of the East; they are both double and single edged. Slightly curved blades belong, as a rule, to the third class.

Swords sharp on the concave side, like the yatagan, have a large part of their weight beyond the center of percussion (roughly at one-third of the length from the point) which makes it possible to give a more powerful blow with them than with any other type of sword. On the other hand they have the disadvantage of being nearly useless for either the thrust or the drawcut. Many of the lighter races of the East have carried this principle to excess and concentrate the greater part of the weight near the point. The Gurka kora is probably the extreme example of this.

Swords intended solely for thrusting always have straight blades. The section of the earlier ones was either a very flat diamond or was bounded by two arcs of circles of opposite curvature meeting at the edges. In many cases they were lightened by grooves on the sides of the blades. Later the triangular and diamond-shaped blades with concave faces were adopted to give the maximum of stiffness with the minimum of weight. The colichemarde of the last half of the 17th century often had the grooved triangular section for about a third of its length from the hilt and suddenly changed to a very light section bounded by two slightly curved faces. It was extremely light and one of the best fencing weapons ever made. Blades of all kinds were frequently lightened by grooves arranged in a great variety of ways. Many of the sections so formed proved unsuitable and were abandoned.

Swords intended for both cutting and thrusting were never as efficient for either as those made for a single purpose, but are often more generally useful than the more specialized forms. They may have either straight or slightly curved blades. The former are generally double-edged, except when the form of the hilt makes it impossible to use them for a sweeping cut in more than one direction, in which case they usually have a false edge. About the only strongly curved sword that can be used for thrusting is the Turkish kilij, the back of which is straight near the point and has a false edge. While it can be used for thrusting it is neither convenient nor efficient for the purpose.

For the early European swords see fig. 761.

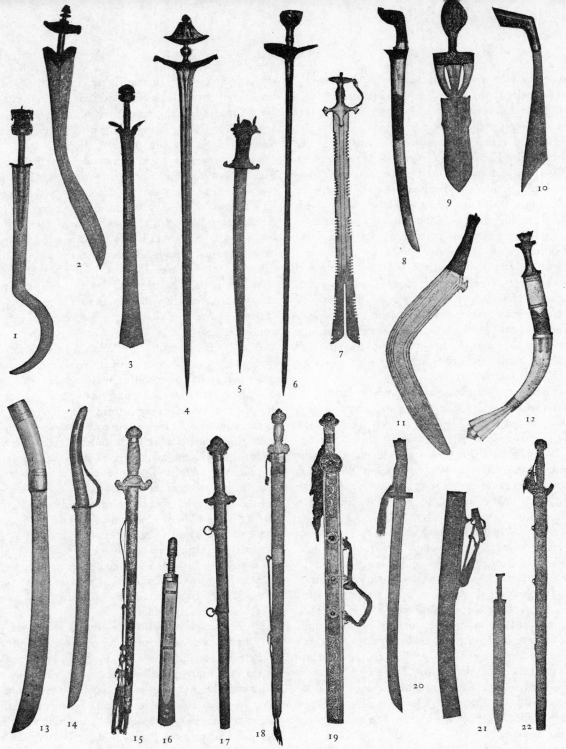

FIGURE 762. *Miscellaneous Swords.* 1. *Malabar. All steel. The top of the pommel is hung with small swinging pieces. All black steel. Length 2 feet 9 inches.* 2. *Malabar, 18th century. The square piece at the upper part of the hilt is of wood, the remainder of iron.* 3. *Malabar. Blade 26.5 inches long. Steel hilt.* 4. *Malabar, 18th century. Double-edged, ribbed and grooved blade 3 feet 6.25 inches long. Broad elliptical guard, doubly curved. Hilt silver plated.* 5. *India. Blade of T section, 26 inches long. Ebony and steel hilt, deeply engraved and inlaid.* 6. *Malabar, 17th century. Spanish rapier blade 3 feet 7 inches long. The plate guard is 5.5 x 6.5 inches; the end of the ricasso next the guard is a monster's head supported by two griffons. The entire hilt and guard are covered with gold lac.* 7. *India. Blade 29 inches long, silver plated hilt.* 8. *Malayan. Blade 23.5 inches long. Carved horn hilt set in silver.* 9. *Upper Congo. Wood hilt, the lower part wound with cane, the upper covered with leopard skin.* 10. *Executioner's sword, Celebes. Blade 18 inches long, ebony handle.* 11. *Upper Congo. Wood hilt, the upper part wound with wire and the lower with woven cord.* 12. *Abyssinia. Much curved blade 18.375 inches long from hilt to point in a straight line. Horn hilt with a fluted silver pommel. Leather scabbard with a large silver locket and chape; the latter has a long fluted silver ornament on the end.* 13. *Siam. Executioner's sword. Blade 32 inches long. Ivory grip with silver caps.* 14. *Siam. Dha. Long hilt of black horn with a broad finger guard. Hilt and finger guard decorated with embossed gold. The scabbard is covered with finely embossed gold.* 15. *Indo-China. Straight blade 26.5 inches long. Silver guard and pommel. Grip of elephant's tooth. Wood scabbard inlaid with engraved pearl shell.* 16. *Bhotan. Hilt of wood with silver bands. Open sided wooden scabbard with iron and silver straps.* 17. *Korea. Straight, double-edged blade 27 inches long.* 18. *Chinese. Straight, single-edged, grooved European blade 2 feet 8.25 inches long. Hilt of carved white jade. Scabbard covered with green shark skin with a hilt of engraved brass.* 19. *Tibet. Grooved, single-edged blade. Hilt and scabbard mounted with embossed silver set with coral and turquoise.* 20. *Watered Persian blade of typical Chinese shape and mounted in Chinese fashion with plain iron mounts. It was probably made for a Chinese officer who was stationed on the Persian border, and for the first time saw a blade of good steel and had one of Chinese shape made for him by a Persian workman.* 21. *Chinese bronze sword of the Ming period, from about 2,000 to 200 B.C. It has an inscription on one side. It was found in the foundations of a house in southern China. Such blades were frequently buried in this way for luck.* 22. *Chinese, 17th century. Straight, double-edged blade 2 feet 4.5 inches long. Hilt and scabbard mountings of finely chased brass. Grip and scabbard covered with cloisonne dragons and flowers.*

In addition to the swords described under their specific names there are many of which we do not know the names. In China, Tibet and Central Asia the swords are almost entirely cutting weapons with straight or slightly curved blades. The hilts frequently have a disk guard and straight grips. Some have cross guards and counterguards, but always of a simple character. In Central Africa some of the swords are simple, serviceable weapons, but many are of freakish shapes, the utility of which it is difficult to imagine. Some of them appear to have been copied from ancient Egyptian models as they resemble some of the old carvings. The African weapons always have iron blades, the copper ones often seen are intended for currency. These and other swords, the names of which are unknown, are shown in fig. 762.

For the different named swords and their parts see: 'Abbasi, 'Abbasi Talwar, Ahir, Alamani, Allonge, Ama-Goi-Ken, Amakurikara, Ama No Murakumo Tsurugi, Amaoi, Anneau, Aobie, Aoi Tsuba, Aor, Aori, Arame, Arming Girdle, Arming Sword, Ashi, Ashima, Asidevata, Asil, Aswar, Ayda Katti, Babanga, Back Sword, Badelaire, Badik, Balatoe, Ballatau, Bandol, Barong, Baselard, Basket Hilt, Bastard Sword, Beladah, Bhawani, Bilbo, Blunts and Sharps, Boku-To, Bolo, Boshi, Bow, Brand, Braquemar, Broadsword, Campilan, Cannelure, Case of Rapiers, Chacheka, Chalcos, Chape, Charay, Chereb, Chikuto, Chi-Nagasi, Chisa Katana, Chisel-Edge, Choku-To Chundrik, Chura, Cinctorium, Cladibas, Claymore, Cluden, Colichemarde, Coustil a Croc, Craquemarte, Curtana, Cutlas, Daimio Nanako, Dai Seppa, Daisho, Dalwel, Damascus Swords, Danpira, Dao, Das, Datto, Dencho-Zashi, Dha, Dhoup, Djoeloeng, Dodhara, Dogane, Dohong, Dueling Sword, Dukn, Duku, Dusack, Efu No Tachi, Egashira, Elephant Sword, Espadon, Estoc, Falchion, False Edge, Fil, Finger Guard, Firangi, Fist Sword, Flamberge, Fleuret, Flyssa, Foil, Fuchi, Fukura, Fukurokata-Kojiri, Fumbari, Futa-Siji-Hi, Gama Ishime, Gagne Pain, Gauntlet Sword, Gembi, Giandonato, Goddara, Goliah, Gomoku Zogan, Gonome, Grip, Guard, Guddara, Gupti, Gupti Aga, Habaki, Hakase, Hako-Mune, Halab, Hamasti, Han-Dachi, Hand-and-a-Half Sword, Hanger, Hereba, Heyazashi, Hikihada, Hita-Tsurugi, Hoken, Ho-Noki, Hon-Tsukuri, Honzogan, Horimono, Hoso Tachi, Hukim Khani, Ichi-No-Ashi, Ichizuke, Ishime, Itami, Ito Maki Tachi, Ito Zukashi, Japanese Blades, Jauhar, Jigane, Jin-Tachi, Jinto, Ji-Tsuya, Johur, Jumgheerda, Kabja, Kabuto Gane, Kabuzuchi, Kairagi, Kamashimo Zashi, Kamuri Otoshi, Kanagu, Kantschar, Kapee Dha, Karasabi, Kasane, Kashira, Kaskara, Kastane, Katana, Katana Kake, Katana Zutsu, Katti Talwar, Ken, Kenjo Tsuba, Kenuki Gata, Kenuki Gata Tachi, Kenuki Kanemono, Ken, Kenye, Kesso, Khadja, Khanda, Khandoo, Kharga S'hapna, Kharg Bandai, Khrobi, Kilij, Kilis, Kindachi, Kin Same, Kippa, Kiromono, Kissaki, Kledyv, Klewang, Klevang Tjara Atjeh, Knuckle Bow, Knuckle Guard, Kodogu, Kogai, Kohong Kalunan, Koi Guchi, Koi Guchi Kanagu, Kojiri, Kora, Koshiate, Koto, Kozuka, Kubi Kiri, Kuchaku, Kuchi Gane, Kudi Tranchang, Kuge-No-Tachi, Kuri-Jiri, Kurikata, Kuro Tachi, Kusari Tachi, Lading Balajoeng Lamah, Lall-I-Wall, Latchen Blade, Locket, Machera, Magari Kane, Makikate-No-Kashira, Makura Dashi, Malab, Mamori Katana, Mandau, Mandau Pasir, Manople, Masame-Hada, Mekike, Mekugi, Mekugi Ana, Mel Puttah Bemoh, Mentok, Menuki, Metazashi, Mimi, Mitokoro Mono, Mokko Tsuba, Mokume Hada, Monokiri, Moroha, Motagi, Muku Gitai, Mune, Mune-Uchi, Musubi Gane, Mutu Gitai, Nagafukurin, Nagatachi, Nakago, Namral, Namban, Nanako, Nawaz Khani, Neri Tsuba, Netaba, Nijiu Yakiba, Niku-Bori, Nimcha, Ni-No-Ashi, Nioi, No-Dachi, Obi-Tori, Odachi, Ogisaki, Omote, Ondanique, Opi, Orikami, Otoshizashi, Pakayun, Palache, Panabas, Parang, Parang Bedak, Parang Ihlang, Parang Jengok, Parang Kajoelie, Parang Latok, Parang Nabur, Parang Negara, Parang Pandit, Parang Parampoean, Parang Pedang, Pas d'Ane, Pata, Paternoster Blade, Pattisa, Pedang Djawie Besar, Pillow Sword, Pira, Piso Eccat, Piso Gading, Piso Halasan, Piso Podang, Pommel, Pulouar, Quaddara, Quillon, Ragee, Ram Da'o, Ramrod Back Sword, Rapier, Rebated Swords, Ricasso, Rudis, Sabidoro, Sabre, Sage-O, Sage-Obi, Saghri, Saif, Saka-Te, Saki, Salapa, Salawar Yatagan, Same, Samezaya, San-No-Sai, Sapara, Sapola, Saru-Te, Sashi-Zoe, Sauveterre, Saya, Saya-Ate, Sayajiri, Sayamaki Tachi, Schiavona, Schleger, Scymiter, Seax, Sei, Seme, Senankhas Bedok, Seppa, Seppa dai, Setto, Shamshir, Shamshir Shikargar, Shashqa, Shearing Sword, Shells, Shibabiki, Shikome-Zue, Shinai, Shinken, Shinodari, Shinogi, Shinome-Zue, Shinto, Shippo, Shira Saya, Shira Tachi, Shirazaya, Shirmani, Shi-

Shi, Shitagi, Shito, Shitodome, Shitogi Tsuba, Sho-bu-Tsukuri, Shotel, Sica, Side Ring, Sime, Sirohi, Small Sword, Sondang, Soroi, Soritsuno, Soroimono, Sosun, Sosunpattah, Spadone, Spadroon, Spathe, Stock, Sultani, Surai, Swept Hilt, Sword Belt, Sword Breaker, Sword Knot, Sword Stand, Tachi, Tachi Bukuro, Tachi Hanagu, Taga Dhara Shani, Taga Talwar, Taiken, Takahi, Takona-Gatana, Takouba, Talibon, Talwar, Tamashigiri, Tampei, Tang, Tegha, Tetsu Same, Tjoendre, Todunga, Tori-No-Tachi, Trialamellum, Tsuba, Tsuka Ai,

used in conjunction with the rapier in the 16th century, but this seems very doubtful as all of the specimens known are believed to be forgeries.

SWORD KNOT. A loop of soft leather, or cord, fastened to the sword hilt. Before drawing the sword the hand is passed through the loop which is then given a couple of turns to make it secure. A swordsman so equipped cannot be disarmed by an adversary, and could drop his sword and let it hang by the loop. (Art of Defense 14). See Tsuyo-No-O. Fig. 717.

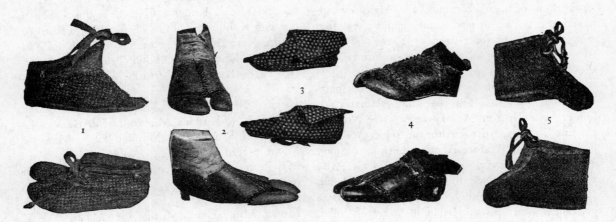

FIGURE 763. *Tabi.* 1. *Mail shoes with soles.* 2. *Steel plates connected by mail.* 3. *Brigandine.* 4. *Lacquered leather on cloth.* 5. *Mail with figured leather borders, no soles. 17th to 19th century.* 2, 3, 4. *Metropolitan Museum. Not to scale.*

Tsuka Gashira, Tsuka Guchi, Tsuka Ito, Tsuka-No-Kanemono, Tsukuri, Tsuyo-No-O, Two-Handed Sword, Udenuki Cord, Umabari, Unokubi Tsurugi, Ura, Uragawara, Urto, Vajra, Verdun, Wafters, Wakizashi, Ward Iron, Wari Kogai, Wasa, Watered Steel, Xiphos, Xiphos-Gladius, Xiphos-Spanish, Yagen Doshi, Yakbandi, Yakiba, Yamagatana, Yasurime, Yatagan, Yorvidoshi, Zafar Takieh, Zu'l Fikar.

SWORD BELT. In many cases a separate belt attached to the scabbard was worn in addition to the ordinary belt of civil life. These belts either fastened around the waist or hung over the shoulder; they varied from simple straps to the most elaborate part of the equipment. See Yakbandi, Sage Obi.

SWORD BREAKER. A weapon with a short, heavy blade with teeth on the back to catch the adversary's blade and break it. It is said to have been

SWORD STAND. See Katana Kake.

SYNGLATON. See Cyclas.

T

TAAVISH, TSUSKIAH. The Tlinket stone axe. The end of the handle is carved to represent a man's head, and the pointed stone blade eight to ten inches long represents the tongue. (Ratzel II, 94).

TABAR. India, a battle-axe. They vary greatly in size and shape. See Axe.

TABAR-I-ZIN. A large two-handed battle-axe; literally a "saddle axe." It is commonly used by the Afghans. (Egerton 748). I have been unable to find any other reference to the use of the axe by the Afghans.

TABARD. A military garment worn over armor in the 15th century. It was rather short with short, open sleeves and had the armorial bearings of the

TABI. (Sandals). Japanese defenses for the feet worn with sandals. They are made of small plates connected by mail, or of mail alone; the plates are

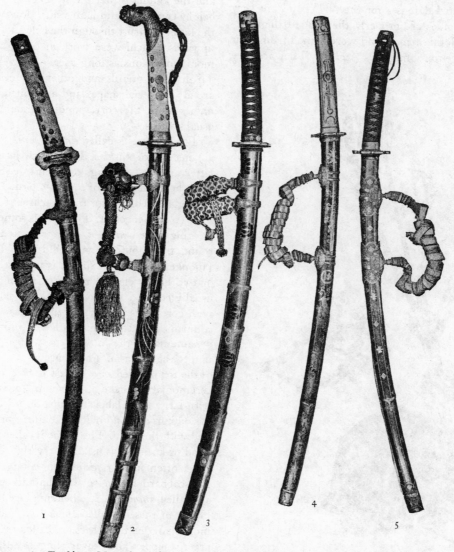

FIGURE 764. *Tachi. 1. Mountings of engraved and gilded copper, shitogi tsuba. Avanturine lacquer scabbard with Honda crests. 2. Blade signed Kaneuji. Shibuichi mounts. The kabuto gane is a ho-o head. Gold lacquer scabbard with ho-o crests. 3. Fine watered blade signed Bizen, Kumotsugu Shoan (1299). Kabuto gane with sarute of actual hands. All the mountings are of shakudo, nanako, decorated with Nabashima crests in gold and shakudo. Scabbard of shell lacquer with Nabashima crests. A court sword of high quality, 18th century. 4. Blade 23.875 inches long by Yukimitsu. Silver hilt with kenukigata menuki. Tsuba and other mounts of silver by Yoshinaga. Old lacquer scabbard. 5. Silver tsuba with pierced dai seppa of shakudo. Other mounts of shakudo and gold, all pierced. The center of each side of the scabbard is of wood with mon in shell, the remainder is lacquered.*

wearer on the front, back and on each sleeve. It is still worn by English heralds on state occasions. (Hewitt III, 413, Planche 496).

of iron or lacquered leather. Most have no soles. They were first worn in the Ashikaga period. (Dean Jap., 32). Fig. 763.

TABURARINGA. See Japururunga.

TACES, TUILLES. These names are frequently used as synonymous with tassets. Taces and tassets are laminated defenses for the thighs and are very similar. Tuilles are properly the pointed thigh defenses of Gothic armor, and were named from their resemblance to roofing tiles (*tuilles*). They are very

FIGURE 765. *Tacula Tefao (helmet) and Bumbewe Tefao (face guard). From U. S. National Museum.*

distinctive of Gothic armor, although other styles of thigh defenses were also worn with it. See Frontispiece.

TA-CHAL. See Nu-Lon.

TACHI. The earliest form of single-edged sword that succeeded the two-edged ken in Japan. The signature is on the opposite side of the tang from that on the katana, that is, it is on the *ura*, the side that is outward when the sword is hung from the belt. The important distinction between the tachi and the katana is that the former is hung from the belt by two slings and hangs edge downwards, while the latter is thrust through the belt and carried edge upwards. Tachi were worn at court and on ceremonial occasions as long as swords were carried in Japan. The guards and other mountings of tachi are all of special shapes and are called by different names from the corresponding mountings on the usual swords.

The pommel is called *kabuto gane* (helmet metal) instead of *kashira*. It is much larger than the latter and has openings on each side. Sometimes it is the head and neck of the *ho-o* bird. It usually has a loop fastened to it for the attachment of the sword knot (*udenuki* cord). This loop is sometimes a simple ring called *musubi gane*, or extends half way round the kabuto gane, and is called the *saru-te* (monkey hands) because it is usually in the shape of two hands clasped monkey fashion. The hilt is usually covered with *same* which is seldom wound with cord. In place of menuki it has *tsuka-ai* (hilt companions). It often also has a number of small ornaments on the hilt called *tawara-byo*, in addition to the tsuka-ai. The guard, tsuba, is frequently of the form called *shitogi*, said to be copied from the ceremonial rice cake of that name, or is an *aoi* tsuba with large and elaborate seppa on it. The scabbard has no kurikata and neither kozuka nor kogai is carried with the tachi. The chape is called *ishi-zuke* instead of kojiri. It is usually very elaborate and very long, often having projections along the edges of the scabbard for more than half its length. These are called *amaoi* and are held in place by bands; the lowest of these is called *shiba-biki*, and if there are more than one the others are called *sei*. Above these are the upper and lower sling bands, *ichi-no-ashi* and *ni-no-ashi*. Each carries a ring, *obi-tori*, for the sling. Collectively the fittings of a tachi, except the guard, are called *kanagu*—the corresponding term for the fittings of an ordinary sword or knife is *kodugu*. Fig. 764.

It is frequently stated that the blades of tachi are more curved than those of katana, but this is very doubtful. Usually they are indistinguishable except for the position of the signature. In 1730 the length of tachi blades was officially fixed as being between 17.5 and 26.5 inches.

There are many varieties of tachi which differ only in the forms and arrangement of their mountings. Some of them are: Hoso Tachi, Ito Maki Tachi, Kazuchi No Tachi, Kenukigata Tachi, Kuge No Tachi, Kuri Tachi, Kusari Tachi, Tachi Hanagu, Tamamaki No Tachi, Tori No Tachi, Shira Tachi.

TACHI BUKURO. A case or box for a tachi, Japan.

TACHI HANAGU. A tachi with mounts of gold, or gilded copper, and the whole scabbard covered with metal ornaments or engraved or punched work of dots and scrolls.

TACK. See Dag.

TACLE. See Takle.

TACULA TEFAO. A helmet used in Nias. It is of steel, bowl-shaped, with a narrow brim, and sometimes a low comb, and on each side projecting ear guards like the Japanese. It is usually decorated with a very large iron ornament like branching plumes. (Modigliani, Nias 225). Fig. 765.

TADA-MASA. A celebrated maker of tsuba who lived in the Akasaka quarter of Yeddo. He introduced iron tsuba with large openings, which are called Akasaka tsuba. His style was continued by his pupils. Much of the work of this school resembles the Higo style, but is more elaborate and not as strong.

TAGA DHARA SHANI. A kind of sabre, India. (Wallace Orient.).

TAGANE. A chisel, also the style of an artist's carving, Japan.

TAGA TALWAR. A sabre with a hukim khani hilt, northern India. (Wallace Orient.).

TAHARAN. The mouthpiece of a Sumatran blowpipe. (Arc. f. Eth. IV, 279).

TAH-I-NISHAN. In India, true damascening. "The steel is warmed to a blue tint, then the subject is designed and cut in with a deep graver. Two-thirds of the diameter of the wire should be the depth of the hollow, and all natural roughness of the steel or iron should be left, so that the precious metal should adhere well. As the channel is hollowed out, the thick gold or silver wire, which should be pure (in the East it is usually without alloy) is introduced into it by a chisel or copper bodkin or probe, and pressed home, after which it is flattened with a plain hammer, or if it is wished to preserve a high relief, with one that is grooved on the face. It is carefully polished with a sweet lime which whitens it, and the color is restored by careful blueing by heat. Sometimes the polishing is done with agate burnishers. This is practically the whole process, although it differs in detail in different places." (Hendley 7). Often the projecting gold is chased or carved. Compare Inlaying.

FIGURE 766. *Tail Guard, Italian, 1550. Metropolitan Museum.*

TAHR LADOK. A Wetter Island hunting spear with the sides of the head decidedly convex for the greater part of their length, but slightly concave near the shaft. (Arc. f. Eth. IV, 75).

TAHR RUAN. A fighting spear with a heavy, barbed head, Wetter Island. (Arc. f. Eth. IV, 75).

TAIAHA. See Hani.

TAIHO. Cannon, artillery, Japan.

TAIKEN. Carrying a sword in the belt, Japan.

TAILPIECE, TAIL GUARD. An arched plate riveted to the crupper of horse armor to protect the root of the tail. (ffoulkes 89, 90). Fig. 766.

TAKA. A falcon, Japan.

TAKA-BORI. Japan, carving in relief. See Niku-Bori.

TAKAGARI. To hunt with a falcon, Japan.

TAKAHI. A sword hilt, Japan.

TAKAMONO. The stand, or perch, for a falcon, Japan.

TAKAJO. A falconer, Japan.

TAKANO. Hawking or hunting grounds, Japan.

TAKA-NO-HA-SODE. See Ha-Sode.

TAKAYA. A room in which hawks are kept, Japan.

TAKA ZOGAN. Inlaying in relief, Japan. That is, inlaying so that the inlaid metal is in relief, and then carving it.

TAKKO. An old name for the obi-tori.

TAKLE, TACLE. A piece of armor of the 13th century about which nothing is known but the

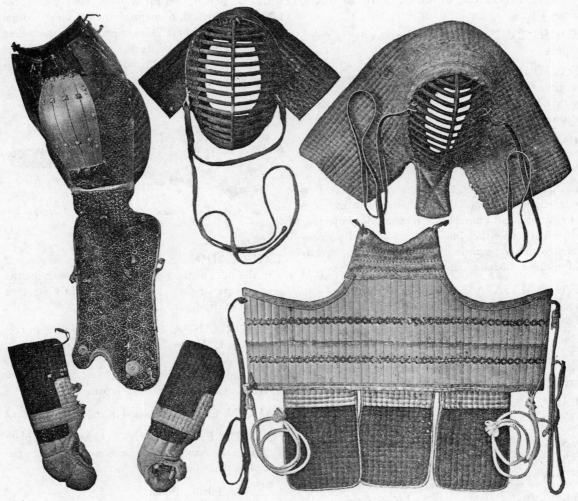

FIGURE 767. *Take Gusoku, Japanese fencing armor. The face guards are of steel, the remainder of padded cloth or of bamboo strips which make a loud noise when a blow lands. Peabody Museum, Salem.*

TAKE-GUSOKU. A bamboo corselet worn when fencing with spears in Japan. Fig. 767.

TAKE-MAKIYE. See Lacquer.

TAKATABA. Fascines of bamboo, Japan.

TAKE-YARI. A bamboo spear, Japan.

TAKSH-ANDAZ. Rockets used by Indian armies in the late 14th century. (Egerton, p. 17).

name. In the 14th century it appears to have meant a kind of arrow. (Planche 500).

An arrow, a name used by Chaucer and others. (Fairholt 610).

TAKO. A blunt arrow tipped with horn, India. It was used for killing birds. (Burton Falconry 32).

TAKONA-GATANA. A bamboo fencing sword, Japan. See Chikuto, fig. 223.

TAKOUBA. The Tuareg sword. It is a straight-bladed, single-edged sword with no guard. There is a crosspiece below the pommel which gives the cruciform effect which so many Tuareg implements show. (Dugald Campbell 104, 156, 260). Fig. 768.

—keen, bright and ready; as many a deep and ghastly cut on Sepoy corpses can testify." (Majendie 153).

The talwar is the commonest sword in India and the blades vary enormously in size, curvature and

FIGURE 768. *Takouba. Straight, double-edged blade 17.75 inches long. No guard, wood and brass hilt with a cross below the pommel.*

TALAWANG. A shield of the Dyaks of Dutch Borneo. (Peralaer 375).

TALIBON. A kind of sword used for fighting by the Christian natives of the Philippines. The blade is very heavy, straight on the back and curved on the edge, with a very long point. The hilt curves sharply towards the edge. (Foreman 485). Fig. 769.

TALOE'I NECHO WANA. A pouch with powder chargers, Nias. (Leiden IV, 52).

TALONS. The claws of all of the hawks of the genus *falco*, those of the short winged hawks are called pounces.

TALVAS, TALLEVAS, TALOCHE. A large shield like the pavis. It was used in the 14th century. (Planche 501).

TALWAR, TULWAR, TULWAUR, TARWAR. The Indian sabre, class name. It includes practically all of the curved swords used in India; but those of very marked curvature are frequently called by their Persian name, shamshir. The members of the fighting castes are almost as careful of their swords and take as much pains to keep them in order as the Japanese. It is a common saying that a really objectionable act is "as disgraceful as having a blunt sword." The moment the native trooper in the British service is off parade his sword is taken from the scabbard and carefully wrapped in oiled muslin, and hung up so that nothing shall dull its edge. They use a number of cuts totally unknown to the European sword exercises. (Baden-Powell 269, 270). "These are Sikh cavalry—who know not steel scabbards—but wear leather sheaths, wherein the swords do not become blunt and dull

quality. The hilts generally have short, heavy quillons and disk pommels. They may or may not have finger guards; some have as many as three. Several other forms of hilt are also used. (Egerton 392, 394 to 397, 644 to 652). Fig. 770.

TAMA. A bullet, Japan.

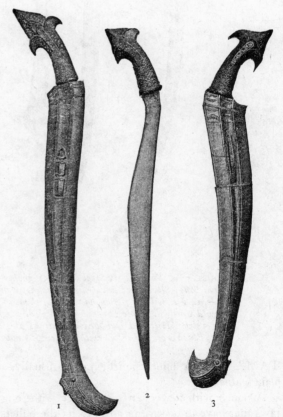

FIGURE 769. *Talibon.* 1. *Blade 21.25 inches long. Well carved horn hilt and scabbard.* 2. *Cebu. Wooden hilt with a braided cane grip.* 3. *Similar to no. 1 but smaller.*

TAMAGOME. The charge for a gun, Japan.

TAMA-GUSURI. Bullets and powder, ammunition, Japan. (Garbutt 153).

TAMANCHA. The Indian pistol. Pistols are quite rare in India, and when found are generally of European make. Matchlock pistols were, however, oc-

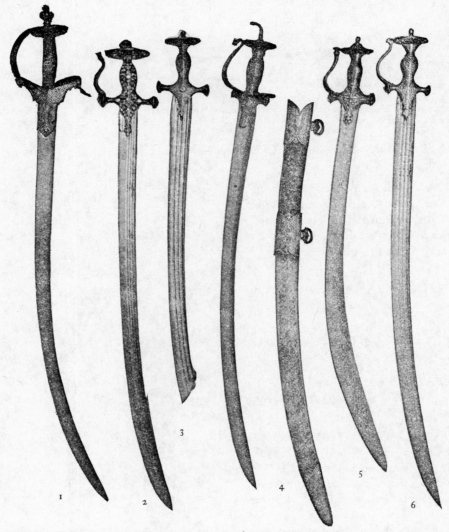

FIGURE 770. *Talwar. 1. Steel blade 31 inches long. Hilt inlaid with gold. 2. Fluted blade 31.5 inches long. Silver hilt covered with transparent green enamel set with white stones. 3. European blade 24 inches long which has been broken off and repointed. Iron hilt with a fine diaper pattern in gold dots. 4. Blade covered with spiral markings and inlaid with gold. Scabbard covered with blue velvet. Hilt and scabbard mountings of steel engraved and pierced. 5. Steel blade 29 inches long. Black iron hilt inlaid with silver. 6. Grooved blade. White metal hilt decorated with bidri.*

TAMA-IRE. A bullet pouch, Japan, usually a plain leather bag.

A pouch with a wooden mouthpiece with long jaws that have to be sprung apart to let the bullets out. It is quite similar to the Battak, Sumatra, pouches. (Joly S. & S. 68).

casionally made and carried, but probably mainly for show. (Egerton 582, matchlock, 660, 661, flint and p. 140). Combinations of matchlock pistols and axes were also made. See Combined Weapons.

TAMARANG. Australian shields made for club

fighting. They are of two entirely different types. The first is a flat piece of hard wood widest in the middle and tapering towards the ends. The hand

TAMASHIGIRI. Testing a sword blade on the bodies of criminals who had been executed, Japan. (Joly S. & S. 3). See Katana for the methods.

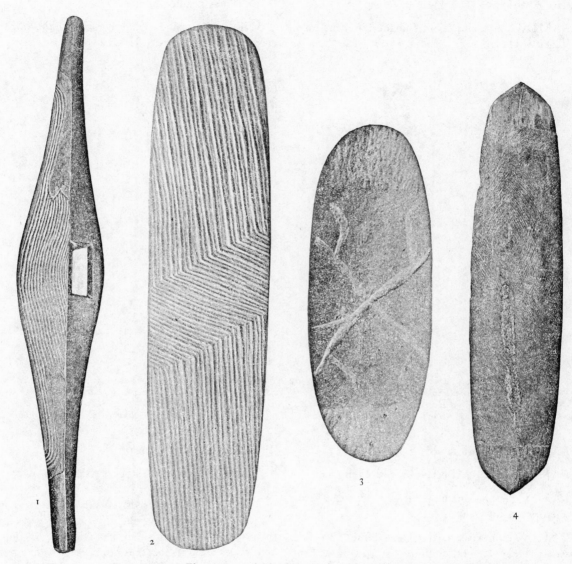

FIGURE 771. *Tamarang.* 1. *First type, 30 inches long, 1.25 wide and 5.25 deep in the middle. The side is shown.* 2, 3, 4. *The second type. Lengths 19 to 24 inches. All are heavy blocks of wood. Nos. 3 and 4 Peabody Museum, Salem. Not to scale.*

hole is in the middle of one edge. The shield is made deep to withstand the shock of the blow, and narrow so as not to obstruct the view. The second type is a heavy block of wood thick in the middle and tapering to ends and edges. The hand hole is cut in the middle of the back. Fig. 771.

TAMBARA, YAMBARRA. A north Queensland club that gradually enlarges from the handle end and then tapers to a point, which is divided into two, three or four prongs. The length is from twenty-eight to thirty-four inches. (Roth, Aust. Mus. VII, 208).

TAMENG. A shield, Java. The earlier Javan shields were long and narrow with curved sides and straight ends. The later ones were small round bucklers with spikes in the center. (Raffles 296 and plate p. 296/297).

TAMING. A round shield, Subanun of Mindanao. (Christie 111).

TANGIRRI. A blowpipe dart with a triangular head, Borneo. (Arc. f. Eth. IV, 279).

TANGO GANE. See Tenjo Gane.

TANJU. A pistol, Japan.

TANKO. A Japanese plate corselet of the fourth century B.C. (M. M. S. II, 222).

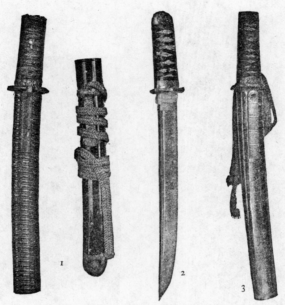

FIGURE 772. Tanto. 1. Blade 8 inches long by Kane-Yuki. Iron guard, lacquered kozuka, other mountings shakudo with silver flowers. Scabbard red lacquer gadrooned. 2. Finely watered blade 12 inches long, silver mountings in bamboo designs. Black lacquer scabbard with birds in low relief. 3. Red bronze guard, other mountings of iron inlaid with gold. Red lacquer scabbard with black crests.

TAMPEI. A short sword, Japan.

TAMPION, TAMPKINGS. See Tompion.

TAMPO. A pad on the point of a Japanese spear when practicing.

TAMUA. Sumbawa, a round shield of buffalo hide with the edge bound with rattan. (Arc. f. Eth. VIII, 9).

TANDA. A north Queensland club that gradually enlarges from the handle end to a globular extremity, the knob being either distinct from, or merged into the shaft. (Roth, Aust. Mus. VII, 208).

TANG. The part of an edged tool or weapon that is inserted in the handle. The Japanese armorers signed the blades of swords, knives and spears and the heads of arrows on the tangs.

TANSOKU. A fuse, Japan.

TANTO. A Japanese dagger, strictly one with a guard. (B. M. Hdbk. 52).

The blade rarely exceeds ten sun (12 inches) in length; it is sometimes straight but is otherwise like the sword blades. It usually has all of the fittings used on swords. In fact it is more likely to have an elaborate kojiri and a soritsuno, and sometimes an extra ornament on the scabbard called a menuki. This must not be confused with the ornaments of the same name used on the hilt. It sometimes has a broad metal band around it on which the kurikata, uragawara and soritsuno are fastened. Being constantly carried, and not being left at the door when paying a visit, it is more apt to be much decorated and to include unusual fittings than the larger swords. Fig. 772. See Japanese Blades and Katana.

The *hamadashi* is a variety of tanto in which the guard is so small that there is not room for the openings for kozuka and kogai, and they become open notches. The *aikuchi*, or dagger without a guard, is also often called a tanto. In fact while tanto has a perfectly definite meaning it is often used as a class name. See Aikuchi and Hamidashi.

TANUKI. See Tomo.

This name as applied to a shield goes back to the 12th century and was used, especially by the Scotch, as late as the early 19th. Targets vary considerably in size but most are about two feet in diameter, though some of the early ones were much larger. In the 16th century some were oval.

The typical Scotch target was about twenty inches in diameter, and was made of wood covered with

FIGURE 773. *Targets. Both Scotch, 17th to 18th centuries. Metropolitan Museum.*

TAO. A Maori spear. It was made of a hard wood and was usually about eight feet long. Occasionally the point was barbed, but in most cases it was plain. It was used in the attack and defense of fortified villages.

TAPER AXE. One of the three forms of axe so much used by northern nations of Europe in early times. The taper axe has a rather narrow, one-edged blade with a curved edge, and was curved top and bottom. (Hewitt I, 45, 47).

TAPUL. The sharp ridge, occasionally rising to a point in the middle line of the breastplates of the latter part of the 16th century. (Dean Hdbk. 70). Fig. 184.

TARBIL. A pellet crossbow, Malay. (Arc. f. Eth. IV, 278).

TARGET, TARGE. A round shield with loops on the back through one of which the arm was passed while the other was grasped by the hand.

leather studded with brass bosses. It had a central spike which was sometimes as much as ten inches long and could be unscrewed and carried in a pocket in the deerskin lining. It usually had two handles, but sometimes three, or a long leather sleeve covering the entire forearm, and having a handle at the end. (Drummond, plate I to VII). Fig. 773.

TARENTINE. The light cavalry of the Greeks; they were not regularly organized. They were sometimes armed with javelins and sometimes with bows and arrows. They charged with sword and axe, and carried a small buckler as a defensive arm and sometimes wore corselets of tanned leather. (Denison 31).

TARENTINARCHIE. See Ile.

TARIAN. Early British bronze shields. The name means "clashers," from the sound they made when coming in collision with an enemy. They were small, round bucklers with a single handle in the center. (Fairholt 9).

TARKASH. A quiver, Central and Northern India. It was cylindrical or elliptical in section and covered with cloth or velvet. (Egerton 369, 601). See Quiver.

TATAMI-GUSOKU. Folding corselets of iron or leather worn by the lower classes of Japanese retainers. (Conder 280).

FIGURE 774. *Tassets. 1. Pair, German, 1530-1550. 2. Italian, about 1570. 3. Italian, 16th century. Metropolitan Museum. Not to scale.*

TARRONIE. The wooden head of a reed spear, Victoria.

TARU. An ancient Egyptian war pike. (Burton Sword 158).

TARWAR. See Talwar.

TASSEL. See Tiercel.

TASSETS. Protections of plate for the thighs made of a single plate, or of several narrow plates flexibly connected by straps and rivets. They were hung from the taces or breastplate by straps and buckles, 16th and 17th centuries. (ffoulkes 69, 81). Fig. 774.

TATAMI-DO. A Japanese folding breastplate, that is, one made of small plates connected by mail. (Dean Jap. 53). Fig. 775.

FIGURE 775. *Tatami-Do. Folding corselet opening at the back (haramaki do). Metropolitan Museum.*

TATAMI JIKU. A kind of folding helmet, Japan. (Garbutt 168).

TATAMI KABUTO. A Japanese helmet made of horizontal rings of steel laced together so that it

FIGURE 776. *Tatami Kabuto. Upper figure open as worn; lower closed for carriage.*

can be closed like an opera hat. (Conder 258). It has an arched piece hinged to the lower part of the sides so that it can be turned up over the top and locked to it by a pin with an eccentric head. Fig. 776.

In the Springfield Art Museum there is a tatami kabuto of unusual construction. It has a small, round plate at the top with a hachimanza. Below this are a number of plates hinged together which form a conical body. One of these plates is fastened to the crown plate; by pulling out one of the hinge pins the others can be folded together into a compact bundle.

TATAMI YOROI. Japanese folding armor. The entire suit, including the helmet was of four-sided plates connected by mail so that it could be folded up compactly for carriage. (Dean Jap. 53). Fig. 777.

TATE. A pavis, or standing shield, supported by a prop, Japan.

TATE, MIMI. A turned over edge (of a tsuba). (Weber I, 204).

TATE-MOCHI. A shield bearer, Japan.

TATE NANAKO. Nanako in straight lines, Japan.

TATE-NASHI-DO. A name given to metal breastplates in Japan because they were believed to give sufficient protection to make shields unnecesary. (Conder 264).

TATENUI. A maker of shields, Japan.

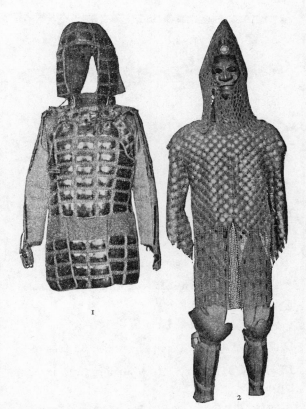

FIGURE 777. *Tatami Yoroi. 1. Small plates of leather lacquered black and connected by mail. 2. The body of small octagonal steel plates connected by mail. The helmet of hexagonal plates connected by mail; the neck guard of mail.*

TATEWARI. A variety of Japanese corselet. (Garbutt 161).

TATSUMA MAKI. See Zara Maki.

TAU-KIEN. Chinese weapons with hilts like swords and heavy square metal bars in place of blades. Whether they were used as weapons or for exercise is uncertain, probably the former as some of them are very well finished. Some weigh as much as ten pounds. Fig. 778.

TEBUTJE. The shark tooth "swords" of the Gilbert Islanders. They are light clubs with shark's teeth lashed to the sides. (Jaehns 194).

The natives of the Gilbert, or Kingsmill, Islands used a variety of weapons made in this way. Figs. 779, 780.

TE-DATE. A hand shield, a buckler, Japan.

TEER. An arrow in Purbati, a Nepalese dialect. Evidently the Indian Tir.

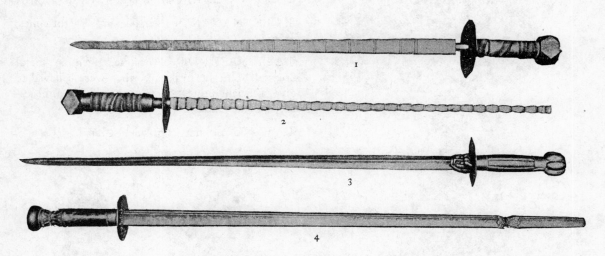

FIGURE 778. *Tau-Kien. 1. Tapered blade of square section, except close to the hilt where it is round and much smaller. Octagonal guard which slides on the small part of the blade. Iron hilt. Length blade 33 inches. 2. Blade of square section with transverse flutes. Length 33 inches. 3. Triangular fluted blade 30 inches long. Octagonal plate guard and bronze mountings. 4. Four sided blade with shallow grooves on each side and beads at each angle. Wooden grip and iron pommel. The guard is of pierced iron similar to the Japanese namban guards. Length of blade 30.75 inches.*

TAWARO BIO Ornaments like nail heads on the hilt of a tachi. They were sometimes used in addition to the tsuka ai. (Gilbertson Dec. 79).

They are said to represent rice balls.

TAWOK. A Javan spear with a diamond-shaped head. (Raffles plate p. 296/297).

TAYUI. A gauntlet, Japan.

TAYU-KOGAI. A split kogai. See Kogai.

TE-BOKO, TE-YARI. A small spear, a javelin, Japan.

TEBUKORO. A glove, Japan. Archer's gloves are sometimes called tebukoro although the proper name is *yu gake.* Tebukoro is the ordinary glove of civil life.

TEGHA. An Indian sabre with a broad, curved blade and a hilt like that of a talwar. It was used by both Mahrattas and Rajputs. (Egerton 398, 399, 534T and p. 105).

TE-GI. A kind of mace formerly carried by the Japanese police.

TE-INGKAJANA. A spatulate club with a rounded end and sharp edges. It was used by the natives near the Pennyfather River, Queensland, to kill fish at night when they were attracted by a light. (W. E. Roth, No. 7, 33).

TELEK. The Tuareg knife. It has a straight, double-edged blade and the pommel is a cross. The entire handle is often wound with brass wire. The leather scabbard has a wide leather ring attached to

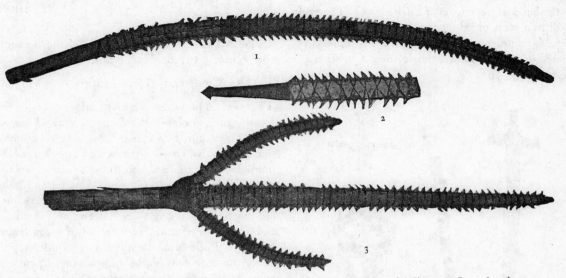

FIGURE 779. *Tebutje.* 1. *Length 3 feet 2.25 inches.* 2. *Colored white with lime.* 3. *Length 2 feet 11.5 inches. Kingsmill Islands.*

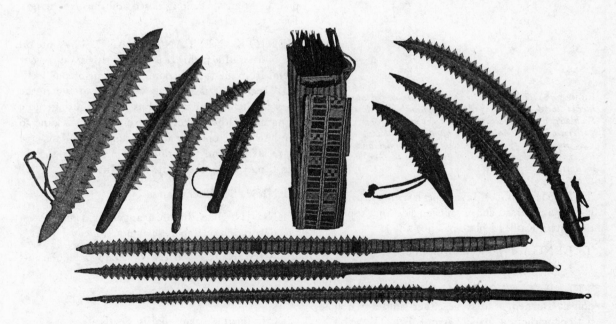

FIGURE 780. *Tebutje. Shark's tooth weapons from the Kingsmill Islands. Peabody Museum, Salem.*

it which is put over the left wrist; the knife lays flat against the inner side of the arm, the handle being in the hand of the wearer. (Furlong 95). The knife is drawn with the right hand. While the Tuaregs are Mahommedans, the cross-shaped pommel is retained, being doubtless a relic of their Christian ancestors. Fig. 781.

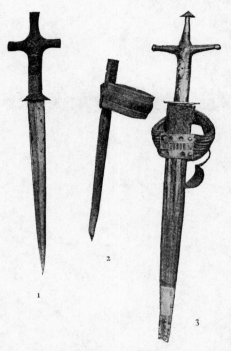

FIGURE 781. *Telek. 1. Straight, double-edged blade 11.5 inches long. Cross-shaped hilt wound with brass wire. Scabbard of brown leather over green, the former with a pattern of round holes. Arm band on scabbard. 2. Blade 14.5 inches long; brass caps on the pommel and ends of the cross. Scabbard of brown and green leather with brass mounts.*

TELEMPANG. A Javan spear with a broad head having a reversed curve on each side and a spike on the butt. (Raffles I plate p. 296/297).

TELENGA. Dyak, a blowpipe quiver. (Leiden II, 101). See Tolor.

TELEP, TELEP ANAK PANAH. A blowpipe quiver, Borneo. It may be either single or double, with or without a cover. (Arc. f. Eth. IV, 279).

TELON. See Ile.

TEMBILAN. The blowpipe quiver of the Tebidah Dyaks. (Leiden II, 95).

TEMOTO. See Habaki Moto.

TEMPET DAMAK. A quiver, Malay. (S. & B.).

TENENTZ. The challengers in a tournament, 16th century. (Hewitt III, 634).

T'ENG. Chinese, stirrups. See Stirrup.

TENGU. The tengu are mythical dwellers in the forests, gnomes classified among the *maya Raikyas*, and divided into two classes: the ordinary human shaped *konoha tengu* with wings and a nose of inordinate length, and the bird-like tengu with a strong beak called *karasu tengu* (crow tengu). The tengu have a ruler, the *dai tengu*, who wears long moustaches and a gray beard descending to his belt, and as a mark of rank carries a fan of seven feathers. He wilfully broke the precepts of Buddha, and in consequence does not belong to either heaven or hell, besides which he is sick three times a day as a penance. (Joly Leg. 364).

The tengu are frequently represented on Japanese armor and sword mountings. Figs. 568, 731.

TENGU. (Menpo). There are two types of menpo called tengu, the long nosed and the crow tengu. Figs. 568, 731.

TENJO KANE, TANGO GANE. The plate on the bottom of a fuchi. It is frequently of a different metal from the ring portion. The name means "ceiling" because it is held above the head when the sword is held point upward as when fighting. The signature of the maker is put on the tenjo kane to the left of the opening for the tang. The date, age or residence, and sometimes the name of a second artist, may be on the right. (Joly Int. 13).

TENKU. See Hachimanza.

TEN-NIN. The Buddhist angel. It is often used as a decoration on Japanese armor. (Dean Jap. 71).

TENTSUKI. A variety of nodowa. (Garbutt 145).

TENUKI O. See Tsuyo No O.

TEOI. Japanese arm guards. See Kote.

TEOKI. A surface prepared for onlaying (false damascening) by cuts and scratches, Japan. (Joly, Naunton xii).

TEPPO. A gun or cannon, firearms, Japan.

TEPPO DAI. A gun carriage, a gunstock, Japan.

TEPPOKAJI. A gunsmith, Japan.

TEPPO YUMI. (Gun crossbow). A light Japanese crossbow made for amusement. The large crossbows used in the castles were called o-yumi

TEREBRA. A spiked beam for boring into the walls of fortresses, 9th century. (Hewitt I, 89).

TERKOEL. A gun, Malay. (Leiden II, 114). Fig. 326.

TERPOLUS. See Tribulus.

TERSELL. See Tiercel.

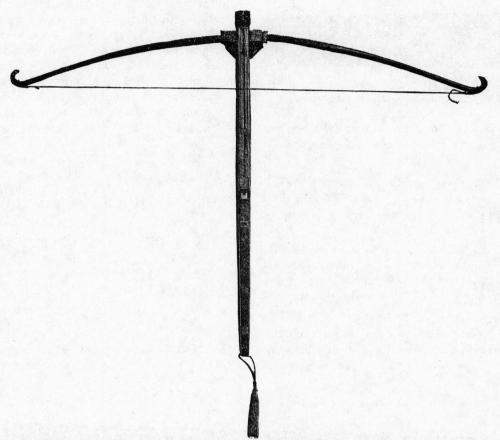

FIGURE 782. *Teppo Yumi. Japanese crossbow with a gun-shaped stock. The bow is of horn in halves, the ends fit in sockets on the sides of the stock. Length of bow 27.75 inches.*

(large bow) on account of their size. The teppo yumi is quite small; the stock is a little more than two feet long and is shaped like a gun. The bow is about as long as the stock. It is made of horn, or whalebone, in halves which fit in sockets on the sides of the stock. Fig. 782.

TEPUS. A blowpipe dart with a plain sharpened point, Borneo. (Arc. f. Eth. IV, 279).

TERCEROLE. A small pocket pistol, probably of Italian origin. (Demmin 71).

TESCHING. A very light gun, a fowling piece, 16th century. (Dean Hdbk. 88).

TESSEN. A fan with an iron frame, Japan. See War Fan.

TESTIERE. Armor for a horse's head. By some authorities it is considered as synonymous with chanfron, others confine it to the plate covering the junction of the chanfron, crinet and jaw plates. (Demmin 349).

TESTUDO. A movable covering to protect be-siegers when attacking a fortress. See Cat and Tortoise.

TETENAULO. Helmets of braided cane worn in Nias. (Modigliana, Nias 228).

TETSU. Iron, Japan.

TETSU-BO. An iron club, Japan.

FIGURE 783. *Tetsu Same. Iron plate carved with waves and inlaid with sea birds in gold and shakudo rocks.*

TETSU-GAI. The plates of iron, or leather, covering the backs of the hands in Japanese armor. (Conder 272). Fig. 475.

TETSU SAME. Iron plates occasionally used instead of shark skin to cover Japanese hilts. They are almost always decorated with carving or inlaying. Fig. 783.

TÈTSU SEN. Folding war fans with ten iron ribs covered with monochrome paper with designs of the red sun and moon. They date from the 12th century, Japan. (Joly Leg. 86). See War Fan.

TEWHA-TEWHA, TAIAHA. One of the most used of New Zealand weapons. It is a long club with a straight shaft pointed at one end and with a quadrant-shaped blade at the other. Unlike most

Maori articles it is usually perfectly plain, or at most, has a narrow band of carving around the middle of the shaft. A bunch of feathers was hung from the blade which was flicked in the face of an adversary when fencing in order to confuse him. The blade was not used for striking, but always the straight side; the point was also used for thrusting. The Maoris had an elaborate system of fencing with both the long and short clubs which was regularly taught the young men. On one occasion an old chief said: "There are but two parts of an opponent that need to be watched, the point of the shoulder if he is using a short club, and the big toe of the advanced foot if he is using a long weapon; the one will twitch and the other dig into the ground the instant before he strikes."

Tewha-Tewha vary greatly in size. Fig. 784.

TE-YARI. A javelin, Japan.

TE-ZUTSU. A pistol, Japan. See Pistol.

THABMOK, THRABMOK. Armor, Western Tibet. See Armor.

THAIR. A spring bow trap used for large game by the wild people of Chota Nagpur. The arrows are poisoned with aconite and snake poison. (Mervin Smith 103, 105).

THAKROO. A quiver, Nepal. It is made of bamboo bound with leather.

THAMI. The Siamese crossbow. "It is about five feet long; it is passed through a stock three or four

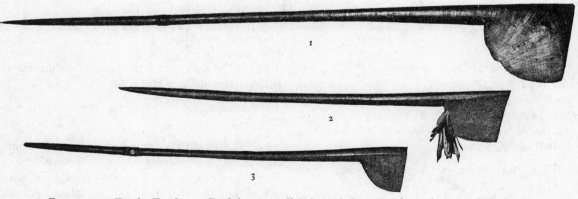

FIGURE 784. *Tewha-Tewha.* 1. *Dark brown, polished wood. Length 5 feet 6 inches; width across the head 9.5 inches.* 2. *Plain brown wood 3 feet 9.25 inches long.* 3. *Dark brown, polished wood with a carved band set with shell. Length 3 feet 8.5 inches. These show about the extremes of size.*

feet long tipped with hard wood or iron. The leaf of a palm supplies the place of feathers to the arrow. The bowstring is drawn to the notch by the united exertions of feet and arms, and the arrow is shot off by a trigger." (Egerton, p. 94).

Mouhot says, p. 161, that their crossbows have

These crossbows are very common in the Hill States in the north of Siam. They vary greatly in size and considerably in construction, although all are powerful weapons, fig. 785. The arrows are very short and are feathered with folded leaves. They are carried in bamboo quivers.

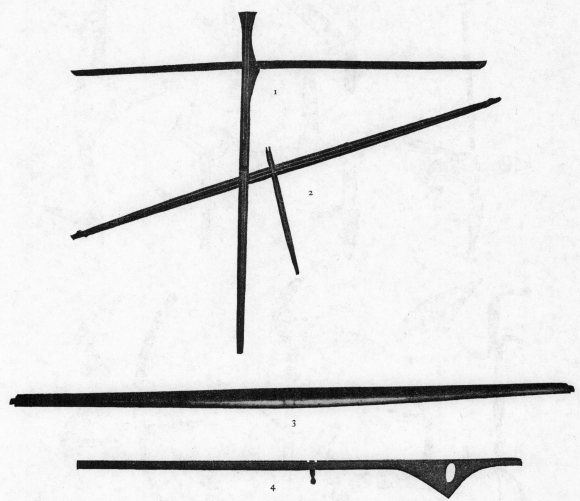

FIGURE 785. *Thami. 1. Very heavy bow of dark brown wood 4 feet 8 inches long. Of elliptical section 2.5 x 0.75 inches in the middle. Stock of wood 3 feet 9 inches long. Wooden trigger. 2. Light bow 4 feet 11 inches long of semi-circular section. Straight stock 20.625 inches long, ivory trigger. 3. The bow of no. 1. 4. The stock of no. 1.*

great power and that they use them very skillfully but rarely at greater distances than fifty paces. The arrows are always poisoned for large animals, and the poison is very active when freshly made. If the arrow hits an elephant, rhinoceros or tiger so as to penetrate the flesh, they are almost sure to find the body within a few hundred yards of where it was hit.

THANG. A crossbow mounted on wheels, China. (Jaehns 333).

THARUMA. A shield, Tjingilli, Umbaia and Gnanji tribes of Central Australia. (Sp. & Gi. 760).

THORAX. The Greek breastplate. (Dean Europe. 15).

FIGURE 786. Throwing Knives. 1. Biskra. All iron. Length 21.375 inches. 2. Congo. Handle covered with woven cord. 3. Congo. Length 17.25 inches. 4. Congo. Engraved blade. 5. Fang (Gaboon). Wood handle wound with brass. 6. Congo. Length 16.5 inches. 7. Congo. Handle covered with copper. 8. Congo. Handle covered with leather. 9. Central Africa. Engraved handle wound with leather of two colors. 10. Congo. Length 17.25 inches. 11. Congo. Handle wound with cord. 12. Congo. Wooden handle. 13. Congo. Slot in body. Handle covered with woven cord. 14. Congo. Handle covered with brass. 15. North Cameroons. Handle covered with hide. Length 28.25 inches. 16. North Cameroons. Engraved blade, hide covered handle. Length 28 inches.

THRABMOK. See Thabmok.

THROWING CLUBS. See Kerrie, Boomerang and Ulas.

THROWING KNIVES. While most knives are occasionally thrown there are many special forms of knife made to be thrown that would be of very little use if handled in the ordinary way. They are used very extensively in Central Africa and are of the most extraordinary shapes. They are thrown horizontally from right to left and may hit with any one of the branches. The trajectory is a curve that inclines towards the right of the thrower. The maximum range is said to be about 100 yards; at 40 to 50 it is quite accurate. "Certain travelers relate that this arm thrown by a skillful hand can cut off a man's leg at 20 metres. Trials at the Musee du Congo Belge showed that when thrown from distances of 15 metres some of these throwing knives would go through a board 15 millimetres in thickness." (Congo, Feb., 1922, p. 1). Fig. 786.

TIERCE. A thrust delivered at the outside of the body over the arm.

TIERCEL, TERCEL, TASSEL, TARSELL. The male of any species of hawk. "The tiercel is said to be so called from being about one-third smaller in size than the falcon (female); by others it is derived from the belief that each nest contained three young birds of which two were females and the third and smallest a male." (Phillott 25 note).

TIGER'S CLAW. See Bagh Nakh.

TIGLUN. An ivory club six or seven inches long, pointed at one end. It is grasped in the hand like a dagger and used for striking blows, and is one of the very few weapons made solely for fighting by the Eskimo of Point Barrow. (Murdoch 191).

TIKA, TIKAGUNG. A hand rest on a harpoon shaft, Cumberland Sound Eskimo. (U. S. N. M. 1900, 261).

TILLER. The stock of a crossbow.

TILLOO. The bone barb of a kind of fish spear called *koanie* in Victoria. (Brough Smyth 306).

TILT, TOILE. The barrier used in jousting. It was originally made of cloth, but later of wood. (ffoulkes Armourer 166).

TILTING CUISSE. See Knee Shield.

TIME. In fencing, "proper time is to reduce the motions of weapon and body to the strictly necessary, both in number and extent, so as to employ the least possible time in attack and parry; secondly to balance these actions carefully with the adversary's in order to seize at once the least opportunity and to reduce the number of chance hits to a minimum." (Castle 8).

TINDIL. A large club that gradually enlarges from the handle and ends in a long point, North Queensland. (Roth, Aust. Mus. VII, 208).

TING KIA. "Armor with nails," brigandine, China. (Laufer 284).

TIR. An arrow, Central India. The Indian arrows have steel heads of a great variety of shapes, with tangs fitting into the shafts, which are generally of reed. The shafts are often painted and gilded elaborately. These arrows have three feathers and bone, or ivory, nocks. (Egerton 603, 604). Figs. 787, 788.

TIRER AU MUR. An exercise in the older French fencing schools consisting in a series of disengagements in all of the lines performed with as much style as possible, which the adversary either parried with equal deliberation and precision, or allowed to be placed on his plastron for the sake of practice. (Castle 166).

The Japanese fencers have an exactly similar exercise.

TIROK, TORAK. A Dyak harpoon with a single barb. (Leiden I, 173).

TIRRER, DA-AAR, DJER-RER, JEE-AOR. Reed spears with round points of hard wood or occasionally bone. The heads are fastened on with sinew covered with resin, Victoria. (Brough Smyth 305).

TJOEDRE. A kind of Malay sword or knife.

TJOMBONG. A bade-bade with openings in the blade.

TJUKULI. A boomerang, Umbaia and Gnanji tribes, Central Australia. (Sp. & Gi. 761).

TJUNKULETTI. Melville Island spears with long, broad barbed heads. The length is from ten

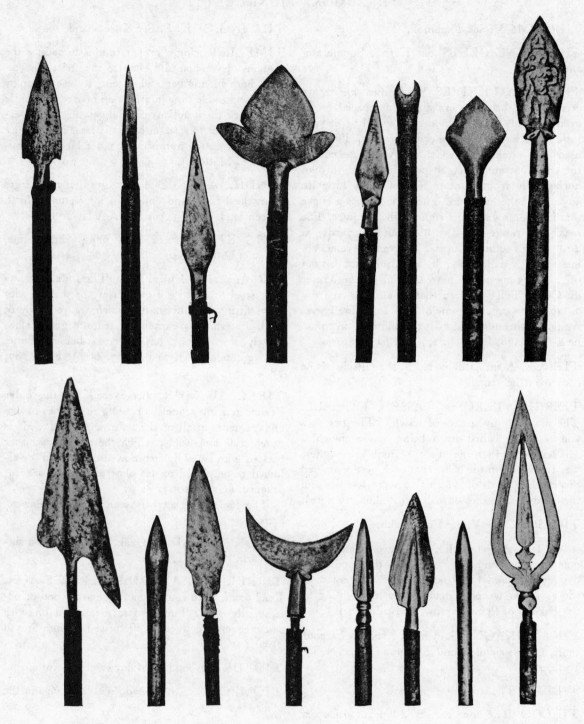

FIGURE 787. *Tir, Mahratta Arrows, 18th century. The heads are of steel and the shafts of reed, originally painted and gilded. The sixth in the upper row is the nock of one of the same lot. The last in the upper row has the figure of Ganesha carved on it. He is the god of luck to whom it is proper to pray when starting any new enterprise. It was possibly intended to be the first arrow fired. The arrows at the ends of the lower row have heads 3.5 inches long.*

to thirteen feet, the head is three or four feet long and from two and three-quarters to four inches wide. Occasionally there are as few as five barbs, but usually a much greater number, from fifteen to thirty-three on a side. If there are but few barbs they are far apart and increase in size as they get further from the point. The heads are decorated in

TOEMBAK. Malay, a spear class name. There are many varieties as T. Tirok, T. Toedoek, T. Sembijang, etc. All are barbed on both sides. (Leiden I, 171, 172, II, 139). Many, in fact most, Malay spears have no barbs.

TOGAI. Food given to a falcon as a reward.

FIGURE 788. *Tir. Arrows of southern India. Finely wrought steel heads. Shafts from twenty-eight to thirty-one inches long, most are covered with sinew. Ivory nocks. The shafts are painted in colors near the nocks and have ferules of silver and brass below the heads.*

red, white and yellow. They are thrown by hand and in a trial by nine natives they threw them from one hundred and four feet three inches to one hundred and forty-three feet five inches, but not accurately. (Spencer, North, Ter. 364).

TOBIYAKI. See Yuhashiri.

TOCK. See Rapier.

TODUNGA. See Ayda Katti.

TOEMBA. Spears, Pare-Pare, Indian Archipelago. (Bock 20).

TOEMBA DJANGAT. A Dyak parade spear with a straight blade set in a brass ornament with branching projections on each side. (Arc. f. Eth. III, 241).

TOGARI-YA. Arrows with pointed heads, Japan. They vary much in width, some being very narrow while others are heart-shaped. (Gilbertson Archery 118). See Ya and Yano-Ne.

TOGATA. The space between the inner and outer gates of a castle, Japan.

TOGGLE IRON. A whaling harpoon with a one-sided head swiveled on the end of an iron shaft. A small hole is drilled through both head and shaft and a wooden peg is placed in it when the harpoon is to be thrown. This keeps the head in line with the shaft and, when a strain is put on the line it shears the peg, allowing the head to swing round at right angles to the shaft, thus forming a toggle which holds it securely in the body of the whale.

The head has two barbs on one side and none on the other. Fig. 789.

The Japanese had similar spears but whether they were of their own invention or copied from

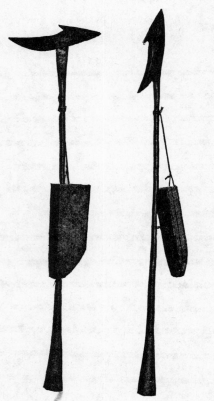

FIGURE 789. *Toggle Iron. It is shown to the right in the position when thrown, and to the left in that which it takes when a strain is put on the line.*

the American is unknown. Many savages use similarly constructed harpoons. Fig. 790.

TOGI-DASHI. See Lacquer.

TOGIDASHI ZOGAN. True inlay of a dark metal in a light one or vice versa. It is rubbed down so that the effect is much the same as that of togi-dashi lacquer. (Joly, Naunton xii). It is often used in the decoration of Japanese sword fittings.

TIGISHI, TOGIYA. A man who sharpens swords, Japan.

TOHO. A spear, class name, Nias. Some are straight and of the usual Malay type, while others are barbed and quite elaborate. (Modigliani, Nias 236).

TOILE. See Tilt.

TOKAGE-GASHIRA. "Lizard head," a form of ornament at the top of the silver plates sometimes found on Japanese helmets. (Conder 259). See Shihojiro.

TO-KAMURI. A Japanese helmet in the form of the ceremonial hat, the *kamuri.* (Conder 257). No. 1, fig. 415.

TOKANG. The toggle head of a harpoon, Cumberland Sound Eskimo. (U. S. N. M. 1900, 262).

TOKI. A stone-headed axe, New Zealand. (Polack II, 30).

TOKI KAKAUROA. A Maori long-handled fighting axe with a European iron head and a wood or bone handle; the latter is often carved. Fig. 791.

Stone axes were not used for fighting by the Maoris.

TO-KIN. A cap worn by Yamabushi (Japanese militant monks). Fig. 792.

TOKI POTO, TOKI POO, TANGATA, PA-TATI. A short-handled fighting axe, Maori. The heads were always of steel and of European make, the handles were of wood or bone, usually carved on the end. Fig. 791.

TOKKO. A vajra of one prong. It forms a spoke of the "wheel of the law," a Buddhistic symbol. Fig. 830.

TOKONOMA. An alcove in a Japanese room. It was the place of honor and racks of swords were frequently placed in it.

FIGURE 790. *Japanese(?) Toggle Iron. Head only with a socket. It has a short piece of rope attached.*

TOKUGAWA. The family that ruled Japan from 1600 to 1868. Iyeyasu, born 1542, raised it to the highest place in Japan which it retained for nearly three hundred years.

TOKUGAWA PERIOD. The period during which the Tokugawa family ruled Japan, 1600-1868. It is the last of the four periods into which Japanese armor is divided. It was a time of peace and prosperity and during it each daimio was required to spend a part of each year at the Shogun's court. The Tokugawa clan was at first a purely feudal organization and the nobles vied with each

TOLOR. The case in which a Dyak carries the poisoned darts for his blowpipe. It is made of a piece of bamboo, a node forming the bottom. The cover

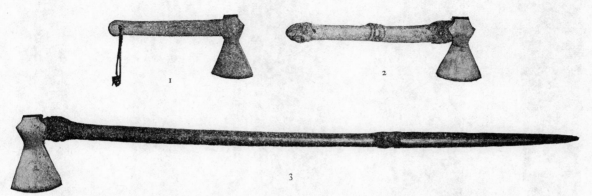

FIGURE 791. *Toki. New Zealand Fighting Axes. 1. Toki Poto. Short, plain bone handle 10.75 inches long. 2. Toki Poto. Carved bone handle 15 inches long. 3. Toki Kakauroa. Wood handle 3 feet 9 inches long, carved and inlaid with shell. All have European steel heads. The stone-headed axes were not used by the Maoris for fighting.*

other in their equipment. Also it was a time of peace and it became the fashion to wear armor of obsolete types copied from celebrated suits kept in the temples. These were called *o-yoroi*. Many were exceedingly elaborate.

is a similar piece with a node forming the top. It has a wooden belt hook fastened to it by two bands of woven cane.

Similar cases are used for the same purpose in the Malay Peninsula. Here the cover is often of an

FIGURE 792. *To Kin. The leather cap worn in place of a helmet by the Japanese fighting monks called Yamabushi. Black leather with a gilt rod around the lower part.*

TOKWAN. A variety of Japanese helmet. (Garbutt 168).

TOL-BOD (DA). An iron-headed arrow, Nicobar Islands. (Man, And. & Nic. 4).

ogival piece of wood or of wickerwork. The Samang quivers are very simple; but those of the Sakai are much more complicated. The latter contain a number of tubes of reed to hold the darts, and also all

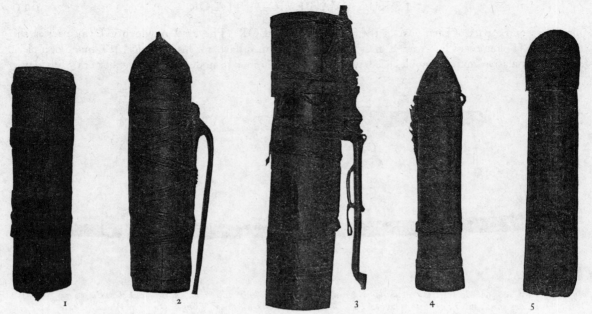

FIGURE 793. Tolor. 1. North Borneo. Bamboo with braided cane bands. 2. Dutch Borneo. Bamboo case 11.5 inches high with a wooden cover. Each dart is in a reed, the whole is wrapped in a furry skin which fits the case. 3. Bamboo case 12.25 inches high with a bamboo cover. There is a band of carving around the bottom of the belt hook which is unusually elaborate. 4. Dutch Borneo. Bamboo case, wooden cover. 5. Sakai. Bamboo engraved, woven cover.

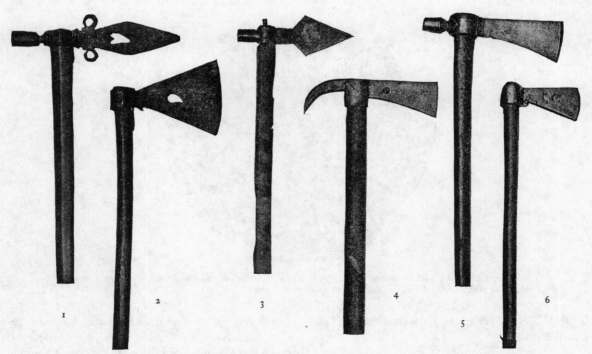

FIGURE 794. Tomahawks. 1. Chippewa pipe tomahawk. 2. Sisseton Sioux. 3. Osage, Oklahoma. 4. Tomahawk with hook. 5. Sioux pipe tomahawk. 6. Ogalala Sioux. Museum of the American Indian. Heye Foundation.

of the requisites for making and poisoning them. Outside it is encircled by two rings of woven cane, one for the attachment of a waist cord, and the other for the hinge of the cover. The latter is shaped like a "Tam o' Shanter," the enlarged upper part being used to hold wadding which is prevented from falling out when the cover is opened by a ring of

ing of the whites. Tomahawks generally have narrow hatchet blades, frequently backed by a pipe bowl. The handles are of wood and hollow, forming the pipestems. They are of two main types, those procured from the English were of much simpler forms than those of French make. They were used for throwing as well as striking. Fig. 794.

FIGURE 795. *Tomo. Black leather with a gilt mon. Broad wrist strap with a heavy pad on it. It is attached to a long, light strap by which it is secured to the wrist. Tokugawa.*

cane. Their quivers are decorated like their blowpipes with complicated incised patterns which have definite meanings. Fig. 793.

TOMAHAWK. The fighting axe of the North American Indians. Originally these weapons had stone heads and short wooden handles. The stone heads gave place to iron ones shortly after the com-

TOMARKI. An ancient type of Russian arrow with a conical point. (Scheremetew 122).

TOMBAT. A variety of boomerang with the concave edge curved and the convex angular, Australia. (Burton Sword 38).

TOMEANG. A composite bow, Malay Peninsula. (Horniman Museum).

TOMINAGA-GOTE. A pair of kote that are connected together by a silk or leather collar instead of being separate as usual.

TOMO, TANUKI. The Japanese bracer. It is a nearly cubical leather pad on a broad strap that fastened around the wrist. It was abandoned in very

weapon than his axe. This little weapon is also used as a projectile, and the Byga will thus knock over hares, peafowl, etc., with astonishing skill." (Forsyth 301).

TONLET, TONNELET. The tonlet suit was used mainly for fighting on foot, but was sometimes

FIGURE 796. *Tonlet. Early 16th century. From the Tower of London, attributed to Henry VIII. Metropolitan Museum. Not to scale.*

early times, the date is very uncertain, when the practice of loosing the hold on the bow and allowing it to turn in the hand became general. The tomo was occasionally carried in Tokugawa times when it was the fashion to wear armor of obsolete type at court. Fig. 795.

TOMPION, TAMPION, TAMPKING. A flanged disk of wood placed in the mouth of a cannon to exclude dirt and water.

The wooden base of a grape shot.

The wooden wad of a petard.

TONGIA. The axe of the Bygas of Central India: "A formidable implement called a *tongia*, with a semicircular blade like an ancient battle-axe in miniature. All of the iron for these weapons, and for their agricultural instruments, is forged from native ore of the hills by a class called Agurias, who seem to be a section of the Gonds. A Byga has been known to attack and destroy a tiger with no other

used in place of other leg armor when jousting at the barrier. It had wide, bell-shaped skirts of plate which were often solid and elaborately fluted with deep vertical folds, fig. 796. Sometimes it was made of horizontal plates connected by sliding rivets so that it could be pulled up and down, 16th century. These skirts were called tonlet, lamboys, jamboys or bases.

TONOE. The guard at the Mikado's gate.

TONOI-BITO. The night guard at the Imperial palace, Japan.

TONOI-NO-HARAMAKI. The armor worn by the lower classes of retainers in Japan in very early times. (Conder 279).

TO-ONO. Long, heavy spears made in two parts, the butt not being more than one-fifth of the length of the head. They were used for hunting in northern Queensland. (Roth, Aust. Mus. VII, 192).

TOOPIN. A matchlock gun, Neman (a dialect of Nepal).

TOOROOM. A long, broad South Indian dagger with many grooves in the blade and a kind of basket hilt. (Egerton, p. 124).

TOP. A helmet, India. It is the same as the Persian kulah khud.

Scudamore suits now in the Metropolitan Museum. (ffoulkes Almain). Laking believes that these suits were made by a different armorer.

TOPI. A cannon, Southern India. (Egerton, p. 34).

TOPOROK, TOPOR. A battle axe, Russia. (Scheremetew 107, 108, 109).

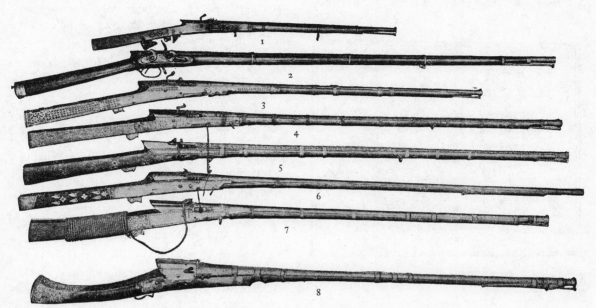

FIGURE 797. Toradar. 1. Central India, 18th century. Gun 3 feet 1 inch long, evidently for a child. All mounts plain, well finished, steel. 2. Early 19th century. Damask barrel inlaid in gold, Sanskrit inscription inlaid on tang. Engraved European flintlock. All mountings of silver. 3. Barrel inlaid with gold, stock inlaid with ivory. Mountings all silver. Length 4 feet 7 inches. 4. Barrel chased in high relief for its entire length. Capucines rawhide bands over silver saddles. Stock painted with colored flowers on a gold ground. Length 5 feet 5 inches. 5. Square barrel 4 feet long, carved in relief and inlaid with gold. Pierced plated capucines. Openwork steel and ivory plates on stock. 6. Damask barrel, fluted muzzle. The pan cover is a clip hung from a string. Stock of brown wood inlaid with ivory ducks and other figures. Length 5 feet 9 inches. 7. Cashmere. Heavy round barrel inlaid with silver. Pan cover like the Japanese. Stock lacquered with patterns in gold. 8. Stock lacquered green with an embossed silver butt cap and fore end. Barrel and side plates gilded. Length 5 feet 6.5 inches.

TOPEE. A hawk's hood, India. See Hood.

TOPF, JACOB. Jacob Topf was born in 1530 and was one of three brothers all of whom were well-known armorers of Innsbruck. In 1581 he worked for the Archduke and his court. He appears to have been away from Innsbruck from 1562 to 1575, and was probably in England during a considerable part of this time. He was for a time master workman at Greenwich and made several decorated suits for English knights. He died in Innsbruck in 1597. He is believed to have made the two

TOPPAI. A Japanese helmet of tall conical form with the sides flattened into a blade shape towards the top. (Conder 257).

TORADAR. India, a matchlock gun (See Banduk). The guns of Central and Northern India belong mainly to two classes, both of which were used throughout these regions. The first has a very slim, straight stock of pentagonal section and quite a light barrel; the second has a curved stock of diamond section and a very heavy barrel much enlarged at the breech. Both have the regular Indian type of lock. The pan cover usually swings on a pin, but is sometimes a loose clamp fitting over and under the pan. Both types have iron reinforcing plates each side of the stock extending for some distance on each side of the lock. In both the barrel is fastened to the stock by coils of wire or rawhide which frequently pass over silver saddles on the barrel. The first type has often the ogival Turkish back sight, but more often an open V. The second nearly al-

FIGURE 798. *Tortoise. A species of movable battering ram. From Colliado.*

ways has a very large open back sight. The muzzles of both are generally reinforced by moulded rings and the front sights are made very long so as to show above them. Sometimes the front sight is the nose of a man or beast carved on the front ring. In many cases the barrels are of fine twist or damask, and the plates by the locks are often of watered steel. The barrels are occasionally square, and some even have square bores. The barrels are frequently carved and inlaid. The stocks are painted, carved and inlaid or mounted with embossed metal inlaid or enameled. Both types generally have a clevis for a sling strap and some have two. The first type is from three to six feet long; the second varies less being always between five and six feet. (Egerton 135 to 137, 411 to 425, 733, 738). Fig. 797. See also Gun.

TORI-KABUTO. A Japanese helmet shaped like a bird's head.

TO-RIL. See Ku-Yan.

TORINO, TSUSHO. The name by which an artist family was known to the public, Japan.

TORI-NO-TACHI. A variety of tachi. It differs only in the style of the mountings.

TORI-TENGU. (Menpo). A menpo with a tengu face with a nose like a bird's beak. 8, fig. 568.

TORMENTUM. An engine of classic times for throwing stones. It was called tormentum because the power was obtained by the reaction of a twisted skein. (Burton Sword 19, 20).

TORTOISE. A movable covering to protect besiegers attacking a fortified place. It often carried a battering ram. Fig. 798.

TOSEI. A variety of Japanese corselet. (Garbutt 142).

TOSEI JIKORO. A variety of Japanese helmet. (Garbutt 168).

TOSHDAN. An ammunition pouch, Northern India. (Burton Lakes 105).

TOSHIBA. The stick on which birds killed by a falcon are carried, Japan.

TOSHIMASA. The first of this name was a very celebrated tsuba maker of about 1800. He was the court carver of the daimio of Kurume. He was succeeded by his son Toshimasa II. (Hara 186).

TOSHINAGA I. One of the three greatest makers of sword mountings of the Nara school. He was a pupil of Toshiharu and died in January, 1737, at the age of seventy. (Hara 187).

TO-SU. A small poniard carried by Japanese nobles as a personal protection. The blade should not be over 125 mm. (Imperial order of the 15th century); actually it varies between 50 and 220. Often several were put in one scabbard. It was often mounted with a kurikata and soritsuno, or with a hole in the kojiri for a knotted cord. (Weber II, 414).

TOTOCHIMALLI. Mexican shields of the better class, indicating the military rank and achievements of the chiefs. They were usually round and made of parallel strips of cane or wood reinforced by heavier crosspieces. They had two handles and the fronts were decorated with designs in feather work. (Arc. f. Eth. V, 53). See Chimalli.

TOTOSUBAI. A helmet, Japan. Obsolete.

TOUCH BOX. A primer or case for priming powder from which the pan and touchhole could be filled. See Primer.

TOURNAMENT. "The imitation of war as an amusement in peace must be as old as war itself. War dances are common among all savage tribes. Horsemanship in arms was practiced as an amusement in peace by the Persians, Arabs, Moors and Indians. The Greeks had pyrrhic dances and races in armor, the Romans their Salian dance and *Ludus Troiae*, from which some derive the word *Torneamentum*. . . . The Goths of the 6th century held games of mimic warfare. The earliest historical instance recorded (by Nithard, a contemporary) is at a meeting at Strasburg between Charles the Bald and Lewis the German, sons of Lewis the Pious, on the occasion of their dividing between them the kingdom of their brother Lothar in 878, at which the vassals of both kings engaged in contests on horseback. Henry the Fowler (876-936) is said to have brought the tourney from France into Germany, or to have invented it in his own country, . . . Geoffrey of Preuilli (1056), a Breton lord, is also credited with the invention: 'Torneameanta inventit': i.e. (we may surmise) drew up the rules of the game.

"It appears probable that tournaments were first in regular use in France, and Mathew Paris calls them *conflictus Gallaci*. We hear of them in England as early as the reign of Stephen, who was accused of 'softness' (mollities) because he could not or would not hinder them. Henry II forbade them and his knights who wanted to joust had to go over seas, . . . Richard also got money for the crusade by granting licenses to hold tournaments in certain lawful places, and fined Robert Mortimer 'quod torniaverat sine licentia.' This shows that the fashion had already taken root in England.

"The tournament, which may have been invented or regulated in the ninth or tenth century, was in full operation in the twelfth in every part of Europe, in spite of the opposition of the Church; and was the favorite pastime of nobles and gentlemen throughout the Edwardian period, and until the beginning of the sixteenth century, when it suffered a brilliant eclipse in the blaze of knightly and royal display which preceded the age of the reformation and the close of the feudal era." (Cornish 91).

Originally the tournament was the charge of a party of horsemen, who turned back to acquire the momentum necessary for a fresh attack. Similarly the joust was the charge of a single horseman against a single antagonist. Both terms have had their meaning stretched to cover all of the military exercises in the form of combats that were so important a feature of life in the middle ages. Hastiludes is the proper name for the entire group; it means spear play.

At first the tournament was strictly a preparation for war and was the best, and was almost the only possible training as long as the single armed horseman was the principal military unit. As tactics changed he became less important; armor became less necessary and was worn more for display; and the tournament degenerated from simple hard fighting, which only stopped short of killing or maiming the opponent, to a more and more complicated and artificial game. By the 16th century the favorite was the joust, which was less dangerous and gave a better chance to exhibit individual skill. There were many forms of it, each having its own rules and requiring its own forms of armor. The Germans in particular recognized a very large number, most of which bore no more resemblance to actual fighting than their students' duels do.

The melee was a combat for life and death, closed only by the defeat of one party, or by the herald, or the king, giving the word to cease, which he did by throwing down his warder (truncheon).

The tourney was between two groups of combatants who first charged on horseback, and then dismounted and continued to fight on foot with swords, maces or axes. The joust was between a single pair of mounted men. If the courses were run in an open enclosure it was called a tilt. If "at the barrier," a joust. The barrier was a heavy timber fence as high as the waist, or sometimes as high as the neck, of a man on horseback, which ran lengthwise of the lists. The knights rode alongside the barrier with their left sides toward it and their lances pointing diagonally across it. The height of the barrier and the position in which the lances were held account for the lack of leg armor, and the extremely unsymmetrical design of the suits intended for this form of joust. Figs. 48, 49.

The behourde, or bourde, is variously described as an exercise with lance and target, and as the assault of a wooden castle. The *pas d'armes* was when a pass (*clusa*, *clausura*) was to be held against all comers. Round Tables were jousts where a party of knights engaged in single combats, or in parties of equal numbers, and afterwards dined at a round table. In the later days of the tournament the last act was frequently the attack of the "castle of love" garrisoned by ladies and attacked by knights in full armor, the only weapons being flowers. It always ended in the capitulation of the fortress and the carrying off of its defenders as prisoners by the victorious knights.

"The lists, an oval enclosure, were pitched with rows of seats and covered galleries all round. At the middle of the longer side was placed a seat of honor for the Queen of the Tournament. The pavilions of the challengers were pitched at either end, each with a shield of arms hung at the tent door. . . . The ground was kept by squires, who had their own trials of arms the day before (les vepres du tournoy); and all of the arrangements were ordered by kings-of-arms and heralds, who acted as judges (diseurs) in case of any breach of the rules. The knights were armed by ladies and received love tokens from them, to be worn in their honour. The Queen of Beauty and of Love gave the 'gree,' or meed of valour, which might be a chaplet of flowers or leaves, a coronet or jewel, or arms besides such trophies as the helmet of the conquered knight, his arms and horse, or any badge worn by him." (Cornish 101).

"The rules and ceremonies of tournaments were arranged by heralds according to the strictest ritual, and differed little if at all in different countries. The challengers rode forward to the barriers, and touched the shields of the knights with whom they wished to joust. The challenger *a outrance* struck his opponent's shield with the sharp end of his lance. Some knights offered themselves to meet 'all comers'; others reserved themselves to meet particular opponents, and might, without reflection on their valour, decline to meet any individual adversary." (Ibid. 102). "When the lists were cleared the jousting began. The squires or poursuivants saw to their master's arms and horses, and stood in readiness to render help in every way short of joining in the contest, which was only allowed in the *melee*. . . . The object of each was to strike his opponent either on the head, the more effectual but more difficult aim, or on the body. The shock of the heavy-armed man and horse often dismounted both contestants. If

both sat firm the lances were generally shivered, but it often happened that horse and man fell together; and whether the arms were blunt or sharp, ribs or necks might be broken. If the horses did not swerve, and the lances did not break, and either knight held his lance firm, mortal wounds were often given. If both knights were unhurt and kept their seats, they wheeled their horses about and charged again with fresh lances, until one or both were unhorsed. The victor also dismounted and the combat was continued on foot with swords. Two men completely encased in mail or plate might slash at each other for a long time without much harm done to either." (Ibid. 104).

In England prizes were given: 1st. To him who bore another from his saddle or overthrew horse and man. 2nd. He who twice struck "cournal to cournal," point to point. 3rd. He that struck another three times in the vue. 4th. "Item, if there be any man who fortuneth in his wise, which shall be deemed to have abiden longest in the field healmed, and to have run the fairest course, and to have given the greatest strokes, and to have holpen himself best with his speare." 5th. He who broke the greatest number of spears.

Broken spears were allowed: 1st. A spear broken between the saddle and the hinge of the visor counted one. 2nd. A spear broken above the hinge of the visor counted two. 3rd. "Who breaketh a spear, so as to strike his adversary down, or put him out of his saddle, or disarmeth him in such wise as hee may not run the next course after, or breaketh his spear cournell to cournell, shall be allowed three speares." Broken spears could be disallowed for breaking a spear on the saddle, or for breaking a spear on the toyle (barrier) two were lost, and for doing it a second time, three.

The prize could be lost by striking a horse, by striking a man with his back turned or deprived of his spear, or by hitting the toyle three times. Or "who unhealmeth himself two times shall have no prize, unless his horse fail him." (Cripps-Day, Appendix IV, xxviii)

Tournaments were originally intended to train men for battle and the varieties corresponded to the different kinds of fighting that they would be called upon to engage in during war. They gave, however, such magnificent opportunities for display that the original purpose was often lost sight of. The fighting was both on foot and mounted, and the most used arms were lances, swords, two-handed swords and axes. Extra pieces of armor were generally worn and special suits were made for certain forms of joust. The jousting helmets were always special and useless for ordinary fighting. In the 16th century a suit of armor sometimes had as many as one hundred extra pieces to be worn in the different kinds of combat in the lists.

TO-WARA. See Dekara.

TOWERS, MOVABLE. Movable towers, sometimes several stories high, were frequently used at sieges to raise the attackers to the level of the walls. They were fitted with bridges to reach the top of a wall with a sloping face. Battering rams were often worked in the lower part of these towers. They were usually made of wood covered with green hides to prevent their being set on fire. See Belfrey.

TOYLE. "A contrivance fixed over the right cuisse to hold the lance when carried upright; a lance bucket." (ffoulkes Armourer 167). Compare Tilt.

TO-ZAMA. (Outside lords). The third class of Japanese nobles during the Tokugawa Period. See Daimio.

TRABEI KLIT KLAU. The wooden shield of the Sea Dyaks. It is about three feet long and twenty inches wide, and made of the wood of the plye or jelutong. (Ling Roth II, 138). See Kliau.

TRABUTIUM. See Trebuchet.

TRAGA. A form of suicide among the Kattees of Guzerat much like the hari-kiri among the Japanese. Among the Kattees no agreement was considered binding unless guaranteed by the mark of the katar, and on the failure or breach of contract they inflicted *traga* on themselves (committed suicide) or, in extreme cases, carried out the murder of relatives with the katar. (Egerton, p. 137).

TRAIL. The inclined stock of a gun carriage or the extension of the stock that rested on the ground when in action.

TRAIN. A live bird or animal used to teach hawks what to fly at. (Phillott 69). It was sometimes used in catching wild hawks.

TRAMAZONE. See Stramazone.

TRAPPER OF MAIL. Mail armor for a horse.

It covered the entire body, head and neck; 13th century. (ffoulkes 87).

TREBUCHET, TRABUTIUM. A class of machines for throwing large stones by means of a heavy weight hung from one end of a pivoted beam, a sling to contain the object to be thrown being attached to the other, and much longer, end. They were used more generally than any other engine during the middle ages. They were of four kinds: those with fixed weights, those with a movable weight, with two weights, one fixed and one movable, those without weights but operated by cords fastened to the short arm of the lever. The last could not throw as heavy objects as the others but could be operated much more rapidly. The projectiles were stones, barrels of Greek fire, dead animals and occasionally even living men. (Hewitt I, 349; Payne-Gallwey, Throwing Engines 27). Fig. 799.

TRELLICE COAT. A kind of armor worn in the 12th century. It was apparently of leather reinforced by straps and studs of metal. The exact construction is not known. (ffoulkes 16).

TREYTZ of MUEHLIN near INNSBRUCK. A family of armorers of the 15th century. The oldest is known to have worked about 1460 and died in 1469. His sons Georg and Christian carried on the work; and his grandson Adrian, the son of Georg who was born in 1470 and died in 1517, was the most famous of the family. Between 1460 and 1500 forty-five historical suits are recorded as having been made by them. (Laking Armour I, 212).

TRIALAMELLUM. A triangular blade deeply grooved on all three sides. This was very often used with the small sword as it is light and stiff. It was at one time called the Biscayan shape. (Burton Sword 135).

TRIARII. The third line of the Roman legion. (Burton Sword 247).

TRIDENT, TRIDENS. A spear with three parallel points. It was used by Roman gladiators and has been used by many nations in many parts of the world since. It was common in China, Korea, Japan and Java and was used in Persia and India. Fig. 800.

FIGURE 799. *Trebuchets, from Payne-Gallwey, Projectile Throwing Engines, p. 28.*

TRIGGER, TRICKER. The lever by which a gun, pistol or crossbow is discharged.

TRIGGER GUARD. A guard to prevent the trigger from being caught and accidentally dis-

FIGURE 800. *Tridents. 1. Persian. Watered steel spearhead inlaid with gold. 2. Korean. Steel 18.25 inches long including socket. A bronze dragon's head where the blades meet. 3. Chinese tiger spear. Head 2 feet 6 inches long and 15.5 across the points. All steel. 4. Java. The straight center point is double-edged and 10 inches long; the side ones are 8.5 inches. 5. Java. The center point is square and 12.5 inches long; the side ones are flat and single-edged, and 4 inches long.*

TRIGGER, FOLDING. Folding triggers were quite common on pocket pistols in the 18th and early 19th centuries. When not in use the trigger is folded forward into a recess in the stock, when the hammer is raised to full cock the trigger springs out ready for use. Fig. 801.

charging the weapon. They are almost universally found on European firearms and are often highly ornamental; this is especially the case with Italian weapons of the 16th and 17th centuries. With the flintlocks used in the East a trigger guard is unnecessary as the cock is securely held by a safety catch.

FIGURE 801. *Folding Triggers. Pocket pistols, damascus barrels, ebony stocks. Length 7 inches. The one on the right shows the hammer raised and the trigger out; that on the left shows the hammer down and the trigger folded up.*

In Assam a lump of resin is sometimes stuck on the lower side of the stock in front of the trigger to act as a guard.

TRILHOENS. Swivel guns carried by elephants and camels in the Mogul armies of the 17th and

TRIPANTUM. A trebuchet with two weights, one fixed to the beam and the other movable. (Hewitt I, 349).

TRISUL. The trident of Mahadeo. (Sherring 47).

TRISULA. An arrow of the Javan gods. It has a

FIGURE 802. *European Trousses. 1. German blade dated 1678. 2. German, 1700. Metropolitan Museum. Not to scale.*

18th centuries. They were always fired towards the rear, never over the animal's head. (Manucci 61).

TRIMACRESIE. Groups of three or four Gaulish horsemen who acted as a unit. Pausanius says the intention was that if the horse of the chief soldier was killed he could replace it by one of those ridden by an attendant. This is somewhat similar to the lance fournie of the middle ages. (Denison 90).

TRIMARKESIA. The cavalry of the Gauls. (Burton Sword 269).

trident head made up of a straight point and a crescent. (Raffles I, 295 and plate p. 296/297).

TROMBASH. A Tookroori (Abyssinia) throwing stick. "It is a piece of flat, hard wood, about two feet long. The end turns up sharply at an angle of thirty degrees." (Baker, Nile Trib. 528).

TRONT. A rocket, Burma. (Egerton, p. 94).

TROUSSE. A sheath carrying a hunting knife, knives and forks and sometimes instruments for cutting up game, 16th century and later. (Dean Hdbk. 103). Fig. 802.

The Chinese and Koreans carry similar cases containing a knife, chopsticks, pickle spear, tooth-

TRUNCHEON. A stick or club. The baton of a commanding officer is often called a truncheon.

FIGURE 803. Oriental Trousses. 1. Manchuria. Silver mounted case. Horn handled knife, bone chopsticks. Large belt loop. 2. China. Shagren case with brass and silver mounts. Knife with a handle of horn and bone. Ivory chopsticks and pickle spear. 3. China. Shagren case with silver mounts. Jade handled knife and tortoise-shell chopsticks with silver ends. 4. China. Case with silver caps, shark skin ends and engraved ivory middle. Knife with wood handle and ivory pommel. Pair of ivory chopsticks and pickle spear with silver caps. 5. China. Case with ends of embossed and gilded metal; middle of engraved white ivory inlaid with green. Knife handle of green ivory with embossed and gilded pommel. Two very long gilded chopsticks. 6. Korea. Wood case with white metal mounts.

picks and ear spoons, all of which are freely used at and after meals. Many of them are beautifully made with ivory or jade handles for the knives. Fig. 803.

TRUMELIERES, TRUMULIERES. See Greaves.

TRUNNIONS. Cylindrical projections from the sides of cannon on which it rests, and which form an axis about which it can be revolved in a vertical plane.

TRUSS, TRUSSING. See Bind.

TSCHEKAN. A war hammer, Russia. (Schere-metew 111).

TSCHEREWZA. The Russian name for the short wrist plate of the Oriental arm guard. (Scheremetew 38). See Bazu Band.

TSCHEU. A wall crossbow, China. Some of them were very large with bows as much as twelve feet long. (Jaehns 333).

of shakudo and shibuichi, and then those of copper, brass, silver and gold. Tsuba were occasionally made of wood or ivory; these were mainly for special kinds of swords.

The different parts of the tsuba have names. The edge is the *mimi* and is treated in various ways, each of which has its own name. The center, about the opening for the tang, is called the *seppa dai*, and is very rarely decorated except in the type called

FIGURE 804. *Tschinke, German, 17th century. Wheel-lock gun with a "hind's foot" stock. Metropolitan Museum.*

TSCHINKE. A wheel-lock gun with the butt placed diagonally and the trigger guard indented for the fingers. (Tower 40, p. 134). Fig. 804.

TSUBA. The guard of a Japanese sword. The tsuba was the earliest fitting used with the sword and is the only one that is essential; the others are for convenience or ornament. It has always been rightly considered by the Japanese as the principal one and is always referred to by name, while the other fittings are known collectively as *kanagu*, if for a tachi, and as *kodugu*, if for any other kind of sword or knife.

The tsuba is a plate of metal through which the tang passes. In the majority of cases it is elliptical, though many are nearly rectangular with slightly curved sides and rounded corners. The four-lobed shape, called *mokko*, is also quite common, and many other shapes are occasionally met with. Fig. 805.

The earliest tsuba are found in the burial mounds of the 8th century and earlier. They are kite-shaped and usually pierced so as to leave a rim and a center plate connected by straight bars, fig. 806. Some very early guards were made of a plate of steel between two pieces of leather, or one of leather between two of steel, the whole lacquered to protect it from the weather. These are known as *neri tsuba*. The great majority of tsuba now in existence are made of iron or steel; next in number come those

namban. There are often openings called *riobitsu* at the sides of the seppa dai for the knife and head pin. Quite often these are filled up with pieces of a different metal from the guard. These plugs are occasionally decorated, but are more often plain.

The Japanese tsuba have gone through the same cycle as European armor — the first were simple, thin plates of steel purely for utility. The makers soon began to vary the texture of the surface and edges by skillful hammer work, and some of the effects so produced are remarkably good. At times the guard was made by welding together steels of different hardness, then twisting the bar in various ways so that when lightly etched it had the appearance of the grain of wood (*mokume hada*). Others pierced their guards with simple but effective designs. In the Kamakura period particularly, guards were pierced and decorated with designs in very low relief. Some of the early makers paid particular attention to the edges, turning them over, raising them or causing the metal to flow back on the body of the guard, thereby producing very interesting and attractive effects.

It was not, however, until the 16th century that any distinguished maker of guards as a specialty appeared. In this century Kaneiye, Nobuiye and Umetada lived and made iron guards that have never been equalled. Kaneiye was the first to inlay guards with gold and silver, which, however, he used very sparingly. His landscapes and figures in low relief slightly touched with the precious metals are charming and fairly hypnotize the beholder, who sees in them things that are only faintly suggested.

About this time, or slightly later, the Higo and Akasaka schools produced very characteristic guards. They are pierced in designs of animals and foliage,

wards broke away and founded schools of their own. It is hardly too much to say that the Goto were the inspirers of most of the magnificent decorative work done by the later tsuba makers. Many of the schools differed totally from the Goto in their designs and in the style of their work, but the technique and fundamental methods were Goto.

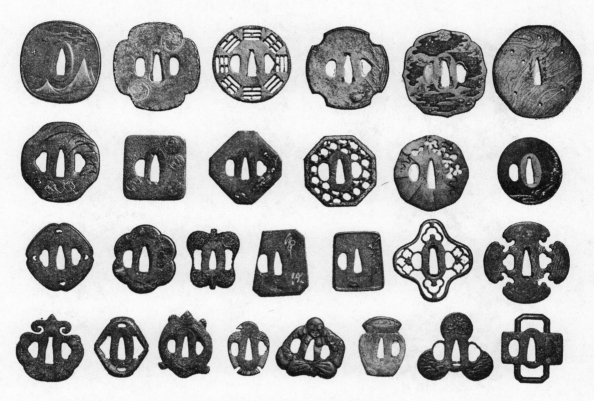

FIGURE 805. *Tsuba — shapes. The commoner forms are shown in the two upper lines; most of those in the lower ones are rare.*

simple and strong in composition. With little or no detail of modeling or engraving, they give a wonderful impression of strength and suitability for their purpose. To many they are the most satisfactory of the Japanese tsuba.

The Goto family began its work in the 15th century, but did not make guards until much later. The work of this school was confined mainly to ornaments in gold and bronzes. The Goto were wonderful workmen and developed the technique of working metals to probably the highest point ever reached; and, such being the case, naturally attracted a number of pupils. Many of these afterwards

One of the principal of these offshoots was the Nara school which was started by Toshiteru in the early 17th century. His work was far excelled by at least three of his successors—Toshinaga (Toshinaga Tahei, 1667-1737), a very skillful chaser in high relief, or entirely in the round. His best pupil, Shozui, founded the Hamano school. Sigura Joi (1700-1744) did marvelous work in engraving and low relief. Many of his subjects are very humorous. Tsuchiya Yasuchika (1668-1744) worked mainly with purely decorative designs and was most successful. This school continued but gradually changed its style. The Nara school as a whole did pictorial subjects in a freer and less conventional manner than the Goto.

In the 17th century guards were made in what was called the Chinese or *Namban* style. In its most characteristic form it consists of elaborate interlaced scrolls and dragons in pierced work. It is undoubtedly due directly to Chinese influence and indi-

fortunately this style was very popular and a host of imitators arose, many of whom did very inferior work which gave the school a bad name.

In the end of the 17th century Soyo I, guard maker to the Shogun, founded the Yokoya school. He was one of the most celebrated of Japanese artists. His successor and adopted son, Somin II, has

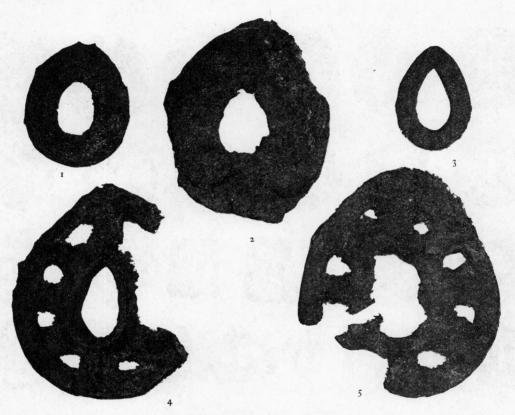

FIGURE 806. *Prehistoric Japanese sword fittings. 1. A seppa. 2. A solid tsuba. 3. A seppa. 4. A pierced tsuba with a raised flange resembling a fuchi. 5. A pierced tsuba. All of iron and not later than the 7th century. Collection of Mr. R. H. Rucker.*

rectly to Portuguese. The best of it is very good, but it was for a time very popular and much of the work done was of inferior quality.

Much of the same can be said of the work of the Soten school. The subjects were generally scenes from the civil wars, and the guards are crowded with figures in high relief, or in the round, minutely carved and inlaid. The work of the founder and best artists of this school is excellent, the different figures being full of life and individuality; but un-

an even higher reputation. He was equally celebrated for his work in high relief and for his engraving. The Yokoya school produced as beautiful guards as any other, and while they were very elaborate they are never unsuitable for use.

The Kinai masters lived in Echizen and this school worked from the 17th to the 19th century. Their best work is very delicate pierced carving with little or no gold inlay. The Kinai dragons are famous and the delicacy and accuracy of the carving of the principal masters could hardly be equalled.

In the 18th century the Hosono school founded by Hosono Masamori did wonderful pictures in very fine flat inlay. A kozuka may have a picture of a bridge with a procession crossing it, each figure of which is perfectly distinct and individual when seen under a magnifying glass. This style also had many imitators.

During the 18th and 19th centuries schools and styles of work multiplied enormously; while the best of it is extremely good, much of it was not. In many cases guards were made that were so over elaborate, delicate, or in such high relief that they were totally unsuitable for use. There were, of course, many makers who followed saner courses and produced guards that were beautiful and still serviceable. Among these Jakushi, a painter of Chinese pictures, who lived in Nagasaki, was conspicuous. He copied his own pictures in low relief and gold inlays, always on iron. His own work and that of his son and immediate followers is most attractive; but many imitators tried to copy his style and failed. Ichinomiya is the name given to the school founded by Setsune Nagatsune (1719-1789) who became dissatisfied with the somewhat stiff style of the Goto. He and his followers produced wonderful pictures in color by a combination of carving and inlaying. The masters of the Ishiguro—Masatsune, Koretsune and Koreyoshi—did some of the most beautiful and natural carving and inlaying that has ever been done. Joly aptly describes its work as a "happy blending of the classical Goto with the more elastic methods of the Nara and Yanagawa families."

Every variety of technique was used, modeling in high, low and medium relief, as well as carving in the round; pierced work in simple silhouette or more or less elaborately modeled; engraving and inlaying in many metals, and even colored stones, ivory, pearl and amber. The inlay was sometimes flat, but more often in relief delicately chiseled. Lacquer was imitated in metals and metals in lacquer. Pieces of various metals and alloys were soldered together and twisted and deformed in various ways and cut into thin plates which were then used alone or as backgrounds for further decoration. This last is called *mokume* (wood grain) because in many cases it suggests the grain of wood.

The most used alloys are *shakudo* and *shibuichi*. The former is a bronze containing gold, at least four per cent. of which is necessary to give the desired dead black or blue black, which it acquires when properly pickled. It sometimes contained much more than four per cent. of gold. Shibuichi means four parts, one of which was understood to be silver; the others might be copper, tin, lead or zinc. The composition varied greatly, the silver being from ten to ninety per cent. It is a much harder alloy than shakudo, and when used for fine carving was generally finished with a smooth polished background. Some of the varieties when properly treated to give the desired patina are of great beauty. All of the metals and alloys were treated with pickles to develop colors and patina. By varying the pickles different colors could be produced with the same base.

The surfaces are frequently polished, *jimigaki*, particularly when the object was made of one of the harder metals. One of the most popular backgrounds was *nanako*, fish roe surface. It is raised dots made by a cupped punch. When we consider that the dots are often not more than one one-hundredth of an inch in diameter, and that they are accurately arranged in straight or concentric lines, it does not seem possible that anyone could acquire the delicacy of touch required to make them. There are also special forms of nanako. One in which a smaller dot is raised on each of the main ones; another in which three dots are superimposed on each other; one in which the dots are rather widely separated and the background stamped with flowers so small that they can only be seen with a rather strong magnifying glass. Sometimes the nanako was with the dots arranged in patterns of lozenges with plain surfaces between the groups. Nanako was considered as the only background proper for the mountings of court swords. This style of background was usually done on the softer metals, gold, copper and shakudo, rarely on shibuichi or iron. Practically all other kinds of surface decoration are called *ishime* (stone surface), of which there are many varieties.

The Japanese define a good guard as one that has the four qualities—good design, good materials, good workmanship and good condition; which very completely covers the requisites.

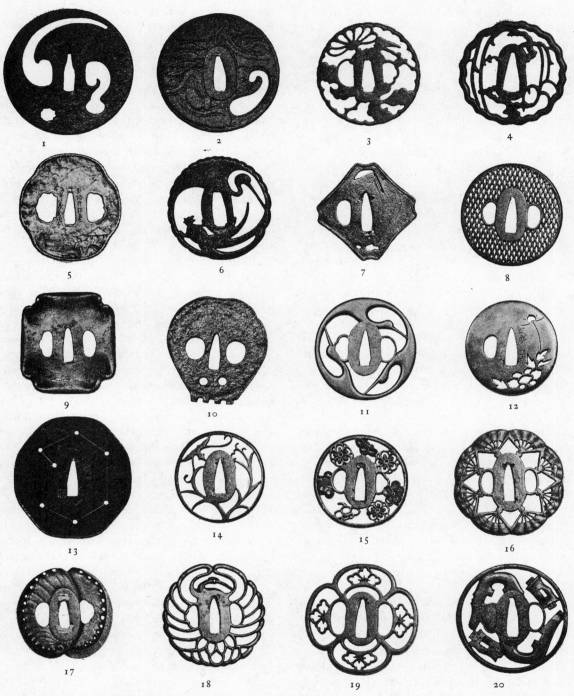

FIGURE 807. *Tsuba*. 1. *Iron. Kamakura type, pierced with a magatama (mythical jewel), 14th century.* 2. *Iron. Kamakura type, a pagoda in low relief, 15th century.* 3. *Iron. Pierced, Akasaka type. Chrysanthemum and leaves, 17th century.* 4. *Iron. Higo type, pierced, a willow tree, 17th century.* 5. *Iron. Kaneiye style, a landscape. Signed Yokuyo-Din.* 6. *Iron. Pierced, a crane and tortoise; the emblems of long life. Akao School.* 7. *Iron. Signed Nobuiye.* 8. *Iron. Ami-gata (net design).* 9. *Iron. Uchikayeshi (turned back and folded over).* 10. *Iron. A skull.* 11. *Iron. Three heraldic geese. Kinai School.* 12. *Copper. Pierced peony flower, itozukashi. Signed Kofuju Tsuneyuki, 18th century.* 13. *Iron. Mokume (wood grain) and a constellation. Signed Tobu ju Masanobu, 17th century.* 14. *Iron. Pierced, a butterfly and flower. Signed Akao.* 15. *Iron. Pierced blossoms.* 16. *Iron with brass inlay, eight folding fans.* 17. *Iron. Two ablona shells.* 18. *Iron. An heraldic crane. Miochin School, 17th century.* 19. *Iron. Pierced mons. The edge is inlaid with a vine in silver.* 20. *Iron. Pierced. The four pieces of a saddle tree.*

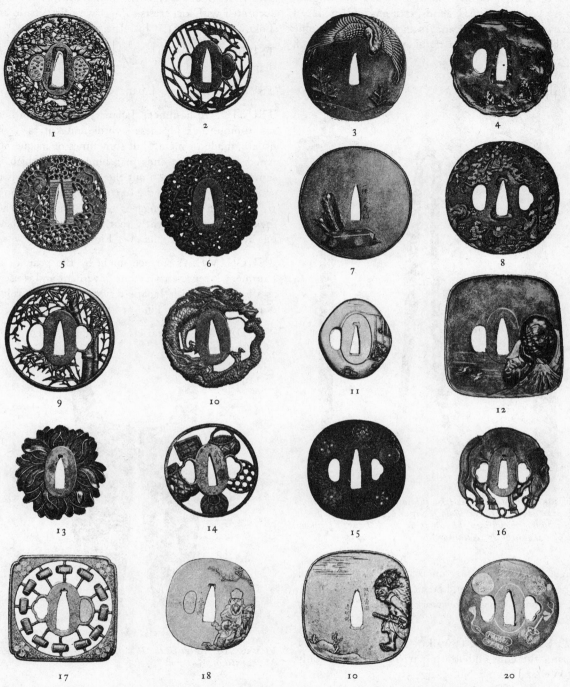

FIGURE 808. *Tsuba.* 1. *Iron. Pierced and inlaid with gold, silver and copper. Warriors. Signed Soheisi Niudo Soten, 17th century.* 2. *Iron. Pierced. Geese flying in the rain.* 3. *Shibuichi. Flying crane and pine tree. Signed Soriuken Masayuki, 19th century.* 4. *Copper. Carved and inlaid. The seven sages in the bamboo grove.* 5. *Iron. Pierced scrolls and dragons, namban style.* 6. *Sentoku. The thousand monkeys. Signed Hishu Yagami ju Mitsuhiro, 18th century.* 7. *Iron. A box and peacock's feathers inlaid to imitate lacquer. Signed Ichiriu Tomohisa, 19th century.* 8. *Iron. Inlaid gold. The meeting of the Emperor Wu Ti and Seibo, 18th century.* 9. *Iron. Pierced bamboo.* 10. *Iron. A coiled dragon. Kinai School.* 11. *Shibuichi. The interior of a kitchen. Signed Den Rausai Yoshinori.* 12. *Sentoku. Toshitoku looking down from Mount Fuji. Signed Nara Yoshimasa, late 18th century.* 13. *Sentoku. A chrysanthemum carved in the round. Signed Tozui, 19th century.* 14. *Iron. Baskets pierced and carved in the round.* 15. *Iron. Ishime, surface resembling crushed morocco. Inset panels of enamel. Signed Furukawa Mitsuyoshi.* 16. *Bronze. Pierced, a horse. Signed Kanse 3rd Tetsugendo.* 17. *Iron. Square shape inlaid with vines at the corners. A water wheel.* 18. *Shibuichi. The three vinegar tasters, carved and inlaid. Signed Konkwan.* 19. *Iron. Warrior and demon in relief and inlay. Signed Kiyoaki, 19th century. Copied from Toshihisa.* 20. *Sentoku. Fans very finely worked in flat inlay of various metals.*

A collection of fine guards illustrates the religion, history, mythology, legends, customs and modes of artistic thought of Japan. As an artist friend of mine once said: "I know of nothing that gives so much

FIGURE 809. *Tsuchi.* 1. *Iron inlaid with silver, the punch is attached by a silver chain. Length 6.25 inches.* 2. *Brass, the punch screws into the top of the head. Length 5 inches. No. 1 from the collection of Mr. T. T. Hoopes.*

in such a small space, composition, drawing, modeling, color, diversity and beauty of materials and surfaces with superlative workmanship." Figs. 807, 808.

TSUBAME-BO. (Swallow face). A menpo covering the chin and lower part of the cheeks only. (Weber II, 20). No. 4, fig. 567.

TSUBA-SHI. A maker of tsuba.

TSUBO ABUMI. "Bag-shaped" stirrups, Japan. Stirrups with a sharp ridge across the front.

TSUBO-ITA. See Waki-Date.

TSUBO KASA KIRI. Menuki in the form of hats decorated with kiri crests. They were first made by Tokujo, 1543-1631. (Joly Int. 15).

TSUBO-YANAGUI. A Japanese quiver in the shape of a long jar.

TSUBURA. A fort, Japan.

TSUCHI. A hammer, Japan. A small hammer for dismounting Japanese swords and knives. It is usually made of metal, but sometimes of lacquered wood. The handle ends in a blunt point which is sometimes used to push out the mekugi. There is a small pin screwed into the top of the handle or hung from it by a chain which is used to drive out the mekugi if it fits so tightly that it cannot be pushed out by the end of the handle. Fig. 809.

TSUCHIME. A surface made by the pean of a hammer; it represents a stone pavement and is used as a background on Japanese sword fittings. (Joly, Naunton xii). It is a kind of ishime.

TSUDZUMI. A variety of Japanese corselet. (Garbutt 161).

FIGURE 810. *Tsugi-Gote, Japan, 17th to 18th centuries. Metropolitan Museum.*

TSUGI GOTE. A form of kote in which the upper arm is protected by a wide plate like a sode loosely fastened to the shoulder. The rest of the arm is of the ordinary type. (Conder 273). Fig. 810.

TSUGI-WAKE. (Spliced, or patched, division). Making the back of a kozuka or kogai of two metals; they may meet in a straight line down the center or in a diagonal one.

FIGURE 811. *Tsuka-No-Kanamono. Shibuichi. Daruma seen through a broken wall. On the other piece the inscription "Facing the wall for nine years." The seal reads, Nagamori, the maker.*

TSUJIGIRI. Killing in the street to test a new sword, Japan.

TSUKA. Japanese, a hilt. See Katana. (B. M. Hdbk. 52).

TSUKA AI. The ornaments that take the place of menuki on a tachi. (Joly Int. 14).

TSUKA GASHIRA, KABUTO GANE. The pommel of a tachi. It is usually much larger than the kashira used on other swords and has large openings in the sides. Fig. 416.

TSUKA GUCHI. See Fuchi.

TSUKA-ITO. The silk cord or braid wound round the hilt of a Japanese sword or knife. It generally passes through the openings (shitodome-ana)

in the kashira and holds the latter in place. In one form of mounting it is crossed over the kashira. There are many ways of winding the tsuka-ito.

TSUKA-NO-KANAMONO. Japan. Metal plates covering the sides of the hilt of a sword or knife instead of the usual shark skin. Fig. 811. See also Gin Same and Tetsu Same.

TSUKU-BO. A Japanese pole arm with a cross-shaped head with teeth on it. It was kept in a rack in the guardhouse at the gate of a castle.

TSUKURA. A bundle of straw used as a target, Japan.

TSUKURI. The ornaments of a sword, Japan.

TSUKURI-SORI. A strongly curved blade, Japan. (Lyman 7).

TSUKURI-SUGU. A very slightly curved blade, one that is almost straight, Japan. (Lyman 7).

TSUKUSHI-BOKO. Large two-edged bronze spearheads, primitive Japan. They are characteristic of the region of Tsuchima. (Dean Notes 11). Fig. 812.

TSUKUSHI NAGINATA. An early form of naginata in which the shaft fits in an eye on the back of the blade. Fig. 588.

TSUMAGURO. An arrow, the feathers of which are partly black, Japan.

TSUNOGI. An arrow tipped with horn or bone, Japan.

TSURA, TSURAO, TSURU. A bowstring, Japan. The Japanese bowstrings are made of sinew or of silk cord. For the ceremonial bows they are of silks of several colors.

FIGURE 812. *Tsukushi-Boko. Bronze spearhead from the Island of Tsuchima, probably antedating the Christian era, i.e., earlier than the period of the tumuli. Metropolitan Museum.*

TSURASASHI. A maker of bowstrings, Japan.

TSURUGI. See Ken.

TSURUMAKI. A reel of basketwork or leather for carrying bowstrings, Japan. The basketwork reels are sometimes plain and sometimes lacquered, the leather ones are almost always lacquered. Fig. 813.

TSUTSU-GOTE. A special form of kote in which the whole is covered with mail and the outer portion of the upper and lower arm are further protected by splints or curved metal plates sewn on so

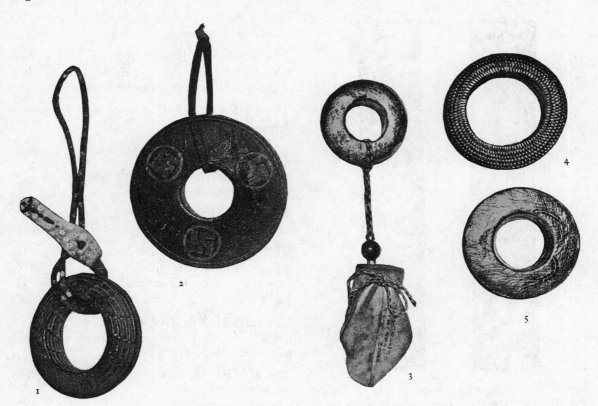

FIGURE 813. *Tsurumaki.* 1. *Heavy, dark basketwork 5.25 inches in outside diameter. Sling of printed leather.* 2. *Black leather with a gilt border and mon. Diameter 6.5 inches.* 3. *Gilded leather with stamped flowers. Diameter 3.75 inches. Attached is a heavy leather pouch.* 4. *Gold lacquered basketwork. Diameters — outside 5 inches, inside 3 inches.* 5. *Gold lacquered leather with a mukade in black and white. Diameter 4.75 inches.*

TSURUMAKI GATAME NO SHI TO. An old method of carrying a sword and dagger, Japan. The sword is horizontal and the knife vertical and passed through a tsurumaki. Fig. 428. (Joly S. & S. 3).

TSURUSUBERI. (The path for the bowstring). A leather guard to cover the breast of the armor to give a smooth surface on which an archer can draw his bow, Japan. Fig. 814.

TSUSHO. See Torino.

TSUSKIAH. See Taavish.

TSUTSU. A gun barrel, Japan.

as to leave the elbow free and only covered by the mail. (Conder 273).

TSUTSU KOSHIATE. See Koshiate.

TSUTSU-SUNE-ATE. Japanese greaves composed of two curved metal plates hinged together and worn over padded leggings. The knee cop is not fixed to this type but separate ones were sometimes worn with it. (Conder 276).

TSUYO-NO-O, TENUKI O, KAKE. A variety of sword knot. In the Nara period it was made of leather, a fashion that was retained for the ceremonial sword (tachi). It had metal tags called *tsuyo* and clamps called *kohaze*. Fig. 717. (Joly S. & S. 47).

TSUYO OTOSHI NO KUBO. "Dew dropping tube." A tube on the chin of a menpo to allow the perspiration to run out.

FIGURE 814. *Tsurusuberi. A pad of printed leather to cover the front of the breastplate to give a smooth surface for drawing the bow.*

TSUZUMI. A drum, Japan. Two forms of drum were used in Japan. One was barrel-shaped with parchment heads; the other had a body shaped like an hourglass and flat metal heads much larger in diameter than the body and laced together outside it.

TUAGH-GATHA. The battle-axe of the early Scotch Highlanders. (Campbell 95).

TUBA. The long Etruscan trumpet. (Burton Sword 248).

TUBAK. A gun, Tibet. See Me-Da.

TUBAK-I-TIKLI. A gun wad, Western Tibet. (Ramsay-Western).

TUBA KNIFE. A Moro knife with the cutting edge straight and the back curved. The hilt is at right angles to the edge. The scabbards are open on one side. Fig. 815.

TUCK, TOCKE, TOCK. See Rapier.

TUFANG-I-CHAMAQUI. Persian, a rifle like those used in the Caucasus, but with a curved stock much like an Afghan jezail. (Moser XXXVIII). See Gun.

Persian, a gun. This name was given to matchlocks by Tippoo. (Egerton, p. 34).

TUGALIN. Arrows used for shooting large birds, Point Barrow. The heads are of walrus ivory five or six inches long, usually five sided, but occasionally triangular, with a rounded tang inserted in the shaft. They have rather blunt points and one or more barbs on one side only. (Murdoch 206).

TUILLES. The pointed Gothic thigh guards worn hung from the breastplate. Their name comes from their resemblance to roof tiles. See Frontispiece.

TUKAK. Spikes planted in the paths by the Dyaks to delay the approach of an enemy. See Panji and Ranjau.

TULA. A flint knife, especially used for circumcision, Australia. (Howitt 654). See Kira.

TULUP. A blowpipe, Java. The Javan blowpipe is a straight tube of wood or cane about five feet long. It never has a spearhead attached to it.

The blowpipe has not been used in war in Java for centuries. (Raffles I, 296 and plate p. 296/297).

The Ball blowpipe is called by the same name. It is of ironwood and has a spearhead. (Arc. f. Eth. IV, 279).

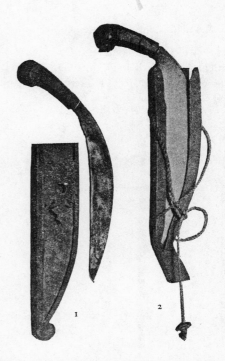

FIGURE 815. *Tuba Knives. 1. Blade 10.25 inches long, wooden hilt. Wood scabbard with an iron piece across the open side. 2. Zamboanga. Hilt of carved black wood.*

TULUPAN. A Javan blowpipe made of the long-jointed bamboo. (Arc. f. Eth. IV, 279).

TULWAR, TULWAUR. See Talwar.

TUMBA. A one-piece spear, Flores. (Arc. f. Eth. VIII, 7).

FIGURE 816. *Tungi. Plain head and handle. Length —*
edge 9.5 inches, handle 14.5 inches.

TUMBAK. A spear, Java. This is the ordinary Malay spear. The head may be of any one of several forms, either straight or waved. (Raffles plate p. 296/297).

TUMBOK LADA. A kind of Malay knife.

TUMPULING. Java, a spear with a barbed head. Some have two barbs, others have only one. (Raffles plate p. 296/297).

TUN. A shield, China. (Laufer 187).

TUNDIWUNG. A boomerang much curved in a sharp angle with a handle at one end. Kurnai tribe, Southeast Australia. (Howitt 265). Compare Liangel.

TUNGI. The Khond fighting axe. (Forbes, Canara and Gangam 252). Fig. 816.

TUNIC. A short linen shirt reaching to just above the knee. It was worn next the body under armor in the 11th century. (ffoulkes 22, 38).

TUNINASHA. A variety of koftgari work (false damascening). (Wallace Orient.).

TURAL. See Ku-Yan.

TURAS. A species of field fortification made of branches of trees interwoven like basket work, 16th century. Mogul India. (Invasions of India 29).

TURNING PINS. Revolvable pins with eccentric heads. They were fastened to one plate of a piece of armor and passed through slots in another to which it was to be fastened. When the pin was turned it could not be withdrawn until turned back so that the head was in line with the slot. (ffoulkes 59).

TURNMUNG. An Australian shield used for club fighting. It is either a flat piece of wood with a handle in one edge, or a short and heavy block of wood of elliptical section and plain, with a handle carved in the back. (Howitt 337, 347). See Tamarang, fig. 771.

TURUP. A guarded katar with a chain or bar joining the tops of the handlebars. (Wallace Orient).

TUSAKI. See Sageo.

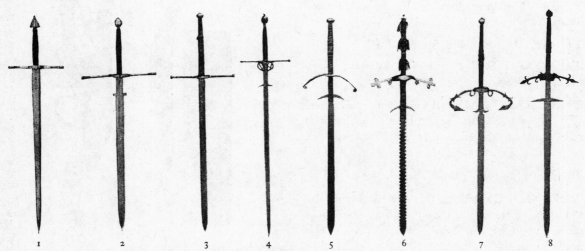

FIGURE 817. *European Two-Handed Swords.* 1. *Swiss(?),* 1515. 2. *Swiss,* 1550. 3. *Italian, about*
1540. 4. *Spanish, 1540. Blade signed Tomas Ayala.* 5. *German, 1550.* 6. *German, 1540-1570.* 7.
Brunswick, 1550. 8. *German, 1540. Metropolitan Museum. Not to scale.*

TUU. An ivory pick on the butt of an Eskimo spear, Port Barrow. (U. S. N. M. 1900, 280).

Swiss used it almost exclusively until the latter part of the 15th century. In 1499 it was decided "to

FIGURE 818. *Oriental Two-Handed Swords. 1. China, an executioner's sword. Hilt and scabbard covered with black leather. All of the mountings are of iron in namban style, partly gilded. Length overall 4 feet. 2. China, all iron. Handle wound with silk cord. Length 5 feet 1 inch. 3. China. Handle wound with blue cord. Length 32 inches. 4. Assam, brass mounted. Length 4 feet 0.25 inch. 5. Assam. Length 3 feet 3.75 inches. 6. Assam. Length 2 feet 8.25 inches. 7. Central India. Brass mounted. Length, blade 2 feet 9.625 inches; overall, 4 feet 10 inches.*

TWO-HANDED SWORD. Any sword heavy enough to require the use of both hands. It was long a favorite weapon in many parts of Europe. The

suppress completely the two handed swords and, instead, to arm the pikemen and halbardiers with a sword or war axe." (L'Armee Suisse). It was, however, retained by the Swiss Papal Guard until the middle of the 19th century, if not later. Fig. 817.

The Japanese katana, or fighting sword, was frequently used with both hands; and the Japanese also had very large two-handed swords. See O-Dachi. The Chinese also used two-handed swords but mainly for executions. Like all Chinese weapons they are clumsy with broad falchion blades and, usually, long, straight iron handles terminating in a ring. The handles are generally wound with cord. Another type is also used; it is carried in a scabbard and the hilt and scabbard mounts are in the namban style.

In India among the Rajputs and Mahrattas two-handed swords were sometimes used. They had rather short blades and very long hilts decorated with three fluted brass balls, the guards were very small with very short quillons curving sharply towards the blade. These hilts are frequently hollow and serve as sheaths for small knives. In the south a different type was used. It had two plate guards. See Mel Puttah Bemoh.

The Nagas of Assam used two quite different forms of two-handed swords. The commoner has a single edged blade, straight and about thirty inches long, and a long iron hilt with two cross guards, one about eight inches from the pommel and the other about eighteen. The upper is the longer. The

FIGURE 819. *Uchi-Ne.* 1. *Head 2.875 inches long. Lacquered shaft. No feathers. Tassel of purple and white silk on the shaft. Red lacquer sheath with a gilt mon. 2. Head 3.5 inches long. Lacquered shaft with large feathers. No sheath. Length 12 inches. 3. Head 5.875 inches long. Lacquered shaft with feathers. Ivory ferule and nock. Gold lacquered sheath.*

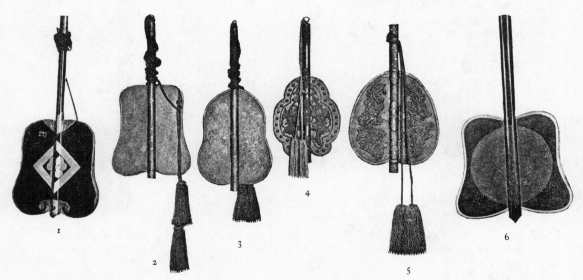

FIGURE 820. *Uchiwa.* 1. *Fine lacquer, a gold mon on black. Reverse inscriptions giving accounts of matches. Mountings of engraved silver. A wrestler's fan; the rest are for officers. 2. Iron with dragons in gold and silver on one side and an inscription and constellation on the other. 3. Iron with warriors in gold and silver on one side and the sun, moon and an inscription on the other. 4. Lacquered handle; body of metal with applied brass ornaments. Length 14.5 inches. 5. Iron very finely embossed with dragons on one side and clouds on the other. 6. Lacquered black with a silver border, a red sun on one side only. Length 19.75 inches.*

other form is much shorter and has but one guard. The blade has a sharp reverse curve close to the hilt which throws it about three inches out of line with the latter but parallel to it. Fig. 818.

TYINDUGO. See Kerrie.

was worn by the lower classes of retainers in Japan. (Conder 280).

UCHI BARI. See Uke Bari.

UCHIDASHI. Hammered work, embossed work.

FIGURE 823. *Ulu. Eskimo women's knives. Steel blades and wooden handles. Museum of the American Indian, Heye Foundation.*

TYRAL. See Kuyan.

TYRRIT. A swivel. It was placed between the jesses and leash of a hawk to keep them from tangling. (Harting 231).

U

UBU-DZUTSU. A variety of kote. (Garbutt 140).

UCHI-AWASE-GUSOKU. A lacquered leather corselet made of two pieces, front and back, tied together with cords. It has short taces attached and

This name is applied to all work bossed out from the inside so that the pattern is shown in relief; this is then chased, inlaid or otherwise ornamented, Japan. (Joly, Naunton xii).

UCHI GANE. The hammer of a gun, the serpentine of a matchlock, Japan.

UCHIKABUTO. The inside of a helmet, Japan. In examining a helmet belonging to another it is considered very rude to look at the inside.

UCHI-KAGI. A grapnel for holding two ships together when fighting, Japan.

UCHI-NE. A short javelin with feathers, Japan.

They are very short, but heavy; and were carried for defense when traveling in a litter. Fig. 819.

UCHIWA. A flat fan that does not fold up. The war fan carried by the higher officers as a sign of command in Japan was of this type. These fans were made of iron embossed or inlaid, or of wood or leather lacquered. They were used for signaling

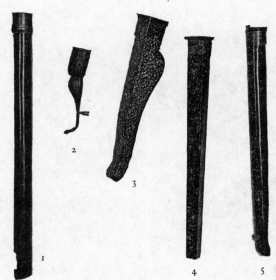

2

3

1

4   5

FIGURE 821. *Uked-Zutsu. 1. Wood lacquered red. Length 16.75 inches. 2. Bronze very finely chased with a vine in relief. 3. Wood lacquered gold. Length 10.75 inches. 4. Wood, square section, lacquered black. 5. Wood, round section, fine black lacquer. The ferule at the top is of shakudo with a vine in gold. Length 14 inches.*

to guard with and as weapons. Similar fans were carried before wrestlers when entering the ring. Fig. 820.

UDENUKI CORD. The Japanese sword knot. It was passed through two openings in the guard of a katana, or fastened to a loop of metal on the pommel of a tachi. (Joly, Naunton xxi). Fig. 416.

UDENUKI TSUBA. A Japanese sword guard with two holes for the udenuki cord (sword knot). One hole is usually considerably larger than the other. (Joly, Naunton xxi).

UDLIMAU. An adze, Point Barrow. (Murdoch 165).

U-DO. Cormorant bronze, shakudo. The blue black variety which has a sheen like cormorant's feathers. (Weber II, 430).

UCHI MAKI. "Wrapped within." A method of making Japanese blades in which a plate of iron is welded to one of steel and the resulting plate is doubled to bring the iron inside. This method was used in making the sword sent to the French Exhibition of 1867 by the Prince of Satsuma, and dissected by Colonel le Clerc. (Gilbertson Blades 192).

This method would not be likely to produce a first-class blade.

UKE BARI, UKE URA, UCHI BARI. A soft cap of quilted silk or cloth forming the lining of a Japanese helmet. It was firmly fastened to the lower edge of the helmet and was not as deep as the latter so that the metal did not press directly on the head. It was strengthened by crossed straps on the inside, which were called *chikara-gawa.* (Conder 262).

UKED ZUTSU, UKI MOCHI. The lower staff holder for a sashimono. It was fastened to the back of the corselet at the waist. (Garbutt 173, Conder 267). Fig. 821.

1   2

FIGURE 822. *Ulas. Fiji throwing clubs of carved wood. 1. Is of the more characteristic shape. Length 16 inches. 2. Carved with the Polynesian pattern.*

UKE-GUSARI. See Kusari Gama.

U-KIN. (Cormorant gold). The blue black shakudo. See U-Do.

UKIRAN, DEDER. A carved kris hilt, Java. (Arc. f. Eth. XIX, 93).

UKUMALITA. The foreshaft of an Eskimo harpoon, Point Barrow. (U. S. N. M. 1900, 280).

dle is at the end. (Mason, U. S. N. M. 1890, 411). Fig. 823.

ULUBALANG, OOOLOBALONG. Malay, a chosen warrior, a champion. Men chosen for an especially dangerous duty or as guards for a king. (Hobson-Jobson 639).

ULOWA, KAM-MA. Different names given to

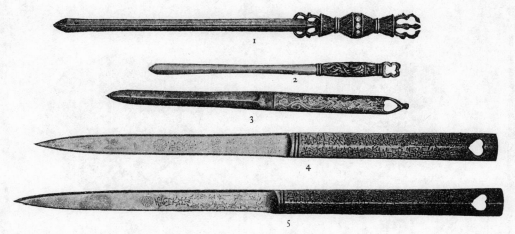

FIGURE 824. *Umabari.* 1. *Iron with gold inlay. A temple sword with a vajra hilt.* 2. *Silver with a gold dragon in waves. Length 4.625 inches.* 3. *Iron inlaid with gold.* 4. *Iron covered with inscriptions.* 5. *Like no. 4 but larger, it has the same inscriptions. Length 8.75 inches.*

ULAPA. A self bow convex on the back and concave on the belly, Surinam. (Arc. f. Eth. XVII, Sup. 115).

ULAS. A Fiji throwing club. (Horniman Museum 21). The Fiji throwing clubs are short with very large carved heads. They are about eighteen inches long and some of the heads are as much as six inches in diameter. Fig. 822.

ULQUITA. A shield, Arunta tribe, Australia. (Sp. & Gi.).

ULTUP. A blowpipe, Battak (Sumatra). (Arc. f. Eth. IV, 280).

ULU. A hilt, Malay.

ULU, OOLOO. An Eskimo woman's knife. In the earlier form it was a sharp-edged stone with a handle on the back; sometimes it was made of bone. The more recent ones have iron blades. In some cases a branch from the back of the blade connects it to the handle, giving it the shape of an ordinary kitchen chopping knife. In some rare cases the han-

reed spears with wood or bone heads, Victoria. (Brough Smyth 308).

UMABARI. (Horse needle). A small double-edged knife with a blade of flattened triangular or quadrangular section, and a hilt forged in one piece with the blade. It was only used in the province of Higo (Japan) and was carried in the side or edge of the sword scabbard in place of the kogai. "It was used to stab horses in the legs to produce a peculiar excitation of the muscles." (Joly Int. 17). Fig. 824.

UMA JIRUSHI. (Horse ensign). A huge fan with sticks five feet long, covered with silk and mounted on a pole about fifteen feet long. It was used as an ensign by the Tokugawa Shoguns. (Joly Leg. 66).

Any standard too large to be carried by a single man.

UMA SASHIMONO. A standard carried on a pole. They are of many shapes and sizes but all are too large to be worn on the back. Fig. 825.

UMA YOROI. Japanese horse armor. See Bard-ings.

UMA YUMI. A bow used for shooting from horseback. Japan.

UMBRIL, IMBER. A movable brim projecting over the eyes from the front of a helmet, 17th century. Some had nasals fastened to them, some of which were movable. (Dean Hdbk. 97, ffoulkes 83). Figs. 201, 202.

FIGURE 825. *Uma Sashimono.* 1. *Gilded shinto papers on a bamboo shaft 7 feet long.* 2. *A gilt war fan with pictures of foliage and inscriptions in black. Length 16.5 inches.* 3. *Wood, sheathed trident in black and gold lacquer. Shell lacquer shaft. Length 3 feet 2 inches.* 4. *Fan-shaped, of black lacquer with an ideograph in gold on one side, and the sun, moon and clouds in gold and silver on the other.* 5. *Single ended tokko of gilded wood on a short shaft with a socket on the lower end. A short shaft of shell lacquer is below the socket.*

UMBO. A central boss on a shield to give room for the hand. It was a prominent feature of the Danish and Gaulish shields, and in many cases is the only part that has been preserved. The early Norman kite-shaped shields retained it though it was of no use with a shield carried on the arm. In many savage and Malayan shields it is a prominent feature, being carved from the solid. Fig. 826.

UMBUL-UMBUL. A Javan standard made of a palm leaf which is trimmed off close to the mid-rib on one side and quite close on the other, a long streamer being left at the extreme end. (Raffles I, plate p. 296/297).

UMETADA of OWARI. One of the most celebrated of the early Japanese makers of sword mountings. His work is generally very fine carving in hard metal. He frequently signed his work with a rebus —a gold plum blossom (*ume*) and the character *tada*.

UM-KONTO. The Kaffir throwing spear. See Assegai.

FIGURE 826. *Umbo. 1. Umbo. 2. Grip. From a Merovingian cemetery near Vermand, Northern France, 5th to 7th centuries. Metropolitan Museum.*

UMLA. A vegetable poison used for arrows in New Guinea. (Ratzel I, 234).

UNA, UNAK, UNAHK, UNAN, UNANG, IMAKPUK, OONAK. A long, light Greenland harpoon with a bone knob on the butt. (U.S.N.M. 1900, 240).

A light Eskimo spear with a foreshaft of narwhal horn on which is a head loosely attached by a line. (Ratzel II, 113).

UNARMED. Not wearing armor. The word was always used in this sense as long as armor was worn. A man equipped with any number of weapons was not "armed" unless wearing armor.

UNCHANA ODOSHI. Armor laced with white and green cords, Japan. The name comes from *unchana* (Deutzia Serabra) which has white blossoms and green leaves.

UNCIN, ONCIN. A pick with one point. (Planche 511).

UNDER-COUNTER. "After you have overlapped your adversary's sword, in this you must go quite *under* his sword, turning your hand in Terce, and bring up his sword, giving him a thrust, as when you play the *Single Feint* at the head." (Castle 194).

UNIBER. "The face guard of a helmet, combining visor and bever." (Fairholt 613).

UNOKUBI TSURUGI. "Cormorant's head shaped," a blade with a blunt back edge for at least a part of its length, Japan.

UNTEI. A tower used at sieges, Japan.

UPPER POURPOINT. A padded garment worn over the hauberk in the 14th century. (ffoulkes 38).

URA. The side of the tang of a Japanese sword that is outward when it is slung edge downward. Tachi are signed on this side, katana on the opposite one. (Joly, Naunton xvii). See Temoto.

URAGAWARA, URAKAWARA. The strip of metal protecting the opening of the pocket for the kozuka in a Japanese scabbard. Frequently it is simply lacquered like the scabbard, but usually it is of metal decorated like the other fittings. Generally it is a straight bar, but occasionally it is of a very irregular shape. A band is sometimes placed around the scabbard with a ring on one side. This takes the place of both the kurikata and uragawara. A broad band may be placed on the scabbard to which the kurikata, soritsuno and uragawara are fastened. Fig. 827.

URAHAZU. The ends of a bow, Japan.

URAHOKIN. "Backed with gold." The Japanese description of a kozuka or kogai, the back of which is of gold and the face of some other metal.

URAMANTA. A boomerang, Arunta tribe, Australia. The boomerang of the Arunta is rather long and slim, and often has a slight reverse curve at one end. It is sometimes decorated with roughly incised lines, often arranged in rude patterns. It is always plentifully smeared with red ochre. (Sp. & Gi. 702, 705).

URR-CHE-RA. See Yirmba.

URTO. A sword in San Ch'uan Chinese.

USAKAWASA. A kind of scabbard fitting. Probably the uragawara.

USAYUZURU. An extra string for a bow, Japan.

USH. An arrow, Salar.

USHIRODATE. A large crest worn on the back of a Japanese helmet.

UTONARI. A corps of ninety men who formed the bodyguard of the Mikado when he went out.

UTSOBO. A Japanese quiver (Yadzutsu) covered with fur or leather. (Gilbertson Archery 117).

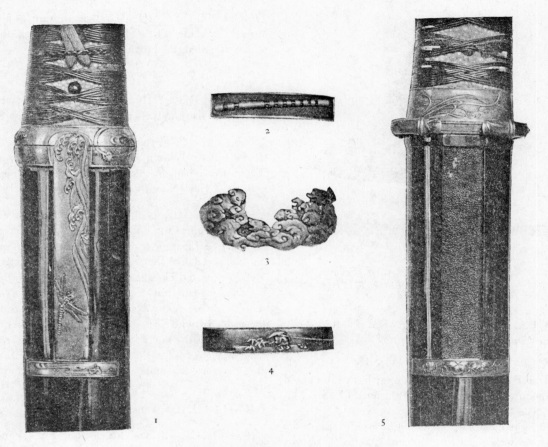

FIGURE 827. *Uragawara.* 1. *Uragawara and kozuka in place. Silver, 19th century.* 2. *Shakudo and gold, a flute in relief. Goto School, 18th century.* 3. *Silver and gold, oni in waves.* 4. *Sentoku and gold, a man towing a boat.* 5. *Uragawara in place showing the pocket for the kozuka. Silver, 18th century.*

USTED KABIR. A celebrated gunmaker of the court of Akbar. (Egerton, p. 62).

USUGANE-NO-YOROI. Iron armor, Japan, 9th century. (Conder 256).

USU-NIKU-BORI. Carving in low relief, Japan.

UTAP. The long form of Dyak shield as distinguished from the *pricei*, or round shield. (Ling Roth II, 139). It is made of bark, rounded at one end and pointed at the other. It is strengthened by strips of wood down the center and at the edges. Fig. 828.

UTTFA. A curious standard of the Bedouins of Northern Arabia. It is a huge case of bamboo covered with ostrich feathers and carried by a camel. "In it a girl is placed, whose business it is to sing during the fight, and encourage the combatants by her words. She needs to be stout-hearted as well as stout-lunged, for the battle generally groups itself round her in attack and defense. The Roala have a superstitious feeling about her defense, and the enemy a corresponding desire to capture her, for it is a belief that with the loss of the *uttfa* the Roala tribe would perish. Formerly every large Bedouin tribe had one of these. Perhaps from the scarcity of ostrich feathers and the difficulty of renewing them, the *uttfa* and the custom attached to it have disap-

down and placed in the groove, and the latter set up against it with a blunt punch or chisel to hold it in place. If the ornament is not of gold but one of the cheaper metals a recess the size and shape of the

FIGURE 828. *Utap. The shield of the Seribas Dyaks. Bark and wood with a cane edge. Length* 30.5 *inches.*

peared, except among the Roala and, I believe, the Ibn Haddal." (Blunt 351).

UTTORI IROYE. "Riveted plating." A method of attaching gold ornaments to sword mountings much used by the earlier Goto. The outline of the piece is cut as a dovetailed groove in the piece to be decorated. The edges of the ornament are bent

ornament is cut in the base and the ornament set in and secured as before.

Properly this should be called *uttori zogan,* which means inlay, and not *iroye,* which means "of several colors," and is only applicable when the inlay is of several metals.

U'U. The war club of the Marquesans. It is the

largest and finest club used anywhere. It is long, heavy and has a large carved head. (O'Brien 337). Fig. 829.

UWA-OBI. The outside belt worn with armor in Japan.

VANE. A broad flag carried by a knight at a tournament in the time of Edward I. (Fairholt 614).

VARVELS. Small, flat rings of silver with the owner's name engraved on them which were fastened

FIGURE 829. *U'U. Marquesas Club. Detail of head. Width 7 inches, thickness at the top 4.5 inches. Length 4 feet 7.75 inches. For the entire club see fig. 232.*

UWAR. See Mendaq.

UWARSHIKI. A cloth spread over a saddle, Japan.

V

VAJRA, DORGE, TOKKO. The first name is Sanskrit, the second Tibetan and the third Japanese. The Buddhist symbol of the thunderbolt. It may have a single prong at each end, or three or five. In Japanese the names are tokko, sanko and goko. The single pronged form makes a spoke of the wheel of the law. The vajra, usually one of three prongs, is used as a hilt on temple swords; and is frequently carved on Japanese blades. Figs. 830, 831.

VAMBESIUM. See Aketon.

VAMBRACE. Armor for the forearm. At first, about 1230, it was worn under the hauberk, but about the middle of the century, over it. Later the mail was discarded and the plate worn alone. (ffoulkes 38, 50, 58). Fig. 832. See also Bazu Band.

VAMPLATE, AVANT PLAT. The large conical guard fixed on the shaft of a lance to protect the hand in the 16th and 17th centuries. (ffoulkes 59, 76). Fig. 833. See Lance.

to a hawk's jesses. The leash was passed through them instead of being attached to a swivel. (Harting 231).

VEECHAROVAL. A scythe-shaped weapon of Southern India. (Egerton 97).

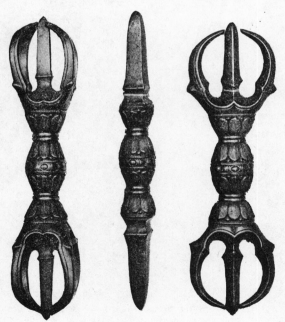

FIGURE 830. *Vajra. The Japanese names for the three varieties are: single-pronged, tokko; three-pronged, sanko; five-pronged, goko. Collection of Mr. R. H. Rucker.*

VELATI. Roman light infantry. They formed the advance force in action. (Burton Sword 245).

VENENTZ. Those who came to fight the challengers (tenentz) in a tournament. (Hewitt III, 633).

FIGURE 831. *Vajra hilt on a Japanese temple sword, 16th century. Metropolitan Museum.*

VENMUROO. A battle-axe with a crescent-shaped blade, Malabar. (Egerton 89, 90).

VENTAIL. The piece covering the lower part of the face on 16th-century helmets. (Dean Hdbk. 70). When the face guard was made of three pieces the middle one was called the ventail. (ffoulkes 60).

VERDUN. A rapier with a very long blade of lozenge or square section. It was used only for duelling in the 16th century. (Castle 235).

VERICULUM, VERETRUM. A light Roman javelin. (Burton Sword 246).

VERVELLES. Staples on a basinet through which the lacing that held the camail was passed. (ffoulkes 41). Fig. 206.

VEXILLARII. Old soldiers who worked the artillery in the Roman army. (Burton Sword 249).

VEXILLUM. A Roman standard of a square piece of cloth fastened to a crossbar at the top of a spear. Sometimes it had a fringe all around, sometimes only at the bottom, and at others no fringe, but was draped at the sides. (Macgeorge 24).

FIGURE 832. *Vambrace, Spanish, about 1550. Metropolitan Museum.*

VIF DE L'HARNOIS, DEFAUT DE LA CUIRASSE. The openings between the plates at the armpit where the body was protected only by mail in the 14th century.

VINCHU. "The scorpion," a Mahratta dagger "shaped like one side of a pair of shears, and worn without a sheath, but concealed in the sleeve. I have one a foot long and double-edged; but the commonest form is not more than half this size, and is stiletto-shaped, i.e., has no edge." (Sinclair, I. A. 216).

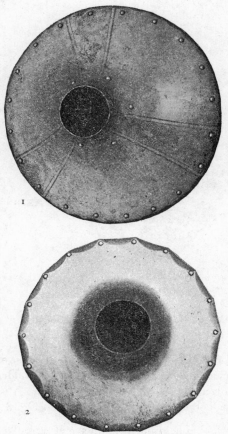

FIGURE 833. *Vamplates. 1. German, about 1500. 2. English, 1585. Metropolitan Museum. Not to scale.*

VINGTNERS. Officers commanding squads of twenty men in the English army from the time of Edward I to that of Henry VII. (Grose I, 182).

VIRATON, VIRETON. A bolt for a crossbow with spiral feathers to cause it to rotate in its flight. (Planche 515).

VIRES, VIROUX. Crossbow bolts used for game; the heads were of a great variety of shapes. (Laking Armour III, 144).

VISOR, VISIERE. The piece attached to a helmet to protect the face. It originated in the 12th century by joining the earflaps and the nasal; in this early form it was fixed. Later the name was applied to the movable piece covering the face. When the face guard was composed of two or three pieces the uppermost was called the visor. (ffoulkes 26, 42). Compare Vue.

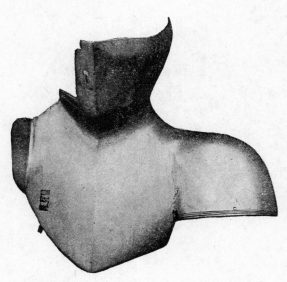

FIGURE 834. *Volant Piece. Probably French, about 1550. Metropolitan Museum.*

VISWACARMA. The Vulcan of Hindu mythology. (Tod I, 184).

VOLANT PIECE. A reinforcing piece worn in tournaments. It covered the chest, left shoulder and the lower part of the face, 16th century. It is substantially the same as the grand guard. Fig. 834.

VOLET. The rondelle of an armet. (ffoulkes Armourer 167).

VOLT-COUP. A feint in a given line followed by a thrust in the most directly opposite one. (Castle 194).

VOLTE. A sudden movement, or leap, to avoid a thrust.

VOULGE, BOULGE, BOUGE. A pole arm with a broad, axe-like head with a spike on the end. It is held to the shaft by two eyes. Some have a slightly curved hook held by a separate eye. In some of the earlier forms the hook was welded to the

head, in others a socket took the place of eyes. The halbard was evolved from the voulge. Some of the

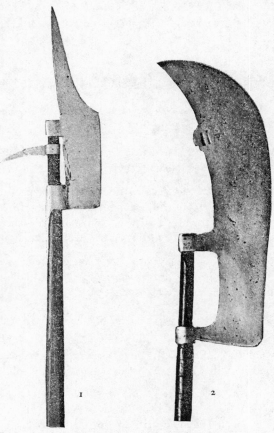

FIGURE 835. *Voulges.* 1. *Swiss, end of the 14th century.* 2. *French, 18th century. A Breton peasant weapon. Metropolitan Museum. Not to scale.*

later peasant weapons with broad, heavy blades, carried by two arms with eyes for the shaft, are also called voulges. Fig. 835.

FIGURE 836. *Wage. A large knob on a Japanese helmet to hold the short pigtail formerly worn.*

VOYDERS, VUIDERS, VUYDERS, GUIDERS. Gussets of mail fastened under the armpits and at the bend of the elbow by laces, or arming points, early 16th century. (ffoulkes 62).

Straps for fastening together the parts of armor. (Fairholt 615).

VOYS, JACQUES. An armorer of Brussels who worked for Philip the Fair, late 16th century. (Laking Armour II, 106).

VUE. When there were three movable pieces on a helmet to protect the face the uppermost was called the vue; if there were but two the upper was called the visor. (ffoulkes 60). Compare Visor.

W

WADDY. Australian clubs with enlarged heads of various shapes, usually pointed. (Burton Sword 38).

A general name for club, Australia.

WADNA. A boomerang. (Ratzel I, 358).

WAFTERS, WASTERS. Swords for practice. They either had wooden blades or the blades were

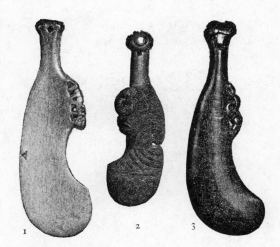

FIGURE 837. *Wahaika. 1. Made of the bone of a sperm whale. Length 17.25 inches. 2. Dark wood very finely carved with scrolls and figures, the latter with shell eyes. Length 14 inches. 3. Dark, heavy wood 16.75 inches long. Carved handle and figure.*

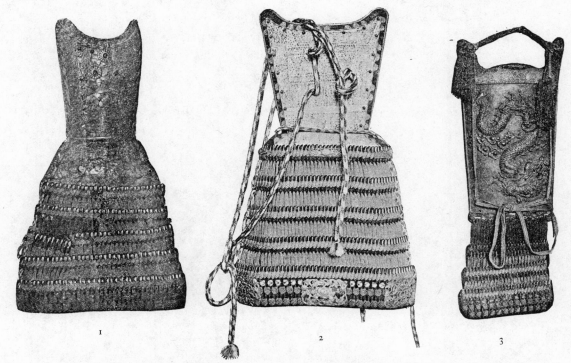

FIGURE 838. *Wai Date. 1. Upper plate covered with leather, lower laced lames, 17th century. 2. From an 18th-century o-yoroi. Side plate covered with printed leather, lacings of green, except the cross stitches on the lower edge, which are of red. Ornaments of gilded metal finely carved and pierced. 3. Iron plate embossed with a dragon in high relief. Lacings of black, green and red, 17th century.*

so set in the hilts that the blow was struck with the flat. (Planche 519, Castle 202, 247).

WAGE. (Topknot). A knob on top of a Japanese helmet, fig. 836. It was probably meant as a pocket to hold the short pigtail worn in early times.

FIGURE 839. *European Waistcoat Armor, Italian, second half of the 17th century. Metropolitan Museum.*

WAGHNAKH, WAGNUK. See Bagh Nakh.

WAHAIKA. A Maori club of irregular shape, made of wood or bone. It is the most elaborately carved of New Zealand weapons. When made of bone it is generally simpler than when of wood. Fig. 837.

WAHAR-NUK. See Bagh Nakh.

WAI-DATE, TSUBO-ITA. The plate forming the right side of a Japanese corselet. It was often a separate piece and was tied around the body by cords before the other parts were put on. When it was not a separate piece it was frequently made of two parts which were hinged to the front and back plates. In some corselets (generally late) both waki-ita and wai-date are made in halves and hinged to the front and back plates and connected by cords. (Conder 266). Fig. 838.

WAINIAN. A stone-headed spear, Mara tribe, Australia. The stone heads were generally made of quartzite, and are very similar to the knives (kira), but are occasionally made of slate. In the far north carefully chipped heads of opaline quartzite are sometimes used. In all cases the stone heads are fastened to the shafts by resin and cord. The shafts are of wood or cane and may be as much as ten feet long. (Sp. & Gi. 674).

WAIRBI. A woman's fighting club, North Australia. (Spencer, North. Ter. 311).

WAISCO-DUSA. A harpoon, Mosquito Coast. It has a short, hollow shaft with a barbed iron head fastened to a line passing through rings on the side

FIGURE 840. *Oriental Waistcoat Armor. 1. Northern India, 17th century. Four heavy leather plates decorated in colors. Each is connected to two others by hinge bars of metal. 2. Persian, 18th to 19th centuries. Five light steel plates gilded and decorated with figures in relief. 3. Persian, 18th century. Five steel plates covered with etched decoration.*

of the shaft and wound on a light wooden float. (U. S. N. M. 1900, 220).

WAISTCOAT ARMOR. A cuirass made of three or more plates hinged together at the sides and opening down the breast, 16th century. Fig. 839.

be put up. Only hawks of the genus *falco* can be taught to do this.

WAKERTI, WAKIDI. A kind of club used by some of the tribes living near Port Essington. The Kakadu call it *kadimango*. It is paddle-shaped, wid-

FIGURE 841. *Waki Biki.* 1. *Embossed steel.* 2. *Plates and laced lames.* 3. *Vertical plates laced.* 4. *Gilded plates and mail.* 5. *Gilded plates and mail, printed leather binding.* 6. *Leather covered plates and laced lames.* 7. *Lacquered plates and mail. The first three Metropolitan Museum. The last four only are to scale.*

Similar armor was worn in Persia and India where it was made of steel or leather. Generally it consisted of five plates—one for the back, two for the sides and two meeting in the middle of the front. Sometimes it was made of four plates hinged together and opened by pulling out one of the hinge pins. Occasionally there was an extra hinge bar at each joint, making the hinges double. Fig. 840.

WAITING ON. For a hawk to fly nearly over the head of the falconer when waiting for game to

ening gradually from the handle, and narrowing again to a round point. The length is about three feet six inches, and the width about five inches. It is decorated with patterns in red and white. See also Mabobo.

WAKI-BIKI, WAKI-DATE. Japan, pieces to protect the armpits. They were pads covered with mail, plates or scales laced together, and worn under the armor. (Conder 277). They should not be confused with the small plates often hung in front of the armpits for the same purpose. Fig. 841.

The waki-biki is either an armored garment like a short vest, fig. 842, or two pieces fitting under and around the arms. In either case it was worn

FIGURE 842. *Wakibiki (after Garbutt). Short vest-like garment of brigandine covered with deerskin and lined with silk damask. Bound with printed leather.*

under the corselet. It is often made of mail, *kusari-wakibiki*; or brigandine or jazerant. Wakibiki are also classified according to the method of fastening, as *botan-gake*, with buttons, *kohaze-gake*, with hooks, and *himo-tsuki*, with cords. (Garbutt 142).

An extra piece to guard the opening in a Japanese cuirass that opens at the side. (Dean Jap. 5, 29). Compare Wai-Date.

WAKI-DATE. A pair of crests worn on the sides of a Japanese helmet. (Conder 261). Figs, 252, 536.

WAKIDI. See Mabobo.

WAKI-ITA, IMUKE. The portion of a Japanese corselet covering the left side. It was usually fastened to the front and back plates by cords and hinges. (Conder 268).

WAKIZASHI, SASHI-ZOE. The shorter of the two swords carried by the Japanese samurai. The

blade was about eighteen inches long. In general it is like the long sword but the fittings are often more elaborate as it was more constantly carried and was taken into the house and laid on the floor by the owner when making a call, while the long sword was left at the entrance. It nearly always has both kozuka and kogai, while the long sword rarely has the latter and often has neither. It is also more often fitted with the soritsuno. The kojiri is more apt to be large and elaborate. It was sometimes called by its owner "the guardian of his honor."

The wakizashi was used as a supplementary arm in fighting, and also for ceremonial suicide, *hari-kiri* or *seppuku*, although in later times the dagger was usually preferred for this purpose. Fig. 843. See Japanese Blades.

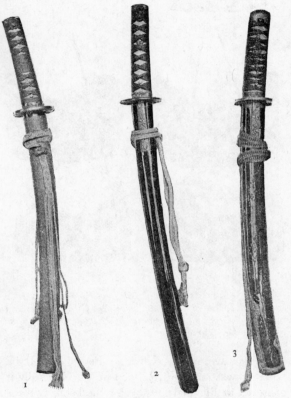

FIGURE 843. *Wakizashi.* 1. *Blade 18 inches long, signed Bushiu Osafune Suketada. All of the mountings are of carved ebony; the tsuba has a shakudo rim.* 2. *Blade 18.375 inches long by Kunekani, about 1650. Mountings of shakudo inlaid with various metals by Goto Junjo. Scabbard of black lacquer.* 3. *Very heavy blade 18.75 inches long, engraved with Fudo and the amakuraken, signed Munehiro. Mountings of shakudo carved and inlaid, fuchi signed Jafudo Shinzui. Scabbard lacquered to imitate the bark of a tree.*

WAL. See Mongile.

WALL GUNS, WALL PIECES. Heavy guns fired from swivels supported on a wall. They have been used in almost all countries using firearms and are generally like the shoulder guns but heavier and larger. Fig. 844.

See also Sher Bacha.

is of wood fastened on with beeswax or resin. It is usually made of some light, soft wood, but occasionally of a dark, heavy one such as acacia. It is the most widely distributed type in Australia. The first of the names is used by the Warramunga tribe, the second by the Larakia, and the third by the Worgait. (Spencer, North. Ter. 376). Fig. 744.

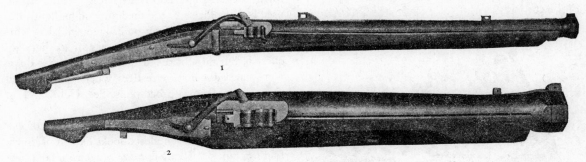

FIGURE 844. *Japanese Wall Guns.* 1. *Iron barrel covered with bronze; bore* $\frac{11}{16}$ *inch. The crest of the daimio of Otaki is inlaid in silver on the barrel. Length 3 feet 6.25 inches. Weight 17 pounds 14 ounces. 2. Barrel 1.75 inches bore. Total length 3 feet 1 inch. Weight 48 pounds 4 ounces. There is a brass lined mortise in the stock for a swivel.*

WALLUNKA. A kind of spear used by the Melville Islanders. It is made of a single piece of wood and has small barbs on one side only. The barbs are widely separated; nine barbs, the usual number, occupying a length of from seventeen to twenty-one inches. The length of the spear is from seven to twelve feet. It is generally decorated with bands of red, white and yellow. (Spencer, North. Ter. 360).

WAMBAIS, WAMBESIUM. See Aketon.

WAMMERA, WOMMERA. A variety of Australian spear thrower. This is the name most used by the white Australians for all spear throwers. See Spear Thrower.

WAMS. See Aketon.

WANAGOSHIATE. (Loop loin pad). A variety of koshiate. (Garbutt 167).

WA-NGAL. The generic name for boomerang on the Lower Tully River, Queensland. (Roth, Aust. Mus. VII, 201).

WANMAIIA, BLETTA, KALLUM. A kind of Australian spear thrower. It is a straight, flat piece of wood rounded at both ends and narrower at one than at the other. Near the wide end it is cut away on both sides to form the handle. The point

WANNA. A woman's fighting stick, also used for digging, and sometimes thrown as a spear, Wonunda-Minung tribe, Australia. (Vic. Mus. 31).

WA-NO-O. The front loop of a helmet cord, Japan. (Garbutt 147, 170).

WARAJI. Straw or hemp sandals worn with armor, Japan. Fig. 845.

WARAWAZURA. "Young boy's face," one of the types of Japanese menpo. (Dean Jap. 67).

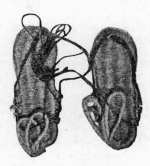

FIGURE 845. *Waraji. Hemp sandals worn with armor.*

WARAYANG. An arrow used by the Javan gods. It has a broad, triangular, barbed head. (Raffles I, 295 and plate p. 296/297).

WARBI. A large fighting club, Kakadu tribe, Australia. (Spencer, North. Ter. 298).

WAR BONNET. The fighting headdress of the North American Indians, particularly those of the Plains. It is a cap, or band, of cloth or skin, fitting tightly to the head, with a broad strip hanging down the back. It is decorated with upright eagle's feathers, horns, colored fur and beads of various kinds. Fig. 846.

FIGURE 846. War Bonnet. Cap of blue and yellow sheepskin hanging from which is a strip of red flannel with a line of erect eagle's feathers and a string of beads with a tassel on the lower end. Hanging below the headdress is a Winnebago beaded bag.

WAR CARTS. They were of two kinds. The first was a cart with a conical cover which protected two cannon that projected through openings in the small end; the gunners were covered by the large end of the shield. The second was a movable fortress large enough to contain a number of men.

WAR CHARIOT. See Chariot.

WARD. Guard, both noun and verb.

WARD IRON. The finger guard of a sword or knife. (Art of Defense 15).

WAR FAN. The fan as an article of military equipment is confined to Japan. Special kinds of fans were carried by Japanese officers as a mark of rank, and were used for signalling and as weapons. They are of two types. The first is the ceremonial form, *uchiwa*, and does not open and shut. It was used by the officers of the medium and higher ranks. It is made of metal, iron or bronze, inlaid or embossed. Some of the early ones are of leather lacquered; but most of the lacquered fans of this shape were carried before wrestlers when they entered the ring in formal processions. See Uchiwa. Fig. 820.

The second type was carried by officers of the lower ranks and when closed looks like an ordinary folding fan. It is called *tetsu-sen* (iron fan). At least the outer sticks, and sometimes all, are made of steel. They are very effective parrying weapons, and the heavier ones are dangerous clubs. They are covered with parchment and have the sun of Japan on a ground of a different color; the usual combinations are of red, black and gold. Some are simply heavy iron clubs shaped like folded fans. Fig. 847.

Similar fans with the outer ribs of iron were carried at night by civilians as a protection, as they could be used to guard with until the user had a chance to draw his sword.

WAR HAMMER. See Hammer.

WAR HAT. See Chapel de Fer and Iron Hat.

WARI-HA. A method of making Japanese blades in which the edge of a bar of iron was split and a piece of steel welded in the opening. The whole was then forged into a blade, the steel forming the edge. This method was only used for inferior blades. (Gilbertson Blades 193, plate I, no. 12).

WARI-ISHIME. Literally "a surface opened up." A method of decorating the background of metal fittings for Japanese swords. (Joly Int. 35).

WARI JIKORO. A variety of shikoro. (Garbutt 168).

WARI KOGAI, HASHI. A split kogai. See Kogai.

WAR-PA. See Ku-Yan.

WARRA-WARRA, WORRA-WORRA. A kind of club used in Victoria. It is made from a young tea tree (*Melaleuca Ericifolia*). The trunk forms the handle and the root is trimmed down to a round head. When fighting with it in their duels a shield is not allowed. (Brough Smyth I, 301).

WAR WOLF. An engine of the 14th century. Its exact nature is not known. (Grose I, 382).

WATERED STEEL. The Eastern steel that shows peculiar markings is known by a great variety of names: Damascus, Wootz, Jauhar, Ondanique, Andanicum, Alkinde, Hundwani and many others. It is often called Damascus, though the steel made there has very indistinct watering. The name was given because Damascus was the point at which the caravans from the West and East met, and from

FIGURE 847. *Folding War Fans. 1. Iron outer sticks 17.5 inches long. It is covered with black paper. 2. Outside sticks of iron 10 inches long. Cover of white paper. 3. Very heavy outer sticks of iron 11.5 inches long. Cover of black parchment with a red sun on each side. 4. Light iron club in the shape of a folded fan. Length 12.25 inches. 5. Very heavy iron club shaped like a folded fan. 6. Carved wood sticks 14.25 inches long, covered with paper with a red sun on a gold ground on one side, and a gold sun on a red ground on the other.*

WASA, WASSAW. A kind of sword, Central Africa. (Burton Sword 168).

WASTERS. See Wafters.

WATAGAMI. The plate at the side of a Japanese cuirass that could be removed to admit the body of the wearer. (Dean Hdbk. 120). Compare Waki-Biki and Wai-Date.

WATA-KUSI. "Tear flesh," a barbed arrow, Japan. They vary much in size and shape. (Gilbertson Archery 119). See Yano-Ne.

which this kind of steel first reached Europe. Damascus was not well situated for making steel as the only available ore was from small deposits in the Lebanon which have long since been exhausted.

In the early days steel was made by the same process everywhere. The ore was smelted in small furnaces much like blacksmith's forges. The product was very irregular as the temperature was not high enough to melt it and make it homogeneous; and it produced a mass ranging from cast iron at the bottom, then hard steel, soft steel, wrought iron and burnt iron on top. This was broken in small pieces and the smiths selected the quality they wanted by eye; welded similar pieces together and forged the articles they desired. In Europe there was a demand could control the watering and make recognizable patterns. There were also places having the advantage of supplies of ores differing in composition, that is, contained different impurities, the presence of

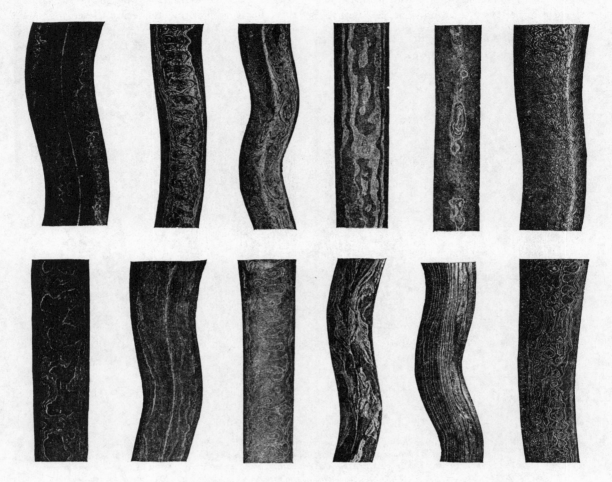

FIGURE 848. *Watered Steel, Malayan. Kris blades showing different kinds of watering with pamir (meteoric iron).*

mand for many qualities and almost all of the product from the smelting could be used for one or the other.

In the East iron and steel were not used for nearly as many purposes and the rejections were very large. Some observant individual noticed that he could get almost any variety that he desired by welding together hard and soft pieces and doubling and welding them several times. Such bars when etched are watered steel. In time the smiths found that by mixing certain particular kinds and welding and doubling the bars in definite ways they

which greatly affected the appearance of the steel. These differences in conditions are the reasons that watered steel was made in the East but not in Europe.

In India and Turkey the watering is almost entirely due to the difference in hardness of the steels used. All of these steels show watering of different shades of gray. In Persia the watering is due, in part at least, to differences in composition. In Khorasan the steel is called kara Khorasan (black Khorasan) and the watering is gray. In Ispahan the steel is, and is called, yellow, that being the prevail-

FIGURE 849. *Watered Steel.* 1, 2, 3. *Japanese.* 4, 5, 6. *Persian.*

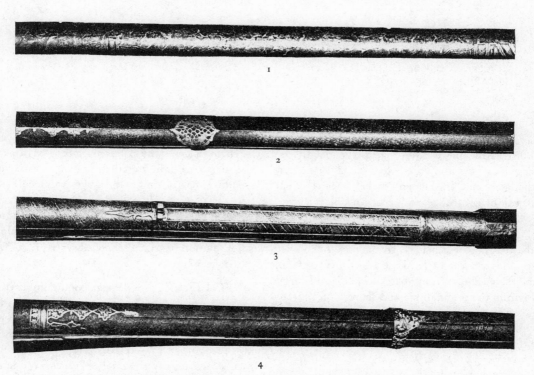

FIGURE 850. *Watered Steel Gun Barrels.* 1 and 3. *Persian.* 2 and 4. *Indian. In all cases they are made of steels of different compositions which when etched either show as different colors (1, 3) or are of different solubility so that one shows in relief (2, 4). The latter are usually called Damascus by Western gun makers although similar work is unknown and was never made there.*

ing tint. The appearance of the two is quite different; and this is not due to the materials or methods of etching. I have a knife, the blade of which is half black and half yellow, the half next the edge being black and the two meet in a straight line the entire length of the blade. The most brilliant watering is in the better Malayan blades which are made by piling alternate layers of mild steel and an alloy of iron and nickel containing about three per cent of the latter. These are welded, twisted in various ways

lines; *Kara Taban*, brilliant black with larger watering and more gray in the tone; *Kirk Narduban*, the ladder pattern, which has more or less distinct transverse markings at fairly regular intervals. It represents the ladder on which the faithful ascend to heaven, fig. 849. See also Jauhar, fig. 403. *Sham*, or simple damask, includes all of the other varieties.

In India they recognize all of the Persian and also *Zinjir*, or chain damask, consisting of prominent

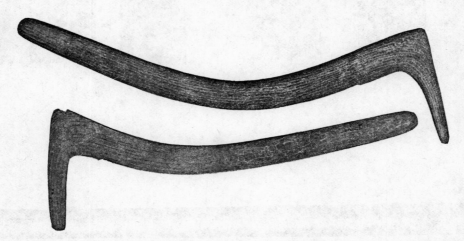

FIGURE 851. *Watilikiri, Beaked Boomerang. Grooved surfaces painted with red ochre. Extreme lengths* 31.875 *and* 29.25 *inches.*

and etched with a mixture of lime juice and arsenious acid. This makes the steel a brilliant black and leaves the nickel alloy like silver. In the old blades the nickel alloy was meteoric iron; in some of the later ones it is Krupp's nickel steel. The patterns can be controlled with recognizable accuracy. Fig. 848.

The finest steel ever produced is found in some of the old Japanese blades. In making it the smith first welded a bar of hard steel to a very soft one and doubled the resulting bar, welded it and forged it down to the original size and shape, and repeated these operations many times. Some of the Japanese blades are said to have over 4,000,000 layers in one less than a quarter of an inch in thickness. By forging in various ways very delicate and beautiful watering was obtained. Fig. 849.

In Persia four main patterns are recognized: *Kara Khorasan*, nearly black with fine undulating

and brilliant lines between parallel bands of plain damask and several others.

In most cases the patterns cannot be seen until the surface is lightly etched. It can be removed by grinding, or rubbing with emery, and be brought back by etching. The surface must be thoroughly cleaned and all grease removed. The commonest etching reagent is an impure native ferric sulphate, a hot solution of which is applied with a rag. Almost any acid will do.

WATILIKRI. The beaked boomerang, Warramunga tribe, Australia. The beaked boomerang is much like the ordinary form but has a sharp point, or beak, projecting from one end of the convex side. It is thrown with the convex side forward and, if it hits a man on the shoulder, it turns over and the point strikes him in the back. (Sp. & Gi. 712). Fig. 851.

WAZNA-I-BARUT. Persian, a powder measure. It is a tube with a close fitting plunger on the end of a graduated stem. The stem is drawn out to give the desired charge, and the tube above the plunger is filled with powder, which is then poured into the gun. The stream of powder is guided into the bar-

princes. It has a blade shaped like that of the ordinary jungle knife but much shorter and broader; the handle is straight and fits into a socket on the end of the blade. The sheath is of wood and has a very large horn belt hook on the back. It is carried at the back on the right.

FIGURE 852. Wazna-I-Barut. 1. Octagonal steel measure inlaid with silver. Length 5 inches. 2. Round measure of watered steel inlaid with gold. 3. Octagonal measure of steel inlaid with silver. It has the original leather sling attached. 4. Persian, 17th century. Ten-sided measure very finely inlaid with chased gold in a flower pattern. 5. Octagonal steel measure inlaid with silver. 6. Round measure covered with pierced and engraved silver. 7. Round measure of engraved brass. The plunger rod has loops on the sides and the end is hollow and threaded on the inside.

rel by a lip on the end of the tube. There is generally a loop on the end of the stem by which to hang the measure from the belt. The outside of the tube is sometimes round, but more often polygonal; and it is decorated with carving and inlaying. These measures are used throughout Persia and Turkey. Fig. 852.

WEDONG. A Javan ceremonial knife carried at court by all persons of position below the rank of

This knife is considered as symbolical of the willingness of the wearer to cut a way through the jungle for his king. (Raffles I, 91, 296). Fig. 853.

WEERBA. A large club made of some heavy wood and used by the natives of the northwest coast of Australia.

WEET-WEET, WONA. A throwing club with a spindle-shaped head and a long and very slim handle. It is only used as a toy, western Victoria. It is called *wona* by the Dieri tribe. (Hewitt 265).

WELSH HOOK, GLAIVE, or BILL. A variety of bill used in the 14th century. Its exact nature is not known.

WENDAT. A sling, New Caledonia. It is merely a long thong with a pouch in the middle made of two crossed cords. The stone is wetted in the mouth before being placed in the pouch so that it will not slip. (Wood 884).

WERRANNEE. The sinews of a kangaroo used to fasten the head of the reed spear, called *uluwa*, to the shaft. (Brough Smyth I, 306).

FIGURE 853. *Wedong. 1. Fine pamir blade 9.25 inches long. Wood scabbard with a large horn belt hook, four horn bands and a silver ornament. 2. Its scabbard. 3. Plain blade 7.5 inches long. Wood scabbard with a horn belt hook and thirteen bands of braided cane.*

WHALING GUN. The earlier form was a short, heavy shoulder gun for firing a bomb lance, fig. 854. The later is a swivel gun mounted on the bow of a boat. It usually fires both harpoon and bomb lance at once. See Bomb Lance.

WHEEL LOCK. A kind of lock invented in Germany about 1520. In it the flint, or more often a piece of pyrites, is held in the jaws of a cock and

pressed against a rough-edged wheel that projects up into the bottom of the pan holding the priming powder. This wheel is revolved by a spring and links which are released when the trigger is pulled. The shaft of the wheel projects through the lock plate and has a square shank for the spanner by which it is wound or set. In very rare cases the lock is set by throwing the cock over and back. The wheel lock was a vast improvement on the matchlock and replaced it wherever its necessarily higher cost did not interfere, fig. 855. At first combination locks that could either be fired by a match or wheel were used. Similarly when the flintlock appeared combinations of it and the wheel lock were quite common for a time.

Repeating wheel-lock guns were made with several locks, one in front of the other, all fired by a single trigger so arranged that it fired the locks in order, the front one first. The gun had as many loads as locks, spaced so that the powder charges came opposite the pans. It is said that there is one in existence with seven locks; several are known with two.

WHYFFLER. A two-handed swordsman who cleared the way for a procession. (ffoulkes Armourer 167).

WHINGER, WHINYARD. See Hanger.

WHINYARD. A Scotch name for a dagger. (Planche 521).

WHIP-PISTOL. Combinations of a whip and a pistol were occasionally made and used as late as the 18th century, particularly for postilions. (Greener 93). They were also made in India in the 19th

FIGURE 854. *Whaling Gun. Made by Grudchos and Eggers, New Bedford. Half octagon barrel 20 inches long, 1 inch bore and 0.25 inch thick at the muzzle. Length 3 feet, weight 15 pounds. A bomb lance is shown hanging on the right-hand support.*

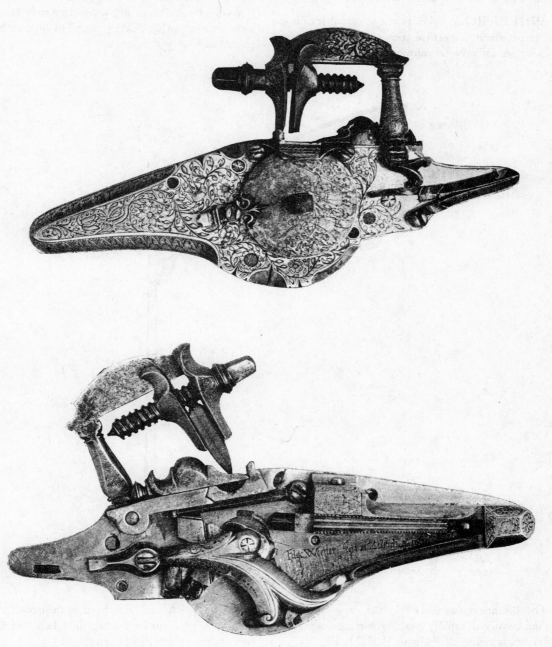

FIGURE 855. *Wheel lock, Swiss. Signed Felix Weeder, Zurich, 1630. Metropolitan Museum. Not to scale.*

century with percussion locks and folding triggers, much like those of a bomb lance. Fig. 856.

WHIRLIGIG. A cylindrical cage capable of being rotated about a vertical axis. It was formerly a common military punishment for minor offenses.

Some of them are very large with heads four inches in diameter and shafts four feet long. The bows used with them are proportionately large; I have seen them in Peking and Tokyo that had a pull of at least 150 pounds.

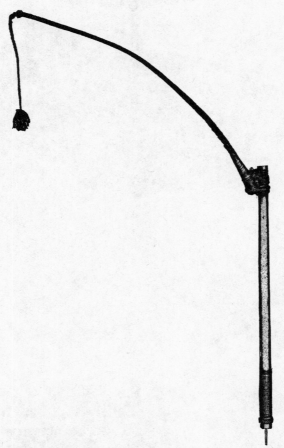

FIGURE 856. *Whip-Pistol, Oriental. The steel handle 19.25 inches long is the pistol. It unscrews to allow of capping, and is cocked by pulling the small rod at the end. When cocked a flat, folding trigger projects from one side. The lash is covered with red leather and wound with silver cord.*

The offender was placed in the cage which was then revolved rapidly making him, or sometimes her, extremely sick. (Grose II, III). Fig. 857.

WHISTLING ARROW. An arrow with a large hollow head with openings in the front and sides; when fired the air rushing through these openings made a whistling noise. They are believed to be a Chinese invention and are still used for signaling in China, and until quite recently, in Japan. Fig. 858.

WHITE ARMOR. Bright or burnished armor as distinguished from that which had been blackened or russeted. (Hewitt III, 493, 702).

WHITTLE. A knife. Sheffield whittles are mentioned by Chaucer. (Fairholt 617).

WILAH. A kris blade, Java.

WILDFIRE. See Greek Fire.

WIN-BREAD. See Gagne-Pain.

WINDLASS. The windlass and tackles used to draw the largest crossbows.

WIRE ARMOR. Mail made of wire rings, 14th and 15th centuries. (Hewitt II, 109, 223).

WIRKA. A two-pronged club used on the Tully River, Queensland. It is a round stick, largest at the handle end. It terminates in two short parallel points. (Roth, Aust. Mus. VII, 207).

WONGALA. A variety of fighting boomerang, Queensland. (Vic. Mus. 26).

WONGUIM. The returning boomerang, Woewurong tribe, Victoria. (Vic. Mus. 19). They vary greatly in size and shape.

WOODEN HORSE. See Riding the Wooden Horse.

FIGURE 857. *Whirligig, Grose II, p. 108.*

WITTOO-AH-WILL. The returning boomerang, a name used by the natives near Kulkyne on the Murray River. (Brough Smyth I, 313).

WI-VALLI. A heavy, clumsy spear seven or eight feet long, made of a single piece of wood. It has a spatulate tip covered with *ngobi* gum, and a tapering butt, Lower Tully River, Queensland. (Roth, Aust. Mus. VII, 317).

WOLF OF LANDSHUT. A celebrated German armorer of the 16th century whose work greatly resembles that of Coloman. (Laking Armor III, 317).

WOMMERA. See Wammera.

WONA. See Weet-Weet.

WONDOUK. A variety of Australian spear thrower. (Earl 205).

WOONDA. The West Australian shield. It has parallel sides and ogival ends and is strongly convex from end to end. The center of the back projects to make room for the hand hole. The front is decorated with grooved lines which are parallel to the sides near the ends, and diagonal in the middle. The grooves are stained with red ochre and the rest with white clay. It is about two feet nine inches long and six inches wide. (Brough Smyth I, 338).

WOOTZ. Indian steel made direct from the ore in Catalan forges. See also Watered Steel.

WORDAN. A spear thrower, Yerkla-Minung tribe, Australia. (Howitt 762).

WORMEGORAM. A fishing spear with two straight points of hard wood lashed to a shaft so that the whole is Y shaped, Victoria. (Brough Smyth 306).

WOR-POI. Spears with long grass-tree shafts and single barbed heads of acacia, North Queensland. (Roth, Aust. Mus. VII, 094).

WORRAN. See Barkur.

WORRA-WORRA. See Warra-Warra.

WRANGKA. See Sarongan.

the 2nd century. (Burton Sword 256). Apparently it was much like the Greek sword but shorter.

XIPHOS, SPANISH. A long two-edged sword of the 2nd century. (Burton Sword 256).

XYSTON. "So at the battle of the Ships, Homer studs a great sea-fighting Xyston (pole), twenty

FIGURE 858. *Whistling Arrows. 1, 2. Japanese wood. 3, 4. Japanese horn. 5. Japanese wood. Length 5.75 inches. Diameter 2.375. 6, 7. Chinese wood. 8. Chinese iron. It forms an efficient head as well as a whistle. 9. Chinese bone. 10. Chinese wood with an iron point, largest section 1.5 x 2.25 inches. 11. Lacquered wood head 2.25 inches in diameter and 6 inches long. 12. Chinese wood 4 inches in diameter and 6 inches long. The arrow is 4 feet 2 inches long.*

WREATH. The wreath as a decoration for the helmet first appeared in the latter part of the 14th century. Jeweled wreaths were favorite ornaments during the next century. The wreath continued in use during the 16th century. (Hewitt II, 204, III, 377, 397, 587).

WYFFLERS. Officers in the English army of the 16th century of about the grade of modern sergeants. (Grose I, 208). Compare Whifflers.

X

XENAGIE. See Ile.

XIPHIDION. The diminutive of xiphos. (Burton Sword 222).

XIPHOS. One of Homer's names for the sword. (Burton Sword 222). It had a double-edged blade widest at about two-thirds of its length from the point and ended in a very long point.

XIPHOS-GLADIUS. A short Roman sword of

cubits long, with spikes of iron." (Burton Sword 222).

Y

YA. An arrow, Japan. See Yano-Ne and Arrow. A bow in Salar, a Tibetan dialect. (Rockhill Jour.).

YABA. A place for practicing archery, Japan.

YA-BAKO. An arrow case, Japan.

YABANE. The feather of an arrow, Japan. Japanese arrows have either three or four feathers; if four, two are usually narrower than the other two.

YA-BUMI. A letter fastened to an arrow to be shot, Japan.

YABUSAME. To shoot with a bow at a target from horseback while the horse is running.

YABUSUMA. A volley of arrows, Japan.

YACHI. An Australian weapon intermediate between the lil-lil and the boomerang. (Arc. f. Eth. X, 11).

FIGURE 859. *Yadate. A bronze cylinder 3 inches in diameter and 15 inches high. It is decorated with a long inscription and a carp in low relief. It is made from a cartridge shell of European or American make.*

YA-DANE. The supply of arrows in a quiver, Japan.

YADATE. A cylindrical metal stand to hold arrows while shooting at a target. It fits into a special quiver for carriage, Japan. Fig. 859.

YADOME. (Bring arrow to stop). Projecting flanges on the cheeks of a menpo to stop arrows. See 1, 6, fig. 568.

YADZUTSU, UTSUBO. An arrow case, Japan. It is a long box with a short cover on one side near the end. It is very awkward to get the arrows in and out of, but it completely protects them from rain and wet. It is frequently carried in a frame with a pair of bows. Fig. 860.

YAG. A bow, Turkish. (Rockhill Jour.). The Turkish bows are the finest made as they are small, light and exceedingly powerful. See Bow.

YA-GAKARI, YAGORO. A bowshot, Japan.

YAGARA. The shaft of an arrow, Japan. It is usually of reed.

FIGURE 860. *Yadzutsu. Black lacquer inlaid with a vine in pearl.*

YAGEN DOSHI. A short, heavy sword for smashing armor, Japan. See also Metazashi.

YA-HAKI. A fletcher, an arrow maker, Japan.

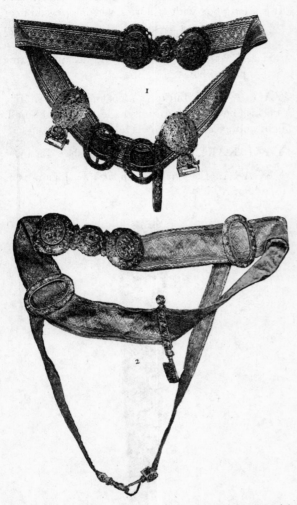

FIGURE 861. *Yakbandi. 1. Belt of gold brocade with mountings of enameled silver. 2. Belt of gold brocade lined with pink velvet. Mountings of enameled and jeweled silver.*

YA-HAZU, YA-HARU. The nock of an arrow, Japan.

YAJIRI. The head of an arrow, Japan. See Yano-Ne.

YAKBANDI. A sword belt, India. (Egerton, p. 23). It is usually a belt with slings for the sword and a hook to hang it from when on foot. Sometimes it is a baldric. Fig. 861.

YAKIBA. Near the edge a Japanese blade is of a misty gray (*ha-tsuya*, edge lustre), while the remainder has a mirror-like polish (*ji-tsuya*, ground lustre). The junction of the two is called the yakiba. In fine blades it shows as a bright line. It is the limit of the part that has been hardened. Its outline can be varied by changing the shape of the edge of the clay cover that is put on the blade when it is heated for hardening. On the older blades it is usually nearly parallel to the edge; while in the later ones it is often exceedingly elaborate. Occasionally a blade shows a double line called *nijiu yakiba*. On a well made blade it is quite close to the edge near the hilt, otherwise the blade would be weak; but near the point it is wider, as hardness rather than strength is required there.

Some of the common patterns are: *Sugu*, straight; *Notare*, wavy; *Midare*, irregular; *Gunome*, regular scallops; *Nokogiri*, saw-toothed; *Yahazu*, like the nock of an arrow; *Hyotan*, gourd-shaped; *Ashi*, rat's leg; *Choji*, like cloves laid side by side; *Hitotsuri*, covering the blade in irregular blotches. These patterns are often combined as: *Notare-Midare*, *Sugu-Ni-Ashi*, etc.

The yakiba and other markings on the blade made in hardening it are often characteristic of the makers and localities where the blades were made; and great weight is given to their appearance by the Japanese experts when judging blades.

See Joly Sword and Same p. 89 et seq. and Weber II, 453.

YAKI-NAOSHI-MONO. See Boshi-Mono.

YALMA. A special form of play boomerang in the form of a cross, Northern Queensland. (Vic. Mus. 21).

YAMABUSHI. Literally "mountain warriors," Japanese militant monks. The order was founded by Shoho, 853-910, in the Enryakuji temple. They wore a characteristic dress, partly military and partly monkish. In place of helmets they wore polygonal caps and carried a traveling box or basket, besides a sword, rosary and a trumpet made of a conch shell. They became very powerful and caused much trouble until they were destroyed by Nobunaga in the 16th century. (Joly Leg. 392). For their armor see fig. 81, no. 2.

YAMA GANE. An alloy of copper with zinc and tin. It was used by the Goto. (Weber II, 458).

YAMA-GATA. A form of kokudzuri. (Conder 276).

A mound behind a target to stop arrows.

YAMAGATANA. A hunting knife.

YAMBARA. See Tambara.

YANAGI-HA, YANAGI-BA. "Willow leaf," a type of Japanese arrowhead. It is usually straight

YANO-NE. An arrowhead, Japan. The four main classes are: *Yasagi-Ha*, or willow leaf, straight sided and pointed. *Togari Ya*, pointed but wider than the previous, and often heart-shaped. *Karimata*, or forked arrow. They vary greatly in size, being from a little over an inch to six and a half inches across the points. They are sometimes called "rope cutters." *Watakusi*, or "flesh tearers," barbed arrows.

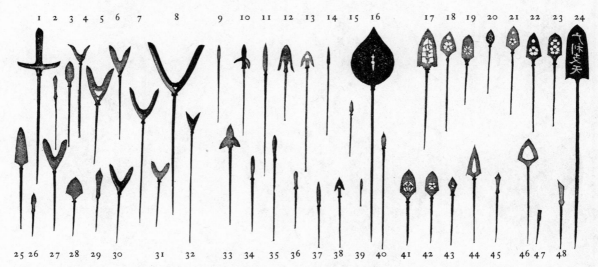

FIGURE 862. *Yano-Ne. Nos. 9, 11, 15, 34 to 37, 39 and 40 are of the type called Yanagiha (willow leaf). It is the commonest form of fighting arrowhead, and is usually of square or lozenge section and from 0.75 to 2.5 inches long. Nos. 3, 17 to 26, 28, 41 to 44, and 46 are of the type called Togari. They are from 0.25 to 2.5 inches wide and from 1 to 6 inches long. This type of arrowhead is more apt to be pierced with figures or inscriptions than any other. Nos. 4 to 8, 27, and 30 to 32 are called Karimata. They vary from 1 to 6 inches across the points. Nos. 10, 12, 13, 33 and 38 are the barbed arrows, Watakusi (tear flesh). They also vary greatly in size, shape and decoration. In addition to these class names each variety has its specific name. Among these are: 2, 29, 45, Tsurugi Kashira (sword's point); 13, Shinogi (protector); 26, 28, Tsube me guchi (sparrow's bill); 33, Omodake (water plantain); 43, Kengata (sword shape); 44, Rinzetsu (dragon's tongue). No. 10 has movable barbs which take the position shown on the right when in flight, but swing to that shown on the left, and no further, if an attempt is made to withdraw the arrow from the wound. Nos. 1, 8 and 16 are much too heavy to be shot from any bow drawn by hand. 1 is 4 x 4.75 x 0.25 inches, 9 is 5.5 inches wide and 5 long, 16 is 4 x 6 inches; it has the signs of the zodiac on it. No. 24 has the name Marishiten, the goddess of archery, in negative silhouette. No. 17 is pierced with an inscription in positive silhouette to the effect that it never hits any good and virtuous person.*

sided and of diamond section, but varies considerably in size and shape. (Gilbertson Archery 118). See Yano-Ne.

YANAGI, YANAGI TO BA. A kind of open quiver, Japan.

YANO. The shaft of an arrow, Japan.

YA-NO-HA. The feathers of an arrow, Japan. (Weber I, 176).

They also vary greatly in size and shape. Fig. 862.

There are a number of other shapes made for parade; nearly all of the arrows made for fighting were yanagi-ha. Some of the parade arrows were made by celebrated artists and are carved and inlaid. Fig. 863.

YANTRAMUKTA. The ancient Hindu divided all weapons into four classes, the first of which is the *mukta* or missiles. The first division of this class is the *yantramukta*, or weapons thrown by machines. (Burton Sword 214). See Amukta.

YAOCHIMALLI. A plain war shield, ancient Mexico. (Arc. f. Eth. V, 53).

ter so as to let it move more freely. It should be worn at the right side." (Garbutt 150).

Some are quite small and made of leather. They were fastened to the leg or stirrup. Fig. 865.

FIGURE 863. *Decorated Yano-Ne. The three are contained in an old wooden box with a document which reads: "On the 11th day of the 10th month of Genbun (1737) these treasures are most reverently offered to the shrine. The Daijin has immediately accepted them and made them safe against foreign invaders forever." All are signed Umetada of Joshu, Yamashiro province. He was the Taiko's swordsmith, and very celebrated, 16th century. 1. Emblems of prosperity and longevity; the pine, bamboo, crane and turtle. On the point is a landscape inlaid in gold. 2. Two figures under a plum tree. 3. Sekko and Chorio. The latter is shown recovering the shoe from the dragon.*

YA-OMOTE. A bow shot, Japan.

YARAK. When a hawk is in such condition that "she shows evident signs of eagerness and excitement, and is obviously on the *qui vive*—attentive to every sight and sound which she may suppose to indicate the presence of quarry or the hope of a flight." (Michell 31).

YARI. A spear, generic name, Japan. Fig. 864.

YARI-ATE, YARI-HASAMI, YARI-SASHI. Japan, a spear rest. "When on horseback carry it (the spear) resting upon the *yari-hasami* (spear rest), which is made of iron or copper. The best type of *yari-sashi* (or *yari-hasami*) has a hinge in its cen-

FIGURE 865. *Yari-Ate. Black leather pocket with a gilt mon on a leather pad 7.25 inches long.*

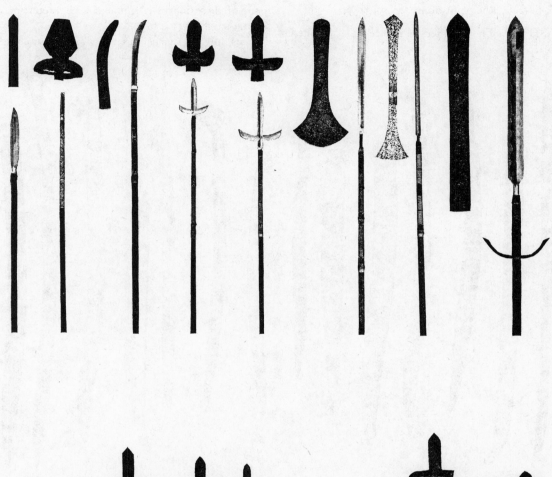

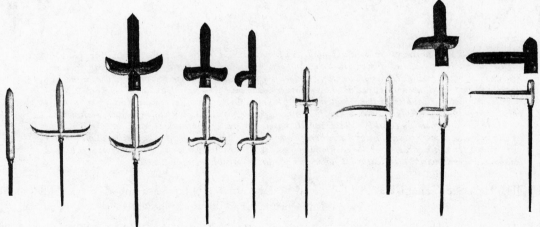

FIGURE 864. *Yari, Japanese Spears, 16th to 19th centuries. The figure gives an idea of the variety of shapes and sizes of the spears and their sheaths. Metropolitan Museum.*

YARI-KAKE. A spear rack, Japan.

YARI-SAKI. The point of a spear, Japan.

YA-SAKI. The point of an arrow, Japan.

YASHIKI. The fortified residence of a Japanese noble.

YASURIME. File marks on the tang of a Japanese blade; they were purposely left rough to keep it from slipping in the hilt. The style and arrangement of these marks is frequently characteristic of the maker. Fig. 401.

Cuts and file marks imitating rain and used as a

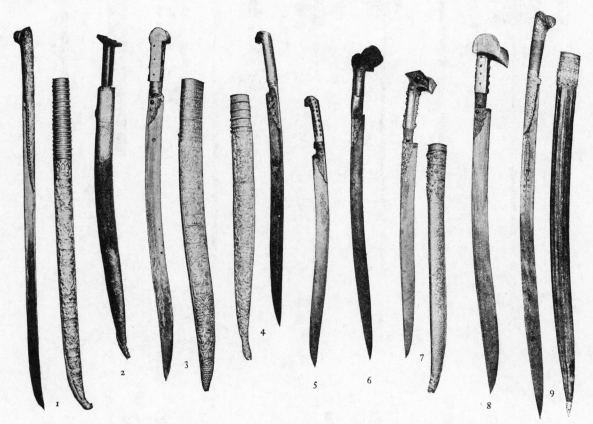

FIGURE 866. *Yatagans. 1. Gold inlaid blade 27.8 inches long with a round reinforcing plate of chased silver. Heavy chased silver hilt and scabbard. 2. Horn hilt with a straight cross pommel. Brass mountings. 3. Blade 23.5 inches long, inlaid with scrolls and inscriptions in silver. Bone hilt set in gilt metal inlaid with coral. Embossed silver scabbard. 4. Engraved blade, silver hilt decorated with niello. Embossed silver scabbard. 5. Blade 19 inches long, ivory hilt inlaid with brass point work. 6. Blade inlaid with inscriptions and scrolls. Horn hilt with very broad, thin wings. 7. Blade 20.5 inches long finely inlaid for its entire length on both sides with inscriptions and scrolls in gold. Heavy silver hilt and scabbard chased and set with coral. 8. Engraved blade with a gilt mount set with coral, very large ivory wings. 9. Engraved blade 30.25 inches long. Fluted scabbard covered with black leather. Chased silver hilt and scabbard mounts.*

YASSAGHI-HA. See Yanagi-Ha. A kind of arrowhead.

YASUCHIKA. There were six tsuba makers of this name. Tsuchiya Yasuchika (1669-1744) was the first, and greatest. He has been called one of the three greatest artists of the Nara school, and one of the four greatest artists of the Tokugawa period.

decoration on Japanese metal work. The name means a "drizzling shower."

YATAGAN, YATAGHAN. A kind of sabre with an incurved blade which was very popular in Turkey and the adjoining countries and North Africa. Burton says of it: "The yatagan, whose beautiful curved line of blade coincides accurately with the action of the wrist in cutting. . . . (it has) the forward weight, so valuable in cutting the hand." The hilt has no guard and the pommel spreads out in large wings. The blades are frequently etched, or inlaid, with texts from the Koran. The tang is flat and the two pieces forming the grip are riveted to it. The latter are often of ivory and the edges of the tang are covered with silver filigree set with coral. Often the entire hilt is of silver. The scabbards are made of wood covered with leather, velvet or silver. They have no sling loops, being carried thrust through the belt. Often there is a small loop near the top through which a cord can be passed to fasten it to the belt. Frequently the scabbard was thrown away when going into a fight, the owner considering that if he won he would have ample time to hunt it up, and if he lost he would not care what became of it.

While yatagans are found over a wide area and differ considerably in form and fittings, these variations seldom seem to be typical of the localities where it is found. The reason probably is that the yatagan was originally a Turkish weapon and the Turkish Empire was made up of a great variety of races and it has been carried wherever the Turks have gone. Fig. 866.

Sabres with blades like those of yatagans are not uncommon in India, but the hilts are of the usual Indian types. Fig. 867.

YA-TSUGI. Fixing an arrow to the bow, Japan.

YA-ZAMA. An embrasure from which to shoot with a bow, Japan.

YA-ZUKA. A bundle of arrows, Japan.

YA-ZUTSU. A quiver, Japan.

YEAMBERREN, MOONOE, MUN-NUP. A club with a conical head much larger than the handle, New South Wales. (Vic. Mus. 29).

YEBIRA. See Ebira.

YEBOSHI. A cap worn under the helmet, Japan. (Garbutt 149).

YECHIU-HAI-DATE. Japanese cuisses that cover both the front and back of the thighs. The upper portion is of plaited silk, and the lower is covered with small plates and mail. There are bands of leather on the sides to stiffen the whole and support the heavy lower portion. There are several varieties. (Conder 275). See Hai-Date.

YEN-II. See Yodare-Kake.

YERI-MAWARI. A Japanese garment of padded cloth or leather worn on the shoulders to support the weight of the armor. The portion around the

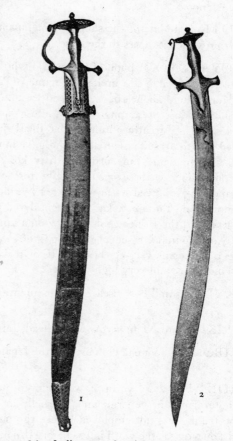

FIGURE 867. *Indian swords with yatagan blades.* 1. *Hilt and blade inlaid with gold. Length blade 25 inches. Scabbard covered with green velvet, mounts pierced and gilded.* 2. *Fine watered blade. Hilt inlaid with gold.*

neck was often covered with metal plates or shark skin. (Conder 277).

YERIPUL, MIKUL. A wooden spear used on Melville Island and the adjacent coast. The barbs are indicated by holes cut through the blade but the edge is left intact. (Spencer, North. Ter. 358).

YERMA NETCHTE. A matchlock, Salar. The Salar use Tibetan guns. See Meda.

YETCHIU-GOTE. See Shino-Gote.

YIRMBA, GURRPAN, KARANJA, LARMA, LU-YO, PUR-TA, URR-CHE-RA. Fishing spears with several barbed points fastened to the end of a light shaft. (Roth, Aust. Mus. VII, 19).

YODARE-KAKE, YODARE-GANE, YEN-II. The laminated neck guard of a Japanese menpo. See Menpo.

YOKOTE. The line of the shinogi of a Japanese blade from which it tapers to the edge.

YOKOYA SOYO. A pupil of Goto Injo who established himself at Yedo under the name of Yokoya Mori-Tsugo about 1640. He made a kozuka for Prince Todo representing a falcon and a squirrel. This was so greatly admired that the Prince attached him to his suite as an artist and gave him a pension, at the same time ordering fifty kozuka. The completion of these occupied him for some years and was followed by an order for five hundred more; and these kozuka were considered the highest reward the Prince could bestow on a samurai. Yokoya founded a school of makers of sword fittings that became very celebrated. His own work is extremely rare and very highly valued.

YO-KYU. A small bow used for amusement, Japan.

YOPPIKI. To draw an arrow to the head, Japan.

YORIBO. A six foot oak club used by the Japanese police.

YOROI. "The word yoroi, now commonly used to denote armor in general, and especially armor for the trunk, was not employed before the Yenji period (901-923), the word in use before this being *Kawara*. This word, now used for roof-tile, is the same originally with *Kora*, the word used for the scales of a tortoise shell. Thus the ancient word used to indicate armour implies the scales or shell of the body." (Conder 255). This explanation seems rather far-fetched. The scales were probably called by the same name as roof tiles because they resembled them. Like tuilles in English.

Yoroi is generally used by the Japanese as the equivalent of the English word armor.

YOROI-HARAMAKI. A name given to a kind of armor used by the common soldier in Japan. It was made of lacquered leather and opened at the back. Unlike the better armor called haramaki it had no separate piece to close the opening. (Conder 280).

YOROI HITATARE. A Japanese surcoat. There are a number of varieties resembling the coats of civil life. There were no regulations concerning them. They should not be confused with the jimbaori. (Garbutt 159).

YOROI KAYESHI. A variety of Japanese corselet. (Garbutt 142).

YOROI SEI. An armorer, a maker of armor, Japan.

YOROI TOSHI, METAZASHI. A kind of dagger used for cutting through armor, Japan. The ancient standard of length was nine and a half bu (11.4 inches), later it was made shorter, seven and a half bu (9 inches). The earlier way of carrying it was thrust vertically through the back of the belt; later it was carried at the right side, with the hilt towards the front, and the edge upwards. This gives it the second name, *metazashi*, "right side wear." (Garbutt 168).

YORVIDOSHI. A short, thick blade, Japan.

YOSHIMICHI. One of the "three great Miochins." He was celebrated both as a maker of armor and tsuba. He lived in the early part of the 16th century.

YOSHIMITSU. One of the most celebrated of the sword makers of Japan in the 15th century. There are several later sword makers of the same name.

YOZEME. A night attack, Japan.

YSGWYD. A Welsh shield. (Planche 623).

YUBUKURO. A bag, or case, for a bow, Japan.

YUDAME, YUMIDAME. An appliance used by the Japanese bow makers to give a bow its permanent reversed curves. It was a large wooded block with grooves in the side and was braced to floor and roof. Fig. 868.

YU GAKE. Japanese archer's gloves. They are of several kinds. Those worn by the higher classes are much like ordinary gloves with long gauntlets; the second and third fingers are usually of a different color and made of softer leather than the rest and the right thumb has a double thickness of leather on the inside to take the wear of the bow string. They have long straps by which to fasten them securely at the wrist. Some have heart-shaped openings in

YUGO. A wooden spear used by the natives of Melville Island. It is said to be well shaped of hard wood, and to be thrown with a thrower. It appears to be only used for duels and not for general fighting. (Earl 205).

FIGURE 868. *Yu-Dame. A modern Japanese bow maker giving a bow its permanent curve in an old yu-dame. The block is 5.375 x 7.75 inches in section and 5 feet 6.75 inches long. One end rests on the floor and the other is raised by a leg 1 foot 8.75 inches long. There is also a strut from the lower end to the roof.*

the palm for ventilation. The ordinary archer wore a glove on the right hand only. It covered the thumb and one or two fingers only. The fingers are connected to a broad wrist band which is held by a long strap tied around the wrist. The thumb is lined with some hard material to take the place of the archer's ring used in most eastern countries. A third type of archer's glove is occasionally found. It is worn on the left hand and looks like an ordinary glove, but the back of the hand and gauntlet are of cloth lined with mail to protect the hand when holding the bow. Fig. 869.

YU-GOTE, YU-KOTE. Japanese archer's sleeves. Sometimes a pair is worn and sometimes a single one.

If a pair is worn they are shaped like the ordinary armor sleeves and hung from the shoulders in the same way. They are made of brocade, usually without any protection. Some have a few small iron plates quilted in; others are lined with leather plates making a brigandine. Fig. 870.

The single sleeves are made of some light material and put on before the armor. They cover the

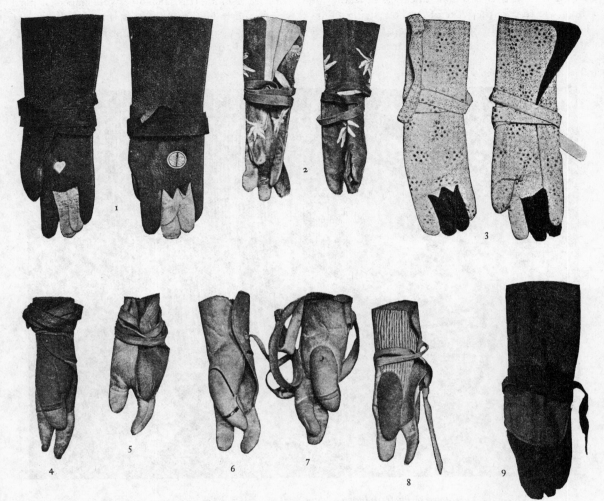

FIGURE 869. *Yu Gake.* 1. *A pair, brown leather except for two fingers which are softer and of the natural color. Gold Inagaki mon on the back and heart-shaped ventilators in the palms. 2. Very old pair of yellow leather with white dragon flies. 3. White leather printed with patterns in red, blue and brown mon embroidered on the backs. Two fingers of each are of soft brown leather. 4. Heavy glove of two kinds of leather; two fingers and a lined thumb. 5. Light glove with one finger and an unlined thumb. 6. Heavy glove with two fingers and a lined thumb. 7. Like 6. 8. Glove of two kinds of figured leather; two fingers and a heavy lined thumb. 9. Palm and fingers of soft black leather, back of hand and gauntlet of cloth lined with mail. For the left hand for holding the bow.*

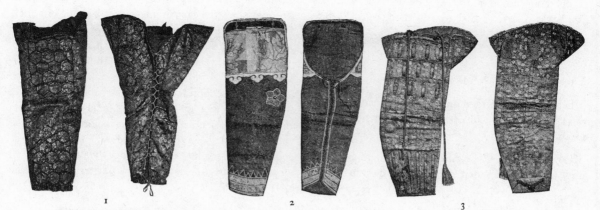

FIGURE 870. *Yu Gote, Pairs.* 1. *Brigandine of hexagonal plates covered with brocade, 18th century.* 2. *The body of the sleeves is of plain cloth, the ends of brocade, 19th century.* 3. *Gold brocade with steel splints quilted in, 17th century.*

FIGURE 871. *Yu-Gote, single.* 1. *Sleeve of reddish brown silk embroidered with gold.* 2. *Red silk printed with gold flowers.* 3. *Red and black silk sleeve with gold mon.*

right arm, shoulder and a good part of the chest and back. They are tied around the body. Fig. 871.

YUHASHIRI. Bright bands of hard metal in a Japanese blade.

YU-HAZU. The ends of a bow, Japan.

YUJO. The founder and most celebrated master of the Goto school of makers of sword fittings. See Goto.

YUKAERI, YUKAESHI. The turning of the bow in the hand when the arrow is discharged. As same width but vary in thickness from half an inch to one inch; the larger ones are all about one inch in thickness and vary from one to two inches in width. Unlike any other bow the handle is placed much below the center so that the upper limb is about twice as long as the lower, but is of the same cross section. This was probably because the old archers shot mainly from horseback or kneeling, and could not have used such long bows if the handles had been in the middle. The Japanese bows were made to shoot very heavy arrows to moderate distances with a very flat trajectory. The

FIGURE 872. *Yumi Yari. Spearhead with socket to fit on the end of a bow, triangular blade* 3.75 *inches long. Total length* 9 *inches.*

the arrow leaves the bow a Japanese archer loosens his hold on the bow which turns in his hand and the string flies round and strikes the outside of the arm after it has expended most of its force. For this reason the Japanese archer neither uses, nor needs, a bracer.

YUKI. A quiver, Japan.

YU-LUN. A North Queensland club with one or more beak-like projections from the head. Sometimes the beaks are colored white and the intervening parts red. (Roth, Aust. Mus. VII, 208).

YOLWAR BUNDI. See Kharg Bandai.

YUMI. A bow, Japan. Japanese bows vary greatly in length, being from about two to nearly eight feet long. Some of the smaller ones are made of horn or whalebone, but the large bows were always made of wood.

The war bow was built up of a strip of hard wood, usually sumac, between two of bamboo. The natural skin of the bamboo shows on both back and belly. These bows have no notches for the string but both sides are cut back to form shoulders which slope from the back to the belly. The string goes around the projecting end of the bow and rests on the shoulders. The bows are usually from seven feet to seven feet two inches long. The lighter bows are all of the arrows are about three feet long exclusive of the head, are made of reed and have usually three feathers. The war heads are quite small but some of the parade arrows have huge heads, some of which weigh nearly half a pound.

See Bow.

YUMI BUKURO. A bag in which to keep a bow, Japan.

YUMI DAME. An instrument for giving a bow its permanent curves, Japan. See Yu-Dame.

YUMI-GOTE, IGOTE. See Yu-Gote. (Garbutt 167).

YUMI GUMI. A company of bowmen, Japan.

YUMI MATO. A target for archery, Japan.

YUMI NO TSURU. A bowstring, Japan.

YUMI SHI. A bow maker, Japan.

YUMITORI. An archer, Japan. Literally "the holder of the bow," a warrior of rank in old Japan. The bow and long sword were the weapons of the noble; the common soldier used the spear and short sword. (Ogawa).

YUMI YARI. Spearheads to fit on the end of the bow. They had triangular blades about three or four inches long on the end of a socket shaped to fit the bow. Between the socket and head were sloping shoulders for the bowstring to rest on. Fig. 872.

YUMI ZIRA. A bowstring, Japan.

YUNDE. "The hand that holds the bow," the left, Japan. The Japanese always give the left hand the precedence.

YUZUKA. The handle of a Japanese bow.

YUZURU. A bowstring, Japan.

Z

ZAFAR TAKIEH, ZAFAR TAKIEH SALAPA. Literally "the cushion of victory." A short

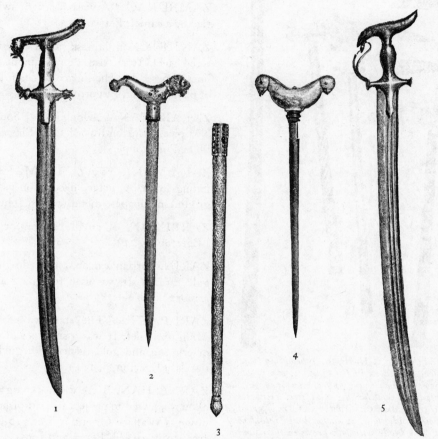

FIGURE 873. *Zafar Takieh.* 1. Blade 20.25 inches long; brass hilt with guard, finger guard and crutch pommel. Zafar Takieh Salapa. 2. Watered blade 15.75 inches long inlaid with gold. Jade hilt set with jewels and with a lion's head of gold on the end. 3. Its scabbard; embossed gold set with jewels. 4. Tanjore, 17th century. European rapier blade 15.5 inches long. Ivory crutch hilt of two parrot's heads. 5. Slightly curved, grooved blade 23.75 inches long. Steel crutch hilt with a bird's head on the end of the finger guard.

YURAL-BARA. A boomerang that swerves to the right when thrown, Lower Tully River, Queensland. (Roth, Aust. Mus. VII, 201).

YURIGI-ITO. The cords that connected the Japanese corselet to the tassets and the lames of the latter to each other. (Garbutt 163).

sword with a crutch-shaped pommel which is also the hilt. It was carried by Indian princes when seated on the masnad (cushion) giving audiences. They are of two kinds—one with a regular hilt with a guard and finger guard, the pommel reaches across to form the rest. The other is a simple crutch at right angles to the blade. Being made for kings to use in public, many are works of art, the hilts and scabbards being of gold and jade set with jewels. (Egerton 393 and p. 162, Wallace Orient.). Fig. 873.

FIGURE 874. *Zaghnals. 1. Heavy steel head 9.75 inches long, ringed steel handle 22 inches long. 2. Heavy blade deeply carved with animals and figures. An open pagoda opposite the blade. Wood handle with steel reinforcing plate. 3. Northern India, 18th century. Narrow grooved blade inlaid with gold, shaft 21 inches long, inlaid with silver. 4. Very long blade with two beasts in the round at the base and an elephant standing on the pean. Spirally fluted handle 21 inches long, silver plated, 17th century. 5. Thin blade 6.5 inches long. The cube on the shaft, the ornament at the back and that on the end of the shaft are engraved and the designs filled in with red, except on one side of the cube, where there is an inscription. Modern handle.*

ZAGAYE. A lance used by the Venetian estradiots. It had a shaft twelve feet long pointed at both ends with iron. (Planche 523).

ZAGHNAL. An axe with one or two heavy curved knife-like blades, India. (Kaemmerer XXXIX). Fig. 874.

ZAI. A commander's baton, Japan. See Saihai.

ZAIMAI. Having the maker's name inscribed, as a sword, Japan.

ZAKANE. See Seppa.

ZAMAN. A celebrated sword maker of Ispahan in the early 17th century. He was a pupil of Assad Ullah. (Egerton, p. 530).

ZAMBURAQ. "A wasp," a light swivel gun carried by a camel, Persia.

ZANJIR. Chain damask, a variety of Indian watered steel. It consists of prominent and brilliant lines disposed like the links of a chain between lines of plain damask. (Egerton, p. 62).

ZARABATANA. A long, heavy South American blowpipe. (Burton Sword 14). This name is Spanish or Portuguese.

ZARA MAKI, ATAZUMA MAKI. Ishime imitating stone. A surface decoration used as a background in Japanese metal work. (Joly Int. 35).

ZARBUZAN. A small cannon or swivel gun. (Egerton, p. 21).

ZARIN. Persian kincob, a brocade with silver and gold threads. It was used for lining and trimming armor and shields.

ZARI-PATTA. The standard of Ragoba, the Mahratta chief. It was a small swallow-tailed flag of crimson and gold tissues with gold fringes and tassels. (Egerton, p. 114).

ZARNESHAN. True damascening in which the alloy is allowed to project instead of being flattened down. (Wallace Orient.). The projecting inlay is frequently carved, Persia and India.

FIGURE 875. *Zirah Bouk. (Mail piercer.) Very heavy blade 6.5 inches long; the half next the point is of square section.*

ZENSHOZAN. "Fore-peak mountain," a style of Japanese helmet.

ZHOO. A bow, Western Tibet. (Ramsay-Western).

ZIN. A saddle, Bokhara. It is of the ordinary Persian type. (Moser XLI).

ZIRA, ZIRAH. Persian mail. It is of the international type with each link passing through four others.

ZIRAH BAKTAH. The Indo-Persian coat of mail. They vary much in size and weight. Some have short sleeves and reach only to the wrist, while others have sleeves long enough to cover the hands and skirts that reach well below the knees. Many have small plates on the back and breast. Figs. 57, 61.

ZIRAH BOUK, ZIRAH BONK. "Mail piercer," Persian. A knife with the point thickened so that it is strong enough to be forced through mail. The name is given to any knife with the point reinforced. Fig. 875.

ZIRAH KORTA SAKTOU. Mail of iron links with patterns worked in with links of brass, copper or both. It is very commonly used in India and Persia for the capes of helmets and collars of mail coats. Sometimes entire suits are made in this way, fig. 57. The patterns are generally geometrical but are sometimes inscriptions in Arabic letters, fig. 543. Mail of this kind is always of unriveted links.

ZOGAN. Inlay, Japan. *Honzogan* is true damascening in which the metal is set in grooves cut in the ground; *numone* is false damascening in which the precious metals are pressed on to roughened surfaces. The Japanese also distinguish between *hira-zogan*, flat inlay, and *taka-zogan*, in which the inlay is in relief. See Inlaying.

ZUBOSHI. The black spot in the center of a target, Japan. The bull's-eye of a Japanese target is always black.

ZUDATE. A badge worn on a Japanese helmet. (Garbutt 156).

ZUIJIN. Palace guards, Japan. (Gilbertson Archery 117).

ZU'L-FIKAR. "Lord of cleaving." The sword given by the archangel Gabriel to Mahomed, and by him to his son-in-law Ali bin Ali Talib. (Burton Sword 141).

ZUMBAI. A sling, Japan.

ERRATA

Page 206 Line 22: should read "when the caps that were held in place".

Page 277 Line 5: explanation of Fig. 346, "pipe" should read "pine".

Page 466 Should include the following paragraph:
NARACHANA. A noose formed of a rope with a metal ring on the end. It was included in Ceylon in the "five weapons of war," the others being swords, spears, javelins and bows. (Tennent I, 499).

Page 467 Omit last paragraph of first column.

Page 484 Should contain paragraph on PASHKOHU now appearing on page 490.

Page 490 Paragraph on PASHKOHU should appear on page 484.

Page 498 In paragraph on PICKET, the word "waist" should read "wrist".

Page 649 Paragraph 1, top of second column: "at the head" should be in italics.

PUBLISHER'S NOTE — In this book the pages containing full-page illustrations have not been numbered, contrary to Mr. Stone's instructions, as it is not customary to place numbers on pages with scant or varying margins, and is in accordance with our standards of fine printing. Also certain full-page illustrations are out of position, although close to their natural sequence, for the reason that when a small amount of text occurs, it is obviously impossible to allocate these illustrations to their proper place.

The printer's errors on pages 206, 277, 466, 467, 484, 490, 498, 649, were discovered by Mr. Stone after the forms had gone to press.

Bibliography

Reference	*Title and Author*
Amiot.	Amiot, P. (translator). L'Art Militaire des Chinois. Paris, 1772.
Art of Defence.	Anonymous. The Art of Defence on foot with the Broad Sword and Sabre. London, 1798.
	Anonymous. Catalogue of the Fire-Arms Collection, United States Cartridge Co. Lowell, Mass., n.d.
Hermitage.	Anonymous. Collection d'Armes de l'Hermitage Imperial. St. Petersbourg, 1908.
	Anonymous. Illustrations of the History and Practices of the Thugs. London, 1837.
Invasions of India.	Anonymous. Invasions of India from Central Asia. London, 1879.
	Anonymous. La Caccia Coll'Archibugio a Pietra ed a Polvere Fulminante. Rome, 1830.
Arc. f. Eth.	Archiv fur Ethnographie. Leiden, 1893-1927.
	Armandi, le Chevalier P. Histoire Militaire des Elephants. Paris, 1843.
Ashdown.	Ashdown, Charles Henry. Arms and Armour. New York, n.d.
	Baddeley, John James. A Guide to the Guildhall of the City of London. London, 1898.
Baden-Powell.	Baden-Powell, Sir Robert. Indian Memories. London, 1915.
Baker, Albert Nya.	Baker, Sir Samuel White. The Albert Nyanza. London, 1866.
Baker, Nile Trib.	Baker, Sir Samuel White. Exploration of the Nile Tributaries of Abyssinia. Hartford, 1868.
	Baker, Sir Samuel White. Ismailia. New York, 1875.
Moorish Literature.	Basset, Rene. Moorish Literature. New York, 1901.
Batchelor.	Batchelor, Rev. John. The Ainu of Japan. New York, n.d.
	Bezancourt, Le Baron de. Les Secrets de l'Epee. Paris, 1876.
	Bernier, Francis (Irving Bock, translator). Travels in the Mogul Empire. London, 1926.
	Bevan, Theodore F. Toil, Travel and Discovery in British New Guinea. London, 1890.
	Bickmore, Albert S. Travels in the East Indian Archipelago. New York, 1869.
	Birdwood, Sir George C. M. Indian Art at Marlborough House. London, 1892.
	Blanch, H. J. A Century of Guns. London, 1909.
	Blumentritt, Ferdinand. The Native Tribes of the Philippines. Washington, Smithsonian Reports, 1899.
Blunt.	Blunt, Lady Anne. Bedouin Tribes of the Euphrates. New York, 1879.
Bock.	Bock, Carl. The Head Hunters of Borneo. London, 1881.
	Boeheim, Wendelin. Handbuch der Waffenkunde. Leipzig, 1890.
	Bonnet, Hans. Die Waffen der Volker des Alten Orients. Leipzig, 1926.
Boutell.	Boutell, Charles. Arms and Armour. London, 1872.
Bowes.	Bowes, James Lord. Japanese Marks and Seals. London, 1882.
Brand.	Brand, John. Observations on Popular Antiquities. London, 1900.
	Brinkley, Captain F. A History of the Japanese People. New York and London, 1915.
Brinkley.	Brinkley, Captain F. Japan, its History, Arts and Literature, vol. VII.
Brit. Mus.	British Museum labels.
B. M. Hdbk.	Handbook to the Ethnographical Collections of the British Museum. London, 1910.
Brown, Mel. & Pol.	Brown, George. Melanesians and Polynesians. London, 1910.
Burton Falconry.	Burton, Richard F. Falconry in the Valley of the Indus. London, 1852.
Burton Sword.	Burton, Richard F. The Book of the Sword. London, 1884.
Burton Lakes.	Burton, Richard F. The Lake Regions of Central Africa. New York, 1860.
Cabaton.	Cabaton, A. Java, Sumatra and other Islands of the Dutch East Indies. New York, 1911.
Calvert.	Calvert, Albert F. Spanish Arms and Armour. London, 1907.
Campbell, Tuareg.	Campbell, Dugald. On the Trail of the Veiled Tuareg. Philadelphia, n.d.
Campbell.	Campbell, Lord Archibald. Highland Dress, Arms and Ornament. London, 1899.
	Campbell, John. Narrative of Major-General John Campbell of the Operations in the Hill Tracts of Orissa. London, 1861.
Castle.	Castle, Egerton. Schools and Masters of Fence. London, 1885.
Catlin.	Catlin, George. Illustrations of the Manners, Customs and Conditions of the North American Indians. London, 1841.
Cayley-Webster.	Cayley-Webster, H. Through New Guinea and the Cannibal Countries. London, 1898.
	Chalmers, James and Gill, W. Wyatt. Work and Adventure in New Guinea. London, 1885.
Christie.	Christie, Emerson Brewer. The Subanuns of Sandringham Bay. Manila, 1909.
Clarke.	Clarke, Sir Purdon. Arms and Armour at Sandringham. London.
Clifford, Court and Kampong.	Clifford, Sir Hugh. In Court and Kampong. London, 1896.

Reference	*Title and Author*
Clifford, Malay Mono.	Clifford, Sir Hugh. Malayan Monochromes. New York, 1913.
Clifford, Since the Begin.	Clifford, Sir Hugh. Since the Beginning. London, 1898.
Clifford, Brown Human.	Clifford, Sir Hugh. Studies in Brown Humanity. London, 1898.
Cloman.	Cloman, Lt.-Col. Sidney A. Myself and a Few Moros. New York, 1923.
Codrington.	Codrington, O. Mussulman Numismatics. London, Royal Asiatic Society, 1904.
Colliado.	Colliado, Luigi. Practtica Manuale dell'Artiglieria. Milan, 1606.
	Collman, Leonard. Guide to Windsor Castle. London, 1899.
Colombari.	Colombari, Colonel F. Les Zamboureks. Le Spectateur Militaire, 2d. Ser. V.
	Colquhoun, Archibald Ross. Amongst the Shans. London and New York, 1885.
Compton.	Compton, Herbert. The European Military Adventurers of Hindustan. London, 1893.
Conder.	Conder, Josiah. The History of Japanese Costume, II. Armour. Trans. Asiatic Society of Japan. 1881.
Cornish.	Cornish, F. Warre. Chivalry. London and New York, 1911.
Cowper.	Cowper, H. S. The Art of Attack and Development of Weapons. Ulverston, 1906.
	Crawfurd, John. A Descriptive Dictionary of the Indian Islands. London, 1856.
Embassy to Ava.	Crawfurd, John. Embassy to the Court of Ava. London, 1834.
	Crawfurd, John. Embassy to Siam. London, 1830.
Cripps-Day.	Cripps-Day, Francis Henry. The History of the Tournament in England and France. London, 1918.
Cubas.	Cubas, Antonio Garcia. (O. E. Henderson, translator). The Republic of Mexico. Mexico City, 1876.
D'Albertis.	D'Albertis, L. M. New Guinea. Boston, 1881.
Dean Europ.	Dean, Bashford. Catalogue of European Arms and Armor. Metropolitan Museum of Art. New York, 1905.
Dean Jap.	Dean, Bashford. Japanese Armor. Metropolitan Museum of Art. New York, 1903.
	Dean, Bashford. Catalogue of a Loan Collection of Arms and Armor. Metropolitan Museum of Art. New York, 1911.
Dean Hdbk.	Dean, Bashford. Handbook of Arms and Armor. Metropolitan Museum of Art. New York, 1915.
	Dean, Bashford. Helmets and Body Armor in Modern Warfare. New York, 1920.
Dean Notes.	Dean, Bashford. Notes on Arms and Armor. New York, 1916.
De Cosson.	De Cosson, the Baron and Burgess, W. Helmets and Mail. London, 1881.
	De Lacoste de Bouillane. Around Afghanistan. New York, 1909.
	De la Gironiere, Paul P. Twenty Years in the Philippines. New York, 1854.
	De la Nieppe, Edgar de Prelle. Catalogue des Armes et Armures de la Porte de Hal. Brussels, 1902.
	De la Vaulx, Compte Henri. Voyage en Patagonie. Paris, 1901.
Demmin.	Demmin, August. (C. C. Black, translator). An Illustrated History of Arms and Armor. London, 1877.
	Demmin, August. Die Kriegswaffen. 4th edition. Leipzig, 1893.
Denison.	Denison, Lieut.-Col. George T. A History of Cavalry. London, 1877.
	De Valencia, el Conde Don Juan. Catalogo de la Real Armeria de Madrid. Madrid, 1898.
De Wit.	De Wit, Augusta. Java Facts and Fancies. Philadelphia, 1906.
Tower.	Dillon, Viscount. Illustrated Guide to the Armouries, Tower of London. London, 1910.
Dodge.	Dodge, Col. Richard Irving. Our Wild Indians. Hartford, 1885.
Dorsey.	Dorsey, James Owen. Omaha Dwellings, Furniture and Implements. U. S. N. M. 1891-2.
Drummond.	Drummond, James. Ancient Scottish Weapons. Edinburg, 1881.
John Rutherford, the White Chief.	Drummond, James, Editor. John Rutherford, the White Chief. Wellington, Melbourne and London, 1908.
Du Chaillu.	Du Chaillu, Paul B. Explorations and Adventures in Equatorial Africa. New York, 1862.
Earl.	Earl, George Windsor. Papuans. London, 1853.
Egerton.	Egerton of Tatton, Lord. A Description of Indian Armor. 2d edition. London, 1896.
	Ehrenthal, M. v. Fuehrer Durch das Koenigliche Historische Museum zu Dresden. 3d edition. Dresden, 1899.

Reference	Title and Author

Elmer. Elmer, Robert P. Archery. Penn Publishing Co. Philadelphia, 1916.

Encyc. v. Nederland India. Vol. IV, p. 685. Wapens der Inlandische Bevolking.

Endle, Rev. Sidney. The Kacharies. London, 1911.

Erben, Wilhelm and John, Wilhelm. Katalog des K. und K. Heeresmuseums Wien. 4th edition. Vienna, 1903.

Evans, John. The Ancient Stone Implements, Weapons and Ornaments of Great Britain. New York, 1872.

Fairholt. Fairholt, F. W. Costume in England, a History of Dress. London, 1846.

ffoulkes, Almain. ffoulkes, Charles. An Almain Armourer's Album. London, 1905.

ffoulkes. ffoulkes, Charles. Armour and Weapons. Oxford, 1909.

ffoulkes, Armourer. ffoulkes, Charles. The Armourer and his Craft. London, 1912.

ffoulkes, Armouries. ffoulkes, Charles. The Armouries of the Tower.

ffoulkes, Charles. European Arms and Armour in the University of Oxford. London, Edinburg and Oxford, 1912.

Field Museum. Field Museum of Natural History, Chicago Labels.

Forbes, Canara & Gangam. Forbes, Gordon S. Wild Life in Cañara and Gangam. London, 1885.

Forbes. Forbes, Henry O. A Naturalist's Wanderings in the Eastern Archipelago. New York, 1885.

Foreman. Foreman, John. The Philippine Islands. New York, 1906.

Forsyth. Forsyth, Capt. John. The Highlands of Central India. New York, 1920.

Furlong. Furlong, Charles Wellington. The Gateway to the Sahara. New York, 1909.

Furness. Furness, William Henry III. The Home Life of the Borneo Head Hunters. Philadelphia, 1902.

Furness, William Henry III. The Island of Stone Money. Philadelphia, 1910.

Fytche, Lieut.-Col. Albert. Burma Past and Present. London, 1878.

Garbutt. Garbutt, Matt. Japanese Armor from the Inside. Trans. Jap. Soc. XI. London.

Garbutt, Matt. Military Works of Old Japan. Trans. Jap. Soc. XVI. London.

Gardner, J. Starkie. Armor in England. London, 1898.

Gelli, Jacopo. Guida del Raccorglitore e dell' Amatore di Armi Antichi. Milan, 1900.

Gerard. Gerard, Sir Montague Gilbert. Leaves from the Diary of a Soldier and Sportsman. New York, 1903.

Gessi, Romolo. Seven Years in the Soudan. London, 1892.

Gilbertson, Dec. Gilbertson, Edward. Decoration of Swords and Sword Furniture. Trans. Jap. Soc. London, 1894.

Gilbertson, Genealogy. Gilbertson, Edward. Genealogy of the Miochin Family. Trans. Jap. Soc. London, 1893.

Gilbertson, Archery. Gilbertson, Edward. Japanese Archery and Archers. Trans. Jap. Soc. London, 1897.

Gilbertson, Blades. Gilbertson, Edward. Japanese Sword Blades. Trans. Jap. Soc. London, 1897.

Goddard, Pliny. The Indians of the Southwest. New York, 1913.

Goddard, Pliny. Indians of the Northwest Coast. New York, 1924.

Gomes. Gomes, Edwin H. Seventeen Years among the Sea Dyaks of Borneo. Philadelphia, 1911.

Greener. Greener, W. W. The Gun and its development. 9th edition. London, 1910.

Greey. Greey, Edward. The Bear-Worshipers of Yedo. Boston, 1884.

Grose. Grose, Edward. Military Antiquities Respecting a History of the English Army. London, 1801.

Gubbins, J. H. A Samurai Manual. Trans. Jap. Soc. Vol. IX. London.

Guillemarde. Guillemarde, F. H. H. The Cruise of the Marchesa to Kamchatka and New Guinea. London, 1889.

Gunsaulus. Gunsaulus, Helen C. Japanese Sword Mounts in the Collections of the Field Museum. Chicago, 1914.

Gurdon, Lieut.-Col. P. R. T. The Khasis. London, 1914.

Guy, Compte de Passage. Catalogue, Exposition de la Venerie Francaise. Paris, 1923.

Hammer-Purgstall, Freiherr. Ueber Bogen und Pfeil. Denkschrifften der K. Akademie der Wissenschaften. Wien, 1853.

Hansard. Hansard, George Agar. The Book of Archery. London, 1841.

Hara. Hara, Shinkichi. Die Meister der Japanischen Schwertzierathen. Hamburg, 1902.

Hardy, Norman and Elkington, E. Way. The Savage South Seas. London, 1907.

Harrison, A. P. The Science of Archery Shewing its Affinity to Heraldry. London, 1834.

Reference	Title and Author
	Hart, Capt. Locker Willis. Character and Costume of Afghanistan. London, 1845.
Harting.	Harting, James Edmund. Bibliotheca Accipitaria. A Catalogue of Books Relating to Falconry. London, 1891.
	Hastings, Thomas. The British Archer. London, 1831.
	Hawker, Lieut.-Col. P. Instructions to Young Sportsmen in all that relates to Guns and Shooting. Philadelphia, 1846.
	Helms, Ludvig Verner. Pioneering in the Far East. London, 1882.
Hendley.	Hendley, T. Holbein. Damascene Work in India. London, 1892.
Hewitt.	Hewitt, John. Ancient Armor and Weapons in Europe. Oxford and London, 1855-60. Three volumes.
Hiller & Furness.	Hiller, H. M. and Furness, W. H., III. A trip to the Veddahs. Philadelphia, 1906.
Hime.	Hime, Henry W. L. The Origin of Artillery. London, 1915.
Hdbk. Amer. Ind.	Hodge, Frederic W., editor. Handbook of the American Indians North of Mexico. Washington, Smithsonian Institute, 1910.
	Hodson, T. C. The Meitheis. London, 1908.
Hodson.	Hodson, T. C. The Naga Tribes of Manipur. London, 1911.
	Hoffman, Walter James. The Graphic Art of the Eskimo. Washington, 1897.
Hoffmeister.	Hoffmeister, W. Travels in Ceylon and India. Edinburg, 1846.
	Holdich, Col. Sir. Thomas. Tibet the Mysterious. New York, 1906.
Holstein.	Holstein, P. Contribution a l'Etude des Armes Orientales. Two vols. Paris, 1931.
Horniman Mus.	Horniman Museum, Forest Hill C. E. A Handbook of Weapons of War and the Chase.
Hose.	Hose, Charles and McDougall, William. The Pagan Tribes of Borneo. London, 1912.
Hough.	Hough, Walter. Catalogue of the Ethnological Exhibit at Madrid, from the U. S. National Museum. Washington, 1904.
	Hough, Walter. Primitive American Armor. U. S. N. M., 1893.
Howitt.	Howitt, A. W. The Native Tribes of South-Eastern Australia. London, 1904.
Hoyt.	Hoyt, E. Practical Instructions for Military Officers. — A Military Dictionary. Greenfield, 1811.
	Hubback, Theodore R. Elephant and Seladang Hunting in Malaya. London, 1905.
	Huc (W. Hazlitt, translator). Travels in Tartary, Thibet and China during the years 1844-5-6. 2nd edition. London, n.d.
Jap. Ex.	Huish, M. B. and Holme, C. Catalogue of an Exhibition of the Arms and Armor of Old Japan. The Japan Soc. London, 1905.
	Huish, Marcus B. The Influence of Europe on the Art of Old Japan. Jap. Soc. London, 1893.
Hutton.	Hutton, Capt. Alfred. Old Sword Play. London, 1892.
	Hutton, Capt. Alfred. The Sword and the Centuries. London, 1901.
	Hutchinson, H. N., Gregory, J. W. and Lydecker, R. The Living Races of Mankind. London, n.d.
	Ichenhauser, Julius D. Collection of Turture Instruments, etc. From the Royal Castle of Nuremberg. New York, 1893.
Inglis.	Inglis, James. Tent Life in Tigerland. London, 1892.
Jaehns.	Jaehns, Max. Entwicklungsgeschichte der Alten Trutzwaffen. Berlin, 1899.
	Jenkins, L. The Hawaiian Portion of the Polynesian Collections in the Peabody Museum of Salem. Salem, 1920.
Jenks.	Jenks, Albert Ernest. The Bontoc Igorot. Manila, 1905.
Joly Int.	Joly, Henri L. Introduction a l'Etude des Montures de Sabres Japonais. Paris, n.d.
Joly Naunton.	Joly, Henri L. Japanese Sword Fittings; Naunton Collection. London, 1912.
Joly Hawkshaw.	Joly, Henri L. Japanese Sword Mounts; Hawkshaw Collection. London, 1910.
Joly Leg.	Joly, Henri L. Legend in Japanese Art. London, 1918.
Joly S. & S.	Joly, H. L. and Inada, Hogitara. The Sword and Same. London, privately printed, 1913.
Jubinal.	Jubinal, A. La Armeria Real ou Collection des Principales Pieces du Musee d'Artillerie de Madrid. Paris, n.d. (about 1840).
Kaemmerer.	Kaemmerer, Georges de. Arsenal de Tsarskoe-Selo ou Collection d'Armes de sa Majeste l'Empereur de Toutes les Russies. St. Petersburg, 1869.
Kepple.	Kepple, Henry. The Expedition to Borneo of H. M. S. Dido. London, 1846.
King.	King, W. J. Harding. A Search for the Masked Tawareks. London, 1903.
Kirkpatrick.	Kirkpatrick, Col. An Account of the Kingdom of Nepal. London, 1811.

Reference	Title and Author
	Knox, Robert. An Historical Relation of Ceylon. (Reprint). London, n.d.
Koop & Inada.	Koop, Albert J. and Inada, Hogitaro. Japanese Names and How to Read Them. London, 1923.
Windsor.	Laking, Sir Guy Francis. The Armoury of Windsor Castle, European Section. London, 1904.
	Laking, Sir Guy Francis. A Catalogue of the Arms and Armour in the Armoury of the Knights of St. John of Jerusalem, Malta. London, n.d.
Laking Armour.	Laking, Sir Guy Francis. A Record of European Armour and Arms. London, 1920.
Wallace Orient.	Laking, Sir Guy Francis. Oriental Arms and Armour in the Wallace Collection. London, 1914.
	Lala, Ramon Reyes. The Philippine Islands. New York, 1899.
	Lane, Edward William. An Account of the Manners and Customs of the Modern Egyptians. London, 1846.
	Lange, Algot. In the Amazon Jungle. New York, 1912.
Laufer.	Laufer, Berthold. Chinese Clay Figures. Prologomena on the History of Defensive Armor. Chicago, 1914.
R. U. S. M.	Leetham, Lieut.-Col. and Sargeant, B. E. Official Catalogue of the Royal United Service Institute, Whitehall S.W. 3rd edition. London, 1908.
Leiden.	Catalogus van's Rijks Ethnographisch Museum. Leiden, 1910-1933.
	Lensi, Alfredo. Il Museo Stibbert. Florence, 1917.
Scheremetew.	Lenz, E. von. Die Waffensammlung des Grafen S. D. Scheremetew in St. Petersburg. Leipzig, 1897.
	Libouille, N. Petit Guide de l'Amateur d'Armes de Chasse et de Tir. Brussels, 1882.
	List, Camillo. Amtlicher Katalog der Ausstellung von Muhammedanischer Kunst, Muenchen 1910. Munich, 1910.
	Loftie, W. J. and Dillon, Viscount. Authorized Guide to the Tower of London. London, 1897.
	Low, Hugh. Sarawak, Its Inhabitants and Productions. London, 1848.
Lumholtz.	Lumholtz, Carl. Among Cannibals. London, 1889.
Lyall.	Lyall, Sir Charles and Stack, E. The Mikies. London, 1908.
Lyman.	Lyman, B. S. Japanese Swords. Numismatic and Antiquarian Soc. Philadelphia. Philadelphia, 1890.
Macgeorge.	Macgeorge, A. Flags, Some Account of their History and Uses. London, Glasgow and Edinburgh, 1881.
Maes.	Maes, J. Armes de Jet des Populations du Congo Belge. Congo. Revue de la Colonie
Congo.	Belge. Brussels, Feb., 1922.
	Maes, J. Les Sabres et Massues des Populations du Congo Belge. Congo. Revue de la Colonie Belge. Brussels, March, 1923.
	Maindron, R. G. Maurice. Les Armes. Paris, 1890.
Majendie.	Majendie, Vivian Dering. Up Among the Pandies. London, 1859.
	Malcolm, Lieut.-Col. Sketch of the Sikhs. London, 1812.
Man, And. & Nic.	Man, Edward Horace. Andamanese and Nicobarese Objects. Jr. Anthrop. Inst. London, 1889.
Man Nic.	Man, Edward Horace. The Nicobar Islanders. Jr. Anthrop. Inst. London, 1889.
Manucci.	Manucci, Nicolao. A Pepys of Mogul India. 1683-1708. New York, 1913.
Marco Polo.	Marco Polo. The Book of Ser Marco Polo. Edited by Sir Henry Yule. London, 1926.
	Mares, Leon. Des Nouvelles Armes a Feu Portative Propre a la Guerre. Montpelier, 1857
Maryatt.	Maryatt, Frank S. Borneo and the Indian Archipelago. London, 1848.
Mason.	Mason, Otis T. The Ulu, or Woman's Knife, of the Eskimo. U. S. N. M., 1890.
	McClatchie, Thomas R. H. The Sword of Japan. Trans. Asiatic Soc. of Japan, 1873-4.
	Mercer, Henry C. Chipped Stone Implements in the Columbian Historical Exposition at Madrid. Washington, 1892.
M. M. S.	Metropolitan Museum Studies. New York.
	Meyer, A. B. and Foy, W. Schwerter von des Celebes See. Dresden, 1899.
	Meyer and Parkinson. Papua-Album, II. Dresden, 1900.
Meyer and Uhle,	Meyer, A. B. and Uhle, M. Seltener Waffen aus Afrika, Asien und Amerika. Leipzig
Seltener Waffen.	1885.
	Meyer, Herrmann. Bogen und Pfeil in Central-Brazilien. Leipzig, n.d.

Reference	*Title and Author*
	Meyrick, Sir Samuel Rush. A Critical Inquiry into Ancient Armour. London, 1824.
Skelton.	Meyrick, Sir Samuel Rush and Skelton J. Engraved Illustrations of Antient Armour from the Collection at Goodrich Court. London, 1854.
Michell.	Michell, E. B. The Art and Practice of Hawking. London, 1900.
	Miller, Edward Y. The Bataks of Palawan. Manila, 1905.
Modigliani Batachi.	Modigliani, Elio. Fra Batachi Independenti. Rome, 1921.
Modigliani Nias.	Modigliani, Elio. Un Viaggio a Nias. Milan, 1890.
Modigliani Engano.	Modigliani, Elio. Viaggio ad Engano. Milan, 1894.
	Montague, L. A. D. Weapons and Implements of Savage Races. London, 1921.
Morier.	Morier, James. The Adventures of Hajji Baba of Ispahan. London, 1895.
Morse.	Morse, Edward S. Ancient and Modern Methods of Arrow-Release. Bul. Essex Inst. 1885.
Morse.	Morse, Edward S. Additional Notes on Arrow-Release. Peabody Museum, Salem, 1922.
	Mosely, Walter Michel. An Essay on Archery. Worcester, 1717.
Moser.	Moser, Henri. Collection Henri Moser-Charlottenfels. Oriental Arms and Armour. Leipzig, 1912.
Mosle.	Mosle, Alexander G. The Sword Ornaments of the Goto Shirobei Family. Trans. Jap. Soc. VIII. London.
Mouhot.	Mouhot, H. Voyage dans les Royaumes de Siam, etc. Paris, 1868.
	Mountney-Jephson, A. J. Emin Pasha and the Rebellion at the Equator. New York, 1890.
	Mourier, J. L'Art au Caucase. Brussels, 1907.
	Muensterberg, Oskar. Japanische Kunstgeschichte. Braunschweig, 1907.
	Mumford, Ethel Watts. The Japanese Book of the Ancient Sword. Jr. Amer. Orient. Soc., 1905.
Murdoch.	Murdoch, John. Ethnological Results of the Point Barrow Expedition. U. S. N. M., 1892.
	Nelson, Edward William. The Eskimo about Behring Strait. U. S. N. M., 1896-7.
	Nouvelle, Arthur. L'Arquebuserie Francaise. Paris, 1885.
O'Brien.	O'Brien, Frederick. White.Shadows in the South Seas. New York, 1919.
Ogawa.	Ogawa, K. Military Costume in old Japan.
Payne-Gallwey, Cross-Bow.	Payne-Gallwey, Sir Ralph. The Cross-Bow, Medieval and Modern, Military and Sporting.
Payne-Gallwey, Throwing Engines. Oriental Bows.	Payne-Gallwey, Sir Ralph. Projectile Throwing Engines with a Treatise on the Turkish and other Oriental Bows. London, 1907.
	Pennel, T. L. Among the Wild Tribes of the Afghan Frontier. Philadelphia, 1909.
Perelaer.	Perelaer, M. T. H. Ran Away from the Dutch, or Borneo from South to North. New York, 1887.
Phillot.	Phillot, D. C. (translator). A Persian Treatise on Falconry, Baz-Nama-Yi Nasari. London, 1908.
Planche.	Planche, James Robinson. A Cyclopedia of Costume or Dictionary of Dress. New York, 1877.
Polack.	Polack, J. S. Manners and Customs of the New Zealanders. London, 1840.
Pollard.	Pollard, H. B. C. A History of Firearms. London, 1926.
Pope.	Pope, Saxton P. Bows and Arrows. University of California. Berkeley, Cal., n.d.
Powell.	Powell, Wilfred. Wanderings in a Wild Country. London, 1884.
Raffles.	Raffles, Sir Thomas Stamford. The History of Java. London, 1817.
Ramsay-Western.	Ramsay-Western. Tibet, A Dictionary of the Language and Customs. Lahore, 1890.
Ratzel.	Ratzel, Friedric (A. J. Butler, translator). The History of Mankind. London, 1896.
	Reade, William Allen. Negritos of Zambales. Manila, 1904.
	Reibisch, F. M. Koenigliche Saechische Ruestkammer. Revised edition. Dresden, 1826.
	Rijnhart, Susie Carson. With the Tibetans in Tent and Temple. New York, 1901.
	Rivers, W. H. R. The Todas. London, 1906.
	Robert, L. and Bernadac, F. Catalogue des Collections Composant le Musee d'Artillerie. Paris, 1889-1901.
	Roberts, Field Marshal Lord. Forty-One Years in India. London, 1898.
	Robinson, Charles Henry. Nigeria, Our Latest Protectorate. London, 1900.
Rockhill Jour.	Rockhill, William Woodville. Diary of a Journey through Mongolia and Tibet. Washington, Smithsonian Inst., 1894.
Rockhill.	Rockhill, William Woodville. The Land of the Lamas. London, 1891.

Reference	Title and Author
Rockhill Eth.	Rockhill, William Woodville. Notes on the Ethnology of Tibet. U. S. N. M., 1893.
Rockstuhl.	Rockstuhl. Musee de Tsarskoe Selo, ou Collection des Armes Rares, Anciennes et Orientales de sa Majeste l'Empereur de Toutes les Russies. St. Petersburg and Carlesruhe, 1835-1853.
	Rodenbough, Theo. F. The Catalogue of the Museum (Governor's Island, N. Y.). New York, 1884.
	Rucker, Robert Hamilton. Catalogue of the Goda Collection, Metropolitan Museum. New York, 1924.
Ling Roth.	Roth, W. Ling. The Natives of Sarawak and British North Borneo. London, 1896.
Roth, W. E.	Roth, Walter E. North Queensland Ethnography. Brisbane, 1901-1906.
Roth, Aust. Mus.	Roth, Walter E. North Queensland Ethnography: Records of the Australian Museum. Sidney, 1907-8-9-10.
Sanderson.	Sanderson, George P. Thirteen Years Among the Wild Beasts of India. 6th edition. Edinburgh, 1907.
	San-Marte (A. Schulz). Zur Waffenkunde des Alteren Deutschen Mittelalters. Quedlinburg and Leipzig, 1867.
	Sergeant, B. E. Weapons. London, 1908.
	Sawyer, Charles Winthrop. Fire Arms in American History. Boston, 1910.
	Schmeltz, J. D. E. Indonesian Ornamental Weapons. Leiden.
Schmidt.	Schmidt, Rodolphe. Les Armes a Feu Portatives. Geneva, Basle, Lyons, 1877.
	Schoen, J. Geschichte der Handfeuerwaffen. Dresden, 1858.
	Schwarzloser, Friedrich Wilhelm. Die Waffen der Alten Araber aus ihren Dichter dargestellt. Leipzig, 1886.
Schweinfurth.	Schweinfurth, Georg. The Heart of Africa. New York, 1874.
	Scidmore, Eliza Ruhamah. Java the Garden of the East. 1898.
Scidmore.	Scidmore, Eliza Ruhamah. The Japanese Yano-Ne. Trans. Jap. Soc. London, 1904.
	Seyssel d'Aix, Vittorio. Armeria Antico e Moderna di S. M. Carlo Alberto. Turin, 1840.
	Shakspear, Lieut.-Col. J. The Lushi Kuki Clans. London, 1912.
Sheldon.	Sheldon, M. French. Sultan to Sultan. Boston, 1892.
Shaw.	Shaw, Henry. Dresses and Decorations of the Middle Ages. London, 1858.
Sherring.	Sherring, Charles A. Western Tibet and the British Border-Land. London, 1906.
Sinclair.	Sinclair, W. F. A List of Weapons used in the Dakhan and Khandish. Ind. Antiquary, vol. II.
Skeat & Blagden.	Skeat, Walter William and Blagden, Charles Otto. Pagan Races of the Malay Peninsula. London, 1906.
Smith, Mervin.	Smith, A. Mervin. Sport and Adventure in the Indian Jungle. London, 1904.
Smyth, Brough.	Smyth, R. Brough. Aborigines of Victoria. Melbourne and London, 1878.
South Kensington.	South Kensington Museum, labels.
	Speke, John Hanning. Journal of the Discovery of the Source of the Nile. New York, 1864.
Spencer & Gillen.	Spencer, Baldwin and Gillen, F. J. The Northern Tribes of Central Australia. London, 1904.
	Spencer, Baldwin and Gillen, F. J. Native Tribes of Central Australia. London, 1899.
Vic. Mus.	Spencer, Sir Baldwin. Guide to the Australian Ethnological Collection, National Museum of Victoria, Melbourne, 1915.
Spencer, North. Ter.	Spencer, Sir Baldwin. Native Tribes of the Northern Territory of Australia. London, 1914.
	Spitzer Sale Catalogue of Arms and Armour. Paris, 1914.
	Stack, E. The Mikies. London, 1908.
	Stephan, Emil. Sudseekunst. Berlin, 1907.
	Stevens, Joseph Earl. Yesterdays in the Philippines. New York, 1898.
	St. John, Spencer. Life in the Forests of the Far East. London, 1862.
	Stocklein, Hans von. Orientalische Waffen, Ethnographischen Museum, Muenchen. Munich, 1914-15.
	Strohl, Hugo Gerard. Japanisches Wappenbuch. Vienna, 1906.
Sugimoto.	Sugimoto, Etsu Inagaki. A Daughter of the Samurai. New York, 1925.
	Swanton, John R. Indian Tribes of the Lower Mississippi Valley. Washington, Smithsonian Institute, 1911.
	Swettenham, Frank. British Malaya. London and New York, 1907.
	Sykes, C. A. Service and Sport on the Tropical Nile. London, 1903.

Reference	Title and Author
Tennent.	Tennent, Sir James Emerson. Ceylon. London, 1859.
	Thimm, Carl. A Bibliography of Fencing and Duelling. London and New York, 1896.
Tijdschrift T-L-V.	Tijdschrift voor Taal, Land, en Volkenkunde. Batavia and the Hague, 1909.
Tod.	Tod, Col. James. Annales and Antiquities of Rajaat'han. London, 1905.
	Various. Beitrage zur Geschichte der Handfeuerwaffen. Dresden, 1905.
	Vauthier, P. Japanische Stickblaetter und Schwertzierraten. Sammlung Georg Oeder Dusseldorf. Berlin about 1915.
	Villiari, Luigi. Fire and Sword in the Caucasus. London, 1906.
	Violet le Duc. Dictionaire du Mobilier Francaise. Paris, 1858.
Violet le Duc, Hist.	Violet le Duc. Histoire d'une Forteresse. Paris, n.d.
	Virchow, Rud. The Peopling of the Philippines. Washington, Smithsonian Institute, 1899.
	Von Sacken, Edouard Freih. Die K. K. Ambraser-Sammlung. Vienna, 1855.
Walcott.	Walcott, Arthur S. Java and her Neighbors. New York, 1914.
Wallace.	Wallace, Alfred Russell. The Malay Archipelago. 10th edition. London, 1906.
	Warburton, Sir Robert. Eighteen Years in the Khyber. London, 1900.
Weber.	Weber, F. V. Ko-Ji Ho-Ten. Paris, 1923.
	White, John Claude. Sikkim and Bhutan. New York, 1909.
	White, John R. Bullets and Bolos. New York and London, 1928.
	Williams, Thomas. Fiji and the Fijians, vol. I. Calvert, James. vol. II. London, 1860.
Winstead.	Winstead, R. O. Malaya. London, 1923.
	Wissler, Clark. North American Indians of the Plains. New York, 1927.
	Wissler, Clark. Indian Costumes of the United States. New York, 1926.
	Wolf, Walther. Die Bewaffnung des Altaegyptischen Herres. Leipzig, 1926.
Wood.	Wood, Rev. J. G. The Uncivilized Races of Men. Hartford, 1878.
Woodford.	Woodford, Charles Morris. A Naturalist Among the Head-Hunters. London, 1890.
	Worcester, Dean C. The Philippine Islands and their People. New York, 1912.
	Wright, Arnold and Reid, Thomas H. The Malay Peninsula. New York, 1912.
	Wyon, Reginald and Prance, Gerald. The Land of the Black Mountain. London, 1903.
	Younghusband, Major G. J. The Philippines and Round About. New York, 1899.
Hobson-Jobson.	Yule, Col. Henry and Burnell, A. C. Hobson-Jobson. A Glossary of Anglo-Indian Words and Phrases. London, 1903.